AF692575

Understanding and Proving International Sex Crimes

Morten Bergsmo, Alf Butenschøn Skre and Elisabeth J. Wood (editors)

2012
Torkel Opsahl Academic EPublisher
Beijing

This and other books in the FICHL Publication Series may be openly accessed and downloaded through the Forum website (www.fichl.org). This site uses Persistent URLs (PURLs) for all publications it makes available. The URLs of these publications will not be changed. Printed copies may be ordered from distributors such as www.amazon.co.uk. This book was first published on 25 April 2012.

© Torkel Opsahl Academic EPublisher, 2012

All rights are reserved. You may read, print or download this book or any part of it from www.fichl.org for personal use, but you may not in any way charge for its use by others, directly or by reproducing it, storing it in a retrieval system, transmitting it, or utilizing it in any form or by any means, electronic, mechanical, photocopying, recording, or otherwise, in whole or in part, without the prior permission in writing of the copyright holder. Enquiries concerning reproduction outside the scope of the above should be sent to the copyright holder. You must not circulate this book in any other cover and you must impose the same condition on any acquirer. You must not make this book or any part of it available on the Internet by any other URL than that on www.fichl.org.

ISBN 978-82-93081-29-6

Dedicated to the memory of the victims of international sex crimes during World War II

SERIES PREFACE

The Torkel Opsahl Academic Epublisher is pleased to release this anthology on *Understanding and Proving International Sex Crimes*. It addresses the gap between international standard-setting prohibiting international sex crimes and actual accountability for individuals who are responsible for such crimes. The book provides detailed analysis of the legal requirements of international sex crimes and types of fact that can be used to meet these requirements. It includes a unique knowledge-base that digests international case law on such crimes. The anthology also contains several studies of institutional and evidentiary challenges in the prosecution of international sex crimes.

The book adds significantly to the study of proving international sex crimes. This is an area of critical importance as the international community moves from awareness-generating activities through the United Nations Security Council and other political arenas, to actual implementation of international legal standards.

The publisher places on record its appreciation for the assistance of Audrey WONG Siew Ming, LAU Yu Don, Elaine LIM Mei Yee, NG Pei Yi, and Nikolaus Scheffel in the preparation of this volume.

Morten Bergsmo
Editor-in-Chief, TOAEP

CHEAH Wui Ling
Editor, TOAEP

Alf Butenschøn Skre
Senior Editorial Assistant, TOAEP

Kiki A. Japutra
Editorial Assistant, TOAEP

FOREWORD

The criminalisation of sexual violence in wartime, whose different features this collection of essays is aimed at exploring and discussing, is a recent but extremely significant development of both international humanitarian law and international criminal law. It is for me a distinguished honour and pleasure to present this book to the public. My pleasure is only increased as it appears in the series of the Forum for International Criminal and Humanitarian Law, whose publisher is named after the eminent Norwegian law professor Torkel Opsahl, a dear colleague and friend. Professor Opsahl was my mentor in the early years of operation of the Human Rights Committee, established under the International Covenant on Civil and Political Rights of 1966, when it first occurred to me to participate in an international mechanism responsible for the protection of human rights. The Human Rights Committee's alphabetical seating order gave me the privilege of sitting next to Professor Opsahl during the years when he acted as rapporteur. His advice served as extremely precious guidance for me on countless occasions. What struck me most about him was the combination of profound legal thinking, firm moral principles, and refined politeness and manners with which he submitted his vision of human rights. Professor Opsahl never made any concession or accepted any compromise that might have gone to the detriment of the protections enshrined in the Covenant. Rather, he always strived for a more protective approach. It is not surprising that he enjoyed the highest respect by the members, including those who did not share his views. Several of the achievements of the Human Rights Committee, in particular in, but not limited to, the field of individual complaints, are due to his firm commitment and untiring efforts to improve the degree of protection of human rights.

The gender dimension is of course one of the basic features of such protection, which ensues from the Covenant's prohibition of all discrimination. It follows from the jurisprudence of the Committee established under the Convention on the Elimination of All Forms of Discrimination against Women of 1979, that 'discrimination' is at the core of and encompassed any form of violence against women. All human rights monitoring bodies, however, have refrained from dealing with such violence in wartime. The partition between humanitarian and human rights law was still perceived as a main feature of international law, and human rights bodies therefore did not venture into this unfamiliar area. This approach did not contribute to developing a culture against sex crimes in wartime, as would have been desirable. In particular in the context of non-international armed conflicts, monitoring human rights bodies could have considered referring to humanitarian law in order to assess the legality of the behaviour of States when derogations were made under the relevant conventions in times of public emergency. This action would have been even more desirable, because international humanitarian law itself did not pay adequate attention to sex crimes and required a progressive interpretation in order to take them into account appropriately. The Geneva Conventions of 1949 do not specifically mention the gender dimension when listing the grave breaches which entail an obligation of criminal prosecution. Common Article 3(1) of the Geneva Conventions of 1949 refers to it only in general terms, under the principle of non discrimination. An interpretation by the human rights monitoring bodies would have positively contributed to better defining the scope of the Geneva Conventions of 1949 from the gender perspective; thus helping the later established international tribunals in their application of international humanitarian law.

It is only with the establishment of the International Criminal Tribunal for the former Yugoslavia (ICTY) and the International Criminal Tribunal for Rwanda (ICTR), whose statutes expressly prohibit sex crimes, that such crimes were given the place they deserve in international criminal law. However, given that the *ad hoc* tribunals were created after the onset of the relevant conflicts and after crimes had been committed, the formal mention of these crimes in their statutes required the judges to interpret their elements as clearly recognized in applicable treaties or customary international law. In such a context, prosecutors often charged sex crimes, and particularly rape, as 'torture' or 'inhuman acts', which were clearly established in the Geneva Conventions of 1949, rather than, more appropriately, as the specific sex crime of 'rape'. Thus, only when the charge of 'rape' was alternatively brought before the court, it was for the competent benches to assess whether the specific sex crime charged was warranted under the Geneva Conventions of 1949 or, more generally, under customary international law.

Such an assessment could have been carried out by the *ad hoc* tribunals by simply determining that sex crimes are a specification of other crimes, such as torture or inhuman acts, without an independent standing of their own. The ICTY went further and established, in the *Kunarac et al.* case heard in 2000, that rape had to be regarded, under international criminal law, as a distinct crime from torture; the distinguishing element being sexual penetration, which is not comprised in the definition of torture. Such a conclusion by no means implies that torture may be regarded as an included crime in the definition of rape. Rather, the distinguishing element of torture is to inflict pain for obtaining information or for other purposes, an element which is not present in the definition of rape. This definition allowed the Trial Chamber to cumulatively convict the accused for both crimes. Besides clarifying the test to be applied for cumulative convictions, this judgement, subsequently upheld by the Appeals Chamber, paved the way to recognise that sex crimes are specific crimes, which deserve independent status and weight.

In a different perspective, the ICTR elaborated on the idea that sex crimes may serve as a means of genocide and, in the *Akayesu* judgement, declared that rape, when accompanied by the intent to commit genocide, may be evidence of that crime. This case law has been affirmed by number of subsequent judgments and has become established jurisprudence of the Tribunal. However, in the more recent *Rukundo* case, the conviction for sexual assault constituting genocide was set aside by the Appeals Chamber, which defined the sexual assault imputable to the perpetrator as merely opportunistic. This position was impossible for me to share, leading me to write a firm dissenting opinion in favour of the view adopted by the lower chamber, which correctly distinguished between motive and intent – following an approach already expressed by the ICTY in *Kunarac et al.* – and maintained that an opportunistic motivation could not exclude the existence of the intent to commit the crime.

The jurisprudential developments briefly referred to show how far the *ad hoc* tribunals have gone in addressing sex crimes. It also shows that further steps are desirable in order to confirm the current achievements and prevent them from being eroded or mitigated. The essays collected in the present book form an outstanding contribution to identifying the issues still open, to exploring and discussing ways and means to clarify sex crimes, to giving suggestions and guidelines for a better understanding of the role of sexual violence as a means of war, and for efficiently investigating and prosecuting sexual war crimes before international and domestic courts. As such, these essays deserve the highest attention of all international and criminal lawyers.

Fausto Pocar
Appeals Judge and former President of the International Criminal Tribunal for the Former Yugoslavia

TABLE OF CONTENTS

1

Towards a More Comprehensive Understanding and Effective Proving of International Sex Crimes

Morten Bergsmo* **and Alf Butenschøn Skre****

1.1. Understanding and Proving International Sex Crimes: Between Standard-Setting and Effective Prosecution

The Statute of the International Criminal Court ('ICC') clarifies the criminalisation of international sex crimes in international law. This progress in standard-setting has been accompanied by an increased political awareness of gender crimes in armed conflicts as reflected through, *inter alia*, UN Security Council resolutions 1325 and 1888.[1] But the enforcement of criminal responsibility for international gender crimes remains weak, especially at the national level. In addition, reference is frequently made at the international and national levels to the legal and evidentiary challenges of proving such crimes.

This anthology brings together experts from different disciplines with the aim of facilitating a conversation on the understanding and proving of international sex crimes. Among others, it addresses the following questions: What are the legal requirements for such crimes for the different forms of participation in their commission? Which requirements are conduct-specific, and which refer to the context in which the conduct occurred? How have the different legal requirements been proved in cases? Where do the main difficulties lie?

---

* **Morten Bergsmo** serves as an academic in China, Europe and North-America. He is Visiting Professor, Peking University Law School (2012 and 2013); Visiting Professor, Georgetown University (2010-); Senior Researcher, University of Oslo; and Visiting Fellow, Stanford University. He is also an ICC Consultant and Co-ordinator of the ICC Legal Tools Project.

** **Alf Butenschøn Skre** is Executive Adviser of the Forum for International Criminal and Humanitarian Law. He has a Bachelor's Degree in Political Science, and is currently pursuing a Master of Laws degree at the University of Oslo. He is an Assistant to the Co-ordinator of the ICC Legal Tools Project.

1 See United Nations Security Council resolution 1325, 31 October 2000, U.N. Doc. S/RES/1325; and resolution 1888, 30 September 2009, U.N. Doc. S/RES/1888.

By undertaking an open-minded and rigorous examination of these questions, this anthology's authors explore the space that rests between standard-setting and the prosecution of international sex crimes. They investigate, *inter alia,* the content and the distinction between different legal and evidential standards, the practical challenges encountered in the collection and analysis of evidence, and the common assumptions influencing the prosecution of international sex crimes. Several chapters also aim to further our understanding of interational sex crimes by analysing them within their institutional environment, comparing their contextual settings, and studying the perspective of those involved.

This anthology's authors come from a variety of disciplinary backgrounds. The nature of international sex crimes, and their prosecution, is nuanced and complex. By drawing on the insights and methods of different disciplines, our understanding of these crimes may be enhanced. Our improved understanding of these crimes may in turn assist in the design and implementation of more effective prosecutions. By starting a focused but multi-perspective discussion on the complex issues that stand between standard-setting and prosecution, this anthology aims to contribute to the discourse on international gender crimes by addressing one of its weakest links: the effective enforcement of individual criminal responsibility for such violations, in particular with respect to those with higher responsibility.

1.2. Chapter Contributions: History, Legal and Evidentiary Requirements, and Sociological Perspectives

Chapters 2 and 3 expand the foundation of this anthology by examining how the prosecution of international sex crimes has historically evolved, and the common challenges encountered in their prosecution. In Chapter 2, David Cohen offers an overview of how the prosecution of international sex crimes has developed over the years that begins with Second World War ('WWII') war crimes prosecutions, especially the International Military Tribunal for the Far East ('IMTFE'). As Cohen notes, "[w]hile crimes of sexual violence were not treated to any significant degree in either the International Military Tribunal ('IMT') or the subsequent proceedings at Nuremberg, rape, enforced prostitution, and sexual slavery were all the subject of serious investigation and prosecution at the [IMTFE], the Asia-Pacific Theater counterpart of Nuremberg. Defendants at Tokyo were convicted for all of these offenses".

The IMTFE did not, however, define the elements of these crimes. Thus, the Trial Chamber of the International Criminal Tribunal for Rwanda ('ICTR') had no precedents to turn to when trying to define rape as an international crime in the ground-breaking *Akayesu* case. Cohen goes on to explore the different approaches to defining rape and sexual violence that have been taken at the ICTY, ICTR, and the Special Court for Sierra Leone ('SCSL') in the context of contemporary international criminal law. Finally, Cohen examines, through a case study of the Special Panels for Serious Crimes in East Timor, how institutional factors, as well as the conduct and attitudes of investigators and prosecutors, can result in the failure to prosecute widespread and systematic occurrences of sexual violence.

Though there has been significant progress in the prosecution of international sex crimes, it continues to be commonly associated with a number of challenges. An overview of these challenges is provided and analysed by Petra Kneuer and Patricia Wildermuth in Chapter 3. As noted by the authors, the practical problems faced by prosecutors in sex crimes cases are quite often "the very same challenges that are presented in cases in which non-gender violations are charged: investigations and evidence collections hampered by location and situation; a lack of detailed memory of potential witnesses; security concerns and considerations; insufficient numbers of trained court staff and professionals; reluctant witnesses; and insufficient funding". There are however some challenges that are amplified when dealing with sex crimes cases, as a result of the very nature of the offences. One such challenge is to resist the temptation of submitting an indictment involving other charges for confirmation until all relevant leads on sexual violence are exhausted and have been documented.

One particular challenge resulting from the nature of sexual violence is that the victim is usually an essential and material witness to establish the offence. At the same time, victims of such crimes are often reluctant to testify without sufficient support from skilled personnel and in the absence of mechanisms in place to provide them protection from harassment and ostracisation. As observed by Kneuer and Wildermuth, the ICTY and the ICTR established extensive substantive and procedural protections for victim witnesses, and these have been expanded by the ICC, through its Statute and its Rules of Procedure and Evidence. However, as the authors note, "it is unclear whether these mechanisms provide sufficient protection", both inside the courtroom and in the local community of the witness. The re-traumatization of witnesses has created some scepticism towards the tribunals and the ICC, and in some cases survivor organisations and potential witnesses have been reluctant to co-operate with the tribunals and the ICC, which can constitute a significant challenge to prosecuting sexual violence charges.

Faced with such challenges, Kneuer and Wildermuth argue that it is necessary to ensure "that investigators, prosecutors, and their advisors fully comprehend that every investigative activity has an impact directly or indirectly on the prosecution of the accused throughout the entire judicial process". Moreover, while it is useful to establish specialised units within the office of the prosecutor, it is also necessary to "mainstream" knowledge on international sex crimes, so that such crimes become part of every investigation, in the same way that murder and other predicate offences are investigated.

Despite these challenges, the international community's commitment to the prosecution of international sex crimes is reflected in the wide range of standard-setting activities aimed at substantively defining the content of these crimes. Chapters 4 to 6 of this anthology examine the legal standards applicable to international sex crimes, their rationale, and their means of proof. Focusing on the ICC Statute, Chapter 4 seeks to explain and critically analyse the legal elements of international sex crimes as well as their underlying guiding principles. As the author Kai Ambos notes, sexual violence has traditionally been implicitly criminalized as a violation of the dignity and honour of the victim, on the national level and in international humanitarian law. In contrast to the statutes of the *ad hoc* international criminal tribunals, the ICC Statute explicitly criminalizes sexual violence, under the headings of crimes against humanity and war crimes. As Ambos points out, the definitions of these crimes, except that of forced pregnancy, are gender-neutral, that is, they apply equally to both female and male victims. With regard to rape, a key issue, Ambos argues, is what role consent on the part of the victim could play in terms of excluding criminal responsibility. Given the general coercive circumstances in the context of armed conflict, Ambos contends that there is a "presumption of non-consent", which entails that this defence could only be brought forward by the defence counsel in exceptional circumstances.

Using the crime of rape as an anchor for analysis, Marina Aksenova, in Chapter 5, examines the scope of complicity as provided in the ICC

Statute and in the jurisprudence of the ICTY, ICTR and the Special Court for Sierra Leone (SCSL). Aksenova emphasises the need for well-defined criteria for different forms of liability in international criminal law. Through a review of relevant jurisprudence, Aksenova explores the requirements, and limitations, of different modes of criminal participation with regard to rape as an international crime.

The questions of how these various definitional legal standards are given further interpretation and how they relate to one another are addressed in Chapter 6. In this chapter, Sangkul Kim provides a detailed analysis of the means of proof of the international sex crimes of rape, forced marriage, and sexual slavery. Defining 'means of proof' as "evidence assessed and decided by the judges as satisfying an element of a crime", Kim argues that by analysing such information, practitioners obtain a "clearer understanding of how those elements manifest themselves in the real world". A significant challenge faced by prosecutors in charging and prosecuting international sex crimes is, according to Kim, their "every-varying characteristics". Using the jurisprudence on forced marriage at the SCSL as an example, Kim explores the consequences, with regard to means of proof, of choices made by prosecutors in drafting the indictment when there is an absence of specific provisions for the offence: "Is there any difference in terms of evidence to be adduced depending on the Prosecution's charging decision in one way or the other between the two options of 'other inhumane acts' and 'any other form of sexual violence'?". Both in the interest of establishing clear legal foundations for future prosecutions of international sex crimes, and strengthening the principle of legality in international criminal law, Kim sees the need for "active codification of new types of sexual violence".

While clear standards defining the crime and individual liability are crucial to the prosecution of any offence, no less important is evidence proving that this crime took place and linking an individual perpetrator to the crime. As already mentioned in Chapter 3, international sex crimes are commonly associated with a number of evidentiary challenges. Chapters 7–10 analyze several of these challenges in different contexts. In Chapter 7, Xabier Agirre Aranburu argues that, "the old deep-seated forces of taboo and denial, and the new assumptions and dogmas of the feminist and human rights movements", are still a hurdle to criminal investigations of international sex crimes. While the feminist movement in international criminal law has since the 1970s made a significant contribution to the fight against impunity for international sex crimes, and its critique of a male-dominated system is still needed, its influence has, according to the author, "together with other factors [...] favored some notions that may need to be critically discussed". Amongst these notions are: the concept of use of rape as a weapon of war; the notion that sexual violence is universally under-reported; the claim that sexual violence is prevalent in all armed conflicts; and the one-sided focus on sexual violence as a "disregard of the bodily integrity of women", which entails a disregard of sexual violence suffered by male victims.

Agirre Aranburu goes on to discuss the utility of pattern evidence in sex crimes cases, a topic that is further elaborated by Amelia Hoover Green in Chapter 8. Despite their evidentiary potential, Green notes that "numerical data on sexual violence, perhaps still more than numerical data on other human rights violations, may prove difficult or impossible to use effectively in international legal settings". According to the author, there is a need to address both (a) inferential problems, that is, sources of statistical bias and observational error; and (b) institutional problems, including such factors as the adversarial information environment, and a lenient standard in assessing expert witnesses' credentials. In the near term, the author argues, it is less than certain that "the (potential) benefits of using statistics in prosecutions involving wartime sexual violence will outweigh the risks inherent in presenting these complex inferences in court". However, as the quality of sexual violence data is likely to improve over time, and as the ICC adopts an inquisitorial system of fact-finding, in contrast to the adversarial system used at the ICTY, the author concludes with a more hopeful observation.

In Chapter 9, Michele Leiby analyses the methodological obstacles experienced when conducting research on political violence. Through careful examination of the supplementary materials published by the truth commissions in El Salvador and Peru, the author demonstrates how strategic choices made in the collection and analysis of statistical data greatly influence what we know about the perpetration of wartime violence. With regard to sexual violence that occurred during civil war in El Salvador and Peru, Leiby observes that there is significant variation in the number of reported cases of sexual violence depending on the data source, that men were more often victimized sexually than previously thought, and that sexual humiliation and torture were common practices of state armed forces during the conflicts.

Shifting to the operational perspective of an international investigator, William H. Wiley contends in Chapter 10 that "the alleged indifference shown historically to gender-based offences by male-dominated institutions" should not be given weight as an explanation when rape and related sexual violence charges do not make their way into indictments. A more compelling explanation, Wiley argues, is that "rape, amongst other crimes of a sexual nature, is a disproportionately difficult offence to investigate". Underlying the difficulties in investigating international sex crimes, is, according to Wiley, the fact that "the nature of the offence compels investigators to rely disproportionately upon victim-witness testimony to establish both the crime base and the basic linkage aspects of the case". As a consequence, scarce investigative and prosecutorial resources will often be invested in dealing with equally serious offences, such as unlawful killing, often with a greater likelihood of success, if there is no overarching strategy directing the resources to investigate sex crimes.

Various authors in this anthology, at some point, make reference to the particular nature of international sex crimes when discussing the legal and evidentiary challenges associated with their prosecution. The authors of Chapters 11–14 interrogate commonly accepted beliefs about the nature of international sex crimes by applying different disciplinary approaches and methods to various aspects of international sex crimes. In Chapter 11, Elisabeth J. Wood notes that "many common beliefs about wartime sexual violence are unsubstantiated, or at best, only partially true", such as the belief that rape is inevitable during war. As Wood demonstrates, there is in fact significant variation in both the amount and the form of sexual violence in armed conflicts. In order to further understand such variation, with a view to strengthening the efforts of ending impunity for such crimes, Wood advances a theoretical framework that focuses on the different parameters of armed groups and their surroundings: the individual combatants; leadership strategy; institutions for socialization of recruits; wartime dynamics; and the discipline and indoctrination of the group. As Wood notes, it is not unheard of that leaders of armed groups may have reasons (be they moral, practical or strategic) to prohibit the perpetration of sexual violence by their troops on the civilian population, and find effective ways of enforcing such policies.

Chapter 12 studies the dynamics of international sex crimes perpetrated by military members and the potential of addressing these crimes through military justice systems. The author, Elizabeth L. Hillman, argues that although military justice systems have in the past failed to hold military personnel accountable for war crimes, there are situations where military courts might be better equipped than international tribunals to prosecute military sexual violence. One reason for this is that military justice systems routinely deal with complex issues such as command responsibility. Moreover, Hillman points to a number of reforms, both institutional and in the social, political and legal frameworks that military justice systems operate within, which may make them better suited than in the past. Focusing on accountability efforts for sexual violence in the United States military, Hillman notes, *inter alia*, that while reforms have in recent years improved the military justice system's ability to deter and prosecute sexual violence (for example by the placing of probative burden on the defendant if the defence of consent is brought forward in rape cases), an increased transparency in, and the centralization of, prosecutorial activity would help standardize charging and sentencing.

The authors of Chapter 13, Alejandra Azuero Quijano and Jocelyn Kelly, examine how our understandings of sexual violence are constructed by undertaking an examination of the narratives employed by news agencies, the UN, NGOs, and governments in their public communications and reports regarding sexual violence in the armed conflicts of Colombia and the Democratic Republic of the Congo. The authors argue that although these two cases are significantly different from each other in terms of their nature, extent and intensity of the violence, they are described in the same narrative language in the sources surveyed. An explanation for this, the authors argue, is that a meta-narrative has emerged, which operates in official and public accounts of sexual violence in war. With the establishment of what the authors describe as a sexual-violence-in-war "formula", this development could "ultimately occlude more nuanced understandings of the multiple realities that can be framed as sexual violence in armed conflict".

Inger Skjelsbæk turns in Chapter 14 to the problem of conceptualizing perpetrators of sexual violence in armed conflicts. In the literature on wartime sexual violence, Skjelsbæk observes, the subject of analysis is most often the victim, while the perpetrator has the role of "a secondary character whose intentions and motivations are assumed but unexamined". In order to advance the understanding of international sex crimes, and strengthen efforts of accountability, Skjelsbæk argues that it is necessary to "incorporate empirical data that bring the perceptions and voices of the perpetrators into the equation", and to conceptualise the perpetrator at the level of an individual, group, and social category. According to the author, an analysis of the perpetrator's motivations should pose the following questions: How is the perpetrator of sexual violence in wartime different from the perpetrator of the same crimes in peace? How does the perpetration of sexual violence in armed conflict pertain to other forms of crimes in armed conflict, an what does this tell us about the perpetrator? How does masculinity and militarism intersect and form the perpetrator identity?

In the final Chapter, which makes up more than 360 pages of the present volume, Magali Maystre and Nicole Rangel develop an innovative comprehensive digest of the jurisprudence of the ICTY, ICTR and SCSL on international sex crimes. The digest is set out in International Sex Crimes Charts that form a substantive knowledge base for those involved in the analysis, investigation and prosecution of international sex crimes. It is also a research and reference tool for other actors in the field. As the first of its kind, the digest shows that there is great variety in the way that international sex crimes have been charged and adjudicated by the tribunals and SCSL, in terms of legal classifications, modes of liability, and features of the defendants and victims, such as gender and role played in the armed conflict that surrounded the perpetrated crimes. As noted by the authors, the digest provides opportunities for researchers to "distil some of the lessons learned about investigating and prosecuting international sex crimes before the ICTY, ICTR and SCSL, and to establish best practice guidelines for investigating and prosecuting international sex crimes".

1.3. Further Inquiry

While the idea of prosecuting international sex crimes has been gradually mainstreamed over time, these crimes are still widely considered as harder to prove in comparison with other core international crimes. The constructive analyses undertaken by the authors of this anthology question the myth that this is always the case, while acknowledging that in certain contexts and under certain circumstances, it may be true. By introducing the groundbreaking resource of International Sex Crimes Charts developed by authors Magali Maystre and Nicole Rangel, and by critically examining the potential of legal and evidentiary tools, such as statistical methods and the ICC Means of Proof Digest, this anthology aims to showcase tools that can 'demystify' and facilitate more effective prosecution of international sex crimes in a practical manner. More importantly, as pointed out by Xabier Agirre Aranburu in his chapter, it is important to avoid "dogmas" and "assumptions" in our further efforts in this area, even as we continue to emphathise with the sufferings of victims. Precisely because these crimes can become so emotionally charged, it is important that we proceed with a dispassionate and yet engaged attitude that will enable us to study and analyse these issues in a professional and technically rigorous manner.

Much like other areas of international criminal law, research on international sex crimes has tended to focus on the development of substantive norms that define these criminal acts. Through their analysis of principles of liability, means of proof, and evidential challenges, the authors of this anthology have sought to bring present-day discussions beyond substantive criminalisation. This is important as substantive norms need to be operationalized through prosecutions, during which the commission of such criminal acts by individual defendants will need to be proven: (1) the criminal act needs to be linked to a particular defendant through principles of liability; (2) relatively abstract legal requirements need to be interpreted and linked to factual scenarios; (3) the case and its material facts need to be pleaded at court; and (4) specific pieces of evidence need to be identified, presented, and evaluated.

The anthology sets the foundation for further research within the multi-tiered framework outlined above. For example, further research on forms of participation in the realisation of international sex crimes, such as that undertaken by Marina Aksenova in her chapter, can provide valuable assistance to ICC judges given the generality of the ICC Statute's provisions on liability, and the fact that the ICC Elements of Crimes do not address other modes of liability than perpetration. Moreover, Sangkul Kim's chapter, which builds on the conceptual structure of the ICC Means of Proof Digest, contributes to our understanding of the in-between interpretative stage, where formal legal requirements are linked with actual factual scenarios. This is an area that should also be further pursued in the context of international sex crimes. Finally, another yet to be explored line of research would be to empirically analyze and compare how different cases have approached the proving of international sex crimes at the level of specific pieces of evidence. Such mapping may be done through an analysis of court documents and records.

By framing the relevant issues, and identifying future directions for research, it is hoped that this anthology will encourage younger researchers and advance academic discourse in an inclusive manner. That is in accordance with the fundamental objectives of the Torkel Opsahl Academic EPublisher and the Forum for International Criminal and Humanitarian Law.

2

Prosecuting Sexual Violence from Tokyo to the ICC

David Cohen*

The prosecution of sexual violence has been one of the most dynamic areas in the development of international criminal law over the past decade and a half since the creation of the International Criminal Tribunal for the former Yugoslavia ('ICTY') and the International Criminal Tribunal for Rwanda ('ICTR'). When the judges of the ICTR Trial Chamber considering the *Akayesu* case[1] first confronted the issue of defining rape as an international crime, they found that they had no precedents to turn to in terms of a delineation of the elements of that offense. The same was true for subsequent cases before international tribunals that considered other crimes of sexual violence such as sexual enslavement, forced marriage, or other forms of misconduct that were characterized as "other inhumane acts" or "outrages upon personal dignity". The *Akayesu* case was also the first to consider the relation of rape as a crime against humanity to the crime of torture as a crime against humanity, or whether rape could be considered as a genocidal act sufficient to ground liability for the crime of genocide.

Within this relatively short period since the *Akayesu* Judgment was handed down in 1998, divergent approaches have been staked out by different tribunals and within tribunals as to the contours and definition of the group of crimes associated under the rubric of sexual violence or "gender based crimes". This paper will consider several areas related to

---

* **David Cohen** is director and founder of the War Crimes Studies Center, and Sidney and Margaret Ancker Distinguished Professor for the Humanities at U.C. Berkeley, Senior Fellow in International Humanitarian Law and the Director of the Asian International Justice Initiative at the East-West Center in Honolulu, Hawaii. He is the author of numerous publications and directs an international project on the WWII war crimes trials in Asia, the Pacific, and Europe. He has also monitored and reported on the East Timor trials before the Serious Crimes Panel in Dili and the *Ad Hoc* Human Rights Court in Jakarta.

1 ICTR, *Prosecutor v. Akayesu*, Case No. 96-4, Judgment, 2 September 1998 ("*Akayesu* Trial Judgment").

the development of approaches to the investigation, prosecution, and adjudication of such crimes. The first section of the paper will discuss the historical backdrop of the Second World War ('WWII') war crimes prosecutions in which crimes such as rape, enforced prostitution, and sexual slavery were first prosecuted before an international tribunal. The next section will turn to the groundbreaking ICTY and ICTR cases that first attempted to define the elements of such crimes. In particular, that section will consider the divergences in approaches to sexual violence in armed conflict that emerged in a body of early case law and how those divergences were resolved in the jurisprudence of the ICTY and ICTR. The next two sections will focus on the development of two other forms of sexual violence as international crimes, sexual slavery and forced marriage, and the efforts to delineate their relation to the general category of enslavement as a crime against humanity and to each other. This will involve examination of a group of cases from the Special Court from Sierra Leone ('SCSL') and the *Katanga* case from the International Criminal Court ('ICC'). The final section of the paper will turn to consideration of the way in which the establishment of prosecutorial and investigative priorities, as well as other factors, influence what kinds of cases the judges of a tribunal will have an opportunity to consider. In looking at the Judgments and Indictments we see a reflection of only a part of the work that leads to adjudication of crimes of sexual violence. This final section of the paper will view the process of seeking accountability in East Timor from the standpoint of the investigations that uncovered evidence of systematic sexual violence, and will consider how prosecutors and investigators dealt with this kind of evidence in light of other priorities that the prosecution unit had already established.

2.1. World War II Foundations

It has often been maintained that sexual violence was not prosecuted in the WWII war crimes trials. Sometime the claim is that crimes involving sexual violence were not prosecuted at all; sometimes that rape was occasionally prosecuted, but systematic crimes of sexual violence such as those involved in the Japanese so-called "comfort women" system were ignored. The fact is that such generalizations are in themselves quite dangerous given the diversity of the various national war crimes programs, and given the fact that so much primary research remains to be done in regard to most of them.

While crimes of sexual violence were not treated to any significant degree in either the International Military Tribunal ('IMT') or the subsequent proceedings at Nuremberg,[2] rape, enforced prostitution, and sexual slavery were all the subject of serious investigation and prosecution at the International Military Tribunal for the Far East ('IMTFE'), the Asia-Pacific Theater counterpart of Nurmberg. Defendants at Tokyo were convicted for all of these offenses. For a variety of reasons, the record of what actually occurred at Tokyo has, until quite recently, remained relatively unknown to all but a few specialists in Japan.[3]

At the national level, while American trials in Asian and the Pacific did largely focus on crimes committed against American prisoners of war ('POW'), there were also some important cases that dealt extensively with sexual violence. The best known of these is the trial of General Yamashita Tomoyuki in Manila, where the prosecution led at length evidence of sexual violence in multi-day closed sessions and also submitted forensic medical evidence in support of the witness testimony.[4] General Yamashita was convicted on a theory (however flawed in its articulation) of command responsibility for the systematic mass rapes, sexual torture, murder, looting, and destruction that was collectively known as the Rape of Manila. In a three-day rampage approximately 20–30,000 women were raped and sexually tortured in Manila by the Japanese Naval forces that Yamashita had repeatedly ordered to withdraw but who had decided to disobey and fight to the last man. Subsequent trials in Manila also dealt with some of these events.[5]

While British and Australian trials focused to a significant degree on Allied POW and civilian internees, they also prosecuted crimes against local non-western populations to a much greater degree than was the case with the U.S. program. Although rape was one of the war crimes specifically included on the Australian war crimes questionnaire, the number of

---

2 I refer here to the 12 follow-on trials before the National Military Tribunals (NMT) conducted by the United States at Nuremberg.

3 Yuma Totani has published pathbreaking work on this topic. See for example *The Tokyo War Crimes Trial: The Pursuit of Justice in the Wake of World War II*, Harvard University Asia Center, Cambridge, Mass., 2008.

4 United States Military Commission, Manila, *Trial of General Tomoyuki Yamashita*, Case No. 21, Judgment, 1945 ("*Yamashita* Trial Judgment").

5 For a discussion of the *Yamashita* Case, see Cohen, "Beyond Nuremberg: Individual Responsibility for War Crimes," in Hesse and Post (eds.), *Human Rights in Transition*, Zone Press, 1999, pp. 53–92.

such prosecutions was relatively small.[6] The same is the case with the British trials that took place in locales ranging from Hong Kong to Singapore to Burma. There are a variety of likely reasons for this, but it is certainly the case that cases of sexual violence were not made a priority for Australian, British, or American war crimes investigators. In the Dutch East Indies, on the other hand, prosecutors did pursue a number of cases involving rape, forced prostitution and sexual enslavement, and also brought to the Tokyo Tribunal evidence of enforced prosecution and sexual enslavement involving the so-called "comfort women" in venues as far away as Portuguese East Timor. There were also Chinese prosecutions of Japanese personnel for rape and enforced prostitution, but further research is required to document these cases more fully.

As seen in the prosecution of General Yamashita, individuals were convicted of rape at all levels of command from the actual perpetrators to military commanders and, in perhaps the most interesting case, the trial of Hirota Koki, Foreign Minister of Japan (and later Prime Minister) at the Tokyo Tribunal.[7] Since that court was the only international tribunal to pass judgment on crimes of sexual violence until the establishment of the ICTY and ICTR, it will be the principle focus of attention in this section.

2.1.1. The Jurisprudence of the Tokyo Tribunal ('IMTFE')

To understand the way in which sexual violence was prosecuted at the Tokyo Tribunal, one must frame it within the general context of prosecution strategy. It must first be remembered that each of the national prosecution teams from the 11 participating nations was responsible for preparing the case involving crimes committed within their territory or against their nationals. A chaotic presentation was to be avoided by an overriding strategy, which was to demonstrate to the judges that Japanese war crimes

[6] Rape was listed as an independent category of war crime on the Australian investigative questionnaire and was not subsumed under a catch-all category like outrages to dignity or the like. These questionnaires were to be filled out by all returning POW and other personnel, indicating whether they had witnesses any of the enumerated offenses. This provided a basis for investigators to identify and map war crimes offenses in territory that had been occupied by the Japanese.

[7] R. John Pritchard (ed.), *The Tokyo Major War Crimes Trial: The Records of the International Military Tribunal for the Far East with an Authoritative Commentary and Comprehensive Guide*, Edwin Mellen Press, 1998–2005 ("Tokyo Tribunal Judgment").

over a 13-year period and throughout their far-flung Asia-Pacific empire had followed similar patterns. This, it was believed, would demonstrate that the crimes were not a product of the personalities or indiscipline of local commanders, but reflected policies and orders originating at the highest level in Tokyo. Defendants were selected to represent different institutions and constituencies within the national leadership echelons.

A similar strategy of establishing patterns of criminality so as to impute liability to commanders had been used by the Americans in the trial of General Yamashita. There, the Manila Military Commission concluded that the crimes were so widespread and so similar in the patterns of their commission that they must have been "secretly ordered or willfully permitted" by the accused.[8] This prosecution worked at the kangaroo court in Manila and, with a far firmer evidentiary base, also persuaded the judges of the IMTFE. One of the 15 patterns of crimes which the Tokyo prosecution listed in an attachment to the Indictment was rape.[9] Sexual enslavement was also a category in an additional enumeration of the particulars of offenses, where it was alleged as a common practice used by the Japanese military against populations under their control.[10]

Following this general strategy, evidence of systematic sexual violence was presented particularly by prosecutors from China, the Philippines, and the Netherlands, though others presented some evidence as well. While the Philippine prosecutor provided evidence on the rape of Manila, the Dutch prosecutor led evidence amassed in the national trials on rape, sexual enslavement, and forced prostitution. He argued that this was one of the widespread patterns of criminal activity that could be traced back to the leadership echelons in Tokyo.[11] Why is it not better known that such evidence formed an important part of the case documenting systematic Japanese atrocities?

---

8 *Yamashita* Trial Judgment, see *supra* note 4.

9 Tokyo Tribunal Judgment, see *supra* note 7. See "Annex 6" of the Indictment, which lists rape in a number of separate categories, including rape of female POW, rape of female civilian internees, and rape of nurses. Under section 12 on civilian populations of territory occupied by the Japanese armed forces, it states, "Large numbers of the inhabitants of such territories were murdered, tortured, raped and otherwise ill-treated, arrested and interned without justification, sent to forced labour, and their property destroyed or confiscated".

10 Totani, 2008, see *supra* note 3.

11 For the best available discussion of the development of the prosecution, see *ibid.*

There are a variety of reasons, but perhaps the most salient is that because of the enormous amount of time that the trial was consuming, after the presentation of what was considered the priority case, which was crimes against peace, it was decided to abbreviate the presentation of the evidence of atrocities. This was done by not reading the exhibits into the record but merely briefly summarizing what was in them.[12] In other words, the massive extent of the evidence is not indicated by what is in the transcript; it is necessary to look at the Exhibits themselves. The transcript itself has proved an obstacle to most researchers because it is 42,000 pages in length. The Exhibits, which are only available on microfilm, are, to say the least, voluminous. The generalizations that are usually made about the Tokyo trial's failures in regard to sexual violence are, then, based upon the Judgment rather than the actual trial record. How then was sexual violence treated in the Judgment?

The majority Judgment is some 500 printed pages in length. It is one of the tragedies of the IMTFE that the judges who wrote the majority opinion chose to devote the bulk of it to the conspiracy to commit crimes against peace. The part of the Judgment that considers the war crimes and crimes against humanity counts is greatly condensed and constitutes a relatively small part of the whole. The result is that the evidence tends to be categorized in general and enumerated in bare lists of events from around the Japanese empire whose similarity in perpetration was alleged to reveal underlying patterns that would link these disparate crimes to the highest levels of military and civilian authority. Rape is dealt with several times, particularly in regard to China and the Philippines, but it is not emphasized by the majority decision that devotes more time to massacres and mistreatment of POW. This is perhaps understandable given the 18 categories of crimes for which the Judgment found that the prosecution had established a common pattern and the compressed nature of this whole section. There are portions of the Judgment, however, that do present the kind of vivid evidence of rape on which the judges relied. In discussing the occupation of Nanking, for example, they state:

> There were many cases of rape. Death was frequently a penalty for the slightest resistance on the part of a citizen or the members of her family who sought to protect her. Even girls of tender years and old women were raped in large numbers

[12] See *ibid.* on the impact of time pressure on the presentation of the prosecution case on conventional war crimes.

> throughout the city, and many cases of abnormal and sadistic behaviour in connection with these rapings occurred. Many women were killed after the act and their bodies mutilated. Approximately 20,000 cases of rape occurred within the city during the first month of the occupation.[13]

The real problem is not that rape was not emphasized, but that its systematic nature throughout Japanese occupied territory was not explained, that it was not linked to other forms of sexual violence that were also systematically employed, and, above all, that the kind of extremely detailed presentation of evidence that takes up the more than 300 pages of the Judgment devoted to the conspiracy to wage aggressive war is completely lacking in the war crimes section of the Judgment. Also lacking is any attempt to conceptualize the crimes themselves, or to define their elements.

In the end, the Judgment finds that the prosecution did succeed in establishing common patterns in regard to 18 patterns of specific crimes, including rape. The opening paragraph of the War Crimes section of the Judgment states:

> The evidence relating to atrocities and other Conventional War Crimes presented before the Tribunal establishes that from the opening of the war in China until the surrender of Japan in August 1945, torture, murder, **rape** and other cruelties of the most inhumane and barbarous character were

[13] Tokyo Tribunal Judgment, see *supra* note 7, p. 1012. See also the powerful quotation adduced by the Judgment (p. 1023) in regard to the order given to Japanese troops returning from China to stop speaking of the atrocities they witnessed or perpetrated there:

> These secret orders detailed the objectionable conduct of returning soldiers which was to be corrected. It was complained that the soldiers told stories of atrocities committed by them on Chinese soldiers and civilians; some of the stories commonly heard were cited as follows: "One company commander unofficially gave instructions for raping as follows; 'In order that we will not have problems, either pay them money or kill them in some obscure place after you have finished'."; "If the army men who participated in the war were investigated individually, they would probably all be guilty of murder, robbery or rape."; "At […] we captured a family of four. We played with the daughter as we would with a harlot. But as the parents insisted that the daughter be returned to them we killed them. We played with the daughter as before until the unit's departure and then killed her."; "In the half year of battle, about the only things I learned are rape and burglary.".

> freely practiced by the Japanese Army and Navy. During a period of several months, the Tribunal heard evidence, orally or by affidavit, from witnesses who testified in detail to the atrocities committed in all theaters of war on a scale so vast, yet following so common a pattern in all theaters, that only one conclusion is possible – the atrocities were either secretly ordered or willfully permitted by the Japanese Government or individual members thereof and by the leaders of the armed forces. (my emphasis)[14]

While rape was linked in this way to the central command apparatus, the majority makes no such finding in regard to sexual enslavement. They do, however, find that it was a war crime: "They [the Japanese forces] recruited women labor on the pretext of establishing factories. They forced the women thus recruited into prostitution with Japanese troops". While this was true of the way in which sexual enslavement was practiced in some places, the evidence led by the Dutch prosecution, for example, showed that recruitment was often by outright force rather than coercive deceit. Perhaps because the evidence on sexual slavery was not presented by as many teams as was the case with other crimes, and perhaps because it was not as systematically documented, the lack of finding an underlying pattern meant that this crime, unlike rape, was not attributed to the national leadership. What the Judgment fails to provide, however, is a discussion of the evidence and a reasoned conclusion as to why it fails to meet that test. This kind of defect, however, characterizes the Judgment as a whole and is by no means limited to sexual enslavement and forced prostitution.

We can take two convictions for rape as a war crime as exemples of the approach by which the majority linked sexual violence to specific accused. General Matsui, commander of the forces that occupied Nanjing, was found guilty on a theory of command responsibility because he must have known of the atrocities and did nothing to stop or prevent them. The same case was made against General Muto for the Rape of Manila, as he was Chief of Staff under General Yamashita. Neither of these individuals operated at the national command level in regard to the crimes of which they were accused.

For various of the accused convicted of war crimes, the Judgment is imprecise as to exactly which crimes they may have been guilty of. At the

14 *Ibid.*, p. 1001.

level of senior field commanders, for example, while Dohihara was in command in various locales where the Judgment found that crimes were systematically perpetrated, the Judgment makes specific findings only in regard to the mistreatment of POW, and even these findings are extremely abbreviated. Or, in regard to General Hata, the Judgment makes a finding that he was responsible for numerous war crimes, but their nature is not specified. The total finding in regard to Hata for war crimes is as follows:

> In 1938 and again from 1941 to 1944, when HATA was in command of expeditionary forces in China, atrocities were committed on a large scale by the troops under his command and were spread over a long period of time. Either HATA knew of these things and took no steps to prevent their occurrence, or he was indifferent and made no provision for learning whether orders for the humane treatment of prisoners of war and civilians were obeyed. In either case, he was in breach of his duty as charged under Count 55.[15]

The same was true in the case of General Kimura, where the findings also do not specify the crimes. From this perspective, some of these convictions may have been intended to include crimes of sexual violence under "atrocities committed on a large scale", but the complete lack of specificity in the findings makes it impossible to determine whether this is the case.

At the national policy level, there appears to be similar confusion and inconsistency in the Judgment. Hirota was Foreign Minister during the Rape of Nanjing. Although he had absolutely no *de jure* or *de facto* authority in regard to the Japanese forces there, he was nonetheless convicted for the crimes they perpetrated in Nanjing. The Court was well aware that civilian Cabinet officials were utterly powerless in regard to the policies being initiated or carried out by the Army. On what basis, then, was Hirota convicted of rape as well as other war crimes committed in Nanjing? The Verdict on Hirota has only this account of the Tribunal's reasoning:

> As to Count 55, the only evidence relating him to such crimes deals with the atrocities at Nanking in December 1937 and January and February 1938. As Foreign Minister, he received reports of these atrocities immediately after the entry of the Japanese forces into Nanking. According to the Defence, evidence credence was given to these reports and

[15] *Ibid.*, p. 1155.

> the matter was taken up with the War Ministry. Assurances were accepted from the War Ministry that the atrocities would be stopped. After these assurances had been given, reports of atrocities continued to come in for at least a month. The Tribunal is of opinion that HIROTA was derelict in his duty in not insisting before the Cabinet that immediate action be taken to put an end to the atrocities, failing any other action open to him to bring about the same result. He was content to rely on assurances which he knew were not being implemented while hundreds of murders, violations of women, and other atrocities were being committed. His inaction amounted to criminal negligence.[16]

What the Judgment appears to hold here is that Hirota, as Foreign Minister was in personal possession of information about the atrocities in Nanjing. As a member of the Cabinet he had the duty to do everything within his power to prevent them. Even though any statements he made to the Cabinet or any protests to the Army would have been routinely ignored, he nonetheless had the duty to "insist before the Cabinet". Despite the ineffectiveness of his previous protests, and despite the meaninglessness within the Japanese context of "insisting" to the Cabinet, he was negligent in regard to his duty as he did not do this.[17] He was convicted and sentenced to death. This conclusion, and other parts of the Judgment, lead to the conclusion that the theory of liability employed here was what we might call "cabinet responsibility". In this implicit theory, the Cabinet, as the principle policy organ of the Japanese government (at least in theory), bore responsibility for the policies carried out by that government in waging war in China and elsewhere. Not uncharacteristically for the IMTFE majority judgment, that standard was not consistently applied to other defendants.

For example, when one examines the verdicts on certain other accused, one is hard pressed to explain the conclusion about Hirota's culpa-

16 *Ibid.*, p. 1160.

17 One may wonder whether what the Judgment really meant was that he had to do everything including insisting to Hirohito that something be done. Because of their tacit agreement to leave the Emperor untouched, the majority may have refrained from stating what they really meant. Since they recount in great detail in the Crimes Against Peace section of the Judgment how the Cabinet was powerless in the face of the Army, they are well aware that Hirohito alone could have influenced or stopped the army's conduct of the war in China.

bility. Take the case of Kido. All the Judgment says about his liability as a Cabinet member for war crimes is that:

> As to war crimes, KIDO was a member of the Cabinet when the atrocities were committed at Nanking. The evidence is not sufficient to attach him with responsibility for failure to prevent them.[18]

The Judgment thus provides no explanation of what distinguishes his case from that of Hirota, who at least protested repeatedly to the Army. Perhaps the fact that the information came directly to Hirota in the form of protests from foreign governments distinguished the case in the minds of the majority. Their reasoning remains opaque. Also troubling is the failure of the Judgment to link crimes of sexual violence directly to Tojo, the War Minister and later also Prime Minister. As the dominant figure in Japanese war policy, they find him guilty of war crimes but they mention only crimes against POW (and to a lesser degree of emphasis, civilian internees) to which he, given his position of military leadership, was directly linked through his duty to ensure that adequate policies for the treatment of POW were promulgated and carried out effectively. The court thus fails to base its verdict on the mistreatment of civilian populations through rape, murder, forced labor, and other forms of mistreatment they found to have been widespread throughout occupied territory. Neither the Rape of Manila nor the Rape of Nanjing is mentioned in the verdict on Tojo. Since the overarching theory of liability for war crimes was to make an inference from pattern to policy so as to establish the liability of government in Tokyo, one would have thought that considering the case of the powerful War Minister and head of that government would have required making that case explicitly in regard to all of the categories of crimes for which the court held a pattern to have been established. In the end, then, it is the Foreign Minister alone who at the Cabinet level is found to be responsible for the systematic sexual violence perpetrated by Japanese forces. And even then, this conviction is only for Nanjing. No one at the national level is explicitly convicted for the broader pattern of rape which the Judgment finds the prosecution to have successfully established.

---

[18] Tokyo Tribunal Judgment, see *supra* note 7, p. 1173.

2.2. Defining Rape and Sexual Violence at the ICTY and the ICTR

While rape was prosecuted at the IMTFE, as we have seen, it was never defined nor its elements elaborated. Rape was no exception here, for in general the WWII courts did not define the elements of offenses. When the next generation of tribunals (the International Criminal Tribunal for the Former Yugoslavia and the International Criminal Tribunal for Rwanda) began their work in the mid-1990's, it thus fell to them to define the contours of rape and to begin the work of distinguishing it from the general category of sexual violence and its various specific forms. The result was a series of ICTY and ICTR decisions in which sharply contrasting definitions of rape were arrived at until the *Kunarac* Appeal Judgment attempted to resolve the discrepancies in approach.[19] While to a significant degree it succeeded, some subsequent cases again raised doubts about definitional issues. The evolving jurisprudence of this body of cases which we will now examine is important not just for clarifying the technical elements of rape, but more importantly because it reveals different fundamental understandings of the way in which sexual violence in armed conflict should be apprehended.[20]

The two different approaches emerge in the first two cases taken up by the ICTY and the ICTR respectively: *Akayesu* and *Furundžija*.[21] The difference in approach to sexual violence arises out of opposing convictions about how to define crimes of sexual violence in the absence of any previous definitions in international law. The answer posed by the *Akayesu* court is to focus "on the conceptual framework of State sanctioned violence". That is, the *Akayesu* Judgment, as we will see, proceeds from the presupposition that sexual violence in the context of armed conflict is different than sexual violence in the domestic context. What follows from this for the Trial Chamber in the *Akayesu* case is that a definition of rape or sexual violence adequate for international criminal law must be developed through a conceptual understanding of the nature and

19 ICTY, *Prosecutor v. Kunarac, Kovač, and Vuković*, Case Nos. IT-96-23 and IT-96-23/1-A, Judgment, 12 June 2002 ("*Kunarac* Appeal Judgment").

20 It also reveals very different understanding as to how to establish the definition and elements of an international customary law norm.

21 ICTY, *Prosecutor v. Furundžija*, Case No. IT-95-17/1-T, Judgment, 10 December 1998 ("*Furundžija* Trial Judgment"); *Akayesu* Trial Judgment, see *supra* note 1.

role of sexual violence in such situations of armed conflict or state sanctioned violence. The Trial Chamber's reasoning is as follows:

> The Tribunal considers that rape is a form of aggression and that the central elements of the crime of rape cannot be captured in a mechanical description of objects and body parts […] The United Nations Convention Against Torture and Other Cruel, Inhuman and Degrading Treatment or Punishment does not catalogue specific acts in its definition of torture, focusing rather on the conceptual framework of state-sanctioned violence. The Tribunal finds this approach more useful in the context of international law. Like torture, rape is used for such purposes as intimidation, degradation, humiliation, discrimination, punishment, control or destruction of a person. Like torture, rape is a violation of personal dignity, and rape in fact constitutes torture when it is inflicted by or at the instigation of or with the consent or acquiescence of a public official or other person acting in an official capacity.[22]

Having indicated its conceptual understanding of rape and the way that it is employed in state sanctioned violence, the court proposes its definition:

> 688. The Tribunal defines rape as a physical invasion of a sexual nature, committed on a person under circumstances which are coercive. The Tribunal considers sexual violence, which includes rape, as any act of a sexual nature which is committed on a person under circumstances which are coercive.[23]

The importance of the coercive nature of the context of conflict is built into the definition. The definition takes account of the fact that in contexts like Rwanda, "physical invasions" may take other forms than conventional sexual penetration. Further, the definition also takes account of the difficulty imposed upon traumatized witnesses by forcing them to testify as to such intimate anatomical details as required to prove actual penetration. As the Judgment puts it,

> The Tribunal also notes the cultural sensitivities involved in public discussion of intimate matters and recalls the painful

[22] *Akayesu* Trial Judgment, see *supra* note 1, para. 687.

[23] *Ibid.*, para. 688.

> reluctance and inability of witnesses to disclose graphic anatomical details of sexual violence they endured.[24]

The court goes on to discuss the way in which coercion is implicit in the circumstances of armed conflict, where the context of omnipresent armed force and an atmosphere of fear and desperation vitiate the very possibility of consent. Going beyond the conventional idea of the "threat of force" embodied in the definitions of many national jurisdictions, the Judgment states,

> The Tribunal notes in this context that coercive circumstances need not be evidenced by a show of physical force. Threats, intimidation, extortion and other forms of duress which prey on fear or desperation may constitute coercion, and coercion may be inherent in certain circumstances, such as armed conflict or the military presence of Interahamwe among refugee Tutsi women at the bureau communal.[25]

The *Akayesu* approach to sexual violence was pathbreaking in the fundamental respect that it recognized the incommensurability of conventional notions of rape in domestic jurisdictions from the way in which rape is employed systematically in many conflicts for a wide range of destructive purposes, aiming at the terrorization or destruction of the civilian population. It implicitly argues that, in order to define rape adequately, it must be understood in this broader conceptual context and must also take into account the nature of victimization. On this basis, the court finds that rape may form the basis of a genocide conviction under the ICTR statute. It also explicitly analogizes rape to torture and finds that rape as a crime against humanity in fact also *per se* constitutes the crime against humanity of torture.

This innovative approach to the understanding of sexual violence in the context of genocide and armed conflict appears to have been difficult for judges in some other cases to accept. In the next international prosecution for rape, the *Akayesu* approach and the definition adopted by the court are explicitly rejected by the ICTY Trial Chamber in the *Furundžija* case:

---

24 *Ibid.*; see the Dissenting Opinion of Judge Arlette Ramoroson in the Kajelijeli Trial Judgment (ICTR, *Prosecutor v. Kajelijeli*, Case No. 98-44A, 1 December 2003) who recounts at para. 98 how one of the witnesses had to be carried out of the courtroom on a stretcher after collapsing while testifying

25 *Akayesu* Trial Judgment, see *supra* note 1, para. 688.

> The Trial Chamber therefore considers that, to arrive at an accurate definition of rape based on the criminal law principle of specificity (*Bestimmtheitgrundsatz*, also referred to by the maxim "*nullum crimen sine lege stricta*"), it is necessary to look for principles of criminal law common to the major legal systems of the world. These principles may be derived, with all due caution, from national laws.[26]

Referring to the principle of certainty or specificity, the *Furundžija* court rejects the *Akayesu* conceptual definition as too vague and as not based on the common principles of major legal systems. The court embarks upon a discussion of the "common denominators" in the various national systems' approaches to rape. What they conclude on this basis is that:

> It is apparent from our survey of national legislation that, in spite of inevitable discrepancies, most legal systems in the common and civil law worlds consider rape to be the forcible sexual penetration of the human body by the penis or the forcible insertion of any other object into either the vagina or the anus.[27]

But what is a "common denominator"? In its surveys of national jurisdictions the court finds that they differ as to questions as fundamental as whether rape can be perpetrated only against a female victim, whether it can include oral penetration, and whether force or non-consent is the crucial factor. The court conflates this important distinction in its effort to show that there is an underlying commonality: "Furthermore, all jurisdictions surveyed by the Trial Chamber require an element of force, coercion, threat, or acting without the consent of the victim".[28] Lumping all of these definitional factors together obscures, for example, the very important differences between jurisdictions requiring proof of force from those requiring only proof that the victim did not consent. The court, in fact, further obscures this conceptual divide when it drops the issue of consent out of its own definition:

> Thus, the Trial Chamber finds that the following may be accepted as the objective elements of rape:
>
> (i) the sexual penetration, however slight:

[26] *Furundžija* Trial Judgment, see *supra* note 21, para. 177.

[27] *Ibid.*, para. 181.

[28] *Ibid.*, para. 180.

(a) of the vagina or anus of the victim by the penis of the perpetrator or any other object used by the perpetrator; or

(b) of the mouth of the victim by the penis of the perpetrator;

(ii) by coercion or force or threat of force against the victim or a third person.[29]

What ensues from the *Furundžija* decision is a situation of uncertainty where various decisions involving sexual violence follow one path or the other.

In 2001 at the ICTY, the *Kunarac* case presented the opportunity to re-evaluate the issue, for that case centrally focused upon sexual violence in the context of the protracted detention of Bosnian Muslim women for the purpose of sexual enslavement. In reviewing the decision in *Furundžija*, the Trial Chamber finds that "the *Furundžija* definition, although appropriate to the circumstances of that case, is in one respect more narrowly stated than is required by international law". That narrowness has to do with *Furundžija*'s holding that force or coercion is required to convict for rape. According to the *Kunarac* court, this ignores "other factors which would render an act of sexual penetration *non-consensual or non-voluntary* on the part of the victim […]".

The *Kunarac* court then embarks on its own survey of national jurisdictions and attempts to reconcile the wide divergence between those which require a showing of force and those who conceptualize rape as a sexual act without the consent of the victim. It does so by identifying an underlying common concept, that of sexual autonomy: "[…] the true common denominator which unifies the various systems may be a wider or more basic principle of penalising violations of sexual *autonomy*". Avoiding saying that the Trial Chamber was wrong in the *Furundžija* case, the *Kunarac* Judgment tries to reconcile the two approaches by stat-

---

[29] *Ibid.*, para. 185. The court goes on to state the following (para. 186):

> As pointed out above, international criminal rules punish not only rape but also any serious sexual assault falling short of actual penetration. It would seem that the prohibition embraces all serious abuses of a sexual nature inflicted upon the physical and moral integrity of a person by means of coercion, threat of force or intimidation in a way that is degrading and humiliating for the victim's dignity. As both these categories of acts are criminalised in international law, the distinction between them is one that is primarily material for the purposes of sentencing.

ing that the two decisions are really in agreement because force or the threat of force may provide *evidence* of the lack of consent or voluntary participation.[30] The result is that the *Kunarac* Judgment adopts the same mechanical definition as *Furundžija* but drops the element of force and adds that,

> such sexual penetration occurs without the consent of the victim. Consent for this purpose must be consent given voluntarily, as a result of the victim's free will, assessed in the context of the surrounding circumstances.[31]

Subsequent cases such as *Kvočka* tried to reconcile the various elements of *Furundžija*, *Akayesu*, and *Kunarac*, or just followed one of them.[32] The ICTY Appeals Chamber, in the *Kunarac* Appeals Judgment, addressed the issue in what is now the leading case on the definition of sexual violence, including rape and enslavement.

The *Kunarac* Appeals Judgment endorses the Trial Chamber's mechanical definition, but indicates that further clarification is required on the issue of the element of non-consent as opposed to force. The Appeals Chamber reiterates the Trial Chamber's claim that it is not rejecting "the Tribunal's prior definitions of rape" but is rather merely clarifying the relationship between force and consent. More significantly, however, the Appeals Chamber explains why what it terms a narrow focus on force could permit perpetrators to evade liability for non-consensual sexual acts. This situation would arise where the perpetrator took advantage of "coercive circumstances without relying on physical force".[33]

---

30 ICTY, *Prosecutor v. Kunarac et al.*, Case No. IT-96-23-T, Trial Judgment, 22 February 2001 ("*Kunarac* Trial Judgment"), para. 458: "In practice, the absence of genuine and freely given consent or voluntary participation may be *evidenced* by the presence of the various factors specified in other jurisdictions – such as force, threats of force, or taking advantage of a person who is unable to resist.".

31 *Ibid.*, para. 460.

32 ICTY, *Prosecutor v. Kvočka et al.*, Case No. IT-98-30/1.

33 *Kunarac* Appeals Judgment, see *supra* note 19, para. 129. In the Decision on the Confirmation of Charges in the *Katanga* Case (ICC, *Prosecutor v. Katanga and Chui*, Case No. ICC-01/04-01/07, "*Katanga* case") at the ICC, the Court defined rape as a war and as a crime against humanity in a way that runs counter to the development of the ICTY/ICTR jurisprudence on this issue. The *Katanga* decision focuses on force or coercion as the required element rather than the lack of consent:

> The war crime of rape, under article 8(2)(b)(xxii)-l of the Elements of Crimes, requires that: (i) the perpetrator must invade the body of a person by conduct resulting in penetration, however slight, of any part of the body

It emerges that the Appeal's Chamber central point is to reaffirm the unique nature of the kind of context in which the *Kunarac* case arose. That is to say, it is in a way implicitly returning to the issue raised by *Akayesu*, but without revisiting the issue of mechanical *versus* conceptual definitions. The Appeals Chamber recalls that,

> […] it is worth observing that the circumstances giving rise to the instant appeal and that prevail in most cases charged as either war crimes or crimes against humanity will be almost universally coercive. That is to say, true consent will not be possible.[34]

That is, the very context in which rape as a war crime or crime against humanity arises prevents consent from even being possible. Applying this general insight to the case at hand, the Appeals Chamber concludes that,

> [f]or the most part, the Appellants in this case were convicted of raping women held in *de facto* military headquarters, detention centres and apartments maintained as soldiers' residences. As the most egregious aspect of the conditions, the victims were considered the legitimate sexual prey of their captors. Typically, the women were raped by more than one perpetrator and with a regularity that is nearly inconceivable […] Such detentions amount to circumstances that were so coercive as to negate any possibility of consent […]
>
> In conclusion, the Appeals Chamber agrees with the Trial Chamber's determination that the coercive circumstances present in this case made consent to the instant sexual acts by the Appellants impossible.[35]

This conclusion seems very akin to the reasoning followed by the *Akayesu* decision, but with an important difference. The *Akayesu* Judgment maintains that the unique circumstances of armed conflict do not merely compel recognition that the opportunity for consent is vitiated but

---

of the victim or of the perpetrator with a sexual organ, or of the anal or genital opening of the victim with any object or any other part of the body; and (ii) the invasion must be committed by force, or by threat of force or coercion, such as that caused by fear of violence, duress, detention, psychological oppression or abuse of power, against such person or another person, or by taking advantage of a coercive environment, or the invasion was committed against a person incapable of giving genuine consent.

34 *Kunarac* Appeals Judgment, see *supra* note 19, para. 130.

35 *Ibid.*, paras. 132–133.

also that the nature and definition of the offense itself must be rethought. What *Akayesu* implicitly argues is that once one recognizes the nature of sexual violence in situations of armed conflict, one cannot then simply carry over a definition formulated in a completely different context. For *Akayesu*, recognizing the nature of sexual violence in situations of state sanctioned violence or armed conflict means recognizing the inadequacy of conventional mechanical definitions. This step the *Kunarac* Appeals Chamber was not prepared to take. Indeed, one might ask why the *Kunarac* Appeals Chamber should articulate a definition of rape as a crime against humanity with non-consent as its central element when it explicitly finds that the circumstances in which crimes against humanity occur make consent impossible.

What is also lost in all of these subsequent decisions is the *Akayesu* case's insight about the burden that the mechanical definition places upon vulnerable witnesses; a burden which is likely to lessen the possibility of effective prosecution because witnesses will either avoid testifying, will emotionally not be able to testify fully enough to meet the required level of proof, or will be re-traumatized by the experience. This, the *Akayesu* judges knew well enough from the testimony and cross-examination that victim-witnesses like JJ notoriously had to endure in their courtroom.

While for most subsequent trials at the ICTY and ICTR the *Kunarac* Appeals Chamber decision resolved this issue, in the *Muhimana* case, the Trial Chamber returned to the conceptual definition of *Akayesu*.[36] While the Trial Chamber notes that the *Semanza*,[37] *Kajelijeli*,[38] and *Kamuhanda*[39] cases followed *Kunarac* in employing "only physical elements of the act of rape", it goes on to argue that in following *Kunarac* it is not necessary to discard the conceptual approach of *Akayesu*:

> The Chamber takes the view that the *Akayesu* definition and the *Kunarac* elements are not incompatible or substantially different in their application. Whereas *Akayesu* referred broadly to a "physical invasion of a sexual nature", *Kunarac* went on to articulate the parameters of what would constitute a physical invasion of a sexual nature amounting to rape.

---

36 ICTR, *Prosecutor v. Muhimana*, Case No. ICTR-95-1B-T, Judgement and Sentence, 28 April 2005 (*Muhimana* Trial Judgement).

37 ICTR, *Prosecutor v. Semanza*, Judgement and Sentence, ICTR-97-20-T.

38 ICTR, *Prosecutor v. Kajelijeli*, Case No. ICTR-98-44A-T ("*Kajelijeli* Trial Judgment").

39 ICTR, *Prosecutor v. Kamuhanda*, Case No. ICTR-99-54A-A.

> On the basis of the foregoing analysis, the Chamber endorses the conceptual definition of rape established in *Akayesu*, which encompasses the elements set out in *Kunarac*.[40]

This is an ingenious argument, the kind that lawyers are trained to make. The *Muhimana* court tries to maintain the viability of the *Akayesu* approach by arguing that the *Kunarac* case only specifies the content of the *Akayesu* definition. But the argument again misses the fundamental point of *Akayesu*, which is that a definition so restrictive is not adequate for the nature of the activity prohibited. What *Akayesu* asks us to do, and which none of the subsequent Judgments has attempted, is to rethink the very category of sexual violence and its meaning in situations of ethnic cleansing, genocide, and other forms of state sponsored violence and armed conflict. While the *Kunarac* Appeals Chamber took one step towards considering the importance of an understanding of that context for defining the elements of rape, it was unwilling to take the next step on the path to which the *Akayesu* decision pointed.

2.3. Defining Forced Marriage and Sexual Slavery at the Special Court for Sierra Leone: *AFRC*, *RUF*, and *CDF* Cases

The SCSL has now completed its final trial, that of Charles Taylor, in the Hague. Each of the three other cases tried by the SCSL focused on one of the three organizations that were the main parties to the conflict: the two rebel groups – Revolutionary United Front ('RUF') and the Armed Forces Revolutionary Council ('AFRC') – and the Civil Defence Forces ('CDF'), which fought to restore the government deposed by the rebels.[41] As is

---

40 *Muhimana* Trial Judgment, see *supra* note 36, para. 550–1. The *Kajelijeli* Trial Judgment, see *supra* note 38, para. 915, explicitly rejects *Akayesu* and adopts the *Kunarac* standard:

> Given the evolution of the law in this area, culminating in the endorsement of the *Furundžija/Kunarac* approach by the ICTY Appeals Chamber, the Chamber finds the latter approach of persuasive authority and hereby adopts the definition as given in *Kunarac* and quoted above. The mental element of the offence of rape as a crime against humanity is the intention to effect the above described sexual penetration, with the knowledge that it was being done without the consent of the victim.

The Kajelijeli Trial Judgment is in many ways deeply flawed, as pointed out by the Dissenting Opinion of Judge Arlette Ramaroson.

41 SCSL, *Prosecutor v. Fofana and Kandewa*, Case No.SCSL-04-14 ("*CDF* case"); SCSL, *Prosecutor v. Sesay, Kallon, and Gbao*, Case No. SCSL-04-15 ("*RUF* case");

well known, extreme forms of sexual violence characterized much of the civil war in Sierra Leone. Sexual violence figures in the *CDF* case by its absence, and in this section we will first consider how this came to be the case. The *AFRC* case, on the other hand, does focus on sexual violence and we will consider in particular the difficulties the judges encountered in trying to legally characterize one of the common forms that sexual violence took in the conflict: the abduction of women and girls to serve the rebel groups in their jungle camps. This practice, known widely in Sierra Leone as the taking of "bush wives", formed the basis for the first prosecution of forced marriage as a crime against humanity. The Trial Chamber and Appeals Chamber, while in full agreement on the factual description of this form of sexual violence, disagreed sharply on whether it should be prosecuted as "forced marriage" or as "sexual slavery". Examination of why and how they differed reveals the difficulty courts may encounter in interpreting local cultural practices and subsuming them under international criminal law categories.

2.3.1. "Silencing Sexual Violence" in the *CDF* Case[42]

In the *CDF* case, the prosecution sought leave to amend the indictment to include rape, sexual slavery, outrages upon human dignity as a war crime and other inhumane acts as crimes against humanity. The leave was not granted, Judge Boutet dissenting, on the grounds that it would have constituted undue delay and abuse of process. The Appeals Chamber dismissed this ground of appeal as an "academic exercise" because the prosecution had acknowledged that it would not be "practicable" to seek any remedy other than its request that the Appeals Chamber note that the refusal to allow amendment was an error of law on the part of the Trial Chamber.[43] The Appeals Chamber also noted that nothing would preclude the prosecution from filing a new indictment against the accused on the crimes of sexual violence that had not been included in the indictment.[44]

SCSL, *Prosecutor v. Brima, Kamara, and Kanu*, Case No. SCSL-04-16 ("*AFRC* case").

42 The phrase "silencing sexual violence" is taken from the title of the report by Staggs and Kendall, see *infra* note 46.

43 SCSL, *Prosecutor v. Fofana and Kandewa*, Case No.SCSL-04-14, Judgment, 28 May 2008 ("*CDF* Appeals Judgment"), para. 427.

44 *Ibid.*, paras. 410-427.

After rejecting the prosecution's request for leave to amend, the Trial Chamber, Judge Boutet again vigorously dissenting, also refused to allow any evidence on sexual violence to be led. The prosecution sought to introduce evidence on sexual violence under Count 3 of the Indictment, Other Inhumane Acts as a crime against humanity and Count 4:

> violence to life, health and physical or mental well-being, in particular cruel treatment, a violation of Article 3 common to the Geneva Conventions and of Additional Protocol II, punishable under Article 3.a. of the Statute.[45]

When the prosecution sought to introduce testimony on forced marriage and other forms of sexual violence, Justices Itoe and Thompson made an oral ruling that such evidence could not be led under Count 3 of the indictment because their ruling refusing leave to amend the indictment precluded it. Justice Boutet argued against this position to no effect. Justices Itoe and Thompson repeatedly refused to allow any testimony that even mentioned any form of sexual violence, even when it was being led for a different purpose. This oral decision was followed later by a written decision, against which Judge Boutet again dissented. The prosecution sought urgent leave to appeal this written decision and that leave was denied by Judges Itoe and Thompson, Judge Boutet dissenting.[46]

The Appeals Chamber held that the Trial Chamber erred in doing so because by the time the prosecution filed its motion the accused had had "timely and consistent notice" for more than 1 year about allegations by the prosecution of sexual violence. They noted that sexual violence can constitute "other inhumane acts" under Count 3 or "cruel treatment" under Count 4. They concluded that while the indictment was defective in not specifying gender-based crimes in these counts, that under established international jurisprudence that defect can nonetheless be cured "if the Prosecution provides the accused with timely, clear and consistent information detailing the factual basis underpinning the charge".[47] Such notice

[45] SCSL, *Prosecutor v. Fofana and Kandewa*, Case No.SCSL-04-14, Judgment, 2 August 2007 ("*CDF* Trial Judgment").

[46] *Ibid.* For a detailed account, see Sara Kendall and Michelle Staggs, "Silencing Sexual Violence: Recent Developments in the CDF case at the Special Court for Sierra Leone", WCSC Thematic Reports, 2005, available at http://socrates.berkeley.edu/~war crime/Papers/Silencing_Sexual_Violence.pdf, last accessed at 20 March 2012.

[47] *CDF* Appeals Judgment, see *supra* note 43, para. 443.

was provided in the pre-trial brief, other documents, and in the prosecution's opening statement.

The intransigence of the Trial Chamber in the case, and some of the reasons for it, have been documented and the lack of a strong legal basis for their position is made clear both by the caustic dissenting opinions of Judge Boutet and the Appeals Judgment.[48] What precipitated all of this time consuming activity, however, was that the Prosecution, in spite of massive evidence of systematic sexual violence, did fail to allege those crimes in the indictment. This omission seems at the very least surprising, and despite the fact that the Trial Chamber could have remedied this situation and chose not to, the lack of importance attached to gender-based crimes may well have played a role in the Rrosecution's omission of this vital aspect of its case. The Prosecution also could have, as the Appeals Chamber suggested, filed a new indictment against the accused. While there were clear practical reasons for not doing so given the financial pressure being exerted by the Management Committee, the fact is that ultimately it is the failing of the Prosecution that sexual violence was not adjudicated in the *CDF* case.

2.3.2. The *AFRC* Trial Chamber Judgment

Sexual violence did, however, figure prominently in the *AFRC* and *RUF* cases. The focus here will be upon the treatment of the novel offense of "forced marriage" as charged in these two cases and particularly in the *AFRC* case. Sexual slavery, rape, and forced marriage were all charged as crimes against humanity, the latter falling under the residual category of "other inhumane acts". As the Appeals Chamber Judgment in the *AFRC* case appeared before either the trial or appeals judgments in the *RUF* case, the *AFRC* Appeals Judgment will be the primary focus here.

In regard to rape, the Trial Chamber in the *AFRC* case adopts a mechanical definition:

> 1. Non-consensual penetration, however slight of the vagina or anus of the victim by the penis of the perpetrator or by any other object [...]

[48] See Staggs and Kelsall, 2005, *supra* note 46, for the best account of the background and implications of the dispute in the Trial Chamber over this issue.

> 2. The intent to effect this penetration and the knowledge that it occurs without the consent of the victim. [...] Force or the threat of force is not an element.[49]

This definition stays very close to the ICTY jurisprudence as articulated in the *Kunarac* Appeals Judgment, rejecting force as a required element of the offfense. Given its conventional approach, it is not surprising that the Judgment devotes scarcely any space whatsoever to discussing the nature of sexual violence in armed conflict. It is striking, however, that in one paragraph the Trial Chamber seems to display some unease about the applicability of such a definition to the context of an armed conflict where sexual violence in multiple forms was a central element of the terrorization of the civilian population.[50] The Court acknowledges that its definition of rape is "restrictive" and, hence, "difficult to satisfy" by the "very specific circumstances of an armed conflict where rapes on a large scale are alleged to have occurred, coupled with the social stigma which is borne by victim of rape in certain societies". This very abbreviated discussion seems to gesture towards the approach of the *Akayesu* Trial Judgment in its recognition of the unique character of such an armed conflict and the stigma that may accrue to women who testify about it.

Of relevance for its subsequent discussion of forced marriage, when defining rape, the Court states that consent must be given voluntarily "*assessed in the context of the surrounding circumstances*" (my emphasis).[51] Commenting on this issue of the context of conflict, the Court states that "in condition of armed conflict or detention, coercion is almost universal".[52] Perhaps with this understanding of the context in mind, the majority of the Trial Chamber rejects the notion of forced marriage as an independent offense. The Court discusses at some length the apprehension of sexual violence and sexual slavery under "other inhumane acts" or "outrages to personal dignity". While Judge Doherty dissented on this point, the majority found that forced marriage is subsumed within sexual slavery. This issue was then taken up on appeal.

---

49 SCSL, *Prosecutor v. Brima, Kamara, and Kanu*, Case No. SCSL-04-16, Judgment, 20 June 2007 ("*AFRC* Trial Judgment"), para. 693.

50 *Ibid.*, para. 695.

51 *Ibid.*, para. 694.

52 See SCSL Rule 96 (1): "Consent cannot be inferred [...] where force, threat of force, coercion, or taking advantage of a coercive environment undermined the victim's ability to give voluntary and genuine consent.".

2.3.3. Forced Marriage in the *AFRC* Appeals Judgment

The Appeals Chamber rejected the Trial Chamber's finding on the relation of sexual enslavement to forced marriage.[53] In doing so it defined the features of that offense, which distinguish it from sexual enslavement sufficiently to make it an independent offense under "other inhumane acts" as a residual category of crimes against humanity. The Trial Chamber had relied on the argument that the essence of the behavior described by the prosecution as "forced marriage" was in fact the exercise of ownership over the victim. They pointed to facts such as the transfer by some perpetrators of their "wives" to other men. They also argued that what distinguished the harm endured by the victims was not the conjugal categorization of their captivity, but rather being treated as property owned by the perpetrators. The Appeals Chamber reviews the evidence discussed by the Trial Chamber and comes up with a completely different interpretation of the facts, an interpretation that emphasizes the significance of the coercive conjugal bond itself rather than the kind of ownership that characterizes sexual enslavement.[54]

One of the key elements of the difference of opinion between the Trial Chamber and the Appeals Chamber was whether forced marriage was a "sexual crime". In finding that forced marriage was subsumed under sexual slavery, the Trial Chamber implicitly maintained that the elements of sexual enslavement (exercise of ownership, restriction of liberty, sexual acts) were what also characterized forced marriage. The Prosecution, on the other hand, argued that the essence of forced marriage was neither ownership nor domestic/sexual slavery, for these features might not be present in some cases of forced marriage. Rather, they argued that the essence of the offense was the perpetrator forcing the victim into a conjugal bond: "forcing a person into the appearance" of a conjugal relation by "threat, physical assault, or other coercion".[55] Thus the prosecu-

---

53 SCSL, *Prosecutor v. Brima, Kamara, and Kanu*, Case No. SCSL-04-16, Judgment, 22 February 2008 ("*AFRC* Appeals Judgment"), para. 184 notes that Inhumane Acts has been held to include a wide variety of sexual acts including forcing women to undress and walk naked in front of others or in public, forcing women to exercise naked in front of others, sexual violence perpetrated on dead bodies, sexual violence, humiliation, harassment and psychological abuse.

54 *Ibid.*, paras. 187-196.

55 *Ibid.*, para. 189.

tion could argue that forced marriage was not "a sexual crime". This is the position that the Appeals Chamber endorses.

In stating that forced marriage is "not ***predominantly*** a sexual crime" (my emphasis) the Appeals Chamber finds that the evidence unequivocally indicates that the conjugal association rather than the exercise of "an ownership interest" is what characterizes the kind of behavior and practices referred to in the indictment as "forced marriage". They hold that one of the characteristic features of the conflict in Sierra Leone was that girls and women were systematically abducted from their homes and "compelled to serve as conjugal partners for AFRC soldiers".[56] In this context they were "coerced to perform a variety of conjugal duties including regular sexual intercourse, domestic labour such as cooking and cleaning for the 'husband,' endure forced pregnancy, and to care for and bring up the children of the 'marriage'".

Paradoxically, the Trial Chamber relied upon exactly the same evidence to find that the idea of "conjugal association' was a sham and that the reality was the exercise of ownership. They pointed out that ownership was manifested through control of the victim's sexuality, movement, and labor. The Trial Chamber also noted that none of the victims who testified indicated that they had felt "married" because their abduction and captivity was referred to as "marriage". The Trial Chamber found that although the ownership was asserted as exclusive, the victim could be "passed on or given to another rebel at the discretion of the perpetrator".[57]

In reaching its concusion on forced marriage, the Appeals Chamber particularly relied upon the testimony of a prosecution expert (Zainab Bangura) who explained what forced marriage meant in the Sierra Leonean cultural context: He stated that the phenomenon referred to as "bush wives" was one of the most devastating forms of abuse suffered by Sierra Leonean women victims. He opined that the "use of the term 'wife' by the perpetrator was deliberate and strategic". It demonstrated control over the victim and the expectation of sexual exclusivity that characterized marriage (for women) and that would result in severe beating or death if violated. He stated that 'bush wives' were expected to demonstrate love, affection, and loyalty, and that what they received in return was physical, sexual, and psychological abuse before, during, and after pregnancy, that

[56] *Ibid.*, para. 190.

[57] *Ibid.*, para. 712.

demonstrated the husband's "control".[58] One might well ask here what distinguishes that "control" manifested through constant coercion in a number of forms from the "exercise of ownership" that characterizes sexual enslavement.

Given the description of forced marriage, which is replete with aspects of the sexual nature of the so-called "conjugal association" ("regular sexual intercourse", coerced "sexual exclusivity", the combination of "sexual, physical, and psychological abuse", forced pregnancy) one must ask how different this is from the kind of ongoing, long term sexual enslavement accompanied by similar expectations of domestic labor, care, and displays of affection, that appeared in the *Kunarac* case. Indeed, more than one of the three defendants in that case alleged that a victim was his "girlfriend" or was in love with him. Is all that is missing in the Bosnian context the distinctive Sierra Leonean cultural tag of "bush wife"?

This depends, I think, on how seriously one takes the strategic deployment of the term "marriage" as alleged by the expert witness on whom the Appeals Chamber heavily relies. He states that this term was used strategically by perpetrators because it enabled "psychological manipulations of her [the "bush wife's"] feelings that rendered her unable to deny his wishes". This seems inherently contradictory to the rest of his description that represents the relation as characterized by compliance through sheer terror: "bush wives" would be killed or severely beaten if they were not sexually faithful. Even if they were, perpetrators nonetheless maintained control, he states, through unremitting abuse in the form of physical battering, sexual abuse, and "psychological terrorization". But how is psychological terrorization compatible with strategic psychological manipulation of *feelings* to induce compliance because a woman called "wife" by the perpetrator feels "unable to deny his wishes"?

What the Appeals Chamber concludes from this, and from its review of the dissenting opinion of Judge Doherty, is that forced marriage is not subsumed within sexual slavery because it has distinctive features that center on the imposed conjugal relation. What are these features? Conceding that forced marriage shares with sexual slavery the elements of "deprivation of liberty and non-consensual sex", the Appeals Chamber claims that it is distinguished: (1) by compelling a person into a forced conjugal association that results in great suffering or physical or mental injury; (2) and that unlike sexual slavery, forced marriage involves sexual exclusivi-

58 *Ibid.*, para. 192.

ty, the breach of which may be punished. These two distinctions, according to the Appeals Chamber, render forced marriage as not "predominantly" a sexual crime and it is therefore not subsumed under sexual enslavement.[59]

The second of the "distinguishing" features seems particularly problematic. The so-called "exclusivity" is one-sided and coerced. As the Trial Chamber noted, the evidence showed that so-called "husbands" sometimes passed their "wives" on to other men and took new ones. The women that were abducted were sometimes gang raped or passed around within the camp until someone decided to claim her as his "bush wife". This is hardly the context of marital sexual exclusivity and can just as well characterize sexual slavery where the one exercising ownership wants exclusive exploitation of his "property".

In the Bosnian context, where there are long-term residential contexts of sexual enslavement, one also may find such "exclusivity", temporary as it may often be, and women who were claimed as exclusive property would also be punished for violating the mandate of her "owner".

The first distinguishing feature is also troubling. Why is this concededly coercive arrangement a "conjugal association"? Is it "conjugal" because it involves sexual services and domestic labor that is uncompensated, involuntary, and enforced with psychological terrorization and extreme physical and sexual brutality and cruelty? Is it because it is labeled by perpetrators as such? Is it because it is a culturally recognized category in Sierra Leone? If it is, how is this form of "conjugal association" really any different than domestic and sexual slavery? The conclusion that it is not "predominantly" a sexual offense must rest on this feature, rather than on the second, which is itself a sexually defined category, but the Appeals Judgment hardly spells out exactly what it is about this arrangement that distinguished it from enslavement, apart from what the perpetrators choose to call it.[60] As we will see, at the ICC, the Decision in the *Katanga* case attempted to clarify and resolve just these issues.

---

[59] *Ibid.*, para. 195.

[60] In the RUF (Sesay) case, the Appeals Chamber took up the issue of forced marriage again and held that the circumstances in which the victims found themselves vitiated the possibility of consent for marriage so that conjugal relations under these circumstances were necessarily coercive so as to constitute forced marriage:

> As found by the Trial Chamber, 'given the violent, hostile and coercive environment in which these women suddenly found themselves […] the

This case is interesting because it demonstrates the difficulty that tribunals may have in grappling with the divergent cultural understandings of the local context. What sometimes appears to result is a misplaced attempt to respect these cultural understandings without fully interrogating them. We have already noted a case in East Timor where a Serious Crimes Unit ('SCU') investigator noted that before proceeding any further into the investigation of the repeated rape of a 12-year old girl, one would have to inquire whether such conduct with very young girls was part of local custom. Once a decision has been made to prosecute international crimes, why should local custom play a part in analyzing such offenses? If local custom is determinative, shouldn't the conduct be charged under national rather than international norms?

One factor that seems to connect the East Timor case with the *AFRC* and *CDF* cases in Sierra Leone is that if investigators and prosecutors do not have a clear understanding of the legal categories of sexual violence and the elements required to prove them, then effective prosecution is unlikely. But even with clarity about the elements, if there is not sufficient political will to prioritize such crimes and investigate fully the context in which they were committed, then mere token prosecutions are the likely result.

2.4. Sexual Slavery and Forced Marriage in the *Katanga* Case at the ICC

In the *Katanga* case arising from the systematic perpetration of sexual violence in the Democratic Republic of the Congo (DRC), sexual slavery was charged as a war crime as follows:

> For the war crime of sexual slavery under article 8(2)(b)(xxii)-2 of the Elements of Crimes, the perpetrator must: (i) exercise any or all of the powers attaching to the right of ownership over one or more persons, such as by purchasing, selling, lending, or bartering such a person or persons, or by imposing on them a similar deprivation of liberty; and (ii) cause such person or persons to engage in one or more acts

sexual relations with the rebels […] could not [be], and was, in [the] circumstances, not consensual because of the state of uncertainty and subjugation in which they lived in captivity.' Such captivity in itself would have vitiated consent in the circumstances under consideration. (para. 736)

> of sexual nature. The instances cited under the first element above do not constitute an exhaustive list.[61]

The definition of sexual slavery adopted by the ICC Pre-Trial Chamber in *Katanga* would seem to fit the circumstances of forced marriage, or so-called "bush marriage" as considered by the Appeals Chamber of the SCSL in the *AFRC* and *RUF* cases. Indeed, the factual circumstances of sexual enslavement in *Katanga* seem highly similar to those considered by the Trial and Appeals Chambers in the *AFRC* and *RUF* cases. For example, the Court stated that it relied on the following kind of evidence in making its finding:

> a. Witness 249 is a Hema civilian woman [REDACTED]. She was abducted, undressed, and raped by an Ngiti combatant at the village of Bogoro. Following death threats, she became the 'wife' of an Ngiti combatant, and was repeatedly raped. She had a child as a result of these rapes during her captivity.[62]

The *Katanga* Court took up the same issue as had been adjudicated in the *AFRC* and *RUF* cases as to the relation of forced marriage to sexual slavery. In *Katanga*, however, the Court took a very different stand on this issue, one much closer to the *AFRC* Trial Chamber holding that was rejected by the SCSL Appeals Chamber. In *Katanga*, the Court explicitly found that forced marriage, whether as a war crime or as a crime against humanity, was properly charged as sexual slavery.

---

61 *Katanga* case, see *supra* note 33, para. 343.

62 *Ibid.*, para. 353.The factual circumstances in subsequent paragraphs underscore the similarity of the conduct in the Katanga/DRC context with that which was considered in the *AFRC* and *RUF* cases (para. 434):

> The Chamber finds that there is sufficient evidence to establish substantial grounds to believe that before and in the aftermath of the joint FRPI/FNI attack against the village of Bogoro on 24 February 2003, combatants from the FRPI [...] (i) abducted women and/or girls from villages or areas surrounding the camps for the purpose of using them as their "wives"; (ii) forced and threatened women and/or girls to engage in sexual intercourse with combatants and to serve as sexual slaves for combatants and commanders alike; and (iii) captured and imprisoned women and/or girls to work in a military camp servicing the soldiers. More specifically, there are substantial grounds to believe that during the attack on Bogoro, women were captured, raped and subsequently abducted by Ngiti attackers. The women were taken to camps where they were kept as prisoners in order to provide domestic services, including cooking and cleaning, and to engage in forced sexual acts with combatants and commanders.

Likewise, in regard to sexual slavery as a crime against humanity, the court explicitly found that criminal acts such as forced marriage are all subsumed under the category of sexual slavery as a crime against humanity. The Chamber found that sexual slavery is "a particular form of enslavement". They referred to the Supplementary Convention on the Abolition of Slavery, the Slave Trade, and Institutions and Practices Similar to Slavery of 1956 which provides that practices including "debt bondage, serfdom, forced marriage practices and forms of child labour" constitute particular forms of enslavement.[63]

In explicitly addressing the relation of forced marriage to sexual slavery, the *Katanga* Court reasoned that "sexual slavery also encompasses situations where women and girls are *forced into 'marriage'*, domestic servitude or other forced labour involving compulsory sexual activity, including rape, by their captors". They gave as examples a variety of practices involving sexual enslavement, some of which are more like forced prostitution, and some of which may involve a form of "marriage":

> [...] the detention of women in 'rape camps' or 'comfort stations', forced temporary 'marriages' to soldiers and other practices involving the treatment of women as chattel, and as such, violations of the peremptory norm prohibiting slavery.[64]

For the *Katanga* Court, unlike the Appeals Chamber of the SCSL the underlying common feature of this wide range of practices was treating women as chattels, rather than as autonomous human beings, accompanied by sexual abuse. This approach focuses on the underlying conceptual foundation of the victimization of those subjected to these practices and from this perspective there is no point in distinguishing between them for the purposes of accountability for crimes against humanity or war crimes.

This decision in *Katanga* seems sounder and more fitting to the reality of sexual subjugation in situations of armed conflict than the reliance of the SCSL Appeals Chamber on the uniqueness of the so-called "conjugal relation" conjured up by the imposition of "bush marriage" upon an unwilling victim. The ICC, both in its Statute (and The Elements of Crimes) and its jurisprudence is staking out its own path in regard to the apprehension of sexual violence. The Decision on the Confirmation of

[63] *Ibid.*, para. 430.

[64] *Ibid.*, para. 431.

Charges in the *Katanga* case indicates that in regard to the definitions of rape and sexual enslavement, as well as the status of forced marriage as an independent offense, the ICC will be an important focus for the further development of international criminal law on sexual violence. How national jurisdictions or other future international hybrid tribunals will make sense of the divergence of approaches among the ICTY, ICTR, SCSL, and the ICC remains to be seen.

2.5. The Special Panels for Serious Crimes in East Timor

The Special Panels for Serious Crimes ('SPSC') in East Timor may have made relatively little contribution to the jurisprudence of sexual violence, but they offer an important example of the critical role that the establishment of prosecutorial and investigative priorities plays in seeking accountability for such crimes. The forms of sexual violence systematically perpetrated in East Timor during the violence in 1999 included rape, sexual slavery, forced marriage, and other kinds of sexual humiliation or mistreatment that would fall under categories such as other inhumane acts as a crime against humanity. Yet none of the many trials conducted before the Special Panels considered the systematic nature of sexual violence and how it figured as part of a more general pattern of terrorizing that part of the civilian population associated by the perpetrators with the movement that sought independence from Indonesia. One reason that so few cases came to trial was because the higher-level perpetrators were all in West Timor, the Indonesian part of the island of Timor. The refusal of the Indonesian government to co-operate with the UN in the trials before the SPSC, and their insistence to try such individuals before a national human rights court in Jakarta, was an important reason for this failure of accountability, but so was the lack of political will on the part of the international community to pressure Indonesia into cooperation. Yet, as will be seen, there were other reasons why so few cases of sexual violence reached the trial stage in East Timor. A consideration of the way in which the prosecution arm of the UN justice effort dealt with the investigation of sexual violence may thus offer insight into the dynamics that can determine what kinds of cases ultimately come before the judges of a tribunal.

The UN Special Panels for Serious Crimes operated from 2000-2005 in Dili, East Timor. During that period, and on an astonishingly slim budget, they completed 55 trials and indicted more than 400 individuals.[65] At the abrupt termination of their mandate in May 2005, approximately 400 investigative files remained open, approximately 100 of which were ready, or almost ready, for trial. The mandate of the SPSC and SCU were limited to crimes that occurred during the violence in 1999 preceding and following the referendum ("popular consultation") that resulted in Timorese independence. Leaving aside what had occurred during the preceding 24 years of Indonesian occupation, systematically perpetrated crimes of sexual violence appear to have occurred on a massive scale in 1999. Why, especially given the very large number of cases tried and investigated by the SCU, do I say "appear to have occurred"? The following example may indicate the underlying problem.

During my work as Advisor from 2006–2008 for the bilateral truth commission for Indonesia and Timor Leste (The Commission on Truth and Friendship or 'CTF'), my research team and I were given access to all of the records, including the investigative files, of the Serious Crimes Unit, the prosecution arm of the UN justice process in East Timor. One SCU case file for a murder investigation contains evidence regarding a rape committed by the same suspect. A memorandum in the file provides both evidence of why the rape charge was not pursued as well as insight into the policies of the SCU. This memo, from Prosecutor G. to the investigator complains that there is "superfluous evidence" in the file. He is referring to the evidence about rape that emerged during the investigation and which had been included when the file was forwarded to the prosecutor. The memo further states that evidence of rape is not relevant to the investigation and might not "be called priority offenses at all".[66] In this case the failure not to pursue the rape is particularly puzzling because the perpetrator had actually confessed to raping a young woman. He was a pro-Indonesian militia (Aitarak) platoon commander and, significantly for the prosecution, he was also a member of the Indonesian Army ('TNI'), serving with one of the most notorious Indonesian units (Batallion 744). The rape occurred while he was transporting the young woman and her family and could have been prosecuted as a crime against humanity be-

[65] In total they issued 95 indictments that included allegations against 440 individuals. Both East Timorese and Indonesians were indicted. However, of those accused, 339 were living outside of East Timor's geographic jurisdiction, mostly in Indonesia. When the SCU closed in 2005, 87 defendants had been tried in a total of 55 cases. Eighty-four of these 87 defendants were convicted.

[66] 14 September 2004 DI 108 99 SC.

cause it was clearly part of the widespread and systematic terrorization and displacement of hundreds of thousands of Timorese civilians. Despite the confession and the evidence already obtained, there was no further investigation or indictment.

If senior SCU prosecutors could rebuke their investigators for providing evidence of rape occurring in the context of the violence they were investigating because such crimes were "superfluous" and not a "priority", this is indicative of why so few sexual violence cases came to trial. It was not for lack of evidence indicating that a broad investigation was required. As we will see, through evidence that repeatedly emerged during murder investigations, and through the work of a small team of female prosecutors, the SCU was well aware that gender-based crimes had been systematically perpetrated. They were also aware that these crimes included, in addition to rape, forced prostitution, forced marriage, and sexual enslavement. Yet it was only in the *Lolotoe* case[67] (Jose Cardoso) that rape as part of the larger context of political violence, terror, and repression was successfully prosecuted. It is in all likelihood not coincidental that the Carodoso case was prosecuted by a female prosecutor who had led the gender crimes investigation.

Every prosecution unit must, of course, establish priorities so as to best allocate limited resources. The SCU did establish priorities in 2 ways. First, it is clear that murder was the top priority category of crime- not just murder as a crime against humanity, but also simple cases of murder prosecuted under the Indonesian penal code, which was the applicable domestic law for these purposes. Indeed, only 9 of the 55 trials involved charges of crimes against humanity (for reasons that are not always clear). Second, the SCU early on announced that it was pursuing a number of specific occurrences of murder as "priority cases". At first there were 5 of these, later 10. Which occurrences were included also changed over time, but in general we can say that these were the most notorious cases of murder, typically involving multiple victims. As one participant in the process put it, however, in the first two years of its operation the public announcement of "priority cases" was more of a public relations exercise than a reality.[68] Most cases that in fact came to trial during this period

[67] Special Panel for Serious Crimes in East Timor (SPSC), *Prosecutor v. Jose Cardoso,* Case No. 04/2001, Judgment, 5 April 2003.

[68] Interview with the SCU head of Public Affairs, Ms. Julia Alinho, 28 March 2005, in Dili, Timor Leste.

were not "priority cases" and not crimes against humanity indictments, but rather simple murder cases involving one lowest level perpetrator, prosecuted under Indonesian Criminal Code Section 338 for intentional homicide.

The process that led to so few gender-based crimes being brought to trial may serve as a case study of the way in which prosecutorial strategies were developed, resources allocated, and of the other kinds of obstacles that may impede the work of tribunals in post-conflict settings. The 10 SCU priority cases in general followed the 14 priority cases identified by a preceding Indonesian report by the investigative commission ('KPP HAM') set up under the new Indonesian human rights law.[69] That the KPP HAM report was regarded as influential and authoritative by the SCU is indicated by the fact that in every crime against humanity they brought to trial at the Special Panels, the SCU introduced no documentary evidence or witness testimony to establish the chapeau elements; they merely introduced the KPP HAM report.[70]

The Timorese national truth commission, CAVR, also undertook to document the crimes committed both in 1999 and from 1974, eventually completing a 2700 page report.[71] Both KPP HAM and CAVR prioritized gender-based violence in their investigations. It is revealing that the SCU for the most part followed the KPP HAM report in regard to the identification of "priority cases," but did not similarly prioritize sexual violence.[72] None of these SCU 10 priority cases were identified as focusing on sexual violence.

---

69 Law 26/2000.

70 The irony is that they never introduced, and may not even have possessed the full report of the KPP HAM or the document and other evidentiary appendices that accompanied it. They only introduced the executive summary. The KPP-HAM's Executive Summary of is Report on the Investigation of Human Rights Violations in East Timor, released on 31 January 2000, is available at http://www.etan.org/news/2000a/3exec.htm, last accessed at 8 April 2012. In most cases they also introduced one or two other reports, such as that of the UN Commission of Inquiry,but the KPP HAM report was by the far the best documented.

71 Commision for Reception, Truth and Reconciliation in East Timor (CAVR), *Chega! The CAVR Report*, April 2006, available at http://www.cavr-timorleste.org/en/chegaReport.htm, last accessed at 8 April 2012.

72 KPP HAM relied on a report prepared by the Indonesian National Commission Against Violence for Women (Komnas Perempuan) which documented several major cases of sexual violence. This report was also available to the SCU.

When a new Deputy Prosecutor General for Special Crimes ('DPGSC'), Ms. Siri Frigaard from Norway, took over leadership of the SCU in January 2002, some 2 years into its mandate, she immediately introduced a much-needed reorganization of the office. Under her leadership, the SCU began to operate much more effectively and to define its priorities more clearly. One of the key changes introduced by DPGSC Frigaard was to focus a substantial amount of investigative resources on investigation and indictment of Indonesian military personnel, and particular commanders. The core of this effort was the so-called "national" indictment against General Wiranto, as well as other high-level commanders.[73] The objective here was to refocus efforts away from solely prosecuting individual low-level Timorese militia members and to seek accountability for the role of the Indonesian military authorities for the perpetration of crimes against humanity against the Timorese civilian population. Rape or other forms of sexual violence were not, however, included in the Wiranto indictment.

One of the changes that DPGSC Frigaard did make, however, was to appoint a gender crimes investigation team in the SCU. This team took as its starting point the report on gender-based crimes that had been prepared by the NGO Fokuppers. There does not appear to have been a significant shift in prosecutorial priorities as a result of their work, for the end result was not a significant body of indictments for sexual violence. Only one of the sexual violence cases that were in fact brought to trial was representative of the more serious systematic crimes that had been widely perpetrated. That case focused originally upon three accused and then subsequently solely upon Jose Cardoso, whose activities had been limited to the sub-district of Lolotoe. In those cases where gender-based violence was actually indicted, it was usually as an adjunct to a murder prosecution where the investigation had coincidentally turned up evidence of rape or other crimes. Some of these instances led to further investigation of sexual violence, but in almost all such cases this investigation did not result in prosecution.[74]

[73] Wiranto was commander in-chief of the TNI during the 1999 violence.

[74] In total the SCU issued eight indictments (out of 95) involving gender-based crimes. Six of these indictments charged rape as crimes against humanity but only one case went to trial. This case, however, was actually relatively minor in terms of the number of victims, the nature, severity, and duration of the violence, *etc*. Other forms of sexual violence apart from rape were never indicted by the SCU despite numerous cases

As noted above, the problem was not a lack of evidence. The investigations that were undertaken, for example, in connection with the murder prosecutions for the Suai Church Massacre (one of the 10 priority cases) unearthed very strong and credible testimony from numerous victims (discussed below). Further, several of these key witnesses had indicated to investigators that they were willing to testify in court as to their experience as victims of sexual violence. If the evidence was there, why then did the SCU not pursue this as a prosecutorial priority?

The examination of the SCU investigative files undertaken by our research team for the two CTF Expert Advisor's reports indicates that gender-based violence seems to have been consistently overlooked in many SCU investigations until the end of the period of investigations in 2004.[75] This section began, for example, with a memorandum from an SCU Prosecutor stating that rape is not relevant to the investigation and should not be 'called priority offenses at all'.

Our research also revealed that the SCU failed to include charges of sexual violence in several other cases where very substantial and weighty evidence of horrific crimes was already in the case file. Some of these cases seem to reveal a lack of understanding of gender-based crimes on the part of investigators prosecutors. For example, in one case the prosecution seems to have been reluctant to proceed because the perpetrator claimed that the victim was a prostitute. The investigator seemed to find persuasive that this claim by the suspect might be supported by the fact that when the alleged perpetrator, an armed militia leader, left the home of the 12-year old child he had just raped in the presence of her mother, he threw a 20,000 Rp. (approximately 2 U.S. Dollars) note on the ground. He returned regularly to her home to rape her again.[76] There was absolutely no other support in the case file for his allegation that she was a prostitute,

that included evidence of abduction, enslavement or forced marriage targeted against women either because of their own political activities or the political affiliations of men to whom they were related.

75 David Cohen, Leigh-Ashley Lipscomb and Aviva Nababan, "Seeking Truth and Responsibility: Report of the Exert Advisor to the CTF", 2008; and "Seeking Truth and Responsibility Part II: Addendum to the Report of the Expert Advisor to the CTF", 2008.

76 That there are other more obvious explanations for his behavior is indicated by the testimony of Witness AA in the Suai investigations (see Appendix 1 below) where there is absolutely no question about the fact that it was rape that occurred: "On 9 September she was raped by a militia who took her to a room where a policeman stood outside the door during the rape. After he raped her he threw 10,000Rp at her".

which she and her family steadfastly denied. The most striking thing, however, is that the investigators and prosecution appear not to have found it relevant that at the time of the alleged sexual violence the victim was 12 years old and, hence, under the age of consent. The investigators went to the trouble of verifying the age of the victim and affirmed that she was in fact 12 years old at the time. The alleged perpetrator, who had admitted having sexual relations with her at her home, was released based on a "lack of evidence". A telling fact in the case file is a note by the investigator that if they were going to proceed with the case they should inquire into local customs about sexual relations with children of this age.

As noted above, indictments were issued by the SCU for rape as crimes against humanity, involving four instances of systematic attacks resulting in large number of victims: multiple women raped from Suai,[77] multiple women raped in Cailaco,[78] multiple women raped from Lolotoe,[79] and multiple women raped in Atabae.[80] Other indictments involve individual cases of rape followed by murder. All of these cases indicate that women were targeted for sexual violence precisely because of their pro-independence affiliations. The sexual violence was thus not random, but rather a weapon directed at political intimidation and repression.[81]

The problem, however, was that the accused in nearly all of these indictments, both Indonesian military personnel and Timorese militia leaders, had fled to Indonesia. For this reason, and because prosecutions were not pursued against perpetrators who were still in East Timor, only one case of rape as a crime against humanity was brought to trial, and there was only one additional conviction for a single act of rape under the Indonesian criminal code. While numerous investigations uncovered evidence of abduction, enslavement, and forced marriage, none of these crimes were investigated or prosecuted.

77 See Indictment, Case #9/2003.

78 See Indictment, Case #15/2003.

79 The *Lolotoe* cases were tried in three separate trials. See Indictments and Judgments for Case #'s: 4a/2001, 4b/2001, 4c/2001.

80 See Indictment, Case #8/2002.

81 The acts alleged in these indictments occurred across multiple districts (3 in these indictments) and within West Timor, and within multiple communities within these districts (3 different locations in Bobonaro and 2 in Covalima) and were perpetrated by different militia groups (Laksaur, Mahidi, Halilintar, DMP, KMP) and by members of the Indonesian armed forces.

To convey an idea of the kind of evidence that was available and that did not lead to prosecution of the perpetrators, we may take the investigations surrounding the Suai Church massacre. In the aftermath of the defeat in the referendum in which 78% of those voting elected for independence from Indonesia, the campaign of terror against the Timorese population, particularly in areas associated with the independence movement, escalated in order to drive communities into exile in Indonesian West Timor. Some 250-350,000 persons, or a quarter to a third of the population were displaced in this manner. Burning of villages, physical violence, and rape were among the weapons used to promote this displacement. In Suai, more than 200 individuals from the surrounding area sought refuge in the church. The church was attacked by Timorese militias with the assistance, acquiescence, and in the presence of Indonesian military officers and personnel. At least 23 victims were killed, and the survivors of the attack were taken into detention as pro-independence supporters.

The SCU investigation into the murders that took place at the Suai Church revealed that the women survivors were systematically separated from the male population, held in several detention centers in Suai, and the systematically and repeatedly raped while in the custody of Indonesian police, military, and civilian officials. The same was true for women who were detained in the surrounding area when they were fleeing, or who were captured in their villages. The evidence also made clear that these women were targeted as either themselves being supporters of independence or being related to men who supported independence. This did lead to some further investigation of the sexual violence, but the evidence from those investigations is contained in investigative files that never led to prosecution. Reading through this evidence, one can only wonder why at least some of the cases, involving perpetrators that had been clearly identified, did not lead to indictment and, at least in some cases, to trial.

Many of the women who were taken to detention centers from the Suai church stated that they saw the Regent (Bupati), Herman Sedyono, at the site where they were separated from the men. Some testified that they heard him order that they be taken to the military HQ (Kodim). Others were taken to a school building and a camp at Betun where other women had already been detained after being taken during sweeping operations. After being held in these centers, and in many cases repeatedly raped there, they were forcibly taken to West Timor. Many of them also reported a continuation of sexual violence in West Timor, including rape and forced marriage.

Extracts from the vivid testimony of the many Suai victims of sexual violence interviewed by investigators are provided below in Appendix 1. We may summarize that testimony by indicating the systematic manner in which the victims were typically raped. They were held in groups in rooms in the various detentions centers. At night militia would come and choose women from the groups. They would take them into adjacent rooms and rape them, sometimes repeatedly. Armed Indonesian police or other militia typically stood guard outside the door of the room where the rape occurred. The entire facility was, of course, guarded by armed police, militia, or military. These occurrences were repeated night after night until the women were forcibly transported to detention camps in West Timor. In some cases militia claimed one of the detained women to be his "wife" in West Timor. The context and the explicit testimony of the victims make clear that this sexual violence was retaliation for the perceived political affiliations of the women.

Such violence did not only occur at Suai, but because it was more intensively investigated there, we can form a clearer picture of what occurred there than in other parts of East Timor. Sexual violence in other places took the form of sexual enslavement, where women linked to the independence movement were brought to militia camps and held there as domestic and sexual slaves. Sometimes they were claimed by an individual; sometimes they were raped by numerous individuals. They were also forcibly taken to militia "parties" where they were expected to dance and to provide sex for the militia members. The full scale of these many forms of sexual violence in East Timor may never be known because of the lack of a systematic investigation of this pattern of conduct across the principal places of conflict. While 'CAVR' did compile witness testimony about sexual violence, it was also not produced by a systematic investigation or subjected to the scrutiny involved in a judicial process. Because the current government of Timor Leste has no interest in pursuing prosecutions, perpetrators, including those living in Timor Leste, continue to enjoy impunity and the truth of what happened to the many victims of sexual violence in East Timor has never been established.[82]

[82] The most comprehensive compilation and examination of the evidence regarding sexual violence is that contained in the CTF Report, *Per Memoriam ad Spem*, and in

Appendix 1: Evidence from Suai on Sexual Violence

One woman (AA) described her experience of being raped during detention. She stated that she was raped by both militia and police. She was in the church at Suai during the attack. Afterwards she was brought to the school detention center SMP2. While detained there she said the militias would come at night and pull the blankets off the women. If they liked them they would take them with them. On 9 September she was raped by a militia who took her to a room where a policeman stood outside the door during the rape. After he raped her he threw 10,000 Rp. at her. On 12 September, she and the other women were taken to the Kodim and told that they would be taken to West Timor. At the Kodim, a militaman gave her to a policeman who took her to his house and raped her. His rifle was next to them while he raped her. He gave her 10,000 Rp. afterwards. She was taken to West Timor on September 15. AA testified that, "Militia came to us in the middle of the night and withdrew the blankets from our faces and looked at us. If they liked a woman they just pulled her away into another room […] I told the policeman that I was three months pregnant. He didn't care […] we were taken at the same time and raped in different rooms".

Another victim (BB) explicitly describes the political context:

> Militia in Suai went from house to house and looked for people who were supporting CNRT and the independence of E. Timor. […] I was a pro-independence supporter. One of my tasks at that time was to explain to the villagers all about the elections. As I said everyone knew I was a pro-independence supporter and the niece of *CNRT leader* [redacted] […]
>
> The militia who caught me then forced me to go to the Indonesian Military station in Suai town called Kodim. *The perpetrator* [redacted] threatened me and my uncle actually the whole family all the time because we were pro-independence. […] He cut my t-shirt with the knife he pointed at my chest. My upper body was naked […] I tried all the time to kick. I actually thought he would kill me so I gave

the 2 reports of the CTF Expert Advisor referenced above. These reports review the evidence from the Indonesian investigation (KPP HAM), the Timorese Truth Commission (CAVR), the trials before the Special Panels for Serious Crimes, the *Wiranto* Case File, the investigative files of the SCU, and other sources.

> up. I also cried permanently after he raped me but he didn't care, he would just continue what he was doing. He threatened to kill me if I told anyone what he did.

Another victim (CC) describes her experience in the detention center and explains how the detention of the men as suspected independence supporters made the women vulnerable to assault:

> About midnight [redacted] and [redacted] came into my house and grabbed myself and [redacted] and took us outside. I struggled against [redacted] but could not make him let go of me. My father could not help me as he had been taken forcibly to the militia headquarters [...] a few hours earlier.

DD describes the entire process of how the TNI surrounded the church and after the attack forced forced people to go to the Kodim. She testified that after a few days many of the women were then forcibly removed to West Timor: "My daughter was kidnapped by the militia from Suai church. The militia took my daughter to W. Timor to become [redacted]'s wife".

EE describes the forced displacement and the accompanying sexual violence. She was not detained at the church, but captured by the militia in Suai under the command of [redacted]. After being forced into a camp in Betun she described how women were raped night after night by the militiamen, usually at the same time each night. It is also clear that she believed she was targeted for political affiliation: "The situation was very dangerous because of TNI and militia. Myself and also other men from Suai hid in the forest because we were known independence supporters and were afraid of getting killed".

The participation of TNI in these attacks was also described by many other witnesses. Some of them explained that they had fled to the church because of such attacks. Witness EE continued:

> [Redacted] and 4 other men arrived at our place (in the camp). [Redacted] and one other man were armed with rifles [...] I only recognized [redacted]. The others had black hoods over their heads I could see only their eyes. They came with a blue pickup truck. [Redacted] was wearing military trousers and a white shirt. The others wore TNI uniforms.

She then describes the rapes which she witnessed:

> [Redacted] tore [redacted]'s shirt apart so her upper body was naked […] she was lying on her back. He then raped her for a few minutes. [She] tried as much as she could to escape. When [redacted] pushed her to the ground she was able to get up and run away. The soldiers ran after her and caught her. The whole situation was very dangerous and [redacted] didn't have any chance to escape […] [Redacted] threatened all of us and told us he would kill us if we told anyone what happened to her later on.

Another witness (FF) describes how she was taken to a camp in Betun after the violence at the church in Suai. She too had fled to the church because of militia attacks against her community. During the course of these attacks, testified, she was raped by TNI and militia.The militia had burned all the houses in her village, including her own. Then a Laksaur militia member by the name of [redacted] and a uniformed TNI soldier forced her to go to a wooden area where she testified she was raped and assaulted. Another female by the name of [redacted] was there to witness this. On a previous occasion, members of the militia came to her house and accused her of being a pro-independence supporter and had given her the choice of sex or death: "We will bring you to Koramil not to meet the Koramil, but we want to rape you". She also describes how, once they reached the women's detention camp Betun, rapes occurred every night: "[…] each night the militia would come into the room and switched off the light and take a girl with them. This would happen usually around 8 pm […] We were guarded at all times by the militia".

The SCU conducted an extensive investigation of a few of the cases in the aftermath of Suai. Case SU-56-01-SC, for example, involved the alleged rape of 2 sisters (HH and JJ). They describe how they fled to the church after an attack on their house by militia and TNI (individuals named). Their house was targeted because of their pro-independence activities. Their mother (GG) described in great detail the arrest and detention of her husband and other men by TNI and militia. Her husband was taken away because of his pro-independence activities and when he was brought back several days later he had sustained very severe injuries from beatings and torture (his lower lip had been cut off). He was thereafter under house arrest. She did not witness the rapes of the 2 victims, HH and JJ. HH describes how she and her husband left their village because they were afraid of the Mahidi. They went to Suai and stayed in the house of GG. On 12 March, they fled to the Church because of the attack on the village by Laksaur militia. They were later asked to leave the church by the nuns and priest out of fear that the church would be attacked (confirmed by GG). They left and on April 14 they were attacked again by militia and TNI (individuals of both groups named) who were looking for HH's uncle. In the aftermath of this event she was repeatedly sexually assaulted, but claims that she was not raped. The investigator appears to believe that she might have been raped but is reluctant to say so. She had no information about the alleged rape of JJ because she says her sister did not talk about it.

JJ was also questioned by investigators and her statement was also taken. She testified that she was raped but said that she does not know if her sister was raped because although her sister was visibly very upset after being taken away and was afterwards crying at night, she did not want to talk about what had happened to her. JJ clearly identified and described the perpetrator and asked the SCU that he be arrested because everyone in her village knew that she was raped and it "[did] not look good" for her if he was allowed to go free. She identified him as [redacted] and stated that he was known to her in her village. He was a member of the Laksaur militia and he came to her family's house and said, "You are Fretilin people. We will kill you". He later came to her house at midnight with [redacted], who went with her sister. Their father could not protect them because he had been taken away by militia that evening. Her assailant threatened her with death, knocked her down, and raped her. She asked for protective measures if the case came to court.

The father of HH and JJ was also interviewed. He described the attack on their village by TNI and militia in which he was arrested. He named Laksaur militia members and said that several of them always wore TNI uniforms.[83] He was taken away in the attack after he and several other men were dragged out of their homes and beaten and struck with machetes. He was taken to the Kodim in a Hino military vehicle, where they were interrogated by TNI. They were asked if they were hiding Falantil members. After two priests came, they were released and then

83 See also the very detailed statement of Cipriano Da Silva Gusmao (Case number SA-38-99 SC, in 3300 WE. IM), Interview of 2 August 2004). He was a driver taking TNI officers and militia on one of the operations where they were rounding up people for forced deportation. He describes in detail who was involved, co-perpetration by TNI and militia, and violence that accompanied the operation. 5259WE. IM contains additional documentation and testimony about transfers and role of TNI.

taken to the hospital for treatment and then to the Suai church. He then returned home on April 14 and described the attack that then occurred, during which he was again severely beaten and tortured. The assailants, who were militia and TNI (and some belonged to both) wanted to know whether arms were hidden in the church. At this time, his daughters were sexually assaulted but not raped. He thinks they were not raped but only sexually assaulted because this is what they told him after the attack[84]

One witness testified that he thought the sexual violence was used to punish supporters of independence.[85] He stated that his wife, [redacted] was raped repeatedly by TNI and militia to punish him for his pro-independence political activities. As he had escaped, "she was an easy target".

Case SU-030-99-SC also involves the aftermath of the Suai church attack. The file consists of three witness statements. They indicate (as do other statements in other case files reviewed above) the way in which the women were separated from the men after the attack on the church and were taken to the Kodim. This particular case involve a victim, II, the daughter of KK, who was claimed as a "prize" by one of the militia members after the attack. Witness NN testifies in detail as to this as she was present. She explains how the victim was taken to the Kodim and how the perpetrator forcibly took her away, put a necklace around her neck, and stated that she was now his "wife". She was later taken to West Timor. At the time of the completion of the investigation in March 2005, the investigator states that she and her assailant are still in West Timor and that she is still being kept there against her will. Witness KK testifies in great detail about the events leading up to the attack, the attack itself, and the aftermath. She names various TNI and militia members who were involved, including the local TNI commander, Lt. X, whom she claimed took a leading role in the attack itself. Her 10-year old child was killed in the attack. She testified about how they were taken to the Kodim by TNI in Kijangs after the attack and how on the night of September 7 she saw several women being raped, including her daughter.[86] She named 2 of the

84 The details of the attack on the village were corroborated by other witnesses, who also named names of the assailants, including both TNI and militia (commanded by a TNI Lt.). This included details such as the Hino truck used to transport them from their village from their village to the Kodim, and how they were beaten on the way.

85 18 May 2001, Suai Case File 1706 WE. IM

86 The witness statement of MM has good information about dual membership in Laksaur militia and TNI but does not pertain to sexual violence. MM was detained and

perpetrators corroborating other testimony in other cases that identifies them as involved in rapes at the Kodim. One of them was a Laksaur commander. She stated that the rapes she saw were perpetrated by militia and that the TNI saw what was happening but did nothing. She stated that she complained to the TNI the next day and did not see rapes after that.[87]

Witness LL testified to the detention and forced transfer and to the sexual violence that occurred after they arrived in West Timor. She relates how she and her two young children left the church on September 5 because they were too afraid to stay there. Fleeing from Suai, they were detained by militia and taken to the high school in Suai. They were guarded there by Kontigen Lorosae and Laksaur. They were told that they were going to be taken to West Timor. She stated that she did not want to go to West Timor "but was forced to". In West Timor she was held with others in a warehouse. There she was raped by Laksaur militia (whom she named, and to one of whom she was related. She asked him how he could do this when she was related to his wife and he said that he was not going to tell his wife).

In the case of the rape of Witness SCA the connection of the violence to [political affiliation is particularly clear. She was a CNRT campaigner for independence. She took refuge in the church because militia were hunting for CNRT in Suai and she was afraid. She was taken to the Kodim after the attack and they were told that they would be taken to West Timor. They were guarded by militia and their names were checked every morning at 8am. She was then taken to an orphanage building in Suai, guarded by four TNI with rifles. She was raped there by a militia member and told that she would be killed if she resisted. She was then brought to West Timor. Her assailant attempted again but she was with her family and successfully resisted.

Witness SCB was also taken along with the others to West Timor and was raped there in the camp. After the men of her village in Suai had fled to the mountains, Laksaur militia rounded up the women and took them to West Timor. SCC was her cousin and was beaten when she was apprehended by Laksaur militia. She was forcibly taken to a camp in Be-

repeatedly beaten and severely tortured. Among others, she was tortured by female militia members.

87 See also Interview of 2 June 2000, Suai File 1706 WE IM.

tun, along with her cousin, SCB. At the warehouse in Betun a militia came and asked for SCB. He raped her in the presence of SCC.

SCD reported that her village was attacked by Laksaur militia in April 1999 and they burned many houses. She fled to the jungle. In June she sought refuge in the Suai church. On 1 September she left the church to go to her sister's place but militia told her to go back because people who went to the jungle "would be killed". After the attack on September 6, she was forcibly rounded up with the other women and take to the Kodim. She was beaten that night and saw how militia took girls out of the sleeping quarters at night. She was transported to West Timor and was raped in the refugee camp there by militia members. On the occasion she was raped she saw another woman being raped at the same time close by.

SCH was also at the Suai church and was taken to the Kodim after the attack. At the Kodim she was informed that her daughter had been forced to become the "wife" of a militia leader. She did not see rapes but she heard the militia guards shouting that they should all be raped because they were pro-independence. They were brought against their will to Betun on 14 September in a truck with two armed TNI guards. At Betun they were told that if they tried to go back they would be killed. She saw her daughter there and all her daughter could do was cry.

SCJ said that she went to West Timor voluntarily. On 6 September she was in warehouse in Betun. On 16 September three armed militia came to the warehouse and one approached her. She said she was married and had a baby. He later raped her.

Witness SCP testified to the cooperation of TNI and militia. Her testimony was very specific and identified both militia and TNI as having raped her. Eight militia came to the house of SCP. Two of them wore TNI uniforms and were carrying rifles. [redacted] and [redacted] told her she had to go to the school building in Zumalai Villa. She went there with [redacted], who was also ordered to go there. At the school there were many TNI members, from KORAMIL who threatened them. There were seven women altogether, and the TNI told the women to sleep in the classrooms. TNI told them they would have to pay Rp. 400,000 to be taken to West Timor. The night before they left, SCP and [redacted] were told to sleep in separate rooms from the others. Militia and TNI raped them that night.

SCV fled to the forest because of threats from Laksaur Militia. She was in the Suai Church on September 6, 1999 and was taken to KODIM

Suai. On 15 September 1999 she was taken from Kodim to Atambua by truck. She was taken to an elementary school in Nualaran where she stayed for 2 months. While there, on September 24, 1999, she was raped by [redacted] who took her to Wemasa Village and raped her there. Her friend [redacted- Witness SCD] was raped by [redacted], and she saw this incident herself.

SCW's house had been burned by militia so she took refuge in the church at Suai. She tried to flee during the attack but was caught and was beaten by a militia member. Another militia interrupted and said "Don't kill her because the Chief of District ordered women to be taken to Kodim". On the way to the Kodim they passed Herman Sedyono and the militia said to him, "We took these from the church" and Herman said "take them to the Kodim". At the Kodim all were women. They were made to cook at the Kodim. On September 14 they were taken to West Timor by TNI. The TNI just left them on the road where there were many militia. On the night of 15 or 16 September, the militias came to them and said "If you don't give us a girl, tonight we will kill you all". There were three militias. Then they took SCW in a car. They stopped the car on the road, and she was dragged to the jungle and was raped by one, then brought to a house and then was raped by another [redacted] who forcibly gave her his necklace, thereby claiming her as his "wife". The next morning she got someone to take her to POLSEK by motorbike, so she was able to escape from [redacted], who was pursuing her. She was protected by the police and the police arranged for her to be brought back to West Timor by UNHCR on October 13, 1999.

Witness statements in the Wiranto case file also deal with the perpetration of sexual violence in Suai connected to the terrorization of the civilian population and the subsequent forced transfers. Witness 90 testified that: "On 9 September 1999 I saw Alberto Amaral, a Laksaur militia, attempt to rape my sister, Alita Marcal on the school grounds of SMP2 school. He threw her down and held a large knife to her side and didn't stab her but pricked her with the point to make her submit to him. I could see them but I was so scared I was afraid to do anything. He would have raped her but an Indonesian policeman from Aceh, Sumatra stopped him. He made Alberto stop and Alberto left. I was afraid to help because Alberto was armed with a long knife and I had no weapons of any kind". She also testified that militia members [whom she then names] shouted at them, "Leave or die!". This group forcing people to leave "had been involved in murder, rape, burning of houses and every form of intimidation used by the militia to force us to leave our homes and friends in East Timor".[88]

SCX was living in Nanu village with her father and step mother during the day and during the night she stayed with an old woman in the village who asked for her company. She was raped the first time at the old woman's place, in the middle of the night by [redacted] who was in Laksaur milita but, she said, always wore a TNI uniform. He was a DANTON at Fohorem. He threatened to kill her and he raped her, which she reported to her father and stepmother. She was raped repeatedly until he went back to West Timor in August 1999. On February 6, her village was forced to go to West Timor by Militias and TNI soldiers. 33 families all together were brought to Laktutus village where they were guarded by militias and TNI soldiers. While in West Timor, she realized she was pregnant. Her baby was taken from her by [redacted]. As she was living with Laksaur militia, she could not get the baby back.

SCY was taken from Suai and on 7 September brought to Betun. She testified that she and the other women she was with wound up in the government refugee center where militias also lived. They were not allowed to leave the camp. In the camp she was raped by four men on different occasions. The first was in January or February of 2000 by a TNI named [redacted] who came to her room and said "your husband is Anti Integration so we can use you freely". She was raped over the next months by three other men, one of whom wore a TNI uniform and another who was Laksuar commander [redacted]. She returned to East Timor in January 2001. Physical force and threats were used against her on all these occasions. She testified, "They just came one by one. It was like a game for them. They were playing with me like with a ball [...] They just came and took me. I did not have any choice".

The experiences of women detained after Suai were different. Not all were raped, though all were aware of the imminent threat of sexual violence. One woman testified that the group of women she was with at the KODIM were not raped, despite being threatened with rape and verbally abused by Laksaur militia commander [redacted] and in constant fear of rape by the militias.[89] She felt that the East Timorese TNI guarding them protected them from the militia who wanted to rape them. The rest

[88] Wiranto Case File P. 160109

[89] Interview of 12 April 2000.

of her story is consistent with that of others: she sought refuge at the church, was taken to KODIM by force, held there against her will, guarded to prevent escape, and taken against her will to West Timor. She testified as to the political context and her fear of reprisals because she and other women were affiliated with CNRT. Her testimony also confirms the close cooperation of militia and TNI personnel, including Indonesian TNI officers, in all of these events connected to the attack on the church and the detention and deportation of the women.

Some cases of rape by Laksaur militia were not connected to the forcible transfer. Witness 70, for example, described her repeated rape by a Laksaur militia member. She testified that:

> I was an independence supporter. [...] I was not a Clandestine member. I didn't cook or physically support Independence. Everyone in the village knew that I was an Independence supporter […] When I got raped the first time by Marcel Moruk I was staying already with the old lady in the house…. I saw him the first time when he came to rape me. I did not know his name, neither where he was from. [… He said], if you don't open this door I will kill you with this machete. I then got up and opened the door. Certainly I was scared to do so but I was more scared not to follow the order. A man was standing in front of the door. He wore a black shirt with "LAKSAUR" written on it. Further I could see the Indonesian flag at the front and at the back of his shirt. At the front of his shirt I read the name Marcel Moruk. He wore military trousers. He held a machete in his hand, but he didn't carry a gun. The man immediately entered. He then grabbed my arm and said to me, "If you do not want me I will kill you." I knew immediately what he wanted, it was to rape me. He still held the machete in his hand. […] From then on he came 2 or 3 times in a week for many months. Each time he raped me. He never raped me more than one time a night. He came, raped me and left […] My parents knew that he raped me all the time but they were too scared to do anything. [...] The last time he raped me was on the 17th of August 1999 […]. I was so happy that he didn't come back. I never wanted to have sexual intercourse with him. He raped me all the time. He threatened me that he would kill

> me if I did not take him. I didn't have a choice . I was very scared of him."[90]

SCU investigators interviewed many other women who had been at the center to corroborate the testimony they received. Another witness, testified that she was among the group taken to a school building (SMP2) and that there she saw one [redacted] of the group of women taken out (a woman from Zumalai whom she knew) by a militia member.[91] When the woman was brought back she told the witness that she had been raped. She also testified that they were ordered to go to the KODIM by the Bupati. (Interview of 16 June 2001, same case file) Despite the scope of this investigation, rape was clearly not a priority of some of the investigators, who were apparently only interested in the murders at the church. One witness testifies at the end of her story that she was raped in Betun by a militia but there are no details of any kind because apparently she was not asked to explain any of the circumstances. The testimony is so general and vague that it is virtually useless, because the investigator was not interested in this part of her story. Other times the corroborative testimony is quite useful because the investigators focused their questioning on this issue. For example, the testimony of RR confirms that about 50 women taken from the church were identified as pro-independence and were held at the school for 8 nights and then taken to West Timor.[92] In the continuation of her interview on June 6, she identifies two women (HH and JJ) that she saw being taken away to be raped at the school by militia. She identified the two men who took them away). She did not see them being raped and they did not tell her. But by their demeanor and the way they were crying and pale when they were brought back, she was certain they had been raped. Another witness was also able to corroborate these events.[93] She testified that the group of women of which she was a part, were forcibly detained, locked in a room, and then taken to West Timor. She was not raped but was beaten (she was about 38 at the time of the attack). She said that HH and JJ were "sexually abused" and that they told her about what had happened to them.

90 Wiranto Case File P. 160010 – 160015, Statement of 2/25/2001.

91 Suai File 1706 WE. IM

92 Interview of 5 June 2001 Suai Case File 1814 WE. IM.

93 Interview of 19 September 2001, Suai File 1824 WE. IM

3

Addressing the Challenges to Prosecution of Sexual Violence Crimes before International Tribunals and Courts

Patricia Wildermuth and Petra Kneuer*

3.1. Introduction

> One hundred years ago, when the world first commemorated International Women's Day, gender equality and women's empowerment were largely radical ideas. On this centenary [commemorated on 8 March 2011], we celebrate the significant progress that has been achieved through determined advocacy, practical action and enlightened policy making.
>
> Yet, in too many countries and societies, women remain second-class citizens. [...] And in many conflict zones, sexual violence is deliberately and systematically used to intimidate women and whole communities.
>
> My UNiTE to End Violence Against Women campaign, along with its Network of Men Leaders, is working to end impunity and change mindsets.
>
> Secretary General to the United Nations, Ban Ki-moon, "Secretary-General's Message on Women's Day, 8 March 2011"[1]

Over the past century, the role of women in society has gradually emerged and gained present international prominence alongside the growing

* **Patricia Wildermuth** is a Judicial Affairs Officer with the United Nations Assistance Mission in Afghanistan. **Petra Kneuer** is a Senior Trial Lawyer at the Office of the Prosecutor, International Criminal Court. The authors would like to thank Jamila Zoubir-Afifi, Eric Iverson, and Dana Bucy for their valuable comments, advice, and assistance. The views expressed in this chapter are those of the authors alone and do not necessarily reflect the views of the Office of the Prosecutor, International Criminal Court, or the US Department of State.

1 United Nations, "Message of the UN Secretary-General Ban Ki-moon", available at http://www.unwomen.org/news-events/international-womens-day/messages/#sg, last accessed on 9 May 2011.

recognition that the establishment and protection of women's basic rights are critical if women are to assume a fully participatory role in society and governance.[2] However, in too many countries, this is not yet a reality.[3] Moreover, in many conflict zones women are sexually brutalized in cultures of impunity. Sexual violence[4] employed as a weapon in armed conflict has proven to be extremely effective in breaking the enemy's morale.[5] In the context of post-conflict recovery, widespread and systematic sexual violence undermines social cohesiveness and sustained peace.[6] Further, the failure of a State to bring perpetrators of sexual violence to justice materially undermines the rule of law and the foundations of effective governance.[7]

---

2 United Nations Commission on Human Rights Resolution 1994/45 Question of Integrating the Rights of Women into the Human Rights Mechanisms of the United Nations and the Elimination of Violence Against Women, 4 March 1994, available at http://www.unhchr.ch/Huridocda/Huridoca.nsf/TestFrame/401503e99f333b03802567 360041e65c?Opendocument, last accessed on 9 April 2011 (appointing the Special Rapporteur on violence against women, including its causes and consequences, in view of the alarming growth in the number of cases of violence against women throughout the world); Beijing Declaration and Platform for Action, The Fourth World Conference on Women, U.N Doc. A/CONF.177/20 and U.N. Doc. A/CONF.177/20/Add., 15 September 1995, available at http://www.un.org/womenwa tch/daw/beijing/pdf/BDPfA%20E.pdf, last accessed on 9 May 2011 ('Beijing Platform').

3 Mary Deutsch Schneider, "About Women, War and Darfur: The Continuing Quest for Gender Violence Justice", in *North Dakota Law Review*, 2007, vol. 83, no. 3, pp. 915, 917–919 (noting that instances of sexual violence in armed conflict have occurred in over thirty-seven countries and regions worldwide).

4 This Chapter employs the term 'sexual violence' to refer to and emphasize the sexual element of crimes committed against a victim based on gender. This term is to be distinguished from gender based violence, which may or may not constitute a criminal act or be of a sexual nature. Anne-Marie de Brouwer, *Supranational Criminal Prosecution of Sexual Violence: The ICC and the Practice of the ICTY and ICTR*, Intersentia, 2005, p. 27.

5 Schneider, 2007, pp. 921–924, see *supra* note 3 (surveying the historical uses of gender-based violence).

6 See, *e.g.*, Elize Delport, "Social Cohesion and Gender: Raising Issues of Human Rights and Policy Frameworks Relevant to Women in Africa", available at http:// www.e-cofi.net/fichero.php?id=188&zona=1, last accessed on 9 May 2011 (stating that social justice is a required component of social cohesion and effective governance).

7 Anne-Marie Goetz and Rob Jenkins, "Sexual Violence as a War Tactic - Security Council Resolution 1888: Next Steps", *UN Chronicle*, 9 April 2010, available at

One of the strongest methods to support, promote and protect women's rights is the international community's commitment to accountability; a commitment to bring to justice those who violate and commit gender atrocities against women. The United Nations ('UN') and the world's States have exhibited a commitment to ending impunity for sexual violence in conflict as evidenced by the above-mentioned words of the Secretary General and the passage of several UN Security Council Resolutions addressing women in conflict and establishing criminal forums to hold offenders accountable for their actions.[8]

The road to accountability for sexual atrocities is lined with challenges, some real and some illusory. The practical problems associated with bringing sexual crime perpetrators to justice are often the very same challenges that are presented in cases in which non-gender violations are charged: investigations and evidence collections hampered by location and situation; a lack of detailed memory of potential witnesses; security concerns and considerations; insufficient numbers of trained court staff and professionals; reluctant witnesses; and insufficient funding.[9] However, several of these challenges are exacerbated while other challenges emerge based on the very nature of these sexual offenses.

This chapter identifies and explores the practical challenges of bringing sexual offense perpetrators to justice. Our aim as international prosecutors is to reaffirm the significance of prosecuting sexual offense

---

http://www.un.org:80/wcm/content/site/chronicle/home/archive/issues2010/empoweringwomen/sexualviolencewartacticscr1888, last accessed on 9 May 2011.

8 United Nations Security Council Resolution 1820, 19 June 2008, U.N. Doc. S/RES/1820 ("S/RES/1820"); United Nations Security Council Resolution 1888, 30 September 2009, U.N. Doc. S/RES/1888 ("S/RES/1888); see also International Women's Tribune Center, "United Nations Security Council Resolution 1820: A Preliminary Assessment of the Challenges and Opportunities", 2009, available at http://www.iwtc.org/1820blog/1820_paper.pdf, last accessed on 9 May 2011.

9 See generally Carla Del Ponte, "Investigation and Prosecution of Large-Scale Crimes at the International Level", in *Journal of International Criminal Justice*, 2006, vol. 4, no. 3, p. 539; Okechukwu Oko, "The Challenges of International Criminal Prosecutions in Africa", in *Fordham International Law Journal*, 2008, vol. 31, no. 2, p. 343; Lt. Colonel Robert T. Mounts, Douglas W. Cassel, Jr., and Jeffrey L. Bleich, "Panel II: War Crimes and Other Human Rights Abuses in the Former Yugoslavia", in *Whittier Law Review*, 1995, vol. 16, no. 2, p. 387; Stephanie Bibas and William W. Burke-White, "International Idealism Meets Domestic-Criminal-Procedure Realism", in *Duke Law Journal*, 2010, vol. 59, no. 4, p. 637.

cases and to demonstrate that these practical challenges are not insurmountable.

3.2. International Focus on Sexual Violence Offenses

The legal concept of accountability for sexual violence based on criminal acts of an international character is not new. Although the International Military Tribunal ('IMT') Charter did not contain any explicit reference to rape or other sexual offenses,[10] Control Council Law No. 10 included rape as a crime against humanity[11] and, notwithstanding that rape was not charged in the indictments, several convictions were returned that included sexual offenses as the factual basis for inhumane acts as crimes against humanity.[12] In addition, although the Charter for the International Military

---

10 Charter of the International Military Tribunal, 8 August 1945, available at http://www.icls.de/dokumente/imt_statute.pdf, last accessed on 9 May 2011 (not including sexual offenses); see also Jocelyn Campanaro, "Women, War, and International Law: The Historical Treatment of Gender Based War Crimes", in *Georgetown Law Journal*, 2001, vol. 89, no. 8, pp. 2557, 2561 (reiterating that neither "rape" nor "sexual assaults" were mentioned in the IMT Charter, despite the numerous instances of rape and sexual violence documented in the transcripts); but see Eileen Meier, "Prosecuting Sexual Violence Crimes During War and Conflict: New Possibilities for Progress", in *International Legal Theory*, 2004, vol. 10, pp. 83, 90.

M. Cherif Bassiouni remarks that rape was implicitly included in both the Nuremberg and Tokyo Charters as a crime against humanity by being subsumed within the words "or other inhumane acts", and that rape and sexual violence "clearly constitute 'inhumane acts.'". He further asserts that rape was also implicitly included as a war crime by being encompassed by the term "ill treatment". Cherif Bassiouni, *Crimes against Humanity in International Criminal Law*, Kluwer Law, The Hague, 1999 (second edition), pp. 164, 344, 348.

11 Control Council Law No. 10, Punishment of Persons Guilty of War Crimes, Crimes Against Peace and Against Humanity, 20 December 1945, Official Gazette Control Council for Germany, 1946, vol. 3, pp. 50–55 ("Control Council Law No. 10").

12 See Control Council Law No. 10, Article II(1)(c), see *supra* note 11 (listing rape committed against the civilian population as a crime against humanity); see also Kelly D. Askin, "Prosecuting Wartime Rape and Other Gender-Related Crimes Under International Law: Extraordinary Advances, Enduring Obstacles", in *Berkeley Journal of International Law*, 2003, vol. 21, no. 2, pp. 288, 301 n. 67; Patricia Viseur Sellers, "Rape", in Dina L. Shelton (ed.), *Genocide and Crimes Against Humanity, Vol. 2*, Gale Cengage, 2005, available at http://www.enotes.com/genocide-encyclopedia/rape, last accessed on 9 May 2011.

For documentation of sexual violence in the transcripts of cases under Control Council Law No. 10, see generally *Trials of War Criminals Before the Nuremburg Military Tribunals Under Control Council Law No. 10*, Nuremburg, October 1946 –

Tribunal for the Far East ('IMTFE') did not include sexual offenses,[13] rape was included in several indictments as war crimes and prosecuted.[14]

The lack of numerous charges for sexual offenses, particularly in the Far East where widespread and systematic sexual offenses occurred, is possibly explained on the basis of the speed in which these cases were tried, the reliance on documentary evidence, and the focus on "traditional" war crimes. It is helpful to recall that the Allied Powers initially were not in agreement regarding the mechanism to bring alleged perpetrators to justice and the establishment of a criminal tribunal was not a foregone conclusion.[15] The record also suggests that the prosecutions at Nuremberg and the IMFTE for rape and sexual offenses were *ad hoc* because these offenses were not institutionalized by statute or charter, thus contributing to the failure to fully address the range and scope of sexual atrocities that had been committed.[16]

Since Nuremburg, the international community has become increasingly focused on women's rights and gender based violence against wom-

April 1949, U.S. G.P.O., Washington, 1949-53, vol. 2 U.S. v. Brandt (citing instances of castration and forced sterilization); vol. 4–5, U.S. v. Greifelt (recounting instances of genocide, gender and ethnic persecutions, reproductive crimes and forced abortion); and vol. 5, U.S. v. Pohl (noting the use of concentration camp brothels and forced abortion). For instances of sexual violence in the transcripts of the IMT, see *Trial of The Major War Criminals Before the International Military Tribunal*, vol. 6, pp. 211–214 (Forty-Fourth Day, Monday, 28 January 1946) and pp. 404–407 (Forty-Seventh Day, 31 January 1946, discussing rape and looting).

13 International Military Tribunal for the Far East Charter, 19 January 1946, available at http://www.jus.uio.no/english/services/library/treaties/04/4-06/military-tribunal-far-east.xml, last accessed on 10 May 2011.

14 R. Pritchard and S. Zaide (eds.), *The Tokyo War Crimes Trial: The Complete Transcripts of the Proceedings of the International Military Tribunal for the Far East*, 1981, pp. 31, 111–117 (reproducing documents of the Tokyo Trials).

15 See Devin Owen Pendas, *The Frankfurt Auschwitz Trial, 1963–1965*, Cambridge University Press, Cambridge, 2006, p. 8 ("[T]here remained considerable disagreement among the Allied leaders for the remainder of the war as to how exactly such war criminals should be handled, whether through criminal trials or via summary executions" that is, executions without trial.).

16 According to Kelly D. Askin, "whether it was out of shyness, prudishness, reserve, ignorance, revulsion, confusion, or intentional omission, the lack of both public documentation and official prosecution gave impetus to the notion that sexual assaults were less important crimes". Kelly D. Askin, *War Crimes against Women: Prosecution in International War Crimes Tribunals*, Martinus Nijhoff Publishers, The Hague, 1997, p. 97.

en. This focus is evidenced by a growing number of treaties and United Nation Security Council Resolutions urging states to publicly recognize and implement their obligations towards women and women's rights, and demanding that states hold accountable those who violate women and children in conflict.[17] Further, the UN established several situation-specific international criminal forums[18] and Member States joined together to sign the Rome Treaty in June 2002, establishing the permanent International Criminal Court ('ICC').[19] As a result of these forums, an institutionalized international criminal law framework has been established within which numerous sexual offenses are set forth specifically, procedural and substantive victim/witness protections are provided, and a body of applicable case law has been and continues to be developed.

3.2.1. International Tribunals and Sexual Violence Offenses

Accountability for sexual offenses against women committed during conflict is inextricably linked to a means to enforce such accountability. Most notably, the ICC is the only standing permanent international criminal court with jurisdiction over gender based atrocities committed after the

[17] See, *e.g.*, United Nations Security Council Resolution 1325, 31 October 2000, U.N. Doc. S/RES/1325 ("S/RES/1325"); S/RES/1820, see *supra* note 8; S/RES/1888, see *supra* note 8; United Nations Security Council Resolution 1889, 5 October 2009, S/RES/1889 ("S/RES/1889"); International Covenant on Civil and Political Rights, 16 December 1966, available at http://www2.ohchr.org/english/law/ccpr.htm, last accessed on 10 May 2011 ("ICCPR"); Convention on the Elimination of All Forms of Discrimination Against Women, 18 December 1979, available at http://www.un.org/womenwatch/daw/cedaw/text/econvention.htm, last accessed on 10 May 2011 ("CEDAW").

[18] United Nations Security Council Resolution 808, 22 February 1993, U.N. Doc. S/RES/808 ("S/RES/808") (establishing the International Criminal Tribunal for the Former Yugoslavia); United Nations Security Council Resolution 955, 8 November 1994, U.N. Doc. S/RES/955 ("S/RES/955) (establishing the International Criminal Tribunal for Rwanda); United Nations Security Council Resolution 1315, 14 August 2000, U.N. Doc. S/RES/1315 ("S/RES/1315") (establishing the Special Court for Sierra Leone); United Nations General Assembly Resolution 228B, 22 May 2003, U.N. Doc. A/RES/57/228B (establishing the Extraordinary Chambers in the Cambodia Courts); United Nations Security Council Resolution 1664, 29 March 2006, U.N. Doc S/RES/1664 (establishing the Special Tribunal for Lebanon).

[19] United Nations, Rome Statute of the International Criminal Court, 17 July 1989, U.N. Doc. A/CONF.183/9 ("Rome Statute").

entry into force of the Rome Statute.[20] Although some sexual offense specific law has evolved from the Special Court of Sierra Leone ('SCSL')[21] and other international courts, the majority of case law that informs the ICC on sexual crimes was developed by the largest and oldest situation specific tribunals, the International Criminal Tribunal for the Former Yugoslavia ('ICTY')[22] and the International Criminal Tribunal for Rwanda ('ICTR').[23] Although faulted for a failure to fully investigate and prosecute those who allegedly committed sexual offenses, the ICTY and ICTR have developed an enormous wealth of exceptional substantive and procedural jurisprudence in the area of international sexual offenses.

The establishment of international tribunals was based, in part, on explicitly expressed concerns about the treatment of women and the need to prosecute those responsible for serious violations of international humanitarian law, including sexual offenses.[24] The UN Security Council described the rapes in the former Yugoslavia as "massive, organized and systematic".[25] In tasking the ICTY with responsibility for prosecuting "serious violations" while expressing "grave concern" over the "treatment of Muslim women in the former Yugoslavia", the UN characterized sexual offenses as serious violations in their own right.[26] The UN Security Council in a similar fashion expressed concerns about sexual offenses in establishing the ICTR and other international criminal forums.

In addition to establishing international criminal forums, the international community joined together to specifically focus on women's rights and the protection of women in conflict. The UN Member States'

---

20 Rome Statute, Article 11, see *supra* note 19 (establishing *jurisdiction ratione temporis* only with respect to crimes committed after the entry into force of the Rome Treaty, 1 July 2002).

21 S/RES/1315, see *supra* note 18.

22 S/RES/808, see *supra* note 18

23 S/RES/955, see *supra* note 18.

24 See S/RES/808, see *supra* note 18 (noting "grave concern" over the "treatment of Muslim women in the former Yugoslavia"); S/RES/955, see *supra*, note 18; see also ICTY, *Prosecutor v. Furundžija*, Judgement, 21 July 2000, IT-95-17/1-A, para. 201 ("*Furundžija* Appeal Judgment") (stating "the general question of bringing justice to the perpetrators of crimes [such as rape] was one of the reasons that the Security Council established the Tribunal").

25 United Nations Security Council Resolution 798, 18 December 1992, U.N. Doc. S/RES/798 ("S/RES/798").

26 *Ibid.*

commitment is evidenced by passage of the Declaration on the Elimination of Violence against Women[27] in 1993 followed by a series of UN Security Council Resolutions addressing women, peace, and security: 1325, 1820, 1888, 1889, and 1960.[28]

UN Security Council Resolution 1325, passed on 31 October 2000, focuses on women in conflict and

> [c]*alls on* all parties to armed conflict to take special measures to protect women and girls from gender-based violence, particularly rape and other forms of sexual abuse, and all other forms of violence in situations of armed conflict [... and] *Emphasizes* the responsibility of all States to put an end to impunity and to prosecute those responsible for genocide, crimes against humanity, and war crimes including those relating to sexual and other violence against women and girls [...].[29]

This Resolution also calls on all Member States to implement the requirements of the Resolution. The subsequent passage of Security Council Resolutions 820, 1325, 1889, and 1960 expressed renewed and ongoing commitments to ending acts of sexual violence against women in conflict and holding perpetrators accountable under international criminal law for "rape and other forms of sexual violence [... as] war crimes, crimes against humanity or a constitutive act with respect to genocide".[30]

---

[27] United Nations General Assembly, Declaration on the Elimination of Violence against Women, 20 December 1993, U.N. Doc. A/RES/48/104.

[28] See *supra* note 17; United Nations Security Council Resolution 1960, 16 December 2010, U.N. Doc. S/RES/1960; see also Beijing Platform, see *supra* note 2; United Nations Security Council Resolution 1612, 26 July 2005, U.N. Doc. S/RES/1612 (Children and Armed Conflict); ("S/RES/1612"); United Nations Security Council Resolution 1674, 28 April 2006, U.N. Doc. S/RES/1674 (Protection of Civilians in Armed Conflict) ("S/RES/1674").

[29] S/RES/1325, see *supra* note 17.

[30] S/RES/1820, see *supra* note 8 (on acts of sexual violence against civilians in armed conflicts). The Resolution also "*calls upon* Member States to comply with their obligations for prosecuting persons responsible for such acts, to ensure that all victims of sexual violence, particularly women and girls, have equal protection under the law and equal access to justice, and *stresses* the importance of ending impunity for such acts as part of a comprehensive approach to seeking sustainable peace, justice, truth, and national reconciliation.".

In September 2009, the U.N. passed S/RES 1888 to strengthen S/RES 1820, requesting the appointment of a Special Representative to coordinate all UN efforts within the framework of the inter-agency initiative, "United Nations Action Against

To date, the implementation of Security Council Resolution 1325 by Member States is less than encouraging, with fewer than twenty states establishing national action implementation plans.[31] Despite numerous calls by the UN Security Council for renewed focus on, prevention of, and accountability for sexual violence against women in conflict, the record of egregious sexual brutality and violations continues,[32] underscoring the need for effective use of mechanisms of accountability.

The ICC's jurisdiction covers many existing situations involving sexual offenses as genocide, crimes against humanity, and war crimes. Further, the Rome Statute and ICC Rules of Procedure and Evidence ('RPE') arguably are the most legally sophisticated to date in regard to sexual offenses.[33] The Rome Statute and RPE include many of the safe-

Sexual Violence in Conflict", and urging that a team of gender and other experts be employed and deployed to specific areas of concern within two years. One month later, S/RES 1889 was passed addressing the same topics and concerns as presented in S/RES 1820 and 1888, and providing for increased reporting by the UN Secretary-General to the Security Council, specifically "within 6 months, for consideration, a set of indicators for use at the global level to track implementation of S/RES 1325 (2000), which could serve as a common basis for reporting by relevant United Nations entities, other international and regional organizations, and Member States, on the implementation of S/RES 1325 (2000) in 2010 and beyond". One month after S/RES 1889, the UN passed S/RES 1960, again reiterating concerns and urging compliance.

31 See S/RES/1325, see *supra* note 17. As of 8 March 2011, only a handful of countries (approximately twenty) have developed action plans for implementation of S/RES/1325. Most notably, the United States and many European States have not fully developed such plans. See also U.N. Women Website, http://www.un-instraw.org, last accessed on 9 May 2011.

32 See "Rapes are reported in Eastern Congo", *The New York Times*, 25 February 2011, available at www.nytimes.com/2011/02/26/world/africa/26congo.html, last accessed on 9 May 2011 (noting that rapes continued in Eastern Congo despite trials and convictions for gang rapes of 30 July 2010).

33 Rome Statute, see *supra* note 19; International Criminal Court Rules of Evidence and Procedure, 9 September 2002, Official Records ICC-ASP/1/3 ("ICC RPE"); see also Fatou Bensouda, "Gender and Sexual Violence under the Rome Statute", in Emmanuel Decaux *et al.* (eds.), *From Human Rights to International Criminal Law: Studies in Honour of an African Jurist, the Late Judge Laïty Kama*, Martinus Nijhoff Publishers, Leiden, 2007, pp. 409–411 (remarking that for the first time, gender crimes have been classified as both crime against humanity and war crimes; the gravity of sexual violence in both international and internal armed conflicts has been acknowledged; and that the Rome Statute recognizes a spectrum of gender crimes in addition to rape).

guards found in the ICTR and ICTY Statutes and RPE, but also include additional articles and rules that identify and clarify several sexual offenses, and provides for procedural safeguards for the admissibility of evidence and the protection of victims and witnesses.[34]

Furthermore, F. Bensouda observes that the Rome Statute is the first international treaty establishing an international criminal court in which principles of female representation and gender expertise have been explicitly incorporated. She also notes that the Rome Statute is revolutionary because it codifies the mandate for the Court to adopt specific investigative, procedural, and evidentiary mechanisms that are essential to ensure gender justice. *Ibid.*

34 See Rome Statute, Articles 7–8, see *supra* note 19; ICC RPE, see *supra* note 33. These provisions define war crimes and crimes against humanity and include a subparagraph listing a broad spectrum of gender specific crimes, namely: rape, sexual slavery, enforced prostitution, forced pregnancy, enforced sterilization and any other form of sexual violence also constituting a grave breach/serious violation of the Geneva Conventions regarding war crimes (Articles 8(2)(b)(xxii) and 8(2)(e)(vi)) or other forms of sexual violence of comparable gravity regarding crimes against humanity (Article 7(1)(g)). Moreover, two other gender-specific crimes have been listed under crimes against humanity: the crimes of gender persecution (Article 7(1)(h) and the crime of "enslavement"(Article 7(2)(c)). Article 6(b) defines the crime of genocide to include causing serious bodily or mental harm to members of the group and the Elements of Crimes explicitly stipulate that this may include rape and sexual violence. Part 4 of the Statute foresees the creation of a Victim and Witness Unit ('VWU') within the Registry to provide protective measures and security arrangements, counseling and other appropriate assistance for witnesses and victims including staff with expertise in trauma related to crimes of sexual violence (Article 43(6), Article 68, and Rules 16- 19 of the RPE). Article 68 requires the Court to take appropriate measures to protect the safety, physical and psychological well-being, dignity, and privacy of victims and witnesses particularly where the crimes involve sexual or gender crimes. The same provision specifies the rights of victims to participate. The safeguards and protections in Article 68 are echoed in other provisions and in the ICC RPE: Article 54(1)(b) (mandating that the Prosecutor investigate crimes of sexual and gender violence); Article 64 (requiring the Trial Chamber to ensure that the trial is conducted with due regard for the protection of victims and witnesses); Rule 63(4)(b) (dispensing with any corroboration requirement); Rule 70 and 71 (prohibiting evidence of prior or subsequent sexual conduct of a victim or witness); Rule 71 (limiting defense of consent); Rule 112(4) (questioning via audio or video-recorded devices to reduce any subsequent trauma). Articles 36(8)(b) and 44(2) provide for the necessity of including staff with legal expertise on violence against women or children. The Prosecutor is explicitly required to appoint advisers with legal expertise on these issues (Article 42(9)). To this effect, the Gender and Children's Unit ('GCU') was created to provide advice and assistance on sexual and gender-based crimes-related issues. See Bensouda, 2007, pp. 413–14, see *supra* note 33 (describing the GCU's mandate).

3.3. The Prosecutorial Framework

3.3.1. The Hybrid Nature of International Criminal Tribunals and the ICC

International criminal tribunals are a hybrid construct that borrows from both civil and common law legal systems,[35] building on the structural and procedural legacy of the IMT at Nuremburg. The Allied Powers established the IMT using a civil law model for admissibility of evidence that incorporated certain aspects of common law, such as the presentation of evidence and courtroom procedure, as a means of compromise and to expedite cases that were primarily "paper cases".[36] The drafters of the Rome Statute also adopted aspects of both systems, as evidenced in the core legal texts of the ICC.[37]

Preparing and prosecuting cases before international courts arguably differs from domestic state practice,[38] particularly at the ICC,[39] and prosecutors from both common and civil law systems must often adapt their methods to meet the realities of the hybrid structure and procedures of international tribunals.

---

35 But see Geert-Jan Knoops, *Theory and Practice of International and Internationalized Criminal Proceedings*, Kluwer Law International, The Hague, 2005, p. 8 (positing that the ICTR and ICTY adopted the "best" elements of common and civil law systems, whereas the ICC is a true hybrid court).

36 See Richard May and Marieke Wierda, "Trends in International Criminal Evidence: Nuremburg, Tokyo, The Hague and Arusha", in *Columbia Journal of Transnational Law*, 1999, vol. 37, no. 3, pp. 725, 729–731, 748-753.

37 Rome Statute, see *supra* note 19; ICC RPE, see *supra* note 33; see also Knoops, 2005, p. 8, see *supra* note 35 (indicating that the ICTY and ICTR are predominantly common law courts with civil law aspects, and concluding that the ICC departs from that model in employing a predominantly civil law model).

38 But see Nina Bang-Jensen *et al.*, "Tribunal Justice: The Challenges, The Record, and the Prospects", in *American University International Law Review*, 1998, vol. 13, no. 6, pp. 1541, 1549 (noting that the differences are inconsequential and complementary at the investigative stage). This chapter addresses only prosecutorial challenges and does not address specifically the issues at the investigative stage.

39 The Rome Statute and ICC RPE establish a Court with predominantly civil law features, whereas it could be argued that the ICTY and ICTR incorporated many more common law features. See, *e.g.*, Robert Cryer *et al.*, *An Introduction to International Criminal Law and Procedure*, Cambridge University Press, Cambridge, 2010 (2nd ed.), pp. 467–68 (discussing the civil and criminal law characteristics of the different tribunals as they relate to issues of guilt and plea bargaining).

A significant feature of the ICC is its organizational structure that empowers the Pre-Trial Chambers to assert a significant degree of control over investigations, disclosure, and pre-trial matters. At the trial stage, the ICTY and ICTR adopt a common law approach to the presentation of evidence, in which the prosecutor presents and questions prosecution witnesses, cross-examines defense witnesses, and prepares a rebuttal case. It is unclear whether the ICC will lean towards the civil law model at the trial stage, with the trial court exercising control over the proceedings and presentation of evidence, or the ICTY/ICTR common law model where the prosecutor and defense attorneys present their respective cases and the court's day-to-day role is reduced.

Another significant feature of these international courts is the free admissibility of evidence,[40] a practice grounded in civil law, coupled with

---

[40] See Rome Statute, Article 69(4), see *supra* note 19. The Court may rule on the relevance or admissibility of any evidence, taking into account, *inter alia*, the probative value of the evidence and any prejudice that such evidence may cause to a fair trial or to a fair evaluation of the testimony of a witness, in accordance with the Rules of Procedure and Evidence. Although Article 69(4) of the Rome Statute is framed in a permissive formulation ("may"), it establishes the principles for the admission of evidence before the Court. The threefold test – relevance, probative value and prejudicial effect – reflects an attempt to merge different legal traditions, setting out the significance of "relevance", which is the fundamental criterion of continental legal systems without elaborate rules of evidence, and "admissibility", which is the starting point from the common law perspective. Trial Chamber I in the *Lubanga Dyilo* case notes that it "must ensure that the evidence is prima facie relevant to the trial, in that it relates to the matters that are properly to be considered by the Chamber in its investigation of the charges against the accused and its consideration of the views and concerns of participating victims. Second, the Chamber must assess whether the evidence has, on a prima facie basis, probative value. In this regard there are innumerable factors which may be relevant to this evaluation [...]. Third, the Chamber must, where relevant, weigh the probative value of the evidence against its prejudicial effect. Whilst it is trite to observe that all evidence that tends to incriminate the accused is also "prejudicial" to him, the Chamber must be careful to ensure that it is not unfair to admit the disputed material [...]". ICC, *Prosecutor v. Lubanga Dyilo*, Decision on the Admissibility of Four Documents, 13 June 2008, ICC-01/04-01/06-1399, paras. 27–31. Evidence is deemed relevant if it has "probative value". See ICC, *Prosecutor v. Bemba*, Decision Pursuant to Rule 61(7)(a) and (b) of the Rome Statute on the Charges of the Prosecutor Against Jean-Pierre Bemba Gombo, 15 June 2009, ICC-01/05-01/08-424, para. 46 ("*Bemba* Confirmation Decision"). The Chamber in the *Katanga* case notes that it must look at the intrinsic coherence of any item of evidence and declare inadmissible those items of evidence of which probative value is deemed prima facie absent after such an analysis. Any other assessment of the probative value will be made

the common law practice of formally admitting evidence into the record for consideration by the trial chamber, and later, by the appeals chamber. In the civil system, the case file, or dossier, is developed by a judicial investigator under the direction of an investigative judge. Generally, this case file is considered in its entirety by the trial and lay judges[41] and, unlike the common law system, a party is neither bound to formally enter documents into "evidence" nor observe detailed rules of evidence.[42] Indeed, in early cases at the ICTR, civil law based judges, defense attorneys and prosecutors were unfamiliar with the practice of common law prosecutors to include documents in the record of trial by moving to admit them into evidence.[43] As the common and civil law systems harmonized over time, these difficulties were resolved by adopting the common law procedural approach.

The free admissibility of evidence creates additional challenges when there are few rules of evidence and the application of these rules for admissibility is unclear.[44] Admissibility of evidence is strictly controlled

in light of the whole body of evidence. ICC, *Prosecutor v. Katanga et al.*, Decision on the Confirmation of Charges, 30 September 2008, ICC-01/05-01/07-716, para. 77 ("*Katanga* Confirmation Decision"). Finally, Rule 64 of the ICC RPE makes it clear that issues about relevance or admissibility should be raised when evidence is submitted and that a Chamber must give reasons for any rulings on evidentiary matters. ICC RPE, Rule 64, see *supra* note 33.

41 See Kenneth Williams, "Do We Really Need the Federal Rules of Evidence?", in *North Dakota Law Review*, 1998, vol. 74, no. 1, pp. 1, 13–14 (explaining that under the civil law system there is a preliminary stage where the hearing judge is assigned, then the hearing judge creates a summary record of the information and evidence which is then transmitted to the decision-making judge).

42 See James P. Carey, "Reflection on Criminal Justice Reforms in Chile", in *Loyola University Chicago International Law Review*, 2004–05, vol. 2, no. 2, pp. 271, 273 (remarking that "[t]raditionally, civil law systems are not bound by a plethora of evidence rules").

43 See ICTR, *Prosecutor v. Semanza*, Minutes of Proceedings, Trial Day 25, 29 March 2001, ICTR-97-20-T, p. 1 (proposing to tender deposition into evidence at time presented to Chamber); See also ICTR, *Prosecutor v. Semanza*, Minutes of Proceedings, Trial Day 27, 23 April 2001, ICTR-97-20-T, p. 1 (noting that the Chamber would consider the deposition as it would "any other testimony at the appropriate time" and failing to admit the deposition into evidence).

44 This led and will continue to lead the Court to develop a rich body of case law in its determinations of whether or not evidence should be admissible within the framework of Article 69(4) of the Rome Statute and Rule 64 of the ICC RPE. In the *Katanga* Confirmation Decision, the Pre-Trial Chamber acknowledged that although the RPE

in the common law system due, in part, to the perceived risk of lay jurors being unable to sort through evidence and assign weight in the fact-finding process. Thus, only certain evidence is admitted, as determined by a judge who interprets and applies extensive and detailed rules for admissibility of evidence.[45] The international courts' permissive rules of evidence provide that the court "shall apply rules of evidence which will best favour a fair determination of the matter before it and consonant with the spirit of the Statute and the general principles of the law".[46] The respective RPEs of the tribunals have fleshed this out a bit, and provide for admissibility of evidence that is probative and relevant,[47] and the exclusion

did not impose a requirement of corroboration pursuant to Rule 63(4), "The Chamber may, pursuant to Article 69(4) of the Statute, determine that the evidence will have a lower probative value if the Defence does not know the witness's identity and only a summary of the statement, and not the entire statement, may be challenged or assessed." *Katanga* Confirmation Decision, para. 159, see *supra* note 40. The Pre-Trial Chamber in the *Bemba* case considered that "more than one piece of indirect evidence having low probative value is required to prove an allegation made" despite the terms of Rule 63(4). *Bemba*, Confirmation Decision, para. 46, see *supra* note 40.

45 See, *e.g.*, United States, Federal Rules of Evidence, 2010, available at http://www.law.cornell.edu/rules/fre/, last accessed on 9 May 2011 ("U.S. Federal Rules of Evidence").

46 ICTY Rules of Procedure and Evidence, as amended, Rule 89(b), 8 December 2010, U.N. Doc. IT/32/Rev.45, available at http://www.icty.org/x/file/Legal%20Library/Rules_procedure_evidence/IT032Rev45_en.pdf, last accessed on 9 May 2011 ("ICTY RPE"); ICTR Rules of Procedure and Evidence, as amended, Rule, 1 October 2009, U.N. Doc ITR/3/Rev. 19, available at http://69.94.11.53/ENGLISH/rules/080314/080314.pdf, last accessed on 9 May 2011 ("ICTR RPE"); Special Court for Sierra Leone Rules of Procedure and Evidence, as amended, Rule 89(b), 28 May 2010, available at www1.umn.edu/humanrts/instree/SCSL/Rules-of-proced-SCSL.pdf ("SCSL RPE").

47 ICTR RPE, Rule 89(c), see *supra* note 46. ("A Chamber may admit any evidence which it deems to have a probative value"); Rome Statute, Articles 64, 69(4), see *supra* note 19; ICC RPE, Rule 63(2), 64, see *supra* note 33 ("A Chamber shall have the authority […] to assess freely all evidence submitted in order to determine its relevance or admissibility in accordance with article 69."); see ICTR, *Prosecutor v. Musema*, Judgement (Trial), 27 January 2000, ICTR-96-13-T, para. 56 ("*Musema* Trial Judgement"); ICTR, *Prosecutor v. Rutaganda*, Judgement (Appeal), 26 May 2003, ICTR-96-3-A, para. 216 ("*Rutaganda* Appeal Judgement"); ICTR, *Prosecutor v. Bagosora*, Decision on Admission of Tab 19 of Binder Produced in Connection with the Appearance of Witness Maxwell and Nkole, 13 September 2004, ICTR-96-7, para. 8; ICTY, *Prosecutor v. Brđanin and Talic*, Order on the Standards Governing the Admission of Evidence, 15 February 2002, IT-99-36, para. 18; ICTY, *Prosecutor v. Delalić*, Appeals Chamber Decision on Application of Defendant Zejnil Delalić for

of evidence if "its probative value is substantially outweighed by the need to ensure a fair trial".[48]

The international courts' free admissibility of evidence may have contributed to the infamous Chamber "tittering" in the *Kajelijeli* case before the ICTR.[49] In that case, the Chamber permitted the defense attorney to question the rape victim about when she had last bathed prior to the sexual assault and, when the defense attorney proceeded on with additional questions in the same vein over the objection of the prosecutor, the Chamber judges started laughing.[50] The record failed to disclose how this line of questioning was probative or relevant to the issue of either the victim's credibility or the substance of her testimony that she had been raped.

Amendments to the RPE of the ICTY and the ICTR, and the current Rome Statute and ICC RPE, suggest a retreat from ungoverned admissibility of evidence by providing additional rules of evidence addressing, in

---

Leave to Appeal Against the Decision of the Trial Chamber of January 19, 1998 for the Admissibility of Evidence, 4 March 1998, IT-96-21, para. 18.

48 See ICTY RPE, Rule 89(d), see *supra* note 46; ICTR RPE, Rule 89(d), see *supra* note 46; but see SCSL RPE, Rule 89, see *supra* note 46 (permitting admissibility of any evidence without the limitations of a rule comparable to Rule 89(D) found in the RPEs of the ICTY and the ICTR, but providing for applicability of the Sierra Leone Criminal Law). See also Rome Statute, Articles 64, 69(4), see *supra* note 19; ICC RPE, Rules 63(2), 64, see *supra* note 33. The fairness of a trial may encompass considerations that are broader than the rights of the accused and other participants, and may require a balancing process of the factors mentioned in article 64(2), or alternatively in the concept of "fair evaluation of the testimony of a witness," mentioned in Article 69(4). In that regard, it was held in the *Katanga* Confirmation Decision that 'the Chamber may, pursuant to Article 69(4) of the Statute, determine that the evidence will have a lower probative value if the Defence does not know the witness' identity and only a summary of the statement, and not the entire statement, may be challenged or assessed." *Katanga* Confirmation Decision, para. 159, see *supra* note 40.

49 See ICTR, *Prosecutor v. Kajelijeli*, Judgement and Sentence (Trial), 1 December 2003, ICTR 98-44A-T ("*Kajelijeli* Trial Judgement").

50 See Binaifer Nowrojee, ""Your Justice is Too Slow" Will the ICTR Fail Rwanda's Rape Victims?", United Nations Research Institute for Social Development, 2005, Occasional Paper 10, available at http://www.unrisd.org/80256B3C005BCCF9/(httpAuxPages)/56FE32D5C0F6DCE9C125710F0045D89F/$file/OP10%20Web.pdf, last accessed on 9 May 2011, pp. 23–24 (recounting the laughter by trial judges during the cross-examination of a rape victim in the *Butare* case).

part, live testimony,[51] pre-recorded testimony,[52] and agreements as to evidence.[53] Nonetheless, the civil law tradition underpinnings of the ICC give weight to the view that rules for admissibility of evidence will be interpreted and applied permissively.[54]

In terms of cases involving sexual offenses, liberal rules for admissibility of evidence coupled with sufficient victim protections both on and off the stand[55] arguably better serve a search for truth than rigid and for-

---

51 ICTR RPE, Rule 92 *bis*, see *supra* note 46 (providing for admissibility of written statements in lieu of oral testimony if certain conditions are met); ICC RPE, Rule 69(2), see *supra* note 33 (requiring in court testimony of a live witness unless the conditions of Article 68 or the RPE are met).

52 ICTR RPE, Rule 92 *bis*, see *supra* note 46; ICC RPE, Rule 68(a), see *supra* note 33 (allowing admissibility of a pre-recorded testimony if both the prosecutor and defense attorney had the opportunity to examine the witness during the recording).

53 ICC RPE, Rule 69, see *supra* note 33 (authorizing chamber to require full presentation of facts in the interests of justice or the victims where facts are nonetheless agreed upon by both the Prosecutor and Defence).

54 Rome Statute, Article 69(2), see *supra* note 19 (allowing the "introduction of documents or written transcripts"). This gives an indication as to the admissibility of such materials, which departs from the approach adopted by common law tribunals. See Donald Piragoff, "Article 69", in Otto Triffterer, *Commentary on the Rome Statute of the International Criminal Court: Observer's Notes, Article by Article*, Hart Publishing, 2008 (2d ed.), pp. 1301–1336, 1317.

The Pre-Trial Chamber in the *Katanga* case admitted in evidence a transcript of an interview with a deceased witness, for the purposes of the confirmation hearing. ICC, *Prosecutor v. Katanga*, Décision relative à l'admissibilité, aux fins de l'audience de confirmation des charges, des transcriptions de l'entretien avec le témoin 12, aujourd'hui décédé, 18 April 2007, ICC-01/05-01/07-716; see also *Katanga* Confirmation Decision, para. 109, see *supra* note 40. The ICC Trial Chamber in the *Lubanga* case responded to the Prosecutor's application for filing or producing documents that "the sole issue in this regard of consequence is whether or not the particular piece of evidence surmounts the applicable admissibility and relevance threshold. Once this issue is resolved, as a general proposition, the exact manner of introduction is unlikely to involve a dispute of substance, and it should be dealt with by reference to the circumstances of the situation". ICC, *Prosecutor v. Lubanga*, Decision on the status before the Trial Chamber of the evidence heard by the Pre-Trial Chamber and the decisions of the Pre-Trial Chamber in trial proceedings, and the manner in which evidence shall be submitted, 13 December 2007, ICC-01/04-01/06-160, para. 7 ("*Lubanga* Evidence Decision").

55 See generally, Rome Statute, Articles 43, 54.1(b), 57(3)(c), 64(6)(e), 68, 93(1)(j), see *supra* note 19; ICC RPE, Rules 16–19, 70, 86–88, see *supra* note 33. Article 68(1) of the Rome Statute provides that the Court shall take appropriate measures to protect the safety, physical and psychological well-being, dignity and privacy of victims and

malized rules of evidence. This is particularly true given that there are often no witnesses to the actual sexual assault or violence, and proof of these acts may be based on hearsay or other evidence that would be inadmissible under common law rules of evidence.

A further significant feature of international criminal tribunals is open and full disclosure, including the requirement that the prosecutor provide the defense all witness statements and, upon the defense's request, all evidence that the prosecutor intends to use as evidence.[56] This

witnesses. Article 68(2) creates an exception to the right of the accused under article 67 to a public hearing. Article 68(5) provides the Prosecutor with the option to rest his case on summary evidence at the confirmation stage to protect the security of a witness or his family. Restrictions to disclosure of evidence for the protection of victims and witnesses are also dealt with in Rule 81. Article 54(3)(f) provides further that the Prosecutor shall take necessary measures, or request that necessary measures be taken, in order to ensure the protection of any person. Article 54(1)(b) binds the Prosecutor to respect, during the investigation, the interests, personal circumstances, and any special needs of victims and witnesses. Article 43 requires the Registrar to set up a Victims and Witnesses Unit within the Registry to provide protective measures and security arrangements, counseling and other appropriate assistance for witnesses, victims who appear before the Court, and others who are at risk on account of testimony given by witnesses. Rules 16–19 of the ICC RPE cover the responsibilities of the Registrar and the VWU. Specific provision is made for the support, comfort, and protection of victims, their security and rights in Rule 17. Rules 87 and 88 provide that the Chamber may grant protective and special measures, which usually cover measures to facilitate the testimony of a vulnerable victim or witness. Rule 70 set out principles of evidence by which the court shall be guided in case of sexual violence. Rule 86 recalls to the Chamber the necessity of taking into consideration the needs of all victims and witnesses when making any direction or order. Articles 57(3)(c) and 64(6)(e) of the Statute provide the Court with a general legal basis for ensuring the protection of witnesses and victims. Article 93(1)(j) of the Statute specifically provides for the cooperation of State Parties to permit effective witness protection, while Rule 16(4) of the Rules stipulates that agreements on relocation of victims and witnesses may be negotiated with States by the Registrar on behalf of the Court.

56 See ICC RPE, Rule 76–84, see *supra* note 33. The ICC RPE establishes a thorough regime of disclosure, applicable with important distinctions to both the Prosecutor and the defence (Rules 76–84). Pursuant to Rule 76 the Prosecutor shall provide the defence with the names of the witnesses it intends to call at trial together with copies of their statements, subject to possible applicable protective measures. Rule 79 establishes a corresponding obligation for the defence, but which applied only to witnesses expected to support specific defences. Rule 77 and 78 require both sides to allow the other to inspect any material in their possession or control which they intend to use as evidence, while the Prosecutor is also required to disclose any such items that may assist the defence. Rule 84 empowers the Trial Chamber to make necessary orders for

disclosure necessitates a vigilant prosecutor who employs all appropriate provisions for victim/witness protection to ensure that information potentially harmful to a sexual assault victim is released in the proper form to a defendant at the appropriate time.[57]

Lastly, the role and rights afforded to victims at the ICC is dramatically increased compared to the ICTY and ICTR, as well as most common law systems.[58] The ICC stands alone among international forums in providing victims a near "open door" to the court. This approach is consistent with several civil law models where the criminal case also serves as the first civil case and attorneys present at the trial pursue the reparation interests of the victim.[59]

3.3.2. The Role and Function of the Prosecutor

The role of the prosecutor in international courts differs from the roles of prosecutors in domestic jurisdictions due to three main factors: the hybrid nature of international tribunals, the novelty of international criminal law, and the complexity of cases. These factors tend to impact a prosecutors' role to a greater degree in cases in which sexual crimes are charged.

The hybrid nature of international tribunals requires prosecutors to set aside their domestic jurisdiction practices and to understand their role within the legal regime of the relevant court. As is the case in all domestic systems, a prosecutor must be considered first-and-foremost an officer of the court in the court's search for truth and justice.[60] Although the concept

the disclosure of documents or information not previously disclosed and for the production of additional evidence.

57 See *supra* note 56 (outlining victim protections provided by the Rome Statute and ICC RPE).

58 See ICC RPE, Rules 85–99, see *supra* note 33 (providing the definition of victims, victim protections, the role of victims in proceedings, and reparations for victims).

59 See generally, Liesbeth Zegveld, "Victims' Reparations Claims and International Criminal Courts: Incompatible Values?", in *Journal of International Criminal Justice*, 2010, vol. 8, no. 1, p. 79.

60 See, *e.g.*, Supreme Court of the United States, *Berger v. United States*, 1935, 295 U. S. pp. 78, 88 ("[A Prosecutor] is the representative not of an ordinary party to a controversy, but of a sovereignty whose obligation to govern impartially is as compelling as its obligation to govern at all, and whose interest, therefore, in a criminal prosecution is not that it shall win a case, but that justice shall be done. As such, he is in a peculiar and very definite sense the servant of the law, the two-fold aim of which is that guilt shall not escape or innocence suffer. He may prosecute with earnestness and

of the prosecutor as an officer of the court is similar to both common and civil law domestic systems, in practice differences arise out of the unique procedures before international tribunals.

In international tribunals, the judges generally take a more active role in managing the trial. Witnesses and evidence do not belong to any party or participant in the proceeding, but rather, belong to the court itself. Nonetheless, prosecutors are responsible for presenting the case, including examining (direct and redirect examination) of sexual assault victims, zealously guarding and protecting the rights of the such witnesses by appropriate motions and objections, and, if necessary, rehabilitating the victim on redirect by thoughtful and considered questioning. Prosecutors must remain flexible to the backgrounds and styles of judges from varying legal traditions. This requires prosecutors to remain both open-minded and creative in their pleadings before the court and the presentation of the evidence of sexual offenses.

The novelty of international substantive and procedural criminal law creates some uncertainty in prosecutorial decisions ranging from charging a defendant to motions practice and to witness examination. Due to this uncertainty, prosecutors must understand how his or her actions can impact the substantive and procedural jurisprudence. A prosecutor must pay particular attention to issues that may be beneficial to the instant case but detrimental to cases in the future and assess the risks and benefits of a particular course of action. It cannot be overstated that in international tribunals prosecutors cannot simply implement or impose their national legal systems. International courts benefit from prosecutors who – while applying the relevant statues and rules – interpret and complement international legal regimes by way of integrating their best practices and the rationale behind specific national legal concepts, such as disclosure, incriminatory and exculpatory material, modes of liability, and theories of intent. This approach assists international courts in advancing their jurisprudence, as seen in the motions practice by international prosecutors and legal advisors in a series that resulted in the current jurisprudence regarding the element of consent for the charge of rapes.

vigor – indeed, he should do so. But, while he may strike hard blows, he is not at liberty to strike foul ones. It is as much his duty to refrain from improper methods calculated to produce a wrongful conviction as it is to use every legitimate means to bring about a just one.").

The complexity and length of cases in international criminal law also impacts the role and functions of prosecutors. The disclosure of evidence is one of the core functions of a prosecutor to ensure a fair trial to the accused and to establish the truth. The large volume of documents and other evidence subject to disclosure requires a high degree of attention to ensure that all incriminatory evidence to be used at trial, all potentially exonerating evidence, and all information material to the preparation of the defense, is disclosed in an orderly fashion to the defense.

In cases involving sexual offenses, every international prosecutor – whether civil or common law trained – faces the challenge of straddling the fence between protecting a victim's privacy and meeting the disclosure requirements to ensure defendant's fair trial rights. This balancing act can require a great deal of advance planning and the preparation of motions to the court for victim protection in the form of redacted statements or other protective measures. This balancing act is fraught with problems as many an international prosecutor can attest – often a victim statement that has been redacted sufficiently to protect the victim may be of little use to a defendant in preparing his case and the timing of the disclosure of an unredacted statement can be critical.

3.4. Sexual Violence Crimes: An Overview

3.4.1. From the ICTR to the ICC

Sexual violence crimes and their elements set forth in the respective statutes of the ICTY, ICTR and ICC are not identical and can cause confusion for a practitioner. The ICTR and the ICTY were established to address context-specific situations and the jurisdictional basis and cognizable offenses listed in their respective statutes reflect this.[61] The ICTR stat-

---

61 See Statute of the International Tribunal for Rwanda, 2007, available at http://untreaty.un.org/cod/avl/pdf/ha/ictr_EF.pdf, last accessed on 20 March 2011, Article 4 ("ICTR Statute") ("The International Tribunal for Rwanda shall have the power to prosecute persons committing or ordering to be committed serious violations of Article 3 common to the Geneva Conventions of 12 August 1949 for the Protection of War Victims, and of Additional Protocol II thereto of 8 June 1977."). See also Statute of the International Criminal Tribunal for the Former Yugoslavia, 25 May 1993, available at www.icty.org/x/file/Legal%20Library/Statute/statute_sept08_en.pdf, Article 5 ("ICTY Statute") ("The International Tribunal shall have the power to prosecute persons responsible for the following crimes when committed in armed conflict,

ute also reflects shifts in customary law not included in the ICTY statute, most notably the absence of the requirement of an armed conflict as an element of crimes against humanity.[62] The ICC adopted the element of "widespread or systematic" set forth in the ICTY and ICTR statutes;[63] current jurisprudence establishes that the requirement is applied in the disjunctive.[64] Further, the ICC as a permanent standing court includes an expansive, although arguably not exhaustive, list of offenses, some of which are grounded in customary international law and others of which are grounded in treaty law.[65] The jurisprudence of other tribunals demonstrates that the lack of enumeration of a specific offense will not bar an otherwise successful prosecution of sexual offenses under other enumerated criminal offenses.[66] Thus, a practitioner should not be hesitant, but

whether international or internal in character and directed against any civilian population [...]").

62 Compare ICTY Statute, Article 5, see *supra* note 61(requiring that crimes against humanity be committed in armed conflict) with ICTR Statute, Article 3, see *supra* note 61 (providing that the ICTR "shall have the power to prosecute persons responsible for the following crimes when committed as part of a widespread or systematic attack against any civilian population" and deleting the requirement of an armed conflict).

63 ICTR Statute, Article 3, see *supra* note 61 (allowing prosecution for crimes against humanity when "committed as part of a widespread or systematic attack against any civilian population").

64 In the *Bemba* Confirmation Decision, para. 82, see supra note 40 the Chamber noted that:

> the terms "widespread" and "systematic" appearing in the chapeau of Article 7 of the Statute are presented in the alternative. The Chamber noted that it need not consider whether the attack was systematic if it finds the attack to be widespread. Therefore, the Chamber confined itself to examining only the requirement that the attack be "widespread."

65 Many argue that the ICC overstepped itself in several areas and for this reason the phrase "grounded in customary international law and others in treaty law" is employed to characterize the list of offenses. See David L. Nersessian, "Comparative Approaches to Punishing Hate: The Intersection of Genocide and Crimes Against Humanity", in *Stanford Journal of International Law*, 2007, vol. 43, no. 2, pp. 221, 241 (noting that although the ICC expanded the categories of crimes to include "grounds that are universally recognized as impermissible under customary international law", the ICC has created additional elements that render it narrower than customary international law); ICTY, *Prosecutor v. Kupreskic*, Judgement (Trial), 14 January 2000, IT-95-6-T, p. 581 (refusing to adopt the ICC approach within the ICTY because "article 7(1)(h) is no consonant with customary international law").

66 See *infra* notes 131, 132 (citing to examples of ICTR and ICTY jurisprudence charging sexual violence offenses not enumerated under the respective Statute).

should move forward deliberately and methodically, to capture the character of an otherwise non-enumerated offense when warranted.[67]

3.4.2. Genocide, Crimes Against Humanity, and War Crimes

The crimes within the jurisdiction of the ICC are limited to genocide, crimes against humanity, war crimes, and aggression.[68] Genocide is defined in a manner comparable to that of the ICTR and ICTY and does not specifically list sexual violence as a genocidal act.[69] Rape, sexual slavery, enforced prostitution, forced pregnancy, enforced sterilization, or any other form of sexual violence of comparable gravity are enumerated and defined as crimes against humanity.[70] Rape, sexual slavery, forced prostitution and any other form of sexual violence are listed and defined as serious violations of Common Article 3 of the four Geneva Conventions.[71] Sexual violence is listed and defined as a war crime in conflicts characterized as either international or non-international.[72]

---

67 See, *e.g.*, SCSL, *Prosecutor v. Brima and 2 others*, Judgement, 10 June 2007, SCSL-04-16-T ("*AFRC* Trial Judgement"); SCSL, *Prosecutor v. Brima and 2 others*, Judgement, 22 February 2008, SCSL-04-16-A ("*AFRC* Appeal Judgement"); SCSL, *Prosecutor v. Sesay and 2 others*, Judgement, 2 March 2009, SCSL-04-15-T ("*RUF* Trial Judgement").

68 See Rome Statute, Article 5(1)(d), see *supra* note 19 (identifying the crime of aggression as a chargeable offense). Although the crime of aggression is within the jurisdiction of the ICC, states parties have yet to agree on a definition and elements); see also Mauro Politi and Giuseppe Nesi, *The International Criminal Court and the Crime of Aggression*, Ashgate, 2004 (examining the history of the crime of aggression and the related definitional and jurisdictional questions).

69 However, the Rome Statute defines the crime of genocide to include causing serious bodily or mental harm to members of the group, and the Elements of Crimes make an explicit reference to rape and sexual violence. See ICC, Elements of Crimes, 9 September 2002, ICC-ASP/1/3(part II-B), Article 6(b) n. 3 ("Elements of Crimes"); see also Convention on the Prevention and Punishment of the Crime of Genocide 1948, 9 December 1948, available at www.preventgenocide.org/law/convention/text.htm, last accessed on 10 May 2011.

70 Rome Statute, Article 7(1)(g), see *supra* note 19.

71 See Rome Statute, Articles 8(2)(b)(xxi) and 8(2)(e)(vi), see *supra* note 19; see also Knut Dörmann, "War Crimes under the Rome Statute of the International Criminal Court, with a Special Focus on the Negotiations Elements of Crimes", in A. von Bogdandy and R. Wolfrum (eds.), *Max Planck Yearbook of United Nations Law*, *Volume 7*, 2003, Koninklijke Brill N.V., the Netherlands, pp. 341–407 (explaining the development of legal elements of crimes under the Rome Statute).

72 Rome Statute, Article 8, see *supra* note 19.

The elements of each offense include the specific predicate act and the contextual requirements. A charge of rape as genocide thus requires proof of not only the predicate act of rape, meaning an act that caused serious bodily or mental harm, or other applicable predicate crimes under genocide,[73] but also the contextual elements that render an isolated act of rape for personal reasons an act of genocide;[74] the rape must be committed against a person belonging to "a particular national, ethnical, racial or religious group", with an "intent to destroy, in whole or in part, that national, ethnical, racial or religious group".[75]

In addition, the prosecutor must establish the contextual element that the conduct took place "in the context of a manifest pattern of similar conduct directed against that group or was conduct that could itself effect such destruction".[76] Unlike crimes against humanity in which numerous predicate acts may make up the "attack",[77] the predicate act in genocide must stand alone and meet the requirement of a manifest pattern of similar conduct, thus setting a high bar for establishing rape or other sexual offenses as genocide.

Likewise, in crimes against humanity, the rape, or other criminal predicate gender based acts, and contextual elements must be established. The contextual elements require that the "the conduct was committed as part of a widespread or systematic attack directed against a civilian population"[78] and that the perpetrator knew that the conduct was part of or intended the conduct to be part of a widespread or systematic attack directed against a civilian population.[79] The predicate act, such as rape and other sexual violence need not be widespread or systematic, but must be a part of a widespread or systematic attack.[80]

---

73 Rome Statute, Article 6, see *supra* note 19.

74 These elements are also referenced as "chapeau" elements.

75 Rome Statute, Article 6, see *supra* note 19.

76 Elements of Crimes, Article 6, see *supra* note 69.

77 See ICTR, *Prosecutor v. Gacumbitsi*, Judgement (Appeal), 7 July 2006, ICTR 2001-64-A, para. 102 ("*Gacumbitsi* Appeal Judgement") ("At the outset, it bears noting that it is not rape *per se* that must be shown to be widespread or systematic, but rather the attack itself (of which the rapes formed part)").

78 Rome Statute, Article 7, see *supra* note 19.

79 *Ibid.*

80 See *Gacumbitsi* Appeal Judgement, see *supra* note 77.

War crimes under the ICC are listed in differing categories in Articles 8(2)(a) through (e), based on the characterization of the conflict, as either international or non-international, and the corresponding Geneva Conventions, including the Protocols.[81] For any war crime charged, the prosecutor must establish the chapeau requirement of an armed conflict and, if the offenses charged are specific to either an international or non-international conflict, the prosecutor must establish the characterization of the conflict. One category of war crimes, offenses under Article 8(2)(b), does not require that the prosecutor provide evidence of the characterization of the armed conflict. Lastly, the contextual element for a war crime is that "the conduct took place in the context of and was associated with an international armed conflict"[82] and "the perpetrator was aware of factual circumstances that established the existence of an armed conflict".[83]

3.4.3. Modes of Responsibility

The modes of individual responsibility under the ICC include: commits whether alone, jointly or through another; orders, solicits or induces; aids

---

81 See Rome Statute, Article 8(2), see *supra* note 19.

82 Elements of Crimes, Article 8(2)(b)(i), see *supra* note 69; see also ICTR Statute, Article 4, see *supra* note 61. Under Article 4 and relevant jurisprudence, there must be a direct connection between the actions of the accused and the armed conflict. Compare ICTR, *Prosecutor v. Kayishema and Ruzindana*, Judgement, 21 May 1999, ICTR-95-1-T (holding that the genocide and the armed conflict in Rwanda were distinct and acquitting the accused of war crimes because of a lack of nexus with the armed conflict) ("*Kayishema* Trial Judgement") with ICTR, *Rutaganda* Appeal Judgement, paras. 569–580, 583, see *supra* note 47 (finding a direct link between the defendant's role as a member of the *Interahamwe* and the armed conflict itself in adopting the legal test enunciated in the ICTY Appeal Judgement in the case of *Prosecutor v. Kunarac* that "if it can be established [...] that the perpetrator acted in furtherance of or under the guise of the armed conflict [...] it would be sufficient to conclude that his acts were closely related to the armed conflict" and explaining that "'under the guise of the armed conflict' does not mean simply 'at the same time as the armed conflict' and/or 'in any circumstances created in part by the armed conflict'" but requires consideration of all of the Kunarac factors , including "the fact that the perpetrator is a combatant; the fact that the victim is a non-combatant; the fact that the victim is a member of the opposing party; the fact that the act may be said to serve the ultimate goal of a military campaign; and the fact that the crime is committed as part of or in the context of the perpetrator's official duties."). ICTY, *Prosecutor v. Kunarac*, Judgement (Appeal), 12 June 2002, ICTR 96-23-A, paras. 57–59 ("*Kunarac* Appeal Judgement").

83 Elements of Crimes, Article 8(2)(b)(i), see *supra* note 69.

and abets; commits by common purpose; and attempts. In addition, one mode of liability is applicable only to genocide: "directly and publicly incites others to commit genocide".[84] It bears note that "common purpose" is not identical to joint criminal enterprise ('JCE'), a theory of responsibility adopted by both the ICTR and ICTY.[85]

In addition to individual criminal responsibility, the ICC also sets forth the responsibility of commanders and other superiors in a separate article.[86] The ICC distinguishes between military commanders and other superiors, holding the military leader responsible for acts of subordinates if the commander "knew, or should have known, that his forces were committing or had committed criminal acts and fail[ed] to take specific action".[87] A superior who is not a military commander will be held responsible only if he or she "knew, or consciously disregarded information that clearly indicated that the subordinates were committing or about to commit such crimes" and "the crimes concerned activities that were within the effective responsibility and control of the superior".[88]

The ICC establishes a number of defenses, including mental disease, involuntary intoxication, self-defense and defense of others, duress,

84 Rome Statute, Article 25(1)–(4), see *supra* note 19.

85 ICC Pre-Trial Chambers adopted literal and contextual approaches to interpret Article 25(3)(a) of the Statute to include leaders and organizers who do not physically perpetrate the criminal act, within the concept of commission. See ICC, *Prosecutor v. Lubanga*, Decision on the Confirmation of Charges, 29 January 2007, ICC-01/04-01/06-803, paras. 334–335 ("*Lubanga* Confirmation Decision"); ICC, *Prosecutor v. Al Bashir*, Decision on the Prosecution's Application for a Warrant of Arrest against Omar Hassan Ahmad Al Bashir, 4 March 2009, para. 210 ("*Al Bashir* Arrest Warrant"). "Under this 'control over the crime' paradigm, an individual is deemed a co-perpetrator if he or she has 'joint control' as a result of an 'essential contribution' to its commission. See William A. Schabbas, *The International Criminal Court, A Commentary on the Rome Statute*, Oxford University Press, 2010, p. 428. In the ICC case law the concept of "co- perpetration" has been distinguished from the joint criminal enterprise approach to liability endorsed by the *ad hoc* tribunals, considered as subjective, in that 'principals to a crime are not limited to those who physically carry out the objective elements of the offence, but also include those who, in spite of being removed from the scene of the crime, control or mastermind its commission, because they decide whether and how the offence will be committed.' *Ibid. at* para. 332; see also *Katanga* Confirmation Decision, para. 485, see *supra* note 40.

86 Rome Statute, Article 28, see *supra* note 19.

87 *Ibid.*

88 Rome Statute, Article 28(b)(i)(ii), see *supra* note 19.

and mistake of fact.[89] Additionally, the ICC provides for a defense based on superior orders; however, this defense applies only to war crimes and requires that the perpetrator was under a legal obligation to obey the order and that she or he acted without knowledge that the order was illegal.[90]

3.5. The Indictment: The Legal Roadmap

The indictment outlines the charges the prosecutor will pursue and the facts that the prosecutor will establish to support the charged offenses. It is the roadmap for the case and arguably the single most important document in the prosecutor's toolkit.[91] The indictment must contain all charges the prosecutor intends to prosecute including the mode of responsibility,[92] and set forth sufficient detail of the facts upon which the charges and mode or responsibility are based.[93]

3.5.1. Legally and Factually Sufficient Indictments

The indictment is subject to initial review for judicial confirmation and the prosecutor must establish a *prima facie* case on the basis of the in-

---

89 Rome Statute, Articles 31 and 32, see *supra* note 19.

90 Rome Statute, Article 33, see *supra* note 19. The defense as worded provides no defense for war committed pursuant to an unlawful order. See, *e.g.*, United States, Uniform Code of Military Justice, 10 USC 892, Art. 92 (criminalizing violation of a *lawful* order) (emphasis added); See generally, United States, "Military Orders: To Obey – or Not to Obey", available at http://usmilitary.about.com/cs/militarylaw1/a/obeyingorders_2.htm, last accessed on 10 May 2011.

91 See ICTR, *Prosecutor v. Uwinkindi*, Decision on Defense Application for Certification to Appeal Decision on Preliminary Motion Alleging Defects in the Form of the Amended Indictment, 28 March 2011, ICTR-01-75-PT, para. 7 (noting that the "scope, content and clarity of an indictment are factors that can significantly affect the fair and expeditious conduct of the proceedings or the outcome of the trial").

92 The civil law system generally requires charging of all defendants for all offenses allegedly committed for which they are believed responsible. However, the ICTR, ICTY, and ICC recognize prosecutorial discretion in charging based on the recognition that it is not possible to adopt this civil law model as applied to international crimes and defendants. See generally Hassan B. Jallow, "Prosecutorial Discretion and International Criminal Justice", in *Journal of International Criminal Justice*, 2005, vol. 3, no. 1, p. 145.

93 See ICTR Statute, Article 47(c), see *supra* note 61 ("The indictment shall set forth the name and particulars of the suspect, and a concise statement of the facts of the case and of the crime with which the suspect is charged."); see also *ibid.* at Article 20(4)(a).

dictment and the supporting materials.[94] Few indictments charging sexual offenses at international tribunals or courts have faced difficulties at the confirmation stage; however this is likely attributable to the low evidentiary standard required for confirmation.[95] Arguably, a failure at the confirmation stage may be preferable to a later determination by the trial chamber that the charges as drafted do not conform to the available evidence, are characterized incorrectly, or are defective in some other manner.[96]

Among the significant challenges to the successful prosecution of sexual offense cases before the ICTR and ICTY are indictments that do not contain sexual offense charges or do not contain specific and sufficient facts to support the sexual offenses as charged. If a confirmed indictment fails to include sexual charges or facts, it will be difficult if not impossible for the prosecutor to bring a perpetrator to justice for sexual offenses depending on the stage of the proceedings – as the prosecution draws closer to trial, leave to amend the confirmed indictment may be limited or unavailable.[97] As noted by the Appeals Chamber in the case of *Prosecutor v. Muvunyi*,

---

94 ICTR Statute, Article 17(4), see *supra* note 61 ("Upon a determination that a *prima facie* case exists, the Prosecutor shall prepare an indictment containing a concise statement of the facts and the crime or crimes with which the accused is charged under the Statute. The indictment shall be transmitted to a judge of the Trial Chamber"). Although the ICTR's Statute and RPE do not require additional information, it is practice that the indictment moves forward to review/confirmation proceedings with the witness statements attached. See also Rome Statute, Article 61(5), see *supra* note 19 (requiring that the prosecutor at the indictment confirmation hearing support each charge with sufficient evidence, including summaries and statements, to establish "substantial grounds" that the person committed the crime); ICC, Regulations of the Court Regulation, as amended, 18 December 2007, Court Regulation 52, Official Document ICC-BD/01-02-07 ("ICC Regulations") (clarifying the requirements of the indictment).

95 *Ibid.*; but see *Katanga* Confirmation Decision, paras. 576, 577, 578, see *supra* note 40 (confirming sexual slavery and rape as war crimes but declining to confirm crimes of inhuman treatment and outrages upon personal dignity as war crimes); see also *Bemba* Confirmation Decision, paras. 189–209, 289–300, 301–313, see *supra* note 40 (failing to confirm torture as a crime against humanity and war crimes).

96 See, *e.g.*, ICTR, *Prosecutor v. Renzaho*, Judgement (Appeal), 1 April 2011, ICTR-97-31A, paras. 111–129 (reversing defendant's convictions for rape because of failure to sufficiently plead the factual basis for the mode of responsibility in the indictment or to cure the deficient indictment).

97 See *infra* Section 3.5.2.

> [d]efects in an indictment may come to light during the proceedings because the evidence turns out differently than expected; this calls for the Trial Chamber to consider whether a fair trial requires an amendment of the indictment, an adjournment of proceedings, or the exclusion of evidence outside the scope of the indictment. In reaching its judgment, a Trial Chamber can only convict the accused of crimes that are charged in the indictment.[98]

Although the number of ICTR indictments challenged by defense attorneys for failure to provide adequate information and details to prepare a defense is high,[99] there is no indication that the charges of sexual offenses lacked specificity to any greater degree than other charged offenses. The difficulties in providing details such as date, time, and place when indictments are drafted routinely many years after the events charged appear to apply indiscriminately across the board to all charges. However, if the indictment is not legally sufficient because of lack of specific or sufficient facts, the court has exhibited a willingness to dismiss sexual offense charges, or, in the alternative, render a verdict of not guilty.[100] In *Prosecutor v. Semanza*, four women testified to being raped and, although finding that the rapes occurred, the ICTR Trial Chamber found the defendant not guilty of rape as a crime against humanity, holding that the indictment was impermissibly vague as to date, place, and time.[101]

In addition to impermissibly vague indictments, numerous sexual offense cases before the ICTR resulted in withdrawal of charges, dismissals, or acquittals because of unavailable or insufficient evidence to sup-

---

98 ICTR, *Prosecutor v. Muvunyi*, Judgement (Appeal), 29 August 2008, ICTR-00-55A-A, para. 18 ("*Muvunyi* Appeal Judgement").

99 A review of ICTR cases prior to 2008 indicates that a motion analogous or similar to a motion for additional facts, or a motion to dismiss for lack of specificity was filed in the majority of cases. One might correctly assume that in cases in which a motion was not filed and charges were dismissed at the end of the case for lack of evidence that the defense attorney took a tactical decision not to file such a motion, thereby foreclosing the prosecution from providing additional evidence to support the indictment.

100 Rome Statute, Article 67(1)(a), (b), see *supra* note 19; ICTR Statute, Article 20(4)(a), (b), see *supra* note 61; see also, *e.g.*, ICTR, *Prosecutor v. Semanza*, Judgement and Sentence (Trial), 15 May 2003, ICTR-97-20-T, paras. 51, 52, 54, 61, 251 ("*Semanza* Trial Judgement").

101 See *Semanza* Trial Judgement, paras. 51, 52, 54, 61, 251, see *supra* note 100.

port the charges or the facts set forth in the indictments.[102] In other cases, the prosecution led evidence of sexual assaults that did not relate to the charged offenses.[103]

Arguably, many of the early ICTR and ICTY indictments were deficient because the ICTR and ICTY investigative teams and their advisors were neither focused on sexual crimes[104] nor "married" to the prosecution team assigned to the case,[105] resulting in incomplete investigations, poorly drafted indictments, and gaps and inconsistencies between the indictment and available evidence. As ICTR prosecution and investigative staff

---

[102] See, *e.g.*, ICTR, *Prosecutor v. Bizimungo*, Decision on Defence Motions Pursuant to Rule 98 *bis*, 31 October 2005, ICTR 99-50 (acquitting defendants on sexual-violence allegations in mid-trial after prosecution led no evidence on these charges); ICTR, *Prosecutor v. Bikindi*, Judgement (Trial), 2 December 2008, ICTR-01-72-T ("*Bikindi* Trial Judgement") (acquitting defendant on sexual related charges because no evidence was led except as to one victim and no evidence linked this victim to the defendant); ICTR, *Prosecutor v. Ndindabahizi*, Judgement (Trial), 15 July 2005, ICTR 01-71 ("*Ndindabahizi* Trial Judgement") (withdrawing the charge of rape as a crime against humanity for lack of evidence); *Semanza* Trial Judgement, see *supra* note 100 (dismissing certain rape charges based on lack of evidence presented and a defective indictment); ICTR, *Prosecutor v. Muhimana*, Judgement and Sentence (Trial), 28 April 2005, ICTR-95-1B-T, para. 556 ("*Muhimana* Trial Judgement") (finding that the prosecution failed to plead a material fact of accurate dates of crime and finding the defendant not responsible for specific rapes based on a defective indictment).

[103] See *Semanza* Trial Judgement, paras. 250, 251, see *supra* note 100 (finding defendant not guilty of rape charged on basis of only one hearsay witness supported by testimony of four rape victims who did not establish that they were raped during the specific attacks set forth in the indictment).

[104] See Kelly Dawn Askin, "Gender Crimes Jurisprudence in the ICTR: Positive Developments", in *Journal of International Criminal Justice*, 2005, vol. 3, no. 4, pp. 1007, 1008 (noting that many indictments at the ICTR failed to include sexual violence charges because there was "little genuine and rigorous investigation of the crime by the Prosecutor's office"); see also Beth van Schaack, "Obstacles on the Road to Gender Justice: The International Criminal Tribunal for Rwanda as Object Lesson", in *American University Journal of Gender, Social Policy and the Law*, 2009, vol. 17, no. 2, pp. 361, 372–73 (noting that under the leadership of Prosecutor Carla Del Ponte the ICTR did not focus on sexual crimes).

[105] This is typical in the United Kingdom where solicitors handle the cases up to trial and then hand over the file to a barrister for trial. In the early days of the tribunals, there was a significant number of investigative staff from the United Kingdom and other countries with similar bifurcated legal systems.

gained experience, and the ICTR as an institution focused on these types of offenses,[106] these deficiencies were gradually addressed.

The role of the prosecutor at the investigative and indictment drafting stage is critical to a legally sufficient indictment that adequately sets forth a well drafted and supported sexual crimes charges, accurately captures a defendant's alleged conduct, and effectively guides the prosecution and the court in their pursuit of justice. Prosecutors should be involved from the very beginning of the opening of an investigation; it is essential that investigators, prosecutors, and their advisors fully comprehend that every investigative activity has an impact directly or indirectly on the prosecution of the accused throughout the entire judicial process, including drafting the indictment, presenting evidence at trial, engaging in motions practice, and setting the record for appeal.

3.5.2. Corrective Action after Confirmation

If evidence of uncharged sexual offenses or additional facts to support charged sexual offenses come to light after the confirmation of the indictment, the prudent course of action is to undertake a prosecutorial motion to amend the indictment.[107] If evidence comes to light during the trial,

---

[106] Prosecutor Hassan Bubacar Jallow assumed the role of Prosecutor following Carla del Ponte in 2003 and focused on gender crimes to include sexual offenses, moving to amend indictments to add charges of sexual offenses in several cases. See Emma Founds, "Dateline: Tanzania, Prosecution of Rwanda Gender Crimes at the ICTR", *Jurist Legal News and Research*, 6 August 2010, available at http://jurist.org/dateline/2010/08/tanzania-prosecution-of-gender-crimes-in-rwanda.php, last accessed on 10 May 2011.

[107] See *Lubanga* Evidence Decision, para. 39, see *supra* note 54. By virtue of Article 61(8) and (9) of Rome Statute, see *supra* note 19, when a charge was not confirmed by the Pre-Trial Chamber, the Prosecutor can request the Pre-Trial Chamber to confirm the charge again if he obtains additional supporting evidence. The Prosecutor can still amend the charges 'before the trial has begun', upon the Pre-Trial Chamber's permission and after giving notice to the person charged. Pursuant to Rule 128 (3) of the ICC RPE, see *supra* note 33, a new hearing must be held when the Prosecutor seeks to add additional charges or to substitute more serious charges before the PTC. According to TC I, in the *Lubanga* case, the reference in Article 61(9) to the term "before the trial has begun" means "the true opening of the trial when the opening statements, if any, are made prior to calling of witnesses".

[107] See, *e.g.*, ICTR, *Prosecutor v. Bizimana and Nzabonimana*, Decision on Prosecution Motion for Severance and Amendment of Indictment, 7 November 2008, ICTR 98-44-I (granting prosecution amendment, noting that the request was made well before

the prosecutor or chamber may also move to amend the charges to conform to the evidence.[108]

The tribunals are reluctant to amend an indictment to charge previously uncharged sexual offenses or include additional facts, particularly as the trial nears or during trial, because of justifiable concerns about the rights of the defendant to a fair trial coupled with the need for expediency.[109] Both the ICTY and ICTR have adopted the general approach that indictments will not be amended at trial to add offenses that are not based on facts alleged in the confirmed indictment.[110] The ICC appears to have accepted this same approach.[111] However, the ICTR has permitted the Prosecutor leave to amend before trial in numerous cases, particularly when a motion is filed well in advance of trial.[112]

---

trial); ICTR, *Prosecutor v. Bizimungo*, Indictment filed in Conformity with Trial Chamber II Decision, 25 Sept 2002, ICTR-00-56-I, para. 5.66 (amending indictment to include allegations of sexual violence in advance of trial).

108 ICTR RPE, see *supra* note 46; ICTY RPE, see *supra* note 46.

109 See ICTR Statute, Article 19(1), see *supra* note 61 ("The Trial Chambers shall ensure that a trial is fair and expeditious and that proceedings are conducted in accordance with the rules of procedure and evidence, with full respect for the rights of the accused with due regard for the protection of victims and witnesses"); ICTR RPE, Rule 46, see *supra* note 46. Compare ICTR, *Prosecutor v. Bizimungu*, Decision on Prosecutor's Interlocutory Appeal against Trial Chamber II Decision of 6 October 2003 Denying Leave to File Amended Indictment, 12 February 2004, ICTR 99-50-AR5, para. 21 (affirming trial court order denying leave to amend a few months before trial because of substantial prejudice to accused) with ICTR, *Prosecutor v. Kabiligi and Ntabakuze*, Decision on the Prosecutor's Motion to Amend the Indictment, 8 October 1999, ICTR 97-34-I and ICTR 97-30-I, paras. 29, 66 (granting motion to amend indictment to add a count of rape as a crime against humanity well in advance of trial, occasioning no delay or prejudice to defendant).

110 See ICTR, *Prosecutor v. Bagambiki*, Judgement and Sentence (Trial), 25 February 2004, ICTR-97-36 ("*Bagambiki* Trial Judgement").

111 See ICC, *Prosecutor v. Lubanga*, Decision giving notice to the parties and participants that the legal characterisation of the facts may be subject to change in accordance with Regulation 55(2) of the Regulations of the Court, 14 July 2009, ICC/04-01/06-T, ICC-01/04-01/06-2049 ("*Lubanga* Legal Characterisation Decision").

112 See, *e.g.*, *Ndindabahizi* Trial Judgement, see *supra* note 102 (granting leave to amend the original indictment prior to trial to include a charge of rape as a crime against humanity); ICTR, *Prosecutor v. Nizeyimana and Hategekimana*, Decision on the Prosecutor's Motion for Severance and Leave to Amend the Indictment Against Idelphonse Hategekimana, 25 September 2007, ICTR-00-55-I (granting leave to amend indictment prior to trial to include a charge of sexual violence as genocide and rape as a crime against humanity); ICTR, *Prosecutor v. Ndindiliyimana, et al.*, Decision on

Notwithstanding this general approach, Trial Chamber 1 of the ICTR under the leadership of the Presiding Judge Navanathem Pillay[113] exercised judicial discretion in the case of *Prosecutor v. Akayesu* to stay the trial to amend the indictment to include charges of sexual offenses based on previously unknown facts adduced at trial during witness testimony, and to provide the defence with adequate time to prepare its defence against these additional charges.[114] These charges provided the foundation for the ground breaking international jurisprudence on rape as genocide.[115] This case is unique and appears to be perhaps the only case at the ICTR in which the Chamber authorized an amendment of the indictment to add sexual offense charges during a trial that proceeded to judgment on those charges.

Another possible remedy to address newly discovered evidence of sexual crimes at trial is to conform the charges to the evidence at the close of the trial in accordance with the *jura novit curia* principle, under which a judge is authorized to recharacterize the charges based on existing facts.[116] An extension of this principle to make amendments outside the scope of facts set forth in the indictment implicates defendant's right to a fair trial and the corollary right to defend against the charges and is problematic.

Prosecutor's Motion Under Rule 50 for Leave to Amend the Indictment, 28 January 2000, ICTR-00-56 (granting leave to amend prior to trial); ICTR, *Prosecutor v. Kabiligi and Ntabakuze*, Decision on the Prosecutor's Motion to Amend the Indictment, 8 October 1999, ICTR-97-34 (granting to leave to amend the indictment prior to trial).

113 Judge Navanathem Pillay, an expert on women's rights, presently serves as the United Nations Commissioner for Human Rights. When appointed to the ICTR, she was the only female judge – a situation that was not rectified for over four years. In an interview after the *Akayesu* judgement, Judge Pillay stated, "[f]rom time immemorial, rape has been regarded as spoils of war. Now it will be considered a war crime. We want to send out a strong signal that rape is no longer a trophy of war." Bill Berkeley, "Judgment Day", in *Washington Post Sunday Magazine*, 11 October 1998, p. W10.

114 See ICTR, *Prosecutor v. Akayesu*, Leave to Amend the Indictment, 11 June 1997, ICTR-96-4-T.

115 *Ibid.* at paras. 596–598, 731–734.

116 See ICC Regulations, Regulation 52(c), see *supra* note 94 (requiring that the indictment contain, in part, "[a] legal characterisation of the facts to accord both with the crimes under articles 6, 7 or 8 and the precise form of participation under articles 25 and 28").

The case of *Prosecutor v. Lubanga Dyilo*[117] poignantly illustrates these problems. During the *Lubanga Dyilo* trial phase, the prosecution submitted evidence of rape and sexual slavery. The representatives of the victims in that case moved under Court Regulation 55(2) to amend the charges to include these offenses, as well as cruel and inhumane treatment.[118] Regulation 55(1) authorizes the Trial Chamber to conform the charges to the evidence adduced at trial if the facts upon which the new charges were fully presented in the indictment and other conditions are met.[119] The Trial Chamber found Regulation 55(1) inapplicable and ruled that Regulation 55(2) provided a procedural basis for the trial chamber to amend the indictment to include sexual violence offenses without the limitations of 55(1).[120] The prosecutor and defense appealed this decision,

117 ICC, *Prosecutor v. Lubanga*, ICC/04-01/06.

118 ICC, *Prosecutor v. Lubanga*, Joint Application of the Legal Representatives of the Victims for the Implementation of the Procedure under Regulation 55 of the Regulations of the Court, ICC/04-01/06-T, ICC-01/04-01/06-1891; see also *Lubanga* Legal Characterisation Decision, para. 1, see *supra* note 111.

119 See ICC Regulations, Regulation 55(2), see *supra* note 94:

> 1. In its decision under article 74, the Chamber may change the legal characterisation of facts to accord with the crimes under articles 6, 7 or 8, or to accord with the form of participation of the accused under articles 25 and 28, without exceeding the facts and circumstances described in the charges and any amendments to the charges.
>
> 2. If, at any time during the trial, it appears to the Chamber that the legal characterisation of facts may be subject to change, the Chamber shall give notice to the participants of such a possibility and having heard the evidence, shall, at an appropriate stage of the proceedings, give the participants the opportunity to make oral or written submissions. The Chamber may suspend the hearing to ensure that the participants have adequate time and facilities for effective preparation or, if necessary, it may order a hearing to consider all matters relevant to the proposed change.

120 See ICC Regulations, Regulation 55, see *supra* note 94; see also *Lubanga* Legal Characterisation Decision, paras. 29, 31, 35, see *supra* note 111. Trial Chamber I, by majority opinion, ruled that the present case is governed by Regulations 55 (2) and (3) and the limitations of Regulation 55(1) are not applicable to the present case. Regulation 55 sets out the powers of the trial chamber in relation to two distinct stages, and the powers of the trial chamber pursuant to Regulation 55(1) are distinct from the powers conferred by Regulation 55(2): One stage is defined in Regulation 55(1) by referring expressly to Article 74 of the Statute, which sets out the requirements for the trial chamber's final judgement. In harmony with Article 74, Regulation 55(1) confers on the Chamber, in that final stage, the power to change the legal characterization of facts "without exceeding the facts and circumstances described in the charges and any amendments to the charges". In contrast to Regulation 55(1), Regulations 55(2) and

and the Appeals Chamber reversed, indicating that Regulation 55 did not expand the *jura novit curia* principle to permit amendments at trial to conform to facts not contained in the confirmed indictment.[121]

3.5.3. Practical and Strategic Considerations

The failure to draft a legally sufficient, accurate and supportable indictment that provides the defendant with sufficient notice of sexual violence charges and the mode of responsibility may materially impact the defend-

55(3) apply at "any time during the trial" and do not include the same limitation as Regulation 55(1) as to facts and circumstances included in the indictment. Judge Fulford dissented from the Majority, noting Regulation 55, created an indivisible or singular process; the Statute left control over framing and affecting any changes to the charges (under Article 61(9)) exclusively to the Pre-Trial Chamber. It follows that a modification to the legal characterization of the facts under Regulation 55 must not constitute an amendment to the charges, an additional charge, a substitute charge or a withdrawal of a charge, because these are each governed by Article 61(9). Judge Fulford considers then, that the procedure set out in Regulation 55 of giving notice of a proposed change to the legal characterization of the facts has not been engaged by this application because the victims seek to add five additional charges, and no other relevant proposed changes have been formulated and disseminated and, under these circumstances, the application should be dismissed.

121 See *Lubanga* Legal Characterisation Decision, see *supra* note 111; see also ICC, *Prosecutor v. Lubanga*, Judgement on the appeals of Mr. Lubanga Dyilo and the Prosecutor against the Decision of Trial Chamber I of 14 July 2009, 8 December 2009, ICC-01/04-01/06-2205. The Appeals Chamber considered two issues in its judgement. First, whether in Regulation 55 subsections (2) and (3) can be read separately from subsection (1) and whether subsections (2) and (3) permit a change in the legal characterisation beyond the charges. In deciding this first issue, the Chamber addressed several incompatibilities between Regulation 55, the Rome Statute, and international law that were raised by the Defence. Second, it considered whether Trial Chamber I erred in holding that the legal recharacterisation sought by the victims' representative in *Lubanga* may be sought. The Appeals Chamber found that the possibility for a Trial Chamber to modify the legal characterisation of the facts is not inherently incompatible with the Rome Statute or general principles of international law. Furthermore, it is not incompatible with the rights of the accused as long as he is given an adequate opportunity to prepare an effective defence to the new legal characterisation in the charges against him. However, the Appeals Chamber stressed that when using Regulation 55, a Trial Chamber shall not exceed the facts and circumstances described in the charges and any amendments thereto. To do so would result in a breach of article 74(2) of the Statute. The Appeals Chamber highlighted that it is the Prosecutor who is tasked with the investigation of crimes under the jurisdiction of the Court and to proffer charges against suspects.

ant's right to mount a defense[122] and the prosecutor's ability to successfully prosecute an otherwise prosecutable sexual violence charge.[123]

Although the mandate to confirm indictments at an early stage is compelling, thought should be given to ensuring that the investigation has exhausted all leads on sexual offenses and has documented each incident that has come to light prior to submitting any indictment for confirmation. Ideally, there should be no cases in which new or additional evidence of sexual offenses is submitted at the trial of a defendant. Having noted this, current rulings at the ICC prohibiting "proofing" of a witness[124] may in fact result in cases in which the court and the prosecution learn of sexual offenses at trial, underscoring the need for full investigations of sexual offenses. This is discussed more fully later in this Chapter.[125]

The sexual offense charges reflected in an indictment ultimately focus the prosecution and court's attention and mold the case at trial.[126] The charging choices involve appropriate characterization of the predicate offense, the international offense (genocide, crimes against humanity, or war crimes) and the mode of responsibility.[127]

Characterizing the predicate offense is straightforward unless there is no specific conduct enumerated in the respective statute. In such an instance, the prosecutor must characterize the act within the scope of enumerated predicate acts in the respective statute. Thus, sexual slavery cannot be charged directly as a predicate offense under crimes against

---

[122] Rome Statute, Article 19, see *supra* note 19.

[123] See *supra* notes 99–121; see *infra* note 143.

[124] See ICC, *Prosecutor v. Lubanga*, Decision on the Practices of Witness Familiarisation and Witness Proofing, 8 November 2006, ICC-01/04-01/06-679, p. 1 ("*Lubanga* Decision on Witness Familiarisation").

[125] See *infra* Section 3.6.1.2. of this Chapter.

[126] See Tamara F. Lawson, "A Shift Towards Gender Equality in Prosecutions: Realizing Legitimate Enforcement of Crimes Committed Against Women in Municipal and International Criminal Law", in *Southern Illinois University Law Journal*, 2009, vol. 33, no. 2, pp. 181, 214 (noting the shift in international tribunals regarding the use of prosecutorial discretion to prosecute crimes against women).

[127] For an overview of the elements of the different charges, see generally Women's Initiatives for Gender Justice, "Sexual Violence and International Criminal Law: An Analysis of the Ad Hoc Tribunal's Jurisprudence and the International Criminal Court's Elements of Crimes", September 2005, available at http://www.iccwomen.org/publications/resources/docs/Overview_Sexual_Violence_and_International_Criminal_Law.doc, last accessed on 10 May 2011.

humanity at the ICTY[128] as is permissible at the SCLS,[129] but can and has been characterized and successfully tried at the ICTY as "enslavement" under crimes against humanity.[130] Additionally, other acts of sexual violence for which there is no corresponding specified predicate offense may be characterized, dependent on the available evidence, as "other inhumane acts", "torture", "enslavement", or "persecution" as crimes against humanity[131] and "outrages upon personal dignity" in relation to war crimes.[132]

A defendant may be charged with all three types of offenses – genocide, crimes against humanity, and war crimes – for the same sexual act, even if arising out of the same set of facts, if all the elements of each offense are met and differ from each other. The test for prohibited cumulative charging is whether the offense charged contains an element not contained in the others.[133] Thus, a charge contained within another cannot be charged (that is, lesser included offenses) except in the disjunctive.[134]

---

[128] See ICTY Statute, Article 5, see *supra* note 61 (listing cognizable offenses as crimes against humanity, not including sexual slavery).

[129] See Statute of the Special Court for Sierra Leone, available at http://www.sc-sl.org/LinkClick.aspx?fileticket=uClnd1MJeEw%3D&, last accessed on 10 May 2011, Article 2(g) (listing sexual slavery as a crime against humanity).

[130] See Patricia Viseur Sellers, "Wartime Female Slavery: Enslavement?", in *Cornell International Law Journal*, 2011, vol. 44, no. 1, pp. 115, 125–26 (examining the *Foča* case, the first international criminal case from the ICTY in which there was a crimes against humanity conviction for enslavement that included sexual slavery); see also *Kunarac* Appeal Judgement, paras. 5, 9, 11, 13, and Section XII, see *supra* note 82 (upholding convictions for enslavement based on sexual slavery as a crime against humanity).

[131] See, *e.g.*, ICTR, *Prosecutor v. Bagosora*, Judgement, 18 December 2008, ICTR-98-41-T, paras. 2218–2221 (finding that inserting a bottle into the vagina of a woman and stripping women publicly of their clothes constitute other inhumane acts) ("*Bagasora* Trial Judgement").

[132] See, *e.g.*, ICTY, *Prosecutor v. Furundžija*, Judgement and Sentence (Trial), IT-95-17/1-T, para. 295 ("*Furundžija* Trial Judgement") (convicting defendant of outrages upon personal dignity for watching a women being raped and humiliated); *Kunarac* Appeal Judgement, para. 33, see *supra* note 82 (convicting defendant of outrages upon personal dignity for forcing women to dance nude on a table with others present).

[133] See Karim A.A. Khan and Rodney Dixon (eds.), *Archbold International Criminal Court: Practice, Procedure, and Evidence*, Sweet and Maxwell, London, 2005 (2d ed.), pp. 206–209 ("Archbold") (articulating the basic rule on cumulative charging and the conditions to be met to assert cumulative charges in the ICTR and ICTY); see also Patricia M. Wald, "Genocide and Crimes Against Humanity", in *Washington*

Sexual offenses as genocide must meet certain requirements as set forth in the elements of this crime in the relevant tribunal or court statutes. The judgment in the *Akayesu* case, the leading case on rape as genocide, stated findings that supported all elements of the offense of genocide.[135]

University Global Studies Law Review, 2007, vol. 6, no. 3, pp. 631–32 (discussing strategic uses of multiple convictions and citing *Kvočka*). For the approaches of the tribunals to cumulative charging, see, *e.g.*, ICTY, *Prosecutor v. Delalić*, Judgement (Appeal), 20 February 2001, IT-96-21-A, para. 400 ("*Delalić* Appeal Judgement") (confirming the use of cumulative charging and stating: "Cumulative charging is to be allowed in light of the fact, prior to the presentation of all of the evidence, it is not possible to determine to a certainty which of the charges brought against an accused will be proven. [...] In addition, cumulative charging constitutes the usual practice of both this Tribunal and the ICTR."); ICTR, *Prosecutor v. Akayesu*, Judgement (Trial), 2 September 1998, ICTR-96-4-T, para. 468 (asserting that under certain circumstances "the Chamber concludes that it is acceptable to convict the accused of two offences in relation to the same set of facts") ("*Akayesu* Trial Judgement"); see also *Bemba* Confirmation Decision, paras. 189–205, see *supra* note 40 (rejecting the cumulative charging approach of the Prosecutor and declining to confirm count 3 of torture as a crime against humanity within the meaning of Article 7(1)(f) of the Statute). The ICC Pre-Trial Chamber in *Bemba* opined that the prosecutorial practice of cumulative charging is detrimental to the rights of the Defence since it places an undue burden on the Defence. The Chamber considered that, as a matter of fairness and expeditiousness of the proceedings, only distinct crimes may justify a cumulative charging approach and, ultimately, be confirmed as charges. This is only possible if each statutory provision allegedly breached in relation to one and the same conduct requires at least one additional material element not contained in the other. The Chamber considered that in this particular case, the specific material elements of the act of torture, namely severe pain and suffering and control by the perpetrator over the person, are also the inherent specific material elements of the act of rape. However, the act of rape requires the additional specific material element of penetration, which makes it the most appropriate legal characterization in this particular case. The Chamber therefore considered that the act of torture was fully subsumed by the count of rape.

134 See Archbold, 2005, p. 207, see *supra* note 133 (elaborating on the conditions for cumulative charging as developed through tribunal case law); ICTY, *Prosecutor v. Kupreskić*, Judgement (Trial), 14 January 2000, IT-96-16T, para. 727 ("The Prosecution [...] should charge in the alternative rather than cumulatively whenever an offence appears to be in breach of more than one provision, depending on the elements of the crime the Prosecution is able to prove. [...] Indeed, in case of doubt it is appropriate from a prosecutorial viewpoint to suggest that a certain act falls under a stricter and more serious provision of the State, adding however that if proof to this effect is not convincing, the act falls under a less serious provision.").

135 See *Akayesu* Trial Judgement, paras. 731–733, see *supra* note 133:

> [...] as to "rape and sexual violence, the Chamber wishes to underscore the fact that in its opinion, they constitute genocide in the same way as any

As a practical matter, these facts may not be present in most cases and the

---

other act as long as they were committed with the specific intent to destroy, in whole or in part, a particular group, targeted as such. Indeed, rape and sexual violence certainly constitute infliction of serious bodily and mental harm on the victims and are even, according to the Chamber, one of the worst ways of inflict harm on the victim as he or she suffers both bodily and mental harm. In light of all the evidence before it, the Chamber is satisfied that the acts of rape and sexual violence described above, were committed solely against Tutsi women, many of whom were subjected to the worst public humiliation, mutilated, and raped several times, often in public, in the Bureau Communal premises or in other public places, and often by more than one assailant. These rapes resulted in physical and psychological destruction of Tutsi women, their families and their communities. Sexual violence was an integral part of the process of destruction, specifically targeting Tutsi women and specifically contributing to their destruction and to the destruction of the Tutsi group as a whole.

[...] This sexualized representation of ethnic identity graphically illustrates that tutsi women were subjected to sexual violence because they were Tutsi. Sexual violence was a step in the process of destruction of the tutsi group - destruction of the spirit, of the will to live, and of life itself.

[...] [T]he Chamber finds that in most cases, the rapes of Tutsi women in Taba, were accompanied with the intent to kill those women. Many rapes were perpetrated near mass graves where the women were taken to be killed . A victim testified that Tutsi women caught could be taken away by peasants and men with the promise that they would be collected later to be executed. Following an act of gang rape, a witness heard Akayesu say "tomorrow they will be killed" and they were actually killed. In this respect, it appears clearly to the Chamber that the acts of rape and sexual violence, as other acts of serious bodily and mental harm committed against the Tutsi, reflected the determination to make Tutsi women suffer and to mutilate them even before killing them, the intent being to destroy the Tutsi group while inflicting acute suffering on its members in the process.

[...] [T]he Chamber finds firstly that the acts described *supra* are indeed acts as enumerated in Article 2 (2) of the Statute, which constitute the factual elements of the crime of genocide, namely the killings of Tutsi or the serious bodily and mental harm inflicted on the Tutsi. The Chamber is further satisfied beyond reasonable doubt that these various acts were committed by Akayesu with the specific intent to destroy the Tutsi group, as such.

See also Suzanne Chenault, "And Since Akayesu? The Development of ICTR Jurisprudence on Gender Crimes: A Comparison of Akayesu and Muhimana", in *New England Journal of International and Comparative Law*, 2008, vol. 14, no. 2, p. 221 (examining the Tribunal's approach to gender crimes in *Akayesu* and its refinement and clarification of the approach in *Muhimana*).

preferable charging choice for the prosecutor may be crimes against humanity and/or war crimes.

Many sexual offenses can be characterized as both a crime against humanity and war crime if there are sufficient facts to establish an armed conflict and, if during that conflict, a civilian population is targeted. The facts must include the existence of an armed conflict[136] and the sexual act must be linked, that is, closely related to the armed conflict to establish a sexual offense as a war crime.[137] The establishment of the linking requirement ensures that the act in question is not one that is more appropriately characterized as a domestic sexual violence offense.[138] Thus, rapes as part of weapons searches were not considered to be "individual domestic crimes" by the ICTY in the case of *Prosecutor v. Brđanin*.[139] In addition, as previously noted, a sexual act charged as a crime against humanity need only form part of a widespread or systematic attack directed against a civilian population; the sexual act charged need not be widely or systematically employed.[140]

136 See Rome Statute, Articles 8(a)–(e), see *supra* note 19 (setting forth offenses under each category of conflict).

137 See *Rutaganda* Appeal Judgement, paras 569–70, see *supra* note 47 (adopting the legal test enunciated in the ICTY Appeal Judgement in the case of *Prosecutor v. Kunarac* that "if it can be established [...] that the perpetrator acted in furtherance of or under the guise of the armed conflict [...] it would be sufficient to conclude that his acts were closely related to the armed conflict" and explaining that "'under the guise of the armed conflict' does not mean simply 'at the same time as the armed conflict' and/or 'in any circumstances created in part by the armed conflict'" but requires consideration of all of the Kunarac factors, including "the fact that the perpetrator is a combatant; the fact that the victim is a non-combatant; the fact that the victim is a member of the opposing party; the fact that the act may be said to serve the ultimate goal of a military campaign; and the fact that the crime is committed as part of or in the context of the perpetrator's official duties.").

138 *Ibid.*

139 See ICTY, *Prosecutor v. Brđanin*, Judgement (Appeal), 3 April 2007, ICTY-99-36-A, para. 256.

140 See ICTR, *Prosecutor v. Nahimana*, Judgement (Appeal), 28 November 2007, ICTR-99-52-A, para. 924 (stating "The Appeals Chamber considers that, except for extermination, a crime need not be carried out against a multiplicity of victims in order to constitute a crime against humanity. Thus an act directed against a limited number of victims, or even against a single victim, can constitute a crime against humanity, provided it forms part of a widespread or systematic attack against a civilian population.") ("*Nahimana* Appeal Judgement").

A prosecutor is not only instrumental in developing a case and bringing alleged perpetrators to justice, but serves as an officer of the court and assists in the development of jurisprudence. An indictment, although primarily a technical tool, is indispensible as a jurisprudential tool. Thus, even though instances of sexual violence as genocide, crimes against humanity, or war crimes may be difficult to prove, if the facts suggest this is a correct characterization of a defendant's actions and there is sufficient evidence to support a *prima facie* case, it may be incumbent on the prosecutor to charge these offenses.[141]

In determining the appropriate mode of responsibility to charge in the indictment, the courts have permitted charging under both individual and derivative (command) responsibility, but have ruled that a defendant may be found guilty under only one mode of responsibility for a finding entered for "the same count and the same set of facts".[142] The courts have scrutinized indictments that do not specifically mention JCE, finding that specific reference to this mode is not required only if the facts presented in support of the indictment or in the pre-trial brief clearly establish that the prosecutor was relying on this mode to establish responsibility and provide the defendant adequate and timely notice.[143]

The challenges of charging the mode of responsibility in a legally and technically sufficient manner, particularly in regard to pleading JCE,[144] and setting forth a sufficient factual basis to support the specific, alleged mode of responsibility[145] are best met by employing highly skilled and experienced trial attorneys, assisted by attorney advisors working as part of an investigative team.

---

141 See generally Xabier Agirre Aranburu, "Sexual Violence beyond Reasonable Doubt: Using Pattern Evidence and Analysis for International Cases", in *Leiden Journal of International Law*, 2010, vol. 23, no. 3, pp. 609–27 (urging forth new statistical methods for establishing proof of systematic sexual offenses).

142 ICTR, *Prosecutor v. Renzaho*, Judgement (Appeal), 1 April 2011, ICTR-97-31A, para. 564 ("*Renzaho* Appeal Judgement").

143 See *Gacumbitsi* Appeal Judgement, paras. 161–178, see *supra* note 77 (restating and applying the law applicable to properly pleading JCE).

144 *Ibid.*

145 See, *e.g.*, ICTR, *Renzaho* Appeal Judgement, paras. 111–129, see *supra* note 142 (reversing defendant's convictions for rape because of defective pleading of the factual basis for the mode of responsibility in the indictment that was not cured).

3.6. Evidentiary Challenges at Trial

Prosecutions of sexual offenses differ in some respects from other offenses and thus face unique, albeit not necessarily more difficult, evidentiary challenges. Among the greatest evidentiary challenges to effective prosecution of sexual offenses are: investigative barriers inherent to uncovering sexual offenses;[146] the need for credible, reliable, accurate, and complete information from sexual assault victims;[147] problems of obtaining sufficient circumstantial evidence of the facts and the perpetrator in cases in which there are no eyewitnesses;[148] establishing corroboration of hearsay evidence or unreliable witnesses;[149] and linking evidence to establish defendant's legal responsibility.[150]

The ICTR's success in overcoming most of these challenges is illustrated by its historical record of sexual offense prosecutions. Of a total of 89 cases indicted by the ICTR,[151] sexual offenses were charged in almost half.[152] Of the total number of indicted cases, 35 have been complet-

---

146 See, *e.g.*, UN Sub-Commission on the Promotion and Protection of Human Rights, Working paper by Françoise Hampson on the criminalization, investigation and prosecution of acts of serious sexual violence, 20 July 2004, E/CN.4/Sub.2/2004/12, available at http://www.unhcr.org/refworld/docid/4152ebe14.html, last accessed on 10 May 2011; see also Binaifer Nowrojee, "We can do better Investigating and Prosecuting International Sexual Crimes", available at http://www.womensrightscoalition.org/site/publications/papers/doBetter_en.php, last accessed on 10 May 2011 (noting that historically there has been a silence surrounding the sex crimes against women that downplays their suffering and renders them invisible).

147 See, *e.g.*, *Semanza* Trial Judgement, see *supra* note 100 (finding that several rape victim/witnesses failed to provide sufficient information to base a finding of guilt of defendant); *Prosecutor v. Muvunyi*, Judgement and Sentence (Trial), 12 September 2006, ICTR-2000-55A-T, paras. 378–401 ("*Muvunyi* Trial Judgement") (finding that it was members from a camp that was not under Muvunyi's control that committed the acts forming the basis for the charge); see also Dianne Luping, "Investigation and Prosecution of Sexual and Gender-Based Crimes Before the International Criminal Court", in *American University Journal of Gender, Social Policy and the Law*, 2009, vol. 17, no. 2, pp. 431, 486 et seq. (focusing on interview techniques to elicit thorough and accurate information from sexual crimes' victims).

148 See *infra* note 159; see also *infra* Sections 3.6.1.2. and 3. of this Chapter.

149 See *infra* Section 3.6.1.3. of this Chapter.

150 See *infra* Section 3.6.3. of this Chapter.

151 See ICTR, Status of Cases, available at http://www.unictr.org/Cases/StatusofCases/tabid/204/Default.aspx, last accessed on 10 May 2011 ("Status of ICTR Cases").

152 This number is based on best available information. In some cases, it is not possible to determine multiple iterations of indictments. This number includes cases that con-

ed through appeal and are considered herein.[153] Of these completed 35 cases, sexual offenses were charged or referenced in the indictment as a basis of a charge in approximately half of the cases.[154] The indictments that proceeded to judgment included about 220 counts of non-sexual violence crimes and 30 counts based on sexual violence. The confirmed judgments resulted in a verdict of guilty in about 82 counts of nonsexual crimes and 13 counts of sexual violence. These statistics establish a conviction rate of 0.37 for nonsexual violence offenses and 0.43 for sexual violence offenses to date at the ICTR. The total number of sexual violence based counts is deceptively low because many cases that were amended under the leadership of Prosecutor Jallow have not yet been completed and are not considered herein.

In nearly all cases before the ICTR in which a victim has testified that a sexual crime was committed, the tribunal found that the predicate sexual act was committed.[155] In those few cases in which the victim did not testify, the prosecution generally was not successful in establishing a

tained sexual crimes offenses at any time after confirmation. See de Brouwer, 2005, pp. 334–35, 335 n. 84, see *supra* note 4 (noting that around half of the indictments brought before the ICTR have included crimes involving sexual violence, including the indictments of Akayesu, Bagambiki, Bagilishema, Barayagwiza, Bisengimana, Bikindi, Bizimana, Gacumbitsi, Gatete, Imanishimwe, Kajelijeli, Kabuga, Karemera, Karera, Kamuhanda, Mpambara, Mpiranya, Muhimana, Musema, Nahimana, Ngeze, Ngirumpatse, Niyitegeka, Nyiramasuhuko, Nzabarinda, Nzabondimana, Nzirorera, Renzaho, Rusatira, Rugambarara, Rwamakuba, Sagahutu, Semanza, and Serushago).

153 A total of 46 cases have been completed through appeal, including 1 for perjury, 1 for contempt of court, and 9 guilty plea cases that are not considered herein, leaving a total of 35 cases. The 9 guilty plea cases are not included in this number because they do not reflect on evidentiary challenges at trial. See Status of ICTR Cases, see *supra* note 151.

154 Sexual acts are also referenced in the indictments or amended indictments in the following cases in which judgement and/or sentence has been rendered by the ICTR through appeal: *Akayesu*, *Barayagwiza*, *Gacumbitsi*, *Kamuhanda*, *Muhimana*, *Musema*, *Muvunyi*, *Nahimana*, *Ndindabahizi*, *Ngeze*, *Niyetegika*, *Renzaho*, *Rukundo*, *Semanza*, and *Kabiligi*.

155 See, *e.g.*, *Akayesu* Trial Judgement, see *supra* note 133; ICTR, *Prosecutor v. Gacumbitsi*, Judgement and Sentence (Trial), 17 June 2004, ITCR-2001-64-T ("*Gacumbitsi* Trial Judgement"); *Prosecutor v. Hategekimana*, Judgement and Sentence (Trial), 6 December 2010, ICTR-00-55 ("*Hategekimana* Trial Judgement"); *Kajelijeli* Trial Judgement, see *supra* note 49; *Muhimana* Trial Judgement, see *supra* note 102; *Prosecutor v. Rukundo*, Judgement (Trial), 27 February 2009, ICTR-2001-70-T ("*Rukundo* Trial Judgement"); and *Semanza* Trial Judgement, see *supra* note 100.

specific sexual assault unless the witnesses provided direct eyewitness testimony or uncontroverted circumstantial evidence.[156]

In a number of cases, prosecutors withdrew sexual offense charges because of a lack of evidence of the predicate sexual offense,[157] or led no evidence of charged predicate sexual offenses resulting in a verdict of not guilty.[158] In most cases of acquittal in which the prosecutor led evidence on the specific sexual crime charged, the basis for a resulting acquittal was the lack of evidence linking the defendant to the crime and establishing his responsibility for the sexual predicate act.[159] The tribunal entered

---

[156] See *Semanza* Trial Judgement, paras. 257–262, 476, see *supra* note 100 (concluding there was insufficient circumstantial evidence to infer that Victim B was raped despite testimony of witnesses that the accused directed men to rape Tutsi women, that men then entered Victim A's house, Victim A saw two men take her cousin, Victim B, outside her home while one man remained who raped her, that Victim A heard Victim B screaming she would rather be dead and, Victim B's body was later discovered); *Muhimana* Trial Judgement, paras. 18, 19, 32, see *supra* note 102 (finding that although the witness was not an eyewitness to the rape, the rape could be inferred on the basis that the witness saw the accused take the girls into his house, heard the girls screaming his name and shouting that they "did not expect him to do that", and seeing the girls being led out of the house naked and walking with their legs apart).

[157] See, *e.g.*, ICTR, *Prosecutor v. Ndindabahizi*, Indictment, 8 July 2003, ICTR 2001-71-I; ICTR, *Prosecutor v. Ntuyahaga*, Decision on the Prosecutor's Motion to Withdraw the Indictment, 18 March 1999, ICTR 98-40-T.

[158] See, *e.g.*, ICTR, *Prosecutor v. Mpambara*, Decision on the Defence's Motion for Judgement of Acquittal, 21 October 2005, ICTR 2001-65-T; *Semanza* Trial Judgement, see *supra* note 100.

[159] See, *e.g.*, *Akayesu* Trial Judgement, see *supra* note 133 (finding insufficient evidence of defendant's responsibility for certain sexual violence offenses); *Hategekimana* Trial Judgement, see *supra* note 155; *Kajelijeli* Trial Judgment, see *supra* note 49 (finding insufficient evidence to hold defendant responsible for sexual acts that were established by the evidence); ICTR, *Prosecutor v. Mpambara*, Judgement and Sentence (Trial), 20 September 2006, ICTR 01-65-T ("*Mpambara* Trial Judgement") (finding insufficient evidence of defendant's responsibility for sexual offenses); *Muhimana* Trial Judgement, paras. 534–563, see *supra* note 102 (finding insufficient evidence of defendant's responsibility for several sexual crimes counts), *rev'd in part*, Judgement (Appeal), 21 May 1997, ICTR 95-1B-A ("*Muhimana* Appeal Judgement"); *Gacumbitsi* Appeal Judgement, see *supra* note 77 (finding evidence of defendant's responsibility for acts of rape committed by others insufficient); *Muvunyi* Trial Judgement, para. 159, see *supra* note 147 (noting that the appellate court set aside all convictions and sentencing, save for one count which was sent back for retrial). But see ICTR, *Prosecutor v. Kamuhanda*, Judgement (Trial), 22 January 2004, ICTR 95-54A-T (acquitting on the rape counts because evidence consisted solely of hearsay witnesses); ICTR, *Prosecutor v. Niyitegeka*, Judgement and Sentence (Trial), 16 May 2003, ICTR

verdicts of not guilty in a few cases in which evidence of sexual violence was led but the indictment was defective.[160] In every case before the ICTR in which sexual crimes had been charged in the indictment and the defendant later entered a guilty plea, the sexual crimes were withdrawn from the final indictment to which the defendant plead guilty.[161] It is also noteworthy that the ICTR has allowed evidence at trial relating to uncharged sexual violence offenses, a practice not provided for in the Statute or the RPE.[162]

96-14-T ("*Niyitegeka* Trial Judgement") (rejecting hearsay testimony evidence to establish act of rape, but accepting and relying on testimony of one eye witness to establish the same); *Gacumbitsi* Appeal Judgement, paras. 141–145, see *supra* note 77 (disagreeing with the trial chamber finding that there was no superior authority and exploring requirements of *de facto* authority but concluding that there was no evidence that defendant exercised "direct control" over those committing the acts); *Bikindi* Trial Judgement, paras. 339–350, see *supra* note 102 (finding witnesses unreliable on the basis of inconsistencies between witnesses' testimony as time and circumstances of the rape and murder of alleged victim and holding that the evidence failed to establish that anyone under defendant's command committed rape or murder).

160 See *Semanza* Trial Judgement, see *supra* note 100; see also *Renzaho* Appeal Judgement, paras. 111–129, see *supra* note 142 (reversing defendant's convictions for rape because of failure to sufficiently plead the factual basis for the mode of responsibility in the indictment or to cure the deficient indictment).

161 See, *e.g.*, ICTR, *Prosecutor v. Nzabirinda*, Trial Chamber Sentencing Judgement (Trial), 23 February 2007, ICTR 2001-77-T ("*Nzabirinda* Trial Judgement"); ICTR; *Prosecutor v. Rugambarara*, Decision on the Prosecution Motion to Amend the Indictment, 28 June 2007, ICTR 2000-59-I, para. 2; ICTR, *Prosecutor v. Bisengimana*, Judgement and Sentence (Trial), 13 April 2006, ICTR 00-60-T, paras. 7, 12 ("*Bisengimana* Trial Judgement"); and ICTR, *Prosecutor v. Serushago*, Sentence (Trial), 5 February 1999, ICTR-98-39 ("*Serushago* Trial Judgement").

162 See, *e.g.*, *Kayishema* Trial Judgement, see *supra* note 82 (allowing evidence of uncharged sexual violence); ICTR, *Prosecutor v. Rutaganda*, Judgement and Sentence (Trial), 6 December 1999, ICTR-96-03-T ("*Rutaganda* Trial Judgement") (allowing testimony of although the indictment charged no sexual offenses or set forth any facts of sexual violence); ICTR, *Prosecutor v. Ntakirutimana*, Judgement and Sentence (Trial), 21 February 2003, ICTR-96-17-T ("*Ntakirutimana* Trial Judgement") (accepting testimony about the rape of three women, even though neither defendant was charged with nor linked to the rapes); ICTR, *Prosecutor v. Nahimana, Barayagiza and Ngeze*, Judgement and Sentence (Trial), 3 December 2003, ICTR-99-52-T ("*Nahimana* Trial Judgement") (allowing testimony of defendant encouraging rapes and other sexual violence through propaganda although the indictment charged no sexual violence offenses); *Ndindabahizi* Trial Judgement, see *supra* note 102 (referencing evidence of uncharged sexual violence); *Muvunyi* Trial Judgement, paras. 270, 301,

3.6.1. Evidence Weighing and Fact Finding

Trial judges are confronted by a staggering mass of evidence as they face deliberations on the findings, judgment, and sentence in any given case.[163] Prosecutors and defense attorneys assist the court by providing closing briefs in which the parties summarize the evidence presented in support of the respective party.[164] Unfortunately, the adversarial system does not lend itself to an exacting and objective evaluation of the evidence by the parties and thus the value of these briefs is diminished. Prosecutors best serve the interests of justice and the court by understanding the challenges and methodology employed by the court in its fact-finding function, particularly in sexual assault cases. This understanding enables a prosecutor to select appropriate witnesses and documents to substantiate the charges as well as assist in the development of applicable jurisprudence.

3.6.1.1. Admissibility of Evidence

The RPE of each tribunal provide for admissibility of relevant and probative evidence[165] and most proffered evidence is admitted; thus, many prosecutors are perhaps less than diligent in critically examining the weight of available evidence to support charged sexual violence offenses,

see *supra* note 147 (allowing testimony of sexual violence and entering findings of rape although no sexual offenses were charged and no sexual violence facts were set forth in the indictment). But see, ICTR, *Prosecutor v. Kanyarukiga*, Decision on Defense Motion for a Stay of the Proceedings or Exclusion of Evidence Outside the Scope of the Indictment, 15 January 2010, ICTR-2002-78-T (granting defense motion to exclude evidence, in part, based on findings that the defendant objected in a timely manner at trial and the prosecution failed to provide sufficient notice of the facts in the indictment, pre-trial brief or opening statement); and ICTR, *Prosecutor v. Ntagerura*, Decision on the Application to File an Amicus Curiae Brief, 24 May 2001, ICTR 99-46-T, paras. 23–24 (noting that the Chamber must exclude evidence of uncharged crimes).

163 See *Bagasora* Trial Judgement, see *supra* note 131 (admitting testimony from over 242 witnesses during the course of a trial that lasted over three years); see also ICTR, Press Release, "Bagosora, Ntabakuze and Nsengiyumva given life sentence; Kabiligi acquitted", 18 December 2008, ICTR/INFO_9-2-582.EN, available at http://69.94.11.53/ENGLISH/PRESSREL/2008/582.html, last accessed on 11 May 2011.

164 See ICTR, "Practice Directions on Length and Timing of Closing Briefs and Arguments", 3 May 2010, available at http://www.unictr.org/Legal/PracticeDirections/tabid/96/Default.aspx, last accessed on 10 May 2011.

165 ICTR Statute, Rule 89(c), see *supra* note 61 (permitting admission of any relevant evidence that the chamber finds to be probative).

leaving the job of sorting out volumes of testimony and documentary evidence to trial chambers. In common law systems in which there is concern that jurors might be unable to properly assess information,[166] the rules of evidence establish stringent safeguards to ensure that evidence is relevant, probative and reliable, is not unduly prejudicial to the defendant, and has been obtained without violating any of the defendant's rights.[167] The ICTY in the *Mucić* case commented on "reliability" and noted that the rule for admissibility was unambiguous and thus declined to add "reliability" as an additional provision to the applicable rule as a condition of admissibility.[168]

As cases progressed and the tribunals matured, the need for permissive authentication of documents – that is, the authority of the court to request that the party proffering a document into evidence establish that the document is indeed what it is purported to be – became more pronounced.[169] Authentication provides initial indicia of reliability and prevents questionable documents from being admitted into evidence and considered in deliberations. Under the civil law system, trial judges may request additional witnesses as a matter of right; however, the common law procedural law system adopted at the ICTY and ICTR does not provide the tribunal authority to independently call non-expert witnesses;

166 See, *e.g.*, Steven I. Friedland, "On Common Sense and the Evaluation of Witness Credibility", in *Case Western Law Review*, 1989–90, vol. 40, no. 1, p. 165 (highlighting concerns over the average jurors ability to assess witness credibility); Joe S. Cecil, Valerie P. Hans, and Elizabeth C. Wiggins, "Citizen Comprehension of Difficult Issues: Lessons from Civil Jury Trials", in *American University Law Review*, 1991, vol. 40, no. 2, p. 727 (surveying juror competence in common law civil trials).

167 See, *e.g.*, U.S. Federal Rules of Evidence, Rules 401–403, see *supra* note 45 (establishing criteria for relevance, probative value, and reliability to be admissible).

168 See ICTY, *Prosecutor v. Delalić et al.*, Decision on Prosecutor's Oral Requests for the Admission of Exhibit 155 into Evidence and for an Order to Compel the Accused, Zdravko Mucić, to Provide a Handwriting Sample, 19 January 1998, ICTY- 96-21-T, para. 32 (distinguishing the *Tadić* Hearsay Decision of 5 August 1996 that focused on the importance of reliability from the requirements for admissibility under existing RPE); see also ICTR, *Prosecutor v. Musema*, Judgement and Sentence (Trial), 27 January 2000, ICTR-96-13-T, para. 56 ("*Musema* Trial Judgement") ("The reliability of evidence does not constitute a separate condition of admissibility; rather, it provides the basis for the findings of relevance and probative value required under Rule 89(c) for evidence to be admitted.").

169 See ICTR RPE, Rule 92*bis*, see *supra* note 46 (as amended); see also Bang-Jensen, 1998, pp. 1541, 1548–49, see *supra* note 38 (noting that many of the documents that the Tribunal receives can be used as evidence if authenticated).

thus, this rule fills the "gap" between the common and civil law procedures at those tribunals.

As a practical matter, a trial chamber hears all testimony, sees all documents, assesses reliability, and assigns weight based on the totality of information available at the close of the case at the trial stage. Thus, it is not uncommon for a trial chamber to admit most evidence, including the prior statements of a witness[170] and to note in the judgment evidence that was afforded little or no weight.[171] Nonetheless, evidence and documents that are otherwise relevant and probative but would deprive a defendant of a fair trial are inadmissible;[172] for example, pre-trial statements of witnesses that fail to meet the requirements of the ICTR RPE have been ruled as inadmissible by the ICTR and as depriving the defendant of a fair trial.[173]

---

170 See, *e.g.*, *Hategekimana* Trial Judgement, see *supra* note 155; ICTR, *Prosecutor v. Gacumbitsi*, Judgement and Sentence (Trial), 17 June 2004, ICTR-01-64 ("*Gacumbitsi* Trial Judgement"); ICTR, *Prosecutor v. Kabiligi*, Judgement and Sentence (Trial), 18 December 2008, ICTR-97-34 ("*Kabiligi* Trial Judgement").

171 See, *e.g.*, ICTY, *Prosecutor v. Delalić*, Judgement (Trial), 16 November 1998, IT-96-21, paras. 709, 710, 711, 713, 714 ("*Delalić* Trial Judgement") (providing various reasons why no weight would be given to particular items of documentary evidence).

172 ICTR Statute, Article 14, see *supra* note 61; ICTR RPE, Rules 70(f), 89, 92*bis*(A)(ii)(b), see *supra* note 46; see, *e.g.*, ICTR, *Prosecutor v. Karemera*, Decision on Reconsideration of Admission of Written Statements in Lieu of Oral Testimony and Admission of the Testimony of Prosecution Witness Gay, 28 September 2007, ICTR 98-44, p. 13 (allowing certain written statements regarding sexual violence to be admitted into evidence); see also ICTR, *Prosecutor v. Karemera*, Decision on Prosecution Motion for Admission of Evidence of Rape and Sexual Assault Pursuant to Rule 92*bis* of the Rules and Order for Reduction of Prosecution Witness List, 11 December 2006, ICTR-98-44, paras. 3, 20 (denying motion of prosecution to admit 63 statements of purported rape victims and transcripts of 8 rape witnesses from previous tribunal cases on basis that the must testify because the evidence was "pivotal" to the Prosecution's case and defendant would be unduly prejudiced if denied the right to cross-examine the witnesses).

173 See ICTR, *Prosecutor v. Nizeyimana*, Decision on Prosecution Motion to Admit into Evidence the Statement of General Marcel Gatsinzi, 6 October 2010, ICTR-2000-55C (ruling a pre-trial statement of a prosecution witness inadmissible where witness would not be providing oral testimony, finding that the witness statement addressed a "pivotal" element of the case and admissibility of the statement without oral interrogation would be highly prejudicial to the accused).

3.6.1.2. Assessing Credibility and Reliability

One of the most difficult tasks of the tribunal is assessing and assigning appropriate weight to the testimony of a witness to international crimes, particularly if that witness is also a victim. One review of ICTR cases reveals that witnesses testified inconsistently with their pre-trial statement in over 50% of cases.[174] At the ICC, one might expect this rate to be higher because proofing is prohibited. Because of the number of cases in which credibility and reliability of witnesses is in issue, it is helpful to know those factors upon which the tribunals have relied on in reaching factual determinations, with specific focus on sexual crimes cases. These factors can provide guidance to a prosecutor and also inform a prosecutor's efforts to move forward with a case in which the credibility or reliability of a material witness has come into question.[175]

The tribunals focus on several factors in assessing the testimony of a witness, including the emotional trauma experienced by a sexual assault victim as witness,[176] inconsistencies in the testimony and pre-trial statements,[177] the investigative methodology used to obtain pre-trial state-

[174] See Nancy Armoury Combs, *Fact-Finding Without Facts, The Uncertain Evidentiary Foundations of International Court Convictions*, Cambridge University Press, Cambridge, 2010, pp. 106–118 (noting that such inconsistencies include differing facts as well as additional, material information presented at trial that were not included in the pre-trial statement).

[175] The classic method to rehabilitate a witness whose credibility has been called into question is to present a prior consistent statement or character evidence. See, *e.g.*, U.S. Federal Rules of Evidence, Rules 608, 613, see *supra* note 45 (allowing character evidence and prior statements that are consistent with trial testimony as a means of rebuttal to impeachment attempts). To date, international prosecutors have not submitted evidence of this nature, perhaps assuming that prosecution witnesses relevant to sexual crimes charges did not need to be rehabilitated.

[176] See, *e.g.*, ICTR, *Prosecutor v. Kajelijeli*, Trial Transcript, 2 December 2001, ICTR98-44A, p. 16 ("*Kajelijeli* Trial Transcript") (testifying that she did not address rape in the pre-trial statement as it was something she did not need to discuss); ICTR, *Prosecutor v. Gacumbitsi*, Trial Transcript, 6 August 2003, ICTR-01-64, p. 9–10 ("*Gacumbitsi* Trial Transcript") (allowing victim/witness to testify to event by writing during trial because she could not speak the words); *Rutaganda* Trial Judgement, para. 22, see *supra* note 162 (noting that many witnesses had been traumatized by the events they witnessed and suffered).

[177] See, *e.g.*, *Muhimana* Trial Judgement, para. 27, see *supra* note 102 (finding that the discrepancy in name of the rape victim, Goretti Mukashyaka in the pre-trial statement and Immaculee Mukakayiro in testimony was adequately explained by the witness at trial); see also *Hategekimana* Trial Judgement, para. 171, see *supra* note 155 (noting

ments,[178] the educational background of the witness,[179] cultural norms,[180] translation challenges,[181] characterization of the witness's testimony,[182] corroboration,[183] and motivation to fabricate or lie.[184]

---

that discrepancies between a witness's trial statement and testimony regarding identification of defendant's escorts raised doubts about the reliability of the witness).

178 Nearly all witnesses who failed to include a material fact in the pre-trial statement stated at trial that the investigator did not inquire into the matter. See, *e.g.*, ICTR, *Prosecutor v. Karera*, Judgement (Trial), 7 December 2007, ICTR 01-74, para. 115 ("*Karera* Trial Judgement") (noting that the investigator did not ask about the issue in question). In addition, witnesses were often illiterate and investigators did not read the statements back to the witness prior to obtaining a signature. See, *e.g.*, ICTR, *Prosecutor v. Ntakarutimana*, Trial Transcript, 24 September 2001, ICTR-96-10, p. 113 (testifying that the he, the investigator, did not read the statement back to the witness prior to obtaining a signature).

179 Many victim/witnesses in ICTR sexual assault cases were illiterate or had limited schooling. Witnesses often referenced this when they did not answer a question posed by the prosecutor at trial. See, *e.g.*, ICTR, *Prosecutor v. Ndindabahizi*, Trial Transcript, 15 September 2003, ICTR-01-71, p. 10 (noting lack of education as explanation for inability to answer questions).

180 Rwandans live in an oral tradition, in which the line between hearing about an event and direct observation of that event are conflated. See *Akayesu* Trial Judgement, para. 155, see *supra* note 133. In addition, taboos about speaking about sexual offenses resulted in unwillingness of victims to come forward, and testimony that there were no rapes in Rwanda. United Nationals Department of Peacekeeping Operations, "Review of the Sexual Violence Elements of the Judgements of the International Criminal tribunal for the Former Yugoslavia and the International Criminal Tribunal for Rwanda, and the Special Court For Sierra Leone in the Light of Security Council Resolution 1820", 2009, available at http://www.unrol.org/files/32914_Review%20of%20the%20Sexual%20Violence%20Elements%20in%20the%20Light%20of%20the%20Security-Council%20resolution%201820.pdf, last accessed on 11 May 2011, p. 57 (citing the *Semanza* judgements and noting that "[a]t trial the accused denied any knowledge of the rapes, explaining that "[i]n Rwandan tradition or culture, rape has never existed"").

181 Many languages, including the Kinyarwanda language in Rwanda, do not have a word for "rape" and the act must be described in detail. Many witnesses are unable to do this, requiring the prosecutor to "lead" the witness and provide language that will meet the required elements of the crime of "rape". See, *e.g.*, ICTR, *Prosecutor v. Semanza*, Trial Transcript, 19 March 2001, ICTR-97-20, paras. 47–48 (describing the act of rape and asking victim/witness if this is what happened: "Did the defendant insert his penis into your vagina?").

When this fails, the court has recognized colloquial terms and euphemisms when supported by expert testimony. See, *e.g.*, *Akayesu* Trial Judgement, paras. 152–154, see *supra* note 133; ICTR, *Prosecutor v. Musema*, Trial Transcript, 11 March 1999, ICTR-96-13, p. 50.

The tribunals painstakingly scrutinize witness statements within the context of all evidence to assess reliability and assign weight. It has been argued that this scrutiny and the weight afforded to evidence in sexual assault cases is applied by the tribunals in a more exacting fashion than that in non-sexual violence cases.[185] An overview of ICTR

---

182 Witnesses who testify may be characterized as eye witnesses (witnessed an act or event directly) or hearsay witnesses (heard about the act or event). In addition, the substance of the testimony may be characterized as direct (witnessing the specific act or event alleged) or circumstantial (witnessing acts or events giving from which one might infer the existence of the act or event alleged). The evidence generally afforded the greatest credibility is eye-witness testimony of direct facts; the least, hearsay and circumstantial.

183 See ICTR RPE, Rule 96, see *supra* note 46 ("In cases of sexual assault [...] no corroboration of the victim's testimony shall be required"); ICTY RPE, Rule 96, see *supra* note 46 (same); ICC RPE, Rule 63, see *supra* note 33 ("[A] Chamber shall not impose a legal requirement that corroboration is required in order to prove any crime within the jurisdiction of the Court, in particular, crimes of sexual violence"). Although corroboration is not required to establish a sexual predicate offense, corroboration is assessed in the fact-finding process when reliability or credibility of a witness is at issue. Where the defendant has put forth an incontrovertible alibi, the reliability of a witness who testifies otherwise generally is considered unreliable and afforded no weight. See, *e.g.*, *Kabiligi* Trial Judgement, paras. 1969–1986, see *supra* note 170 (finding unreliable the testimony of several witnesses placing Kabiligi at roadblocks and elsewhere in Rwanda at times in which the defendant's passport clearly showed him traveling outside the county and the Defense presented first-hand information corroborated by five defense witnesses as well as a co-defendant); see also *Bagasora* Trial Judgement, paras. 1722–33, 1729, see *supra* note 131 (finding the uncorroborated testimony of a second-hand and otherwise unreliable witness insufficient to support findings of rape, and noting that the Chamber declined to accept the testimony "without corroboration").

184 Despite testimony suggesting that witnesses may have a motive to lie, the tribunals have assessed this in very few cases, preferring not to characterize a witness's testimony that conflicts with their previous statements as perjured testimony. See *Akayesu* Trial Judgement, para. 442, see *supra* note 133 (failing to comment in judgement on evidence that women who had not previously disclosed rape were coming forward with these allegations at a later time as a means to blackmail defendants and others); but see ICTR, *Prosecutor v. GAA*, Judgement and Sentence, 4 December 2007, ICTR-07-90-R77 (pleading guilty to false testimony submitted in an evidentiary hearing on the appeal of conviction and sentence of Jean de Dieu Kamuhanda).

185 See Kate Fitzgerald, "Problems of Prosecution and Adjudication of Rape and Other Sexual Assaults under International Law", in *European Journal of International Law*, 1997, vol. 8, no. 4, pp. 638, 646 (reiterating the longstanding opinion that "rape must be examined with greater caution than any other crime as it is easy to charge and difficult to defend").

judgments does not appear to support this argument.[186] However, the private nature of sexual crimes often involves a lack of direct witnesses, perhaps giving rise to a greater reliance on circumstantial evidence and hearsay, resulting in what might appear to be a raised bar for evidentiary requirements for sexual crimes cases.

3.6.1.3. Corroboration

In assessing witness reliability, the tribunal appears to examine all of the factors noted above, relying on corroboration when the credibility or reliability of a witness is in question.[187] The tribunal has rejected uncorroborated second-hand (hearsay) testimony of witnesses in sexual offenses and other cases.[188] This approach is well grounded in law, such as in common law systems where admissibility of hearsay is extremely limited.[189]

Thus, although corroboration is not required to prove sexual offenses, it nonetheless may play a critical role in establishing the elements of a charged offense.[190] Establishing the predicate offense of rape or other

186 See, *e.g.*, *Bagasora* Trial Judgement, see *supra* note 131 (citing over 75 times to a need for witness corroboration to overcome issues with witness reliability relevant to all charges).

187 *Ibid.*

188 *Ibid.*; see, *e.g.*, ICTR, *Prosecutor v. Kamuhanda*, Judgement (Trial), 22 January 2004, ICTR 95-54A-T (acquitting the defendant of rape because the only evidence was hearsay; witnesses testified they heard girls were abducted and one was raped and although the defendant appealed convictions on other counts, the prosecutor did not appeal the acquittals; see also ICC RPE, Rule 63(4), see *supra* note 33.

189 See U.S. Federal Rules of Evidence, Article 8, see *supra* note 45 (establishing detailed requirements for admissibility of hearsay).

190 ICC RPE, Rule 63(4), see *supra* note 33 (" [...] a Chamber shall not impose a legal requirement that corroboration is required in order to prove any crime within the jurisdiction of the Court, in particular, crimes of sexual violence".); see also *Bemba* Confirmation Decision, para. 53, see *supra* note 40; *Katanga* Confirmation Decision, para. 159.

It should be noted as a practice note that although corroboration is not required to prove crimes of sexual violence, as with any charge before the court, the court will look to corroboration if a witness is not found to be credible or reliable, or the evidence of the sexual act is based on hearsay. As a general practice, the SCSL, ICTY, and ICTR have admitted and assessed the weight of hearsay evidence under the general rules of admissibility as contained in the ICTR RPE Rule 89, when the relevance and probative value can be established. See Archbold, 2005, p. 452–54, see *supra* note 133; ICTY, *Prosecutor v. Galić*, Decision on Interlocutory Appeal Concerning

sexual offenses when there are no witnesses to the act and the victim is unavailable to testify will be difficult if not impossible to prove on the basis of uncorroborated hearsay.[191] Presenting a sexual offense case without corroborating as many facts as possible fails to recognize trial chambers' difficult task of fact-finding and their reliance on corroboration. To assist the Court in this function, a prosecutor should identify and present corroborating evidence to support all witnesses that are presenting on ultimate issues of fact or law, particularly if the prosecution is relying on one witness.

3.6.2. The Sexual Assault Victim as a Material Witness

The cases before the tribunals suggest that the victim, if available, is an essential and material witness to establish the predicate sexual offense.[192] Historically, sexual crime victims are reluctant to disclose and discuss sexual offenses, particularly rape, without sufficient community and court

Rule 92*bis*(C), IT-98-29, para. 27; *Prosecutor v. Tadić*, Decision on Defence Motion on Hearsay, 5 August 1996, IT-94-1, para. 7; ICTY, *Prosecutor v. Blaškić*, Decision on Standing Objection of the Defence to the Admission of Hearsay with no Inquiry as to its Reliability, 21 January 1998, IT-95-14; ICTY, *Prosecutor v. Milošević*, Decision on Testimony of Defence Witness Dragan Jasovic, 15 April 2005, IT-99-37, p. 5; ICTR, *Prosecutor v. Semanza*, Decision on the Defence Motion For Exclusion of Evidence on the Basis of Violations of the Rules of Evidence, Res Gestae, Hearsay and Violations of the Statute and Rules of the Tribunal, 23 August 2000, ICTR-97-20.

191 See ICTR RPE, Rule 93, see *supra* note 46 ("Evidence of a consistent pattern of conduct relevant to serious violations of international humanitarian law under the Statute may be admissible in the interests of justice."); ICTY RPE, Rule 93, see *supra* note 46 (same); see also Aranburu, 2010, p. 855, see *supra* note 141 (discussing the use of pattern evidence to establish incidence of sexual violence and urging that pattern evidence utilizing impartiality, legality, and evidence standards has greater potential than heretofore seen in international sexual violence prosecutions); John Hagan, Richard Brooks, and Todd J. Haugh, "'Reasonable Grounds' Evidence Involving Sexual Violence in Darfur", 2010, available at http://www.lexglobal.org/?q=node/91&nid=91, last accessed on 11 May 2011 (addressing comments presented at the Interdisciplinary Colloquium on Sexual Violence as International Crime: Interdisciplinary Approaches to Evidence, June 16, 2009, and exploring the use of pattern and statistical evidence in lieu of the testimony of victims in sexual violence cases).

192 See Patricia M. Wald, "Dealing with Witnesses in War Crimes Trials: Lessons from the Yugoslav Tribunal", in *Yale Human Rights and Development Law Journal*, 2002, vol. 5, pp. 217, 219 (discussing the important nature of witness testimony and characterizing witnesses as "the lifeblood of ICTY trials").

support,[193] and are unwilling to testify in court without significant levels of protection from harassment and embarrassment.[194] Many victims and witnesses suffer from medical conditions that interfere with lengthy travel and have no available childcare providers at home during the time they must be away from home to testify.[195] These practical considerations for women who are asked to be witnesses in court to horrific events can pose serious challenges to a successful prosecution.

3.6.2.1. Protecting and Supporting the Sexual Crime Victim as Witness

The ICTR and ICTY Statutes and RPE include extensive substantive and procedural protections to victim witnesses.[196] The ICC expanded and crystallized these protections and included others in an integrated and

---

[193] See LaShawn R. Jefferson, "In War as in Peace: Sexual Violence and Women's Status", in *Human Rights Watch World Report*, 2004, available at http://www.hrw.org/legacy/wr2k4/download/wr2k4.pdf, last accessed on 11 May 2011, pp. 325, 343–54 (addressing the challenges of sexual violence victims regarding social integration post-conflict and how without adequate social support and community programs, the ensuing stigma may prevent them from seeking redress); see generally Eric Stover, *The Witnesses: War Crimes and the Promise of Justice in the Hague*, 2005, University of Pennsylvania Press, Philadelphia. However, admissibility does not establish the weight that will be afforded such evidence during deliberations on findings and judgement. See *infra* Section 3.7.1. of this Chapter for discussion of assessing weight of the evidence.

[194] Amnesty International, "'Whose Justice?' The Women of Bosnia and Herzegovina are Still Waiting", 2009, available at http://www.amnesty.org/en/library/info/EUR63/006/2009, last accessed on 11 May 2011 ("Many survivors told Amnesty International that they agreed to be witnesses as a result of their determination to see those responsible for the crimes against them brought to justice, risking their personal safety and exposing themselves to re-traumatization, only to discover that, upon the conclusion of the trial, all support to them ended despite their continued need for support and protection.").

[195] International tribunals may not fully understand the unique requirements of women victims as witnesses. See, *e.g.*, ICTR, *Prosecutor v. Rukundo*, Judgement (Appeal), 20 October 2010, ICTR01-70-A, para. 224 (noting that the defense witness indicated she "could not leave her family for a long period of time" and finding that these concerns could be addressed by "appropriate planning and travel arrangements").

[196] See, *e.g.*, ICTY Statute, Article 22, see *supra* note 61; ICTY RPE, Rules 69, 75, see *supra* note 46; ICTR Statute, Article 21, see *supra* note 61; ICTR RPE, Rules 34, 69, 75, see *supra* note 46.

holistic approach to protection of victims and victim witnesses, with specific focus on protection of sexual crimes victims.[197]

Article 68(1) of the Rome Statute mandates the ICC to take all "appropriate measures to protect the safety, physical and psychological well-being, dignity, and privacy of victims and witnesses".[198] Additional articles ensure that the ICC is empowered to meet this mandate by establishing a Victims and Witnesses Unit ('VWU')[199] that "may advise the Prosecutor and the Court on appropriate protective measures, security arrangements, counseling and assistance",[200] authorizing camera proceedings as an exception to the principle of public hearings, and allowing the presentation of evidence by electronic or other special means when necessary to protect witnesses, particularly in the case of a victim of sexual violence.[201] Further, information that may endanger the victim may be withheld from the defendant before trial[202] and the victim may present testimony by video, audio or written recordings.[203]

These protections are implemented and supplemented by specific Rules and Regulations of the ICC that include authorizing the presence of a "lawyer, legal representative, psychologist, or family" during the vic-

---

197 See, *e.g.*, Rome Statute, Article 68(2), see *supra* note 19 (referencing victims of sexual violence); see also, Rome Statute, Article 43(6), see *supra* note 19; ICC RPE, Rules 16–19, see *supra* note 33 (outlining the responsibilities, functions and expertise of the Victim Witness Unit ('VWU')).

198 Rome Statute, Article 68(1), see *supra* note 19.

199 See Rome Statute, Article 43(6), see *supra* note 19.

200 See Rome Statute, Article 68(4), see *supra* note 19.

201 See Rome Statute, Article 68(2), see *supra* note 19; see also ICC RPE, Rule 87(3), see *supra* note 33 (allowing for in camera reviews of evidence for redaction to prevent the witness' identity from becoming a part of public records); ICC, Regulations of the Registry, Regulation 94, ICC-BD/03-01-06, 2006 ("ICC Registry Regulations") (listing various protective measures that may be ordered pursuant to Rule 87, including pseudonyms, facial and voice distortions, private sessions, closed sessions, videoconferences, expunction from the public record of the person's identity, and any combination of protective measures that are technically feasible).

202 Rome Statute, Article 68(5), see *supra* note 19.

203 Rome Statute, Article 69(2), see *supra* note 19; see also ICC RPE, Rule 87(1), see *supra* note 33 (providing for protective measures); ICC RPE, Rule 112(4), see *supra* note 33 (allowing for the recording of questioning for later introduction as evidence at trial to reduce victim witness's trauma).

tim's testimony,[204] and "controlling the manner of questioning a witness or victim to avoid any harassment or intimidation, paying particular attention to attacks on victims of crimes of sexual violence".[205] The RPE provide that consent cannot be inferred by certain acts or omissions of the victim in a sexual crimes case.[206] The ICC RPE provide that the "[c]redibility, character or predisposition to sexual availability of a victim or witness cannot be inferred by reason of the sexual nature of the prior or subsequent conduct of a victim or witness",[207] and evidence of prior or subsequent sexual conduct of the victim is inadmissible.[208] The Pre-Trial Chamber is vested with the authority and responsibility to ensure the protection and privacy of victims and witnesses[209] by providing for a number of witness protection tools, including the use of pseudonyms, the redaction of witness statements, and the timing of disclosure of witness statements.

However, it is unclear whether these mechanisms provide sufficient protection. Interviews with rape victims suggest that those who testified before the ICTR were re-traumatized and hold deep feelings of bitterness towards the tribunal.[210] In early 2002, difficulties with the failure to charge sexual crimes coupled with the experience of sexual crimes' victims as witnesses reached a point where several victims' groups refused to

---

204 See ICC RPE, Rule 88(1), (2), see *supra* note 33 (permitting the Chamber to order special measures for to facilitate the victim's testimony).

205 ICC RPE, Rule 88(5), see *supra* note 33.

206 The jurisprudential evolution of the applicability of the concept of consent in international prosecution of rape cases is evidenced in ICTR, *Prosecutor v. Renzaho*, Judgement and Sentence, 14 July 2009, ICTR-97-31A, para. 791 (noting that consent is assessed within the context of the surrounding circumstances and that force or threat of force provides clear evidence of non-consent lack of consent, but force is not an element *per se of rape)* citing to *Bagosora et al.* Trial Judgement para. 2199, citing *Kunarac et al.* Appeal Judgement, paras. 127–133; and *Semanza* Trial Judgement, para. 344, see *supra* note 100.

207 ICC RPE, Rule 70(d), see *supra* note 33.

208 ICC RPE, Rule 71, see *supra* note 33.

209 Rome Statute, Article 57(3)(c), see *supra* note 19.

210 See Nowrojee, 2005, p. 21, see *supra* at note 50; see also, Elizabeth Neuffer, *The Key to My Neighbor's House, Seeking Justice in Bosnia and Rwanda*, Picador, New York, 2001, pp. 377–384 (recounting experiences of several sexual offense victims as witnesses at the ICTR).

continue to co-operate with the ICTR.[211] Certain protections have proven to be less than effective, including mechanisms to protect identity[212] and to ensure a victim is not harassed or humiliated on the stand.[213] Further, protection methods that implicate a defendant's rights may be unavailable. In the case of *Prosecutor v. Tadić*[214] the ICTY granted anonymity as a protective measure to a sexual assault victim as a witness. The resulting outcries from the international and legal communities that the defendant had been deprived of his right to a fair trial[215] resulted in a reluctance of

---

211 See van Schaack, 2009, pp. 361, 372–73, see *supra* note 104 (noting the difficulties in amending claims to include sexual violence charges, even when supported by women's coalitions and the Prosecution); see also Victor Peskin, *International Justice in Rwanda and the Balkans: virtual trials and the struggle for state cooperation*, Cambridge University Press, Cambridge, 2008, pp. 200–01 (highlighting that IBUKA, and an umbrella organization for survivor associations in Rwanda, and AVEGA, the Association of the Widows of Rwanda, boycotted support for the ICTR because of humiliating treatment and threats to victim witnesses by Hutu genocide suspects employed by the ICTR).

212 See *ibid.* at p. 401 (noting that although protective mechanisms exist at the ICTR, they are not always used effectively and have resulted in the identities of witnesses becoming public leading to threats and harassment of witnesses).

213 See Natasha Price, Kate Grady, and Rachel Ibreck, *Injustice after Sexual Violence, Problems in Practice at the International Criminal Tribunal for Rwanda*, University of Bristol, 2010, p. 12 (noting repeated and invasive interrogation of rape victim by defense attorneys at trial).

214 See ICTY, *Prosecutor v. Tadić*, Judgement (Appeal), 15 July 1999, IT-94-1-A; ICTY, *Prosecutor v. Tadić*, Opinion and Judgement (Trial), 7 May 1997, IT-94-1-T ("*Tadić* Trial Judgement"); see also ICTY, *Prosecutor v. Tadić*, Decision on the Prosecutor's Motion Requesting Protective Measures for Victims and Witnesses, 10 August 1995, IT-94-1-T, para. 46.

215 Compare ECHR, *Kostovski v. The Netherlands*, Judgement, 20 November 1988, Case No. 10/1988/154/208, para. 42 ("If the defence is unaware of the identity of a person it seeks to question, it may be deprived of the very particulars enabling it to demonstrate that he or she is prejudiced, hostile or unreliable. Testimony or other declarations inculpating an accused may well be designedly untruthful or simply erroneous and the defence will scarcely be able to bring this to light if it lacks the information permitting it to test the author's reliability or cast doubt on his credibility. The dangers inherent in such a situation are obvious.") with 4 ALL ER 571 CA, R. v. Davis, Appeal, 2006 (reviewing the jurisprudence of the ECHR and concluding that the ECHR accepts the right to witness anonymity under certain conditions that include cross-examination by an advocate and other protections to ensure the trial is fair); *and* ECHR, *Baegen v. the Netherlands*, 1994, App. No. 16696/90, para. 77 (finding that defendant's rights were not violated where the defendant was afforded an opportunity to confront, but not question, the sexual crime victim).

the tribunals to grant this protective measure in subsequent cases.[216] Despite the reluctance of the ICTR and ICTY to grant witness anonymity as a protective measure, the Rome Treaty delegates agreed not to agree on this issue and drafted RPE 88(1) in a permissive manner, electing to leave witness anonymity as a witness protective measure to the discretion of the court.[217]

Outside of the courtroom, there may be insufficient effective local community protection and support programs for sexual crimes' victims.[218] The ICC's most recent investigations into sexual offenses committed in Sudan and Congo underscore these continued difficulties. The reluctance of rape victims to speak to Court personnel, coupled with continued insecurity in remote locations, has resulted in most investigations occurring outside of Sudan, materially hampering investigation of sexual atrocities.[219] The ICC has fared no better in Congo where horrific and recurring

[216] Since *Prosecutor v. Tadić*, neither the ICTY nor the ICTR has provided a witness complete anonymity. See ICTR, *Prosecutor v. Rutaganda*, Decision on the Preliminary Motion submitted by the Prosecutor for Protective Measures for Witnesses, 26 September 1996, ICTR-96-3-T (granting a number of protective measures for the witness, but not allowing full anonymity); see also Karin N. Calvo-Goller, *The Trial Proceedings of the International Criminal Court: ICTY and ICTR Precedents*, 2006, Martinus Nijhoff Publishers, Leiden, pp. 91–93, 280–291 (distinguishing witness anonymity from witness confidentiality and noting that the former raises issues of fairness to the accused in the trial); Amanda Beltz, "Prosecuting Rape in International Criminal Tribunals: The Need to Balance Victim's Rights with the Due Process Rights of the Accused", in *St. John's Journal of Legal Commentary*, 2008, vol. 23, no. 1, pp. 167, 190–95.

[217] See Carsten Stahn and Goran Sluiter, *The Emerging Practice of the International Criminal Court*, Brill, 2009, pp. 626–634 (discussing witness anonymity, current case law and the ICC).

[218] See Stover, 2005, pp. 92–109, see *supra* note 193 (highlighting the difficulties for witnesses in returning home after testifying and noting local authorities provided little support for returning witnesses).

[219] In his Third Report to the Security Council since the case was referred to the ICC in March 2005, Prosecutor Louis Moreno-Ocampo noted that investigators are hampered by the precarious security situation in the countryside, and must be able to ensure that witnesses are able to testify without fear of reprisals. Moreover, many rape victims may opt to remain silent at the risk of being ostracized and rebuked. The Report further noted, "[t]he continuing insecurity in Darfur is prohibitive of effective investigations inside Darfur, particularly in light of the absence of a functioning and sustainable system for the protection of victims and witnesses". As a result, the ICC is conducting the bulk of its investigation from outside Sudan. ICC, "Third Report of The Prosecutor of the International Criminal Court to the UN Security Council pursuant to

sexualized attacks on civilians occurred and continue to occur with disturbing frequency.[220] The need for community and international support and outreach programs persists and sexual crimes investigations in remote, isolated, and dangerous locations will continue to be extremely difficult until this challenge is addressed.[221]

3.6.2.2. The Victim's Pre-Trial Statement and Testimony at Trial

Often a sexual crime victim's first contact with an international tribunal or court is an investigator. At the end of an interview process with an investigator, the victim generally is asked to sign a statement prepared by the investigator detailing what the victim has told the investigator. This statement is part of the indictment package that moves forward to confirmation, is disclosed prior to trial to the defense team to assist in preparation for trial,[222] and is generally considered by the tribunals at trial.[223] The

UNSCR 1593 (2005)", 14 June 2006, available at http://www.amicc.org/docs/OTP_ReportUNSC_3-Darfur_English.pdf, last accessed on 11 May 2011.

220 United Nations Security Council, Report of the Secretary-General on the United Nation Organization Stabilization Mission in the Democratic Republic of the Congo, 8 October 2010, U.N. Doc. S/2010/512 (recounting continuing attacks involving among other crimes, rape and other forms of sexual violence).

221 However, the SCSL has been praised uniformly for its outreach and community support programs. See Mohamed Suma, "The Charles Taylor Trial and Legacy of the Special Court for Sierra Leone", in *ICTJ Briefing*, September 2009, available at http://www.ictj.org/static/Publications/bp_suma_impunity_rev3.pdf, last accessed on 11 May 2011, p. 1 (commenting that the "SCSL's innovative outreach program, focusing on improving domestic understanding of the court's activities, served as a model for future tribunals").

222 See *supra* note 56 (discussing the ICC disclosure regime); see also ICC, *Prosecutor v. Lubanga*, Decision on the Final System of Disclosure and the Establishment of a Timetable, 15 May 2006, ICC-01/04-01/06-102; ICC, *Prosecutor v. Bemba*, Decision on the Evidence Disclosure System and Setting a Timetable for Disclosure between the Parties, 31 July 2008, ICC-01/05-01/08-55; ICTR RPE, Rules 66, 73*bis*, see *supra* note 46.

223 This process reflects the civil law based evidentiary rules; generally, in a common law jurisdiction, prior statements of witnesses are admitted to impeach or to rebut allegations of recent fabrication. See U.S. Federal Rules of Evidence, Rule 613, see *supra* note 45 (providing for admissibility of prior inconsistent statement of a witness), Rule 801(d) (characterizing as non-hearsay the prior consistent statement of a witness if offered at trial for specific reasons, including rebutting implied charges of recent fabrication). There appears to be a shift to greater reliance on in-court testimony and use of prior statements only as a discovery mechanism prior to trial or impeachment mecha-

substance of the pre-trial statements shapes the charges that are set forth in the indictment and also sets the stage for the trial testimony of the victim.

To date, many if not most pre-trial statements of sexual assault victims fail to contain all relevant details about the offense,[224] or contain information that is inconsistent with the victim's testimony at trial. Assuming the victim at trial adds details and relevant information, or offers a correction to the pre-trial statement, the judges are faced with assessing the credibility of a witness in light of a prior inconsistent statement.[225]

In evaluating victim witness testimony in light of inconsistent statements, the ICTR applies the same rigorous analysis as that applied to witness statements in general.[226] However, although victims' motives might well result in perjured testimony, to date there has been little suggestion that a victim committed perjury regarding the act itself.[227] Nonetheless, the ICTR has found victim testimony relating to the perpetrator's identity to be less than reliable and has acquitted on that basis.[228]

One practice in place at the ICTR and ICTY to assist in bridging potential inconsistencies between a witness's pre-trial statement(s) and trial testimony is the practice of "proofing" prior to trial;[229] that is, the practice of the prosecutor reviewing the witness statement with the witness prior to trial to refresh the recollection of the witness and to determine if the witness concurs with the statement as written.[230] In nearly

nism as trial; nonetheless, prior statements continue to be admitted for substantive purposes at trial if the witness testifies. See ICTR RPE, Rule 73*bis*, see *supra* note 46.

224 See generally Nancy Armoury Combs, "Testimonial Deficiencies and Evidentiary Uncertainties in International Criminal Tribunals", in *UCLA Journal of International Law and Foreign Affairs*, 2009, vol. 14, no. 1, p. 235.

225 *Ibid.*

226 See *supra* Sections 3.4.1.2–3 of this Chapter; see also Combs, 2009, pp. 235, 263, see *supra* note 174.

227 See, *e.g.*, *Rukundo* Trial Judgement, para. 376, see *supra* note 155 (accepting without inquiry victim's testimony as to an attempted rape by defendant although the witness admitted she knew that defendant wanted her deceased relative killed and she had not mentioned the sexual assault to anyone).

228 See, *e.g.*, *Kabiligi* Trial Judgement, paras. 1969–1986, see *supra* note 170.

229 See B. Don Taylor III, "Witness Proofing in International Criminal Law: Is Widening Procedural Divergence in International Criminal Tribunals a Cause for Concern?", available at http://www.isrcl.org/Papers/2008/Taylor.pdf, last accessed on 18 March 2011.

230 *Ibid.*

every case before the ICTY and ICTR, a witness has provided the statement years previously and has had no contact with the court or prosecutor since that time.

The ICTR Appeals Chamber affirmed the Trial Chamber ruling in *Prosecutor v. Karemera* by denying a defense motion to prohibit the prosecution from "proofing" witnesses,[231] noting that as long as the practice did not constitute manipulating the evidence,[232] the practice could incorporate several permissible activities.[233] The Appeal Chamber noted that the defense could explore witness coaching or tampering on cross-examination.[234] As a practice note, proofing enables the prosecution to identify additional or inconsistent information and disclose this information to the defense team prior to trial.[235] Properly conducted, "proofing" not only eliminates surprise at trial and provides the defendant an opportunity to better defend,[236] but enables the prosecutor to establish a level of trust with the victim, placing the victim at greater ease and reducing the trauma of testifying at trial.[237]

---

[231] ICTR, *Prosecutor v. Karemera*, Decision on Interlocutory Appeal Regarding Witness Proofing, 11 May 2007, ICTR-98-44-AR73.8.

[232] *Ibid.* at para. 15

[233] *Ibid.* at para. 23 (noting that permissible activities consist of "comparing statements made by a witness, detecting differences and inconsistencies in recollection of the witness, allowing a witness to refresh his or her memory in respect of the evidence he or she will give, inquiring and disclosing to the Defence additional information and/or evidence of incriminatory and exculpatory nature in sufficient time prior to the witness' testimony").

[234] *Ibid.* at para. 15.

[235] *Ibid.* at para. 17.

[236] *Ibid.*

[237] See ICTY, *Prosecutor v. Limaj*, Decision on Defence Motion on Prosecution Practice of "Proofing" Witnesses, 10 December 2004, IT-03-66-T, p. 3 (upholding the practice of witness proofing before the ICTY, noting that the practice of proofing has been practiced at the ICTY since its inception, the practice is widespread in jurisdictions where there is an adversary procedure, and the practice has a number of advantages including assisting a witness to better cope with the testifying); SCSL, *Prosecutor v. Sesay*, Decision on the Gbao and Sesay Joint Application for the Exclusion of the Testimony of Witness TF1-141, 26 October 2005, SCSL 04-15-T, para. 33 (finding that "proofing witnesses prior to their testimony in court is a legitimate practice that serves the interests of justice [...] especially so given the particular circumstances of many of the witnesses in this trial who are testifying about traumatic events in an environment that can be entirely foreign and intimidating for them").

In the case of *Prosecutor v. Lubanga*, the ICC rejected the ICTR approach, specifically noting the Courts' concerns relative to sexual crimes victim/witnesses and finding that the prosecution had failed to establish an accepted practice of witness proofing in domestic systems.[238] The civil law system does not identify a witness with a party and thus prosecutors in civil systems do not proof witnesses. However, the ICC has adopted an adversarial trial methodology and although many have urged that the ICC adopt greater indicia of a civil law system, prohibiting proofing may not be the most appropriate starting point and this ruling may very well result in collateral issues,[239] including increased delays during trial.[240]

In addition to issues involving substance, many sexual assault witnesses have indicated that testifying at trial rose to the level of what they perceived to be an attack on their credibility and a feeling that they were placed on trial.[241] In trials at the *ad hoc* international tribunals and ICC, the witness is expected to clarify and expand on information contained in the pre-trial statement, either on direct or cross-examination, and through this process provide information to the court by which the court can assess the content of the testimony and the credibility of the witness. Unfortunately, the role of the defense counsel in the adversarial model includes vigorous examination of material prosecution witnesses to assess credibility and reliability. Thus, given the current model, it is critical that sexual crimes victims understand the international court system and how this system operates so they are prepared for the ordeal of testifying.[242] This

---

238 See *Lubanga* Decision on Witness Familiarisation, p. 42, see *supra* note 124 (stating that if any general principle of law could be drawn from a survey of the national laws of the world's various legal systems, witness proofing would be prohibited).

239 See van Schaack, 2009, p. 400, see *supra* note 104 (noting that the prohibition "may also disparately impact women and particularly victims of sexual violence," re-traumatizing them because they are ill prepared to fully understand the need for invasive questions and the right of defense to vigorously cross-examine).

240 See ICTR, *Prosecutor v. Karemera*, Decision on Defence Motions to Prohibit Witness Proofing, 15 December 2006, ICTR 98-44-T, para. 17 (noting that proofing reduces "surprise" at trial and the delays that could result).

241 Price, 2010, pp. 10–12, see *supra* note 213.

242 The ICC ruling on proofing did not include a prohibition on court familiarization. However, unless this familiarization is conducted by the prosecutor who will lead this witness, the effectiveness of such familiarization is in dispute. See ICC, *Prosecutor v. Lubanga*, Decision Regarding the Practices Used to Prepare and Familiarise Witness-

aspect of the adversarial model has been assessed in the context of international prosecutions and found lacking by several experts who urge the ICC to adopt a civil trial model with increased judicial involvement and with respect to the mode of presentation of the case.[243]

3.6.3. Establishing Accountability

The mandate of the tribunals and the ICC is to bring to justice those most responsible for the commission of those international crimes within the jurisdiction of each respective court – leaders, planners, and organizers.[244] Although several officials and individuals involved in the senior levels of criminal activity personally commit predicate sexual violence acts, current ICC investigations suggest this may be less likely in cases of the most senior – and potentially most culpable – military commanders and leaders.[245] This difference in the fact pattern between sexual offenses and other types of offenses places significant focus on the defendant's responsibility for sexual acts committed by others. Despite this, the indictments and findings in the ICTR cases to date suggest that the prosecutor relies most heavily on establishing a defendant's responsibility under Article 6(1) of the ICTR Statute, that is, individual criminal responsibility,[246] and includes Article 6(3) of the ICTR Statute, that is, command and superior

es for Giving Testimony at Trial, 30 November 2007, ICC-01/04-01/06, para. 22 (indicating the Registry will conduct witness familiarization).

243 See William Pizzi, "Overcoming Logistical and Structural Barriers to Fair Trials at International Tribunals," in *International Commentary on Evidence*, 2006, vol. 4, no. 1, article 4.

244 ICTR Statute, Articles 5, 7, 8, see *supra* at note 61; ICTY Statute, Articles 6, 8, 9, see *supra* note 61; Rome Statute, Article 5, see *supra* note 19.

245 See, *e.g.*, *Bemba* Confirmation Decision, see *supra* note 40 (indicting defendant on basis of command responsibility for sexual violence crimes of subordinates); *Katanga* Confirmation Decision, see *supra* note 40 (indicting Katanga, the *de facto* leader of the FRPI, and Chui, the *de facto* leader of the FNI as co-perpetrators for acts of sexual violence committed by others); ICC, *Prosecutor v. Mbarushima*, Decision on the Prosecutor's Application for a Warrant of Arrest Against Callixte Mbarushima, 28 September 2010, ICC-01/04-01/10 (issuing an arrest warrant for defendant, Mbarushima, under theory of common plan and common purpose for acts of sexual violence not personally committed by defendant).

246 ICTR Statute, Article 6(1), see *supra* note 61 ("A person who planned, instigated, ordered, committed or otherwise aided and abetted in the planning, preparation or execution of a crime referred to in articles 2 to 4 of the present Statute, shall be individually responsible for the crime.").

responsibility,[247] as a "back up" rather than a primary means of establishing responsibility. More recently, following in the footsteps of the ICTY's success in holding senior defendants responsible under the theory of joint criminal enterprise ('JCE'),[248] ICTR prosecutors have displayed a preference for this theory in lieu of command responsibility under Article 6(3).[249] As discussed below in Section 3.6.3.2., this may be the result of the inflexible and stringent application of the elements required to establish responsibility that is appropriately characterized as command responsibility.

Irrespective of prosecutorial maneuvering to select a theory of responsibility that can be established with the available evidence, prosecutors continue to struggle to establish defendant responsibility in sexual crimes cases at trial. A review of several ICTR cases resulting in acquittals suggests that the successful prosecution of sexual offense cases requires prosecutors to identify specific evidentiary requirements to establish a defendant's responsibility and present specific evidence to meet these requirements.[250]

---

247 ICTR Statute, Article 6(3), see *supra* note 61 ("The fact that any of the acts referred to in articles 2 to 4 of the present Statute was committed by a subordinate does not relieve his or her superior of criminal responsibility if he or she knew or had reason to know that the subordinate was about to commit such acts or had done so and the superior failed to take the necessary and reasonable measures to prevent such acts or to punish the perpetrators thereof.").

248 See Patricia Viseur Sellers, "The Prosecution of Sexual Violence in Conflict: The Importance of Human Rights as Means of Interpretation", 2007, available at http://www2.ohchr.org%2Fenglish%2Fissues%2Fwomen%2Fdocs%2FPaper_Prosecution_of_Sexual_Violence.pdf, last accessed on 4 April 2011; *Tadić* Trial Judgement, para. 536, see *supra* note 214; *Furundžija* Appeal Judgement, see *supra* note 24; ICTY, *Prosecutor v. Krstić*, Judgement (Trial), 2 August 2001, IT-98-33-T, para. 2; ICTY, *Prosecutor v. Kvočka*, Judgement (Appeal), 22 March 2006, IT-97-24-A, para. 85.

249 But see Rome Statute, Article 25(3)(d), see *supra* note 19 (rejecting the wholesale importation of the theory of joint criminal enterprise into the Rome Statute adopting instead the theory referenced as "common purpose").

250 See, *e.g.*, *Kabiligi* Trial Judgement, see *supra* note 170; *Hategekimana* Trial Judgement, see *supra* note 155; *Kajelijeli* Trial Judgement, see *supra* note 49; *Muvunyi* Trial Judgement, see *supra* note 147.

3.6.3.1. Individual Criminal Responsibility

Article 6(1) of the ICTR Statute establishes individual responsibility for the planning, instigating, ordering, committing or otherwise aiding and abetting in the planning, preparation or execution of any crime within the jurisdiction of the tribunal.[251] It is an unusual case in which military superiors "order" rape and sexual offenses; a large number of sexual crimes cases before the ICTR include aiding and abetting, and instigating as the primary grounds of direct responsibility.[252] In those cases resulting in acquittals, the prosecution failed to present evidence linking the defendant to the individual acts of others in sufficient detail with respect to the time, date and location to establish the defendant's responsibility for the act. In *Semanza*, although there was testimony as to certain rapes, the prosecution failed to establish that these particular rapes occurred in the location charged and the court dismissed those counts.[253] Similarly, in *Gacumbitsi*, the court found that the defendant instigated rape by use of a megaphone calling for rape of Tutsi women but that the evidence did not sufficiently

---

[251] See ICTR Statute, Article 6(1), see *supra* note 61; ICTY Statute, Article 7(1), see *supra* note 61; Rome Statute, Articles 25(3)(a)–(f), see *supra* note 19; see also Sellers, 2007, see *supra* note 248.

[252] See ICTR Statute, Article 6, see *supra* note 61 (defining the required elements of "ordering" within a command structure as including a duty of the subordinate to obey). Characterizing rapes or sexual offenses during armed conflict as resulting from "orders" is generally not accurate and tends to blur the lines between differing modes of responsibility, such as instigation, command responsibility, and common purpose. See ICTR, *Prosecutor v. Nyiramasuhuko and Ntahobali*, Indictment, 3 February 2001, ICTR 97-21-I (indicting Nyiramasuhuko for rape as CAH on the basis of telling her subordinates to rape Tutsi women before killing them); see also *Semanza* Trial Judgement, see *supra* note 100 (holding defendant responsible for instigating a rape occurring after he encouraged others to rape Tutsi women). But see, Tracy Fehr, "In unprecedented decision, Congo sentences military officer for ordering rape", in *Christian Science Monitor*, *Africa Monitor*, 25 February 2011, available at http://www.csmonitor.com/World/Africa/Africa-Monitor/2011/0225/In-unprecedented-decision-Congo-sentences-military-officer-for-ordering-rape, last accessed on 11 May 2011 (noting that several military officers were found guilty and sentenced to not more than 20 years for ordering rapes in Congo with 49 rape victims testifying and the number of rapes estimated at over 8000). The facts of the case established that nearly all women and children, some as young as only several months old, in specific villages were raped and sexually assaulted, but not killed, by military personnel over a short period of time are compelling and unique).

[253] *Semanza* Trial Judgement, see *supra* note 100.

link defendant's actions to rapes that occurred in the nearby areas.[254] In *Muvunyi*, the court found that rapes had occurred but that the group that committed the rapes was not the same as those referenced in the indictment, and that the evidence failed to establish a relationship between the defendant and the group.[255]

It is unclear whether the required evidence was unavailable or available but not presented. In cases where the missing link is time and location, a greater focus on these requirements at the investigative stage may have yielded the required evidence. In the case of *Gacumbitsi*,[256] the missing evidence possibly could have been provided by a witness who could place the defendant at a certain time in the vehicle with the megaphone. Such witnesses provide additional facts that buttress other witnesses' testimony and fill in the gaps in the prosecution's case. Likewise, establishing location generally does not require a reliance on the witness's ability to read maps. In *Semanza*,[257] perhaps a painstaking examination to assist the rape victims in recalling how long they walked, whether a witness recognized the location of where the assault occurred, what the assailant was wearing and what the assailant might have said would have provided some indication of location, time or date. Because this type of evidence does not go directly to an element of the offense itself, this is the type of material information that often is not contained in a pre-trial statement and not led or presented in evidence by a prosecutor. These types of witnesses who can corroborate certain facts and add "missing" information are often overlooked when the prosecutor is compiling a final witness list.[258]

---

[254] *Gacumbitsi* Trial Judgement, see *supra* note 155.

[255] *Muvunyi* Trial Judgment, see *supra* note 147.

[256] *Gacumbitsi* Trial Judgement, see *supra* note 155.

[257] *Semanza* Trial Judgement, see *supra* note 100.

[258] This is an enormous task for a prosecutor particularly in courts where proofing is not permitted, investigations are not thorough, time has passed between the statement and trial, and number of witnesses is limited by the court. In such courts, it will be nearly impossible for a prosecutor to identify evidentiary "gaps" prior to trial and he or she may be required to amend the witness list throughout trial to meet evidentiary requirements.

3.6.3.2. Holding Senior Officials Responsible for Acts of Subordinates

Historically, rape and other sexual offenses have been regarded as "spoils of war".[259] The remnants of this historical backdrop are still with us today as seen in the difficulties in establishing derivative responsibility of senior officials and military personnel for sexual offenses under the theory of command or superior responsibility.[260] Under the theory of command and superior responsibility, superiors are held responsible for acts of a subordinate if certain requirements are met.[261] The focus of the courts has been on the degree of control the superior exercised and whether the superior knew or should have known that the subordinate was about to commit or had committed criminal acts.[262]

---

[259] See generally Noma Bar, "Violence Against Women: War's Overlooked Victims", in *The Economist*, 13 January 2011, available at http://www.economist.com/node/17900482, last accessed on 11 May 2011; Larry J. Siegel, *Criminology*, Thomson Wadsworth, 2008, p. 291.

[260] See generally Joakim Dungel, "Command Responsibility in International Criminal Tribunals", Paper Presented at the National Consultative Summit on Extrajudicial Killings and Enforced Disappearances – Searching for Solutions, Manila, 16–17 July 2007, available at http://sc.judiciary.gov.ph/publications/summit/Summit%20Papers/Dungel%20-%20Command%20Responsibility%20in%20ICT.pdf, last accessed on 11 May 2011. For cases discussing command responsibility, see SCSL, *Prosecutor v. Brima*, Judgement (Trial), 20 June 2007, SCSL-04-16-T, paras. 779-800; ICTY, *Prosecutor v. Blaškić*, Judgement (Trial), 3 March 2000, IT-95-14-T, para. 721-32. However, the *Blaškić* conviction for sexual violence was overturned on appeal. ICTY, *Prosecutor v. Blaškić*, Judgement (Appeal), 29 July 2004, IT-95-14-A, para. 613 (finding that the actions giving rise to the charge were beyond the appellant's control); *Nahimana* Trial Judgement, see *supra* note 162.

[261] See generally Richard P. Barrett and Laura E. Little, "Lessons of Yugoslav Rape Trials: A Role for Conspiracy Law in International Tribunals", in *Minnesota Law Review*, 2003, vol. 88, no. 1, p. 30; Nicole Laviolette, "Commanding Rape: Sexual Violence, Command Responsibility, and the Prosecution of Superiors by the International Criminal Tribunals for the Former Yugoslavia and Rwanda", in *Canadian Yearbook of International Law*, 1998, vol. 35, p. 93.

[262] Angela M. Banks, "Sexual Violence and International Criminal Law: An Analysis of the Ad Hoc Tribunal's Jurisprudence and the International Criminal Court's Elements of Crimes", in *College of William and Mary Law School Faculty Papers*, 2005, Paper 305, available at http://scholarship.law.wm.edu/facpubs/305, last accessed on 1 May 2011, pp. 59–62 (setting for the approaches of the *ad hoc* tribunals and the ICC to the concept of superior responsibility); Rome Statute, Article 28, see *supra* note 19 (discussing the circumstances under which a superior can be held criminally liable for the acts of subordinates).

Successful prosecution at the ICTR under this mode of responsibility has been problematic for a number of reasons. The court appears to have applied a "rigid and highly technical approach to the law of superior responsibility"[263] requiring findings of "effective control" that are outdated and that have failed to keep pace with developments in command structures in ongoing military, paramilitary and warlord operations in armed conflicts.[264] Although the ICTR has recognized *de facto* authority as a "flexible template" for analysis of evidence, the requirements of "effective control" remain high and the prosecutor is required to link a particular defendant to the specific individual who committed the sexual act.[265] In addition, the ICTR has interpreted and applied the requirement of "knows or should have known" as requiring near-direct evidence, raising the evidentiary bar for sexual offense cases based on command responsibility.

In the *Kajelijeli* case, the ICTR Trial Chamber found that the prosecutor failed to establish that the defendant knew or should have known about his subordinates' sexual crimes although the prosecutor submitted evidence of widespread rapes by his subordinates over the course of a few days in a limited geographic area.[266] The Court rejected the circumstantial evidence, noting that the defendant was not at the scene of any of the rapes[267] and that there was no evidence he ordered the rapes.[268] It is unclear whether the Trial Chamber conflated the two distinct modes of responsibility, ordering and superior responsibility, in reaching their findings. In this situation, statistically sound pattern evidence may assist in establishing these requirements and, if available, should be put forward by the prosecutor.[269]

---

263 See Michael Newton and Casey Kuhlman, "Why Criminal Culpability Should Follow the Critical Path: Reframing the Theory of 'Effective Control'", in I.F. Dekker and E. Hey (eds.), *Netherlands Yearbook of International Law*, Cambridge University Press, Cambridge, 2009, vol. 40, p. 12.

264 *Ibid.*

265 *Ibid.* at p. 13.

266 *Kajelijeli* Trial Judgement, paras. 937–39, see *supra* note 49.

267 *Ibid.*

268 *Ibid.*

269 See Aranburu, 2010, p. 855, see *supra* note 141 (discussing the use of pattern evidence).

The Trial Chamber in *Prosecutor v. Gacumbitsi* convicted the defendant of eight rapes but acquitted him of certain other rapes where the Trial Chamber found that the rapes had taken place, but that the defendant did not exercise authority "over the *conseillers*, gendarmes, soldiers, and *Interahamwe* in Rusumo Commune at the time of the events".[270] On appeal, the prosecution argued, in part, that the Trial Chamber erred in failing to find defendant responsible for the rapes under Article 6(3) of the ICTR Statute.[271] The Appeal Chamber found that Trial Court erred in failing to find that the defendant exercised *de facto* authority; however, it found that the prosecution failed to establish the relationship between the accused and the specific persons who committed the rapes.[272] Although the "link" between the defendant and the perpetrators would appear to have been established by proving the position of the defendant and the identity of at least one of the perpetrators as someone over which the defendant exercises *de facto* authority, Conseiller Karagame, the Trial and Appeal Chamber found this evidence insufficient. Thus, a prosecutor should be ever mindful that specific evidence may be required to establish a defendant's effective control in cases involving sexual offenses, and ensure that witness lists include witnesses that can address these issues thoroughly.

3.6.3.3. Common Purpose as a Sister of Joint Criminal Enterprise

Prosecutors at both the ICTY and ICTR have relied increasingly on the theory of JCE to overcome the challenges of linking the defendant to the predicate criminal act.[273] Joint criminal enterprise has been an effective

---

270 *Gacumbitsi* Appeal Judgement, paras. 141–42, see *supra* note 77 (citing to Judgement (Trial), ICTR-01-64-T, 17 June 2004, para. 243).

271 *Ibid.* at paras. 141–46.

272 *Ibid.* at paras. 144–45.

273 See Rebecca L. Haffajee, "Prosecuting Crimes of Rape and Sexual Violence at the ICTR: The Application of Joint Criminal Enterprise Theory", in *Harvard Journal of Law and Gender*, 2006, vol. 29, no. 1, p. 201; Banks, 2005, pp. 53–58, see *supra* note 262 (summarizing the *Tadić* decision and explaining the three different categories of actions that qualify as joint criminal enterprise).

Joint Criminal Enterprise (also known simply as 'JCE') was developed and urged forward at the ICTY to address the recurrent challenges to establishing responsibility of senior leaders. JCE, known as "Just Convict Everyone" in international prosecutorial circles, was not adopted in its entirety as a mode of responsibility by the ICC. The competing tensions between accountability of senior leaders for acts of those under

tool for prosecuting cases of senior leaders where evidence fails to establish a direct link between the defendant and the individual committing the predicate act.[274] However, JCE could be used to establish culpability in attenuated circumstances, a practice that borders on strict liability based on organization membership that was rejected in practice at Nuremberg[275], and although some fully urge the use of JCE to ease evidentiary requirements for gender based crimes,[276] thought should be given to employing JCE judiciously.[277] Since the ICC has not adopted the theory of joint criminal enterprise (substituting instead the "common purpose" mode of responsibility), challenges to establishing defendant's responsi-

their control and holding such leaders accountable for all foreseeable acts of subordinates (strict liability) have not fully been resolved.

274 See, *e.g.*, ICTR, *Prosecutor v. Mpambara*, Amended Indictment, 27 November 2004, ICTR-2001-65-I, para. 20 (charging defendant sexual offenses as genocide on the basis of JCE where the charged acts were a reasonably foreseeable consequence of executing the JCE, in the absence of allegations or facts supporting a superior/subordinate relationship or link between the defendant and those who committed the acts); see also ICTY, *Prosecutor v. Krštić*, Judgement (Appeal), 19 April 2004, IT-98-33-A; ICTY, *Prosecutor v. Krajišnik*, Judgement (Appeal), 17 March 2009, IT-00-39-A, paras. 162–175.

275 See Raha Wala, "From Guantanamo to Nuremberg and Back: An analysis of Conspiracy to Commit War Crimes under International Humanitarian Law", in *Georgetown Journal of International Law*, vol. 41, no. 3, pp. 683, 696–97 (noting that the Nuremberg judges did not apply strict membership liability but required a *mens rea* determination and further stating that "[m]ost of the defendants sufficiently used their control and authority in connection with war crimes to be convicted, but the IMT's treatment of Hess showed that the tribunal was reticent to establish liability where a defendant's connection to the substantive war crimes was too tenuous").

276 See Patricia Viseur Sellers, *Individual('s) Liability for Collective Sexual Violence*, in Karen Knop (ed.), *Gender and Human Rights*, Oxford University Press, 2004, pp. 153, 182–185 (examining specific ICTY cases and arguing that foreseeability of sexual violence crimes renders a defendant responsible under JCE for sexual assaults in wartime). "Sexual violence as a natural and foreseeable consequence of other crimes comes close to being the legal description of the inevitable wartime sexual violence". *Ibid.* at p. 192.

277 Haffajee, 2006, p. 202, see *supra* note 273 (noting concerns with broad application of JCE and arguing "for the targeted use of JCE theory in effectively prosecuting crimes of rape and sexual violence").

bility in prosecution of sexual crimes before the ICC under the mode of "common purpose" are unclear.[278]

3.7. The Appeal

3.7.1. Setting the Record

For many prosecutors, setting or establishing the record for appeal is not a primary concern as they present a case at trial; however, including appellate considerations in trial preparation assists the prosecutor in not only identifying trial issues, but resolving these in advance of trial.

Common law attorneys are often not adept at preserving prosecution appellate issues regarding the civil law based right of the prosecutor to appeal a verdict of not guilty.[279] This right to appeal an acquittal may influence the manner in which a prosecutor establishes a record for appeal at trial.

The prosecutor should make a record at trial for appeal of all exhibits[280] and witnesses[281] that the prosecutor moves forward at trial, but are not admitted or permitted to be called, respectively. The preferred manner in which this is done is through a written motion at the time that the court rules the document inadmissible or excludes a witness.[282] The motion should append the document if it has not been excluded prior to trial and is not in the trial record.

---

278 But see *Lubanga* Confirmation Decision, paras. 334–335, see *supra* note 85; *Al Bashir* Arrest Warrant, para. 210, see *supra* note 85 (discussing modes of responsibility in context of confirmation proceedings).

279 ICTR Statute, Article 24(1), see *supra* note 61 (providing for appeals from "persons convicted by the Trial Chambers or from the Prosecutor"); Rome Statute, Article 81(a), see *supra* note 19.

280 Exhibits can include documents, video tapes, audio tapes, pictures, maps, victim's clothing and any other tangible items. See Archbold, 2005, pp. 994–995, see *supra* note 133.

281 See ICTR, *Prosecutor v. Bagosora*, Decision on Aloys Ntabakuze's Interlocutory Appeal on Questions of Law Raised by the 29 June 2006 Trial Chamber I Decision on Motion for Exclusion of Evidence, 18 September 2006, ICTR-98-41-AR73.

282 ICC RPE, Rule 64(1), see *supra* note 33; ICTR RPE, Rule 72, see *supra* note 46 (providing for preliminary motions and establishing requirements); see also ICTR RPE, Rule 73, see *supra* note 46 (providing for motion practice and establishing requirements).

For documents introduced at trial, the prosecutor should move the document forward to the court by identifying it to the court and requesting that it be "identified for the record". Often, prosecutors will move a document forward with one witness who can testify to the document's authenticity and relevancy in part, and the prosecutor will indicate that he will complete the process through another witness who will be called at a later time. After the witness testifies at a later time, the prosecutor will then move to admit the document into evidence. The prosecutor should ensure that the grounds on which a document was excluded are noted by the trial chamber and should make a short statement on the record addressing any deficiencies noted if the record is not clear on what basis the prosecutor sought to introduce the document. If the deficiency is authentication, the prosecutor should strive to cure this deficiency at a later time in trial by reserving the right to establish this later during the trial. In any given case, there will be documents marked and submitted to the court for identification that are not admitted into evidence. These documents assist the Appeals Chamber in establishing whether there are certain grounds for appeal, and ruling appropriately on these issues.

Witness testimony that is excluded after a witness answers a question is generally not problematic unless the purpose of the prosecutor's line of questioning is unclear. In that instance, the prosecutor should state the purposes for the line of questioning on the record. If the witness has not answered and the line of questioning is unclear, the prosecutor should clarify this by means of a short statement on the record and, if known, what was the expected response. On occasion, a party seeks information from a witness, encounters difficulty in eliciting that information, and the trial court truncates the line of questioning.[283] In this situation, the prosecutor should place on the record the expected answer and the basis for why the prosecutor expects this answer. The trial chamber may require that this be done out of hearing of the witness, and the prosecutor might elect to establish the record after the witness has left the stand. Likewise, if a witness is excluded, the prosecutor should move into evidence the summary of the witness's statement submitted in the pre-trial brief, or offer a summary of expected testimony orally into the record. Without this information about the expected testimony of a witness, the appellate

[283] See, *e.g.*, ICTR, *Prosecutor v. Semanza*, Transcript, 14 November 2000, pp. 48–49 (terminating line of questioning from a defense counsel regarding distance).

chamber is forced to reach outside the record to the pre-trial briefs and admitted witness pre-trial statements to resolve whether there was an error in refusing to call a witness.

The ICTR and other international tribunals tend to hold the parties to rigid pre-trial witness lists and consider several factors in determining whether to grant a motion to vary that list.[284] The prosecutor is well-advised to inform the tribunal of a need to call additional witnesses as soon as these needs become known.[285] A refusal of the trial court to allow

---

[284] See ICTR Statute, Articles 54, 71, 73, 73*ter*, 92*bis* and 93*bis*, see *supra* note 61; see also ICTR, *Prosecutor v. Karemera and Ngirumpatse*, Decision Relative a la Requete de Mathieu Ngirumpatse aux fins de Modification De Sa Liste De Noms De Temoins Et En Consideration, *Articles 54,* 71, 73 *et 73ter,* 28 December 2010, ICTR-98-44-T (noting several factors for determining whether to grant leave to modify a witness list, including the complexity of the issue at hand, prejudice to either party, the stage of the proceedings, existence of corroboration, and any delays that might result); see also *ibid.* at p. 4 n. 12:

> 12. *Le Procureur c. Bagosora et consorts*, affaíre n° ICTR-98-41-T, Decìsìon on Prosecution Motion for Addition of Witnesses Pursuant to Rule 73 *bis* (E), 26 juin 2003, par. 14-22; Decision on Prosecutor's Motion for Leave to Vary the Witness List Pursuant to Rule 73 *bis* (E), 21 mai 2004, par. 8-14. *Le Procureur c. Pauline Nyiramasuhuko, Arsène Shalam Ntahobali, Sylvain Nsabimana, Alphonse Nteziryayo, Joseph Kanyabashi and Élie Ndayambaje*, affair n° ICTR-98-42-T, Decision on Prosecutor's Motion for Leave to Add a Handwriting Expert to His List of Witnesses, 14 octobre 2004, par. 11; *Le Procureur c. Ferdinand Nahimana, Jean-Bosco Barayagwiza and Hassan Ngeze* ("Media Case"), affaire n° ICTR-99-53-T, Decision on the Prosecutor's Oral Motion for Leave to Amend the List of Selected Witnesses, 26 juin 2001, par. 17; *Le Procureur c. Aloys Simba*, affaire no° ICTR-01-76-1, Decision on the Prosecution's Motion to Vary the Witness List, 27 août 2004, par. 7; *Le Procureur c. Augustin Ndindiliyimana, Augustin Bizimungu, François-Xavier Nzuwonemeye and Innocent Sagahutu*, affaire no° ICTR-00-56-T ("*Ndindiliyimana et al.*"), Decision on Sagahutu's Motion to Vary his Witness List, 26 mai 2008, par. 5; *Ndindiliyimana et al.*, Decision on Augustin Bizimungu's Motion to Vary his Witness List, 24 octobre 2007; *Ndindiliyimana et al.*, Decision on Nzuwonemeye's Motion to Request to Vary his Witness List, 31 janvier 2008, par. 3; *Le Procureur c. Rukundo*, affaire n° ICTR-2001-70-T, Decision on the Defence Motions for Additional Time to Disclose Witness' Identifying Information, to Vary its Witness List and for Video-Link Testimony and on the Prosecution's Motion for Sanctions, 11 septembre 2007, par. 10.

[285] On ICC disclosure regime, see *supra* note 56. See Rome Statute, Article 64(9)(a), see *supra* note 19 (the trial chambers shall have the power on application of a party or its own motion to rule on the admissibility or relevance of evidence); ICC Regulations, Regulation 35, see *supra* note 94; ICTR RPE, Rule 67(A)(i), see *supra* note 46 (requiring the Prosecutor to notify "the Defence of the names of the witnesses that he intends to call to establish the guilt of the accused and in rebuttal of any defence plea of

the prosecution to hear the testimony of a corroboration witness whose need becomes known only during trial may deprive the prosecution of their right to fully present the case. Given that no proofing is permitted by either party at the ICC, it might be prudent for the prosecution to list all possible witnesses and summaries of testimony in the witness list, and identify those that the prosecution expects to call, reserving the right to call any additional witnesses as required. This practice adopted at the ICTR reduces the risk of "surprise" to a defendant; however, it does not address a situation where both the prosecution and defense are caught unawares by a witness's testimony at trial and, as a result, desire to call additional witnesses.

A proper, transparent record is the responsibility of all parties and the trial chamber. The prosecutor can assist in this process by a well-reasoned, deliberate preparation and presentation of the case. In the case of sexual offenses, this approach supports the expansion of sexual crimes jurisprudence at the appellate level by providing the appeals court a clear record and thus the tools to appropriately address complex, substantive issues raised at trial.

3.8. Gender Mainstreaming

The ICC's framework includes many provisions that assist and support a gender mainstreaming approach to address what many have identified as a failure of international courts to investigate and charge sexual offenses.[286]

Importantly, Article 54 of the Rome Statute of the ICC specifically provides that in order to ensure the effective investigation and prosecution of the crimes under the jurisdiction of the Court, the Prosecutor shall "take into account the nature of the crime, in particular where it involves sexual violence, gender violence or violence against children".

---

which the Prosecutor has received notice in accordance with Sub-Rule (ii)"); ICC RPE, Rule 67(D), see *supra* at note 46 ("If either party discovers additional evidence or information or materials which should have been produced earlier pursuant to the Rules, that party shall promptly notify the other party and the Trial Chamber of the existence of the additional evidence or information or materials.").

286 See Solange Mouthaan, "The Prosecution of Gender Crimes at the ICC: Challenges and Opportunities", *University of Warwick School of Law*, 2010, Legal Studies Research Paper No. 2010-17, available at http://papers.ssrn.com/sol3/papers.cfm?abstract_id=1652790#%23, last accessed on 10 May 2011, pp. 18–20.

At the pre-investigative stage, the ICC focuses on methods of investigation particularly as they relate to women and children.[287] The Gender and Children's Unit ('GCU') was established to provide assistance related to sexual and gender-based crimes to the Office of the Prosecutor ('OTP') and others at the ICC.[288] The GCU supported the OTP in developing victim questionnaires and interview techniques designed to reduce trauma while eliciting accurate and thorough information. Charging documents reflect a focus on sexual crimes with nearly all ICC indictments including sexual crimes charges as appropriate.[289] Furthermore, Article 42(9) of the Statute requires the Prosecutor to appoint advisers with legal expertise on specific issues, including on sexual and gender violence. In this light, Professor Catharine MacKinnon was appointed as Special Gender Adviser.

However, mainstreaming requires not only a focus on gender offenses, but a holistic approach where sexual crimes are part of every investigation in the same way that murder and other predicate offenses, as well as modes of responsibility, are investigated.[290] Simply focusing on the victim and the predicate act without sufficient supporting investigation into modes of responsibility and linking evidence will result in the same technical and evidentiary deficiencies seen to date at the ICTR and other tribunals. Thus, as per regular practice of the OTP of the ICC, the investi-

---

[287] See Office of the Prosecutor, *Report on Prosecutorial Strategy*, ICC, The Hague, 14 September 2006, pp. 5, 7; see also Regulations of the Office of the Prosecutor, 23 April 2009, ICC-BD/05-01-09 (providing in Regulation 34 that: "[i]n each provisional case hypothesis, the joint team shall aim to select incidents reflective of the most serious crimes and the main types of victimization – including sexual and gender violence and violence against children – and which are the most representative of the scale and impact of the crimes.").

[288] Bensouda, 2007, pp. 401, 416, see *supra* note 33.

[289] See ICC, *Prosecutor v. Katanga*, Document Summarising the Charges Confirmed by the Pre-Trial Chamber, 3 November 2009, ICC-01/04-01/07-1588-Anx1; ICC, *Prosecutor v. Bemba*, Corrected Revised Second Amended Document Containing the Charges, 10 October 2010, ICC-01/05-01/08-950-Red-AnxA; see also ICC, *Prosecutor v. Al Bashir*, Prosecution's Application Under Article 58, 14 July 2008, ICC-02/05-157-AnxA.

[290] ICTR, "Best Practices Manual for the Investigation and Prosecution of Sexual Violence Crimes in Situations of Armed Conflict: Lessons from the International Criminal Tribunal for Rwanda", 2008, available at http://www.unictr.org/Portals/0/english/news/events/nov2008/en/best-practices-manual-sexual-violence.pdf, last accessed on 10 May 2011, pp. 5–7.

gative and prosecutorial teams should maintain an integrated approach to prosecution of sexual crimes, investigating and charging these crimes as part of an overall situation.

3.8.1. Staffing and Gender Representation

Although the ICTR benefited from some of the best and brightest judges from throughout the world,[291] there was a lack of gender representation in the early days of the tribunal. The appointment of women judges to the ICTR heralded significant advances in legal jurisprudence regarding sexual crimes.[292] Judge Pillay, the president of the trial chamber that rendered the *Tadić* decision, was singularly instrumental in ensuring that indictment was amended to include rape as genocide, laying the foundation for the ground breaking decision establishing the definition of rape – previously a lacunae in international law. Unfortunately, despite such focus and a renewed determination to establish appropriate gender representation at the mid to senior levels at the ICTR and ICC, this goal has arguably not been reached. It is difficult to understand why international courts have been unable to achieve the goal of adequate gender representation in their staffing[293] when over half of all lawyers and judges in developed states are women.[294] Possibly, this lack of gender representation offers an

[291] Many of these judges have gone on to serve on the ICTY/ICTR Appeals Chamber and/or now hold significant positions in the international community or their home states. See, *e.g.*, Judge Navanethem Pilay (named as the UN High Commissioner for Human Rights in 2008, after serving as the President of the ICTR and assigned as a judge to the International Criminal Court); Judge Erik Møse (named as Supreme Court Justice in Norway in 2008 after serving as President of the ICTR).

[292] Haffajee, 2006, pp. 201, 205 n. 28 (and accompanying text), see *supra* note 273.

[293] The ICTR has been unable to reach effective gender representation at the senior levels. See *supra* note 113. This underrepresentation is possibly explained on the basis of required geographical representation and gender inequality in developing states. Consideration should be given to a waiver for geographical representation until such time as gender representation can be met without such waiver.

[294] See, *e.g.*, Statement by H.E. Ambassador Zhang Yesui, Permanent Representative of the People's Republic of China at the General Assembly of the United Nations Commemorative of the 15th Anniversary of the International Conference on Population and Development, New York, 12 October 2009, available at http://www.china-un.org/eng/hyyfy/t619994.htm, last accessed on 10 May 2011 (noting that gender inequality still plagues "the development of the world population, especially the people in the developing countries").

explanation for the deficiencies in ICC investigations and charging relative to gender based offenses.[295]

3.9. Conclusion

Rape and sexual offenses as genocide, crimes against humanity, and war crimes are among the most serious of criminal acts and fall within the jurisdiction of international courts. The international community of states recognizes the far reaching effects of prosecuting international sexual offenders; however, the prosecution of these cases has been hampered by a lack of overall strategic planning, resulting in a failure to focus on sound and thorough investigations, to draft informed and legally sufficient indictments, and to present available and material evidence of the sexual act and defendant's responsibility at trial.

Prosecuting international sexual violence crimes is unlike prosecuting domestic sexual offenses where the focus often is on establishing that an act of sexual violence occurred and that a charged accused personally committed that act. The prosecution of international criminal offenses has been and is limited to the most serious of offenders, including leaders and planners who may not have personally committed the charged sexual act. Although the practical problems associated with prosecuting international sexual crimes are very often the same challenges present in cases in which non-gender violations are charged, locating and presenting sufficient evidence on the issue of mode of responsibility and criminal culpability of a senior leader for sexual offenses presents additional challenges. The greatest prosecutorial challenge facing international prosecutors often is not establishing that the sexual assault took place – as is the case in most

295 See Katy Glassborow, "ICC Investigative Strategy Under Fire", in Caroline Tosh and Yigal Chazan (eds.), *Special report: Sexual Violence in the Democratic Republic of the Congo*, Institute for War and Peace Reporting, 2008, pp. 8–9 (noting that early investigations at the ICC commenced "before sufficient planning had been done", resulting in less than effective investigations and charging); see also ICC, *Prosecutor v. Katanga and Chui*, Decision on Evidentiary Scope of the Confirmation Hearing, Preventive Relocation and Disclosure under Article 67(2) of the Statute and Rule 77 of the Rule, 25 April 2008, ICC-01/04-01/07, para. 399 (excluding statements of two sexual offense witnesses who had not been provided witness protection). Exclusion of witness statements at the pre-trial stage for failure to provide statutory witness protections and subsequent dropping of charges of sexual slavery (later cured) suggests a lack of coherent prosecutorial strategy.

domestic jurisdictions – but, rather, proving that a particular defendant is legally responsible.

These challenges can only be addressed by skilled, knowledgeable, and dedicated court personnel, including linguists, investigators, legal advisors, prosecutors, judges, and judicial and registry staff, working together from the beginning of an investigation with the common goal of holding defendants responsible for sexual offenses. Mainstreaming gender as an integrated part of an overall prosecutorial strategy to effectively investigate, charge, and prosecute these types of cases is the single most material factor to ensuring the effective prosecution of senior leaders for sexual crimes.

As noted by a career international criminal prosecutor,

> [y]ou cannot later graft additional sexual offense charges to an indictment that was originally crafted with little regard to sexual offenses and based on the extensive investigation of a pervasive genocide – that subsumed sexual offenses – as a subset of the more vicious genocide. You will not succeed. The host indictment will reject the grafted afterthought.[296]

[296] Interview with Ibukunolu Alao Babajide (IBK), a 12-year career prosecutor at the ICTR, now serving as the senior legal advisor at United Nations Mission in Sudan (UNMIS), 27 March 2011.

4

Sexual Offences in International Criminal Law, With a Special Focus on the Rome Statute of the International Criminal Court

Kai Ambos*

This chapter intends to explain and critically analyse the legal elements of the sexual offences in international criminal law ('ICL'), with a special focus on the Rome Statute. Thus, the starting point is the Rome System, including the growing, albeit incipient, case law of the International Criminal Court ('ICC'). The case law of the *ad hoc* tribunals will be taken into account as far as it provides basic definitions of sexual offences. The chapter focuses on the explicit criminalizations, that is, the offences codified explicitly as sexual acts (Section 4.2.). Implicit criminalizations will only be dealt with in a complimentary manner (Section 4.3.). Before starting with the legal analysis, some general remarks on the integration of sexual violence in ICL and international crimes in general are necessary (Section 4.1.).

4.1. International Criminal Law, International Crimes and Sexual Violence

Sexual violence may be *criminalized explicitly* or *implicitly*.[1] A classical implicit criminalization constitutes the classification of a sexual offence as an offence against the honor or dignity of the victim. Indeed, in national law rape and other forms of sexual violence are, in part, still considered

* **Kai Ambos** is Chair of Criminal Law, Criminal Procedure, Comparative Law and International Criminal Law at the Georg-August-Universität Göttingen. He is also judge at the District Court in Göttingen.

1 Generally on the status of sexual violence in international law, see Ntombizozuko Dyani, "Sexual Violence, Armed Conflict and International Law in Africa", *African Journal of International and Comparative Law*, 2007, vol. 15, pp. 234 *et seq*. Equally distinguishing between explicit and implicit criminal provisions, see Dianne Luping, "Investigation and Prosecution of Sexual and Gender-Based Crimes before the International Criminal Court", 2009, in *American University Journal of Gender, Social Policy & the Law,* vol. 17, no. 2, pp. 431 *et seq*.

as offences against dignity[2] although there is a clear tendency to qualify them as offences against sexual integrity or autonomy.[3] Older definitions of rape in International Humanitarian Law also focus on the attack on the woman's honor.[4] After the issue of sexual violence was almost non-existent in the trials following World War II[5] (sexual crimes have even

---

2 Criminalization of rape and sexual violence has experienced several changes worldwide, closely linked to the current understanding of gender-equality and rights. As described in Dipa Dube, *Rape Laws in India,* LexisNexis, New Delhi 2008, pp. 1–2, 11–15 and 161 *et seq.*, and similarly in Christina Müting, *Sexuelle Nötigung; Vergewaltigung (§ 177 StGB). Reformdiskussion und Gesetzgebung seit 1870*, De Gruyter, Berlin, 2010, pp. 8 *et seq.*, rape was previously considered as an offence against property or the honor of third parties (the women's owner, husband and/or family members), before it was later considered as an offence against the honor of the actual female victim. See, for example, the Indian Penal Code of 6 October 1860 (reprinted in K G Kannabiran (ed.), *Halsbury's Laws of India. 5(2). Criminal Law-II*, LexisNexis Butterworths, New Delhi 2006, p. 193), where rape is incorporated in Section 375, Chapter 12 under 'Offences against Women'. Dipa Dube, *op. cit.*, describes rape in Indian law as "violence of the private person of the woman" (p. 1) and welcomes developments in the Indian jurisprudence until 2003 as "the recognition of the rights of rape victims [which] have enabled women to secure their dignity and honor" (p. 135). See also Uruguay, where rape is criminalized, unmodified since 1933, by Art. 272 of the Código Penal under the heading of "good customs and family order ("Titulo X: De los delitos contra las buenas costumbres y el orden de la familia"). According to a Draft law, rape shall be punished as a crime against the sexual liberty (the draft is available at http://www.presidencia.gub.uy/sci/noticias/2010/12/2010121301.htm, last accessed on 30 March 2011).

3 For examples, see *infra* note 16.

4 See, *e.g.*, Art. 27 Geneva Convention (IV) relative to the Protection of Civilian Persons in Time of War, 12 August 1949, United Nations Treaty Series ('U.N.T.S.'), vol. 75, p. 287, entered into force 21 October 1950 (women "shall be especially protected against any attack on their honor, in particular against rape, enforced prostitution, or any form of indecent assault") and Art. 75(2)(b) Additional Protocol to the Geneva Conventions of 12 August 1949, and relating to the Protection of Victims of International Armed Conflicts (Protocol I), 8 June 1977, U.N.T.S., vol. 1125, p. 3, entered into force 7 December 1979 ("AP I"). See further Machteld Boot and Christopher K. Hall, in Otto Triffterer (ed.), *Commentary on the Rome Statute*, Beck, Munich, 2008 (second edition), Art. 7 marginal number ('mn.') 42, 48 with fn. 246; Michael Cottier, in Triffterer (ed.), *op. cit.*, Art. 8 mn. 202, 209. On further international laws and instruments with relevance to sexual violence and gender crimes, see Kelly D. Askin, "Crimes against women under international criminal law", in Bartram S. Brown (ed.), *Research handbook on international criminal* law, Edward Elgar, Cheltenham, 2011, pp. 86 *et seq.*

5 For an assessment of the Nuremberg and Tokyo trials, see Alison Cole, "International criminal law and sexual violence", in Clare McGlynn and Vanessa E. Munro (eds.),

been labeled "the 'forgotten' crimes in international law"[6]), it has meanwhile received increasing attention.[7] In the negotiations leading to the Rome Statute ('ICC Statute')[8] the first war crimes proposals linked sexual offences to outrages upon personal dignity, and it was not before December 1997 that the Preparatory Committee created a separate category in its own right for sexual offences.[9] Today, sexual violence is explicitly criminalized under the heading of crimes against humanity and war crimes (see Section 4.2.). Apart from that, one may also read sexual offences implicitly into several other crimes against humanity and war crimes, in particular those referring to acts against the bodily integrity and right to reproduction.[10] In ICL such a criminalization *latu sensu* exists with regard to the crime of outrages upon personal dignity and torture (see *infra* 4.3.1.), genocide (see *infra* 4.3.2.) and to persecution as a crime against humanity (see *infra* 4.3.3.).

The use of criminal law as an instrument of social control presupposes that the conduct criminalized actually causes *harm* to legal interests (*Rechtsgüter*) which a given society considers important enough to be protected by means of criminalizations.[11] While international crimes con-

Rethinking Rape Law. International and Comparative Perspectives, Routledge-Cavendish, Abingdon 2010, pp. 48–50, and pp. 58–59.

6 See Christine Chinkin, "Gender-related Violence and International Criminal Law and Justice", in Antonio Cassese (ed.), *The Oxford Companion to International Criminal Justice*, Oxford University Press, Oxford, 2009, p. 76; Kelly D. Askin, "Women and International Humanitarian Law", in Kelly D. Askin and Dorean M. Koenig (eds.), *Women and international human rights law, Vol. 1*, Transnational Publishers, Ardsley NY, 2001, p. 64. In a similar vein, see Nimah Hayes, "Creating a Definition of Rape in International Law: The Contribution of the International Criminal Tribunals", in Shane Darcy and Joseph Powderly (eds.), *Judicial Creativity at the International Criminal Tribunals*, Oxford University Press, Oxford, 2010, p. 129 ("extraordinarily little appetite historically to prosecute the crime, in part due to the continuing perception that sexual violence was simply one of the 'spoils of war'.").

7 For an enlightening summary of the approaches to sexual violence before the different institutions of ICL, see Cole, 2010, pp. 48 *et seq.*, see *supra* note 5.

8 Rome Statute of the International Criminal Court, 17 July 1998, U.N.T.S., vol. 2187, p. 3, entered into force on 1 July 2002 ("ICC Statute").

9 Reproducing Art. 75(2)(b) AP I (*supra* note 4), see Cottier, 2008, Art. 8 mn. 203, see *supra* note 4.

10 For cross-references as to war crimes, see *ibid.*, Art. 8 mn. 203 *in fine*, 204.

11 The underlying harm principle, or *Rechtsgutslehre*, is a core question of criminal law theory that has been extensively treated in several academic writings, in particular with a view to the anticipated criminalization of preparatory acts. See, *e.g.*, Jens

stitute a threat to the collective legal interests of international peace and security,[12] national crimes concern more concrete legal interests such as life, bodily integrity, liberty and personal autonomy.[13] As to international sexual offences international peace and security is also invoked,[14] but

Puschke, "Grund und Grenzen des Gefährdungsstrafrechts am Beispiel der Vorbereitungsdelikte", in Roland Hefendehl (ed.), *Grenzenlose Vorverlagerung des Strafrechts?*, Berliner Wissenschafts-Verlag, Berlin, 2010, pp. 9–39, at 23–24 calling for a strictly limited criminalization of preparatory acts with a view to their potential to violate *Rechtsgüter*; see also Larry Alexander and Kimberly Kessler Ferzan, *Crime and Culpability. A Theory of Criminal Law,* Cambridge University Press, Cambridge, 2009, pp. 289–90, criticizing overcriminalization, *i.e.*, punishing "conduct that does not risk harm to any interest the criminal law might wish to protect" in the form of a too early intervention of criminal law ("only [...] attenuated connection to legally protected interests") or its "overinclusiveness". For the same twofold approach, see the recent Resolution of the *XVIII AIDP International Congress of Penal Law* (Istanbul, 20–27 September 2009) calling for strict conditions to consider the punishment of preparatory offences and autonomous acts of participation as legitimate, reprinted in *Zeitschrift für die gesamte Strafrechtswissenschaft* ('*ZStW*'), 2010, vol. 122, pp. 474–475; see, on the discussions of the respective section I (General Part), Tim Müller, "Bericht über die Verhandlungen der I. Sektion: Strafrecht Allgemeiner Teil: erweiterte Formen der Vorbereitung und der Teilnahme", *ZStW*, 2010, vol. 122, pp. 453 *et seq.* For a general critique of "overcriminalization", see Douglas Husak, *Overcriminalization. The Limits of Criminal Law*, Oxford University Press, Oxford, 2008, proposing internal and external constraints (at pp. 55 *et seq.*, 120 *et seq.*) and arguing that offences of risk prevention may be acceptable under certain conditions in that the criminal law may also be employed to reduce the "risk of harm" (pp. 159–60).

12 See the Preamble of the ICC Statute, para. 3, see *supra* note 8.

13 The question of which *Rechtsgut* to protect with the criminalization of sexual violence depends on the understanding of sexual violence, which has differed widely from ancient times up to now, and still seems to be developing. Most important for the modern understanding of sexual violence and its meaning was, with a rather sociological perspective on rape, Susan Brownmiller, *Against Our Will. Men, Women and Rape,* Bantam Books, New York, 1976 (dealing with rapes in wartimes at pp. 23 *et seq.*).

14 This is recognized in United Nations Security Council ('UNSC') Resolution 1820, 19 June 2008, U.N. Doc. S/RES/1820, para. 1; UNSC Resolution 1880, 30 September 2009, U.N. Doc. S/RES/1880, para. 1; and UNSC Resolution 1960, 16 December 2010, U.N. Doc. S/RES/1960, all stating that "sexual violence [...] may impede the restoration of international peace and security". Previous resolutions referred to sexual violence in conflict situations, without linking this to international peace and security: UNSC Resolution 820, 17 April 1993, U.N. Doc. S/RES/820, para. 6, condemned the "massive, organized and systematic [...] rape of women" in the former Yugoslavia's conflict (see Anne-Marie L.M. de Brouwer, *Supranational Criminal Prosecution of Sexual Violence. The ICC and the Practice of the ICTY and the ICTR*, Intersentia, Antwerpen and Oxford, 2005, p. 16 who emphasizes that this resolution is

more concretely they protect the physical or mental integrity,[15] the dignity and the personal (sexual) autonomy.[16] The issue is not only of academic nature since the protected legal interest offers often the only rational criterion to delimitate the scope of the criminalization. We will come back to this if we discuss the specific sexual offences.

All international crimes have so called *context elements* or "chapeaus".[17] The specific conduct must be related or linked to these elements, that is, in the case of genocide, it must take place "in the context of a manifest pattern of similar conduct directed against" a protected group or "could itself effect" its destruction,[18] in the case of crimes against hu-

---

the first that explicitly recognized rape as having taken place in conflict); see also UNSC Resolution 1325, 31 October 2000, U.N. Doc. S/RES/1325, calling upon conflict parties to protect women's rights and in this context (in paras. 10–11) calling on all parties to armed conflict to "take measures to protect women and children from gender-based violence".

15 See Wolfgang Schomburg and Ines Peterson, "Genuine Consent to Sexual Violence Under International Criminal Law", in *The American Journal of International Law* ('*AJIL*'), 2007, vol. 101, p. 126.

16 *E.g.*, in the German Criminal Code, sexual offences are contained in Chapter 13 as "Offences against sexual self-determination", see German Criminal Code ("German StGB") in the version promulgated on 13 November 1998, Federal Law Gazette [Bundesgesetzblatt] I, p. 3322, last amended by Art. 3 of the Law of 2 October 2009, Federal Law Gazette I p. 3214. With regard to the U.K., the Sexual Offences Act 2003, Chapter 43, 20 November 2003, is designed to protect several interests, among them to punish non-consensual sexual activity. Thus, sexual offences on adults each include the element that the victim 'does not consent to', see Sexual Offences Act 2003, Part 1: 1 Rape (1)(b), 2 Assault (1)(c), 3 Sexual Assault (1)(c), 4 Causing Sexual Activity without Consent (1)(c). See also Richard Card, Alisdair A. Gillespie and Michael Hirst, *Sexual Offences*, Jordans, Bristol, 2008, para. 1.14.

17 See Gerhard Werle, *Principles of International Criminal Law*, TMC Asser Press, Berlin, 2009 (second edition), pp. 32–33; Schomburg and Peterson, 2007, p. 128, see *supra* note 15; moreover, for a critical approach, arguing for a revival of state policy as an element of international crimes, see William Schabas, "State Policy as an Element of International Crimes", in *The Journal of Criminal Law and Criminology*, 2008, vol. 98, no. 3, pp. 953 *et seq.*

18 This Element is not explicitly phrased in the ICC Statute, but in the ICC Elements of Crimes, ICC-ASP/1/3(part II-B), entered into force on 9 September 2002, ("Elements of Crimes"), Element 4 to Art. 6(b) 4; Element 5 to Art. 6(c); Element 5 to Art. 6(d). As described elsewhere, the need and legality of this element has been questioned in several contexts and was a disputed issue in the *ad hoc* tribunal's jurisprudence (where the context has not been recognized as a requirement for the crime of genocide

manity, it must be committed "as part of a widespread or systematic attack directed against a civilian population"[19] and, in the case of war crimes, it must take place "in the context of and was associated with" an (international or non-international) armed conflict.[20] A single act of sexual violence may suffice in this regard if a linkage between the act and the context exists.[21] Yet, the existence of such a context implies a general climate of violence and coercion, which in most cases excludes the possibility of a free choice of the victim and therefore her genuine consent.[22] This is the big difference between sex crimes in armed conflict and in times of peace and thus between international and national law where consent if often a valid defence. We will come back to this in the following, especially when discussing the definition of rape.[23]

With regard to the *mental element*, Article 30 applies, according to which the perpetrator must have committed the act "[...] with intent and knowledge" in order to be criminally responsible.[24] With regard to the context element a specific awareness is required, that is, as to the conduct being part of "a widespread or systematic attack directed against a civilian

but as an important indication for a given intent to destroy, see Kai Ambos, *Internationales Strafrecht*, Beck, 2011 (third edition), § 7 mn. 140 with further references.

19 See Elements of Crimes, Element 3 to Art. 7, Introduction; Element 3 to Art. 7(1)(g)-1; Element 3 to Art. 7(1)(g)-2, Element 3 to Art. 7(1)(g)-3, Element 2 to Art. 7(1)(g)-4, Element 3 to Art. 7(1)(g)-5, Element 4 to Art. 7(1)(g)-6, see *supra* note 18; see also Stefan Kirsch, "Two Kinds of Wrong: On the Context Element of Crimes Against Humanity", in *Leiden Journal of International Law* ("LJIL"), 2009, vol. 22, pp. 525 *et seq*.

20 See Elements of Crimes, Introduction to the Elements of Art. 8, third subpara. and respectively the second last para. of the elements to each single war crime, see *supra* note 18. Recently, sexual violence committed by UN peacekeeping soldiers has become a cause for concern, see Muna Ndulo, "The United Nations Responses To The Sexual Abuse And Exploitation Of Women And Girls By Peacekeepers During Peacekeeping Missions", in *Berkeley Journal of International Law*, 2009, vol. 27, no. 1, pp. 127 *et seq*. However, such sexual violence may typically not amount to international crimes, due to a lack of the contextual element (apparently contrary to Ndulo, *ibid*., p. 156).

21 See also Dyani, 2007, p. 233, see *supra* note 1.

22 Schomburg and Peterson, 2007, pp. 124 *et seq.*, see *supra* note 15.

23 See *infra* Section 4.2.1. (Rape), third paragraph.

24 Werle, 2009, pp. 325, 326, 392, 394, see *supra* note 17.

population"[25] or as to the "factual circumstances that established the existence of an armed conflict".[26]

Notwithstanding these important legal questions one must not overlook the *cultural conditionality* of criminal prohibitions that becomes particularly obvious in the context of sexual offences.[27] As the respective conflicts are normally not taking place in the highly developed industrial societies, but rather in underdeveloped or developing countries[28] (especially in Sub-Saharan Africa[29]), ICL is confronted with highly traditional, sometimes even archaic conceptions, according to which sexual offences are primarily considered as attacks on the honor – yet not of the female

25 See ICC Elements of Crimes, Element 4 to Art. 7, Introduction, Element 4 to Art. 7(1)(g)-1, Element 4 to Art. 7(1)(g)-2, Element 4 to Art. 7(1)(g)-3, Element 3 to Art. 7(1)(g)-4, Element 4 to Art 7(1)(g)-5, Element 5 to Art. 7 (1)(g)-6, *supra* note 18.

26 See ICC Elements of Crimes, as a general rule for war crimes: Art. 8 Introduction, third indent, Element 4 to Art. 8(2)(b)(xxii)-1, Element 4 to Art. 8(2)(b)(xxii)-2, Element 4 to Art. 8(2)(b)(xxii)-3, Element 3 to Art. 8(2)(b)(xxii)-4, Element 4 to Art. 8(2)(b)(xxii)-5, Element 5 to Art. 8(2)(b)(xxii)-6, Element 4 to Art. 8(2)(e)(vi)-1, Element 4 to Art. 8(2)(e)(vi)-2, Element 4 to Art. 8(2)(e)(vi)-3, Element 3 to Art. 8(2)(e)(vi)-4, Element 4 to Art. 8(2)(e)(vi)-5, Element 5 to Art. 8(2)(e)(vi)-6, *supra* note 18.

27 Generally on human rights in different cultural contexts, see Udo Di Fabio, "Menschenrechte in unterschiedlichen Kulturräumen", in: Nooke, Lohman, and Wahlers (eds.), *Gelten Menschenrechte universal?*, 2008, available at http://www.kas.de/wf/de/33.14437/, last accessed on 12 June 2011, pp. 63 *et seq*. See also *supra* note 2.

28 For a worldwide study on sexual violence in conflict, see Francesch *et al.*, "Alert!, Report on conflicts, human rights and peacebuilding", 2009, available at http://escola pau.uab.cat/img/programas/alerta/alerta/alerta10i.pdf, last accessed on 18 May 2011: "During 2009 sexual violence was used as a weapon of war in the majority of armed conflicts, especially in DR Congo, Somalia, Sri Lanka (east), Colombia, Myanmar, India (Jammu and Kashmir) and Iraq" (p. 139). On sexual violence in Colombia, see Oxfam, "Sexual Violence in Colombia, Instrument of War, Briefing Paper", September 2009, available at http://www.oxfam.org/en/policy/sexual-violence-colombia, last accessed on 1 April 2011; and Amnesty International, Colombia, "Scarred bodies, hidden crimes: Sexual Violence against women in the armed conflict", AMR 23/040/2004, October 2004, available at http://www.amnesty.org/en/libr AMR23/040/2004/en, last accessed on 12 June 2011.

29 For a critique of the focus on Africa, see Alexis Arieff, "Sexual Violence in African Contexts", November 2010, available at http://www.fas.org/sgp/crs/row/R40956.pdf, last accessed on 12 June 2011, p. 3: "The issue of sexual violence in conflict is far from confined to Sub-Saharan Africa [...] and it has not been a salient feature of all African conflicts".

victim but of her male partner.[30] Thus, the rape of a woman is considered as the emasculation of her male guardian who failed to accomplish his protective function.[31] Additionally, there are numerous reports of cases where men left their raped women after those "consented" to being raped to save their men from being killed.[32] It is clear that the understanding of gender equality and rights that lies beneath such attitudes amplifies the harm that victims of sexual violence suffer, and may even hinder the imposition of adequate punishment. Also, the obvious secondary rank accorded to women in a male dominated society entails the playing down of sexual violence and the risk of a secondary victimization of the respective women.[33]

4.2. Explicit Criminalization of Sexual Violence

For the first time and in contrast to the *ad hoc* tribunals' statutes,[34] the ICC Statute includes explicit penalizations of sexual violence (Articles 7(1)(g), 8(2)(b)(xxii), and 8(2)(e)(vi)).[35] It distinguishes between several forms of perpetration or conduct:

---

30 On rape as an offence against the property and honor of a third person (the female's owner, husband and/or her relatives), see Dube, 2008, pp. 1 *et seq.*, 11 *et seq.*, 161 *et seq.*, see *supra* note 2; see also Müting, 2010, pp. 8 *et seq.*, see *supra* note 2.

31 Statement of a participant of the international master's programme "transcrim" of the University of Western Cape and the Humboldt University Berlin, during a lecture by the author on 9 March 2011.

32 Statement of a participant at the above mentioned lecture, see *supra* note 31.

33 See, on the perception of women and the role of sexual violence in the Democratic Republic of Congo, Omanyondo Ohambe *et al.*, "Women's Bodies as a Battleground, Sexual Violence Against Women and Girls During the War in the Democratic Republic in Congo (South Kivu 1996–2003)", 2005, available at www.grandslacs.net/doc/4053.pdf, last accessed on 18 May 2011, pp. 25 *et seq*.

34 For the legal position in these Statutes, see Chinkin, 2009, pp. 76 *et seq.*, see *supra* note 7.

35 According to Kathrin Anastasia Gabriel, "Women's Issues. Engendering the International Criminal Court: Crimes based on Gender and Sexual Violence", in *Eyes on the ICC*, 2004, vol. 1, no. 1, p. 47, the ICC Statute "contains an impressive list of sexual gender crimes" and therefore constitutes a "landmark in codifying crimes of sexual and gender violence"; the provisions are described as a milestone in the criminalization of sexual violence in the context of conflicts by Zimmermann and Geiß, in Otto Lagodny (ed.), *Münchener Kommentar zum Strafgesetzbuch. Band 6/2 – Nebenstrafrecht III, Völkerstrafgesetzbuch*, Beck, Munich 2009, § 8 VStGB mn. 139; similarily, see Chinkin, 2009, pp. 77, see *supra* note 6; On gender issues during the

- Rape
- Sexual Slavery
- Enforced Prostitution
- Forced Pregnancy
- Enforced Sterilization
- Other forms of sexual violence

Notwithstanding the commission of these offences within the broader context of crimes against humanity or war crimes (in international or non-international armed conflict) they are defined identically. The ICC Statute does not in itself provide definitions of these forms of conduct (except for forced pregnancy[36]). Definitions are laid down in the Elements of Crimes, which shall, pursuant to Article 9(1) of the ICC Statute, assist the Court in the interpretation and application of the crimes.[37] Furthermore, some previous jurisprudence regarding the former Yugoslavia ('ICTY')[38], Rwanda ('ICTR')[39] and Sierra Leone ('SCSL')[40] will be considered.[41] All forms of sexual offences (except forced pregnancy[42]) are gender-neutral, applying equally to male and female victims.[43]

---

negotiations of the ICC Statute, see Barbara Bedont and Katherine Hall-Martinez, "Ending Impunity for Gender Crimes under the International Criminal Court", in *The Brown Journal of World Affairs,* 1999, vol. VI, Issue 1, pp. 66 *et seq*.

36 According to Art. 7(2)(f) ICC Statute, see *supra* note 8, this is to be understood as "the unlawful confinement of a woman forcibly made pregnant, with the intent of affecting the ethnic composition of any population or carrying out other grave violations of international law. […]".

37 ICC Elements of Crimes, see *supra* note 18.

38 International Criminal Tribunal for the former Yugoslavia, see http://www.icty.org/.

39 International Criminal Tribunal for Rwanda, see http://www.unictr.org/.

40 Special Court for Sierra Leone, see http://www.sc-sl.org/.

41 For a throughout report on sexual violence considered at ICTY, ICTR and SCSL, see UN Department of Peacekeeping Operations, *Review of the Sexual Violence Elements of the Judgments of the International Criminal Tribunal for the Former Yugoslavia, the International Criminal Tribunal for Rwanda, and the Special Court for Sierra Leone in the Light of Security Council Resolution 1820*, 2010, United Nations, New York (hereinafter: "UN Report Review Sexual Violence Elements"); see also chapter 15 in the present publication. See further, for an interesting study on the prosecutions at the ICTY, Gabriela Mischkowski *et al.*, ""… and that it does not happen to anyone anywhere in the world" – The Trouble with Rape Trials – Views of Witnesses, Prosecutors and Judges on Prosecuting Sexualised Violence during the War in the former Yugoslavia", Medica Mondiale, Cologne, December 2009, esp. pp. 15 *et seq.*, available at: http://www.medicamondiale.org/fileadmin/content/07_Infothek/Gerechtigkeit/

4.2.1. Rape

Rape has not been statutorily defined,[44] but the Elements provide for a definition:[45]

> 1. The perpetrator invaded the body of a person by conduct resulting in penetration, however slight, of any part of the body of the victim or of the perpetrator with a sexual organ,

---

medica_mondiale_Zeuginnenstudie_englisch_december_2009.pdf accessed 12 June 2011. For an analysis of contributions the *ad hoc* tribunals made to substantial criminal law, see Mohammed Ayat, "Quelques apports des Tribunaux pénaux internationaux, ad hoc et notamment le TPIR, à la lute contre les violences sexuelles subies par les femmes durant les genocides et les conflits armés", in *International Criminal Law Review*, 2010, vol. 10, pp. 787, 807 *et seq.*; Askin, 2010, pp. 94 *et seq.*, see *supra* note 4; and Alica Gil Gil, "Derecho penal en contextos de graves violaciones a los derechos humanos. La violación como arma de Guerra y su persecución como crimen internacional", in Andrés Fernando Ramírez Moncayo *et al.* (ed.), *Realidades y tendencias del derecho en el siglo XXI. Derecho penal. Tomo III,* Editorial Temis, 2010, pp. 11 *et seq*., and on the ICC Statute's provisions at *ibid.*, pp. 17 *et seq.* See also on the several forms of sexual offences in the ICC Statute, with a special focus on previous laws and jurisdictions: Luping, 2009, pp. 452 *et seq,* see *supra* note 1.

42 Art. 7(2)(f) ICC Statute, see *supra* note 8.

43 See also Art. 7(3) Statute, *supra* note 8: "For the purpose of this Statute, it is understood that the term 'gender' refers to the two sexes, male and female, within the context of society. […]". On gender neutrality, see also Cottier, 2008, Art. 8 mn. 203 *in fine*, see *supra* note 4. A gender neutral application of international sexual crimes conforms to the fact that not only women, but also children and men are victims of sexual violence in conflict, see UN Report Review Sexual Violence Elements, 2010, para. 53, see *supra* note 41. On the controversies regarding the gender definition in the ICC negotiations, see Chinkin, 2009, pp. 77, see *supra* note 7.

44 For relevant previous decisions of the tribunals for Rwanda and the former Yugoslavia, see Hayes, 2010, pp. 129 *et seq*., see *supra* note 7; William A. Schabas, *The International Criminal Court: A Commentary on the Rome Statute*, Oxford University Press, 2010, Art. 7, p. 171; Werle, 2009, pp. 323 *et seq.*, see *supra* note 17; Schomburg and Peterson, 2007, see *supra* note 15, pp. 132–138; Luping, 2009, pp. 448 *et seq.*, see *supra* note 1; and Ayat, 2010, pp. 809 *et seq*., see *supra* note 41. For relevant decisions of the SCSL, see Valerie Oosterveld, "Gender Jurisprudence of the Special Court for Sierra Leone: Progress in the Revolutionary United Front Judgment", in *Cornell International Law Journal,* 2011, vol. 44, pp. 49 *et seq.*

45 Elements of Crimes, *supra* note 18, for Arts. 7(1)(g)-1, 8(2)(b)(xxii)-1, and 8(2)(e)(vi)-1 of the ICC Statute. The same definition was used at the SCSL in the 'RUF' trial judgment, see SCSL, *Prosecutor v. Sesay et al*., Case No. SCSL-04-15-T, Judgment, 2 March 2009, ("*Sesay et al.* Trial Judgment"), paras. 145, 146 (whereby the Trial Chamber abstained from using the further – here not reproduced – Elements on intent and coercion, see Oosterveld, 2011, p. 57, see *supra* note 44).

> or of the anal or genital opening of the victim with any object or any other part of the body.
> 2. The invasion was committed by force, or by threat of force or coercion, such as that caused by fear of violence, duress, detention, psychological oppression or abuse of power, against such person or another person, or by taking advantage of a coercive environment, or the invasion was committed against a person incapable of giving genuine consent.

The Elements provide for a gender-neutral,[46] requiring a physical invasion of *any* part of the victim's body (penetration) *and* force or coercion.[47] Paragraph 1 refers to the (objective) conduct of the perpetrator, paragraph 2 to the opposing will of the victim. From this the sexual integrity and free will (personal autonomy) can be deduced as the legal interests protected by the criminalization of rape.[48] As to the former, *any penetration*, be it in the classical sense (as forced sex meaning penetration of the male penis into the vagina) or in any other sense (insertion of the perpetrator's sexual organ into other body cavities, oral and anal penetration, or insertion of other parts of the perpetrator's body or of objects into the vagina or the anus) is covered.[49] In other words, every sexual penetration may constitute rape, whereas sexual behaviour falling short of a penetration is not covered.[50] The definition in the Elements of Crimes was originally influenced by the ICTY's and ICTR's jurisprudence,[51] although it

46 Fn. 15 to the Elements of Crimes, *supra* note 18: "The concept of 'invasion' is intended to be broad enough to be gender-neutral". de Brouwer, 2005, p. 133, see *supra* note 14, greets this as an improvement compared to some national legislations, which still refer to female victims and male perpetrators.

47 Boot and Hall, in Triffterer (ed.), Art. 7 mn. 45, see *supra* note 4.

48 Werle, 2009, pp. 323 *et seq.*, see *supra* note 17, sees a definitional shift from the focus on the perpetrator's objective conduct to the victim's opposing will.

49 See similarly Zimmermann and Geiß, 2009, § 8 VStGB mn. 142, see *supra* note 35; for a broader understanding of the definition see Werle, 2009, p. 323, see *supra* note 17; Cottier, 2008, Art. 8 mn. 206, see *supra* note 4. For a critique, see de Brouwer, 2005, p. 132, see *supra* note 46, who takes issue with a confusing wording in the Elements and points out, that the Elements' definition does not seem to cover the penetration of the mouth of the victim with an object, probably due to a then missing sexual aspect of the act.

50 See similarly de Brouwer, 2005, p. 132, see *supra* note 14.

51 See *ibid.*, p. 130. de Brouwer sees the Elements' definition as most close to that applied in ICTY (Trial Chamber), *Prosecutor v. Furundžija,* Judgment, 10 December

later deviated from it in some instances.[52] An ICC decision on the particular requirements of rape has not yet been rendered.

As rape infringes upon the (sexual) autonomy, the key issue is what role a "genuine" *consent* may play. While consent is a classical defence in criminal law in offences against the personal autonomy – it is logically impossible to violate personal autonomy if the person affected voluntarily renounces it by "consenting" to the agent's intrusion – it certainly plays a minor rule in rape committed as a crime against humanity or war crime in armed conflict situations. In fact, in the existing jurisprudence the view prevails that the existing climate of coercion and violence in an armed

1998, Case No. IT-95-17/1-T ("*Furundžija* Trial Judgment"), para. 185, where the objective elements of rape have been defined as follows:

(i) the sexual penetration, however slight:

(a) of the vagina or anus of the victim by the penis of the perpetrator or any other object used by the perpetrator; or

(b) of the mouth of the victim by the penis of the perpetrator;

(ii) by coercion or force or threat of force against the victim or a third person."

See, similarly, Oosterveld, 2011, p. 55, see *supra* note 44 (distinguishing between four approaches to the definition of rape).

52 Another, broader, definition on rape was given in ICTR, *Prosecutor v. Akayesu*, Case No. 96-4-T, Judgment, 2 September 1998 ("*Akayesu* Trial Judgment"), paras. 598, 688 (defining rape as a "physical invasion of a sexual nature, committed on a person under circumstances who are coercive"), which also seems to cover, *e.g.*, enforced masturbation and sexual mutilations; see also de Brouwer, 2005, p. 133, see *supra* note 14. Vanessa E. Munro calls this approach a 'conceptual' rather than a 'cataloguing' one in "From consent to coercion. Evaluating international and domestic frameworks for the criminalization of rape", in McGlynn and Munro (eds.), 2010, p. 17, see *supra* note 5. Decisions by the *ad hoc* tribunals passed after the drafting of the Elements of Crimes often referred to this decision, see, *e.g.*, ICTY, *Prosecutor v. Kvočka et al.*, Case No. IT-98-30/1-T, Judgment, 2 November 2001 ("*Kvočka et al.* Trial Judgment"), para. 175; endorsed by ICTR, *Prosecutor v. Muhimana*, Case No. ICTR-95-1B-T, Judgment and Sentence, 28 April 2005 ("*Muhimana* Trial Judgment"), para. 551. On the development, see de Brouwer, 2005, pp. 105–129 (on *ad hoc* tribunals' definitions) and pp. 131–137 (on the Element's definition), see *supra* note 14. On the relevant ICTR jurisprudence, see also Kelly D. Askin, "Gender Crimes Jurisprudence in the ICTR. Positive Developments", in *Journal of International Criminal Justice* ("*JICJ*"), 2005, vol. 3, pp. 1007 *et seq.*; for a critique of the related ICTR jurisprudence, see Doris Buss, "Learning our lessons? The Rwanda Tribunal record on prosecuting rape", in McGlynn and Munro (eds.), 2010, see *supra* note 5, pp. 61 *et seq.* (regretting that the jurisprudence following *Akayesu* has not fully applied this approach).

conflict makes a "genuine" consent impossible.[53] This is, as in the above cited paragraph 2 of the Elements, also implied by the term "coercive environment".[54] By no means does this imply, however, that consent, as a

53 See, originally, *Akayesu* Trial Judgment, paras. 598, 688 ("committed on a person under circumstances who are coercive"), see *supra* note 52. In the same vein, see ICTY, *Prosecutor v. Kunarac et al.*, Case No. IT-96-23 & IT-96-23/1-A, Judgment, 12 June 2002 ("*Kunarac et al.* Appeals Judgment"), para. 130: "[…] crimes against humanity will be almost universally coercive. […] true consent will not be possible"; and the *Muhimana* Trial Judgment, para. 546 ("vitiating true consent"), see *supra* note 52; *Sesay et al.* Trial Judgment, para. 1577, see *supra* note 45. In a similar vein Schomburg and Peterson, 2007, pp. 138, 140 ("make genuine consent by the victim impossible"), see *supra* note 15; Xabier A. Aranburu, "Sexual violence beyond reasonable doubt: using pattern evidence and analysis for international cases", in *LJIL* 2010, vol. 23, p. 617 ("unlikely to carry any weight in a context of mass coercion and violence."); and Zimmermann and Geiß, 2009, § 8 VStGB mn. 143, see *supra* note 35, arguing that in a situation of armed conflict and presence of armed units and/or groups, normally a coercive situation will exist that excludes genuine consent. See also Amnesty International, "Rape and Sexual Violence. Human Rights Law and Standards in the International Criminal Court", IOR 53/001/2011, March 2011 ("AI Report Rape"), available at http://www.amnesty.org/en/library/info/IOR53/001/2011/en, last accessed on 12 June 2011, pp. 6, 16 *et seq.* (differentiating between several situations of force and threat), pp. 29 *et seq*. Contrary to this, some criticise this presumption of coercion, as it makes consensual sexual relationships *per se* "legally impossible, in some sets of circumstances", see Karen Engle, "Feminism and Its (Dis)contents: Criminalizing Wartime Rape in Bosnia and Herzegovina", in *AJIL*, 2005, vol. 99, no. 4, p. 804. For a more general discussion (partly referring to the above mentioned *Akayesu* Trial Judgment) about the relationship and effect of consent and coercion see, *e.g.*, Munro, 2010, pp. 17 et seq. (calling for a "consent-plus" approach, pp. 22 *et seq.*), see *supra* note 52. On possible justification of a penetration with consent in general, see Jonathan Herring and Michelle Madden Dempsey, "Rethinking the criminal law's response to sexual penetration. On theory and context.", in McGlynn and Munro (ed.), 2010, pp. 30 *et seq.*, see *supra* note 5. On the meaning of the *Akayesu* Trial Judgment's approach in this regard, see also Cole, 2010, pp. 54–55, see *supra* note 5.

54 On the negotiations in this regard, see Cottier, 2008, Art. 8 mn. 207, see *supra* note 4. Further, see Rule 70 of the ICC Rules of Procedure and Evidence, ICC-ASP/1/3 (Part. II-A), 9 September 2002:

> In cases of sexual violence, the Court shall be guided by and, where appropriate, apply the following principles:
>
> (a) Consent cannot be inferred by reason of any words or conduct of a victim where force, threat of force, coercion or taking advantage of a coercive environment undermined the victim's ability to give voluntary and genuine consent;
>
> (b) Consent cannot be inferred by reason of any words or conduct of a victim where the victim is incapable of giving genuine consent;

ground excluding criminal responsibility, is an "outdated concept";[55] rather, consent is recognized in ICL, as a matter of principle, but the necessary circumstances for an armed conflict normally entail the (actual) absence of any consent.

Clearly, the domestic concept of consent[56] cannot be "transplanted" without further ado to the international arena but this only confirms the truism in comparative law methodology that "legal transplants" from one to another jurisdiction are not possible or at least not functional.[57] In any case, only a "genuine" consent, that is, a consent not obtained through any act excluding the free will of the person affected, for example through deception or coercion, may exclude the unlawfulness of the act.[58] A person may also be incapable of giving genuine consent if affected by natural, induced or age-related incapacity.[59] In practice, the case law infers the

---

(c) Consent cannot be inferred by reason of the silence of, or lack of resistance by, a victim to the alleged sexual violence;

(d) Credibility, character or predisposition to sexual availability of a victim or witness cannot be inferred by reason of the sexual nature of the prior or subsequent conduct of a victim or witness.

55 As suggested by Boot and Hall, 2008, Art. 7 mn. 45, see *supra* note 4. For the same result, see Luping, 2009, p. 474, see *supra* note 1, who sees the rape definition as "not based on concepts related to the consent of the victim".

56 As an example of national law precluding consent in case of force or threat, see Art. 120(t)(14) US Uniform Code of Military Justice (United States Code, Title 10, Subtitle A, Part II, Chapter 47, hereinafter: 'US UCMJ'): "The term 'consent' means words or overt acts indicating a freely given agreement to the sexual conduct at issue by a competent person. [...] Lack of verbal or physical resistance or submission resulting from the accused's use of force, threat of force, or placing another person in fear does not constitute consent. [...]."

57 See the seminal work of Alan Watson, *Legal transplants: an approach to comparative law*, University of Georgia Press, Athens, 1993 (second edition), esp. pp. 95 *et seq.*; see, for a recent assessments on legal transplants, Margit Cohn, "Legal Transplant Chronicles: The Evolution of Unreasonableness and Proportionality Review of the Administration in the United Kingdom", in *American Journal of Comparative Law*, 2010, vol. 58, no. 3, pp. 583, 587 *et seq.*; and Cynthia Alton, "Plea Bargaining as a Legal Transplant: A Good Idea for Troubled Criminal Justice Systems", in *Transnational Law and Contemporary Problems*, 2010, vol. 19, no. 2, pp. 355 *et seq.*

58 As to deception, see also fn. 20 to the Elements of Crimes, *supra* note 18: "It is understood that 'genuine consent' does not include consent obtained through deception".

59 Elements of Crimes, *supra* note 18, see fn. 16 to Art. 7(1)(g)-1: "It is understood that a person may be incapable of giving genuine consent if affected by natural, induced or age-related incapacity." This footnote also applies to the corresponding elements of

lack of consent from the normally coercive environment in an armed conflict and thus relies, as in other cases, on circumstantial evidence.

From this perspective one may speak of a *presumption of non-consent*,[60] which converts the traditional defence of consent in an affirmative one to be brought forward by the defence and only admissible in exceptional circumstances.[61] This also entails that the classical mistake of fact problem – the perpetrator argues that he thought that the victim consented to sexual intercourse[62] – cannot be credibly brought up by the ac-

Art. 7 (1) (g)-3, 5 and 6. See also identical fn. 51 applying to Art. 8(2)(b)(xxii)-1, 8(2)(b)(xxii)-3, 8(2)(b)(xxii)-5, 8(2)(b)(xxii)-6; and identical fn. 63 applying to Art. 8(2)(e)(vi)-1, 8(2)(e)(vi)-3, 8(2)(e)(vi)-5, 8(2)(e)(vi)-6.

60 See also Cottier, 2008, Art. 8, mn. 207, p. 440 (referring to the *Kunarac et al.* Appeals and the *Furundžija* Trial Judgments) and mn. 208, p. 444 (referring to sexual slavery), see *supra* note 4. In the *Kunarac et al.* Appeals Judgment, the ICTY Appeals Chamber notes that "[…] the circumstances […] will be almost universally coercive. That is to say, true consent will not be possible" (para. 130), and concludes after a comparative view to some national legislations on a "need to presume non-consent here" (para. 131), see *supra* note 53. Similarly, Boot and Hall, 2008, Art. 7 mn. 46, see *supra* note 4, speak of a "concept of non-consent"; see also Schomburg and Peterson, 2007, p. 138, see *supra* note 15.

61 In this vein, see ICTR, *Prosecutor v. Gacumbitsi,* Case No. ICTR-2001-64-A, Judgment, 7 July 2006, paras. 151–157. See, similarly, Schomburg and Peterson, 2007, p. 139, see *supra* note 15.

62 See the notorious case of the boxer Mike Tyson who was convicted in Indianapolis, U.S.A., in 1992 (confirmed by the Indiana Court of Appeals in 1993) for having raped the 18 year old Desiree Washington, although he invoked the victim's consent in his defence, see Hereto Rosanna Cavallaro, "A Big Mistake: Eroding the Defence of Mistake of Fact About Consent in Rape", in *The Journal of Criminal Law and Criminology*, 1996, vol. 86, no. 3, pp. 815 *et seq*. (on the Tyson case in fn. 90). The US UCMJ, see *supra* note 55, explicitly contains a provision on "mistakes of fact as to consent" in Art. 120(t)(15):

> (15) **Mistake of fact as to consent.** The term "mistake of fact as to consent" means the accused held, as a result of ignorance or mistake, an incorrect belief that the other person engaging in the sexual conduct consented. The ignorance or mistake must have existed in the mind of the accused and must have been reasonable under all the circumstances. To be reasonable the ignorance or mistake must have been based on information, or lack of it, which would indicate to a reasonable person that the other person consented. Additionally, the ignorance or mistake cannot be based on the negligent failure to discover the true facts. Negligence is the absence of due care. Due care is what a reasonably careful person would do under the same or similar circumstances. The accused's state of intoxication, if any, at the time of the offense is not relevant to mistake of fact. A mistaken belief that the other person consented must be that

cused. A mistake of law defence referring to the scope of the defence of consent or, more radically, to an alleged right to sexual assault in armed conflict would border on the absurd and, in any case, be irrelevant since it would not negate the mental element (Article 32(2) of the ICC Statute).[63]

The requirement of coercion was quite broadly defined by the ICC Pre-Trial Chamber III in the *Bemba* Confirmation Decision, which held:[64]

> With regard to the term 'coercion', the Chamber notes that it does not require physical force. Rather, threats, intimidation, extortion and other forms of duress which prey on fear or desperation may constitute coercion, and coercion may be inherent in certain circumstances, such as armed conflict or military presence.

Apart from this decision, the Court confirmed the charge of rape in the *Katanga* case.[65] In addition, several warrants of arrest[66] and summons

---

which a reasonably careful, ordinary, prudent, sober adult would have had under the circumstances at the time of the offense.

63 Assuming that a possible consent does not exclude the objective elements of the offence (the so called "actus reus" or *Tatbestand*), but operates as a ground excluding responsibility (more precisely as a cause of justification). On the delicate provision on mistake in Art. 32 ICC Statute, see Ambos, 2011, § 7 mn. 97 *et seq*., see *supra* note 18.

64 ICC, *Prosecutor v. Jean-Pierre Bemba Gombo*, Decision Pursuant to Article 61(7)(a) and (b) on the Charges against Jean-Pierre Bemba Gombo, ICC-01/05–01/08, 15 June 2009, ("*Bemba* Confirmation Decision"), p. 57, para. 162; for a similar interpretation, see *Akayesu* Trial Judgment, see *supra* note 52, para. 688.

65 ICC, *Prosecutor v. Katanga et al.*, Decision on the Confirmation of the Charges, ICC-01/04-01/07, 30 September 2008, ("*Katanga* Confirmation of Charges"), paras. 442–444.

66 See, *e.g.*, ICC, *Prosecutor v. Kony et al.*, Warrant of Arrest for Joseph Kony issued on 8 July 2005 as amended on 27 September 2005, Public redacted version, ICC-02/04-01/05-53 ("*Kony* Warrant of Arrest"), Count 2,3 on pp. 12–13; ICC, *Prosecutor v. Kony et al.*, Warrant of Arrest for Vincent Otti, Public redacted version, ICC-02/04-01/05-54, 8 July 2005, ("*Otti* Warrant of Arrest"), Count 3 on p. 13; ICC, *Prosecutor v. Harun and Kushayb*, Warrant of Arrest for Ali Kushayb, ICC-02/05-01/07-3, 27 April 2007 ("*Kushayb* Warrant of Arrest"), Count 13, 14, 42, 43 on pp. 8–9 and 14–15; ICC, *Prosecutor v. Harun and Kushayb*, Warrant of Arrest for Ahmad Harun, ICC-02/05-01/07-2, 27 April 2007 ("*Harun* Warrant of Arrest"), Count 13, 14, 42, 43 on pp. 8–9 and 13–14; ICC, *Prosecutor v. Al Bashir*, Warrant of Arrest for Omar Hassan Ahmad Al Bashir, ICC-02/05-01/09-1, 4 March 2009 ("*Bashir* First Warrant of Arrest"), p. 6 (considering thousands of rapes) and para. vii on p. 8 (charge of rape as crime against humanity in indirect perpetration).

to appear[67] include charges of rape, and allegations of rape are also under investigation in the situation in Libya.[68]

4.2.2. Sexual Slavery

Sexual Slavery is a specific form of enslavement within the meaning of Article 7(1)(c) of the ICC Statute.[69] It may be committed by one or more persons as a part of a common criminal purpose.[70] It is defined in the Elements of Crimes as follows:[71]

---

67 The ICC summons to appear in the case regarding the Kenyan 'post election violence' for the suspects Muthaura, Kenyatta and Ali include the allegation, that "Muthaura and Kenyatta are criminally responsible as indirect co-perpetrators in accordance with article 25(3)(a) of the Rome Statute for the crimes against humanity of murder, forcible transfer, rape, persecution and other inhumane acts.", see ICC Press Release, "Pre-Trial Chamber II delivers six summonses to appear in the Situation in the Republic of Kenya", ICC-CPI-20110309-PR637, 9 March 2011, available at http://www.icc-cpi.int/menus/icc/press%20and%20media/press%20releases/news%20and%20highlights/pre_trial%20chamber%20ii%20delivers%20six%20summonses%20to%20appear%20in%20the%20situation%20in%20the%20republic%20of%20kenya?lan=en-GB, last accessed on 12 June 2011.

68 See ICC Prosecutor, "Statement to the United Nations Security Council on the situation in the Libyan Arab Jamahiriya, pursuant to UNSCR 1970 (2011)", 4 May 2011, para. 12, available at http://www.icc-cpi.int/menus/icc/structure%20of%20the%20court/office%20of%20the%20prosecutor/reports%20and%20statements/statement/statement%20to%20the%20united%20nations%20security%20council%20on%20the%20situation%20in%20the%20libyan%20arab%20jamahiriya_%20pur, last accessed on 12 June 2011.

69 Cottier, 2008, Art. 8 mn. 208 (p. 442), see *supra* note 4; Schabas, 2010, Art. 7 p. 172, see *supra* note 44; Werle, 2009, p. 325, see *supra* note 17; see also *Katanga* Confirmation of Charges, para. 430, see *supra* note 65; and SCSL, *Prosecutor v. Brima et al.*, Case No. SCSL-04-16-T, Judgement, 20 July 2007, ("*Brima et al.* Trial Judgment"), para. 706.

70 See fn. 17 of the Elements of Crimes, see *supra* note 18: "Given the complex nature of this crime, it is recognized that its commission could involve more than one perpetrator as a part of a common criminal purpose".

71 Elements of Crimes, see *supra* note 18, for Arts. 7(1)(g)-2, 8(2)(b)(xxii)-2, and 8(2)(e) (vi)-2 of the ICC Statute; the same definition was used in the *Sesay et al.* Trial Judgment, para. 158, see *supra* note 45; and in the *Brima et al.* Trial Judgment, para. 708, see *supra* note 69. Dyani, 2007, p. 237 in fn. 69, see *supra* note 1, sees this definition elaborating on the slavery definition as contained in the Slavery Convention from 1926 (Slavery Convention, 25 September 1926, U.N.T.S., vol. 60, p. 254, entry into force on 9 March 1927); Luping, 2009, p. 477, see *supra* note 1, sees parallels to the supplementary slavery convention (Supplementary Convention on the Abolition

> 1. The perpetrator exercised any or all of the powers attaching to the right of ownership over one or more persons, such as by purchasing, selling, lending or bartering such a person or persons, or by imposing on them a similar deprivation of liberty.
>
> 2. The perpetrator caused such person or persons to engage in one or more acts of a sexual nature.

Ownership ("chattel slavery") and *deprivation of one's autonomy* are the essential elements of the offence.[72] The powers of ownership as listed in paragraph 1 of this definition are non-exhaustive.[73] Deprivation of liberty may include extracting forced labour or otherwise reducing a person to servile status.[74] In cases of sexual slavery, the deprivation of the victim's autonomy is intensified by the sexual acts (paragraph 2 of the above definition), which need not necessarily amount to rape.[75] Given the deprivation of liberty element sexual slavery constitutes a continuing offence.[76]

Forms of sexual slavery can, for example, be practices such as the detention of women in 'rape camps'[77], 'comfort stations' (as set up by the Japanese army during World War II) or in a private house.[78] Sexual slavery may also encompass forced temporary 'marriages' to soldiers and

---

of Slavery, the Slave Trade, and Institutions and Practices Similar to Slavery, 7 September 1956, U.N.T.S., vol. 266, p. 3, entry into force on 30 April 1957).

72 See also Cottier, 2008, Art. 8 mn. 208, see *supra* note 4.

73 *Brima et al.* Trial Judgment, para. 709, see *supra* note 69.

74 *Ibid.* See also fn. 18 of the Elements of Crimes, *supra* note 18:

> It is understood that such deprivation of liberty may, in some circumstances, include exacting forced labour or otherwise reducing a person to a servile status as defined in the Supplementary Convention on the Abolition of Slavery, the Slave Trade, and Institutions and Practices Similar to Slavery of 1956. It is also understood that the conduct described in this element includes trafficking in persons, in particular women and children.

75 Luping, 2009, p. 477, see *supra* note 1.

76 Boot and Hall, Art. 7 mn. 49, see *supra* note 4.

77 ICTY, *Prosecutor v. Gagović (Foča),* Case No. IT-96-23-1, Indictment, 26 June 1996, paras. 1.5 and 4.8.

78 As prosecuted in ICTY, *Prosecutor v. Kunarac et al.*, Case No. IT-96-23-T, Judgment, 22 February 2001, ("*Kunarac et al.* Trial Judgment", also known as "Foča"), para. 744. It should be noted, that the ICTY Statute does not contain a special provision on sexual slavery. Therefore, the conviction was based here on crimes against humanity in the form of rape and enslavement (Art. 5(c) and (g) ICTY Statute).

other practices involving the treatment of women as chattel thereby violating the peremptory norm prohibiting slavery.[79] In this respect, especially (temporary) forced marriages were discussed. The SCSL was the first ICL institution that addressed sexual slavery and forced marriages.[80] Thus, in the '*AFRC* case' (*Brima* et al.), the Trial Chamber considered forced marriages as covered by the crime of sexual slavery;[81] yet, it was overruled by the Appeals Chamber which considered forced marriages as a distinct crime against humanity in form of an 'other inhuman act' (Article 2(i) of the SCSL-Statute).[82] The Chamber held:

> While forced marriage shares certain elements with sexual slavery such as non-consensual sex and deprivation of liberty, there are also distinguishing factors. First, forced marriage involves a perpetrator compelling a person by force or threat of force, through the words or conduct of the perpetrator or those associated with him, into a forced conjugal association with a another person resulting in great suffering, or serious physical or mental injury on the part of the victim. Second, unlike sexual slavery, forced marriage implies a relationship of exclusivity between the 'husband' and 'wife', which could lead to disciplinary consequences [sic!] for

79 *Katanga* Confirmation of Charges, para. 431, see *supra* note 65.

80 See Oosterveld, 2011, pp. 61 *et seq*., see *supra* note 44; and Sara Wharton, "The Evolution of International Criminal Law: Prosecuting 'New' Crimes before the Special Court for Sierra Leone", in *International Criminal Law Review* 2011, vol. 11, pp. 217 *et seq.* (esp. pp. 230 *et seq.* on the possibility of residual crimes constituting 'new' crimes, in relation to the principle of *nulla poena sine lege*).

81 *Brima et al.* Trial Judgment, paras. 703–713, see *supra* note 69; see also Wharton, 2011, pp. 227 *et seq.*, see *supra* note 80.

82 SCSL, *Prosecutor v. Brima et al.*, Case No. SCSL-04-16-A, Judgment, 22 February 2008 ("*Brima et al.* Appeals Judgment"), paras. 181–203, esp. 195 and 202. This view was welcomed in the literature, see, *e.g.*, Neha Jain, "Forced Marriage as a Crime against Humanity: Problems of Definition and Prosecution", in *JICJ*, 2008, vol. 6, no. 5, pp. 1013, 1022 ("long overdue"); see, similarly, Teresa Doherty, "Developments in the Prosecution of Gender-Based Crimes – The Special Court for Sierra Leone Experience", in *Journal of Gender, Social Policy and the Law*, 2009, vol. 17, no. 2, pp. 331 *et seq.*; see also Cole, 2010, p. 57, see *supra* note 5; Wharton, 2011, pp. 228 *et seq.*, see *supra* note 80; and Michael P. Scharf and Suzanne Mattler, "Forced Marriage: Exploring the Viability of the Special Court for Sierra Leone's New Crime Against Humanity", Case Research Paper Series in Legal Studies Working Paper 05-35, October 2005, p. 6, available at http://papers.ssrn.com/sol3/papers.cfm?abstract_id=824291, last accessed on 12 June 2011.

> breach of this exclusive arrangement. These distinctions imply that *forced marriage is not predominantly a sexual crime*.[83]

The issue of forced marriages was also addressed by the SCSL Trial Chamber in the 'RUF' case. It held that the RUF has been using 'bush wives' – which were forced into marriage by means of threat and duress – deliberately and strategically to enslave and psychologically manipulate civilian women and girls.[84] The accused were convicted, cumulatively, for sexual slavery as well as for forced marriages (as an crime against humanity of 'other inhumane acts').[85]

In contrast, in the view of ICC Pre-Trial Chamber I, sexual slavery also encompasses forced "marriage" situations, domestic servitude or other forced labour involving compulsory sexual activity, including rape.[86]

As to the *mens rea*, the SCSL required that the perpetrator intended to engage in the act of sexual slavery or in the reasonable knowledge that it was likely to occur.[87]

The charge of sexual slavery has been confirmed by the ICC, without further substantial considerations, in the Katanga-case[88] and included in two warrants of arrest against members of the LRA in the Ugandan case[89].

4.2.3. Enforced Prostitution

Enforced Prostitution is defined in the Elements of Crimes as follows:[90]

> 1. The perpetrator caused one or more persons to engage in one or more acts of a sexual nature by force, or by threat of

83 *Brima et al.* Appeals Judgment, para. 195, see *supra* note 82 (emphasis added).

84 *Sesay et al.* Trial Judgment, paras. 1465–1473, see *supra* note 45; see Oosterveld, 2011, pp. 52 *et seq.*, esp. 66, see *supra* note 44.

85 *Sesay et al.* Trial Judgment, para. 2307, see *supra* note 45.

86 *Katanga* Confirmation of Charges, para. 431, see *supra* note 65. See also Cottier, 2008, Art. 8 mn. 208, see *supra* note 4.

87 *Brima et al.* Trial Judgment, para. 708, see *supra* note 69.

88 *Katanga* Confirmation of Charges, para. 436, see *supra* note 65.

89 *Kony* Warrant of Arrest, Count 1 on p. 12; *Otti* Warrant of Arrest, Count 1 on p. 12, see *supra* note 66.

90 Elements of Crimes, *supra* note 18, for Art. 7 (1)(g)-3, Art. 8 (2)(b)(xxii)-3, Art. 8 (2)(e)(vi)-3 of the ICC Statute.

> force or coercion, such as that caused by fear of violence, duress, detention, psychological oppression or abuse of power, against such person or persons or another person, or by taking advantage of a coercive environment or such person's or persons' incapacity to give genuine consent.
>
> 2. The perpetrator or another person obtained or expected to obtain pecuniary or other advantage in exchange for or in connection with the acts of a sexual nature.

The first non-contextual element constitutes a quite broad definition of causing one or more persons to engage in sexual acts by any form of coercion, including a "coercive environment". According to the second non-contextual element the perpetrator's expectation as to a financial or other advantage, not the victim's perspective is of relevance.[91] It is thus clear that the sexual conduct is not initiated by the person engaging in the sexual acts, as may be the case with "national" prostitution, but by the perpetrator.[92] Similarly, it is possible to delimitate the offence from "sexual enslavement" countering a criticism that it diminishes this latter offence if such conduct is characterized "only" as enforced prostitution.[93] In fact, enforced prostitution captures "those situations that lack slavery-like conditions"[94] and thus has a residual function. Enforced prostitution contains an element of continuity since the victim may be under "force" for a certain period of time; in this sense it can be a continuing offence. On the other hand it may also constitute a separate offence of result if it only consists of one act of a sexual nature.[95]

---

91 See for a similar national provision § 181a German StGB, see *supra* note 16. On the delimitation between enforced prostitution and national elements of the crime of prostitution, see Boot and Hall, 2008, Art. 7 mn. 49, see *supra* note 4:

> The second non-contextual element makes clear that this crime is entirely different in nature from the ordinary crime of prostitution under national law, because it includes expectation by the perpetrator who coerced the victim to engage in one or more acts of a sexual nature, not an expectation of advantage by the person engaging in those acts.

92 See for an insofar incorrect criticism Boot and Hall, 2008, Art. 7 mn. 48, see *supra* note 4; see also Cottier, 2008, Art. 8 mn. 209, see *supra* note 4.

93 *Ibid.* For the relationship see also Cottier, 2008, Art. 8 mn. 203 in fine, see *supra* note 4.

94 Bedont and Hall-Martinez, 1999, p. 73, see *supra* note 35; see also Boot and Hall, 2008, Art. 7 mn. 49, see *supra* note 4.

95 *Ibid.*, Art. 7 mn. 50; Cottier, 2008, Art. 8 mn. 209, see *supra* note 4.

4.2.4. Forced Pregnancy

Forced Pregnancy is the only conduct defined explicitly in the ICC Statute, Article 7(2)(f):

> 'Forced Pregnancy' means the unlawful confinement of a woman forcibly made pregnant, with the intent of affecting the ethnic composition of any population or carrying out other grave violations of international law.

The definition in the Elements[96] reads in the relevant part:

> 1. The perpetrator confined one or more women forcibly made pregnant, with the intent of affecting the ethnic composition of any population or carrying out other grave violations of international law.

The offence encompasses both *(en)forced impregnation* (pregnancy as a result of rape or of a illegal medical procedure) and *(en)forced maternity* (being forced to carry the pregnancy).[97] It has no historical precedents.[98] Unlawful confinement is any form of deprivation of physical liberty contrary to international law and standards.[99] The force used in bringing about pregnancy ("forcibly made pregnant") "does not necessarily require the use of violence, but includes any form of coercion".[100] The female victim may have been "made pregnant" before the actual confinement since the crime only requires the "unlawful confinement of a woman [...] made pregnant", that is, earlier by another person or during confinement.[101]

The perpetrator has to act with the "intent of affecting the ethnic composition of any population or carrying out other grave violations of

96 Elements of Crimes, *supra* note 18, for Art. 7 (1)(g)-4, Art. 8 (2)(b)(xxii)-4, Art. 8 (2)(e)(vi)-4 of the ICC Statute.

97 There are no precedents for forced pregnancy in ICL. On the development of the provision, see de Brouwer, 2005, pp. 143 *et seq.*, see *supra* note 14. See also Cottier, 2008, Art. 8 mn. 210, see *supra* note 4.

98 For the provision's development, see de Brouwer, 2005, pp. 143 *et seq.*, see *supra* note 14; see also Cottier, 2008, Art. 8 Rn. 210, see *supra* note 4.

99 Boot and Hall, 2008, Art. 7 mn. 111, see *supra* note 4.

100 *Ibid.*, Art. 7 mn. 112, see *supra* note 4, stating that the act of forcibly making a woman pregnant might be covered by the crime of rape or 'any other form of sexual violence of comparable gravity'.

101 Werle, 2009, p. 326, see *supra* note 17.

international law". This has been interpreted as a "specific"[102] or "special intent".[103] This is not entirely convincing since the term "intent" is, at best, ambiguous and may also be understood in a cognitive sense.[104] Thus, if the drafter wanted to require a special intent, why did they not explicitly say so? In any case, the "speciality" of the intent required consists in the conduct's orientation towards the ethnic composition of the population affected. In other words, what is "special" about the intent is that it goes beyond the normal intent regarding the "ordinary" *actus reus* (*in casu* the unlawful confinement) requiring an ulterior intent (a surplus of intent) with a view to the change in the ethnic composition of the attacked population.[105] The (other) violations of international law referred to include genocide, crime against humanity, war crimes, torture and enforced disappearances.[106]

The ICC Statute's clarification in Article 7(2)(f), that the definition "shall not in any way be interpreted as affecting national laws relating to pregnancy" ensures that national policies against abortion may not be promoted under the guise of policies against forced pregnancy.[107]

4.2.5. Enforced Sterilization

Enforced sterilization is defined in the Elements of Crimes as follows:

> 1. The perpetrator deprived one or more persons of biological reproductive capacity.
>
> 2. The conduct was neither justified by the medical or hospital treatment of the person or persons concerned nor carried out with their genuine consent.

According to a footnote in the Elements the "deprivation is not intended to include birth-control measures which have a non-permanent

102 Boot and Hall, 2008, Art. 7 mn. 113, see *supra* note 4.

103 Cottier, 2008, Art. 8 mn. 210, see *supra* note 4.

104 See Kai Ambos, "What does "intent to destroy" in genocide mean?", 2009, in *ICRC-Review*, vol. 91, pp. 842–43.

105 Gabriel, 2004, p. 49, see *supra* note 35, note with regard underlying cultural conditions: "the rapist is a person of different ethnicity and belongs to a culture, society, or religion in which the ethnicity of the father is considered to determine the ethnicity of the child".

106 Boot and Hall, 2008, Art. 7 mn. 113, see *supra* note 4.

107 *Ibid.*, Art. 7 mn. 51, 114; on the position of the Holy See, see Cottier, 2008, Art. 8 mn. 210 (pp. 449–450), see *supra* note 4.

effect in practice".[108] It has been questioned, however, whether this footnote is consistent with international law since such measures may amount to genocide and, in any case, violates different fundamental rights related to one's personal autonomy.[109] Also, such measures always, even if applied temporarily, constitute a grave restriction of one's self-determination.[110] Classical examples of the crime are policies of "racial hygiene" and medical experiments on prisoners, both practices known from the Nazi regime.[111] "Enforced" implies that a (genuine and informed) consent excludes the crime (see also paragraph 2 of the Elements).[112]

4.2.6. Other Forms of Sexual Violence

Articles 7(1)(g), 8(2)(b)(xxii) and (e)(iv) confirm that the list of forms of sexual conduct is not exhaustive by criminalizing "any other form of sexual violence of comparable gravity" or "any other form of sexual violence also constituting a grave breach of the Geneva Conventions" or "a serious violation of Article 3 common to the four Geneva Conventions". This residual conduct is defined identically in the Elements on the Crimes against humanity and War crimes as follows:

> 1. The perpetrator committed an act of *a sexual nature* against one or more persons or caused such person or persons to engage in an act of a sexual nature by force, or by threat of force or coercion, such as that caused by fear of violence, duress, detention, psychological oppression or abuse of power, against such person or persons or another person, or by taking advantage of a coercive environment or such person's or persons' incapacity to give genuine consent.

As always in cases of residual or fall back liability defined by imprecise terms, the question of legal certainty arises. It can only be achieved by a restrictive interpretation guided by the other specific conduct that the residual category refers to. *In casu*, the "other form of sexual

108 Elements of Crimes, fn. 18, see *supra* note 18. See also Cottier, 2008, Art. 8 mn. 211, see *supra* note 4.

109 See Boot and Hall, 2008, Art. 7 mn. 52, see *supra* note 4.

110 *Ibid.*

111 Werle, 2009, p. 327, see *supra* note 17; Boot and Hall, 2008, Art. 7 mn. 52, see *supra* note 4.

112 For a discussion see Cottier, 2008, Art. 8 mn. 211, see *supra* note 4.

violence" must be of "comparable gravity" to the forms of conduct defined in Article 7(1)(g) and the grave breaches or the serious violations of common Article 3.[113] This is an objective test[114] introducing a *minimum threshold of (comparable) gravity* and thereby excluding lesser forms of sexual violence[115] (which may anyway be covered by the implicit criminalizations, see Section 4.3.). Against this background I have some doubts whether acts that do not even require physical contact – take the example from *Akayesu*[116] of physical exercises naked and in front of a crowd – can be considered "sexual violence of comparable gravity".[117] After all, they can be punished as outrages upon personal dignity.

According to the Elements, the sexual act could be directly committed by the perpetrator or the victim caused to engage in such an act. The victim may be caused to do that by different forms of force or coercion, including "taking advantage of a coercive environment" or the victim's "incapacity to give genuine consent". The former formulation shows, as already said above, that a broad concept of coercion is used, similar to the one of the ICTR in the *Akayesu* case.[118]

4.3. Other Implicit Criminalization of Sexual Violence

4.3.1. Outrages upon Personal Dignity and Torture

Rape has been considered by both ICTR and ICTY as torture and a violation of personal dignity. Thus, the *Akayesu* Trial Chamber[119] held:

> […] Like torture, rape is used for such purposes as intimidation, degradation, humiliation, discrimination, punishment, control or destruction of a person. Like torture, rape is a vio-

[113] See respective Element 2 to Art. 7 (1)(g) and to Art. 8 (2) (b) (xxii)-1 and (e) (vi)-1.

[114] Boot and Hall, 2008, Art. 7 mn. 53 *in fine*, see *supra* note 4.

[115] See, for a good account of the drafting history Cottier, 2008, Art. 8 mn. 212 (p. 452 *et seq.*), see *supra* note 4; for a restrictive interpretation, see also Zimmermann, 2008, Art. 8 mn. 316, see *supra* note 4.

[116] *Akayesu* Trial Judgment, para. 688, see *supra* note 52.

[117] In favour, see Boot and Hall, 2008, Art. 7 mn. 53, see *supra* note 4; contrary, apparently, see de Brouwer, 2005 pp. 159 *et seq.*, see *supra* note 14.

[118] *Akayesu* Trial Judgment, para. 598, see *supra* note 52; Boot and Hall, 2008, Art. 7 mn. 53, see *supra* note 4.

[119] *Akayesu* Trial Judgment, para. 597, see *supra* note 52; see, similarly, *Furundžija* Trial Judgment, para. 595, see *supra* note 51.

> lation of personal dignity, and rape in fact constitutes torture when it is inflicted by or at the instigation of or with the consent or acquiescence of a public official or other person acting in an official capacity.[120]

In same vein, the *Semanza* Trial Chamber, stated

> Noting, in particular the extreme level of fear occasioned by the circumstances surrounding the event and the nature of the rape of Victim A, the Chamber finds that the perpetrator inflicted severe mental suffering sufficient to form the material element of torture […].[121]

Laurent Semanza, the *bourgemestre* of Bicumbi commune in Kigali-Rural prefecture, was finally convicted, *inter alia*, for having instigated a crowd to rape Tutsi women and, concurrently, for his personal participation in torturing and killing one victim.[122]

Similar approaches can be observed at the ICTY. Thus, for example, in the *Čelebići* case, rape and other forms of sexual violence were considered to possibly constitute torture.[123] The *Furundžija* Trial Chamber held that rape can amount to torture and can be related to a violation of human dignity and physical integrity of women.[124] In the *Foča* case, acts of forced nudity, inter alia, were qualified as outrages upon personal dignity.[125] The SCSL also punished sexual offences as offences against dignity.[126]

Yet, the issue of the relationship between these crimes and sexual crimes only became the object of a more sophisticated analysis in the *Bemba* case before the ICC. Pre-Trial Chamber II noted in the respective confirmation decision:

> that also in the context of outrages upon personal dignity the Prosecutor presented the same conduct, related mainly to

---

120 *Akayesu* Trial Judgment, para. 687, see *supra* note 52.

121 ICTR, *Prosecutor v. Semanza*, Case No. ICTR-97-20-T, Judgment and Sentence, 15 May 2003, para. 482.

122 *Ibid*., para. 586.

123 ICTY, *Prosecutor v. Delalić et al.*, Case No. IT-96-21, Judgment, 16 November 1998, paras. 495–496 (also known as "Čelebići"). On the relevant findings of the *Čelebići* case, see Askin, 2010, pp. 96 *et seq.*, see *supra* note 4.

124 *Furundžija* Trial Judgment, para. 595, see *supra* note 51.

125 *Kunarac* Trial Judgment, paras. 773–774, see *supra* note 78.

126 See, *e.g.*, *Brima et al.* Trial Judgement, para 705, see *supra* note 69.

> acts of rape, under different legal characterisations, namely articles 8(2)(c)(ii) and 8(2)(e)(vi) of the Statute. In the opinion of the Chamber, most of the facts presented by the Prosecutor at the Hearing reflect in essence the constitutive elements of force or coercion in the crime of rape, characterising this conduct, in the first place, as an act of rape. In the opinion of the Chamber, the essence of the violation of the law underlying these facts is fully encompassed in the count of rape.[127]

and therefore,

> in this particular case the count of outrage upon personal dignity is fully subsumed by the count of rape, which is the most appropriate legal characterisation of the conduct presented.[128]

The Chamber referred also to torture when it considered,

> that in this particular case, the specific material elements of the act of torture, namely severe pain and suffering and control by the perpetrator over the person, are also the inherent specific material elements of the act of rape.[129]

It concluded that torture (as a crime against humanity) and outrages against personal dignity (as a war crime) are "fully subsumed" by rape (as a crime against humanity),[130] since this act requires, compared to torture, only one additional element, namely the act of penetration,[131] and, compared to outrages, "reflect in essence the constitutive elements of force or coercion".[132] While this is, in principle, correct,[133] the Chamber's considerations can only be fully understood if one refers to the theory of *con-*

[127] *Bemba* confirmation decision, para. 310, see *supra* note 64.

[128] *Ibid.*, para. 312.

[129] *Ibid.*, para. 204 (fn. omitted).

[130] *Ibid.*, paras. 205, 312.

[131] *Ibid.*, para. 204.

[132] *Ibid.*, para. 310.

[133] For a different view (albeit without detailed reasoning), see Prosecution's leave to appeal, see *supra* note 64, paras. 16, 17; and ICC, *Prosecutor v. Bemba Gombo*, Public Redacted Version of the Amended Document containing the charges filed on 30 March 2009, ICC-01/05-01/08-395-Anx3, 30 March 2009, Count 3 on p. 35 (as to rape and torture).

cours, which is the other side of the coin of cumulative charging.[134] In any case, while rape may be "the most appropriate legal characterization"[135] in cases of torture with an (additional) act of penetration the Prosecutor must charge torture for those acts where the element of penetration is lacking.[136] In any case, notwithstanding the correct rules of *concours*, this discussion confirms that rape encompasses torture and, indeed, frequently constitutes torture.[137]

4.3.2. Genocide

Sexual violence can be part of three forms of genocidal conduct (Article 6 of the ICC Statute):[138]

> (b) Causing serious bodily or mental harm to members of the group;
>
> (c) Deliberately inflicting on the group conditions of life calculated to bring about its physical destruction in whole or in part;
>
> (d) imposing measures intended to prevent births within the group;

Serious bodily harm means non-fatal physical violence causing disfigurement, and serious injuries to external or internal organs or senses,[139]

---

[134] See Kai Ambos, "Critical Issues in the Bemba Confirmation Decision", in *LJIL*, 2009, vol. 22, p. 723 with further references.

[135] *Bemba* confirmation decision, para. 204, see *supra* note 64. In case of a penetration still calling for an additional charge of torture: AI Report Rape, pp. 38 *et seq.*, see *supra* note 53.

[136] See *in casu Bemba* confirmation decision, paras. 206 *et seq.*, see *supra* note 64.

[137] See also Boot and Hall, 2008, Art. 7 mn. 44, see *supra* note 4: "criminal acts aimed at the physical and mental integrity of a person […], more often than not, constitute torture."; see also mn. 55 for case law references.

[138] In the existing jurisprudence, only the ICTR has linked sexual violence to the genocide offence (see references in subsequent footnotes, esp. 139, 140, 141, 145). For a detailed assessment of rape as genocide, with a focus on Bosnia and Herzegovina and from a feministic perspective, see Engle, 2005, pp. 792 *et seq.*, *supra* note 53. See also Schomburg and Peterson, 2007, pp. 128–129, see *supra* note 15. On the ICTR's approaches to label acts of rape as genocide, see Ayat, 2010, pp. 809 *et seq.*, see *supra* note 41. On implicit criminalization as genocide (art. 6(b), (d)), see also Sabine Gless, *Internationales Strafrecht*, Helbing Lichtenhahn, Basel, 2011, mn. 813, 815–816.

[139] ICTR, *Prosecutor v. Seromba*, Case No. 2001-66-I, Judgment, 12 March 2008, para. 46; Werle, 2009, pp. 265 *et seq.*, see *supra* note 17, with additional references from

not necessarily in an irremediable manner[140]. This may include sexual violence, which causes serious bodily and mental injury.[141] Causing serious *mental harm* does not require a physical attack or any physical effects of mental harm.[142] The destructive psychological effects of crimes of sexual violence are thus granted the same importance as the physical consequences of the acts.[143] Similarly, serious mental harm can be construed as some type of impairment of mental abilities, or harm that causes serious injury to the mental state of the victim.

Sexual violence may also amount to the bringing about "*destructive conditions of life*" (Article 6(c)). This provision prohibits death measures, which are conducted not to immediately kill, but ultimately to bring about the physical destruction of group members.[144] Thus, for example, mass rapes are not 'conditions of life' as such, but they may amount to such conditions if inflicted systematically and repeatedly, perhaps in connection with other measures.[145]

Measures intended to prevent births (Article 6(d)) include measures targeting the biological existence of the group.[146] They may be carried out

---

the international case law; see also Schomburg and Peterson, 2007, p. 129, see *supra* note 15.

140 ICTR, *Prosecutor v. Gacumbitsi*, Case No. 2001-64-T, Judgment, 17 June 2004 ("*Gacumbitsi* Trial Judgment"), para. 291.

141 This was held by ICTR Trial Chamber I in *Akayesu* Trial Judgment, paras. 706, 731, see *supra* note 52, which was the first judgment considering sexual violence as part of the Rwandan genocide. See, similarly, ICTR, *Prosecutor v. Kayishema and Ruzindana*, Case No. ICTR-95-1-T, Judgment, 21 May 1999 ("*Kayishema and Ruzindana* Trial Judgment"), para. 108, where Trial Chamber II held in the context of genocide, that "acts of sexual violence, rape, mutilations and interrogations combined with beatings, and/or threats of death, were all acts that amount to serious bodily harm". See also *Gacumbitsi* Trial Judgment, paras. 291–293, see *supra* note 140; and Werle, 2009, pp. 265 *et seq.*, see *supra* note 17, with additional references.

142 Werle, 2009, p. 266, see *supra* note 17.

143 *Akayesu* Trial Judgment, para. 731, see *supra* note 52; Werle, 2009, p. 266, see *supra* note 17.

144 *Akayesu* Trial Judgment, para. 505, see *supra* note 52; Werle, 2009, p. 267 with additional references, see *supra* note 17.

145 *Kayishema and Ruzindana* Trial Judgment, para. 116, see *supra* note 141; Werle, 2009, p. 268, see *supra* note 17.

146 Luping, 2009, p. 455, see *supra* note 1, considers this as a crime that explicitly punishes sexual violence.

in a physical or psychological (mental) manner,[147] for example through enforced sterilization within the meaning of Article 7(1)(g),[148] and/or forced birth control.[149] Rape may fall under this definition, for example if in the aftermath the victim desists from reproduction due to the trauma suffered.[150] Rape was moreover found to exist if committed with the purpose of changing the ethnic composition of a group, as, for example, in patriarchal societies, where children are regarded to belong to the father's ethnic group.[151]

4.3.3. Crime Against Humanity of Persecution

Qualifying widespread and systematic sexual offences as persecution within the meaning of Article 7(1)(h) of the ICC Statute would require that the victims were persecuted as an "identifiable group" on one of the grounds mentioned, and that the persecution took place "in connection" with other acts contained in Articles 5–8 of the ICC Statute. While the grounds requirement is relatively easy to prove, in particular because of the residual reference to "universally recognized" grounds (which includes gender grounds),[152] it is more difficult to argue that the normally female victims of sexual offences are a sufficiently "identifiable" group –

---

147 *Akayesu* Trial Judgment, para. 508, see *supra* note 52:

> measures intended to prevent births within the group may be physical, but can also be mental. For instance, rape can be a measure intended to prevent births when the person raped refuses subsequently to procreate, in the same way that members of a group can be led, through threats or trauma, not to procreate.

148 Boot and Hall, 2008, Art. 7 mn. 52, see *supra* note 4.

149 *Akayesu* Trial Judgment, para. 507, see *supra* note 52:

> measures intended to prevent births within the group, should be construed as sexual mutilation, the practice of sterilization, forced birth control, separation of the sexes and prohibition of marriages.

150 *Akayesu* Trial Judgment, para. 508, see *supra* note 52; see also Werle, 2009, p. 268, see *supra* note 17.

151 *Akayesu* Trial Judgment, para. 507, see *supra* note 52; see also Werle, 2009, p. 268, see *supra* note 17. Similarly, considering a policy of systematic impregnation as genocide by systematic rape, see Engle, 2005, pp. 792 *et seq.*, see *supra* note 53.

152 See Boot and Hall, 2008, Art. 7 mn. 69, see *supra* note 4, referring to the special meaning of "gender grounds" in the ICC Statute (Art. 7(3)) and considering the universally recognized grounds as fulfilled. Such a recourse does not seem to be necessary, however, because Art. 7(1)(h) expressly includes "gender" and this term is, pursuant to Art. 7(3), to be understood as gender-neutral.

notwithstanding an objective or subjective perspective[153] – given that the gender criterion is, arguably, less precise than the other grounds. Moreover, persecutions committed in a macro-criminal overall event are mostly not "only" targeted against the victims of sexual offences, but rather part of a persecution of a group identifiable by other attributes and are committed in a context with other crimes (killings, plundering, and so on).[154]

Two ICC warrants of arrest include charges of persecution as a crime against humanity based on alleged sexual violence.[155]

153 *Ibid.*, Art. 7 mn. 60.

154 Thus, in *Kvočka et al.* Trial Judgment, see *supra* note 52, the ICTY found a crime against humanity of persecution whereby the persecuted group has been identified as "non-serbs" (para. 196), persecuted for ethnic reasons (paras. 195–197). The acts of persecution, committed in the notorious prison camp Omarska, consisted of killings, torture, rapes, beatings and other forms of physical and mental violence (para. 197). Similarly, see also Boot and Hall, 2008, Art. 7 mn. 72 (mentioning rape), see *supra* note 4.

155 *Kushayb* Warrant of Arrest, Count 10 at p. 8 and Count 39 at p. 14, see *supra* note 66; *Harun* Warrant of Arrest, Count 10 at p. 8 and Count 39 at p. 13, see *supra* note 66. Both charges relate to persecutions of members of the Sudanese regional population group "Fur" which were allegedly committed in the towns of Bisindi (Count 10) and Arawala (Count 39), each time through several conducts (killings, rapes, raids, *etc.*).

5

Complicity in Rape in the Jurisprudence of the *ad hoc* Tribunals and the Special Court for Sierra Leone

Marina Aksenova*

5.1. Introduction

The concept of complicity in international criminal law raises many questions. What is the exact scope of the concept? Is it sufficient to describe an accomplice as someone "who associates himself in an offence committed by [an]other",[1] or is there more to this term? Does participation in a crime pursuant to a common design qualify as complicity? What are the consequences of distinguishing between a primary perpetrator and an accomplice in international criminal law? What is the connection between complicity as a form of responsibility and the substantive crimes? This contribution aims at answering these questions using the crime of rape as an anchor for the analysis.

The International Criminal Tribunal for the Former Yugoslavia ('ICTY'), the International Criminal Tribunal for Rwanda ('ICTR'), and the Special Court for Sierra Leone ('SCSL') have treated the definition of crimes and the modes of liability for crimes as separate questions.[2] As will become clear from the case studies below,[3] the tribunals and the court chose to discuss the substantive crimes and the forms of individual criminal responsibility for these crimes in different parts of the judgments. Both substantive crimes and modes of liability, including various forms of

---

* **Marina Aksenova** is a PhD Researcher at the European University Institute. The author would like to thank Professor Morten Bergsmo for his comments on an earlier draft of this chapter, and, in particular, for highlighting the importance of distinguishing between the elements of crimes and the legal requirements of individual criminal responsibility.

1 ICTR, *Prosecutor v. Akayesu*, Case No. 96-4-T, Trial Chamber Judgment, 2 September 1998 ("*Akayesu* Trial Judgment"), para. 527.

2 Alexander Zahar and Goran Sluiter, *International Criminal Law: A Critical Introduction*, Oxford University Press, 2008, p. 220.

3 See Section 5.5.

complicity, consist of elements. In order to secure a conviction, the Prosecution has to prove both sets of elements. To further complicate matters, the Prosecution must also establish the existence of the so-called *chapeaux* elements or the "general" or "preliminary" conditions characteristic of the certain type of offence (for example, the existence of an armed conflict for war crimes).[4]

Ambos stresses the importance of developing a comprehensive theory of individual criminal responsibility in international criminal law: he argues that, despite the fact that the concept of individual criminal responsibility for violations of humanitarian and human rights norms is universally recognized, the elements of this responsibility are not sufficiently discussed in the literature.[5] Establishing a comprehensive theory of individual criminal responsibility entails the careful spelling out of its various forms (commission, aiding and abetting, and so on), a description of the legal requirements of each form of responsibility, and the establishment of links between the respective form of responsibility and the substantive offences to which this particular form attaches. The interaction between complicity as a mode of liability and rape as a substantive crime will be explored in this chapter.

A few preliminary issues are discussed in Section 5.2. Section 5.3. deals with the theoretical foundations of complicity. This part explains complicity from the perspective of municipal law. It clarifies the scope of the concept and seeks to dissolve the confusion in terminology created by the double sets of elements: one set of elements for complicity and one for substantive offences. The evolution of the concept of complicity in international criminal law is briefly discussed in Section 5.4. Section 5.5. is devoted to case law analysis with a special focus on complicity in rape in the jurisprudence of the ICTY, the ICTR, and the SCSL. Section 5.6. synthesizes theoretical foundations of complicity and its practical application to the crime of rape in international criminal law. Some conclusions are drawn in Section 5.7.

---

4 Guenael Mettraux, *International Criminal and Ad Hoc Tribunals*, Oxford University Press, 2005, p. 30.

5 Kai Ambos, "Individual Criminal Responsibility", in Gabrielle Kirk McDonald and Olivia Swaak-Goldman (ed.), *Substantive and Procedural Aspects of International Criminal Law*, Kluwer Law International, The Hague/Boston/London, 2000, p. 6.

5.2. Preliminary Observations

There are three preliminary issues that need to be addressed prior to starting the analysis of complicity. Firstly, the list of cases selected for this chapter is not exhaustive; it includes, however, some of the most important pronouncements on the crime of rape in international criminal law. It must be noted here that apart from rape, this chapter touches upon other offences, not necessarily of a sexual nature, committed in Rwanda, former Yugoslavia, and Sierra Leone. This has to do partially with the principle of cumulative charging, whereby different offences are charged based on the same events, and partially with the fact that sometimes rapes form a part of a systematic attack consisting of various atrocious acts, thus making it difficult to distil rape from other crimes committed in the course of the attack. Similarly, the chapter mentions other forms of responsibility, different from complicity, in order to better illuminate the concept and draw its borders.

Secondly, the sentencing considerations for each of the cases discussed in this chapter are spelled out in some detail. This is done because the sentence is a reflection of the gravity of the offence committed by the accused,[6] and in assessing the gravity the *ad hoc* tribunals and the SCSL take into account the particular circumstances of the case as well as *the nature and degree of the accused's participation* in the crimes.[7] Consequently, the sentences handed down for complicity in rape should in theory differ from the sentences received for the commission of rape. In practice, however, Cassese notes that international criminal law is rudimentary in nature when it comes to explaining the consequences attached to different classes of participation.[8]

Finally, the technicality with which complicity in rape is discussed in this chapter in no way diminishes the horrendous nature of crimes committed in the context of the warfare. It is hardly possible to make

6 Statute of the International Criminal Tribunal for the Former Yugoslavia, adopted on 25 May 1993, U.N. Doc. S/RES/827 ("ICTY Statute"), Article 24; Statute of the International Criminal Tribunal for Rwanda, adopted on 8 November 1994, U.N. Doc. S/RES/955 ("ICTR Statute"), Article 22; Statute of the Special Court for Sierra Leone, adopted on 14 August 2000, U.N. Doc. S/RES/1315 ("SCSL Statute"), Article 19.

7 ICTR, *Prosecutor v. Muhimana*, Case No. 95-1B-T, Trial Judgement, 28 April 2005, para. 591, emphasis added.

8 Antonio Cassese, *International Criminal Law*, 2nd ed., Oxford University Press, 2008, p. 188.

sense of the violence committed in war and the force driving a person to commit this violence, but this is exactly why it is important to study the correlation between the crime and the way in which the individual becomes involved in it.

5.3. Law of Complicity: Theoretical Foundations

5.3.1. Theories of Attribution

International criminal law is ultimately based on national criminal law – it represents a blend of different legal systems with some international flavour to it. Complicity as a form of criminal participation exists in countries with both common and civil law traditions.[9] The approach to complicity, however, differs to some extent from one country to another depending on the country's general view on the attribution of responsibility for criminal acts.

The different theories of attribution are discussed in some detail by Fletcher, who draws a conceptual distinction between wrongdoing and attribution in criminal law. He notes that the question of wrongdoing is dealt with under the set of primary legal norms prohibiting or requiring particular acts. The question of attribution, on the other hand, "is resolved under an entirely distinct set of norms, which are directed not to the class of potential violators, but to judges and jurors charged with the task of assessing whether individuals are liable for their wrongful acts".[10]

There exists a tension between the normative theory of attribution, which views the process of attribution as a judgment about whether the accused can be fairly held accountable for his wrongful act, and the descriptive theory, which implies that there is some single feature of all criminal conduct that serves to link the actor to the wrongful act thus justifying liability.[11] Fletcher notes that the countries with an Anglo-American tradition have sought to suppress the normative aspect of accountability and pack the problems of attribution into the concept of re-

9 See ICTR, *Prosecutor v. Akayesu*, Case No. 96-4-T, Trial Chamber Judgment, 2 September 1998, para. 527; Markus D. Dubber, "Criminalizing Complicity. A Comparative Analysis", in *Journal of International Criminal Justice*, 2007, vol. 5, no. 4, p. 977; George Fletcher, *Rethinking Criminal Law*, Little, Brown & co., Boston, 1978, pp. 634–682.

10 Fletcher, 1978, pp. 491–492, see *supra* note 9.

11 *Ibid.*, pp. 492–495.

sponsibility by focusing on the status and capacity of the actor, while the German tradition has favoured the normative approach to attribution.[12]

In line with this division, the countries adhering to a continental law tradition, like Germany or Russia, tend to adopt a nuanced approach to participation in crimes by distinguishing between, for example, different degrees of assistance. The common law tradition, on the other hand, draws just one fundamental distinction between perpetrators (called principals) and accomplices (all secondary parties).[13] Another consequence of the different approach to attribution is that, in countries with a common law tradition, the degree of participation is reflected in the sentencing stage rather than in the attribution stage as in many continental law systems.[14] Thus, in many continental law countries it is stipulated by law that accomplices get more lenient sentences than primary perpetrators, while in common law countries the reflection of the degree of participation of the accused is left to the discretion of the judges.[15]

5.3.2. The Causation Problem and the Nature of Complicity

The principle of individual autonomy underlies the concept of complicity as a form of responsibility. Ashworth clarifies that at the heart of the principle of autonomy lies the idea for respect of individuals as rational, choosing persons[16] who are "sovereigns of their own actions".[17] Consequently, the decision to support another in the commission of the crime and the realization of this decision in the form of assisting is culpable and deserves criminal sanction.[18] This is in line with the retributive or 'just deserts' philosophy implying that the punishment for crime must be pro-

12 *Ibid.*, 1978, pp. 496–497, see *supra* note 9.

13 For the description of different models of participation in crimes, see Elies van Sliedregt, *The Criminal Responsibility of Individuals for Violations of International Humanitarian Law*, TMC Asser Press, 2003, p. 61.

14 *Ibid.*

15 Andrew Ashworth, *Principles of Criminal Law*, Clarendon Law Series, second edition, Oxford University Press, 1995, p. 412.

16 *Ibid.*, p. 83.

17 Stanford H. Kadish, "Complicity, Cause and Blame: A Study in the Interpretation of Doctrine", in *California Law Review*, 1985, vol. 73, no. 2, p. 330.

18 Ashworth, 1995, p. 409, see *supra* note 15.

portionate to its relative seriousness, which is measured by the harm produced by the crime and the culpability of the offender.[19]

At first glance, it may seem illogical to infer the accomplice's culpability based on the actions of the principal when it is presumed that the principal's actions are fully voluntary, and the accomplice may not be said to have caused these actions.[20] Indeed, Fletcher points out that complicity is a field of attribution which falls outside the standard of causation.[21] Kadish explains this phenomenon by the derivative (or indirect) nature of accomplice liability. He submits that an accomplice is culpable not because he caused certain events (as would be the case with the primary perpetrator) and not because he caused the perpetrator to commit a crime, but because the accomplice is to be blamed for the conduct of another person. As Kadish puts it:

> […] whether I am to be blamed for the other person's action would not be assessed by asking whether I caused his action in the same sense that his lighting the match caused the fire. Rather, my responsibility would be determined by asking whether my persuasion or help made me accountable for the other person's actions and what they caused.[22]

It may seem that complicity casts its net too wide by not requiring that the act of accomplice caused the principal to act. Ashworth, however, points out that the loose conduct requirements of complicity are narrowed down by more stringent fault requirements: a small act of assistance may suffice, but only if it is done with intent to assist or encourage the commission of the principal's crime.[23]

There are other competing views on complicity emerging in the modern literature: Kutz argues that our current practices of accountability (the term he uses to refer to responsibility) are relational and positional rather than individualistic and retributivist. Accountability, he continues, shall be understood through the relationship between an agent (an indi-

---

19 Andrew von Hirsch, "Proportionate Sentences: A Desert Perspective" in Andrew von Hirsch, Andrew Ashworth and Julian Roberts (ed.), *Principled Sentencing*, 3rd ed., Hart Publishing, 2009, p. 115–123.

20 Kadish, 1985, p. 327, see *supra* note 17.

21 Fletcher, 1978, p. 492, see *supra* note 9.

22 Kadish, 1985, p. 332, see *supra* note 17. On the nature of derivative liability see also Fletcher, p. 583.

23 Ashworth, 1995, p. 409, see *supra* note 15.

vidual causing harm) and the respondent (the victim).[24] The individualistic approach to accountability fails to reflect the special nature of associative wrongdoing, in particular the culpability of the agent in the context of his relationship with the respondent. For Kutz, criminal responsibility of accomplices for their confederates' acts is defensible only if viewed in relation to the actions of the respondent, and if the individual differences in culpability are taken into account.[25]

5.3.3. Definitions

The general observations on complicity furnished in the previous two subsections provide some understanding about the nature of complicity, but they do not answer the vital question: what is the exact scope of complicity? This question calls for a separate extensive analysis. The only reasonable way to approach it in this chapter is to provide a list of terms associated with complicity and to define each of these terms, highlighting the peculiarities of common and civil law traditions along the way. Fletcher's categorization of crime participants is adopted here as a starting point of the analysis.[26]

A 'perpetrator' (a 'principal' in common law) is someone whose liability can be established independently of all other parties. The perpetrator's liability is direct and not derivative of someone else's conduct.[27]

a. A *primary perpetrator* (a 'principal in the first degree' in common law) is an actor who "commits the criminal act himself" (as defined by the German Penal Code).[28] In other words, he "directly" or "at first hand" commits the criminal act (as defined in the Russian Penal Code).[29] Smith and Hogan define the principal as someone whose act is the most immediate cause of the *actus reus*.[30]

---

24 Christopher Kutz, *Complicity: Ethics and Law for a Collective Age*, Cambridge University Press, 2000, pp. 17–19.

25 *Ibid.*, pp. 8 and 16.

26 Fletcher, 1978, pp. 637–649, see *supra* note 9.

27 Fletcher, 1978, p. 637, see *supra* note 9.

28 Strafgesetzbuch, adopted on 15 May 1871 ("StGB"), Article 25(1).

29 Ugolovnii Kodeks Rossiskoi Federacii (The Criminal Code of Russian Federation), adopted by the State Duma on 24 May 1996, adopted by the Federation Council on 5 June 1996 ("Ugol. Kod."), Article 33(2).

30 J.C. Smith and Brian Hogan, *Criminal Law*, 10th ed., Butterworths, 2002, p. 142.

b. A *co-perpetrator* (a 'principal in the second degree' in common law) is a person who commits the offence jointly with others.[31] The problematic aspect of co-perpetratorship is that sometimes the conduct of one or more co-perpetrators does not satisfy the objective elements of the substantive crime.[32] Ashworth explains that the English law allows holding two or more persons as co-principals (co-perpetrators) if each of them satisfies some part of the conduct element of a substantive crime, and if each of them has the required mental element.[33] This is when the joint enterprise concept comes into play.[34]

c. A *perpetrator-by-means* (a 'principal in the first degree' in common law) is a principal who commits the offence through another (as per the German definition),[35] or "the person who committed the offence by using other persons, not subject to criminal responsibility due to their age, insanity or other factors" (as per the Russian definition).[36] The American Model Penal Code offers another definition: perpetrator-by-means "causes an innocent or irresponsible person to engage in the proscribed conduct".[37]

'Accessories' (an 'accessory before the fact' in common law) are all those who are held derivatively liable for another's committing the offence. This category includes instigators as well as aiders-and-abettors.[38] Unlike civil law, the Anglo-American common law does not recognize a distinction between different types of accessories.[39] Ashworth clarifies that the accomplice in English law (sometimes called 'an accessory' or a secondary party) is anyone who aids, abets, counsels or procures a principal.[40] Accessories incur secondary liability.

---

[31] StGB, Article 25(2), see *supra* note 28; Ugol. Kod., Article 33(2), see *supra* note 29.

[32] Fletcher, 1978, p. 638, see *supra* note 9.

[33] Ashworth, 1995, p. 410, see *supra* note 15.

[34] Smith and Hogan, 2002, p. 162, see *supra* note 30.

[35] StGB, Article 25(1), see *supra* note 28.

[36] Ugol. Kod., Article 33(2), see *supra* note 29.

[37] The Model Penal Code (MPC), developed by the American Law Institute in 1962 ("MPC"), Article 2.06 (2)(a).

[38] Fletcher, 1978, p. 637, see *supra* note 9.

[39] *Ibid.*, 1978, p. 644.

[40] Ashworth, 1995, p. 410, see *supra* note 15. See also Accessories and Abettors Act 1861, as amended by s.65(4) Criminal Law Act 1977.

a. An *aider and abettor* in German law is "any person who intentionally assists another in the intentional commission of an unlawful act"[41] or "a person who assisted in the commission of the offence by supplying counsel, directions, information or the means for the commission" in Russian law.[42]
b. An *instigator* in Germany is "any person who intentionally induces another to intentionally commit an unlawful act" [43] and "a person who induced another to commit a crime through persuasion, bribery, threat or any other means" in Russia.[44]
c. An *organizer*: the Russian law recognizes this additional type of accessory as someone who "planned the commission of the offence or took charge in the commission of the offence". [45]

An 'accomplice', per Fletcher's definition, is any partner in crime – a co-perpetrator or an accessory. [46] Ashworth uses the term 'accomplice' more narrowly, as a synonym for an accessory, to contrast the accomplice with the principal.[47]

'Conspiracy' is a distinct offence, which is consummated upon entering into the agreement to commit the offence. Conspiracy also generates a standard for holding each conspirator complicitous in the crimes of fellow conspirators, but unlike complicity, which is a category of accessorial liability, conspiracy functions as a test of what it means to be a co-perpetrator.[48] In *Pinkerton v. United States*, the U.S. Supreme Court held that each member of a conspiracy can be liable for substantive offences carried out by co-conspirators in furtherance of the conspiracy, even when there is no evidence of their direct participation in, or knowledge of such offences, provided they were "reasonably foreseen as a necessary or natural consequence of the unlawful agreement".[49] In German law, "a person who declares his willingness or who accepts the offer of another or who agrees with another to commit or abet the commission of a felony shall be

41 StGB, Article 27(1), see *supra* note 28.
42 Ugol. Kod., Article 33(5), see *supra* note 29.
43 StGB, Article 26, see *supra* note 28.
44 Ugol. Kod., Article 33(4), see *supra* note 29.
45 *Ibid.*
46 Fletcher, 1978, p. 637, see *supra* note 9.
47 See the definition of 'accessory' above.
48 Fletcher, 1978, p. 646, see *supra* note 9.
49 *Pinkerton v. United States* (1946) 328 US 640.

liable under the same terms". Withdrawal from the plan or an earnest attempt to prevent the completion of the crime suffices to exempt such a participant from liability.[50] The Russian law is similar to German law in that it punishes only the agreement to commit a felony (and not minor offences). The commission of an offence with a prior agreement is also an aggravating factor at sentencing.[51]

'Joint enterprise' (or 'common design') seems to be recognized to some extent by both civil and common law countries. In German law, the joint enterprise could be roughly equated with the notion of 'co-perpetratorship' in some instances. A co-perpetrator is a person who commits an offence jointly with others on the basis of a common plan.[52] It is not necessary that all co-perpetrators be present at the actual commission of the crime, but what is important is that they act intentionally regarding the crime itself, the common plan, and the form of co-operation.[53] Similarly, under Russian law the co-perpetrators are not liable for the so-called 'excess of the perpetrator' when the principal commits crimes not intended by other members.[54] From the English law perspective, Ashworth notes that most complicity cases involve some kind of agreement, but historically it is unclear whether common purpose, or joint enterprise, amounts to an additional form of complicity liability (beyond aiding, abetting, counselling or procuring), or if it is merely attached to each of them. The English courts have tended to use the doctrine to address the question of unexpected turn of events.[55] Unlike the Russian law, where the members of the group are not responsible for the 'excess of the perpetrator', the English courts, relying on the *Chan Wing-Siu* case,[56] appear to hold the member of the joint enterprise responsible if the jury is satisfied that

50 StGB, Articles 30(2) and 31, see *supra* note 28.

51 Ugol. Kod., Articles 30(2), 35(7), see *supra* note 29.

52 StGB, Article 25(2), see *supra* note 28.

53 Kai Hamdorf, "The Concept of a Joint Criminal Enterprise and Domestic Modes of Liability for Parties to a Crime. A Comparison of German and English Law", in *Journal of International Criminal Justice*, 2007, vol. 5, no. 4, p. 212.

54 Ugol. Kod., Article 36, see *supra* note 29.

55 Ashworth, 1995, p. 429, see *supra* note 15.

56 *Chan Wing-Siu v. The Queen* (1985) A.C. 168.

the defendant contemplated that there was a real possibility that one member of the joint enterprise might go beyond the agreement.[57]

With respect to constituent elements of crimes, Smith and Hogan clarify that it is the general principle of criminal law that a person may not be convicted of a crime unless it is proved beyond reasonable doubt that he has caused a certain event or that responsibility is to be attributed to him for the existence of a certain state of affairs (*actus reus*), and that he had a defined state of mind in relation to the causing of the event or the existence of the state of affairs (*mens rea*).[58]

a. *Actus reus*: Smith and Hogan suggest that *actus reus* includes all the elements in the definition of the crime except the accused's mental element.[59] Thus, *actus reus* is made up generally of the conduct (which includes acts or omissions) and sometimes its consequences, and also the circumstances in which the conduct took place. An example of the 'circumstances' would be the absence of the consent of the rape victim.[60] *Actus reus* is sometimes referred to as a 'conduct element' of the crime, but as follows from the definition, *actus reus* can be broader than just conduct. The German Criminal Code simply states that the act is 'unlawful' if it fulfils all the elements of the criminal provision.[61]
b. *Mens rea:* for the crime to attract criminal liability, *actus reus* must be committed with the requisite state of mind. Smith and Hogan use the term '*mens rea*' to mean the state of mind, intention or recklessness required by the particular crime. They suggest that the term 'negligence', while being a manifestation of fault in English law in addition to the intention and recklessness, falls outside the scope of *mens rea*, if properly understood, for it is not a state of mind but ra-

57 Ashworth, 1995, p. 432. See also Marianne Giles who argues that the basis of liability for secondary participation, developed in *Chan Wing-Siu*, is based on a defendant's realisation of the risk that the principal will act with the required *mens rea*, and his acceptance of that risk. Giles suggest that such liability is based on the 'principle of implied authorization'. Marianne Giles, "Complicity - the Problems of Joint Enterprise", in *Criminal Law Review*, 1990, Jun, pp. 383–393.

58 Smith and Hogan, 2002, p. 28, see *supra* note 30.

59 Smith and Hogan, 2002, p. 30, see *supra* note 30.

60 Smith and Hogan, 2002, p. 31, see *supra* note 30.

61 StGB, Article 11, see *supra* note 28.

ther a failure to comply with a standard conduct.[62] The German Criminal Code adopts an even more narrow definition of the requisite state of mind by saying that "[u]nless the law expressly provides for criminal liability based on negligence, only intentional conduct shall attract criminal liability".[63]

With respect to the legal requirements of complicity, it is important to distinguish the constituent elements of the offence and the constituent elements of the mode of responsibility used in conjunction with this offence. In cases when the crime is committed solely by the primary perpetrator (the principal), it is not necessary to discuss separately his mode of liability because his conduct fully satisfies the *actus reus* for the defined crime and he acted with the requisite *mens rea*. However, when talking about various forms of complicity, one needs to differentiate between the *actus reus* and *mens rea* of the substantive offence committed by the principal and the *way* in which the accomplice was involved in this act. Consequently, there exists a separate set of requirements for the various forms of complicity designed to help the judge or the juror decide whether the accomplice's involvement in a crime entails criminal responsibility or not. In the literature and the judgments, the terms '*mens rea*' and '*actus reus*' are often used in relation to both the substantive offences and complicity. However, for the sake of clarity, the elements of complicity (as opposed to the elements of the crime) will be referred to as the "legal requirements" in this chapter.

a. *Conduct requirements of complicity* differ depending on the type of complicity involved, but, as noted above, the common feature is that the law of complicity does not require causation,[64] thus even a small act of assistance may suffice in entailing the liability of an accomplice.
b. *The fault requirement of complicity* has two dimensions: first, the accomplice must intend to do whatever acts of assistance or encouragement that are done, and must be aware of his ability to assist or encourage the principal; secondly, the accomplice must know the circumstances of the offence.[65] The fault requirement serves as a

[62] Smith and Hogan, 2002, pp. 69–70, see *supra* note 30.
[63] StGB, Article 15, see *supra* note 28.
[64] See Section 5.3.2.
[65] Ashworth, 1995, p. 423, see *supra* note 15.

"guidepost" limiting accomplice liability, as the conduct requirement allows for a very broad application of the concept.[66]

It appears from the definitions provided above that the law of complicity in national jurisdictions is full of subtle differences that create some room for ambiguous interpretations.[67] Nonetheless, each legal system defines complicity in one way or another and attaches certain consequences to its application.

An observation by Dubber can serve as a good conclusion to this section: after having studied in some detail the concept of complicity in German and American law, he suggests that national legal systems shall serve as no more than a mere guidepost for the development of the concept of accomplice liability in international criminal law, which strives to strike a balance between a broader view of accomplice liability urged by the enormity of the crimes involved and a more narrow view of complicity based on the considerations of the principle of legality.[68] It is hard to argue with his conclusion. The next section aims to understand the scope of complicity in international criminal law and the extent to which the concept draws from national legal systems.

5.4. Complicity in International Criminal Law

5.4.1. Historical Perspective

The principle of individual criminal responsibility in international criminal law implies that even those who do not physically commit the crime in question are still liable for other forms of participation.[69] This principle started to develop following the Nuremberg trials.[70] Clapham describes the Nuremberg trials as a paradigm shift, going beyond the obligations of

[66] See *ibid.*, p. 410.

[67] See *ibid.*, p. 439.

[68] Dubber, 2007, p. 1001, see *supra* note 9. For a similar view see also Ambos, 2000, p. 30, see *supra* note 5.

[69] ICTY, *Prosecutor v. Delalić et al. (Čelebići)*, Case No. IT-96-21-T, Trial Judgment, 16 November 1998 ("*Čelebići* Trial Judgment"), para. 319 as discussed by Karim Khan and Rodney Dixon (ed), *Archbold: International Criminal Courts. Practice, Procedure and Evidence*, Sweet and Maxwell, 2005, p. 502.

[70] Sliedregt, 2003, p. 39, see *supra* note 13; Khan and Dixon, 2005, p. 502, see *supra* note 69.

states and attaching duties to individuals.[71] Article 6 of the Nuremberg Charter established by the London Agreement on 8 August 1945[72] called for individual responsibility for crimes against peace, violations of the laws and customs of war, and crimes against humanity. This provision specifically called for the liability of accomplices participating in the execution of a common plan or conspiracy to commit any of the foregoing crimes.

Despite the explicit reference to different modes of participation in the Charter, when preparing the *Nuremberg* judgment,[73] the International Military Tribunal in Nuremberg did not distinguish between primary perpetrators and other crime participants, adopting instead a rather fact-based approach to attributing responsibility. As Ambos points out, "the Nuremberg approach can be called pragmatic rather than dogmatic".[74]

The judgment is divided into three distinct parts: the first part discusses in detail the factual circumstances of Germany's aggression against several countries; the second part outlines the crimes against peace, war crimes, and crimes against humanity committed by German forces; and the third part deals with reasons for the declaring guilt or innocence of the 24 accused standing trial. It is odd that the third part of the *Nuremberg* judgment dealing with individual criminal responsibility does not attempt to 'label' the behaviour of the accused with any legal terms. There is no analysis as to the elements of crimes or the legal requirements of complicity. There is no distinction drawn between perpetrator and accessory.[75] This part simply discusses the position of the accused in the Nazi regime and the specific events in which the accused took part. The offenders' role

---

71 Andrew Clapham, "Issues of Complexity, Complicity and Complimentarity: from Nuremberg Trials to the Dawn of the Next International Criminal Court", in P. Sands (ed.), *From Nuremberg to the Hague: The Future of International Criminal Justice*, Cambridge University Press, 2003, p. 33.

72 United Nations, *Charter of the International Military Tribunal - Annex to the Agreement for the Prosecution and Punishment of the Major War Criminals of the European Axis ("London Agreement")*, 8 August 1945.

73 *The Trial of the Major War Criminals before the International Military Tribunal Sitting at Nuremberg Germany*, dated 1 October 1946.

74 Ambos, 2000, pp. 7–8, see *supra* note 5; Sliedregt, 2003, p. 39, see *supra* note 13.

75 Ambos, 2000, pp. 7–8, see *supra* note 5.

in the commission of crimes was to some extent acknowledged in the sentencing part of the *Nuremberg* judgment.[76]

5.4.2. Jurisprudence of the *ad hoc* Tribunals

A more differentiated approach to joint criminal participation has been adopted by the ICTY, the ICTR and the SCSL. Article 7(1) of the ICTY Statute and Article 6(1) of the ICTR and the SCSL Statutes[77] provide for the following modes of criminal participation: planning, instigating, ordering, committing, aiding and abetting in the planning, preparation or execution of a crime.[78]

Schabas notes that apart from 'committing', all of the other modes of participation fit within the notion of 'complicity' in international criminal law.[79] This view is in line with the derivative (or indirect) nature of accomplice liability discussed in the previous section of this chapter:[80] planning, ordering, instigating, as well as aiding and abetting, all imply the culpability of an accomplice not because he caused certain events but

76 For example, the Reich Marshall Hermann Göring, who is described as the most prominent individual in the Nazi regime after Hitler, received a death sentence. In contrast, the Minister of Foreign Affairs and Reich Protector of Bohemia and Moravia Konstantin von Neurath was sentenced to only fifteen years of imprisonment because his participation in the crimes committed by Nazi Germany was mostly limited to attending the conferences and negotiations.

77 *Op. cit.*, see *supra* note 6.

78 In the Draft Code of Crimes Against the Peace and Security of Mankind adopted by the International Law Commission in 1996 (Report of the ILC to the General Assembly, Forty-Eighth Session, U.N. GAOR, 51st Sess., Supp. No. 10 U.N. A/51/10 (1996)), the International Law Commission created a similar list of modes of criminal participation (even though with a more detailed description attached to each liability mode). Article 2(3) of this Draft Code includes, *inter alia*: intentionally committing a crime; ordering the commission of a crime; knowingly aiding, abetting or otherwise assisting, directly and substantially, in the commission of a crime; directly participating in planning or conspiring to commit a crime; directly and publicly inciting another individual to commit a crime. Even though the 1996 Draft Code became more or less redundant following the adoption of the Rome Statute of the International Criminal Court on 17 July 1998, A/CONF./183/9 ("ICC" and "Rome Statute"), it still serves as the evidence of customary international law and has been used by the ICTY and ICTR in various judgments. For more discussion, see Ian Brownlie, *Principles of Public International Law*, 7th ed., Oxford University Press, 2008, p. 589.

79 William Schabas, *The U.N. International Criminal Tribunals: The Former Yugoslavia, Rwanda and Sierra Leone*, Cambridge University Press, 2006, p. 305.

80 See Section 5.3.2.

because his conduct assisted in some way the commission of the crime by the primary perpetrator. It should be noted, however, that 'complicity' in international criminal law is sometimes understood in a more narrow sense as encompassing aiding and abetting only. Judge Keith, in his separate declaration to the *Genocide* judgment, examined various definitions of 'complicity' and came to the conclusion that "complicity is often equated in whole or in part with aiding and abetting".[81]

The ICTY has to some extent recognized the narrow and the wide meanings of complicity in its jurisprudence: in *Krnojelac* the ICTY Appeals Chamber pointed out that the term 'accomplice' has different meanings depending on the context and may refer to a co-perpetrator or an aider and abettor.[82] Similarly, in *Tadić*, the Trial Chamber came up with a two-pronged test to establish accomplice liability: the first element of the test being "intent, which involves awareness of the act of participation coupled with a conscious decision to participate by planning, instigating, ordering, committing, or otherwise aiding and abetting in the commission of a crime"; and the second, that the conduct of the accused must have contributed to the commission of illegal act. Consequently, the Trial Chamber has adopted a wide outlook on what comprises 'complicitous conduct'. However, while discussing the two elements of complicity in international criminal law, the Trial Chamber in *Tadić* has on several occasions substituted the term 'complicity' with the term 'aiding and abetting'. Thus, the Trial Chamber in *Tadić*, while mostly referring to 'complicity' in a broader sense, did not rule out the possibility of using 'complicity' in a more narrow sense to describe 'aiding and abetting.'[83]

The Chambers' varying approach to complicity and its scope may be explained by the fact that the modes of participation are not defined in the ICTY, the ICTR and the SCSL Statutes. Thus the *ad hoc* tribunals and the court defined the legal requirements of the various forms of liability mentioned in their statutes on a case-by-case basis, relying on existing

[81] ICJ, *The Application of the Convention on the Prevention and Punishment of the Crime of Genocide (Bosnia and Herzegovina v. Serbia and Montenegro)*, case 91, Judgment, 26 February 2007, Declaration of Judge Keith, p. 353.

[82] ICTY, *Prosecutor v. Krnojelac,* Case No. IT-97-25-A, Appeal Judgment, 17 September 2003 ("*Krnojelac* Appeal Judgment"), para. 70.

[83] ICTY, *Prosecutor v. Tadić*, Case No. IT-94-1-T, Trial Judgment, 7 May 1997 ("*Tadić* Trial Judgment"), paras. 674 and 688.

customary international law.[84] The findings of the *ad hoc* tribunals are summarized below.

'Planning' implies "that one or several persons contemplate designing the commission of a crime at both the preparation and execution phases".[85] The Trial Chamber in *Akayesu* clarified that in order for a person to incur liability under the heading of 'planning', the crime that had been planned must have been executed.[86] Planning a crime also serves as an aggravating factor in the sentencing of the actual perpetrator. The level of participation of the accused in the planning of the crime must have been "substantial" enough.[87]

'Instigation' presupposes "urging, encouraging, or prompting" another person to commit a crime.[88] It is not necessary that these actions be perpetrated in public,[89] but it is vital that they have a causal relationship to the commission of the crime.[90]

'Ordering' entails "a person in a position of authority using that position to convince another to commit an offence".[91] Neither the form of the order (explicit or implicit) nor its legality is a decisive factor in the attracting of liability for ordering a crime.[92]

84 See, for example, *Celibici* Appeal Judgment, para. 178, as quoted by Mettraux, 2005, p. 270, see *supra* note 4.

85 *Akayesu* Trial Judgment, para. 480 as discussed by Khan and Dixon, 2005, p. 503, see *supra* note 69.

86 *Ibid.*, para. 473.

87 Mettraux, 2005, p. 280, see *supra* note 4.

88 *Prosecutor v. Semanza*, ICTR Case No. 97-20-T, Trial Judgment, 15 May 2003, para. 381; *Akayesu* Trial Judgment, para. 482 as discussed in Khan and Dixon, 2005, p. 503, see *supra* note 69.

89 ICTR, *Prosecutor v. Akayesu*, Case No. 96-4-A, Appeal Judgment, 1 June 2001 ("*Akayesu* Appeal Judgment"), paras. 478-482.

90 *Prosecutor v. Bagilishema*, ICTR Case No. 95-1A-T, Trial Judgement, 7 June 2001, par 30.

91 *Akayesu* Trial Judgment, para. 483 as quoted by Mettraux, 2005, p. 270, see *supra* note 4.

92 ICTY, *Prosecutor v. Blaškić,* ICTY Case No. IT-95-14-T, Trial Judgment, 3 March 2000 ("*Blaškić* Trial Judgment"), para. 281 as quoted by Cassese, 2008, p. 230, see *supra* note 8.

Finally, an 'aider or abettor' is one who provides "practical assistance, encouragement, or moral support" to the principal.[93] These actions must have had a substantial effect on the perpetration of a crime.[94] There is a slight semantic difference between the terms 'aiding' and 'abetting': aiding has been described by international criminal tribunals as meaning "giving somebody assistance", whereas 'abetting' stands for "facilitating the commission of an act by being sympathetic thereto".[95] The contribution of the aider or abettor may be provided at any stage of a criminal process, including planning, preparation, and execution.[96] Moreover, it may take the form of either a positive act or an omission. Even mere presence at the scene of the crime could constitute aiding and abetting when "it is demonstrated to have significant encouraging effect on the principal offender".[97]

The fault requirement for liability in the form of planning, instigating or ordering is criminal intent.[98] For aiding and abetting, it must be shown that the accused "knew (in the sense he was aware) that his own acts assisted the commission of the specific crime in question by the principal offender".[99] The fact that the aider and abettor may not have shared the intent of the principal offender generally lessens his culpability compared to that of a principal, or compared to that of an accused acting pur-

93 ICTY, *Prosecutor v. Delalić et al. (Čelebići)*, Case No. IT-96-21-A, Appeal Judgment, 20 February 2001, para. 352, *Prosecutor v. Tadić*, ICTY Case No IT-94-1, Appeals Chamber Judgment, 30 July 2002 *("Tadić* Appeal Judgment"), para. 229 as quoted by Mettraux, 2005, p. 284, see *supra* note 4.

94 ICTY, *Prosecutor v. Furundžija*, Case No. IT-95-17/1-T, Trial Judgment, 10 December 1998 ("*Furundžija* Trial Judgment"), paras. 223, 224, 249; *Blaškić* Appeal Judgment, para. 48 as discussed by Mettraux, 2005, p. 284, see *supra* note 4; Cassese, 2008, p. 188, see *supra* note 8.

95 ICTY, *Prosecutor v. Kvočka et al.*, Case No. IT-98-30/1-T, Trial Judgment, 2 November 2001, par 254; *Akayesu* Trial Judgment, para. 484 as discussed by as discussed by Khan and Dixon, 2005, p. 505, see *supra* note 69.

96 *Tadić* Trial Judgment, para. 677, see *supra* note 83.

97 ICTY, *Prosecutor v. Vasiljevic*, Case No. IT-98-32-T, Trial Judgment, 29 November 2002 ("*Vasiljevic* Trial Judgment"), para. 70; *Furundžija* Trial Judgment, para. 232 as discussed by Mettraux, 2005, p. 285, see *supra* note 4.

98 *Blaškić* Trial Judgment, para. 31, para. 280, para. 282 as discussed Cassese, 2008, p. 225, see *supra* note 8.

99 *Vasiljevic* Trial Judgment, para. 71, see *supra* note 97; ICTY, *Prosecutor v. Aleksovski*, Case IT-95-14/1-A, Appeal Judgment, 24 March 2000 ("*Aleksovski* Appeal Judgment"), para. 162 as discussed by Mettraux, 2005, p. 286, see *supra* note 4.

suant to a joint criminal enterprise[100] who does share the intent of the principal offender.[101]

Finally, it is important to note that the ICTY displayed its autonomous understanding of the concept of direct and indirect liability by holding in *Čelebići* that the modes of participation listed in Article 7(1) of the ICTY Statute represent the forms of direct liability by virtue of dealing with positive conduct, while the concept of command responsibility enshrined in Article 7(3) of the Statute is a form of indirect liability for it aims to punish the failure to prevent crimes committed by subordinates.[102] This understanding of direct and indirect liability is different from the understanding deriving from municipal law.[103]

The superior (or command) responsibility under Article 7(3) of the ICTY Statute and Article 6(3) of the ICTR and SCSL Statutes does not qualify as complicity for the purposes of this paper, but merits a short discussion because it resembles some forms of complicity enshrined in Article 7(1) and 6(1) of the Statutes. Command responsibility requires a three-pronged test for liability to be proved: first, there should exist a superior-subordinate relationship between the accused as a superior and a perpetrator of the crime; second, the superior should have known or have reason to know that the crime was about to be or had been committed; and, finally, the accused should have failed to take reasonable and necessary measures to prevent the crime or punish the perpetrators.[104] It follows that the accused need not be in such proximity to the crime as he would otherwise have to be in order to stand convicted under various modes of liability listed in Article 7(1) and 6(1) of the Statutes; nonetheless, this less stringent requirement of proximity to a crime is compensated by the superior-subordinate link that the Prosecution has to prove.

[100] See Section 5.4.3.

[101] ICTY, *Prosecutor v. Vasiljevic*, Case No. IT-98-32-A, Appeal Judgment, 25 February 2004 ("*Vasiljevic* Appeal Judgment"), para. 181–182; ICTY, *Prosecutor v. Krstić*, Case No. IT-98-33, Appeal Judgment, 19 April 2004 ("*Krstić* Appeal Judgment"), para. 268 as quoted by Mettraux, 2005, p. 287, see *supra* note 4.

[102] *Čelebići* Trial Judgment, paras. 333–334 as quoted by Sliedregt, 2003, p. 60, see *supra* note 13

[103] See Section 5.3.3.

[104] *Čelebići* Trial Judgment, para. 346, see *supra* note 69.

5.4.3. The ICC Take on Complicity and Joint Criminal Enterprise

The Rome Statute represents the future of international criminal law as it was drafted after the creation of the ICTY and the ICTR, and makes use of their experience when defining different modes of participation. It also takes into account the Draft Code of Crimes against the Peace and Security of Mankind adopted by the International Law Commission in 1996.[105] Article 25(3) of the Rome Statute presents modes of participation in a systemic way, indicating, in the opinion of some academics,[106] the degree of individual guilt relevant for sentencing purposes. Article 25(3) reads as follows:

> In accordance with this Statute, a person shall be criminally responsible and liable for punishment for a crime within the jurisdiction of the Court if that person:
>
> (a) Commits such a crime, whether as an individual, jointly with another or through another person, regardless of whether that other person is criminally responsible;
>
> (b) Orders, solicits or induces the commission of such a crime which in fact occurs or is attempted;
>
> (c) For the purpose of facilitating the commission of such a crime, aids, abets or otherwise assists in its commission or its attempted commission, including providing the means for its commission;
>
> (d) In any other way contributes to the commission or attempted commission of such a crime by a group of persons acting with a common purpose. Such contribution shall be intentional and shall either:
>
> (i) Be made with the aim of furthering the criminal activity or criminal purpose of the group, where such activity or purpose involves the commission of a crime within the jurisdiction of the Court; or
>
> (ii) Be made in the knowledge of the intention of the group to commit the crime;

---

105 See *supra* note 78.

106 See Gerhard Werle, "Individual Criminal Responsibility in Article 25 Rome Statute", in *Journal of International Criminal Justice*, 2007, vol. 5, no. 4; and Hector Olasolo, "Complementarity Analysis of National Sentencing", in *Roelof Haveman* and Olaoluwa *Olusanya* (ed.), *Sentencing and Sanctioning in Supranational Criminal Law,* Intersentia, Antwerp-Oxford, 2006, p. 55.

[…]

This Article of the Statute provides for a slightly different set of modes of participation as compared with the ICTY, the ICTR and the SCSL Statutes: planning is omitted; instigating is replaced by soliciting and inducing; and aiding and abetting is preceded by the words "for the purpose of facilitating the commission of a crime". It is rather surprising that the requirement of 'substantial contribution', widely relied on by the ICTY and ICTR in their case law, is not in any way reflected in the description of aiding and abetting in the Rome Statute. It remains to be seen whether the ICC interprets this as an "omission" and continues applying the test for aiding and abetting as developed by the previous tribunals, or whether it will lower the threshold for holding an individual complicit in crimes and no longer require that contribution to the crime be 'substantial'.[107]

Schabas notes that complicity is addressed in subparagraphs (b) and (c) of the Article.[108] Subparagraph (a) covers both the commission of the crime, perpetration-by-means and perpetration of the crime through the joint criminal enterprise. The expression 'jointly with another' refers to both co-perpetration and the perpetration in the joint criminal enterprise.[109] This latter mode of participation is not new in international criminal law. Even though not explicitly mentioned in the ICTY or the ICTR Statutes, it is part of customary international law and has been widely used by the *ad hoc* tribunals and the SCSL.

Three particular forms of the joint criminal enterprise have been developed by the international tribunals:[110]

- The first category involves cases where all participants are acting pursuant to a common purpose and share the same criminal intent;
- The second category refers to instances of systemic ill-treatment in organized institutions, such as concentration camps;

[107] Clapham in P. Sands (2003), p. 56, see *supra* note 71; William Schabas, "Enforcing International Humanitarian Law: Catching the Accomplices", in *International Review of the Red Cross*, 2001, vol. 83, no. 842, p. 448.

[108] William Schabas, *An Introduction to the International Criminal Court*, 3rd edn. Cambridge University Press, 2009, p. 213.

[109] Cassese, 2008, p. 212, see *supra* note 8.

[110] *Tadić* Appeal Judgement, paras. 195–226 as discussed by Schabas, 2006, p. 309–310, see *supra* note 79.

- The third category, called the 'extended form' of the joint criminal enterprise, entails liability of the members of the group for the acts which occur as a 'natural and foreseeable consequence' of carrying out the common purpose.[111]

The ICTY Appeals Chamber has pointed out that the joint criminal enterprise constitutes a form of 'commission'.[112] However, the legal requirements of the joint criminal enterprise are similar to those of certain forms of complicity, namely aiding and abetting.[113] This similarity prompted the ICTY Appeals Chamber to distinguish joint criminal enterprise from aiding and abetting.[114] The major differences between the two forms of participation is that the aider and abettor *knowingly* commits acts specifically directed at assisting the perpetration of a particular crime, while members of the joint criminal enterprise perform acts in some way directed to the furtherance of common design with the *intent* to pursue this design.

On a conceptual level, it appears that the joint criminal enterprise can be said to constitute a somewhat "borderline" case, lying between complicity and the actual commission of an offence: on the one hand, the acts of the participants are attributed to all members of the group as if each participant has committed these acts himself; on the other, the members of the group do not directly perpetrate these acts, thus their liability is derivative. The concept of the joint criminal enterprise seems to be borrowed from the English law, with the difference that in England the joint enterprise is a creation designed to deal for the most part with the unexpected turn of events, while in the jurisprudence of the *ad hoc* tribunals it became an independent mode of liability, standing on its own. The joint criminal enterprise also seems to resemble some features of the national law concepts of co-perpetration and conspiracy.[115]

Subparagraph (d) of the Rome Statute also introduces the new category of criminal participation, namely "contributing to the commission of

---

111 Ibid., para. 204.

112 *Vasiljevic* Appeal Judgment, para. 95, see *supra* note 101; *Tadić* Appeal Judgement, para. 188, see *supra* note 110; *Krnojelac* Appeal Judgement, para. 29; Mettraux, 2005, p. 288, see *supra* note 4.

113 Schabas even considers joint criminal enterprise as a form of participation *or* complicity, see Schabas, 2006, p. 319, see *supra* note 79.

114 *Tadić* Appeal Judgment, para. 229, see *supra* note 93.

115 See Section 5.3.3.

a crime by group acting with a common purpose". The views have been expressed that subparagraph (d) explicitly addresses the concept of the joint criminal enterprise.[116] However, the joint enterprise requires membership in the enterprise, whereas subparagraph (d) discusses contribution made by the outside contributor. This mode of participation differs from aiding and abetting in that the individual's contribution is made to the whole group.[117]

5.5. Case Studies

5.5.1. The ICTY Jurisprudence

5.5.1.1. The *Furundžija* Case

Factual Background

Anto Furundžija served as a local commander of the Croatian Defence special unit in one of the municipalities in Bosnia and Herzegovina. At one point during the conflict he subjected a Bosnian Muslim woman to interrogation in the nude in front of forty soldiers. After this interrogation the woman was taken to another room where she was raped in the presence of the accused, who did nothing to stop the sexual violence.

Case Analysis

The Prosecution charged Furundžija with one instance of rape and torture without specifying the mode of liability, thus leaving it to the Trial Chamber to determine.[118] This lack of clarity regarding the nature of the participation of the accused prompted the Trial Chamber to examine the difference between participating in the joint criminal enterprise and aiding and abetting a crime, using torture and rape as examples for its analysis. Based on a review of the post-Second World War jurisprudence, the Trial Chamber concluded that the conduct requirement of aiding and abetting consists of practical assistance, encouragement, or moral support which has a substantial effect on the perpetration of the crime, whereas the fault requirement is the knowledge that these acts assist the commission of the

[116] Schabas, 2009, pp. 211-213, see *supra* note 108.

[117] Cassese, 2008, p. 213, see *supra* note 8. See also Sliedregt, 2003, p. 72, see *supra* note 13.

[118] *Furundžija* Trial Judgment, para. 189, see *supra* note 94.

offence.[119] In contrast with aiding and abetting, the notion of common design presupposes the conduct requirement, which consists of participation in a joint criminal enterprise, and the fault requirement is intent to participate.[120]

When applying these principles to the case, the Chamber concluded that to be guilty of torture as a co-perpetrator, the accused must have participated in an integral way in the torture and with the intent to obtain a confession or to punish and humiliate the victim.[121] In contrast, to be guilty as an aider and abettor, the accused must assist in some way which had a substantial effect on the torture and with the knowledge that torture is taking place.[122] Following this line of argument, the Chamber noted that aiding and abetting torture may only happen in very limited instances.[123]

With regards to rape, the Chamber held that it is indisputable that rape in armed conflict attracts individual criminal responsibility, but there is no definition of rape in international law. [124] Thus, the tribunal felt compelled to provide its own definition of rape. In order to be guilty of rape as a perpetrator or as a co-perpetrator the accused must have satisfied the elements of the crime of rape developed by the Trial Chamber:

> (i) the sexual penetration, however slight:
>
> (a) of the vagina or anus of the victim by the penis of the perpetrator or any other object used by the perpetrator; or
>
> (b) of the mouth of the victim by the penis of the perpetrator;
>
> (ii) by coercion or force or threat of force against the victim or a third person.[125]

Based on these considerations the Trial Chamber concluded that the interrogation of the Bosnian woman was an integral part of torture, and

---

[119] *Furundžija* Trial Judgment, para. 191 as quoted by Cassese, 2008, p. 217, see *supra* note 8.

[120] *Furundžija* Trial Judgment, para. 249 as quoted by Schabas, 2006, p. 307, see *supra* note 79.

[121] *Ibid.*

[122] *Furundžija* Trial Judgment, para. 245 as quoted by Schabas, 2006, p 307, see *supra* note 79.

[123] *Furundžija* Trial Judgment, para. 257, see *supra* note 94.

[124] *Ibid.*, paras. 169, 175.

[125] *Ibid.*, para. 185.

thus the accused was guilty of torture as a co-perpetrator.[126] At the same time, the Chamber found that the accused merely aided and abetted rape because he himself did not commit the act, as defined by the Chamber, but by virtue of being present at the scene of the crime and holding the position of authority, he encouraged sexual violence to take place.[127] Thus, Furundžija was found guilty of aiding and abetting rape.[128]

Sentencing

The Trial Chamber sentenced Furundžija to ten years of imprisonment for torture and eight years of imprisonment for aiding and abetting rape, with both sentences to be served concurrently.[129] The Chamber did not explicitly discuss the effect of the mode of participation on sentencing; it has, however, made it clear that the accused's role in torture as a fellow perpetrator is an aggravating factor as he is as responsible for the crime as the person actually inflicting pain.[130] Given that both torture and rape are equally reprehensible crimes, the slightly more lenient sentence for aiding and abetting rape confirms the relative weight the Trial Chamber assigned to the mode of the accused's participation in crimes. The Appeals Chamber confirmed the sentence.[131]

5.5.1.2. The *Kunarac et al.* Case

Factual Background

Dragoljub Kunarac, Radomir Kovač and Zoran Vuković were all members of the Bosnian Serb forces fighting against Bosnian Muslims in the Foča region in 1992. Following the takeover of the Foča municipality, many Muslim women and girls were detained in houses and apartments, where they were mistreated and sexually abused.[132] Kunarac on at least

[126] *Ibid.*, para. 267.

[127] *Furundžija* Trial Judgment, para. 273–275 as discussed by Cassese, 2008, p. 218, see *supra* note 8.

[128] *Furundžija* Trial Judgment, para. 275, see *supra* note 94.

[129] *Ibid.*, p. 112.

[130] *Furundžija* Trial Judgment, paras. 281–282 by Khan and Dixon, 2005, p. 822, see *supra* note 69.

[131] ICTY, *Prosecutor v. Furundžija*, Case No. IT-95-17/1-A, Appeal Judgment, 21 July 2000 ("*Furundžija* Appeal Judgment"), para. 254.

[132] ICTY, *Prosecutor v. Kunarac et al.*, Case No. IT-96-23/1-A, Appeal Judgment, 12 June 2002 ("*Kunarac* Appeal Judgment"), para. 3.

two occasions took girls to his headquarters, where he raped one of the girls, while allowing his soldiers to rape the other girls in the adjacent rooms. Kunarac also detained two girls in one of the houses in Foča for a prolonged period of time. He treated them as his property, forcing them to perform household chores, regularly raping one of the girls and allowing another soldier to rape the other girl.[133] Kovač committed similar crimes: at one point during the conflict, he assumed control over four girls: he detained them in his apartment, where the girls were regularly raped, humiliated and forced to perform household chores. [134] Vuković, together with another soldier, raped a young girl on one occasion in July 1992.[135]

Case Analysis

Similarly to *Furundžija*, the Prosecution charged the accused with participation in the crimes pursuant to Article 7(1) of the ICTY Statute without specifying the particular mode of liability. Based on the evidence, the Trial Chamber decided that 'committing' and 'aiding and abetting' are the two appropriate heads of responsibility in the case at issue.[136] The Chamber went on to define both modes of liability, holding that 'commission' entails either a physical perpetration of a criminal act or a culpable omission of a rule of criminal law. There can be several perpetrators of the crime provided that the conduct of each one of them fulfils the requisite elements of the definition of the substantive offence.[137] With regards to 'aiding and abetting', the Chamber adhered to the *Furundžija* formula,[138] pointing out that, unlike the 'commission', 'aiding and abetting' is a form of accessory liability.[139]

Kunarac was found guilty of perpetrating as well as aiding and abetting rapes, enslavement, and torture.[140] The Trial Chamber ruled, in particular, that bringing the girls to the house and leaving them to the sol-

---

133 *Ibid.*, paras. 5–10.

134 *Ibid.*, paras. 11–18.

135 *Ibid.*, para. 21.

136 ICTY, *Prosecutor v. Kunarac et al.*, Case No. IT-96-23-T, Trial Judgment, 22 February 2001 ("*Kunarac* Trial Judgment"), paras. 388-389.

137 *Kunarac* Trial Judgment, para. 390 as quoted by John R.W.D. Jones and Steven Powles, *International Criminal Practice*, third edition, Oxford University Press, 2003, p. 415.

138 See Section 5.5.1.1.

139 *Kunarac* Trial Judgment, para. 391, see *supra* note 136.

140 *Kunarac* Appeal Judgment, paras. 6–9, see *supra* note 132.

diers in the knowledge that they would rape them "constituted an act of assistance which had a substantial effect on the acts of torture and rape later committed by his men". Thus, the court found Kunarac guilty of rape as a principal perpetrator with respect to the girls he personally raped, and as an aider and abettor with respect to the girls raped by his men in the adjacent rooms.[141]

The incidents relating to the prolonged detention of girls in the accused's house were charged in the indictment as enslavement and rape. The Trial Chamber endorsed this approach: it entered convictions for two statutory crimes – rape and enslavement – in respect of the same incident.[142] The Chamber held that Kunarac was a primary perpetrator of the rape and enslavement of one of the girls he held captive in his house, while he also aided and abetted the same crimes in respect of another victim detained in the same house and sexually assaulted by another soldier.[143]

Kovač was found guilty of rape, enslavement and outrages upon personal dignity.[144] The Chamber held that Kovač exercised *de facto* ownership over the girls held captive in his apartment.[145] In addition to raping and subjecting the captives to slavery, the Chamber established that Kovač substantially assisted the other soldiers in raping those girls by allowing the soldiers to visit the apartment and by handing the girls to the solders in the knowledge that they would rape them.[146]

Vuković was found guilty in respect of one instance of torture and rape.[147]

Both Kunarac and Kovač perpetrated rapes over an extended period of time with victims who did not necessarily show explicit signs of resistance due to their young age or fear of being killed. Thus, the *Kunarac* Trial Chamber had to modify the definition of rape introduced in *Furundžija* in order to match it with the circumstances of the case and the conduct of the accused:[148] the Chamber ruled that the element requiring "co-

[141] *Kunarac* Trial Judgment, paras. 636–656, 670, see *supra* note 137.

[142] *Kunarac* Amended Indictment, 1 December 1999.

[143] *Kunarac* Trial Judgment, para. 728 *et seq.*, see *supra* note 137.

[144] *Kunarac* Appeal Judgment para. 11., see *supra* note 132.

[145] *Kunarac* Trial Judgment, para. 749 *et seq.*, see *supra* note 137.

[146] *Ibid.*, para. 759.

[147] *Kunarac* Appeal Judgment para. 21., see *supra* note 132.

[148] See Section 5.5.1.1.

ercion or force or threat of force against the victim or a third person" is too restrictive and may not encompass other factors that would render the sexual act non-consensual.[149] Consequently, the Chamber held that sexual penetration lacking genuine consent in the context of the surrounding circumstances shall constitute rape.[150]

Sentencing

The Trial Chamber sentenced Kunarac, Kovač and Vuković to a single sentence of twenty-eight, twenty and twelve years of imprisonment, respectively.[151] These sentences were confirmed on appeal.[152] It is somewhat unfortunate for the purposes of comparing direct perpetration of rape and complicity in rape that the Trial Chamber chose to impose a single sentence without specifying the length of imprisonment for each particular conviction. Nonetheless, the fact that Kunarac received the longest sentence of all the accused is indicative of the fact that the Trial Chamber took due account of his extensive participation in rapes both as a perpetrator and as an accomplice. Moreover, the Trial Chamber explicitly noted that his influence over other perpetrators as well as the fact that he aided and abetted several rapes aggravates his guilt.[153]

5.5.2. The ICTR Jurisprudence

5.5.2.1. The *Akayesu* Case

Factual Background

Jean-Paul Akayesu, a father of five, served as a teacher in the Rwandan municipality of Taba. He was a well-respected leader of his local commune. He even held the position of mayor for some time in 1993 and 1994, overseeing the local economy, police and law in the village. After the Rwandan genocide began, Akayesu actively urged the population to kill Tutsis. Akayesu knew that the local radical militia members took away and raped Tutsi women seeking refuge in the premises of the bureau communal.[154] On several occasions he made comments alluding to acts of

---

149 *Kunarac* Trial Judgment, para. 438, see *supra* note 137.

150 *Ibid.*, para. 460.

151 *Ibid.*, paras. 883–890.

152 *Kunarac* Appeal Judgment, pp. 125–127, see *supra* note 132.

153 *Kunarac* Trial Judgment, paras. 863, 866, see *supra* note 137.

154 *Akayesu* Trial Judgment, paras. 419–448, see *supra* note 85.

sexual violence against women, such as "[n]ever ask me again what a Tutsi woman tastes like". He also encouraged militia to perpetrate rapes by pointing at girls and saying "take them".[155]

Case Analysis

The *Akayesu* judgment is of utmost importance in international criminal law as it contains the world's first conviction of the defined crime of genocide. *Akayesu* describes the crime of genocide and the sexual offences in the context of different provisions of the ICTR Statute: the former covered by Article 2 (genocide), and the latter, by Articles 3 (crimes against humanity) and 4 (war crimes).[156] However, there is a link between the two crimes: the acts of sexual violence against Tutsi women formed, in the opinion of the Trial Chamber, the factual elements of genocide and evidenced Akayesu's genocidal intent to destroy the Tutsi group.

It is noteworthy that the Prosecution charged Akayesu, *inter alia*, with both genocide and complicity in genocide,[157] but the Trial Chamber disagreed with the Prosecutor's decision to charge both modes of participation, stating that an individual cannot be at the same time the principal perpetrator of a particular crime and the accomplice thereto.[158] The Trial Chamber held that Akayesu's acts, including sexual violence against Tutsi women, constitute factual elements of the crime of genocide. He incurs individual criminal liability for "having ordered, committed, or otherwise aided and abetted in the preparation or execution of the killing of and causing serious bodily or mental harm to members of the Tutsi group".[159] Such an extensive participation in genocidal acts led the Chamber to conclude that Akayesu possessed specific genocidal intent and thus was responsible for genocide and not merely for complicity in genocide.[160]

In contrast with genocide, the Trial Chamber did not find Akayesu guilty of 'committing' rape or other acts of sexual violence as there was

155 *Ibid.*, para. 452.

156 The Trial Chamber found no nexus between the acts of the Accused and the armed conflict, consequently, no conviction was entered with respect to Article 4 of the ICTR Statute. See *Akayesu* Trial Judgment, para. 643.

157 ICTR Statute, Articles 2(3)(a) and 2(3)(e), see *supra* note 6.

158 *Akayesu* Trial Judgment, paras. 468, 532 as discussed by Kriangsak Kittichaisaree, *International Criminal Law*, Oxford University Press, 2002, p. 237.

159 *Akayesu* Trial Judgment, paras. 705–706 as discussed by Cassese, 2008, p. 217, see *supra* note 8.

160 *Akayesu* Trial Judgment, para. 734, see *supra* note 85.

no evidence that he himself had perpetrated these crimes.[161] There was evidence, however, that Akayesu was present on the compound where the rapes happened. When discussing the ways in which Akayesu was involved in rapes, the Trial Chamber faced the lack of clarity in the definition of rape in international law.[162] Thus it felt compelled to define rape for the purposes of international criminal law. The court held that rape constitutes a form of aggression, and, akin to torture, must be understood conceptually rather than as a set of certain acts. Consequently, the ICTR adopted a wide definition of rape "as a physical invasion of a sexual nature, committed on a person under circumstances which are coercive".[163]

The *Akayesu* Trial Chamber held that Akayesu incurred accomplice liability for rapes in three different ways: first, he "by his own words, specifically ordered, instigated, aided and abetted" certain rapes; [164] second, Akayesu aided and abetted several rapes by being present on the premises of the bureau communal in his position of authority and allowing the rapes to take place, *inter alia*, by his words of encouragement in other sexual acts happening at that time;[165] third, Akayesu aided and abetted several rapes by allowing rapes to happen while being in a position of authority and having a reason to know that sexual violence was occurring.[166]

The border line between finding Akayesu responsible for ordering, instigating and aiding and abetting rapes on the one hand, and solely aiding and abetting rapes, on the other, lay in Akayesu's verbal encouragement of the rapes in the former case, and his tacit approval thereof in the latter.[167]

There is a discrepancy between the trial judgment and the sentencing decision regarding the exact mode of Akayesu's participation in sexual violence: while the trial judgment mentions aiding and abetting along

[161] *Ibid.*, para. 450.

[162] *Ibid.*, para. 686.

[163] *Ibid.*, paras. 687–688. See also Anne-Marie de Brouwer, "Gacumbitsi Judgement" in Goran Sluiter and Andre Klip (ed.), *Annotated Leading Cases of International Criminal Tribunals: The International Criminal Tribunal for Rwanda*, Intersentia, Antwerp/Oxford/Portland, 2005–2006.

[164] *Akayesu* Trial Judgment, para. 692, see *supra* note 85.

[165] *Ibid.*, para. 693.

[166] *Ibid.*, para. 694.

[167] *Ibid.*, paras. 452, 692–694.

with instigating and ordering acts of sexual violence, the sentencing decision only talks about aiding and abetting sexual crimes.[168]

Sentencing

The Trial Chamber sentenced Akayesu to life imprisonment for genocide and incitement to commit genocide, and fifteen years of imprisonment for rape.[169] In arriving at such a conclusion, it assessed his personal role in the crimes committed in the municipality of Taba. In particular, the tribunal noted that Akayesu was in a position of authority in a local municipality and was under the duty to protect the population, whose confidence he had betrayed.[170] The Trial Chamber pointed out that Akayesu's relatively low ranking in the government of Rwanda could have served as a mitigating factor at sentencing, but his deliberate choice to participate in killings and rapes of Tutsi population through orders and tacit encouragement constitutes a powerful aggravating factor, one which clearly outweighs the mitigating one.

At the sentencing stage, the tribunal placed the magnitude of the crime at the centre of its considerations. Life imprisonment for genocide stands in contrast to the fifteen years of imprisonment for all other crimes committed by Akayesu, including rape.[171] Nonetheless, the mode of participation did not play a peripheral role in this case: the Trial Chamber spent a significant amount of time determining whether the accused was responsible for merely aiding and abetting genocide or whether he was indeed the primary perpetrator. This analysis helped in determining the sentence of the accused. Without compromising the importance of individual circumstance in each case, one may suggest that should the Trial Chamber have found Akayesu guilty of merely aiding and abetting the genocide, he could have received a shorter sentence.[172] With respect to crimes other than genocide, the mode of participation did not seem to

168 *Akayesu* Trial Judgment, sentencing decision dated 2 October 1998.

169 *Ibid.*

170 *Ibid.*

171 Sentences were ordered to be served concurrently.

172 Radislav Krstić and Dragan Nikolić have both been sentenced by the ICTY to 35 years of imprisonment for aiding and abetting the genocide. In contrast, Popovic and Beara, just like Akayesu, have been sentenced to life imprisonment following their conviction of genocide. See *Krstić* Appeal Judgment, see *supra* note 102; and ICTY, *Prosecutor v. Popovic et al.*, Case No. 05-88-T, Trial Judgement, 10 June 2010.

make an impact on sentencing – at least not in the rhetoric of the Trial Chamber.

5.5.2.2. The *Musema* Case

Factual Background

Alfred Musema served as the director of a public enterprise (the tea factory) at the time when the atrocities happened in Rwanda. In 1994 Musema was involved in attacks against Tutsi refugees in the area surrounding his factory. Amongst various violent acts against Tutsis, the Trial Chamber held that Musema, in concert with four other men, raped a young Tutsi woman, brought to him by the others. Musema allegedly raped the victim with the words "[t]he pride of the Tutsi is going to end today"; he was then followed by four other men encouraged by his behaviour.[173] The Appeals Chamber reversed this particular conviction for rape in the light of new evidence adduced at the appeal stage, highlighting, however, that the Trial Chamber did not err in the assessment of the available evidence.[174] Thus, the arguments of the Trial Chamber relating to modes of participation in sexual offences merit discussion in this chapter.

Case Analysis

The Prosecution brought various charges against Musema including rape as a crime against humanity, genocide, or, alternatively, complicity in genocide.[175] The Trial Chamber upheld the cumulative charging approach whereby multiple offences were charged on the basis of the same facts.[176] In line with this approach, the rape committed by Musema qualified as one of the elements of the crime of genocide, namely, the causing of serious bodily or mental harm to members of the group.[177] The tribunal inferred the specific intent to destroy the Tutsi group from, *inter alia*,

[173] ICTR, *Prosecutor v. Musema*, Case No. 96-13-A, Trial Judgement, 27 January 2000 ("*Musema* Trial Judgment"), para. 907.

[174] *Ibid.*, paras. 176, 193, 194.

[175] *Ibid.*, para. 149, 168, 218, 220. The Prosecution also charged Musema with violation of Article 4 of the ICTR Statute (war crimes), including rape but similarly to the *Akayesu* case, the Trial Chamber failed to establish the nexus between the acts of the accused the armed conflict. See *ibid.*, para. 974.

[176] *Ibid.*, para. 297.

[177] *Ibid.*, para. 907.

Musema's humiliating utterances that he pronounced before the rape.[178] Consequently, Musema was found guilty of the crime of genocide and not merely complicity in genocide.

Apart from using the instance of rape to establish the elements of the crime of genocide, the Trial Chamber discussed rape as a separate crime in the context of Article 3(g) of the ICTR Statute – rape as a crime against humanity. As a preliminary matter, the *Musema* Trial Chamber reiterated the broad conceptual definition of rape as "a physical invasion of a sexual nature, committed on a person under circumstances which are coercive", as introduced by *Akayesu*.[179] In particular, the tribunal stressed the evolving nature of the definition of rape in international law, which justified abandoning the mechanical definition in favour of the conceptual one.[180] Consequently, the Trial Chamber, when discussing rape as a crime against humanity, did not elaborate much on the technical details but rather referred to the factual part of judgment describing the event. The tribunal also ensured that the Prosecution established the contextual (legal prerequisite or *chapeaux*) elements common to all crimes falling under Article 3 of the ICTR Statute (such as Musema's knowledge of the widespread attack on the civilian population).[181] The tribunal did not elaborate much on Musema's mode of participation in rape because the witness testified that he was the primary perpetrator. The Trial Chamber, nonetheless, added that Musema also incurred individual criminal responsibility for having abetted the others in the rape of the same victim by virtue of the example he had set.[182]

The Trial Chamber also discussed a different incident, whereby Musema ordered the rape and mutilation of another Tutsi woman. With regard to this event, however, there was no conclusive evidence that the order was executed and that these acts were in fact perpetrated. Therefore, Musema did not incur individual responsibility for having ordered this crime.[183]

Sentencing

---

178 *Ibid.*, para. 933.
179 *Ibid.*, para. 967.
180 *Ibid.*, para. 228.
181 *Ibid.*, paras. 966.
182 *Ibid.*, paras. 908.
183 *Ibid.*, paras. 828, 829.

The Trial Chamber sentenced Musema to a single sentence of life imprisonment. The rape of the young Tutsi woman served as an aggravating factor at sentencing.[184] Despite the reversal of the rape conviction, Musema's life sentence for all other convictions was confirmed on appeal.[185] This is an important indicator that the rape was not an indispensable element of the crime of genocide in this particular case, and even in the absence of this particular element, Musema still stood convicted of genocide.

5.5.3. The SCSL Jurisprudence

5.5.3.1. The *AFRC* Case

Factual Background

Alex Tamba Brima, Ibrahim Bazzy Kamara and Santigie Borbor Kanu were former leaders of the Armed Forces Revolutionary Council ('AFRC'), which seized power from the elected government of Sierra Leone in the 1997 *coup d'état*.[186] Following the power takeover, the AFRC was not immediately able to exercise control over the whole territory of Sierra Leone. Consequently, it had to resort to multiple military operations.[187] The AFRC fell in 1998 but widespread atrocities continued throughout the territory of Sierra Leone until the cessation of hostilities in early 2002.[188] In their capacity as members and leaders of the AFRC, Brima, Kanu and Kamara committed various crimes, including extermination, murders, act of terrorism, outrages upon personal dignity, sexual slavery and rape.[189]

Case Analysis

The Prosecution charged rape under two separate counts in the indictment: rape as a crime against humanity under Article 2(g) of the Statute;

184 *Ibid.*, para. 1008.

185 ICTR, *Prosecutor v. Musema*, Case No. 96-13-A, Appeal Judgement, 16 November 2001 ("*Musema* Appeal Judgment"), para. 399.

186 SCSL, *Prosecutor v. Brima, Kamara and Kanu* (*AFRC* Case), SCSL-04-16-T, Trial Judgment, 20 June 2007 ("*AFRC* Trial Judgment"), paras. 285, 332, 434, 509.

187 SCSL, *Prosecutor v. Brima, Kamara and Kanu* (*AFRC* Case), SCSL-04-16-T, Appeal Judgement, 22 February 2008 ("*AFRC* Appeal Judgment"), para. 8.

188 *Ibid.*, para. 11, 12.

189 *AFRC* Trial Judgment, paras. 2113–2123, see *supra* note 186.

and rape as an outrage upon personal dignity in the context of war crimes under Article 3(e) of the Statute.[190] When discussing rape as a crime against humanity, the *AFRC* Trial Chamber did not elaborate much on the definition of rape, pointing out that rape has been sufficiently defined by the jurisprudence of the ICTY and ICTR. Without any further explanations, the Trial Chamber adopted the technical *Kunarac* definition of rape.[191]

With regard to rape as an outrage upon personal dignity, the Trial Chamber held that rape is just one act in the non-exhaustive list of conduct that amounts to treatment that is degrading of human dignity.[192] The Trial Chamber refrained from further elaborating on the definition of rape in the context of the provision on war crimes, ruling that rape as a crime against humanity is, in fact, an outrage upon personal dignity.[193] Consequently, the Trial Chamber used the same factual findings in relation to rape[194] when entering convictions on both counts, distinguishing between the different *chapeaux* elements of crimes against humanity and war crimes.[195] In addition to this, the Trial Chamber found that the sexual slavery occurring during the war also fell under the category of outrages upon personal dignity in the context of war crimes.[196] Thus, this latter category appeared to be broader than rape and also included the crime of sexual slavery. Sexual slavery is similar to rape in the sense that the perpetrator causes the victim to engage in conduct of a sexual nature without the consent of the victim, with the distinction lying in the continuous nature of sexual slavery and the relationship of ownership between the perpetrator and his victim.[197]

The Trial Chamber, when discussing the modes of individual responsibility of the accused, turned the count relating to the outrages upon personal dignity essentially into a 'sexual slavery' rather than a 'rape' count and dealt with it along with the other enslavement crimes of conscripting children to participate in hostilities and enslavement (including

[190] *Ibid.*, paras. 691, 715.
[191] *Ibid.*, paras. 692, 693.
[192] *Ibid.*, para. 715.
[193] *Ibid.*, paras. 715, 718.
[194] *Ibid.*, paras. 1026, 1041, 1068.
[195] *Ibid.*, paras. 1070, 1188.
[196] *Ibid.*, paras. 1109, 1133, 1145, 1170, 1187.
[197] *Ibid.*, paras. 708–709.

forced labour) as a crime against humanity.[198] The court stressed the continuous nature of sexual slavery as opposed to rape, which can be seen as a crime fixed in time.[199]

The Prosecution pleaded individual criminal responsibility of all three accused on the basis of Articles 6(1) and 6(3) of the Statute.[200] Article 6(1) covers the commission of the crime as well as various forms of complicity, while 6(3) deals with superior responsibility for the acts of subordinates. All three accused were convicted of rape as a crime against humanity under Article 6(3) and not under Article 6(1) of the Statute.[201]

The Trial Chamber held Brima responsible for rapes under Article 6(3) of the Statute based on the finding that several of his subordinates beat and gang-raped two civilians in the town of Rosas, Bombali district.[202] In line with the three-pronged test for command responsibility,[203] the court inferred a superior-subordinate relationship from Brima's position as the overall commander of the AFRC forces that committed crimes in Bombali region.[204] The Chamber held that the systematic nature of attacks and Brima's close physical proximity to the crimes justified establishing his knowledge about the crimes based on the circumstantial evidence.[205] Finally, the Chamber held that Brima failed to punish perpetrators and prevent crimes because despite the existence of a functioning disciplinary system in the AFRC, it was not employed to punish or prevent rapes of the civilians. Only rapes of soldiers' wives were deemed worth punishing.[206]

Kamara and Kanu were found responsible under Article 6(3) for the same crimes committed in Rosas, Bombali district.[207] The court was less elaborate, however, on the legal requirements of command responsibility – it held that Kanu was responsible due to his position as a commander of

198 See *ibid.*, paras. 1919, 1981.

199 See, for example, *ibid.*, para. 1720 (Corrigendum to *AFRC* Trial Judgment).

200 *Ibid.*, paras. 1635, 1636.

201 *AFRC* Appeal Judgment, para. 23, see *supra* note 187.

202 *AFRC* Trial Judgment, paras. 1031-1035, see *supra* note 186.

203 See Section 5.4.2.

204 *AFRC* Trial Judgment, para. 1723, see *supra* note 186.

205 *Ibid.*, paras. 1730–1733.

206 *Ibid.*, paras. 1739–1741.

207 SCSL, *Prosecutor v. Brima, Kamara and Kanu* (*AFRC* Case), SCSL-04-16-T, Sentencing Judgment, 19 July 2007, paras. 74, 96.

troops attacking the region[208] and, Kamara, as a deputy commander of the AFRC troops in the Bombali region.[209]

With regard to the responsibility of the accused under Article 6(1) of the Statute, the Trial Chamber went through each form of liability listed in this provision and evaluated whether the Prosecution had adduced sufficient evidence for that particular form of liability.[210] Analysing every mode of liability with respect to every crime listed in the indictment led to a lengthy discussion in the judgment, also because various crimes were grouped around different geographical locations, and for each location the Trial Chamber had to repeat itself with respect to each of the accused.

Of particular importance for this chapter is the conviction of all three accused of planning the commission of outrages upon personal dignity in the form of sexual slavery.[211] The Trial Chamber suggested that 'planning' implies that one or more persons contemplate the commission of a crime at both the preparatory and execution phases.[212] It further held that circumstantial evidence may provide proof of the existence of a plan, and an individual may incur responsibility for planning when his level of participation is substantial, even though the crime may have actually been committed by another person.[213]

Upon establishing that a system existed whereby an unknown number of women and girls were abducted and used as sex slaves by the members of the AFRC in various regions of Sierra Leone,[214] the Trial Chamber concluded that the only reasonable inference from such a systemic nature of enslavement crimes in general, and sexual slavery in particular, is that these crimes were planned.[215] Thus the court ruled that Brima and Kanu were responsible for designing the commission of enslavement crimes, including sexual slavery, and that although these

---

208 *AFRC* Trial Judgment, para. 2041, see *supra* note 186.

209 *Ibid.*, paras. 1923, 1927.

210 See, for example, *ibid.*, paras. 1646–1650.

211 *AFRC* Sentencing Judgment, paras. 41, 70, 94, see supra note 207.

212 *AFRC* Trial Judgment, para. 765, see *supra* note 186.

213 *Ibid.*

214 *Ibid.*, paras. 1109, 1110, 1133, 1145, 1170.

215 *Ibid.*, paras. 1823, 1826, 2090.

crimes were largely committed by their subordinates, the contribution of the three men accused was substantial.[216]

The Appeals Chamber upheld the convictions on the planning of sexual slavery, and added that the Prosecution had adduced sufficient evidence to warrant Kanu's conviction on the basis of aiding and abetting this crime due to the fact that Kanu was specifically responsible for girls and women in one of the forced labour camps: Kanu provided practical assistance to a system of sexual slavery and knew that his acts would assist the implementation of this system.[217] The Appeals Chamber, however, fell short of actually convicting Kanu of aiding and abetting sexual slavery, holding that the question of aiding and abetting does not arise in the light of the conviction for planning.[218]

Apart from individual criminal responsibility under Articles 6(1) and 6(3) of the Statute, the Prosecution also charged the accused with participation in the joint criminal enterprise, the objective of which was to take any action necessary to gain and exercise political power and control over the territory of Sierra Leone and, in particular, the diamond mining areas.[219] The Trial Chamber found, however, that the Prosecution failed to define the criminal objective of the enterprise; thus, the Trial Chamber did not consider joint criminal enterprise as a mode of participation when determining the responsibility of the accused.[220] The Appeals Chamber subsequently overturned this particular finding.

In a not entirely convincing line of arguments, the Appeals Chamber held that "the criminal purpose underlying the joint criminal enterprise can derive not only from its ultimate objective, but also from the means contemplated to achieve that objective".[221] The Appeals Chamber then suggested that even though gaining and exercising political power over the territory of Sierra Leone may not be a crime itself, the criminal actions taken to reach this goal are a means to achieve the objective. Consequently, the indictment read as a whole provides that the crimes within the Statute committed by the AFRC qualify as actions contemplated as a

216 *Ibid.*, paras. 1827, 2095, 2096.
217 *AFRC* Appeal Judgment, paras. 302, 305, see *supra* note 187.
218 *Ibid.*, para. 306.
219 *Ibid.*, para. 15.
220 *AFRC* Trial Judgment, para. 1639, see *supra* note 186.
221 *AFRC* Appeal Judgment, para. 76, see *supra* note 187.

means to achieve that objective.[222] In the interests of justice, the Appeals Chamber decided not to rule on factual findings in the light of the existence of the joint criminal enterprise.[223] One possible interpretation of this decision is that the Appeals Chamber was satisfied with the overall sentences imposed on the accused by the Trial Chamber and thought it was unnecessary to revisit the questions of culpability of the accused.

Sentencing

The Trial Chamber sentenced Brima and Kanu each to a single term of imprisonment of fifty years, and Kamara to a single term of imprisonment of forty-five years.[224] These sentences have been confirmed on appeal.[225] When determining the sentences, the Trial Chamber took into account the gravity of the offence and the individual circumstances of the convicted persons.[226] The court reiterated the case law previously established by the ICTY and ICTR by stressing that the form and degree of the participation of the accused as well as the role played by the accused in the commission of the crimes are relevant for determining the gravity of the offence.[227] The mode of participation in the offences appeared to play a relative role in the determination of sentences – for each of the convicted persons, the Trial Chamber listed with great prudence all the crimes for which he stood convicted and modes of participation thereof.[228]

Superior responsibility under Article 6(3) seemed to aggravate the Trial Chamber's perception of the crimes committed by the convicted persons.[229] The vulnerability of young girls subjected to sexual crimes was another aggravating factor.[230] Kanu's Defence attempted to mitigate his responsibility for rape pursuant to Article 6(3) by stating that his involvement in this crime as a superior was limited to his failure to punish the perpetrators. The court rejected this argument by noting that, indeed, Kanu was convicted pursuant to Article 6(3) (command responsibility)

222 *Ibid.*, paras. 81-84.
223 *Ibid.*, para. 86.
224 *AFRC* Sentencing Judgment, p. 36, see *supra* note 207.
225 *AFRC* Appeal Judgment, p. 105, see *supra* note 187
226 *AFRC* Sentencing Judgment, para. 11, *op.cit.*
227 *Ibid.*, para. 19.
228 See, for example, *ibid.*, paras. 41 and 43.
229 *Ibid.*, para. 73.
230 *Ibid.*, paras. 53 and 55.

and not Article 6(1), but this distinction did not mitigate in his favour.[231] It should be noted also that the Trial Chamber delivered the sentences on the general pretext that Brima, Kamaru and Kanu had been found responsible for some of the most heinous, brutal and atrocious crimes ever recorded in human history.[232]

5.5.3.2. The *RUF* Case

Factual Background

Issa Hassan Sesay, Morris Kallon and Augustine Gbao were all leaders of the Sierra-Leonean Revolutionary United Front ('RUF'), a military organization originating from Liberia, which started its operations in the territory of Sierra Leone in 1991.[233] It later joined the AFRC and transformed itself into a political party.[234] In the mid-nineties, RUF gained control of large territories in Sierra Leone, including the major towns and diamond mines.[235] The seizure of power and control was accompanied by ongoing hostilities and attacks against the civilian population.[236]

Case Analysis

The Prosecution charged the accused with participation in the first category of joint criminal enterprise with the broadly-defined common criminal purpose of taking power and control of Sierra Leone, in particular mining areas.[237] The Trial Chamber followed the Prosecution's approach and convicted all three accused of war crimes and crimes against humanity stemming from their participation together with the AFRC members in a single joint criminal enterprise with a common criminal purpose to seize control over Sierra Leone by committing crimes such as terrorism, rape,

---

[231] *Ibid.*, paras. 117 and 118.

[232] *Ibid.*, para. 34.

[233] SCSL, *Prosecutor v. Sesay, Kallon and Gbao* (RUF Case), SCSL-04-16-A, Appeal Judgement, 26 October 2009 ("RUF Appeal Judgment"), paras. 4,5.

[234] *Ibid.*, para. 9.

[235] *Ibid.*, paras. 6, 10.

[236] *Ibid.*, para. 17.

[237] RUF Indictment, paras. 36, 38, 39. For a description of the three categories of joint criminal enterprise, see Section 5.4.3.

enslavement, murder, attacks on UN personnel, forced marriages and recruitment of child soldiers.[238]

This judgment stands out as one of the most controversial judgments in modern international criminal law. Its disputable nature lies, *inter alia,* in the extension of the concept of the joint criminal enterprise, which becomes most apparent when one scrutinizes the conviction of the accused Gbao.

Gbao was found guilty pursuant to the basic form of joint criminal enterprise for crimes that he did not intend to commit: both the Trial and the Appeals Chambers held that so long as the accused had agreed to the common criminal purpose, he was responsible for all the natural and foreseeable consequences flowing from the execution of that purpose, however remote they might have been from the defendant's own intentions.[239] Thus the SCSL eliminated the requirement of shared intent from the concept of the joint criminal enterprise. This inference, coupled with an excessively wide definition of the criminal purpose, has attracted significant criticism of the *RUF* judgment.[240]

The Trial Chamber's creative approach to the definition of rape also deserves some discussion. Following the finding that rape is part of customary international law,[241] the Trial Chamber came up with a lengthy set of elements, which in the view of the Chamber are the constituent elements of rape.[242] It appears that the Chamber decided not to borrow the fixed definition of rape from the case law of international criminal tribunals, but rather master its own detailed definition containing a combination of elements of rape coming from a variety of different sources. The *mens rea* requirement for rape is particularly complex and excessive as

238 SCSL, *Prosecutor v. Sesay, Kallon and Gbao* (RUF Case), SCSL-04-16-T, Trial Judgment, 2 March 2009 ("RUF Trial Judgment"), paras. 1979–1985, 2070.

239 RUF Appeal Judgment, para. 492, see *supra* note 233; RUF Trial Judgment, para. 2109, see *supra* note 238

240 For criticism of RUF Judgments see Guenael Mettraux, "'Joint Criminal Enterprise' has Grown Another Tentacle!" available at International Criminal Law Bureaux, http://www.internationallawbureau.com/blog/?p=944, last accessed on 17 May 2011); and Wayne Jordash, "Joint Criminal Enterprise at the Special Court for Sierra Leone", available at International Criminal Law Bureaux, http://www.internat ional-lawbureau.com/blog/?p=950, last accessed on 17 May 2011.

241 RUF Trial Judgment, para. 144, see *supra* note 238.

242 *Ibid.*, para. 145.

the Chamber ruled that the accused must have intended to effect sexual penetration or acted in the reasonable knowledge that this was likely to occur, and must have known or had a reason to know that the victim was not consenting.[243]

The judgment is structurally organized around the geographical areas where the crimes happened during the time that RUF was in control. With regard to sexual crimes, and in particular rapes, the Trial Chamber established that they were committed in the Kono district together with other crimes over a period of several months in 1998. This time corresponds with the existence of the AFRC/RUF joint criminal enterprise.[244] The Chamber further held that the Prosecution failed to establish that any of the accused personally committed crimes in the Kono district.[245] Thus, the court turned to the joint criminal enterprise.

The Chamber established that following the loss of power in early 1998, the RUF/AFRC alliance had to regain control over the territory of Sierra Leone through the commission of unlawful killings, rapes, sexual slavery, 'forced marriages', mutilations, enslavement, pillage and the enlistment, conscription and use of child soldiers.[246] Sesay, Kallon and Gbao, together with several other leaders of the RUF/AFRC, were found to be members of the joint criminal enterprise.[247]

The Chamber then evaluated the role of each of the accused in the joint criminal enterprise. The court held that Sesay contributed to the joint criminal enterprise by virtue of being a senior commander in the RUF forces, and through his close personal relationship to the *de facto* leader Bockarie.[248] Sesay instructed the RUF/AFRC fighters to kill the civilians and burn their houses in the Kono district. Sesay had knowledge of the events in the Kono district through regular radio reports as well as his bodyguards, who, unlike Sesay, were physically present in Kono.[249] Similarly, the court found that Kallon was an important and influential commander in the RUF/AFRC hierarchy in the Kono district, and he was present at the meeting when Sesay gave instructions to the RUF/AFRC fight-

243 *Ibid.*
244 *Ibid.*, para. 2063.
245 *Ibid.*, para. 2066.
246 *Ibid.*, paras. 2067–2070.
247 *Ibid.*, para. 2077.
248 *Ibid.*, para. 2089.
249 *Ibid.*, paras. 2084–2085.

ers to kill the civilians.[250] Women were raped by RUF fighters during food-finding missions ordered by Kallon.[251]

The Trial Chamber used the same rhetoric with respect to both Sesay and Kallon when discussing their contribution to the joint criminal enterprise. It held that Sesay and Kallon contributed significantly to the furtherance of the common purpose in the knowledge that their actions were part of the widespread and systematic attack against the civilian population. They intended to take power and control over the territory of Sierra Leone, and actively participated in the furtherance of this common purpose. By their participation they significantly contributed to crimes, including rapes, committed by RUF/AFRC fighters in Kono district in 1998.[252]

Gbao's participation in and contribution to the joint criminal enterprise was largely "inferred" by the court. In particular, the Trial Chamber held that its findings in respect of Gbao's participation and contribution to the joint criminal enterprise in some other districts of Sierra Leone apply *mutatis mutandis* to Kono district.[253] The Chamber inferred from his "important role and oversight functions" that Gbao knew or had reason to know that sexual violence was intended by members of the joint criminal enterprise in order to further the goals of the joint criminal enterprise.[254] The Chamber failed to establish Gbao's intent in relation to crimes committed in Kono. It did, however, find him responsible for these crimes based on the fact that "he willingly took the risk that the crimes [...] might be committed by other members of the joint criminal enterprise or persons under their control".[255] It is important to note that during the time that hostilities happened in Kono, Gbao was permanently stationed elsewhere in Sierra Leone.[256]

Sentencing

At sentencing, the Trial Chamber took the familiar path established by the ICTY and ICTR, noting that the sentence must reflect the totality of the

250 *Ibid.*, paras. 2093–2094.
251 *Ibid.*, para. 2099.
252 *Ibid.*, paras. 2089–2092, 2100–2103.
253 *Ibid.*, para. 2105.
254 *Ibid.*, para. 2107.
255 *Ibid.*, para. 2109.
256 *Ibid.*, para. 2077.

criminal conduct of the offender, including the circumstances of the case and the degree of the participation of the accused.[257] The SCSL elaborated on these criteria in great detail.[258]

First, the Trial Chamber systematically enumerated all of the offences for which the accused stood convicted, concluding in each case that the inherent gravity of these offences was "exceptionally high".[259] With respect to rapes, the court held in particular that "the crimes of sexual violence for which the accused stand convicted are of extremely serious nature and were committed in a conspicuously brutal manner".[260] These rapes were committed publicly in order to instil fear in civilians.[261] The court also added that using rapes and forced marriages to terrorise the population further aggravates the underlying offence for sentencing purposes.[262]

Second, the court assessed the involvement of each of the accused in these offences, finding that Sesay's level of participation in the joint criminal enterprise was vital to the furtherance of its objectives; therefore his culpability was of the highest level.[263] Similarly, Kallon's involvement in the design and maintenance of the system of recruitment of child soldiers and his participation in the joint criminal enterprise as a senior commander raised his culpability to the highest level.[264] In contrast, the Trial Chamber found Gbao's involvement in the overall scheme to be more limited than that of his co-defendants, thus decreasing his level of culpability for sentencing purposes. In particular, the Chamber noted that Gbao was a functionary of the RUF whose major contribution to the joint criminal enterprise was ideological instruction and enslavement of civilians.[265] Consequently, Gbao received the lowest sentence of the three men accused.

---

[257] *Prosecutor v. Sesay, Kallon and Gbao* (RUF Case), SCSL-04-16-T, Sentencing Judgment, 8 April 2009 ("RUF Sentencing Judgment"), para. 18.

[258] *Ibid.*, paras. 101–102.

[259] *Ibid.*, paras. 116 et seq.

[260] *Ibid.*, para. 123.

[261] *Ibid.*, para. 121.

[262] *Ibid.*, para. 131.

[263] *Ibid.*, para. 215.

[264] *Ibid.*, paras. 236 and 240.

[265] *Ibid.*, paras. 268, 270, 271.

Sesay, Kallon and Gbao were sentenced to fifty-two, forty and twenty-five years imprisonment respectively,[266] with Gbao's sentence reduced to twenty years' custody after the Appeals Chamber had acquitted him of attacks on UN personnel.[267] At sentencing, the Trial Chamber imposed a separate sentence for each count that the accused had been found guilty of. Sesay received forty-five years for rape as a crime against humanity; Kallon, thirty five years; and Gbao, fifteen years.[268]

5.6. Complicity in Rape: Comparative Approach

It follows from the cases discussed in this chapter that the ICTY, the ICTR and the SCSL employed different modes of liability in respect of rape. The *ad hoc* tribunals and the court held that Furundžija aided and abetted rape; Kunarac perpetrated and aided and abetted rapes committed in the context of sexual slavery; Akayesu encouraged sexual violence by verbal and tacit approval; and Brima, Kamara, and Kanu incurred command responsibility for rapes perpetrated by their subordinates. Additionally, the concept of joint criminal enterprise made it possible to hold Sesay, Kallon, and Gbao responsible for the rapes perpetrated by other RUF fighters during food-finding missions. What is common in these cases is that, with the exception of Kunarac, the defendants did not directly perpetrate the rapes. Consequently, they incurred accomplice liability in the sense that it is based on the conduct of others, and thus derivative in nature. This finding is not surprising, for international criminal law mostly deals with high-level perpetrators removed from the actual commission of the crime.[269] These figures, distant from the crime scene, still have to face punishment in accordance with the principle of individual criminal responsibility developed at Nuremberg.

Another common feature of the case law discussed in this chapter is the level of sophistication involved in the process of attributing responsibility for complicity in rape. The *ad hoc* tribunals and the court had to perform the complex task of establishing the following: first, the *chapeaux* elements characteristic of a certain category of crimes; secondly,

266 *Ibid.*, p. 92.

267 RUF Appeal Judgment, p. 189, see *supra* note 233.

268 RUF Sentencing Judgment, p. 93, 95, 97, see *supra* note 257.

269 Jones and Powles, 2003, pp. 410–411 *supra* note 137; and Zahar and Sluiter, p. 221, see *supra* note 2.

the substantive elements of rape, namely *mens rea* and *actus reus*; and finally, the legal requirements of complicity. As was discussed in the chapter, rape can fall under the category of war crimes and crimes against humanity. It can also be one of the manifestations of genocide. Thus, the Prosecution often has to prove different *chapeaux* elements in respect of the same offence. The matter is further complicated by the absence of a fixed definition of rape as a substantive crime and, consequently, its ever changing *mens rea* and *actus reus.* The fact that rape can also constitute torture or sexual slavery under certain circumstances expands the substantive elements of the offence even further. This complexity creates many challenges for judges in the process of attributing responsibility for various forms of complicity in rape.

The *ad hoc* tribunals and the court each adopted their individual approach to the attribution of responsibility for complicity in rape. The ICTY appears to have the most cautious stance by holding Furundžija an aider and abettor of rape based on the consideration that his physical presence at the scene of a crime, coupled with his position of authority, encouraged its commission. Furundžija was not a co-perpetrator of rape because he did not physically fulfil the *actus reus* of the offence, nor did he share 'a purpose' behind it. Similarly, in *Kunarac* the ICTY Trial Chamber was cautious to find the defendant guilty of only those rapes that he directly perpetrated or aided and abetted by explicit encouragement and support. In *Akayesu*, the ICTR adopted a less restrictive approach to the legal requirements of complicity. The Trial Chamber held, *inter alia*, that Akayesu incurred criminal responsibility for aiding and abetting rapes by virtue of allowing them to happen while being in a position of authority and having reason to know about the sexual violence happening in the local municipality. The SCSL adhered to the most relaxed approach in the attribution of responsibility for rapes and other mass atrocities. Instead of focusing on particular crimes, the Ccourt chose to group a number of offences around various geographical areas in Sierra Leone and infer the defendants' responsibility for these crimes based on either the doctrine of command responsibility (the *AFRC* case) or joint criminal enterprise (the *RUF* case).

It is submitted here that some level of discrepancy in the standards for attributing responsibility for complicitous conduct adopted by the ICTY, ICTR and SCSL is acceptable and could be explained by the geographical differences and nature of the conflict. It is important, however, to define the clear legal requirements of each mode of accomplice liability and apply them in a consistent manner to the substantive crime.

For the purposes of this chapter, it is instructive to compare the two divergent approaches to attributing responsibility for involvement in rape: the most restrictive ICTY's approach in *Furundžija* and the relaxed method adopted by the SCSL in the *RUF* and *AFRC* cases.

Furundžija is a good example of how the legal requirements of the different liability modes interact with elements of substantive crimes. The ICTY Trial Chamber developed the definition of rape and found that Furundžija satisfied the legal requirements for aiding and abetting this offence. Furundžija's presence at the scene of the crime, coupled with his position of authority, encouraged the rape to occur. Further, the Accused was aware of this fact. At the same time, the Chamber found Furundžija guilty of torture as a co-perpetrator. The Accused satisfied the legal requirements for co-perpetration in the joint criminal enterprise by virtue of having participated in an integral part of torture with the intent to obtain confessions and humiliate the victim. Consequently, the Chamber accurately reflected the degree of Furundžija's involvement in both crimes by combining the definition of crimes (elements of crimes) and the legal requirements of a particular mode of liability.

The *Furundžija* case also demonstrates the contrast between the derivative nature of accomplice liability and the direct nature of liability incurred by virtue of co-perpetratorship in the joint criminal enterprise. On one hand, Furundžija cannot be said to have caused the rape, but his acts certainly encouraged the primary perpetrator to commit this crime. On the other hand, Furundžija can be said to have caused torture in the sense that he participated in its integral part – namely interrogation. On might claim, however, that the *Furundžija* case stands in great contrast with many other international criminal law cases due to its rather limited scope; *Furundžija* deals with just one accused and two charges.

The SCSL, on the other hand, mostly tries cases involving multiple accused, many geographical locations, and numerous charges. The distinction between the legal requirements of the different liability modes and the elements of crimes seems to be diluted by the magnitude of cases heard before the SCSL. The SCSL, in the *RUF* case, expanded the notion of joint criminal enterprise originally developed by the ICTY in *Tadić*. It adopted the loose fault requirement by abandoning the requirement of "necessary intent to further the objective of the joint criminal enterprise" in favour of recklessness. In addition, the *RUF* Trial Chamber did not require that the acts of the participants of the joint criminal enterprise directly caused any particular crimes to occur; it was only required that the accused participated in furtherance of the common purpose. Thus, the SCSL treated participation in the joint criminal enterprise as a form of derivative, rather than direct, liability. Such a relaxed approach to the requirement of fault, coupled with no requirement of causation characteristic of all forms of derivative liability, created an over-expansive and over-inclusive mode of liability.[270] The SCSL Appeals Chamber stretched the notion of joint enterprise even further by holding in the *AFRC* case that the objective of the enterprise does not necessarily have to be criminal, so long as the means of achieving the objective are. This reasoning defeats the whole purpose of the joint enterprise, which is aimed, *inter alia*, at punishing the faulty choice to become a member of a group pursuing the criminal purpose.

The approach adopted by the SCSL inferring the defendant's involvement in crimes from their position in a military structure or membership in a certain group fails to respect the core principle of individual criminal responsibility – the principle of individual autonomy, which views persons as rational beings responsible for their own actions.

The bodies applying international criminal law must be particularly careful with the doctrine of joint criminal enterprise. Joint criminal enterprise has an instrumental function in national law and addresses, for the most part, the issue of unexpected events when the principal commits crimes beyond what has been previously agreed.[271] International criminal law appears to utilize this doctrine as a self-sufficient mode of liability, which the ICTY Appeals Chamber defined as a 'form of commission.' While being a form of commission, the doctrine of joint enterprise, in most instances, entails derivative liability of its members for the conduct of others. This ambiguity calls for a careful application of the doctrine.

It is true that some problems with the attribution of liability in an over-expansive manner can be cured at the sentencing stage by allowing for the mitigation of sentence based on the level of contribution and individual circumstances of the convicted person. The SCSL took such an approach with the defendant Gbao. It does not, however, seem satisfacto-

[270] See Section 5.3.2.

[271] See Section 5.3.3.

ry to patch the holes in the attribution of liability by decreasing the sentence of the convicted person, as these are two separate issues that need to be dealt with separately.

In sum, international criminal law has several modes of traditional accomplice liability – such as aiding and abetting or ordering at its disposal – which are far more precise and nuanced than the doctrine of joint criminal enterprise. However, these traditional modes of participation may be harder to prove than joint criminal enterprise, especially in relation to such a complex crime as rape, which entails very specific conduct in very specific circumstances. This conclusion is somewhat paradoxical in the light of the fact that the *ad hoc* tribunals view the aider or abettor as less culpable than the member of the joint criminal enterprise.[272]

The traditional forms of derivative liability are designed in such a way that they require proof of the constituent elements of each specific offence prior to finding the responsibility of accomplices. This is so because accomplice liability is based on the act of another person. Consequently, in order to prove complicity, one needs to be sure that the act in question indeed took place and that the accomplice was at least aware of this act and intended to influence its commission in one way or another. As has been shown above, aiding and abetting, for example, requires the accused's action to have a substantial effect on the perpetration of the specific crime, coupled with the awareness that his acts contribute to the commission of this offence. With the perpetrator being removed from the scene of the crime – as it often the case where individuals stand trial for mass atrocities – these two criteria appear to be harder to prove than contribution to a broadly-defined joint criminal enterprise. In addition, individuals convicted pursuant to the joint criminal enterprise can bear responsibility for the acts of unknown perpetrators, who are not even members of this enterprise.[273]

5.7. Conclusion

Both common and civil law systems distinguish between complicity and primary perpetration. The extent to which complicity is defined in national law depends on the general approach to the attribution of responsibility adopted in a particular country and the extent of the judges' discretionary

[272] See Section 5.4.2.

[273] See Section 5.5.3.2.

powers. Nonetheless, complicity appears to have some defined content in both common and civil law countries. In national criminal law, which has been developing over a much longer period than international criminal law, the concept is applied to relatively small cases involving few participants. In international criminal law, complicity appears to be a nebulous concept without clear borders; it requires more definition as to the nature of accomplice liability, its scope, and its legal requirements.

This chapter has attempted to illuminate certain aspects of complicity in relation to the crime of rape. Like complicity, rape has been recognized by customary international law, but lacks a fixed definition in modern international criminal law. As discussed above, rape falls under different categories of offences recorded in the Statutes of the *ad hoc* tribunals and the SCSL. Rape also forms the basis of other crimes documented in the Statutes. This makes the attribution of responsibility for rape a complicated and multi-layered task. The level of complexity associated with cases heard by the *ad hoc* tribunals and the SCSL suggests that international criminal law would benefit from the definition of different forms of complicity and "bordering" concepts like joint criminal enterprise. These concepts seem to be replacing the traditional forms of complicity in cases where the actual perpetrator cannot be identified or the accused is far removed from the scene of the crime. This latter trend requires more justification than is currently available in international criminal law.

As argued in this chapter, the nuances of the defendant's level of contribution to the crime can certainly be reflected at the sentencing stage, even without clear guidelines as to the scope and legal requirements of complicity. Nonetheless, for the purposes of legal certainty, it is important to have well-defined criteria for different forms of liability in international criminal law. Such criteria can assist judges in the determination of the defendant's guilt.

6

The Means of Proof of International Sex Crimes

Sangkul Kim[*]

6.1. Introduction

The term 'means of proof' means 'probative evidence'. The term indicates evidence in respect of which a positive evaluation has been completed by adjudicators – 'positive' in the sense of substantively supporting the establishment of an element of a crime. This definition originated from the Office of the Prosecutor of the International Criminal Court ('ICC') when it designed the conceptual structure of the Means of Proof Digest. Contrary to the usages in some national jurisdictions, "means of proof", for the purpose of this chapter, does not carry any procedural connotation of being a *form* of evidence – for example, evidence being adduced either in the form of affidavit or of testimony.[1] Instead, in this chapter, the concept of the 'means of proof' functions only in the substantive law context. When the Trial Chamber in the *Sikirica et al.* case of the International Criminal Tribunal for the former Yugoslavia ('ICTY') stated that "[…] his evidence may constitute a means of proof of an element of the genocide […]",[2] the Chamber shared the author's understanding of the term 'means of proof' – that is, evidence assessed and decided by the judges as satisfying an element of a crime.

---

* **Sangkul Kim** is Researcher at the Legal Research Institute of the Korea University Law School (Seoul); S.J.D. Candidate at Georgetown University Law Center (Washington DC); and former Associate Legal Adviser at the Office of the Prosecutor of the International Criminal Court (The Hague, 2004-2008). The views expressed in this article are those of the author's alone, and do not necessarily reflect the views of the Office of the Prosecutor of the International Criminal Court.

1 See, *e.g.*, Rule 44(a)(2)(C) "Other Means of Proof" of the U.S. Federal Rules of Civil Procedure.

2 International Criminal Tribunal for the former Yugoslavia, *Prosecutor v. Sikirica et al.*, Case No. IT-95-8-T, Decision on Prosecution's Application to Admit Transcripts under Rule 92*bis*, 23 May 2001, para. 11.

Manifesting itself in the form of a specific fact, means of proof can be considered as a graphic expression of an element of a crime. Such graphic function of means of proof is realised in two distinctive manners: 'concretisation' for 'descriptive elements' on the one hand, and 'transformation' for 'normative elements' on the other. That is, the means of proof of the 'descriptive elements' (such as 'conduct', 'consequence' and 'circumstance' as specified in Article 30 of the ICC Statute) are cognitively produced by the concretisation process. For instance, with regard to the contextual element of crimes against humanity, the descriptive element of the 'widespread or systematic attack' can be concretised into the means of proof of the 'scale of the attack', the 'pattern of the attack', and the 'organized nature of the attack'. On the other hand, the 'normative elements' such as the 'gravity' requirement concerning 'other inhumane acts' as a crime against humanity undergoes the process of 'transformation'. That is, in order to assist the evidentiary assessment to be performed in the mind of the adjudicator, the normative element of 'gravity' must be transformed into graphic images contained in the relevant means of proof. Hence, through the transformation process taken by the judges, the 'normative element' of 'gravity' is to be transformed into the graphic images of a 'lasting social stigma', the 'vulnerable status of the victim being a woman, child or the sick', and an 'atmosphere of violence surrounding the perpetrator's conduct'.[3] In sum, through all these cognitive processes producing concrete factual pictures of means of proof, the elements are understood and found to be established.

Since the above-mentioned 'normative elements' are rarer amongst the elements of core international crimes, this chapter will mostly address the means of proof of 'descriptive elements'. The main sources of the relevant means of proof are the jurisprudence of the ICTY, the International Criminal Tribunal for Rwanda ('ICTR') and the Special Court for Sierra Leone ('SCSL'). It should be noted at the outset that, for the purpose of this chapter, the means of proof of material elements (as opposed to mental elements) will be the main object of research.

3 See *infra* section 6.3.3.3.

6.2. Rape

6.2.1. Elements: 'Sexual Invasion (Conduct)' and 'Coercive Circumstances (Circumstance)'

There are two material elements of rape recognized by the statute and jurisprudence of international criminal tribunals: (i) sexual invasion; and (ii) coercive circumstances.[4] At the *ad hoc* tribunals, it appears that there has been a divide in the case law as to whether the absence of the victim's consent is an element of rape. While the *Kunarac et al.* Appeals Chamber of the ICTY answers in the affirmative, the ICTR Trial Chamber in the *Akayesu* case states that a showing of the coercive circumstance would suffice. As a matter of practice, however, this legal confrontation seems to be illusive because most of the relevant case law acknowledges that the general circumstances – that is, facts constituting the 'contextual elements' of a genocidal campaign (genocide); a widespread or systematic attack against a civilian population (crimes against humanity); or an armed conflict (war crimes) – surrounding a specific rape incident in the context of international criminal law are so inherently coercive as to vitiate any possibility of consent.[5] In other words, from the standpoint of a

---

4 See International Criminal Court, Elements of Crimes, ICC-ASP/1/3, art. 6, U.N. Doc. CNICC/2000/1/ Add.2, 10 September 2002 ("ICC Elements of Crimes"), art. 7(1)(g)-1; art. 8(2)(b)(xxii)-1; and art. 8(2)(e)(vi)-1. They provides the same material elements respectively as follows:

1. The perpetrator invaded the body of a person by conduct resulting in penetration, however slight, of any part of the body of the victim or of the perpetrator with a sexual organ, or of the anal or genital opening of the victim with any object or any other part of the body.
2. The invasion was committed by force, or by threat of force or coercion, such as that caused by fear of violence, duress, detention, psychological oppression or abuse of power, against such person or another person, or by taking advantage of a coercive environment, or the invasion was committed against a person incapable of giving genuine consent.

5 International Criminal Tribunal for Rwanda, *Prosecutor v. Gacumbitsi*, ICTR-2001-64-A, Judgement,7 July 2006 ("*Gacumbitsi* Appeals Judgement"), para. 155 ("The answers both Tribunals have given to this second question resolve as a practical matter the objections raised by the Prosecution with respect to the elements approach. The Prosecution can prove non-consent beyond reasonable doubt by proving the existence of coercive circumstances under which meaningful consent is not possible. As with every element of any offence, the Trial Chamber will consider all of the relevant and admissible evidence in determining whether, under the circumstances of the case,

it is appropriate to conclude that non-consent is proven beyond reasonable doubt. But it is no necessary, as a legal matter, for the Prosecution to introduce evidence concerning the words and conduct of the victim or the victim's relationship to the perpetrator. Nor need it introduce evidence of force. Rather, the Trial Chamber is free to infer non-consent from the background circumstances, such as an ongoing genocide campaign or the detention of the victim. Indeed, the Trial Chamber did so in this case."); International Criminal Tribunal for the former Yugoslavia, *Prosecutor v. Kunarac et al.*, IT-96-23/1-A, Judgement, 12 June 2002 ("*Kunarac et al.* Appeals Judgement"), paras. 130–132 ("[…] it is worth observing that the circumstances giving rise to the instant appeal and that prevail in most cases charged as either war crimes or crimes against humanity will be almost universally coercive. That is to say, true consent will not be possible […] German substantive law contains a section penalizing sexual acts with prisoners and persons in custody of public authority. The absence of consent is not an element of the crime. Increasingly, the state and national laws of the United States – designed for circumstances far removed from war contexts – support this line of reasoning. [A state's] legislature reasonably recognized the unequal positions of power and the inherent coerciveness of the situation which could not be overcome by evidence of apparent consent. […] Such jurisdictions have established these strict liability provisions to protect prisoners who enjoy substantive legal protections […] highlights the need to presume non-consent here. […] Such detentions amount to circumstances that were so coercive as to negate any possibility of consent."); International Criminal Tribunal for Rwanda, *Prosecutor v. Akayesu*, ICTR-96-4-T, Judgement, 2 September 1998 ("*Akayesu* Trial Judgement"), para. 688 ("The Tribunal notes in this context that coercive circumstances need not be evidenced by a show of physical force. […] coercion may be inherent in certain circumstances, such as armed conflict or the military presence of Interahamwe among refugee Tutsi women at the bureau communal."); International Criminal Tribunal for Rwanda, *Prosecutor v. Muhimana*, ICTR-95-1B-T, Judgement and Sentence, 28 April 2005 ("*Muhimana* Trial Judgement"), para. 546 ("Accordingly, the Chamber is persuaded by the [Kunarac] Appellate Chamber's analysis that coercion is an element that may obviate the relevance of consent as an evidentiary factor in the crime of rape. Further, this Chamber concurs with the opinion that circumstances prevailing in most cases charged under international criminal law, as either genocide, crimes against humanity, or war crimes, will be almost universally coercive, thus vitiating true consent."); Special Court for Sierra Leone, *Prosecutor v. Brima et al.*, SCSL-04-16-T, Judgement, 20 June 2007 ("*AFRC* Trial Judgement"), para. 694 ("[…] [I]n situations of armed conflict or detention, coercion is almost universal."). A recent decision of the ICC Pre-Trial Chamber in *Bemba* case seems to share the same view. See International Criminal Court, *Prosecutor v. Bemba*, ICC-01/05-01/08-424, Decision Pursuant to Article 61(7)(a) and (b) of the Rome Statute on the Charges of the Prosecutor Against Jean-Pierre Bemba Combo, 15 June 2009 ("*Bemba* Confirmation of Charges Decision"), para. 162 ("With regard to the term 'coercion' [in the 2nd element of the ICC Elements of Crimes], the Chamber notes that it does not require physical force. Rather, 'threats, intimidation, extortion and other forms of duress which prey on fear

prosecutor who is obligated to prove the 'contextual elements' of the core international crimes, the legal problem of whether the absence of the victim's consent is an element of rape or not becomes moot because the problem is already destined to be solved when he or she proves those 'contextual elements'. Consequently, such contextual circumstances of core international crimes proven by the prosecutor might simultaneously satisfy the second material element of rape – that is, "coercive circumstances" – and the absence of consent be presumed.[6]

6.2.2. Means of Proof

6.2.2.1. Means of Proof of 'Sexual Invasion (Conduct)'

As regards the three prongs of descriptive material elements (*actus reus*) under the legal framework of the ICC Statute ('conduct,' consequence,' and 'circumstance'),[7] it should be noted at the outset that the crime of rape requires proof of 'conduct' (sexual invasion) and 'circumstance' (coercive circumstance) only. That is, rape as defined in the jurisprudence of *ad hoc* tribunals and the ICC Elements of Crimes does not require any 'consequence' (or 'result') of the underlying criminal 'conduct' of invasion. As shared by academic views expressed in connection with the crime of rape under national criminal jurisdictions,[8] rape as an international crime should be classified as a 'conduct crime' (as opposed to a 'result crime') in the sense that the Prosecution is not required to prove any 'result/consequence' of the conduct of sexual invasion. In this context, the phrase "resulting in penetration"[9] as provided in the first element of rape in the ICC Elements of Crimes seems to serve no purpose other

or desperation may constitute coercion, and coercion may be inherent in certain circumstances, such as armed conflict or military presence.'").

6 In relation to enslavement as a crime against humanity, see *Kunarac et al.* Appeals Judgment, see *supra* note 5, para. 120.

7 See ICC Statute, art. 30(2) and art. 30(3). ICC Elements of Crimes, see *supra* note 4, General Introduction, paras. 2 and 7.

8 See George P. *Fletcher, Basic Concept of Criminal Law*, Oxford University Press, 1998, pp. 59–62; Albin Eser, "The Principle of Harm in the Concept of Crime: A Comparative Analysis of the Criminally Protected Legal Interests", in 4 *Duquesne University Law Review*, 1965, pp. 389–90; Eugene Milhizer, "Justification and Excuse: What They Were, What They Are, and What They Ought To Be", in 78 *Saint John's Law Review*, 2004, p. 805.

9 See *supra* note 4.

than to cause unnecessary confusion. Furthermore, the legal value of evidence regarding the effects of rape ('trauma') should be assessed based on the precise understanding of the crime of rape classified as a 'conduct crime'.[10]

The following means of proof circumstantially[11] support the factual establishment of sexual invasion: (i) scream from pain during penetration of the victim's sexual organ or anus or a part of a body;[12] (ii) bleeding of the victim's sexual organ or anus or a part of a body;[13] (iii) medical treatment administered to the victim after the sexual invasion, such as the treatment of the victim's wound on anus with a compress, or the victim being provided with tranquillisers;[14] (iv) perpetrator's ejaculation on a part of the victim's body;[15] (v) trace of sperm left on the bed;[16] (vi) after a

---

10 See *infra* section 6.2.2.3.

11 *AFRC* Trial Judgement, see *supra* note 5, para. 695 ("The Trial Chamber acknowledges that the very specific circumstances of an armed conflict where rapes on a large scale are alleged to have occurred, coupled with the social stigma which is borne by victims of rape in certain societies, render the restrictive test set out in the elements of the crime difficult to satisfy. Circumstantial evidence may therefore be used to demonstrate the *actus reus* of rape."). See also other decisions from the *ad hoc* tribunals sharing the same view: *Gacumbitsi* Appeals Judgement, see *supra* note 5, para. 115 ("It is well established that, as a matter of law, it is permissible to base a conviction on circumstantial evidence and/or hearsay evidence."); International Criminal Tribunal for Rwanda, *Prosecutor v. Kamuhanda*, Case No. ICTR-99-54A-A, Judgement, 19 September 2005, para. 241 ("Nothing prevents a conviction being based on circumstantial evidence."); International Criminal Tribunal for the former *Yugoslavia, Prosecutor v. Kupreskić*, Case No. IT-95-16-A, Appeal Judgement, 23 October 2001, para. 303 ("The case against Vlatko Kupreskić at trial was wholly dependent upon circumstantial evidence. The Appeals Chamber first notes that there is nothing to prevent a conviction being based upon such evidence. Circumstantial evidence can often be sufficient to satisfy a fact finder beyond reasonable doubt.").

12 International Criminal Tribunal for the former Yugoslavia, *Prosecutor v. Delalić et al.*, Case No. IT-96-16-T, Judgement, 16 November 1998 ("*Delalić et al.* Trial Judgement"), para. 960.

13 *Ibid.*, para. 960; International Criminal Tribunal for Rwanda, *Prosecutor v. Gacumbitsi*, ICTR-2001-64-T, Judgement, 17 June 2004 ("*Gacumbitsi* Trial Judgement"), para. 208 ("A branch slightly longer than a meter was driven into her genitals, wounding her and causing her to bleed profusely.").

14 *Delalić et al.* Trial Judgement, see *supra* note 12, para. 960.

15 *Ibid.*, paras. 958, 960, 961; International Criminal Tribunal for the former Yugoslavia, *Prosecutor v. Kunarac et al.*, Case No. IT-96-23-T, Judgement, 22 February 2002 ("*Kunarac et al.* Trial Judgement"), para. 99.

16 *Delalić et al.* Trial Judgement, see *supra* note 12, para. 937.

gang-rape, the victim was barely able to walk;[17] (vii) perpetrator put the victim's face down on the bed (and penetrated her vagina with his penis);[18] (viii) perpetrator subsequently turned her over on to her back (and again penetrated her vagina with his penis);[19] (ix) perpetrator ordered the victim to turn around and kneel (before penetrating her anus).[20] In this context, it should be noted that the relevant rules of the ICTY and the ICTR do not require any corroboration of the testimony of the victim who is often the only person present at the crime scene besides the perpetrator.[21]

6.2.2.2. Means of Proof of 'Coercive Circumstances (Circumstance)'

The relevant evidence constituting the element of 'coercive circumstances' can be categorized into three groups: (1) evidence from the perpetrator's side: his utterance and deed; (2) evidence from the victim's side: her response before, after and during the sexual invasion; and (3) evidence of surrounding circumstances.

---

17 *Kunarac et al.* Trial Judgement, see *supra* note 15, para. 650.

18 *Delalić et al.* Trial Judgement, see *supra* note 12, para. 937.

19 *Ibid.*, para. 937.

20 *Ibid.*, para. 960.

21 Rule 96(i), Rules of Procedure and Evidence of the ICTY and ICTR that provides, "[i]n case of sexual assault, no corroboration of the victim's testimony shall be required." Judges of the ICTY and ICTR are quite willing to find that a rape was committed, based solely on the testimony of a victim-witness. See International Criminal Tribunal for the former Yugoslavia, *Prosecutor v. Duško Tadić*, Case No. IT-94-1-T, Opinion and Judgment, 7 May 1997, para. 563 and *Akayesu* Trial Judgement, see *supra* note 5, para. 134 (Rule 96(i) "accords to the testimony of a victim of sexual assault the same presumption of reliability as the testimony of victims of other crimes, something long been denied to victims of sexual assault by the common law."); See also, *e.g.*, *Delalić et al.* Trial Judgement, see *supra* note 12, para. 957 ("The Trial Chamber finds Ms. Antic's testimony as a whole compelling and truthful, particularly in light of her detailed recollection of the circumstances of each rape and her demeanour in the court room in general and, particularly, under cross-examination."); *Gacumbitsi* Trial Judgement, see *supra* note 13, para. 218 ("As to the rape and subsequent killing and [sic] of Witness TAO's wife in the ruins of his grandfather's house, the Chamber finds that the witness is credible and his account of events reliable, even without corroboration, because he was an eyewitness and the circumstances of the events were peculiar, in particular, the relationship between the witness and the victim of the rape and murder.").

Means of Proof from the Perpetrator's Side

Needless to say, evidence of the perpetrator's use of force or threat to the victim will satisfy the second material element of 'coercive circumstances', be it made orally or physically.

First, as to evidence of *oral* threat or coercion, the judges of the *ad hoc* tribunals have thus far taken into account the following means of proof: (i) perpetrator's threatening utterance against the victim, such as a threat not to cry, shout, or make noise;[22] (ii) perpetrator's cursing remark against the victim;[23] (iii) perpetrator's mocking and taunting utterance;[24] (iv) perpetrator's expression of hatred against a particular group;[25] (v) perpetrator's instruction to the victim not to speak or report about the rape.[26] In this context, it should be noted that a threat against a third person (for example, the victim's family member) can also satisfy the 'coercive circumstance' element.[27]

Secondly, in respect of the perpetrator's deed, the following means of proof have been given credit as constituting the element of 'coercive circumstances': (i) perpetrator or accomplice's acts of violence directed against the victim;[28] (ii) perpetrator or accomplice's acts of violence directed against another person;[29] (iii) perpetrator's physical assaults against the victim;[30] (iv) perpetrator used his knife to tear off the victim's clothes;[31] (v) perpetrator pointing a rifle at the victim while she took her

22 *Delalić et al.* Trial Judgement, see *supra* note 12, para. 958 ("He […] told her that if she did not do whatever he asked she would be sent to another camp or she would be shot.").

23 *Ibid.*, paras. 958 and 959 ("He then said to her "why are you crying? This will not be your last time.").

24 *Akayesu* Trial Judgement, see *supra* note 5, para. 430; *Gacumbitsi* Trial Judgement, see *supra* note 13, para. 203 ("[T]he attackers asked her if the child she was bearing was a boy or a girl, for he would have disembowelled her in order to kill the child if it was a boy."); *Ibid.*, para.208 ("The attackers were saying that in the past Tutsi women and girls hated Hutu men and refused to marry them, but that now they were going to abuse the Tutsi girls and women freely.").

25 *Kunarac et al.* Trial Judgement, see *supra* note 15, para. 711.

26 *Delalić et al.* Trial Judgement, see *supra* note 12, para. 937.

27 *Kunarac et al.* Trial Judgement, see *supra* note 15, para. 711.

28 *Delalić et al.* Trial Judgement, see *supra* note 12, para. 937 (the accused slapped the victim).

29 *Kunarac et al.* Appeals Judgement, see *supra* note 5, para. 301.

30 *Gacumbitsi* Trial Judgement, see *supra* note 13, para. 208.

31 *Muhimana* Trial Judgement, see *supra* note 5, para. 297.

clothes off;[32] (vi) perpetrator forced the victim to undress;[33] (vii) perpetrator stripped the victim by tearing their clothes;[34] (viii) perpetrator forced the victim to undress in public;[35] (ix) perpetrator forced the victim to walk, run and exercise while being naked.[36]

Means of Proof from the Victim's Side

In terms of the proof of the second material element of 'coercive circumstances', the victim's responses *before, after, and during* the conduct of sexual invasion have been an important reference point for judicial fact-findings of the international criminal tribunals. Needless to say, those means of proof of the victim's response *during* the sexual invasion can also support the establishment of the first element of 'sexual invasion'.

The means of proof found in international judgements with regard to the victim's response *before* the conduct of sexual invasion are: (i) the victim pleaded not to touch her;[37] (ii) the victim told the perpetrator that she was sick;[38] (iii) the victim's mother begged the perpetrator to kill her daughters rather than to rape them in front of her;[39] (iv) the victim started to cry;[40] (v) the victim tried to escape.[41] These means of proof clearly remind us of those words "fear of violence", "duress", and "psychological oppression" as provided in the second element of rape of the ICC Elements of Crimes.

Second, the means of proof of the victim's response *after* the conduct of sexual invasion that was considered by the judges as indicative of

32 *Delalić et al.* Trial Judgement, see *supra* note 12, para. 958.

33 *Ibid.*, paras. 937, 958, 960; *Gacumbitsi* Trial Judgement, see *supra* note 13, para. 202.

34 *Gacumbitsi* Trial Judgement, see *supra* note 13, para. 202.

35 *Akayesu* Trial Judgement, see *supra* note 5, para. 688; *Muhimana* Trial Judgement, see *supra* note 5, paras. 609–611.

36 *Akayesu* Trial Judgement, see *supra* note 5, para. 694.

37 *Delalić et al.* Trial Judgement, see *supra* note 12, paras. 958 and 961; *Kunarac et al.* Trial Judgement, see *supra* note 15, para. 99.

38 *Delalić et al.* Trial Judgement, see *supra* note 12, paras. 960–1.

39 *Akayesu* Trial Judgement, see *supra* note 5, para. 430 ("[Witness] said her mother begged the men, who were armed with bludgeons and machetes, to kill her daughters rather than rape them in front of her, and the man replied that the "principle was to make them suffer" and the girls were then raped […] She said her sister was raped by the other man at the same time, near her, so that they could each see what was happening to the other. Afterwards, she said she begged for death.").

40 *Delalić et al.* Trial Judgement, see *supra* note 12, para. 960.

41 *Kunarac et al.* Trial Judgement, see *supra* note 15, para. 99.

the 'coercive circumstances' can be grouped into two categories: the 'victim's utterance after the rape' and the 'victim's behavior after the rape'. For example, the evidence that the victim cursed God and protested to God for his inaction would fall into the first category of the 'victim's utterance after the rape' and demonstrates at least the "psychological oppression" that rendered the victim insulted and incapacitated in terms of her broken chastity.[42] On the other hand, the latter category of the 'victim's behavior after the rape' would encompass those facts that (i) the victim began crying each time upon seeing the perpetrator;[43] and (ii) the victim appeared to be terrified.[44] The means of proof of the victim's response after the rape can also have an impact on the adjudicator's decision on cumulative conviction and sentencing as they can be clear indications of the suffering and trauma caused by rape.[45]

Lastly, evidence of the victim's response *during* the conduct of sexual invasion can also contribute to establishing the element of 'coercive circumstances'. An example would be facts that the victim vomited while being raped,[46] or that the victim screamed from pain during the penetration of her anus.[47] What if a victim took part in the sexual intercourse actively, for instance, by taking off the trousers of the man and kissed him all over his body? This was what happened in the *Kunarac et al.* case.[48] In this incident, the victim was threatened by one of the Kunarac's subordinates that, if she failed to satisfy the desires of Kunarac, she would be killed.[49] During the trial, Kunarac claimed that he did not know that the victim was under threat and that she did not have sex with him on her own free will.[50] The Trial Chamber however found that whether Kunarac knew of the threat against the victim made by his subordinate was "irrelevant" because it was "highly improbable that the accused

42 *Delalić et al.* Trial Judgement, see *supra* note 12, para. 959 ("[After the rape by the accused] she was brought back to her room in building A in tears, where she stated that she exclaimed, "Oh, fuck you, God, in case you exist. Why did you not protect me from this?").

43 *Ibid.*, para. 959.

44 *Kunarac et al.* Trial Judgement, see *supra* note 15, para. 650.

45 See *infra* section 6.2.2.3.

46 *Gacumbitsi* Trial Judgement, see *supra* note 13, para. 203.

47 *Delalić et al.* Trial Judgement, see *supra* note 12, para. 960.

48 *Kunarac et al.* Trial Judgement, see *supra* note 15, para. 644.

49 *Ibid.*, para. 645.

50 *Ibid.*, para. 644.

Kunarac could realistically have been confused by the behavior of [the victim], given the general context of the existing war-time situation and the specifically delicate situation of the Muslim girls detained in Partizan or elsewhere in the Foča region during that time".[51] It is noteworthy that the Chamber also took into account the general religious culture of Muslim women *vis-à-vis* their sexual chastity. Apart from the question of whether the ICTY Trial Chamber actually applied the Rule 96(ii)(a),[52] from this decision, we can clearly see that the general circumstances of war and detention is becoming a significant reference point in determining the factual establishment of the second material element of rape – that is, 'coercive circumstances'.

Means of Proof of Surrounding Circumstances

In addition to 'evidence from the perpetrator's side' and 'evidence from the victim's side', 'evidence of surrounding circumstances' have contributed to international judges' findings of the element of 'coercive circumstances'. We can split the 'evidence of surrounding circumstances' into two categories of (i) immediate circumstances of fear/terror at the site of rape; and (ii) general circumstances of a coercive nature.

As to the first category of 'immediate circumstances of fear/terror at the site of rape', the relevant case law acknowledges the following means of proof: (i) the victim saw another victim being killed/quartered;[53] (ii) the victim was approached by attackers who killed her mother some minutes ago;[54] (iii) gang-rape: victim being raped by a number of persons;[55] (iv) rape in public: victim being raped in the presence of other men;[56] (v) per-

51 *Ibid.*, para. 646.

52 International Criminal Tribunal for the former Yugoslavia, Rules of Procedure and Evidence, IT/32/Rev. 45, 8 December 2010, Rule 96(ii)(a): "consent shall not be allowed as a defence if the victim (a) has been subjected to or threatened with or has had reason to fear violence, duress, detention or psychological oppression, […]". In this incident, the victim was raped by three men in a row immediately before having the sexual intercourse with Kunarac. Thus, the Trial Chamber might have just rejected the Kunarac's defense of ignorance of the fact that the victim did not have sex from her own free will by just invoking the Rule 96(ii)(a) of the ICTY Rules of Procedure and Evidence, without explaining the substantive reasons it specified in paragraph 646 of the judgement.

53 *Gacumbitsi* Trial Judgement, see *supra* note 13, para. 204.

54 *Ibid.*, para. 208.

55 *Kunarac et al.* Trial Judgement, see *supra* note 15, para. 653.

56 *Delalić et al.* Trial Judgement, see *supra* note 12, para. 937.

petrator being armed with weapons;[57] and (vi) the victim being raped while the perpetrator's weapon was placed on the table.[58] On the other hand, in relation to the second category of means of proof concerning 'general circumstances of a coercive nature', the jurisprudence of *ad hoc* tribunals accepts the followings as constituting the second element of rape: (i) the victim being detained legally or illegally;[59] (ii) the victim being in captivity; and (iii) the victim's being interrogated.[60] At this juncture, it should be reminded that the relevant case law discussing the evidentiary value, for the purpose of rape, of general circumstances such as a widespread or systematic attack or an armed conflict, attempts to address the question of whether the absence of consent is an element of rape or not. To sum up, what the case law states is that the existence of an armed conflict, for example, can be relied upon for the purpose of presuming the 'absence of the victim's consent', but not the 'coercive circumstances'. Put differently, the prosecution cannot invoke the existence of an armed conflict in order to shift the burden of proof on the element of 'coercive circumstances' to the accused. That is because the element of 'coercive circumstances' is not to be presumed by the existence of an armed conflict. The burden of proof to establish the second element of rape stays with the prosecution no matter how strong the evidence of armed conflict may be. Only the absence of consent is to be presumed by the evidence of contextual elements of core international crimes.[61]

---

[57] *Kunarac et al.* Trial Judgement, see *supra* note 15, para. 640; *Delalić et al.* Trial Judgement, see *supra* note 12, paras. 960–1.

[58] *Kunarac et al.* Trial Judgement, see *supra* note 15, para. 724.

[59] *Delalić et al.* Trial Judgement, see *supra* note 12, paras. 937 and 955.

[60] *Ibid.*, para. 937 ("Ms. Cecez was interrogated by Mr. Delić who asked her about the whereabouts of her husband […]"); para. 955.

[61] In the same vein, the SCSL Trial Chamber in the RUF case states as to the crime of forced marriage, "[…] the Chamber is of the opinion and so holds, that in hostile and coercive circumstances of this nature, there should be a presumption of absence of genuine consent to […] contracting marriages with the said RUF fights". See Special Court for Sierra Leone, *Prosecutor v. Sesay et al.*, Case No. SCSL-04-15-T, Judgement, 2 March 2009 ("RUF Trial Judgement"), para. 1471.

6.2.2.3. Means of Proof of the 'Effects of Rape/Trauma (Consequence)'?

As briefly explained above,[62] rape is a conduct crime (as opposed to result crime) in the sense that it does not require any material element of 'result'/'consequence'. In other words, the 'conduct' of invasion and the 'circumstance' of coercive circumstance suffice for the constitution of the crime. Thus, for the satisfaction of the elements of rape, the prosecution is not required to adduce any evidence showing the physical or psychological effects of rape against the victim or his or her family after the rape. The international judges however generally pay attention to the sufferings of rape victims and describe them in their judgements.[63] Though the effects of rape are legally irrelevant to whether the crime of rape to be constituted, the facts concerning thereof are legally relevant in two respects. First, facts of the adverse effects of rape can play the role of means of proof for the offence of torture cumulatively charged on the basis of the same conduct of rape.[64] Not only does each of the offences of rape and

---

62 See *supra* notes 8–10 and their accompanying texts.

63 See, *e.g.*, *Delalić et al.* Trial Judgement, see *supra* note 12, paras. 938 and 957.

64 As to the issue of cumulative charging and cumulative conviction under the ICC law, paragraph 9 of the Introduction to the ICC Elements of Crimes provides, "[a] particular conduct may constitute one or more crimes". Note that the ICC Pre-Trial Chamber in its confirmation of the charge decision in *Bemba* rejects the Prosecution's cumulative charging practice *vis-à-vis* rape and torture. The reasons explained in the decision, however, seem odd. While the Pre-Trial Chamber endorses the different element test adopted by the *Delalić et al.* Appeals Chamber of the ICTY, it declines to approve the cumulative charges of rape and torture, mistakenly considering that torture is a sort of a lesser included offence of rape. This result is caused by the Pre-Trial Chamber's incorrect assessment of the different element test. Instead of comparing the *elements (law)* of torture and the *elements (law)* of rape, the Chamber compares the *elements (law)* of torture and the *potential effects (fact)* of rape. This clearly violates the underlying principle in applying the different element test as set forth in the *Delalić et al.* Appeals Judgement and the U.S. jurisprudence on the Blockburger test from which the *Delalić et al.* Appeals Chamber copied the different element test – *i.e.*, the principle of comparing the law only, not facts. More specifically, the *Bemba* Pre-Trial Chamber seems to make a mistake when it takes into account severe pain and suffering of a rape victim (that is, legally speaking, only an acoompanying *fact* of rape, but not an element as such) for its assessment of the different element test. Namely, since severe pain and suffering is not an element of rape, it must not be considered in comparing the elements of rape and another offence for the purpose of the different element test. Yet, the *Bemba* Pre-Trial Chamber concludes that torture is fully subsumed within the offence of rape because severe pain and suffering is an "*in-*

herent specific material elemen[t]" of rape. This is simply wrong. Severe pain and suffering is an *inherently accompanying fact* of rape, but not an element. Since it is not an element, severe pain and suffering should not play any role for the application of the different element test. The Pre-Trial Chamber seems to have confused the concepts of 'element' with 'fact' that can possibly accompany the proof of an element. Legally speaking, a conviction of rape is still possible where the victim of rape did not experience any severe pain and suffering. Summing up, contrary to the *Bemba* Pre-Trial Chamber's understanding, severe pain and suffering is not an element of rape. The Prosecution cannot charge the extermination and murder cumulatively based on the same conduct because the latter does not have a materially distinct element not included in the former. Yet, it can charge rape and torture cumulatively as *each* offence has a materially distinct element from the other – *i.e.*, the element of 'severe pain of suffering' of torture not included in the elements of rape; and the element of 'invasion' of rape not included in the elements of torture. See *Bemba* Confirmation of Charges Decision, see *supra* note 5, paras. 202–5 ("[…] The Chamber considers that, as a matter of fairness and expeditiousness of the proceedings, only distinct crimes may justify a cumulative charging approach and, ultimately, be confirmed as charges. This is only possible if each statutory provision allegedly breached in relation to one and the same conduct requires at least one additional material element not contained in the other. […] The Chamber considers that in this particular case, the specific material elements of the act of torture, namely severe pain and suffering and control by the perpetrator over the person, are also the inherent specific material elements of the act of rape. However, the act of rape requires the additional specific material element of penetration, which makes it the most appropriate legal characterization in this particular case. […] The Chamber therefore considers that the act of torture is fully subsumed by the count of rape."); International Criminal Tribunal for the former Yugoslavia, *Prosecutor v. Delalić et al.*, Case No. IT-96-21-A, Judgement, 20 February 2001, paras. 412–3 ("Having considered the different approaches expressed on this issue both within this Tribunal and other jurisdictions, this Appeals Chamber holds that reasons of fairness to the accused and the consideration that only distinct crimes may justify multiple convictions, lead to the conclusion that multiple criminal convictions entered under different statutory provisions but based on the same conduct are permissible only if each statutory provision involved has a materially distinct element not contained in the other. An element is materially distinct from another if it requires proof of a fact not required by the other. Where this test is not met, the Chamber must decide in relation to which offence it will enter a conviction. This should be done on the basis of the principle that the conviction under the more specific provision should be upheld. Thus, if a set of facts is regulated by two provisions, one of which contains an additional materially distinct element, then a conviction should be entered only under that provision."); *Blockburger v. United States*, 284 US 299, 304 (1932), as cited in International Criminal Tribunal for the former Yugoslavia, *Prosecutor v. Kupreskić et al.*, Case No. IT-95-16-T, Judgement, 14 January 2000, para. 681. ("The applicable rule is that where the same act or transaction constitutes a violation of two distinct statutory provisions, the test to be applied to determine whether there are two offences or only one, is whether each provision requires torture include a materially distinct element from the other ('severe pain and suffering' of torture; and 'physical invasion' of rape);[65] the interests protected by rape (sexual autonomy) also differ from that protected by torture (physical and mental integrity).[66] Second, such facts of a rape victim's short-term or long-term sufferings would have a significant impact on the determination of sentence pursuant to Rule 145(1)(c) of the ICC Rules of Procedure and Evidence that provides,

> In its determination of the sentence [...], the Court shall [...] give consideration, *inter alia*, to the extent of the damage caused, in particular the harm caused to the victims and their families [...].

---

proof of an additional fact which the other does not."). For more about the *Blockburger* test and the charging considerations for international sex crimes, see David Luban, Julie O'Sullivan and David Stewart, *Transnational and International Criminal Law*, Aspen Publishers, 2010, pp. 1178–1189.

65 *Kunarac et al.* Trial Judgement, see *supra* note 15, para. 557. Note however that other judgements of the *ad hoc* tribunals took a bit different position. Namely, the ICTY Appeals Chamber in *Kunarac* and the ICTR Trial Chamber in *Semanza* found the element of 'prohibited purposes' to be the materially distinct element of torture *vis-à-vis* rape. See *Kunarac et al.* Appeals Judgement, see *supra* note 5, para. 179; International Criminal Tribunal for Rwanda, *Prosecutor v. Semanza*, Case No. ICTR-97-20-T, Judgement and Sentence, 15 May 2003, para. 506. In the context of the ICC law, however, this jurisprudence can be relevant only for torture as a war crime because the ICC Elements of Crimes keeps the 'prohibited purposes' element only for torture as a war crime, but not for torture as a crime against humanity.

66 International Criminal Tribunal for the former Yugoslavia, *Prosecutor v. Kupreskić et al.*, IT-95-16-T, Decision on Defence Challenges to Form of the Indictment, 15 May 1998, p. 1. ("CONSIDERING FURTHER that the Prosecutor may be justified in bringing cumulative charges when the Article of the Statute referred to are designed to protect different values and when each Article requires proof of a legal element not required by the others"); International Criminal Tribunal for the former Yugoslavia, *Prosecutor v. Naletilić et al.*, Case No. IT-98-34-T, Decision on Vinko Martinović's Objection to the Amended Indictment and Mladen Naletilić's Preliminary Motion to the Amended Indictment, 14 February 2001 ("Reference was made to the principles distilled in the Kupreskić Judgement of 14 January 2000,17 namely that cumulative charges will be permitted where each offence requires proof of an element that the other does not (the "different elements" test), or alternatively, where each offence protects substantially different values (although this would seldom be used as an independent ground for permitting cumulative charges.).").

Relevant sentencing judgements of the *ad hoc* tribunals take into consideration the impact of rape on victims as an aggravating circumstance.[67]

6.3. Forced Marriage as Other Inhumane Act

6.3.1. Prosecutorial Choice due to the Absence of a Specific Provision of Forced Marriage

The SCSL is the first ever international institution that has developed jurisprudence on the crime of forced marriage. The innate difficulty however in bringing the accused to account for this offence was the absence of a specific provision of 'forced marriage' in the statutes of international criminal tribunals. Faced with this situation, the Prosecution of the SCSL chose the 'other inhumane acts' as a crime against humanity for the prosecution of this offence,[68] instead of another candidate in its statute: 'any other form of sexual violence'.[69] As discussed by the relevant case law, what if the Prosecution charged the offence of 'forced marriage' invoking the catch-all sexual crime provision of 'any other form of sexual violence'? Is there any difference in terms of evidence to be adduced depending on the Prosecution's charging decision in one way or the other between the two options of 'other inhumane acts' and 'any other form of sexual violence'? The answer is yes in a significant sense. The Prosecution's charging decision in this regard would change the legal nature of the offence of 'forced marriage'. That is, if the Prosecution charged 'forced marriage' as 'any other form of sexual violence', the Prosecution would not be required to prove any 'consequence' as a material element of the offence of 'forced marriage'. To the contrary, the Prosecution's

[67] See, *e.g.*, International Criminal Tribunal for the former Yugoslavia, *Prosecutor v. Bralo*, Case No. IT-95-17-S, Sentencing Judgement, 7 December 2005, para. 39.

[68] Statute of the Special Court for Sierra Leone, ("SCSL Statute"), art. 2(i). In this connection, note that the Closing Order of the Case 002 of the Extraordinary Chambers in the Courts of Cambodia also charges 'forced marriage' as 'other inhumane acts'. See Extraordinary Chambers in the Courts of Cambodia, Case File No. 002/19-09-2007-ECCC-OCIJ, Closing Order, 15 September 2010.

[69] *Ibid.*, art. 2(g). Note that, contrary to the view of the *AFRC* Trial Chamber, the *AFRC* Appeals Chamber held that 'forced marriage' is a crime distinct from 'sexual slavery'. The Appeals Chamber also clarified that 'forced marriage' is a crime of non-sexual nature. This position was followed by subsequent RUF case, which ultimately resulted in the first conviction of the crime of 'forced marriage'.

decision to charge 'forced marriage' as an 'inhumane act' would shift the legal nature of the offence of 'forced marriage' to being a 'result crime' as the element of 'great suffering or serious injury' is required to be proven.[70] In short, the Prosecution's charging decision in this context would make a significant difference in terms of the means of proof needed to secure the conviction of 'forced marriage', which might have a considerable impact on the management of judicial resources. The key question would be how the future development of relevant international jurisprudence will treat the victims' sufferings caused as a result of the imposition of forced conjugal association. If such sufferings are to be recognized as a necessary legal component of the offence of 'forced marriage', the option of charging it under the heading of 'any other form of sexual violence' would disappear. On the other hand, if future international judges think that the *conduct* of imposing forced conjugal association in a war time situation or during an attack on civilians is itself grave enough for the imposition of criminal sanctions, 'consequence of the conduct' ('sufferings') might not be needed as an element of 'forced marriage'.[71] If this is the case, the offence of 'any other form of sexual violence' would still remain as a viable option in charging the offence of 'forced marriage'. The point is that it is unclear whether the judges at the SCSL included great suffering as one of the elements of 'forced marriage' because 'other inhumane acts' requires it, or because they thought great suffering is an inherent and essential legal requirement of 'forced marriage'.[72]

---

70 The elements of the offence of 'other inhumane acts' in the jurisprudence of the SCSL are the same as those provided in the ICC Elements of Crimes. See Special Court for Sierra Leone, *Prosecutor v. Brima et al.*, SCSL-2004-17-A, Judgment, 22 February 2008, ("*AFRC* Appeals Judgement"), para. 198; *AFRC* Trial Judgement, see *supra* note 5, para. 698; RUF Trial Judgement, see *supra* note 61, para. 168.

71 An example of this changing jurisprudence in terms of elements of a crime would be that of the war crime of 'attacking civilian population' as provided in articles 8(2)(b)(i) and 8(2)(e)(i) of the ICC Statute. While the jurisprudence of the *ad hoc* tribunals was generally of the view that the consequence of the attack (*e.g.*, civilians being killed) is an element of the crime, the ICC Elements of Crimes does not require any such consequence. Note however that the ICC Elements of Crimes enhanced the level of mental element by requiring that the perpetrator *intended* civilians to be the object of the attack.

72 See *infra* note 76 and the accompanying texts. See, *e.g.*, *AFRC* Appeals Judgement, see *supra* note 70, para. 193 ("[Judge Doherty, in her Partly Dissenting Opinion] further considered that [forced marriage] satisfied the elements of "Other Inhumane Acts" because victims were subjected to mental trauma by being labeled as rebel

6.3.2. Elements: 'Imposing Forced Conjugal Association (Conduct)', 'Physical or Mental Suffering (Consequence)' and 'Gravity'

The SCSL Appeals Chamber in the *AFRC* case defines 'forced marriage' as "a situation in which the perpetrator through his words or conduct, or those of someone for whose actions he is responsible, compels a person by force, threat of force, or coercion to serve as a conjugal partner resulting in severe suffering, or physical, mental or psychological injury to the victim".[73] The pertinent jurisprudence of the SCSL is of the view that there are two elements of 'forced marriage': (i) imposition of forced conjugal association;[74] and (ii) great suffering or serious injury.[75] It should be noted that the process of drawing the elements of 'forced marriage' at the SCSL was to a significant extent influenced by the facts of the conflict at Sierra Leone.[76]

6.3.3. Means of Proof

6.3.3.1. Means of Proof of 'Imposing Forced Conjugal Association (Conduct)'

The means of proof in relation to the material element of 'conduct' of the offence of 'forced marriage' – that is, 'imposition of forced conjugal association'[77] – are to be discussed below in accordance with the pattern of

---

"wives"; further, they were stigmatized and found it difficult to reintegrate into their communities."). What this portion of the judgement seems to say is that *facts* of forced marriage satisfy the *elements* of 'other inhumane acts".

73 *AFRC* Appeals Judgement, see *supra* note 70, para. 196.

74 RUF Trial Judgement, see *supra* note 61, para. 1295. Note that, following the explanation of the *AFRC* Appeals Chamber, the RUF Trial Judgement specify the element of 'forced conjugal association' one step further by stating, "forced conjugal association based on *exclusivity* between the perpetrator and victim." (emphasis added). See *AFRC* Appeals Judgement, see *supra* note 70, paras. 191–5; RUF Trial Judgement, see *supra* note 61, para. 2306.

75 *AFRC* Appeals Judgement, see *supra* note 70, paras. 195–6; RUF Trial Judgement, see *supra* note 61, para. 1296.

76 Note, *e.g.*, that some paragraphs discussing what are the elements of 'forced marriage in the *AFRC* Appeals Chamber start with the phrases "[i]n light of all the evidence at trial," or "[b]ased on the evidence on record,". See *AFRC* Appeals Judgement, see *supra* note 70, paras. 193 and 195.

77 RUF Trial Judgement, see *supra* note 61, para. 1295 ("In relation to Count 8, the Chamber is satisfied that the conduct described by numerous reliable witnesses that

the "bush wife" phenomenon as found by the SCSL Trial Chamber in the RUF case. The *RUF* Trial Judgement in which the accused was convicted of the offence of 'forced marriage' for the first time in the history of international criminal tribunals explains the pattern of the "bush wife" phenomenon as follows:

> The Chamber concludes from the evidence […] that a consistent pattern of conduct existed towards women who were forced into conjugal relationships. These "wives" were "married" against their will, forced to engage in sexual intercourse and perform domestic chores, and were unable to leave their "husbands" for fear of violent retribution. The Chamber is satisfied that the "husbands" were aware of the power exercised over their "wives" and therefore were aware that their "wives" did not genuinely consent to the "marriage" or perform conjugal "duties" including sexual intercourse and domestic labour of their own free volition.[78]

The means of proof for the element of the 'imposition of forced conjugal association' in the *RUF* case fits well into this factual pattern as set out below under the subsections of: (i) "wives" being captured/abducted and "married" against their will (factors of force, threat, coercion, violence and oppression); (ii) performing household chores; (iii) the victims unable to escape their "husbands" (for fear of violent retribution); and (iv) rape and other sexual activities. Together with the means of proof related to the 'detention' part of subsection (i) as explained below, subsections (ii) to (iv) are taken from the facts during the extended period of "living together" with "husbands".

Means of Proof of "Wives" being Captured/Abducted and "Married" against their Will (Factors of Force, Threat, Coercion, Violence and Oppression)

For this subsection, we can spot the following means of proof from the SCSL jurisprudence: (i) widespread and regular practice/pattern of abduction of women for the purpose of having them serve as "wives" of commanders;[79] (ii) the victims being forcibly taken from their husbands, par-

rebels captured women and "took them as their wives" in Koidu and Wendedu satisfies the *actus reus* of 'forced marriage,' namely the imposition of a forced conjugal association.").

78 *Ibid.*, para. 1293.

79 *Ibid.*, paras. 1409–11.

ents, and home villages;[80] (iii) most of the young girls captured beingforced to be the 'wives' of commanders;[81] (iv) the victims, especially beautiful women, becoming wives of commanders;[82] (v) a family member begging for the release of a girl about to be taken by rebels as a wife of a commander, and the rebels responding by saying, "your life, your sister, which of the two do you want?";[83] (vi) the victim being asked to marry by a rebel;[84] (vii) the victim accepting an offer to marry a rebel because she did not want to die;[85] (viii) the victims having no option but to submit to a 'husband' as they were in no position to negotiate their freedom;[86] (ix) the absence of parental and family consent to the so-called "marriage";[87] (x) a 16 year-old-girl being captured and declared to be a commander's wife, and the commander agreeing on the spot;[88] (xi) rebels claiming that captured women were their "wives" (commander's claims that captured women were their wives, stating, "there is no wedlock from the family. Just because of gun, you've taken her to be your wife, using her as your wife.");[89] (xii) rebels distributing the female captives among themselves, with each rebel saying "this is my own wife";[90] (xiii) rebels fighting each other over a woman;[91] (xiv) the victim being expected to show loyalty to

80 *Ibid.*, paras. 1155, 1406–7, 1412 and 1460; *AFRC* Trial Judgement, see *supra* note 5, para. 711.

81 *Ibid.*, para. 1565.

82 *Ibid.*, paras. 1155 and 1408

83 *Ibid.*, para. 1178.

84 *Ibid.*, para. 1408.

85 *Ibid.*, para. 1408.

86 *Ibid.*, para. 1412.

87 *Ibid.*, para. 1469 ("The Defence also contends that the marriages which were so contracted were conducted with the requisite consent of the parties involved. The Chamber observes, however, that parental and family consent to the so-called marriages of these sexually enslaved and abused women was conspicuously absent."). Note here that the Chamber use the Sierra Leone tradition of arranged marriage in responding to the Defence's submission.

88 *Ibid.*, para. 1178 ("One of the Junta boys then captured TF1-217's 16-year old sister and declared "This is Captain Bai Bureh's wife". Bai Bureh said, "Yes, this is a beautiful lady".)

89 *Ibid.*, para. 1179.

90 *Ibid.*, para. 1211.

91 *Ibid.*, para. 1408. This means of proof can be considered indicative of the exclusive nature of the relationship between a rebel "husband" and a female captive. See *supra* note 74.

her "husband";[92] (xv) soldiers who captured civilians having a right to rape them and make them their wives;[93] (xvi) none of the victims giving evidence that they considered themselves to be in fact "married";[94] (xvii) the victims' repeated assertion that they had been "taken as wives";[95] (xviii) a victim's testimony that she did not consent to the conjugal arrangement;[96] (xix) the absence of evidence that the victims stayed with their rebel "husbands" after the war;[97] (xx) the victim's status as a married woman being no bar for her to become one of the 'bush wives';[98] (xxi) the general war time atmosphere/environment of violent, hostile, and coercive nature;[99] (xxii) the victim wife and rebel husband living together in the same house/place;[100] (xxiii) the duration of captivity/detention as a "wife";[101] and (xxiv) a rebel husband taking a victim ("wife") together with him when he moved to another place/area/region where the "wife" continued working for him and continued being forced to have intercourse with him.[102]

---

92 *Ibid.*, para. 1413.

93 *Ibid.*, para. 1562.

94 *AFRC* Trial Judgement, see *supra* note 5, para. 712. This example, together with (xix), shows that the judges also considered the 'absence of positive evidence' *vis-à-vis* the 'existence of the victim's genuine consent'. Note that the 'absence of genuine consent' is not an element of 'forced marriage', and thus the Prosecution does not bear the burden of proof thereof. See also *infra* texts accompanying the note 103.

95 *Ibid.*, para. 712.

96 RUF Trial Judgement, see *supra* note 61, paras. 1179 and 1211 ("[It was] not my wish, because somebody is not your husband and you are just taken and given to the person. I was not really happy about it.").

97 *AFRC* Trial Judgement, see *supra* note 5, para. 712.

98 RUF Trial Judgement, see *supra* note 61, para. 1412.

99 *Ibid.*, para. 163 ("The Chamber subscribes to the statement of the ICTY Appeals Chamber [in Kunarac case] that "circumstances which render it impossible to express consent may be sufficient to presume the absence of consent, […].""); *Ibid.*, paras. 1466 ("The Chamber finds that acts of sexual violence were intentionally committed against women and girls in the context of a hostile and coercive war environment in which genuine consent was not possible. The Chamber also finds that when the rebels forcefully took victims as 'wives' they intended to deprive them of their liberty.").

100 *Ibid.*, paras. 1212 and 1406.

101 *Ibid.*, paras. 1213 ("TF1-016 was held captive with Kotor for a period of one year and three months."); *Ibid.*, 1406 ("From 1994 to 1998, TF1-314 was in Buedu as part of the Small Girl Unit ("SGU")).''; *Ibid.*, 1460 ("from 1994 to 1998").

102 *Ibid.*, paras. 1213, 1408 and 1561; *AFRC* Trial Judgement, see *supra* note 5, para. 711.

For this subsection, the relevant means of proof generally contain the feature of force/coercion, and are therefore considered by the judges as indicative of the absence of genuine consent from the wives to the "marriage". In cases before the SCSL, the basic fact pattern of abduction and subsequent period of 'living together' during which various forms of both the sexual and non-sexual violence were inflicted upon victims was obvious. Thus the accused's preferred line of defence was that the 'marriage' was in fact not forced and not against the victim's will. The answer of the SCSL judges to this assertion was the presumption of an absence of genuine consent, following the same logic explained by the relevant case law of the ICTY and the ICTR *vis-à-vis* rape.[103] The *AFRC* Trial Chamber, for instance, held that despite the fact that a victim "had been married to her husband in a ceremony […] no consent could be inferred given the environment of violence and coercion".[104]

Means of Proof of Performing Household Chores

In the jurisprudence of the SCSL, the second subsection of means of proof for 'imposing forced conjugal association' can be identified under the heading of 'performing household chores'. In this respect, the following means of proof are mentioned in the *RUF* Trial Judgements: (i) the victim being forced to do cooking;[105] (ii) the victim being forced to pound rice;[106] (iii) the victim being forced to do washing/cleaning;[107] (iii) the victim being forced to do laundering;[108] and (iv) the victim being forced to carry the possessions of her "husband" when he was deployed.[109]

---

[103] See *supra* note 99. See also Special Court for Sierra Leone, Rules of Procedure and Evidence, Amended on 28 May 2010, Rule 96(i) ("[c]onsent cannot be inferred by reason of any words or conduct of a victim where force, threat of force, coercion or taking advantage of a coercive environment undermined the victim's ability to give voluntary and genuine consent.").

[104] *AFRC* Trial Judgement, see *supra* note 5, para. 712.

[105] RUF Trial Judgement, see *supra* note 61, paras. 1154–5, 1212, 1406–7, 1408, 1561 and 1565.

[106] *Ibid.*, para. 1212.

[107] *Ibid.*, para. 1212.

[108] *Ibid.*, paras. 1406–8.

[109] *Ibid.*, para. 1413.

Means of Proof of Restriction of Movement/Escape and Various Punishments[110]

The third subsection of means of proof for the element of 'imposing forced conjugal association' includes: (i) the victim being too afraid to attempt an escape because armed rebels were everywhere around;[111] (ii) the victim being unable to escape because civilians who attempted to escape were liable to be killed or fall into the hands of killers;[112] (iii) the victim attempting to escape was punished with beatings;[113] (iv) the victim being summoned, accused and threatened to be killed for inciting other captives to attempt to escape;[114] (v) the victim not making any attempt to talk to other civilians outside of her house, because it was not permitted and the rebels punished such behaviour by death;[115] (vi) the victim being sent to the front line as a punishment for trying to escape;[116] and (vii) the victim being unable to escape as her "husband" ordered an armed guard to watch her.[117]

Means of Proof of Rape and Other Sexual Activities

The forth subsection of means of proof concerning the element of 'imposing forced conjugal association' is related to rape and forced sexual violence. The Trial Chamber in the *RUF* case noted the following means of proof in its judgement: (i) the victim being forced to have sex with the "husband" (on a regular basis);[118] (ii) the victim becoming pregnant;[119] (iii) the victims being forced to "serve the commanders as their wives", meaning that the rebels used the women for sexual purposes.[120] In particular, the judges took into account the following means of proof in finding the forced nature of such sexual intercourse: (i) the victims being raped;[121]

110 *Ibid.*, para. 1212 ("If we attempt to go somewhere, they will do something bad with us.").

111 *Ibid.*, para. 1212.

112 *Ibid.*, paras. 1407, 1412 and 1460.

113 *Ibid.*, para. 1561.

114 *Ibid.*, para. 1213.

115 *Ibid.*, para. 1213.

116 *Ibid.*, para. 1467.

117 *Ibid.*, para. 1561.

118 *Ibid.*, paras. 1212, 1406–7, 1408, 1413, 1460, 1560–2 and 1565.

119 *Ibid.*, para. 1413.

120 *Ibid.*, para. 1155.

121 *Ibid.*, paras. 1154–5, 1406, 1408, 1460 and 1564.

(ii) the victim's direct resistance and expression of non-consent to rebel husbands (for example, attempts from the victim to tell the "husband" that she does not consent to sexual intercourse;[122] women in the camp screaming at night "leave me, leave me, leave me alone. You did not bring me for this. I'm not your wife.";[123] and victims complaining to the "husband" about forcible sexual intercourse[124]); (iii) the victim being sent to the frontline as a punishment for refusing sexual intercourse with her "husband";[125] and (iv) general wartime atmosphere/environment of violent, hostile and coercive nature.[126]

6.3.3.2. Means of Proof of 'Physical or Mental Suffering (Consequence)'

Before embarking on a detailed overview of the relevant means of proof concerning the 'consequence' element of 'forced marriage' ('physical and mental sufferings'), it should be borne in mind that, generally speaking, the means of proof for the first element of 'imposing forced conjugal association' as set out in the previous section were also considered pertinent. In this respect, the *RUF* Trial Chamber held,

> The Chamber concludes that TF1-093 was taken after the rainy season of 1996 to Kailahun District where she was forced into an exclusive conjugal relationship with Superman and was forced to become his 'wife'. The Chamber is satisfied that TF1-093 was incapable of giving her genuine consent and became Superman's 'wife' because she feared she would have been killed. As Superman's wife, she cooked and did laundry for him and had sex with him, *all of which caused her to endure physical and mental suffering.*[127] (emphasis added)

Compared with the means of proof set out in the previous section, the means of proof of physical and psychological sufferings in this section are generally of a nature of having long-term effects.

---

122 *Ibid.*, para. 1212.

123 *Ibid.*, para. 1179 (Those women later told other captured civilians that "they were forced to have sex with the rebels at night.").

124 *Ibid.*, para. 1212.

125 *Ibid.*, para. 1413.

126 *Ibid.*, paras. 1470 and 1471. See also *supra* note 99.

127 *Ibid.*, para. 1463.

Means of Proof of Physical Suffering

The *RUF* Trial Judgement takes note of the following means of proof in its findings of physical suffering of 'wives': (i) physical injuries caused by forced sexual intercourse;[128] (ii) most of the victims experiencing miscarriages without receiving any medical attention;[129] (iii) the victim experiencing diverse medical problems such as severe stomach pains; some having their uterus removed; menstrual cycles becoming irregular; some being infected with sexually transmitted diseases and others testing HIV positive;[130] (iv) the victim being physically battered during and after pregnancies;[131] (v) the victim being injured from forced labour;[132] (vi) the victim being attacked by rebels;[133] (vii) the victim being habitually given drugs, including cannabis sativa, tablets and also gunpowder to eat.[134]

Means of Proof of Mental Suffering

As regards the mental suffering of victims, the following means of proof were accepted by the judges of the *RUF* Trial Chamber: (i) the victim being psychologically terrorized by their 'husbands' who thereby demonstrated their control over their wives;[135] (ii) psychological manipulations of the victim's feelings caused by deliberate and strategic use of the term 'wife', which rendered the victim unable to deny the 'husband's wishes;[136] (iii) the victim being psychologically traumatized by being forced to watch the killing and mutilation of close family members (before becoming 'bush wife').[137]

Means of Proof of Social Stigma

We can draw the following means of proof from the *RUF* Trial Judgement in relation to the Chamber's finding of victims' suffering from the

---

128 *Ibid.*, para. 1296.

129 Special Court for Sierra Leone, *Prosecutor v. Sesay et al.*, Case No. SCSL-04-15-A, Judgment, 26 October 2009 ("RUF Appeals Judgement"), para. 192.

130 *Ibid.*, para. 192.

131 *Ibid.*, para. 192.

132 RUF Trial Judgement, see *supra* note 61, para. 1212 ("I did everything […] I used to do all this work up to an extent all my hands were all blistered.").

133 *Ibid.*, para. 1408.

134 *Ibid.*, paras. 1408 and 1463 ("The Chamber also finds that Superman gave drugs to TF1-093 which reflects his intention to further abuse and exercise control over her.").

135 RUF Appeals Judgement, see *supra* note 129, para. 192.

136 *Ibid.*, para. 192.

137 *Ibid.*, para. 199.

social stigma of being 'wives' of rebels: (i) long-term social stigmatisation suffered by both victims and their children in cases of victims becoming pregnant from the forced marriage;[138] (ii) lasting social stigma attached to the forced conjugal association;[139] (iii) the victim's recovery being hampered by a lasting social stigma;[140] (iv) the victim's reintegration into society being hampered by a lasting social stigma.[141]

6.3.3.3. Means of Proof of 'Gravity'

Since the Prosecution charged 'forced marriage' under the heading of 'other inhumane acts' as a crime against humanity as provided in article 2(i) of the SCSL Statute, the *RUF* Trial Chamber also considered the gravity of the relevant conduct of 'forced marriage'.[142] In deciding the degree of gravity, the Trial Chamber mainly drew on the means of proof related to the consequence of 'forced marriage' – that is, the victims' suffering – especially the long-term social stigma inflicted upon the 'wives'. It states,

> The Chamber observes that the conjugal association forced upon the victims carried with it a lasting social stigma which hampers their recovery and reintegration into society. This suffering is in addition to the physical injuries that forced intercourse commonly inflicted on women taken as "wives". The Chamber thus finds that the perpetrators' actions in taking "wives" in Koidu inflicted grave suffering and serious

---

138 *Ibid.*, para. 199.

139 RUF Trial Judgement, see *supra* note 61, para. 1296.

140 *Ibid.*, para. 1296.

141 *Ibid.*, paras. 1296, 1351. See also *RUF* Trial Judgment, note 2514.

142 *Ibid.*, para. 168 set out the elements of 'other inhumane acts' as a crime against humanity as follows:

(i) The occurrence of an act or omission that inflicts great suffering or serious injury to body, or to mental or physical health;
(ii) The act or omission is sufficiently similar in gravity to the acts referred to in Article 2(a) to Article 2(h) of the Statute;
(iii) The Accused was aware of the factual circumstances that established the character of the gravity of the act; and
(iv) The Accused, at the time of the act or omission, had the intention to commit inhumane act or acted in the knowledge that this would likely to occur.

See also *supra* note 70.

> injury to the physical and mental health of the victims, and that the perpetrators were aware of the gravity of their actions.[143]

On the same subject of gravity assessment, the means of proof examined by the *AFRC* Appeals Chamber were broader in scope. In addition to the 'consequence' of 'forced marriage', it also took into account (i) the nature of the perpetrators' conduct; (ii) the atmosphere of violence in which victims were abducted; and (iii) the vulnerability of women and girls, especially those of a very young age.[144]

6.3.3.4. Means of Proof of Mental Element for 'Gravity'

While the *RUF* Trial Chamber did not specify the means of proof in this regard, the *AFRC* Appeals Judgement specifically addressed the issue. The Judgement inferred the perpetrator's knowledge from the following means of proof:[145] (i) the systematic and forcible abduction of the victims of forced marriage; (ii) the prevailing environment of coercion and intimidation; and (iii) the fact that the acts described as forced marriage may have involved the commission of one or more international crimes such as enslavement, imprisonment, rape, sexual slavery, and abduction among others.[146]

6.4. Sexual Slavery in the SCSL Jurisprudence

6.4.1. Overview

The *RUF* Trial Judgement in the SCSL is the only international case law in which the accused have been found guilty of the offence of 'sexual slavery' *per se*.[147] It should be noted however that the accused in the *AFRC* case have also been found guilty of 'outrages upon personal dignity' based on the evidence of sexual slavery. That is, though the Trial

[143] RUF Trial Judgement, see *supra* note 61, para. 1296.

[144] *AFRC* Appeals Judgement, see *supra* note 70, para. 200.

[145] Note that the 'gravity' as a normative element of a crime is not an object of the mental element of 'intent'.

[146] *AFRC* Appeals Judgement, see *supra* note 70, para. 201.

[147] ICC Statute and the SCSL Statute are the only two statutes of international criminal tribunals in which the crime of 'sexual slavery' is independently provided. See ICC Statute, Arts. 7(1)(g), 8(2)(b)(xxii), 8(2)(e)(vi); and the SCSL Statute, see *supra* note 68, Art. 2(g).

Chamber in the *AFRC* case dismissed count 7 (sexual slavery and any other form of sexual violence) for duplicity, the Trial Chamber still considered relevant evidence of sexual slavery under the charge of 'outrages upon personal dignity' (count 9) for the purpose of deciding whether the offence of sexual slavery had been constituted.[148] This is evident from the fact that, in the section on 'outrages upon personal dignity', the *AFRC* Trial Chamber repeatedly uses the phrase "the elements of sexual slavery are established".[149] In short, in the *AFRC* case, though the charge of sexual slavery was dismissed on its face, evidentiary analysis in respect of the elements of sexual slavery was still performed by the Trial Chamber. Thus, the 'outrages of personal dignity' section of the *AFRC* Trial Judgement is still a source from which we can find the means of proof of sexual slavery.

In the *RUF* case, the Trial Chamber concluded that all the four charges of sexual violence – that is, 'rape' (count 6), 'sexual slavery' (count 7), 'other inhumane act (forced marriage)' (count 8) and 'outrages upon personal dignity' (count 9) – were proven. Particularly, it deserves our attention that the judges found the accused guilty of the charges of sexual slavery and 'forced marriage (as 'other inhumane act')' on the basis of the same factual basis of the widespread pattern of the "bush wife" phenomenon. Thus, those means of proof set out in the previous section on 'forced marriage' (most of which were based on the "bush wife" phenomenon) also serve as reference point for finding the means of proof of sexual slavery. In the *RUF* Trial Judgement, evidentiary examination of incidents of the "bush wife" phenomenon is performed in the same location under the heading of "Sexual Slavery and 'Forced Marriage'".[150] That is to say, the Chamber invariably holds that *both* the ele-

[148] *AFRC* Trial Judgement, see *supra* note 5, para. 1069 ("The Trial Chamber is satisfied that the acts of rape and sexual slavery are encompassed by the definition of outrages on personal dignity and will consider evidence to this effect presently.").

[149] *AFRC* Trial Judgement, see *supra* note 5, paras. 1109, 1133, 1145, 1170 and 1187.

[150] See the headings of the following sections in the RUF Trial Judgement: "5.1.2.6. Sexual Slavery and 'Forced Marriages'"; "5.1.4.4. Sexual Slavery and 'Forced Marriages'"; "5.2.2.2. Sexual Slavery and 'Forced Marriages' (Counts 7 and 8)"; "6.2.2.1. Sexual Slavery and 'Forced Marriage' of TF1-314"; "6.2.2.2. Sexual Slavery and 'Forced Marriage' of TF1-093"; and "6.2.2.3. Sexual Slavery and 'Forced Marriages' of other civilians". See also, RUF Trial Judgement, see *supra* note 61, para. 1464 ("Based upon the foregoing, the Chamber finds that the elements of sexual slavery and of 'forced marriage' as an other inhumane act have been established beyond rea-

ments of sexual slavery and 'forced marriage' are established based on the same set of facts.[151] In other words, as to a given set of facts, conviction is always made cumulatively in the *RUF* case *vis-à-vis* the charges of sexual slavery and forced marriage.[152]

To sum up, both the *AFRC* Trial Judgement and the *RUF* Trial Judgement are sources for spotting the means of proof of 'sexual slavery'. On the basis of the same fact pattern of the "bush wife" phenomenon, the two judgements are different only in terms of their legal reasoning. Namely, whilst the *AFRC* Trial Chamber linked the means of proof of 'forced marriage' to the element of the 'right of ownership' (sexual slavery),[153] the judges in the *RUF* case linked the same means of proof to the elements of both the 'right of ownership' ('sexual slavery') and the 'infliction of forced conjugal relationship' (forced marriage as an inhumane act).[154] The *AFRC* Trial Chamber held by majority that 'forced marriage' is a sexual crime and consequently the "evidence" of 'forced marriage' is "completely subsumed by the crime of sexual slavery".[155] In this context,

---

sonable doubt. We therefore find that the 'forced marriage' of TF1-093 constitutes sexual slavery and an other inhumane act, as charged under Counts 7 and 8 of the Indictment."). See also *Ibid.*, paras. 1461, 1473 and 1581–2.

151 Thus the Chamber's finding on the elements of 'exercising powers attaching to the right of ownership (sexual slavery)' and 'imposing forced conjugal relationship (forced marriage) is made together in relation to a given set of facts. See, *e.g.*, RUF Trial Judgement, see *supra* note 61, para. 1461 ("Based on the foregoing, the Chamber is satisfied that the Commander intended to exercise powers attaching to the right of ownership over TF1-314 and that he deliberately forced her into a conjugal partnership. The Chamber thus finds tha the elements of sexual slavery and the other inhumane act of 'forced marriage' have been established, as charged under Counts 7 and 8 of the Indictment.") See also, *Ibid.*, paras. 1293–4, 1473; and 1582.

152 RUF Trial Judgement, see *supra* note 61, para. 2307 ("Therefore a conviction on both Counts 7 (sexual slavery) and 8 (other inhumane acts) is permissible.").

153 *AFRC* Trial Judgement, see *supra* note 5, paras. 1105 ("indicative of [...] the exercise of ownership [...]"), 1114, 1126 ("exclusive relationships of ownership"), 1126, 1130, 1141, 1159, 1165 and 1183.

154 See *supra* note 151.

155 *AFRC* Trial Judgement, see *supra* note 5, para. 713. Note that, in paragraph 713, the *AFRC* Trial Chamber made the same mistake as the ICC Pre-Trial Chamber in *Bemba*. That is, the *AFRC* Trial Chamber compared the "evidence adduced by the Prosecution [concerning 'forced marriage']" and the element of sexual slavery. This practice of comparing *fact* and *law* violates the basic principle of the different element test adopted by the *Delalić et al.* Appeals Chamber (and its original form in the *Blockburger* test). Although Justice Doherty disagreed with the majority's view that "the

it should be noted that this legal interpretation was reversed by the *AFRC* Appeals Chamber which held that 'forced marriage' is not predominantly a sexual crime, and that the *AFRC* Trial Chamber "erred in holding that the evidence of forced marriage is subsumed in the elements of sexual slavery".[156]

6.4.2. Elements: 'Exercising Powers of Right of Ownership (Conduct)' and 'Sexual Acts (Conduct)'

The SCSL jurisprudence shares the same elements of 'sexual slavery' with the ICC Elements of Crimes.[157] As summarized by the *RUF* Trial Chamber, the crime of 'sexual slavery' has two elements: (i) exercising powers attaching to the right of ownership (enslavement element), and (ii) sexual acts (sexual act element).[158] The elements of 'sexual slavery' as provided in the ICC Elements of Crimes are:

> 1. The perpetrator exercised any or all of the powers attaching to the right of ownership over one or more persons, such as by purchasing, selling, lending or bartering such a person or persons, or by imposing on them a similar deprivation of liberty.
>
> 2. The perpetrator caused such person or persons to engage in one or more acts of a sexual nature.

---

evidence pleaded by the Prosecution was completely subsumed by the crime of sexual slavery", she engaged in the same mistaken analysis of comparing *facts* as evident from her statement, "[h]aving considered the *evidence*, I respectfully disagree." (emphasis added). See *AFRC* Trial Judgement, Trial Judgement, see *supra* note 5, Partly Dissenting Opinion of Justice Doherty on Count 7 (Sexual Slavery) and Count 8 ('Forced Marriage'), paras. 14 *seq*. For more detailed explanation, see *supra* note 64.

156 *AFRC* Appeals Judgement, see *supra* note 70, para. 195. Note that the *AFRC* Appeals Chamber seems to perform an assessment of 'different element test' in para. 195. It deserves our note that the *AFRC* Appeals Chamber specifies the element of a "relationship of exclusivity" into the legal definition of 'forced marriage, and the subsequent RUF Trial Judgement follows this definition of 'forced marriage'. See *supra* note 74.

157 *AFRC* Trial Judgement, see *supra* note 5, para. 708; RUF Trial Judgement, see *supra* note 61, paras. 158.

158 RUF Trial Judgement, see supra note 61, para. 159.

6.4.3. Means of Proof

6.4.3.1. Means of Proof of 'Exercising Powers of Rights of Ownership (Conduct)'

As mentioned above, both the *AFRC* Trial Chamber and the *RUF* Trial Chamber relied on the same fact pattern of 'forced marriage' in reaching the conviction of 'sexual slavery in the name of outrages upon personal dignity' (count 9 of the *AFRC* Trial Judgement) and 'sexual slavery' (count 7 of the *RUF* Trial Judgement) respectively. Hence, for the purpose of satisfying the element of 'exercising powers attaching to the right of ownership', the means of proof taken by both Trial Chambers are the same (means of proof of 'forced marriage'). Since we have already examined the means of proof of 'forced marriage' in the *RUF* case in the previous section, only the means of proof of 'forced marriage' addressed in the *AFRC* case will be reviewed below. As will be immediately noted by readers, they are almost the same as those spotted in the *RUF* case.

Means of Proof of "Wives"[159] being Captured/Abducted and "Married" against their Will[160]

The *AFRC* Trial Chamber considered the following means of proof in its findings that the elements of sexual slavery had been established: (i) women were captured/abducted;[161] (ii) the captured women were placed under the full control of commanders and became their "wives";[162] (iii) rebels asked a person to turn over 15- and 17-year old girls to them to be their "wives";[163] (iv) a former rebel member testified that, in a certain area, if "they" saw a young girl they would hold her and turn her into their

159 *Ibid.*, para. 1466.

160 *Ibid.*, paras. 1154, 1178, 1211, 1558 and 1562.

161 *AFRC* Trial Judgement, see *supra* note 5, para. 1105 ("The Trial Chamber is of the opinion that witness TF1-334's testimony that women were captured; that captured civilians who tried to escape were executed; that captured women were place[d] under the "full control" of commanders and became their "wives"; and that these women cooked for the commanders and other soldiers is indicative of the deprivation of the captured women's liberty and the exercise of ownership over them by members of the AFRC."); see also, *Ibid.*, paras. 1114, 1165, 1183, and 1184.

162 *Ibid.*, para. 1105.

163 *Ibid.*, para. 1106 ("The Trial Chamber is of the opinion that girls aged 15 and 17 years of age, in the context of coercion and violence, could not have validly consented to "marriage".).

wife;[164] (v) the captor considered the victim to be his "wife";[165] (vi) the captor used the term "wife"; (vii) a commander told a victim that one of his subordinates was the victim's husband from that time on;[166] (viii) the victim agreed that a rebel became her "husband" because she had no other option;[167] (ix) the victim was taken with the troops as they moved/traveled from one place to the other;[168] (x) the murder of a victim's parents in her presence established a context of fear and violence;[169] (xi) the victim's fear that she too would be killed if she did not have sex with the captor;[170] (xii) detention of the victim with the troops for a number of months;[171] (xiii) a rebel wanting to give a victim to his commander as a "wife";[172] (xiv) a rebel threatening to kill the victim upon her refusal to be a "wife" of his commander;[173] (xv) the victim being wounded by a rebel with a bayonet upon her refusal to be a "wife" of his commander;[174] (xvi) the use of the term "wife", in this context a label of possession;[175] (xvii) the victims being placed in exclusive relationships of ownership by certain rebels;[176] (xviii) the victims being punished with physical violence if the exclusive sexual relationship was violated;[177] (xix) rebels recording/registering the names of captured female civilians so that they would not go missing;[178] (xx) the victims captured by rebels being distributed to soldiers to be their "wives";[179] (xxi) the victims being subjected to physical and psychological violence as a form of punishment;[180] and (xxii) the

[164] *Ibid.*, para. 1107.
[165] *Ibid.*, para. 1113.
[166] *Ibid.*, para. 1169.
[167] *Ibid.*, para. 1169.
[168] *Ibid.*, paras. 1113, 1126, 1159 and 1184.
[169] *Ibid.*, para. 1114.
[170] *Ibid.*, para. 1114.
[171] *Ibid.*, paras. 1113–4 (four to five months); para. 1120 (seven months); para. 1126, para. 1127 (three months), para. 1159 (seven menths); para. 1183 (less than a month).
[172] *Ibid.*, para. 1117.
[173] *Ibid.*, para. 1117.
[174] *Ibid.*, para. 1117.
[175] *Ibid.*, paras. 1126, 1159 and 1183.
[176] *Ibid.*, para. 1126.
[177] *Ibid.*, para. 1126.
[178] *Ibid.*, paras. 1128 and 1130.
[179] *Ibid.*, para. 1141.
[180] *Ibid.*, para. 1141.

victim as the "wife" of a Colonel being accorded certain status and benefits, for example, not being forced to cook or clean and being deferentially called "De Mammy", was not considered exculpatory.[181]

Means of Proof of Performing Household Chores

The means of proof in this category are: (i) the captured women cooking for the commanders and other soldiers;[182] (ii) the captured women transformed into "wives" being sent to spy for the rebels or to find food;[183] (iii) doing laundering, cooking and other chores;[184] and (iv) the victim being forced to carry a load/luggage.[185]

Means of Proof of Restriction on Movement/Escape

The following means of proof appear to be especially close to the element of 'exercising powers attaching to the right of ownership': (i) the captured civilians who tried to escape were executed;[186] (ii) the victims who were captured being well secured so they could not escape;[187] and (iii) the victim's thought/feeling that she cannot escape for fear of what her rebel husband might do to her.[188]

6.4.3.2. Means of Proof of 'Sexual Act (Conduct)'

The means of proof in this category are: (i) the captured women being "used sexually" for the purpose of sexual intercourse;[189] (ii) the victim being raped upon capture by rebels;[190] (iii) the victim being repeatedly raped by a rebel;[191] (iv) the victims being raped at the hands of her rebel "husbands";[192] (v) the victims being raped at the hands of other soldiers;[193] (vi) the victim becoming pregnant;[194] (vii) the victim miscarrying

[181] *Ibid.*, para. 1160.
[182] *Ibid.*, paras. 1105 and 1165.
[183] *Ibid.*, para. 1107.
[184] *Ibid.*, paras. 1113, 1114 and 1121.
[185] *Ibid.*, para. 1184.
[186] *Ibid.*, para. 1105.
[187] *Ibid.*, para. 1165.
[188] *Ibid.*, para. 1183.
[189] *Ibid.*, paras. 1105 and 1121.
[190] *Ibid.*, paras. 1116 and 1184.
[191] *Ibid.*, paras. 1113–4, 1127, 1159 and 1184.
[192] *Ibid.*, para. 1141.
[193] *Ibid.*, para. 1141.

as a result of the rape;[195] and (viii) becoming a "wife" being generally understood by captured women and rebels as "whoever you were with would have sex with you" whenever he felt like it.[196]

6.4.4. Open-Ended Nature of Means of Proof of Sexual Slavery

The means of proof listed above in terms of 'sexual slavery' in the SCSL jurisprudence centered around the peculiar fact pattern of the so-called "bush wife" in the Sierra Leone conflict. Yet, as we will see in detail below, the fact pattern found in the *Kunarac et al.* case is quite different from that of the "bush wife" phenomenon. In this context, the following observation made by the *AFRC* Trial Chamber as to the first element of sexual slavery explains the open-ended nature of potential facts of sexual slavery:

> The powers of ownership listed in the first element of sexual slavery are non-exhaustive. There is no requirement for any payment or exchange in order to establish the exercise of ownership. Deprivation of liberty may include extracting forced labour or otherwise reducing a person to servile status. Further, ownership, as indicated by possession, does not require confinement to a particular place but may include situations in which those who are captured remain in the control of their captors because they have no where else to go and fear for their lives. The consent or free will of the victim is absent under conditions of enslavement.[197]

As implied by the phrase "or by imposing on them a similar deprivation of liberty" as provided in the first element of 'sexual slavery' in the ICC Elements of Crimes, what the *AFRC* Trial Chamber meant to say in the quoted paragraph is that it is not advisable or even possible to set a limit on the types of means of proof for the first element of sexual slav-

---

[194] *Ibid.*, paras. 1113–4 and 1184.

[195] *Ibid.*, para. 1184.

[196] *Ibid.*, paras. 1121, 1129 and 1457.

[197] *Ibid.*, para. 709, citing UN Sub-Commission on the Promotion and Protection of Human Rights, Systematic Rape, Sexual Slavery and Slavery-like Practices during Armed Conflict: Update to the Final Report / submitted by Gay J. McDougall, Special Rapporteur, 6 June 2000, E/CN.4/Sub.2 /2000/21, available at: http://www.unhcr.org/refworld/docid/3b00f56310.html, last accessed at 17 May 2011, para. 50.

ery.[198] There is no reason to circumscribe the boundary of means of proof for 'exercising powers attaching to the right of ownership' *in abstracto*. The means of proof of sexual slavery found in SCSL jurisprudence might not be found in any other international case law in the future if the fact pattern of "bush wife" is not to be repeated. In this sense, it should be noted that the means of proof of sexual slavery based on the "bush wife" phenomenon might have limited referential value. At this juncture, let us have a look at the relevant means of proof from a different fact pattern of the conflict in the former Yugoslavia.

6.5. Enslavement Based on Rape in the ICTY Jurisprudence

6.5.1. Overview

In the *Kunarac et al.* case, the Trial Chamber dealt with a set of facts in which the accused detained two women for a number of months in an abandoned house. The accused forced them to do all household chores and subjected them to continued rape and sexual assaults.[199] Though the Prosecution charged 'enslavement' as a crime against humanity under Article 5(c),[200] this legal characterisation is based on a set of facts composed of factual features of both 'enslavement' and 'rape' as the title of the relevant part of the indictment suggests.[201] Thus the means of proof in this case are considered relevant for the purpose of the offence of 'sexual slavery'.[202] Since the means of proof of rape have been extensively dis-

[198] In this respect, note the following view of the *Kunarac et al.* Appeals Chamber: "[c]onsequently, it is not possible exhaustively to enumerate all of the contemporary forms of slavery which are comprehended in the expansion of the original idea; this Judgement is limited to the case in hand." See *Kunarac et al.* Appeals Judgement, see *supra* note 5, para. 119.

[199] *Kunarac et al.* Trial Judgement, see *supra* note 15, paras. 728–745.

[200] The ICTY Statute does not contain an independent provision on 'sexual slavery'.

[201] The title says, "Enslavement and Rape of FWS-186, FWS-191 and J.G.". See International Criminal Tribunal for the former Yugoslavia, *Prosecutor v. Kunarac et al.*, Case No. IT-96-23-T, Amended Indictment, 8 November 1999 ("*Kunarac et al.* Amended Indictment").

[202] For a relevant discussion, see Kelly Askin, "Prosecuting Wartime Rape and Other Gender-Related Crimes under International Law: Extraordinary Advance, Enduring Obstacles", in *Berkeley Journal of International Law*, 2003, vol. 21, p. 340 (opining that the most appropriate legal characterization in this case would have been sexual slavery given that the primary purpose of the enslavement of the women was sexual exploitation).

cussed above, in this section, we will focus on the means of proof concerning the enslavement aspect and see to what extent they overlap with those drawn from a distinctive fact pattern of "bush wife" in the Sierra Leone conflict.

6.5.2. Element: 'Exercising Powers of Right of Ownership (Conduct)'

In the ICC Elements of Crimes, the offences of 'enslavement' and 'sexual slavery' share the same element of 'exercising powers attaching to the right of ownership' verbatim in language.[203] The only difference is that the offence of 'sexual slavery' has an additional element of 'sexual acts'. In this respect, the ICTY jurisprudence on 'enslavement' also identifies the same element:

> Thus, the Trial Chamber finds that the *actus reus* of the violation is the exercise of any or all of the powers attaching to the right of ownership over a person. The *mens rea* of the violation consists in the intentional exercise of such powers.[204]

What are the types of substantive evidence regarding the element of 'exercising powers attaching to the right of ownership' in the *Kunarac* case?

6.5.3. Means of Proof

6.5.3.1. Indicia of 'Exercising Powers Attaching to the Right of Ownership'

It is noteworthy that the *Kunarac et al.* Trial Chamber, on the basis of an extensive examination of international treaties and jurisprudence, enumerates indicia of the element of 'exercising powers attaching to the right

[203] The shared element provides, "[t]he perpetrator exercised any or all of the powers attaching to the right of ownership over one or more persons, such as by purchasing, selling, lending or bartering such a person or persons, or by imposing on them a similar deprivation of liberty." See ICC Elements of Crimes, see *supra* note 4, Arts. 7(1)(c) 'Crime against humanity of enslavement' and 7(1)(g)-2 'Crime against humanity of sexual slavery'.

[204] *Kunarac et al.* Trial Judgement, see *supra* note 15, para. 540. The Appeals Chamber upheld the definition of enslavement found by the Trial Chamber. See *Kunarac et al.* Appeals Judgement, see *supra* note 5, para. 124.

of ownership'.[205] Reviewing the list of the indicia, it seems we might group them into the two categories of: (a) 'owner's control factors'; and (b) 'slave's suffering factors'. This categorisation should not be considered absolute or strict as the 'owner's control' and the 'slave's suffering' are often difficult to distinguish factually. A good example would be sexual exploitation that clearly shows the both the control and suffering factors.

The first category of 'owner's control factors' would include: (i) restriction/control of an individual's autonomy; (ii) restriction/control of freedom of choice; (iii) restriction/control of freedom of movement; (iv) control of physical environment; (v) detention/captivity; (vi) duration; (vii) psychological control; (viii) socio-economic conditions; (ix) measures taken to prevent or deter escape; (x) deception or false promise; (xi) the victim's position of vulnerability; (xii) exploitation; (xiii) assertion of exclusivity; (xiv) force/coercion; (xv) accruing of some gain to the owner; and (xvi) buying, selling, trading or inheriting a person or his or her labours or services.

The second category of 'slave's sufferings factors' would include: (i) subjection to cruel treatment and abuse; (ii) control of sexuality; (iii) forced labour; and (iv) physical hardship.

It is interesting to note that the fact pattern of "bush wife" in the Sierra Leone conflict fits well into these indicia of enslavement. The 'wives' were abducted and kept in captivity for months and years; they were forced to stay with their 'husbands' and measures were taken to restrict their movement and escape; 'husbands' claimed exclusive relationship with their 'wives'; 'wives' had to do all the household chores and were sexually exploited; 'husbands' tried to deceive and manipulate 'wives' by deliberately using the term "wife"; and 'wives' were continuously subject to various forms of mistreatment and abuse. The positive result of this comparison might confirm the general applicability of the indicia of enslavement as set out by the *Kunarac et al.* Trial Chamber.

[205] *Kunarac et al.* Trial Judgement, see *supra* note 15, paras. 542–3.

6.5.3.2. Means of Proof of 'Exercising Powers Attaching to Right of Ownership' from the Specific Facts of *Kunarac et al.* case

The means of proof drawn from the enslavement incident as charged under counts 18–21 of the indictment *vis-à-vis* the accused Kunarac can also be grouped in accordance with the categorisation scheme of the 'owner's control factors' and the 'victim's suffering factor'.

The category of the 'owner's control factors' includes: (i) the victims being kept in a house for five to six months;[206] (ii) the victims not being free to go where they wanted to go;[207] (iii) the victims having no realistic option to flee the house;[208] (iv) the accused inviting a soldier to the house so that he could rape the victim for 100 Deutschmark if he so wished;[209] (v) the accused telling the victim's mother that her daughter was with him and that he would not bring her back;[210] (vi) the victim being allowed to write a letter to her mother at some point;[211] (vii) the accused ordering the victim's mother to give him clothes for her daughter;[212] and (viii) the victim doing anything the accused ordered her to do.[213] In this context, it is to be noted that the Trial Chamber denied the exculpatory value of the fact that the victims were given the keys to the house where they had been kept in captivity.[214] That was because the Chamber noted that the victims had nowhere to go and no place to hide from the accused.[215] In this respect, the Chamber also took into account the general circumstances of war.[216]

The means of proof that belong to the second category of the 'victim's suffering factors' are: (i) the accused continuing to rape the victim

---

206 *Ibid.*, para. 732 ("[T]he Trial Chamber reiterates that specific dates and exact time periods do not require to be proved beyond reasonable doubt due to the specific war context wherein the crimes concerned occurred.").

207 *Ibid.*, para. 740.

208 *Ibid.*, para. 742.

209 *Ibid.*, para. 742.

210 *Ibid.*, para. 737.

211 *Ibid.*, para. 737.

212 *Ibid.*, para. 737.

213 *Ibid.*, para. 742.

214 *Ibid.*, para. 740.

215 *Ibid.*, para. 740.

216 *Ibid.*, para. 740.

for about two months;[217] (ii) that each time the accused came to the house he raped the victim;[218] (iii) that although the accused broke his arm in an accident sometime in September 1992, he nevertheless continued to rape her;[219] (iv) that the accused tried to rape the victim while in his hospital bed, in front of other soldiers;[220] (v) that the accused continuously raped the victim during her five-month stay at the house;[221] (vi) that the victim was obliged to have sexual intercourse with the accused whenever he returned to the house from Montenegro or from the frontlines;[222] and (vii) that the victim performed household chores for the accused.[223] As noted above, the means of proof of sexual assaults can be considered indicative of the 'owner's control factor' as well.

As to another 'enslavement' charge *vis-à-vis* the second accused Kovač, which is based on almost the same set of facts as the equivalent charge of Kunarac,[224] the means of proof noted by the Trial Chamber are: (i) that the accused sold the victims at the price of 500 Deutschmark each;[225] (ii) the daily regime of rapes and other abuses;[226] (iii) that the accused detained the victim for the period of a week to four months;[227] (iv) that the accused detained the victims by locking them up and by psychologically imprisoning them, and thereby depriving them of their freedom of movement;[228] (v) that the accused possessed complete control over the victims' movement, privacy and labour;[229] (vi) that the accused made the victims cook for him, serve him and do the household chores for him;[230] and (vii) that the accused subjected the victims to degrading treatments, including beatings and other humiliating treatments.[231]

217 *Ibid.*, para. 734.
218 *Ibid.*, para. 734.
219 *Ibid.*, para. 734.
220 *Ibid.*, para. 742.
221 *Ibid.*, para. 735.
222 *Ibid.*, para. 735.
223 *Ibid.*, para. 742.
224 *Kunarac et al.* Amended Indictment, see *supra* note 201, paras. 11.1–11.7.
225 *Ibid.*, para. 779.
226 *Ibid.*, para. 777.
227 *Ibid.*, para. 780.
228 *Ibid.*, para. 780.
229 *Ibid.*, para. 780.
230 *Ibid.*, para. 780.
231 *Ibid.*, para. 780.

It is interesting to see that the *Kunarac et al.* Trial Chamber kept using the phrase "treated as personal property" in respect of the enslavement incidents.[232] It is considered however that the use of the concept of "personal property" in the context of discussing evidence of 'enslavement' should be cautious because for now it is not clear what purposes this concept should serve. Is it an element (or a component of the element of 'exercising powers attaching to the right of ownership)? Or, is it just a factual summation of the representative fact pattern of 'enslavement'? The key question seems to be whether it is necessary to introduce the concept of "personal property" in the relevant discussion, be it factual or legal, in addition to that of 'power attaching to the right of ownership' for the purpose of assessing the evidence of enslavement.

6.6. Conclusion

Given its grave impact on victims and the society as a whole to which the victims belong, recent developments in the area of international sex crimes in terms of both the codification and the accumulation of relevant jurisprudence should be welcomed. Despite the fact that we now have extensive provisions in the ICC Statute from 'rape' to the 'other sexual violence', the difficulties and confusion caused by the absence of a specific provision defining the offence of 'forced marriage' at the SCSL demonstrate the ever-varying characteristics of international sex crimes. In view of the importance of the principle of legality and the difficult experiences that the international criminal justice system has undergone in respect thereof, for example, with regard to the offences related to child soldiers at the SCSL and the joint criminal enterprise at the ICTY, the ICTR and the ECCC, active codification of new types of sexual violence should be encouraged. The means of proof of international sex crimes as found by the judges of international criminal tribunals will be of great help to prosecutors and investigators for the preparation of their cases. That is because the means of proof provides them with graphic expressions of legal elements already examined and accepted by international judges. In respect of, for instance, the legal concepts of 'forced conjugal

[232] *Ibid.*, paras. 728, 738, 742, 744(iii) and 781. Note that there is another perpetrator involved in this enslavement incident – *i.e.*, "DP 6". The phrase "treated as the personal property" was originally used by the Prosecution it its indictment. See *Kunarac et al.* Amended Indictment, see *supra* note 201, para. 10.3.

association', 'rights of ownership' and 'gravity', practitioners in the area of international criminal justice would have a much clearer understanding of how those elements manifest themselves in the real world when they refer to the means of proof of international sex crimes as explored in this chapter.

7

Beyond Dogma and Taboo: Criteria for the Effective Investigation of Sexual Violence

Xabier Agirre Aranburu*

7.1. Introduction

Criminal investigations of sexual violence, both at the national and international levels, are struggling to find their way between the old deep-seated forces of taboo and denial, and the new assumptions and dogmas of the feminist and human rights movements. On the one hand, in spite of all the progress made in recent decades, there is still reluctance to confront sexual violence in many areas of our societies and legal systems due to either sexist ideology or mere feelings of shame. On the other hand, advocacy efforts have promoted a focus on the suffering of the female victims, rather than on impartial fact-finding and due process, which may get in the way of the truth that societies afflicted by conflict need.

The purpose of this chapter is to suggest some criteria of methodology to overcome the hurdles of the old taboos and the new dogmas, for more effective criminal investigation of sexual violence. For that matter, with the benefit of feedback received in the seminar and some additional research, this chapter will expand several points taken from a previous

---

* **Xabier Agirre Aranburu** is Senior Analyst at the Office of the Prosecutor ('OTP') of the International Criminal Court ('ICC') since 2004, and previously analyst at the OTP of the United Nations International Criminal Tribunal for the former Yugoslavia ('ICTY', 1997–2004) and has contributed to a number of investigative and training projects on international crimes with different international organizations, universities and NGOs. I am grateful to professors Morten Bergsmo and Elisabeth Wood for the invitation to the seminar and their advice for this chapter, and to Olivia Swaak-Goldman, Eirini Louppi and Shereen Abdul-Baki for their review and corrections. This chapter is based on the presentation that the author gave in the seminar 'Proving International Sex Crimes' co-organized by the FICHL (Forum for International Criminal and Humanitarian Law), Yale University and the University of Cape Town (New Haven, 15–16 October 2010). The views contained in this chapter do not necessarily represent the views of the ICC nor the UN.

piece on the use of pattern evidence and analysis for the investigation of sexual violence.[1]

In the 1970s the feminist movement, particularly in the USA, started denouncing the impunity for rape under a male-dominated system. In 1975 Susan Brownmiller published in New York her classic work *Against Our Will. Men, Women and Rape,* which would set the tone for the feminist critique on this issue.[2] The book is a remarkable piece of research that, in spite of some hyperbolic language, contains an abundance of empirical information and should be mandatory reading for sexual violence investigators. More recent research includes, among others, the findings of Elisabeth Wood and others on comparative analysis of rape, and very useful historical and sociological studies by Joanna Bourke (2007), Gina M. Weaver (2010), Elizabeth D. Heineman (2011) and Véronique Le Goaziou (2011).[3]

The feminist critique reached with some success the public opinion, and then the national jurisdictions, as well as the international institutions and tribunals.[4] The fight against rape was raised by the movement as a

1 See X. Agirre Aranburu, "Sexual Violence beyond Reasonable Doubt: Using Pattern Evidence and Analysis for International Cases", in *Leiden Journal of International Law*, 2010, vol. 23, pp. 609–627.

2 Susan Brownmiller, *Against our Will. Men, Women and Rape*, Fawcett Columbine, New York, 1975. I am grateful to Patricia Viseur-Sellers for sharing her expertise and first bringing to my attention the research of Brownmiller in 1997, in the context of our work at the ICTY. For an overview of the progress made, see P. Viseur-Sellers "Gender strategy is not a luxury for international courts", in *American University Journal of Gender, Social Policy and the Law*, 2009, vol. 17, pp. 301–325. Note also the publications by the renowned feminist author Catharine MacKinnon, who was appointed by the ICC Prosecutor Luis Moreno Ocampo as his Special Gender Advisor in November 2008, see ICC OTP press relsease at http://www.icc-cpi.int/menus/icc/press%20and%20media/press%20releases/press%20releases%20%282008%29/icc%20prosecutor%20appoints%20prof_%20catharine%20a.%20mackinnon%20as%20special%20adviser%20on%20gender%20crimes, last accessed on 26 August 2011.

3 See Joanna Bourke, *Rape: Sex Violence History*, Counterpoint, Berkeley, 2007; G.M. Weaver, *Ideologies of Forgetting. Rape in Vietnam War*, SUNY Press, Albany 2010; Elizabeth D. Heineman (ed.), *Sexual Violence in Conflict Zones. From the Ancient World to the Era of Human Rights*, University of Pennsylvania Press, Philadelphia, 2011; and Veronique Le Goaziou, *Le viol, aspects sociologiques d'un crime*, La Documentation Française, Paris, 2011.

4 For an overview of the international jurisprudence see, among others, Anne-Marie L.M. de Brouwer, *Supranational Criminal Prosecution of Sexual Violence. The ICC and the Practice of the ICTY and the ICTR*, Intersentia, Antwerpen-Oxford, 2005;

major banner to promote its values and empower women. In the words of Patricia V. Sellers:

> Rape was just the beachhead; the proverbial landing at Normandy, so that we could wade ashore at Kigali. It was the enumerated provisional place where we chose to disembark while under fire and while behind enemy lines.[5]

In any event, historically the awareness about rape grew in parallel with the overall awareness of human rights violations, just like the renewed interest in rape in contexts of mass violence starting in the 1990s developed in parallel with the emergence of the new wave of International Criminal Law.

The feminist critique is still needed today to keep adequate awareness and focus on sexual violence. As an experienced practitioner, I have seen professionals refusing to deal with allegations of sexual violence, neglecting the relevant evidence, or setting higher standards of evidence in a number of occasions. When drafting an indictment for an international tribunal in the late 1990s my modest attempt to include a reference to sexual violence under the chapeau of "persecutions" (as a crime against humanity) was stopped by two attorneys senior to me because in their view "there was no sufficient evidence". Later I discussed the issue with one of them and was puzzled when he explained that in his country as a prosecutor he always avoided sexual violence because it was "very annoying and difficult to prove". More recently, when lecturing a group of experienced judges and prosecutors visiting The Hague, references to

---

Kelly D. Askin, *War Crimes Against Women. Prosecution in International War Crimes Tribunals*, Martinus Nijhoff Publishers, Dordrecht, 1997; Kelly D. Askin, "The jurisprudence of International war crimes tribunals: securing gender justice for some survivors", in Helen Durham and Tracey Gurd (eds.), *Listening to the silences: women and war*, Martinus Nijhoff Publishers, Leiden, 2005, pp. 125–153; X. Agirre Aranburu, "Los delitos de agresión sexual en el Tribunal Penal Internacional de Naciones Unidas para la Antigua Yugoslavia", in S. Diaz Luengo, R. Abril Stoffels and S. Sanz Caballero (ed.), *Violencia contra las mujeres en conflictos armados*, Cruz Roja Española, Valencia, 2003, pp. 39–63; Dianne Luping "Investigation and prosecution of sexual and gender-based crimes before the ICC", in *American University Journal of Gender, Social Policy and the Law*, 2009, vol. 17, pp. 433–494; and the periodical reports of the Women's Initiative for Gender Justice, available at http://www.icc women.org/.

5 P. Viseur-Sellers, "Gender strategy is not a luxury for international courts", in *American University Journal of Gender, Social Policy and the Law*, 2009, vol. 17, pp. 301–325, at p. 305.

sexual violence were met with laughter and mocking signs, and I was asked the question of whether international tribunals accepted female investigators, since apparently this was not an option in their country.

Notwithstanding the legacy of *Akayesu* and other landmark cases on sexual violence, the expert on ICTR (International Criminal Tribunal for Rwanda), Binaifer Nowrojee, has assessed the record of this Court as "shameful" because "crimes of sexual violence have never been *fully and consistently* incorporated into the investigations and strategy of the Prosecutor's Office".[6] Concerning both ICTR and ICTY, according to expert assessment, there has been a "tendency to require that the prosecution meet a higher evidentiary standard in cases of sexual violence and gender based crimes".[7] In 2008 the inquiry on the post-electoral violence in Kenya found an "apparent lack of interest of the police in sexual violence" and many allegations of rape that were overlooked by the national police.[8] Still today the most common software for crime analysis utilized by police forces around the world, the British made i2 Analyst's Notebook, does not include rape in the menu of crimes to be analyzed (see figure 1 below).[9]

---

6 B. Nowrojee, "A Lost Opportunity for Justice: Why Did the ICTR Not Prosecute Gender Propaganda?", in A. Thompon (ed.), *The Media and the Rwanda Genocide*, Pluto Press, London, 2007, at p. 370. The critical assessment on ICTR is confirmed by the study by G. Breton-Le Goff, *Analysis of Trends in Sexual Violence Prosecutions in Indictments by the International Criminal Tribunal for Rwanda (ICTR). From November 1995 to November 2002*, available at http://www.womensrightscoalition.org/site/advocacyDossiers/rwanda/rapeVictimssDeniedJustice/analysisoftrends_en.php; and Beth Van Schaak "Obstacles on the road to gender justice: the international criminal tribunal for Rwanda as object lesson", in *American University Journal of Gender, Social Policy and the Law*, 2009, vol. 17, pp. 362–406.

7 See Susana SaCouto and Katherine Cleary, "The importance of effective investigation of sexual violence and genderbased crimes at the ICC", in *American University Journal of gender, Social policy and the Law*, 2009, vol. 17, pp. 338–358, at 356.

8 See CIPEV, *Report of the Commission of Inquiry into Post-Election Violence*, 15 October 2008, p. 249, available at http://www.communication.go.ke/documents/CIPEV_FINAL_REPORT.pdf, last accessed on 2 January 2010.

9 For commercial information see http://www.i2group.com/template1.asp?id=5 (accessed 2 Jan. 2010).

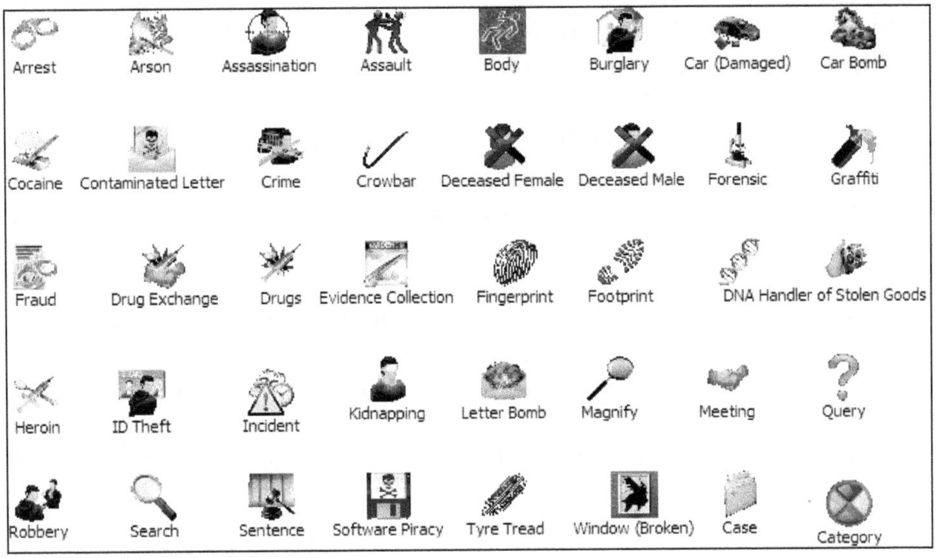

Figure 1: The "crime"category of the i2 Analyst Notebook software commonly used for criminal investigations: rape is absent from the menu of crimes to be analyzed.

The reluctance to investigate sexual violence appears to result from two main factors: lack of awareness and sensitivity in teams usually led by senior male officers, and a certain taboo or embarrassment when dealing with intimate aspects of our bodies and minds. Researchers from the field of cognitive psychology could test these two causal factors as hypotheses, and they could assist in suggesting corrective measures (the most obvious ones being evaluation at the recruitment stage, specific training, clear policies and standards, appointment of designated specialized staff and gender balance in the teams). Research in this field could follow the precedents of the cognitive psychologists that reviewed the practice of the UK police in the 1980s and developed the standards for "cognitive interviewing", as well as others that have developed "investigative psychology" or "psychology of law" as specific fields of research on the psychological factors affecting the perception of the evidence and the rules by investigators and judges. Simulations and surveys could help for this research, as well as qualitative analysis of judicial records of the kind that professor Nancy A. Combs developed in her recent book on the evidence of international tribunals.[10]

It is clear that investigators and judges are subject to the influence of different ideological trends, also at the international level, which in turn may affect their interpretation of the facts and the law.[11] For example, the Nuremberg proceedings were influenced, among other factors, by Marxist ideology, which had gained renewed credit after the capitalist debacle of 1929. This influence was most apparent among the Soviet prosecutors and judges, with their emphasis on characterizing the Nazi crimes as a matter of class struggle. A softer version of Marxist thinking was in the mind of Franz Neumann, the senior analyst that assisted Justice Jackson's team in preparing the cases. He was a former labor lawyer trained in the Frankfurt school, a moderate Marxist blend of law and social sciences. In his classic study of the Nazi State Neumann explained Nazism as a new phase in the development of capitalism, and he argued that the industry was one of the fundamental pillars of the Nazi state. It appears that this analysis influenced the choice of the prosecution to focus on some of Hitler's senior business associates.[12] Neumann's socialist interpretation of the Nazi regime conflicted with the Zionist interpretation focused on the distinct suffering of the Jews, and subsequently Zionist authors have criticized him for underestimating the "uniqueness" of Jewish suffering in the Holocaust.[13] That the proceedings in Nuremberg would be influenced to some extent by Marxism is understandable in that historical context, just like the Eichmann case in Israel was affected by Zionist ideology, and these days feminist ideology is having an influence consistent with the expectations of the societies that sponsor international justice.

---

[10] Nancy A. Combs, *Fact-Finding Without Facts*, Cambridge University Press, Cambridge, 2010.

[11] For an analysis of ideological influences on domestic criminal law, including references to the influence of the new social movements, see Massimo Pavarini, *Control y dominación: teorías criminológicas burguesas y proyecto hegemónico*, Siglo XXI, Mexico, 1983 (translation of the original in Italian of 1980). For an analysis of the historical evolution of the perception of sexual behavior under the law, see Richard Green, *Sexual Science and the Law*, Harvard University Press, Cambridge, 1992.

[12] See F. Neuman Behemoth, *The structure and practice of national socialism*, Oxford University Press, Oxford, 1942.

[13] For an overview on the Zionist interpretation of the holocaust by an author closer to Neumman's views see, N.G. Finkelnstein, *The Holocaust Industry: Reflections on the Exploitation of Jewish Suffering*, Verson, London, 2000.

Justice for international crimes is not free of ideological influences, and there is a need to identify and discuss openly such influences so that victims, society, and judicial operators are better informed in their choices. While the feminist movement must be credited for its contribution in fighting impunity for sexual violence, its influence, together with other factors, has favored some notions that may need to be critically discussed. Sections 2 to 5 below will discuss some of these aspects, while section 6 will try to assist in developing the best evidence for investigating patterns of sexual violence.

7.2. Strategy, Opportunity and Other Factors

In the context of an armed conflict it has become a common line for media and advocacy groups to claim that sexual violence and rape result from a strategic choice to use them as a "weapon of war".[14] The sad reality is that it does not take much strategy for rape to take place on a large scale. As Susan Brownmiller observed already in 1975:

> After the fact, the rape may be viewed as part of a recognizable pattern of national terror and subjugation. I say 'after the fact' because the impulse to rape does not need a sophisticated political motivation beyond a general disregard for the bodily integrity of women.[15]

In social sciences the term "opportunity structure" is used to refer to the set of autonomous factors that favor the emergence of a social or criminal trend, whether related to population trends, ideology, politics or other. Given the right opportunity structure sexual violence may occur, and it does occur, in a rather large scale without needing any comprehensive plan or strategy.

Numerous examples of widespread rape in the absence of armed conflict illustrate this point. Hundreds of women have been raped and killed in Ciudad Juarez and other cities in Mexico, as a result of the opportunity created by the exposure of thousands of young female workers commuting through areas of pervasive and very violent crime, dysfunc-

[14] For an example of this kind of literature, see Karima Guenivet, *Violences Sexuelles. La nouvelle arme de guerre*, Éditions Michalon, Paris, 2001. Among others, the author sees strategic motivation for the rapes in Bosnia, Rwanda and Algeria, to achieve ethnic cleansing, genocide and the imposition of Islamic theocracy.

[15] See Brownmiller, 1975, p. 37, see *supra* note 2.

tional law enforcement and other underlying social factors.[16] Still in Mexico, reportedly some 60% of the female illegal immigrants that transit through the country northwards are raped: it is so frequent that many take contraceptives before the journey in anticipation of the rape.[17] Sexual violence against women increased in the aftermath of hurricane Katrina in 2005, apparently as a result of law enforcement breakdown, vulnerability of displaced population, and pre-existing risk factors. Members of the Catholic clergy have been accused of sexual crimes in a number of countries around the world, allegedly taking the opportunity given by their position of authority, the vulnerability of young victims, and the cover-up by their superiors.[18] Rape is so endemic in South Africa that women can purchase a self-defense product called Rape Axe: a latex tube with razor-sharp barbs on the inside, to be worn by the woman like a tampon, so that the penis of the rapist would get trapped and injured.[19] Often the perpetrators of common rape are known and close to the victim (for example, around 70 to 80% of reported cases in France, Australia and China fit this description), which excludes any dimension of conflict between different groups.[20] The same applies to the rape of soldiers within the U.S. military,

16 See, among others, the report of the Inter-American Commission of Human Rights of 7 March 2003, "Situación de los derechos de la mujer en Ciudad Juárez México: El derecho a no ser objeto de violencia y discriminación", available at http://www.cidh.org/annualrep/2002sp/cap.vi.juarez.htm, last accessed on 26 August 2008.

17 See interviews with victims and social workers in the documentary "Los Invisibles", available at http://www.youtube.com/watch?v=XMrU0jelMoY&feature=channel, last accessed on 5 January 2011.

18 For an overview on this issue see Geoffrey Robertson, *The case of the Pope*: *Vatican Accountability for Human Rights Abuse*, Penguin Global, London, 2010.

19 See the commercial site of Rape Axe at http://www.antirape.co.za/index.php?option=com_content&view=article&id=6&Itemid=18, last accessed on 16 July 2011. On rape in South Africa, see Lisa Vetten, "Paradox and Policy: addressing rape in post-apartheid South Africa", in N. Westmarland and G. Gangoli (eds.), *International Approaches to Rape*, The Policy Press, Bristol, 2011, pp. 169–192.

20 On France see Le Goaziou, 2011, p. 32, see *supra* note 3; on Australia see Patricia Easteal, "Sexual assault law in Australia: contextual challenges and changes", in Westmarland and Gangoli (eds.), 2011, pp. 13–34, at p. 15, see *supra* note 19; and on China see Qihua Ye, "Introduction to the issue of rape in China as a developing country", in Westmarland and Gangoli (eds.), *op. cit*, pp. 57–77, at p. 62.

which is not uncommon and, far from being a "weapon of war" resembles abuse by fellow warriors void of any ulterior purpose.[21]

Rhonda Copelon warned that "it is critical to overcome 'conflict exceptionalism'", the false image that sexual violence is something distinctive of armed conflicts, but it might be that the emphasis on strategic causation theories is reinforcing such "conflict exceptionalism".[22]

The emphasis on strategic theories seems to follow from a kind of *post-hoc* fallacy, that is, assuming that the consequences of an act must constitute its cause or motivation. Sexual aggression, like any other form of aggression, may cause long-term damage to the victim and his or her community, which needs to be seriously taken into account to assess the gravity of the conduct, but this does not necessarily mean that such consequence was the motive of the aggressor. The same applies for looting, which may have devastating effects, but that is not necessarily the motivation of looters, who were perhaps instead guided by their own greed.

Different factors contribute to the proliferation of claims of strategic rape "as a weapon of war". First, at a general level, there is the Roussonian assumption that human beings are good by nature and evil must spring from some higher instance alien to them. As Potts and Hayden have explained, Roussonian assumptions have influenced the understanding of both war and sexual violence, at the expense of overlooking other dimensions of human behavior.[23]

Secondly, the victims may favor strategic explanations because it helps them rationalize their traumatic experience. To think that your suffering was triggered by some powerful actor, following some deeper agenda, may be psychologically more comforting than to think that it derives from some banal decision that could have been easily avoided. The thought processes of victims, which may be part of their healing process-

[21] See information of the US Department of Veteran Affairs on "Miltitary Sexual Trauma" ('MST') at http://www.ptsd.va.gov/public/pages/military-sexual-trauma-general.asp, last accessed on 15 July 2011. MST is defined as "experiences of sexual assault or repeated, threatening acts of sexual harassment" that take place within the military, and reportedly it affects 1 of 5 women and 1 of 100 men in the U.S. military.

[22] See R. Copelon "Toward Accountability for Violence Against Women in War", in Heineman (ed.), 2011, pp. 222–256, at p. 255, see *supra* note 3.

[23] Malcom Potts and Thomas Hayden, *Sex and War*, Benbella Books, Dallas, 2008, pp. 18–20.

es, need to be respected, but their knowledge of the perpetrators may be insufficient to assess their functioning and strategies.

Thirdly, media and advocacy groups, whether human rights activists, feminist or parties to the conflict, may find the strategic argument rhetorically convenient to highlight the gravity of the crime and to affect public opinion. Advocacy groups and authors don't like to hear about "opportunistic" sexual violence because they fear this may justify or under-estimate the gravity of the crimes. These fears are justified, as references to opportunism are frequently used with dismissive undertones. For example, in the 1990s in El Salvador and South Africa the commissioners of the truth commissions excluded from their reports cases of rape committed in the context of the conflict because they found them opportunistic in a way that rendered them "non-political" and hence irrelevant to the political violence under investigation.[24] This narrow interpretation is mistaken in separating individual or opportunist acts of violence from the broader context that caused or enabled them, and it seems to have fallen in disuse in view of the evolution on this subject over the last twenty years.

And yet sexual violence often presents aspects of opportunism that cannot be ignored when analyzing objectively the evidence. To begin with, it is clear that the rapist often gets an orgasm from his crime, and this personal reward may be the main motive for his decision to rape, just like many looters are motivated by their personal profit. Rape is often a crime of the youth, taking into account the age of both the victims and the direct perpetrators. For example, a recent survey of rape in France shows an average of 17 years old for victims and 31 for perpetrators, and: "This is now an established fact: young age is a risk factor for sexual aggression. Multiple national and international surveys show without contradiction that young adults, adolescents and children are those most affected".[25] This young profile is not uncommon in war-related rape where, although many advocacy reports like to underline that the victims includ-

---

[24] See Priscilla B. Hayner, *Unspeakable Truths. Transitional Justice and the Challenge of Truth Commissions*, Routledge, New York, 2011 (second edition), pp. 87–88, chapter 7 "The truth about women and men".

[25] Le Goaziou, 2011, pp. 41 and 42, see *supra* note 3. The average age of the victims reported (mean value) is conditioned by the very young average age of the cases of child rape within families included in the survey (9 years old), without which the average of victims would be closer to 25.

ed "women of all ages", the rapist most often targets young victims. More research is needed for a more precise assessment of the age factor, since victim and perpetrator profiles within the age span of greater sexual drive and appeal may be an indicator of opportunistic behavior.

As in the old military motto "beauty and booty", rape in wartime is often committed as a kind of sexual looting, the main motive of the aggressor being his immediate sexual satisfaction. In the words of Brownmiller, "[…] beyond the shiny patina of ideological excuse, it was also rape amid the levity and frivolity of men having a good time".[26] Such is the banality of rape, which does not mean that rape of this kind is any less grave, just like when Hannah Arendt referred to "the banality of evil" to explain the conduct of Eichmann, which did not prevent her from requesting the capital punishment for his "banal" crimes.[27]

The most truthful approach to this issue would be to acknowledge the elements of opportunism when the evidence indicates so, and then ascertain whether still higher levels of authority may be accountable for such crimes under different provisions. The existing positive law and emerging international jurisprudence allows for different modes and scenarios of liability for such cases: a) Deliberate inducement, if the leaders create deliberately the opportunity to rape by giving *carte blanche* to do so or by setting the example with their own conduct or with notorious and persistent tolerance after the fact; b) Responsibility as a matter of *dolus eventualis*, if the crime was a natural and foreseeable result from actions triggered by the leaders, which may well be the case in many scenarios of opportunistic rape; c) Command responsibility if the leaders, whether civilian or military, knowingly failed to prevent or repress crimes committed by their subordinates (as per Article 28 of the ICC Statute).[28]

---

26 See Brownmiller, 1975, p. 139, see *supra* note 2. For a historical example of this kind of rape in my native city, see Javier Sada, *El Asalto a la Brecha. Crónica de la destrucción de San Sebastián en 1813*, Txertoa, Donostia, 2010, including testimony of witnesses and victims or rape in the chapter "Juicio popular: Hablan los donostiarras", pp. 99–128.

27 See Hannah Arendt, *Eichmann in Jerusalem: A Report on the Banality of Evil*, Viking, New York, 1963 (revised edition 1968).

28 On the investigation of senior leaders, see Xabier Agirre Aranburu, "Prosecuting the most responsible for international crimes: Dilemmas of definition and prosecutorial discretion", pp. 381–404, in J. Gonzalez (ed.), *Protección Internacional de Derechos Humanos y Estado de Derecho*, Grupo Editorial Ibáñez, Bogotá, 2009.

The *Bemba* case at the ICC has prompted useful discussions on this subject, starting from the decision of the pre-trial chamber in June 2009 to amend the mode of liability alleged by the prosecution and charge Bemba under Article 28 rather than Article 25 of the Statute (different forms or causation) for the rapes and other crimes committed by his subordinates.[29] This is the first trial before the Court that concerns command responsibility, and the prosecution alleges that Bemba failed his responsibility to prevent or punish his troops from raping and attacking civilians. Hopefully the findings of the ICC judges in this case will warn military commanders around the world about their active duty to prevent and punish sexual violence and other crimes.

The discussions of "opportunistic vs. strategic" in the investigations of sexual violence echo the broader theoretical debate on the etiology of rape. Authors closer to feminist advocacy have emphasized the aspects of social construction and cultural inducement.[30] Authors from the field of evolutionary biology have argued a deeper biological predisposition of men towards violent sex that would explain cross-cultural prevalence of rape.[31] These and other theories should not be seen as mutually exclusive since each of them may carry valuable insight on the different dimensions of the crime. The investigator will be best served by learning about the

[29] See ICC, *Prosecutor v. Jean-Pierre Bemba Gombo*, Case No. 01/05-01/08, Decision Pursuant to Article 61(7)(a) and (b) of the Rome Statute on the Charges of the Prosecutor Against Jean-Pierre Bemba Gombo, 15 June 2009, available at http://www.icc-cpi.int/iccdocs/doc/doc699541.pdf, last accessed on 26 August 2011.

[30] For an overview of feminist theories and bibliography on rape, relying mainly on USA authors, see the entry "Feminist perspectives on rape" (2009) of the *Stanford Encyclopedia of Philosophy*, available at http://plato.stanford.edu/entries/feminism-rape/#Oth. For different feminist interpretations of war-time rape, see Darius M. Rejali, "After Feminist Analyses of Bosnian Violence", in *Peace Review: A Journal of Social Justice*, vol. 8, no. 3, 1996, pp. 365–371, available at http://academic.reed.edu/poli_sci/faculty/rejali/articles/bosnia96.html, last accessed on 26 August 2011. For a focus on gender and genocide see the "Gendercide Watch" project at http://www.gendercide.org/. For a well-informed network of legal researchers and practitioners, see the blog http://intlawgrrls.blogspot.com/. All above links last accessed on 2 January 2010.

[31] For this sort of Darwinian-Hobbessian approach from evolutionary biology, see Randy Thornhill and Craig T. Palmer, *A Natural History of Rape. Biological Bases of Sexual Coercion*, MIT Press, Cambridge, 2000. For a thorough critique of this approach, see Cheryl Brown Travis (ed.), *Evolution, Gender and Rape*, MIT Press, Cambridge, 2003.

different theories and keeping an open mind for different types and causal hypotheses of the crime.[32]

There are clearly different types of sexual violence in wartime, from the more "opportunistic" kind to the more "strategic" one and many variants. Factual typologies of sexual violence were defined for example by the reports of the UN Commission of Experts on the Former Yugoslavia (1994) and the Commission of Inquiry on the Post-Election Violence in Kenya (2008).

The legal definition of the offences needs to be taken into account, particularly for what concerns the most advanced provisions of Articles 7 and 8 of the ICC Statute including the following 6 types of sexual violence: "Rape, sexual slavery, enforced prostitution, forced pregnancy, enforced sterilization, or any other form of sexual violence of comparable gravity". Genital mutilation is not included in this list and it may be worth including in an analytical typology, in view of the gravity and widespread nature of the conduct. Forced abortion was also excluded from this list in the process of drafting the ICC Statute, in spite of the known existence of such criminal acts, apparently because it conflicted with the agenda of advocacy groups committed to promoting abortion rights.

In essence the following appear to be the most common types of sexual violence, when considering the aspects of causation and modus operandi:

- Opportunistic – As discussed above, a kind of sexual looting decided by the direct perpetrator, who takes the opportunity given by the defenselessness of the victim and aims primarily at his own sexual satisfaction.
- Strategic – When used as a means to terrorize, punish, interrogate, expel or subjugate the victimized population. This may become apparent with conduct that may not give direct sexual satisfaction to the perpetrator (sterilization, mutilation, penetration with objects), or when the aggression is publicized with an intent to offend the wider population.
- Captivity – Crimes committed in the context of captivity may combine elements of strategy and opportunity or present a kind of "organized opportunity" for rapists to obtain their primary sexual satis-

[32] For an overview of the different theories, see Jonathan Gottschall, "Explaining Wartime Rape", in *Journal of Sex Research*, 2004, vol. 41, no. 2, pp. 129–136.

faction within schemes or premises strategically organized, including scenarios of abduction, sexual slavery or sexual abuse of child soldiers. Captivity scenarios are usually easier to investigate for what concerns leadership responsibility because of the persistency over time, greater ability of the victims to identify perpetrators and commanders, commission within hierarchically organized structure, and coincidence of multiple victims on the same premises. The landmark cases of sexual violence of ICTY focused on captivity scenarios (rapes in the Čelebići detention camp, rape and torture by Furundžija, sexual enslavement in Foča, genital mutilation in the Omarska detention camp).

Sexual behavior comprises multiple variants and factors, even when used for criminal purposes, so that typologies help for the analysis but the reality will often be more complex. For example, in the case of the Lord's Resistance Army ('LRA') the opportunistic rape in the courses of attacks on villages was forbidden, the reason being that the soldiers had orders to capture the women and surrender them to their commanders, for them to have the privilege of choosing their personal sexual slaves who would serve them for years in their base camps. The LRA commanders enforced this system while operating in Northern Uganda, but it seems that when operating in other areas they allowed the most basic scheme of tolerating opportunistic rape by their soldiers, together with killings, mutilations and any kind of violence against civilians. The combination of opportunistic rape followed by highly systematic and strategic cover-up has been observed in several other situations.

7.3. Reporting Issues: Under, Hyper and False

The advocacy literature emphasizes that sexual violence is under-reported, which is true, but it is not entirely the truth. It is clear that sexual violence is usually under-reported due to factors that include fear of retaliation, distrust and dysfunction of the criminal justice system, a sense of shame and rejection from partners, society and the "marriage market". Studies on different situations and contexts have indicated reporting rates between 5 to 25% of the total of committed rapes or sexual assaults: Up to

25% of common rape reported in Australia;[33] 18% reported for the victims of sexual violence from the Rift Valley of Kenya during the post-election violence of 2007–2008;[34] some 15% for the female victims of rape in the USA;[35] up to 10% for victims of rape in France;[36] 8% for female victims of sexual assault in Canada;[37] and 5% for male victims of prison homosexual rape in the U.S.[38]

At the same time instances of hyper-reporting and false reporting are also known from historical and forensic evidence. As Susan Brownmiller observed, rape has been widely reported and highlighted for reasons of political expediency or "atrocity propaganda" in a number of cases, including the following examples of propagandistic exaggeration or false reports: the prominent reports in Belgian media of the rape of white nuns in the Democratic Republic of the Congo at the time of the independence; propagandistic reports of rape of white women by Native Americans in the wars of the XIX century USA; the portrayal of German forces as rapists by the war propaganda in WWI;[39] the false rumors of rape committed by the Vietcong spread by the U.S. military intelligence in Vietnam; false allegations of rape of white women used by the KKK and others for lynching black innocent males in the USA; the promotion

[33] See Patricia Easteal, "Sexual assault law in Australia: contextual challenges and changes", in Westmarland and Gangoli (eds.), 2011, pp. 13–34, at p. 15, see *supra* note 19.

[34] CIPEV, 2008, p. 246, see *supra* note 8.

[35] See Dean Kilpatrick and Jenna McCauley, *Understanding National Rape Statistics.* National Online Resource Center on Violence Against Women, September 2009, available at http://new.vawnet.org/Assoc_Files_VAWnet/AR_RapeStatistics.pdf, last accessed on 3 January 2010.

[36] See Nathalie Bajos, Michel Bozon and the team of the CSF (Contexte de la Sexualité en France) survey, "Les violences sexuelles en France : quand la parole se libère", in *Population et Sociétés*, May 2008, no. 445, available at http://www.ined.fr/fichier/t_publication/1359/publi_pdf1_pop_soc445.pdf (accessed 30 July 2011). Other authors quote lower reporting rates for France.

[37] See Lee Lakeman, "Ending rape: the responsibility of the Canadian State", in Westmarland and Gangoli (eds.), 2011, pp. 35–56, at p. 38, see *supra* note 19 (estimate for 2004).

[38] See Brownmiller, 1975, p. 265, see *supra* note 2. Estimate on the Philadelphia prison system (USA, 1968).

[39] For a detailed analysis on how true crimes were utilized for war propaganda in WWI see Nicoletta F. Gullace, "War Crimes or Atrocity Stories? Anglo-American Narratives of Truth and Deception in the Aftermath of World War I", in Heineman (ed.), 2011, pp. 105–121, see *supra* note 3.

of victims of rape as national heroes in Bangladesh after the independence in 1973.[40]

Figure 2: World War I, recruitment poster of the USA army.

False allegations of sexual violence are a reality, just like with any other crime, due to personal or political motivation. Their extent is difficult to assess but in all known situations of mass violence they appear to be at a lesser or anecdotal scale *vis-à-vis* the very large number of truthful allegations.[41] The collector of statistical data should be careful to avoid prompting false allegations from sources who, in certain contexts, may want to please the interviewer, or may anticipate some advantage from the claim. As the UN WHO (World Health Organization) recommended in 2007:

> Information gatherers need to make sure they are not overly influencing participants with their authority, attitude, or demeanour […] Experience shows that respondents may misunderstand the purposes of interviews and/or misunderstand

[40] See Brownmiller, 1975, pp. 41–44, 78, 87, 132–133, 140–153 and 222–224, see *supra* note 2.

[41] See, among others, Robert R. Hazelwood and Ann W. Burgess, *Practical Aspects of Rape Investigation. A Multidisciplinary Approach*, CRC Press, Florida, 2001, chapter X "False rape allegations", pp. 177–197; and F.D. Jordan, *Sex Crime Investigations. The complete Investigator's Handbook*, Paladin Press, Boulder, 1996, chapter V "False allegations", pp. 79–103.

whether interviews will lead directly to an increase in or personal access to services.[42]

7.4. Analysis of Variations and Prevalence Factors

It is often said that sexual violence is frequent and prevalent in all armed conflicts. What empirical research shows is that there are very large variations across conflicts and actors, so that in many armed conflicts sexual violence is very prevalent and in others much less so.[43] For example, Susan Brownmiller observed a remarkable absence of sexual violence on the part of the Vietcong forces during the Vietnam War, which in her view was due mainly to strict prohibition enforced from the senior command, as well as to the presence of women in the fighting force.[44]

The comparative research of Elisabeth Wood shows that "while sexual violence occurs in all wars, its extent varies dramatically", so that the conflicts of Bosnia, Rwanda, Sierra Leone, Darfur and the Soviet occupation of Germany are among examples with a high prevalence of sexual violence, while Palestine, El Salvador and Sri Lanka have a much lower prevalence.[45] While research associated with advocacy projects typically focuses on the cases of high prevalence, Wood has taken an interest in researching the cases of low sexual violence in order to identify inhibiting factors and show how such crimes are far from unavoidable in war time. For example, in her analysis of the Tamil guerrilla of Sri Lanka it appears that minimal sexual violence is the result of a certain puritanical ethos, the strategic need to co-opt the civilian population, and the fact that "the organization prohibits sexual violence and effectively enforces that

42 WHO Department of Gender, Women and Health, *Ethical and safety recommendations for researching, documenting and monitoring sexual violence in emergencies*, 2007, p. 22, available at http://www.who.int/gender/documents/violence/9789241595681/en/index.html, last accessed on 1 March 2012.

43 For an overview of research bibliography on multiple situations, see Alliance for Direct Action against Rape in Conflicts and Crises, *Documenting Sexual Violence in Conflict: Data and Methods - An Annotated Bibliography*, 2006, available at http://www.alliancedarc.org/downloads/news/Annotated_Bibliography_on_sexual_violence_in_conflict.pdf, last accessed 3 January 2010.

44 See Brownmiller, 1975, pp. 90–91, see *supra* note 2.

45 Elisabeth J. Wood, "Sexual violence during war: toward an understanding of variation", in I. Shapiro, S. Kalyvas and T. Masoud (eds.), *Order, Conflict and Violence*, Cambridge University Press, Cambridge, 2008, pp. 321–351, at p. 321.

decision through a tightly controlled military hierarchy in which punishment is swift and severe".[46]

It is difficult to identify at a general level the factors that affect the level of sexual violence because of the diversity of armed conflicts and types of sexual violence. The contributing factors that seem most relevant include: opportunity for the perpetrator, related to the availability of vulnerable population in the given territory and timeline; strategic agenda of the armed groups to punish, or conversely to co-opt, the civilian population; sexual and ethical culture of the fighting force; prohibition and enforcement from senior command levels; and presence of women in the fighting force.

7.5. Male Victims: the Last Taboo

A point in feminist analysis and advocacy literature which needs to be corrected is their reductionist focus on female victims. The problem is not limited to, in the words of Brownmiller, the "disregard for the bodily integrity of women": human integrity is equally disregarded in the many cases of sexual violence against the will of men.

Common rape of men, in the absence of armed conflict, is well-known and widespread around the world, among others, in the context of prisons, and the subjugation of young males to religious authorities as, among others, within the Catholic Church. Wartime rape of men is also a rather frequent phenomenon. Field research by Lynn Lawry and her team has found an extensive pattern of sexual abuse among male soldiers in Liberia.[47] The investigations of the UN Commission of Experts and ICTY found a number of cases of male rape in former Yugoslavia, just like the ICC investigations did in Central African Republic, among other war situations. That U.S. military personnel sexually abused male prisoners in the Abu Ghraib prison, Iraq, in 2003–2004, is a fact established by disciplinary and judicial investigations.[48] Similar incidents of male sexual victim-

[46] Elisabeth J. Wood, "Armed Groups and Sexual Violence: When Is Wartime Rape Rare?", in *Politics & Society*, vol. 37, no. 1, March 2009, pp. 131–162, at p. 152.

[47] See interview with Lynn Lawry, "Sexual abuse of male soldiers common in Liberian war", available at http://www.newscientist.com/article/dn14522-sexual-abuse-of-male-soldiers-common-in-liberian-war.html, last accessed on 6 January 2010.

[48] See a summary of several investigation reports produced by the U.S. military at http://www.globalsecurity.org/intell/library/reports/2004/intell-abu-ghraib_ar15-6.pdf, last accessed 17 July 2011.

ization are known in the armed conflicts or political persecutions in Chile, Argentina, Greece, Sri Lanka, El Salvador, Iran, Kuwait, and the former Soviet Union, among others.[49]

And yet male victimization remains the most under-reported, or suppressed in advocacy literature, like the last taboo in the world of sexual violence. In the words of UN Office for the Co-ordination of Humanitarian Affairs ('OCHA'), "there is an extremely limited awareness of, and knowledge about, sexual violence against men and boys in conflict among the humanitarian and sexual violence research community".[50] A survey of more than 4,000 NGOs that deal with war-related sexual violence has indicated that only 3% mention male victims in their reports.[51] In the region of the Great Lakes of central Africa the focus of relief and advocacy groups on female victims have come together with a near suppression of the experience of male victims, as the Refugee Law Project from Uganda has found in their remarkable field and research work.[52]

As Lara Stemple has observed, there is not a single instrument of human rights law that mentions sexual violence against men, in contrast with the more that one hundred uses of the term "violence against women" – defined to include sexual violence – in U.N. resolutions, treaties, and other sources of human rights law: "The international instruments that contain the most comprehensive and meaningful definitions of sexual violence exclude men on their face, reflecting and embedding the assumption that sexual violence is a phenomenon relevant only to women and girls".[53] In spite of all the available information, male victims are entirely

49 See Sandesh Sivakumaran, "Sexual Violence Against Men in Armed Conflict", in *European Journal of International Law*, 2007, vol. 18, no. 2, pp. 253–276.

50 See the UN OCHA discussion paper "The Nature, Scope and Motivation for Sexual Violence Against Men and Boys in Armed Conflict", June 2008, p. 2, available at http://ochaonline.un.org/OchaLinkClick.aspx?link=ocha&docId=1092305, last accessed 15 Aug. 2011).

51 See Augusta DelZotto and Adam Jones, "Male-on-Male Sexual Violence in Wartime: Human Rights' Last Taboo?", paper presented to the Annual Convention of the International Studies Association (ISA), New Orleans, 23–27 March 2002, available at http://adamjones.freeservers.com/malerape.htm, last accessed on 17 July 2011.

52 See the documentary produced by the Refugee Law Project *Gender Against Men*, 2009, available at http://www.forcedmigration.org/video/gender-against-men/media/ last accessed on 17 July 2011.

53 Lara Stemple, "Male rape and human rights", in *Hasting Law Journal*, 2009, vol. 60, at p. 619, available at http://uchastings.edu/hlj/archive/vol60/Stemple_60-HLJ-605 .pdf last accessed on 17 July 2011.

ignored in the key resolutions adopted by the UN Security Council in relation to sexual violence in armed conflicts (resolutions 1325, 1820, 1888 and 1889, adopted between 2000–2009).

Several factors are contributing to the taboo of male sexual victimization. Firstly, it seems clear that the number of female victims of sexual violence is greater, and thus it justifies greater attention. Secondly, men may be particularly reluctant to report the crime because of the effect of humiliation and challenge of their power status, as well as severe stigma in homophobic societies. Very low reporting rates for male victims are known from peace-time rape, such as a 0.6% in France, compared to up to 10% for female victims.[54] Thirdly, male victims may be seen as an inconvenient truth for those advocacy groups and donors dedicated to distinctively highlighting the suffering of women.[55]

The taboo on male victims is an impediment for establishing the truth about sexual violence, it is unfair to those victims that happen to be men, and furthermore it may promote a stereotypical view of women as perpetual victims that does not necessarily help the cause of their empowerment. For all these reasons, researchers, advocates and investigators should not be allowed anymore to ignore sexual violence when committed against the will of men.

7.6. Pattern Evidence and Analysis

The following pages will refer only briefly to the methodology for using pattern evidence and analysis in the investigation of sexual violence, since this issue has already been explained in detail in a previous article.[56] Patterns are key elements of international crimes, which usually consist of large series of incidents that share common causes and features. The investigation of international crimes often will need determine whether a large series of incidents have enough elements in common to be considered as a relevant pattern or crime. The relevance of patterns is acknowledged in several legal instruments, such as the concept of "Evidence of

[54] Le Goaziou, 2011, p. 42, see *supra* note 3.

[55] On the position of aid agencies on this issue see the report, see The Observer, "The rape of men", 17 July 2011, available at http://www.guardian.co.uk/society/2011/jul/17/the-rape-of-men, last accessed on 17 July 2011.

[56] See Xabier Agirre Aranburu, "Sexual Violence beyond Reasonable Doubt: Using Pattern Evidence and Analysis for International Cases", in *Leiden Journal of International Law*, 2010, vol. 23, pp. 609–627.

Consistent Pattern of Conduct" considered in Rule 93 of the Rules of Procedure and Evidence of ICTY and ICTR, the reference to a "Context of a manifest pattern of similar conduct" in the definition of genocide of the Elements of the Crimes of the ICC, and extensive international case law.[57]

Large number of incidents can be characterized as a pattern as long as they show common features on the following aspects: a) The profile of the perpetrators; b) The profile of the victims; c) The geographical and chronological distribution of the crime; d) The modus operandi in the commission of the crime. Pattern evidence and analysis have been used successfully mainly for killings and mass destruction and displacement, but its use for sexual violence charges has been remarkably more limited. As Susana SaCouto and Katherine Cleary have observed:

> Unfortunately, while the ad hoc tribunals have used circumstantial or pattern evidence to establish that an accused ordered certain crimes, a review of sexual violence and gender-based cases before these tribunals indicates that they appear more reluctant to do so in these types of cases.[58]

Concerning criminal investigations the pattern of the crime is an element of the case that will need to be proved before the chamber of trial, ultimately up to a standard of "beyond reasonable doubt", further to due process, and including the following requirements: a) Disclosure: the pattern data may be subject to disclosure at the trial stage as a requirement of law, or at a specific request from the defense or the judges, which needs to be taken into account at the collection stage in order to either collect anonymous data, or sanitize the data to protect the identity of providers, or obtain informed consent from the provider for the eventual disclosure of their personal data.[59]; b) Credentials: In case of expert testimony the judges and the defense may well raise questions about the professional credentials and neutrality of the witness, or the data collectors, which is not uncommon.[60]; c) Scientific methodology: Pattern evidence, whether

---

[57] For definitions of Crime Pattern Analysis in domestic jurisdictions see, among others, http://www.macrimeanalysts.com/articles/IdentifyingCrimePatterns.pdf, last accessed on 18 July 2011, and the EUROPOL *Analytical Guidelines*.

[58] SaCouto and Cleary, p. 353, see *supra* note 7.

[59] For a detailed protocol on informed consent see WHO, 2007, section 6 "Informed consent", pp. 22–23, see *supra* note 42.

[60] For a comparative analysis of expert evidence across different national systems, see Lirieka Meintjes-Van der Walt, *Expert Evidence in the Criminal Justice Process. A Comparative Perspective*, Rozenberg Publishers, Amsterdam, 2001. On the qualifica-

statistical or other, will need to be produced following standard scientific methodology, accepted by the scientific community, subject to peer review, and properly sourced and justified; d) Defense expertise: The accused is likely to bring experts to challenge the pattern evidence presented by the prosecution, as it has happened in numerous cases before international tribunals (for example, in the *Galić* and *Milutinović* cases before ICTY concerning crime statistics); e) Cross-examination: Experts or investigators presenting pattern evidence are likely to be subject to adversarial cross-examination by the defense, who may want to raise doubts on any of the above issues.

Different kinds of data should be considered in the investigations of sexual violence patterns:

- Surveys – Victimization data collected through sampling surveys. Provided scientific consistency, data from specifically designed surveys could provide with the best pattern evidence. Examples include surveys conducted in Sierra Leone, Liberia and among refugees from Darfur in Chad.[61]
- Medical data – Data on medical treatment of the victims, provided that the victims did seek medical assistance, the providers did record adequately their services, and eventual biases (due to uneven access to medical services, political factors or other) can be identi-

tions of data collectors, see WHO, 2007, section 7 "Information gathering team", pp. 24–25, see *supra* note 42. On the experience and skills of investigators and interpreters collecting statements of victims, see Patricia Viseur-Sellers "The other voices: Interpreters and investigators of sexual violence in international criminal prosecutions", in Durham and Gurd (eds.), 2005, pp. 155–164, see *supra* note 4.

61 See L.L. Amowitz *et al.*, "Prevalence of War-Related Sexual Violence and Other Human Rights Abuses Among Internally Displaced Persons in Sierra Leone", in *Journal of the American Medical Association* ('*JAMA*'), 2002, vol. 287, no. 4; S. Swiss *et al.*, "Violence against women during the Liberian civil conflict", in *JAMA*, 1998, vol. 279, no. 8, pp. 625–629; and Physicians for Human Rights, *War-Related Sexual Violence in Sierra Leone. A Population-Based Assessment*, 2002. See also the survey conducted by the Atrocities Documentation Team ('ADT') in Darfur, as documented in the book by S. Totten and E. Markusen (eds.), *Genocide in Darfur: Investigating the Atrocities in the Sudan*, Routledge, New York, 2006. See the questionnaire utilized by the ADT, including references to rape, available at http://conference.cedat.be/sites/default/files/Pfunderheller_ADT%20questionnaire.pdf, last accessed on 3 January 2010.

fied and controlled.[62] The privacy rights of the victims need to be respected, by means of informed consent as a pre-condition for data collection, or alternatively by inviting the holder of the data (hospitals or other institutions) to produce generic statistics without disclosure of personal data. For example, the data on sexual violence provided by different hospitals in Kenya was used by the inquiry on the post-election violence in 2007–2008.[63]

- Public reports – Reports from news agencies and other open sources, provided adequate coverage and source reliability, have a great potential, particularly in view of the rapid development of electronic media. Examples include the monitoring for crime reports in Darfur and Iraq, as well as the new options explored by the Ushahidi project with web-based user-generated contents since 2008 in Kenya, DRC, Gaza and elsewhere.[64]
- Crime reports – Data collected by law enforcement or human rights agencies based on the allegations presented by victims. For example, the data on rape collected by the UN in Central African Republic contributed greatly to assess the pattern related to the armed conflict in this country 2002–2003.[65]

---

62 See S. Swiss and J.E. Giller, "Rape as a crime of war. A medical perspective", in *JAMA*, August 4, 1993, vol. 270, no. 5, pp. 612–615.

63 See CIPEV, 2008, pp. 247–248, see *supra* note 8. See also The Centre for Rights Eudcation and Awareness, *Women Paid the Price! Sexual and Gender-based violence in the 2007 post-election conflict in Kenya*, Nairobi, 2008, available at http://creawkenya.org/index.php?option=com_content&view=article&id=100&Itemid=127 last accessed on 5 March 2010. On rape as a common crime in Kenya, see Connie Kisuke, *Rape. A Critical Analysis*, Uzima Publishing House, Nairobi, 2008.

64 See for Darfur, with a focus on mortality but also including data on rape, A.H. Petersen and L. Tullin, *The Scorched Earth of Darfur: Patterns in death and destruction reported by the people of Darfur. January 2001-September 2005*, Copenhagen: Bloodhound, Copenhagen, 2006, available at http://www.bloodhound.se/06_04_26_DARFUR_report.pdf; On Irak, with a focus on violent deaths, see the Irak Body Count project at http://www.iraqbodycount.org/, and for Ushahidi see http://www.ushahidi.com/, last accessed on 3 January 2010.

65 See FIDH Report International investigative mission War crimes in the Central African Republic "When the elephants fight, the grass suffers", 2003, available at http://www.fidh.org/IMG/pdf/FIDH_Report_WarCrimes_in_CAR_English_Feb2003.pdf, last accessed on 3 January 2010. For an attempt to estimate the number of victims of rape in Rwanda see C. Bijleveld, A. Morssinkhof and A. Smeulers, "Counting the

- Internal records – In some cases the perpetrators and their systems generate valuable data about their own crimes, or the administration of their resources and premises, which could be available in cases of systematic captivity or sexual enslavement.
- Perpetrator data – Information on the profile, behavior and rules of the perpetrators may be highly relevant to analyze patterns, as proved by the pioneering research of Elisabeth Wood. This may include information on the utterances by perpetrators when committing the crime or on the rules adopted formally or informally by the attacking force.
- Proxy data – Data related to the consequences of sexual violence may be valuable as leads or circumstantial evidence, including outliers in pregnancy, sexually transmitted infections, traumatic symptoms, abortion, consumption of certain drugs or tests. For example, in 1993 a UN team found in the former Yugoslavia 119 pregnancies due to rape within a limited sample and, assuming conservatively that 1% of intercourses result in pregnancy, they estimated 11,900 rapes as an indicator of the large scale of the pattern.[66] Mental health indicators have been also explored to analyze sexual violence in the aftermath of hurricane Katrina.[67] Like any other form of circumstantial evidence, proxy data should be considered cautiously, mainly for corroboration purposes.[68]

In criminal investigations information cannot be taken at face value and the above-mentioned types of data shall be subject to standard methods of source evaluation by criteria of credibility, reliability, and so on. When working with data of limited quality, which is most often the case, it will be necessary to acknowledge such limitations, operate with approx-

---

Countless Rape Victimization During the Rwandan Genocide", in *International Criminal Justice Review*, 2009, Vol. 19, No. 2, pp. 208–224.

66 See Swiss and Giller, 1993, p. 613, see *supra* note 62.

67 L. Lawry, M.P. Anastario and R. Larrance, "Using mental health indicators to identify postdisaster gender-based violence among women displaced by hurricane Katrina", in *Journal of Women's Health*, 2008, vol. 17, no. 9, pp. 1437–1444.

68 For an overview of the kind of data on sexual violence that can be found in displaced populations see Jeanne Ward, "Addressing Gender-Based Violence in Refugee, Internally Displaced and Post-Conflict Settings", Reproductive Health for Refugees Consortium, 2002, available at http://www.rhrc.org/resources/gbv/ifnotnow.html, last accessed on 3 January 2010.

imate ranges and confidence intervals, and present the findings accordingly.

The available data will need to be registered in a relational database designed with adequate analytical standards and technical requirements. From the field of human rights investigations very useful database models have been developed and implemented in multiple situations since the 1990s, such as the model *Who Did What to Whom?* of the American Association for the Advancement of Science (AAAS) and the HURIDOCS model.[69] The more advanced database models should provide for object-relational applications (links to the original electronic files containing the information or scanned images of the original paper records), descriptive statistics, graphics, and web-based or remote access. The choice of the most suitable database model will depend on the available human and technical resources.

To the question of whether statistics can be used as evidence of sexual violence patterns in leadership cases, the answer is yes: similar methods have already been used successfully for other offences in international tribunals, and for various other matters in a number of national jurisdictions.[70] Descriptive statistics can make a unique evidentiary contribution for the most accurate and objective assessment of the crime pattern. This has been the experience of the ICTY Prosecutor since 2000

69 Patrick Ball, *Who Did What to Whom? Planning and Implementing a Large Scale Human Rights Data Project*, AAAS, Washington, 1996; and P. Ball, H.F. Spirer, and L. Spirer (eds.), *Making the Case. Investigating Large Scale Human Rights Violations Using Information Systems and Data Analysis*, available at http://shr.aaas.org/mtc, last accessed 3 January 2010; J. Dueck *et al.*, *HURIDOCS Standard Formats: A Tool for Documenting Human Rights Violations*, HURIDOCS, Oslo, 1993; and J. Dueck, A.M. Noval *et al.*, *HURIDOCS Standard Formats: Supporting Documents*, HURIDOCS, Oslo, 1993.

70 See, among others, J.L. Gastwirth (ed.), *Statistical Science in the Courtroom*, Springer-Verlag, New York, 2000. For epidemiology statistics, see *ibid.*, chapter XIII by S. Loue, "Epidemiological causation in the legal context: Substance and procedures", pp. 263–280; and the publications of the Centre for Research on the Epidemiology of Disasters at http://www.cred.be/. See also C. Aitken and F. Taroni, *Statistics and the Evaluation of Evidence for Forensic Scientists*, Wiley, Chichester, 2004 (second edition); and J. Asher, D. Banks and F.J. Scheuren (eds.), *Statistical Methods for Human Rights*, Springer, New York, 2008.

with the use of statistics for the description of crime patterns.[71] The expertise originated mainly from the field of demography, led by Helge Brunborg and Ewa Tabeau, using data from multiple sources (census data, exhumation records, ICRC data on missing persons, data provided by NGOs, and so on).[72] This evidence was accepted by the judges and contributed to convictions in the cases of Krstić, Blagojević and Jokić (for the mass killings in Srebrenica in July 1995), Galić (for the siege of Sarajevo and the resulting injuries and deaths of civilians 1992–1995) and Brđanin (for persecutions in the Bosnian Krajina including thousands of killings). Most of this work relied on different techniques of counting, matching and managing existing individual records which, as long as the records are reliable, makes a relatively safe and robust approach.

Since 2004 the Prosecutor of the ICC has used descriptive statistics in all investigations, both internally for purposes of situation and case selection (including assessments of crime gravity and degrees of responsibility among leaders) and to support applications for warrants of arrest before the judges (from the application on Kony and others in Uganda to the application on President Bashir of the Republic of Sudan).

Crime mapping is the standard term for the use of GIS (Geographic Information Systems) in crime analysis. It may take from basic manual drawing to computerized cartography through geo-coding, geo-databases (matching descriptive data with geometric data) and geo-statistics.[73] Provided sufficient accuracy of the geographic and other data, crime mapping should be used for analyzing patterns of sexual violence just as much as it

---

[71] For an overview of ICTY statistical evidence as of 2006 see the paper by Boris Mijatovic "Statistical Evidence for the Investigation of International Crimes", available at http://www.ssm.lu/pdfs/2006_2_12.pdf, last accessed on 31 December 2009.

[72] Dr. Helge Brunborg is a demographer employed by the ICTY OTP, starting in 1997. For the Krstić case he testified and presented the team's "Report on the Number of Missing and Dead from Srebrenica". Prof. Ewa TABEAU is a demographer heading the Demographic Unit of the ICTY OTP and for the Galić case she testified on the basis of her report "Population Losses in the 'Siege' of Sarajevo – 10 September 1992 to 10 August 1994". See Dr. Brunborg's recommendations for the ICC OTP in his paper of April 2003, "Needs for demographic and statistical expertise at the Inter-national Criminal Court", available at http://www.icc-cpi.int/iccdocs/asp_docs/library/organs/otp/brunborg.pdf, last accessed on 16 December 2009.

[73] On domestic crime mapping standards, see, among others, K. Harries, *Mapping Crime: Principle and Practice*, Crime Mapping Research Center, Washington, 1999, available at http://www.ncjrs.gov/pdffiles1/nij/178919.pdf, last accessed on 1 March 2012.

has been used for other crimes in national and international jurisdictions. Since 2004 the Prosecutor of the ICC has used crime mapping techniques in all investigations, including in presentations before the judges, whether plotting incidents and relevant events in still maps, using animations to show the flow of events over the relevant areas, analyzing and coding satellite imagery, or using remote sensing data for three-dimensional topography. In the case of Bemba, data on rape and other crimes were plotted in animated maps to analyze the correlation with military operations. In the case of Bashir, crime and tribal population data were plotted to analyze correlations indicative of specific intent. In both cases such maps were presented before the judges.

Using pattern witnesses, those who have an overall view of multiple incidents, is rather common practice before international tribunals. Precedents are known since the Tokyo trials, when missionaries that witnessed the "rape of Nanking" were called as witnesses for the Prosecution, since they were able to move through the city when the rapes and other crimes were taking place.[74] The testimony of Binaifer Nowrojee before the ICTR is also a valuable precedent.[75] Witnesses of this kind may include field workers, researchers, journalists, international observers or local leaders and authorities, provided this is done with their agreement, reliability, and no impeding conflict with their primary responsibilities. Often the testimony of these witnesses is supported by the reports that they produced at the relevant time (a technique already utilized in the Tokyo trials and greatly exploited before the different international tribunals).

---

[74] See Z. Khaiyuan (ed.), *Eyewitnesses to Massacre: American Missionaries Bear Witness to Japanese Atrocities in Nanjing*, East Gate Book, M.E. Sharp Inc., New York, 2001. Some of them were qualified scholars in Chinese culture and had reported to the Japanese Embassy in a series of letters.

[75] Nowrojee produced, in 2004, the report "Sexual Violence Crimes during the Rwandan Genocide" for the ICTR OTP, and she gave expert testimony in several ICTR cases, basing her assessment on her direct access to the evidence and a comprehensive review of the ICTR jurisprudence. See B. Nowrojee, *Shattered lives: sexual violence during the Rwandan genocide and its aftermath*, Human Rights Watch, New York, 1996; her reports "We Can Do Better Investigating and Prosecuting International Crimes of Sexual Violence", 2004, and "'Your Justice is Too Slow'. Will the ICTR Fail wanda's Rape Victims?", 2005, both available at http://www.coalitiondroitsdesfemmes.org/site/publications/index_en.php, last accessed on 18 July 2011.

7.7. Conclusions: the Way Forward

The fight against the taboos and impunity for sexual violence has advanced greatly in recent decades thanks to the influence of the feminist movement and other advocacy efforts. At this stage it is time to acknowledge this progress, gather lessons learned and best practices, and further advance towards a more complete and empirically rigorous understanding of sexual violence. The axiomatic assumption that sexual violence must be prevalent in every conflict has been disproved by extensive empirical research showing large variations related to multiple factors of population, opportunity and strategy. The assumption that war-related rape must always follow from strategic design "as a weapon of war" is over-simplistic, and it should give way to broader typologies considering both opportunistic and strategic factors.

It is true that sexual violence is under-reported, as indicated by numerous studies in peace and wartime. There is a need to bring to light the very large "dark figure" of sexual crimes that remain unknown with advanced methods of data collection and pattern analysis. Specific victimization surveys may produce the most suitable evidence, for which proper methodology and resource allocation is needed. Perpetrator-focused evidence will always be critical for successful criminal investigations. Proxy data should also be considered, to the possible and reasonable extent. Specific training is clearly advisable for the originators and collectors of the data.

It is also true that there are instances of hyper-reporting or false reporting due to political or personal interest and, furthermore, factors of under-reporting and hyper-reporting may be present simultaneously and working at cross-purposes at the same time in the same given situation. The victimization of men seems to be the last taboo in relation to sexual violence, affecting even advocacy groups and international institutions, which needs to be addressed on behalf of those victims that should not receive any less attention simply because they happen to be male.

These criteria should guide investigations operating in the best interest of all victims of sexual violence, while making sure that criminal law is a tool to serve not only the victims, but also the rights of the suspects to have an impartial process, and furthermore to let the truth set free the societies that suffered the conflict.

8

Statistical Evidence of Sexual Violence in International Court Settings

Amelia Hoover Green[*]

8.1. Introduction

Conflict-related sexual violence presents a serious challenge to international legal structures for a number of reasons. Sexual violence is under-reported as a general rule, and is particularly under-reported via 'official' processes (for example, law enforcement and courts).[1] Consequently, documentary and testimonial evidence of individual cases may be too sparse to support accusations that armed group leaders "knew or should have known" of a "plan or policy" to commit widespread and/or systematic sexual violence. Nevertheless, non-governmental and intergovernmental organizations ('NGOs' and 'IGOs') advocate international prosecutions as a means of ending impunity for the practice of sexual violence, and prosecutors at the International Criminal Tribunal for the Former Yugoslavia ('ICTY'), the International Criminal Tribunal for Rwanda ('ICTR') and the International Criminal Court ('ICC') have sought convictions for sexual violence and sexual violence related crimes.[2]

---

[*] **Amelia Hoover Green** is a Ph.D. Candidate in the Department of Political Science at Yale University, and a Consultant to the Human Rights Data Analysis Group at Benetech, Inc. During the summer of 2010 and academic year 2010–2011, she is finishing her dissertation, which documents and attempts to explain micro-level variations in the types – as distinct from the levels – of violence against non-combatants. More generally, her research interest lies in how, and how effectively, behavioral norms get transmitted through hierarchical organizations.

[1] Francoise Roth, Tamy Guberek and Amelia Hoover Green, *Using Quantitative Data to Assess Conflict-Related Sexual Violence in Colombia: Challenges and Opportunities*. Human Rights Data Analysis Group, 2011. Available at http://www.hrdag.org/resources/publications/SV%20report%20april%2026,%202011.pdf, last accessed on 1 June 2011; Dean Kilpatrick and Jenna McCauley, "Understanding National Rape Statistics", in *VAWnet Applied Research Forum*, 2009, available at http://www.vawnet.org/Assoc_Files_VAWnet/AR_RapeStatistics.pdf, last accessed on 1 June 2011.

[2] See review in K. Alexa Koenig, Ryan Lincoln and Lauren Groth, *The Jurisprudence of Sexual Violence*, University of California Berkeley Human Rights Center, 2011.

While these prosecutorial moves are laudable, they represent prosecutions for only a small fraction of wartime sexual violence, typically the most well-documented and/or clearly systematic cases. Ending the prevailing climate of impunity for sexual violence in most conflicts requires significantly more evidence than is typically thought to be available via "standard" (documentary and testimonial) legal sources.

Given this problem, a key question is the extent to which numerical data can be used as the basis of factual determinations in international courts. Numerical data has gained increasing power in courtrooms as courts have moved beyond purely individual-level issues (Person X sues Person Y; the State accuses Person Y of Crime Z) to consider "social issues" affecting large classes of people (a group of female employees alleges that Corporation M uses sex-discriminatory hiring practices; a group of African American plaintiffs alleges that racial discrimination is *per se* harmful). Prosecution for war crimes and crimes against humanity typically fall under the latter category. Conviction, especially of higher-level leaders, requires proving not only that crimes occurred, but that those crimes were directed, or known of and tolerated, by such leaders. Patterns and trends that appear at the level of whole populations can – in theory, at least – provide this broader view.

The evaluation of "patterns and trends" is frequently associated with quantitative data. In theory, statistical evidence of sexual violence can connect armed group leaders to patterns of widespread and/or systematic sexual violence even in the absence of massive documentary or testimonial evidence. Yet numerical data on sexual violence, perhaps still more than numerical data on other human rights violations, may prove difficult or impossible to use effectively in international legal settings. As will be discussed in the present chapter, statistical evidence has yet to form a significant part of an international prosecution, largely for two reasons, one inferential and one institutional.

The inferential problems with numerical data on sexual violence (and especially war crimes of sexual violence) are well known.[3] The incidence and prevalence of sexual violence are notoriously difficult to measure, even in ideal circumstances (for example during peacetime, when populations are relatively stable, the rule of law is well established and the threat of retaliation is relatively low). For example, in the United States a

[3] See review in Roth, Guberek and Hoover Green, 2011, *supra* note 1.

majority of rape victims do not report their experiences to law enforcement or other authorities; many do not even disclose an experience of sexual violence in the context of a confidential survey investigation.[4] In consequence, correctly inferring specific patterns and trends of sexual violence in a wartime population may prove impossible, at least in the short term. At the very least, the well-known difficulty of measuring such phenomena may prove beneficial for defense attorneys seeking to discredit prosecution theories. Below, I discuss several sources of statistical bias that stand in the way of inferring population-level patterns and trends in sexual violence.[5]

The institutional problems with statistics in international legal settings are perhaps less well known. In a previous paper, I argued that the ICTY's adversarial information environment, as well as other institutional characteristics, played an important role in the judges' decision not to rely upon the Prosecution's statistical evidence in trials related to killing and forced migration in Kosovo.[6] Here I explore the extent to which these insights apply to data on sexual violence, hypothesizing that the cognitive biases that affected data on mortality and migration in *Milutinović et al.*[7] should be expected to affect sexual violence data still more strongly. In line with conclusions in Roth, Guberek and Hoover Green,[8] I argue that sexual violence data should not be used in isolation; rather, numerical data should be used only to complement qualitative information in the evaluation of (both legal and social scientific) hypotheses.

---

4 Mary P. Koss, "Detecting the Scope of Rape: A Review of Prevalence Research Methods", in *Journal of Interpersonal Violence*, 1993, vol. 8, no. 2, pp. 198–222; Bonnie Fisher, "The Effects of Survey Question Wording on Rape Estimates", *Violence Against Women*, 2009, vol. 15, no. 2, p. 133; Sarah L. Cook, Christine A. Gidycz, Mary P. Koss and Megan Murphy, "Emerging Issues in the Measurement of Rape Vitimization", *Violence Against Women*, 2011, vol. 17, no. 2, p. 201.

5 My view is perhaps less optimistic than that of Agirre. See his chapter in the present volume and also Xabier Agirre Aranburu, "Sexual Violence beyond Reasonable Doubt: Using Pattern Evidence and Analysis for International Cases", in *Law and Social Inquiry*, 2010, vol. 35, issue 4, pp. 855–879.

6 Amelia Hoover Green, "Learning the Hard Way at the ICTY: Statistical Evidence of Human Rights Violations in an Adversarial Information Environment", in Alette Smeulers (ed.), *Collective Violence and International Criminal Justice: An Interdisciplinary Approach*, Intersentia, Antwerp, 2010.

7 International Criminal Tribunal for the Former Yugoslavia, *Prosecutor v. Milan Milutinović et al.*, Case No. IT-05–87, 2009. Hereafter referred to as *Milutinović*.

8 See *supra* note 1.

To be clear, this chapter is written from the perspective of a statistical analyst who may be asked to defend claims in an international court setting, rather than from a legal perspective. While legal issues are considered, they are considered only in light of their effects on statistical reasoning.

8.2. Inferential Problems

8.2.1. Biased Samples

Roth, Guberek and Hoover Green define statistical bias non-technically, as "the difference between a sample measurement (for example the number of reported cases of sexual violence) and the true population value, that is, the real but unknowable number of cases of sexual violence in the population".[9] To be clear, while "bias" frequently refers to cognitive phenomena such as prejudice or preference, this type of "bias" is a statistical, not a cognitive, phenomenon, and I discuss it as such.

Sampling bias occurs when the subjects measured (for example, patients at medical clinics) are not representative of the population of interest (the population of a particular area). When a sample is biased (for example, when the "sample" only includes people who presented to the clinic), statistics that describe the sample ("50% of patients at clinic X reported experiencing sexual violence") cannot be generalized to the population of interest ("50% of people in region Y suffered sexual violence"). Samples may also be biased by the level of training, ethnicity, sex, or other characteristics of interviewers or survey enumerators. For example, in a nationwide survey, if survey enumerators (workers who ask questions of survey respondents) were better-trained in one location than another – or if enumerator ethnicity matched subject ethnicity in one region, but not another – then these locations may falsely appear to be experiencing different amounts of violence.

A second key source of bias in sexual violence data is the reporting process; hence, this type of bias is known as reporting bias.[10] The fundamental problem in the sexual violence reporting process can be boiled

---

9 Roth, Guberek, and Hoover Green, 2011, p. 19, see *supra* note 1.

10 See, *e.g.*, Joseph Catania, "A Framework for Conceptualizing Reporting Bias and Its Antecedents in Interviews Assessing Human Sexuality", *Journal of Sex Research*, 1999, vol. 36, no. 1., pp. 25–38.

down to just one dynamic: some victims are more likely to report than others. For example, if urban, educated women are more likely to report sexual violence than women from rural areas with little access to education, then data on sexual violence may *erroneously* show that urban women suffered more sexual violence, when in fact the observation is the result of different rates of reporting. The true danger of reporting bias, from the point of view of an analyst attempting to build a legal case against an institutional perpetrator, resides in its unevenness. Consider an example in which prosecutors theorize that an armed group targeted a particular ethnic identity for sexual violence, and support this theory with statistical evidence. Defense attorneys (and defense experts) would be likely to attack the representativeness of these statistical findings, arguing that victims from the ostensibly targeted ethnic group were more likely to *report* having been victimized, not more likely to have been victimized.

To take one example, it is frequently argued that wartime and post-conflict sexual violence in Liberia targets socially taboo groups such as elderly women and very young children specifically.[11] However, there is no reliable evidence to suggest that this is the case; witnesses may simply be more likely to report sexual violence against young victims. In addition, claims regarding the targeting of very young or very old victims do not withstand controlling for the age and sex distribution in the Liberian population. In other words, although there may be more child victims than adult victims, this is more likely to be a function of the overrepresentation of children in the Liberian population than of targeting by armed actors.[12]

Disclosure bias (also known as "fear of disclosure bias") presents another significant barrier to the representativity of sexual violence data.[13] Disclosure bias occurs when respondents fear disclosure of their full and honest answer, and consequently answer incompletely or falsely. Among

---

[11] Nicholas Kristof, "After War, Mass Rape Persists", *New York Times*, 21 May 2009, reviewed in Dara Cohen and Amelia Hoover Green, "Dueling Incentives: Sexual Violence in Liberia and the Politics of Human Rights Advocacy", manuscript on file with the author.

[12] Kristen Cibelli, Amelia Hoover and Jule Krüger, *Descriptive Statistics from Statements to the Truth and Reconciliation Commission of Liberia*, Human Rights Data Analysis Report to the Truth and Reconciliation Commission of Liberia, 1 September 2009. Available at http://www.hrdag.org/resources/publications/Benetech-TRC-descri ptives-final.pdf, last accessed on 1 June 2011.

[13] Paul Biemer and Lars Lyberg, *Introduction to Survey Quality*, John Wiley and Sons, Inc., 2003, p. 145.

victims, the potential costs of disclosure vary significantly. For example, in communities in which public gang rapes occurred, there is no additional cost of disclosure, because the status of respondents as rape victims is already known to neighbors who witnessed the event. If, on the other hand, most rapes occurred in private, victims may have the option to keep the incidents secret, protecting themselves against subsequent stigma.[14] From the analyst's perspective, this means that reporting rates may vary with the modus operandi of the perpetrator, creating an unmeasurable but critical bias in the relative proportions of public versus private sexual violence. Any quantitative analysis of sexual violence will be heavily influenced, even determined, by the immensely complex combination of factors which influence each victim's decision about whether it is to her benefit to report or conceal the violence done to her.[15]

8.2.2. Definitions

Issues of definition frequently plague empirical studies of sexual violence. For example, when conducting interviews with survivors or service providers, question wordings may or may not accurately represent the definition of sexual violence that legal proceedings later consider. Leiby notes, for example, that the legal definition of rape influenced how testimonials were classified in the Peruvian Truth Commission; survivors who were forced to marry their rapist were not seen as victims of rape, and male victims of sexual abuse were commonly viewed as victims of torture, rather than sexual violence.[16] In the Democratic Republic of the Congo (DRC), the World Health Organization found that sexual violence for

---

14 According to some UN personnel serving in the Democratic Republic of Congo (DRC), this dynamic appears to play a significant role in reporting bias, causing over-estimates of the proportion of rapes that had multiple perpetrators and/or occurred in public.

15 Ethical considerations demand that investigators respect victims' choices regarding reporting, although these decisions may play havoc with evidentiary considerations. Victims and witnesses make conscious decisions to keep their experience private. Simply insisting on more testimonies places pressure on victims – and does little to mitigate the biases inherent in unsystematically gathered data. See Shana Swiss and Peggy Jennings, *Documenting the Impact of Conflict on Women Living in Internally Displaced Persons' Camps in Sri Lanka: Some Ethical Considerations*, Women's Rights International, 2006.

16 Michele Leiby, "Digging in the Archives: The Promise and Peril of Primary Documents", *Politics and Society*, vol. 37, no. 1, p. 75.

which no witness would testify to the use of force was not recorded as such, even when the victim reported the assault directly.[17] All these definitional issues may continue to plague statistical findings when they are introduced in legal settings.

Perhaps more troubling to prosecutors than the definition of sexual violence is the extent to which conflict-related sexual violence and non-conflict-related sexual violence are intertwined. In some cases, conflict-relatedness is clear; in many others, it is difficult or impossible to demonstrate that sexual violence actually increased during the conflict period, because no "baseline" statistics exist.

In some settings, conflict dynamics indicate clear differences between conflict-related and non-conflict-related sexual violence. Cases from the Central African Republic, now before the International Criminal Court, exemplify this dynamic. Here, a high incidence of rape and other acts of sexual violence, perpetrated by armed individuals, appears to have been "a central feature of the conflict" in 2002–2003, and was clearly associated with armed groups, rather than with non-combatant perpetrators.[18] This clarity is reinforced by the fact that the perpetrators came to villages only for a short while, to commit violent acts, and then left. Some types of associated conduct may also connect sexual violence unambiguously with a conflict. For example, when military personnel use sexual violence in the course of military operations, such as attacks, massacres, looting, detention or interrogation, the association between conflict and sexual violence is clear.

However, these clear cases are rare, relative to the total amount of sexual violence perpetrated during, and therefore potentially associated with, armed conflict. Occasionally, the modus operandi of the crimes provides a clue: for example, gang rape and public sexual violence are frequently associated with wartime rape.[19] The endemic nature of sexual violence across cultures, and associated endemic under-reporting, present

---

[17] Mendy Marsh, MS Purdin and S. Navani, "Addressing Sexual Violence in Humanitarian Emergencies", *Global Public Health*, vol. 1, no. 2, p. 133–146.

[18] Office of the Prosecutor, International Criminal Court, "Background: Situation in the Democratic Republic of the Congo", 22 May 2007. Available at http://www.icc-cpi.int/NR/rdonlyres/B64950CF-8370-4438-AD7C-0905079D747A/144037/ICCOTPBN20070522220_A_EN.pdf, last accessed on 15 December 2010.

[19] Dara Kay Cohen, *Explaining Sexual Violence in Civil War*. Ph.D. Thesis, Stanford University, 2010.

a serious challenge to prosecutors attempting to draw a bright line between rape and sexual violence perpetrated during a conflict and sexual violence perpetrated *because of* a conflict. For example, while wartime rape is a significant feature of the conflict in the Democratic Republic of the Congo, rape by soldiers (or indeed, rape by anyone other than the respondent's partner) represented only a minority of cases reported in the Demographic and Health Survey for DRC in 2008.[20]

8.2.3. Comparing Data Sources

In determining the utility of a source of quantitative information, it is vital to distinguish between two main types of data: surveys and convenience data. In this piece, "survey data" refers to data that was gathered as part of a systematic sample survey, drawn to represent relevant population strata proportionally. A carefully drawn sample survey may provide the most defensible route via which to make inferences from a data collection to population-level patterns and trends. However, even survey data – the current "gold standard" – frequently reach conflicting results and are subject to serious criticisms. For example, even if relevant sub-populations are carefully sampled in order to ensure representativity in the subject pool, this does not "protect the data" against criticism charging that, for example, Group X is more likely to report sexual violence than Group Y, and that therefore findings comparing prevalence between these groups are invalid.

The most common way to collect data on conflict-related sexual violence is through testimonies or other forms of direct contact with victims of violence. However, such accounts are likely to be biased when considered in the aggregate – not in the sense of being incorrect or untrue, but in the sense of reflecting individual victims rather than populations. This is unsurprising: qualitative accounts' particular strength is in their ability to convey the particularities of individual experience, rather than reducing victims to a population of "like units".

However, when the question concerns a population (for example, "How many individuals suffered sexual violence in this area?"), what is necessary is precisely the sort of representativity that individual testimo-

20 Amber Peterman, Tia Palermo and Caryn Bredenkamp, "Estimates and Determinants of Sexual Violence Against Women in the Democratic Republic of Congo", *American Journal of Public Health*, vol. 101, no. 6, pp. 1060–1067.

nies cannot provide – unless the testimonies were collected from randomly-selected respondents. As discussed in the previous section, patterns in a population can only be estimated from a carefully drawn random sample or other probability-based model. From a sampling perspective, most collections of testimonies, case files or media mentions known to an individual organization are called convenience samples or non-random samples. A key difference between convenience data and (most) survey investigations is that many self-reports and testimonies are open-ended narratives, whereas surveys frequently ask specific, closed-ended questions.

Convenience data sources may include many types of information. Some of the most common are coded transcripts of focus groups or individual oral histories, records and observations from service providers, vital statistics registries, and other non-survey demographic information. In some cases, focus groups and narrative interviews have helped frame the focus of a quantitative analysis, as well as increasing the capacity of community leaders to acknowledge and address the issue.[21]

Records and observations from service providers, such as health facilities, provide a rich source of data on sexual violence in armed conflict.[22] For example, MSF has published numerous reports detailing cases of sexual violence observed at clinics located in conflict areas, using med-

---

21 Ruth Ojiambo Ochieng, "The efforts of non-governmental organizations in assessing and documenting the violations of women's human rights in situations of armed conflict: The Isis-WICCE experience", in *Violence against women: Statistical overview, challenges and gaps in data collection and methodology and approaches for overcoming them*, Expert group meeting, United Nations Division for the Advancement of Women, 2005. Available at http://www.un.org/womenwatch/daw/egm/vaw-stat-2005/docs/expert-papers/Ochieng.pdf, last accessed on 15 June 2011; Sydia Nduna and Lorelei Goodyear, *Pain too deep for tears: assessing the prevalence of sexual and gender violence among Burundian refugees in Tanzania*, International Rescue Committee, 1997.

22 Jamila Kerimova *et al.*, "High Prevalence of Self-Reported Forced Sexual Intercourse Among Internally Displaced Women in Azerbaijan", *American Journal of Public Health*, vol. 93, no. 7, p. 1068; Physicians for Human Rights and United Nations Assistance Mission in Sierra Leone, "War-related sexual violence in Sierra Leone: A population-based assessment", 2002. Available at http://physiciansforhumanrights.org/library/report-sierraleone-2000.html, last accessed on 15 June 2011. See also Lynn Amowitz *et al.*, "Prevalence of War-Related Sexual Violence and Other Human Rights Abuses Among Internally Displaced Persons in Sierra Leone", *Journal of the American Medical Association*, 2002, vol. 287, no. 4, pp. 513–521.

ical records.[23] The United Nations Population Fund (UNFPA) conducted a review of health centers in the DRC in 2007, finding about 50,000 reported cases of rape since 2003.[24] However, service provider data is a poor source for population level assessments. In particular, the ethical obligation to keep victims' personal information confidential means that it is impossible to determine when the same victim presents in several different clinics. Furthermore, victims who are multiply-counted are likely to be systematically different from the victims who present only once, perhaps because the multiply-counted require more serious medical assistance, are relatively wealthier, or have better access to transportation.

Of course, many, perhaps most victims are never seen at any clinic, so service provider and other convenience data both overcount (due to undetected multiple reports of the same events) and undercount (due to stigma, disclosure bias and other factors).[25] Where resources are available to conduct systematic sample surveys, these are the data most likely to be representative of patterns and trends in the population. However, surveys, like convenience data, suffer from inferential problems that seriously problematize efforts to tie individual leaders to crimes by their subordinates using quantitative data alone.

8.3. Institutional Problems[26]

In a previous article, I discussed the judicial response to statistical evidence introduced by the Prosecution in *Milutinović et al.*[27] While this case

[23] Medecins Sans Frontieres, *Civilians Still the First Victims: Permanence of Sexual Violence and Impact of Military Operations*, Medecins Sans Frontieres, Geneva, 2007.

[24] W. Wakabi, "Sexual Violence Increasing in Democratic Republic of Congo", *The Lancet*, 2008, vol. 378, no. 9606, pp. 15–16.

[25] Roth, Guberek and Hoover Green (2011, see *supra* note 1) describe the possibilities for using multiple systems estimation (MSE) to create reliable and valid population estimates of sexual violence in the absence of survey data. MSE is a demographic technique that uses the overlap between multiple convenience data sources to estimate the number of cases not counted by any source. However, Roth, Guberek and Hoover Green argue that MSE is not currently usable for estimating sexual violence, largely because sexual violence data tends to lack the type of identifying information that would allow researchers to determine overlap.

[26] Portions of this section are directly inspired by an earlier piece. See Hoover Green, 2010, see *supra* note 6.

[27] *Milutinović*, see *supra* note 7.

did not involve sexual violence, it tested the ability of prosecutors, defense attorneys and the ICTY Chamber to assess statistical evidence tying individual leaders to patterns of war crimes.

The statistical issue in *Milutinović et al.* concerned responsibility for deaths and migration during the conflict in Kosovo, in particular the period of highest violence, roughly March through June 1999. In particular, the prosecution argued that Milan Milutinović, then President of Serbia, and his co-defendants planned and executed a campaign of ethnic cleansing in which approximately 10,000 Kosovar Albanians were killed, and hundreds of thousands forced to leave their homes. Prosecution statistician Patrick Ball used a number of data sources to reconstruct patterns of deaths and migration, arguing in two parts: (1) that patterns of killing and migration were similar over time and across regions of Kosovo; and (2) that neither NATO air strikes nor Kosovar separatist militias (the KLA) could have been responsible for the observed patterns.[28] The Defense hired a business economist, Eric Fruits. Fruits stated in an interview that he had never done work in the international court system or dealt with human rights issues previously.

The ICTY Chamber's Judgment in *Milutinović et al.*, ultimately rendered in 2009, contained only a brief section relevant to the statistical findings of Ball *et al.* and Fruits.[29] Two paragraphs lay out the prosecution and defense hypotheses regarding the statistical evidence. Paragraph 23 reviews what the Chamber viewed as "five key issues" concerning this evidence:[30] "Ball's potential bias; Fruits' alleged lack of qualification; the integrity and completeness of the underlying data; the soundness of the applied methodology; and, most importantly, the persuasiveness of the conclusion reached". On all but the first of these issues, the Chamber sided with the Defense expert, Fruits, in his assessment of the evidence.

Before discussing the implications of *Milutinović et al.*, for human rights statistics in general and sexual violence statistics in particular, it is important to acknowledge the possibility that the Kosovo cases are outliers, that is, that "lessons learned" from these are inapplicable to other uses

28 Patrick Ball, Wendy Betts, Fritz Scheuren, Jana Dudukovich, and Jana Asher, "Killings and Refugee Flow in Kosovo, March-June 1999", Report to the International Criminal Tribunal for the Former Yugoslavia, 2002.

29 *Milutinović*, see *supra* note 7, p. 27166–27170.

30 *Milutinović*, see *supra* note 7, p. 27172.

of statistics in human rights law. I wish to suggest that this is not the case – that adversarial legal institutions (including, for example, both American courts and the ICTY, but *not* the International Criminal Court) use fundamentally similar styles of reasoning that present particular challenges for statistical evidence. Given the difficulties of making accurate inferences from data on sexual violence in particular, I speculate that the dynamics I discuss below would be aggravated, rather than mitigated, if the data at issue had been sexual violence statistics. However, there has as yet been no opportunity to test these speculations.

8.3.1. Complexity and Heuristics

In an extremely polarized and complex information environment, a statistically inexpert judge must determine for her(him)self where the truth lies. There exist cases in which common sense, logic and legal wherewithal are sufficient to make this type of determination. In these cases, the question at hand concerns a specific narrative about a specific individual, with little or no role for randomness (for example, "On date X, did he or did he not steal the car?"). Psychological research shows that most juror decisions are framed around a particular narrative or story,[31] which allows for easier testing of facts ("Does this fact fit the story I'm considering?"). However, in the case of abstract or indirect "actions" (such as instituting, or ignoring, a policy of sexual violence during time of war), concrete stories are more difficult to discern. Moreover, statistical evidence may rely on techniques that are highly specialized, extremely technically demanding, complex, or non-intuitive.

Findings from social and cognitive psychology suggest that high-volume, highly polarized information environments are inhospitable to complex understandings, and to facts derived from non-intuitive processes. Allison, for example, noted that high-stakes decision-making led many members of the Kennedy administration to become extraordinarily inflexible during negotiations over the Cuban missile crisis, adhering to "implicit conceptual models" even after those models were proven ineffec-

[31] Pennington and Hastie, "Explaining the Evidence: Tests of the Story Model for Juror Decision-Making", *Journal of Personality and Social Psychology* 1992, vol. 62, no. 2, pp. 189–206.

tive.[32] Janis found that decision-makers facing stress or threat, including expert decision-makers, become less flexible in their thinking.[33] Staw outlines a number of seminal works in social and cognitive psychology in which individual and group problem-solving capability are undermined by threats, including "threats" such as increasing the pace at which problems are solved.[34]

In a key critique of rationalist models of decision-making, Tversky and Kahneman discuss the prevalence of several modes of heuristic thinking, showing "that people rely on a limited number of heuristic principles which reduce the complex tasks of assessing probability and predicting values to simpler judgmental operations.[35] In general, these heuristics are quite useful, but sometimes they lead to severe and systematic errors".[36] Tversky and Kahneman outline several common heuristics, the most relevant of which in the court setting is cognitive accessibility: items or instances that are easy to recall (for any of several reasons) are typically judged as more common or likely. Familiarity with concrete items or instances leads to increased recall of those items and, crucially in the present context, "imaginability" leads to increased judgment of likelihood for abstract concepts.[37] This well-replicated finding suggests that counter-intuitive information will be more difficult to store, more difficult to retrieve (less accessible) from memory, and consequently more difficult to employ in making judgments.

More recently, Lau and Redlawsk showed that heuristic use increases with information complexity and volume.[38] Lau and Redlawsk's subjects were political decision-makers. Each was presented with an

---

32 Graham Allison, "Conceptual Models and the Cuban Missile Crisis", *American Political Science Review*, 1969, vol. 63, no. 3, pp. 689–718.

33 Irving Janis, *Victims of Groupthink: A Psychological Study of Foreign Policy Decisions and Fiascoes*. Boston: Houghton Mifflin, 1972.

34 Staw, Standelands and Dutton. "Threat Rigidity Effects in Organizational Behavior: A Multilevel Analysis", *Administrative Science Quarterly* 1981, vol. 26, no. 4, pp. 501–524.

35 Amos Tversky and Daniel Kahneman, "Judgment Under Uncertainty: Heuristics and Biases", *Science, New Series*, 1974, vol. 185, no. 4157, pp. 1124–1131.

36 *Ibid.*, p. 1124.

37 *Ibid.*, p. 1127.

38 Lau and Redlawsk, "Advantages and Disadvantages of Cognitive Heuristics in Political Decision Making", *American Journal of Political Science*, 2001, vol. 45, no. 4, pp. 951–971.

overwhelming amount of information about a policy option on which they had previously specified a preferred goal. The subjects were also presented with several potential sources of heuristic information, including subject-matter experts, as a means toward judging which option would satisfy their goal. Heuristic use *increased* the accuracy of well-informed subjects' judgments, but *decreased* the accuracy of novices' judgments, actually magnifying their lack of expertise. The implication for statistical experts presenting complex information to inexpert judges is clear.

The complexity of the debate over statistics in the Kosovo cases, as well as the sheer volume of information considered at trial, negatively affected the Chamber's capacity to assess the statistical evidence. In particular, the Chamber failed to determine which Defense criticisms of the Ball *et al.* analyses were substantively important (or potentially substantively important) and which were irrelevant – to say nothing of which were accurate and which were erroneous. The Judgment suggested that the court had closely considered several criticisms of the statistical evidence that are demonstrably irrelevant to the major substantive findings of Ball *et al.*[39]

These criticisms were damaging to the Prosecution largely because the Prosecution bears the burden of proof. A defense expert need offer no exonerating evidence; he need only show that the Prosecution's conclusions are overhasty or potentially vulnerable to criticism. Ball *et al.* did not prepare an extensive arsenal of statistical proofs, instead relying (sometimes necessarily, sometimes unnecessarily) on novel hypothesis testing methods of which the court was suspicious. The court attentively considered statistical criticisms that were demonstrably irrelevant largely because results actually demonstrating their irrelevance were never produced.

8.3.2. Expert Credentialing

Compounding its failures to determine which criticisms were substantive and which were not, the Chamber adopted a relatively lenient standard in assessing expert witnesses' credentials. In particular, the court took no notice of differences in training and expertise between Ball, the Prosecution's key expert witness, and Fruits, for the Defense. While both hold Ph.D.'s in the social sciences, Ball had served as a statistical expert for

[39] Ball *et al.*, 2002, see *supra* note 28.

numerous large-scale documentations of human rights abuses. Fruits, on the other hand, is a business economist who had never taken or taught a course in statistical demography or dealt with human rights matters prior to this case. Over the Prosecution's objection, the court held that Fruits was a suitable expert because "he [...] taught a higher education course concerning the problems associated with linear regression analysis, [...] consulted on projects involving statistical analyses of demographic data, and [was] admitted as a statistical expert in courts in the U.S".[40]

The ICTY relies on the American standard for expert witnesses, laid out in *Daubert v. Merrill Dow Pharmaceutical*.[41] In *Daubert* the Justices overturned the previous standard ("generally accepted practice", *Frye vs. United States*[42]) for expert witnesses, charging trial judges with conducting "far-ranging" inquiries into the potential expert's qualifications. As has been extensively discussed in both scientific and legal forums,[43] *Daubert* asks that Judges assess potential experts' credibility and qualifications, despite their own lack of expertise.[44]

As discussed at length in Hoover Green 2010, Fruits' credentials were appropriate for his previous testimony (in other words, entirely appropriate to statistical testimony in cases involving insurance matters in the US courts). However, such economic analyses differ considerably from the demographic statistics that are necessary in human rights statistics. Using already-corrected demographic data in an econometric investigation, as Fruits had, involves different skill sets than making corrections to raw demographic data, the practice at issue in *Milutinović et al.* Be-

40 *Milutinović,* see *supra* note 7, p. 27168, para. 25.

41 United States Supreme Court, *Daubert v. Merill Dow Pharmaceutical,* 509 U.S. 579, 1993.

42 United States Court of Appeals, District of Columbia Circuit, *Frye v. United States*, 293 F. 1013, 1923.

43 S. Jasanoff, "Law's Knowledge: Science for Justice in Legal Settings", *American Journal of Public Health*, vol. 95, no. S1, pp. S49–S58; H.H. Kaufman, "The Expert Witness: Neither *Frye* nor *Daubert* Solved the Problem. What Can Be Done?" *Science and Justice*, vol. 41, pp. 7–20; Ronald W. Tochterman, "Daubert: A (California) Trial Judge Dissents", *University of California Davis Law Review*, vol. 30, p. 1013.

44 For a more general (pre-*Daubert*) account of problems with adversarial expert evidence, see Samuel R. Gross, "Expert Evidence", *Wisconsin Law Review*, 1991, p. 1113. Gross argues for the appointment of impartial experts and notes that complicated evidence is unlikely to be correctly assessed in an adversarial setting.

cause of the lenient expertise requirement adopted by the ICTY, the defense expert was able to state, honestly but incorrectly, that the statistical analyses of Ball *et al.* were "ad hoc" and "not standard practice".

The lenient expert credentialing standard set by the ICTY Chamber magnified errors in judgment by the Chamber resulting from the use of cognitive accessibility heuristics, and underlined differences between legal expertise and subject matter expertise.

8.3.3. Legal *versus* Statistical Reasoning

Comparing the information environment at the ICTY to the style of argumentation in statistics or academic social science is instructive.[45] Arguments between experts in statistics and social sciences, though not necessarily civil, typically focus on one or a few key disputes. At best, interlocutors carefully explain the extent to which the criticisms present damage to the key conclusions of the research, and separate minor empirical quibbles from major theoretical disagreements or methodological critiques. The "judges" in the academic setting are fellow experts, whose background knowledge (again, in a best-case scenario) permits judgment based on the merits of the work, rather than on heuristics such as the perceived trustworthiness of the source.

In addition, while not every academic interlocutor is well-intentioned, nearly all face incentives to engage other experts in a collegial manner, and with a clear recognition of which criticisms are important and appropriate to the venue and substantive questions. Arguments are situated in (or in relation to) long-standing lines of research and theory, which help other experts organize and prioritize their disagreements. Not so in the courtroom, where judges are situated in long-standing lines of *legal* research and theory, but must rapidly assimilate the facts (including technical facts and statistical arguments) of each individual case anew.

Reviewing the institutional bases of the difficulties encountered by the use of human rights statistics in *Milutinović et al.* provides some basis for considering the problems that the statistical analyses of sexual violence might face. In their Judgment, the *Milutinović et al.* Chamber made three major missteps. First, the judges relied implicitly on several factors that were cognitively accessible but potentially irrelevant or misleading.

45 Note, however, that the ICTY's adversarial fact-finding system is quite different from the inquisitorial system in use at, for example, the International Criminal Court.

Second, the judges appear to have used both explicit and implicit heuristics, including expert trustworthiness and concept accessibility, in considering their decision. Finally, the Chamber set a low bar for expert credentialing. One might argue that these dynamics would be irrelevant to sexual violence data, given that a greater number of *valid* critiques of (most) sexual violence data are available. I speculate, on the contrary, that valid criticisms would be more difficult to separate from invalid criticisms, in some sense intensifying these problems. Again, however, such speculation remains, for the moment, untestable.

8.4. Conclusion

Given the difficulties faced by statistical expert witnesses in human rights trials, one might be tempted to argue that statistical evidence should play little or no role in international legal settings, and/or that their use should be restricted to issues simpler than wartime sexual violence. Certainly, non-expert judges in adversarial settings will find it exceptionally difficult to reach a nuanced or abstract judgment based on incomplete information. Still, there are lessons to be drawn from the experience of statistical experts in *Milutinović et al* that can and should be applied to the presentation of statistics on sexual violence. Yet the fact remains that sexual violence is in some sense a special case. Whereas numerical data may stand alone in some other prosecutions, numerical data alone cannot be used for inferences about sexual violence. Below, I revisit general principles for the introduction of human rights data in international courts and expand these ideas to data on sexual violence.

Effective presentation of background knowledge may be the most challenging piece of the statistical expert's extremely difficult puzzle. Human rights statistics are seldom well-suited to traditional modes of analysis and therefore often rely on methods that are unfamiliar, counter-intuitive, or both. It is important, then, to make the case for those methods simply and convincingly, in advance. In the case of sexual violence data, "background knowledge" must include a clear exposition of the usual extent of under-registration and the inadvisability of inferring directly from any data source. Statistical experts should illustrate clearly the ways in which convenience data are biased, and the effectiveness of survey techniques as alternatives.

In the case of sexual violence specifically, background knowledge also must take on common presumptions regarding sexual violence (especially sexual violence in conflict): that only extremely violent rape is "really" rape, for example, or that conflict-related sexual violence is endemic and therefore inevitable or even "natural". The frequent presumption that accusations of sexual violence are false or that victims are complicit in their victimization must be explicitly addressed; moreover, it must be addressed in the context of data analysis, as an argument for the validity of survey and other inferential techniques.

Given the cognitive constraints of the environment, the point is – for better or worse – less to convince judges of the merits of the techniques at issue, and more to give a clear statement of the intellectual pedigree of each method. Recall that judges, consciously or unconsciously, will be using credentialing (of both experts and information) and concept familiarity as heuristics in their judgments.

Another key strategy is redundant, exhaustive hypothesis testing. Whereas judgments of hypothesis tests in the academic environment are made at least ostensibly on the basis of shared expert knowledge (that is, many hypotheses are implicitly ruled out), this is not the case in court. Many simple hypothesis tests should be presented alongside any large or complex analysis. Moreover, and especially in the case of sexual violence data, "exhaustive hypothesis testing" includes drawing connections between qualitative and quantitative information. While their audience is primarily advocacy-based rather than legal, Roth, Guberek and Hoover Green focus extensively on this requirement, stating that quantitative data on sexual violence should *never* be used to test hypotheses outside of specific (qualitatively described) contextual information.[46]

Two final strategic suggestions – transparency of the analysis process and increased training for statisticians in legal settings – require little explanation. Transparency in analysis is a fundamental requirement of quantitative academic analyses, and a key factor in assessing the merit of statistical work. In that light, one advantage to using simpler or more simplistic analytical techniques is the ease with which one's interlocutors can reproduce them. Lastly, both expert witnesses in this case noted the importance of training for experts who need to present complex, detailed technical information in an adversarial environment.

As with most work undertaken in the aftermath of conflict or human rights abuses, statistical analyses of violence carry extremely high

[46] Roth, Guberek, and Hoover Green, 2011, see *supra* note 1.

stakes. Incorrect analyses can and do lead to counterproductive policies and misallocations of resources, which cost lives. In court cases involving human rights abuses, incorrect analysis may allow extremely bad actors to avoid responsibility – or it may lead to wrongful convictions. Unfortunately, the formal and informal institutions of legal reasoning may make it exceptionally difficult for statisticians to present their work accurately in court.

The obvious question is whether the (potential) benefits of using statistics in prosecutions involving wartime sexual violence will outweigh the risks inherent in presenting these complex inferences in court. In the near future, the state of sexual violence data and the institutional difficulties associated with legal argumentation suggest a negative answer. However, the quality of sexual violence data improves over time, as does understanding of its implications. In a number of war-affected countries, surveys on the incidence and prevalence of sexual violence have now been performed a number of times; to the extent that these surveys reach broadly similar conclusions about population patterns and trends, they may prove extremely useful in reasoning about population trends and patterns. On the other hand, it is also possible to exploit even small differences in studies that generally agree.[47]

A more hopeful observation concerns the institutional differences between the ICTY, which heard *Milutinović* and which suffers from a highly adversarial information environment, and the ICC, which uses an inquisitorial system of fact-finding. Presumably, a less adversarial information environment such as that encountered at the ICC would provide a stronger basis for judging complex statistical claims. However, whether a less adversarial information environment could correctly judge information as emotionally laden and incomplete as sexual violence data remains to be seen.

[47] The defense in *Milutinović* did just this, arguing that the work of Ball *et al.* was "incorrect" and ad-hoc because it did not reach precisely the same number of estimated deaths as another study.

9

The Promise and Peril of Primary Documents: Documenting Wartime Sexual Violence in El Salvador and Peru

Michele Leiby*

9.1. Introduction

Accounts of wartime rape, sexual torture, forced impregnation, and sexual slavery have been reported in Liberia, Bosnia and Herzegovina, Rwanda, East Timor, Iraq, and Sierra Leone in the last ten years alone. Sexual violence is one of the most horrific and intimate forms of nonlethal violence during war. Victims of sexual violence may suffer chronic health problems, face social stigma and isolation, and often confront inordinate obstacles to obtaining justice and reparation. The urgency of documenting the occurrence and understanding the causes of wartime sexual violence should not be underestimated, as stories of such atrocities continue to surface in the Sudan, the Democratic Republic of the Congo, and most recently, Libya.

Emerging research on the patterns and determinants of wartime sexual violence represents one of the most exciting developments in the political violence and human rights literatures. Scholars are making significant advancements in documenting the prevalence and patterns of sexual violence and identifying the determinants of its use in civil and international conflicts.[1] Employing different methodological approaches

* **Michele Leiby** is Ph.D. Candidate at the University of New Mexico. The author would like to thank Kathryn Hochstetler, Marie Manrique and Elisabeth Wood for their very helpful comments on previous drafts of this article. An earlier version of this paper, "Digging in the Archives: The Promise and Perils of Primary Documents" was published in *Politics and Society* vol. 37 no. 1, pp. 75–100.

[1] See Jeffrey Burds, "Sexual Violence in World War II 1939–1945", in *Politics and Society*, 2009 vol. 37, no. 1; Dara Cohen, "Evaluating the Causes of Sexual Violence by Insurgents during Civil War: Cross-National Evidence (1980–1999)", paper presented at the annual meeting of the American Political Science Association, Boston, August 28–31, 2008; Elisabeth Wood, "Variation in Sexual Violence during War", in *Politics & Society*, 2006, vol. 34, no. 3, pp. 307–41; and Elisabeth Wood, "Armed

and research designs, they are developing new theories to explain individual, group and state, or conflict-level variation, in sexual violence. However, research on wartime sexual violence is faced with unique practical, ethical and methodological obstacles. Using El Salvador and Peru as illustrative case studies, this article discusses the challenges of collecting and coding data on wartime sexual violence and offers suggestions for overcoming them. I argue that the methods employed to date by truth commissions, including in how cases of sexual violence are defined and counted, are too narrow, and may ultimately miss or misrepresent 'the truth'.

This article is organized as follows. In the section below, I will provide a brief overview of the civil conflicts in El Salvador and Peru, and the subsequent work of the Truth Commissions in each country (abbreviated as 'CVES' in El Salvador and 'CVR' in Peru). I then discuss the four most common methodological obstacles confronted by scholars of political and sexual violence. I compare the figures on rape reported in the Commissions' final reports with those I have found after a careful reading of the final reports and published supplementary materials. I also compare these figures to those in my sample of original testimonies from victims and witnesses of violence.[2] Doing so provides a unique opportunity to examine the processes through which reports of human rights abuse are collected, information sorted, and statistics transmitted. I show that what we know about wartime violence depends greatly on the choices we make in designing our investigations. Specifically, I find that (1) the number of reported cases of sexual violence varies significantly depending on the data source; (2) men were more often the targets of sexual violence than previously thought; and (3) sexual humiliation and sexual torture were common practices of state armed forces during the conflicts.

Groups and Sexual Violence: When Is Wartime Rape Rare?", in *Politics & Society*, 2009, vol. 37, no. 1.

2 The terms 'victim' and 'perpetrator' are used throughout to refer to attributions of identity at a particular moment in time as it relates to the violation of an individual's human rights. These identities are fluid and dynamic, as are the concepts of 'innocence' and 'guilt'. The same individual that may at one moment be an agent of violence, and thus a perpetrator, can at another moment be a victim of human rights abuse. Particularly with regard to sexual violence, my use of the term 'victim' is not intended to reinforce the stigma of an individual who has suffered sexual violence, nor is it to deny or minimize the agency, power and resistance of the person.

9.2. Civil War in El Salvador and Peru

9.2.1. El Salvador

Emblematic of class-based conflicts, the Salvadoran civil war was rooted in long-standing economic and political divisions in society. For generations, a small elite class successfully marginalized the rural peasant population and monopolized the country's already limited arable land, such that three percent of all landowners controlled 56 percent of the country's arable land. Between 1961 and 1980, the rural landless grew from 11 to 51 percent.[3] As a result, 76 percent of rural families lived in poverty; 55 percent lived in extreme poverty.[4]

Rampant electoral fraud and political corruption signaled to those already beginning to organize in the 1970s that while occasional promissory carrots might be extended to abate discontent, there would be no restructuring of economic or political relations in El Salvador. The political opposition was systematically blocked from assuming power in 1972, 1974, and 1977.[5] Those already frustrated by an economic system that promoted inequality were galvanized to support small guerrilla groups advocating the armed overthrow of the state. In 1980, five such groups unified under the umbrella of the *Frente Farabundo Martí para la Liberación Nacional* ('FMLN', Farabundo Marti National Liberation Front).[6]

---

3 Tommie Sue Montgomery, *Revolution in El Salvador: From Civil Strife to Civil Peace*, Westview Press, Boulder, 1994, p. 23.

4 Elisabeth Wood, *Insurgent Collective Action and Civil War in El Salvador*, Cambridge University Press, New York, 2003, p. 24.

5 In 1972, the *Unión Nacional de Oposición* ('UNO', National Union of Opposition) candidate, José Napoléon Duarte, was prevented from assuming office by the military. Another UNO victory was blocked in 1974, when the government simply declared that the *Partido de Conciliación Nacional* ('PCN', National Conciliation Party) had won. Amidst accusations of fraud and violence against voters, the PCN candidate, General Carlos Humberto Romero, assumed power as the president.

6 The five factions of the Farabundo Marti National Liberation Front ('FMLN') were: (1) the *Fuerzas Populares de Liberación Farabundo Martí* ('FPL', Popular Liberation Forces Farabundo Martí), (2) the *Ejército Revolucionario del Pueblo* ('ERP', People's Revolutionary Army), (3) the *Resistencia Nacional* ('RN', National Resistance), (4) the *Partido Revolucionario de los Trabajadores Centroamericanos* ('PRTC', Revolutionary Part of Central American Workers, and (5) the *Partido Comunista de El Salvador* ('PCS', Salvadoran Communist Party. The FMLN gets its namesake from Augustín Farabundo Martí, who led a 1932 peasant uprising in El Salvador. The re-

Marxist in ideological orientation, the FMLN had strong ties to the Communist governments in Russia and Cuba. The FMLN received a massive amount of international aid, in terms of arms, training and money, from abroad.[7] Reflecting its varied composition, the FMLN employed a mix of military tactics and warfare strategies. This flexibility allowed it to respond quickly and effectively to different combat situations and ultimately contributed to its battlefield successes.[8] After the failed 1981 "final offensive", the FMLN shifted away from urban guerrilla warfare and retreated to the countryside where they prepared for a prolonged 'people's war'.

The military-led government, aided by millions of dollars in American assistance, carried out a policy of widespread repression to defeat the armed insurgency. Unable, and in some cases unwilling, to distinguish between FMLN combatants and its wide civilian support network, the armed forces disappeared or executed tens of thousands of civilians between 1979 and 1981 alone.[9] Rather than weaken the rebels, the State's campaign of indiscriminate violence outraged local populations, providing a new pool of potential recruits and supporters for the FMLN.

The only significant shift in the State's counterinsurgency strategy came in 1984 after sustained American pressure on the armed forces to improve its human rights record. The Salvadoran government was forced to understand, after a visit by then Vice President George H. W. Bush, that the withdrawal of American military support, particularly air support, would almost certainly mean defeat. While the overall level of lethal violence declined, the armed forces' rapid reaction battalions continued to arbitrarily detain and torture those suspected of subversion.[10]

---

volt was quickly and violently crushed by the state military under the direction of Maximiliano Hernandez.

7 The FMLN also had significant ties to the governments in Nicaragua and Vietnam: see José Angel Moroni Bracamonte and David E. Spencer, *Strategy and Tactics of the Salvadoran FMLN Guerrillas: Last Battle of the Cold War, Blueprint for Future Conflicts*, Praeger Publishers, Westport, CT, 1995.

8 *Ibid.*

9 Mark Peceny and William D. Stanley, "Counterinsurgency in El Salvador", in *Politics and Society*, 2010 vol. 38, no. 1, pp. 67–94.

10 During this time, the state began to pursue social welfare programs, such as the construction of schools and medical facilities, in areas where the FMLN boasted support. In comparison to its investment in violent repression, civic action programs of this sort were never a significant component of the state's counterinsurgency strategy.

Despite its repressive efforts, the armed forces were unable to militarily defeat the FMLN. Locked in a stalemate, the two sides began to negotiate a settlement in January 1990. Two years later, the FMLN and the Salvadoran government signed the Chapultepec peace accords, ending 12 years of civil war.

9.2.2. Peru

On May 17, 1980, a small group of armed persons broke into the local election board offices in Chuschi and burned the ballot boxes to be used the following day in the country's first democratic elections in twelve years. With this, the insurgent organization Sendero Luminoso ('Shining Path'), declared war against the Peruvian state and began the most violent period of conflict in the country's history.[11]

Centered around a personality cult of leader Abimael Guzmán, the Shining Path combined the politico-military ideology of Mao Zedong and the Chinese Communist Party with the teachings of Guzmán and called for immediate action to overthrow the existing imperialist system of power and realize the revolution. Unlike other leftist rebel groups in Latin America, including the FMLN in El Salvador, the Shining Path did not accept violence as simply necessary, but celebrated its use.[12] Common tactics employed by the group included sabotaging radio towers; bombing police stations, banks, and other commercial buildings; destroying electrical pylons; systematically killing local authorities and community leaders; and coercing the support of the civilian population (often using them as protective shields) through the threat and use of violence.

11 However flawed the democratic system may have been, between 1980 and 1992, the country held free local and national elections and enjoyed freedom of the press. The Shining Path never intended to inject itself into the existing political system, but rather to destroy it and create a new government in which Abimael Guzmán would exercise supreme authority. In addition to the Shining Path, the state faced a second opposition organization, the *Movimiento Revolucionario Túpac Amaru* ('MRTA', Tupac Amaru Revolutionary Movement). The MRTA initiated its armed struggle against the state in 1984. The MRTA is responsible for less than two percent of human rights violations documented by the CVR, including its most famous act of violence, in which insurgents stormed the Japanese Embassy and held dozens of people hostage for months.

12 Gustavo Gorritti, *The Shining Path: A History of the Millenarian War in Peru*, University of North Carolina Press, Chapel Hill, 1998.

The initial response of the State was inadequate to confront the threat posed by the Shining Path. The armed group established itself in the southern Andes, a region of the country that historically has been ignored by government officials and institutions. The relative absence of authorities made it easier for the Shining Path to take control and more difficult for the State to gather intelligence on the movement. The State underestimated the strength of the guerrilla army and poorly understood its organizational versatility and military tactics.

Unable to distinguish between the civilian population and combatants who did not wear uniforms, the armed forces and the police responded with indiscriminate violence.[13] This violence was not reducible to the excesses of a few individuals, but rather, at certain times and places, amounted to a generalized and systematic practice of illegal detention often accompanied by torture during interrogations, extra judicial executions, and forced disappearance.[14] As the police and armed forces acquired a better understanding of the Shining Path, it refined its strategy to include more targeted actions that distinguished among friendly, neutral, and enemy populations. This policy shift led to a reduction in abuses against the civilian population, even as the conflict continued to intensify.[15]

In 1992, the *Dirección Nacional Contra El Terrorismo* (National Anti-terrorism Police Task Force, 'DINCOTE') carried out intelligence operations which led to the capture of key leaders of the Shining Path, among them, Guzmán. Internal fractures within the organization and the arrest of its principal leader dealt a significant blow to the armed opposition. While combatants continue to carry out subversive operations in the country, they are sporadic and small in scale.

---

[13] The police were the first sent in to respond to the security threat. Under the state of emergency, the police were subordinated to the armed forces and particularly to the political-military commands. As such, officers answered to military commanders and not to civilian authorities.

[14] Ernesto de la Jara Basombrío, *Memoria y Batallas en Nombre de los Inocentes: Perú 1992–2001*, Instituto de Defensa Legal, Lima, Peru, 2001; Comisión para la Verdad y Reconciliación ('CVR'), *Hatun Willakuy: Versión Abreviada del Informe Final de la Comisión de la Verdad y Reconciliación*, Comisión de Entrega de la Comisión de la Verdad y Reconciliación, Lima, Peru, 2004.

[15] CVR, 2004, see *supra* note 14.

While the civil wars in El Salvador and Peru are different in ways potentially significant to the comparative prevalence of wartime sexual violence, the present analysis focuses on how these crimes were reported.[16] The following section discusses the availability of data on sexual violence in each conflict. It begins with a discussion of the reporting organizations in each country.

9.3. Confronting the Past: Truth Commissions and Human Rights NGOs

While there are several transitional justice mechanisms, the establishment of temporary investigative bodies known as truth commissions has become an increasingly popular choice for States moving from periods of violence conflict and authoritarian rule toward democracy.[17] Below I will briefly describe the work of each commission (see Table 1 for a comparative overview of key characteristics).

9.3.1. El Salvador

On January 16, 1992, the representatives of the Salvadoran government and the FMLN signed the Chapultepec Accords, ending 12 years of brutal violence and war. Both parties agreed to establish a truth commission, moderated by the United Nations, which would "investigat[e] serious acts of violence that have occurred since 1980 and whose impact on society urgently demands that the public should know the truth".[18] The *Comisión de la Verdad para El Salvador* ('CVES') was also to issue recommenda-

[16] For a comparative analysis of the prevalence of wartime sexual violence in El Salvador and Peru, see Michele Leiby, *Why Soldiers Rape: Understanding the Causes of Wartime Sexual Violence in Latin America*, unpublished manuscript.

[17] Among others, States in transition may offer reparations to the victims and their families; try those responsible for criminal acts in the national court system or establish a special war crimes tribunal; remove individuals, including members of the armed forces, judges, or political leaders, from their posts or offices; and may issue a formal national apology to those who suffered.

[18] Comisión de la Verdad para El Salvador ('CVES'), *From Madness to Hope: the 12-year War in El Salvador: Report on the Truth for El Salvador*, 1993, UNSC S/25500, p. 18, available at http://www.usip.org/files/file/ElSalvador-Report.pdf, last accessed on 2 May 2011. All Spanish texts were translated by the author.

tions to prevent future human rights abuses and to promote national reconciliation.[19]

As a UN-sponsored truth commission, the executive committee was governed entirely by internationals.[20] While all were well-respected leaders in their professions, the exclusion of national scholars and experts from the Salvadoran truth commission was a point of contention and sets it apart from its predecessors in Argentina and Chile as well as subsequent commissions in Guatemala and Peru. The decision was made in large part to guarantee the commission's objectivity and impartiality, and to overcome concerns that lingering insecurity would impede Salvadoran nationals' ability to frankly investigate and publish findings on their country's violent past. The CVES had an additional staff of 25 lawyers, sociologists and forensic scientists, but was still comparatively small in size for a truth commission.[21]

The CVES was given six months (later extended to eight months) to complete its investigations and issue its final report. It began its work in July 1992. Announcements about the Commission's work flooded radio, television and print media outlets, encouraging all individuals, groups and organizations with information on acts of violence to testify before the Commission. Individuals could make statements at the Commission's main office in San Salvador or any one of its satellite offices, established in each department throughout the country. Individuals were reassured that all testimonies and procedures of the CVES were confidential. In the end, the Commission collected more than 2,000 testimonies detailing acts of violence against more than 7,000 victims and survivors.[22]

---

19 This was the first time the United Nations sponsored such a truth commission.

20 Belisario Betancur, a former President of Colombia, served as the Chairman with Reinaldo Figueredo Planchart, a former Foreign Minister of Venezuela and Thomas Buergenthal, a former Judge and President of the Inter-American Court of Human Rights, as members.

21 Priscilla Hayner, *Unspeakable Truths: Confronting State Terror and Atrocity*, Routledge, New York, 2001.

22 The Commission also relied on indirect sources of information from various international and domestic organizations, including the American Association for the Advancement of Science, Americas Watch, Amnesty International, the United Nations Working Group on Forced and Involuntary Disappearances, the *Comité de Familiares de Víctimas de las Violaciones de Derechos Humanos de El Salvador "Marianella Garcia Villas*, CODEFAM (Committee of Relatives of Victims of Human Rights Violations in El Salvador), the *Comisión de Derechos Humanos de El Salvador*,

In its final report, the CVES estimated that 75,000 people were killed during the civil war in El Salvador between 1980 and 1992. Between 1980 and 1983, state violence was widespread and less discriminate, targeting entire communities on the basis of suspected geographic proximity to rebel bases.[23] Thousands of peasants were massacred in the now well-known massacres at the Sumpul river in 1980, the Lempa river in 1981, and in El Mozote, Morazán in 1981. Lethal acts of violence began to decrease in 1984 when the American government threatened to terminate military aid if the country's human rights record did not improve. At the same time, however, less visible forms of violence, including arbitrary detention, torture, and sexual violence, continued.[24] Eighty-five percent of all of these acts of violence were attributed to state security agents; the FMLN was judged responsible for less than five percent of all human rights violations.[25]

The truth commission in El Salvador did not investigate cases of sexual violence. It argued that because there was no evidence of orders or a policy of rape, such acts were apolitical, interpersonal violence and as such did not fall within its mandate.[26] Because of this executive decision, the Commission did not define the parameters of sexual violence, and made no attempt to explain these violations in the narrative of its final report. This is true even for well-known cases where sexual violence was reported. In the case of four American churchwomen who were kidnapped, raped and murdered in 1980 by the *Guardia Nacional* ('GN', National Guard), the Commission reported, but did not investigate the motives behind, the rapes.[27] Another publicized case involved the kidnapping, torture and murder in 1982 of four Dutch journalists. In addition to other forms of torture and physical mutilation, the victims also endured

CDHES (Salvadoran Human Rights Commission), Tutela Legal, and Socorro Jurídico, the Salvadoran Armed Forces, and the FMLN (for a complete list see Appendix II, CVES, 1993). The testimonies it received from other indirect sources covers 18,462 unique events of violence and 18,455 individual victims: see CVES, 1993, pp. 23 and 45, see *supra* note 18.

23 Approximately 50 percent of the denunciations recorded by the CVES concerned human rights violations that occurred in 1980 and 1981; an additional 20 percent occurred in 1982 and 1983: see CVES, 1993, p. 37, see *supra* note 18.

24 CVES, 1993, see *supra* note 18.

25 CVES, 1993, see *supra* note 18.

26 Hayner, 2001, see *supra* note 21.

27 CVES, 1993, see *supra* note 18.

trauma to their genitals, which was not reported in the Commission's final report.[28] The Commission's disparate reporting suggests it had an implicit working definition of sexual violence as the rape of women.

In the annex to its final report, the CVES published a list of victims of sexual violence based on its compilation of testimonies. Where permitted, the Commission documented the individual's name, the date and location of the human rights violation, the type of violation, including rape, and the suspected perpetrator group. Of the 7,357 cases recorded, only 270 (3.7 percent) included rape.[29] Not all victims were identified by name to protect their wishes for anonymity. Based on those who were, it appears that the truth commission only identified cases of rape against women, and did not include sexual violence against men, such as sexual torture.[30] Moreover, the annex does not include demographic information on the victims, or contextual information about the crimes, such as how it unfolded, the sequencing of acts, who was present at the time, and so on. Absent this data, it would be almost impossible to conduct a rigorous analysis on the motives of wartime sexual violence in El Salvador. Due to an agreement between the national government and the United Nations sealing the records of the CVES until 2042 (50 years after the completion of its work),[31] it is not possible at this time to conduct an independent analysis of sexual violence using the commission's testimonies. Instead, data will be used from two non-governmental human rights organizations: *Socorro Jurídico Cristiano* ('SJC', Christian Legal Aid) and *Tutela Legal del Arzobispado* (The Archbishop's Legal Aid). The CVES used the original testimonies collected by both organizations to supplement its own documentation and analysis.

SJC was founded in 1975 by the Archdiocese in San Salvador as a nongovernmental human rights group to provide social and legal aid to those in need. After the 1979 coup, Socorro's work focused on providing

28 Gloria Valencia-Weber and Robert J. Weber, "El Salvador: Methods Used to Document Human Rights Violations", in *Human Rights Quarterly*, 1986, vol. 8 no. 4, pp. 731–770; Dutch Ministry of Foreign Affairs, *Report of Dutch Government to Foreign Affairs Committee of the Lower House of the Dutch Legislature*, 14 April 1982.

29 CVES, 1993, Appendix II, p. 8, see *supra* note 18.

30 There was one case of rape against an individual identified as male by his name.

31 Access to documents of this nature, which include sensitive and private information on witnesses, victims and perpetrators of violent crimes, is often limited to protect those whose identity is contained within.

assistance to victims of political violence and documenting those abuses. It collected first-hand testimonies under oath from witnesses and victims of political violence, submitted *habeas corpus* petitions on all disappearances, and issued monthly statistical reports on the human rights situation in the country. After the murder of Archbishop Romero and the installation of Apostolic Administrator Arturo Rivera y Damas, disagreements emerged between the Archdiocese and SJC regarding the Archdiocese's suspicion of SJC's political bias and inattention to abuses perpetrated by the FMLN.[32] As a result, Tutela Legal was created in 1982 to replace SJC, which continued to operate and report on human rights issues outside the purview of the Archbishop's office.

Like its predecessor, Tutela Legal aimed to collect systematic information on the nature of violence and human rights abuses as a tool to wield pressure on those who were committing these abuses. Its methodology also mirrored that of SJC, but was expanded to include reporting on all abuses by all perpetrators where verification of the event was possible.[33] It dispatched teams (comprised mostly of lawyers and university students) to suspected sites of violence, including state prisons and military bases. Its investigators collected oral testimony from witnesses and victims of violence and their loved ones. Individuals interested in speaking with a representative from Tutela Legal could visit the main office, located in the chancery offices of the Archdiocese of San Salvador, or visit their local Catholic church, which would coordinate contact with the nearest representative or regional branch of Tutela Legal.[34]

Despite significant opposition from the Salvadoran and American governments, Tutela Legal was considered by most international experts to be one of few credible sources of evidence on human rights violations in El Salvador.[35] The United Nations relied on and cited data collected by

---

32 The accusations of political bias against the Christian Legal Aid were fair. As a matter of policy, the Christian Legal Aid did not report on abuses committed by the FMLN. However, subsequent investigations by independent nongovernmental organizations and the Salvadoran commission found that the FMLN was responsible for a small percentage (about five percent) of all human rights violations during the conflict.

33 Valencia-Weber and Weber, 1986, see *supra* note 28.

34 Lic. Ovidio Mauricio González's personal interview, 19 March 2009. All interviews were conducted in Spanish and subsequently translated.

35 A prominent example of this disagreement is the case of the massacre of more than 500 civilians in El Mozote, Morazán. Even after mass graves of women, children and the elderly were discovered, the Salvadoran government, American embassy and

Tutela in its repeated resolutions condemning the government's violation of international human rights and humanitarian law and its apparent unwillingness to investigate and prosecute offenses perpetrated by the armed forces or paramilitary groups.

Examining the testimonies collected by Tutela Legal and SJC reveals two primary patterns of sexual violence during the Salvadoran civil war: (1) the rape of women in rural communities by state forces before both the men and the women of the community were executed; and (2) the rape, sexual humiliation, and torture of political prisoners in state-run detention facilities. One hundred and twenty-three acts of sexual violence were recorded in the dataset and represented one percent of all human rights violations. The most frequently reported types of sexual violence were as follows: sexual humiliation (41 percent), rape and gang rape (24 percent), sexual torture (18 percent), attempted and threatened acts of sexual violence (12 percent) and sexual mutilation (four percent). According to the reports, 53 percent of victims of sexual violence were men. This is the first time that a conflict has ever registered more male than female victims of sexual violence. Confirming the general asymmetry of violence during the war, the State was responsible for 96 percent of all sexual abuses. Finally, sexual violence was most frequent in San Salvador and Cuscatlán.[36]

These data are limited in several respects and thus must be interpreted with caution until independent confirmation is possible. Tutela Legal and SJC collected denunciations of human rights violations *during* the conflict. Denunciations were typically filed within days of the event

State Department contested reports by Tutela Legal describing the incident as a massacre, arguing instead that the deaths resulted from a battle between State armed forces and rebels. The disagreement focuses on differing conceptions of 'civilian' and 'combatant' and how each is categorized under the concept of 'victim'. American officials expressed particular concern over Tutela's treatment of civilian noncombatants who lived in close proximity to guerrilla camps: see Valencia-Weber and Weber, 1986, see *supra* note 28. However, Article 13 of Protocol II of the Geneva Conventions clearly asserts that unless directly participating in hostilities, civilians cannot be attacked or targeted for violence: see Protocol Additional to the Geneva Conventions of 12 August 1949, and Relating to the Protection of Victims of Non-International Armed Conflicts (Protocol II), 8 June 1977, Article 13, available at http://www1.umn.edu/humanrts/instree/y6pagc.htm, last accessed on 15 May 2011.

36 The distribution of violations across departments is likely skewed towards San Salvador, where most human rights organizations were based.

occurring. The case files of Tutela Legal and SJC read much like missing persons reports. At the time the deponent files the report, s/he has incomplete information on the event. "*My wife never returned home form work*". "*We were on our way to school when some guys with guns jumped out of a car and grabbed my friend*". The victim may later be released from prison or be found dead. However, unless this updated information is transmitted to the original reporting institution, the record of the event will remain incompletely coded as a kidnapping or arbitrary detention. As a result, particular *types* of violence – torture, sexual violence and extra-judicial execution – are probably under-represented.

While this method of contemporaneous data collection minimizes the effects of memory formation processes or memory loss that is inherent in post-hoc investigations, it may also severely limit who is willing to speak openly and what they are willing to divulge about their experiences. Many may deem it too dangerous to travel to a regional human rights office or be seen speaking with foreign investigators, journalists or human rights activists. Because of the fluidity of battle lines in civil wars and the targeting of those attempting to document and report on war-related events, researchers, investigators and journalists often find themselves at a risk similar to that experienced by the populations they are aiding.[37] Indicative of this climate of violence and fear, the armed forces required Tutela Legal's investigators to sign waivers of responsibility for their physical safety while operating in contested regions of the country.[38] As a result, both Tutela Legal and Socorro Jurídico often limited their investigations to urban areas where violence was less widespread.[39]

37 The State carried out an explicit campaign of repression against journalists in El Salvador. The *Comité de Prensa de las Fuerzas Armadas de El Salvador*, COPREFA (Armed Forces Press Office) repeatedly threatened those who 'distorted' the image of the Salvadoran state and government with 'drastic measures'. Journalists' names also figured prominently on death squad 'hit lists' in the early 1980s. See Valencia-Weber and Weber, 1986, see *supra* note 28.

38 González, 2009, see *supra* note 34.

39 Neither organization, for example, reported on key massacres in rural areas in the early 1980's because they were unable to obtain independent sworn testimony from eyewitnesses or individual victims at the time of their occurrence: see Lic. Ovidio Mauricio González, Lic. Wilfredo Medrano and Hector Rivera, author interviews, 2009. In some cases, this is not just the result of widespread violence in the area, but also because the totality of the massacres left behind no survivors or witnesses to relate their experiences. After the signing of the peace accords, the Archbishop's Legal Aid and the Salvadoran commission conducted in-depth forensic investigations, in-

Findings based on the data from Tutela Legal and SJC should be interpreted with caution. In particular, it would be inappropriate at this time to conclude that sexual violence was more prevalent in San Salvador than in other parts of the country, or that sexual violence and torture comprised only one percent and ten percent, respectively, of all human rights violations during the war. It is not likely, however, that the contemporaneous data collection procedures of Tutela Legal and SJC affected the relative likelihood of a particular *type* of sexual violence being reported. Nor is it likely that this process more adversely affected female victims than male victims of sexual violence.

9.3.2. Peru

The Peruvian government established the *Comisión para la Verdad y Reconciliación* ('CVR') on June 4, 2001.[40] It was modeled in part after the commission in El Salvador, but also drew lessons from previous commissions in Argentina, Chile, Guatemala and South Africa. The CVR learned from the successes and failures of these truth commissions, reflected in its decision to investigate a broad range of human rights violations and hold public hearings throughout the country.[41]

The CVR was charged with:

> clarifying the process and facts [of what] occurred, as well as the corresponding responsibilities, not only of those who ex-

cluding the exhumation of mass graves, of well-known massacres in rural zones. See, for instance, CVES, 1993, see *supra* note 18, and Tutela Legal, *El Mozote: Lucha por la Verdad y la Justicia: Masacre a la Inocencia*, Tutela Legal del Arzobispado de San Salvador, San Salvador, El Salvador, 2008.

40 Valentín Paniagua, "*Creación de la Comisión de la Verdad en el Perú*" (Creation of the Peruvian Truth Commission) *Decreto Supremo* No. 065-2001-PCM (Supreme Decree No. 065-2001-PCM), 2 June 2001, Lima, Peru.

41 The truth commissions in Argentina, Chile, and Uruguay have been criticized for restricting their investigations to deaths (either extrajudicial executions or torture that results in death) and forced disappearances, a choice which underestimates the level and potentially mischaracterizes the nature of violence. In Uruguay, for example, the truth commission did not investigate illegal detentions, which was later discovered to be the most frequently experienced human rights violation. Conversely, the significant role of public hearings in South Africa's Truth and Reconciliation Commission led to their inclusion in the Peruvian model (a first for Latin American truth commissions). For a list of recent truth commissions and a critical overview of their structure and efficacy, see Priscilla Hayner, "Truth Commissions: A Schematic Overview", *International Review of the Red Cross*, 2006, vol. 88 no. 862, pp. 295–310.

> ecuted them, but also who ordered or tolerated them, while at the same time, proposing initiatives to strengthen peace and reconciliation among all Peruvians.[42]

This included investigating assassinations and massacres, forced disappearances, torture, sexual violence, forced recruitment, violence against children, and violations of the collective rights of indigenous peoples. To complete its work, the CVR was awarded a staff of more than five hundred people, including twelve Peruvian commissioners, and a budget of $11 million. Although sizeable and comparatively well financed, the CVR had only twenty-four months to document twenty years of civil conflict and violence.[43]

At regional offices throughout the country, members of the CVR team collected 16,917 testimonies from witnesses, victims and perpetrators of violence, and approximately 1,700 photographs documenting individuals' varied experiences during the war.[44] It held public hearings where survivors were invited to denounce the violence they experienced. The hearings, which were broadcast on national television and radio stations, covered 318 cases and 422 testimonies (see the Appendix for a detailed description of the CVR's work and the documents available at their documentation center in Lima, Peru). On August 28, 2003, the CVR released its twelve-volume final report. In it, the CVR estimated that 69,280 people were killed or had disappeared during the conflict.[45] Violence was concentrated in the south-central region of the country, particularly in the department of Ayacucho where the Shining Path initiated the 'people's

[42] Alejandro Toledo, "*Creación de la Comisión de la Verdad en el Perú*" (Creation of the Peruvian Truth Commission) *Decreto Supremo* No. 101-201-PCM (Supreme Decree No. 101-201-PCM), 31 August 2011, Lima, Peru.

[43] Hayner, 2006, see *supra* note 41.

[44] The Commission opened twenty-six regional offices. Each department had at least one office; Apurímac and Cusco each had two. The number of testimonies collected in each department are as follows: 5,313 Ayacucho; 1,444 Apurimac; 1,154 Huancavelica; 316 Cusco; 2,441 Huánuco; 209 Ucayali; 735 San Martín; 579 Puno; 2,308 Junin-Pasco; 1,174 Lima-Callao; 1,295 Other: see CVR, *Informe Final y Los Anexos de la Comisión para la Verdad y Reconciliación,* 2003, p. 382, available at http://www.cverdad.org.pe, last accessed on 11 May 2011. Photographs were donated by individuals, community and social organizations, churches, and various state agencies. More than two hundred of these photographs are on display at the Museo de la Nación in Peru. The exhibition, entitled *Yuyanapaq: Para Recordar*, will be on display until 2011.

[45] CVR, 2004, p. 17, see *supra* note 14.

war'. Peasants who spoke indigenous languages, such as Quechua, Aymara and Asháninka, and received little or no formal education, were disproportionately targeted for violence.[46] According to the CVR, while both the State and non-state armed actors perpetrated horrific acts of violence against the civilian population, more than half (54 percent) of all deaths and disappearances were attributed to the Shining Path.[47]

Due largely to the advancements forged by the International Criminal Tribunals for the former Yugoslavia and Rwanda (established in 1993 and 1994, respectively), the CVR operated in a more gender-aware climate than the CVES in El Salvador and other similarly early truth commissions. At the urging of feminist scholars and activists in Peru, the CVR appointed a gender unit to investigate the varied roles and experiences of men and women during the civil conflict. They also lobbied to increase the overall gender consciousness within the Commission and in all of its work. While the unit's influence was limited, its work is best reflected in the CVR's final report, which includes a historical analysis of gender inequality in Peru, the role of women in civil society organizations and armed organizations, and the patterns of wartime sexual violence.[48]

Unlike the truth commission in El Salvador, the CVR interpreted sexual violence as falling within its mandate to investigate cases of torture, serious abuses and injuries, and other cases that constitute grave violations of human rights.[49] While defining sexual violence broadly to include such abuses as forced prostitution, forced marriage, sexual slavery, forced abortion, forced impregnation, rape, and sexual torture, it investigated and reported only cases of rape and made only occasional references to these other forms of sexual abuse in its final report. The CVR found that rape was widespread, but accounted for 1.53 percent of all human rights violations registered. The majority of victims were young women (between the ages of 10 and 29), housewives, and peasants who

---

46 *Ibid.*, pp. 21–23.

47 *Ibid.*, p. 18.

48 Julissa Mantilla, personal interview, 5 February 2009. See CVR, 2003, chps. 2 and 6; Narda Ayín Henríquez, *Cuestiones de Género y Poder en el Conflicto Armado en el Perú*, Concejo Nacional de Ciencia, Tecnología e Innovación, Lima, Peru, 2006. In particular, the absence of a gender-sensitive approach within the national reparations program has been noted. For further discussion of the role of the gender unit within the CVR, see Henríquez, 2006.

49 CVR, 2003, see *supra* note 44.

spoke Quechua as their primary language and completed only primary-level education.[50] Of the 538 documented cases, 527 (98 percent) were perpetrated against women and only 11 (two percent) were perpetrated against men. Contrary to patterns of other forms of violence, the State was responsible for the overwhelming majority (83 percent) of sexual abuses and 100 percent of sexual violence against men.[51] Finally, the CVR found that sexual violence was most frequent in Ayacucho, Huancavelica, and Apurímac, between 1984 and 1990.[52]

Any large-scale human rights data collection program, like those described above in El Salvador and Peru, confronts numerous practical and methodological obstacles in its work. For example, because of time and resource constraints, only 70 percent of the testimonies received by the CVR were ever coded for nonlethal acts of violence and included in its final estimates. The testimonies themselves are complex and highly detailed, requiring time on the part of interviewers, translators, coders and data entry staff. Often, truth commissions overestimate the capacity of their research teams and underestimate the demand by the population for denunciations.[53] The following section addresses additional obstacles faced by truth commissions or other investigative bodies when documenting and analyzing sexual violence in conflict situations.

---

50 *Ibid.*

51 State security agents include the armed forces, police, civil defense organizations, and paramilitary groups. The Dirección Nacional Contra El Terrorismo and Sinchis counterterrorism forces within the National Police were singled out as particularly frequent perpetrators of sexual violence. Although sexual violence was prohibited by both the Shining Path and the Tupac Amaru Revolutionary Movement, the Commission found that both groups (the MRTA to a lesser degree) participated in the sexual victimization of the civilian population.

52 CVR, 2003, see *supra* note 44.

53 David Sulmont, "Evaluación del Trabajo de Testimonios", internal document of the *Comisión Para la Verdad y Reconciliación*, Document No. 140306, *Centro de Información para la Memoria y los Derechos Humanos*, Lima, Peru, 2002.

	El Salvador		Peru
	CVES	**Tutela Legal and SJC**	**CVR**
Timing	Post-hoc, 9 months.	Contemporaneous, duration of the civil war.	Post-hoc, 25 months.
Mandate	Investigate select crimes of a political nature between 1980-1991; and make binding recommendations to secure national peace and reconciliation.	Document denunciations of human rights abuse.	Investigate human rights abuses and violent attacks between 1980-2000.
Resources	Entirely externally funded.[54]	Predominantly internally funded.	Predominantly internally funded.
Sponsor	United Nations.	Catholic Church.	Peruvian Government.
Staff	Three international commissioners, all men, appointed by Secretary General of UN.	Between 12-25 local investigators, mostly lawyers and university students.	12 Peruvian commissioners, 10 men and two women.
Report	Three volumes, released March 15, 1993.	None.	10 volumes, released August 28, 2003.
Treatment of Sexual Violence	None.	No formal definition is provided, although documented cases span the full spectrum of sexual abuses.	Sexual violence is defined broadly, but investigation is limited to incidents of rape and gang rape.
Limitations of the Data	Memory loss may limit/distort what individuals report.	Less complete coverage of violations that occur *after* initial	Memory loss may limit/distort what individuals re-

54 A special $2.5 million fund was administered by the United Nations. Funds were donated from willing members States, included the United States, the Netherlands, Norway and Sweden and other western European countries.

	Less accurate reporting of time and date when event occurred. Less accurate reporting of location where event occurred.	capture.	port. Less accurate reporting of time and date when event occurred. Less accurate reporting of location where event occurred.
Strengths of the Data	More complete oral histories of individuals' experiences during conflict.	Very accurate reporting of time and date when event occurred. Very accurate reporting of location where event occurred.	More complete oral histories of individuals' experiences during conflict.

Table 1: Comparison of Human Rights Reporting Institutions in El Salvador and Peru.

9.4. Data Availability and Victim Underreporting

The greatest impediment to advancements in our understanding of sexual violence is the absence of systematic data on its occurrence. The limitations of the data come from victims' reluctance to report sexual crimes, as well as institutional decisions that lead to the underreporting of the true prevalence of sexual violence. The factors that lead to the relative (under)reporting of sexual violence vary over time and across societies and groups of people within those societies. As a result, caution should be taken when interpreting statistics on wartime sexual violence, as observed variation in its prevalence and patterns of perpetration may simply be the result of differential biases in its documentation.[55]

[55] In this chapter, I will make reference mostly to the factors that lead to the underreporting of wartime sexual violence. However, there are some who warn of the risk of overreporting that results from the misguided efforts of individuals who lodge false complaints of sexual violence or non-governmental organizations who misrepresent statistical evidence in order to raise international attention and resources to this humanitarian crisis: see Evlan Isikozlu and Ananda S. Millard, "Wartime Rape and Post-Conflict Research", Bonn International Center for Conversion, Bonn, Germany, 2009. This study relies on the direct testimony of victim's and survivors of violence. I have never come across a case in either of the two research sites where the veracity of a victim's testimony of sexual violence has been called into question. It is conceivable that an individual could falsely claim to be the victim of rape, or any other human

Survivors of sexual violence, whether in conflict situations or in times of 'peace', rarely report the offense to the authorities. In the United States, for instance, it is estimated that only 26 to 36 percent of all sexually motivated crimes are reported to the police.[56] Reporting sexual offenses varies greatly across countries and cultures, the sex of the victim, and the type of sexual crime. In societies where patriarchal norms are particularly strong, survivors may be disinclined to report sexual offenses because they feel ashamed or fear being blamed, stigmatized and isolated from their community.[57] After being raped by a lieutenant from the local military base, whom she characterized as "crazy looking for women in the community", one woman in Peru described her pain as follows:

> [...] I was suffering and I wished the ground would open up and swallow me to end my embarrassment. Because of the shame, no one knows about this, only myself and my husband.[58]

In Peru, Andean culture is based on mutually supportive relationships and reciprocity. Couples' social recognition or prestige within the community is relative to their combined contributions to community life. "In the Andean world, 'being two' is part of what it means to be a community member and a peasant".[59] One woman, married with six children, relates her experience and the trauma she suffered after discovering she was pregnant from her rapist:

---

rights violation, if they believed that such a claim would result in their receipt of financial reparations. However, given the strong stigma of victims of sexual violence and the abundant evidence of victim's silence regarding these crimes, it is unlikely that there exists a significant number of false allegations in my dataset.

56 Callie Marie Rennison, "Rape and Sexual Assault: Reporting to Police and Medical Attention, 1992–2000", Bureau of Justice Statistics, 2002, available at http://bjs.ojp.us doj.gov/content/pub/pdf/rsarp00.pdf, last accessed on 21 February 2010.

57 While most discussions of rape statistics focus on the pervasive underreporting issue, it is also possible for false reports to be injected into the data. This is of greater concern in political conflicts where either side may encourage the intentional fabrication and reporting of abuses to human rights agencies to demonize their opposition. Because of the high costs to individuals and the stigma attached to rape victims, I do not expect this kind of over-counting to affect my data on sexual violence.

58 Comisión para la Verdad y Reconciliación ('CVR 1'), *Collection of Individual Testimonies*: *No. 200920*, Centro de la Información para la Memoria Colectiva y los Derechos Humanos, Lima, Peru.

59 CVR, 2003, Tomo VIII, p. 75, see *supra* note 44.

> A husband knows when he can get you pregnant and when he can't. My period didn't come and I said nothing until I told him and he was surprised because he had calculated the days. Weeping and in pain, I told him what happened and since then I have lived a terrible hell. Having been abused, my husband who was drinking all the time, insulted me, saying I was a whore.[60]

Similarly, another woman recounts how she was rejected and abandoned by her husband after he discovered she had been raped. The victim was raped in her home on multiple occasions by unknown armed men wearing ski masks. She never went to the police and did not report it to any human rights organizations out of fear that she or her family would suffer more. When her husband found out that she was pregnant as a result of the rapes, he left her. The victim describes how her family fell apart. Her husband remarried and abandoned her and their two children.[61]

Similar norms governing gender and sexual relations can be found in El Salvador, where both men and women's beliefs regarding sexual violence are laced with moral judgment and prejudice. Victims are often blamed for conducting themselves in a way that put them at risk for sexual assault.[62] Although fictional in nature, the story told in 'La Honra' accurately captures the attitudes that still dominant Salvadoran society today. In the story, a young peasant girl, Juanita was raped while bathing at a water hole near her home. She ran home, crying. When she told her father what happened, he lashes out at her with contempt and disgust: "why were you so stupid to have lost your honor; how could you lose the only valuable thing you had?"[63]

Victims may also anticipate ineffective or unsupportive responses from the authorities. The police may be unable or unwilling to adequately protect victims of sexual violence and prosecute their offenders. This is of particular concern in conflict situations where state security agents bear responsibility for many sexual violations. In such cases, survivors may

60 JL de Fernandez and C Wurst, "Sexual Violence against Women: Psycho-Juridical Approach", in *Torture,* 2007, vol. 17 no. 2, p. 171.

61 CVR 1, *Collection of Individual Testimonies: No. 203354*, see *supra* note 58.

62 Mo Hume, "It's as if You Don't Know, Because You Don't Do Anything About it": Gender and Violence in El Salvador", in *Environment and Urbanization,* 2004, vol. 16, no. 2, pp. 63–72.

63 Salarrué, *Cuentos de Barro,* Consejo Nacional para la Cultura y el Arte, San Salvador, El Salvador, 1999, p. 10.

fear retributive violence if they report the crime and denounce the perpetrator.

One deponent in Peru recounts how she told the soldiers at the barracks about the rape of her cousin by members of the *Movimiento Revolucionario Túpac Amaru* ('MRTA', Tupac Amaru Revolutionary Movement):

> The soldiers told her that her cousin should come to the barracks to help them find the perpetrators. When she arrived, her hands and feet were tied. She was beaten and thrown on top of a desk and *offended* by one official and five soldiers. The deponent told her cousin that she shouldn't say anything to anyone about what happened.[64]

A review of testimonies collected by the CVR in Peru revealed that 31 percent of all human rights violations had been reported to state security authorities or a human rights or assistance agency. While it is impossible to isolate the reporting rate of sexual crimes from other human rights violations, I suspect it to be much less. The most commonly cited reasons for not denouncing a crime include fear (76%), a sense of futility and disillusionment in the justice system (10%), because the individual did not know how (either due to age, literacy or unfamiliarity with the system) (9%), a lack of resources (time and/or money) to travel to the appropriate institution (3%), and so on.[65]

Even if victims are willing to report acts of violence, war-torn societies may lack the necessary resources and infrastructure to do so. Roads and bridges may be destroyed, making travel more difficult. Hospitals, community organizations, and police stations may have been bombed, and personnel killed. Access to social services is not uniform within societies. Disadvantaged populations, whether based on socio-economic class, race, ethnicity, or geography, often experience greater difficulty in accessing state institutions and services. As judicial and political authorities in El Salvador and Peru fled the violence in rural communities and relocated to departmental capitals, those without the resources to travel the hours or days necessary were left with no representation or contact with the State.

---

64 CVR 1, *Collection of Individual Testimonies: No. 300578*, see *supra* note 58. Italics were added.

65 The interview and information collection process for human rights organizations in El Salvador differed from those of the CVR in Peru. As a result, similar reporting statistics are not available in El Salvador.

Individuals living in the most rural and isolated of communities may have no awareness of the activities of aid organizations and/or possess intense skepticism and distrust of 'outsiders'. This was a prominent concern of the truth commission in Peru. Before dispatching its teams of investigators, the CVR sent volunteers to outlying communities to establish a rapport with community members and familiarize them with the objectives and work of the truth commission.[66] To the extent that such subgroups within the population are affected by political and sexual violence differently, unequal access to reporting mechanisms may distort not only the overall level of violence reported, but also the types of violations and patterns of violence reported.

There are some measures that can be implemented to encourage victims of sexual violence to come forward, such as guaranteeing victims' anonymity, creating special female police units to handle cases of sexual abuse, increasing protective services, and providing physical and mental health services to victims. For the most part, however, such initiatives are beyond the purview and capabilities of social science scholars. In the section below, I will discuss a number of decisions that researchers make, often without thoughtful consideration, and the consequences they have on data and findings on wartime sexual violence.

9.5. What Is Sexual Violence: Legal Statutes and Social Norms

Concept formation is central to the research process. It is inextricably linked to theory building, operationalization of variables, and measurement.[67] Despite this, social scientists often pay insufficient attention to conceptualization in their analyses. Studies of sexual violence are no exception. What is understood as sexual violence varies widely across ethnic, religious, and social groups. For example, not all societies recognize marital rape as a criminal offense. Cases where the victim does not show obvious signs of a violent attack, where the perpetrator did not use a weapon to coerce the victim, or where sexual violence is perpetrated to restore family honor, may not be prosecuted.[68] How institutions and re-

---

[66] Emilio Salcedo, personal interview, 27 January 2009.

[67] Gary Goertz, *Social Science Concepts: A User's Guide*, Princeton University Press, Princeton, 2005.

[68] Patricia D. Rozée, "Forbidden or Forgiven? Rape in Cross-Cultural Perspective", in *Psychology of Women Quarterly*, 1993, vol. 17, no. 1, pp. 499–514.

searchers define the parameters of sexual violence determines which offenses are 'counted' and how statistics on their reported frequency should be interpreted.

How societies define and codify sexual offenses in national penal codes greatly determines how individuals conceptualize such acts and ultimately whether they are reported to the police.[69] In their 1980 study based on the United States, Skelton and Burkhart found that the most significant factor affecting a victim's likelihood of reporting sexual abuse was whether s/he understood what happened to be a crime, an issue complicated by changing cultural norms and legal statutes of domestic and sexual violence. However, national laws do not only affect the victim's perceptions of sex relations and violence; they also shape the attitudes and beliefs of those who document and prosecute criminal offenses. In her study of wartime rape in Peru, Boesten found that legal codes strongly shaped the perceptions of the survivors of rape, their family members, and those working for the Truth Commission.[70]

The following excerpt from an interview by a CVR staff member discusses the case of Anna,[*] a fifteen-year-old girl raped by a soldier stationed at the military base in her community. At the behest of her mother, Anna later signed a contract saying that she had sexual relations with the soldier and that she would marry him. After subsequent sexual relations, Anna discovered she was pregnant and gave birth to the soldier's baby. The case is illustrative of the social, cultural, and legal understanding of rape, consent, and violence from the perspectives of Anna, her mother, the captain of the military base who arranged for the marriage contract, and the CVR interviewer.

> *Interviewer*: So it is more probable that you, that your daughter who was born on 18 October was, well, was born as a result of the sexual relations that you had with your hus-

---

69 For example, both men and women will be less likely to report sexual assaults when by doing so, they may risk criminal charges and punishment. In societies where adultery or engaging in same sex acts is illegal, male and female rape survivors may avoid reporting the crime when they fear they will be unable to demonstrate that they did not consent to the sex act, which is necessary to prove that they themselves did not break the law.

70 Jelke Boesten, "Marrying Your Rapist: Domesticating War Crimes in Ayacucho, Peru", in Donna Pankhurst (ed.), *Gendered Peace: Women's Search for Post-war Justice and Reconciliation*, Routledge Press, London, 2007.

* All names have been replaced.

> band, with your consent, in January. That would make for the nine months, which it normally takes in pregnancy, is that not true *mamita*? When I took your declaration earlier, you did not tell me this. You said that as a result of the rape, you had a baby; that is what you said. And your daughter was not born as a result of this rape, as we were discussing earlier, rather, she was conceived later, when you had relations with your consent, when there was no violence, is that not true? So that means that there was no violence involved in conceiving your child, so why did you tell me that she was the product of violence?
>
> *Anna*: But if it was not for this rape, I would not have had my daughter.[71]

Signing the contract not only changed the social and legal understanding of any subsequent sexual relations Anna and the soldier had; it worked retroactively as well to declare the original act legal and consensual in the eyes of the state and community. The sexual act that resulted in the birth of Anna's daughter was framed as consensual and nonviolent, despite the highly coercive and violent context within which it occurred. It is clear from the excerpt above that human rights organizations, truth commissions, and international criminal tribunals cannot assume that their investigators share the same understanding of sexual violence.

At the time of Anna's case, the Peruvian Penal Code allowed individuals accused of rape to avoid prosecution and punishment if they proposed to marry the victim.[72] In cases of gang rape, all of the alleged perpetrators would be exempt from punishment if the victim agreed to marry one of them.[73] In 1997, Congress repealed the law, but still maintained that criminal charges would be withdrawn if the issue was resolved 'privately'.[74] Subsequent testimonies collected by the CVR revealed individuals' uncertainty in identifying rape cases and reluctance to denounce them as crimes due to changes in national rape statutes.

---

71 CVR, 2003, pp. 30–31, 402–403, see *supra* note 44.

72 Lucero B. Merino, *Matrimonio y Violación: El Debate del Artículo 178 del Código Penal Peruano*, Movimiento Manuela Ramos, Lima, Peru, 1997.

73 *Código Penal de Perú, Capítulo* IX: *Violación de la Libertad Sexual* (Penal Code of Peru, Chapter IX: Rape and Sexual Freedom), *Articulos* 170–178.

74 Lisa Sharlach, *Sexual Violence as Political Terror*, Ph.D. dissertation, Department of Political Science, University of California, Davis, 2001.

El Salvador, on the other hand, has had a stable legal tradition with respect to rape and other sexual violence cases. Rape is defined as "any form of violence in which there was penetration of the vagina or anus by another person" and is punishable by six to 10 years in prison.[75] Other forms of sexual aggression that do not meet the requisites of rape are sanctioned with three to six years in prison.[76] Accordingly, victims of sexual violence in El Salvador may be more likely to view their experiences as criminal acts, to report them to the police, and seek judicial reparations than their counterparts in Peru, *ceteris paribus*.

In addition to the law, social and cultural norms, particularly regarding masculinity and heterosexuality, complicate the meaning of sexual violence. Men are less likely to report sexual violence and less likely to describe it as *sexual* violence if it threatens their identity as strong, capable, virile, heterosexual men:[77]

> Societies' constructs of masculinity play an important role in…non-reporting. Society often equates manhood with 'the ability to exert power over others, especially through the use of force.' Thus, victimization and masculinity may be considered incompatible in the belief that men cannot be victims.[78]

Moreover, there is what Sivakumaran calls the 'taint' of homosexuality for the victims of male/male rape.[79] Victims of male/male rape often question their own sexuality after the assault. According to surveys cited

---

75 *Código Penal de El Salvador* (Penal Code of El Salvador), 1997.

76 *Ibid.* Prison terms for rape or other sexual crimes against a minor are longer.

77 The underreporting of male sexual violence may be further compounded in ethno-nationalist conflicts in which the power of the state is symbolically linked to images of the virility, power, and heterosexuality of its men. For instance, despite evidence of rape and castration of men in camps in the former Yugoslavia, the Croatian media reported only one story of male sexual violence, namely, the rape of a Muslim man. There was no mention of Croatian men either having suffered sexual violence or having perpetrated it during the conflict. The image of a powerful and righteous state is defended through the denial or suppression of stories of Croatian men having been the object or perpetrator of sexual assault: see Dubrakva Zarkov, "Sexual Violence and War in the Former Yugoslavia", Speech made at the Cordaid Debate on Gender-based War Crimes: A Future after Humiliation, 11 January 2005, available at http://www.cordaid.nl/Overice/Extra_pop_up/Index.aspx?mid=9593&sid=292, last accessed on 1 May 2011.

78 Sandesh Sivakumaran, "Male/Male Rape and the 'Taint' of Homosexuality", in *Human Rights Quarterly*, 2005, vol. 27 no. 4, p. 1289.

79 *Ibid.*, p. 1289.

by the author, victims of male/male rape often report wondering if they possessed a certain homosexual trait that attracted the perpetrator to them.[80] Failure to recognize such cultural constructs of victimhood, masculinity, and sexuality can result in the underreporting of sexual violence against men.[81] Scholars and policy makers believe that the majority of victims of sexual violence are women and girls. However, the proportion of male to female victims can change according to how sexual violence is understood and recorded.

Confirming the finding that many men were subjected to sexual violence during the Salvadoran civil war, a survey of political prisoners at La Esperanza men's prison (commonly known as La Mariona) revealed that 76 percent had suffered sexual abuse during their incarceration.[82] The study was carried out in 1986 by members of the non-governmental *Comisión de Derechos Humanos de El Salvador* (El Salvador Human Rights Commission) who were also being held at the prison on suspicion of committing subversive acts. The most commonly reported forms of sexual violence are as follows: forced nudity (58 percent), genital beatings (20 percent), electric torture (14 percent)[83], rape (0.5 percent) and threats of rape (15 percent).[84] Men were often kicked, punched, or beaten on their testicles with guns or sticks as a form of punishment or coercion during detention and interrogation. While similar beatings on other parts of the

80 *Ibid.*

81 See Augusta del Zotto and Adam Jones, "Male-on-Male Sexual Violence in Wartime: Human Rights' Last Taboo?", paper presented at the annual meeting of the *International Studies Association*, New Orleans, LA., 23–27 March 2002. The authors examined the informational materials of 4,076 non-governmental organizations that address sexual violence in conflict situations and found 1.4 percent of the reports expressly framed the issue as one that affects only women and girls. An additional 25 percent of the organizational literature denied that sexual violence against men and boys was a problem. Only three percent of the materials specifically mentioned the experience of male victims and survivors of sexual violence.

82 Most incidents of sexual violence occurred before the detainee was transferred to Mariona, while in the custody of state security agents: see *Comisión de Derechos Humanos de El Salvador* ('CDHES'), *La Tortura Actual en El Salvador*, CDHES, San Salvador, El Salvador, 1986.

83 Because the report does not differentiate between cases where electricity was applied to the genitalia and those where electricity was applied to the ears, fingertips, feet, and so on, there is no way to know how many of these instances should be categorized as *sexual* torture.

84 CDHES, 1986, see *supra* note 82.

body were a common experience in detention and reported as such by human rights groups, few activists, medical care providers, or victims interpreted the specific genital attacks as *sexual* torture or assault.[85]

The following case illustrates a common pattern of sexual torture against men in El Salvador. A young man, age 23, was waiting at a bus stop when an unmarked car pulled up and six armed men in civilian clothes approached him. They threatened to shoot him if he ran or made a scene. They pushed him into the car, blindfolded him, and took him to what he later discovered was the Polícia de Hacienda ('PH', Treasury Police) in San Salvador. While detained, the man was interrogated and tortured in an attempt to extract a confession of his affiliation with the guerrillas. He was forced to do exercises, beaten all over his body, including his testicles, until he passed out. The police doused him with cold water to revive him, and repeated the process. He was ultimately forced to sign blank papers (presumably a "confession" used as evidence of his guilt) and then transferred to Mariona prison.[86] From the case description, it appears that genital beatings were one of several repressive techniques used against suspected guerrillas and not necessarily distinct in motive. To determine if this is true of all forms of sexual violence perpetrated against both men and women throughout the civil war, researchers must distinguish sexual violations from other human rights abuses so that their patterns of perpetration may be compared and their distinct motivations (if any) identified.

---

85 See Eric Stener Carlson, "The Hidden Prevalence of Male Sexual Assault during War: Observations of Blunt Trauma to the Male Genitals", in *British Journal of Criminology*, 2005, vol. 46 no. 1, pp. 16–25. The author argues that victims' and researchers' reticence to categorize blunt trauma to the male genitalia as sexual torture is related to "peacetime" conceptions of similar episodes. He writes:

> being hit in the testicles during peacetime activities is generally considered a 'normal' occurrence. For example, men's testicles are hit in soccer, American football and in many other contact sports, where players are expected to 'take it like a man.' Some martial arts instructors even purposely hit their students in the testicles as a form of punishment, and some college fraternities have been known to pour hot wax on their pledges' testicles as a form of initiation. Furthermore, a woman kicking a man in the groin has become a stereotyped form of sexual rejection […]. (*op. cit.*, p. 20)

86 Tutela Legal, *Collection of Individual Testimonies: No. CV-3700*, Archives Department, University of Colorado, Boulder, Colorado.

Preliminary research evaluating both the published records as well as the primary documents of the CVR reveals that the percentage of male victims of sexual violence in Peru is higher than commonly expected *and* higher than previously reported.[87] Rather than the two percent cited in the Commission's final report, I found that 29 percent of events of sexual violence listed in the published annexes of the report included male victims.[88] My work in the archives, accessing the original victim and witness testimonies, similarly indicates that 29 percent of victims of sexual violence were men. One reason for the discrepancy between my and the CVR's figures is our different conceptualization and operationalization of 'sexual violence'. While defining sexual violence broadly to include such abuses as forced prostitution, forced marriage, sexual slavery, forced abortion, forced impregnation, rape, and sexual torture, the CVR investigated and reported only cases of rape and made only occasional references to other forms of sexual violence in the narrative of its final report. As a result, the Commission overlooked the multiple ways in which men and women were sexually victimized. Examining the primary documents shows that the most frequent form of sexual abuse suffered by men was sexual humiliation (54 percent) followed by sexual torture (18 percent), sexual mutilation (13 percent), and rape (seven percent).[89]

---

87 There was only one case of sexual violence against a man reported by the CVR. The case does not appear exceptional in any regard that would indicate its inclusion in the CVR's database when similar violations were excluded. In this case, the victim describes how he was attacked two years after his father, sister and two others were killed by the military. He was at a party at a relative's house and was intoxicated. The military arrived. They entered the house and captured the victim, putting a hood over his head and tying his hands behind his back. They detained him at a military base, where he was tortured for 10 days and violently raped. See CVR, *Collection of Individual Testimonies: No. 407532 and 425187*, see *supra* note 58.

88 Michele Leiby, "Wartime Sexual Violence in Guatemala and Peru", in *International Studies Quarterly*, 2009, vol. 53 no. 2, pp. 445–468. This study was conducted using he published annexes of the Truth Commission, which are available on the CVR's website at http://www.cverdad.org.pe. The annexes provide very brief descriptions of cases presented to the Commission. I read each summary and collected data on events of sexual violence. An 'event' can include multiple victims, violations and/or perpetrators. I recorded 695 events of sexual violence, and 913 individual sexual violations. Of the 695 events, 30 percent included male victims (25 percent of these included only male victims and five percent included both male and female victims).

89 Of the cases of sexual torture against men, two-thirds are beatings of the victim's genitals, which some may argue should be excluded as a form of *sexual* torture and

Security forces, for instance, often used electricity applied to the genitals to punish or elicit information or a confession from male detainees. Linking the testimonies with the CVR's database reveals that sexual torture against both men and women is often coded as torture.[90] The rape of men is treated inconsistently: it is coded as either sexual violence or torture, and sometimes not recorded at all. Sexual violence perpetrated by non-state actors was also misleadingly documented. One tactic employed by the Shining Path to punish men suspected of betraying the revolution was to forcibly strip them in public and remove their testicles and/or penis. Failing to report such abuses as *sexual* violence, or failing to report them at all, misrepresents the nature and patterns of violence during the war.

Consider the following example. In February 1984, a group of thirty soldiers entered and searched the home of a suspected member of the Shining Path. While interrogating the suspect's grandmother, the soldiers severely beat her and burned her vagina and anus. They later poured kerosene on her body and set her on fire. The soldiers also beat and interrogated the suspect. They accused him of terrorism, stripped him, and cut off his penis.[91] The CVR's database (herein referred to as 'BDCVR') captures the detention and torture of each victim. However, neither the sexual torture of the grandmother nor the mutilation of the grandson was recorded as sexual violence. Each act was coded as torture. I argue, however, that these forms of violence are qualitatively different from other forms of torture. They attack the victim's gender and sexual identity, cause deep physical and psychological scars, and degrade and humiliate the person in ways that beatings, water boarding, or other forms of torture do not. In addition to being used to punish or extract information from individuals, sexual torture also may be used explicitly, and perhaps solely, for the purpose of attacking and destroying the individual's sense of self as a man or woman, a father or mother, or a spouse.

A similar comparison of the primary and published records of the CVES, Tutela Legal or Socorro Jurídico is not possible because none of

characterized as just torture. It is conceivable that the motive behind such abuse is to cause the victim pain, rather than to attack his sexual or gender identity.

90 Individual testimonies can be matched to observations in the database according to the testimony number, the event number, the observation number, and the victim ID number.

91 CVR, *Collection of Individual Testimonies: No. 201444*, see *supra* note 58.

these institutions conducted an analysis of sexual violence during the war. However, it is unlikely that these institutions, working in a less gender-sensitive context, would have done a better job than that of the CVR in Peru.

Scholars of wartime sexual violence need to understand the legal statutes and socio-cultural norms regarding sexual abuse that operate within the country. These norms influence not only what survivors of sexual violence are willing to report to investigators, but also *how* they report it as well. Care must also be taken to adequately train investigators so that their own perception and internalization of these norms does not interfere with taking a witness or survivor's statement.

9.6. Building on International Human Rights Norms to Create Analytical Concepts

The academic literature has similarly struggled with conceptualizing and operationalizing sexual violence. Much of the literature either poorly specifies the dependent variable or limits it to rape and gang rape.[92] Green observes incidents of "collective rape", which she defines as "a pattern of sexual violence perpetrated on civilians by agents of the state or political civil group".[93] Sharlach uses rape and sexual violence interchangeably and defines them as "any sexual penetration of a female by a male (or with an object) that takes place without her consent".[94] The dependent variable of her study, however, is a State's "rape policy", which can range from the State's use of rape as an act of genocide, torture, or terror, to its failure to prosecute rape perpetrated by civilians, or to the State's due diligence in prosecuting and preventing rape.[95] While each author defines the dependent variable, these are concepts not easily operationalized or empirically measured. Moreover, they are limited to acts of penetrative rape, and in the latter case, only when perpetrated against a woman by a man. The decision to focus exclusively on cases of rape may be driven by

[92] Dara Kay Cohen, *Explaining Sexual Violence during Civil War*, PhD diss., Department of Political Science, Stanford University, 2010; Jennifer Green, *Collective Rape: A Cross-National Study of the Incidence and Perpetrators of Mass Political Sexual Violence, 1980–2003*, PhD diss., Department of Sociology, Ohio University, 2006; Sharlach, 2001, see *supra* note 74.

[93] Green, 2006, p. ii, see *supra* note 92.

[94] Sharlach, 2001, p. 11, see *supra* note 74.

[95] *Ibid.*, pp. 7–8.

the limitations of the data. While there exists ambiguity across and within societies about what constitutes rape, it is more easily identified than other forms of sexual violence.

Collecting data on the various forms of sexual violence requires corresponding definition and operationalization. Isolating the unique attributes of different sexual abuses is not easy. What constitutes sexual torture and how does it differ from sexual mutilation? Should forced nudity be considered sexual violence? These are questions without straightforward answers. The International Criminal Court ('ICC') recognizes rape, sexual torture and mutilation, sexual slavery, enforced prostitution, enforced sterilization, and forced pregnancy in its definitions of sexual violence as a war crime and a crime against humanity. The ICC does not recognize sexual humiliation as a crime.[96]

In the interest of creating social science concepts to be used in analyses of the underlying causes of wartime sexual abuse, I argue for a broader interpretation of sexual violence than that currently used by the ICC. Here, the term includes all forms of sexual violence recognized by the ICC, and adds sexual humiliation and sexual coercion. I hypothesize that armed groups that commit rape, mutilation, and other forms of sexual violence recognized by the ICC also will be inclined to use sexual humiliation and coercion.[97] Therefore, understanding the causes of one may help us to understand the causes of all forms of wartime sexual violence.[98] Collecting data on the varied forms of sexual violence and maintaining the disaggregation of these violations will allow researchers to examine

96 Rome Statute of the International Criminal Court, 17 July 1989, U.N. Doc. A/CONF.183/9 ("Rome Statute"), Article 8(2)(e)(vi)(2000).

97 Some of the same causal processes, such as a disdain for women and societal disregard for their rights, could explain both armed groups' willingness to perpetrate rape and other forms of sexual violence on the "battlefield" and the forced sterilization of women by health care professionals, policymakers, and others in the health care community. Others, such as how these social norms are imbedded and transmitted through military institutions, and how state armed forces frame their national security and react to threats to it, are distinct and require separate analysis.

98 It may be the case that even those forms of sexual violence recognized by the ICC – rape, sexual slavery, forced prostitution, forced pregnancy, forced sterilization, and mutilation – occur under different behavioral constraints and institutional contexts. Similarly, groups that engage in one or more of these abusive practices may not use them all.

additional hypotheses regarding the perpetration of sexual violence during war.

I adopt the ICC's definition of rape, as outlined in Article 8(2)(e)(vi) of the Rome Statute: "the invasion of the body of a person by conduct resulting in penetration, however slight, of any part of the body of the victim or of the perpetrator with a sexual organ, or of the anal or genital opening of the victim with any object or any other part of the body".[99] Gang rape, then, is any rape perpetrated by more than one person.[100]

Although usually involving multiple and repeated rapes, sexual slavery and forced marriage are conceptually distinct. The ICC defines enslavement as "the exercise of any or all of the powers attaching to the right of ownership over a person", and includes "the exercise of such power in the course of trafficking persons, in particular women and children (Article 7(2)(c) of the Rome Statute). Sexual slavery is described as "when women and girls are kidnapped against their will and converted into the property of one or more people who demand sexual services from them, and often other forms of domestic service as well".[101] Forced marriage can take many different forms, including when fathers or other guardians give a woman to be married without her consent or ability to refuse. I included sexual slavery and forced marriage as a separate analytical category and assigned it a distinct code in the database. However, I

---

[99] Rome Statute, see *supra* note 96.

[100] I only coded a rape as gang rape if it was clear from the testimony that more than one perpetrator actively participated in the rape of the victim. This includes cases where multiple, but an unspecified number of, persons committed the act: "Las terroristas me violaron/The terrorists raped me". Both the subject and the verb of the statement suggest more than one perpetrator participated in the rape. Testimonies of events involving more than one victim and violation are complex. Often the details of each case are lost or aggregated. Therefore, I only coded reports of multiple rapes against multiple victims by multiple perpetrators as gang rape if the testimony indicated that more than one perpetrator was involved in each attack against each individual victim. The following hypothetical case would be recorded as rape, not gang rape: Los soldados abusaron varias mujeres de la comunidad/The soldiers raped various women in the community

[101] Agnés Callamard, *Documentar las Violaciones de Derechos Humanos por los Agentes del Estado: Violencia Sexual,* Centro Internacional de Derechos Humanos y Desarrollo Democrático, Montreal, 2002.

found no reports of either crime during the civil wars in either El Salvador or Peru.[102]

Following the United Nations Special Rapporteur on Torture, I argue that any form of sexual violence that causes severe pain and suffering to the victim, whether physical or psychological, should be considered sexual torture. Sexual torture can, but does not always, result in permanent damage or scars that affect future sexual function. Beyond the physical pain inflicted, often the purpose of sexual torture is to attack and destroy an individual's identity as a man/woman, sexual partner, parent, and so on. It can be perpetrated during interrogation to intimidate or punish the victim, obtain information, or coerce a confession from the victim or a third party.[103] The Inter-American Commission of Human Rights ('IACHR') further argued that in accordance with Article 5 of the Inter-American Convention on Human Rights, sexual offenses do not have to be perpetrated in official centers or institutions in order to be considered torture.

In the case of *Fernando and Raquel Mejía vs. the Republic of Peru*, the IACHR found that the rape of individuals in their home by state security agents was an act of torture.[104] This decision was significant in recognizing the environment in which irregular and counterinsurgent conflicts are often fought. To create mutually exclusive categories of sexual violence, I use 'sexual torture' to refer to those abuses that satisfy the criteria for torture, but which are not covered in the ICC's definition of rape.[105] This includes, but is not limited to, the application of electricity, beatings, or other injuries to the breasts, genitals, and in the case of pregnant women, the abdomen. These acts of violence need not result in permanent sexual dysfunction or even visible bruises or scars to constitute sexual torture. Physical assaults to the breasts or genitalia always involve an attack

---

[102] Chapter 2 of the CVR *Informe Final* discusses cases of sexual slavery and forced marriage perpetrated against the Asháninka, however, no such cases were found in the sample of testimonies included in this study.

[103] United Nations, *United Nations Document* UN E/CN.4/1992/SR.21 United Nations, New York, 1999.

[104] Inter-American Commission on Human Rights (IACHR), *Informe N 5/96 Case 10.970 Fernando y Raquel Mejía vs. Peru*, IACHR, Washington, DC, 1999.

[105] United Nations, *Convention against Torture and Other Cruel, Inhuman or Degrading Treatment or Punishment*, United Nations, New York, 1994, available at http://www.hrweb.org/legal/cat.html, last accessed on 25 February 2010.

on the individual's sexual identity by embedding within the psyche of the victim an association between sexuality and fear, pain and violence.[106]

To the extent that they are targeted against different population groups and occur in contexts different from rape, excluding cases of sexual torture will result in our misunderstanding of the nature of wartime sexual violence. It may be, for instance, that rape is perpetrated more often when soldiers are dispatched in the field where supervising officers may have less control over their subordinate troops. Sexual torture (many forms of which are grotesquely elaborate and require access to specialized equipment) may be more common in detention facilities where perpetrators have more control over the environment and more time to plan and execute the crimes. Suggesting variation within the category of sexual violence, the CVR found that of the 118 individual testimonies collected from the Establecimiento Penal de Régimen Cerrado Especial de Mujeres de Chorrillos II (Women's Maximum Security Prison in Chorrillos), 96 inmates (81 percent) reported being the victims of sexual violence, but only 30 (25 percent) indicated rape as the offense.[107]

Sexual mutilation, while similar, can be distinguished from sexual torture in that it involves the removal or permanent damage and scarring of reproductive organs, and may be accompanied by sterilization. In Peru, both the state armed forces and the Shining Path perpetrated sexual torture and mutilation. Moreover, compared with rape, these offenses followed different patterns of perpetration. They were often carried out in public or during interrogation, targeted both men and women, and resulted in visible scars or signs of abuse, perhaps serving to terrorize others in the community.[108] The use of these offenses to send a message to a broader audience, combined with their brutality, warrants their treatment as a separate category of sexual violence.[109]

---

106 See Inger Agger and Søren Buus Jensen, "The Psychosexual Trauma of Torture" in John P. Wilson and Beverly Raphael (eds.), *International Handbook of Traumatic Stress*, Plenum Press, New York, 1986; and Carlson, 2005, see *supra* note 85. State security agents have been reported to beat pregnant women's abdomens in order to induce labor or forcibly abort the fetus or otherwise damage the woman's reproductive organs.

107 CVR, 2003, see *supra* note 44.

108 Leiby, 2009, see *supra* note 88.

109 Publicity is not a characteristic unique to sexual mutilation. Rape and gang rape, sexual humiliation, and even sexual torture may, and often are, committed in public settings. In such cases, these other forms of sexual violence may also be used to ter-

I define sexual humiliation as any offense of a sexual nature whose primary goal is to humiliate and debase the victim, but which does not use direct physical force and which does not result in physical injury. Examples of sexual humiliation include forcible or compulsory nudity, forced stripping or dancing naked in public, and mocking an individual's genitalia. In societies where nudity is not the norm, the naked body is imbued with gendered and sexed meanings, suggestive of an individual's sexual availability, promiscuity and vulnerability. Being stripped and forced to remain naked has the intention of not just subjecting an individual to the elements (cold, rain, and so on), but of humiliating them, making them aware of their powerlessness and terrorizing them by provoking fears of an impending sexual assault. Examining the original testimonies collected by Tutela Legal and Socorro Jurídico reveals that sexual humiliation comprised 41 percent of all sexually-based offenses during the Salvadoran civil war. Similarly, examining the original testimonies collected by the CVR reveals that 33 percent of all sexual violations in Peru were incidents of sexual humiliation.

Sexual coercion involves the threat of sexual violence to pressure or force individuals to do something against their will, such as inform on the political activities of a neighbor or confess to committing a crime. According to these definitions, the following would be categorized as sexual coercion and sexual humiliation:

> On November 24, 1987, 60 soldiers arrived by helicopter and detained three people in the community of Nuevo San Miguel, district of Jepelacio, province of Moyobamba, department of San Martín. They gagged, bound and detained the victims at the local school. The soldiers hung and beat the three men on their backs with the butts of their guns. The soldiers then brought the men's wives and children into the school, stripped them and threatened to burn them alive. The soldiers also threatened to "abuse" the wives. One of the victims' faces was cut four times. Later, they were taken to the military base in Moyobamba where they were given food and attended to by doctors. [...] They were then taken to the base in Tarapoto where they were accused of belonging to the PCP-SL (Partido Communista del Peru-Sendero Luminoso, Community Party of Peru-Shining Path). Finally, they

rorize entire families or communities, making their distinction from sexual mutilation less clear.

> returned to Nuevo San Juan and were freed on November 28, 1987.[110]

The case is more complex than its presentation in the CVR database, which reports the three male victims as having suffered detention and torture. The men were not only subject to hangings and beatings. The soldiers intentionally used the sexual victimization of their wives and children (by forcibly stripping them) *and* the threat of further sexual violence (suggested by the use of *abusar*), perhaps to coerce the men to comply with their orders, or simply to punish them for their suspected subversive affiliations.

This was also a common strategy used by security agents in El Salvador to manipulate the civilian population. In one case, uniformed soldiers from the 2nd Infantry Brigade stormed a village in Coatepeque, Santa Ana in 1990. They went first to the local agricultural cooperative, where they captured five men, and then began to raid each house and detain those found inside. The soldiers gathered the men of the community together in the street and told them that they would not detain or *touch* their women if they answered their questions and agreed to co-operate.[111] Threats of sexual violence against women may be particularly effective in coercing men to comply with the demands of their captors. Such threats attack a man's sense of self and expose his inability to protect "his" woman in times of war.

Recording realized, attempted, and threatened acts of sexual violence gives the researcher a larger sample of cases to analyze the repertoires of violence of armed actors. Understanding in what contexts armed forces threaten or attempt sexual violence and how or why they were unable or unwilling to carry it out provides insight into the underlying causes of wartime sexual violence.

Understanding how victims and reporting agencies conceptualize sexual violence is crucial to understanding exactly what is captured in reported statistics on sexual violence and its use in war. I am proposing one model here with specific definitions for various forms of sexual abuse, including violations that have not been recognized by international law. While some may draw the lines in different places, it is important to clearly define our concepts and open a dialogue in which academic and

[110] CVR, *Informe Final*, Case No. 1012572, see *supra* note 44.

[111] Tutela Legal, *Collection of Individual Testimonies: No. CV-7686*, see *supra* note 86.

human rights communities can build a consensus regarding what constitutes sexual violence.

9.7. Who Counts: Estimating the Number of Sexual Violence Victims

After deciding what sexual violence is, human rights organizations and scholars must determine what constitutes a victim. One common point of disagreement is the treatment of anonymous or unnamed victims. The truth commissions in El Salvador and Peru only collected data on victims identifiable by first and last name.[112] Including only named victims is a method commonly employed by large-scale database management projects. However, in studies and databases of sexual violence, there are likely to be numerous unnamed or unidentified victims. Because of the fear and stigma associated with being sexually violated, victims often report their attacks in the third person, as an event they witnessed or that happened to someone they know.

Despite, and perhaps due to, the reluctance of individuals to report personal sexual traumas, the CVR states that many of the testimonies it received make general reference to and provide stories of sexual abuse: "I heard that other girls had been raped, but not me".[113] Working with the archived testimonies, I have been able to identify 249 incidents of sexual violence that were not included in the CVR's database because the victims' full name was unknown or withheld (there were 222 unidentified victims of sexual violence, some of whom suffered more than one violation). The most frequent forms of sexual violence against unidentified victims were rape and gang rape (56 percent), sexual humiliation (29 percent), and sexual torture, sexual mutilation and unspecified forms of sexual violence or the threat of sexual violence (5 percent each). Given the CVR's operationalization of sexual violence as rape or gang rape, it is not surprising that the latter cases were not captured in the database.

If events of violence including unnamed victims are qualitatively different from those where individuals can be identified, excluding anon-

[112] The annex to the CVES' final report includes victims by their first and last name, as well as those who were identified only by their initials. However, the report does not include any information on victims who wished to remain completely anonymous or who could not be identified by the deponent.

[113] CVR, *Collection of Individual Testimonies: No. 700021*, see supra note 58.

ymous accounts may underestimate a particular subgroup within the population of victims: specifically those who have been attacked in the context of larger events of political violence where there were numerous victims. Massacres, battles between armed groups, or mass detentions are contexts particularly vulnerable to having "missing" victims of sexual violence. It may be the case that there are no surviving witnesses to the attack. Even if there are a few survivors, it may be that they do not know the names of everyone in the razed village. The massacre in El Mozote, Morazán in December 1981 is typical in this regard. The soldiers of the Atlacatl battalion separated the men from the women and the children of the community. The women were taken to the nearby hills where they were raped (perhaps gang raped) before all of the residents were systematically executed. The single witness to the event, Rufina Amaya Mírquez was 11 years old at the time of the attack. Until her recent death in 2007, Ms. Amaya repeatedly recounted the details of the massacre before the foreign media, heads of state and international human rights organizations. However, she did not know the number of women and girls who were raped, nor the names of all of those who were killed. It is common during community raids, massacres, and battles for there to be multiple, but an unspecified number of, unnamed victims. Excluding these cases from our analyses will bias our findings against identifying the patterns associated with mass, indiscriminate acts of violence.

Another illustrative case considers the use of sexual violence against fellow members of subversive organizations. Although officially prohibited, sexual violence, particularly forced marriage and sexual slavery, have been reported amongst the ranks of the Shining Path. Individuals sequestered or forcibly recruited by the Shining Path may have witnessed this violence and reported it to the CVR. Because it is a clandestine organization, little is known about the identity of individual members. Witnesses can provide little, if any, information on the victims' names, ages, family members, or where they lived. Rather than excluding all victims of violence who belong or used to belong to subversive organizations, I treat them as "unnamed Shining Path" or "unnamed MRTA" and record as many details about the event as possible.

When the deponent does not provide a specific number or some other quantitative descriptor of the number of victims, I record two victim-violation observations. Often witnesses will refer to "many", "a lot", or even "everyone" being subjected to political violence during a particular event. Also likely are statements such as "among those killed, was my husband". In these cases we know that more than one person died, but exactly how many more is indeterminable. Erring on the side of conservative estimate, while again risking mischaracterizing the level and patterns of violence, is warranted since we can make no reasonable judgment of the number of victims. Employing this strategy, I have identified a minimum of 224 cases of sexual violence against unknown individuals.[114]

Adding unnamed victims to datasets of political violence introduces its own potential biases. In this case, there is a risk of distorting the patterns of violence by over-counting cases that are duplicated within the dataset. Most cases are sufficiently unique to allow duplicate records to be matched and eliminated based on the context and description of the violation, the sequencing of events, and where and when the event occurred. However, this presumes that victims and witnesses remember the events accurately and similarly. Even if we accept this as true, the matching process is time-consuming, difficult and imperfect. There is an obvious trade-off when making the methodological decision to focus on both named and unnamed victims of violence. At the very least, full disclosure of these trade-offs is warranted.

9.8. Prioritization of Human Rights Violations

Quantifying sexual violence, as well as other human rights violations, is no easy task. This is particularly true when victims suffer multiple or repeated violations. Much of the human rights field employs a "one victim equals one violation equals one perpetrator" approach to recording abuses, but most cases of human rights abuse do not conform to such a narrow model.[115] The single coded violation is usually the one implicitly judged to be most severe. Imposing this restriction distorts reality and limits our ability to examine variation in the repertoires of violence employed by different armed actors. Knowing whether sexual violence is perpetrated in combination with other forms of human rights abuse, and the order in which these offenses are perpetrated, is useful to understanding motive.

114 That there were only two unidentified victims of sexual violence in El Salvador is likely due to the nature of the data. The denunciation reports filed by Tutela Legal and SJC do not reflect complete conflict narratives such as those collected by the CVES or the CVR in Peru.

115 Patrick Ball, *Who Did What to Whom?,* American Association for the Advancement of Science, Washington, DC, 1996.

Using this model, with its simplification of offenses and the coding of only the purportedly most important or severe violation, creates a situation in which particular abuses are systematically excluded or underreported. Even when truth commissions do not employ this model, staff may nonetheless neglect to systematically investigate and document "lesser" offenses.

This is of concern not only because it underreports the level of sexual violence, but also because it rests on a presumed hierarchy of human rights violations. As Audre Lourde has said, "there is no hierarchy of oppressions".[116] Many victims appear to feel that sexual violence is not less severe than prolonged detention, beatings or even death. Because of the unique long-term effects of sexual violence – the potential for becoming pregnant, contracting a sexually transmitted disease, losing one's spouse – victims sometimes report wishing they had not survived their attack. In one testimony, a young woman detained at a military base in Abancay, Peru, tells how she witnessed a number of sexual attacks. She could hear the women screaming and begging to be killed.[117] Another woman describing her own sexual abuse while in detention says, "I always thought to myself that rape was the worst thing that could happen to a woman, and if it happened at least I would be able to kill myself".[118] Cases like these, where survivors report suffering deep depression or suicidal thoughts following a sexual attack, are not uncommon and suggest that for some, sexual violence is among the most destructive violence suffered by women and men in times of war. Recording only a single violation rather than the set of violations serves no analytical purpose in studies of the uses and causes of violence, and inevitably results in the loss of valuable data regarding the repertoires of violence.

9.9. Linguistic and Cultural Variation in Victim Reporting

By accessing the original testimonies, researchers can pay close attention to the nuances in the language used by victims in recounting violence and traumatic events. Victims may not use direct language when discussing human rights violations, particularly those of an intimate nature, or simply

[116] Audre Lourde, *Homophobia and Education*, Council on Interracial Books for Children, New York, 1983.

[117] CVR, *Collection of Individual Testimonies: No. 205316*, see *supra* note 58.

[118] CVR, *Collection of Individual Testimonies: No. 700225,* see *supra* note 58.

may not have the same concepts in their native tongue. In Quechua communities in Peru, survivors often spoke of *sassachacuy tiempu*, "the difficult times", and the *llaki*, "grief and sorrow", or *lukuyasca*, literally translated as the "craziness" that individuals suffered.[119]

The reporting of sexual violence is particularly affected by cultural norms regarding sexuality, purity and gender. In native communities, it may be considered highly inappropriate for women to talk about their bodies, sex or violence. As a result, women (and men) avoided the use of direct language to describe the assault. In El Salvador and Peru, the Spanish word for "to rape" (violar) was rarely used. Instead, roundabout phrases or words such as "they bothered me" (molestar, fastidiar), "they were with me" (estar), "they harassed me" (acosar), "they abused me" (maltratar), "they took me" (sacar), "they committed private crimes", "they did 'el largo' to me",[120] "they took advantage of me" (aprovechar), "they touched me" (tocar), or "I surrendered" (capitular). The literal translation of these words and phrases may not point to acts of sexual abuse. However, by examining the context within which they appear, such as the removal of the victim's clothing or indications of subsequent health problems, researchers can usually determine the intended meaning of the speaker.

For example, a woman in Ayacucho who was accused of participating in subversive activities was subjected to repeated detentions and torture. In 1984, she was detained and transferred to the military base in Cangallo. The soldiers asked her about her involvement in a previous attack that resulted in a number of deaths, including a few soldiers. She denied participating in or knowing anything about the event. She was later transferred to the *Policía Investigativa de Perú* (PIP; Peruvian Investigative Police), where she was repeatedly interrogated by an officer (identified by name). After being released, the officer continually broke into the woman's home, beating and "bothering" (from the verb *molestar*) her. As a result of these events, the victim reported to the Commission having

[119] Duncan Pedersen, Jacques Tremblay, Consuelo Errazuriz, and Jeffrey Gamarra, "The Sequelae of Political Violence: Assessing Trauma, Suffering and Dislocation in the Peruvian Highlands", in *Social Science and Medicine,* April 2008, pp. 1–13.

[120] "El largo" refers to a process whereby soldiers rub their weapons against the body of the victim, who is often blindfolded to intensify the fear and anticipation of the violence, and then rape him/her with the weapon.

chronic pain in her ovaries.[121] Other women would describe their "condition as women" or their "dignity" or how a neighbor suddenly changed, became withdrawn, or had trouble with her husband. One woman simply said: "I didn't have the strength to defend myself and I was really affected".[122] Because these nuances will vary across countries and cultures, investigations of wartime sexual violence must be rooted in case-based knowledge and sufficient field experience at the research site.

9.10. Constructing a New Database on Wartime Sexual Violence in El Salvador and Peru

Using the original denunciations collected by *Tutela Legal and Socorro Jurídico Cristiano*, I created a new dataset on sexual and other forms of political violence in El Salvador. I read all of the testimonies collected by Tutela Legal and those collected by SJC between 1978 and 1983. In total, this amounts to 60 boxes of records and includes approximately 8,000 unique testimonies.

Using the original testimonies of the CVR, I created a new dataset on political violence in Peru. The dataset directly builds on the work done by the CVR, adding greater detail to its database on violent events. Cases that were previously not included in the CVR's database, either because they fall within the 5,000 testimonies that were not coded for nonlethal violence or because the victims were not identified by name, were added. Cases of sexual violence such as sexual torture that were overlooked or misrepresented in the CVR's work were also added. Reading almost 17,000 testimonies with great attention to detail and context would require far more time and resources than are available to the individual researcher. My database, therefore, is based on a random sample of approximately 2,500 testimonies. I sampled according to the event or case number (a number assigned at the time the case was entered into the CVR database), reading the testimonies for every tenth event. Since this captures only those cases that were originally included in the CVR's database, I then oversampled from the range of cases that Commission staff did not code for nonlethal acts of violence.

[121] CVR, *Collection of Individual Testimonies: No. 201476*, see *supra* note 58.

[122] CVR, *Collection of Individual Testimonies: No. 700906*, see *supra* note 58. Emphasis added.

For all testimonies read, I included information on cases of detention, disappearance, extrajudicial execution, death as a result of armed combat, injury, forced recruitment, kidnapping, torture, and multiple forms of sexual violence, including rape and gang rape, sexual torture, sexual mutilation, sexual humiliation, sexual coercion, forced abortion, forced impregnation, sexual slavery, and a general category for unspecified forms of sexual violence. Additional details, such as descriptions of preceding events and the contexts in which the violence was perpetrated, were recorded for each case. I paid particular attention to such key facts as how the victim came to be targeted for violence, what he or she was doing at the time of the attack, who was present during the commission of the violence, and exactly where the violence was perpetrated. I documented whether the victim or his or her family or friends were previously targeted for violence. I also recorded language used by the perpetrators during the assault. Evidence of sexist or racist language can be particularly insightful in determining motive or demonstrating small-group norms regarding the use of violence.

To summarize, Table 2 presents descriptive statistics on wartime sexual violence in Peru and El Salvador according to the methods employed by the Truth and Reconciliation Commission, those found after re-examining the Commission's published documents with a broader definition of sexual violence and a more inclusive counting of victims, and finally those found after accessing the primary documents and employing these same methodological guidelines.

EL SALVADOR		
CVES Final Report	**Published Documents**	**Primary Documents**
• 270 individual cases of rape (3.7% of all human rights violations) • 99% of victims were women; less than 1% of victims were men • 100% of cases of sexual violence were rape • 97% of cases of sexual violence were		• 123 cases of sexual violence • 45% of victims were women; 53% of victims were men; 2% of victims' gender was unreported • 41% of cases of sexual violence were sexual humiliation; 18% were sexual torture; 17% were rape; 12%

perpetrated by State armed forces		were sexual coercion; 7% were gang rape
PERU		
CVR Final Report	**Published Documents**	**Primary Documents**
• 538 individual cases of rape (1.53% of all human rights violations) • 98% of victims were women; 2% of victims were men • 100% of cases of sexual violence were rape • 83% of sexual violence cases were perpetrated by State armed forces	• 695 events of sexual violence • 71% included female victims; 24% included male victims; 5% included both male and female victims • 48% of events of sexual violence included rape; 22% sexual humiliation; 6% sexual torture	• 800 cases of sexual violence • 67% of victims were women; 22% of victims were men; 10% of victims' gender was unreported • 40% of cases of sexual violence were rape; 27% sexual humiliation; 10% gang rape; 10% sexual torture; 5% sexual mutilation

Table 2: Comparison of Figures on Wartime Sexual Violence in El Salvador and Peru. NOTE: The unit of analysis in the CVR's final report and in the analysis of the primary documents is the victim-violation. In other words, a "case" is an observation of one human rights violation against one victim. In Leiby, 2009, the unit of analysis is a violent event. An event may include more than one victim, more than one type of violation, and more than one perpetrator. "Primary documents" refer to the original testimonies collected by the CVR in Peru and Tutela Legal and SJC in El Salvador.

Table 3 provides additional figures from the primary documents on the patterns of wartime sexual violence. It highlights the findings that men are more often the targets of sexual violence than previously reported and that, unlike women, men are more often the victims of sexual humiliation, mutilation, and torture than rape or gang rape. Lastly, it reports the number and types of sexual violations suffered by unidentified victims.

EL SALVADOR		
Most Frequent Sexual Violations	**Victim Gender and Most Frequent Sexual Violations**	**Unidentified Victims and Most Frequent Violations**
• Sexual humiliation (40%)	• Women comprised 45% of victims of sex-	• Only 2 cases of sexual violence against unidenti-

• Sexual torture (18%) • Rape (17%) • Sexual coercion (12%) • Gang Rape (7%) • Sexual mutilation (4%)	ual violence o Rape and gang rape (53%) o Sexual humiliation (27%) o Sexual coercion (11%) o Sexual torture (4%) o Sexual mutilation (4%) • Men comprised 53% of victims of sexual violence[123] o Sexual humiliation (48%) o Sexual torture (24%) o Sexual coercion (13%) o Rape and gang rape (10%) o Sexual mutilation (6%) • Gender was unreported for 2% of victims of sexual violence	fied victims; both were cases of sexual humiliation
PERU		
Most Frequent Sexual Violations	**Victim Gender and Most Frequent Sexual Violations**	**Unidentified Victims and Most Frequent Violations**
• Rape (40%) • Sexual humiliation (27%) • Gang rape (10%) • Sexual torture (10%) • Sexual mutilation (5%) • Sexual coercion	• Women comprised 67% of victims of sexual violence o Rape and gang rape (64%) o Sexual humiliation (15%) o Sexual torture (8%) o Sexual coercion and attempted sex-	• 249 cases of sexual violence against unidentified victims o Rape and gang rape (56%) o Sexual humiliation (29%) o Sexual torture (5%) o Threat of sexual violence (5%)

[123] If one were to exclude cases of sexual humiliation, the percentage of male victims of sexual violence would fall to 35 percent.

(5%)
• Unspecified forms of sexual violence (3%)
	ual violence (8%)
	  ○ Sexual mutilation (2%)
	• Men comprised 22% of victims of sexual violence
	  ○ Sexual humiliation (46%)
	  ○ Sexual mutilation (20%)
	  ○ Sexual torture (15%)
	  ○ Rape (15%)
	• Gender was unreported for 10% of victims of sexual violence
		○ Unspecified forms of sexual violence (5%)

Table 3: New Findings on Wartime Sexual Violence in El Salvador and Peru from the Archives.

9.11. Conclusion

There are a number of methodological obstacles researchers confront when analyzing political violence. Accurately capturing the historical record is no small feat. When focusing on sexual violence in conflict situations, the obstacles become more frequent and complex. Underreporting is so pervasive that statistically estimating the total number of victims is likely impossible.[124] As victims themselves are reluctant to report sexual abuse, we must be particularly careful to not "lose" their stories when recording, coding or manipulating the data.

In this article, I discussed four methodological decisions that researchers must make when collecting and reporting statistics on the occurrence of sexual violence. These include: (1) how to define and measure sexual violence; (2) whether to include only named or both named and unnamed victims of sexual violence; (3) how to treat cases where victims suffer multiple forms of human rights abuse; and (4) how to treat ambiguous language in victims' statements. Above, I argue for a broad definition

[124] See Amelia Hoover, "Sexual Violence and 'Variation in Covariation'", paper presented at the Yale University Workshop on Wartime Sexual Violence, New Haven, CT, 2–4 November 2007 for a discussion of the possibilities of using multiple systems estimation for nonlethal acts of violence, including sexual violence.

of sexual violence, the disaggregated coding of all forms of sexual violence, the inclusion of unnamed victims, the creation of a victim-violation database that does not force the researcher to rank or limit human rights abuses, and special attention to be paid to the linguistic nuances in reporting sexual violence. There are trade-offs associated with each decision, and ultimately, how one proceeds depends on the individual researcher, the resources available to him or her, and the goals of the study.

Scholars are implementing innovative strategies and methods to document and analyze wartime sexual violence. In this article, I present an argument for the use of existing primary documents. Access to original sources allows researchers to choose their own parameters of study and make their own decisions regarding concept formation, measurement, the unit of analysis, and the construction of their database. Moreover, primary sources allow the researcher to do all of this without re-interviewing and potentially stigmatizing or re-traumatizing survivors and witnesses of political violence. My goal in writing this article is not only to increase awareness of two underutilized and extremely rich human rights archives, but also to demonstrate how the use of primary documents may aid researchers in overcoming some of the methodological obstacles that plague the literature on wartime sexual violence.

Appendix: Guide to Collections of Archived Human Rights Documents in El Salvador and Peru*

In 1997, Socorro Jurídico Cristiano and Tutela Legal gifted copies of the testimonies they collected to the University of Colorado, Boulder, which has since served as a secondary depository and safe house for the organizations' records. The collection includes 64 boxes of case files on victims and survivors of political violence. Each file contains a standardized intake form used by staff to record demographic information on the individual making the statement and the victim, and contextual information on the incident being reported, the alleged perpetrators involved and any measures taken by those involved to file a criminal charge or denunciation regarding the case. Some files include additional information on the case, such as news reports, letters and petitions to the Supreme Court from the families of the victims, letters to state security agencies and the FMLN from Tutela Legal or SJC (acting on behalf of the victims and their loved ones) requesting information on the case, demanding the release of those captured, and/or demanding the prosecution of those involved in human rights violations, as well as responses to those letters from state security and judicial institutions.

The University also has the archived testimonies collected by the non-governmental Comisión de los Derechos Humanos de El Salvador. The collection includes the individual testimonies of witnesses and victims of violence during the civil war, as well as supplemental secondary materials gathered by the CDHES during their investigations between 1974 and 1992. Each case file contains biographical information about the victim, the date and place of the attack, the alleged perpetrator(s), and a narrative description of the circumstances surrounding the attack. There are 36 boxes of case files in the collection. In additional to the testimonial records of Tutela Legal, SJC and the CDHES, the University also holds archived materials from the National Security Archives in Washington, DC, and Amnesty International relevant to the war in El Salvador and the peace process.

* Special thanks to the dedicated staff of the University of Colorado at Boulder Archives Department and the Centro de Información para la Memoria Colectiva y los Derechos Humanos in Peru for the important work that they do in preserving the historical record so that we may never forget the extraordinary costs of civil war.

Due to budgetary cutbacks, the collections remain in the original state as when they first arrived at the University. The contents of the collections has not been evaluated or systematically catalogued. The materials are not digitized. Particularly in the case of the National Security Archives materials and the SJC testimonies, there are a significant number of duplicated documents in the collections, which remain largely unorganized. Despite this, the wealth of information available and the knowledgeable staff make the Archives Department at the University of Colorado, Boulder an invaluable research site for scholars of the Salvadoran civil war.

The *Centro de Información para la Memoria Colectiva y los Derechos Humanos* ('CIMCDH', The Center for Information on Collective Memory and Human Rights) in Lima holds the complete records of the Comisión para la Verdad y Reconciliación (CVR, Commission for Truth and Reconciliation), files from former district attorneys and special prosecutors, and files from the Defensoría del Pueblo (Office of the Ombudsman) and the human rights branch of the *Ministerio Público* (Public Prosecutor) of the Peruvian state. Among its primary sources are internal reports, memoranda, and photographs documenting the institutional history of the CVR and news articles and photojournalistic accounts of the conflict as it unfolded. In addition, the CIMCDH has a collection of approximately 3,500 secondary sources on topics related to human rights, political violence, and transitional justice in Peru, as well as other countries (pre-dominantly in Latin America). Included in this library are all the secondary materials the CVR used in conducting its analyses and writing the final report.

The gem of the archive, however, is the 16,917 testimonies collected by teams of investigators throughout the country, which document the most violent period in Peruvian history as seen through the eyes of its citizens. The testimony files are of tremendous value to scholars. Each file contains the original intake forms used by field workers to record demographic information on the interview, the deponent, and the victims and perpetrators of violence. These forms are accompanied by a transcription of the deponent's statement describing the event. In addition, files may hold various supplemental documents, such as pictures to identify victims who have disappeared or copies of previous denunciations filed by the victim's family.

In addition to victim and witness denunciations of violence, the Center also holds statements made to the Commission by alleged or confessed perpetrators. For the most part, these exist only in audio or video formats, and have not been transcribed. These interviews provide incredible insight into individuals' command posts throughout the war, military policy and operations, military training practices, and degrees of cooperation between branches of the state security apparatus, as well as officials' understanding of the nature of the opposition threat and prospects for a negotiated settlement to the conflict.

Staff at the Center can search the database of testimonies according to the name of the victim, the deponent (or person who gave the testimony), or the date or location of the violent event. This is an invaluable tool for researchers. For instance, someone interested in a particular region or community, such as Accomarca in Ayacucho, can ask the staff to search the database and pull all testimonies that discuss violence in Accomarca and/or all testimonies that were taken in Accomarca. More specifically, someone wanting to investigate the massacre in Accomarca on August 14, 1985, can ask the staff to search the database according to the location and date of the massacre. Unfortunately, the database is not searchable according to the type of violation coded by the Commission. However, because all of the testimonies have been digitalized, staff can conduct keyword searches to circumvent this setback. The latter scenario is in fact preferable for researchers who may be concerned about the criteria used to code human rights abuses, as I have discussed may be the case with sexual violence.

10

The Difficulties Inherent in the Investigation of Allegations of Rape before International Courts and Tribunals

William H. Wiley[*]

10.1. Introduction

The modern era of international criminal justice has witnessed the establishment, since 1994, of numerous bodies – international, domestic and hybrid (that is, joint international–domestic institutions) – whose primary purpose is the application of International Criminal Law in both conflict and post-conflict situations. An extraordinary body of academic literature as well as human-rights advocacy has been written parallel to the development of the myriad adjudicative institutions, much of it evidently designed to influence prosecutorial policy. Taken as a whole, this collection of literature and advocacy has frequently had the effect of placing considerable pressure on prosecutorial and investigative divisions to apply significant human as well as material resources to addressing allegations of rape and other forms of sexual violence. Setting aside for a moment the question of whether the purpose of investigating and prosecuting allegations of rape is to render "comprehensively and sensitively […] justice to women victims"[1] – as opposed to, for instance, achieving the goal of re-

---

* Dr. **William H. Wiley** is Director of Tsamota Ltd., a UK-based consultancy that specialises *inter alia* in the provision of justice- and security-sector reform projects. He was the first investigator retained by the International Criminal Court (2003–2005) and has likewise served in investigative and intelligence-analytical posts with the Canadian war-crimes programme (1997–1999) as well as the Rwanda and Yugoslavia Tribunals (2000–2003). Additionally, Wiley was International Law Advisor to the Iraqi High Tribunal (2006–2008) and he currently provides investigative support to defence counsel appearing before the ICC and other international bodies. He is a CMN Senior Adviser.

1 B. Nowrojee, "We Can Do Better: Investigating and Prosecuting International Crimes of Sexual Violence", paper presented at the Colloquium of Prosecutors of International Criminal Tribunals in Arusha, Tanzania, 25–27 November 2004, available at http://www.womensrightscoalition.org/site/publications/papers/doBetter_en.php, last accessed on 17 October 2011.

moving from communities those who pose a threat thereto, and ensuring when so doing that suspected and accused perpetrators are afforded a scrupulously fair hearing – the bulk of scholarly writing and advocacy which concerns itself with rape as an international crime tends to overlook the complexity of investigating allegations of rape according to the necessary evidentiary standard(s). As one long-time international practitioner recently noted, with what is taken here to be a measure of understatement, "the logic of the [criminal] investigation may differ from the logic of [the] advocacy of social movements".[2]

Indeed, until very recently much of the scholarship-*cum*-advocacy to which reference is here made took as its starting point the canard, which would appear to have emerged in the 1970s, that "sexual assaults were less important crimes".[3] More curious still was the assertion made in 2002 by Richard Goldstone, the first Prosecutor of the *ad hoc* Tribunals for the former Yugoslavia and Rwanda – the International Criminal Tribunal for the Former Yugoslavia ('ICTY'), and the International Criminal Tribunal for Rwanda ('ICTR'). Goldstone claimed (incorrectly) that "for many centuries domestic and international legal systems [...] ignored gender-related crimes".[4] This same authority went on to blame his male-dominated investigative team for paying insufficient attention at the outset of his term to allegations of rape made in the context of the Balkan conflict[5] – strangely ignoring the fact that each and every one of the frequently shoddy investigators in the employ of the ICTY during its formative phase had been retained or otherwise arrived in The Hague during the tenure of Judge Goldstone. That noted, when confronted with claims of rape, the difficulty facing the ICTY investigators at the start was less a question of their collective competence (or the lack thereof), rather than the sheer volume of allegations juxtaposed against the then-limited human and material resources. As one member of the Commission of Experts that examined the conflict *in situ* opined when later called to testify by the

2 X. Agirre Aranburu, "Sexual Violence beyond Reasonable Doubt: Using Pattern Evidence and Analysis for International Cases", in *Leiden Journal of International Law*, vol. 23, p. 612.

3 K.D. Askin, *War Crimes Against Women: Prosecution in International War Crimes Tribunals*, Martinus Nijhoff Publishers, 1997, p. 98.

4 R.J. Goldstone, "Prosecuting Rape as a War Crime", in *Case Western Reserve Journal of International Law*, Fall 2002, p. 280.

5 *Ibid.*

ICTY in 1996, "the Commission had reason to state that sexual assault and rape were committed [...] widely", but that difficulties had been experienced in determining "the true stories from the false ones".[6]

The challenge facing investigators (and, by extension, prosecutors) assigned to enquiries arising from allegations of rape as an international crime is not the alleged indifference shown historically to gender-based offences by male-dominated institutions – a fallacy recently demolished by Dianne Luping, a practitioner employed with the Office of the Prosecutor ('OTP') of the International Criminal Court ('ICC').[7] Nor, as a general rule, are knuckle-dragging investigators a factor standing in the way of effective investigations into crimes involving sexual violence. When rape allegations have not been pursued "with the same seriousness as other war crimes", the root of this ostensible fact is unconnected to "a silence surrounding the sex crimes against women that downplays their suffering and renders them invisible".[8] Rather, when rape and related sexual-violence charges have not made and do not make their way into indictments, the reason for this is invariably rooted in the particular complexity of gathering sufficient evidence to warrant charging one or more specific individuals with the relevant war crime(s), crime(s) against humanity and even genocide. Put another way, rape, amongst other crimes of a sexual nature, is a disproportionately difficult offence to investigate. The nature of these difficulties shall constitute the focus of the remainder of this chapter.

10.2. Investigative Plans and Objectives

Investigations of alleged international offences as well as the suspected forms of individual-criminal liability are (or ought to be) undertaken in accordance with a detailed investigation plan rooted explicitly in the constituent elements of the crimes and modes of participation set out in International Criminal Law. Properly constituted, investigative plans take into

6 Office of the Prosecutor, International Criminal Tribunal for the former Yugoslavia, *Prosecutor v. Dragoljub Kunarac and Radomir Kovač*, IT-96-23-PT, Prosecutor's Submission of Expert Witness Statement under Rule 94*bis*, Testimony of Mrs Christine Cleiren, 02 July 1996.

7 D. Luping, "Investigation and Prosecution of Sexual and Gender-Based Crimes before the International Criminal Court", in *American University Journal of Gender, Social Policy and the Law*, 2009, vol. 17, pp. 436–443.

8 Nowrojee, 2004, see *supra* note 1.

account the moral-ethical (and, at the ICC, legal[9]) duty of investigators to seek inculpatory as well as exculpatory information. What investigative plans do not – and cannot – do is to take into account social constructs such as victim-centric and other variations on restorative justice.

Stated succinctly, a collection plan is a tool that is employed by investigators in order to determine whether or not sufficient evidence can be, and is being, collected in accordance with the elements of the crimes as well as the legal requirements of the modes of liability established in law. The focus of an investigation, particularly at the start, on the collection and analysis of both inculpatory and exculpatory information is rooted in the demands of procedural fairness for suspects and accused persons. Invariably, an investigation will focus in the first instance upon determining the *prima facie* veracity of whatever claims have been made – typically in the public domain by advocacy groups through media channels – to the effect that murder, rape and other offences have been perpetrated, generally (when rape is concerned) in the context of an armed conflict. Here, the focus is on what is known as the 'crime base'. Once the crime base has been established to a reasonable, albeit less-than-prosecution-ready standard, the investigative effort will tend to be channelled towards two largely distinct, albeit parallel objectives: the buttressing of the crime base to the necessary evidentiary requirements, and, secondly, the establishment of linkages between the crime base and a particular organisation, invariably an armed group. Whilst the crime base must generally be built in the main upon witness testimony, a 'linkage' case is established whenever possible upon documentary materials generated by the organisation(s) and individual(s) responsible in fact for the perpetration of the underlying acts; gaps in the documentary record are normally filled later with information collected from persons associated with the body that has fallen under suspicion. More advanced linkage investigations proceed, in turn, to establish the leadership structures of the perpetrating bodies, with a particular eye to individual suspects. As will be noted later in this paper, rape investigations tend to give rise to necessary, and complicated, deviations in the methodology normally applied to linkage investigations.

---

9 Rome Statute of the International Criminal Court, 17 July 1989, U.N. Doc. A/CONF.183/9 ("Rome Statute"), art. 54(1)(a), pmbl.

International prosecutions are rooted in law. However, the overwhelming bulk of the human, material and temporal resources of any investigative-prosecutorial body are invested in the collection of information which is, in turn, transformed into evidence through analytical processes undertaken within the context of the relevant substantive law. Put another way, the overwhelming focus of international investigations and prosecutions is on factual matters, rather than legal niceties – a fact which is, unfortunately, not yet reflected in the enormous body of scholarly literature concerning itself with questions of International Criminal Law.

International criminal law provides for a wide range of offences, and these offences differ markedly from one another in the degree to which criminal enquiries are likely to draw upon investigative and analytical resources. It will also be noted that the difficulty of investigating a given offence is not in every case commensurate with the seriousness of that offence. For instance, offences such as murder and wilful killing can be, and generally are, easier to investigate than certain relatively minor crimes such as pillaging. Rape as a war crime and a crime against humanity are very serious offences, and the pursuit of rape allegations is among the most resource-draining undertakings in which an investigation division can engage. Prosecutors rather than investigators – because international investigation divisions are invariably run by prosecutors – will frequently, when not subjected to public pressure, forego the investigation of allegations of rape. They do so for two principal reasons. Firstly, rape is almost never a stand-alone crime: that is, rapes are invariably accompanied by forms of unlawful killing which are easier to investigate than rape and, in the event of a conviction, will give rise to significant custodial sentences whether or not a parallel conviction on one or more rape charges is registered. Secondly, it has already been noted that rape investigations draw heavily on available resources and, more often than not, an investigative team will lack sufficient resources to investigate *to the necessary evidentiary standard* sexual offences as well as, say, allegations of unlawful killing. As one female prosecutor noted, rape "is difficult to convict and prosecutors, especially when time constraints are present, prefer to prosecute other crimes as they want […] a conviction".[10] Judges

[10] G. Mischkowski and G. Mlinarević, *The Trouble with Rape Trials – Views of Witnesses, Prosecutors and Judges on Prosecuting Sexualised Violence during the War in the former Yugoslavia*, Medica Mondiale e.V., 2009, p. 65.

are likewise aware of this fact, one going so far as to state that "When I see rape charges, I'm instantly concerned [with] how the prosecutor is going to prove it".[11]

From a *purely legal-conceptual point* of view, rape – or at any rate, mass rape – is not terribly difficult to establish to the necessary evidentiary standard.[12] It remains to be seen whether the *de facto* evidentiary standard applied to rape charges differs from that employed by judges when they hear evidence of other offences. In particular, there is a great deal of difference in opinion between interested persons on the question of whether international judges have tended to raise or lower the evidentiary bar when they find themselves adjudicating rape counts. SáCouto and Cleary have recently argued that the trial chambers of the *ad hoc* Tribunals have been less inclined to enter convictions when sexual violence has been alleged on the grounds of a certain collective reluctance to accept inferential evidence relating to the knowledge of the accused of the underlying acts. For her part, Combs, in something of an indictment – albeit a very well-argued one – of international criminal justice, has concluded that convictions are routinely registered on the basis of insufficient evidence, although one hastens to add that Combs did not concern herself with rape allegations *per se*.[13] However, Chinkin has noted the willingness of international judges to register rape convictions, notwithstanding inconsistencies in the testimony of rape victims.[14]

For these and other reasons, international practitioners, including the author of this paper, tend towards the view that international judges are for the most part inclined to lower the evidentiary bar when dealing with sexual violence counts; and certain of the rules of evidence in place at, for instance, the ICC would tend to proffer support to this seeming

---

11 *Ibid.*, p. 71.

12 Agirre makes a similar point: Agirre, 2004, pp. 616–617, see *supra* note 2.

13 S. SáCouto and K. Cleary, "The Importance of Effective Investigation of Sexual Violence and Gender-Based Crimes at the International Criminal Court", in *American University Journal of Gender, Social Policy and the Law*, 2009, vol. 17, pp. 454–458; N.A. Combs, *Fact-Finding Without Facts: The Uncertain Evidentiary Foundations of International Criminal Convictions*, Cambridge University Press, 2010.

14 C. Chinkin, "Gender-Related Crimes: A Feminist Perspective", in R. Thakur and P. Malcontent (eds.), *From Sovereign Impunity to International Accountability: The Search for Justice in a World of States*, United Nations University Press, 2004, p. 126.

inclination.[15] Nonetheless, it ought not to be concluded that judges remove the bar in its entirety when sexual-violence charges are concerned. More to the point, should it be anticipated that judges will lower the evidentiary standard when rape is formally alleged by a prosecutor, the fact remains that investigating rape allegations even to a lower standard of proof is very difficult. The roots of the difficulties found at the base of any rape investigation are not, in the main, tied to the elements of rape as a war crime and a crime against humanity. Rather, the problem confronting investigators and, in turn, prosecutors is that virtually all rape investigations and prosecutions rest, when compared to other offences, disproportionately upon witness testimony rather than documentary evidence. What complicates matters further is the fact that the overwhelming number of witnesses needed to establish both the crime base and the linkage case are likely to be women and men who maintain that they have been victimised – and, in the vast majority of cases, these claims will be correct. The challenges to be overcome when investigators are forced to rely heavily upon victim-witnesses are myriad and the remainder of this chapter shall focus primarily on this issue.

10.3. Security and Logistics

In September 2010, the United Nations mission in the Democratic Republic of the Congo ('MONUSCO') issued a preliminary report alleging that roughly three-hundred women, men and children had been raped during the period 30 July to 2 August 2010 along the axis Kibua-Mpofi in the territory of Walikale, North Kivu. The report maintained that the perpetrators were linked to irregular militia which MONUSCO claimed remained present in the wider region and, in particular, that these militia had been fighting in the Kibua-Mpofi area during the period at which the sexual offences were perpetrated.[16] The veracity of the MONUSCO report is not relevant to this chapter. What might be considered here are the initial problems that would face an investigative team despatched to collect information on potential evidential quality in support of an international

15 International Criminal Court, Rules of Procedure and Evidence, Rules 63(4) and 73, U.N. Doc. PCNICC/2000/1/Add.1 (2000).

16 MONUSCO-OHCHR, *Rapport preliminaire de la mission d'enquete*, 24 September 2010, available at http://www.ohchr.org/documents/countries/zr/Rapport_preliminaire_viols_massifs.pdf, last accessed on 17 October 2011.

prosecution, for instance the prosecution of Callixte Mbarushimana, a Rwandan national currently in ICC custody whom the Prosecutor has claimed is a leading figure in one of the militia named in the aforementioned report.

Walikale is situated roughly one hundred kilometres *as the crow flies* from Goma, a regional centre that can be accessed with relative ease through Rwanda. However, to access Walikale by (uneven) road, one must cover a distance of roughly 250 kilometres, much of it running through militia-controlled or otherwise militia–infested territory. The Kibua-Mpofi axis runs approximately eighty kilometres in a west-northwesterly direction from Walikale through Congolese bush, and it would at any rate be very difficult to traverse this area by vehicle. Aside from the poor (or non-existent) roads, the territory is not under the effective control of any party: like in the rest of North Kivu, a number of armed groups hostile to the ICC can be found roaming the area. Given the threat posed to international investigators, and the difficulty of the terrain, there are only two ways in which witness testimony could be collected in such a case by ICC investigators: (1) the investigative team would need to descend on the area by helicopter, and move from village to village by this means or by foot; or conversely, (2) the witnesses could be brought out of the bush to a central location for processing.

The significant pitfalls of gathering witnesses in a single location away from their homes will be discussed below. When the first option is concerned – the use of an airlift to access crime scenes in, for instance, the Eastern DRC – there are a number of major disadvantages to be considered, not the least of which is the complete lack of operational discretion arising when helicopters land in remote areas. More specifically in this instance, air activity of such a sort would run the risk of provoking the presumed perpetrators, in turn giving rise to the possibility of an immediate armed attack on the perimeter established around the investigative team. Additionally, or in the alternative, the perpetrators could and would, after the departure of the international dog-and-pony show, again enjoy sufficient freedom of movement to return unhampered to the scene of earlier crimes in order to threaten and even kill persons prepared to cooperate with any and all investigations. Finally, even in the unlikely event that these risks were assessed by the ICC-OTP as being acceptable and witness testimony was taken *in situ*, should charges focussed on these particular crime scenes be brought later by the ICC Prosecutor, it would prove impossible for the defence investigative team to secure access to the alleged crime scene(s) in order to seek exculpatory evidence in support of the accused. Suffice it to say that the ICC does not possess the resources to facilitate such a mission on its own, and it is inconceivable that MONUSCO would make these resources available to defence representatives. Such a state of affairs would give rise not only to the customary generalised concerns about the equality of arms in international criminal litigation, but likewise raise legitimate questions with respect to the fairness of any proceedings when the prosecution had access to a crime scene as well as witnesses, whereas the defence did not.

Moving dispossessed and largely illiterate peasants to locations more easily accessed by investigators is likewise an option that offers significant disadvantages. The most obvious of these is that the investigative team is forced to rely on local middlemen who, for a fee, escort the witnesses to a centralised and secure point in order to be interviewed. Careful observers of the *Lubanga* proceedings at the ICC will know that the use of similar methodology during the investigation of that case ultimately gave rise to the production of false witnesses – an eventuality that ought to have been foreseen within the ICC-OTP and, indeed, was foreseen and presented to management by the author of this paper when he was still in the employ of the Court. The other problems likely to arise are perhaps only slightly less obvious. For instance, Congolese peasants do not tend to wander far from their villages as a matter of routine (unless, of course, they have been forced to do so); as such, a succession of villagers disappearing for several days at a time will assuredly raise suspicions within an oral culture where news of unusual occurrences travels very quickly to indifferent as well as hostile ears. Whilst witnesses that are subsequently threatened can be taken into the witness-protection programme overseen by the ICC Registry, spaces within the programme are very limited, owing to the extraordinary cost of relocating witnesses and, more often than not, their extended families. Here, it is worth recalling that, at one point during *Lubanga*, no additional witnesses could be offered institutional (that is, ICC) protection – whatever the threat posed to them – because the witness-protection budget had been badly overrun. Responsibility for this debacle rested squarely with the OTP, which by that point in its life had lost much of its experienced staff and was relying upon increasingly young personnel, whose considerable intellect and enthusiasm was matched only by their collective ignorance of sound investigative methodology in high-threat environments.

Finally, when the protection of witnesses is concerned, several additional challenges need to be considered. For instance, it can be very difficult to find language assistants who speak highly-localised dialects and who can be counted upon without reservation to maintain the confidentiality of the investigative process – most especially if the interpreters have been retained locally. What is more, the identities of witnesses must be disclosed to accused persons, who may or may not engineer reprisals against those prepared to speak against them. A still greater problem is the utter incapacity of international investigative institutions to operate on a strictly need-to-know basis, with the result that interested outside parties are frequently well-briefed with respect to operational plans and investigative detail, even to the point of seeking to influence improperly specific investigations. This was most certainly a problem at the ICTR and the ICTY when the author of this paper was employed in those institutions; and there are strong indications that similar difficulties are being experienced at the OTP of the ICC, in no small measure owing to the professionally-irresponsible decision of the ICC-OTP investigative management to employ nationals of interested States on investigations targeting prominent figures in those States. Unsurprisingly, the ICTR-OTP internal working paper on the investigation and prosecution of sexual-violence cases notes explicitly the risk that the identities of victims of sexual violence will be leaked – and witnesses must therefore be warned clearly of this possibility.[17] ICC-OTP witnesses would likewise benefit from a similar admission of the OTP's frailties in this respect, as evidenced by the enormous sums being expended by the Registry to protect OTP witnesses whose identities have come to the attention of suspects as well as hostile intelligence agencies in the Great Lakes Region.

Investigations being undertaken in the midst of an ongoing conflict should, for the reasons set out above, proceed with care. When crimes have been perpetrated and there is a demonstrable social benefit to be realised in the event of the removal of the alleged perpetrators from the

[17] ICTR-OTP, *Best Practices Manual for the Investigation and Prosecution of Sexual Violence Crimes in Situations of Armed Conflict: Lessons from the International Criminal Tribunal for Rwanda*, para. 54, 2008, available at http://www.endvawnow.org/uploads/browser/files/Best%20Practices%20Manual%20Sexual%20Vio%20Int%20Criminal%20Manual%20Rwanda.pdf, last accessed on 17 October 2011.

midst of the conflict, it is necessary to proceed with extreme caution when determining what offences will be investigated. Here, it is worth reiterating that the most difficult challenges inherent in any pursuit of rape charges stems from the fact that rape cases, in contrast to certain other equally deleterious offences, must invariably be built largely upon the testimony of victim-witnesses. Setting aside the problem of protecting prosecution and even defence investigators in a conflict zone, serious reservations need to be registered when there is a possibility that the investigation itself will put witnesses at risk. It is here that the consideration of security matters ceases to become a purely logistical issue and, in turn, takes on the characteristics of an ethical question which imposes moral responsibilities upon those charged with initiating as well as undertaking investigations.

The World Health Organization has summarised succinctly the relationship between security and ethics with a handful of rules which ought to be considered immutable by the ICC-OTP and any other investigative body:

> 1. The benefits to respondents or communities of documenting sexual violence must be greater than the risks to respondents and communities.
> 2. Information gathering and documentation must be done in a manner that presents the least risk to respondents, is methodologically sound, and builds on current experience and good practice.
>
> […]
>
> 4. The safety and security of all those involved in information gathering about sexual violence is of paramount concern, and in emergency settings, in particular, should be continuously monitored.
> 5. The confidentiality of individuals who provide information about sexual violence must be protected at all times.[18]

The long experience of this author of international investigations would suggest that, where the first guideline is concerned, it is inconceivable this requirement can be met in any situation where (1) a conflict is

[18] World Health Organization, *WHO Ethical and Safety Recommendations for Researching, Documenting and Monitoring Sexual Violence in Emergencies*, WHO, 2007, p. 9.

ongoing, and (2) the confrontation lines are not clearly fixed as well as unlikely to change. Applying this evident lesson to the current caseload of the ICC-OTP, the pursuit of rape charges in the midst of an ongoing conflict such as that in the DRC creates an unacceptable degree of risk to the witnesses required by the prosecution in order to secure a conviction on one or more rape charges. When the ethical balance might be tipped in favour of the pursuit in such charges is in situations where the conflict has been (or largely has been) resolved, for instance, in Kenya and in Northern Uganda.

10.4. Establishment of the Crime Base – Witnesses

Broadly speaking, there are three means by which the crime base can be established in a rape case:

1. through the direct recruitment of victim and eye witnesses by the investigative-prosecutorial body;
2. by means of what is sometimes referred to as pattern evidence, which is presented at trial by expert witnesses, who may or may not be analysts employed by the investigative-prosecutorial body; and
3. through a combination of victim witnesses, eye witnesses and expert witnesses.

One of the greatest problems bedevilling international investigative bodies pursuing heavily witness-reliant offences is the lack of a coherent and consistent methodology when the establishment of crime bases is concerned. Whilst it is understandably necessary to proceed on a case-by-case basis, established policies – for instance, at the ICC-OTP – would foster the building of long-term working relationships with civil-societal and international-governmental organisations, and these relationships could be calibrated to enhance the volume and quality of information coming from the field whilst concomitantly lessening the pressure on limited investigative resources. In the event, the unchannelled advocacy efforts of CSOs and IGOs serve not infrequently to undermine international investigations and prosecutions. This point shall be addressed below in more detail.

When rape as a war crime or a crime against humanity is suspected and a prosecution appears to be warranted, there is invariably a requirement to identify and interview victim-witnesses who might testify at some future trial. Leaving aside questions of security and logistics, the greatest challenge facing investigators in this respect is the need to locate what might be termed untainted witnesses. Succinctly stated, untainted witnesses are persons who have not been interviewed previously, who have not shared their experiences with counsellors and who, most especially, have refrained from comparing their experiences with other potential witnesses. The methodological foundations of such an approach are well established: witnesses who have discussed what they saw and experienced with persons other than investigators – in particular, fellow victims – frequently develop a narrative in their own minds which may or may not correspond to the factual circumstances present at the crime scene. Equally deleterious from a prosecutoral perspective are situations when the testimony of a given witness mirrors that of other witnesses to a degree likely to arouse the suspicion of judges. Skilled defence counsel will invariably sense when memories have been enhanced in a group setting (or worse, by investigators) and, in turn, create confusion in the minds of witnesses with respect to what they saw, experienced and later heard.[19] When this occurs, the effect is to undermine the prosecution case in part and, if the investigative lapses are sufficiently serious and widespread, as a whole. These observations point to an ethical dilemma which lies at the heart of the problem of victim-witness recruitment in rape cases: the best victim-witness is invariably a witness who has been afforded little, if any, professional support.

The tendency of CSO and IGO representatives to descend on scenes of alleged mass rape, in particular in Central Africa, is likewise counterproductive when seen from an admittedly positivistic point of view, that is, the point of view of the investigator needing untainted victim-witness testimony in order to build a criminal case. For its part, the WHO has noted "the risk that sexual violence is being 'over-researched,'" criticising in particular the problem of "multiple sexual violence inquiries [being] conducted in the same place, by different organizations or individuals, with little or no information sharing or coordination".[20] Where the conflict in the former Yugoslavia is concerned, prosecutors have noted the fact that some victim-witnesses "testify so often they become professional witnesses", and other sources have pointed to the difficulties that arise

---

19 Inexplicably and inexcusably, the Institute for International Criminal Investigations (IICI) suggests that service providers such as rape-crisis centres might be used to identify potential witnesses. See IICI, *Investigator's Manual*, IICI, 2002, p. 242.

20 WHO, 2008, p. 7, see *supra* note 18.

when the same witnesses are interviewed repeatedly.[21] Remaining with the Balkan conflict, it might additionally be noted that many victims of sexual violence were questioned by security and intelligence agencies during or immediately after the war. The statements taken during these sessions "often contain sweeping exaggerations and inaccuracies that contaminate the credibility and reliability of later evidence"[22] – a phenomenon frequently seen by the author of this paper during his own service with the ICTY investigations division.

Whilst investigators require untainted witnesses, investigators likewise have a duty of care towards those witnesses imposed by professional ethics and, at the ICC, the Rome Statute.[23] In rape and other cases in which individual witnesses are likely to have experienced significant physical and mental trauma, it is very difficult in the majority of instances to reconcile the need for the care of an individual victim with the requirements of a criminal investigation, given that the investigative dynamic requires investigators to entreat the individual as a witness first and, only secondarily, as a victim. The principal need of, say, a victim of rape will be, in most cases and when available, psycho-social counselling rather than whatever catharsis might be gained from participation as a witness in lengthy investigative-prosecutorial proceedings. Nonetheless, as has been noted already, the exposure of a victim-witness to counselling, in particular when the counselling involves other victims of the same, or a parallel, offence, runs the risk of undermining the utility of that witness. The view taken here is that only in rare cases can the unique – and dare one say competing – needs of the witness and the investigator be reconciled with one another, no matter how well-trained the investigator may be in the legal as well as emotional particularities of sexual-assault investigations.

When the managerial decision is taken to move forward with a rape investigation, despite all the problems set out above, additional considerations need to be taken into account, not the least of which is that investigators will frequently find themselves confronted by false testimony from self-identified victims. The falsehoods might be intentional or unintentional. Unintentional errors arise with all forms of witness testimony ow-

[21] ICTR-OTP, 2008, paras. 13 and 31, see *supra* note 17.

[22] Medica Mondiale, 2009, pp. 68–69, see *supra* note 10.

[23] Rome Statute, art. 68(1), see *supra* note 9.

ing (broadly speaking) to the frailty of human memory. It is for this reason that the most methodologically-sound international criminal investigations are founded upon contemporaneously-generated documentary materials generated by the organisations and individuals implicated in the offences under investigation and, in rape cases, medical reports prepared immediately after the perpetration of the underlying acts. Unfortunately, such materials are in the main unavailable, especially in support of the establishment of the crime base. Hence, investigators find themselves disproportionately dependent upon victim-witness testimony – and the invariable absence of documentary foundations in rape cases makes it that much more difficult for investigators to recognise instances of false testimony.

The phenomenon of deliberate false testimony in rape cases has never been studied systematically, and consequently the incidences thereof are difficult to measure. However, international practitioners of longstanding stature are familiar with the problem of untruthful utterances, in particular, those personnel who are engaged in fieldwork – because field personnel deal with much larger pools of witnesses than those seen later by litigators.[24] Whilst the vast majority of persons who self-identify as victims in rape cases have indisputably been subjected to sexual violence of some form, false claims to this effect are not rare. In some cases, in particular in the former Yugoslavia, witnesses were manipulated by domestic intelligence services into making knowingly-untruthful claims as part of a wider effort to demonise opposing States and armed forces.[25] More commonly, false claims of victimisation are motivated by a desire on the part of the claimant to access social services and other forms of support, should such support be available. Anecdotal evidence, in particular from Africa, would suggest that when this motivation is present, it is more likely to be seen amongst female witnesses when the false witness has lost her partner and has one or more children for whom she is having difficulty providing. The (re-)marriage prospects of these women are frequently poor, and it may be that the social stigma that too often befalls rape victims is of little or no relevance in instances such as these, when a

[24] See, for instance, Wanda Akin cited in report on Colloquium on Sexual Violence as International Crime: Interdisciplinary Approaches to Evidence, 17 June 2010, available at http://lexglobal.org/files/Colloquium%20-%20WGR%20C_0.pdf, last accessed on 17 October 2011.

[25] For instance, refer to the Cleiren testimony, see *supra* note 8.

woman's desire to provide for her children and herself will overcome the instinct to conform to social convention. Criminal investigators must be aware of these as well as related phenomena, and undertake accordingly interviews with self-identified rape victims. In practice, investigators should approach self-identified victims without assuming that their claims are true or that they are false. Good interpreters – when interpretation is required, which is almost always the case – will pick up quickly on likely falsehoods on the basis of word selection; investigators can focus on the fact patterns being presented by witnesses and, if sufficiently aware culturally, body language. Article 54(1)(a) suggests that it is necessary that ICC investigators cross-examine witnesses, however gently; it might be said to follow from this that it is inappropriate to empathise with self-identified victims, at least until an interview has been completed. As the lead prosecutor in *Taylor* has noted correctly, objectivity is essential to the success of the interview.[26]

The ethical requirement to protect witnesses from retaliation has been touched upon above. In both published works and public addresses, several practitioners have identified the imperative to select witnesses on a needs-only basis and to maintain contact with these witnesses after their testimony has been taken in order to ensure, *inter alia*, the witnesses' ongoing safety.[27] Indeed, the ICC Prosecutor was compelled by the Pre-Trial Chamber in *Katanga and Chui* to drop sexual-slavery allegations on the grounds that inadequate measures had been put in place to protect the witnesses; the charges were restored only when the said witnesses were taken into the witness protection programme.[28] When one considers the trauma invariably suffered by the majority of witnesses who self-identify as sexual-assault victims, and the inescapable requirement that investigators take victims carefully through this trauma in order to satisfy the particular elements of the crime of rape, a great deal of patience is required on the part of investigators, who must also be prepared to distance them-

[26] Brenda Hollis, cited in Colloquium on Sexual Violence, see *supra* note 24.

[27] *Ibid.*; see also Luping, 2009, p. 489, see *supra* note 7.

[28] ICTY, Decision on Evidentiary Scope of the Confirmation Hearing, Preventive Relocation and Disclosure under Article 67(2) of the Statute and Rule 77 of the Rules, para. 39 (25 April 2008); Decision on Prosecution's Urgent Application for the Admission of the Evidence of Witnesses 132 and 287, paras. 6–7 (28 May 2008); Submission of Amended Document Containing the Charges Pursuant to Decision, paras. 32–33 (26 June 2008), *Prosecutor* v. *Katanga and Chui*, Case No. ICC-01/04-01/07.

selves emotionally from what is frequently wrenching testimony, in particular to satisfy the element requiring evidence of penetration of a sexual nature.[29] At the ICC-OTP, there is especial pressure on investigators to conduct exceedingly good interviews from the outset, given the stringent disclosure requirements in place at the Court and the fact that OTP litigators are, for all intents and purposes, not permitted to question witnesses on the eve of their testimony – a practice permitted by other international institutions which serves as an important last-minute corrective to poor fieldwork. In the event, the tendency of the ICC-OTP for the past several years, at least as far as can be determined by the author of this paper, has been largely to avoid having OTP staff interview rape victims. Instead, this responsibility is largely outsourced, under the guise of the principle of complementarity, to non-governmental and international-governmental organisations. The upshot of this tendency is to put pressure on the analytical arm of the OTP to transform into something of evidential quality the oftentimes shoddy, and invariably inadequate (from a criminal-law point of view), information collected by NGO and IGO personnel. This process will be touched upon in the next section.

10.5. Establishing the Crime Base – Pattern Evidence

In this volume and elsewhere, the subject of pattern evidence has been covered in detail by Xavier Agirre Aranburu; there is consequently no requirement to revisit the subject in any detail.[30] A few remarks germane to this chapter shall suffice.

Broadly speaking, pattern evidence is employed in an effort to establish crime bases with the minimum number of witnesses, in particular, victim-witnesses; this approach has been used with mixed degrees of prosecutorial success at the *ad hoc* Tribunals for a number of years, and the practice will presumably become more in evidence at the ICC as additional cases come to trial. The difficulty with pattern evidence, which is based in the main upon open-source materials – principally the reports of ostensible experts employed in the field by NGOs and IGOs – is that the

[29] This point is made in P. Viseur-Sellers, "The Other Voices: Interpreters and Investigators of Sexual Violence in International Criminal Prosecution", in H. Durham and T. Gurd (eds.), *Listening to the Silences: Women and War*, Martinus Nijhoff Publishers, 2005, pp. 162–163.

[30] Agirre, 2004, see *supra* note 2.

materials on which pattern evidence are based have generally been collected according to a human-rights-advocacy, rather than a criminal-law-prosecution, standard. The author of this paper, along with a colleague, has written on the subject of how the differences between the human-rights-based and criminal-law approaches might be bridged.[31] Such arguments are rare; and what is currently lacking at the ICC-OTP is a coherent as well as standardised practice with respect to how to co-operate with partner organisations (principally NGOs and IGOs) with strong field presences which are seen as potential sources of crime-base data. Until coherent practices are put into place by the ICC Prosecutor – an unlikely prospect in the near future given the long history of investigative mismanagement by Luis Moreno Ocampo – the OTP will more often than not continue to establish pattern evidence on the basis of sub-standard external work product, with a concomitant effect upon the strength of ICC-OTP prosecutions.

10.6. Establishing Linkages

It was noted earlier in this chapter that all international criminal prosecutions are built upon two pillars: the crime base and the linkage case. The linkage case is that part of an investigation and prosecution in which the underlying acts are tied to suspects and accused persons through reference to the modes of liability found in International Criminal Law, in particular, Articles 25 and 28 of the Rome Statute. In most, but not all, instances the suspects in rape cases are not the physical authors of the underlying (sexual) acts. It is for this reason that the identities of the physical perpetrators do not need to be identified. Nevertheless, it is crucial in rape cases to determine with absolute clarity the organisations – typically armed groups – to which the physical perpetrators belonged. An investigation will then work through chains of command to arrive at higher-level perpetrators that are more properly the subject of international-criminal investigations.

When compared to most offences of concern to international courts and tribunals, there are significant differences in rape cases in the manner

[31] M. Bergsmo and W. Wiley, "Human Rights Professionals and the Criminal Investigation of Suspected Violations of International Criminal Law", in Norwegian Centre for Human Rights, *Manual on Human Rights Monitoring: An Introduction for Human Rights Field Officers*, 2008, Chapter 10.

in which linkages are established between the crime base and physical perpetrators on the one hand, and higher-level suspects and accused on the other. These differences are most commonly present in situations where the alleged rapes were perpetrated in the midst of conflicts characterised by fluid confrontation lines involving a multiplicity of poorly-outfitted armed groups. This sort of confusion is very typical of conflicts in Africa, for instance, in the Eastern DRC. It follows from this fact that there is more often than not in such cases a requirement to seek information concerning the likely affiliations of the physical perpetrators from victim-witnesses – raising, in turn, many of the same problems experienced when relying upon victim-witnesses to establish the crime base.

The reliance on witnesses – and most especially victim-witnesses – to identify perpetrators is fraught with peril in both rape and other cases. There are several reasons for this, the most relevant being that civilians frequently have trouble remembering with clarity the details of uniforms (if any) worn by attackers. Worse still, victimised individuals are extremely vulnerable to suggestions from other victims, as well as investigators, on the question of what group was responsible for their victimisation.

If only briefly, this point might be illustrated through reference to a 2009 Human Rights Watch Report (HRW) on the problem of sexual violence in the DRC.[32] In the said report, HRW alleged that members of 14 Brigade of the *Forces Armées de la République Démocratique du Congo* (FARDC) had perpetrated a number of rapes in the Kivu provinces; for the most part, the affiliation to 14 FARDC Brigade of the unknown physical perpetrators was made by HRW on the basis of witness testimony which offered that the physical perpetrators had worn uniforms with purple epaulettes.[33] Given that the victims in these cases were rural peasants, the first question that springs to the mind of any criminal investigator with Africa experience is whether the victim-witnesses would necessarily have a word for 'purple', given that purple is a colour that is unlikely to appear naturally in the region in question. And even if the witnesses had a broad range of colours in their vocabularies, other troubling questions ought to be raised by the extracts from victim-witness testimony that appear in the report. For instance, a seventeen-year-old female victim is quoted as hav-

32 Human Rights Watch, *Soldiers Who Rape, Commanders Who Condone: Sexual Violence and Military Reform in the Democratic Republic of the Congo*, HRW, 2009.

33 *Ibid.*, pp. 12–13.

ing told the human-rights monitors that the perpetrators "were two soldiers of the 14th Brigade, with purple epaulettes".[34] Another victim offered suspiciously similar testimony: "They were two soldiers from the 14th Brigade […] They had purple epaulettes".[35] These sorts of similarities in the witness testimony point either to corroboration between the witnesses with respect to the identity of their attackers or to inappropriate suggestions having been made by the person(s) who collected the testimony. The pitfalls of relying on information collected in such a slipshod manner are obvious not only from a linkage perspective, but also when an investigative body (for example, the ICC-OTP) chooses to rely on reports of this quality in building pattern evidence. On the positive side, when the problem of the initial identification of the organisational affiliation of physical perpetrators can be overcome, the remainder of the linkage case – that is, the linking of the physical perpetrators to higher-level suspects – can be undertaken just as with any other offence, that is, through an investigation targeting documentation generated by the said organisation and the recruitment of insider-witnesses affiliated thereto.

10.7. Concluding Remarks

Rape as a war crime and a crime against humanity is frequently very difficult to investigate consistent to the necessary evidentiary standards required for a successful prosecution; this truism stems less from the complexity of the elements of the offences and more from the fact that the nature of the offence compels investigators to rely disproportionately upon victim-witness testimony to establish both the crime base and the basic linkage aspects of the case. Aside from the problems that arise from the natural fallibility of all witnesses, given the tendency of witness testimony towards mistakes of fact and even outright lies, victim-witnesses in rape cases are particularly exposed psychologically, and, in the midst of ongoing conflicts, they are vulnerable to reprisals. The upshot of these considerations is that rape investigations are, with rare exceptions (generally limited to investigations in which physical perpetrators are being targeted in a post-conflict setting), exceedingly draining of scarce investigative and prosecutorial resources which can be invested, with a greater likelihood of success, in dealing with equally serious allegations involving

[34] *Ibid.*, p. 27.
[35] *Ibid.*, p. 28.

offences concerned with unlawful killing. It is for this reason, rather than on the grounds of prosecutorial indifference and gender-based prejudice, that investigators and prosecutors, when left to their own devices, are frequently loath to deal with rape allegations.

11

Rape During War is Not Inevitable: Variation in Wartime Sexual Violence

Elisabeth J. Wood *

Wartime sexual violence varies dramatically across wars and sometimes, across armed groups fighting in the same war. During the conflict in Bosnia-Herzegovina, the sexual abuse of Bosnian Muslim women by Bosnian Serb forces was so systematic and widespread that it qualified as a crime against humanity under international law. In Rwanda, the widespread rape of Tutsi women comprised a form of genocide, according to the International Criminal Tribunal for Rwanda. In such settings, sexual violence frequently takes place in public, in front of family and community members. Other notable cases include the Janjaweed militias in Darfur, the Soviet and Japanese armies in World War Two, and the various armed groups in the eastern Democratic Republic of the Congo ('DRC').[1]

Yet, in some conflicts, sexual violence by some armed groups is remarkably limited despite their engaging in other violence.[2] Some armed groups, such as the Salvadoran insurgency, appear to have successfully prohibited their combatants from engaging in sexual violence against civilians. Even in some cases of ethnic conflict, such as the Israeli–Palestinian conflict, sexual violence is limited.

---

* **Elisabeth Jean Wood** is Professor of Political Science at Yale University and Professor at the Santa Fe Institute.

1 This chapter draws on the work of a new generation of social scientists working on wartime sexual violence (cited herein), as well as my own. I am grateful for comments from Dara Kay Cohen, Amelia Hoover Green, Michele Leiby, and Elizabeth Starr; for research support from the Harry Frank Guggenheim Foundation, the United States Institute of Peace, the MacMillan Center for International and Area Studies of Yale University; and the Santa Fe Institute; and for research assistance from Molly Daniell, Tess Lerner-Byars, Molly O'Grady, Elizabeth Starr, and Kai Thaler.

2 Elisabeth Jean Wood, "Variation in Sexual Violence During War", in *Politics and Society*, 2006, vol. 34, no. 3, pp. 307–341; Elisabeth Jean Wood, "Armed Groups and Sexual Violence: When Is Wartime Rape Rare?", in *Politics and Society*, 2009, vol. 31, no. 1, pp. 131–161.

When sexual violence does occur, the pattern varies in targeting, form, purpose, as well as frequency. Some armed groups target women and girls who belong to 'enemy' groups during ethnic or political cleansing. Some groups target only females, while others target males as well. The form of sexual violence also varies. Although sexualized torture and gang rape are particularly common, sexual violence sometimes takes on other forms, such as forced prostitution or sexual slavery. In some settings, patterns of wartime sexual violence appear to be a magnification of peacetime cultural practices; in others, they are wartime innovations. In some conflicts, the pattern of sexual violence is symmetric, with all parties to the war engaging in sexual violence to roughly the same extent. In other conflicts, it is very asymmetric, as one armed group does not respond in kind to sexual violence by the other party. Despite the challenges of gathering data on this sensitive topic, the variation does not appear to be a product of inadequately reported violence: there are well-documented cases where sexual violence is rare (including those mentioned above) as well as frequent.

Sexual violence varies in frequency, targeting, and form among civil wars as well as interstate wars, among ethnic wars as well as non-ethnic, among secessionist conflicts, among state armies, and among non-state actors.[3] Until recently, with some exceptions, both the policy and academic literature focused on cases with patterns of widespread rape of girls and women, as in Bosnia, Rwanda, Sierra Leone, and the DRC. Common explanations for wartime rape reflect that emphasis: rape is an effective strategy of war, particularly of ethnic cleansing; rape is one form of atrocity and occurs alongside other atrocities; war provides the opportunity for widespread rape and many male soldiers will take advantage of it. Yet many armed groups, including both state militaries and non-state armed groups, do not engage in widespread rape despite frequent interaction with civilians. Indeed, some armed groups, including the Sri Lankan insurgency, engage in ethnic cleansing, which is often seen as the classic setting for widespread rape, without engaging in sexual violence.

Focusing on a few patterns instead of the full spectrum of variation, including the absence of wartime rape, misses the opportunity to leverage

[3] Wood, 2006, see *supra* note 2; Elisabeth Jean Wood, "Sexual Violence during War: Toward an Understanding of Variation", in Kalyvas *et al.* (eds.), *Order, Conflict, and Violence*, Cambridge University Press, Cambridge, 2008; and Wood, 2009, see *supra* note 2.

variation for a better understanding of wartime sexual violence. The observed variation raises several questions: Under what conditions do armed groups not engage in sexual violence? Under what conditions do they engage in rape as a strategy of war? Sexual torture? Sexual slavery? When is widespread rape better understood as a practice, namely, a form of violence that is not ordered but tolerated by commanders (defined more precisely below), rather than a strategy?

The observed variation in wartime sexual violence, particularly the relative absence of wartime sexual violence by many armed groups, also has important policy implications. In particular, rape is not, as is sometimes claimed, inevitable in war. The absence of sexual violence by some armed groups reinforces the argument that commanders of armed groups that do engage in it should be held accountable.

Social scientists are increasingly documenting and analyzing the variation in the patterns of wartime sexual violence, particularly temporal variation of the form, frequency, targeting and purpose of such violence. I first introduce key concepts, including distinctions among different dimensions of violence. I then briefly summarize recent research documenting patterns of wartime sexual violence. After showing that many approaches in the published literature do not account for the observed variation – indeed, many predict *more* sexual violence than the tragic levels observed – I advance a theoretical framework that focuses on the internal dynamics of armed groups. I then analyze the conditions under which armed groups do not engage in rape, those under which they engage in strategic rape, and those under which rape emerges as a practice – namely, a pattern that is not ordered, but is tolerated, by commanders, and that occurs where there are no strategic benefits as well as where there are. Throughout the chapter, I draw on recent findings from social science literature, some of which is not yet published. I conclude with some tentative policy implications of this analysis.

11.1. Concepts and Definitions

By 'absence of sexual violence', I mean that sexual violence by a group is very rare, but not necessarily completely absent. Throughout, 'armed groups' refers to both state and non-state groups.

In accordance with recent international law, by 'rape', I mean the penetration of the anus or vagina of the victim with any object or body part, or the penetration of any body part of the victim or perpetrator's body with a sexual organ, either by force, or by the threat of force or coercion, or by the taking advantage of a coercive environment, or against a person incapable of giving genuine consent.[4] Thus rape can occur against men as well as women. 'Sexual violence' is a broader category that includes rape, non-penetrating sexual assault, sexual mutilation, sexual slavery, enforced prostitution, enforced sterilization, and forced pregnancy.[5] The term 'sexual violence' is frequently used as if aggregating this variety of form is a sound basis for analysis, but the underlying causal processes may be very different. For example, those factors that make strategic rape more probable on the part of an armed group are very likely distinct from those that make sexual mutilation or forced sterilization more probable. In what follows, I focus my usage of the term on rape and sexual torture, but employ the aggregate meaning of the term where appropriate or when the literature does so.

Essential to understanding any pattern of violence against civilians by an armed group, including any particular form of sexual violence, are three dimensions of violence.

The first dimension is the *frequency* of that form of violence by a particular armed group: does it occur very frequently, moderately often, occasionally, or very rarely? This of course begs the question: relevant to what? In the literature, the reference of the comparison is often not made explicit. The comparison is often to other units or armed groups in the same conflict, and sometimes to other conflicts. Throughout, I focus on patterns on the part of armed groups, comparing the frequency of particular forms of sexual violence on the part of one group to those of other groups in the same and other conflicts. The appropriate measure of frequency varies depending on the focus: the number of events (rapes, for

4 See International Criminal Court ('ICC'), Elements of Crimes, ICC Doc. No. ICC-ASP/1/3(part II-B), 9 September 2002, Articles 7(1)(g)-1 and 8(2)(b)(xxii)-1, available at http://www.icc-cpi.int/NR/rdonlyres/336923D8-A6AD-40EC-AD7B-45BF9DE73D56/0/ElementsOfCrimesEng.pdf, last accessed on 1 December 2011.

5 *Ibid.* Note that sexual humiliation, including forced nudity, is not explicitly listed with rape, sexual slavery, forced prostitution, forced pregnancy, and forced sterilization as a distinct crime, but might count as a crime against humanity of sexual violence if it was an act of sexual violence as defined above that was "of a gravity comparable to the other offences" and/or as a war crime of outrages upon personal dignity if the act met the other requirements of the crimes: see *supra* note 4, Articles 7(1)(g)-6 and 8(2)(b)(xxi), respectively.

example), the number of events per member of the referent population (incidence), or the fraction of the referent population that suffered at least one such event (prevalence).[6] Note, however, that 'referent population' begs precision: is it the population of some geographical area, a targeted ethnic group, or the national population? Moreover, available data is often partial, imprecise and not comparable across conflicts, so the comparisons I make are usually qualitative, except where I draw on newly available sources.

Targeting, the second dimension, concerns whom the group targets with violence. 'Selective targeting' is that against an individual because of her behavior, often the provision of support for a rival group or some other refusal to comply.[7] In contrast, 'indiscriminate violence' is violence that is not targeted: indeed, in its proper form, it is random. In between is 'collective targeting', the targeting by an armed group of social groups because of who they are – that is, their identity as members of that group. Examples include ethnic groups, political parties, particular villages thought to support the rival.

The third dimension builds on the distinction between 'strategic sexual violence' and 'opportunistic sexual violence'. I define 'opportunistic sexual violence' as violence carried out for private reasons, not group objectives, and 'strategic sexual violence' as a pattern, or instances, of sexual violence purposefully adopted by commanders in pursuit of group objectives.[8]

It is of course difficult to demonstrate empirically the purposeful adoption of violence: groups where violence such as rape or sexual torture is explicitly ordered are probably rare, but do exist.[9] Following Michele Leiby, I include as strategic any violence whose empirical pattern indicates that the armed group controls its use: namely, the violence occurs

6 There is an additional, sometimes relevant, notion of frequency, which is the frequency of events compared to the number of members of the armed group: 100 incidents of rape, for example, indicate a different level of sexual violence by armed group members if they number 1,000,000 than if they number only 100.

7 Stathis Kalyvas, *The Logic of Violence in Civil Wars*, Cambridge University Press, Cambridge, 2006.

8 Note that if a single commander purposefully adopts rape in pursuit of group objectives, then rape committed by those under his command is strategic. The definition does not presume uniformity across the armed group.

9 See the subsequent content of this chapter.

when it is strategically beneficial (meaning beneficial in terms of group objectives) and does not occur when it is not.[10] Also included are cases where rape of civilians is tolerated by group leaders because it is understood by combatants and/or commanders as a form of compensation.

The distinction between 'strategic' and 'opportunistic' sexual violence is important for both scholarly understanding and prosecution. However, the distinction as used in the literature is often confusing.[11] 'Strategic' sometimes appears to be used as a synonym for 'massive', which conflates the frequency, with the purpose, of violence. Moreover, the existence of a strategy is sometimes inferred, rather than demonstrated, as when widespread rape is followed by social disruption, and the consequence – social disruption – is presumed to be the purpose without further evidence. (Note that while inferring the existence of a strategy from its consequences is problematic, inferring the existence of a strategy from evidence that violence occurs only under control of commanders is not.) Similar concerns arise when a pattern of violence is claimed to be a 'weapon', 'tactic', or a 'tool' of war without further evidence that it was in fact strategic as defined here.

To address these problems, I introduce a third category between 'opportunistic' and 'strategic'. Violence which is not ordered but is tolerated by commanders, and occurs when it is not strategic as well as when it is, I term a 'practice'. Typically, a practice originates on the part of field units as an innovation or an imitation of units of other groups, and then diffuses across units. In the case of sexual violence as a practice, the vio-

---

[10] See Michele Leiby, *State-Perpetrated Wartime Sexual Violence in Latin America*, doctoral dissertation, University of New Mexico, 2011a; and Michele Leiby, "Wartime Sexual Violence as a Weapon of Irregular Warfare: An Analysis of Sub-National Variation in Peru", paper presented to the annual meeting of the American Political Science Association, Seattle, 30 August – 4 September 2011b. Such cases are similar to what Osiel terms "atrocity by connivance". See Mark Osiel, *Obeying Orders: Atrocity, Military Discipline, and the Law of War*, Transaction Publishers, New Brunswick, NJ, 1999. Note that in earlier work, I defined 'strategic' more broadly, including practice as well, but I have come to think it clearer to develop the separate category of practice. See Elisabeth Wood, "Sexual Violence during War: Variation and Accountability", in Alette Smeulers and Elies van Sliedregt (eds.), *Collective Crimes and International Criminal Justice: an Interdisciplinary Approach*, Intersentia, Antwerp, 2010.

[11] See the chapter by Agirre in this volume.

lence is tolerated when it is not strategically beneficial as well as when it is. Thus my definition of 'strategic' is narrower than that of most scholars.

The dimensions as defined are distinct. A practice could be more or less frequent, and targeted more or less narrowly (that is, collectively, or even indiscriminately or selectively). Targeting could be narrow, but with either a high or low frequency, and could be opportunistic, strategic, or the result of a practice.

A final concept also essential in describing variation in sexual violence is that of repertoire. By 'repertoire of violence', I mean the subset of battle deaths, assassination, forced displacement, torture, the various forms of sexual violence, and so on, regularly observed on the part of an armed group.[12] The concept captures important differences in the context of acts: for example, some groups rape and then kill the victim; some rape and then displace the victim; and others do neither. Repertoires can be wide or narrow, and vary sharply across armed groups: for example, in some conflicts, one armed group engages in significant sexual violence but other groups do not. Similarly, the 'repertoire of sexual violence' is the subset of forms of sexual violence in which the group regularly engages, and can be wide or narrow, and varies across groups.

The pattern of sexual violence on the part of an armed group may vary significantly over the course of a conflict. The observed patterns are diverse, including a change in form from rape to sexual slavery, from being a strategy to a practice, from opportunistic events to a practice, as well as becoming more or less frequent, or more or less narrowly targeted. For example, a group may begin to engage in the rape of civilians in response to another group's doing so: it may 'mirror' the other group, either as a strategic decision by commanders, or by individual units wielding violence similar to that which they observe. Or should civilians resist a group's rule, an armed group may turn to rape as a form of punishment, on command or as a result of combatant frustration. Similarly, repertoires of sexual violence also vary over time, sometimes becoming wider (the group engages in more forms of sexual violence, perhaps mirroring another group), but in some cases becoming more narrow.

---

12 James Ron, "Savage Restraint: Israel, Palestine and the Dialectics of Legal Repression", in *Social Problems*, 2000, vol. 47, no. 4, pp. 445–472; and Amelia Hoover Green, *Repertoires of Violence Against Non-combatants: The Role of Armed Group Institutions and Ideologies*, doctoral dissertation, Yale University, 2011.

Note that these distinctions made for the purpose of social science analysis should not be understood as implying distinct legal consequences. In particular, commanders and leaders are responsible for sexual violence as a practice and opportunistic sexual violence, as well as strategic sexual violence, if the usual criteria for command and/or superior responsibility under international law are met.

11.2. Variation in Patterns of Sexual Violence

Recent research on patterns of wartime sexual violence spans the methods of social science, including qualitative, quantitative and historical research. Space constraints prevent an adequate summary of all relevant work, so I focus here on work that is explicitly cross-national either in empirics or in the scope of the theory advanced.

Much of the literature initially focused on sexual violence in Bosnia-Herzegovina and Rwanda, as human rights advocates and legal scholars sought to hold perpetrators of widespread sexual violence responsible under international law. Those works noted variation in targeting, but paid little attention to variation in frequency and made little attempt to distinguish sexual violence as a practice from strategic sexual violence. When other cases were considered, researchers often referred to Susan Brownmiller's sweeping analysis of global and historical patterns in her seminal 1975 book, *Against Our Will*. While Brownmiller acknowledges some variation (for example, the North Vietnamese and Viet Cong appeared to have engaged in little rape of civilians), the overarching argument was that rape during war was ubiquitous, but not inevitable.[13] While the focus on Bosnia and Rwanda contributed to the development of sexual violence as a crime under international law, the question of variation was neglected and the rhetoric of the time emphasized the supposed ubiquity of wartime rape.

That is no longer the case as scholars increasingly focus on variation.[14] The initial work that explicitly documented and analyzed variation across armed groups and conflicts largely drew on careful qualitative

---

13 Susan Brownmiller, *Against Our Will*, Bantam, New York, 1975.

14 Some journalists have picked up on the theme of variation and its implications for policy. See "War's overlooked victims: rape is horrifyingly widespread in conflicts all around the world", The Economist, 13 January 2011; and Jina Moore, "Confronting Rape as a War Crime", in *CQ Global Researcher*, 2010, vol. 4, no. 5, pp. 105–130.

comparison of a few cases, but did not fully leverage the entire spectrum of variation, particularly the existence of groups that did not engage in sexual violence.[15] To address this gap, I chose my initial set of cases to represent the entire spectrum of frequency (including armed groups that engaged in little sexual violence) and showed that the frequency of sexual violence varied across inter-state as well as civil conflicts; ethnic as well as ideological conflicts; and state militaries as well as insurgent groups.[16]

Before proceeding to discuss more recent work, it is important to address a doubt sometimes raised about my claim that sexual violence on the part of some groups is very rare. Given the inadequacy of available data, the observed absence might reflect our ignorance of its actual occurrence rather than its rarity. Indeed, there are many reasons why rape and other forms of sexual violence are under-reported in wartime, including the reluctance of victims to report the crime, the failure of forensic authorities to record sexual violence, and the limited resources available to organizations reporting human rights abuses.[17] The reported variation may reflect different intensities of domestic and international monitoring of conflicts rather than different frequencies; violence in some regions appears to garner more international attention than in others. Nor is it reasonable to assume that it is under-reported to the same degree across conflicts, parties and regions, as there is often regional, class and partisan bias in both reporting and data collection. Reporting rates may also vary across forms of sexual violence: rape, particularly the rape of males, is likely less reported than other forms in most settings. Even when sexual violence is documented, available data may only identify the perpetrators as "armed men".[18] Moreover, the description of sexual violence as "widespread and systematic" may reflect an organization's attempt to draw resources to

---

15 Cynthia Enloe, *Maneuvers: The international politics of militarizing women's lives*, University of California Press, 2000; Lisa Sharlach, "Sexual Violence as Political Terror", dissertation, University of California, Davis, 2001; and Mia Bloom, "War and the Politics of Rape: Ethnic versus Non-Ethnic Conflicts", unpublished manuscript, 1999.

16 Wood, 2006, see *supra* note 2; and Wood, 2008, see *supra* note 3.

17 Wood, 2006, see *supra* note 2.

18 For discussion of the challenges of documenting wartime sexual violence, see Francoise Roth, Tamy Guberek and Amelia Hoover Green, Corporación Punto de Vista and Benetech Human Rights Data Analysis Group, "Using Quantitative Data to Assess Conflict-Related Sexual Violence in Colombia: Challenges and Opportunities", 2011, available online at http://www.hrdag.org, last accessed at 1 December 2011.

document sexual violence, whatever its actual level, rather than the pattern of incidents *per se*. And in settings where political violence is ongoing, organizations may feel it prudent to state that all sides engage in sexual violence, whether or not this is shown in their data.

Nonetheless, the variation in the incidence and form of sexual violence is sufficiently large that it clearly exceeds measurement error in the better-documented cases: the existence of very well-documented, low-incidence cases strongly suggests that the claim that some armed groups engage in little sexual violence is not an artifact of ignorance.[19] For example, it is unlikely that the apparent absence of sexual violence in the Israeli-Palestinian conflict is due to under-reporting, given the scrutiny of violence there by domestic human rights groups and international actors. In short, it is unlikely that the level of rape of women and girls was so much less in Bosnia-Herzegovina or that it was so much more in Israel-Palestine, as to confound the observation of significant variation.

Fortunately, more accurate data on wartime sexual violence is becoming available for some conflicts. Michele Leiby, for example, analyzes a random sample of testimonies of victims and witnesses compiled by the Truth and Reconciliation Commission in Peru, coding not only various types of sexual violence but, remarkably, all human rights violations.[20] Among her important findings is that the incidence of sexual torture of male detainees by state forces was much higher than the truth commission had recognized. For the case of El Salvador's civil war, Amelia Hoover Green reconstructed the databases of human rights organizations and the Truth Commission for El Salvador in order to analyze repertoires of violence on the part of distinct state forces and insurgent factions. She shows that El Salvador was an extremely asymmetric conflict: state forces engaged both in rape during military operations early in the war, and in sexual torture of both males and female prisoners throughout the war in moderate to high levels, while the insurgent forces engaged in little sexual violence of any kind.[21]

---

[19] Wood 2006, see *supra* note 3; and Wood, 2008, see *supra* note 3.

[20] See her chapter in this volume as well as Leiby, 2011a, see *supra* note 10; and Leiby, 2011b, see *supra* note 10.

[21] More precisely, she documents a few early incidents of rape as well as other abuse of civilians, in response to which the group transformed its training and socialization institutions such that little sexual violence occurred later. See Hoover Green, 2011, see *supra* note 12.

Moreover, in the last decade or so, researchers have included questions about sexual violence in surveys based on representative samples, in order to estimate the incidence and/or prevalence of certain forms of sexual violence among particular populations (initially, of the refugee camp populations in Liberia, for example; and more recently, of the DRC national population using the national version of the Demographic Household Survey).[22] However, the patterns identified in such surveys are often too aggregate to address many questions of interest at the necessary level of detail, such as when and where rape diffused from one group to another, and whether some units of an armed group engage in sexual slavery more than others.[23] It is rare that perpetrators are identified in other than vague terms such as "armed men", "soldiers", or "rebel". Indeed, the DRC survey asked only whether or not the perpetrator was a sexual partner.

The present state-of-the-art documentation of patterns of rape across civil wars is the work of Dara Kay Cohen (and collaborators: see below).[24] For every conflict between 1980 and 2009, she collected data from the US State Department Human Rights Country Reports, an annual publication that provides detailed data on human rights violation for every country. To address the problem of poor and incomparable data, she coded the relative magnitude of reported rape to construct an index in which no reports was coded as "0", isolated reports as "1", numerous reports as "2" and widespread reports as "3".

---

[22] Lynn L. Amowitz, Chen Reis, Kristina Hare Lyons, Beth Vann, Binta Mansaray, Adyinka M. Akinsulure-Smith, Louise Taylor, and Vincent Iacopino, "Prevalence of War-related Sexual Violence and Other Human Rights Abuses Among Internally Displaced Persons in Sierra Leone", in *Journal of the American Medical Association*, 2002, vol. 287, no. 4, pp. 513–21; and Amber Peterman, Tia Palermo and Caryn Bredenkamp, "Estimates and Determinants of Sexual Violence Against Women in the Democratic Republic of Congo", in *American Journal of Public Health,* 2001, vol. 101, no. 6, pp. 1060–1067.

[23] For an assessment of quantitative analysis based on representative sample surveys, see Hoover Green, 2011, see *supra* note 12; and Roth *et al.*, *Using Quantitative Data*, see *supra* note 16. For discussion of the use of statistical evidence in the prosecution of wartime sexual violence, see Hoover Green's chapter in this volume.

[24] Dara Kay Cohen, "Explaining Sexual Violence during Civil War", doctoral dissertation, Stanford University, 2010; and Dara Kay Cohen, "Causes of Rape during Civil War: Cross-National Evidence (1980–2009)", unpublished paper, 2011a.

Among her most important findings are as follows. Sub-Saharan Africa had a smaller proportion of civil wars with the highest level of rape (10 of 28) than did Eastern Europe (four of nine), thereby belying the imagery of many journalistic reports. Of the conflicts with some non-zero level of rape, in 62 percent of those conflicts, both state and insurgent forces engaged in it; in 31 percent, only state forces did so; and in seven percent, only insurgent groups did.[25] Thus state forces are more often the perpetrators of rape.

Researchers at the Peace Research Institute of Oslo, in collaboration with Cohen, are extending Cohen's approach and data to build a database based on a much broader range of sources, including reports by Amnesty International, Human Rights Watch, and the International Crisis Group, as well as State Department reports. To date, the research group has published the findings from the pilot project, namely, an analysis of conflicts (and the first five years after the conflict where relevant) in 20 African countries.[26] Of the 177 conflicts analyzed, there were no reports of sexual violence in 59 percent of the conflicts, while the highest level of sexual violence ("3") was reported in 11 percent of the conflicts and the next highest, in 16 percent. While the percentage of armed groups that engage in the highest level of sexual violence has not changed, the percentage of those that engage in the 'isolated' and 'numerous' categories ("1" and "2") declined from 2000 to 2009. The study confirms Cohen's earlier finding that it is state forces, not rebel groups, that engage in sexual violence more frequently: the forces of 50 percent of the states analyzed engage in sexual violence at some period, while only 42 percent of rebel groups and 35 percent of militias had done so. According to the pilot study, the targeting of state, rebel and militia forces alike appears to be indiscriminate. Finally, high levels of sexual violence often occur during periods with few killings.

---

[25] Cohen 2011a, see *supra* note 24. This last finding confirmed the earlier work of Jennifer Green, "Uncovering Collective Rape: A Comparative Study of Political Sexual Violence", *International Journal of Sociology*, 2004, vol. 34, no. 1, pp. 97–116. After systematically coding New York Times articles from 1991–2003 for reported episodes of mass rape, Green found that mass rape was carried out by state, not insurgent forces, in approximately two thirds of the cases she identified. However, the New York Times is not as detailed a source as the State Department reports for several reasons: see Cohen, 2010, see *supra* note 24.

[26] Ragnhild Nordås, "Sexual Violence in Armed Conflicts", Center for the Study of Civil War, Oslo, 2011.

11.3. Incomplete Explanations

What might account for the observed variation in wartime sexual violence? In earlier work, I discussed the various explanations, at times implicit, in the literature published to date, and showed that they are at best incomplete.[27] Increased opportunity during war, combined with a presumption (present in some of the literature) that many men will rape if given the opportunity, does not explain variation: many non-state actors who do not engage in sexual violence have ample opportunity to do so as they live close to civilian populations, as was the case of the Salvadoran and Sri Lankan rebel groups. Nor does opportunity explain cases where targeting is narrow: usually the armed groups engaging in such violence have access to civilians that they do not target as well as those they do. In both Bosnia-Herzegovina and Rwanda, perpetrators had roughly equal access to civilians of various ethnicities, yet targeted particular ones.

Nor do increased individual incentives to engage in sexual violence explain the observed pattern. Sexual violence is sometimes said to occur in retaliation for sexual violence previously suffered, or rumored to have been suffered, by co-ethnics. But in many conflicts, at least one armed group does not respond in kind to sexual violence: recall that Cohen found that about 39 percent of conflicts exhibited asymmetry, with one group engaging in sexual violence and the other not. The 'substitution' argument (that wartime rape 'substitutes' for sex with prostitutes, camp followers, female combatants or willing civilians) also does not explain the observed variation. It does not account for the targeting of particular groups of women, the often extreme violence that frequently accompanies wartime rape, or the occurrence of sexual torture. Moreover, if it were adequate as the sole explanation of variation, rape by forces with ample access to prostitutes would not occur, but that is belied by the rape of girls and women by members of the American military in Vietnam[28] and the rape of civilians by the combatants of the Revolutionary United Front of Sierra Leone despite their access to girls and women held as sex slaves. Furthermore, some armed groups with significant numbers of female combatants do engage in high levels of sexual violence; the Revolutionary United Front of Sierra Leone is an example. Additionally, female combat-

[27] Wood, 2008, see *supra* note 3, and Wood, 2009, see *supra* note 2.

[28] Gina Weaver, *Ideologies of Forgetting: Rape in the Vietnam War*, State University of New York Press, Albany, 2010.

ants themselves actively participate in rape in some conflicts: according to Dara Cohen, female combatants participated in 25 percent of the Revolutionary United Front's gang rapes, which comprise about 75 percent of the total.[29]

The militarized masculinity approach argues that societies in war develop, or draw on, institutions and norms that inculcate a highly militarized masculinity based on sharp distinctions between genders: to become men, boys must become warriors. The result is that combatants represent domination of the enemy in highly gendered terms and use specifically sexual violence against enemy populations. The argument thus accounts for the targeting of enemy women and men, and with specifically *sexual* violence.[30] However, the argument does not explain the absence of sexual violence on the part of some very effective insurgent and state armies.

In contrast to the above arguments based on gratification, increased incentives, or a general product of military training, the instrumental argument for sexual violence holds that when it is widespread, it occurs because armed groups engage in it as a strategy. In addition to the oft cited Bosnian Serb militias and Hutu forces in Rwanda, in Guatemala, where state forces engaged in widespread rape during sweeps through indigenous villages, the Truth Commission found direct evidence of commander promotion of rape of civilians in the form of ridicule of combatants who initially declined to participate.[31] Some of the literature in this vein also holds that wartime rape is much more frequent in recent years than in the past. However, high levels of rape by armed groups are not a new phenomenon as some have argued; some militaries in World War Two engaged in rape, sexual slavery and forced prostitution with great frequency.[32]

---

29 Reported in Dara Kay Cohen, "Female Combatants and Violence in Armed Groups: Women and Wartime Rape in Sierra Leone", unpublished paper, 2011b, which analyzes data in Jana Asher, ed., and Human Rights Data Analysis Group of Benetech, "Sierra Leone War Crimes Documentation Survey Database v. 2", unpublished dataset, 2004.

30 Madeline Morris, "By Force of Arms", in *Duke Law Journal*, 1996, vol. 45, no. 4, pp. 651–781; and Joshua Goldstein, *War and Gender. How Gender Shapes the War System and Vice Versa*, Cambridge University Press, New York, 2001.

31 Cited in Michele Leiby, "Wartime Sexual Violence in Guatemala and Peru", in *International Studies Quarterly*, 2009, vol. 53, no. 2, pp. 445–468.

32 Wood, 2006, see *supra* note 2.

Such strategic violence appears to take four broad forms. The first is sexual torture against persons detained by an armed group when it occurs as an immediate strategic benefit. The second is sexual slavery, another form of custodial sexual violence. The third is widespread sexual violence as a form of terror or punishment targeted at a particular group, which frequently takes the form of gang (and often public) rape, most notoriously as part of some campaigns of 'ethnic cleansing' to force the movement of entire populations from particular regions claimed as the homeland, and as part of some genocides. The fourth is the decision, perhaps implicit, by commanders to reward troops for service with rape. (Of course the common response of military and political leaders to accusations of strategic sexual violence by their forces is to claim that the troops were not under their control, an issue I return to in the conclusion.)

However, this argument predicts *more* sexual violence than is observed: if sexual violence is an effective strategy of war, why is it the case that not all armed groups engage in it? The conditions for such instrumental engagement in sexual violence are not well identified in the literature. Some authors suggest that patriarchal culture provides the relevant condition: where armed groups understand sexual violence as a violation of the enemy family and community's honor, they are likely to engage in sexual violence as a weapon of war.[33] However, such beliefs are present in many societies where massive sexual violence on the scale predicted by this argument has not occurred, as in Sri Lanka and Israel-Palestine. Moreover, such broad notions of cultural proclivity do not account for cases where one party to the war promotes sexual violence while the other does not. While devaluation of women is a necessary condition for the occurrence of sexual abuse of women, this general notion of patriarchy is too broad to account for the observed variation: it is not a sufficient condition. Rather than focus on broad notions of culture, many recent scholarly works focus on the culture and institutions of the armed organization.

Thus many of the explanations in the published literature at best explain only part of the observed variation. Indeed, they generally predict more wartime sexual violence than the tragic levels observed. They fail to explain the fact that many armed groups do not engage in even moderate levels of sexual violence.

[33] Enloe, 2000, see *supra* note 15.

11.4. A Theoretical Framework for Explaining Variation in Wartime Sexual Violence

Because such arguments do not explain the observed variation, researchers have turned their focus to the dynamics internal to armed groups. In what follows, I develop a theoretical framework that emphasizes combatant norms, leaders' strategic choices about forms of violence, the dynamics within small units once deployed in war, and armed group institutions.

11.4.1. Individual Combatants

Armed groups draw their members from particular cultural settings, usually a particular patriarchy. Incoming recruits carry with them cultural norms and beliefs concerning the appropriateness of different kinds of violence, including sexual violence, against particular populations. Armed groups may draw from particular sub-groups, for example, a specific ethnic group, precisely for these reasons. Some groups, for example, some paramilitary groups, actively attempt to recruit from criminal populations. In contrast, state militaries often attempt to draw or conscript recruits from a wide range of sub-cultures in order to build national unity. The relevant pool of recruits may also reflect the organization's resource base: those without economic resources may be more likely to attract 'activist' recruits willing to make long term commitments to ideological goals, while those with economic resources may attract 'opportunistic' recruits, an argument that neglects the impact of subsequent socialization of the recruit by the group.[34] Whether or not recruits enter an armed organization with relatively homogeneous norms and beliefs thus depends on the recruiting practices of the organization. Those norms and beliefs are often profoundly altered as recruits are inducted into the group through both formal and informal practices, as discussed below.

---

[34] Jeremy Weinstein, *Inside Rebellion: The Politics of Insurgent Violence*, Cambridge University Press, Cambridge, 2007. However, in his emphasis on contrasting pools of recruits, Weinstein underestimates the power of socialization practices and disciplinary institutions to meld recruits, typically male teenagers, into group members irrespective of their initial motives for joining. Distinct patterns of violence may reflect group strategy concerning training, discipline, and incentives and group ideology rather than distinct pools of recruits. See below, and also Wood, 2009, see *supra* note 2; Hoover Green, 2011, see *supra* note 12; and Francisco Gutiérrez Sanín, "Telling the Difference: Guerrillas and Paramilitaries in the Colombian War, in *Politics and Society*, 2008, vol. 36, no. 1, pp. 3–34.

11.4.2. Leadership Strategy

Military leaders seek to control the repertoire, targeting, and frequency of violence wielded by their combatants, not least because of the fear that weapons wielded by soldiers may be turned against officers. Likely considerations include not only issues of military tactics and strategy, but also implications for the ongoing supply of recruits, intelligence, other necessary 'inputs' to the war effort, and for the legitimacy of the war effort in the eyes of desired supporters (domestic and international alike). Even when an armed group appears to embrace terrorizing civilians, there are decisions to be made about targeting and timing. In particular, military leaders may make explicit decisions to prohibit or to promote sexual violence of different forms, against particular groups. If it occurs at a significant level, leaders who have not yet made an explicit decision may be pressed to do so and may decide to tolerate its occurrence without an explicit decision to prohibit or promote. Commanders may also promote high levels of violence towards civilians without a formal decision to do so, using euphemisms understood as signaling to combatants that they will not be punished. Leaders may further delegate certain forms of violence to groups they claim not to command, for example, militias or death squads. In order to control violence to at least the minimum necessary degree, group leaders or their delegates develop institutions for the socialization and training of recruits and for the discipline of members.[35] To highly varying degrees, those institutions may also attempt to distill group ideology (discussed below).

11.4.3. Institutions for Socialization of Recruits

To build an effective armed group, recruits have to be melded into effective combatants through training and socialization. The military socialization literature argues that combatants hold fast under fire not because of grand concepts such as patriotism or group ideology, but because of their commitments to their 'primary group' of fellow combatants.[36] Training and socialization to the small group take place both formally through group institutions such as boot camp and informally through initiation rituals and hazing. In state militaries, the powerful experiences of endless

---

[35] Hoover Green, 2011, see *supra* note 12.

[36] Edward Shils and Morris Janowitz, "Cohesion and Disintegration in the Wehrmacht in World War II", in *Public Opinion Quarterly*, 1948, vol. 12, no. 2, pp. 280–315.

drilling, dehumanization through abuse at the hands of the drill sergeant, and degradation and then 'rebirth' as group members through initiation rituals typically meld recruits into combatants whose loyalties are often felt to be stronger than those to family.[37] Brutalization of recruits is intended to enhance aggression, which the discipline of drill is intended to control.[38] To the extent that the organization relies on child recruits, training and socialization are particularly likely to re-socialize combatants. These processes occur to a lesser or greater degree; nonetheless, the result is a setting where conformity effects are likely to be extremely strong.

11.4.4. Wartime Dynamics

Combatant norms and practices, both general cultural ones and also those instilled during initial socialization, may evolve dramatically during active engagement. Both the suffering and wielding of violence may bring profound changes to combatants' understanding of the appropriateness of repertoires, targeting, and frequency of violence. The increasing desensitization of combatants to violence and the dehumanizing of victims, the anxiety and uncertainty of combat and the threat of violence, and the displacement of responsibility not only onto the group but onto the enemy who 'deserves what they got' (blame attribution) are powerful wartime processes that may reshape group repertoires towards the wider use of violence: wider both in the sense of wider targeting and a broader repertoire which may include many forms sexual violence.[39] Collective responsibility for atrocities can itself become a source of group cohesion and a

---

37 Donna Winslow, "Rites of Passage and Group Bonding in the Canadian Airborne", in *Armed Forces and Society*, 1999, vol. 25, no. 3, pp. 429–57; and Hank Nuwer, "Military Hazing", in *The Hazing Reader*, Indiana University Press, Bloomington, 2004, pp. 141–46.

38 Dave Grossman, *On Killing. The Psychological Cost of Learning to Kill in War and Society*, Back Bay Books, Little Brown and Company, 1996; and Osiel, 1999, see *supra* note 10.

39 Christopher Browning, *Ordinary Men: Reserve Police Battalion 101 and the Final Solution in Poland*, HarperCollins, New York, 1992; Alexander Hinton, *Why did they kill? Cambodia in the Shadow of Genocide*, University of California, 2005; and Daniel Chirot and Clark McCauley, *Why Not Kill Them All? The Logic and Prevention of Mass Political Murder*, Princeton University Press, Princeton, 2006; and Hoover Green, 2011, see *supra* note 12. For an argument about how an initial pattern of limited sexual violence may escalate to more brutal forms and wider targeting, see Jamie Leatherman, *Sexual Violence and Armed Conflict*, Polity Press, Cambridge, 2011.

bulwark against betrayal.[40] Indeed, small group dynamics can undermine military discipline when small group loyalties and conformity dynamics within the group lead to withholding of information from commanding officers, disobedience, or even to the 'fragging' of officers, as seen in the case of the US Army in Vietnam.[41]

11.4.5. Armed Group Institutions: Discipline and Indoctrination

The strength of the armed group's institution for discipline and ongoing indoctrination determines whether the leadership's choices about the frequency, targeting and repertoire of violence dominate patterns driven by the wartime social psychological dynamics just discussed. Within an armed organization – particularly in the changing and often covert circumstances of irregular warfare – there are a series of relationships down the chain of command in which the superior officer attempts to influence the behavior of those below (who often have different preferences for the level, targeting and form of violence), but without direct access to what those below are, in fact, doing.[42] The challenge applies to insurgent groups as well: leaders attempt to control the violence of their combatants and whether they succeed in doing so depends on the strength of the group's institutions.[43] Armed groups that adopt an irregular warfare strategy face this challenge in particularly sharp form: units may operate inde-

---

40 Osiel, 1999, see *supra* note 10; and Goldstein, 2001, see *supra* note 30.

41 Robert MacCoun, "Unit Cohesion and Military Performance", in *Sexual Orientation and U.S. military personnel policy: Policy options and assessment*, National Defense Research Institute, RAND, Santa Monica, 1993; and Joanna Bourke, *An Intimate History of Killing. Face-to-Face Killing in Twentieth Century Warfare,* Granta Books, London, 1999.

42 Scott Gates, "Recruitment and Allegiance: the Microfoundations of Rebellion", in *Journal of Conflict Resolution*, 2002, vol. 46, no. 1, pp. 111–130; Neil Mitchell, *Agents of Atrocity: Leaders, Followers, and the Violation of Human Rights in Civil War*, Palgrave MacMillan, New York, 2004; Christopher Butler, Tali Gluch, and Neil Mitchell, "Security Forces and Sexual Violence: A Cross-National Analysis of a Principal-Agent Argument", in *Journal of Peace Research*, 2007, vol. 44, no. 6, pp. 669–687; Hoover Green, 2011, see *supra* note 12; and Leiby, 2011, see *supra* note 10.

43 Humphreys *et al.* found that unit cohesion and discipline, rather than the level of contestation, social structure such as community or ethnic ties, or the existence of a local economic surplus, best explained patterns of civilian abuse across armed groups in Sierra Leone: see Macartan Humphreys and Jeremy Weinstein, "Handling and Manhandling Civilians in Civil War", in *American Political Science Review*, 2006, vol. 100, no. 3, pp. 429–47.

pendently for significant periods of time with little direct contact with superiors, with the result that superiors know little about the practices on the ground and have little opportunity to punish infractions.

Amelia Hoover Green argues that there are, in principle, two ways in which armed groups resolve this 'commander's dilemma', as she terms the tension between needing both to produce and to control violence.[44] The first is through strong disciplinary institutions: combatants obey orders because they are punished if they do not. Given the challenges of organizing and controlling violence toward group goals, armed groups tend to be hierarchical, in varying degrees.[45] The ability of the hierarchy to enforce decisions depends on the flow of information concerning those patterns up the chain of command and the willingness of superiors to hold those below them accountable.

Military sociologists stress the importance of discipline, but often argue that disciplinary institutions are insufficient. Strong identification with group units above and with the armed group as a whole ('secondary group cohesion') is one way to resolve such tensions and ensure a strong hierarchy.[46] When military superiors are seen as legitimate authorities, the likelihood of obedience even in the wielding of extreme violence is enhanced.[47] Such cohesion and legitimacy enhances the probability that information about infractions of group rules and norms is passed up the chain of command, so that the need for a disciplinary response is recognized. Maintaining discipline through the vagaries of combat often requires the development of strong internal intelligence institutions to ensure the flow of such information. For example, the Liberation Tigers of Tamil Eelam insurgency in Sri Lanka deployed a parallel chain of command dedicated to internal intelligence.[48]

According to Hoover Green, the second way in which organizations may, in principle, resolve the 'commander's dilemma' is through institu-

44 Hoover Green, 2011, see *supra* note 12.

45 Samuel Huntington, *The Soldier and the State. The Theory and Politics of Civil-military Relations*, Belknap Press of Harvard University Press, Boston, 1957; and Guy Siebold, "Core issues and theory in military sociology", in *Journal of Political and Military Sociology*, 2001, vol. 29, pp. 140–59.

46 Siebold, 2001, see *supra* note 45.

47 Stanley Milgram, *Obedience to Authority; An Experimental View*, Harper, New York, 1974; and Grossman, 1996, see *supra* note 38.

48 Wood, 2009, see *supra* note 2.

tions which inculcate recruits so strongly that they internalize group ideology and norms, an argument that calls for indoctrination stronger than that of the 'secondary cohesion' just described. Through ongoing, intensive political education, the group instills an understanding of the purpose of the conflict, and an understanding that some forms of violence undermine that purpose. In the ideal case, combatants thus come to internalize the leadership's choices about violence and implement it with little need for discipline. In practice, armed groups inculcate group ideology to highly varying degrees. Some armed groups, often leftist groups that understand the conflict is likely to continue over many years and perhaps decades, go to impressive lengths to inculcate group ideology and identification long after the initial training period. Note that this discussion raises the question of what accounts for the particular institutions developed by the armed group, a discussion that would take us too far afield.

11.5. When is Wartime Rape a Strategy or Practice of War? When is it Rare?

This theoretical framework is of course relevant for the analysis of all forms of violence, not just the various forms of sexual violence. In what follows, I focus on the implications that are especially relevant for analysis of patterns of rape, particularly for the absence of rape on the part of the group, rape as a strategy of war, and rape as a practice of war. Throughout I draw on relevant unpublished works (with permission of the authors), as well as other sources.

Before doing so however, what happens when the orders of superiors and the intentions of combatants about sexual violence collide? If indoctrination of combatants is complete, in principle, no conflict will arise. When conflicts do arise, if disciplinary and internal intelligence institutions are sufficiently strong, the choice of the leadership will prevail, whether it is promotion, prohibition, or tolerance of rape of civilians. For example, if leaders judge sexual violence to be counterproductive to their interests and if the group's institutions are sufficiently strong, little sexual violence will be observed. In the contrasting case, an organization with strong institutions could judge sexual violence as in its interest and effectively enforce such violence by its combatants. If organizational strength is insufficient, individual and unit norms will dominate, with the organization unable to deter or occasion behavior it would rather prevent or promote, respectively. Thus under some probably rare conditions, the prevalence of sexual violence may be low without relying on hierarchical discipline, namely, when sufficiently many combatants have themselves internalized norms against sexual violence (see below). More frequent is the other case of an organization's prohibiting sexual violence, but without the hierarchy or will to effectively do so.

The strength of armed group institutions – the ability of the hierarchy to enforce decisions taken by the leadership through disciplinary and/or through ongoing indoctrination – is thus central to the theoretical framework and its implications. For the framework to be useful in analyzing patterns of sexual violence, the degree of organizational strength must be observable apart from those patterns. Observable indicators include the ability to effectively tax the civilian population and to channel the resulting resources throughout the organization with low levels of corruption; the organization's routine punishment of combatants who break rules and norms other than those governing rape, a sufficient but not a necessary condition for strong institutions, as indoctrination may be so strong that combatants never break the rules; and the organization's capacity to carry out widespread and/or complex offensive or defensive maneuvers that require extensive coordination of multiple units.

11.5.1. Explaining the Absence of Sexual Violence

What considerations would lead commanders and leaders to attempt to effectively prohibit sexual violence by combatants? An armed group's leadership may prohibit sexual violence for strategic, normative, or practical reasons.[49] Many armed groups fear the consequences of uncontrolled violence by their combatants: such forces may be unready to counter a surprise attack, they may prove difficult to bring back under control, and they may even turn their sights on their commanders;[50] the unintended consequences may be severe, such as the entry of an ally of the enemy into the fray. That aside, if an organization aspires to govern the civilian population, leaders will probably attempt to restrain combatants' engagement in sexual violence against those civilians (though perhaps endorsing

[49] Wood, 2009, see *supra* note 2.

[50] Gutiérrez Sanín, 2008, see *supra* note 34. The Salvadoran insurgency attempted to shape individual longings for revenge toward a more general aspiration for justice because revenge-seeking by individuals would undermine insurgent discipline and obedience. See Elisabeth Jean Wood, *Insurgent Collective Action and Civil War in El Salvador*, Cambridge University Press, New York, 2003.

it against other civilian groups) for fear of undermining support for the group. Similarly, if an armed group is dependent on civilians for supplies or high quality intelligence, the latter of which is difficult to coerce,[51] leaders will probably attempt to restrain sexual violence against those civilians.

Reasons for prohibiting sexual violence may reflect normative concerns as well as practical constraints. Leaders of a revolutionary group seeking to carry out a social revolution may see their group as the disciplined bearer of a new, more just social order for all citizens, and therefore prohibit sexual violence because such violence violates the norms of the new society or because its prohibition legitimizes its ideology both to members and to its likely constituents. Despite systematic celebration of martyrdom in pursuit of victory, the Salvadoran insurgency did not endorse suicide missions and effectively prohibited sexual violence.[52] Nationalist and anti-colonial insurgencies may prohibit sexual violence and seek female cadres as part of its ideological commitment to becoming a modern state army.[53] Leninist groups may suppress sexual violence as part of a general emphasis on discipline and self-sacrifice, and of its commitment, in varying degrees, to gender equality. Leaders may regulate sexual relations on the part of its combatants as part of a general norm of self-sacrifice and effectively prohibit sexual violence as well. For example, the Sri Lankan insurgency engaged in little sexual violence toward civilians, even when it engaged in the ethnic cleansing of Muslims from the northern part of the country in 1990 and also killed thousands of civilians in the course of assassinations by suicide bombing and collective reprisals.[54] Relatedly, in conflicts where one party engages in massive violence against civilians, the other party may not do so as an explicit strategy to demonstrate moral superiority. A norm against sexual violence may take a distinct form: sexual violence across ethnic boundaries may be understood by leaders as polluting the instigator, rather than harming and humiliating the targeted individual and community. Finally, leaders may prohibit sexual violence out of deference to international law for various

[51] Wood, 2003, see *supra* note 50.

[52] *Ibid.*; and Hoover Green, 2011, see *supra* note 12.

[53] Armed groups that rely on female combatants may have additional reasons to restrain sexual violence on the part of their troops. See Wood, 2009, see *supra* note 2.

[54] Wood, 2009, see *supra* note 2.

reasons, perhaps because they aspire to some sort of international recognition or because they fear financial backers may curtail funding.

Whether or not the decision to prohibit sexual violence is effectively implemented depends on the strength of the group's institutions. If disciplinary and internal intelligence institutions are sufficiently strong, combatants will not engage in it if prohibited. However, given the strength of the social psychological processes during war that tend to widen repertoires, and the challenges of continued access by superiors to detailed information about the behavior of combatants, Hoover Green argues that these institutions are necessary, but that alone they are not sufficient to ensure an absence of sexual violence.[55] Rather, an armed group must also develop strong institutions for ongoing political education of combatants, so that they develop and maintain internalized norms against rape. (Disciplinary institutions remain necessary as alignment of norms of all combatants with those of the leadership is not likely to occur). In her analysis of contrasting repertoires of violence on the part of the various insurgent factions and state military organizations during El Salvador's civil war, Hoover Green demonstrates that armed groups that employ both strong disciplinary systems and consistent political education institutions use narrower repertoires of violence and, in particular, engage in little sexual violence.

If commanders prohibit sexual violence or promote it, but institutions are too weak to enforce that policy, whether or not combatants engage in sexual violence depends on individual and small unit norms. If individual combatants and their units endorse and enforce norms against sexual violence, little sexual violence by those combatants will occur. Such norms may take the form of internalized cultural norms whereby in the case of some ethnic conflicts, combatants themselves understand that sexual relations with civilians associated with the enemy is polluting to the perpetrator or, for other reasons, is normatively prohibited. However, as Hoover Green argues, the conditions for such shunning of sexual violence by combatants are demanding.[56] The wartime processes of brutalization, desensitization, and dehumanization discussed above must not have eroded such normative constraints. And given the powerful influ-

[55] Hoover Green, 2011, see *supra* note 12.

[56] Amelia Hoover, "Disaggregating Violence during Armed Conflict: Why and How", unpublished manuscript, 2007; and Hoover Green, 2011, see *supra* note 12.

ence of small group dynamics in armed units, all or nearly all combatants must endorse the norm, and enforce it against the few who attempt to transgress it. The likelihood that combatants continue to adhere to such a norm is significantly higher if the armed group itself endorses and attempts to reinforce such norms.

11.5.2. Explaining Rape as a Strategy of War

As we saw above, sexual violence may be adopted by commanders as a strategy of war against particular populations, as in the case of sexual torture of political prisoners or the public rape of members of particular groups as they are "cleansed" from an area; as a form of collective punishment (usually in the context of orders to terrorize civilians); or as a form of compensation. The conditions for its top-down emergence as a strategy are the inverse of those for the absence of sexual violence: commanders must perceive the benefits of the strategy – a terrorized detainee, community or population; a territory not only 'cleansed' of the targeted population, but with memories making return unlikely; and troops compensated by rape of civilians – as outweighing its costs – less disciplined troops who may engage in rape in contexts where it is not strategically beneficial; decreased civilian loyalty and cooperation; and violation of domestic and international norms. In this case, combatants are never punished for engaging in sexual violence; indeed, there may be evidence of punishment for failing to do so, as in the case of Guatemala (mentioned above). If strategic, the overall pattern should be that sexual violence occurs when strategically beneficial, and is absent when not.

Michele Leiby analyzes rape as a counterinsurgency strategy on the part of states engaged in irregular warfare.[57] In this case, where and when rebel forces are visibly active, but not strong enough to engage the state in frequent combat, state forces engage in sexual torture and rape (as well as other forms of violence) against purported and potential supporters, as well as rebels, to extract information but also to punish and terrorize. If such efforts fail and the rebel organization gains sufficient strength to engage in numerous attacks in the area, state forces abandon strategic violence against civilians in favor of combat. Using the Peruvian data she compiled as the dependent variable in a statistical analysis, she shows that

[57] Leiby, 2011a and 2011b, see *supra* note 10.

sexual violence on the part of state forces conforms to the pattern predicted by her analysis of rape as counterinsurgency, and was thus strategic.

Maria Eriksson Baaz and Maria Stern analyze how soldiers of the DRC state military understand the widespread rape of civilians by the group. In the context of deeply inadequate salaries that often go unpaid for extended periods, many of the 200 soldiers interviewed by the authors linked the high rates of rape with the frustration and anxiety occasioned by the failure to live up to masculine ideals of establishing and providing for a family. Soldiers also distinguished (but not sharply, and with some ambivalence) between what they see as 'lust' rapes – namely, rape involving forced sexual intercourse born out of frustration, but without mutilation and gratuitous violence – and what they term 'evil' rapes – namely, rape involving both forced sexual intercourse as well as mutilation and gratuitous violence. The former were rapes that are "somehow more 'ok,' morally defendable, ethically palatable and socially acceptable (and therewith, arguably not really rapes in their eyes), and those that are 'evil,' and not acceptable – but still 'understandable'".[58] While sexual violence does not appear to have been ordered, it appears to be broadly tolerated by the military, arguably as a form of compensation. (On the other hand, it could be the case that the hierarchy tolerates the violence as a practice whose curtailment would be too costly. More evidence is needed for a definitive judgment.)

11.5.3. Explaining Rape as a Practice of War

Rape may emerge as a practice of war – that is, unordered and occurring even when not providing a strategic benefit – for a number of reasons explored in current literature. When commanders tolerate rape as a practice by combatants, they do so not because they perceive the benefits of rape as outweighing the costs, but because they perceive the costs of effective prohibition as too high. Such costs may include the diversion of scarce resources to strengthen relevant institutions, particularly disciplinary and intelligence institutions, or the consequences of moving against

58 Maria Eriksson Baaz and Maria Stern, "Why Do Soldiers Rape? Masculinity, Violence, and Sexuality in the Armed Forces in the Congo (DRC)", *International Studies Quarterly*, 2009, vol. 53, p. 497. See also Jocelyn Kelly, "Rape in War: Motives of Militia in DRC", USIP Special Report, 2010, no. 243.

the practice, for instance, the loss of experienced field commanders were they held accountable for rape.

Dara Kay Cohen argues that gang rape reinforces cohesion in groups that rely on forced recruitment and thus have to create cohesion among hostile and bewildered recruits. Gang rape effectively built cohesion, she argues, because it was an act understood by participants to be very costly in terms of the breaking of local social norms and the likelihood of venereal disease, which might go untreated. Drawing on the literature on urban and prison gangs, she argues that it was effective in creating cohesion precisely because of its costliness: public gang rape broke recruits' ties to their communities and cemented new ones to the group. Cohen does not argue that rape in these cases is ordered or purposefully adopted by the group's leadership. Rather, senior members of small units insist that new recruits also rape, and it occurs in non-strategic as well as strategic settings. Thus according to her theory (in the terms of this paper), gang rape is a practice.

Cohen shows that gang rape played this role in the Revolutionary United Forces of Sierra Leone.[59] The Revolutionary United Forces was heavily reliant on forced recruitment: 87% of combatants reported being forced to join. The pattern of gang rape was understood as costly, according to her interviews with perpetrators, and was enforced by members of small units. Indeed, in analyzing a household survey of wartime violence, she finds that female combatants participated in approximately a quarter of gang rape events.[60] In the analysis of her cross-national data on wartime sexual violence, Cohen shows that non-state armed groups that practice abduction are more likely to engage in high levels of sexual violence, as are state militaries that engage in press-ganging of conscripts.[61] Her forced recruitment explanation explains more of the observed variation than the other theories that she tests. However, it is not yet clear whether the mechanisms of gang rape as socialization is as general as she suggests, as there are other causal processes that may link gang rape with forced recruitment.

---

59 Cohen, 2011a, see *supra* note 24; and Cohen, 2011b, see supra note 28.

60 Cohen, 2011b, see *supra* note 28.

61 Cohen, 2011a, see supra note 24, in her analysis of Asher, 2004, see *supra* note 29.

11.6. Conclusion: Policy Implications

The variation in patterns of wartime rape and other forms of sexual violence documented and analyzed here suggests that many common beliefs about wartime sexual violence are unsubstantiated, or at best, only partially true. Rape of civilians is not, throughout history, ubiquitous in war or committed by all armed groups, as is sometimes asserted. The victims of wartime sexual violence are not always overwhelmingly female; men and boys suffer high levels of rape and sexual torture by some armed groups. An armed group may engage in frequent rape without it being a strategy of war. Conflicts with high levels of rape, as measured by the percentage of conflicts characterized by such high levels, are not more frequent in Sub-Saharan Africa than other regions. Nor is it likely the case that wartime rape is more frequent today than historically.

Most importantly, rape is not inevitable during war. Recognition that some armed groups do not engage in sexual violence should strengthen efforts to hold accountable those groups that do, whenever the usual criteria for command and/or superior responsibility under international law are met, irrespective of which analytical (not legal) category best describes the pattern of violence (strategic, opportunistic, or as a practice).[62] The existence of such groups demonstrates that it is possible for armed groups to build institutions that inculcate and enforce norms against rape, sexual slavery, forced prostitution, sexual torture, and other forms of sexual violence of civilians.

Thus recent analysis by social scientists of variation in patterns of wartime sexual violence, including variation in form, frequency, and targeting, may help policy-makers establish accountability for sexual violence. In the hope that the argument presented here may strengthen the efforts of policymakers who seek to end sexual violence and other violations of the laws of war – be they government, military, or insurgent leaders, United Nations officials, or members of non-governmental organizations – I here offer some tentative policy implications of this analysis.

It would be rash to suggest that policy-makers try to compel armed groups to copy the institutions of those groups that do not engage in sexual violence. Nonetheless, some more implementable policy implications follow from this discussion. Policy-makers can point to the existence of

62 Wood 2008, see *supra* note 3; and Hoover Green, 2011, see *supra* note 12.

the latter groups to bring together two constituencies that often hold dramatically different presumptions about wartime sexual violence, namely, feminist advocates and military commanders. The fact that some of the armed groups prohibiting sexual violence are strong, professional state or rebel armies should undermine any notion that a truly professional group need not concern itself with such 'soft' issues. Effective fighting forces, that is, excellent 'warriors', need not engage in the profoundly misogynistic rituals too often celebrated as 'masculine' values.

Of course it is precisely in the settings where change is most needed, namely where group members are already engaged in wartime rape and other forms of sexual violence as a strategy or practice, that resistance to changing institutions is likely the most strong. Appeal to the normative condemnation of rape under traditional teaching, for example, is not likely to be successful where armed groups have displaced and sharply undermined the authority of traditional leaders. Lessons could perhaps be learned from campaigns against the practice of female genital cutting, the success of which often depends not on persuasion of individual family members, but on widespread community pledges not to require cutting as a condition of marriageability of daughters.[63] Ideally, reinforcing traditional norms against sexual violence would be possible without also reenforcing gender inegalitarian practices and beliefs.

A distinct approach is to address the historical impunity of wartime leaders for sexual violence: the prosecution of commanders as well as perpetrators would increase the costs to the armed group, strengthening incentives to effectively prohibit its occurrence. (See the many relevant chapters of this volume.) Prosecution of sexual violence as a war crime; as a crime against humanity, which is possible only where the sexual violence is part of widespread or systematic attack on civilian population; or as genocide, would likely increase those costs more than its prosecution under other relevant law. The same argument applies to groups where

63 Gerry Mackie, "Ending Footbinding and Infibulation: A Convention Account", in *American Sociological Review*, 1996, vol. 61, no. 6, pp. 999–1017; Gerry Mackie, "Female Genital Cutting: The Beginning of the End", in Bettina Shell-Duncan and Ylva Hernlund (eds.), *Female Circumcision in Africa: Culture, Controversy and Change*, Lynne Rienner Publishers, Boulder, 2000, pp. 253–281; and Elizabeth Levy Paluck and Laurie Ball, *Social norms marketing aimed at gender based violence: A literature review and critical assessment*, International Rescue Committee, New York, 2010.

sexual violence is a practice: increasing the costs of toleration by commanders would strengthen their incentives to punish combatants for sexual violence. In short, the implication is to strengthen commander incentives to build strong disciplinary institutions and possibly, strong political education institutions, to effectively prohibit sexual violence.

Direct indicators of strategic sexual violence includes copies of orders, credible combatant or witness reports of such orders, credible reports that combatants who refused to participate were punished, and the abrogation from above of attempts to curtail the practice. Such direct evidence is increasingly unlikely as international and perhaps domestic prosecution of sexual violence occurs more frequently. Commands that use euphemisms for general terror may support a claim of sexual violence as a strategy of war: for example, commands such as 'total war' or 'all forms of vengeance', when they are unqualified by any phrase such as 'against enemy troops' or where they explicitly include violence against civilians. Such commands establish a climate of tolerance for human rights violations, in the same way that allowing a hostile workplace climate that is permissive of harassment supports charges of sexual harassment in some countries.

More realistically, perhaps the approach advocated here – to document and analyze patterns of sexual violence – should contribute to proving command responsibility for sexual violence in the absence of direct proof. In the absence of such evidence and in the face of leaders' claims that they did not exercise control of troops, how might the 'effective control' necessary to show command responsibility be documented? This discussion suggests some indicators of an effective chain of command. First, the ability of leaders to command combatants into harm's way is itself evidence of effective command: a key indicator of loss of command is the refusal of troops to engage in combat (and to fire weapons at commanders). Evidence of effective control is still stronger in the case where the armed group carries out offensive or defensive maneuvers over an extended area or period, because orders must be transmitted down the chain of command, and information about present position and capacity, as well as intelligence about enemy position, must travel up the chain of command. And it is stronger still if such movements require coordination across many different units. Second, analysis of local patterns of where and when sexual violence occurs may help establish the purposeful adoption of sexual violence, as suggested by the analysis of sexual violence by state forces in Peru discussed above. If prosecutors can show that rape occurred only where and when it was strategically beneficial, and did not occur where and when it was not, a charge of command or superior responsibility should be more credible.

Third, an armed group that is able to gather and distribute financial resources across various branches of its organization without substantial 'deviation' of those resources for private purposes demonstrates a cohesive command structure. Fourth, if an armed group routinely punishes its members for breaking rules other than those nominally prohibiting sexual violence, it could also punish combatants for sexual violence.

Other indirect indicators that sexual violence occurs under an effective chain of command include the occurrence of sexual violence in military bases, prisons, or state-run facilities (that is, sites that are evidently under commander control); against political opponents, when commanding officers are present; under order of commanding officers; or when commanding officers themselves participate in sexual violence.[64] In some contexts, evidence of collective targeting of particular groups implies purposeful engagement in sexual violence, as it suggests that commanders successfully prohibit sexual violence against groups not so targeted.

Rape is not an unavoidable collateral damage of war. Its victims, women and men of all ages, were not brought down by cross-fire or an errant missile. They were intentionally violated. As Neil Mitchell emphasized, "[…] rape is not done by mistake".[65] Is anyone beyond the immediate perpetrator responsible for the crime? Armed groups, whether they are non-state actors or state militaries, often choose to prohibit sexual violence by their members and do so effectively. The fact that many armed groups do not engage in sexual violence should help to strengthen accountability for wartime sexual violence and to put the stigma of sexual violence on the perpetrators, rather than on the victims themselves.

64 Leiby, 2009, see *supra* note 31.

65 Neil Mitchell, *Agents of Atrocity: Leaders, Followers, and the Violation of Human Rights during Civil War*, Palgrave MacMillan, New York, 2004, p. 50.

12

Sexual Violence in State Militaries

Elizabeth L. Hillman*

12.1. Introduction

The prosecution of military sexual violence by international criminal tribunals has brought hope to many frustrated by the historic failures of state militaries to investigate and prosecute sexual violence during armed conflict. The history, limits, and challenges that face international criminal lawyers in this fraught arena have long engaged scholars and advocates eager to expand the capacity of international tribunals to fill a major gap in military justice. That gap was created by military leaders unwilling to spend resources to investigate, military lawyers without enough experience or interest to prosecute, and military laws that lacked sufficient rigor and specificity.

That gap, however, is narrower than it once was. This essay suggests that in some situations state military justice systems might be better equipped than international tribunals to prosecute military sexual violence. It seeks to understand state military prosecution as a potential means of redress when sexual violence flares during armed conflict or occurs during times of relative peace. Despite a past of overlooking wartime sexual violence as either impossible to prevent or unworthy of attention, state militaries now often operate within social, political, and legal frameworks that make investigation and prosecution of these crimes possible. Because they accompany military forces wherever they might be deployed and routinely manage complex issues of command responsibility, state military justice systems may be more effective than either international tribunals or civilian domestic courts in holding military personnel accountable for crimes of sexual violence. The development and capacity of domestic legal systems is also of import to the jurisdiction of international criminal tribunals themselves, since their jurisdiction is comple-

---

* **Elizabeth L. Hillman** is Professor of Law, University of California Hastings College of the Law and President, National Institute of Military Justice. The author is grateful to Morten Bergsmo, Alf Butenschøn Skre, Eugene R. Fidell, Beth Stephens, and Jean Marie Lutes for their comments and encouragement. All errors remain her own.

mentary to that of state courts and only arises where domestic legal systems, including military justice systems, have failed.

In order to explore the capacity of state militaries to prosecute sexual violence, this essay assesses global trends in military justice alongside national efforts to encourage more aggressive prosecution of sexual violence. It first examines the international convergence of military justice systems around broadly accepted principles of human rights, and then assesses the United States' exceptional practices, which have involved extending military jurisdiction, revising statutes, and preserving the discretion of military prosecutors, in efforts to enhance its ability to prosecute military sexual violence. Together, these global trends and U.S.-style practices signal that state militaries may be increasingly capable of enforcing laws prohibiting sexual violence. State military justice systems can, in some cases, be viable sites for investigating and prosecuting military sexual violence. Greater awareness of the threat that military sexual violence poses to the success of military missions has increased the likelihood that state militaries can, and perhaps will, prosecute sexual violence within their ranks.

12.2. Sexual Violence as an International War Crime

Revelations of widespread sexual violence in some armed conflicts over the last two decades reinforced doubt over the ability and willingness of state militaries to protect populations against sexual violence during war. Advocates and survivors exposed sexual violence in the former Yugoslavia, Rwanda, Haiti, Sierra Leone, the Democratic Republic of Congo, and elsewhere, "surfacing" wartime sexual violence and triggering increased recognition of rape as an international crime and crime of war.[1] Set against a global history of impunity for most perpetrators and *de minimis* legal redress for most survivors of wartime sexual violence, these grim incidents of military sexual violence confirmed for many observers that state militaries were unlikely to either deter or prosecute sexual violence committed by military forces.[2]

---

[1] Rhonda Copelon, "Surfacing Gender: Re-engraving Crimes Against Women in Humanitarian Law", *Hastings Women's Law Journal*, 1994, vol. 5, p. 243.

[2] Elizabeth D. Heineman (ed.), *Sexual Violence in Conflict Zones From the Ancient World to the Era of Human Rights*, University of Pennsylvania Press, Philadelphia, 2011.

As a result, both *ad hoc* and permanent international criminal tribunals were created to investigate and prosecute incidents left unaddressed by internal military justice systems. These include *ad hoc* courts such as the International Criminal Tribunals for the former Yugoslavia and Rwanda, the permanent International Criminal Court, the hybrid Special Court for Sierra Leone, where national and international judges share the bench, and a special sex crimes-only court in Liberia.[3] These courts have crafted legal means to implement a new political commitment to policing human rights violations.

International organizations have also adopted clear statements of intent that deplore sexual violence and seek to hold its perpetrators accountable.[4] Since 2008, when the United Nations Security Council unanimously adopted Resolution 1820 (SCR 1820), the UN's highest decision-making body has made ending the use of rape and sexual violence as tactics of war an explicit part of its mandate. SCR 1820 built on the Security Council's unanimous adoption of SCR 1325 in 2000, which recognized that women must be included in peace and security efforts.[5]

Despite this progress toward greater accountability, advocates of international women's rights remain concerned that world leaders deem efforts to stop sexual violence in armed conflict "hopeful endeavors rather than necessary actions".[6] Critics point to the limited success of international courts in prosecuting gender violence, the tendency of tribunals to preserve patterns of gender privilege and hierarchy, and the persistence of political and practical barriers to effective prosecution.[7] "[L]ingering mis-

---

3 Beth van Schaack and Ronald C. Slye, *International Criminal Law and Its Enforcement Cases and Materials,* 2d ed. 2010, Foundation Press, pp. 41–80; Sara Kuipers Cummings, "Liberia's 'New War': Post-Conflict Strategies for Confronting Rape and Sexual Violence", in *Arizona State Law Journal*, vol. 43, pp. 223, 239.

4 Susana SáCouto, "Victim Participation at the International Criminal Court and the Extraordinary Chambers in the Courts of Cambodia: A Feminist Project?", in *Michigan Journal of Gender and the Law*, 2012, vol. 18, p. 297, 298; Kelly D. Askin, "Prosecuting Wartime Rape and Other Gender-Related Crimes Under International Law: Extraordinary Advances, Enduring Obstacles", in *Berkeley Journal of International Law*, 2003, vol. 21, p. 288.

5 Rachel Schreck, "Rhetoric Without Results: United Nations Security Council Resolutions Concerning Rape During Armed Conflict", in *Penn State International Law Review*, 2009, vol. 28, pp. 83, 83–95.

6 *Ibid.*, p. 100.

7 Beth van Schaack, "Obstacles on the Road to Gender Justice: The International Criminal Tribunal for Rwanda as Object Lesson", in *American University Journal of Gender, Society, Policy, and Law,* 2009, vol. 17, p. 364; Katherine M. Franke, "Gendered

conceptions and a need for greater gender expertise within prosecutorial and judicial offices" have proven difficult to resolve even within an atmosphere of heightened attention to sexual violence as an international crime.[8] As a result, few observers or participants are satisfied with the contemporary capacity of international courts to police gender violence during war.

12.3. Global Convergence in Military Justice

State military justice systems have heard and reacted to this crescendo of international criminal law regarding sexual violence and other human rights violations.[9] Much like the significant variance in the actual incidence of sexual violence within armed conflict, the wide range of state military justice systems across continents and conflicts defies simple categorization.[10] Yet virtually every contemporary armed force has been forced to deal publicly with allegations that it fails to adequately deter or respond to military sexual violence. The problem of preventing and prosecuting sexual violence affects highly structured armed forces as well as irregular and poorly resourced militias.

Like other state and international courts, military courts must prosecute claims of sexual violence with vigor and transparency because sexual violence represents one of the most egregious violations of human rights and dignity. However, additional reasons apart from the primary human rights rationale also support the prosecution of sexual violence in military courts, even those of state militaries that do not consider protection of human rights paramount. For states in which the military is subject to robust civilian control, soldiers who rape are more than a sign of deficient discipline. They are also a liability that can provoke domestic and international censure. Sexual violence is an unwelcome sign of indiscipline, an

Subjects of Transitional Justice", *Columbia Journal of Gender and Law*, 2006, vol. 15, p. 813; Beth Stephens, "Humanitarian Law and Gender Violence: An End to Centuries of Neglect?", in *Hofstra Law and Policy Symposium*, 1999, vol. 3, p. 87.

8 Valerie Oosterveld, "Atrocity Crimes Litigation: Year in Review, 2010", in *Northwestern University Journal of International Human Rights*, 2010, vol. 9, p. 325, 328.

9 Peter Rowe, *The Impact of Human Rights Law on Armed Forces*, Cambridge University Press, 2006, at 225.

10 Elisabeth J. Wood, "Sexual Violence during War: Variation and Accountability", in Alette Smeulers and Elies van Sliedregt (eds.), *Collective Crimes and International Criminal Justice: an Interdisciplinary Approach*, 2010, Intersentia, Antwerp.

embarrassment to professional soldiers, and a potential criminal and civil liability. For example, in 2011, more than two dozen women and men filed a civil suit against the United States for sexual assaults that took place during their military service. Although the case was dismissed 11 months later by a district court judge who found that the military environment of the claim constituted "a special factor counseling hesitation," the suit was widely reported in international media.[11] Scandals follow accusations of sexual assault whether or not investigations and prosecutions ensue, but especially when cover-ups are revealed, allegations are not followed up, or officials become complicit in protecting alleged perpetrators and avoiding the sullying of the military's reputation.[12] Many military leaders, like their civilian counterparts, have confronted the high operational and political consequences of sexual violence during both periods of war and relative peace.[13]

In order to limit the potential for human rights violations to undermine military missions, commanders in States that place military forces under civilian control have largely accepted the legalization of military operations.[14] A critical aspect of that legalization involves shared norms of substance and process in military justice that make the prosecution of sex crimes possible at the same time they protect due process rights. As Canadian Forces Colonel Michael R. Gibson has argued, military courts can be fair and even preferable to civilian courts if they are "subject to constitutional restraints and the supervisory jurisdiction of civilian appel-

---

11 Ashley Parker, "Lawsuit says military is rife with sexual abuse", in *New York Times*, 15 February 2011; *Cioca v. Rumsfeld*, U.S. District Court for the Eastern District of Virginia, 14 December 2011, available at http://lawprofessors.typepad.com/conlaw/2011/12/sexual-violence-in-the-military-not-a-judicial-matter.html, last accessed on 12 February 2012.

12 Megan Schmid, "Combating a Different Enemy: Proposals to Change the Culture of Sexual Assault in the Military", in *Villanova Law Review*, 2010, vol. 55, pp. 475, 480–83.

13 Lucy Broadbent, "Rape in the U.S. military: America's dirty little secret", in *The Guardian*, 9 December 2011, available at http://www.guardian.co.uk/society/2011/dec/09/rape-us-military, last accessed on 10 February 2012; U.S. Department of Defense Sexual Assault Prevention and Response Office Annual Reports, available at http://www.sapr.mil/, last accessed on 12 February 2012.

14 Michael A. Newton, "Modern Military Necessity: The Role and Relevance of Military Lawyers", *Roger Williams University Law Review*, 2007, vol. 12, p. 877; Elizabeth L. Hillman, "Mission Creep in Military Lawyering", in *Case Western Reserve Journal of International Law*, 2011, vol. 43, p. 565.

late courts as in Canada, the United Kingdom, Australia, New Zealand, and the United States".[15]

Military justice systems that lack such supervision and procedural constraints, whether because of a "dysfunctional model of civil-military relations" or a corrupt or ineffective government, are unlikely to investigate or prosecute military sexual violence. Defects in justice have been as rampant as horrific incidents of sexual violence in the Democratic Republic of Congo (DRC), for instance.[16] But even in such situations, state military justice systems may eventually offer a potential avenue of prosecution. In the DRC in 2011, mobile courts funded by outside organizations brought several army officers to trial and won convictions and lengthy sentences for crimes that included rape.[17] For irregular forces that lack structure and training, or for forces led by leaders who reject the principles of international human rights, sexual violence is still sometimes seen as part of the spoils of war or as a military tactic. Yet it has become a tactic with an increasingly salient risk of post-conflict reckoning, investigation, and prosecution. In such unstable situations, the Geneva Centre for the Democratic Control of Armed Forces and other organizations have worked to establish a baseline of military criminal procedure and substantive law because of the potential importance of state military justice capacity in transitional justice.[18] The success of such efforts remains limited, however. State military justice prosecutions of sexual violence will not be effective in States where the practice of military justice protects neither victim nor accused.

Greater worldwide military awareness of, and accountability for, human rights violations has also been accelerated by an increase in combined humanitarian and military operations. Sexual violence in peace-

---

15 Michael R. Gibson, "International Human Rights Law and the Administration of Justice through Military Tribunals: Preserving Utility While Precluding Impunity", in *Journal of International Law and International Relations*, 2008, vol. 4, p. 1, 4.

16 International Bar Association/International Legal Assistance Consortium, *Rebuilding courts and trust: An assessment of the needs of the justice system in the Democratic Republic of Congo*, August 2009, available at http://www.ibanet.org/Human_Rights_Institute/DRC.aspx, last accessed on 12 February 2012.

17 Ruth Collins, "The Struggle for Africa", in *IBA Global Insight*, 2011, vol. 65, no. 4, p. 43.

18 Geneva Centre for Democratic Control of the Armed Forces, "The Gender Security Sector Reform Training Resource Package", available at http://www.dcaf.ch/, last accessed on 12 February 2012.

keeping operations has been exposed and condemned by the United Nations and human rights organizations.[19] Training materials on best practices in preventing, and responding to, sexual violence during peacekeeping operations have proliferated, seeking to establish norms that minimize opportunities for sexual violence while undermining presumptions about the sexual availability of women among occupying and other military forces.[20]

Military leaders who seek to maintain high morale and mission effectiveness among military personnel realize that in multi-national humanitarian operations, individuals from many states, accustomed to different disciplinary mechanisms and standards, must work together. This practical reality has led to convergence across previously disparate systems, bringing "national military justice systems into much closer alignment than in the past".[21] This convergence has spurred legal reforms that address, if indirectly, States' shared interest in deterring and mitigating the costs of military sexual violence. Reforming national legal systems and imposing accountability on perpetrators from military and law enforcement organizations are explicit recommendations of a 2005 report on gender violence by the Geneva Centre for the Democratic Control of Armed Forces, echoing the conclusions of other human rights advocates.[22]

Many, but not all, of such reforms have come about through extra-military judicial review. For example, a 1997 opinion of the European Court of Human Rights that held that the United Kingdom failed to maintain an independent and impartial military judiciary led to extensive structural reform in British military justice.[23] National civilian courts, as well as international courts, have reined in state military justice procedures. In

---

19 Oosterveld, 2010, p. 328, *supra* note 8.

20 UNIFEM, United Nations Department of Peacekeeping Operations, UN Action against Sexual Violence in Conflict, *Addressing Conflict-Related Sexual Violence – An Analytical Inventory of Peacekeeping Practice,* 2010, available at http://www.unifem.org/materials/item_detail.php?ProductID=172, last accessed on 14 February 2012.

21 Eugene R. Fidell, Elizabeth L. Hillman, and Dwight H. Sullivan, *Military Justice Cases and Materials*, LexisNexis, 2012, p. ix. *See also* Eugene R. Fidell, "A World-Wide Perspective on Change in Military Justice", in *Air Force Law Review*, 2000, vol. 48, p. 195.

22 Marie Vlachová and Lea Biason (eds.), *Women in an Insecure World: Violence Against Women: Facts, Figures and Analysis*, 2005, Geneva Centre for the Democratic Control of Armed Forces, Geneva, p. 24; Gibson, 2008, p. 42, *supra* note 15.

23 *Findlay v. United Kingdom*, 1997, *European Human Rights Reporter*, vol. 24, p. 221.

2009, the High Court of Australia ruled the Australian Military Court unconstitutional in a case that began with sexualized horseplay among navy recruiters – itself a sign that sexual violence is not only a problem for civilian women who encounter military forces, but also a barrier to morale and good order for men and women within military services – and ended in the dismantling of an entire judicial system.[24] New Zealand and Ireland have also opted to substantially revise their military justice systems rather than abolish them in favor of civilian-only criminal jurisdiction.[25] External supervision of state military justice has been an essential aspect of human rights reform within military tribunals.

The threat that sexual violence poses to human rights, as well as military legitimacy and effectiveness, has also triggered reforms that increase civilian control over military prosecution, and restrict military jurisdiction over sexual violence and other human rights violations. Limits on military jurisdiction have shifted authority for many potential violations to civilian, rather than military, courts. Austria, Spain, and France try all offenses in civilian courts except in times of war.[26] The Inter-American Commission on Human Rights has sharply limited military jurisdiction in States with defective procedural guarantees, relying on the lack of independent, impartial tribunals and the checkered human rights history of many Member States.[27] In a series of cases decided in the last decade, the Inter-American Court rejected Peruvian military jurisdiction over civilians, held that the Mexican military lacked authority to prosecute human rights violations, and restricted the Argentinian military from trying a captain in the military for criminal offenses.[28] The Mexican cases

---

24 *Lane v. Morrison*, 2009, 29 C.L.R. 230.

25 Panagiotis Kremmydiotis, "Military Justice and Human Rights", paper presented to the *International Society for Military Law and the Law of War Conference*, September 2011, Rhodes, Greece (on file with the author), pp. 2, 14.

26 *Ibid.*, p. 6.

27 Christina M. Cerna, "The Inter-American System for the Protection of Human Rights and the Emerging Trend Towards the Abolition of Military Jurisdiction", paper presented to the *International Society for the Study of Military Law and the Law of War Conference*, September 2011, Rhodes, Greece (on file with the author).

28 *Ibid.*, citing I/A Court H.R., *Loayza Tamayo v. Peru*, Judgment of September 17, 1997; *Castillo Petruzzi v. Peru,* Judgment of 30 May 1998; *Cantoral Benavides v. Peru*, Judgment of 18 August 2000; *De La Cruz Flores v. Peru*, Judgment of 18 November 2004 and *Lori Berenson- Mejia v. Peru*, Judgment of 25 November 2004; I/A Court H.R., *Radilla-Pacheco v. Mexico*, Judgment of 23 November 2009; IACHR,

are especially notable because they involved rapes of civilian indigenous women by Mexican soldiers.

These limits on military jurisdiction reflect a primary concern with protecting human rights, but they may also operate to protect civilian offenders from military prosecution in cases in which the possibility of civilian prosecution is remote. Sharp limits on civilians being charged by military courts can be found in many states, including Italy, Spain, Austria, and the DRC, which recognize no exceptions under which civilians can be charged in military courts.[29] The United Kingdom, Belgium, Tunisia, and Turkey also impose limits on civilian vulnerability to military prosecution.[30] Not all countries follow this trend, of course. The U.S., Egypt, Switzerland, Syria, Chile, Uruguay, China, and Russia permit some civilians to be tried by military courts.[31] Much like the range of due process and degree of potential human rights vindication varies across state military justice systems, the capacity of those systems to prosecute individual acts of sexual violence depends in part on domestic law governing civil-military relations.

Judges and prosecutors in military courts are also now more likely to be civilians than military members. Placing civilians in positions of authority in military justice has been a key structural reform of domestic military courts. The presence of civilian judges and prosecutors hedges the risk that the impartiality and effectiveness of military-only legal officers will be corrupted by concerns of protecting military institutions, resources, and missions over human rights. In the United Kingdom, there have been almost only civilian judges, except in summary courts, since 1947.[32] In Denmark, Canada, and Bulgaria, "military" judges are civilians who wear a uniform at work and a robe when on the bench.[33] Germany, Hungary, Azerbaijan, Latvia, Estonia, the Czech Republic, Norway, North Korea, and Poland also have civilian judges.[34] In Turkey, Estonia,

Friendly Settlement Report N° 15/10, Petition 11.758, *Rodolfo Correa Belisle v. Argentina*, 16 March 2010.

29 Kremmydiotis, 2011, p. 12, *supra* note 25.

30 *Ibid.*

31 *Ibid.*

32 *Ibid.*, p. 6.

33 *Ibid.*

34 *Ibid.*

and Tunisia, military prosecutors act independently from defense ministries or federal bodies.[35]

Taken together, these reforms have made prosecuting military sexual violence in either state military or domestic courts more likely to succeed than in the past. Trends toward more fair and just criminal procedures, more robust civilian control, and greater evidence of accountability have begun to change the nature of military justice practices in many state militaries.

12.4. Sexual Violence in the United States Military

While other States have increasingly placed civilians in positions of authority within their military justice systems, most notably as judges and prosecutors, the U.S. has maintained its historical practice of relying on commanding officers, with the advice of staff judge advocates (senior military lawyers), to wield prosecutorial discretion, and on military lawyers to serve as judges at courts-martial and military commissions.[36] Military officers' resistance to the civilianization of U.S. military justice has combined with civilian judicial deference to the U.S. military to insulate U.S. military justice from reforms common in other States.[37]

Despite this divergence from worldwide military justice trends, the U.S. military has faced challenges similar to other state militaries in struggling to control military sexual violence.[38] Military sex scandals began to appear in the U.S. regularly in 1991, when the Tailhook convention of naval aviators inaugurated the current era of military sexual violence.[39] In 2004, when stories of servicewomen being raped by other military per-

[35] *Ibid.*, p. 7.

[36] Fidell, Hillman, and Sullivan, 2012, *supra* note 21, Chapter 3, "The Role of the Commander", and Chapter 12, "Military Judges".

[37] Catherine M. Grosso, David C. Baldus, and George Woodworth, "The Impact of Civilian Aggravating Factors on the Military Death Penalty (1984–2005): Another Chapter in the Resistance of the Armed Forces to the Civilianization of Military Justice", 2010, in *University of Michigan Journal of Law Reform*, vol. 43, p. 569; Diane H. Mazur, *A More Perfect Military: How the Constitution Can Make Our Military Stronger*, 2010, Oxford University Press.

[38] Helen Benedict, *The Lonely Soldier: The Private War of Women Serving in Iraq*, Beacon Press, 2009.

[39] Jean Zimmerman, *Tailspin: Women at War in the Wake of Tailhook*, Doubleday, 1995.

sonnel during deployments in Iraq appeared in the media, the Department of Defense created a new office to centralize responses to military sexual assault. That office became the permanent Sexual Assault Prevention and Response Office, a clearinghouse for data, training, and education on sexual assault.[40] At the same time, Congress adopted stricter reporting and oversight guidelines for the disclosure of military sexual assaults.[41] Rates of reported sexual assault rose in the tracking measures put in place after these efforts, but observers disagree about whether the collected data is a valid indicator of the incidence of assault, and if so, whether higher reporting rates indicate success in convincing victims to report or failure in deterring actual assaults.[42] U.S. efforts to restrain and punish sexual violence by military personnel, and by civilians who accompany military forces, reveal additional means by which a state military justice system can attempt to address military sexual violence as both a violation of human rights and an issue of military discipline. U.S. military courts may not in fact be best equipped to deal with military sexual violence, given their history and precedents.[43] Nonetheless, official efforts toward reform are worth close examination for the insight they provide into potential means of redress.

Unlike the global trend towards sharp restriction of military jurisdiction, particularly in the realm of alleged human rights violations by military personnel, the U.S. has expanded the jurisdiction of its military justice system in recent years. In 2006, the U.S. Congress expanded military jurisdiction to subject to court-martial "those serving with or accompanying an armed force in the field" during a "contingency operation" as well as during "a time of declared war".[44] Intended to enhance the accountability of private military contractors, this change sought to ensure that crimes committed by contractors in theaters of conflict and occupa-

[40] U.S. Department of Defense, Sexual Assault Prevention and Response Office, available at http://www.sapr.mil/, last accessed on 14 February 2012.

[41] Schmid, 2010, p. 483, *supra* note 12.

[42] U.S. Government Accountability Office, *Report to Congressional Requesters, Military Personnel: DoD's and the Coast Guard's Sexual Assault Prevention and Response Programs Face Implementation and Oversight Challenges*, 2008, available at http:// www.gao.gov/new.items/d08924.pdf, last accessed on 14 February 2012.

[43] Elizabeth L. Hillman, "Front and Center: Sexual Violence in U.S. Military Law", 2009, in *Politics and Society*, vol. 37, p. 101.

[44] Uniform Code of Military Justice, 2006, U.S. Code, Title 10, Section 802a(10).

tion could be tried in U.S. courts.[45] Prosecutions under this provision have been extremely rare, just as there have been a vanishingly small number of prosecutions under the related Military Extraterritorial Jurisdiction Act (MEJA).[46] Yet the adoption of these jurisdiction-expanding statutes reflect high-level concern not only with the general misconduct of private military contractors, but with the sexual violence, sexualized torture, and other infamous human rights violations that contractors committed in Iraq and Afghanistan, including at Abu Ghraib.[47] Congress was finally spurred to close a long-ignored gap in federal criminal jurisdiction because of a desire to increase state capacity to prosecute sexual violence. That capacity has not yet been fully utilized, as many critics have pointed out, but it exists only because of the pressure created on legislators by the existence of military-related sexual violence.[48]

In addition to altering the jurisdiction-granting provisions of the U.S. military code, the U.S. Congress has re-written entirely the military rape statute in recent years. In 2007, a new military sexual assault statute, codified in Article 120 of the Uniform Code of Military Justice (UCMJ), took effect. Judicial interpretations of military sexual assault law had already partially modernized the prosecution of rape in U.S. military justice, but Congress went beyond existing parameters to craft a lengthy, comprehensive sexual assault statute.[49] It includes a series of fourteen specified offenses, sets out careful definitions of its terms, and endorses a much-challenged shift of the burden of proving consent to the accused, with both consent and mistake of fact becoming affirmative defenses.[50] The

---

45 Chia Lehnardt, "Private Military Companies and State Responsibility", in Simon Chesterman and Chia Lehnardt (eds.), *From Mercenaries to Market: The Rise and Regulation of Private Military Companies*, Oxford University Press, New York, 2007, p. 139; Martha Minow, "Outsourcing Power: Privatizing Military Efforts and the Risks to Accountability, Professionalism, and Democracy", in Jody Freeman and Martha Minow (eds.), *Government by Contract: Outsourcing and American Democracy*, Harvard University Press, Cambridge, 2009, p. 110.

46 Eugene R. Fidell, "Criminal Prosecution of Civilian Contractors by Military Courts", in *South Texas Law Review*, 2009, vol. 50, p. 845.

47 Angela Snell, "The Absence of Justice: Private Military Contractors, Sexual Assault, and the U.S. Government's Policy of Indifference", in *University of Illinois Law Review*, 2011, pp. 1125, 1125–28.

48 *Ibid.*, pp. 1128–29.

49 Timothy W. Murphy, "A Matter of Force: The Redefinition of Rape", in *Air Force Law Review*, 1996. vol. 39, p. 19.

50 United States Code, Title 10, Section 920 (2006).

law was enacted over the objections of an official military advisory group, the Joint Service Committee on Military Justice, which had recommended no changes in the UCMJ's rape statute.[51] Although its terms have been criticized by advocates as well as practitioners, this greatly elaborated 21st-century version of the old Article of War version of the U.S military's rape law confirms that Congress and the U.S. military share an interest in finding better prosecutorial means of mitigating the harms of military sexual violence.

Despite this progress, the U.S. military has stopped short of making more extensive sexual violence-related reform to its military justice system. While Department of Defense policies and statutory reform have been adopted, proposals for structural reform on how sexual violence is prosecuted under U.S. military justice have not taken hold. For example, specialized prosecution units for sexual assault have been used with success in some U.S. civilian jurisdictions and could be a model for special military sexual violence units.[52] A legislative proposal that would remove prosecutorial discretion from commanders in favor of a dedicated civilian expert was introduced by Congresswoman Jackie Speiers in November 2011 and has attracted considerable support as well as ardent critics.[53] Especially doubtful of this proposal are judge advocates and commanding officers, not least because they are accustomed to a system in which prosecutorial discretion rests in the hands of ranking military officers rather than with civilians.

More systemic reform in military justice overall would likely have a positive impact on the effectiveness of investigation and prosecution for military sexual violence as well. Centralization of prosecutorial authority would advance attempts to standardize and rationalize charging and sentencing in all military criminal prosecutions, not only those involving sexual violence. Given the frequency of allegations that commanders of-

51 Jack Nevin and Joshua R. Lorenz, "Neither a Model of Clarity nor a Model Statute: An Analysis of the History, Challenges, and Suggested Changes to the 'New' Article 120", in *Air Force Law Review*, 2011, vol. 67, p. 269.

52 Mitsie Smith, "Adding Force Behind Military Sexual Assault Reform: The Role of Prosecutorial Discretion in Ending Intra-Military Sexual Assault", in *Buffalo Journal of Gender, Law and Social Policy*, 2011, vol. 19, p. 147.

53 Soraya Chemali, "'The Invisible War' Takes On Sexual Assault in the Military", in *The Huffington Post*, 17 January 2012, available at http://www.huffingtonpost.com/soraya-chemaly/the-invisible-war_b_1205741.html, last accessed on 14 February 2012.

ten fail to pursue claims of sexual assault, a high degree of institutional transparency would also improve the legitimacy of military justice by providing data to observers seeking to track the disposition of military cases.[54] Yet U.S. military justice remains "opaque," according to Yale law school professor Eugene R. Fidell, in part because of "the decentralized character of the system, in which commanders around the world" control investigation and prosecution".[55] Media coverage of military justice is likewise hindered by lack of access to updated, coherent information.[56] More robust theories of accountability for higher-ranking officers who neglect or condone military sexual violence would also advance the prosecution of military sexual violence.[57] When considering the legal mechanisms of a system as singular as the U.S. military justice system among contemporary military justice regimes, advocates of human rights would do well to consider reforms that would alter the entire system, not only those aspects that bear on the investigation and prosecution of military sexual violence.

12.5. Conclusion

> "The past is never dead. It's not even past."
> - William Faulkner, *Requiem for a Nun*, 1951

No historian with even a modest command of facts can dispute that the armed forces of state militaries have been responsible for the worst sexual violence of our shared past. Nor is there any doubt that military justice has failed to call soldiers to account for the full scale of inhumanity that crimes of war reveal. These undeniable realities foster deep suspicion of contemporary military efforts to eradicate sexual violence, especially

[54] Broadbent, 2011, *supra* note 13.

[55] Eugene R. Fidell, "Transparency", in *Hastings Law Journal*, 2009, vol. 61, pp. 457, 467–68.

[56] Lucy A. Dalglish *et al.* (eds.), *Military Dockets: Examining the Public's Right of Access to the Workings of Military Justice*, 2008, Reporters Committee for Freedom of the Press, available at http:// www.rcfp.org/militarydockets/whitepaper.pdf, last accessed on 31 January 2012.

[57] Melissa Epstein Mills, "Brass-Collar Crime: A Corporate Model for Command Responsibility", in *Willamette Law Review*, 2010, vol. 47, p. 25 ("Yet in modern military times, the United States has never subjected one of its own commanders to criminal prosecution on a true command responsibility theory, and indeed there is no effective legal mechanism by which to do so".); Schmid, 2010, p. 479, *supra* note 12.

when those efforts appear to be superficial, calculated for public affairs effect, or forced upon reluctant officers by external judicial mandates. Yet that undeniable past also imposes upon governments and their militaries a responsibility to prevent recurrences of historical horrors with every means available. For all their limitations, state military justice systems have gained much greater capacity to try crimes of military sexual violence in recent years. Social and cultural change has accompanied this legal evolution, with women as well as gay men and lesbians becoming an increasingly significant part of global military forces themselves. These demographic shifts, as uneven as they might be across States and regions of the world, increase the likelihood that militaries might be able to shed the weight of past injustice in favor of clear-eyed enforcement of contemporary human rights principles. In assessing our collective capacity to deter, investigate, and prosecute international sex crimes, the ongoing development of state military justice systems deserves a place among alternative domestic and international systems of accountability and justice.

13

A Tale of Two Conflicts: an Unexpected Reading of Sexual Violence in Conflict through the Cases of Colombia and Democratic Republic of the Congo

Alejandra Azuero Quijano* **and Jocelyn Kelly****

13.1. Introduction

This chapter is set in the context of ongoing conversations among social science researchers and prosecutors, defense lawyers, and activists about the increasing relevance of social science research in the production of evidentiary methods for holding leaders accountable for sexual violence as a war crime, a crime against humanity and genocide.[1] It is a product of the ongoing conversation between a social scientist and a lawyer who have been investigating the dynamics of sexual violence in Africa and

---

* **Alejandra Azuero Quijano** has an LL.B. degree from Universidad de los Andes (Colombia) and an LL.M. degree from Harvard Law School, where she is currently SJD Candidate.

** **Jocelyn Kelly** is Director of the Women in War Program, Harvard Humanitarian Initiative, MS from Harvard School of Public Health.

The authors would like to thank Morten Bergsmo, Elisabeth Wood and Alf Butenschøn Skre for accepting this collaborative contribution to the volume. We would also like to thank Beth Maclin at the Harvard Humanitarian Initiative for her invaluable contributions in coding the sources analyzed in the chapter. We are grateful to the Undisciplined Women Writers from Cambridge for their insightful and timely comments.

1 Social science research is at the core of contemporary debates about prosecutorial strategies for sex crimes committed in contexts of armed conflict. Some of the most recent examples of this trend are the 2010 and 2011 FICHL seminars (held in New Haven and Cape Town) and the 2009 and 2011 Hague Colloquiums sponsored by the Center for Globalization. The topics of each group of events have played a role in the social sciences by fostering innovations in evidence gathering strategies. Behind this agenda lies an assumption common to ever-growing efforts to criminalize crimes committed against civilians in war: evidentiary methods are key steps in holding leaders accountable for sexual violence as war crimes, crime against humanity and genocide (Hague Colloquium I).

Latin America for the past four years. This chapter serves as the first stage of a broader effort to compare the way sexual violence is narrated and represented in different locales around the globe while trying to engage with some of the key issues that arose during the two-day conference held in New Haven under the auspices of the Forum for International Criminal and Humanitarian Law.

The Democratic Republic of the Congo ('DRC') has been called "the rape capital of the world" while Colombia was known in the late 1990s as "the murder capital of the world". What do these *capitals of crime* have in common? Both countries have been plagued by conflict-related violence, including sexual violence. This chapter will serve as a comparative study to explore how such different cases – situated at different points on the spectrum in terms of prevalence and attention received – are still described using the same narrative language. In both cases, sexual violence is described as "widespread and systematic". In both cases, the perpetrators are men, the victims are women, and descriptions rely on strikingly similar narrative structures, formulas and metaphors. The authors argue that by reading these two cases together, we can learn about the assumptions and master narratives that define the way we talk about sexual violence in conflict. We argue that, despite significant differences in the nature, extent and intensity of the violence, there is a common template to describe both cases. This contributes to the creation of a sexual-violence-in-war "formula" that may ultimately occlude more nuanced understandings of the multiple realities that can be framed as sexual violence in armed conflict ('SVAC').

The DRC and Colombia have different profiles of SVAC in terms of the frequency and extent of perpetration. The DRC has an extraordinarily high prevalence of rape, while Colombia would be situated on the lower to moderate frequency levels, despite the fact that there is evidence showing that the number of cases is significant. The DRC has become an iconic case that portrays the horrors of sexual violence in contemporary armed conflict. Not surprisingly, it also appears to receive the most attention from United Nations ('UN') agencies, international governments, and the international press. Colombia lags behind the DRC in frequency and intensity of sexual violence in the context of the country's ongoing armed conflict. Nonetheless, campaigning by local and international non-governmental actors in Colombia has been significant. Partly due to the effective political action of non-governmental organizations ('NGOs') in

2008, the Colombian Constitutional Court ruled that sexual violence committed in the midst of Colombia's armed conflict ought to be considered widespread and systematic in nature.[2] Despite the fact that considerable amounts of funding from international donors have been allocated to promote research, litigation, and policy reform initiatives, when compared to the DRC, the statistics of sexual violence committed by parties in the armed conflict against civilians appear minimal.

A comparison between the two cases could focus on describing the differences across these countries, and on the possible explanatory frameworks that could allow us to understand their variation.[3] If we took this approach, one could suggest that the disparity in attention given to the DRC and Colombia in mainstream global discourse about sexual violence in war could be explained by the disparity between the numbers of cases from one conflict to the other.[4] The situation in the DRC, defined by highly frequent and intense violence, combined with a non-existent response on the part of the State, would not only explain, but justify, the prioritization of limited political and economic resources.

---

2 For a discussion on the relevance of the decision made by the Court in Auto 092, see CODHES, "Survivors Matter: The Experience of Women in the Massacres of Chengue and Tigre", 2010, p. 8.

3 Elisabeth Jean Wood, "Variation in Sexual Violence during War", in *Politics and Society*, 2006, vol. 34, no. 3, pp. 307–342; Michele L. Leiby, "Wartime Sexual Violence in Guatemala and Peru", in *International Studies Quarterly*, 2009, vol. 53, p. 445–468; Amelia Hoover Green, "The Commander's Dilemma and the Repertoire of Violence: A Theory", in *Repertoires of Violence Against Noncombatants: The Role of Armed Group Institutions and Ideologies*, Ph.D. dissertation, Yale University, 2011.

4 In 2002 when the ICC started operating, the Prosecutor, Luis Moreno, had two cases in mind, Colombia and the DRC. In Moreno's narrative, impunity in DRC was a key element for the ICC to decide to open an investigation in the DRC. In Colombia, the action of the judiciary, although still imperfect, did not amount to the same degrees of impunity. The DRC is the iconic case that portrays the sexual horrors of sexual violence in war (the representation of this case has given it its place as rape capital of the world). Meanwhile, Colombia illustrates those cases that have traditionally remained on the margins of the international responses to the phenomenon of sexual violence in war. This has shaped the disparity in international responses. See Council on Foreign Relations, "Pursuing International Justice: A Conversation with Luis Moreno-Ocampo", available at http://www.cfr.org/human-rights/pursuing-international-justice-conversation-luis-moreno-ocampo/p21418, last accessed on 3 June 2011 ("The worst cases were Colombia and Congo. But in Colombia there were national prosecutions; nothing in Congo. So we decided it's Congo.").

Instead, we argue in this chapter that, regardless of the position of the DRC and Colombia within the prevalence spectrum, both cases are narrated with recourse to the same meta-narrative. The chapter develops two different but interrelated arguments. First, based on an argument made previously by one of the authors,[5] we argue there is a meta-narrative[6] operating in official and public accounts of sexual violence in war. Furthermore, we argue that the meta-narrative defines at least four elements: victimhood, perpetration, categorization of the violence and use of metaphoric language, which remain constant in local and international accounts of sexual violence in the DRC and Colombia despite the fact that, due to variations in frequency and intensity, both cases are usually represented as standing in opposite sides of the prevalence spectrum. By comparatively analyzing these elements during a four-year period, we arrive at the second argument of the chapter. The theoretical assumptions that sustain those constant narrative elements in official/public accounts of SVAC in the DRC and Colombia stand in tension – and oftentimes in contradiction – with some of the key arguments that have led social researchers to be considered "key players" in reshaping our understanding of sexual violence in war and helping to build international criminal law institutions.[7]

We set out to explore public accounts of sexual violence in the DRC and Colombia produced locally and/or internationally by asking the following questions: against whom is the violence happening? Or *who are*

5 Alejandra Azuero Quijano, "The Girl Who Cried Wolf: A History of Sexual Violence Activism in Colombia", presented at the Fourth Annual Toronto Group Conference, January 2011.

6 "[According to Jean Francois Lyotard a] metanarrative is meta in a very strong sense. It purports to be a privileged discourse capable of situating, characterizing, and evaluating all other discourses but not itself to be infected by the historicity and contingency which render first-order discourses potentially distorted and in need of legitimation", Linda J. Nicholson, *The Play of Reason: From the Modern to the Postmodern*, Cornell University Press, 1999, p. 102. For Lyotard's development of the argument at large see *The Postmodern Condition: A Report on Knowledge*, University of Minnesota Press, 1979.

7 We borrow these words from statements made at a recent conference on SVAC by Navanethem Pillay. Office of the United Nations High Commissioner for Human Rights, "Statement: by Ms. Navanethem Pillay, United Nations High Commissioner for Human Rights, 'Women, Peace and Security: from Resolution to Action'", available at http://www.peacewomen.org/portal_initiative_initiative.php?id=506, last accessed on 1 May 2011.

the victims? Who is responsible for the violence? Or *who are the perpetrators?* What are the concrete forms of the violence? Or *how is the violence described?* How is the violence represented? Or *what metaphors are deployed?*

Using these four elements, we identify them within the narrative structure and follow them over a period of four years (2007 through 2010). To explore the meta-narrative, we identify different national and international actors that shape and reinforce the global discourse. These include the popular press, the UN, international NGOs, local NGOs, national governments, and the United States ('U.S.') government. Specific sources within each of these categories were chosen because they were engaged in writing on sexual violence in each context during the period of analysis and thus serve as "thought leaders" and active participants in the international dialogue around these issues. The sources chosen for analysis are detailed in Table 1 below.

Sources	DRC	Colombia
Press	BBC, Agence France Presse, New York Times, Washington Post, IRIN	BBC, Christian Science Monitor, Reuters
United Nations	United Nations Population Fund, United Nations Refugee Agency, United Nations Development Fund for Women	Office of the High Commissioner for Human Rights, UN Committee Against Torture, United Nations Development Fund for Women, UN Committee on Economic, Social and Cultural Rights
International NGOs	Amnesty International, Human Rights Watch, Oxfam	Amnesty International, Human Rights Watch, International Center for Transitional Justice, Oxfam, MADRE
Local NGOs	Panzi Hospital, HEAL Africa	Colombian Commission of Jurists, Mesa Mujer y Conflicto Armado, Ruta Pacifica de la Mujer,

		HUMANAS, Corporación Sisma Mujer, Mesa de Seguimiento al Auto 092
National government	Congolese national legislation, statements from Congolese government officials	National Institute of Forensic Medicine, Constitutional Court, Ombusdman Office
United States government	U.S. State Department, United States Agency for International Development	

Table 1: Sources used for analysis 2007–2010.

The results of this close reading within and across cases are presented in Part I of the chapter. We argue that regardless of the position of the DRC and Colombia within the prevalence spectrum, both cases are narrated with recourse to a common narrative structure. The master narrative is heavily influenced by the language and practice of prosecuting sex crimes as crimes against humanity ('CAH'), and specifically those aspects of the language that have to do with how to produce evidence for proving CAH. In Part II of the chapter, we will explore how the master narrative (and here is the paradox) appears to be in tension with some of the most recent trends of social science research on sexual violence in armed conflict.

13.2. Part I: Close Reading of SVAC Public Narratives in Colombia and the DRC

In this section, we do a comparative close reading of official/public narratives and tease out four elements that come forward by asking the following questions:

- Violence against whom? (Victimhood)
- Violence by whom? (Perpetration)
- Violence described how? (Descriptions of violence)
- Violence compared to what? (Widespread/systematic formula)

Our agenda in asking these questions is the following: the first two questions try to bring to the foreground the production of victimhood: who are the victims and who are the perpetrators of sexual violence in the DRC and Colombia. The third question attempts to trace two moves within and across narratives: conceptualization (abstraction) and description (concretization) of the events of sexualized violence. Finally, the fourth question seeks to underscore the use of metaphoric language to capture the reality of the phenomenon and, in particular, the use of the words *widespread* and/or *systematic* as two terms that serve to qualify the violence to make it relevant as an international crime. For the purpose of the chapter, the formula is seen as a metaphor.[8]

13.2.1. Victims

It is not new to state that women and girls are the archetypal victims in contemporary narratives of SVAC. The DRC and Colombia are no exceptions to this trend. In the DRC, UN agencies[9] as well as the Congolese government[10] held firm to this portrayal of victimhood throughout the four-year period studied in this chapter. The following statement by a MONUC officer illustrates the female subjectivity that increasingly appears in SVAC narratives, that of the endangered woman: "[i]t is more dangerous to be a woman than to be a soldier right now in Eastern

8 Evelyn F. Keller, *Reflections on Gender and Science,* Yale University Press, 1985.

9 UNHCR and UNFPA consistently did not include men and boys as victims in the publications used for examination during the four-year period.

10 The Congolese government passed a comprehensive law on sexual violence in 2006 expanding the definition of what constitutes sexual violence and making it clear that both women and men can be victims. Despite the passage of this law, the discourse around victimhood for conflict-related violence still largely focused on women and girls throughout all the years of analysis. Statements made by the DRC's Minister for Gender, Family and Children, Marie-Ange Lukiana Mufwankol in 2009 and 2010 described the Congolese Government's desire to protect victims of sexual violence, defined as women and children. In 2009, according to a HRW report, the Minister for Gender, Family Affairs and Children also announced the creation of a fund for the protection of women and children, and the creation of an agency for the fight against sexual violence; the mandate of this agency has not yet been defined publicly. According to the minister, the agency will be operational, providing victim assistance (Human Rights Watch, "Soldiers Who Rape, Commanders Who Condone: Sexual Violence and Military Reform in the Democratic Republic of Congo", available at http://www.hrw.org/sites/default/files/reports/drc0709web.pdf, last accessed on 4 April 2012).

DRC".[11] In contrast, international NGOs ('INGOs') and popular media narratives[12] shifted towards the inclusion of men and boys as victims during the second half of the period.[13] It is of particular interest that UN agencies did not explicitly acknowledge men and boys as victims of sexual violence in the DRC.[14] However, we found that gendering victims was not the only narrative strategy available. When victims were not openly gendered as girls, teenagers or adult women, INGOs chose gender-neutral categories such as "civilians"[15], "IDPs"[16], "populations"[17] and "civilian population"[18]. The absence of male victimization from local NGO accounts is particularly heightened among those organizations that have

---

11 Major General Patrick Cammaert, former Deputy Force Commander, MONUC.

12 BBC News, "Clinton demands end to Congo rape", 11 August 2009 ("Men have also been the victims of rape, Oxfam said"); New York Times, "Symbol of Unhealed Congo: Male Rape Victims", 4 August 2009 ("Aid workers struggle to explain the sudden spike in male rape cases. The best answer, they say, is that the sexual violence against men is yet another way for armed groups to humiliate and demoralize Congolese communities into submission"); BBC News, "DR Congo rapes 'defy belief', says UN", 24 September 2010 ("The preliminary report, issued by the UN Joint Human Rights Office, said that three groups of armed militia raped 235 women, 52 girls, 13 men and three boys - many "multiple times" - looted more than 900 houses, and abducted 116 people"); New York Times, "Rape Victims in Congo Raid Now More Than 240", 2 September 2010 ("Thousands of women, and hundreds of men, have been sexually assaulted by the various armed groups warring in eastern Congo", "Rape Victims in Congo Raid Now More Than 240"); IRIN Africa, "Analysis: Rethinking sexual violence in DRC", 6 August 2010 ("Nearly 40 percent of women and more than 23 percent of men surveyed reported having suffered sexual assault, mostly rape").

13 INGOs recognized this fact while still emphasizing that women and girls are by far the most affected, while the popular press in 2010 seemed to emphasize male victimization almost as much as female victimization.

14 In contrast to UNHCR reports on DRC, in Colombia the Committee's 2007 report referred to young girls, women, and boys [who] were victims of different forms of sexual violence perpetrated by leftist guerrilla groups and the state's security forces. The report also referred to sexual violence committed "by members of the FARC-EP against young girls in their ranks". In 2008, UNHCHR continued to affirm that boys were victimized along with women and girls.

15 UNHCR, "Six years in the East", in *Refugees*, 2007, no. 145, iss. 1, page 9.

16 UNHCR Global Report 2008, "Democratic Republic of the Congo (DRC)", available at http://www.unhcr.org/4a2d21992.html, last accessed on 4 April 2012.

17 *Ibid.*

18 UNHCR Global Report 2009, "Democratic Republic of the Congo (DRC)", available at http://www.unhcr.org/4c08f1f29.html, last accessed on 4 April 2012.

been vocal advocates for women's rights as victims of political violence.[19] In such accounts, which explicitly focus on sexual violence against women as a distinct phenomenon in the context of armed conflict analysis, gender-neutral terms give way to the words *women* and *girls.*

The absence of references to male victimization in dominant narratives of SVAC is not simply the byproduct of the absence of data. For example, data from a 2010 population-based study in the eastern DRC supports the importance of registering the experience of male victimization – 23.6% of randomly sampled men reported experiencing sexual violence.[20] In Colombia, according to the National Forensic Medicine Institute, the number of men who experienced sexual violence in 2008 was significant (14%).[21] In both Colombia and the DRC, the process of inclusion or exclusion of male victimization from narratives requires further investigation. For example, when UNHCR's 2007 report is read against La Mesa's[22] report from the same year, we found that the latter included men as victims while the former only mentioned girls, female adults and

19 Sexual violence is deeply rooted in shame. An act of violence that is extremely shameful for women to report may be even more difficult for men to disclose. Often, the rape of men is seen by both victim and perpetrator as the ultimate shaming and "feminizing" of the victim. The reporting of rape is often extremely low for both sexes, and most services related to sexual violence are geared towards women, making it difficult for those men who may want to report the crime to come forward.

20 Kirsten Johnson, Jennifer Scott, Bigy Rughita, Michael Kisielewski, Jana Asher, Ricardo Ong, and Lynn Lawry, "Association of Sexual Violence and Human Rights Violations With Physical and Mental Health in Territories of the Eastern Democratic Republic of the Congo ", in *Journal of the American Medical Association*, 2010, vol. 304, no. 5, pp. 553–562.

21 The National Forensic Medicine Institute (Instituto Nacional de Medicina Legal, 'INML') reported a total of 52 cases of sexual violence committed by armed actors. From the total of cases, 85% of the victims were women, and the 11 cases involving males were allegedly committed by state security forces. Despite the fact that only 11 cases involve male victimization, this number is particularly relevant when taking into consideration that the predominant perpetrator of SVAC in Colombia – against males and females – are the state's security forces. Instituto Nacional de Medicina legal y Ciencias Forenses, "Forensis 2008", Bogotá, p. 159, available at http://www.medicinalegal.gov.co/images/stories/root/FORENSIS/2008/Delitosexual.pdf, last accessed on 5 April 2012.

22 La Mesa de Trabajo Mujer y Conflicto Armado is a coalition of Colombian NGOs that has produced yearly reports on the situation of violence against women and girls in the context of the country's ongoing conflict since 2001.

elderly women.[23] This contrast persisted in 2008. Male victims were also absent from INGO accounts in Colombia during the first half of the period.[24] These results give rise to two observations: UN agencies are not consistent in their inclusion of males as victims across countries; and within countries there is tension between UN narratives (for example, that of UNHCR) and local NGO accounts.

A trend across Colombian NGO accounts that was particularly observable in 2009 and 2010 is the development of theories involving *double* and *triple* victimization of women. For example, Oxfam reported in 2009 how the aggravated violence that women experience during armed conflict was considered worse for those women already vulnerable in times of peace because of their ethnic and racial identities. As the report noted, "Afro-Colombian and indigenous women are most vulnerable to sexual violence given the triple discrimination that they suffer due to their gender, their ethnicity and the poverty in which they live". Feminist theories that explain sexual violence in war as a continuum of the violence women endure in times of peace have proved influential in shaping dominant narratives of SVAC. Although tracing the influence of feminist theory in SVAC narratives is beyond the scope of this chapter, noting how this particular explanatory framework for sexual violence has permeated specific accounts proves relevant in trying to understand the absence or presence of men and boys in specific narratives. As we stated earlier in this section, our view is that the absence of male victimization in dominant narratives of SVAC is not simply the byproduct of the absence of data. In

---

23 Other local NGOs only reported cases involving women and girls (CCJ reported 10 cases of sexual violence, all of them against women, 5 of them girls, 2 of them adult women, 3 of them of unknown age).

24 In 2008 Human Rights Watch published a report entitled, "Breaking the Grip? Obstacles to Justice for Paramilitary Mafias in Colombia". The report described that 91 women had "reportedly filed complaints of sexual violence in the context of the Justice and Peace process [for the demobilization of paramilitary units in the country.]" Amnesty International ('AI') published reports in 2007 and 2008, and neither mention men or boys. In 2007, AI found that "women who are most often the victims of such acts are those who play leadership roles or are emotionally involved with members of the security forces or illegally armed groups". Later, in 2008, AI published "Leave us in Peace: Targeting Civilians in Colombia's Internal Armed Conflict", affirming that girls and women, and particularly displaced women, were victims of sexual violence. There was no mention of adult men or boys in the report.

Colombia, Oxfam's 2009[25] and 2010[26] reports illustrate the engagement of particular INGOs with the theory of continuity of violence against women[27] and how this particular template impedes the consideration of men as victims of sexual violence.

Another interesting aspect of Oxfam's 2009 report, which highlights how the theory of continuity links sexual violence to a specific gender order, is their mention of sexual violence committed against women, both civilians and combatants. This symmetric move to include women on both sides of the armed conflict spectrum contrasts with the absence of INGO and NGO accounts of SVAC in Colombia addressing – or even naming – the victimization of men (civilians or combatants), or the role of females as perpetrators.[28] Similarly, we observe how this underlying gendered dimension of victimization is also present in accounts that highlight SVAC against girls but neglect boys as victims of sexual violence. In 2010, an overarching concern among UN agencies in Colombia was the increase of cases against girls in which the alleged perpetrators were members of the State's security forces. For example, in 2010 the Office of the High Commissioner for Human Rights ('OHCHR') reported that it was "of particular concern [for the Office] that in almost 86 per cent of these cases [of sexual violence victimization both within and without armed conflict] the victims were girls, most of whom were between 10 and 14 years (31.5 per cent)". This statistic was reiterated in the Human Rights Committee Observations for Colombia's 6th Periodic Report, which reported "grave concern about cases, mostly involving young girls".[29]

---

25 Oxfam, "Sexual Violence in Colombia: Instrument of War", available at http://www.oxfam.org/sites/www.oxfam.org/files/bp-sexual-violence-colombia.pdf, last accessed on 1 May 2011.

26 Oxfam, "Sexual Violence in Colombia: First Survey of Prevalence", available at http://publications.oxfam.org.uk/display.asp?K=e2010121610383507, last accessed on 1 May 2011.

27 In the case of Oxfam, this might be explained by the fact that the two local NGOs that are its main partners in Colombia are the two most vocal advocates of the continuum theory among NGOs working on women's rights in the country.

28 The focus on women and girls (both civilians and combatants) as victims of sexual violence continued to be emphasized in 2010. For further analysis on the element of perpetration on SVAC narratives in DRC and Colombia, see *infra* section 13.3.2.

29 United Nations Human Rights Committee, "Sixth Periodic Report: Colombia", available at http://www.ccprcentre.org/doc/HRC/Colombia/CCPR.C.COL.6_En.pdf, last

We observed an important variation between Oxfam and Amnesty International narratives in Colombia and the DRC.[30] In Colombia, these INGOs do not include male victimization in their accounts. However, in the DRC, we observed increasing attention to men and boys as victims during the second half of the period. We read this variation from the dominant theme of *victims as females*, which is predominant in both countries, not as an exception, but as a trend towards the inclusion of men and boys as victims in the DRC that has been amplified, iterated and thus validated in journalistic accounts. In 2007 and 2008, only two articles in the popular media mentioned male survivors of sexual violence in the DRC.[31] In

accessed on 1 May 2011. A dimension in which the theory of continuity has proved to be productive is in its efforts to understand SVAC in connection to the phenomenon of forced displacement. Thus, between 2009 and 2010 there was a growing link between sexual violence as a cause of forced displacement. As Oxfam noted in 2009: "sexual violence is one of the main causes of the forced displacement of women in Colombia, with 2 of 10 displaced women forced to flee because of these types of crimes". La Mesa's report for the same year disaggregates the victims and includes 9 cases of sexual violence against internally displaced women. More so, it explicitly presents "sexual violence as a direct cause of forced displacement of women and their families". Inter-American Commission on Human Rights, "Violence and Discrimination against Women in the Armed Conflict in Colombia", available at http://www.cidh.oas.org/annualrep/2009eng/Chap.V.4.htm, last accessed on 8 June 2011.

30 In contrast, Oxfam and AI took a more nuanced approach to understanding victimhood. AI introduced the concept of men and boys as victims of sexual violence in 2008 when they wrote, "In North Kivu, members of armed groups and government security forces continue to rape and commit other sexual abuse against women and girls, and in a smaller number of cases, men and boys", see *supra* note 24. In 2009, Oxfam also listed men and boys as victims, saying, "Some of the most widespread and brutal sexual violence against women, children and men was reported in parts of northern South Kivu" (Oxfam, "Waking the devil: the Impact of Forced Disarmament on Civilians in the Kivus", available at http://www.oxfam.org/sites/www.oxfam.org/files/bn-waking-the-devi-drc-0907.pdf, last accessed on 4 April 2012.). Both of these organizations included men as victims in their descriptions of sexual violence in 2010. Human Rights Watch was the only of the INGOs analyzed that did not include men and boys in any of the reports published in the four-year span.

31 IRIN, "DRC: Sexual Violence - the Scourge of the East", 16 October 2007, available at http://www.irinnews.org/Report.aspx?ReportID=74801, last accessed on 1 May 2011 ("'There is no age differentiation in the rape,' Lavand'Homme said. 'Very young girls and even young boys are raped'".); IRIN, "DRC: Rape Crisis Set to Worsen amid Kivu Chaos", IRIN, 19 November 2008, available at http://www.irinnews.org/Report.aspx? ReportID=81549, last accessed on 1 May 2011 ("With the recent surge in fighting between the government army and rebels led by renegade gen-

2009, there was a substantial shift, with three of the five press sources describing the phenomenon of men as victims of sexual violence.[32] Additionally, in 2010, four of the five press sources wrote on the issue of men as victims of sexual violence.[33] The following text was featured in the *New York Times* article, "Symbol of Unhealed Congo: Male Rape Victims":

> For years, the thickly forested hills and clear, deep lakes of eastern Congo have been a reservoir of atrocities. Now, it seems, there is another growing problem: men raping men […] Brandi Walker, an aid worker at Panzi hospital in nearby Bukavu, said, "Everywhere we go, people say men are getting raped, too." But nobody knows the exact number. Men here, like anywhere, are reluctant to come forward. Several who did say, they instantly became castaways in their villages, lonely, ridiculed figures, derisively referred to as "bush wives".

The absence of male rape victims in SVAC narratives remains dominant in Colombia, while in the DRC, accounts from INGOs have moved towards the inclusion of men and boys. This trend has had visible influence in mediatized accounts related to the DRC, a phenomenon that can be explained – at least partly – by the fact that INGOs are some of the most frequent sources for journalists of the international press. Nonethe-

eral Laurent Nkunda, many more women – and some men – will likely have fallen victim to Congo's notorious reputation for the use of rape as a weapon of war.").

32 BBC News, 2009, see *supra* note 12; New York Times, 2009, see *supra* note 12; Agence France Presse, "Sexual Violence, Torture Surging in Congo: Oxfam", 14 July 2009 ("The survey found sexual violence had dramatically increased since the offensive began. Women were most likely to be the victims but children and men had also been targeted.").

33 BBC News, 2010, see *supra* note 12 ("The preliminary report, issued by the UN Joint Human Rights Office, said that three groups of armed militia raped 235 women, 52 girls, 13 men and three boys – many "multiple times" – looted more than 900 houses, and abducted 116 people"). New York Times, 2010, see *supra* note 12 ("Thousands of women, and hundreds of men, have been sexually assaulted by the various armed groups warring in eastern Congo".). IRIN, 2010, see *supra* note 12 ("The results confirm the widespread use of sexual violence against civilians – including males – since war broke out in the area in the mid-1990s. Nearly 40 percent of women and more than 23 percent of men surveyed reported having suffered sexual assault, mostly rape."). Agence France Presse, 2010, see *supra* note 12 ("'The known victims include 235 women, 52 girls, 13 men and three boys,' detailed the probe, following the team's visit to 13 affected villages in the Walikale region in Nord-Kivu province").

less, accounts also deviate from dominant narratives. In each move, narrative strategies are deployed that either abide by or deviate from the narrative canon that associates female with victim. They can relate to particular theories and explanatory frameworks of SVAC or be the mere product of mimesis or iteration of bites of information considered truthful (as in the case of journalistic accounts of the DRC). However, we argue that narrative strategies that vindicate women as the ultimate victims of sexual violence not only reinforce stereotypical narratives about gender roles in armed conflict, but occlude forms of victimization that involve men enduring forms of sexualized violence in war.[34] As we will further analyze in Section 13.2.2., these narratives stand in tension *vis-à-vis* current social research on male victimization and the vulnerability that certain forms of masculinity (for example male homosexuality) entail for men in contexts of armed conflict.

13.2.2. Perpetrators

The most salient feature of the victimhood narrative in the DRC and Colombia is that of the gender of the perpetrators.[35] It appears as a tacit gendering, a product of the conflation of armed actors with men. We argue that this tacit sexual ordering of the perpetrators is a key aspect of the contemporary master narrative of SVAC. Across all the sources studied during the four-year period in both the DRC and Colombia, not once is a reference made to women as perpetrators of sexual violence, despite evidence that this is an important dynamic to examine.

In fact, a 2010 population-based study found high rates of female perpetration of sexual violence in the DRC.[36] In Colombia, women have

---

[34] Sexualized violence against men in conflict may be under different categories. For instance, torture of men in detention can classify as sexualized violence (*e.g.*, insertion of objects into a man's anus, forced nudity, forced masturbation). In Colombia, research by political scientist Viviana Quintero has shown how cases of men who had been victims of sexualized violence during episodes of torture by armed groups (particularly state security forces) had been coded in NGO and government databases for human rights violations as *torture*.

[35] "Rape is a man's act, whether it is a male or a female man and whether it is a man relatively permanently or relatively temporarily; and being raped is a woman's experience, whether it is a female or a male woman and whether it is a woman relatively permanently or relatively temporarily". Susan Brownmiller, *Against our Will: Men, Women and Rape,* Fawcett Books, 1975, p. 5.

[36] Johnson *et al.*, 2010, see *supra* note 20.

achieved high rank, and sometimes make up a significant proportion of combatants in some groups. Despite evidence that female combatants can play an important role in armed groups in our countries of interest, there is almost no discussion of how they reinforce, change or challenge small group dynamics, especially around the perpetration of violence. Work from Sierra Leone by Dara Kay Cohen suggests that female combatants can be as violent as men in perpetrating SVAC.[37] She goes on to show the ways in which women fighters participated in violence with their male counterparts on a widespread scale. The work of Cohen and others, as well as data from Colombia and the DRC, strongly challenges the dominant assumptions in our case studies that females are not perpetrators of SVAC.

Besides the gendered dimension in the representation of the perpetrators of sexual violence in the DRC and Colombia, a second dominant trait across sources and cases is the lack of differentiation amongst armed groups relating to their perpetration of sexual violence against civilians. All groups in the conflict are cataloged as maniacal perpetrators of SVAC, without attempts at differentiation as to their motivations, backgrounds or levels of perpetration. The following quotes highlight this key trait of "undifferentiation":

> Several groups are involved in the sexual violence, including government soldiers, guerrillas of the National Congress for the Defense of the People (CNDP) led by renegade general Laurent Nkunda, local Mai Mai militia allied to the government, and Rwandan rebel group Forces Democratiques de Liberation du Rwanda.[38]
>
> In almost all the reported cases, the culprits are described as young men with guns, and in the deceptively beautiful hills

[37] As Cohen notes "the survey data indicate that women participated in one in four of the reported incidents of gang rape [by the RUF], or nearly one in five of the reported incidents of the total rape. In interviews, I found that women in the RUF were active participants in gang rape, mainly through holding down the victim. There were also reports of women participating actively in rape, through the use of bottles and sticks". See Dara Kay Cohen, "Causes of Sexual Violence During Civil War: Cross-National Evidence (1980-2009)", Presented at the Minnesota International Relations Colloquium (28 March, 2011), p. 33, available at http://www.humansecuritygateway.com/documents/HSPA_UM_CausesofSexualViolenceDuringCivWar.pdf, last accessed on 5 April 2012.

[38] Wairagala Wakabi, "Sexual violence increasing in Democratic Republic of Congo", in *The Lancet,* 2008, vol. 371, no. 9606, pp. 15–16.

> here, there is no shortage of them: poorly paid and often mutinous government soldiers; homegrown militias called the Mai-Mai who slick themselves with oil before marching into battle; members of paramilitary groups originally from Uganda and Rwanda who have destabilized this area over the past 10 years in a quest for gold and all the other riches that can be extracted from Congo's exploited soil.[39]
>
> Rape of women and girls by government security forces or armed groups remained widespread in all areas of the DRC.[40]
>
> Over the past decade, fighters from many different groups have ranged up and down the eastern provinces of the Democratic Republic of the Congo slaughtering people, robbing and destroying property – and also raping tens of thousands of women and girls.[41]

The three main armed actors in Colombia in 2007 were the guerrilla, paramilitary groups and the states security forces (police and military personnel).[42] As in Congo, there is no distinction drawn between the three groups when analyzing their use of sexual violence *vis-à-vis* other forms of violence inflicted upon the civilian population. In 2007, both Amnesty and a coalition of local NGOs (La Mesa) referred to armed groups broadly, with the former saying, "[a]ll parties to the conflict – the security forces and army-backed paramilitaries as well as guerrilla groups, mainly the Revolutionary Armed Forces of Colombia (Fuerzas Armadas Revolucionarias de Colombia, FARC) and the smaller National Liberation Army (Ejército de Liberación Nacional, ELN) – continued to abuse human rights and breach international humanitarian law",[43] and the latter saying,

---

39 New York Times, "Rape Epidemic Raises Trauma of Congo War", 7 October 2007.

40 AI, "Amnesty International Report 2007: Democratic Republic of Congo", available at http://archive.amnesty.org/report2007/eng/Regions/Africa/Democratic-Republic-of-Congo/default.htm, last accessed on 1 May 2011.

41 Sarah Russell, "Sheer Brutality: HIV May Compound the Suffering of the Women Raped in the Eastern DRC", available at http://www.unhcr.org/cgi-bin/texis/vtx/home/opendocPDFViewer.html?docid=45b0930f2&query=HIV%20may%20compound%20the%20suffering%20of%20women%20raped%20in%20the%20eastern%20DRC, last accessed on 1 May 2011.

42 See AI's yearly report referring to soldiers, guerrilla and paramilitaries as perpetrators of rape.

43 AI, "Colombia-Amnesty International Report 2007", available at http://www.amnesty.org/en/region/colombia/report-2007, last accessed on 1 May 2011.

it "can almost never be established if the perpetrator belongs to any armed group [in particular].[44]

Journalistic accounts are useful when trying to underscore elements of the narrative structure. Journalism at its core tends to be mimetic – reiterating, reproducing and amplifying the strands of UN and INGO accounts that respond to the question: *violence by whom?* In all four years examined in both the DRC and Colombia, the media repeatedly stated that all armed parties associated with the conflict – whether militia, rebels or the national army – were seen as perpetrators of sexual violence.[45] These men are often portrayed as beyond human, and acts of extreme deprivation are described to support this. The media's portrayal of violence will be discussed further in the next section.

In the DRC, the involvement of civilians as perpetrators of SVAC has been a growing trend in public narratives. This is a point of departure *vis-à-vis* the Colombian narrative on perpetration, where the stress from UN agencies, INGOs, and local NGOs remained on armed actors as perpetrators throughout the four-year period. This departure is relevant insofar as it highlights a shift in the narrative: sexual violence is considered conflict-related even when committed by civilians against civilians. Hence, formalist legal doctrine on the civilian/combatant distinction – central to international humanitarian law and international criminal law – loosens its grip in order to incorporate a different angle on the issue of perpetration: namely, that civilians also commit sexual violence with political ends. The tendency among rebel groups to exploit civilians, and the demobilization of these groups or their incorporation into the Congolese army, could also explain this trend in DRC narratives.[46]

[44] Mesa de Trabajo Mujer y Conflicto Armado (hereinafter 'La Mesa'), "VI Informe sobre violencia sociopolítica contra mujeres, jóvenes y ni as en Colombia 2002–2006", available at, http://www.mujeryconflictoarmado.org/informes/mca_6to_informe_2002_2006.pdf, last accessed on 10 June 2011.

[45] Media narratives emphasized this throughout the period. Militia members, national army troops, and other men in uniform such as police were indistinctively referred to as perpetrators of sexual violence in DRC.

[46] The rapid and poorly organized integration resulted in a national army composed of poorly trained rebel troops that often retained their original command structures and behaviors (including the exploitation of civilians).

By 2008, both the UN and INGOs kept stressing that all armed groups in the DRC were implicated in rape,[47] while highlighting that increasing numbers of civilians perpetrated rape as well.[48] As an example of how this movement is produced in the DRC narrative, we observe how UNFPA's report in 2008[49] inserts a temporary shift by means of differentiating between what happened *initially* and what happens *now* ("now" referring here to the year in which the report was written).

> Initially, rape was used as a tool of war by all the belligerent forces involved in the country's recent conflicts, but now sexual violence is unfortunately not only perpetrated by armed factions but also by ordinary people occupying positions of authority, neighbors, friends and family members.

While some recognition of the role of civilians appeared in UNFPA[50] documents in 2008,[51] the U.S. State Department[52] placed further stress on the implication of the national military in perpetrating human rights abuses, with particular emphasis on their involvement in sexual violence cases. This trend is accompanied by stronger recourse to impunity as the key argument that explains the increasing and sustained number of cases of sexual violence.

---

47 AI, "Amnesty International Report 2008: State of the World's Human Rights: Democratic Republic of the Congo", available at http://archive.amnesty.org/air2008/eng/regions/africa/democratic-republic-of-the-congo.html, last accessed on 1 May 2011. UNFPA, "The Humanitarian Response Newsletter: Democratic Republic of Congo", available at http://www.unfpa.org/emergencies/newsletter/frontlines_mar2008.pdf, last accessed on 1 May 2011.

48 Starting in 2008 and continuing in 2009, the UN, INGOs, and media recognized the increasing role of civilians in perpetrating rapes in the DRC.

49 UNFPA, see *supra* note 47.

50 UNHCR in 2009 emphasized the role of the national army noting, "The DRC's armed forces, or FARDC, have often been seen as perpetrators of gross human rights violations, including sexual violence." (UNHCR Global Report 2009, "Democratic Republic of the Congo (DRC)", see *supra* note 18.

51 UNFPA, see *supra* note 47.

52 U.S. State Department, "2009 Human Rights Report: Democratic Republic of the Congo", available at http://www.state.gov/g/drl/rls/hrrpt/2009/af/135947.htm, last accessed on 6 May 2011.

In Colombia, there has been a tendency not to differentiate between armed actors in local NGO[53] accounts; we have labeled this trend as the "*all parties in conflict*" formula. Meanwhile, UN agencies (as seen in UNHCHR reports for 2008, 2009 and 2010) have utilized a detailed list of the different actors involved, but do not distinguish perpetration dynamics across groups or within them (that is, between different structures within one group). This is illustrated in the case of the Human Rights Committee General Observations to Colombia in 2010[54]:

> [The Human Rights Committee is] concerned about the number of such violations attributed to members of the Fuerzas Armadas Revolucionarias de Colombia – Ejército del Pueblo (Revolutionary Armed Forces of Colombia – People's Army) (FARC- EP) and illegal armed groups that have emerged from the demobilization of paramilitary organizations.

The dominant perpetrator narrative operates under a *non-distinction principle;* in what follows, we present some of its manifestations in the Colombian case.[55] First, there is no distinction among leftist guerrilla groups, in most cases *la guerrilla* (the guerrilla) is the standard category to refer to the FARC-EP and ELN, which are different groups of leftist insurgency. Second, the absence of differentiation admitted the inclusion of a new actor of armed conflict violence as perpetrator (during the second half of the period) in the aftermath of paramilitary demobilization.[56]

---

53 La Mesa, "IX Informe sobre violencia sociopolítica contra mujeres, jóvenes y ni as en Colombia 2009", available at, http://www.mujeryconflictoarmado.org/informes/IX%20informe%20Mesa.pdf, last accessed on 8 June 2011.

54 The greatest concerns for the Human Rights Committee are those cases involving state security forces and perpetrated against girls. However, they list all armed actors involve in internal conflict, including armed groups post paramilitary demobilization.

55 The non-differentiation principle has two main manifestations in the Colombian context: (i) lack of differentiation among leftist guerrilla groups; (ii) distinction across actors is more likely to be introduced when quantitative data is available, which is not very frequent. Hence, distinction appears to be subject to quantitative data.

56 Human Rights Watch elaborates on the idea of successor groups to the paramilitaries as the most recent *new* perpetrators of sexual violence in Colombia's conflict, in its report "Paramilitaries' Heirs: The New Faces of Violence in Colombia", 2010. This is reiterated in Human Rights Watch's country summary of Colombia: "Successor groups to the paramilitaries, often led by mid-level commanders of demobilized paramilitary organizations exercise territorial control in certain regions and are responsible for widespread atrocities against civilians" (Human Rights Watch, "Colombia:

Starting in 2009, new formations of previously demobilized paramilitary groups emerged both in local and international NGO accounts as a new category of perpetrators.[57]

Third, the principle of non-differentiation in the Colombian narrative also admitted a reiterative distinction between sexual violence perpetrated by armed actors associated with the right (paramilitaries and state security forces) and those associated with the left (guerrilla groups). This distinction is based on a measure of the number of cases where the perpetrator was identified as belonging to paramilitary or security forces.[58] Fourth, under the principle of non-differentiation, the most prevalent perpetrators were the State's security forces.[59] Nonetheless, taking into ac-

Country Summary", available at http://www.hrw.org/sites/default/files/related_material/Colombia_English%201-27.pdf, last accessed on 4 April 2012).

57 In the Office of the High Commissioner for Human Right's 2009 and 2010 reports, there is explicit reference to "armed groups that emerged after paramilitary demobilization": "In 2009, OHCHR-Colombia received an alarming amount of information on cases of sexual violence against women and girls that were attributed to members of FARC-EP and the illegal armed groups that emerged after the paramilitary demobilization". The High Commisioner's 2010 report refers to the collaboration between the state security forces and armed groups. This is the only reference to collaboration between paramilitary and state security forces in a joint enterprise as perpetrators of sexual violence: "Armed groups that emerged after the paramilitary demobilization were accused of committing acts of sexual violence and creating networks of prostitution, human trafficking, and sexual slavery, occasionally with the acquiescence and even collaboration of some members of the National Police, particularly in Medellín".

58 In 2007, Comisión Colombiana de Juristas, a local NGO, pointed out that state security forces are the most frequent perpetrators. The Instituto Nacional de Medicina Legal presented data that same year showing that 78.8% of the cases reported to them were committed by state security forces; 21% to the guerrillas: "En su mayoría, los perpetradores de violencia sexual en el marco del conflicto armado contra las mujeres son agentes del Estado". The National Institute of Forensic Medicine is a public institution highly regarded for its yearly statistical report on sexual violence cases. In 2009, INML's report coincided with the local NGO Casa de la Mujer y Ruta Pacífica pointing out the police and military as the two main perpetrators of SVAC. In the same year, UN Committee Against Torture expressed "concern about the rapes reportedly carried out by the security forces, noting the lack of firm action, and the absence of investigations to identify the perpetrators": "La Policía Nacional es el actor armado que aparece como presunto victimario de manera más recurrente con 29 casos, seguida de las Fuerzas Militares con nueve casos; las FARC con seis; los paramilitares con cinco; otros grupos de seguridad privada ocho casos; otras guerrillas con ocho y el ELN con un caso" (2009, p. 160).

59 "The majority of perpetrators of SVAC against women are state agents" (La Mesa 2009). The National Institute of Forensic Medicine is a public institution highly re-

count that NGOs sustain "it can almost never be established if the perpetrator belongs to an armed group [specifically]",[60] the overall reach of distinctions based on quantitative data remains marginal in narratives throughout the period. The dominant trait continues to be the absence of variation in the analysis of dynamics of perpetration among different armed groups through time.

Totalization remains a constant discursive move across the master narrative. In the following excerpts from Oxfam's 2009 report and a publication from a local NGO coalition on SVAC in Colombia, it is possible to observe the totalizing narratives:

> Over almost 50 years of Colombia's armed conflict, sexual violence has been employed as a weapon of war by all of the armed groups – state military forces, paramilitaries, and guerrillas – both against civilian women and their own female combatants. (Oxfam)
>
> In the context of Colombia's armed conflict sexual violence has become a means of attack perpetrated by <u>all</u> actors in the conflict for many years.[61] (La Mesa)

Here, despite being historicized, sexual violence is framed as an ongoing trait of half a century of internal armed conflict in the country, with no distinction of the specific armed groups, nor the position of women as either combatants or civilians. This trait counters trends of empirical research and the narratives that ensue from authors such as Wood, Leiby, and Hoover Green, as we will explore further in Part II. The tendency to use totalizing language when referring to perpetrators (for example the military tactics of all armed groups involved in the conflict) accompanies

garded for its yearly statistical report on sexual violence cases. In 2009 INML's report coincides with Casa de la Mujer y Ruta Pacífica pointing out to the police and military as the two main perpetrators of SVAC. "The National Police is the most recurrent armed actor perpetrating SVAC, 29 cases were reported, followed by the Armed Forces, 9 cases reported, FARC, 6 cases reported; paramilitary groups, 5 cases; other private security groups, 8 cases; other guerrillas 8 cases; ELN, 1 case." (2009, p. 160). In 2010, La Mesa denounced "an increase in the number of cases of sexual violence committed by the state's security forces as a form of torture during the Uribe administration".

[60] La Mesa, see *supra* note 44.

[61] "En el contexto del conflicto armado colombiano, la violencia sexual se ha constituido en un medio de ataque perpetrado por todos los actores del conflicto armado interno, desde hace muchos años."

formulaic jargon and metaphoric language,[62] as we will examine in the following sections.

13.2.3. Descriptions of Violence

The portrayal of women and girls as helpless victims of bestial male combatants emerges strongly in narratives of SVAC in Colombia and the DRC. In both contexts, extremely brutal forms of sexual violence were described within the dichotomized victim/perpetrator construct. In both contexts, there was less qualitative differentiation amongst the types of sexual violence seen in the first year of analysis, with a trend towards becoming more precise and graphic in subsequent years. By the end of the analysis, both cases encompassed the following forms of violence: family members forced to watch rape and killing, rape with objects, and sexual slavery among other forms of violence. In Colombia, there were descriptions of sex trafficking and abuse of reproductive freedoms. In the DRC, there was an emphasis on monstrous and graphic rituals associated with rape, including drinking blood, being forced to eat the flesh of relatives, and forced incest. This expansion and specification of the forms of sexual violence can be read both as an indication of the increased understanding of, and interest in, attempting to characterize SVAC. In both the DRC and Colombia, sexual violence was described with increasing detail and, through this contextualization, SVAC was placed within a larger repertoire of violence that might include murder, displacement and other abuses. However, when taken too far, this tendency has also been object of critique as the sensationalization of particularly inhuman forms of violence (sometimes even labeled as "rape pornography").

The trends toward specification, categorization and explicit illustration of forms of sexual violence are dominant in both cases. In the first year of analysis, all sources in Colombia and the DRC were more likely to refer to "sexual violence", "sexual abuse", and "rape" than to detailed forms of violence. In 2008, there was a significant escalation in the level of detail used to describe the types of sexual violence in the DRC. Much of the language was reminiscent of (and in some cases almost verbatim from) the most-cited journal article on this topic published in 2008, "Sexual Violence Increasing in Democratic Republic of Congo", by Wairagala Wakabi, published in *The Lancet* in January. UN sources moved from

[62] See *infra* section 13.2.4.

describing sexual violence in general terms, to describing how women are "shot and stabbed in the vagina with bullets, bits of broken glass and [corn cobs]; and men being forced to sexually violate their daughters, sisters, and mothers at gun point". While the UN seemed to retreat from using such detailed language in the following years, INGOs escalated their language around the forms of sexual violence in 2007–2010. By 2010, the INGOs emphasized the forms of violence from previous years and added new forms of violence they had recorded. These additions included: gang rape, sexual slavery, genital mutilation, instrumentation with foreign objects, forced rape between victims and rape in the presence of family members, forced marriages, kidnapping and forced pregnancy.

Also illustrating this trend from the general to the categorical and specific, it was not until around 2009 that sources in Colombia began to qualitatively differentiate between types of sexual violence. In 2007, reports generally referred to "rape" or "sexual violence". However, anecdotal descriptions of incidents in Colombia made clear that other forms of violence were being perpetrated, such as being forced to watch other family members being raped and killing associated with rape. As seen in the quotes from Amnesty International: "four of the soldiers reportedly raped her in front of her three-year old son" and "paramilitaries raped and killed a human rights female worker".[63] By 2009, Oxfam and others had begun creating lists of the specific types of SVAC emerging in Colombia – typifying the trends towards specification and classification of SVAC. Amongst the forms of violence in Oxfam's list[64] were: domestic violence, rape, trafficking, forced prostitution, sexual violence in armed conflict, murder, systematic rape, sexual slavery, social and sexual control, forced pregnancy, forced abortion and crimes of honor. A trigger for this shift may be the issuing of decision Auto 092 de 2008 by the Colombian Constitutional Court – the Court includes a typology of sexual violence that mirrors those produced by the the International Criminal Tribunal for the former Yugoslavia ('ICTY') and the International Criminal Tribunal for Rwanda ('ICTR'). Among the types of violence included were: sexual abuse, sexual harassment, sexual slavery, forced prostitution and forced abortions.

63 "Colombia-Amnesty International 2007", available at http://www.amnesty.org/en/region/colombia/report-2007, last accessed on 6 May 2011.

64 "Sexual Violence in Colombia", available at http://www.oxfam.org/sites/www.oxfam.org/files/bp-sexual-violence-colombia.pdf, last accessed on 6 May 2011.

The line between categorizing and specifying sexual violence to engaging in what has been qualified by some observers as "rape pornography" can be seen in the media's increasingly graphic portrayals of sexual violence in the DRC. Rather than focusing on the pervasiveness and dire consequences of SVAC, news outlets engaged in a form of sensational echoism in which a few non-representative but gruesome stories were recounted and embellished upon. In 2007 for instance, the *New York Times* described how "many [women and girls] have been so sadistically attacked from the inside out, butchered by bayonets and assaulted with chunks of wood, that their reproductive and digestive systems are beyond repair".

Also in 2007, three of the five news outlets analyzed in this chapter ran stories about victims of sexual violence being forced to eat human flesh, sometimes of dead relatives. This story was first introduced by Agence France Presse ('AFP'), BBC and the *New York Times,* which wrote, "Militias often force men, at gunpoint, to rape their own mothers, sisters or daughters. In some cases… gangs hold women as slaves and force them to eat excrement or the flesh of their murdered relatives". The original story, of the ones included in the research, was published in July of 2007 by the BBC, then repeated in the *New York Times* in September, and then repeated again, though sourced differently, by AFP in December.

Another illustration of the abandonment of the representation of SVAC as one form of violence in the larger repertoire of armed conflict related violence in favor of detailed and hyperbolic descriptions occurred in 2008. A story was introduced by the *Washington Post* and *New York Times* about the forced abortions and disembowelments of pregnant women. The *New York Times* repeated this story in 2009 along with AFP, whose article said that, "[Hillary] Clinton offered personal comfort to two rape survivors, one of whom was violated when she was eight months pregnant with the fetus ripped out".

One could argue that using such uniquely disturbing cases amplifies the case of sexual violence in the DRC to a wider audience through emoting horror. The effect, however, is an increasing sensationalization, resulting in international organizations and media "competing" with previous conflicts and accounts for grotesque effect. The cases that are located at the most horrific end of the spectrum become the iconic, rather than the exceptional cases. This movement to the more shocking means that other prevalent and representative cases risk becoming devalued as "not shocking enough" to attract attention.

A more constructive trend seen in the discourse about types of violence was the emergence of narratives that provide texture and situate violence within the wider context of war, as in the case of Colombia when SVAC became increasingly linked with internal displacement. In a report from the Colombian Commission of Jurists ('CCJ'), there is reference to vulnerability and risk factors augmenting the situation of IDP women.[65] This assertion is based on a statistic produced by another local NGO (Profamilia) that states that among IDPs, 4% of women were victims of sexual violence. The tendency to associate forced displacement with higher risks of sexual violence is reiterated in Amnesty International's 2008 publication. The relationship between forced displacement and sexual violence is framed both as the cause and/or consequence of forced displacement. In Amnesty International's publication more detailed descriptions appeared to be paired with more complex explanatory frameworks that attempt to portray the connections between the situation of IDPs and the higher risk of being victimized. For instance, Amnesty International noted that "displaced women are at greater risk of being subjected to sexual violence, including rape", and "paramilitaries in the area recruit under-age girls for prostitution […] Many of these girls live in camps for displaced people next to the local military base".[66]

In 2010, Reuters produced a report on Colombia's ongoing conflict, drawing the connection between internal displacement as a consequence of rape among other forms of violence. In sharp contrast with the media attention given to the DRC, this connection is the only reference to sexual violence among international journalistic sources consulted for the period. The OHCHR report in 2010 referred to statistics on sexual violence and pointed out that "they continue to be incomplete and fragmented". The concern for women in situations of forced displacement persists in the concluding observations of the UN Committee on Economic, Social and Cultural Rights: "The Committee is particularly concerned by violence against women in [the] situation of forced displacement due to the armed conflict".

65 Colombian Commission of Jurists CCJ, "Situación de Derechos Humanos y Derecho Humanitario en Colombia, Julio de 2007 a Junio de 2008", 2009.

66 "Amnesty International Report 2009: DR Congo", available at http://report2009.amnesty.org/en/regions/africa/democratic-republic-congo, last accessed on 6 May 2011.

Another trend in the contextualization of SVAC in Colombia is to highlight sexual violence as a way to intentionally punish communities. In 2008, UNHCR reported sexual violence committed by FARC-EP as a "mechanism for pressure or retaliation". This form of violence is only referenced when women are victims – the implication being that rape of women is a way to punish an entire community. This example can be seen as a move towards presenting quantitative data and drawing conclusions that fit into some of the elements of the "sexual violence in conflict formula". We call this phenomenon "overstating of data". The following excerpt from the 2009 report by La Mesa, in which the fact that nine cases of rape were perpetrated by commanders is taken to mean that rape in the Colombian conflict is a "strategy of war".

> In nine cases (24%), women said they were victims of sexual violence by commanders of armed groups (four cases by guerrillas and five cases by paramilitaries), which also implies that this is a strategy through war, promoted from the highest levels of hierarchical structures. Finally, in 13 cases (35%), offenses were committed to accuse the women or her family members of collaborating with an enemy group, which means that sexual violence was perpetrated as an intentional and planned strategy of war rather than as an isolated and prohibited practice within these organizations.

The fact that 13 cases of sexual violence were reported as linked specifically with punishing a women or her family for perceived collaboration with an enemy group is more convincing. However, the overall argument is weakened when the assumption of systematicity is made based on the fact that higher level commanders perpetrate these crimes.

The press in the DRC is especially likely to write about sexual violence as a weapon of war and a way to terrorize communities, but fails to engage in a justification or analysis of the concept. In 2007, the *Washington Post* notes that rape is a "weapon of terror" and a "routine weapon of war". The AFP echoes this, saying that rape is being used "as a weapon of war". The UN, NGOs and the popular press continue to use this formulation of "weapon of war" or "tool of war" throughout the years of analysis – showing the mimetic nature of the discourse around the forms of violence. However, there is no analysis of what this "tool of war" is meant to achieve. Nor is there recognition that the complexity of the conflict in the DRC may mean there is a diversity of motivations for perpetrating sexual violence (both within and across groups). Reasons for raping may include a lack of discipline and use of rape as a reward for troops, rather than the use of this violence as a premeditated "weapon" used to achieve specific objectives. The use of other formulas, specifically those that have legal implications, like the *systematic* and *widespread* phrasing, will be examined further in the next section.

13.2.4. Metaphors and Formulas

In this section we analyze the use of two categories – *widespread* and *systematic* – traditionally associated with the definition of crimes against humanity ('CAH'). We call this the "W/S formula". According to the UN Review of the Sexual Violence Elements in ICTY, ICTR and International Criminal Court ('ICC') case-law: "Any conviction of any crime as crime against humanity – including crimes such as rape – per definition means that *the crime was part of a widespread or systematic attack directed against a civilian population*" (emphasis added).[67] Across the narratives analyzed in this chapter, these two terms are used alternatively, concomitantly, or interchangeably to qualify acts of violence as international crimes. We analyze them as metaphors because of their ability to produce imagery and specific representations of sexual violence. We also analyze the use of alternative metaphors in SVAC accounts (for example rape as a weapon of war, sexual terrorization, weaponization of women's bodies, etc.).

The W/S formula became international treaty law in 1994 when it was included in the definition of CAH (Article 5) of the ICTR statute. In the early 1990s the *ad hoc* international criminal courts for Yugoslavia and Rwanda issued the first judicial decisions arguing that sex crimes committed in the context of a systematic attack against a civilian population ('SAACP') or a widespread attack against a civilian population ('WAAC') were CAH. These decisions and their distinct – and sometimes contradictory – interpretations of the W/S formula gave rise to a doctrinal debate over the content and scope of these two categories in the context of SVAC. Despite ongoing interpretive debates, we argue here – based on an

[67] United Nations, Department of Peacekeeping Operations, Review of the Sexual Elements of the Judgments of the ICTY, the ICTR, and SCSL in the Light of Security Council Resolution 1829, 2009, p. 23 ("*UN Review*").

argument made previously by one of the authors[68] – that any correct reading of the formula includes the assertion of three statements[69]:

1. *Widespread and systematic are not synonymous concepts, but quantitative and qualitative qualifiers (respectively) that cannot be interchangeably used*: The context in which sexual violence occurs is systematic when there is evidence that shows the attack against civilians is organized and/or planned.[70] It is widespread when the attack against civilians involves a large number of violent acts, and among them there is evidence of a single or multiple of episodes of sexual violence.[71]
2. *The formula qualifies the* ***nature of the attack (context)*** *in which one*[72] *or multiple sex crimes take place*: The categories widespread

[68] Quijano, see *supra* note 5.

[69] The UN Review presents a synthesized version of our interpretive statements in the following excerpt: "In the case-law, 'widespread' refers to the large-scale nature of the attack and the number of victims, while "systematic" refers to the organized nature of the acts of violence and the improbability of their random occurrence. Patterns of crimes – that is the non-accidental repetition of similar criminal conduct on a regular basis – are a common expression of such systematic occurrence. Except for extermination, a crime need not be carried out against a multiplicity of victims in order to constitute a crime against humanity. Thus, an act directed against a limited number of victims, or even against a single victim, can constitute a crime against humanity, provided it forms part of a widespread or systematic attack against a civilian population". *Op. cit.*, see *supra* note 67.

[70] The question here is: *did the sex crime occur in the context of an organized plan of violence against civilians?*

[71] See cases *Tadić* (the widespread attack was defined referring to the "big number of victims"); *Kayishema* ("directed against a large number of victims"); *Blaškić* ("a crime can be widespread [...] due to the cumulative effect of a series of inhuman actions or due to the single effect of an inhuman act of a large magnitude"); and *Kunarac* ("the widespread adjective relates the large scale nature of the attack and to the number of victims"). Quoted in Kai Ambos, *Topics of international and European criminal law*, Marcial Pons, Madrid, 2006, p. 188.

[72] *Tadić* Trial Judgment, para. 649, cited in Antonio Cassese, "Crimes Against Humanity", in Antonio Cassese, Paola Gaeta, and John R.W.D. Jones (eds.), *The Rome Statute of the International Criminal Court: A Commentary*, Volume 1, Oxford University Press, New York, 2002, p. 367 ("Clearly, an individual act by a perpetrator taken within the context of a systematic or widespread attack against the civilian population implies an individual criminal responsibility and an individual perpetrator does not need to commit several offences in order to be prosecuted [...] Even an isolated act may constitute a crime against humanity if it is the product of a political system based on terror and persecution.").

and systematic qualify the context in which the sex crimes occur and not the sex crimes themselves. Thus, in order to prove sex crimes as a CAH, prosecutors must produce evidence beyond reasonable doubt that the event of sexual violence occurred in the context of a SAACP or a WAAC.

3. *The two elements of the formula do not need to apply concomitantly but* ***alternatively***: Proving the occurrence of either a SAACP **or** a WAACP is sufficient for the configuration of a CAH, thus, there is no need to prove both the systematic and widespread nature of the context. It is sufficient that the attack be either widespread or systematic for configuration of this element of CAH.[73]

During the first decade of the 21st century, we have witnessed how the doctrine of sex crimes as CAH became part of mainstream international criminal law ('ICL') with the inclusion of several sex crimes in the Rome Statute's definition of CAH under Article 7. In addition, systematic or widespread also became the formulaic statement used by the United Nations Security Council ('UNSC') to describe sex crimes committed in armed conflict as a crime that represents a threat to international security. UNSC resolutions 1820,[74] 1888[75] and 1960[76] reflect this trend. There is no surprise then that the W/S formula has become a cornerstone of advocacy strategies (litigation, legal reform, policy making) by local, international and transnational NGOs as well as international organizations (IOs) trying to address and prevent the use of sexual violence in armed conflict settings.

The UNSC has championed the agenda of SVAC using the W/S formula: resolutions, 1820, 1888 and 1960 attest to this trend. Their narrative is probably the most widely published, diffused and mediatized of all

---

[73] During the drafting of the Rome Statute, the States were divided around the cumulative or alternative nature of the systematic and widespread requirements of the attack. However, at the end, the alternative connection was accepted, on the condition that the definition of the expression "attack against the civilian population", included the implicit political element of the said definition was explicitly included in the text of article 7. *Ibid.*, p. 225.

[74] United Nations Security Council, Committee on Women and peace and security. Res. 1888, UN SCOR, 6195th Meeting, U.N. Doc. S/Res/1820 (2008).

[75] United Nations Security Council, Committee on Women and peace and security. Res. 1888, UN SCOR, 6195th Meeting, U.N. Doc. S/Res/1888 (2009).

[76] United Nations Security Council.Committee on Women and peace and security. Res. 1960, UN SCOR, 6453rd Meeting, U.N. Doc. S/RES/1960 (2010).

contemporary narratives on the topic. As a result, this storyline has been influential in defining a template for talking about sexual violence in war. The DRC is a key feature in the story, as Inés Alberdi, Executive Director of UNIFEM, tells in her 2008 address[77] to the Economic and Social Council (ECOSOC) Chamber, stating how the reason we know that rape today is "no longer an isolated and random element of conflict" is because of past experiences in Bosnia, Rwanda and "now the brutal attacks in Eastern Democratic Republic of Congo".[78] The DRC emerges as the latest link to the theory of SVAC that the Security Council launched with resolution 1820, one that uses the W/S formula to draw the line between sexual violence that is a problem of international security – hence, relevant for the UNSC – and sexual violence that remains to be addressed domestically by national judiciaries. In Alberdi's account, the DRC becomes the next iconic case of SVAC that should be taken up by the Security Council (as in previous situations in which the UNSC has intervened) sexual violence is widespread and systematic:

> We need to be clear that this resolution [1820] addresses sexual violence in conflict situations, not sexual violence in general. The latter is a criminal justice problem, which needs to be addressed by each country's police and judicial systems. But when sexual violence is widespread and used systematically against civilians for military or political gain, it is a matter for the Security Council (emphasis is Alberdi's).

---

77 Statement by UNIFEM Executive Director, Inés Alberdi, on behalf of UN Action during the ECOSOC session on sexual violence against women and children in conflict at the UN-IPU Hearing: "*Towards Effective Peacekeeping and the Prevention of Conflict: Delivering on our Commitment*".

78 *Ibid.* ("Yet too many people shrug their shoulders and say: things are terrible but what can we do? This response comes from the belief that sexual violence is an inevitable part of war, that boys will be boys, and that nothing can stop them. It is precisely this myth of inevitability that stops people from acting. It has obscured the fact that rape is no longer an isolated and random element of conflict – it is organized, it is systematic, it is targeted against specific groups." "We know this from the rape camps of Bosnia, the mass rapes in Rwanda, and now the brutal sexual attacks in Eastern Democratic Republic of Congo. Commanders order or incite troops to rape – to humiliate, terrorize and displace civilians – or else they turn a blind eye to what they know to be war crimes. This is why Resolution 1820 urges all parties to armed conflict to 'debunk the myths' surrounding sexual violence – including the myth of its inevitability").

The trajectory for introducing the use of W/S formula in Colombia and DRC narratives is different.[79] The DRC has been represented by UN agencies and INGOs alike as the iconic portrayal of the *widespread* and *systematic* nature of SVAC. Congolese judiciary and police institutions have played an important part in enhancing this iconic portrayal by means of their inaction regarding sexual violence. Meanwhile, in Colombia the local judiciary (and particularly the Constitutional Court) is the site where local NGOs have found an authoritative discourse that echoes the use of W/S language in describing SVAC in the country.

Despite the fact that UN agencies and INGOs include W/S language when they refer to sexual violence in Colombia, this country remains largely excluded from narratives that serve the purpose of listing and describing exemplary cases of the strategic use of sexual violence in war.[80] In the DRC, local NGOs ground their use of W/S language on authoritative statements made by UNIFEM's executive director, Secretary of State Hillary Clinton, and Special Rapporteur Margot Wallström. Meanwhile, Colombian NGOs are still trying to prove to national judiciary officials that sexual violence in Colombia is not an isolated feature but a strategic part of armed conflict,[81] and thus ought to be addressed as a crime against humanity. Additionally, Colombian NGO narratives emphasize their purpose of raising awareness among the "international community".

Although the use of W/S language in both Colombian and Congolese accounts is iterative and increased during the first half of the period, Colombian narratives shifted to include additional qualifiers of the violence during the second half. We read this as a narrative effort to prove the gravity of the situation. The reports published between 2007 and 2010 by a local coalition of Colombian NGOs (La Mesa) advocating for the prosecution of SVAC as crimes against humanity illustrate these two stages. The first phase is one of incorporation of W/S language into NGO

79 This statement is true, although in both cases this language was adopted locally during the second half of the first decade of the 21st century, approximately 10 years after it had started circulating in international fora.

80 Hence the absence of any references to SVAC in Colombia among the journalistic sources consulted for the period.

81 This observation takes into account the fact that significant amounts of funding from UN agencies (particularly UNIFEM and UNFPA) have been allocated to local NGOs in Colombia with the purpose of documenting SVAC. However, we would like to introduce a distinction between funding flows and the listing of iconic cases and how these affects those *other* cases that are left outside.

and INGO narratives. In 2007, La Mesa's report was the only publication to use the words systematic and widespread (*sistemática* y *recurrente*)[82] without including further metaphoric language. Soon after, the Colombian Constitutional Court made the decision to explicitly describe SVAC as systematic and widespread. La Mesa's 2008 report made a broad interpretation of the content of Auto 092 and affirmed that both SVAC and domestic violence were widespread and systematic. We signal here (and analyze later in the chapter) an important shift in the narrative that demonstrates the blurring of peacetime and wartime distinctions in the use of W/S language:

> [i]t is for La Mesa an honor to deliver this report to the national and international community reflecting that sexual violence in Colombia is a systematic and widespread practice against women and girls, not only in the context of armed conflict, but also in the context of family life, work and social relations.[83]

In 2009, the report published by La Mesa echoes Oxfam's landmark publication for the same year.[84] Both documents include explicit statements that reject the isolated quality of SVAC while reinforcing the use of the W/S formula: "Sexual violence [in Colombia's armed conflict] is not an isolated conduct, but it is characterized by being premeditated, system-

---

82 The systematicity standard is used to refer both to specific criminal conducts (such as rape) and broadly to the violation of women's human rights. The term is used in every chapter of the report and a total of 13 times. Overall, the intention appears to be the denial of the isolated character of sexual violence committed by armed actors in the country's ongoing conflict ("sexual violence is not an isolated fact, but a violation by the paramilitaries that has continued during demobilization").

83 The report denounces the resistance from the General Attorney's Office to investigate sexual violence in Colombia's armed conflict following a prosecutorial strategy aimed at proving the W/S nature of the crimes "despite the reiterated confirmation of its massive occurrence all around the country". It is necessary that the Attorney General's Office deploys a proactive approach that includes within its investigative hypothesis that sexual violence is committed as a systematic and widespread practice.

84 Oxfam's report is entitled "Sexual Violence in Colombia: A Weapon of War". It explicitly frames the violence in formulaic terms and calls for its characterization as a crime against humanity. ("The generalized and systematic existence of sexual violence against women [...] could meet one of the conditions for characterizing this practice as a crime against humanity […] The use of sexual violence is far from sporadic. It has become a generalized and systematic practice; a normal aspect of the armed conflict").

atic, and widespread".[85] Across the two countries, the terms widespread and systematic are used with regularity among INGOs, and increasingly during the first half of the period. In Colombia, both Amnesty International and the International Center for Transitional Justice used the word widespread to describe SVAC in 2008, while the former also used the word systematic.[86]

Another important feature in the use of the W/S formula among Oxfam, Amnesty International and Human Rights Watch in Colombia and the DRC is the interchangeability of the terms. For example, INGOs in the DRC used both terms over the four-year period without explaining the content and differences between them. The following are three examples from the same Human Rights Watch 2009 report[87]:

> Nevertheless, there are some indisputable facts: brutal acts of sexual violence continue on a widespread basis throughout Congo and many of the victims are girls under the age of 18.
>
> [...]
>
> Sexual violence was widespread and sometimes systematic, a weapon of war used by all sides to deliberately terrorize civilians, to exert control over them, or to punish them for perceived collaboration with the enemy.
>
> [...]
>
> Three reports on Congo have since been submitted to the Security Council through the mechanism, each drawing attention to widespread incidents of rape and other sexual violence against children.

---

85 The formula grave, systematic and widespread is used in the text (interesting here to see how the W/S formula appears not to be enough and includes a third qualifier denoting the seriousness of the conduct).

86 AI states, "conflict [in Colombia] has also been marked by […] widespread sexual violence against girls and women", available at http://www.amnesty.ca/colombia/news/view.php?load=arcview&article=1949&c=Colombia+News, last accessed on 8 June 2011. Meanwhile the ICTJ used the formula to describe sexual violence both in Colombia and the DRC ("widespread and systematic sexual abuse of citizens has been a central and often epidemic feature of the conflict"), available at http://ictj.org/our-work/regions-and-countries/colombia, last accessed on 8 June 2011.

87 Human Rights Watch, "Soldiers Who Rape, Commanders Who Condone: Sexual Violence and Military Reform in the Democratic Republic of Congo", available at http://www.hrw.org/en/reports/2009/07/16/soldiers-who-rape-commanders-who-condone-0, last accessed on 6 May 2011.

Amnesty International followed the same tendency to transpose these terms within the same report. This trend remained constant until 2010, as other organizations continued to use both terms interchangeably, alternatively, or concomitantly.[88]

The trend among UN agencies in the DRC was to use alternative metaphors when possible, avoiding the use of W/S language. The United Nations Population Fund (UNFPA) and the OHCHR, both of them UN agencies publishing on the DRC's situation, are examples of this trend. In contrast, in Colombia the Office of the UNHCR has been using terms of the W/S formula – although interchangeably – since 2008. Thus, in its 2008 country report, the Office of the Commissioner states that sexual violence committed by the FARC is a "grave and systematic breach".[89]

Meanwhile, the trend among INGOs was to avoid using metaphors different from W/S to describe violence in the DRC and Colombia.[90] In

88 Amnesty International, "Mass Rapes in Walikale: Still a Need for Protection and Justice in Eastern Congo", available at http://www.amnesty.org/en/library/asset/AFR62/011/2010/en/6394b6fc-226b-49db-b009-36d04b178a1b/afr620112010en.pdf, last accessed on 6 May 2011 ("Since the beginning of the armed conflict in eastern DRC, tens of thousands of women and girls have been victims of systematic, as well as widespread, rape and sexual assault committed by combatants"); Harvard Humanitarian Initiative and Oxfam International, "'Now the World is Without Me': An Investigation of Sexual Violence in Eastern Democratic Republic of Congo", 2010, available at http://www.oxfam.org.uk/resources/policy/conflict_disasters/downloads/rr_sexual_violence_drc_150410.pdf, last accessed on 6 May 2011 ("Although the true extent of the sexual violence is not known, it is estimated that tens of thousands of men have been systematically raped by combatant forces. […] The war and ongoing political instability in Eastern DRC have been marked by extreme violence including widespread rape").

89 The discursive shift is toward a framing of the violence in terms of violations to international humanitarian law, but qualified with being systematic; hence it appears to be a combination of the language of the Geneva Conventions with the definition of CAH.

90 It is relevant to note that INGO's accounts include the use of the terms *widespread* and/or *systematic* to describe sexual violence specifically as well as to describe human rights violations against civilians more broadly. However, it is not rare to observe how the use of the terms in the second situation is later interpreted in other NGO accounts (both local and international) as a qualifier of sexual violence in particular. Thus, for example, in 2010 AI's report uses "widespread" not to describe the nature of SVAC exclusively, but more broadly to describe abuses against civilians by new paramilitary structures: "The successor groups are committing widespread and serious abuses, including massacres, killings, forced disappearances, rape, forced displacement, threats, extortion, kidnappings, and recruitment of children as combat-

our analysis we identified two types of metaphors. The first group uses a language of war, mainly referring to sexual violence as a weapon,[91] the weaponization of the female body,[92] and the female body as a battleground.[93] The second type of metaphors allude to what Carol Harrington has called the medicalization of the discourse of SVAC.[94] They refer to sexual violence as an epidemic[95] and/or as a plague.[96] The use of alterna-

ants". This information bite is iterated in HRW World Report chapter on Colombia: "Like previous paramilitaries, the groups engage in drug trafficking, actively recruit, and commit *widespread* abuses, including massacres, killings, *rape*, and forced displacement".

91 In 2010, the UN Committee Against Torture ('CAT') used the "rape as a weapon of war" metaphor in its concluding observations regarding Colombia: "The Committee is concerned about the high incidence of sexual violence and about its use as a weapon of war [...] The State party should adopt effective and urgent measures to eradicate sexual violence, particularly when used as a weapon of war" (Committee Against Torture, *Report of the Committee Against Torture*, United Nations, Forty-third session (2-20 November 2009) and Forty-fourth session (26 April–14 May 2010), p. 25). In 2010, Oxfam International said: "In DRC however, as in other contemporary conflicts, sexual violence is employed as a weapon of war because it is inexpensive and readily available, but still extremely effective" Harvard Humanitarian Initiative, "'Now the World is Without Me': An Investigation of Sexual Violence in Eastern Democratic Republic of Congo", available at http://www.oxfam.org.uk/resources/policy/conflict_disasters/downloads/rr_sexual_violence_drc_150410.pdf, last accessed on 4 April 2012.

92 Language used in a report published by Oxfam in Colombia in 2009 includes metaphors of instrumentalization of the female body in two ways, by means of making it a weapon of war and by means of producing terror ("terrorizing communities", "broader strategy of terror against the civilian population"), more information available at http://www.oxfam.org.uk/oxfam_in_action/where_we_work/drc.html, last accessed on 8 June 2011. In 2009, Human Rights Watch said: "Sexual violence was widespread and sometimes systematic, a weapon of war used by all sides to deliberately terrorize civilians, to exert control over them, or to punish them for perceived collaboration with the enemy", http://www.hrw.org/americas/colombia, last accessed on 8 June 2011.

93 In 2008, UNFPA said: "As warfare rages on between rebel and government groups, the violence is escalating and women's bodies have literally become a battleground" (UNFPA, "Legacy of War: An Epidemic of Sexual Violence in DRC", available at http://www.unfpa.org/public/cache/offonce/news/pid/1399;jsessionid=0D32FF5EB279C5433061BA35436ABA54, last accessed on 4 April 2012).

94 Carol Harrington, *Politicization of Sexual Violence: From Abolitionism to Peacekeeping*, Ashgate Publishing Limited, 2010, pp. 121–143.

95 In 2010, Oxfam International examined "the relationship between South Kivu's rape epidemic and the region's militarization", see http://www.oxfam.org.uk/oxfam_in_action/where_we_work/drc.html, last accessed on 8 June 2011.

tive metaphors among INGOs seemed to replace elaborate descriptions of the events of violence during the second half of the period. Graphic descriptions of particular events were a trait of SVAC public accounts during the 1990s as well as a narrative element that was later subject to criticisms because some consider it a form of pornography.[97] It is important to point out that this critique has not particularly addressed the use of metaphors in descriptions of SVAC but has focused on the "lists of graphic details"[98] used to depict the violent events.[99]

Further contrasts between Congolese and Colombian NGO narratives emerged in our observations. In the latter, the movement towards metaphoric language has tended to displace detailed descriptions while broadly reducing the amount and types of descriptors used to qualify the violence. There has been a shift towards more formulaic "bytes" of information. Meanwhile, in Colombian narratives the increasing use of W/S language[100] has been accompanied by a trend to *enhance* the descriptions by adding other adjectives to the terms widespread and systematic. This addition has been particularly visible during the second half of the period. In 2009, a report from the coalition of NGOs monitoring the enforcement of the Constitutional Court's Auto 092/2008 included the exact formula

96 In 2008, the UNFPA representative for DRC said: "Sexual violence constitutes a plague in the DRC", see UNFPA, "The Humanitarian Response Newsletter: Democratic Republic of Congo", available at http://www.unfpa.org/emergencies/ newsletter/frontlines_mar2008.pdf, last accessed on 1 May 2011.

97 Kimberly Theidon, "Gender in Transition: Common Sense, Women, and War", in *Journal of Human Rights*, 2007, vol. 6, no. 4, pp. 453–478 ("I am also not interested in presenting a list of horrors – a list of graphic details that may resemble a pornography of violence, and that may well be yet another violation of the women with whom I have worked.").

98 *Ibid.*

99 Whether or not the images that metaphors produce in these listing exercises play a role in amplifying the pornographic quality of the narrative is an issue that has not been explored in the literature.

100 It is important to bring to the foreground one of the findings of Benetech's 2011 report on SVAC in Colombia. They concluded that "the claim that sexual violence is "widespread" or "systematic" in the Colombian internal conflict may be true, but cannot be established on the basis of existing evidence". See Françoise Roth, Tamy Guberek, and Amelia Hoover Green, "Using Quantitative Data to Assess Conflict-Related Sexual Violence in Colombia: Challenges and Opportunities", available at http://www.hrdag.org/resources/publications/SV-report_2011-04-26.pdf, last accessed on 10 June 2011, p. 75.

used in the Court's decision (and was reiterated in most documents that have been published since Auto 092 came out[101]): "*habitual, widespread, systematic and invisible practice*". Formulaic language appears *enhanced* by the adjectives *habitual* and *invisible*. Qualifiers pointing to a heightened sense of strategy behind SVAC were also frequent in 2009 and 2010. For example, La Mesa's 2009 report uses the following list of adjectives to qualify the violence: premeditated, serious, recurring, known and permitted. Read together, these adjectives point to the organized nature of the violence and its inherent rationale being that of producing harm with a purpose in mind.[102]

For the purpose of the argument developed in this chapter, we were particularly interested in observing how the use of metaphoric language appeared to be transforming the narratives of sexual violence in the DRC and Colombia. In one instance, we had metaphors used by INGOs that perform an operation of synthesis by creating a representation of sexual violence usually associated with an image. We observed that in the accounts that used more metaphors, there was less recourse to lists of graphic details. Conversely, accounts that reverted to elaborate descriptions were the ones that used less metaphoric language. INGO accounts reflect the former[103] while UN accounts, the latter.[104]

101 In their 2009 report the coalition of local NGOs that monitors the enforcement of Auto 092 reiterated the statement included in the Court's decision that references the W/S formula: "In 2008 [Colombia's] Constitutional Court recognized that sexual violence against women is a *consistent, widespread, systematic and invisible* practice in the context of Colombia's armed conflict" (emphasis added). Mesa Mujer y Conflicto Armado, "IX informe sobre violencia sociopolítica contra mujeres, jóvenes y niñas en Colombia" available at http://www.mujeryconflictoarmado.org/informes/IX%20informe%20Mesa.pdf, last accessed on 5 April, 2012, pp. 62, 84.

102 The *mens rea* or subjective elements of the conduct are also key in La Mesa's analysis of violence against women as a form of torture. The elements of torture stated are the following: produces pain and physical and mental suffering; is intentionally inflicted; involves either passive or active participation of official authorities. The understanding of sexual violence as torture appears here connected to the need to prove the existence of a specific purpose to produce harm, once again, pointing to the absence of arbitrariness of the violence and instead heightening its strategic nature in the context of internal armed conflict. One could say that this is another trait of the script – to push the narrator to find some rationale in the violence, to be able to explain its purpose and finality, to be able to prove that there was the intent to harm.

103 In reference to the DRC, Human Rights Watch has used imagery focusing on sexual violence as a "weapon […] used by all sides to deliberately terrorize" that has localized war to women's "bodies", Human Rights Watch, 2009, see *supra* note 87. Oxfam

Additionally, we observed that during the second half of the period, the tendency across narratives was to reduce the use of graphic detailing of specific events and replace it with metaphoric language.[105] Even in UN accounts, where the use of W/S metaphors was almost absent, the trend displayed an overall increase in the use of metaphors. Employing the metaphoric use of ICL categories *widespread* and *systematic* was more frequent among NGOs – both local and international – who had a legal advocacy agenda aiming at the recognition and prosecution of SVAC under ICL standards. The UN, on the other hand, avoided using the same language to qualify the violence in a move that needs further exploration but exceeds the scope of this chapter.

The U.S. State Department, a key player in shaping global narratives of SVAC through its annual human rights reports and particularly in

---

International used similar metaphoric language in describing its programs targeting sexual violence in Colombia. See Oxfam International, "Sexual Violence in Colombia: Instrument of War", 2009, available at http://www.oxfam.org/en/policy/ sexual-violence-colombia, last accessed on 6 May 2011.

104 As opposed to likening it to a weapon, UNIFEM has described sexual violence as a "method of warfare". Accounts of sexual violence are more graphic, noting the "aggravated character" of rape, including examples, like "gang-rapes; rapes accompanied with torture, mutilation or branding; rapes with objects; rapes in the presence of family members; or rapes of particularly taboo categories of victim such as men, boys, and the elderly". See UNIFEM, 2010, "Addressing Conflict-Related Sexual Violence: An Analytical Inventory of Peacekeeping Practice", available at http://www.unifem.org/attachments/products/Analytical_Inventory_of_Peacekeeping_Practice_online.pdf, last accessed on 6 May 2011.

105 It is worth noting that we do not argue that these trends are mutually exclusive. For example, NGOs sometimes combine metaphors, W/S categories and are more or less descriptive in their narratives of SVAC. Our point is that those narratives that frequently use metaphors tend to use less descriptive language. A more nuanced analysis of the interaction of these dynamics could be the object of further exploration, but exceeds the purpose of this chapter. For some actors, for example grassroots NGOs, the use of one strategy tends to give place to a combination of the multiple elements in what appears to be an attempt to amplify the denouncing effect by combining all available narrative resources. As an illustration of the point we are trying to make, we found that two local NGOs in DRC, Panzi Hospital and HEAL Africa, describe sexual violence in the "Background" sections of their websites in mostly comparable ways. Both sites exclusively refer to women as victims, while also using W/S metaphors ("rape has been systematically used as a weapon of war") as well as other metaphoric language ("abusing women as an instrument of war"). On the other hand, while Panzi Hospital refrains from using either "widespread" or "systematic" to describe SVAC, HEAL Africa uses both terms interchangeably.

the case of the DRC since Hillary Clinton became Secretary of State,[106] is an illustrative example of a narrative that is highly scripted according to the elements of the dominant narrative of SVAC. Their storyline has been the most consistent one throughout the period, particularly in relation to the use of both metaphoric language and the terms of the W/S formula.[107]

The move towards an increasing use of metaphors in UN and INGO accounts has also permeated international mediatized accounts of SVAC.[108] Parallel analysis of journalistic sources brings to the foreground the ways in which the move from descriptive to metaphoric language permeated popular press descriptions of SVAC in the DRC and facilitated the condensation and synthesizing of information in shorter *bites.*[109] Met-

---

106 During the Obama administration, Hillary Clinton has become an outspoken advocate of ending SVAC in DRC. During a 2009 visit to a SVAC survivors' clinic and a refugee camp in Goma, Clinton made a speech that was widely quoted in the NYT, BBC, and AFP ("It is almost impossible to describe the level of suffering"; "Eastern Congo's rape epidemic, she added, is just horrific"; "We believe there can be more done to protect civilians while you are trying to kill and capture insurgents"; "We believe there should be no impunity for the sexual and gender-based violence committed by so many and that there must be arrests, prosecutions and punishments.").

107 The main deviation from the storyline was the inclusion in the 2010 DRC report of men as victims of SVAC. For a more detailed analysis of victimhood in narratives of SVAC, see *supra* section 13.2.1.

108 All of the press sources consulted over the four years (with the exceptions of AFP in 2008 and IRIN in 2010) used catchphrases that employed metaphoric language to narrate the situation of SVAC in DRC. Among these metaphors, most of them are the same ones used in UN and INGO accounts ("rape as a weapon of war", "rape epidemic", "the battleground is women's bodies", "sexual terrorism") but they also include other metaphors such as "rape capital of the world", "hunting women", and "rape mines of the world".

109 Mediatized accounts (press articles) from the beginning of the period (particularly 2007) are distinct from those located towards the end (2009–2010). In the latter, sexual violence tends to be portrayed in a broader and more elaborate description of cultural contexts and specificities of armed conflict dynamics in the country. The loss of detail and specificity in descriptive language in the following three years can be explained – at least partially – by two distinct but related phenomena. On the one hand, the existence of a wider variety of available metaphors that condense information; and on the other, the fact that these metaphors have informed public consciousness on the topic and so less explanatory *bites* are needed as the audience becomes more familiar with the terms used by the press.

aphors were used throughout the four-year period by the press,[110] though the terms used were not consistent during that period.[111] Iteration plays a large part in turning a new metaphor into a mainstream catchphrase to describe SVAC in journalistic accounts; during the second half of the period, the same metaphors appeared to be repeated with more frequency. For example, the terms widespread and systematic only appeared in five of the 30 press articles reviewed for the 2007–2009 period. Conversely, in 2010, four of the nine articles reviewed used that language.[112]

13.3. Part II: Social Science Literature and the Reshaping of SVAC Narratives

In Part I we argued how at least four elements (victimhood, perpetration, categorization of the violence, and use of metaphoric language) of public accounts of SVAC are observable over time in local and international accounts of sexual violence in the DRC and Colombia. Despite variation and transformation in language used by different sources over time, we also identified several trends in the sources examined – particularly the move towards totalizing narratives of SVAC. We observed how these narrative patterns exist despite drastic variations in frequency and intensity between the cases. Finally, we explored convergences and divergences across narratives in order to bring to the foreground how dominant repre-

[110] Each year, at least half of the articles reviewed included metaphors. 2007 and 2009 had the highest number of articles with metaphors, with six of the ten reviewed articles using them.

[111] The most consistent metaphor repeated over the four years was "weapon of war"; 13 of the 39 articles reviewed included that term in some form, including variations like "weapon of terror", "tool of war", and "deliberate weapon". This phrase was more common in 2007 and trailed off with only one mention in 2010. The opposite trend happened for the most common phrase in 2010, which were metaphors related to location. Three of the five publications used the term "rape capitol of the world", with a fourth publication saying, "the sexual violence in Congo the worst in the world."

[112] BBC News, 2010, see *supra* note 12 ("This incident stands out because of the extraordinarily cold-blooded and systematic way in which it appears to have been planned and executed."); Agence France Presse, "DR Congo mass rapes 'defy belief': UN", 24 September 2010 ("This incident stands out because of the extraordinarily cold-blooded and systematic way in which it appears to have been planned and executed."). Agence France Presse, 5 October 2010, "Sexual violence can destroy DR Congo: UN official" ("Widespread rape."); IRIN, 2010, see *supra* note 12 ("Widespread use of sexual violence against civilians.").

sentations of SVAC prevail regardless of the frequency and intensity of the violence in each setting.

In this section, we offer an interpretation of how social science literature is reshaping narratives and representations of SVAC. Since other authors in this volume will present a review of social science literature to date, we chose to frame our analysis around four topics – pattern-based research; overstating the absence of data; documenting variation; blurring of peacetime-wartime distinctions – that come to the foreground during the analysis. Each topic illustrates specific ways in which SVAC narratives analyzed in Part I of this chapter stand in tension – and often times in contradiction – with current social science research.

Through rigorous methods of data collection and analysis, social science researchers are increasingly providing prosecutors of sexual violence with tools to produce evidence.[113] This fact was at the core of the conversation that took place under the auspices of the Forum for International Criminal and Humanitarian Law (FICHL) in New Haven in October 2010, when social science researchers and legal practitioners discussed the potential of social science research in the production of evidentiary methods and data for holding leaders accountable for sexual violence committed as war crime, a crime against humanity or genocide. What happens then when efforts to prove sexual violence as an international crime using social science methods or data stand in tension *vis-à-vis* dominant elements for narrating and representing sexual violence in war? Stemming from that discussion, we attempt to offer an interpretation of how current social science research is interrogating dominant SVAC narratives produced both inside and outside courtrooms.

13.3.1. Pattern-Based Research

The identification of patterns is a legally relevant issue among prosecutors seeking to prove that sexual violence has been systematic or widespread in a particular setting or within a particular group.[114] In Xabier Agirre's

[113] Xabier Agirre Aranburu, "Sexual Violence beyond Reasonable Doubt: Using Pattern Evidence and Analysis for International Cases", in *Law and Social Inquiry*, 2010, vol. 35, no. 4, pp. 855–879.

[114] The following excerpt is from a summary of Xabier Agirre's comments at the Hague Colloquium: "To do that [successfully prosecute those responsible], said I.C.C. Senior analyst Xabier Agirre, it is necessary to take three steps: to get a level of description of the patterns of a crime; then, to correlate the crime with the working of the com-

words, "it is necessary to take three steps: to get a level of description of the patterns of a crime; then, to correlate the crime with the working of the command structures that produced it; then to explain what caused it". Agirre's efforts have focused on establishing patterns within a particular conflict by a particular armed group, and often by a group under a particular commander. This project differs from a trend that we have identified across SVAC narratives in Colombia and the DRC, namely the tendency to believe that traits of sexual violence in a specific setting only become patterns when they are proven to occur in other locales.

The need to prove patterns is not explicitly included in any definition of crimes against humanity or crimes of war. Nonetheless, dominant SVAC narratives tend to bring to the foreground those cases that *look like* those committed in other settings. We believe this interpretation of the need to prove patterns is connected to the misreading of legal categories such as "widespread" and "systematic". In such accounts, the impulse to legitimate the gravity of SVAC by comparing it to the same phenomenon in other settings fails to be balanced with more nuanced understandings of what it means to prove a pattern and the extent to which patterns will vary across warring countries.[115]

As Amelia Hoover Green poignantly stated during her presentation in New Haven, "in cases that are not Rwanda or Bosnia, patterns vary with a large degree". The idea shared among social science researchers that "levels and patterns of sexual violence vary not only across conflicts, but also within the same conflict over time and across space"[116] stands in tension *vis-à-vis* the dominant trend in SVAC narratives to narrow pattern-based research to comparisons across countries (and particularly taking the Rwandan, Yugoslav and Congolese cases as templates of compari-

mand structures that produced it; then to explain what caused it. To establish the gravity of the crime, he said, we need descriptive statistics to show that the crime is grave, that its scope warrants the intervention of the International Criminal Court which intends to take on only the most serious cases" (American Bar Foundation, "Hague Conference: Social Science Research Seen To Play Key Role In Building Institutions of International Criminal Law", available at http://www.americanbarfoundation.org/news/192, last accessed on 4 April 2012.

115 Kathryn Farr, "No Escape: Sexual Violence against Women and Girls in Central and Eastern African Armed Conflicts", *Deportate, esuli, profughe* (DEP), 2010, no. 13–14, pp. 85–112.

116 Michele Leiby, "Why Soldiers Rape: Wartime Sexual Violence in Latin America", Ph.D. dissertation, University of New Mexico, 2004.

son). During her presentation at the seminar, Inger Skjelsbaek also formulated the importance of distinguishing between the Bosnia and Kosovo conflicts (two different parts of the former Yugoslavia). What is particularly relevant from Inger's statement is that she is pointing to the need to investigate patterns while remaining sensitive to variations in the occurrence of SVAC both at the subnational level and across countries.[117]

If patterns vary with large degree within the same conflict, narratives based on the assumption that patterns can be equated to similarities between sexual violence in the DRC and Colombia will be prone to occlude relevant instances of violence.[118] As Benetech's recently published report on SVAC in Colombia[119] has suggested, the usefulness of statistical indirect evidence depends on the scope of the hypothesis one seeks to generate from the data collected. Thus, when we focus on localized hypothesis of patterning, the stories that emerge either through numbers or qualitative evidence, even when trying to prove patterns, are quite different.

117 Skjelsbæk, Inger, "Outlining a Psychological Research Agenda on Gender and Violence in Peace and Conflict Studies", paper presented at the International Studies Addociation 49th Annual Convention, "Bridging Multiple Divides", 26 March 2008 ("This approach leads to two overarching research questions which can be said to constitute the core of a psychological research agenda in the field, namely the following; (1) How do gender differences and variations on individual and societal levels lead to different manifestations and transformations of war-related violence; and, conversely, (2) how do different forms of war-related violence lead to manifestations and transformations of gender differences and variations on individual and societal levels. In other words a psychological research agenda in this particular field will be characterized by an integrative approach bridging conceptualizations of the individual and the social in order to understand the political").

118 For example, when the pattern investigated is sexual violence against women and girls, the absence of male victimization is particularly acute. This is precisely what we observed in the reports of local NGOs in Colombia.

119 Roth, Guberek and Hoover Green, see *supra* note 100 ("Patterns of sexual violence in Colombia appear to be extremely complex and heterogeneous, although the heterogeneity in the true patterns of sexual violence cannot be definitively distinguished from variations in the reporting. Assessing, and in some cases acknowledging, this heterogeneity is among the most difficult tasks facing human rights advocates in Colombia. As we document above, Colombian organizations have collected a significant amount of data, documenting a number of contexts in which sexual violence occurs. However, not all of these contexts can be tied to conflict, or even to armed actors. In consequence, we can say little regarding national trends or comparisons".).

13.3.2. Overstating the Absence of Data

"Sexual violence, in wartime or in peacetime, is among the most notoriously difficult forms of violence to measure".[120] Underreporting of sexual violence is frequently cited as the reason that it is impossible to collect reliable data regarding the frequency and intensity of sexual violence during conflict. Underreporting is also invoked in order to explain the high levels of impunity. However, explanatory frameworks for sexual violence in war that focus on underreporting are based on the assumption that women's reporting of their cases is the only way to get evidence of it actually happening. As Kimberly Theidon has noted, this statement also places a burden on women as bearers of the responsibility to articulate the narratives that rebuild the memory of sexual violence in the context of armed conflict.[121] On the other hand, Benetech has expressed critical views on the overinterpretation of data on under-registration and framed this trend as "a symptom of a broader impulse to overinterpret data".[122] They express concern about using such powerful statistical and quasi-statistical claims as merely means of argumentation, which "may profoundly affect policy interventions and, via policy interventions, the lives of individuals".[123]

Despite challenges associated with getting reliable data, cases at both the low and high-end of the SVAC spectrum have been documented. Research by social scientists has illustrated how the absence of data ensuing from underreporting can be countered through the inclusion of indirect or secondary indicators of sexual violence.[124] In her chapter, "The Promise and Peril of Primary Documents" in this book, Leiby examines novel ways to examine sexual violence in conflict through archival research. She advocates for techniques that will add texture and detail to reporting of SVAC, including: better capturing multiple violations against one individual; more closely investigating language used in reporting of

[120] *Ibid.*

[121] Theidon, 2007 See *supra* note 99.

[122] Roth, Guberek and Green, see *supra* note 100, p. 59.

[123] *Ibid.*

[124] See for example P. Jennings and S. Swiss, "Statistical information on violence against women during the Liberian civil war", in *Statistics, Development, and Human Rights: Proceedings of the International Association of Official Statistics*, Switzerland, 2000; S. Swiss and J.E. Giller, "Rape as a Crime of War. A Medical Perspective", Journal of the American Medical Association, 1993, vol. 270, no. 5, pp. 612–615.

violations; re-examining who counts as a victims; and concretizing the definitions around sexual violence, sexual torture and sexual humiliation.[125]

Another strategy being explored in this field is the use of perpetrator-related data. For instance, researchers can examine how troop movements or data indicating troop movements may correlate with observed changes in patterns of sexual violence.[126] In addition, interviews with current and former combatants, while posing a myriad of challenges, can illuminate some of the ways that violence is viewed and acted out in armed groups.[127] In the case of the DRC, Maria Stern and Maria Eriksson Baaz were one of the first to bring our attention to the voices of perpetrators.[128] Their groundbreaking report "The Complexity of Violence: A Critical Analysis of Sexual Violence in DRC" published in 2010 "critically explores and convincingly challenges existing stereotypes and narratives about the nature of sexual violence in conflict settings".[129]

---

125 See Michele Leiby's chapter in the present volume.

126 Hoover Green. See *supra* note 3.

127 Kelly, Jocelyn, "Rape in War: Motives of Militia in DRC", available at http://www.usip.org/publications/rape-in-war-motives-militia-in-drc, last accessed on 8 June 2011; see also Cohen, see *supra* note 37.

128 Maria Eriksson Baaz and Maria Stern, "Making Sense of Violence: Voices of Soldiers in the Congo (DRC)", *The Journal of Modern African Studies*, 2008, vol. 46, no. 1, p. 57 (Their critical take on the silence of perpetrators is twofold, on the one hand, it limits our understanding of sexual violence itself, but it also contributes to reinforcing stereotypes about African armed conflict. In their own words this "silence is problematic not only because it limits the ability to understand the violence, but also because the silence itself tends to reinforce the stereotypes of African warring described above. Importantly, our intention is not to offer a reading of how soldiers 'really are' or the 'true' reasons behind violent acts, but to show how the stories of these soldiers unsettle familiar and dominant narratives of Congolese soldiers and combatants, not only in popular media, but also in academic depictions of African warring as somehow chaotic, barbaric, 'traditional' and self-explanatory. We therefore pay attention to the ways in which soldiers seek to make sense of the violence in which they have participated, in recounting their experiences to us".); see also Maria Eriksson Baaz and Maria Stern, "Why Do Soldiers Rape? Masculinity, Violence, and Sexuality in the Armed Forces in the Congo (DRC)", *International Studies Quarterly*, 2009, vol. 53, no. 2, p. 495.

129 By identifying forms of conflict-related violence, and explaining the role of various complex factors, it draws attention to the need for a more nuanced understanding of sexual violence, including its invisible victims. See Maria Eriksson Baaz, and Maria Stern, *La Complexité De La Violence: Analyse Critique Des Violences Sexuelles En*

The absence of reference to male victimization in dominant narratives of SVAC is not simply the byproduct of the absence of data.[130] For example, data from a 2010 population-based study in eastern DRC supports the importance of registering the experiencing of male victimization – 23.6% of randomly sampled men reported experiencing sexual violence.[131] In Colombia, according to the National Forensic Medicine Institute the number of men experiencing sexual violence in 2008 was significant (15%).[132] Evidence of sexualized violence against men may be found in existing data coded under different categories. Torture of men in detention can classify as sexualized violence (for example insertion of objects into a man's anus, forced nudity, forced masturbation). In Colombia, research by social researchers has shown how cases of men who had been victims of sexualized violence during episodes of torture by armed groups (particularly state security forces) had been coded in NGO and government databases for human rights violations as torture.[133]

A striking example of this is found in Leiby's work re-coding data from two Latin American countries. Through her re-analysis of primary documents collected through Truth Commissions, she found that the majority of victims of sexual violence in El Salvador were men (53%) and in Peru, one-fifth of victims were men – a smaller but still substantial proportion. These numbers are in stark contrast to the official Truth Commissions reports in each country, which used the same data but concluded that in El Salvador and Peru, the rates of male victimization were less that 1% and 2%, respectively. In this case, the disparity between these numbers can partially be explained by overly-specific definitions of what constituted sexual violence. In her chapter, Leiby notes these numbers show

République Démocratique Du Congo (RDC), Nordiska Afrikainstitutet, Uppsala, 2011.

130 See *infra* Part II of the chapter, where we further analyze the problematic of overstating the absence of data.

131 Susan A Bartels, Jennifer A Scott, Denis Mukwege, Robert I Lipton, Michael J VanRooyen and Jennifer Leaning, "Research Patterns of Sexual Violence in Eastern Democratic Republic of Congo: Reports from Survivors Presenting to Panzi Hospital in 2006", in *Conflict and Health*, 2010, vol. 4, no. 9.

132 INML, see *supra* note 21.

133 Viviana Quintero, "Capitulo II del Informe de Memoria Historica sobre Genero y Conflicto Armado en el Caribe Colombiano", available at http://www.scribd.com/doc/50835006/46036778-Memoria-en-Tiempos-de-Guerra, last accessed on 8 June 2011.

"that men are more often the targets of sexual violence than previously reported and that, unlike women, men are more often the victims of sexual humiliation, mutilation, and torture than rape or gang rape".[134]

These findings illuminate the extent to which questions may asked, or data may be coded, in a way that leads to confirmation of our assumptions – in this case that only women are victims and only men are perpetrators. In both Colombia and the DRC, the process of inclusion or exclusion of male victimization from narratives needs further investigation. The studies examined here are examples of the way that data can be re-examined and primary and secondary sources can be leveraged to gain new and sometimes unexpected knowledge about SVAC.

13.3.3. Documentation of Variation

"Wartime rape occurs in some scenarios but not in others" – this statement by Ines Alberdi[135] is from 2010. Less than a decade ago, arguments for the variation of sexual violence in war were not frequent, much less popular.[136] This is partly due to the role feminist theories have played in providing and explanatory framework for the phenomenon of SVAC. Indeed, feminist theory has been characterized by explaining this violence through a continuum approach, that is, SVAC is a part of the continuum of violence women endure throughout their lives, whether in times of war or peace. In our comparative reading of narratives in the DRC and Colombia, we observed how the continuum approach has played an important role in defining the identification of males with perpetrators and females with victims. Although tracing the influence of feminist theory in SVAC narratives is beyond the scope of this chapter, noting how this particular explanatory framework for sexual violence has permeated specific accounts proves relevant in trying to understand the absence or presence

[134] Leiby, see *supra* note 125.

[135] Alberdi is the Executive Director of UNIFEM.

[136] Today variation plays an important role in destabilizing the idea of SVAC as inevitable, thus in 2011 the ICRC produced this statement on occasion of International Women's Day: "The widespread perception of sexual violence against women as inevitable in armed conflict is wrong, the International Committee of the Red Cross (ICRC) said today. In the run-up to International Women's Day on 8 March, the ICRC is calling on States and other entities not to relent in their efforts to prevent rape and other forms of sexual violence that harm the lives and dignity of countless women in conflict zones around the world every year".

of men and boys in specific narratives. For example, in Colombia, Oxfam's 2009[137] and 2010[138] reports illustrate the engagement of particular INGOs with the theory of continuity of violence against women[139] and how this particular template impedes the consideration of men as victims of sexual violence.

SVAC narratives grounded on feminist theories have been vocal when criticizing gender-neutrality. The core of their claim is that gender plays a determinant role in defining women as victims of sexual violence. Social science research that documents variation does not deny the underlying argument, that is, the gendered dimensions of SVAC and the patterns of female victimization. However, social scientists have pointed out an element that remains absent from narratives grounded on the continuity approach. They are transforming narratives by means of bringing to the foreground the gendered dimensions of SVAC when males are victims by documenting variation in patterns of victimization (i) between men and women, and (ii) between different groups of men.

Accounts grounded on the feminist doctrine of continuity argue against gender neutrality by maintaining that SVAC is perpetrated by men against women *because* they are women, and that women are victims of multiple forms of sexualized violence across space and time. In terms of this trend, social science arguments are pushing for a different argument against gender neutrality. One that acknowledges how male victimization – despite being less frequent – is also rendered invisible by means of denying that SVAC is perpetrated by men and women against men *because* they are men. An example of such narratives is found in the report published in 2009 by Medica Mondiale, which critically revisits the prosecution of sexualized violence at the ICTY.[140]

---

137 Paula San Pedro, "Sexual Violence in Colombia: Instrument of War", available at http://www.oxfam.org/sites/www.oxfam.org/files/bp-sexual-violence-colombia.pdf, last accessed on 5 May 2011.

138 "Sexual Violence in Colombia: First Survey of Prevalence in Spanish", available at http://publications.oxfam.org.uk/display.asp?k=e2010121610383507&sort=sort_date/d&sf1=cat_class&st1=630&ds=Conflict%20%26%20Security&m=9&dc=357, last accessed on 11 May 2011.

139 In the case of Oxfam, this might be explained by the fact that the two local NGOs that are its main partners in Colombia are the two most vocal advocates of the continuum theory among NGOs working on women's rights in the country.

140 Medica Mondiale, ... *And that it Does Not Happen to Anyone Anywhere Else in the World*, 2009, p. 32.

> Charging male and female sexualized assault as gender-neutral carries the danger that the specific gendered patterns of sexualized war violence and the possible legal implications escape prosecution. This might be important, for example, for the question of the "foreseeability" of rape, which can be crucial in particular in determining the responsibility of high-ranking leaders [...]
>
> As the Report of the Expert Commission had pointed out and as the facts in some indictments show, the gendered pattern of sexualized assaults on men differed significantly from sexualized attacks against women or girls.[141]

Documentation of variation is transforming the production and interpretation of narratives of sexualized violence in war at multiple levels: first, by proposing a critique of gender-neutrality as a pervasive approach for the prosecution of cases that involve either men or women as victims of sexual violence (and not just women); second, by highlighting that documenting differences between gendered patterns of sexualized assaults on men/boys *vis-à-vis* women/girls are as relevant for combating impunity and promoting foreseability as the documentation of continuity across sexualized attacks against women or girls; third, by interpreting as relevant the continuity across patterns of victimization of men that remains occluded in dominant narratives (such as the report written by the Commission of Experts in the Bosnian case); and fourth, by using distinctions

[141] Contrary to what was often written about rape in this war, most of the incidents brought before the ICTY (and to date before the WCC) did not happen in open public spaces, not even necessarily in front of other persons. However, all of the indicted sexualized attacks on men took place in the presence of other prisoners as well as camp guards or soldiers watching. Not surprisingly, none of these cases involves penetration of a male detainee by a captor. The most common kind of sexualized assault against men is either genital mutilation or forcing male prisoners to commit fellatio with each other. The public character of these acts is essential because of the symbolic homosexualisation of the victimised man which is witnessed by others. Symbolic homosexualisation and feminisation can also be achieved through penetration as the sociologist Dubravka Zarkov notes in ... *And that it Does Not Happen to Anyone Anywhere Else in the World*, Medica Mondiale, 2009, at p. 32: "in the Balkan context, [...] there is a difference between these 2 acts of violence. While castration is a symbolic appropriation of the male's phallic power, rape is not. In Balkan norms of sexuality, both men involved in the sexual act are homosexualized. Thus, the drastic difference in the acts of sexual violence performed by the camp guards and the prisoners themselves [...] It seems that prison guards have mutilated and assaulted male prisoners with foreign objects in public, but have not raped them in public".

in circumstances, and modes of perpetration to bring to the foreground how the gendered objectives served by SVAC against men vary and cannot be reduced to feminization (for example the distinction between homosexualization and feminization).

As described in Part I, we observe the absence of variation in dynamics of perpetration as another trait in which current narratives of SVAC resist the variation theory. For example, in Colombia there has been a tendency not to differentiate between armed actors in local NGO[142] accounts; this is the "*all parties in conflict*" formula. Meanwhile, UN agencies (exemplified by UNHCHR reports for 2008, 2009 and 2010) have utilized a detailed list of the different actors involved, but do not distinguish perpetration dynamics across groups or within them (that is, between different structures within one group).

The work of Elisabeth Wood has played an important role in shifting the emphasis of analysis from continuity to variation.[143] Placed within Woods spectrum of variation, the Colombian and Congolese cases fall on different ends of the spectrum in terms of a number of variables. The Congolese case is considered as a high prevalence conflict, while the Colombian case is a low to moderate prevalence one. Making such a statement has material implications when it comes to prioritizing resources for the investigation and prosecution of the crimes, as well as funding initiatives to promote research, legal and policy reform, and advocacy in favor of victims. The Congolese case is redefining what we understand as a high-prevalence conflict. By doing so, it is also redefining the distribution of energy and resources all along the spectrum, leaving cases like Colombia's without much option but to argue in favor of the similarities between both cases (thus renouncing the variation/distinction theory).

Totalization remains a constant discursive move across the master narrative. The tendency to use totalizing language when referring to perpetrators (for example the military tactics of all armed groups involved in the conflict) accompanies formulaic jargon and metaphoric language. One could argue that one of the effects of using this language of gravity has been a move towards a narrative structure that privileges a set of moves:

---

[142] "La Mesa Reiterates the Generalization of All Parties Using Sexualized Violence against Women", available at http://www.cidh.oas.org/annualrep/2009eng/Chap.V.4.htm, last accessed on 8 June 2011.

[143] Wood, 2006, see *supra* note 3.

totalization (over specificity), and metaphors and formulaic language (over characterization). This is connected to the continuity theory in which SVAC is portrayed as continuous through time and across actors in a national conflict (that is, on spatial and temporal axes of continuity).

13.3.4. Peacetime/Wartime Distinctions

The blurring of peacetime/wartime distinctions in narratives of SVAC is a trend that needs to be understood in its relation to the continuum approach described above. Among our observations, we concluded that peacetime and wartime distinctions tend to be scarce in accounts produced by NGOs that argue in favor of the descriptions which emphasize the continuity of sexual violence from pre-conflict to conflict settings. In these accounts, what prevails is the understanding of a difference in degree and intensity of the violence, as well as changes in its purpose.[144]

We argue that in Colombia, the blurring of peacetime/wartime distinctions is also linked to the conceptual framing of sexual violence as domestic violence. This strategy serves the purpose of making the argument of continuity, that is, suggesting that sexual violence as a part of internal armed conflict is first and foremost a manifestation of the deterioration of violence against women in the family. However, as Benetech argued in its 2011 report, "using domestic violence statistics to analyze sexual violence may lead to substantial misinterpretations".[145] Arguing for

---

[144] See Wilches Ivonne, "Lo que hemos aprendido sobre la atención a mujeres víctimas de violencia sexual en el conflicto armado colombiano", Revista de Estudios Socioculturales, Agosto, 2010. In this author's explanatory framework, the importance of the use of the formula lies in the possibility of making a point about the non-isolated nature of sexual violence cases in Colombia. Instead, it is portrayed as being used *intentionally* "with a purpose within war itself". Wilches presents the specific purposes that sexual violence serves in the country's ongoing conflict: to exercise violence against women pointed out as collaborators, informants or lovers of the enemy armed group; heighten the violence exercised in massacres against civilian population; disempower feminine figures of authority and female leaders within a community; and make the presence of the armed group evident in zones of occupation.

[145] Roth, Guberek and Green, see *supra* note 100, p. 20 ("There is no doubt that sexual violence and other types of domestic violence (*e.g.*, battering, psychological abuse, and so on) frequently co-occur, or that domestic sexual violence is common in Colombia and should be considered 'an endemic pathology'" (Interview, Oriéntame, Bogotá, January 2010). However, researchers hoping to fully understand sexual violence in Colombia must look beyond the domestic context, and consider the relationship between the frames that guide data gathering processes and the patterns that ap-

the continuity of peacetime to wartime sexual violence is an important statement for local feminists who are advocating for the VAW agenda. However, careful social science research continues to reveal the fragility of this explanatory framework for explaining and predicting high levels of SVAC.

It is true that in Colombia the distinction between sexual violence against women in times of peace and times of conflict might prove irrelevant given the fact that conflict has been present since the second half of the 20th century. However, we argue that the blurring of this distinction in public narrative serves a different purpose and should be scrutinized. In the DRC, the conflict has also been protracted (lasting for over two decades), making it difficult to go back to draw distinctions between "peacetime" and "wartime" sexual violence. However, in the DRC, many advocates, programmers and researchers assume that the sexual violence seen in the conflict is a straightforward reflection of women's poor status in society before the war. However, this "cultural" explanation is overly simplistic and does not stand up to further research.[146]

In fact, data emerging about the nature of SVAC in the DRC reveals telling differences between types of violence perpetrated before and during conflict. As an illustrative example, 60% of women treated for rape at a regional hospital reported gang rape with sometimes up to ten assailants.[147] In focus groups with Congolese civilians in eastern DRC, respondents repeatedly emphasize that these highly violent forms of rape were "brought" with the war.[148] This is not to say that sexual violence was absent in the DRC pre-conflict, but that armed groups brought forms of violence that were substantially different from anything that occurred pre-conflict. In this case, SVAC cannot easily be characterized as exacerbated

pear in the resulting data. Even in the domestic context, the extent to which armed conflict affects ostensibly "private" violence is unknown, and has not been a major focus of research".

146 Dara Kay Cohen discusses this argument in terms of the Sierra Leone context in her paper, "Explaining Sexual Violence during Civil War: Evidence from the Sierra Leone War (1991–2002)", prepared for the 2007 Annual Meeting of the American Political Science Association, Chicago, Illinois, 16 August 2007.

147 Harvard Humanitarian Initiative and Oxfam International, see *supra* note 88.

148 Kelly, Kabanga, Cragin, Alcayna-Stevens, Haider, and Vanrooyen, "'If your husband doesn't humiliate you, other people won't': Gendered attitudes towards sexual violence in eastern Democratic Republic of Congo", in *Global Public Health: An International Journal for Research, Policy and Practice*, 9 June 2011.

forms of previously existing violence, but rather as new and unprecedented abuses.

Indeed, many contexts exhibit forms of SVAC that are qualitatively distinct from peacetime sexual violence. Unique forms of sexual violence that present in war include: rape of women of all ages, including the very young and very old; forced incest; use of weapons or foreign objects to carry out the rape; rape in public (in front of family or community members); forced impregnation; sexual slavery and impunity for the perpetrators.[149] The continuity argument, which calls on gender subordination and culturally condoned violence against women to explain why wartime rape happens, cannot adequately account for why some forms of SVAC occur that are taboo in most cultures, including forced incest and rape in public among others. It is also worth investigating why there are attempts to examine sexual violence in this way while other forms of conflict-related violence are not subjected to continuity arguments. As Cohen notes, "scholars who study wartime killing are rarely asked to calculate rates of pre-war murder to determine if the culture was especially murderous before the outbreak of conflict".[150]

Some forms of SVAC may in fact be driven by higher rates of peacetime violence, because of increasing impunity and because the opportunity to commit sexual violence is heightened, among other reasons. Other forms of SVAC, however, may be unique to conflict, and can have the aim of terrorizing and subjugating populations. In most contexts, it is true that sexual violence can be exacerbated by women's low status in society and lack of access to punitive systems. While it is important to understand the pre-conflict environment and to examine to what extent it can be used as an explanatory framework, it is also important to acknowledge unique features of SVAC in some conflicts. Just as continuity may inform the ways violence transforms from times of peace to times of conflict, we must also examine how violence changes from conflict to post-conflict periods. For instance, high rates of violence in post-conflict periods may continue through the diffusion of forms of abuse from combatants to civilians, through the demobilization of combatants who continue to exhibit violence behavior, through violent behavior that manifests as a result of war trauma and through other pathways.

---

149 Claudia Card, "Rape as a Weapon of War", in *Hypatia,* 1996, vol. 11, no. 4, pp. 5–18.

150 Personal e-mail communication, 20 May 2011.

13.4. Conclusion

This chapter is an attempt to explore how the "tale of two conflicts" has played out in the amphitheater of new global attention towards, and in efforts to respond to, sexual violence in conflict. In Part I, we investigated narratives from the United Nations, the U.S. and national governments, international NGOs, local organizations and the popular media as they related to the conflicts in Colombia and the DRC. In Part II, we examined how new trends in social science, including recognition of the variation of sexual violence both within and across conflicts, the use of new sources of data, and a more fine-grained understanding of patterns of violence, have brought dominant narratives under scrutiny.

In the readings of the Colombian and DRC cases, we find a recounting of sometimes one-dimensional tales of SVAC. A dominant discourse emerges in both cases despite significant differences in the nature, frequency and intensity of the violence. However, we do find texture within how different players emphasize different aspects of SVAC – often as fits best with their own strategic mission. The UN may avoid language that implicates the international community with a responsibility to respond and may retreat from extremely shocking portrayal of violence. In sharp contrast, popular media can sensationalize extreme cases of rape. International NGOs may take a similar tack for different reasons, trying to emphasize the brutality of a conflict while playing on the sympathy of readers to provoke a response from either the population or policy makers to address the problem.

The victim/perpetrator dichotomy remains at the heart of the dominant discourse. Monstrous perpetrators rape helpless women and girls, creating a simple and emotive moral allegory. The result is a narrative that may occlude the complex reality of violence in war and its changes through time. In the DRC, a 2010 population based study has found remarkably high rates of male victims of sexual violence – with almost a quarter of men reporting this abuse.[151] In Colombia, although one report from the National Forensic Medicine Institute (INML) in 2007 found that 15% of victims were male, hardly any discussion of male victims of rape emerged in the following years. These victims do not fall within an easy understanding of rape in war and so are often left out of reporting, policies and programs.

---

[151] Johnson *et al.*, 2010, see *supra* note 20.

The same 2010 population-based report in the DRC found high rates of female perpetration of sexual violence in the DRC. In Colombia, women have achieved high rank, and sometimes make up a significant proportion of combatants in some groups. However, no attention has been placed on the role of these women in the perpetration, or suppression, of sexual violence. This fits within the broader trend of non-differentiation between perpetrators of violence. In the current understanding, armed men (and to some extent men in general) are *all equally* perpetrators of crime. Similarly, no distinction is made between the behaviors of different armed groups within the same conflict. This is what we call the "*all parties in conflict*" formula – totalizing language is used to refer to perpetrators, barring us from taking a more nuanced and detailed understanding of perpetration.

In both the Colombia and DRC cases, the description of types of violence being used became more detailed and specific after the first year. In both countries, narratives in 2007 put emphasis on the fact that rape and sexual violence were occurring, while remaining general about the types of abuses. In Colombia, it was not until 2009 that the UN, advocacy organizations and local NGOs began specifying types of sexual violence, including trafficking, forced prostitution, sexual slavery, forced pregnancy, forced abortion, and crimes of honor. In the DRC, sexual violence came to be described in ways that emphasize the most atrocious and inhuman cases of rape, leading to an "escalation" – not of violence, but of the *types of violence that must be detailed* in order to shock the international community into a response. The term "rape pornography" has been coined to describe the graphic and detailed ways that sexual violence in war is sometimes portrayed. Anecdotes like this push a rise in lurid narrative – making all cases of conflict compete to seem as terrible as the next to vie for attention and funding. Perhaps to retreat from this trend, later years saw graphic details replaced by echoing of certain metaphors and phrases to symbolize sexual violence in conflict.

The fortification, reiteration and dissemination of these formulas emerge strongly in the analysis. Terms like "weapon of war", "epidemic of violence", "plague", "women's bodies as battlegrounds", and "widespread and systematic" are brought into play. While the trajectory of the "widespread and systematic" formula is different for each country, the same language is used to describe very different phenomena.

In Part II, we explore how some of the key assumptions that sustain the dominant narrative of SVAC are being reshaped by new trends in social science research. The identification of patterns of sexual violence in conflict is fundamental to prosecution of sex crimes, just as it is key to advocating for the allocation of resources for programming and policy. However, the definitions of, motivations behind, and concepts of "systematic and widespread" are considerably different in the popular versus the legal definitions. There is an impulse to legitimate the gravity of SVAC by comparing it to the same phenomenon in other settings. However, this impulse to draw similarities and prove patterns across different cases entails the risk of masking crucial differences.

New methods, tools, and sources of information are bringing to light novel ways of characterizing SVAC and challenging the trope that no accurate data exists on sexual violence during conflicts. The result is that the tendency to "totalize" concepts of perpetration, victimization and motivations for violence is being challenged. Research reveals significant variation both within and across conflicts in the way sexual violence occurs. Evidence-based characterization of SVAC can also bring into dispute historic ways of understanding sexual violence, as in the case of assuming that SVAC is simply an aggravated manifestation of peacetime violence against women.

Current social science research, while strengthening the role of international criminal justice, is also challenging assumptions about SVAC in popular, scientific and legal communities. Today, social science research provides language to measure the gravity of the violence both quantitatively and qualitatively. In doing this, the work done by political scientists, forensic anthropologists, and social psychologists, among others, shapes the sexual violence agenda (and budget) of the UN, the U.S. Department of State and the ICC. In this way, the work of social theory and research has become increasingly important in determining the contexts of impunity in which cases reach the threshold of gravity. Social science researchers have become indirect – and growingly direct – participants in defining the criteria that establish under what circumstances sexual violence is a serious risk that requires international political and/or military intervention. We hope that this chapter will contribute to understanding: first, how metanarratives of SVAC operate in specific contexts; and second, how recent social science research is playing its part in generating new narratives that challenge, interrogate and reshape assumptions of the past.

14

Conceptualizing Sexual Violence Perpetrators in War

Inger Skjelsbæk[*]

The conflicts that followed the breakup of Yugoslavia marked the beginning of what several scholars have called the "new wars".[1] Emerging in the aftermath of the Cold War, such new wars are fought within States,[2] and are characterized by both the absence of legitimate state power[3] and the lack of a clear distinction between civilians and militaries: war and peace are blurred.[4] Whether this type of conflict is actually new or not is open to debate, and is widely contested, but both Øyvind Østerud[5] and Mary Kaldor[6] agree that the so-called new wars share a common characteristic: they are about identity, and they make identities the front lines of conflict. According to Kaldor, the response to these new wars has been a cosmopolitan effort in which transnational institutions intervene to enforce law and order, and to police the streets, in affected countries.[7] Helga Hernes writes that a gender analysis of these new wars shows that

> war suffering is in many ways more gendered than ever before. Women (and civilians more broadly) are forcefully transformed into victims as a consequence of gender-based

* **Inger Skjelsbæk** is Deputy Director and Senior Researcher at Peace Research Institute Oslo (PRIO).

1 Mary Kaldor, *New and Old Wars: Organized Violence in a Global Area*, Polity Press, Cambridge, 1999, p. 1.

2 Stein Tønnesson, "Hva er nytt i krig?" [What Is New in War?], in Hege Skjeie, Inger Skjelsbæk and Torunn L. Tryggestad (eds.), *Kjønn, krig og konflikt* [Gender, War, and Conflict], Pax Forlag, Oslo, 2008, pp. 127-137.

3 Øyvind Østerud, *Hva er krig?* [What Is War?], Universitetsforlaget, Oslo, 2009.

4 Kaldor, 1999, p. 27, see *supra* note 1.

5 Østerud, 2009, pp. 45–75, discusses whether these wars can in fact be called new or simply represent a break with the interstate war pattern and a return to prestate wars, see *supra* note 3.

6 Kaldor, 1999, p. 8, see *supra* note 1.

7 *Ibid.* at p. 3.

> violence and the fact that entire societies collapse and become completely dependent on help from the outside.[8]

The Bosnian War (1992–95) and the international engagement in their aftermaths epitomize these new wars. In these conflicts, rape and sexual violence was documented, prosecuted, and understood in ways never seen before.

As international efforts to rectify a history of silence and inaction regarding such crimes intensify – thanks largely to a set of UN Security Council resolutions[9] – there are still themes that are largely unexplored and the one theme that is most understudied is the transformation of soldiers and men into perpetrators of sexual violence crimes in war. I will argue that we now have a unique opportunity to learn and understand more of perpetrator behavior due to the massive documentation of these particular crimes in a particular context, namely international criminal courts. This chapter discusses how this can be done.

14.1. Ending Impunity and Massive Documentation

One of the most important responses to the massive documentation of rape and sexual violence in the conflict in Bosnia was a resolve that these acts of violence should not and could not be committed with impunity.[10] The perpetrators had to be brought to justice. Up until the early 1990s, the track record for bringing prosecutions in cases of rape and sexual violence in armed conflicts was unimpressive, to put it mildly. It was therefore imperative that the response of the international community to these events consisted not only of help and assistance to the victims but also of criminal prosecution of the perpetrators at the international level. The international community therefore undertook an unprecedented concerted

---

[8] Helga Hernes, "De nye krigene i et kjønnsperspektiv" [The New Wars from a Gender Perspective], in Hege Skjeie, Inger Skjelsbæk and Torunn L. Tryggestad (eds.), *Kjønn, krig og konflikt* [Gender, War, and Conflict], Pax Forlag, Oslo, 2008, p. 31; translated from Norwegian by the author.

[9] Specifically, United Nations Security Council Resolution 1325, 31 October 2000, U.N. Doc. S/RES/1325; United Nations Security Council Resolution 1820, 19 June 2008, U.N. Doc. S/RES/1820; United Nations Security Council Resolution 1888, 30 September 2009, U.N. Doc. S/RES/1888; United Nations Security Council Resolution 1889, 5 October 2009, U.N. Doc. S/RES/1889; United Nations Security Council Resolution 1960, 16 December 2010, U.N. Doc. S/RES/1960.

[10] The similar international response to the atrocities committed during the genocide in Rwanda in 1994 also helped strengthen this resolve.

effort to establish an international criminal prosecution system. On 25 May 1993, the UN Security Council passed resolution 827, which formally established the International Criminal Tribunal for the Former Yugoslavia ('ICTY'). This resolution contained the Statute of the ICTY, which set out the tribunal's jurisdiction and organizational structure, as well as the criminal procedure to be followed in general terms. This date thus marked the beginning of the end of complete impunity for war crimes in the former Yugoslavia. The ICTY was the first war crimes court established by the United Nations, and the first international war crimes tribunal to be set up since the Nuremberg and Tokyo tribunals after World War II. The tribunal is temporary, *ad hoc*, and has limited jurisdiction covering the entire territories of the former Yugoslavia, including Croatia, Bosnia and Herzegovina, Kosovo, and Macedonia. The overall aim of the Tribunal (together with the International Criminal Tribunal for Rwanda, or ICTR, a similar body set up to deal with crimes committed during the 1994 Rwandan genocide)[11] is to hold major perpetrators accountable for the most serious crimes, although low- and mid-level perpetrators have also been prosecuted.[12] The Court was established in order to address all atrocities committed in the region, but the massive documentation of rape and sexual violence served as an additional impetus for its creation. Since its creation, the ICTY has indicted 162 persons, 58 of whom were inter alia charged with having committed acts of sexual violence.[13]

When the tribunal terminates its work, criminal prosecutions will be carried out in national courts. The transition from international criminal prosecution to prosecutions at the national level has been taking place since 2004. Judges and other legal personnel have undergone massive training on how to prosecute international crimes, how to provide witnesses with adequate protection, and how to prioritize cases.

In 1998, some years after the establishment of the *ad hoc* tribunals for the former Yugoslavia and Rwanda, the International Criminal Court ('ICC') became a reality. The aim of this court is to prosecute cases that national courts are unable or unwilling to pursue. Article 5 of the Rome

[11] For further information on the International Criminal Tribunal for Rwanda, see http://www.ictr.org/, last accessed on 2 April 2012.

[12] Anne-Marie de Brouwer, *Supranational Criminal Prosecution of Sexual Violence: The ICC and the Practice of the ICTY and the ICTR*, Intersentia, Antwerp, 2005, p. 15.

[13] *Ibid.* at p. 18.

Statute of the International Criminal Court lists the crimes that fall within the ICC's jurisdiction, which include only the most serious crimes that are of concern to the international community as a whole – in other words, genocide, crimes against humanity, and crimes of aggression.[14] With the noteworthy exception of the United States and China, sixty-six countries have ratified the ICC, and the court became a permanent international body on 1 July 2002.

With the ICC in place, a long legal journey of integrating gender concerns within international criminal law has come to a turning point, as an international criminal system that will also prosecute crimes of sexual violence has been established. According to the Coalition of the ICC – a coalition of more than 2,500 organizations working to strengthen international cooperation with the court – the integration of gender into the work of the ICC can be seen on different levels. First, at the level of witness protection, the ICC ensures that victims of sexual and gender-based violence will be safe both physically and psychologically, and that their dignity will be safeguarded by being spared harassing and intimidating questions in court. In addition, a trust fund for victims and their families has been set up. Second, at the level of rules of evidence, the court cannot take into account the prior sexual history of a victim as part of the case, nor can it speculate about the consent of the victim, as it recognizes the coercive circumstances of the acts constituting the alleged crime. Third, the staff of the ICC is to include legal advisers who specialize in gender-based crimes, and efforts are to be made to ensure that there is a fair balance between men and women among judges, prosecutors, and registrars. Lastly, the ICC makes provision for women to come forward with their stories without necessarily being witnesses, allowing women's voices to be heard even when regular legal proceedings are not taking place.[15] These guidelines are clearly based on experiences from the ICTY and the ICTR. In her account of the supranational criminal prosecution of sexual violence, Anne-Marie de Brouwer writes that:

> the massive scale of the rapes of women thus proved to be one of the impetuses for setting up an international criminal tribunal that was able to try persons on the basis of individual criminal responsibility. For the first time in history, rape

[14] *Ibid.* at p. 19.

[15] This section is based on information from the Coalition of the ICC web page; see http://www.iccnow.org/?mod=gender, last accessed on 16 September 2009.

> was explicitly recognized to have taken place in an armed conflict and, as such, given explicit standing in the ICTY Statute under Article 5(g) as a crime against humanity.[16]

While the court has had many other charges to investigate beyond that relating to sexual violence crimes it is also clear that efforts by the ICTY in this field have been setting precedents for future trials and courts.[17]

The ICC Statute specifies particular forms of gender-based crime within supranational criminal law in ways that are unprecedented. It is now possible to prosecute incidents of rape, sexual slavery, enforced prostitution, forced pregnancy, enforced sterilization, or any other form of sexual violence of comparable gravity as crimes against humanity or war crimes, and a footnote has been added to the 1948 Genocide Conventions to the effect that genocide can include acts of rape and sexual violence.[18]

The work carried out in these tribunals shows that the legal conceptualization of crimes of sexual violence during war is evolving and becoming more nuanced with every new verdict. Future cases involving the criminal prosecution of perpetrators of wartime sexual violence will rest on an increasingly elaborate foundation of verdicts and trials, which will, it is hoped, ensure that more offenders will be prosecuted for such crimes.

What, then, have the criminal prosecutions in the ICTY achieved? The most comprehensive study to date of these cases has been carried out by de Brouwer, who has examined the extent to which the concerns and interests of the victims of sexual violence were integrated into the nascent supranational international law system.[19] While the concerns of the victims of crimes of sexual violence have been the main focus of her work, the perpetrators are also crucial to her analyses. Her study shows that it was the ICTY's aim to try between 128 and 138 individuals by the end of 2010, and 58 of them were expected to be charged, *inter alia*, with crimes involving sexual violence.[20] This "involvement" takes different forms ranging from direct involvement to lack of intervention of a superior.

16 De Brouwer, 2005, p. 16, see *supra* note 12.

17 *Ibid.*

18 *Ibid.* at pp. 20–21.

19 *Ibid.* at p. 427.

20 *Ibid.* at p. 331.

What both the work carried out by the ICTY and the analyses of that work show is that there is a wealth of data available for a research community that wants to learn more about the perpetrators of sexual violence in war. Transcripts from the court hearings, videos, and background documents are all available at the ICTY's web pages.[21] This massive documentation effort is a gold mine not only for legal scholars but also for social science scholars. Through a close examination of these transcripts, it will be possible to critically investigate the question of intent in a social as well as a legal sense. In an article focusing on law's regulation of human trafficking the following statement is made about the relationship between law and public and political concerns: "The law is not only the result of cultural norms, it is also a political and formal process whereby public concern and international obligations are translated into law".[22] This statement also holds true for the development of international legal enforcement measures to meet the challenges that widespread use of sexual violence in war creates and, as will be shown, opens up the possibility of studying the perpetrators in ways which have not yet been done. These efforts to end impunity, and to bring perpetrators to justice, have also opened up the possibility of studying who these perpetrators are, what motivated them to choose sexual violence over other actions in given settings, and what impact punishment has had both on them and on their victims.

14.2. How to Conceptualize the Sexual Violence Perpetrators in War?

There is now a rich literature on crimes of wartime sexual violence in general, but within these analyses it is predominantly the victims who are given a voice and who are being analyzed. The perpetrator is a secondary character whose intentions and motivations are assumed but unexamined. In other words, the ways in which sexual violence in war has been theorized up until now have been based on empirical data from only one of the groups involved in this violent relationship – the victims of such violence. In order to advance our understanding of this area, we need to incorporate empirical data that bring the perceptions and voices of the perpetrators

[21] See http://www.icty.org/, last accessed on 3 April 2012.

[22] May-Len Skilbrei, "Taking Trafficking to Court", in *Women and Criminal Justice*, 2010, vol. 20, p. 42.

into the equation. This is necessary not to somehow justify the actions of the perpetrators but to seek insights into why and how such behavior can be understood as a social practice that constitutes war and gender at the level of individual, group and social category. These will be examined in turn below.

14.2.1. Individual Level Conceptualizations

It is plausible to assume that there is a difference between the perpetrators of acts of sexual violence in war and those who commit acts of sexual violence in times of peace. This means that the existing body of knowledge on perpetrators of sexual violence might have little applicability to the perpetrators of wartime sexual violence. The setting of war represents an extreme break with the norms and values that guide peaceful coexistence between people(s) – as illustrated by the very fact that killing is permissible under certain conditions in war according to the Geneva Conventions (*jus in bello*). The back cover text of a recently published book on Norway's role as an actor on the international military scene states that:

> the soldier's profession is about being able to kill while risking your own life. The use of military forces in international operations since the end of the Cold War has increased the likelihood that on behalf of Norwegian society at large, Norwegian soldiers will kill other people and suffer losses among their own.[23]

Part of the training that soldiers undergo in regular armies is geared towards learning what actions are permissible under international law given particular sets of circumstances. In other words, soldiers are trained to recognize and analyze in which settings certain forms of violence are legitimized. These settings require clear distinctions to be made between civilians and military personnel, and entail a set of parameters that regulate relationships between military forces on the battleground. When a person in a war situation kills without violating the rules of war, he or she is usually not regarded as a murderer in the aftermath of war, and quite likely will never kill again. Likewise, a perpetrator of sexual violence in war may not be a rapist with a history of offenses involving sexual vio-

[23] Håkan Edström, Nils Terje Lunde, Janne Haaland Matlary (eds.), *Krigerkultur i en fredsnasjon* [War Culture in a Peace Nation], Abstrakt forlag, Oslo, 2009; translated from Norwegian by the author.

lence prior to the war, and that violence may have no bearing on behavior after the war. But there is a clear distinction between killing and committing acts of sexual violence in war: killing can be legitimized under certain conditions, whereas sexual violence cannot. However, it is possible to regard sexual violence in war as part of a *repertoire* of actions that appear permissible because the circumstances of war are extraordinary and because it elicits no consequences, punishment, or condemnation from the military leadership.

In addition, in the "new wars" – where the frontlines are blurred, identities are the battleground, and the distinction between military and civilian is unclear – it is likely that the propensity for extreme violence in all its forms increases just because the opportunity for such violence is present. James Waller argues that men are implicated in extreme violence more often than women simply because they find themselves more often in situations where such acts can be carried out, and war presents a wealth of such situations.[24] While this may be true, it is also true that many men ignore these opportunities, and it would be interesting to discover when and why some men do while others do not resort to this kind of violence. The information that the research and policy community needs is precisely what happens in the war setting that transforms far too many ordinary men into perpetrators of sexual violence. In order to get closer to an understanding of this transformation process it is crucial to examine the group pressures that are at play in the context of armed conflict.

14.2.2. Group Level Conceptualizations

Following what has been argued above it is the *contexts* of armed conflict that "produce" perpetrators of sexual violence crimes. In other words, there appears to be a particular logic that applies to a very particular setting. In his study on how ordinary people commit genocide and mass killing, Waller argues that the

> social construction of cruelty – buttressed by professional socialization, group identification, and binding factors of the group – envelops perpetrators in a social context that encourages and rewards extraordinary evil. It reminds us that the normal reaction to an abnormal situation is abnormal be-

[24] James Waller, *Becoming Evil: How Ordinary People Commit Genocide and Mass Killing*, Oxford University Press, Oxford, 2007, p. 265.

> havior; indeed, normal behavior would be an abnormal reaction to an abnormal situation. We must borrow the perspective of the perpetrators and view their evil not as the work of "lunatics" but as actions with a clear and justified purpose – so defined by a context of cruelty.[25]

Maria Eriksson Baaz and Maria Stern have carried out a study of crimes of sexual violence committed by the Forces Armées de la République Démocratique du Congo ('FARDC') in the Democratic Republic of the Congo ('DRC'), focusing on the perpetrators.[26] According to estimates by the UN observer mission in the DRC, the FARDC was responsible for about 40 percent of the sexual violence committed in the first part of 2007.[27] For their study, the authors interviewed 193 people about the army's use of rape, but did not address whether the interviewees themselves had committed such acts. Instead, the interviews focused on what being a good soldier entailed and how sexual violence intersected with these conceptualizations. What the authors found was that the soldiers conceptualized rape in two distinctly different ways. On the one hand were what the soldiers labeled "lust rapes", which were rapes committed against random women owing to an urge to release sexual tension. The soldiers explained this phenomenon as a consequence of a particular context: their military confinement and the war. Soldiers were uncertain about how long they would be in the military and were both poor and hungry. Such rapes were linked directly to the "poor distribution of resources and organization of the military",[28] and they were viewed by the interviewees as more ethically palatable than the second kind of rape, which they labeled "evil rapes". These are seen as being part of what Cynthia Enloe has called the "lootpillageandrape" frenzy: the taking of drugs, the craziness of war, the frustrations and anger of the individual soldier, and the transgressions involved in extreme forms of violence pave the way for the use of sexual violence with no other purpose than the commission of evil acts.[29] Rapes of this type, Baaz and Stern explain,

---

25 *Ibid.* at p. 271.

26 Maria Eriksson Baaz, Maria Stern, "Why Do Soldiers Rape? Masculinity, Violence and Sexuality in the Armed Forces in the Congo (DRC)", in *International Studies Quarterly*, 2009, vol. 53, no. 2, pp. 495–518.

27 *Ibid.* at p. 497.

28 *Ibid.* at p. 509.

29 Cynthia Enloe, *Globalization and Militarism: Feminists Make the Link*, Rowman and Littlefield, Lanham, MD, 2008, p. 108.

occur in the context of other forms of extreme violence. The aim of their study is to demonstrate that the notion that sexual violence is a weapon of war does little to help us understand the "myriad relations of power which make up the context in which sexual violence occurs".[30]

These are important insights. They force us to ask new questions about the nature of the context in which war rapes take place and about what the conceptualization of sexual violence as a weapon of war entails. We need to understand the level of this form of violence as well as the reasoning behind its organized nature. For instance, does the sexual violence manifest itself in the form of organized rape camps where acts of sexual violence are targeted and systemic? Who facilitates such setups, and what do the perpetrators know about the arrangements? When and how does the violence take place – in captivity, in a private home, or in public spaces? What rationales lie behind the different contexts? In what contexts are rape and sexual violence rampant but not systematic, and what does that information tell us about the rationale behind such violence and those committing it? In an article that examines the variations in the use of sexual violence in different armed conflicts, Elisabeth Wood has commented that even in somewhat similar conflicts – such as Sierra Leone and Bosnia, where ethnicity marked the frontlines and sexual violence was widespread – the ways in which sexual violence was used varied. In Bosnia, the use of such violence has been documented as systematic and organized, whereas in Sierra Leone it appears to have been the opposite – random and disorganized.[31]

The perpetrators in question are predominantly soldiers, which calls for an analysis of what military structures "produce" perpetrators of sexual violence. Are such acts of violence most common among paramilitary units with particular ideologies? Is there, for instance, a difference between Marxist-based paramilitary units and other paramilitary groups? What about state militaries and private security companies? All these different military constellations will bring individuals – predominantly men – into extraordinary situations, where new codes and norms of behavior will apply. Because their reference group will be other men in the same setting, it is important that we discover more about which of these (close

---

[30] Baaz and Stern, 2009, p. 514, see *supra* note 26.

[31] Elisabeth Wood, "Variation in Sexual Violence during War", in *Politics and Society*, 2006, vol. 34, no. 3, pp. 307–341.

to) all-male military settings appear more conducive to acts of sexual violence than others – and why. A related issue concerns the status, rank, and age of sexually violent offenders. Is it the case that most perpetrators are young recruits? Is the military leadership involved – either by actively encouraging these acts or by knowingly turning a blind eye and a deaf ear to what might be happening under its command?

14.2.3. Social Category Conceptualizations

The ways in which gender and war are linked has been theorized by numerous scholars since the 1980's. The notion that men and women may have differing understandings, perceptions and experiences of peace and conflict, as well as the argument that traditional approaches to understandings of peace and conflict may gain by incorporating a gender dimension, run through, albeit with diverse nuances, these early publications.[32] In these works war is seen as manifestation, and as constitutive of *hegemonic masculinity*, through an intricate process of *militarization*. Enloe questions whether it is possible for militarization to exist at all without masculinity.[33] She argues that it is especially difficult to envisage demilitarization without conceptualizing any transformation of masculinity. What she implies is that "real" men are militarized men and that it is very hard to create a new space for notions of manhood which can exist outside the militaristic sphere. This has been particularly salient in cases where military bases have been shut down and many men have had to find new jobs and hence redefine themselves, according to Enloe.[34] The connection be-

[32] Jean Bethke Elshtain, Sheila Tobias (eds.), *Women, Militarism, and War*, Rowman and Littlefield, Savage, MD, 1990; Cynthia Enloe, *Does Khaki Become You?: The Militarization of Women's Lives*, Pluto Press, London, 1983; Cynthia Enloe, *Bananas, Beaches & Bases: Making Feminist Sense of International Politics*, University of California Press, Berkeley, CA, 1989; Jan Jindy Pettman, "A Feminist Perspective on Peace and Security", in Michael Salla (ed.), *Essays on Peace: Paradigms for Global Order*, Central Queensland University Press, Rockhampton, 1995, pp. 24–33; Betty Reardon, *Women and Peace: Feminist Visions of Global Security*, State University of New York Press, Albany, 1993; Sara Ruddick, *Maternal Thinking: Towards a Politics of Peace*, Beacon Press, Boston, 1989; Ann J. Tickner, *Gender in International Relations: Feminist Perspectives on Achieving Global Security*, Columbia University Press, New York, 1992; Jeanne Vickers, *Women and War*, Zed Books, London, 1993.

[33] Cynthia Enloe, *The Morning After: Sexual Politics After the End of the Cold War*, University of California Press, Berkeley, CA, 1993, p. 26.

[34] *Ibid.*

tween militarism and masculinity is evident, but this does not imply that all men are militaristic and all women are not. "We must examine how militarism and masculinity – while not identical – have become so entwined", says Peterson.[35] In this process it is important to see that both men and women play a part, and that both men and women may share militaristic values. Although women do not constitute a large proportion of military personnel this does not necessarily mean that they are opposed to the military system. Many mothers encourage their sons to join the military, and many women are proud when their sons, husbands or fathers go off to war. The work they do at home while waiting for them to return becomes their contribution in this system. Enloe has eloquently described how men's and women's lives become militarized in different ways.[36] Her major point is that military systems and militarization must be regarded processes with both a material and an ideological dimension. She argues that this system is dependent on men and women complying with stereotypical norms of masculinity and femininity. When men have to move to a different place in order to do their service in the military system, the system as such is dependent on the fact that someone keeps the home fires burning.[37] This becomes the work of many women; hence women's lives are as much "militarized" as the lives of the male soldier. These processes influence men's and women's lives as much as in times of peace as in times of war, albeit in different ways.

When a young conscript enters the military system, the success of his transformation from a boy to a soldier depends on the degree to which he internalizes the value-system of militarism and accepts the outcome of militarization. It also depends on how his family and friends regard his transformation. Support and encouragement will naturally make the transformation process easier. But there are also other benefits that will ease his transformation. Firstly, the military system is to a large extent based on *camaraderie*. Enloe says that "the glue is camaraderie, the base of that glue is masculinity".[38] She draws on examples from the US military where the recruits often come from the lower strata of society. Meeting

35 Spike Peterson, "Security and Sovereign States: What is at Stake in Taking Feminism Seriously?" in Spike Peterson (ed.), *Gendered States*, Lynne Rienner, Boulder, CO, 1992 p. 48.

36 Enloe, 1983, 1989, 1993, see *supra* notes 32 and 33.

37 Enloe, 1983, pp. 46–91, see *supra* note 32.

38 Enloe, 1993, p. 52, see *supra* note 33.

and socializing with people from other strata and feeling accepted may be one way of retaining the recruits and making them loyal to their superiors and the cause. Whether this is a more or less conscious strategy of the superiors, it is a crucial element in keeping the system operating smoothly. If the soldiers start fighting each other then they will not be effective in fighting against an enemy. This may partly explain why the military has been so reluctant in admitting/accepting homosexual soldiers. Being a homosexual is perceived as a potential threat to the culture of masculine camaraderie. It is also potentially dangerous to include women, because much of the camaraderie culture is based on the antagonistic relation to women. Women and homosexuals represent values, norms, and behavior that are the opposite to those of "real" men. Condescending attitudes towards homosexuals and misogynist views of women may act to create greater masculine cohesion among soldiers and their superiors. Secondly, being a *warrior* means being a real *man*. In Enloe's words, "[i]n most cultures that we know about, to be manly means to be warrior".[39] The trademark of the warrior is his ability to kill. Enloe, who rejects the notion of an essentially male inclination to war, argues that ways of creating new masculinities would be the best way to create better hopes for peaceful solutions to conflicts. She also acknowledges that this would be very difficult because notions of masculinity are so intertwined with notions of militarism. The third point relates to the *privileged* status one achieves as a militarized person. The argument is that these "chosen" men will be role models for a way of thinking and reasoning which is militarized. Being militarized can indeed bear the potential for being privileged.

Hutchings has examined the ways in which this first generation of scholars conceptualized masculinity and how this compares to the current writings on the new wars.[40] Her main argument is that;

> [T]he link between masculinity and war made in both these literatures has nothing to do with the substantive meaning of either *masculinity* or *war*, or with a straightforward casual or constitutive relation between the two; rather, war is linked to masculinity because the formal, relational properties of masculinity as a concept provide a framework through which

[39] *Ibid.*

[40] Kimberly Hutchings, "Making Sense of Masculinity and War", in *Men and Masculinities*, 2008, vol. 10, no. 4, pp. 389–404.

> war can be rendered intelligible and acceptable as a social practice and institution.[41]

The question debated by Hutchings in her article, is whether war provides an arena for hegemonic masculinities to be played out in the interest of state power where alternative masculinities and feminized "others" are defined out? Or, could it be that the so-called new wars, forces us to focus on the "formal, relational properties of masculinity as a concept"?[42] In her presentation of Kaldor's conceptualizations of new wars, Hutchings argues that Kaldor diagnoses the "masculinity of the new warrior as pathological, something that takes a recognizable form of human behavior to new and extreme limits and that needs to be countered by responsible and autonomous action on the part of the cosmopolitan law enforcer".[43] It is the patterns described by Kaldor that is observed in places like Bosnia, Kosovo, Rwanda, the DRC and the Sudan. The nature of war has changed, the display of hegemonic (and militarized masculinity) is seen as pathological, and the response is not a privileged status but potential international criminal prosecution. Which effects might this have for the use of sexual violence in war? What does this new paradigm of war mean for perpetrators of sexual violence crimes? How do they make sense of their actions and their punishment and from which subject positions will they discuss their experiences?

A few examples from personal statements from those who have been convicted of sexual violence crimes in the ICTY and who have pleaded guilty show that gender and military culture is at the forefront of their accounts of their actions and their regrets.

> I tried to be proud of my actions and to think that they were actions of a successful soldier. Today I am ashamed of all that, ashamed of my conduct and ashamed of how I behaved. (Miroslav Bralo)
>
> I am sorry for every man who suffered every family that lost a family member, every child that lost a father. I am sorry for every mother who lost a son. (Damir Došen)
>
> [...] I carried weapons in Susica, I wore uniform; and on the other hand, there is the fact that there were women there [in the Susica concentration camp], aged the same as my moth-

41 *Ibid.* at p. 389.

42 *Ibid.* at p. 390.

43 *Ibid.* at p. 399.

> er, there were children there, there were people who used to be friends of mine, whom I used to see over the years in cafees, on sport fields, and playgrounds, with whom I spent summer vacations. (Dragan Nikolić)

By exploring these relationships and narratives in more detail from the ICTY, ICTR, ICC and other international jurisdictions engaged in prosecution of sexual violence offenders in times of war, it will be possible to learn more about the individual, groups and social category dynamic which transforms soldiers into perpetrators.

14.3. Conclusion

This chapter seeks to map out the conceptual concerns related to studying perpetrators of sexual violence in war. Analyses aimed at creating a better understanding of the perpetrator's motivations for committing these acts should include the following three questions. First, how is the war perpetrator of sexual violence crimes different from the perpetrator of the same crimes in time of peace? Second, how does the perpetration of sexual violence crimes in times of war pertain to other forms of war violence, and what does this tell us about the perpetrator? Third, how does masculinity and militarism intersect and form the perpetrator identity? These questions need be explored in studies in the years ahead.

15

Analytical and Comparative Digest of the ICTY, ICTR and SCSL Jurisprudence on International Sex Crimes

Magali Maystre* **and Nicole Rangel****

15.1. Introduction

This chapter contains a comprehensive digest of the jurisprudence of the International Criminal Tribunal for the former Yugoslavia ('ICTY'), the International Criminal Tribunal for Rwanda ('ICTR') and the Special Court for Sierra Leone ('SCSL') on international sex crimes. It includes international sex crimes charts ('ISCCs') for all ICTY, ICTR and SCSL cases that contain charges and/or convictions for these crimes. More specifically, for each of these cases, the ISCCs review the operative indictment, trial and appeal judgements, and provide both summaries and pertinent quotes of all relevant findings.

The *raison d'être* of the ISCCs is in response to the lack of a comprehensive digest on ICTY, ICTR and SCSL jurisprudence on international sex crimes. The ISCCs seek to disseminate knowledge on, and provide free access to, international sex crimes jurisprudence.

The ISCCs are a comprehensive research and reference tool to assist practitioners, researchers, legal academics, government officials, NGO representatives and others. They are intended to serve as a useful

* **Magali Maystre** holds a *D.E.A.* (post-graduate degree) in international law from the *Institut universitaire de hautes études internationales* in Geneva, Switzerland. She currently works as an Associate Legal Officer in the Appeals Chamber of the International Criminal Tribunal for the former Yugoslavia ('ICTY'). The views expressed herein are those of the author and do not necessarily reflect the views of the United Nations or the ICTY. The principal author would like to thank **Nicole Rangel** for her active involvement in the preliminary research for this chapter and her assistance in the editorial process.

** **Nicole Rangel** holds a J.D. from Mc George School of Law in Sacramento, USA. She currently works as a Legal Assistant for a Defence team appearing before the International Criminal Tribunal for Rwanda ('ICTR') and previously worked as an intern in the Appeals Chamber of the ICTY.

resource to those working with cases of a similar nature at both international and national levels.

The ISCCs are also aimed at advancing the discourse on international sex crimes, and the effective enforcement of individual criminal responsibility for such violations.

15.1.1. International Sex Crimes Charts' Taxonomy

The ISCCs are arranged by jurisdictions, namely the ICTY, the ICTR and the SCSL. The ICTY ISCCs contain 35 cases, the ICTR ISCCs 27 cases and the SCSL ISCCs 4 cases. For each of the tribunals, the cases are organised chronologically by the date of the trial judgements. Each case is analysed in its own chart, divided into five sections.

The first section provides the case's name and number, as well as a short description of the role or position of the accused during the relevant events.

The second section specifies the charges of international sex crimes and modes of liability, as alleged by the Prosecution in the indictment. 'CAH' is the abbreviation for crime(s) against humanity and 'WC' for war crime(s). Both the charge(s) and the mode(s) of liability appear in bold. When no mode of liability appears in bold for charges under Article 7(1) of the ICTY Statute or Article 6(1) of the ICTR or SCSL Statutes, it means that either all modes of liability under this provision are charged in the indictment (namely, planning, instigating, ordering, committing or otherwise aiding and abetting in the planning, preparation or execution of a crime), or that the indictment is unclear as to the mode of liability charged. The footnotes for this section not only provide references to relevant paragraphs, but also to actual quotes of the operative indictment. It is worth noting that, for some cases, such as *Blaškić*, there are no charges or factual allegations of international sex crimes in the operative indictment. In such cases, the second section of the ISCC provides the charges for which the accused was convicted for international sex crimes.

The third section provides a summary of the outcome of the case concerning the international sex crimes charges, including the findings of guilt or innocence with respect to those charges, and the mode(s) of liability under which the accused was found criminally responsible. The charge(s) and the mode(s) of liability under which the accused was found guilty appear in bold. Any dissenting or separate opinions on international sex crimes charges or material facts are also indicated. This section is left blank for the cases for which the trial is in progress or has not yet started, as well as for the cases in which the accused is still at large.

The fourth section provides a summary of the outcome of the appellate proceedings concerning the international sex crimes charges, including any additional convictions entered by the appeals chamber and/or reversals of the convictions originally entered by the trial chamber. This section is left blank when the appellate proceedings are in progress or when the cases were determined by a plea agreement.

Finally, the last section not only provides references to relevant paragraphs, but reproduces the relevant quotes of the legal and factual findings pertaining to international sex crimes, as well as remarks on evidence, as made by the trial and appeals chambers. In that sense, the ISCCs are intended to be as comprehensive as possible, so that the reader does not need to refer to the official judgements. This section is left blank when no trial judgement has yet been issued.

15.1.2. Research Method

For this research, all ICTY, ICTR and SCSL operative indictments, trial and appeal judgements issued before 1 August 2011 were consulted. Reviewing only trial and appeal judgements of cases in which the operative indictment contained international sex crimes charges revealed itself as unproductive as some operative indictments were defective, but trial chambers nonetheless entered convictions for international sex crimes.

ICTY and ICTR cases referred to national jurisdictions pursuant to Rule 11 *bis* of the Rules of Procedure and Evidence of these tribunals (that is, referral of an indictment to a national jurisdiction) were not included in this research as they were – or will be – adjudicated by national courts. Similarly, cases in which the accused passed away before the issuing of the trial judgement were not included nor were the cases in which the Prosecution withdrew international sex crimes charges from indictments pursuant to a plea agreement. Finally, cases containing general factual findings on international sex crimes but no charges and/or convictions on international sex crimes were also not included.

The focus of this research has not only been on completed cases, but also on cases for which the proceedings – whether at trial or on appeal – are ongoing or have not yet started. Moreover, the ISCCs contain cases for which the accused are still at large but whose operative indictments include international sex crimes charges. In that sense, the ISCCs are exhaustive, given that the ICTY, the ICTR and the SCSL will not issue new indictments. The ICTY, the ICTR and the SCSL have yet to complete their work, and accordingly the ISCCs which have been left blank will be completed and updated in due course.

15.1.3. Main Findings

One of the main findings of the ISCCs is that international sex crimes can constitute, or form part of, various crimes. Assuming that all other requirements are satisfied, international sex crimes can constitute genocide, crimes against humanity and war crimes.

International sex crimes can be charged and prosecuted as specific sex crimes, such as rape or sexual slavery as crimes against humanity or rape as a war crime. Moreover, international sex crimes can also be charged and prosecuted as – or as part of – non-specific sex crimes, such as torture or persecutions as crimes against humanity. The ICTY, ICTR and SCSL jurisprudence on international sex crimes reflects the re-conceptualisation of many crimes of the statutes of these tribunals from a sexual perspective. The ISCCs illustrate the full range of the crimes under which convictions for international sex crimes were entered. These crimes include, *inter alia*: (i) rape as a crime against humanity; (ii) rape as a violation of the laws of customs of war; (iii) rape as a violation of Article 3 common to the Geneva Conventions and of Additional Protocol II; (iv) torture as a crime against humanity; (v) torture as a violation of the laws of customs of war; (vi) torture as a grave breach of the Geneva Conventions of 1949; (vii) cruel treatment as a violation of the laws or customs or war; (viii) inhumane acts as a crime against humanity; (ix) inhuman treatment as a grave breach of the Geneva Conventions of 1949; (x) wilfully causing great suffering or serious injury to body or health as a grave breach of the Geneva Conventions of 1949; (xi) humiliating and degrading treatment as a violation of the laws or customs of war; (xii) outrages upon personal dignity as a violation of the laws or customs of war; (xiii) outrages upon personal dignity as a violation of Article 3 common to the Geneva Conventions and of Additional Protocol II; (xiv) violence to health and physical or mental well-being of persons as a violation of Article 3 common to the Geneva Conventions and of Additional Protocol II; (xv) other inhumane acts as a crime against humanity; (xvi) sexual slavery as a crime against humanity; (xvii) enslavement as a crime against humanity; (xviii) persecutions as a crime against humanity; (xix) genocide; (xx) complicity in genocide; (xxi) conspiracy to commit genocide; (xxii) acts of terrorism as a violation of Article 3 common to the Geneva Conventions and of Additional Protocol II; and (xxiii) collective punishment as a violation of Article 3 common to the Geneva Conventions and of Additional Protocol II.

The ISCCs also demonstrate that international sex crimes were charged and prosecuted under all the modes of liability including, *inter alia*, ordering, superior responsibility and joint criminal enterprise.

Finally, it is also worth noting that the ISCCs show that victims of international sex crimes are not limited to women, but also include men. Moreover, in two instances, two women were charged and convicted for international sex crimes. Biljana Plavšić pleaded guilty and was convicted under Article 7(1) of the ICTY Statute (joint criminal enterprise) for persecutions as a crime against humanity for various acts committed against Bosnian Muslims, Bosnian Croats and other non-Serbs, including rapes and sexual violence. Pauline Nyiramasuhuko was found guilty under Article 6(3) of the ICTR Statute (superior responsibility) for rape as a crime against humanity, and outrages upon personal dignity as a violation of Article 3 common to the Geneva Conventions and of Additional Protocol II for ordering *Interahamwe* under her effective control to rape Tutsi women at the Butare prefecture office between the end of April and the first half of June 1994.

15.1.4. Implication for the Future Research Agenda

The ICTY, ICTR and SCSL ISCCs illustrate the significant developments made in the prosecution and enforcement of individual criminal responsibility for international sex crimes.

Whether international sex crimes can be prosecuted and individuals held individually criminally responsible for such crimes is no longer an issue. Even in the absence of a developed gender-oriented legislation, international sex crimes can be investigated and prosecuted under many non-specific sex crimes. Nonetheless, too many international sex crimes remain unpunished and difficulties of proving such crimes are often raised. Therefore, one of the possible consequences of the ISCCs for the future research agenda would be to distil some of the lessons learned about investigating and prosecuting international sex crimes before the ICTY, the ICTR and the SCSL, and to establish best practice guidelines for investigating and prosecuting international sex crimes based on the current ISCC.

15.2. ICTY International Sex Crimes Charts[***]

<table>
<tr><td colspan="2">1. Duško <u>Tadić</u> (Case No. IT-94-1)

President of the Local Board of the Serb Democratic Party (SDS) in Kozarac, in the Republic of Bosnia and Herzegovina.</td></tr>
<tr><td>Indictment[1] (International sex crimes (or related) charges and mode(s) of liability)</td><td>- Persecutions as CAH (count 1) under Article 7(1) of the Statute for various acts including sexual assaults,[2] and torture inflicted through gang-rapes.[3]
- Torture or inhuman treatment as a grave breach of the Geneva Conventions of 1949 (WC) (count 8), Wilfully causing great suffering or serious injury to body or health as a grave breach of the Geneva Conventions of 1949 (WC) (count 9), Cruel treatment as a violation of the laws or customs of war (WC) (count 10) and Inhumane acts as CAH (count 11) under Article 7(1) of the Statute for forcing two prisoners to commit oral sexual acts and for forcing one prisoner to sexually mutilate another prisoner.[4]</td></tr>
</table>

*** Please note that, in the following footnotes, judicial documents will be cited without reference to jurisdiction. Moreover, cross-references from abbreviated citations to the footnote containing the original full citation have been omitted. These small deviations from the standard citation practice of Torkel Opsahl Academic EPublisher have been introduced in the interest of limiting the amount of characters and space used for citations in this section. It is hoped that the systematic structure of the ISCCs will compensate for the somewhat reduced scope of information included in the citations.

1 For the general background to the charges, see *Prosecutor v. Duško Tadić*, Case No. IT-94-1-I, Indictment, 14 December 1995 ("*Tadić* Indictment"), paras. 2.6 (Omarska camp: "Both female and male prisoners were beaten, tortured, raped, sexually assaulted, and humiliated".), 2.7 ("In Trnopolje [camp], female detainees were sexually abused".). It is noteworthy that Counts 2, 3 and 4 of the *Tadić* Indictment, which related to charges of forcible sexual intercourse were withdrawn at trial following a motion by the Prosecution. See *Prosecutor v. Duško Tadić*, Case No. IT-94-1-T, Opinion and Judgment, 7 May 1997 ("*Tadić* Trial Judgement"), para. 27 and references cited therein. These counts included Inhuman treatment as a grave breach of the Geneva Conventions of 1949 (WC) (Count 2), Cruel treatment as a violation of the laws or customs of war (WC) (Count 3), and Rape as CAH (Count 4) for the forcible sexual intercourse with 'F'. See *Tadić* Indictment, para. 5 ("'**F**' was taken to the Omarska camp as a prisoner in early June 1992. Sometime between early June and 3 August 1992, '**F**' was taken to the Separacija building at the entrance to the Omarska camp and placed in a room where **Dusko TADIC** subjected '**F**' to forcible sexual intercourse".).

2 *Tadić* Indictment, paras. 4 ("Between about 23 May 1992 and about 31 December 1992, [...] Serb forces, including **Dusko TADIC**, subjected Muslims and Croats inside and outside the camps to a campaign of terror which included killings, torture, sexual assaults, and other physical and psychological abuse".), 4.2 ("**Dusko TADIC** was also seen on numerous occasions in the three main camps operating within opstina Prijedor: Omarska, Keraterm and Trnopolje. During the period between 25 May 1992 and 8 August 1992, **TADIC** physically took part or otherwise participated in the killing, torture, sexual assault, and beating of many detainees at Omarska camp".).

3 *Tadić* Indictment, para. 4.3 ("**TADIC** also physically took part or otherwise participated in the torture of more than 12 female detainees, including several gang rapes, which occurred both in the [Trnopolje] camp and at a white house adjacent to the camp during the period between September, 1992 and December, 1992".).

4 *Tadić* Indictment, para. 6 ("During the period between 1 June and 31 July 1992, a group of Serbs, including **Dusko TADIC** [... in the large garage building or hangar of Omarska camp, ...] forced two other prisoners,

Trial Judgement	- Guilty of **Cruel treatment as a violation of the laws or customs of war (WC)** (count 10) and **Inhumane acts as CAH** (count 11) under Article 7(1) of the Statute (**aiding and abetting**)[5] for forcing two prisoners to commit oral sexual acts and for forcing one prisoner to sexually mutilate another prisoner. - Not guilty of counts 8 and 9 because the charges brought under Article 2 of the Statute were inapplicable because it was not proved that the victims were protected persons.[6] - Although Duško Tadić was found guilty of persecutions as CAH (count 1), the Trial Chamber found that the Prosecution failed to present any evidence regarding the accused's participation in sexual assault and torture for this charge.[7]
Appeal Judgement	- In addition to the convictions imposed by the Trial Chamber, the Appeals Chamber found Duško Tadić: - Guilty of **Inhuman treatment as a grave breach of the Geneva Conventions of 1949 (WC)** (count 8) and **Wilfully causing great suffering or serious injury to body or health as a grave breach of the Geneva Conventions of 1949 (WC)** (count 9) under Article 7(1) of the Statute (**aiding and abetting**)[8] for the same acts than the ones in counts 10 and 11 for which he was found guilty at trial.
Legal and Factual Findings and/or Evidence	- This is the first case before the ICTY in which sexual assault (of men) was prosecuted. - Factual findings: "After G and Witness H had been forced to pull Jasmin Hrnić's body about the hangar floor they were ordered to jump down into the inspection pit, then Fikret Harambašić, who was naked and bloody from beating, was made to jump into the pit with them and Witness H was ordered to lick his naked bottom and G to suck his penis and then to bite his testicles. Meanwhile a group of men in uniform stood around the inspection pit watching and shouting to bite harder. All three were then made to get out of the pit

'G' and 'H,' to commit oral sexual acts on HARAMBASIC and forced 'G' to sexually mutilate him. KARABASIC, HRNIC, ALIC, and HARAMBASIC died as a result of the assaults. By his participation in these acts, **Dusko TADIC** committed: [...] **COUNT 8:** a **GRAVE BREACH** recognised by Articles 2(b) (torture or inhuman treatment) and 7(1) of the Statute of the Tribunal; and, **COUNT 9:** a **GRAVE BREACH** recognised by Articles 2(c) (wilfully causing great suffering or serious injury to body and health) and 7(1) of the Statute of the Tribunal; and, **COUNT 10:** a **VIOLATION OF THE LAWS OR CUSTOMS OF WAR** recognised by Articles 3 and 7(1) of the Statute of the Tribunal and Article 3(1)(a) (cruel treatment) of the Geneva Conventions; and, **COUNT 11:** a **CRIME AGAINST HUMANITY** recognised by Articles 5(i) (inhumane acts) and 7(1) of the Statute of the Tribunal".).

5 *Tadić* Trial Judgement, para. 237 ("This Trial Chamber is satisfied beyond reasonable doubt from the evidence […] that the accused was present on the hangar floor on the occasion of the assault upon and sexual mutilation of Fikret Harambašić but is not satisfied that he took any active part in that assault and mutilation".). See also *Tadić* Trial Judgement, paras. 670, 692, 726, 730.

6 *Tadić* Trial Judgement, para. 720 and Section VIII (Judgment), pp. 285–286.

7 *Tadić* Trial Judgement, para. 427 ("[…] the Prosecution has failed to present any evidence regarding the accused's participation in sexual assault and torture as alleged in this subparagraph".). See also *Tadić* Trial Judgement, para. 452 (with respect to facts contained in paragraph 4.3 of the *Tadić* Indictment, the Trial Chamber noted that, "[w]ith the exception of the first sentence, the allegations contained in this paragraph were supported only by the testimony of Dragan Opacić, who was originally given the pseudonym 'L'. During trial, aspects of his testimony were revealed which led the Prosecution to state in open court that it did not consider Dragan Opacić a witness of truth and to submit a motion to withdraw these allegations".).

8 *Prosecutor v. Duško Tadić*, Case No. IT-94-1-A, Judgement, 15 July 1999 ("*Tadić* Appeal Judgement"), paras. 171, 327(4). The Appeals Chamber found that "the Trial Chamber erred in so far as it acquitted the Appellant on the sole ground that the grave breaches regime of the Geneva Conventions of 1949 did not apply". See *Tadić* Appeal Judgement, para. 170.

	onto the hangar floor and Witness H was threatened with a knife that both his eyes would be cut out if he did not hold Fikret Harambašić's mouth closed to prevent him from screaming; G was then made to lie between the naked Fikret Harambašić's legs and, while the latter struggled, hit and bite his genitals. G then bit off one of Fikret Harambašić's testicles and spat it out and was told he was free to leave. Witness H was ordered to drag Fikret Harambašić to a nearby table, where he then stood beside him and was then ordered to return to his room, which he did. Fikret Harambašić has not been seen or heard of since".[9]

2. Zejnil **<u>Delalić *et al.*</u>** (Case No. IT-96-21) "***Čelebići Camp***" - Zejnil Delalić: From May 1992 to July 1992, coordinator of the Bosnian Muslim and Bosnian Croat forces in the Konjic area; from June to November 1992, Commander of the First Tactical Group of the Bosnian Army. - Zdravko Mucić: From about May 1992 to November 1992, Commander of Čelebići prison-camp, established by the Bosnian Muslim and Bosnian Croat forces in mid-1992 and located near Konjic in central Bosnia and Herzegovina. - Hazim Delić: From about May 1992 to November 1992, Deputy Commander of Čelebići prison-camp; from about November and December 1992, Commander of the prison. - Esad Landžo: From May 1992 to December 1992, worked as a guard at the Čelebići prison-camp.	
Indictment (International sex crimes (or related) charges and mode(s) of liability)	- **Torture as a grave breach of the Geneva Conventions of 1949 (WC)** (counts 18, 21 and 33) and **Torture as a violation of the laws or customs of war (WC)** (counts 19, 22 and 34) or, in the alternative, **Cruel treatment as a violation of the laws or customs of war (WC)** (counts 20, 23 and 35) under Articles 7(1) and 7(3) of the Statute (**superior responsibility**) for subjecting Grozdana Ćećez to repeated rapes, including gang-rapes and rapes in front of other persons[10] and for subjecting a detainee, Witness A, to repeated rapes and, in the case of Hazim Delić, for raping this detainee himself.[11] Hazim Delić was charged under both Articles 7(1) and 7(3) of the

[9] *Tadić* Trial Judgement, para. 206. See also *Tadić* Trial Judgement, para. 198.

[10] *Prosecutor v. Zejnil Delalić et al.*, Case No. IT-96-21-I, Indictment, 20 March 1996 ("*Zejnil Delalić et al.* Indictment"), para. 24 ("Sometime beginning around 27 May 1992 and continuing until the beginning of August 1992, **Hazim DELIĆ** and others subjected Grozdana ĆEĆEZ to repeated incidents of forcible sexual intercourse. On one occasion, she was raped in front of other persons, and on another occasion she was raped by three different persons in one night. By his acts and omissions, **Hazim DELIĆ** is responsible for: **Count 18. A Grave Breach** punishable under Article 2(b) (torture) of the Statute of the Tribunal; **Count 19. A Violation of the Laws or Customs of War** punishable under Article 3 of the Statute of the Tribunal and recognised by Article 3(1)(a)(torture) of the Geneva Conventions; or alternatively **Count 20. A Violation of the Laws or Customs of War** punishable under Article 3 of the Statute of the Tribunal and recognised by Article 3(1)(a)(cruel treatment) of the Geneva Conventions".). See also *Zejnil Delalić et al.* Indictment, para. 29 ("With respect to the acts of torture committed in Čelebići camp, […] including those acts of torture described in paragraphs twenty-three to twenty-eight, **Zejnil DELALIĆ**, **Zdravko MUCIĆ**, and **Hazim DELIĆ** knew or had reason to know that subordinates were about to commit those acts or had done so, and failed either to take the necessary and reasonable steps to prevent those acts or to punish the perpetrators. With respect to those counts above where **Hazim DELIĆ** is charged as a direct participant, he is also charged here as a superior. By their acts and omissions, Zejnil **DELALIĆ**, **Zdravko MUCIĆ**, and **Hazim DELIĆ** are responsible for: **Count 33. A Grave Breach** punishable under Article 2(b) (torture) of the Statute of the Tribunal; **Count 34. A Violation of the Laws or Customs of War** punishable under Article 3 of the Statute of the Tribunal and recognised by Article 3(1)(a)(torture) of the Geneva Conventions; or alternatively **Count 35. A Violation of the Laws or Customs of War** punishable under Article 3 of the Statute of the Tribunal and recognised by Article 3(1)(a)(cruel treatment) of the Geneva Conventions".).

[11] *Zejnil Delalić et al.* Indictment, para. 25 ("Sometime beginning around 15 June 1992 and continuing until the beginning of August 1992, **Hazim DELIĆ** subjected a detainee, here identified as Witness A, to repeated incidents of forcible sexual intercourse, including both vaginal and anal intercourse. **Hazim DELIĆ** raped her

	Statute (**superior responsibility**) for these acts, while Zejnil Delalić and Zdravko Mucić were charged only under Article 7(3) of the Statute (**superior responsibility**). - Zejnil Delalić, Zdravko Mucić, and Hazim Delić: **Wilfully causing great suffering or serious injury to body or health as a grave breach of the Geneva Conventions of 1949 (WC)** (count 38) and **Cruel treatment as a violation of the laws or customs of war (WC)** (count 39) under Article 7(3) of the Statute (**superior responsibility**) for placing a burning fuse cord around the genital areas of two detainees.[12] - Zejnil Delalić, Zdravko Mucić, and Hazim Delić: **Inhuman treatment as a grave breach of the Geneva Conventions of 1949 (WC)** (count 44) and **Cruel treatment as a violation of the laws or customs of war (WC)** (count 45) under Article 7(3) of the Statute (**superior responsibility**) for forcing detainees to commit fellatio on each other.[13] - Esad Landžo: no charges related to international sex crimes.
Trial Judgement	- Zejnil Delalić: Acquitted of all counts, including the international sex crimes charges, because the Prosecution failed to prove that Zejnil Delalić had superior responsibility over Čelebići prison-camp, its commander, deputy commander or guards.[14] - Hazim Delić: Acquitted of all counts for which he was charged under Article 7(3) of the Statute, because the Prosecution failed to prove that Hazim Delić had superior responsibility over Čelebići prison-camp.[15] Guilty of **Torture as a grave breach of the Geneva Conventions of 1949 (WC)** (counts 18 and 21) and **Torture as a viola-**

during her first interrogation and during the next six weeks, she was raped every few days. By his acts and omissions, **Hazim DELIĆ** is responsible for: **Count 21. A Grave Breach** punishable under Article 2(b) (torture) of the Statute of the Tribunal; **Count 22. A Violation of the Laws or Customs of War** punishable under Article 3 of the Statute of the Tribunal and recognised by Article 3(1)(a)(torture) of the Geneva Conventions; or alternatively **Count 23. A Violation of the Laws or Customs of War** punishable under Article 3 of the Statute of the Tribunal and recognised by Article 3(1)(a)(cruel treatment) of the Geneva Conventions".). See also *Zejnil Delalić et al.* Indictment, para. 29.

12 *Zejnil Delalić et al.* Indictment, para. 31 ("With respect to the acts causing great suffering committed in Čelebići camp, including […] placing of a burning fuse cord around the genital areas of Vukašin MRKAJIĆ and Duško BENĐO […], **Zejnil DELALIĆ, Zdravko MUCIĆ**, and **Hazim DELIĆ** knew or had reason to know that subordinates were about to commit those acts or had done so, and failed either to take the necessary and reasonable steps to prevent those acts or to punish the perpetrators. With respect to those counts above where **Hazim DELIĆ** is charged as a direct participant, he is also charged here as a superior. By their acts and omissions, **Zdravko MUCIĆ** and **Hazim DELIĆ** are responsible for: **Count 38. A Grave Breach** punishable under Article 2(c) (wilfully causing great suffering or serious injury) of the Statute of the Tribunal; and **Count 39. A Violation of the Laws or Customs of War** punishable under Article 3 of the Statute of the Tribunal and recognised by Article 3(1)(a)(cruel treatment) of the Geneva Conventions".).

13 *Zejnil Delalić et al.* Indictment, para. 34 ("With respect to the incidents of inhumane acts committed in Čelebići camp, including forcing persons to commit fellatio with each other […], **Zejnil DELALIĆ, Zdravko MUCIĆ**, and **Hazim DELIĆ** knew or had reason to know that subordinates were about to commit those acts or had done so, and failed either to take the necessary and reasonable steps to prevent those acts or to punish the perpetrators. With respect to those counts above where **Hazim DELIĆ** is charged as a direct participant, he is also charged here as a superior. By their acts and omissions, **Zejnil DELALIĆ, Zdravko MUCIĆ**, and **Hazim DELIĆ** are responsible for: **Count 44. A Grave Breach** punishable under Article 2(b) (inhuman treatment) of the Statute of the Tribunal; and **Count 45. A Violation of the Laws or Customs of War** punishable under Article 3 of the Statute of the Tribunal and recognised by Article 3(1)(a) (cruel treatment) of the Geneva Conventions".).

14 *Prosecutor v. Zejnil Delalić et al.*, Case No. IT-96-21-T, Judgement, 16 November 1998 ("*Zejnil Delalić et al.* Trial Judgement"), paras. 721, 1285. See also *Zejnil Delalić et al.* Trial Judgement, paras. 605–720.

15 *Zejnil Delalić et al.* Trial Judgement, para. 810. See also *Zejnil Delalić et al.* Trial Judgement, paras. 776–809.

	tion of the laws or customs of war (WC) (counts 19 and 22) under Article 7(1) of the Statute (**committing**) for the rape of Grozdana Ćećez[16] and for the multiple rapes of Milojka Antić (Witness A).[17] - Zdravko Mucić: Guilty of **Torture as a grave breach of the Geneva Conventions of 1949 (WC)** (count 33) and **Torture as a violation of the laws or customs of war (WC)** (count 34) under Article 7(3) of the Statute (**superior responsibility**)[18] for the multiple rapes of Grozdana Ćećez and Milojka Antić (Witness A).[19] Guilty of **Wilfully causing great suffering or serious injury to body or health as a grave breach of the Geneva Conventions of 1949 (WC)** (count 38) and **Cruel treatment as a violation of the laws or customs of war (WC)** (count 39) under Article 7(3) of the Statute (**superior responsibility**)[20] for the serious pain and injury inflicted upon Vukašin Mrkajić, a detainee, when Esad Landžo placed a burning fuse cord against Vukašin Mrkajić's bare skin in the genital area.[21] Guilty of **Inhuman treatment as a grave breach of the Geneva Conventions of 1949 (WC)** (count 44) and **Cruel treatment as a violation of the laws or customs of war (WC)** (count 45) under Article 7(3) of the Statute (**superior responsibility**)[22] for when Esad Landžo forced two detainees, Vaso Đorđić and his brother Veseljko Đorđić, to commit fellatio on each other.[23]
Appeal Judgement	- The Appeals Chamber found that "multiple criminal convictions entered under different statutory provisions but based on the same conduct are permissible only if each statutory provision involved has a materially distinct element not contained in the other".[24] Therefore, it upheld Hazim Delić's convictions for Torture as a grave breach of the Geneva Conventions of 1949 (WC) (counts 18 and 21) but **reversed his convictions for Torture as a violation of the laws or customs of war (WC)** (counts 19 and 22). Similarly, the Appeals Chamber upheld Zdravko Mucić's convictions for Torture as a grave breach of the Geneva Conventions of 1949 (WC) (count 33), Wilfully causing great suffering or serious injury to body or health as a grave breach of the Geneva Conventions of 1949 (WC) (count 38) and Inhuman treatment as a grave breach of the Geneva Conventions of 1949 (WC) (count 44) and **reversed his convictions for Torture as a violation of the laws or customs of war (WC)** (count 34), **Cruel treatment as a violation of the laws or customs of war (WC)** (count 39) **and Cruel treatment as a violation of the laws or customs of war (WC)** (count 45).[25]
Legal and Factual Findings	- The Trial Judgement contains the first conviction for rape as torture constituting war crimes (charged as a grave breach of the Geneva Conventions of 1949 and violation of the laws of customs of war) by the ICTY.

16 *Zejnil Delalić et al.* Trial Judgement, paras. 936–943, 1253, 1262, 1285.

17 *Zejnil Delalić et al.* Trial Judgement, paras. 955–965, 1253, 1263, 1285.

18 *Zejnil Delalić et al.* Trial Judgement, paras. 775, 1010–1011. See also *Zejnil Delalić et al.* Trial Judgement, paras. 722–774.

19 *Zejnil Delalić et al.* Trial Judgement, paras. 1010–1011, 1237, 1285.

20 *Zejnil Delalić et al.* Trial Judgement, paras. 775, 1047. See also *Zejnil Delalić et al.* Trial Judgement, paras. 722–774.

21 *Zejnil Delalić et al.* Trial Judgement, paras. 1039–1040, 1047, 1237, 1285. See also *Zejnil Delalić et al.* Trial Judgement, paras. 1035–1038. The Trial Chamber found that the Prosecution did not present evidence in relation to the alleged placing of a burning fuse cord around the genital area of Duško Benđo, the second detainee, as alleged in the *Zejnil Delalić et al.* Indictment. See *Zejnil Delalić et al.* Trial Judgement, paras. 1041–1045, 1047.

22 *Zejnil Delalić et al.* Trial Judgement, paras. 775, 1072. See also *Zejnil Delalić et al.* Trial Judgement, paras. 722–774.

23 *Zejnil Delalić et al.* Trial Judgement, paras. 1062-1066, 1072, 1237, 1285.

24 *Prosecutor v. Zejnil Delalić et al.*, Case No. IT-96-21-A, Judgement, 20 February 2001 ("*Zejnil Delalić et al.* Appeal Judgement"), para. 412.

25 *Zejnil Delalić et al.* Appeal Judgement, para. 427 and Section XV (Disposition), p. 306. See also *Zejnil Delalić et al.* Appeal Judgement, paras. 400–426.

and/or Evidence	- Legal findings: **- Rape:** The Trial Chamber adopted the definition of rape given by the ICTR in the *Akayesu* case:[26] "This Trial Chamber [...] sees no reason to depart from the conclusion of the ICTR in the *Akayesu Judgement* on this issue. Thus, the Trial Chamber considers rape to constitute a physical invasion of a sexual nature, committed on a person under circumstances that are coercive".[27] **- Rape as Torture:** In considering whether rape met each of the elements of the crime of torture, the Trial Chamber examined the relevant findings of other international judicial and quasi-judicial bodies as well as some relevant United Nations reports.[28] The Trial Chamber then concluded that rape and other forms of sexual violence may constitute torture: "The Trial Chamber considers the rape of any person to be a despicable act which strikes at the very core of human dignity and physical integrity. The condemnation and punishment of rape becomes all the more urgent where it is committed by, or at the instigation of, a public official, or with the consent or acquiescence of such an official. Rape causes severe pain and suffering, both physical and psychological. The psychological suffering of persons upon whom rape is inflicted may be exacerbated by social and cultural conditions and can be particularly acute and long lasting. Furthermore, it is difficult to envisage circumstances in which rape, by, or at the instigation of a public official, or with the consent or acquiescence of an official, could be considered as occurring for a purpose that does not, in some way, involve punishment, coercion, discrimination or intimidation. In the view of this Trial Chamber this is inherent in situations of armed conflict. Accordingly, whenever rape and other forms of sexual violence meet the aforementioned criteria, then they shall constitute torture, in the same manner as any other acts that meet this criteria".[29] - Factual findings: - Rape of Grozdana Ćećez: "Ms. Ćećez, born on 19 April 1949, was a store owner in Konjic until May 1992. She was arrested in Donje Selo on 27 May 1992, and taken to the Čelebići prison-camp. She was kept in Building B for the first two nights of her detention and was then taken to Building A on the third night, where she stayed until her release on 31 August 1992. Upon her arrival at the prison-camp she was taken by a driver, Mr. Džajić, to a room where a man with a crutch was waiting, whom she subsequently identified as Hazim Delić. Another man subsequently entered the room. Ms. Ćećez was interrogated by Mr. Delić, who asked her about the whereabouts of her husband and slapped her. She was then taken to a second room with three men, including Mr. Delić. Hazim Delić who was in uniform and carrying a stick, then ordered her to take her clothes off. He then partially undressed her, put her face down on the bed and penetrated her vagina with his penis. He subsequently turned her over on to her back, took off the remainder of her clothes and again penetrated her vagina with his penis. During this time, Mr. Džajić was lying on another bed in the same room and the other man present was standing guard at the door of the room. Mr. Delić told her that the reason she was there

26 ICTR ISCC *Akayesu*, see *infra* p. 649.

27 *Zejnil Delalić et al.* Trial Judgement, para. 479 (internal citation omitted). See also *Zejnil Delalić et al.* Trial Judgement, para. 478.

28 *Zejnil Delalić et al.* Trial Judgement, paras. 480–493.

29 *Zejnil Delalić et al.* Trial Judgement, paras. 495–496.

was her husband, and that she would not be there if he was. Later that evening Zdravko Mucić came to the room where she was being kept and asked about the whereabouts of her husband. He noticed her appearance and asked her whether anyone had touched her. She did not dare to say anything as Delić had instructed her not to do so. However Mr. Mucić 'could notice that I [Ms. Ćećez] had been raped because there was a big trace of sperm left on the bed'. The effect of this rape by Hazim Delić was expressed by Ms. Ćećez, when she stated: '… he trampled on my pride and I will never be able to be the woman that I was'. Ms. Ćećez lived in constant fear while she was in the prison-camp and was suicidal. Further, Ms. Ćećez was subjected to multiple rapes on the third night of her detention in the prison-camp when she was transferred from Building B to a small room in Building A. After the third act of rape that evening she stated '[i]t was difficult for me. I was a woman who only lived for one man and I was his all my life, and I think that I was just getting separated from my body at this time.' In addition, she was subjected to a further rape in July 1992. As a result of her experiences in the prison-camp Ms. Ćećez stated that '[p]sychologically and physically I was completely worn out. They kill you psychologically.' […] The Trial Chamber finds that acts of vaginal penetration by the penis under circumstances that were coercive, quite clearly constitute rape. These acts were intentionally committed by Hazim Delić who was, an official of the Bosnian authorities running the prison-camp. The purposes of the rapes committed by Hazim Delić were, *inter alia*, to obtain information about the whereabouts of Ms. Ćećez's husband who was considered an armed rebel; to punish her for her inability to provide information about her husband; to coerce and intimidate her into providing such information; and to punish her for the acts of her husband. The fact that these acts were committed in a prison-camp, by an armed official, and were known of by the commander of the prison-camp, the guards, other people who worked in the prison-camp and most importantly, the inmates, evidences Mr. Delić's purpose of seeking to intimidate not only the victim but also other inmates, by creating an atmosphere of fear and powerlessness. In addition, the violence suffered by Ms. Ćećez in the form of rape, was inflicted upon her by Delić because she is a woman. As discussed above, this represents a form of discrimination which constitutes a prohibited purpose for the offence of torture. Finally, there can be no question that these rapes caused severe mental pain and suffering to Ms. Ćećez. The effects of the rapes that she suffered at the hands of Hazim Delić are readily apparent from her own testimony and included living in a state of constant fear and depression, suicidal tendencies, and exhaustion, both mental and physical".[30]

- Multiple rapes of Milojka Antić (Witness A):

"The Trial Chamber thus finds that Ms. Antić was raped for the first time on the night of her arrival in the prison-camp. On this occasion she was called out of Building A and brought to Hazim Delić in Building B, who was wearing a uniform. He began to interrogate her and told her that if she did not do whatever he asked she would be sent to another camp or she would be shot. Mr. Delić ordered her to take her clothes off, threatened her and ignored her crying pleas for him not to touch her. He pointed a rifle at her while she took her clothes off and ordered her to lie on a bed. Mr. Delić then raped her by penetrating her vagina with his penis, he ejaculated on the lower part of her stomach and continued to threaten and curse her. She was brought back to her room in Building A in tears, where she stated that she exclaimed, 'Oh, fuck you, God, in case you exist. Why did you not protect me from this?' The following day, Hazim Delić came to the door of the room where she was sleeping and she began crying upon seeing him. He then said to her '[w]hy are you crying? This will not be your last time'. Ms. Antić stated during her testimony 'I felt so miserably [sic], I was constantly crying. I was like crazy, as if I had gone crazy.' […] The second rape occurred when

30 *Zejnil Delalić et al.* Trial Judgement, paras. 937–938, 940–942 (internal references omitted).

Hazim Delić came to Building A and ordered Ms. Antić to go to Building B to wash herself. After doing so, she was led to the same room in which she was first raped, where Delić, who had a pistol and a rifle and was in uniform, was sitting on a desk. She started crying once again out of fear. He ordered her to take her clothes off. She kept telling him that she was sick and asking him not to touch her. Out of fear that he would kill her she complied with his orders. Mr. Delić told her to get on the bed and to turn around and kneel. After doing so he penetrated her anus with his penis while she screamed from pain. He was unable to penetrate her fully and she started to bleed. Mr. Delić then turned her around and penetrated her vagina with his penis and ejaculated on her lower abdomen. After the rape Ms. Antić continued crying, felt very ill and experienced bleeding from her anus, which she treated with a compress, and was provided with tranquillisers. The third rape occurred in Building A. It was daylight when Hazim Delić came in, armed with hand grenades, a pistol and rifle. He threatened her and she again said that she was a sick woman and asked him not to touch her. He ordered her to undress and get on the bed. She did so under pressure and threat. Mr. Delić then pulled his trousers down to his boots and raped her by penetrating her vagina with his penis. He then ejaculated on her abdomen. The Trial Chamber finds that acts of vaginal penetration by the penis and anal penetration by the penis, under circumstances that were undoubtedly coercive, constitute rape. These rapes were intentionally committed by Hazim Delić who was an official of the Bosnian authorities running the prison-camp. The rapes were committed inside the Čelebiči prison-camp and on each occasion Hazim Delić was in uniform, armed and viciously threatening towards Ms. Antić. The purpose of these rapes was to intimidate, coerce and punish Ms. Antić. Further, at least with respect to the first rape, Delić's purpose was to obtain information from Ms. Antić, as it was committed in the context of interrogation. In addition, the violence suffered by Ms. Antić in the form of rape, was inflicted upon her by Delić because she is a woman. As discussed above, this represents a form of discrimination which constitutes a prohibited purpose for the offence of torture. Finally, there can be no question that these rapes caused severe mental and physical pain and suffering to Ms. Antić. The effects of the rapes that she suffered at the hands of Hazim Delić, including the extreme pain of anal penetration and subsequent bleeding, the severe psychological distress evidenced by the victim while being raped under circumstance where Mr. Delić was armed and threatening her life, and the general depression of the victim, evidenced by her constant crying, the feeling that she was going crazy and the fact that she was treated with tranquilizers, demonstrate most emphatically the severe pain and suffering that she endured".[31]

- Forcing two detainees, Vaso Đorđić and his brother Veseljko Đorđić, to commit fellatio on each other:

"[T]he Trial Chamber finds that, on one occasion, Esad Landžo ordered Vaso Đorđić and his brother, Veseljko Đorđić, to remove their trousers in front of the other detainees in Hangar 6. He then forced first one brother and then the other to kneel down and take the other one's penis into his mouth for a period of about two to three minutes. This act of fellatio was performed in full view of the other detainees in the Hangar. The Trial Chamber finds that the act of forcing Vaso Đorđić and Veseljko Đorđić to perform fellatio on one another constituted, at least, a fundamental attack on their human dignity. Accordingly, the Trial Chamber finds that this act constitutes the offence of inhuman treatment under Article 2 of the Statute, and cruel treatment under Article 3 of the Statute. The Trial Chamber notes that the aforementioned act could constitute rape for which liability could have been found if pleaded in the appropriate manner".[32]

31 *Zejnil Delalić et al.* Trial Judgement, paras. 958–964 (internal references omitted).

32 *Zejnil Delalić et al.* Trial Judgement, paras. 1065–1066.

	- <u>Evidence:</u> - **Evidence of prior sexual conduct:** The Trial Chamber was called upon to address the issue of the inadmissibility of evidence concerning the prior sexual conduct of victims of sexual assault. Such evidence is specifically excluded pursuant to Rule 96(iv) of the Rules of Procedure and Evidence. On this basis, the Trial Chamber ordered the redaction from the public record of references made in open court to the prior sexual conduct of a Prosecution witness while testifying to a charge of sexual assault.[33]

3. Anto <u>**Furundžija**</u> (Case No. IT-95-17/1) "***Lašva Valley***" A commander of the "Jokers", a unit of the Croatian Defence Council (HVO); an active combatant in the Vitez municipality in central Bosnia and Herzegovina.	
Indictment (International sex crimes (or related) charges and mode(s) of liability)	- **Torture as a violation of the laws or customs of war (WC)** (count 13), **Outrages upon personal dignity including rapes as a violation of the laws or customs of war (WC)** (count 14) under Article 7(1) of the Statute for being present and not stopping the repeated rapes of Witness A during her interrogation.[34]
Trial Judgement	- Guilty of **Torture as a violation of the laws or customs of war (WC)** (count 13) under Article 7(1) of the Statute (**co-perpetration**), **Outrages upon personal dignity including rape as a violation of the laws or customs of war (WC)** (count 14) under Article 7(1) of the Statute (**aiding and abetting**)[35] for interrogating Witness A, who was naked, while Accused B rubbed his knife on Witness A's inner thighs and threatened to cut out her private parts if she did not tell the truth in answer to the interrogation by Furundžija. Accused B then repeatedly raped Witness A in front of an audience of soldiers. Although Furundžija did not rape Witness A himself, the Trial Chamber found that Furundžija's presence and continued interrogation of Witness A aided and abetted the crimes committed by Accused B.[36]

33 *Zejnil Delalić et al.* Trial Judgement, para. 70.

34 *Prosecutor v. Anto Furundžija*, Case No. IT-95-17/1-PT, Amended Indictment, 2 June 1998, paras. 25 ("On or about 15 May 1993, at the Jokers Headquarters in Nadioci (the 'Bungalow'), Anto FURUNDŽIJA the local commander of the Jokers, [REDACTED] and another soldier interrogated Witness A. While being questioned by FURUNDŽIJA, [REDACTED] rubbed his knife against Witness A's inner thigh and lower stomach and threatened to put his knife inside Witness A's vagina should she not tell the truth".), 26 ("Then Witness A and Victim B, a Bosnian Croat who had previously assisted Witness A's family, were taken to another room in the 'Bungalow'. Victim B had been badly beaten prior to this time. While FURUNDŽIJA continued to interrogate Witness A and Victim B, [REDACTED] beat Witness A and Victim B on the feet with a baton. Then [REDACTED] forced Witnesses A to have oral and vaginal sexual intercourse with him. FURUNDŽIJA was present during this entire incident and did nothing to stop or curtail [REDACTED] actions".).

35 *Prosecutor v. Anto Furundžija*, Case No. IT-95-17/1-T, Judgement, 10 December 1998 ("*Furundžija* Trial Judgement"), paras. 269, 275 and Section IX (Disposition), p. 112.

36 For details on the factual findings, see also *Furundžija* Trial Judgement, paras. 124–126 ("In the Large Room: Witness A was interrogated by the accused. She was forced by Accused B to undress and remain naked before a substantial number of soldiers. She was subjected to cruel, inhuman and degrading treatment and to threats of serious physical assault by Accused B in the course of her interrogation by the accused. The purpose of this abuse was to extract information from Witness A about her family, her connection with the ABiH and her relationship with certain Croatian soldiers, and also to degrade and humiliate her. The interro-

Appeal Judgement	- The convictions were affirmed by the Appeals Chamber.[37]
Legal and Factual Findings and/or Evidence	- This is the first case before the ICTY concentrating entirely on charges of sexual violence. - Legal findings:[38] **- Rape:** The prohibition of rape and serious sexual assaults in armed conflict has evolved in customary international law and entails the individual criminal responsibility of the perpetrators.[39] Rape may amount to torture.[40] "Rape may also amount to a grave breach of the Geneva Conventions, a violation of the laws or customs of war or an act of genocide, if the requisite elements are met, and may be prosecuted accordingly".[41] The Trial Chamber gave the following definition of rape: "the Trial Chamber finds that the following may be accepted as the objective elements of rape: (i) the sexual penetration, however slight: (a) of the vagina or anus of the victim by the penis of the perpetrator or any other object used by the perpetrator; or (b) of the mouth of the victim by the penis of the perpetrator; (ii) by coercion or force or threat of force against the victim or a third person".[42] - Factual and legal findings: "Count 13 is based on what happened in the large room and in the pantry of the Holiday Cottage. The Trial Chamber is satisfied that the accused was present in the large room and interrogated Witness A, whilst she was in a state of nudity. As she was being interrogated, Accused B rubbed his knife on the inner thighs of Witness A and threatened to cut out her private parts if she did not tell the truth in answer to the interroga-

gation by the accused and the abuse by Accused B were parallel to each other. Witness A was left by the accused in the custody of Accused B, who proceeded to rape her, sexually assault her, and to physically abuse and degrade her. Witness A was subjected to severe physical and mental suffering and public humiliation".), 127–130 ("In the Pantry: The interrogation of Witness A continued in the pantry, once more before an audience of soldiers. Whilst naked but covered by a small blanket, she was interrogated by the accused. She was subjected to rape, sexual assaults, and cruel, inhuman and degrading treatment by Accused B. Witness D was also interrogated by the accused and subjected to serious physical assaults by Accused B. He was made to watch rape and sexual assault perpetrated upon a woman whom he knew, in order to force him to admit allegations made against her. In this regard, both witnesses were humiliated. Accused B beat Witness D and repeatedly raped Witness A. The accused was present in the room as he carried on his interrogations. When not in the room, he was present in the near vicinity, just outside an open door and he knew that crimes including rape were being committed. In fact, the acts by Accused B were performed in pursuance of the accused's interrogation. It is clear that in the pantry, both Witness A and Witness D were subjected to severe physical and mental suffering and they were also publicly humiliated. There is no doubt that the accused and Accused B, as commanders, divided the process of interrogation by performing different functions. The role of the accused was to question, while Accused B's role was to assault and threaten in order to elicit the required information from Witness A and Witness D".).

37 *Prosecutor v. Anto Furundžija*, Case No. IT-95-17/1-A, Judgement, 21 July 2000, Section VIII (Disposition), p. 79.

38 For a discussion on rape and other serious sexual assaults in international law, see *Furundžija* Trial Judgement, paras. 165–189.

39 *Furundžija* Trial Judgement, paras. 168–169.

40 *Furundžija* Trial Judgement, paras. 163, 171.

41 *Furundžija* Trial Judgement, para. 172 (internal references omitted).

42 *Furundžija* Trial Judgement, para. 185. See also *Furundžija* Trial Judgement, para. 261.

	tion by the accused. The accused did not stop his interrogation, which eventually culminated in his threatening to confront Witness A with another person, meaning Witness D and that she would then confess to the allegations against her. To this extent, the interrogation by the accused and the activities of Accused B became one process. The physical attacks, as well as the threats to inflict severe injury, caused severe physical and mental suffering to Witness A. The intention of the accused, as well as Accused B, was to obtain information which they believed would benefit the HVO. They therefore questioned Witness A about the activities of members of Witness A's family and certain other named individuals, her relationship with certain HVO soldiers and details of her alleged involvement with the ABiH. The Trial Chamber has found that the accused was also present in the pantry where the second phase of the interrogation of Witness A occurred. Witness D was taken there for a confrontation with Witness A to make her confess as 'promised' by the accused in the large room. Both Witness A and Witness D were interrogated by the accused and hit on the feet with a baton by Accused B in the course of this questioning. Accused B again assaulted Witness A who was still naked, before an audience of soldiers. He raped her by the mouth, vagina and anus and forced her to lick his penis clean. The accused continued to interrogate Witness A in the same manner as he had done earlier in the large room. As the interrogation intensified, so did the sexual assaults and the rape. The intention of the accused, as detailed above, was to obtain information from Witness A by causing her severe physical and mental suffering. In relation to Witness D, the accused intended to extract information about his alleged betrayal of the HVO to the ABiH and his assistance to Witness A and her children. The Trial Chamber finds that in relation to Witness A, the elements of torture have been met. Within the provisions of Article 7(1) and the findings of the Trial Chamber on liability for torture, the accused is a co-perpetrator by virtue of his interrogation of her as an integral part of the torture. The Trial Chamber finds that the accused tortured Witness A".[43] "The rapes committed by Accused B on Witness A were not disputed in any of the details described by the victim and Witness D. What was contested was the presence of the accused, and, to some extent, whether he played any part in their commission. The Trial Chamber has found that Witness A was subjected to rape and serious sexual assaults by Accused B in the course of the interrogation by the accused. The elements of rape [...] were met when Accused B penetrated Witness A's mouth, vagina and anus with his penis. Consent was not raised by the Defence, and in any case, Witness A was in captivity. Further, it is the position of the Trial Chamber that any form of captivity vitiates consent. Under Rule 96 of the Rules, it is clear that no corroboration of the evidence of Witness A is required. The Trial Chamber notes that in any case, the evidence of Witness D does confirm the evidence of Witness A in this regard. The Trial Chamber is satisfied that all the elements of rape were met. Again, the rapes and sexual assaults were committed publicly; members of the Jokers were watching and milling around the open door of the pantry. They laughed at what was going on. The Trial Chamber finds that Witness A suffered severe physical and mental pain, along with public humiliation, at the hands of Accused B in what amounted to outrages upon her personal dignity and sexual integrity. The position of the accused has already been discussed. He did not personally rape Witness A, nor can he be considered, under the circumstances of this case, to be a co-perpetrator. The accused's presence and continued interrogation of Witness A encouraged Accused B and substantially contributed to the criminal acts committed by him. [...T]he Trial Chamber holds that the presence of the accused and his continued interrogation aided and abetted the crimes committed by Accused B. He is individually responsible for outrages upon personal dignity including rape, a violation of the laws or customs of war under Article 3 of the Statute".[44]

43 *Furundžija* Trial Judgement, paras. 264–267.

44 *Furundžija* Trial Judgement, paras. 270–274.

	- Evidence: **- Reliability of a witness suffering from post-traumatic stress disorder (PTSD) following an international sex crime:** The Trial Chamber found that there is no reason why a person suffering from PTSD cannot be a perfectly reliable witness.[45]

4. Tihomir **Blaškić** (Case No. IT-95-14) "***Lašva Valley***" Colonel in the Croatian Defence Council (HVO) and became commander of the HVO in the Central Bosnian Operative Zone on 27 June 1992; promoted to the rank of General and appointed Commander of the HVO at the beginning of August 1994.	
Indictment (International sex crimes (or related) charges and mode(s) of liability)	- There are no factual allegations of international sex crimes in the Indictment. However, the charges for which Tihomir Blaškić was tried for international sex crimes are the following: **Inhuman treatment as a grave breach of the Geneva Conventions of 1949 (WC)** (count 15), **Cruel treatment as a violation of the laws or customs of war (WC)** (count 16) under Article 7(1) (**planning, instigating, ordering or otherwise aiding and abetting**) or, in the alternative, Article 7(3) of the Statute (**superior responsibility**).[46]
Trial Judgement	- Guilty of **Inhuman treatment as a grave breach of the Geneva Conventions of 1949 (WC)** (count 15), **Cruel treatment as a violation of the laws or customs of war (WC)** (count 16) under Article 7(3) of the Statute (**superior responsibility**). The Trial Chamber found that Tihomir Blaškić had reason to know that various crimes, including rapes of Bosnian Muslims detained by the HVO in Rotilj village (Kiseljak municipality) and in Dubravica primary school (Vitez municipality), were committed by the HVO soldiers and Military Police over which he had effective control and he did not take the necessary and reasonable measures to punish the perpetrators (in this specific case, to duly carry out his duty to investigate the crimes and impose disciplinary measures or to send a report on the perpetrators of these crimes to the competent authorities).[47]
Appeal	- The Appeals Chamber upheld Tihomir Blaškić's conviction for Inhuman treatment as

45 *Furundžija* Trial Judgement, para. 109 ("The Trial Chamber bears in mind that even when a person is suffering from PTSD, this does not mean that he or she is necessarily inaccurate in the evidence given. There is no reason why a person with PTSD cannot be a perfectly reliable witness".).

46 *Prosecutor v. Tihomir Blaškić*, Case No. IT-95-14-T, Second Amended Indictment, 25 April 1997, paras. 12–13 ("From January 1993 to January 1994, **Tihomir BLASKIC**, together with members of the HVO, caused Bosnian Muslims to be detained at the following locations: [...] Dubravica Elementary School [...] Rotilj village [...] and planned, instigated, ordered or otherwise aided and abetted in the planning, preparation or execution of the unlawful and inhumane treatment of Bosnian Muslims [...] and, or in the alternative, knew or had reason to know that subordinates were about to do the same, or had done so, and failed to take the necessary and reasonable measures to prevent such acts or to punish the perpetrators thereof **Inhumane and or cruel treatment of detainees:** Bosnian Muslims, who were detained in HVO controlled detention facilities were used as human shields, beaten, forced to dig trenches, subjected to physical or psychological abuse and intimidation, inhumane treatment including being confined in cramped or overcrowded facilities, and deprived of adequate food and water. [...] By these acts and omissions **Tihomir BLASKIC** committed: **Count 15:** a **GRAVE BREACH** as recognised by Articles 2(b), 7(1) and 7(3) (inhuman treatment) of the Statute of the Tribunal. **Count 16:** a **VIOLATION OF THE LAWS OR CUSTOMS OF WAR** as recognised by Articles 3, 7(1) and 7(3) of the Statute of the Tribunal and Article 3(1)(a) (cruel treatment) of the Geneva Conventions".).

47 *Prosecutor v. Tihomir Blaškić*, Case No. IT-95-14-T, Judgement, 3 March 2000 ("*Blaškić* Trial Judgement"), paras. 692, 695, 700, 720–725, 731–734 and Section VI (Disposition), pp. 267–268.

Judgement	a grave breach of the Geneva Conventions of 1949 (WC) (count 15) under Article 7(3) of the Statute (superior responsibility) but **dismissed his conviction for Cruel treatment as a violation of the laws or customs of war (WC) (count 16) as a cumulative conviction.**[48] Although the Appeals Chamber upheld Tihomir Blaškić's conviction under count 15, it found that **Tihomir Blaškić did not exercise effective control over the subordinates responsible for the crimes, including rapes, committed upon the Bosnian Muslims detained in Rotilj village (Kiseljak municipality) and in Dubravica primary school (Vitez municipality).**[49]
Legal and Factual Findings and/or Evidence	- Factual findings: - Rapes in Rotilj: "The prisoners of Rotilj were forced to endure particularly harsh living conditions. The village was overcrowded and the people crammed into those houses which had not been destroyed. They lacked medicines and there was insufficient water and food. The Trial Chamber points to the murders and acts of physical violence, including rape, which occurred in the village".[50] - Rapes in Dubravica primary school: "Located in a municipal building near to Vitez railway station and just over two and a half kilometres from the Hotel Vitez, Dubravica primary school was the billet for the Vitezovi unit and the Ludwig Pavlović Brigade. During the second half of April 1993, the school also served as an HVO detention centre. Two hundred Muslim men, women and children from the villages of Vitez municipality were detained there. They suffered from a lack of food and comfort. Furthermore, the women and children were terrorised and threatened by their guards. Women were raped by HVO soldiers and members of the Military Police".[51]

5. Dragoljub **Kunarac *et al.*** (Case Nos. IT-96-23 and IT-96-23/1) "***Foča***"

- Dragoljub Kunarac: Leader of a reconnaissance unit of the Bosnian Serb Army (VRS), which formed part of the local Foča Tactical Group.
- Radomir Kovač: One of the sub-commanders of the military unit of the Bosnian Serb Army (VRS); a paramilitary leader in Foča town.
- Zoran Vuković: One of the sub-commanders of the military unit of the Bosnian Serb Army (VRS); a member of the paramilitary in Foča town.

48 *Prosecutor v. Tihomir Blaškić*, Case No. IT-95-14-A, Judgement, 29 July 2004 ("*Blaškić* Appeal Judgement"), paras. 633-634 and Section XIII (Disposition), p. 258.

49 *Blaškić* Appeal Judgement, para. 613 ("However, the Appeals Chamber holds that it was reasonable to find that the Appellant knew of the conditions of detention in the Vitez Cultural Centre and the Vitez veterinary hospital. As regards the other facilities: the detainees in Dubravica, and in the SDK building in Vitez, were subject to Vitezovi control and were beyond the Appellant's control; Kaonik Prison in Busovača was controlled by Military Police who were loyal to others and beyond the Appellant's control; Kiseljak was largely isolated, and thus the detention centres there (the former JNA barracks and Rotilj village) were beyond the Appellant's control; and the detentions in various houses in the village of Gačice has already been shown to have been beyond the Appellant's knowledge" (internal references omitted)). See also *Blaškić* Appeal Judgement, paras. 606–612.

50 *Blaškić* Trial Judgement, para. 692.

51 *Blaškić* Trial Judgement, para. 695 (internal references omitted).

Indictment[52] (International sex crimes (or related) charges and mode(s) of	- Dragoljub Kunarac:[53] **Torture as CAH** (count 1), **Rape as CAH** (count 2), **Torture as a violation of the laws or customs of war (WC)** (count 3) and **Rape as a violation of the laws or customs of war (WC)** (count 4) under Articles 7(1) and 7(3) of the Statute (**superior responsibility**) for removing women – including FWS-48, FWS-50, FWS-75, FWS-87, FWS-95 – from Partizan and taking them to his headquarters at Ulica Osmana Đikića no. 16, where he either personally raped them or was present in the house while his soldiers raped them (including gang-rapes and repeated rapes);[54]

[52] For the general background to the charges, see *Prosecutor v. Dragoljub Kunarac and Radomir Kovač*, Case No. IT-96-23-PT, Third Amended Indictment, 2 December 1999, ("*Kunarac and Kovač* Indictment"), paras. 1.2 ("As soon as the Serb forces had taken over parts of Foča town, military police accompanied by local and non-local soldiers started arresting Muslim and Croat inhabitants. Until mid-July 1992 they continued to round up and arrest Muslim villagers from the surrounding villages in the municipality. The Serb forces separated men and women and unlawfully confined thousands of Muslims and Croats in various short and long-term detention facilities or kept them essentially under house arrest. During the arrests many civilians were killed, beaten or subjected to sexual assault".), 1.3 ("The Foča Kazneno-popravni Dom ('KP Dom'), one of the largest prison facilities in the former Republic of Yugoslavia, was the primary detention facility for men. Muslim women, children and the elderly were detained in houses, apartments and motels in the town of Foča or in surrounding villages, or at short and long-term detention centres such as Buk Bijela, Foča High School and Partizan Sports Hall, respectively. Many of the detained women were subjected to humiliating and degrading conditions of life, to brutal beatings and to sexual assaults, including rapes".), 1.5–1.8 ("Living conditions in Partizan were brutal. The detention was characterised by inhumane treatment, unhygienic facilities, overcrowding, starvation, physical and psychological torture, including sexual assaults. Immediately after the transfer of women to Partizan, a pattern of sexual assaults commenced. Armed soldiers, mostly in groups of three to five, entered Partizan, usually in the evenings, and removed women. When the women resisted or hid, the soldiers beat or threatened the women to force them to obey. The soldiers took the women from Partizan to houses, apartments or hotels for the purpose of sexual assault and rape. Three witnesses, identified by the pseudonyms FWS-48, FWS-95 and FWS-50, a 16 year old girl, were detained at Partizan from about 13 July until 13 August 1992. Two others, identified by the pseudonyms FWS-75 and FWS-87, a 15 year old girl, were detained in Partizan from about 13 July until 2 August 1992. Almost every night during their detention, Serb soldiers took FWS-48, FWS-95, FWS-50, FWS-75 and FWS-87 out of Partizan and sexually abused them (vaginal and anal penetration and fellatio). On or around 13 August 1992, most detainees were released from Partizan and deported to Montenegro. The women who left on the 13 August convoy received medical care for the first time in Montenegro. Many women suffered permanent gynaecological harm due to the sexual assaults. At least one woman can no longer have children. All the women who were sexually assaulted suffered psychological and emotional harm; some remain traumatised".), 1.11 ("Besides the above mentioned detention places, several women were detained in houses and apartments used as brothels, operated by groups of soldiers, mostly paramilitary".), 4.8 ("In all counts charging sexual assault, the victim was subjected to or threatened with or had reason to fear violence, duress, detention or psychological oppression, or reasonably believed that if she did not submit, another might be so subjected, threatened or put in fear".). See also *Zoran Vuković*, Case No. IT-96-23/1-PT, Amended Indictment, 7 October 1999 ("*Vuković* Indictment"), paras. 1.2–1.4.

[53] Originally, Dragoljub Kunarac was also charged with enslavement as CAH (count 14), rape as CAH (count 15), rape as a violation of the laws or customs of war (WC) (count 16), outrages upon personal dignity as a violation of the laws or customs of war (count 17) under Articles 7(1) and 7(3) of the Statute (superior responsibility) for the enslavement and repeated rapes of witness FWS-101, who was 7 months pregnant at the time. See *Kunarac and Kovač* Indictment, paras. 9.1–9.3. However, on 3 April 2000, the Prosecution withdrew counts 14 to 17 from the Indictment as witness FWS-101 was not willing to testify. See *Prosecutor v. Dragoljub Kunarac et al.*, Case No. IT-96-23-T and IT-96-23/1-T, Transcript of hearing, 3 April 2000, pp. 1479–1482.

[54] *Kunarac and Kovač* Indictment, paras. 5.1–5.6 ("Several groups of perpetrators assaulted women detained at Partizan. One group, under the command of **DRAGOLJUB KUNARAC**, was a special unit for reconnaissance detail comprising mostly Serb soldiers from Montenegro. This group maintained their headquarters in a house in the Aladža neighbourhood in Foča at Ulica Osmana Đikica no. 16. Usually at nights, **DRAGOLJUB KUNARAC**, accompanied by some of his soldiers, removed women from Partizan and took them to the house Ulica Osmana Đikica no. 16, knowing that they would be sexually assaulted there by soldiers under his command. After taking the women to his headquarters, **DRAGOLJUB KUNARAC** would sometimes stay and take one of the women to a room and rape her personally. Even when **DRAGOLJUB**

liability)	**Torture as CAH** (count 5), **Rape as CAH** (count 6), **Torture as a violation of the laws or customs of war (WC)** (count 7) and **Rape as a violation of the laws or customs of war (WC)** (count 8) under Article 7(1) of the Statute for taking FWS-48 and two other women to the Hotel Zelengora where he raped FWS-48 (vaginal penetration and fellatio) and for taking FWS-48 and FWS-95 to a house in the Donje Polje neighbourhood where he raped FWS-48 (vaginal penetration and fellatio);[55] **Rape as CAH** (count 9) and **Rape as a violation of the laws or customs of war (WC)** (count 10) under Article 7(1) of the Statute for transferring FWS-75, FWS-87 and two other women from Partizan to Miljevina, where the women were detained in an abandoned

KUNARAC did not personally rape one of the women, he often remained at the headquarters or visited it periodically while other soldiers raped and sexually assaulted the women in the house. On at least two occasions between 13 July and 1 August 1992, **DRAGOLJUB KUNARAC** took FWS-87 to his headquarters at Ulica Osmana Đikica no. 16. On both occasions, two Montenegrin soldiers commanded by the accused were present and raped FWS-87. **DRAGOLJUB KUNARAC** took FWS-75 and D. B. several times to his headquarters at Ulica Osmana Đikica no. 16, where his soldiers were housed. On or around 16 July 1992, **DRAGOLJUB KUNARAC**, together with his deputy 'GAGA', took FWS-75 and D. B. to this house for the first time. When they arrived at the headquarters, a group of soldiers were waiting. **DRAGOLJUB KUNARAC** took D. B. to a separate room and raped her, while FWS-75 was left behind together with the other soldiers. For about 3 hours, FWS-75 was gang-raped by at least 15 soldiers (vaginal and anal penetration and fellatio). They sexually abused her in all possible ways. On other occasions in the headquarters, one to three soldiers, in turn, raped her. On 2 August 1992, **DRAGOLJUB KUNARAC** took FWS-75, FWS-87, FWS-50 and D. B. to the headquarters at Ulica Osmana Đikica no. 16. Some women from the Kalinovik women's detention camp were also present. On this occasion, **DRAGOLJUB KUNARAC** and three other soldiers raped FWS-87. Several soldiers raped FWS-75 during the entire night. A Montenegrin soldier raped FWS-50 (vaginal penetration) and threatened to cut her arms and legs and to take her to church to baptise her. On at least two occasions between 13 July and 2 August 1992, **DRAGOLJUB KUNARAC** took FWS-95 out of Partizan to the headquarters at Ulica Osmana Đikica no. 16 for the purpose of rape. The first time, **DRAGOLJUB KUNARAC** took FWS-95 to his headquarters together with two other women. He took her in a room and raped her personally. Then FWS-95 was raped by three more soldiers in this same room. The second time, after **DRAGOLJUB KUNARAC** had taken her to Ulica Osmana Đikica no. 16, FWS-95 was raped by two or three soldiers, but not by the accused himself. By the foregoing acts and omissions in relation to the witnesses FWS-50, FWS-75, FWS-87, FWS-95, and the other women specified above, [...] **DRAGOLJUB KUNARAC** committed: [...] **Count 1**: Torture, a **CRIME AGAINST HUMANITY** punishable under Article 5 (f) of the Statute of the Tribunal. [...] **Count 2**: Rape, a **CRIME AGAINST HUMANITY** punishable under Article 5 (g) of the Statute of the Tribunal. [...] **Count 3**: Torture, a **VIOLATION OF THE LAWS OR CUSTOMS OF WAR**, punishable under Article 3 of the Statute of the Tribunal and recognised by Common Article 3 (1) (a) (torture) of the Geneva Conventions. [...] **Count 4**: Rape, a **VIOLATION OF THE LAWS OR CUSTOMS OF WAR**, punishable under Article 3 of the Statute of the Tribunal".).

55 *Kunarac and Kovač* Indictment, paras. 6.1–6.3 ("On or around 13 July 1992, **DRAGOLJUB KUNARAC** took FWS-48 and two other women to the Hotel Zelengora. FWS-48 refused to go with him and **DRAGOLJUB KUNARAC** kicked her and dragged her out. At Hotel Zelengora, FWS-48 was placed in a separate room and **DRAGOLJUB KUNARAC** and ZORAN VUKOVIĆ, a local military commander, raped her (vaginal penetration and fellatio). Both perpetrators told her that she would now give birth to Serb babies. On or around 18 July 1992, GOJKO JANKOVIĆ, the military commander of another local unit, took FWS-48, FWS-95 and another woman to a house near the bus station. From there, **DRAGOLJUB KUNARAC** took FWS-48 to another house in the Donje Polje neighbourhood where he raped her (vaginal penetration and fellatio). By the foregoing acts and omissions in relation to the witness FWS-48, [...] **DRAGOLJUB KUNARAC** committed: [...] **Count 5**: Torture, a **CRIME AGAINST HUMANITY** punishable under Article 5 (f) of the Statute of the Tribunal. [...] **Count 6**: Rape, a **CRIME AGAINST HUMANITY** punishable under Article 5 (g) of the Statute of the Tribunal. [...] **Count 7**: Torture, a **VIOLATION OF THE LAWS OR CUSTOMS OF WAR**, punishable under Article 3 of the Statute of the Tribunal and recognised by Common Article 3 (1) (a) (torture) of the Geneva Conventions. [...] **Count 8**: Rape, a **VIOLATION OF THE LAWS OR CUSTOMS OF WAR**, punishable under Article 3 of the Statute of the Tribunal".).

	Muslim house called Karaman's house and for raping FWS-87 there (vaginal penetration);[56] **Torture as a violation of the laws or customs of war (WC)** (count 11) and **Rape as a violation of the laws or customs of war (WC)** (count 12) under Article 7(1) of the Statute for gang-raping FWS-183 with two soldiers (vaginal penetration);[57] **Enslavement as CAH** (count 18), **Rape as CAH** (count 19), **Rape as a violation of the laws or customs of war (WC)** (count 20) and **Outrages upon personal dignity as a violation of the laws or customs of war (WC)** (count 21) under Article 7(1) of the Statute for taking FWS-186, FWS-191 and J.G. from the house Ulica Osmana Đikića no. 16 to the abandoned housed of Halid Čedić in Trnovače, where they were raped, and for raping FWS-191 for approximately 6 months and treating FWS-186 and FWS-191 as his personal property.[58] -Radomir Kovač: **Enslavement as CAH** (count 22), **Rape as CAH** (count 23), **Rape as a violation of the laws or customs of war (WC)** (count 24) and **Outrages upon personal dignity as a violation of the laws or customs of war (WC)** (count 25) under Article 7(1) of the Statute for detaining witnesses FWS-75, FWS-87 and two

56 *Kunarac and Kovač* Indictment, paras. 7.1–7.3 ("On or about 2 August 1992, **DRAGOLJUB KUNARAC**, together with Pero Elez, the military commander of a Serb unit based in Miljevina, municipality of Foča, transferred FWS-75, FWS-87 and two other women from Partizan to Miljevina, where they were detained in an abandoned Muslim house called Karaman's house, a place maintained by PERO ELEZ and his soldiers. Sometime in either September or October 1992, **DRAGOLJUB KUNARAC** visited Karaman's house and raped FWS-87 (vaginal penetration). By the foregoing acts in relation to the witness FWS-87, [...] **DRAGOLJUB KUNARAC** committed: [...] **Count 9**: Rape, a **CRIME AGAINST HUMANITY** punishable under Article 5 (g) of the Statute of the Tribunal. [...] **Count 10**: Rape, a VIOLATION OF THE LAWS OR CUSTOMS OF WAR, punishable under Article 3 of the Statute of the Tribunal".).

57 *Kunarac and Kovač* Indictment, paras. 8.1–8.2 ("One night in mid-July 1992, **DRAGOLJUB KUNARAC**, together with two of his soldiers, accused the witness FWS-183 of sending messages out over radio. They looted the witness' apartment and took her to the banks of the Cehotina river in Foča near Velečevo. There, the accused questioned the witness about the money and gold she and other Muslims in her flat were keeping. During the questioning, the witness was threatened with death and that her son would be slaughtered. After the threats, the witness was raped vaginally by all three soldiers. During the rapes, **DRAGOLJUB KUNARAC** humiliated the witness by saying that they (the soldiers) would never know whose son this was. After returning the witness to her flat, the accused robbed her of all the gold and money she had hidden. By the foregoing acts in relation to the witness FWS-183, [...] **DRAGOLJUB KUNARAC** committed: [...] **Count 11**: Torture, a VIOLATION OF THE LAWS OR CUSTOMS OF WAR, punishable under Article 3 of the Statute of the Tribunal and recognised by Common Article 3 (1) (a) (torture) of the Geneva Conventions. [...] **Count 12**: Rape, a VIOLATION OF THE LAWS OR CUSTOMS OF WAR, punishable under Article 3 of the Statute of the Tribunal".).

58 *Kunarac and Kovač* Indictment, paras. 10.1–10.4 ("On 2 August 1992, the accused **DRAGOLJUB KUNARAC**, together with his deputy 'GAGA' and GOJKO JANKOVIĆ, the commander of another Foča unit, took FWS-186, FWS-191 and J. G. from the house Ulica Osmana Đikica no. 16 to the abandoned house of Halid Čedić in Trnovace. There the men divided the girls among themselves and raped them the same night. On that occasion, **DRAGOLJUB KUNARAC** raped FWS-191. FWS-186 and FWS-191 were kept in this house for approximately 6 months, while J. G. was transferred to Karaman's house in Miljevina for the purpose of rape. During the entire time of her detention in Trnovače, GOJKO JANKOVIĆ constantly raped FWS-186, while for at least two months, the accused **DRAGOLJUB KUNARAC** constantly raped FWS-191. Eventually, another soldier protected FWS-191 against further rapes. After 6 months this soldier took both witnesses away from the house. FWS-186 and FWS-191 were treated as the personal property of **DRAGOLJUB KUNARAC** and GOJKO JANKOVIĆ. In addition to the rapes and other sexual assaults, FWS-186 and FWS-191 had to do all household chores and obey all demands. By the foregoing acts and omissions in relation to the witnesses FWS-186, FWS-191 and J.G. [...], **DRAGOLJUB KUNARAC** committed: [...] **Count 18**: Enslavement, a **CRIME AGAINST HUMANITY** punishable under Article 5 (c) of the Statute of the Tribunal. [...] **Count 19**: Rape, a **CRIME AGAINST HUMANITY** punishable under Article 5 (g) of the Statute of the Tribunal. [...] **Count 20**: Rape, a **VIOLATION OF THE LAWS OR CUSTOMS OF WAR**, punishable under Article 3 of the Statute of the Tribunal. [...] **Count 21**: Outrages upon personal dignity, a **VIOLATION OF THE LAWS OR CUSTOMS OF WAR**, punishable under Article 3 of the Statute of the Tribunal".).

	other women, 20-year-old A.S. and 12-year-old A.B., in an apartment, where they had to perform household chores and where he frequently raped them or ordered them to have sexual intercourse with soldiers and for forcing them to take all their clothes off and dance naked on a table and for selling A.B., and FWS-87 and A.S., for 200 and 500 Deutschemarks respectively.[59] -Zoran Vuković: **Torture as CAH** (count 21), **Rape as CAH** (count 22), **Torture as a violation of the laws or customs of war (WC)** (count 23) and **Rape as a violation of the laws or customs of war (WC)** (count 24) under Article 7(1) of the Statute for raping FWS-75 and FWS-87 (vaginal penetration) in a classroom in the Foča High School;[60] **Torture as CAH** (count 33), **Rape as CAH** (count 34), **Torture as a viola-**

[59] *Kunarac and Kovač* Indictment, paras. 11.1–11.7 ("After the accused **DRAGOLJUB KUNARAC** had transferred the witnesses FWS-75 and FWS- 87 to Karaman's house on 2 August 1992, as described in paragraph 7.1, the witnesses together with seven other women were detained there until about 30 October where they had to perform household chores and were frequently sexually assaulted. On or about 30 October 1992, the witnesses FWS-75 and FWS-87 together with two other women, 20-year-old A.S., and 12-year-old A.B., were taken from Karaman's house to Foča by DRAGAN ZELENOVIĆ, GOJKO JANKOVIĆ and JANKO JANJIĆ and were subsequently handed over to the accused **RADOMIR KOVAČ** near the centre of Foča close to the Ribarski fish restaurant. **RADOMIR KOVAČ** detained, between or about 31 October 1992 until December 1992 witness FWS-75 and A.B., and until February 1993 witness FWS-87 and A.S. **RADOMIR KOVAČ** was in charge of an apartment in the Brena block and had taken over the two witnesses together with two other women, A.S., and A.B., whom he had received from DRAGAN ZELENOVIĆ, GOJKO JANKOVIĆ and JANKO JANJIĆ. Their situation was similar to what they had experienced in Karaman's house. They had to perform household chores and were frequently sexually assaulted, as described in paragraphs 11.3, 11.4, and 11.5. During their detention, FWS-75, FWS-87, A.S. and A.B. were also beaten, threatened, psychologically oppressed, and kept in constant fear. FWS-75 and A.B. were detained in this apartment from about 31 October until about 20 November 1992. During that time they had to do household chores and sexually please soldiers. **RADOMIR KOVAČ** and another soldier, Jagos Kostić, frequently raped them. In addition, on an unknown date during this time, **RADOMIR KOVAČ** brought Slavo Ivanović to the flat and ordered FWS-75 to have sexual intercourse with him; when she refused, **RADOMIR KOVAČ** beat FWS-75. Around 20 November 1992, **RADOMIR KOVAČ** took FWS-75 and victim A. B. from the apartment to a house near the Hotel Zelengora. They were kept there for about twenty days, during which time they were frequently sexually assaulted by a group of unidentified Serbian soldiers who belonged to the Brane Čosović group, the same group to which **RADOMIR KOVAČ** belonged. Although the two women were no longer in the Brena apartment, **RADOMIR KOVAČ** still was in charge of them. Around 10 December 1992, FWS-75 and victim A.B. were moved from the house near Hotel Zelengora to a flat in the Pod Masala neighbourhood of Foča. There, they stayed for about fifteen days, together with the same soldiers. FWS-75 and A.B. were frequently raped by these soldiers during those fifteen days. On about 25 December 1992, when FWS-75 and the other women were brought back to the apartment, **RADOMIR KOVAČ** sold A. B. to an unidentified soldier for 200 DM. On about 26 December 1992, FWS-75 was handed over to JANKO JANJIĆ. FWS-87 and A.S. were detained in **RADOMIR KOVAČ**'s apartment from on or about 31 October until about 25 February, 1993. During this entire time, she and A.S. were raped by **RADOMIR KOVAČ** and Jagos Kostić. On an unknown date between about 31 October 1992 and about 7 November 1992 during their detention in **RADOMIR KOVAČ**'s place, FWS-75, FWS-87, A.S. and A.B. were forced to take all their clothes off and dance naked on a table, while **RADOMIR KOVAČ** watched. On or about 25 February, 1993, FWS-87 and A.S. were sold by **RADOMIR KOVAČ** for 500 DM each to two unidentified Montenegrin soldiers, who took them to Montenegro. By the foregoing acts and omissions, **RADOMIR KOVAČ** committed: [...] **Count 22**: Enslavement, a **CRIME AGAINST HUMANITY** punishable under Article 5 (c) of the Statute of the Tribunal. [...] **Count 23**: Rape, a **CRIME AGAINST HUMANITY** punishable under Article 5 (g) of the Statute of the Tribunal. [...] **Count 24**: Rape, a **VIOLATION OF THE LAWS OR CUSTOMS OF WAR**, punishable under Article 3 of the Statute of the Tribunal. [...] **Count 25**: Outrages upon personal dignity, a **VIOLATION OF THE LAWS OR CUSTOMS OF WAR**, punishable under Article 3 of the Statute of the Tribunal".).

[60] *Vuković* Indictment, paras. 6.4–6.7, 6.16 ("Many of the female detainees were subjected to sexual abuse during their detention at the Foča High School. From the second day of their detention, every evening, groups of Serb soldiers sexually assaulted, including gang-rape, some of the younger women and girls in class-rooms or apartments in neighbouring buildings. Among them were witnesses FWS-50, FWS-75, FWS-

	tion of the laws or customs of war (WC) (count 35) and **Rape as a violation of the laws or customs of war (WC)** (count 36) under Article 7(1) of the Statute for raping FWS-48 (vaginal penetration and fellatio)[61] and FWS-50 (vaginal penetration) and gang-raping FWS-87.[62]

87, FWS-95, FWS-74 and FWS-88, as set forth below. The soldiers threatened to kill the women or the women's children if they refused to submit to sexual assaults. Women who dared to resist the sexual assaults were beaten. The above mentioned groups of soldiers consisted of members of the military police. They referred to themselves 'Ćosa's Guards', named for the local commander of the military police Ćosović. The accused [...] **ZORAN VUKOVIĆ** [was] among these groups of soldiers. The physical and psychological health of many female detainees seriously deteriorated as a result of these sexual assaults. Some of the women endured complete exhaustion, vaginal discharges, bladder problems and irregular menstrual bleedings. The detainees lived in constant fear. Some of the sexually abused women became suicidal. Others became indifferent as to what would happen to them and suffered from depression. On or about 6 or 7 July 1992, DRAGAN ZELENOVIĆ in concert with JANKO JANJIĆ and **ZORAN VUKOVIĆ,** selected FWS-50, FWS-75, FWS-87, FWS-95 out of the group of detainees. The accused led them to another classroom where unidentified soldiers stood waiting. Then DRAGAN ZELENOVIĆ decided which woman should go to which man. The women were ordered to remove their clothes. FWS-95 refused to do so and JANKO JANJIĆ slapped her and held her at gun point. Then DRAGAN ZELENOVIĆ raped FWS-75 (vaginal penetration). **ZORAN VUKOVIĆ** raped FWS-87 (vaginal penetration) and JANKO JANJIĆ raped FWS-95 (vaginal penetration) within the same room. One of the other soldiers took FWS-50 to another classroom and raped her (vaginal penetration). Between or about 8 July and about 13 July 1992, in addition to the sexual assaults described under paragraph 6.6, on at least five other occasions DRAGAN ZELENOVIĆ led a group of soldiers that sexually abused FWS-75 and FWS-87. First the women were taken into another classroom in the Foca High School. There **ZORAN VUKOVIĆ** and DRAGAN ZELENOVIĆ raped FWS-75 and FWS-87 (vaginal penetration). [...] By the foregoing acts and omissions in relation to the victims FWS-50, FWS-95, FWS-75 and FWS-87, **ZORAN VUKOVIĆ** committed: [...] **Count 21:** Torture, a **CRIME AGAINST HUMANITY** punishable under Article 5 (f) of the Statute of the Tribunal. [...] **Count 22:** Rape, a **CRIME AGAINST HUMANITY** punishable under Article 5 (g) of the Statute of the Tribunal. [...] **Count 23:** Torture, a **VIOLATION OF THE LAWS OR CUSTOMS OF WAR,** punishable under Article 3 of the Statute of the Tribunal and recognised by Common Article 3 (1) (a) (TORTURE) of the Geneva Conventions. [...] **Count 24:** Rape, a **VIOLATION OF THE LAWS OR CUSTOMS OF WAR,** punishable under Article 3 of the Statute of the Tribunal".).

61 *Vuković* Indictment, paras. 7.9–7.10, 7.15, 7.18, 7.21 ("The same night [on or around 13 July 1992], after JANKO JANJIĆ returned the women to Partizan, Dragoljub Kunarac took the same three women to the Hotel Zelengora. FWS-48 refused to go with him and Dragoljub Kunarac kicked her and dragged her out. At Hotel Zelengora, FWS-48 was placed in a separate room and both Dragoljub Kunarac and **ZORAN VUKOVIĆ** raped her (vaginal penetration and fellatio). Both perpetrators told her that she would now give birth to Serb babies. On or around 14 July 1992, JANKO JANJIĆ again took FWS-48 together with FWS-87 and Z. G. to the Brena apartment block near Hotel Zelengora. When they arrived, **ZORAN VUKOVIC** and an unidentified soldier were waiting. Then, **ZORAN VUKOVIĆ**, raped FWS-48 (vaginal penetration) while the unidentified soldier raped FWS-87 (vaginal penetration) and JANKO JANJIĆ raped Z. G. [...] On or around 15 July 1992, GOJKO JANKOVIĆ led FWS-48 to an empty Muslim house in the Aladža neighbourhood. When FWS-48 arrived, about 14 Montenegrin soldiers were already present. DRAGAN ZELENOVIĆ then arrived with about 8 more soldiers, among them **ZORAN VUKOVIĆ**. DRAGAN ZELENOVIĆ took FWS-48 to a room and threatened to slash her throat if she resisted. Then, DRAGAN ZELENOVIĆ raped FWS-48 (vaginal penetration and fellatio) together with at least other 7 soldiers. **ZORAN VUKOVIĆ** was the 6th man who raped her. During the sexual assault, **ZORAN VUKOVIĆ** bit her nipples a number of times. Although the witness was bleeding from these bites, the 7th man squeezed and pinched her breasts as he raped her. FWS-48 fainted as a result of the pain. [...] The same night [on or around 23 July 1992], after being taken back to Partizan, JANKO JANJIĆ took FWS-48, together with two other women, to the Brena apartment block, where **ZORAN VUKOVIĆ** and a certain Panto were already waiting. Panto raped FWS-48 (vaginal penetration). She heard **ZORAN VUKOVIĆ** and JANKO JANJIĆ, at the same time, sexually assaulting the other women in the next room. [...] After midnight, on the same night [12 August 1992], JANKO JANJIĆ took FWS-48 together with other women to the Brena apartments. While leaving Partizan, a group of soldiers approached the women and tried to pull them away. JANKO JANJIĆ told these soldiers that he needed these women for his own people and that they should go into Partizan and find other women. **ZORAN VUKOVIĆ** and Panto joined them at the Brena apartments. That night, JANKO JANJIC raped

Trial Judgement	-Dragoljub Kunarac: Guilty of **Torture as CAH** (count 1), **Rape as CAH** (counts 2, 9 and 19), **Torture as a violation of the laws or customs of war (WC)** (counts 3 and 11) and **Rape as a violation of the laws or customs of war (WC)** (counts 4, 10, 12 and 20) under Article 7(1) of the Statute (**committing** and **aiding and abetting**) for: (i) taking FWS-75 and D.B. to his headquarters at Ulica Osmana Đikića no. 16, where he raped D.B. and aided and abetted the gang-rape of FWS-75 by several soldiers; (ii) taking FWS-87, FWS-75, FWS-50 and D.B. to his headquarters at Ulica Osmana Đikića no. 16, where he raped FWS-87 and aided and abetted the torture and rapes of FWS-87, FWS-75 and FWS-50 by soldiers; (iii) transferring FWS-95 from Partizan Sports Hall to his headquarters at Ulica Osmana Đikića no. 16, where he raped her; (iv) taking FWS-87 to a room on the upper floor of Karaman's house in Miljevina, where he raped her; (v) threatening to kill FWS-183 and her son while he tried to obtain information or a confession from FWS-183 concerning her alleged sending of messages to the Muslim forces and information about the whereabouts of her valuables and for raping her on that occasion; and (vi) raping FWS-191 and aiding and abetting the rape of FWS-186 by soldiers in an abandoned house in Trnovače.[63] Guilty of **Enslavement as CAH** (count 18) under Article 7(1) of the Statute (**committing** and **aiding and abetting**) for the enslavement of FWS-186 and FWS-191 for a period of six months in a house in Trnovače and for treating them as his property.[64] For counts 1 to 4, although Dragoljub Kunarac was also charged under Article 7(3) of the Statute, the Trial Chamber found that the Prosecution failed to prove that the soldiers who committed the offences were under the effective control of Dragoljub Kunarac at the time they committed the offences and, therefore, found that Dragoljub Kunarac was not responsible as a superior under Article 7(3) of the Statute (superior responsibility).[65] Not guilty of counts 5 to 8 and 21.[66]

FWS-48. During the sexual assault, he mentioned that it would be the last time".). These paragraphs were struck through as, in its Decision on Motion for Acquittal (Rule 98*bis* of the Rules of Procedure and Evidence), the Trial Chamber found that Zoran Vuković had no case to answer in relation to the allegations made by witness FWS-48 in support of counts 33 to 36 as the totality of the evidence did not provide a sufficient basis upon which a reasonable trier of fact could be satisfied beyond a reasonable doubt that it was Zoran Vuković who raped witness FWS-48. See *Prosecutor v. Dragoljub Kunarac et al.*, Case No. IT-96-23-T and IT-96-23/1-T, Decision on Motion for Acquittal, 3 July 2000, paras. 18–26, 28(2).

62 *Vuković* Indictment, paras. 7.10–7.11, 7.13, 7.24 ("On or around 14 July 1992, JANKO JANJIĆ again took FWS-48 together with FWS-87 and Z. G. to the Brena apartment block near Hotel Zelengora. When they arrived, **ZORAN VUKOVIC** and an unidentified soldier were waiting. [...T]he unidentified soldier raped FWS-87 (vaginal penetration) and JANKO JANJIĆ raped Z. G. On or around 14 July 1992, **ZORAN VUKOVIĆ** came to Partizan to remove FWS-50 and FWS-87. As FWS-50 hid, **ZORAN VUKOVIĆ** threatened to kill the other detainees if she did not come out of hiding. FWS-50 then did so. The two girls were taken to an apartment close to Partizan, where an unidentified soldier stood waiting. There **ZORAN VUKOVIĆ** raped FWS-50 (vaginal penetration), while the unidentified soldier raped FWS-87. [...] In July 1992, witness FWS-87 was frequently taken out, and raped (vaginal and anal penetration and fellatio). On one occasion witness FWS-87 was gang-raped by 4 men including DRAGAN ZELENOVIĆ and **ZORAN VUKOVIĆ.** [...] By the foregoing acts and omissions in relation to the victims FWS-48, FWS-50 and FWS-87, **ZORAN VUKOVIĆ** committed: [...] **Count 33:** Torture, a **CRIME AGAINST HUMANITY** punishable under Article 5 (f) of the Statute of the Tribunal. [...] **Count 34:** Rape, a **CRIME AGAINST HUMANITY** punishable under Article 5 (g) of the Statute of the Tribunal. [...] **Count 35:** Torture, a **VIOLATION OF THE LAWS OR CUSTOMS OF WAR,** punishable under Article 3 of the Statute of the Tribunal and recognised by Common Article 3 (1) (a) (TORTURE) of the Geneva Conventions. [...] **Count 36:** Rape, a **VIOLATION OF THE LAWS OR CUSTOMS OF WAR,** punishable under Article 3 of the Statute of the Tribunal".).

63 *Prosecutor v. Dragoljub Kunarac et al.*, Case No. IT-96-23-T and IT-96-23/1-T, Judgement, 22 February 2001 ("*Kunarac et al.* Trial Judgement"), paras. 685–687, 701, 704, 711, 715, 744–745, 883.

64 *Dragoljub Kunarac et al.* Trial Judgement, paras. 742, 744–745, 883.

65 *Dragoljub Kunarac et al.* Trial Judgement, paras. 628–629. See also *Dragoljub Kunarac et al.* Trial Judgement, paras. 626–627.

	- Radomir Kovač: Guilty of **Enslavement as CAH** (count 22), **Rape as CAH** (count 23), **Rape as a violation of the laws or customs of war (WC)** (count 24) and **Outrages upon personal dignity as a violation of the laws or customs of war (WC)** (count 25) under Article 7(1) of the Statute (**committing** and **aiding and abetting**) for: (i) detaining FWS-75 and the 12-year-old girl A.B. in his apartment for about a week and FWS-87 and A.S. for about four months and for treating them as his property; (ii) raping FWS-75, FWS-87 and A.B and for aiding and abetting the rapes of these women and of A.S. by allowing other soldiers to visit or stay in his apartment and to rape them or by encouraging the soldiers to do so, and by handing the girls over to other men with the knowledge that they would rape them; (iii) forcing FWS-87, A.S. and A.B. to strip and dance naked on a table while watching them; and (iv) selling A.B. for 200 Deutschmarks, FWS-87 and A.S for 500 Deutschmarks each and for handing over FWS-75 to other men.[67] - Zoran Vuković: Guilty of **Torture as CAH** (count 33), **Rape as CAH** (count 34), **Torture as a violation of the laws or customs of war (WC)** (count 35) and **Rape as a violation of the laws or customs of war (WC)** (count 36) under Article 7(1) of the Statute (**committing**) for taking FWS-50, a 16-year-old girl, from Partizan Sport Hall to an apartment and raping her.[68] Not guilty of counts 21 to 24.[69]
Appeal Judgement	- The convictions were affirmed by the Appeals Chamber.[70]
Legal and Factual Findings and/or Evidence	- The Trial Judgement contains the first conviction for rape as a crime against humanity before the ICTY. The Trial Judgement also contains the first convictions for sexual enslavement in international criminal law. - <u>Legal findings:</u> **- Rape:** The Trial Chamber agreed that the objective elements established by the Trial Chamber in the *Furundžija* case, if proved, constitute the *actus reus* of the crime of rape in international law.[71] However, the Trial Chamber held that it was necessary to clarify its understanding of the second element in the *Furundžija* definition (i.e. "by coercion or force or threat of force against the victim or a third person") and held that his element is in one respect more narrowly stated than is required by international law and "does not refer to other factors which would render an act of sexual penetration *non-consensual or non-voluntary* on the part of the victim" which, in the opinion of the Trial Chamber, is the accurate scope of this aspect of the definition in international law.[72] Accordingly, the Trial Chamber held that "the *actus reus* of the crime of rape in international law is constituted by: the sexual penetration, however slight: (a) of the vagina or anus of the victim by the penis of the perpetrator or any other object used by the perpetrator; or (b) of the mouth of the victim by the penis of the perpetrator; where such sexual penetration occurs without the consent of the victim. Consent for this purpose must be consent given voluntarily, as a result of the victim's free will, as-

66 *Dragoljub Kunarac et al.* Trial Judgement, paras. 698, 745, 884. See also *Dragoljub Kunarac et al.* Trial Judgement, paras. 688–697, 743.

67 *Dragoljub Kunarac et al.* Trial Judgement, paras. 759, 761, 773–774, 779–782, 886.

68 *Dragoljub Kunarac et al.* Trial Judgement, paras. 817, 822, 888.

69 *Dragoljub Kunarac et al.* Trial Judgement, paras. 798, 889. See also *Dragoljub Kunarac et al.* Trial Judgement, paras. 784–797.

70 *Prosecutor v. Dragoljub Kunarac et al.*, Case No. IT-96-23 and IT-96-23/1-A, Judgement, 12 June 2002 ("*Dragoljub Kunarac et al.* Appeal Judgement"), Section XII (Disposition), pp. 125–127.

71 *Dragoljub Kunarac et al.* Trial Judgement, paras. 437–438, referring to *Furundžija* Trial Judgement, para. 185.

72 *Dragoljub Kunarac et al.* Trial Judgement, para. 438.

	sessed in the context of the surrounding circumstances. The *mens rea* is the intention to effect this sexual penetration, and the knowledge that it occurs without the consent of the victim".[73] The Appeals Chamber concurred with the Trial Chamber's definition of rape.[74] With regard to the role of force in the definition of rape, the Appeals Chamber noted that, "in explaining its focus on the absence of consent as the *conditio sine qua non* of rape, the Trial Chamber did not disavow the Tribunal's earlier jurisprudence, but instead sought to explain the relationship between force and consent. Force or threat of force provides clear evidence of non-consent, but force is not an element *per se* of rape. In particular, the Trial Chamber wished to explain that there are 'factors [other than force] which would render an act of sexual penetration *non-consensual or non-voluntary* on the part of the victim'. A narrow focus on force or threat of force could permit perpetrators to evade liability for sexual activity to which the other party had not consented by taking advantage of coercive circumstances without relying on physical force".[75] **- Enslavement:** The Trial Chamber found "that, at the time relevant to the indictment, enslavement as a crime against humanity in customary international law consisted of the exercise of any or all of the powers attaching to the right of ownership over a person".[76] It further found that "the *actus reus* of the violation is the exercise of any or all of the powers attaching to the right of ownership over a person", and the "*mens rea* of the violation consists in the intentional exercise of such powers".[77] With respect to the *mens rea*, the Appeals Chamber specified that "[i]t is not required to prove that the accused intended to detain the victims under constant control for a prolonged period of time in order to use them for sexual acts".[78] The Appeals Chamber agreed with the Trial Chamber that "that the question whether a particular phenomenon is a form of enslavement will depend on the operation of the factors or indicia of enslavement identified by the Trial Chamber. These factors include the 'control of someone's movement, control of physical environment, psychological control, measures taken to prevent or deter escape, force, threat of force or coercion, duration, assertion of exclusivity, subjection to cruel treatment and abuse, control of sexuality and forced labour'".[79] In addition, the Appeals Chamber further rejected the Appellants' contention that lack of resistance or the absence of a clear and constant lack of consent during the entire time of the detention can be interpreted as a sign of consent. It held: "the Appeals Chamber does not accept the premise that lack of consent is an element of the crime since, in its view, enslavement flows from claimed rights of ownership; accordingly, lack of consent does not have to be proved by the Prosecutor as an element of the crime. However, consent may be relevant from an evidential point of view as going to the question whether the Prosecutor has established the element of the crime relating to the exercise by the accused of any or all of the powers attaching to the right of ownership. In this respect, the Appeals Chamber

73 *Dragoljub Kunarac et al.* Trial Judgement, para. 460. See also *Dragoljub Kunarac et al.* Trial Judgement, paras. 438–459.

74 *Dragoljub Kunarac et al.* Appeal Judgement, para. 128.

75 *Dragoljub Kunarac et al.* Appeal Judgement, para. 129, referring to *Dragoljub Kunarac et al.* Trial Judgement, paras. 438, 458.

76 *Dragoljub Kunarac et al.* Trial Judgement, para. 539.

77 *Dragoljub Kunarac et al.* Trial Judgement, para. 540.

78 *Dragoljub Kunarac et al.* Appeal Judgement, para. 122.

79 *Dragoljub Kunarac et al.* Appeal Judgement, para. 119, referring to *Dragoljub Kunarac et al.* Trial Judgement, para. 543. See also *Dragoljub Kunarac et al.* Trial Judgement, para 542.

	considers that circumstances which render it impossible to express consent may be sufficient to presume the absence of consent. In the view of the Appeals Chamber, the circumstances in this case were of this kind".[80] The Appeals Chamber further clarified that "the duration of the enslavement is not an element of the crime".[81] **- The requirement of pain and suffering in the definition of torture:** "The Appeals Chamber holds that the assumption of the Appellants that suffering must be visible, even long after the commission of the crimes in question, is erroneous. Generally speaking, some acts establish *per se* the suffering of those upon whom they were inflicted. Rape is obviously such an act. The Trial Chamber could only conclude that such suffering occurred even without a medical certificate. Sexual violence necessarily gives rise to severe pain or suffering, whether physical or mental, and in this way justifies its characterisation as an act of torture. Severe pain or suffering, as required by the definition of the crime of torture, can thus be said to be established once rape has been proved, since the act of rape necessarily implies such pain or suffering".[82] **- The subjective elements in the definition of torture:** "The Appellants argue that the intention of the perpetrator was of a sexual nature, which, in their view, is inconsistent with an intent to commit the crime of torture. In this respect, the Appeals Chamber wishes to assert the important distinction between 'intent' and 'motivation'. The Appeals Chamber holds that, even if the perpetrator's motivation is entirely sexual, it does not follow that the perpetrator does not have the intent to commit an act of torture or that his conduct does not cause severe pain or suffering, whether physical or mental, since such pain or suffering is a likely and logical consequence of his conduct".[83] "Furthermore, in response to the argument that the Appellant's avowed purpose of sexual gratification is not listed in the definition of torture, the Appeals Chamber restates the conclusions of the Trial Chamber that acts need not have been perpetrated solely for one of the purposes prohibited by international law. If one prohibited purpose is fulfilled by the conduct, the fact that such conduct was also intended to achieve a non-listed purpose (even one of a sexual nature) is immaterial".[84] - <u>Factual and legal findings:</u> Counts 1 to 4 for Dragoljub Kunarac: - Summary: "In conclusion, the Trial Chamber finds as follows: [...] Dragoljub Kunarac took FWS-75 and D.B. to Ulica Osmana Đikića no 16 where they were raped by several soldiers. Dragoljub Kunarac personally raped D.B. on that occasion. [...] On 2 August 1992, Dragoljub Kunarac took four girls, FWS-87, FWS-75, FWS-50 and D.B., to Ulica Osmana Đikića no 16. FWS-75 and FWS-50 were raped by several soldiers. Dragoljub Kunarac and three other soldiers raped FWS-87. [...] It has been established beyond reasonable doubt that Dragoljub Kunarac personally raped FWS-95 on one occasion [...]. As far as the girls were raped and tortured by other men, Dragoljub Kunarac was aiding and abetting the latter by taking the girls to them in the knowledge that they would rape them and by encouraging them to do so. The Trial Chamber

80 *Dragoljub Kunarac et al.* Appeal Judgement, para. 120.

81 *Dragoljub Kunarac et al.* Appeal Judgement, para. 121.

82 *Dragoljub Kunarac et al.* Appeal Judgement, paras. 150–151.

83 *Dragoljub Kunarac et al.* Appeal Judgement, para. 153 (internal references omitted).

84 *Dragoljub Kunarac et al.* Appeal Judgement, para. 155 (internal references omitted).

	therefore finds the accused Dragoljub Kunarac GUILTY of torture under Counts 1 and 3 and GUILTY of rape under Counts 2 and 4".[85] - Rapes of FWS-75 and D.B.: "Trial Chamber accepts the testimonies of both FWS-75 and D.B. as to being taken out of Partizan by Dragoljub Kunarac and 'Gaga', and to being brought to Ulica Osmana Đikića no 16 where a group of soldiers was already waiting. [...] Dragoljub Kunarac entered the room while FWS-75 was being raped by 'Bane', a soldier who sometimes went on mission with him, and Kunarac told her to get dressed and he took her back to Partizan. She learnt his name upon their return to Partizan after that night. FWS-75 heard his soldiers refer to Kunarac as 'Žaga'. She described him as being 'tall, quite slim, ugly with a sort of curly hair, looking frightening'. The accused Dragoljub Kunarac himself had admitted in his interview with the Prosecution, conducted in March 1998, Ex P67, that he took FWS-75 and D.B. out of Partizan to Ulica Osmana Đikića no 16, and that he spent two and half to three hours with D.B. behind closed doors there. The Trial Chamber is satisfied that, upon D.B.'s arrival at Ulica Osmana Đikića no 16, she was separated from FWS-75, taken to a room and raped first by Jure, then by 'Gaga' and next by a young boy of 15 or 16 years of age. The Trial Chamber is satisfied that it has been proven beyond reasonable doubt that D.B. subsequently also had sexual intercourse with Dragoljub Kunarac in which she took an active part by taking of the trousers of the accused and kissing him all over the body before having vaginal intercourse with him. The accused Kunarac admitted having had intercourse with D.B. in Ulica Osmana Đikića no 16 on this occasion, during his interview with the Prosecution in March 1998, Ex P67. In this same interview, Kunarac had put forward that he was not aware of the fact that D.B. did not have sex with him on her own free will but that she had only complied out of fear. The Trial Chamber, however, accepts the testimony of D.B. who testified that, prior to the intercourse, she had been threatened by 'Gaga' that he would kill her if she did not satisfy the desires of his commander, the accused Dragoljub Kunarac. The Trial Chamber accepts D.B.'s evidence that she only initiated sexual intercourse with Kunarac because she was afraid of being killed by 'Gaga' if she did not do so. The Trial Chamber rejects the evidence of the accused Dragoljub Kunarac that he was not aware of the fact that D.B. only initiated sexual intercourse with him for reasons of fear for her life. The Trial Chamber regards it as highly improbable that the accused Kunarac could realistically have been 'confused' by the behaviour of D.B., given the general context of the existing war-time situation and the specifically delicate situation of the Muslim girls detained in Partizan or elsewhere in the Foča region during that time. As to whether or not he was aware of the threat by 'Gaga' against D.B., the Trial Chambers finds it irrelevant as to whether or not Kunarac heard 'Gaga' repeat this threat against D.B. when he walked into the room, as D.B. testified. The Trial Chamber is satisfied that D.B. did not freely consent to any sexual intercourse with Kunarac. She was in captivity and in fear for her life after the threats uttered by 'Gaga'. On the evidence accepted, the Trial Chamber finds that the Prosecution has proved beyond reasonable doubt that the accused Dragoljub Kunarac took D.B. out of Partizan and drove her to Ulica Osmana Đikića no 16 together with 'Gaga'. The Trial Chamber accepts that D.B. was raped there first by 'Gaga' and two other men and then forced to have sexual intercourse with Dragoljub Kunarac because she had been threatened with death by 'Gaga'. The Trial Chamber is satisfied beyond reasonable doubt that Dragoljub Kunarac had sexual intercourse with D.B. in the full knowledge that she did not freely consent. The Trial Chamber also accepts that the accused Kunarac was fully aware of the rapes inflicted upon D.B. by the other soldiers. The Trial Chamber further accepts the testimony of FWS-75 as to having been gang-raped in the same house, while D.B. was

85 *Dragoljub Kunarac et al.* Trial Judgement, paras. 685–687.

	being raped by the three soldiers and Dragoljub Kunarac. FWS-75 was taken to a separate room by 'Gaga' who ordered her to have sex with a 16-year-old boy nick-named 'Zuca'. The Trial Chamber is satisfied beyond reasonable doubt that FWS-75 was subsequently gang-raped by a group of soldiers, vaginally and orally. She identified most of the rapists as Montenegrins, and she also identified several individuals amongst them, eg Jure Radovic, DP 7 and DP 8. Whereas the Trial Chamber finds that the testimony of FWS-75 already proves the gang-rape of herself charged under paragraph 5.3 to their satisfaction, D.B. stated that, upon their return to Partizan, FWS-75 appeared to be terrified and that she was barely able to walk. The Trial Chamber is also satisfied that Dragoljub Kunarac was aware of the gang-rape of FWS-75 during her stay in the house. Firstly, the Trial Chamber accepts the evidence provided by FWS-75 as to Kunarac entering the room while she was still being raped by 'Bane' and telling her to get dressed because they had to go. Secondly, the witnesses as well as Kunarac in his statement of March 1998, Ex P67, said that the sexual intercourse of D.B. and Kunarac and the gang-rape of FWS-75 by a group of soldiers took place in adjacent rooms. The Trial Chamber is satisfied that Kunarac must have heard sounds caused by this incident. Thirdly, the fact that the accused Kunarac and 'Gaga' took the girls to Ulica Osmana Đikića no 16 in concert makes it highly unlikely, and therefore incredible, that Dragoljub Kunarac would not have known that FWS-75 was brought to the house for the purposes of rape, as was D.B. Finally, the Trial Chamber further accepts as proved that FWS-75 was taken to the house in Ulica Osmana Đikića by Dragoljub Kunarac and raped there by soldiers at least one other time, as was testified by FWS-75. The Trial Chamber is satisfied beyond reasonable doubt that Dragoljub Kunarac was aware that FWS-75 would be subject to rapes and sexual assaults by soldiers at the house in Ulica Osmana Đikića when he took her there. The Trial Chamber is therefore satisfied that the allegations made in paragraph 5.3 of the Indictment have been proved beyond reasonable doubt, namely that Dragoljub Kunarac took FWS-75 and D.B. to Ulica Osmana Đikica no 16 for them to be raped. On this occasion, Kunarac personally had sexual intercourse with D.B. in the knowledge that she did not consent and aided and abetted the gang-rape of FWS-75 at the hands of several of his soldiers by taking her to the house in the knowledge that she would be raped there and that she did not consent to the sexual intercourse. The accused acted intentionally and with the aim of discriminating between the members of his ethnic group and the Muslims, in particular its women and girls. The treatment reserved by Dragoljub Kunarac for his victims was motivated by their being Muslims, as is evidenced by the occasions when the accused told women, that they would give birth to Serb babies, or that they should 'enjoy being fucked by a Serb'. The law does not require that the purpose of discrimination be the only purpose pursued by the offender; it is enough that it forms a substantial part of his *mens rea*. Such was the case with the accused Kunarac. The acts of the accused caused his victims severe mental and physical pain and suffering. Rape is one of the worst sufferings a human being can inflict upon another. This was abundantly clear to the accused Dragoljub Kunarac, as he stated during his testimony concerning the rape of D.B., when he admitted the fact that he had done something terrible, even though he maintained that it had happened with the consent of D.B. By raping D.B. himself and bringing her and FWS-75 to Ulica Osmana Đikica no 16, the latter at least twice, to be raped by other men, the accused Dragoljub Kunarac thus committed the crimes of torture and rape as a principal perpetrator, and he aided and abetted the other soldiers in their role as principal perpetrators by bringing the two women to Ulica Osmana Đikica no 16".[86] - Rapes of FWS-87, FWS-75 and FWS-50: "[On 2 August 1992, t]he Trial Chamber is satisfied that Dragoljub Kunarac […] went

[86] *Dragoljub Kunarac et al.* Trial Judgement, paras. 638, 641–656.

	to Partizan Sports Hall where he took four women out, FWS-87, FWS-75, FWS-50 and D.B. FWS-75 and FWS-87 were taken out by Kunarac that day and driven to Ulica Osmana Đikića no 16, together with FWS-50 and D.B. […] The Trial Chamber accepts the evidence of FWS-87, that she was raped by Dragoljub Kunarac that night in a room next to the kitchen of the house. She was also raped during the night by an older man, whose name she could not recall, and by a certain Toljic. FWS-87 described the accused Kunarac as 'not very tall, not too skinny or too fat and having dark brown hair'. She saw him come to Partizan every third night with other soldiers. She also noticed that he had a cast on his body when he came to 'Karaman's house' and raped her. Apart from the credible identification by FWS-87, the Trial Chamber further notes that the accused admitted having met FWS-87 at Partizan on 3 August and having seen her again at 'Karaman's house'. The Trial Chamber further accepts the evidence of FWS-50, FWS-75 and D.B. who testified that, in the meantime and during the rest of the night, they were raped by Dragoljub Kunarac's men. Upon their arrival at Ulica Osmana Đikica no 16, Dragoljub Kunarac and 'Gaga' abandoned FWS-75 and the other women to the soldiers present there. FWS-75 was first raped by three Montenegrin soldiers, whom she was able to identify as Kontic (nicknamed 'Konta'), DP 7 and DP 8, and she was then locked in a room by DP 8 where he continued to rape her for the rest of the night vaginally, anally and orally. 'Gaga' raped her the next morning. […] The Trial Chamber further accepts FWS-50's testimony about her being raped 'in a beast-like manner' by an old Montenegrin soldier that night who wielded a knife and threatened to draw a cross on her back and to baptise her. […] The rapes resulted in severe mental and physical pain and suffering for the victims. The Trial Chamber is satisfied that the victims were taken to Ulica Osmana Đikica no 16 by Dragoljub Kunarac for the very purpose of rape and that they were chosen for this purpose on the basis only of their Muslim ethnicity. The Trial Chamber is satisfied that, on 2 August 1992, Dragoljub Kunarac went to Partizan Sports Hall where he took out FWS-75, FWS-87, FWS-50 and D.B. and drove them to the house in Ulica Osmana Đikića no 16, where some women who had been taken out of the Kalinovik school had already arrived. The Trial Chamber is also satisfied that Kunarac took these women to this house in the knowledge that they would be raped by soldiers during the night. The Trial Chamber finds that Kunarac took FWS-87 to one of the rooms of the house and forced her to have sexual intercourse in the knowledge that she did not consent. The Trial Chamber also finds that, on that occasion, FWS-75 and FWS-50 were repeatedly raped by other soldiers while Kunarac raped FWS-87. The Trial Chamber further finds that FWS-87 was also raped by other soldiers that same night. The fact that Kunarac took the girls to the house and left them to his men in the knowledge that they would rape them constituted an act of assistance which had a substantial effect on the acts of torture and rape later committed by his men. He therefore aided and abetted in that torture and rape".[87] - Rapes of FWS-95: "[Between 20 July and 2 August 1992, u]pon their arrival at Ulica Osmana Đikića no 16, FWS-95 was separated from FWS-105 and FWS-90, taken to a room and raped there by the accused Dragoljub Kunarac. […] The Trial Chamber is satisfied that Dragoljub Kunarac himself had sexual intercourse with FWS-95 without her consent on the first incident described under paragraph 5.5 of the Indictment while he knew that FWS-95 did not consent".[88] Counts 9 and 10 for Dragoljub Kunarac:

[87] *Dragoljub Kunarac et al.* Trial Judgement, paras. 663–667, 669–670.

[88] *Dragoljub Kunarac et al.* Trial Judgement, paras. 674, 678, 684.

	- Rape of FWS-87: "The Trial Chamber is satisfied that the allegations contained in paragraph 7.1 of the Indictment have been proved beyond reasonable doubt. The Trial Chamber finds that, on or about 2 August 1992, FWS-87, together with FWS-75, D.B. and FWS-50 were taken by the accused Dragoljub Kunarac from the house in Ulica Osmana Đikića no 16 in Foča to Miljevina, where they were handed over to DP 3 and his men who, in turn, transferred them to 'Karaman's house'. The Trial Chamber is also satisfied beyond reasonable doubt that, sometime in either September or October 1992, Dragoljub Kunarac went to 'Karaman's house' and took FWS-87 to a room on the upper floor of the house where he forced her to have sexual intercourse in the knowledge that she did not consent. The accused Kunarac did not dispute that he went to this house at the end of September, nor that he took FWS-87 to a room upstairs. Kunarac claimed, however, that he did not have sexual intercouse with her. The Trial Chamber is of the view that Dragoljub Kunarac's assertion that he simply talked to her is highly improbable, in the light of his total disregard for Muslim women in general, those he raped in particular, and FWS-87 most specifically, whom he had raped on at least one occasion prior to those events while in Ulica Osmana Đikića no 16. The Trial Chamber accepts the evidence of FWS-87. It does not accept that Dragoljub Kunarac's version of events could reasonably have been true, and it holds that the allegations made in paragraph 7.2 of the Indictment have been proved beyond reasonable doubt. The Trial Chamber therefore finds Dragoljub Kunarac GUILTY of rape under Counts 9 and 10".[89] Counts 11 and 12 for Dragoljub Kunarac: - Rape of FWS-183: "The Trial Chamber accepts the testimony of FWS-183 that, in the second half of July 1992, while she was in FWS-61's apartment, three Serb soldiers came and accused her of transmitting radio messages. The Trial Chamber accepts that a soldier she later realised to be 'Žaga' put her in a red Lada, where she had to wait with him for the two other soldiers to return, and who had in the meantime looted her apartment. The three soldiers then took her to the banks of the Cehotina river in Foča near Velečevo, where the accused tried to obtain information or a confession from FWS-183 concerning her alleged sending of messages to the Muslim forces and information about the whereabouts of her valuables while he threatened to kill her and her son. By his attempt to intimidate her, Dragoljub Kunarac also showed his hatred for Muslims, his intention to intimidate her, and his intention to discriminate against Muslims in general, and FWS-183 in particular. All three soldiers raped FWS-183. In the course of the rapes, Kunarac forced her to touch his penis and to look at him. He cursed her. The other two soldiers watched from the car, laughing. While she was raped by Dragoljub Kunarac, FWS-183 heard him tell the other soldiers to wait for their turn. Subsequently, she was raped vaginally and orally by the other soldiers. The rapes resulted in severe mental and physical pain for FWS-183. [...] FWS-61 testified that FWS-183 was taken out from the apartment and that both her apartment and FWS-183's apartment were looted by the soldiers. She saw FWS-183 returned by the same three soldiers who had taken her away. She said that FWS-183 looked confused upon her arrival, as if she had been crying. She further testified that FWS-183 told her that she had to give all her valuables to the soldiers, and that she had been forced to touch them at their 'shameful places' and do 'impossible things'. The Trial Chamber is satisfied that the incident described in paragraph 8.1 of the Indictment has been proved beyond reasonable doubt. The accused Dragoljub Kunarac and the other two soldiers acted as principal co-perpetrators. For these acts, the Trial Chamber finds the accused Dragoljub Kuna-

89 *Dragoljub Kunarac et al.* Trial Judgement, paras. 700–704 (internal references omitted).

	rac GUILTY of torture under Count 11. Likewise, the Trial Chamber finds the accused Dragoljub Kunarac GUILTY of rape under Count 12".[90] Counts 18 to 20 for Dragoljub Kunarac: - Summary: "In summary, the Trial Chamber finds that: […] On 2 August, Dragoljub Kunarac personally raped FWS-191 and aided and abetted the rape of FWS-186 by DP 6. […] For a period of about 6 months, FWS-186 and FWS-191 were kept in the house in Trnovače. For a period of about 2 months, Dragoljub Kunarac sporadically visited the house and raped FWS-191 on those occasions. […] While they were kept in the house in Trnovače, FWS-191 and FWS-186 were treated as the property of Dragoljub Kunarac and DP 6. The Trial Chamber consequently finds the accused Dragoljub Kunarac GUILTY of rape under Counts 19 and 20, GUILTY of enslavement under Count 18 […]".[91] - Rapes of FWS-191 and FWS-186: "The Trial Chamber is satisfied, on the evidence of FWS-191 and FWS-186, that Dragoljub Kunarac, together with 'Gaga' and DP 6, took FWS-186, FWS-191 and J.G. from the house Ulica Osmana Đikića no 16 on 2 August 1992 to an abandoned house in Trnovače, where FWS-186 was raped by DP 6 and FWS-191 was raped by Dragoljub Kunarac. […] FWS-191 and FWS-186 were taken out of Kalinovik School together by Dragoljub Kunarac and 'Gaga' on 2 August 1992, driven by them to a house in the Alad'a area and, from there, to the house in Trnovače. Upon arrival, the girls were told where to sleep. FWS-191 was assigned to Kunarac, he ordered her to undress and he tried to rape her while his bayonet was placed on the table. Kunarac did not entirely succeed penetrating FWS-191 because, as FWS-191 was still a virgin, she was rigid with fear. He succeeded in taking away her virginity the next day. Kunarac knew that she did not consent, and he rejoiced at the idea of being her 'first', thereby degrading her more. […] FWS-186 was raped during this night by DP 6 on the second floor of the Trnovače house. FWS-186 identified the house in Trnovače and recounted her impression that it was owned by DP 6. FWS-186 was sent to a room on the second floor. DP 6 then came, locked the door from the inside and raped her. […] The Trial Chamber finds that the incident described under paragraph 10.1 of the Indictment, apart from the alleged rape of J.G., has been proved beyond reasonable doubt. The Trial Chamber is satisfied that Dragoljub Kunarac was fully aware that the other girls, whom he took out of Ulica Osmana Đikića together with 'Gaga' and DP 6, ie FWS-191, FWS-186 and J.G., were taken to the abandoned house also for the purpose of rape".[92] - Rapes and enslavement of FWS-191 and FWS-186: "The Trial Chamber is satisfied that FWS-191 and FWS-186 were kept in the Trnovače house for five to six months […]. The Trial Chamber is satisfied that Dragoljub Kunarac constantly raped FWS-191 for about two months while she was kept in the house. Kunarac came to the Trnovače house until the end of September, and that each time he came he would rape FWS-191. Although Kunarac broke his arm in an accident sometime in September 1992, he nevertheless continued to rape her. […] FWS-186 was raped by DP 6 continuously during her five-month stay at the Trnovače house. She was obliged to have sexual intercourse with DP 6 whenever he returned to the house from Montenegro or from the frontlines. […] The Trial Chamber accepts the

[90] *Dragoljub Kunarac et al.* Trial Judgement, paras. 710–711, 713-715.

[91] *Dragoljub Kunarac et al.* Trial Judgement, paras. 744–745.

[92] *Dragoljub Kunarac et al.* Trial Judgement, paras. 718, 724–725, 727.

evidence of FWS-191 and FWS-186, and finds that both witnesses were treated as the personal property of Dragoljub Kunarac and DP 6 during their stay in the Trnovače house as described in paragraph 10.3 of the Indictment. The Trial Chamber accepts from FWS-191 that the girls at Trnovače did anything they were ordered to do by the soldiers while being kept there. The testimonies of both FWS-191 and FWS-186 substantiated convincingly that the girls were kept in the house to be used by Dragoljub Kunarac and DP 6 for sexual services whenever the soldiers returned to the house. The Trial Chamber further accepts that the witnesses were not free to go where they wanted to, even if, as FWS-191 admitted, they were given the keys to the house at some point. Referring to the factual findings with regard to the general background, the Trial Chamber accepts that the girls, as described by FWS-191, had nowhere to go, and had no place to hide from Dragoljub Kunarac and DP 6, even if they had attempted to leave the house. The Trial Chamber is satisfied that Kunarac and DP 6, both being Serb soldiers in the Foča area, were fully aware of this fact. The Trial Chamber accepts the evidence of FWS-191 and FWS-186 that the girls performed household chores for the soldiers whilst under captivity. The Trial Chamber is satisfied that it has been proven beyond reasonable doubt that FWS-191 was raped by Dragoljub Kunarac and that FWS-186 was raped by DP 6, continuously and constantly whilst they were kept in the house in Trnovače. Kunarac in fact asserted his exclusivity over FWS-191 by forbidding any other soldier to rape her. The Trial Chamber is satisfied that Kunarac was aware of the fact that DP 6 constantly and continuously raped FWS-186 during this period, as he himself did to FWS-191. It has not been established however that Kunarac provided DP 6 with any form of assistance, encouragement or moral support which had a substantial effect on the perpetration of the individual rapes. Kunarac continued to come to the house for about two months, but it has not been established, apart from the incident charged and described in paragraph 10.1, that he was present while DP 6 raped FWS-186. It has not been shown either how Kunarac's presence or actions would have assisted DP 6 in his raping FWS-186; so loose is the connection between the events at the house and his sporadic presence there, it would stretch the concept of aiding and abetting beyond its limits with respect to the actual rapes by DP 6. The Trial Chamber is satisfied that FWS-191 and FWS-186 were denied any control over their lives by Dragoljub Kunarac and DP 6 during their stay there. They had to obey all orders, they had to do household chores and they had no realistic option whatsoever to flee the house in Trnovače or to escape their assailants. They were subjected to other mistreatments, such as Kunarac inviting a soldier into the house so that he could rape FWS-191 for 100 Deutschmark if he so wished. On another occasion, Kunarac tried to rape FWS-191 while in his hospital bed, in front of other soldiers. The two women were treated as the personal property of Kunarac and DP 6. The Trial Chamber is satisfied that Kunarac established these living conditions for the victims in concert with DP 6. Both men personally committed the act of enslavement. By assisting in setting up the conditions at the house, Kunarac also aided and abetted DP 6 with respect to his enslavement of FWS-186".[93]

Counts 22 to 25 for Radomir Kovač:

- "The Trial Chamber is satisfied that it has been proven beyond reasonable doubt that, on or about 30 October 1992, FWS-75, FWS-87, A.S. and A.B. were taken from 'Karaman's house' and brought by Dragan Zelenović, DP 6 and DP 1 to the Lepa Brena building block in Foča. There, they were handed over to the accused Radomir Kovač. Another man named Jagos Kostic lived in Radomir Kovač's apartment. The Trial Chamber is also satisfied that, while kept in Radomir Kovač's apartment, these girls were constantly raped, humiliated and degraded. They were sometimes beaten, slapped or threatened by one of the occupants of the apartment. The accused Kovač

[93] *Dragoljub Kunarac et al.* Trial Judgement, paras. 732, 734–735, 738–742.

	once slapped FWS-75 because she refused to sleep with a soldier whom he had brought in. Twelve-year old A.B. was sent in her place. Kovač also beat FWS-75 up on other occasions. The Trial Chamber is satisfied that the girls could not and did not leave the apartment without one of the men accompanying them. When the men were away, they would be locked inside the apartment with no way to get out. Only when the men were there would the door of the apartment be left open. Notwithstanding the fact that the door may have been open while the men were there, the Trial Chamber is satisfied that the girls were also psychologically unable to leave, as they would have had nowhere to go had they attempted to flee. They were also aware of the risks involved if they were re-captured. While they were detained in Radomir Kovač's apartment, the girls were required to take care of the household chores, the cooking and the cleaning. The Trial Chamber is satisfied that the girls' diet and hygiene was completely neglected by Radomir Kovač. When the men were in the apartment, the girls would get their left-over food. But Kovač sometimes left the girls behind without making sure that they would have sufficient food while he was away. On some occasions, witness DK, a cousin of the accused Radomir Kovač who lived on the floor below the accused's apartment, passed some food to the girls through the window. Considering that people were organising parties where food and drinks were served, that cafés and shops were open, that supply would be available from Montenegro, and that Kovač received food from the army, the Trial Chamber does not accept that the hunger of the girls while detained in Kovač's apartment was due to general shortage of food in Foča".[94] - "The Trial Chamber is satisfied that it has been proven beyond reasonable doubt that FWS-75 and A.B. stayed for a few days in Radomir Kovač's apartment before being taken away by a Serb soldier named Vojkan Jadzic to another apartment in the vicinity of Hotel Zelengora. The two girls stayed at that apartment for about 15 days, during which they were constantly raped by at least ten or fifteen Serb soldiers. Kovač would come to this apartment from time to time, asking the girls how they were doing and if they had been abused, despite being [...] aware that they were being raped. The two girls were then taken to another apartment near Pod Masala by Serb soldiers, including Vojkan Jadzic. They stayed in that other apartment for about 7–10 days, during which time they continued to be raped. One evening, Vojkan Jadzic took the girls back to Radomir Kovač's apartment where FWS-87 and A.S. were still being kept. [...] The day after they had returned, A.B. and FWS-75 were taken from Radomir Kovač's apartment. A.B. was taken by a man called 'Dragec', who gave Kovač 200 Deutschmarks in the process, while FWS-75 was handed over to DP 1 and Dragan 'Zelja' Zelenovic. The Trial Chamber finds that this sexual exploitation of A.B. and FWS-75, in particular their sale, constitutes a particularly degrading attack on their dignity. The Trial Chamber is satisfied that it has been proven beyond reasonable doubt that, while she was in Radomir Kovač's apartment, FWS-75 was raped by both Kovač and Jagos Kostić. She was once raped together with FWS-87 by Kovač while 'Swan Lake' was playing in the background. In addition, she was raped by several other soldiers who would come to Kovač's apartment, including Vojkan Jadzic [...]. While in Radomir Kovač's apartment, twelve-year old A.B. was raped by, among others, the accused Kovač, Slavo Ivanović and 'Zeljko'. [...] The Trial Chamber finds that FWS-75 and A.B. were detained in Radomir Kovač's apartment for about a week, starting sometime at the end of October or early November 1992. The Trial Chamber finds that the accused Radomir Kovač had sexual intercourse with the two women in the knowledge that they did not consent, and that he substantially assisted other soldiers in raping the two women. He did this by allowing other soldiers to visit his apartment and to rape the women or by encouraging the soldiers to do so, and by handing the girls over to

94 *Dragoljub Kunarac et al.* Trial Judgement, paras. 748–752.

	other men in the knowledge that they would rape them and that the girls did not consent to the sexual intercourse. Finally, the Trial Chamber is satisfied that it has been proven beyond reasonable doubt that, after about a week, Kovač handed the two women over to other soldiers whom he knew would most likely continue to rape and abuse them. Kovač eventually sold A.B. to an unidentified soldier, and handed over FWS-75 to DP 1, in the almost certain knowledge that they would be raped again".[95] - "The Trial Chamber is satisfied that it has been proven beyond reasonable doubt that, while in Radomir Kovač's apartment, FWS-87 was raped by both Kovač and Jagos Kostić. Kovač reserved FWS-87 for himself and raped her almost every night he spent in the apartment. Jagos Kostić constantly raped A.S., and he took advantage of Kovač's absence to rape FWS-87 too. He threatened her that if she reported this to Radomir Kovač he would kill her. Kovač knew at all times that the girls did not consent to the sexual intercourse. Jagos Kostić could rape A.S. because she was held by Kovač in his apartment. Kovač therefore also substantially assisted Jagos Kostić in raping A.S., by allowing Jagos Kostić to stay in his apartment and to rape A.S. there. The Trial Chamber notes that it has not been established beyond reasonable doubt that the accused Kovač aided and abetted the rape of FWS-87 by Jagos Kostić. The evidence indicates that the fact that Jagos Kostić raped FWS-87 was hidden from Kovač. Considering the two men's relationship and Jagos Kostić's threats to FWS-87, it seems very unlikely that Kovač could have envisaged the possibility that Jagos Kostić would rape FWS-87. FWS-87 consistently denied any emotional relationship with the accused Radomir Kovač. The Trial Chamber notes that several Defence witnesses mentioned a letter with a heart drawn on the envelope which was allegedly sent by FWS-87 to Kovač. The Trial Chamber accepts, however, that FWS-87 did not send such a letter, and it notes the fact that, even by their own account, none of the Defence witnesses actually read the content of the letter, but only heard about it from Kovač. The relationship between FWS-87 and Kovač was not one of love as the Defence suggested, but rather one of cruel opportunism on Kovač's part, of constant abuses and domination over a girl who, at the relevant time, was only about 15 years old. Radomir Kovač forced FWS-87 to go to cafés with him, at least once forcing her to wear an insignia of the VRS. The Trial Chamber is also satisfied beyond reasonable doubt that, while in Radomir Kovač's apartment, A.S. was constantly raped by Jagos Kostić. The Trial Chamber is satisfied that FWS-87 and A.S. were held in Radomir Kovač's apartment for a period of about 4 months".[96] - The naked dancing: "The Trial Chamber therefore finds that, sometime between about 31 October 1992 and about 7 November 1992, while in Radomir Kovač's apartment, FWS-87, A.S. and A.B. were forced to strip and dance naked on a table while Kovač watched them from the sofa, pointing weapons at them. The accused Radomir Kovač certainly knew that, having to stand naked on a table, while the accused watched them, was a painful and humiliating experience for the three women involved, even more so because of their young age. The Trial Chamber is satisfied that Kovač must have been aware of that fact, but he nevertheless ordered them to gratify him by dancing naked for him. The Statute does not require that the perpetrator must intend to humiliate his victim, that is that he perpetrated the act for that very reason. It is sufficient that he knew that his act or omission could have that effect. This was certainly the case here".[97]

95 *Dragoljub Kunarac et al.* Trial Judgement, paras. 754–759.

96 *Dragoljub Kunarac et al.* Trial Judgement, paras. 761–765.

97 *Dragoljub Kunarac et al.* Trial Judgement, paras. 772–774.

	- "The Trial Chamber first notes that the Defence did not deny that a financial transaction took place between the accused Radomir Kovač and two Montenegrins shortly before the girls were taken away by these two Montenegrins. They submitted that the transaction was of a different sort, and claimed that it was Kovač who actually paid for the girls to be taken away to Montenegro. In view of the treatment reserved by the accused Radomir Kovač for FWS-87 and A.S., which included an almost daily regime of rapes and other abuses, it is not credible to suggest that, after four months of constant intimidation and mistreatment, the accused suddenly decided to shield these two girls from the risks involved for a Muslim girl to live in Foča at the time and so to pay for them to be taken away. The Trial Chamber does not accept the accused's account. […] The Trial Chamber finds that, sometime in February 1993, two Montenegrins came to Radomir Kovač's apartment. They went together with the accused to the living room while FWS-87 and A.S. were told to go to the kitchen. The two girls crept out of the kitchen into the corridor from where they listened to the conversation before rushing back to the kitchen when they heard the men moving. FWS-87 heard that the two girls were being sold for 500 Deutschmarks each, but A.S. did not hear the exact words of the conversation. Not long after the transaction, possibly the next day, the two Montenegrins came back to take the girls away. While they were in the car with the two Montenegrins, these two men laughed at their being sold for such a small amount of money and, as A.S. recounted, also for a truck-load of washing powder. […] Radomir Kovač detained FWS-75 and A.B. for about a week, and FWS-87 and A.S. for about four months in his apartment, by locking them up and by psychologically imprisoning them, and thereby depriving them of their freedom of movement. During that time, he had complete control over their movements, privacy and labour. He made them cook for him, serve him and do the household chores for him. He subjected them to degrading treatments, including beatings and other humiliating treatments. The Trial Chamber finds that Radomir Kovač's conduct towards the two women was wanton in abusing and humiliating the four women and in exercising his *de facto* power of ownership as it pleased him. Kovač disposed of them in the same manner. For all practical purposes, he possessed them, owned them and had complete control over their fate, and he treated them as his property. The Trial Chamber is also satisfied that Kovač exercised the above powers over the girls intentionally. The Trial Chamber is satisfied that many of the acts caused serious humiliation, of which the accused was aware".[98] Counts 33 to 36 for Zoran Vuković: - Rape of FWS-50: "FWS-50 testified, and the Trial Chamber accepts, that a day or two after she arrived at Partizan Sports Hall she was taken out of Partizan Sports Hall together with FWS-87 by the accused Zoran Vuković and another soldier, and that they were taken to an abandoned apartment. Her mother came to look for her in the toilet of Partizan where she was hiding. FWS-50 testified that the accused Vuković took her to one room of the apartment and raped her. […] FWS-50 gave evidence that she saw the accused Zoran Vuković at Buk Bijela where he had raped her for the first time. This event in Buk Bijela was not charged in the Indictment, and the Trial Chamber will therefore not take it into account for convicting and sentencing, but it does take that event into account for matters of identification. FWS-50 also stated that, when he raped her, Vuković told her that she was lucky in that she was the same age as his daughter, otherwise he would have done much worse things to her. The Trial Chamber notes that Vuković's daughter was approximately of the same age as FWS-50 at the relevant time. The Trial Chamber notes that this incident was the second time that Zoran Vuković raped FWS-50 within a fortnight. He knew of her situation as a Muslim refugee since he had seen

[98] *Dragoljub Kunarac et al.* Trial Judgement, paras. 776–777, 779–781.

	her at Buk Bijela, and he knew that she was about 16 years old at the time, as he told her that she was about the same age as his daughter. The rape led to serious mental and physical pain for the victim. In the Final Trial Brief of the Defence, the accused Zoran Vuković argued that, even if it were proved that he had raped a woman, the accused would have done so out of a sexual urge, not out of hatred. However, all that matters in this context is his awareness of an attack against the Muslim civilian population of which his victim was a member and, for the purpose of torture, that he intended to discriminate between the group of which he is a member and the group of his victim. There is no requirement under international customary law that the conduct must be *solely* perpetrated for one of the prohibited purposes of torture, such as discrimination. The prohibited purpose need only be part of the motivation behind the conduct and need not be the predominant or sole purpose. The Trial Chamber has no doubt that it was at least a predominant purpose, as the accused obviously intended to discriminate against the group of which his victim was a member, ie the Muslims, and against his victim in particular. [...] The Trial Chamber finds that, sometime in mid-July 1992, the accused Zoran Vuković and another soldier came to Partizan Sports Hall looking for FWS-50. She was taken out of Partizan Sports Hall to an apartment and taken to a room by Vuković where he forced her to have sexual intercourse with full knowledge that she did not consent".[99] - Evidence: **- Evidence in cases of sexual assault:** In accordance with Rule 96(i) of the Rules of Procedure and Evidence, the Trial Chamber accepted that, in cases of sexual assault, no corroboration of the victim's testimony shall be required.[100]

6. Dario **Kordić and** Mario **Čerkez** (Case No. IT-95-s14/2) "***Lašva Valley***" - Dario Kordić: One of the leading political figures in the Bosnian Croat community: from 1991 until 1995, President of the Croatian Democratic Union of Bosnia and Herzegovina (HDZ-BiH); from 1992 until 1995, Vice-President and a member of the Presidency of the Croatian Community of Herceg-Bosna (HZ H-B) and later the Croatian Republic of Herceg-Bosna (HR H-B). - Mario Čerkez: Commander of the Vitez Brigade of the Croatian Defence Council (HVO) from its formation in 1992 until at least the end of May 1993, and during the HDZ-BiH/HVO takeover of the municipal functions within the municipality of Vitez.	
Indictment (International sex crimes (or related)	Only one general paragraph in the Indictment refers to the factual allegation of international sex crimes, more specifically to "sexual assaults".[101] However, another paragraph of the Indictment specifies that this allegation is incorporated and realleged in each charge.[102] Thus, the charges incorporating this general allegation of sexual as-

99 *Dragoljub Kunarac et al.* Trial Judgement, paras. 812, 814–817.

100 *Dragoljub Kunarac et al.* Trial Judgement, para. 566.

101 *Prosecutor v. Dario Kordić and Mario Čerkez*, Case No. IT-95-14/2-PT, Amended Indictment, 2 October 1998 ("*Kordić and Čerkez* Indictment"), para. 29 ("Detention and imprisonment were other means used to persecute Bosnian Muslims, who were systematically selected, detained and imprisoned in HZ H-B/ HR-H-B and HVO detention facilities, on political, racial, ethnic or religious grounds. Imprisoned and otherwise detained Bosnian Muslim civilians were subjected to physical and psychological abuse, including beatings and sexual assaults, and suffered inhumane deprivations of basic necessities, such as adequate food, water, shelter and clothing. There was often little or no medical attention, and overcrowded and unsanitary conditions".).

102 *Kordić and Čerkez* Indictment, para. 23 ("The general allegations contained in paragraphs 1 through 22, as well as the allegations in paragraphs 24 through 35 below, are realleged and incorporated in each charge".).

charges and mode(s) of liability)	saults are the following: **Persecutions as CAH** (count 1 for Dario Kordić and count 2 for Mario Čerkez);[103] **Inhumane acts as CAH** (count 10 for Dario Kordić and count 17 for Mario Čerkez); **Wilfully causing great suffering or serious injury to body or health as a grave breach of the Geneva Conventions of 1949 (WC)** (count 11 for Dario Kordić and count 18 for Mario Čerkez); **Inhuman treatment as a grave breach of the Geneva Conventions of 1949 (WC)** (count 12 for Dario Kordić and count 19 for Mario Čerkez); **violence to life and person as a violation of the laws or customs of war (WC)** (count 13 for Dario Kordić and count 20 for Mario Čerkez);[104]

[103] *Kordić and Čerkez* Indictment, paras. 36–37 ("From about November 1991 to approximately March 1994, **Dario KORDIC,** together with various members of the HDZ-BiH, the HZ H-B/HR H-B and HVO and their leaders, armed forces and agents, caused, planned, instigated, ordered or committed, or aided and abetted the planning, preparation or execution of, a crime against humanity, that is, the widespread or systematic persecutions of Bosnian Muslim civilians on political, racial, ethnic or religious grounds, throughout the HZ H-B/HR H-B and the municipality of Zenica, in the territory of Bosnia and Herzegovina. This campaign of widespread or systematic persecutions was perpetrated, executed and carried out by or through the following means: […] (b) killing and causing serious injury or harm to Bosnian Muslim civilians, including women, children, the elderly and the infirm, both during and after such attacks; […] (g) physical and psychological abuse, inhumane acts, inhuman treatment, forced labor and deprivation of basic human necessities, such as adequate food, water, shelter and clothing, against Bosnian Muslims who were detained or imprisoned; […] By these acts and omissions, **Dario KORDIC** committed: **Count 1: a CRIME AGAINST HUMANITY,** as recognised by Articles 5(h), 7(1) and 7(3) (persecutions on political, racial, or religious grounds) of the Statute of theTribunal".), 38–39 ("From about 1 April 1992 to September 1993, **Mario CERKEZ,** together with various members of the HDZ-BiH, the HZ H-B/HR H-B and HVO and their leaders, armed forces and agents, caused, planned, instigated, ordered or committed, or aided and abetted the planning, preparation or execution of, a crime against humanity, that is, the widespread or systematic persecutions of Bosnian Muslim civilians on political, racial, ethnic or religious grounds, in the municipalities of Vitez, Busovaca and Novi Travnik, in the territory of Bosnia and Herzegovina. This campaign of widespread or systematic persecutions was perpetrated, executed and carried out by or through the following means: […] (b) killing and causing serious injury or harm to Bosnian Muslim civilians, including women, children, the elderly and the infirm, both during and after such attacks; […] (f) physical and psychological abuse, inhumane acts, inhuman treatment, forced labor and deprivation of basic human necessities, such as adequate food, water, shelter and clothing, against Bosnian Muslims who were detained or imprisoned; […] By these acts and omissions, **Mario CERKEZ** committed: **Count 2: a CRIME AGAINST HUMANITY,** as recognised by Articles 5(h), 7(1) and 7(3) (persecutions on political, racial, or religious grounds) of the Statute of the Tribunal".).

[104] *Kordić and Čerkez* Indictment, paras. 42 ("From about January 1993 to approximately October 1993, **Dario KORDIC**, together with members of the HZ H-B/HR H-B and HVO and their leaders, armed forces and agents, caused, planned, instigated, ordered or committed, or aided and abetted the planning, preparation or execution of, murders and wilful killings of, and wilful causing and infliction of serious injury and great suffering to body and health, both physical and mental, inhumane acts and inhuman treatment upon and against Bosnian Muslims, in the following cities, towns and villages on about the dates indicated: Busovaca January 1993, Rotilj April 1993, Ahmici April 1993, Nadioci April 1993, Pirici April 1993, Santici April 1993, Vitez April 1993, StariVitez April 1993, Veceriska-Donja Veceriska April 1993, Zenica April 1993, Tulica June 1993, Han Ploca/Grahovci June 1993, Stupni Do October 1993. By these acts and omissions, **Dario KORDIC** committed: […] **Injuries: Count 10:** a **CRIME AGAINST HUMANITY**, as recognised by Articles 5(i) (inhumane acts), 7(1) and 7(3) of the Statute of the Tribunal. **Count 11:** a **GRAVE BREACH**, as recognised by Articles 2(c) (wilfully causing great suffering or serious injury to body or health), 7(1) and 7(3) of the Statute of the Tribunal. **Count 12:** a **GRAVE BREACH**, as recognised by Articles 2(b) (inhuman treatment), 7(1) and 7(3) of the Statute of the Tribunal **Count 13:** a **VIOLATION OF THE LAWS OR CUSTOMS OF WAR**, as recognised by Articles 3, 7(1) and 7(3) of the Statute of the Tribunal and Article 3(1)(a) (violence to life and person) of the Geneva Conventions".), 43 ("During or about April 1993, **Mario CERKEZ**, together with members of the HZ H-B/HR H-B and HVO and their leaders, armed forces and agents, caused, planned, instigated, ordered or committed, or aided and abetted the planning, preparation or execution of, murders and wilful killings of, and wilful causing and infliction of serious injury and great suffering to body and health, both physical and mental, inhumane acts and inhuman treatment upon and against Bosnian Muslims, in the following cities, towns and villages on about the dates indicated: Ahmici April 1993, Nadioci April 1993, Pirici April 1993, Santici April 1993, Vitez April 1993, StariVitez April 1993, Veceriska-Donja Veceriska April 1993. By these acts and omissions, **Mario CERKEZ** committed: […] **In-**

	Inhuman treatment as a grave breach of the Geneva Conventions of 1949 (WC) (count 23 for Dario Kordić and count 31 for Mario Čerkez); **Cruel treatment as a violation of the laws or customs of war (WC)** (count 24 for Dario Kordić and count 32 for Mario Čerkez)[105] under Articles 7(1) and 7(3) of the Statute (**superior reponsibility**).
Trial Judgement	The Trial Chamber's factual and legal findings are extremely unclear. However, it seems that the Trial Chamber found Dario Kordić and Mario Čerkez: Guilty of **Inhumane acts as CAH** (count 10 for Dario Kordić and count 17 for Mario Čerkez) and **Inhuman treatment as a grave breach of the Geneva Conventions of 1949 (WC)** (count 12 for Dario Kordić and count 19 for Mario Čerkez) under Article 7(1) of the Statute for unclear acts of sexual violence.[106]
Appeal Judgement	-Although the Appeals Chamber upheld some of Dario Kordić's convictions under counts 10 and 12, it found that the incidents of sexual assaults were not charged in the Indictment or not proved and, thus, it **reversed Dario Kordić and Mario Čerkez's convictions for the sexual assault of Witness TW21 in Vitez in April 1993 (Inhumane acts as CAH,** Count 10 (Kordić), Count 17 (Čerkez) **and Inhuman treatment**

juries: Count 17: a **CRIME AGAINST HUMANITY**, as recognised by Articles 5(i) (inhumane acts), 7(1) and 7(3) of the Statute of the Tribunal. **Count 18:** a **GRAVE BREACH**, as recognised by Articles 2(c) (wilfully causing great suffering or serious injury to body or health), 7(1) and 7(3) of the Statute of the Tribunal. **Count 19:** a **GRAVE BREACH**, as recognised by Articles 2(b) (inhuman treatment), 7(1) and 7(3) of the Statute of the Tribunal. **Count 20:** a **VIOLATION OF THE LAWS OR CUSTOMS OF WAR**, as recognised by Articles 3, 7(1) and 7(3) of the Statute of the Tribunal and Article 3(1)(a) (violence to life and person) of the Geneva Conventions".).

105 *Kordić and Čerkez* Indictment, paras. 44–45 ("From about 1 January 1993 to approximately 31 March 1994, **Dario KORDIC**, together with members of the HZ H-B/HR H-B and HVO and their leaders, armed forces and agents, caused, planned, instigated, ordered or committed, or aided and abetted the planning, preparation or execution of, the imprisonment, unlawful confinement and inhuman treatment of Bosnian Muslims at about the following locations, in the territory of Bosnia and Herzegovina: Kaonik Prison, Vitez Cinema Complex, Vitez Veterinary Station, SDK Offices in Vitez, The chess club in Vitez, Dubravica Elementary School, Municipal Building in Kiseljak, Kiseljak Barracks, Rotilj village, Nova Trgovina, and Silos. Many Bosnian Muslims were expelled or forcibly transferred from their homes and villages. Bosnian Muslims were detained and beaten, subjected to physical and/or psychological abuse, intimidation and inhuman treatment, including being confined in overcrowded and unsanitary conditions, deprived of adequate food and water, and provided little or no medical attention. By these acts and omissions, **Dario KORDIC** committed: [...] **Inhuman and/or Cruel Treatment of Detainees: Count 23:** a **GRAVE BREACH** as recognised by Articles 2(b) (inhuman treatment), 7(1) and 7(3) of the Statute of the Tribunal. **Count 24:** a **VIOLATION OF THE LAWS OR CUSTOMS OF WAR** as recognised by Articles 3, 7(1) and 7(3) of the Statute of the Tribunal and Article 3(1)(a) (cruel treatment) of the Geneva Conventions".), 50–51 ("From about 1 April 1993 to approximately 31 August 1993, **Mario CERKEZ**, together with members of the HZ H-B/HR H-B and HVO and their leaders, armed forces and agents, caused, planned, instigated, ordered or committed, or aided and abetted the planning, preparation or execution of, the imprisonment, unlawful confinement and inhuman treatment of Bosnian Muslims at the following locations in the territory of Bosnia and Herzegovina: Kaonik Prison, Vitez Cinema Complex, Vitez Veterinary Station, SDK Offices in Vitez, The chess club in Vitez, Dubravica Elementary School. Many Bosnian Muslims were expelled or forcibly transferred from their homes and villages. Bosnian Muslims were detained and beaten, subjected to physical and/or psychological abuse and intimidation, and inhuman treatment, including being confined in overcrowded and unsanitary conditions, deprived of adequate food and water, and provided little or no medical attention. By these acts and omissions, **Mario CERKEZ** committed: [...] **Inhuman and/or Cruel Treatment of Detainees: Count 31:** a **GRAVE BREACH** as recognised by Articles 2(b) (inhuman treatment), 7(1) and 7(3) of the Statute of the Tribunal. **Count 32:** a **VIOLATION OF THE LAWS OR CUSTOMS OF WAR** as recognised by Articles 3, 7(1) and 7(3) of the Statute of the Tribunal and Article 3(1)(a) (cruel treatment) of the Geneva Conventions".).

106 See *e.g. Kordić and Čerkez* Trial Judgement, fn. 1251.

	as a grave breach of the Geneva Conventions of 1949 (WC), Count 12 (Kordić), Count 19 (Čerkez)).[107] The Appeals Chamber further **reversed Dario Kordić's convictions for the alleged rape committed in Nadioci (Inhumane acts as CAH**, Count 10 **and inhuman treatment as a grave breach of the Geneva Conventions of 1949 (WC)**, Count 12).[108] Finally, it **reversed Dario Kordić's convictions for the alleged rape of Adina Jusić (Inhumane acts as CAH**, Count 10 **and Inhuman treatment as a grave breach of the Geneva Conventions of 1949 (WC)**, Count 12).[109] - The Appeals Chamber affirmed Dario Kordić's convictions for the crimes of inhumane acts as CAH (Count 10) and inhuman treatment as a grave breach of the Geneva Conventions of 1949 (WC) (Count 12) in Rotil, in April 1993; however, the alleged rape of the victim was not taken into account in the conviction.[110]
Legal and Factual Findings and/or Evidence	- Factual and legal findings: - Crimes in Vitez and Stari Vitez, in April 1993: "The Trial Chamber also refers to the testimony of Witness TW21 (based on transcripts in the *Blaškić* trial), according to whom armed men came into her house in Vitez looking for weapons, sexually assaulted her and stole her jewellery. A review of the transcript reveals that Witness TW21, a female Muslim inhabitant of Vitez, only answered in the affirmative to the Prosecution's questions as to whether the man who took her upstairs sexually assaulted her and as to whether the second man who came into the room also did so. It is unclear from the witness's testimony whether the perpetrators of these sexual assaults were soldiers and she was not even asked about their ethnicity. She testified that one of the men who assaulted her was wearing civilian clothes and the other camouflage trousers. The Appeals Chamber also takes into account further portions of the witness's testimony. She testified that during the events, a third man stayed downstairs with her younger son, taking some jewellery allegedly needed 'for the army'. She further recounted the conversation she had later that same night with two Croat soldiers who came to her door having heard about the 'rape'. The Appeals Chamber considers that a reasonable trier of fact could have found that Witness TW21 was sexually assaulted. It is clear that the assault caused serious mental suffering to her and constituted a serious attack on her human dignity. In the particular circumstances of the case, a reasonable Trial Chamber could have concluded on the basis of the transcript of her testimony that Witness TW21 was a civilian. The Appeals Chamber considers that since it is unclear who the perpetrators were of this crime, it is not established whether it was civilians or soldiers or which unit these soldiers belonged to. Further, this incident was not charged in the Indictment. Consequently, the Appeals Chamber finds that the Trial Chamber's conclusion that the crime of inhumane acts, Count 10 (Kordić), Count 17 (Čerkez), and inhuman treatment, Count 12 (Kordić) Count 19 (Čerkez) in Vitez/Stari Vitez were established, must be reversed".[111] - Crimes in Nadioci: "The Appeals Chamber notes that the Indictment limits the inhumane acts charged in Count 10 and the inhuman treatment charged in Count 12 to injuries, and the Appeals Chamber will therefore only consider evidence in relation to injuries. The Prosecution directed the Appeals Chamber during the appeals hearing to the evidence of Witness S, on which the Trial Chamber relied in other parts of the Trial Judgement, and which

107 *Prosecutor v. Dario Kordić and Mario Čerkez*, Case No. IT-95-14/2-A, Judgement, 17 December 2004 ("*Kordić and Čerkez* Appeal Judgement"), paras. 462–463 and Section X (Disposition), pp. 296, 299.

108 *Kordić and Čerkez* Appeal Judgement, paras. 491–493 and Section X (Disposition), p. 296.

109 *Kordić and Čerkez* Appeal Judgement, paras. 581–582 and Section X (Disposition), p. 297.

110 *Kordić and Čerkez* Appeal Judgement, paras. 544–546 and Section X (Disposition), p. 297.

111 *Kordić and Čerkez* Appeal Judgement, paras. 462–463.

	are relevant to these charges. Witness S testified to two incidents. First she testified to women who had received injuries from firearms while being held in houses in Novaci. Since Novaci is a part of Vitez, this evidence will not be considered in this respect in relation to Nadioci. Witness S further testified about a crime (rape) (of which she was told of by colleagues) that occurred in 'the Bungalows,' which the Prosecution submits is in Nadioci (the Jokers' headquarters). The Trial Chamber placed the rape in Novaci (Vitez), and found that 'Doctors in Vitez received complaints and examined women who had been held (for purposes of rape) by HVO soldiers in a house in Novaci'. Having reviewed the transcript, even though it is a bit unclear and does mention the Bungalows, the Appeals Chamber is satisfied that from the context no reasonable trier of fact could have found that the crime occurred in Nadioci. Having no other evidence to support the Trial Chamber's finding, the Appeals Chamber reverses the Trial Chamber's findings that inhumane acts (Count 10) and inhuman treatment, Count 12 (Kordić) were established in Nadioci".[112] - Crimes in Rotilj, in April 1993: "The Appeals Chamber notes that the Indictment limits the inhumane acts charged in Count 10 and the inhuman treatment charged in Count 12 to injuries, and the Appeals Chamber will therefore only consider evidence in relation to injuries. Witness Lt.-Col. Landry, referring to Zibiza Skrso, testified that there was blood in the house from her murder, and evidence of her having been raped. He did not elaborate further as to what this evidence was. Witness TW07 stated that Zibiza Skrso's body was found on a table, covered with a sheet and that she had been hit by rifle bullets in the chest area. The Appeals Chamber considers that a reasonable trier of fact could have found that Zibiza Skrso was assaulted and that it was a "serious attack on human dignity" constituting inhumane acts and inhuman treatment. The Appeals Chamber upholds the Trial Chamber's finding that inhumane acts and inhuman treatment, Counts 10 and 12 (Kordić) were established".[113] - Crimes in Han Ploča-Grahovci, in June 1993: "The Trial Chamber relied on Witness TW08 who gave evidence that she had not witnessed rape but that she knew a younger woman from the village of Duhri who was raped. Witness TW08 provided no further information about the incident. She further testified that she had seen Adina Jusić being taken away in a car by Zoran Ljevak, but that she does not know whether anything happened to Adina Jusić. The Appeals Chamber notes that there is no charge relating to the village of Duhri in the Indictment and that therefore evidence relating to Duhri is not before the Chamber. Based on the fact that women were afraid and fled, and Adina Jusić was taken away in a car, the Appeals Chamber considers that no reasonable trier of fact could have found that inhumane acts, Count 10 (Kordić) and inhuman treatment, Count 12 (Kordić), were established, and reverses the Trial Chamber's finding".[114]

7. Stevan **Todorović** (Case No. IT-95-9/1) "***Bosanski Šamac***" From 28 March 1992 until at least 31 December 1993, chief of police and a member of the Serb crisis staff in Bosanski Šamac in north-eastern Bosnia and Herzegovina.	
Indictment	- **Persecutions as CAH** (count 1) under Article 7(1) of the Statute (**committing and**

112 *Kordić and Čerkez* Appeal Judgement, paras. 491–493 (internal references omitted).

113 *Kordić and Čerkez* Appeal Judgement, paras. 544–546 (internal references omitted).

114 *Kordić and Čerkez* Appeal Judgement, paras. 581–582 (internal references omitted).

(International sex crimes (or related) charges and mode(s) of liability)	**aiding and abetting**) and Article 7(3) of the Statute (**superior responsibility**) for the sexual assaults of Bosnian Croats, Bosnian Muslims and other non-Serb civilians detained in various detention camps in and around the Bosanski Šamac municipality.[115] - **Rape as CAH** (counts 16, 19 and 22), **Humiliating and degrading treatment as a violation of the laws or customs of war (WC)** (counts 17, 20 and 23) and **Torture or inhuman treatment as a grave breach of the Geneva Conventions of 1949 (WC)** (counts 18, 21 and 24) under Article 7(1) of the Statute for forcing or ordering prisoners to perform acts of fellatio upon each other, sometimes in the presence of several other prisoners and guards, on various occasions.[116]
Sentencing Judgement	- Guilty of **Persecutions as CAH** (count 1) under Article 7(1) of the Statute (**ordering**) for ordering six men to perform fellatio on each other at the police station in Bosanski Šamac on three different occasions in May and June 1992.[117] - Note: plea agreement: On 29 November 2000, a joint motion was filed on Todorović's behalf with the Office of the Prosecutor informing the Trial Chamber of an

115 *Prosecutor v. Stevan Todorović*, Case No. IT-95-9-PT, Second Amended Indictment, 19 November 1998 ("*Todorović* Indictment"), para. 34(b) ("From on or about 17 April 1992 through at least 31 December 1993, **Stevan TODOROVIĆ,** while serving as Chief of Police of Bosanski Šamac and as a member of the Serb Crisis Staff, committed and aided and abetted the commission of the crime of persecutions as described in paragraphs 29 and 30 above, through his participation in the following acts or omissions, among others: […] (b) the murders, sexual assaults and repeated beatings of numerous Bosnian Croats, Bosnian Muslims and other non-Serb civilians detained in various detention camps in and around the Bosanski Šamac municipality".). See also *Todorović* Indictment, paras. 25, 27, 29–30.

116 *Todorović* Indictment, paras. 44 ("**COUNTS 16-18** (Sexual Assaults): On or about 13 June 1992 in the hallway of the Bosanski Šamac police (SUP) building, **Stevan TODOROVIĆ** forced Witness A and Witness B to perform acts of fellatio upon each other in the presence of several other prisoners and guards. By these actions, **Stevan TODOROVIĆ** planned, instigated, ordered, committed or otherwise aided and abetted the planning, preparation or execution of: **Count 16**: Rape (which includes other forms of sexual assault), a **CRIME AGAINST HUMANITY**, punishable under Articles 5(g) of the Statute of the Tribunal; **Count 17**: Humiliating and degrading treatment, a **VIOLATION OF THE LAWS OR CUSTOMS OF WAR**, punishable under Article 3 of the Statute of the Tribunal and recognised by Article 3(1)(c) of the Geneva Conventions; and **Count 18**: Torture or inhuman treatment, a **GRAVE BREACH**, punishable under Article 2(b) of the Statute of the Tribunal".), 45 ("**COUNTS 19-21** (Sexual Assaults): On or about 10 May 1992, while in an office in the Bosanski Šamac police (SUP) building, **Stevan TODOROVIĆ** ordered Witness C and Witness D to perform fellatio on each other. By these actions, **Stevan TODOROVIĆ** planned, instigated, ordered, committed or otherwise aided and abetted the planning, preparation or execution of: **Count 19**: Rape (which includes other forms of sexual assault), a **CRIME AGAINST HUMANITY**, punishable under Article 5(g) of the Statute of the Tribunal; **Count 20** Humiliating and degrading treatment, a **VIOLATION OF THE LAWS OR CUSTOMS OF WAR**, punishable under Article 3 of the Statute of the Tribunal and recognised by Article 3(1)(c) of the Geneva Conventions; and **Count 21**: Torture or inhuman treatment, a **GRAVE BREACH**, punishable under Article 2(b) of the Statute of the Tribunal".), 46 ("**COUNTS 22-24** (Sexual Assaults): In or about mid-May 1992, while in a room in the Bosanski Šamac police (SUP) building, **Stevan TODOROVIĆ** ordered Witness E and Witness F to perform fellatio on each other. By these actions, **Stevan TODOROVIĆ** planned, instigated, ordered, committed or otherwise aided and abetted the planning, preparation or execution of: Count 22: Rape (which includes other forms of sexual assault), a **CRIME AGAINST HUMANITY**, punishable under Articles 5(g) of the Statute of the Tribunal; **Count 23**: Humiliating and degrading treatment, a **VIOLATION OF THE LAWS OR CUSTOMS OF WAR**, punishable under Article 3 of the Statute of the Tribunal and recognised by Article 3(1)(c) of the Geneva Conventions; and **Count 24**: Torture or inhuman treatment, a **GRAVE BREACH**, punishable under Article 2(b) of the Statute of the Tribunal".).

117 *Prosecutor v. Stevan Todorović*, Case No. IT-95-9/1-S, Sentencing Judgement, 31 July 2001 ("*Todorović* Sentencing Judgement"), para. 9 ("In the Plea Agreement the Prosecution and Stevan Todorović agree on certain facts as being true and constituting the factual basis for the guilty plea. These include […] ordering six men to perform fellatio on each other at the police station in Bosanski Šamac on three different occasions in May and June 1992".). See also *Todorović* Sentencing Judgement, para. 17.

	agreement reached between the parties as to the entry of a guilty plea by the accused to persecutions as a CAH (count 1) and the withdrawal of all ther counts against Todorović. Todorović entered a guilty plea to count 1 of the Indictment on 13 December 2000. The Trial Chamber entered a finding of guilt on 24 January 2001.[118]
Appeal Judgement	N/A
Legal and Factual Findings and/or Evidence	- Factual findings: "In relation to the allegations of sexual assault, Stevan Todorović has accepted the following account of his conduct. Witness A described how he was taken to the police station in Bosanski Šamac, where Stevan Todorović began to beat him and kick him in the genital area. Witness A was then taken over to another man and ordered by Stevan Todorović to 'bit into his penis'. After that he was beaten again and endured further mistreatment. Witness C stated that Todorović had telephoned and had required him to come to the police station in Bosanski Šamac. There, Witness C was beaten for about half an hour. In Witness C's words: 'Only Todorović and me were present at the office and the beating lasted for about half an hour. After that Witness D was brought to the office and he continued beating both of us. The beating lasted for another hour. After that he ordered us to perform oral sex on each other.' Witness E described how he was arrested on 9 or 10 May 1992 and taken to the police station in Bosanski Šamac. There he was beaten by Stevan Todorović, among others, for several hours. Witness E stated that: 'After the beating Todorović ordered us (Witness E and Witness F) to do a blow job on each other. He was laughing when we [were] doing it'".[119]

8. Radislav **Krstić** (Case No. IT-98-33) "***Srebrenica-Drina Corps***" Chief of staff/Deputy Commander of the Drina Corps of the Bosnian Serb Army (VRS); appointed Commander of the Drina Corps on 13 July 1995.	
Indictment (International sex crimes (or related) charges and mode(s) of liability)	- There are no factual allegations of international sex crimes in the Indictment. However, the charge for which Radislav Krstić was tried for international sex crimes is the following: **Persecutions as CAH** (count 6) under Article 7(1) of the Statute or, alternatively, Article 7(3) of the Statute (**superior responsibility**).[120]
Trial	- Guilty of **Persecutions as CAH** (count 6) under Article 7(1) of the Statute (**joint criminal enterprise – third category**) for the incidental rapes committed against the

118 *Todorović* Sentencing Judgement, paras. 4–5, 16–17. See also *Todorović* Sentencing Judgement, paras. 1–15.

119 *Todorović* Sentencing Judgement, paras. 37–40 (internal references omitted).

120 *Prosecutor v. Radislav Krstić*, Case No. IT-98-33-PT, Amended Indictment, 27 October 1999, paras. 29–31 ("**COUNT 6 (PERSECUTIONS)** The Prosecutor re-alleges and reincorporates by reference paragraphs 4, 6, 7, 11, and 22 through 26 above. Beginning on 11 July 1995 and continuing through 1 November 1995, **RADISLAV KRSTIC** committed, planned, instigated, ordered, or otherwise aided and abetted the planning, preparation, or execution of a crime against humanity, that is, the persecutions of Bosnian Muslim civilians on political, racial, or religious grounds, in Srebrenica and its surroundings. The crime of persecutions was perpetrated, executed, and carried out by or through the following means: [...] b. the cruel and inhumane treatment of Bosnian Muslim civilians, including severe beatings; c. the terrorising of Bosnian Muslim civilians; [...]; and, e. the deportation or forcible transfer of Bosnian Muslims from the Srebrenica enclave. By these acts or omissions, and the acts and omissions described in paragraphs 4, 6, 7, 11, and 22 through 26, **RADISLAV KRSTIC** committed: **COUNT 6:** Persecutions on political, racial and religious grounds, a **CRIME AGAINST HUMANITY**, punishable under Articles 5(h), and 7(1) and 7(3) of the Statute of the Tribunal".).

Judgement	Bosnian Muslims as they were natural and foreseeable consequences of the joint criminal enterprise implemented at Potočari on 12 and 13 July 1995.[121]
Appeal Judgement	- The Appeals Chamber affirmed Radislav Krstić's conviction for Persecutions as CAH (count 6) under Article 7(1) of the Statute and dismissed his appeal against his convictions for the opportunistic crimes that occurred at Potočari as natural and foreseeable consequences of his participation in the joint criminal enterprise at Potočari.[122]
Legal and Factual Findings and/or Evidence	- This is the first case before the ICTY establishing a link between rape and "ethnic cleansing". - Legal findings: **- Rape and sexual abuse may cause serious bodily or mental harm:** The Trial Chamber found that rape is among the acts, which may cause serious bodily or mental harm constituting genocide: "In subscribing to the above case-law, the Chamber holds that inhuman treatment, torture, rape, sexual abuse and deportation are among the acts which may cause serious bodily or mental injury".[123] - Factual and legal findings: **- Rapes and joint criminal enterprise – third category:** The Trial Chamber found that the rapes committed against the Bosnian Muslims at Potočari were natural and foreseeable consequences of the joint criminal enterprise implemented at Potočari on 12 and 13 July 1995 and, therefore, that Radislav Krstić incurred liability for the rapes committed in the execution of this joint criminal enterprise at Potočari: "The Trial Chamber is not, however, convinced beyond reasonable doubt that the murders, rapes, beatings and abuses committed against the refugees at Potočari were also an agreed upon objective among the members of the joint criminal enterprise. However, there is no doubt that these crimes were natural and foreseeable consequences of the ethnic cleansing campaign. Furthermore, given the circumstances at the time the plan was formed, General Krstić must have been aware that an outbreak of these crimes would be inevitable given the lack of shelter, the density of the crowds, the vulnerable condition of the refugees, the presence of many regular and irregular military and paramilitary units in the area and the sheer lack of sufficient numbers of UN soldiers to provide protection. In fact, on 12 July, the VRS organised and implemented the transportation of the women, children and elderly outside the enclave; General Krstić was himself on the scene and exposed to firsthand knowledge that the refugees were being mistreated by VRS or other armed forces. In sum, the Trial Chamber finds General Krstić guilty as a member of a joint criminal enterprise whose objective was to forcibly transfer the Bosnian Muslim women, children and elderly from Potočari on 12 and 13 July and to create a humanitarian crisis in support of this endeavour by causing the Srebrenica residents to flee to Potočari where a total lack of food, shelter and necessary services would accelerate their fear and panic and ultimately their willingness to leave the territory. General Krstić thus incurs liability also for the incidental murders, rapes, beatings and abuses committed in the execution of this criminal enterprise at Potočari. Finally, General Krstić knew that these crimes were related to a widespread or systematic attack directed against the Bosnian Muslim civilian population of Srebrenica; his participation in them is undeniable evidence of

121 *Prosecutor v. Radislav Krstić*, Case No. IT-98-33-T, Judgement, 2 August 2001 ("*Krstić* Trial Judgement"), paras. 45–46, 150, 513, 517–518, 616–618, 653, 727.

122 *Prosecutor v. Radislav Krstić*, Case No. IT-98-33-A, Judgement, 19 April 2004, paras. 145–151 and Section VII (Disposition), p. 87.

123 *Krstić* Trial Judgement, para. 513.

	his intent to discriminate against the Bosnian Muslims. General Krstić is therefore liable of inhumane acts and persecution as crimes against humanity".[124] - Conclusions on Radislav Krstić's criminal responsibility: "At this point, the Trial Chamber concludes that General Krstić incurs criminal responsibility for his participation in two different sets of crimes that occurred following the attack of the VRS on Srebrenica in July 1995. Firstly, on the basis of the humanitarian crisis and crimes of terror at Potočari and the forcible transfer of the women, children and elderly from Potočari to Bosnian Muslim held territory, from 11 to 13 July, General Krstić incurs responsibility under Article 7(1) for inhumane acts (forcible transfer, count 8 of the Indictment) and persecution (murder, cruel and inhumane treatment, terrorisation, destruction of personal property and forcible transfer, count 6 of the Indictment)".[125] - Factual findings: - Crimes committed in Potočari on 12–13 July 1995: "That night, a Dutch Bat medical orderly came across two Serb soldiers raping a young woman: '[W]e saw two Serb soldiers, one of them was standing guard and the other one was lying on the girl, with his pants off. And we saw a girl lying on the ground, on some kind of mattress. There was blood on the mattress, even she was covered with blood. She had bruises on her legs. There was even blood coming down her legs. She was in total shock. She went totally crazy.' Bosnian Muslim refugees nearby could see the rape, but could do nothing about it because of Serb soldiers standing nearby. Other people heard women screaming, or saw women being dragged away. Several individuals were so terrified that they committed suicide by hanging themselves. Throughout the night and early the next morning, stories about the rapes and killings spread through the crowd and the terror in the camp escalated".[126] "On 12 and 13 July 1995, upon the arrival of Serb forces in Potočari, the Bosnian Muslim refugees taking shelter in and around the compound were subjected to a terror campaign comprised of threats, insults, looting and burning of nearby houses, beatings, rapes, and murders".[127] - Rape constituting cruel and inhumane treatment as an element of the persecutions inflicted on the Bosnian Muslims: "The Trial Chamber has described in detail the ordeal suffered both by the Bosnian Muslims who fled to Potočari and the Bosnian Muslims captured from the column. More specifically, the Trial Chamber heard reliable evidence concerning the severe beatings and other cruel treatments suffered by the Bosnian Muslim men after they had been separated from their relatives in Potočari. Numerous witnesses further testified about the terrible conditions prevailing both in and outside the UN Potočari compound: lack of food and water which the VRS provided in very limited quantity, thousands of people crammed into a small space. More significantly, rapes and killings were reported by credible witnesses and some committed suicide out of terror. The entire situation in Potočari has been depicted as a campaign of terror. As an ultimate suffering, some women about to board the buses had their young sons dragged away from them, never to be seen again. The Trial Chamber thus concludes that the VRS and other Serb forces imposed cruel and inhumane treatment on a large number of

124 *Krstić* Trial Judgement, paras. 616–618 (internal references omitted).

125 *Krstić* Trial Judgement, para. 653.

126 *Krstić* Trial Judgement, paras. 45–46 (internal references omitted).

127 *Krstić* Trial Judgement, para. 150 (internal reference omitted).

	Bosnian Muslims who were subjected to intolerable conditions in Potočari, cruelly separated from their family members, and, in the case of the men, subjected to the unspeakable horror of watching their fellow captives die on the execution fields, escaping that fate only by chance. The main fact for which the Prosecution alleges inhumane treatment, though, is the forcible transfer of the Bosnian Muslim women, children and elderly outside the enclave of Srebrenica".[128]

9. Miroslav **<u>Kvočka *et al.*</u>** (Case No. IT-98-30/1) "***Omarska, Keraterm & Trnopolje Camps***" - Miroslav Kvočka: Professional police officer attached to the Omarska police station; participated in the operation of the Omarska camp, in north-western Bosnia and Herzegovina, as the functional equivalent of the deputy commander of the guard service. - Dragoljub Prcać: Retired policeman and crime technician mobilised to serve in the Omarska police station on 29 April 1992; administrative aide to the commander of the Omarska camp. - Milojica Kos: Guard shift leader in the Omarska camp from approximately 31 May to 6 August 1992; also known as "Krle". - Mlađo Radić: A professional policeman attached to the Omarska police station and a shift leader of Omarska camp guards from approximately 28 May until the end of August 1992; also known as "Krkan". - Zoran Žigić: A civilian taxi-driver mobilised to serve as a reserve police officer; worked for a short period of time as a guard at Keraterm camp and specifically entered the Omarska and Trnopolje camps for the purpose of abusing, beating, torturing and/or killing prisoners; also known as "Žiga".	
Indictment[129] (International sex crimes (or related) charges and mode(s) of liability)	- All the accused are charged with: **Persecutions as CAH** (count 1), **Inhumane acts as CAH** (count 2) and **Outrages upon personal dignity as a violation of the laws or customs of war (WC)** (count 3) for various acts, including sexual assaults and rapes of Bosnian Muslims, Bosnian Croats and other non-Serbs in Prijedor municipality, including prisoners detained in the Omarska, Keraterm and Trnopolje camps. All the accused were charged under Article 7(1) of the Statute. In addition, Miroslav Kvočka, Dragoljub Prcać, Milojica Kos and Mlađo Radić were also charged under Article 7(3) of the Statute (**superior responsibility**).[130]

[128] *Krstić* Trial Judgement, paras. 517–518 (internal references omitted).

[129] For the general background to the charges, see *Prosecutor v. Miroslav Kvočka et al.*, Case No. IT-98-30/1-T, Amended Indictment, 26 October 2000 ("*Miroslav Kvočka et al.* Indictment"), paras. 9 ("Severe beatings, torture, killings, sexual assault, and other forms of physical and psychological abuse were commonplace at Omarska and Keraterm".), 12 ("In addition, many of the women detained at the Trnopolje camp were raped, sexually assaulted, or otherwise tortured by camp personnel, who were both police and military personnel, and by others, including military units from the area who came to the camp for that specific purpose. In many instances, the women and girls were taken from the camp and raped, tortured, or sexually abused at other locations".).

[130] *Miroslav Kvočka et al.* Indictment, paras. 24–33 ("Between 24 May 1992 and 30 August 1992, **Miroslav KVOČKA, Dragoljub PRCAĆ, Milojica KOS, Mlađo RADIĆ and Zoran ŽIGIĆ** participated in persecutions of Bosnian Muslims, Bosnian Croats and other non-Serbs in the Prijedor area, on political, racial or religious grounds. The persecution included the following means: […] c. the sexual assault and rape of Bosnian Muslims, Bosnian Croats and other non- Serbs in Prijedor municipality, including prisoners detained in the Omarska, Keraterm and Trnopolje camps, amongst whom were those persons listed in Schedules A-E; […] **Miroslav KVOČKA** instigated, committed or otherwise aided and abetted the persecutions of Bosnian Muslims, Bosnian Croats and other non-Serbs in the Prijedor area, on political, racial or religious grounds, as well as the commission of the other crimes charged in this indictment, through his direct participation in crimes and through his approval, encouragement, acquiescence, and assistance in the development and continuation of the conditions in the camp and the on-going commission of crimes as described in paragraph 25 against the prisoners in the Omarska camp, including those set forth in Schedule A. As the Camp Commander and then Deputy Commander, **Miroslav KVOČKA** had the authority to alter the conditions of confine-

	- Mlađo Radić is also charged with **Torture as CAH** (count 14), **Rape as CAH** (count 15), **Torture as a violation of the laws or customs of war (WC)** (count 16) and **Outrages upon personal dignity as a violation of the laws or customs of war (WC)** (count 17) under Article Article 7(1) of the Statute (**committing**) for the rapes and sexual assaults of female prisoners at Omarska camp, including the rape of Witness A

ment that existed in the camps. He had the authority to control the conduct of the guards in the camp and to prevent or control the conduct of any visitors to the camp. He had the authority to set the daily regime of the prisoners and to grant them more freedoms and rights within the camp […]. In addition, as an active duty policeman, **Miroslav KVOČKA** had an independent duty to uphold the laws in force on the territory of Bosnia and Herzegovina and to safeguard the lives and property of civilians. **Dragoljub PRCAĆ** instigated, committed or otherwise aided and abetted the persecutions of Bosnian Muslims, Bosnian Croats and other non-Serbs in the Prijedor area, on political, racial or religious grounds, as well as the commission of the other crimes charged in this indictment, through his direct participation in crimes and through his approval, encouragement, acquiescence, and assistance in the development and continuation of the conditions in the camp and the on-going commission of crimes as described in paragraph 25 against the prisoners in the Omarska camp, including those set forth in Schedule E. As the Deputy Commander of the camp, **Dragoljub PRCAĆ** had the authority to alter the conditions of confinement that existed in the camps. He had the authority to control the conduct of the guards in the camp and to prevent or control the conduct of any visitors to the camp. He had the authority to set the daily regime of the prisoners and to grant them more freedoms and rights within the camp […]. In addition, as a policeman on active duty, **Dragoljub PRCAĆ** had an independent duty to uphold the laws in force on the territory of Bosnia and Herzegovina and to safeguard the lives and property of civilians. **Milojica KOS** and **Mlađo RADIĆ** instigated, committed or otherwise aided and abetted the persecutions of Bosnian Muslims, Bosnian Croats and other non-Serbs in the Prijedor area, on political, racial or religious grounds, as well as the other crimes charged in this indictment, by their direct participation in the various crimes and by their instigation, approval, encouragement, acquiescence, and assistance in the development and continuation of the conditions in the camp and the on-going commission of crimes as described in paragraph 25, against the prisoners in the Omarska camp, including those listed in Schedules B and C. As Shift Commanders in the Omarska camp, **Milojica KOS** and **Mlađo RADIĆ** had the authority to alter the conditions of confinement that existed in the camps during the times they were on duty. They had the authority to control the conduct of the guards assigned to their shifts and to prevent or control the conduct of any visitors to the camp. They had the authority to grant the prisoners more freedoms and rights within the camp […]. In addition, as policemen, **Milojica KOS** and **Mladjo RADIC** had an independent duty to uphold the laws in force on the territory of Bosnia and Herzegovina and to safeguard the lives and property of civilians. **Zoran ŽIGIĆ** instigated, committed or other wise aided and abetted the persecutions of Bosnian Muslims, Bosnian Croats and other non-Serbs in the Prijedor area, including those set forth in Schedule D, on political, racial or religious grounds, as well as the other crimes charged in this indictment, by his direct and continuing participation in the various crimes and his instigation, approval, encouragement, acquiescence, and assistance in the development and continuation of the conditions in the camp and the on-going commission of crimes as described in paragraph 25. In addition, between 24 May 1992 and 30 August 1992, **Miroslav KVOČKA, Dragoljub PRCAĆ, Milojica KOS** and **Mlađo RADIĆ** knew or had reason to know that persons subordinate to them in the Omarska camp were about to participate in the persecution of Bosnian Muslims, Bosnian Croats and other non-Serbs in the Prijedor area, including those persons listed in Schedule A, on political, racial or religious grounds, or had done so, and failed to take necessary and reasonable measures to prevent such acts or to punish the perpetrators. By their involvement in the above acts and omissions, **Miroslav KVOČKA, Dragoljub PRCAĆ, Milojica KOS, Mlađo RADIĆ** and **Zoran ŽIGIĆ** committed: **Count 1:** persecutions on political, racial or religious grounds, a **CRIME AGAINST HUMANITY**, punishable under Articles 5(h) and 7(1) of the Statute of the Tribunal. **Count 2:** inhumane acts, a **CRIME AGAINST HUMANITY**, punishable under Articles 5(i) and 7 (1) of the Statute of the Tribunal; **Count 3:** outrages upon personal dignity, a **VIOLATION OF THE LAWS OR CUSTOMS OF WAR**, as recognised by Article 3(1)(c) of the Geneva Conventions of 1949, punishable under Articles 3 and 7(1) of the Statute of the Tribunal. In addition, **Miroslav KVOČKA, Dragoljub PRCAĆ, Milojica KOS** and **Mlađo RADIĆ**, are criminally responsible for the crimes set forth in **Counts 1 to 3** pursuant to Article 7(3) of the Statute of the Tribunal".). On 15 December 2000, in its Decision on Defence Motions for Acquittal (Rule 98*bis* of the Rule of Procedure and Evidence), the Trial Chamber found that no evidence had been presented as to any role of Miroslav Kvočka, Dragoljub Prcać, Milojica Kos and Mlađo Radić in the Keraterm and Trnopolje camps. See *Prosecutor v. Miroslav Kvočka et al.*, Case No. IT-98-30/1-T, Decision on Defence Motions for Acquittal, 15 December 2000, para. 63(a).

	on five occasions during June and July 1992, the rape of Witness K on one occasion around the middle of July, the sexual assault of Witness E between 22 and 26 June 1992, the sexual assault of Witness F between 1 June and 3 August 1992, the sexual assault of Witness J on several occasions between 9 June and 3 August 1992, and the sexual assault of Witness L between 22 June and 3 August 1992.[131]
Trial Judgement	- Miroslav Kvočka, Dragoljub Prcać, Milojica Kos, Mlađo Radić and Zoran Žigić: Guilty of **Persecutions as CAH** (count 1) under Article 7(1) of the Statute (**joint criminal enterprise**) for various acts, including sexual assault and rape of Bosnian Muslims, Bosnian Croats and other non-Serbs detained in Omarska camp.[132] Not guilty of Inhumane acts as CAH (count 2) and Outrages upon personal dignity as a violation of the laws or customs of war (WC) (count 3) for the same acts.[133] - Mlađo Radić: Guilty of **Torture as a violation of the laws or customs of war (WC)** (count 16) under Article 7(1) of the Statute (**joint criminal enterprise**) for the rape of Witness K, the attempted rape of Witness J and the threat of rape or other forms of sexual violence committed against Witness F, Zlata Cikota and Sifeta **Sušić** in Omarska camp.[134] Not guilty of Torture as CAH (count 14), Rape as CAH (count 15) and Outrages upon personal dignity as a violation of the laws or customs of war (WC) (count 17) for the same acts.[135]
Appeal Judgement	- The Appeals Chamber **reversed the conviction of Miroslav Kvočka for Persecutions as CAH** (count 1) **in so far as his conviction relates to sexual assault and rape** of Bosnian Muslims, Bosnian Croats and other non-Serbs detained in Omarska camp.[136] - The Appeals Chamber also **reversed the conviction of Zoran Žigić for Persecutions as CAH** (count 1) for various acts, including sexual assaults and rapes of Bosnian Muslims, Bosnian Croats and other non-Serbs detained in Omarska camp.[137]
Legal and Factual Findings	- Legal findings: **- Being forced to watch sexual attacks may inflict severe mental harm amounting**

[131] *Miroslav Kvočka et al.* Indictment, para. 42 ("Between 24 May 1992 and 30 August 1992, at the Omarska camp, **Mlado RADIĆ** raped and sexually assaulted female prisoners, including the rape of witness A on five occasions during June and July 1992, the rape of witness K on one occasion around the middle of July, the sexual assault of witness E between 22 June 1992 and 26 June 1992, the sexual assault of witness F between 1 June 1992 and 3 August 1992, the sexual assault of witness J on several occasions between 9 June 1992 and 3 August 1992, and the sexual assault of witness L between 22 June 1992 and 3 August 1992. By the foregoing acts **Mlado RADIĆ** committed: **Count 14:** torture, a **CRIME AGAINST HUMANITY**, punishable under Articles 5(f) and 7(1) of the Statute of the Tribunal; **Count 15:** rape, a **CRIME AGAINST HUMANITY**, punishable under Articles 5(g) and 7(1) of the Statute of the Tribunal; **Count 16:** torture, a **VIOLATION OF THE LAWS OR CUSTOMS OF WAR**, as recognised by Article 3(1)(a) of the Geneva Conventions of 1949 punishable under Articles 3 and 7(1) of the Statute of the Tribunal. **Count 17:** outrages upon personal dignity, a **VIOLATION OF THE LAWS OR CUSTOMS OF WAR**, as recognised by Article 3(1)(c) of the Geneva Conventions of 1949, punishable under Articles 3 and 7(1) of the Statute of the Tribunal".).

[132] ***Prosecutor v.*** *Miroslav Kvočka et al.*, Case No. IT-98-30/1-T, Judgement, 2 November 2001 ("*Miroslav Kvočka et al.* Trial Judgement"), paras. 98–108, 182–183, 197–198, 209, 233–234, 327, 413–419, 466, 468–470, 502–504, 570–578, 684–688, 691, 752, 755, 758, 761, 764.

[133] *Miroslav Kvočka et al.* Trial Judgement, paras. 173–174, 209, 232, 412–420, 570–579, 684–687, 753, 756, 759, 762, 765.

[134] *Miroslav Kvočka et al.* Trial Judgement, paras. 98–108, 158, 546–557, 559–561, 570, 570–578, 761.

[135] *Miroslav Kvočka et al.* Trial Judgement, paras. 158, 173–174, 182–183, 231, 233–234, 546–557, 559–561, 570–579, 762.

[136] ***Prosecutor v.*** *Miroslav Kvočka et al.*, Case No. IT-98-30/1-A, Judgement, 28 February 2005 ("*Miroslav Kvočka et al.* Appeal Judgement"), paras. 329–334, 339 and Section VIII (Disposition), p. 242.

[137] *Miroslav Kvočka et al.* Appeal Judgement, paras. 594–599 and Section VIII (Disposition), p. 243.

and/or Evidence	**to torture:** The Trial Chamber held: "The Trial Chamber notes that abuse amounting to torture need not necessarily involve physical injury, as mental harm is a prevalent form of inflicting torture. For instance, the mental suffering caused to an individual who is forced to watch severe mistreatment inflicted on a relative would rise to the level of gravity required under the crime of torture. Similarly, the *Furundžija* Trial Chamber found that being forced to watch serious sexual attacks inflicted on a female acquaintance was torture for the forced observer. The presence of onlookers, particularly family members, also inflicts severe mental harm amounting to torture on the person being raped".[138] **- Forced public nudity may constitute outrages upon personal dignity:** The Trial Chamber recalls that: "The *Furundžija* and *Kunara*[*c*] Trial Chambers have found that rape and other forms of sexual violence, including forced public nudity, cause severe physical or mental pain and amount to outrages upon personal dignity".[139] **- Rape: definition:** The Trial Chamber adopted the definition of rape given in the *Kunarac et al.* case:[140] "The Trial Chamber agrees with the factors set out by the Trial Chamber in *Kunara*[*c*], defining rape as a violation of sexual autonomy. In order for sexual activity to be classified as rape: (i) the sexual activity must be accompanied by force or threat of force to the victim or a third party; (ii) the sexual activity must be accompanied by force *or* a variety of other specified circumstances which made the victim particularly vulnerable or negated her ability to make an informed refusal; or (iii) the sexual activity must occur without the consent of the victim".[141] The Trial Chamber further held: "In considering allegations of rape, the *Čelebići* Trial Chamber stressed that coercive conditions are inherent in situations of armed conflict. Further, the *Furundžija* Trial Chamber emphasized that 'any form of captivity vitiates consent.' This Trial Chamber endorses these holdings. The *mens rea* of the crime of rape is the intent to effect a sexual penetration and the knowledge that it occurs without the consent of the victim".[142] **- Sexual violence: definition and acts:** The Trial Chamber held: "The *Akayesu* Trial Chamber defined sexual violence as 'any act of a sexual nature which is committed on a person under circumstances which are coercive.' Thus, sexual violence is broader than rape and includes such crimes as sexual slavery or molestation. Moreover, the *Akayesu* Trial Chamber emphasized that sexual violence need not necessarily involve physical contact and cited forced public nudity as an example".[143] "Sexual violence would also include such crimes as sexual mutilation, forced marriage, and forced abortion as well as the gender related crimes explicitly listed in the ICC Statute as war crimes and crimes against humanity, namely 'rape, sexual slavery, enforced prostitution, forced pregnancy, enforced sterilization' and other similar forms of violence. Rome Statute of the International Criminal Court, UN Doc

138 *Miroslav Kvočka et al.* Trial Judgement, para. 149 (internal reference omitted).

139 *Miroslav Kvočka et al.* Trial Judgement, para. 170 (internal reference omitted).

140 ICTY ISCC *Kunarac et al.*, see *supra* p. 528.

141 *Miroslav Kvočka et al.* Trial Judgement, para. 177 (internal reference omitted).

142 *Miroslav Kvočka et al.* Trial Judgement, paras. 178–179 (internal references omitted).

143 *Miroslav Kvočka et al.* Trial Judgement, para. 180 (internal references omitted).

	A/CONF.183/9, 17 July 1998, at Art. 7(1)(g), Art. 8(2)(b)(xxii), and Art. 8(2)(e)(vi)".[144] **- Sexual violence may constitute persecutions:** "Thus far, the Trial Chambers of the ICTY have found that the following acts may constitute persecution when committed with the requisite discriminatory intent: [...] sexual violence".[145] **- Forced prostitution may constitute inhumane acts:** The Trial Chamber held that forced prostitution may constitute inhumane acts.[146] **- Cumulative convictions: concurrent offences characterizing the acts of rapes and sexual assaults:** The Trial Chamber held that, when rapes or sexual assaults constitute both torture as a violation of the laws or customs of war (WC) and outrages upon personal dignity as a violation of the laws or customs of war (WC), "it is not permissible to enter cumulative convictions under both charges of outrages upon personal dignity under Article 3(1)(c) and torture under Article 3(1)(a); if torture is established it must be preferred over the offence of outrages upon personal dignity".[147] The Trial Chamber also held, with respect to international sex crimes constituting persecutions as CAH and international sex crimes constituting other inhumane acts as CAH, "if a persecution charge is upheld, the charge of other inhumane acts on the basis of the same acts must be dismissed".[148] The Trial Chamber further held, with respect to the relationships between persecutions as CAH, torture as CAH and rape as CAH, that: "The offence of rape requires sexual penetration, while the offence of torture requires the infliction of severe pain or suffering for a prohibited purpose. Thus, consistent with the analysis in the *Kunara*[*c*] case, convictions for both are allowed if the requirements of each are met. Nonetheless, the Trial Chamber previously indicated that the crime of persecution requires a materially distinct element, namely the discriminatory intent, vis-à-vis the crime of torture; this same intent also distinguishes persecution from elements of rape. Therefore, in instances where the same act qualifies as rape, torture, and persecution under Article 5 of the Statute, the Trial Chamber may convict the accused for persecution only. To summarize, if the same act qualifies as rape, torture, and persecution, the Trial Chamber may only enter convictions of torture and rape as violations of the laws or customs of war (Article 3(1)(a) and (c) of the Geneva Conventions) and persecution as a crime against humanity (Article 5(h) of the Statute). The other charges covering the same act must be dismissed".[149] - <u>Factual and legal findings:</u> **- Sexual violence and joint criminal enterprise – third category:** "[A]ny crimes that were natural or foreseeable consequences of the joint criminal enterprise of the Omarska camp, including sexual violence, can be attributable to participants in the criminal enterprise if committed during the time he participated in

144 *Miroslav Kvočka et al.* Trial Judgement, fn. 343.

145 *Miroslav Kvočka et al.* Trial Judgement, para. 186 (internal reference omitted).

146 *Miroslav Kvočka et al.* Trial Judgement, para. 186.

147 *Miroslav Kvočka et al.* Trial Judgement, para. 231.

148 *Miroslav Kvočka et al.* Trial Judgement, para. 232.

149 *Miroslav Kvočka et al.* Trial Judgement, paras. 233–234 (internal references omitted).

the enterprise. In Omarska camp, approximately 36 women were held in detention, guarded by men with weapons who were often drunk, violent, and physically and mentally abusive and who were allowed to act with virtual impunity. Indeed, it would be unrealistic and contrary to all rational logic to expect that none of the women held in Omarska, placed in circumstances rendering them especially vulnerable, would be subjected to rape or other forms of sexual violence. This is particularly true in light of the clear intent of the criminal enterprise to subject the targeted group to persecution through such means as violence and humiliation. Liability for foreseeable crimes flows to aiders and abettors as well as co-perpetrators of the criminal enterprise”.[150]

- Factual findings:

- Sexual violence in the Omarska camp:

“Approximately thirty-six of the detainees held at Omarska camp were women. The women detained at Omarska were of different ages; the oldest were in their sixties and there was one young girl. The Trial Chamber heard compelling evidence from several female detainees who testified that it was commonplace for women to be subjected to sexual intimidation or violence in Omarska. For example, Sifeta Susić felt threatened by Željko Meakić when he said to her that someone had ‘asked whether it was true that Sifeta Sušić was raped by 20 soldiers…and I said ‘Yes, it is. I was the 20th in line’.’ Several witnesses told of an occasion when a man approached a female detainee in the eating area, unbuttoned her shirt, drew a knife over one of her breasts, and threatened to cut it off. Many others testified that women were frequently called out from the administration building or the cafeteria at night and were subsequently raped or subjected to other forms of sexual violence. Witness J testified that on one occasion Nedeljko Grabovac, known as ‘Kapitan’, called her out. She was afraid he might kill her and described how he started touching her on her genitals and grabbing her breasts. Despite her pleas, he took out his penis and attempted to rape her, finally ejaculating on her before she managed to escape. The witness incurred bruises on her thighs and breasts as she struggled to get away. Witness F testified that she was often taken away by a guard named Gruban. The witness described how this guard took her on several occasions, at any time of the day or night, to a room upstairs in the administration building where he forced her to have sex with him. Another guard, named Kole, called her out twice during the night where he took her to the same room where Gruban had raped her and then raped her himself. She further testified that she was taken to the ‘Separacija’ building (a kitchen outside the Omarska camp) where she was forced to have sexual intercourse with Mirko Babić and Dule Tadić. Witness U testified that she was detained with another woman in one room of the white house. There they heard cries of pain and terror emanating from male detainees and heard interrogators or guards yelling and cursing at the detainees. On one occasion, a guard prevented other guards at the white house from assaulting the two female detainees. Witness U however also testified that, when she was detained in the administration building with the other women, a guard took her from her room several times at night to a room at the end of the corridor, where she was systematically raped by a string of perpetrators: ‘…He would rape me…He would leave, and then all the time, one after the other, others would come in, I don’t know the exact number…they also raped me.’ She was also taken twice during the day to that same room by another guard, where she was again subjected to repeated rapes by multiple assailants: ‘…First he raped me, and then afterwards again others entered…three or four men who raped me. Q. Did you experience bleeding due to the multiple rapes that you endured at the Omarska camp? A. Yes, throughout [the time] I was there.’ Witness B was taken to one of the offices in the administration building by a young guard who attempted to rape her: ‘He lay on top of me and started physically abusing me. I tried to defend myself, and I did for as

[150] *Miroslav Kvočka et al.* Trial Judgement, para. 327.

	long as my strength lasted, and at one point, he threatened to kill me if I wouldn't let him have his way…I felt a very strong pain in the neck area of my spine…'. Witness B continued to struggle and the guard finally stopped when she said that she would report him to Radić. Nedzija Fazlić testified that on one occasion a guard called Lugar called her to a room at the end of the corridor and ordered her to take off her clothes. She told him that she could not have sexual intercourse with him as she was menstruating. He forced her to prove it to him and then told her that he would sleep with her later. Nedzija Fazlić continued to be threatened by Lugar until she complained to Željko Meakić. The women testified that they spoke little amongst themselves about the sexual violence they were forced to endure. Defense witness Vinka Andić, who cleaned the administration building, testified that the female detainees never complained about mistreatment to her. The Trial Chamber notes however that, as the female detainees were reluctant to talk about the abuses among themselves, it would be unlikely they would discuss it with a cleaning lady of Serb ethnicity employed by the camp authorities. The testimony given by female detainees did suggest that they had their suspicions about what was happening to the other women. Witness J testified that during her stay in the administration building, women were very often called out at night. When they returned, they appeared absent-minded and did not speak to the others. Similarly, Witness F testified that during the time she spent at Omarska, almost every woman from her room was taken out at night. She said that when a woman came back to the room, she would usually be withdrawn or crying. Witness A described an occasion when guards took her and another woman to the 'Separacija' building. The other woman was forced to go off with a man called Mirko Babić and when she returned she was in tears. Witness B reported how one woman would often be taken out for interrogation and when she returned showed signs of 'physical abuse.' Zuhra Hrnić was kept in a room above the cafeteria with seventeen other women and she testified that their 'room leader' was separated from them during the night. The witness later noticed that the 'room leader' had an enormous bruise on her right thigh and that she kept crying all the time. The Trial Chamber finds that female detainees were subjected to various forms of sexual violence in Omarska camp".[151] "Evidence discloses that the detainees were subjected to serious humiliating and degrading treatment through such means as inappropriate conditions of confinement in the Omarska camp. The detainees […] endured the constant fear of being subjected to […] sexual violence in the camp, as described in Part II of this Judgement. The Trial Chamber finds that outrages upon personal dignity within the meaning of Article 3 of the Statute were regularly committed upon detainees in Omarska camp".[152] "The evidence establishes, as demonstrated in Part II of this Judgement, that female detainees in Omarska camp were subjected to forced or coerced acts of sexual penetration, as well as other acts of a sexual nature committed under coercive or abusive circumstances. The Trial Chamber is satisfied that rape and other forms of sexual violence falling within the meaning of Articles 3 and 5 (rape and persecution) of the Statute were committed".[153] "In relation to the facts at hand, the Trial Chamber first notes that virtually all the offences alleged were committed against non-Serb detainees of the camps. The victims were targeted for attack on discriminatory grounds. While discriminatory grounds form the requisite criteria, not membership in a particular group, the discriminatory grounds in this case are founded upon exclusion from membership in a particular group, the Serb group. Based on the totality of the evidence, it is clear that […] rape[s …] were strategically and systematically committed against non-Serbs in Omarska. Most of these atrocities appear to have been committed with a premeditated intent to

151 *Miroslav Kvočka et al.* Trial Judgement, paras. 98–108 (internal references omitted).

152 *Miroslav Kvočka et al.* Trial Judgement, paras. 173–174.

153 *Miroslav Kvočka et al.* Trial Judgement, paras. 182–183.

	create an atmosphere of violence and terror and to persecute those imprisoned. [... S]electively targeting only non-Serbs for [...] sexual violence – these are all examples of discriminatory and demoralizing treatment designed to persecute. [...] The Trial Chamber finds that the elements of persecution as a crime against humanity have been satisfied. There is no doubt that the attacks specifically targeted the non-Serb population of Prijedor and purported to drive this population out of the territory or to subjugate those remaining. The Trnopolje and Keraterm camps appear to have been each established as part of a common plan to effectuate this goal, and the Omarska camp was clearly established to effectuate this goal".[154] "The Trial Chamber finds that inhumane acts falling within the meaning of Article 5 (inhumane acts and persecution) of the Statute were committed in Omarska camp. Evidence discloses that detainees were subjected to [...] sexual violence".[155] - Rape at the Keraterm camp: "The Trial Chamber also heard credible evidence that women were raped in the Keraterm camp".[156] - Criminal responsibility of Miroslav Kvočka for international sex crimes as persecutions: The Trial Chamber held: "The Trial Chamber has previously found that murder, rape, torture, and inhumane acts within the meaning of Article 5 of the Statute were committed in Omarska camp. It also found that these crimes were committed with the intent to persecute non-Serbs detained therein. The Prosecution has charged other crimes, including those alleging violations of Article 5 of the Statute, using the same set of facts as those underlying the persecution count. The Trial Chamber has found Kvočka guilty of persecution as a crime against humanity based on the murder, torture, rape, and other inhumane acts charged in the Amended Indictment and committed as part of the joint criminal enterprise. As discussed *supra*, this conviction for persecution subsumes the other crimes against humanity charges, thus they cannot be the subject of separate convictions and must be dismissed".[157] However, the Appeals Chamber reversed Miroslav Kvočka's conviction for persecutions as CAH (count 1) for the acts of rapes and sexual assaults. The Appeals Chamber held: "The Appeals Chamber notes first that the parties concur on the fact that no conclusive evidence was provided by the Prosecution on the dates on which Witnesses F, J and K were raped and sexually assaulted. The Appeals Chamber then points out that, with the exception of the assaults committed by Nedeljko Grabovac against Witness J, the Trial Chamber did not enter in the Trial Judgement any finding as regards the dates or approximate dates on which these crimes were allegedly committed. In finding the accused liable for sexual violence the Trial Chamber refers to pages 5385 to 5387 of the transcripts. On the review thereof, the Appeals Chamber notes that the witness provides no date or approximate date for the acts of sexual violence committed against her, and that the Trial Chamber could not properly rely on this witness testimony to conclude that these crimes were committed during the time that Kvočka was employed in the camp. The Appeals Chamber finds that the Trial Chamber erred in stating that rape and sexual assault with which Kvočka was charged in the Indictment were committed in Omarska during the time that he was employed there and, consequently, erred in convicting Kvočka of 'persecution for ... sexual assault and

154 *Miroslav Kvočka et al.* Trial Judgement, paras. 197–198.
155 *Miroslav Kvočka et al.* Trial Judgement, para. 209.
156 *Miroslav Kvočka et al.* Trial Judgement, para. 114 (internal reference omitted).
157 *Miroslav Kvočka et al.* Trial Judgement, para. 415 (internal reference omitted).

	rape.' The Appeals Chamber upholds this ground of appeal and quashes this conviction".[158] - Mlađo Radić's personal involvement in sexual violence: "The Trial Chamber heard compelling evidence that Radić was personally involved in the sexual harassment, humiliation, and violation of women in Omarska camp. He would call particular women out from their place of detention and when these women returned, it was apparent to the other women that something terrible had happened to them. Typically, they did not speak to or look at the other women. Witness F testified that Radić took her to one of the rooms (referred to as the 'police room'). Once there, Radić told Witness F that he could help her if she agreed to sleep with him and that she should get out of the room where she was held one night when he was on duty. He then touched the 'female parts' of her body. Sifeta Sušić testified that on one occasion when Radić was having breakfast with the guards and she was clearing the table, Radić grabbed her, put her down on his knees and said: 'It's better for me to rape you than somebody else do it'. Terrified, she ran off. Zlata Cikota testified that the morning after her arrival in the camp, she was told she should go see Radić and take her identity card. Once in the office with Radić, he wrote down her personal details then grabbed her breasts. She was shocked and told him she was an old woman, but Radić said 'Well, you're good, it doesn't really matter'. Zlata Cikota managed to leave the room when another person came in. Nedzija Fazlić testified that Radić once called her into his office after he heard that Lugar, a guard, had tried to have sexual intercourse with her. Radić suggested that he have sex with her in exchange for helping her meet her husband who was also being held at the camp. Nedzija Fazlić was not mentioned among the counts of the Amended Indictment against Radić or in the attached Schedules. The Trial Chamber is satisfied that the testimony can assist in establishing a consistent pattern of conduct in conformity with Rule 93. Radić grossly abused his position and took advantage of the vulnerability of the detainees. On one occasion he called Witness J into his office and told her that he could help her if she had sexual intercourse with him. Later he attempted to rape her. Witness J testified that after finishing her duties in the cafeteria, Radić called her to his office. He pushed her against a wall and started touching her. Witness J testified that although she pleaded with him, telling him that she was menstruating, Radić took out his penis, attempted to penetrate her, and then ejaculated over her: '…He pushed me against a wall, and he started touching me on my breasts and on my bottom … I was pleading with him to let me go, not to touch me, but he was very rough. He was pushing against me, and I was breathless.' The Defense objects to the credibility of this testimony, stating that the description of this rape incident is identical to another rape incident Witness J described involving a man known as 'Kapitan'. The Trial Chamber, however, considers the testimony and the witness credible and finds that both incidents occurred. Three other former detainees, Witnesses K, AT, and A, testified that Radić sexually assaulted them: Witness K testified about an occasion when one of the cleaning ladies in the camp, Vinka Andzić, came to fetch her, saying that Radić needed her. Radić had previously attempted to coerce her into having sex with him by saying that her children would not be killed if she would agree to having sexual intercourse with him. She was led upstairs to the conference room where Radić was waiting. Witness K noticed a foam mattress on the floor, and stated that '[h]e told me that my children would not be harmed ... .Then he attacked me, he assaulted me, and he raped me.' After Radić left, she said that she stayed in the room for a while to try to stop her bleeding, which was due not only to her menstruating but also to the forced penetration of her vagina. The Defense challenged the credibility of Witness K, since during cross-examination, the witness acknowledged she had not mentioned that Radić raped her to a female journal-

[158] *Miroslav Kvočka et al.* Appeal Judgement, paras. 333–334 (internal references omitted).

	ist that interviewed her in Zagreb in 1993, while in the statement given to the Office of the Prosecutor in 1995 she did describe this incident. Furthermore, the Defense pointed out that there were contradictions between the 1995 statement and the testimony of Witness K before the Trial Chamber concerning the time of the day that the rape occurred. However, the Trial Chamber finds the fact that Witness K did not mention this rape incident in 1993 to a journalist is irrelevant, particularly in light of the sexual and intensely personal nature of the crime. This omission does not undermine the credibility of her testimony. Further, any discrepancy that may exist in her two testimonies concerning the time of day the rape occurred is not fatal to the credibility of the testimony. Defense witness Vinka Andić testified that Radić never asked her to bring Witness K, or any other woman, to the conference room. According to Vinka Andić, Radić was a fine man who treated women in a correct manner. The testimony of Vinka Andić is in direct contrast to the evidence of sexual assault and harassment given by a number of witnesses. As such, the Trial Chamber rejects the testimony of Vinka Andić and accepts the testimony of Witness K. Witness AT testified that Radić called her out of her room several times during her 23 days spent in Omarska camp. Like other women, she was taken to a room at the end of the corridor, where a sponge mattress was on the floor. The witness described how, on one such occasion, Radić told her to take her clothes off and forced her to have sexual intercourse with him. She emphasized: 'I defended myself, and I asked him why he was doing that. But I had to, under pressure from him, to take my clothes off and lie down on the foam mattress.' The Defense pointed out that the witness acknowledged, during cross-examination, that Radić had helped her by bringing her food and water and by moving her husband from the white house to the glass house. However, the Trial Chamber does not find that this fact discredits the testimony of the witness in any way. Indeed, the evidence suggests that he regularly attempted to bribe or coerce victims to 'agree' to sexual intercourse in exchange for favors. The Trial Chamber recalls previous holdings by the Tribunal, as well as Rule 96, dealing with evidence in cases of sexual assault, which states that a status of detention will normally vitiate consent in such circumstances. The Defense further stated that the rape of Witness AT was not mentioned either among the counts of the Amended Indictment against Radić or in the attached Schedules. The Trial Chamber agrees with the Defense on this point and considers that out of fairness to the accused, new charges cannot be brought against the accused in mid-trial without adequate notice. The testimony of Witness AT charging Radić with rape will not therefore be considered in the determination of his guilt. However, the Trial Chamber is satisfied that the testimony of this witness is highly credible and can assist in establishing a consistent pattern of conduct in conformity with Rule 93. Witness A was the third witness who testified before the Court that Radić raped her. The Trial Chamber has no difficulty believing that this witness suffered a terrible and traumatizing ordeal. However, her testimony was so confused as to details of the rape that it cannot be relied upon to establish guilt. […] The Trial Chamber finds that Radić raped Witness K and that he attempted to rape Witness J. It recalls the definition of sexual violence established in *Akayesu* as 'any act of a sexual nature, which is committed on a person under circumstances which are coercive'. The Trial Chamber finds that the sexual intimidations, harassment, and assaults committed by Radić against Witness J, Witness F, Sifeta Susić, and Zlata Cikota clearly fall within this definition, and thus finds that Radić committed sexual violence against these survivors. The Trial Chamber further finds that the rape and other forms of sexual violence were committed only against the non-Serb detainees in the camp and that they were committed solely against women, making the crimes discriminatory on multiple levels. Radić did not rape any of the male non-Serb detainees. As recognized in *Čelebići*, raping a person on the basis of sex or gender is a prohibited purpose for the offence of torture. Torture also requires proof of intentional infliction of severe pain and suffering. Based on the testimony above the Trial Chamber concludes that Radić intentionally committed the aforementioned acts. The rape of Witness K and the attempted rape of Witness J

	manifest his intent to inflict severe pain and suffering. Thus, the Trial Chamber also finds that Radić is guilty of the torture of Witness K and Witness J. In considering whether severe pain and suffering was also inflicted upon the other victims of sexual violence, the Trial Chamber takes into consideration the extraordinary vulnerability of the victims and the fact that they were held imprisoned in a facility in which violence against detainees was the rule, not the exception. The detainees knew that Radić held a position of authority in the camp, that he could roam the camp at will, and order their presence before him at any time. The women also knew or suspected that other women were being raped or otherwise subjected to sexual violence in the camp. The fear was pervasive and the threat was always real that they could be subjected to sexual violence at the whim of Radić. Under these circumstances, the Trial Chamber finds that threat of rape or other forms of sexual violence undoubtedly caused severe pain and suffering to Witness F, Zlata Cikota, and Sifeta Susić and thus, the elements of torture are also satisfied in relation to these survivors".[159] - Criminal responsibility of Mlađo Radić for international sex crimes as persecutions as CAH and torture as a violation of the laws or customs of war (WC): "In addition to the crimes charged in conjunction with persecution, Radić was also charged under counts 14 to 17 with rape, torture, and outrages upon personal dignity. There is no indication in the Amended Indictment as to whether the crimes of sexual violence alleged generally under the persecution count are based on the same acts as the individualized charges brought under counts 14–17 of the Amended Indictment. Counts 14–17 do not separately allege persecution for the sexual violence. The Trial Chamber notes that the Defense challenged the form of the Amended Indictment, and Radić complained that the Amended Indictment did not provide him sufficient specific indication about the crimes with which he was charged. The Prosecution was not required to specify whether the sexual violence included within the persecution count formed the basis of the crimes of sexual violence charged separately. The Trial Chamber considers that Radić was not the sole perpetrator of sexual violence in the Omarska camp and notes there is evidence of additional sex crimes in the Factual Findings that do not relate to Radić and thus, there is no reason to infer that the sexual violence underlying the persecution count or committed as part of the joint criminal enterprise is limited to the crimes of sexual violence charged against Radić. Nonetheless, in the circumstances of this case, due to lack of clarity on this issue in the Amended Indictment, the Trial Chamber holds that the conviction for persecution for crimes including sexual violence cover the rape crimes for which Radić is separately charged. Insofar as rape and torture are charged as crimes against humanity under Article 5 of the Statute, the charges will be dismissed as subsumed within the persecution count. There were allegations of sexual violence charged in the Amended Indictment which were not addressed or established at trial. The Trial Chamber proceeds solely on the basis of the evidence before it. The Trial Chamber already concluded that Radić raped Witness K, attempted to rape Witness J, and that he committed sexual violence against Witness J and three other women. The Trial Chamber has found that Radić played a substantial role in the functioning of Omarska camp as a guard shift leader. He remained at the camp for its entire duration never missing a single shift, guard's on his shift were notoriously brutal and he played a role in orchestrating the abuses, and he personally committed crimes of sexual violence against female detainees. Radić is thus a co-perpetrator of the joint criminal enterprise. Radić is charged with torture (count 16) and outrages upon personal dignity (count 17) as violations of the laws or customs of war under Article 3 of the Statute, based on the rapes and other forms of sexual violence committed in Omarska camp. As noted in Part III, B, Cumulative Convictions, it is permissible to enter convictions for rape and torture based on the same acts when

[159] *Miroslav Kvočka et al.* Trial Judgement, paras. 546–557, 559–561 (internal references omitted).

	elements of both crimes have been satisfied. It is not permissible, based upon the same underlying conduct, to enter multiple convictions for torture and outrages upon personal dignity, as torture is the more distinct crime. In sum, the Trial Chamber finds Radić guilty as a co-perpetrator of the following crimes committed as part of the joint criminal enterprise: persecution (count 1) under Article 5 of the Statute; […] and torture ([count] 16) under Article 3 of the Statute. For the reasons set forth previously, the following crimes are dismissed: inhumane acts (count 2), […] rape (count 15) and torture ([count] 14), which were subsumed within the persecution conviction under Article 5 of the Statute; and outrages upon personal dignity (count 3) […], which [was] subsumed within the torture conviction; and outrages upon personal dignity (count 17), which was subsumed within the torture conviction for the sexual violence, under Article 3 of the Statute".[160]

10. Duško **<u>Sikirica *et al.*</u>** (Case No. IT-95-8) "***Keraterm Camp***" - Duško Sikirica: Between 14 June and 27 July 1992, Commander of Security at the Keraterm detention camp, established by Bosnian Serb forces on the site of a ceramics factory on the eastern outskirts of Prijedor in north-western Bosnia and Herzegovina. - Damir Došen: From 3 June to early August 1992, shift leader at the Keraterm camp. - Dragan Kolundžija: From early June to 25 July 1992, shift commander at the Keraterm camp.	
Indictment[161] (International sex crimes (or related) charges and mode(s) of	- All three accused were charged with: **Persecutions as CAH** (count 3), **Inhumane acts as CAH** (count 4) and **Outrages upon personal dignity as a violation of the laws or customs of war (WC)** (count 5) under Articles 7(1) (**instigating, committing or aiding and abetting**) and 7(3) (**superior responsibility**) for the persecutions of Bosnian Muslims, Bosnian Croats and other non Serbs at the Keraterm camp, including through sexual assaults and rapes.[162]

160 *Miroslav Kvočka et al.* Trial Judgement, paras. 572–579 (internal references omitted).

161 For the general background to the charges, see *Prosecutor v. Duško Sikirica et al.*, Case No. IT-95-8-PT, Second Amended Indictment, 3 January 2001 ("*Duško Sikirica et al.* Indictment"), para. 12 ("interrogations were conducted on a daily basis at the Keraterm camp. The interrogations were regularly accompanied by beatings and torture. Severe beatings, torture, killings, sexual assault, and other forms of physical and psychological abuse were commonplace at Keraterm camp".).

162 *Duško Sikirica et al.* Indictment, paras. 35–40, 42 ("Between 24 May 1992 and 30 August 1992, **Duško SIKIRICA, Damir DOŠEN** […and] **Dragan KOLUNDŽIJA** […] participated in the persecution of Bosnian Muslims, Bosnian Croats and other non-Serbs in the Prijedor area, and specifically in the Keraterm camp, on political, racial or religious grounds. The persecutions included the following means: […] (c) the sexual assault and rape of Bosnian Muslims, Bosnian Croats and other non-Serbs in the Prijedor municipality, including those detained in the Keraterm camp; […]. **Duško SIKIRICA** instigated, committed or otherwise aided and abetted the persecutions of Bosnian Muslims, Bosnian Croats and other non-Serbs in the Prijedor area, on political, racial or religious grounds, as well as the commission of the other crimes charged in this indictment, through his direct participation in crimes and through his instigation, approval, encouragement, acquiescence, and assistance in the development and continuation of the conditions in the Keraterm camp and the on-going commission of crimes as described in paragraph 35 against the prisoners in the Keraterm camp, including those described in paragraphs 43 to 50 below. As the Camp Commander **Duško SIKIRICA** had the authority to alter the conditions of confinement that existed in the Keraterm camp. He had the authority to control the conduct of the guards in the camp and to prevent or control the conduct of visitors to the camp. He had the authority to set the daily regimen of the prisoners and to grant them more freedoms and rights within the camp, including access to potable water, reasonable living conditions and hygienic standards, and contact with their families or friends to receive clothing, hygienic supplies, food and medicines. In addition, as a policeman on active duty, **Duško SIKIRICA** had an independent duty to uphold the laws in force on the territory of Bosnia and Herzegovina and to safeguard the lives and property of civilians. **Damir DOŠEN** […] instigated, committed or otherwise aided and abetted the persecutions of Bosnian Muslims, Bosnian Croats and other non-Serbs in the Prijedor area, on political, racial or religious grounds, as well as

liability)	- In addition, Duško Sikirica was charged with: **Genocide** (count 1) and **Complicity in Genocide** (count 2) under Articles 7(1) and 7(3) of the Statute (**superior responsibility**) for various crimes, including **causing serious bodily and mental harm** to the Bosnian Muslim and Bosnian Croats detainees at Keraterm camp by subjecting them to rapes and sexual assaults.[163]

the other crimes charged in this indictment, by their direct participation in the various crimes and by their instigation, approval, encouragement, acquiescence, and assistance in the development and continuation of the conditions in the Keraterm camp and the on-going commission of crimes as described in paragraph 35, against the prisoners in the Keraterm camp, including those described in paragraph 45 below. As Shift Commanders in the Keraterm camp, **Damir DOŠEN** [...] and **Dragan KOLUNDŽIJA** had the authority to alter the conditions of confinement that existed in the Keraterm camp during the times they were on duty. They had the authority to control the conduct of the guards assigned to their shifts and to prevent or control the conduct of visitors to the camp. They had the authority to grant the prisoners more freedoms and rights within the camp, including access to potable water, reasonable living conditions and hygienic standards, and contact with their families or friends to receive clothing, hygienic supplies, food and medicines. In addition, as policemen on active duty, **Damir DOŠEN** [...] and **Dragan KOLUNDŽIJA** had an independent duty to uphold the laws in force on the territory of Bosnia and Herzegovina and to safeguard the lives and property of civilians. [...] In addition, between 24 May and 30 August 1992, **Duško SIKIRICA, Damir DOŠEN** [...] and **Dragan KOLUNDŽIJA** knew or had reason to know that persons subordinate to them in the Keraterm camp were about to participate in the persecution of Bosnian Muslims, Bosnian Croats and other non-Serbs in the Prijedor municipality on political, racial or religious grounds, including the acts described in paragraphs 43 to 50 below, or had done so, and failed to take necessary and reasonable measures to prevent such acts or to punish the perpetrators. By these acts and omissions, the accused **Duško SIKIRICA, Damir DOŠEN** [...] **Dragan KOLUNDŽIJA** [...] committed: **Count 3:** Persecutions on political, racial or religious grounds, a **CRIME AGAINST HUMANITY,** punishable under Articles 5(h) and 7(1) of the Statute of the Tribunal. **Count 4:** inhumane acts, a **CRIME AGAINST HUMANITY**, punishable under Articles 5(i) and 7 (1) of the Statute of the Tribunal; **Count 5:** outrages upon personal dignity, a **VIOLATION OF THE LAWS OR CUSTOMS OF WAR**, as recognised by Article 3(1)(c) of the Geneva Conventions of 1949, punishable under Articles 3 and 7(1) of the Statute of the Tribunal. In addition, the accused **Duško SIKIRICA, Damir DOŠEN** [...] and **Dragan KOLUNDŽIJA** are criminally responsible for the crimes set forth in **Counts 3 to 5** pursuant to Article 7(3) of the Statute of the Tribunal."), 46 ("Around the latter part of June 1992 [subordinates of the accused] and others, repeatedly called a group of detainees, including Emsud BAHONJIĆ and a man named JUSUFAGIĆ a/k/a 'Car' from Room 2 of the camp and severely beat and abused them. During these beatings [a subordinate of the accused] and others forced BAHONJIĆ to engage in various degrading, humiliating and/or painful acts, such as [...] engaging in fellatio on another prisoner and having objects forced into his anus. [A subordinate of the accused] and others also forced JUSUFAGIĆ to engage in various degrading, humiliating and/or painful acts, such as [...] engaging in fellatio on another prisoner, and having objects forced into his anus. Both BAHONJIC and JUSUFAGIC died from injuries received during the beatings and maltreatment".).

163 *Duško Sikirica et al.* Indictment, paras. 30–31 ("The Bosnian Serb military and police personnel in charge of these camps, their staff, and other persons who visited the camps also caused serious bodily and mental harm to the Bosnian Muslim and Bosnian Croat detainees by subjecting them to sexual assaults [...]. The Keraterm, [...] camps were deliberately operated in a manner designed to inflict upon the detainees conditions intended to bring about their physical destruction with the intent to destroy, in part, the Bosnian Muslim and Bosnian Croat peoples as national, ethnic or religious groups. The conditions were abject and brutal. [...] In all camps, including the Keraterm camp, detainees were continuously subjected to or forced to witness [...] rape and sexual assaults [...]".), 33–34 ("Between 24 May 1992 and 30 August 1992, **Duško SIKIRICA**, instigated, committed or otherwise aided and abetted the killing of Bosnian Muslims and Bosnian Croats, causing serious bodily or mental harm to Bosnian Muslims and Bosnian Croats, and deliberately inflicting on the Bosnian Muslims and Bosnian Croats conditions of life calculated to bring about the physical destruction of a part of the Bosnian Muslim and Bosnian Croat populations, with the intent to destroy the Bosnian Muslims and Bosnian Croats, in part, as national, ethnic or religious groups. **Duško SIKIRICA** participated in the above acts through his direct participation in such acts and through his instigation, approval, encouragement, acquiescence, and assistance in the development and continuation of the conditions in the camp and the on-going commission of crimes against the prisoners in the Keraterm camp. Furthermore, between 24 May 1992 and 30 August 1992, **Duško SIKIRICA**, knew or had reason to know that Bosnian Serb and Serb forces under his control at the Keraterm camp were killing Bosnian Muslims and Bosnian Croats, causing serious bod-

Sentencing Judgement	- Duško Sikirica: Guilty of **Persecution as CAH** (count 3) under Article 7(3) (**superior responsibility**) of the Statute for various acts, including the sexual assault of Bosnian Muslims, Bosnian Croats and other non-Serbs detained at the Keraterm camp.[164] - Note: plea agreements: On 31 August 2001, a joint motion was filed on Kolundžija's behalf with the Office of the Prosecutor informing the Trial Chamber of an agreement reached between the parties as to the entry of a guilty plea by the accused to persecutions as CAH (count 3). On 4 September 2001, Kolundžija entered a guilty plea to count 3 of the Indictment and the Prosecution confirmed the formal withdrawal of the remaining counts against Kolundžija. On 7 September 2001, joint submissions were filed on Sikirica and Došen's behalf with the Prosecution informing the the Trial Chamber of an agreement reached between the parties as to the entry of guilty pleas by the accused to persecutions as CAH (count 3) and the withdrawal of all other counts against them. On 19 September 2001, Sikirica and Došen entered guilty pleas to count 3 of the Indictment and the Prosecution confirmed the formal withdrawal of the remaining counts against them.[165] International sex crimes did not form part of Došen and Kolundžija's guilty pleas.[166]
Appeal Judgement	N/A
Legal and Factual Findings and/or Evidence	- Factual findings: "Rapes were also committed in the Keraterm camp. One woman told Witness K that she had been raped in an office at Keraterm by Nedeljko Timarac, and then by other men in turn, all night long. She was then taken outside and told to sit on a rock. At one point a guard walked by and kicked her".[167] "It is admitted that a small number of women were raped at Keraterm. There is no evidence that Sikirica knew of any such incidents or that he was in a position to know of their having happened after the event. He admits that there is evidence that certain detainees were forced to engage in sexual activities against their will".[168]

ily or mental harm to Bosnian Muslims and Bosnian Croats, and deliberately inflicting on the Bosnian Muslims and Bosnian Croats conditions of life calculated to bring about the physical destruction of the Bosnian Muslims and Bosnian Croats in the Keraterm camp, with the intent to destroy the Bosnian Muslims and Bosnian Croats, in part, as national, ethnic or religious groups, or had done so, and he failed to take necessary and reasonable measures to prevent such acts or to punish the perpetrators thereof. By these acts and omissions, **Duško SIKIRICA** committed: **Count 1: GENOCIDE,** punishable under Articles 4(3)(a), 7(1), and 7(3) of the Statute of the Tribunal; and, **Count 2: COMPLICITY TO COMMIT GENOCIDE,** punishable under Articles 4(3)(e), 7(1), and 7(3) of the Statute of the Tribunal".). In its Judgement on Defence Motions to Acquit (Rule 98*bis* of the Rules of Procedure and Evidence), the Trial Chamber found that the specific intent to commit genocide could not be inferred and, therefore, dismissed counts 1 and 2 of the *Duško Sikirica et al.* Indictment in respect of Duško Sikirica. See *Prosecutor v. Duško Sikirica et al.*, Case No. IT-95-8-T, Judgement on Defence Motions to Acquit, 3 September 2001, paras. 97, 172.

164 *Prosecutor v. Duško Sikirica et al.*, Case No. IT-95-8-S, Sentencing Judgement, 13 November 2001 ("*Duško Sikirica et al.* Sentencing Judgement"), para. 18 ("In the Sikirica Plea Agreement the Prosecution and Duško Sikirica agree on certain facts as being true and constituting the factual basis for the guilty plea to the charge of persecution, a crime against humanity, as set forth in paragraph 36 (a) to (e) of the Indictment. It is agreed that the count of persecution encompasses the evidence led by the Prosecution in respect of the Keraterm camp as to the specific allegations in the Indictment of: […] (c) the sexual assault and rape of Bosnian Muslims, Bosnian Croats and other non-Serbs in the Prijedor municipality, including those detained in the Keraterm camp […]".).

165 *Duško Sikirica et al.* Sentencing Judgement, paras. 12–15.

166 *Duško Sikirica et al.* Sentencing Judgement, paras. 26, 32.

167 *Duško Sikirica et al.* Sentencing Judgement, para. 99 (internal reference omitted).

168 *Duško Sikirica et al.* Sentencing Judgement, para. 125 (internal references omitted).

<table>
<tr><td colspan="2">11. Milan <u>Simić</u> (Case No. IT-95-9/2) “Bosanski Šamac”

Between May 1992 and June 1993, member of the Bosnian Serb Crisis Staff and President of the Executive Board in the Municipality Assembly of Bosanski Šamac, located in north-eastern Bosnia and Herzegovina.</td></tr>
<tr><td>Indictment (International sex crimes (or related) charges and mode(s) of liability)</td><td>- Torture as CAH (counts 4 and 7), Inhumane acts as CAH (counts 5 and 8) and Cruel treatment as a violation of the laws or customs of war (WC) (counts 6 and 9) under Article 7(1) of the Statute for: (i) kicking four non-Serb prisoners in their genitals, namely Hasan Bičić, Muhamed Bičić, Perica Mišić and Ibrahim Salkić, and firing gunshots over their heads; and (ii) forcing Safet Hadžialijagić to pull down his pants while one of the perpetrators accompanying Milan Simić brandished a knife and threated to cut off Safet Hadžialijagić’s penis and Milan Simić fired gunshots over his head.[169]
- Persecutions as CAH (count 1) under Article 7(1) of the Statute for the above-mentioned acts.[170]</td></tr>
</table>

169 *Prosecutor v. Blagoje Simić et al.*, Case No. IT-95-9-T, Fourth Amended Indictment, 9 January 2002 (“*Milan Simić* Indictment”), paras. 24–25 (“One night between about 10 June and 3 July 1992, in the hallway of the gymnasium of the Bosanski Šamac primary school, **Milan SIMIĆ,** while serving in the position of President of the Executive Board of the Municipal Assembly of Bosanski Šamac, and a member of the Serb Crisis Staff, and accompanied by other Serb men, beat Hasan Bičić, Muhamed Bičić, Perica Mišić, and Ibrahim Salkić with a variety of weapons. **Milan SIMIĆ** kicked Hasan Bičić, Muhamed Bičić, Perica Mišić, and Ibrahim Salkić in their genitals and fired a gun shot over the heads of Hasan Bičić, Muhamed Bičić, Perica Mišić, and Ibrahim Salkić. By these actions, **Milan SIMIĆ** planned, instigated, ordered, committed or otherwise aided and abetted the planning, preparation or execution of: **Count 4**: Torture, a **CRIME AGAINST HUMANITY,** punishable under Article 5(f) of the Statute of the Tribunal; **Count 5**: Inhumane acts, a **CRIME AGAINST HUMANITY,** punishable under Article 5(i) of the Statute of the Tribunal; **Count 6**: Cruel treatment, a **VIOLATION OF THE LAWS OR CUSTOMS OF WAR,** punishable under Article 3 of the Statute of the Tribunal and recognised by Article 3(1)(a) of the Geneva Conventions”.), 26–27 (“One night in or about June 1992, in the hallway of the gymnasium building of the Bosanski Šamac primary school, **Milan SIMIĆ,** while in the position of President of the Executive Board of the Municipal Assembly of Bosanski Šamac, and a member of the Serb Crisis Staff, and accompanied by other Serb men, kicked Safet Hadžialijagić and beat him repeatedly with a variety of weapons. **Milan SIMIĆ** placed the barrel of his gun in Safet Hadžialijagić’s mouth. During the beating, the other Serb men who accompanied **Milan SIMIĆ** repeatedly pulled down the victim’s pants and threatened to cut off his penis. During the course of the beating, **Milan SIMIĆ** fired gun shots over the head of Safet Hadžialijagić. By these actions, **Milan SIMIĆ** planned, instigated, ordered, committed or otherwise aided and abetted the planning, preparation or execution of: **Count 7**: Torture, a **CRIME AGAINST HUMANITY,** punishable under Article 5(f) of the Statute of the Tribunal; **Count 8**: Inhumane acts, a **CRIME AGAINST HUMANITY,** punishable under Article 5(i) of the Statute of the Tribunal; **Count 9**: Cruel treatment, a **VIOLATION OF THE LAWS OR CUSTOMS OF WAR,** punishable under Article 3 of the Statute of the Tribunal and recognised by Article 3(1)(a) of the Geneva Conventions”.).

170 *Milan Simić* Indictment, paras. 13–14, 16, 19 (“Beginning in or about September 1991 and continuing through at least 31 December 1993, […] **Milan SIMIĆ** […], acting in concert together, and with other Serb civilian and military officials, planned, instigated, ordered, committed, or otherwise aided and abetted the planning, preparation, or execution of a crime against humanity, that is, the persecutions of Bosnian Croat, Bosnian Muslim and other non-Serb civilians on political, racial, or religious grounds, throughout the municipalities of Bosanski Šamac, Odžak and elsewhere in the territory of Bosnia and Herzegovina. The crime of persecutions was perpetrated, executed and carried out by or through the following means: […] c. the cruel and inhumane treatment of Bosnian Croats, Bosnian Muslims and other non-Serb civilians including beatings, torture, forced labour assignments and confinement under inhumane conditions […]. From on or about 17 April 1992 through February 1993, **Milan SIMIĆ**, both prior to and while serving as President of the Executive Board of the Bosanski Šamac Assembly and as a member of the Serb Crisis Staff, acting in concert with others, planned, instigated, ordered, committed, or otherwise aided and abetted the planning, preparation, or execution of the crime of persecutions as described in paragraphs 13 and 14 above, through his participation in the following acts or omissions, among others: […] c. the torture and beating of Bosnian Croats,

Sentencing Judgement	- Guilty of **Torture as CAH** (counts 4 and 7) for kicking four non-Serb prisoners in the genitals, namely Hasan Bičić, Muhamed Bičić, Perica Mišić and Ibrahim Salkić, while gunshots were fired above their heads and for forcing Safet Hadžialijagić to pull down his pants, while one of the men accompanying Milan Simić brandished a knife and threatened to cut off Safet Hadžialijagić's penis and the other assailants were challenging and exhorting the man wielding the knife to cut off Safet Hadžialijagić's penis and for concurrently firing gunshots over his head.[171] - Note: plea agreement: On 13 May 2002, a joint motion was filed by Milan Simić and the Office of the Prosecutor informing the Trial Chamber of an agreement reached between the parties as to the entry of a guilty plea by the accused to torture as CAH (counts 4 and 7) and the the withdrawal of all other counts against him. On 15 May 2002, Milan Simić entered a guilty plea to counts 4 and 7 of the Indictment and the next day the Prosecution confirmed the formal withdrawal of the remaining counts against Milan Simić.[172]
Appeal Judgement	N/A
Legal and Factual Findings and/or Evidence	- Factual and legal findings: "In relation to count 4, the Plea Agreement details the 'instruments' used to beat the victims: the victims were beaten with fists, the leg of a chair, a rod or bar, the butt of a rifle, and were kicked, on various parts of their bodies and especially in the genitals. It further provides that the victims were forced to stand with their arms outstretched, and were ordered to stand with their legs apart in order to receive forceful kicks to their genitals. Safet Hadžialijagić, the victim of torture charged in count 7, in addition to being severely beaten, had to face threats that his penis would be cut off. He had the barrel of a gun pushed into his mouth. The victims of both counts also had to endure gunshots fired over their heads. There can be no doubt that the acts that comprised the

Bosnian Muslims and other non-Serb civilians confined at detention camps, including but not limited to Hasan Bičić, Muhamed Bičić, Perica Mišić, Ibrahim Salkić and Safet Hadžialijagić. By these actions [...] **Milan SIMIĆ** [...]**,** acting in concert together and with others, planned, instigated, ordered, committed or otherwise aided and abetted the planning, preparation or execution of: **Count 1**: Persecutions on political, racial and religious grounds, a **CRIME AGAINST HUMANITY,** punishable under Article 5(h) of the Statute of the Tribunal".).

171 *Prosecutor v. Milan Simić*, Case No. IT-95-9/2-S, Sentencing Judgement, 17 October 2002 ("*Milan Simić* Sentencing Judgement"), para. 11 ("Milan Simić and the Prosecution agreed that the facts and allegations set out in paragraphs 2, 5, 6–12, 24, 25, in respect of count 4, paragraphs 26 and 27 in respect of count 7, and paragraphs 28–30, 32–34 and 36–37 of the Indictment would be proven beyond reasonable doubt were the Prosecution to proceed with further evidence, and these facts were not disputed by Milan Simić. Specifically, Milan Simić acknowledged that: (a) on 30 May 1992 he was appointed President of the Executive Board in the Municipality of Bosanski Šamac; (b) hundreds of Muslim and Croatian men and women were detained within detention centres or prison camps established for civilians in Bosanski Šamac after 16 April 1992; (c) on various occasions during the summer months of 1992, he went, whilst armed and wearing a uniform, accompanied by other armed Serb men, to the primary school in Bosanski Šamac which was serving as a prison camp; (d) on one occasion between 10 June and 3 July 1992, four non-Serb prisoners at the primary school, Hasan Bičić, Muhamed Bičić, Perica Mišić and Ibrahim Salkić, were attacked, brutally beaten and kicked by Milan Simić and the men accompanying him, on various parts of their bodies, and especially in the genitals; during the beating, gunshots were fired above their heads; (e) in an incident in June 1992, Safet Hadžialijagić was severely beaten by Milan Simić and the men accompanying him; it was common knowledge in Bosanski Samac that Safet Hadžialijagić had a heart condition; Safet Hadžialijagić was forced to pull down his pants, and one of the men accompanying Milan Simić brandished a knife and threatened to cut off Safet Hadžialijagić's penis; the other assailants were challenging and exhorting the man wielding the knife to cut off Safet Hadžialijagić's penis; and at one point, the barrel of a handgun was pushed into Safet Hadžialijagić's mouth and Milan Simić fired gunshots over his head, before the victim was released and allowed to return to the gymnasium". (internal references omitted)).

172 *Milan Simić* Sentencing Judgement, paras. 9–10, 19–22.

	particular torture acts for which Milan Simić stands convicted are barbaric and shocking. Although the mistreatment inflicted by Milan Simić upon his victims did not happen over a prolonged period of time, the manner and methods used render them despicable. The sexual, violent, and humiliating, nature of the acts are therefore considered in aggravation, as it would certainly have increased the mental suffering and feeling of degradation experienced by the victims".[173] - <u>Factual findings:</u> "Milan Simić was a member of the Serb Crisis Staff and serving in the position of President of the Executive Board of the Municipal Assembly of Bosanski Šamac when he committed the offences with which he is charged. Milan Simić has admitted that, one night between about 10 June and 3 July 1992, he, along with several other men, beat Hasan Bičić, Muhamed Bičić, Perica Mišić, and Ibrahim Salkić with a variety of weapons. Milan Simić kicked the victims in their genitals and gunshots were fired over their heads. Milan Simić also admitted that he, along with several other men, repeatedly beat Safet Hadžialijagić with a variety of weapons one night in or about June 1992. The barrel of a handgun was placed in Safet Hadžialijagić's mouth. During the beating, Safet Hadžialijagić was forced to pull down his pants and one of the other Serb men who accompanied Milan Simić threatened to cut off his penis while brandishing a knife. During the course of the beating, Milan Simić fired gun shots over the victim's head".[174]

12. Biljana <u>**Plavšić**</u> (Case No. IT-00-39&40/1) "***Bosnia and Herzegovina***" Serbian representative to the collective Presidency of Bosnia and Herzegovina from 11 November 1990 until December 1992; member of the collective and expanded Presidencies of the Bosnian Serb Republic (later Republika Srpska) from May until December 1992; had *de facto* control and authority over members of the Bosnian Serb armed forces.	
Indictment (International sex crimes (or related) charges and mode(s) of	- **Genocide** (count 1) and **Complicity in Genocide** (count 2) under Articles 7(1) (**joint criminal enterprise**) and 7(3) of the Statute (**superior responsibility**) for various crimes, including **causing serious bodily or mental harm** to the Bosnian Muslim and Bosnian Croat detainees in various detention facilities by subjecting them to sexual violence and **deliberately inflicting conditions of life calculated to bring about their physical destruction** through sexual violence.[175]

[173] *Milan Simić* Sentencing Judgement, para. 63 (internal reference omitted).

[174] *Milan Simić* Sentencing Judgement, paras. 53–54 (internal references omitted).

[175] *Prosecutor v. Momčilo Krajišnik and Biljana Plavšić*, Case No.IT-00-39&40-PT, Amended Consolidated Indictment, 7 March 2002 ("*Plavšić* Indictment"), paras. 15–17 ("Between 1 July 1991 and 30 December 1992, **Momčilo KRAJIŠNIK** and **Biljana PLAVŠIĆ**, acting individually or in concert with each other and with Radovan KARADŽIĆ, Nikola KOLJEVIĆ and other participants in the joint criminal enterprise, planned, instigated, ordered, committed or otherwise aided or abetted the planning, preparation or execution of the partial destruction of the Bosnian Muslim and Bosnian Croat national, ethnical, racial or religious groups, as such, in territories within Bosnia and Herzegovina. As alleged in paragraphs 3 to 9, **Momčilo KRAJIŠNIK** and **Biljana PLAVŠIĆ** participated in a joint criminal enterprise. The objective of the joint criminal enterprise was primarily achieved through a manifest pattern of persecutions as alleged in this indictment. In some Municipalities this campaign of persecutions included or escalated to include conduct committed with the intent to destroy in part the national, ethnical, racial or religious groups of Bosnian Muslims and Bosnian Croats as such. In these municipalities a significant section of the Bosnian Muslim and Bosnian Croat groups, namely their leaderships, as well as a substantial number of the members of the groups were targeted by Bosnian Serb Forces and Bosnian Serb Political and Governmental Organs and their agents for intended destruction. The most extreme manifestations of this form of partial destruction of the Bosnian Muslims and Bosnian Croats took place in Bosanski Novi, Brčko, Ključ, Kotor Varoš, Prijedor, and

liability)	- **Persecutions as CAH** (count 3) under Articles 7(1) (**joint criminal enterprise**) and 7(3) of the Statute (**superior responsibility**) of Bosnian Muslims, Bosnian Croats and other non-Serbs through various acts, including sexual violence.[176]
Sentencing Judgement	- Guilty of **Persecutions as CAH** (count 3) under Article 7(1) (**joint criminal enterprise**) of Bosnian Muslims, Bosnian Croats and other non-Serbs through various acts, including rapes and sexual violence.[177] - Note: plea agreement: On 30 September 2002, a joint motion was filed by Biljana Plavšić and the Office of the Prosecutor informing the Trial Chamber of an agreement reached between the parties as to the entry of a guilty plea by the accused to persecutions as CAH (count 3) and the withdrawal of all other counts against her. On 2 October 2002, Biljana Plavšić entered a guilty plea to count 3 of the Indictment and the Prosecution confirmed the formal withdrawal of the remaining counts against her.[178]
Appeal Judgement	N/A
Legal and Factual Findings	N/A

Sanski Most. The destruction of these groups was effected by: […] b. the causing of serious bodily or mental harm to Bosnian Muslims and Bosnian Croats, including leading members of their communities, during their confinement in detention facilities. The detention facilities include those that are specified in **Schedule C.** At these locations, detainees were subjected to cruel or inhuman treatment, including […] sexual violence […]. c. the detention of Bosnian Muslims and Bosnian Croats, including leading members of their communities, in detention facilities under conditions of life calculated to bring about their physical destruction, namely through cruel and inhuman treatment, including […] sexual violence […]. By these acts and omissions, **Momčilo KRAJIŠNIK** and **Biljana PLAVŠIĆ** participated in: **Count 1: GENOCIDE,** punishable under Articles 4(3)(a), and 7(1) and 7(3) of the Statute of the Tribunal; and/or **Count 2: COMPLICITY IN GENOCIDE**, punishable under Articles 4(3)(e), and 7(1) and 7(3) of the Statute of the Tribunal".).

176 *Plavšić* Indictment, paras. 18–21 ("Between 1 July 1991 and 30 December 1992, **Momčilo KRAJIŠNIK** and **Biljana PLAVŠIĆ**, acting individually or in concert with each other and with Radovan KARADŽIĆ, Nikola KOLJEVIĆ and other participants in the joint criminal enterprise, planned, instigated, ordered, committed or otherwise aided and abetted the planning, preparation or execution of persecutions of the Bosnian Muslim, Bosnian Croat or other non-Serb populations of the following municipalities: Banja Luka; Bijeljina; Bileća; Bosanska Krupa; Bosanski Novi; Bosanski Petrovac; Bratunac; Brčko; Čajniče; Čelinac; Doboj; Donji Vakuf; Foča; Gacko; Hadžići; Ilidža; Ilijaš; Ključ; Kalinovik; Kotor Varoš; Nevesinje; Novi Grad; Novo Sarajevo; Pale; Prijedor; Prnjavor; Rogatica; Rudo; Sanski Most; Šipovo; Sokolac; Teslić; Trnovo; Višegrad; Vlasenica; Vogošća and Zvornik ('Muncipalities'). Bosnian Serb Forces and Bosnian Serb Political and Governmental Organs and their agents committed persecutions in the Municipalities upon Bosnian Muslim, Bosnian Croat or other non- Serb populations. The persecutions included: […] c) cruel or inhumane treatment during and after the attacks on towns and villages in the Municipalities including torture, physical and psychological abuse, sexual violence and forced existence under inhumane living conditions; […] g) cruel or inhumane treatment in detention facilities including those listed in **Schedule C**. This treatment included torture, physical and psychological abuse and sexual violence; […] Beginning in March 1992, Bosnian Serb Forces and Bosnian Serb Political and Governmental Organs and their agents attacked and took control of towns and villages in the Municipalities. Before, during and after these attacks, they committed persecutory acts enumerated in paragraph 19 upon Bosnian Muslim, Bosnian Croat or other non-Serb populations. Bosnian Serb Forces and Bosnian Serb Political and Governmental Organs and their agents established and controlled detention facilities in the Municipalities. After the attacks, Bosnian Muslim, Bosnian Croat or other non-Serb populations were detained in those facilities and were subjected to persecutory acts enumerated in paragraph 19. […] By these acts and omissions, **Momčilo KRAJIŠNIK** and **Biljana PLAVŠIĆ** participated in: **Count 3:** Persecutions on political, racial and religious grounds, a **CRIME AGAINST HUMANITY**, punishable under Articles 5(h) and 7(1) and 7(3) of the Statute of the Tribunal".).

177 *Prosecutor v. Biljana Plavšić*, Case No.IT-00-39&40/1-S, Sentencing Judgement, 27 February 2003 ("*Plavšić* Sentencing Judgement"), paras. 5, 8, 15, 126.

178 *Plavšić* Sentencing Judgement, para. 5.

and/or Evidence	

13. Mladen **Naletilić and** Vinko **Martinović** (Case No. IT-98-34) "***Tuta and Štela***" - Mladen Naletilić: Founder and commander of the Bosnian Croat "Kažnjenička Bojna" (Convicts' Battalion), a 200 to 300 strong body of soldiers based around Mostar in south-eastern Bosnia and Herzegovina; also known as "Tuta". - Vinko Martinović: Commander of the "Mrmak" or "Vinko Škrobo" unit of the Convicts Battalion; subordinate to Mladen Naletilić; also known as "Štela".	
Indictment (International sex crimes (or related) charges and mode(s) of liability)	- There are no factual allegations of international sex crimes in the Indictment. However, the charge for which Mladen Naletilić was tried for international sex crimes is: **Wilfully causing great suffering or serious injury to body or health as a grave breach of the Geneva Conventions of 1949 (WC)** (count 12) under Article 7(1) of the Statute (**committing**).[179]
Trial Judgement	- Mladen Naletilić: Guilty of **Wilfully causing great suffering or serious injury to body or health as a grave breach of the Geneva Conventions of 1949 (WC)** (count 12) under Article 7(1) of the Statute (**committing**) for beating a young man named Zilić on the genitals wih his hand at the Tobacco Institute in Mostar on 10 May 1993.[180]
Appeal Judgement	- The conviction was affirmed by the Appeals Chamber.[181]
Legal and Factual	- Factual and legal findings: - Beating of Zilić:

179 *Prosecutor v. Mladen Naletilić and Vinko Martinović*, Case No. IT-98-34-T, Second Amended Indictment, 28 September 2001, paras. 45, 50 ("Beginning in May 1993 and at least through January 1994, **MLADEN NALETILIĆ, VINKO MARTINOVIĆ** and their subordinates tortured or wilfully caused great suffering to Bosnian Muslim civilians and prisoners of war captured by the KB or detained under the authority of the HVO. Severe physical and mental suffering was intentionally inflicted on Bosnian Muslim detainees for the following purposes: to obtain from them information; to punish them; to retaliate due to adverse developments in the front lines; or to intimidate them, based on their ethnicity or religion. Throughout this period, **MLADEN NALETILIĆ** and **VINKO MARTINOVIĆ** repeatedly committed, aided and abetted torture, wilfully caused great suffering, and by their example instigated and encouraged their subordinates to torture or cause great suffering on Bosnian Muslim detainees. […] Throughout this period, the beatings and torture of Bosnian Muslim civilians and prisoners of war became a common practice of the members of the KB. Beatings and torture of Bosnian Muslim civilians and prisoners of war were committed by a large number of members of the KB, including commanders. […] Beatings and tortures were additionally inflicted at several other locations following the capture of prisoners. **MLADEN NALETILIĆ** and **VINKO MARTINOVIĆ** knew, or had reason to know, that their subordinates were about to commit such acts, or had done so, and they failed to take the necessary and reasonable measures to prevent such further acts, or to punish the perpetrators thereof. […] By the acts and omissions alleged in Paragraphs 45 - 50, **MLADEN NALETILIĆ** committed, and by the acts and omissions alleged in Paragraphs 45, 49 and 50, **VINKO MARTINOVIĆ** committed: […] **COUNT 12:** wilfully causing great suffering or serious injury to body or health, a **GRAVEBREACH OF THE GENEVA CONVENTIONS OF 1949**, under Articles 2 (c), 7(1) and 7(3) of the Statute of the Tribunal".).

180 *Prosecutor v. Mladen Naletilić and Vinko Martinović*, Case No. IT-98-34-T, Judgement, 31 March 2003 ("*Naletilić and Martinović* Trial Judgement"), paras. 450, 453–454, 720–721, 728, 763–764.

181 *Prosecutor v. Mladen Naletilić and Vinko Martinović*, Case No. IT-98-34-A, Judgement, 3 May 2006, Section X (Disposition), p. 207.

Findings and/or Evidence	"The Chamber further finds that Mladen Naletilić committed cruel treatment and wilfully caused great suffering when he hit another prisoner in the face with a Motorola at the Tobacco Institute in Mostar on 10 May 1993 (Counts 11 and 12). [...] On the same occasion, Mladen Naletilić threatened a young man named Zilić. After he had allowed his escorts to beat him up with fists and rifle butts Mladen Naletilić himself beat the victim on the genitals with his hand and hit him on the face with his fist before Zilić was further beaten by his men. The Chamber is satisfied that the mistreatment of the prisoner amounts to cruel treatment and wilfully causing great suffering and that Mladen Naletilić bears individual criminal responsibility as a perpetrator pursuant to Articles 2(c), 3 and 7 (1) of the Statute (Counts 11 and 12)".[182]
	- The Trial Chamber made the following important factual finding with respect to acts inflicted upon Nenad Harmandžić; however, it did not enter a conviction for cruel treatment and wilfully causing great suffering or serious injury to body or health for these acts: "Before the war, and until relieved of his duties, Nenad Harmandžić was a police officer with the Ministry of Interior in Mostar. About a month prior to the breakout of the conflict in Mostar, Nenad Harmandžić was verbally abused and threatened by Vinko Martinović and his soldiers on various occasions. [...] On 30 June 1993, Nenad Harmandžić was again arrested and transferred to the Heliodrom. [...] On 12 or 13 July 1993, the Strumpf brothers entered the Heliodrom specifically seeking for Nenad Harmandžić who tried to hide in another room. A co-detainee told the Strumpf brothers where he was hiding and helped them to find him. Nenad Harmandžić was then transported from the Heliodrom to Vinko Martinović's headquarters with a group of 25 prisoners in a blue pick-up truck. [...] Halil Ajanić had the chance to talk to Nenad Harmandžić while they were unloading canned food at the base. Nenad Harmandžić told him that he was very worried he might not return alive from Vinko Martinović's base. While they unloaded the tin cans, Ernest Takač and a man nicknamed Dolma passed by. They both hit Nenad Harmandžić brutally in the crotch several times until he fell down. Nenad Harmandžić was then unable to assist further Halil Ajanić in the unloading of the tin cans because he was in too much pain. Later, when Halil Ajanić was cleaning Martinović's office, Ernest Takač entered the office and informed Martinović that he had brought Nenad Harmandžić who had tried to run away. Nenad Harmandžić denied the accusation and Martinović ordered him to be brought to the basement but not to be beaten. Ernest Takač took Nenad Harmandžić down the stairs and some minutes later, Halil Ajanić heard a loud scream. Halil Ajanić saw five or six soldiers on the stairs to the basement. About half an hour to an hour later, he was called to come downstairs. Vinko Martinović was present with a number of soldiers. He ordered Halil Ajanić to either hit Nenad Harmandžić or to suffer the same treatment himself. Nenad Harmandžić was bloodied at that time. Halil Ajanić first wanted to comply and hit Nenad Harmandžić because he had a little personal grudge against him. However, when he saw his poor condition, he could not bring himself to hit him. Nenad Harmandžić asked him not to hesitate to hit him since Halil Ajanić had many children and since he himself had no chance of surviving this incident anyway. The soldiers laughed at Halil Ajanić and let him go back upstairs from where he could hear Nenad Harmandžić starting to scream again. After a while it stopped and he saw Nenad Harmandžić being taken out of the building by some soldiers to wash a car. The soldiers urinated into emptied cans of beer and forced Nenad Harmandžić to drink. One of them took out his penis, forced it into Nenad Harmandžić's mouth and asked him whether he liked it. This second time he saw Nenad Harmandžić he looked black and blue".[183]

[182] *Naletilić and Martinović* Trial Judgement, para. 450 (internal references omitted).

[183] *Naletilić and Martinović* Trial Judgement, paras. 460–464 (internal references omitted).

	"The Chamber finds that Vinko Martinović bears individual criminal responsibility for the cruel treatment and wilfully causing great suffering or serious injury to body or health of Nenad Harmandžić pursuant to Articles 2(c), 3 and 7(1) of the Statute (Counts 16 and 17)".[184] "Under Counts 13 to 17, the Prosecution has charged Vinko Martinović with murder pursuant to Article 5(a) of the Statute and Article 3 of the Statute and wilful killing pursuant to Article 2(a) of the Statute and with cruel treatment under Article 3 of the Statute and wilfully causing great suffering or serious injury to body or health under Article 2(c) of the Statute. The mistreatment charges (Counts 16 and 17) and the murder charges (Counts 13, 14 and 15) have, however, been charged *in the alternative*. […] The Chamber has found that Vinko Martinović bears individual criminal responsibility for murder and wilful killing. It thus finds that a conviction shall be entered for Counts 13 to 15 of the Indictment. Due to their character as alternative charges, the findings on the alternative Counts 16 and 17 will not be considered".[185]

14. Milomir **Stakić** (Case No. IT-97-24) "***Prijedor***" From 30 April 1992 until 30 September 1992, President of the Serb controlled Prijedor Municipality Crisis Staff and Head of the Municipal Council for National Defence in Prijedor in north-western Bosnia and Herzegovina.	
Indictment (International sex crimes (or related) charges and mode(s) of liability)	- **Genocide** (count 1) or, alternatively, **Complicity in genocide** (count 2) under Articles 7(1) (**joint criminal enterprise**) and 7(3) of the Statute (**superior responsibility**) for various crimes, including **causing serious bodily or mental harm** to Bosnian Muslims and Bosnian Croats detainees in various camps and detention facilities in the Prijedor municipality by subjecting them to – or forcing them to witness – rape and sexual assault.[186] - **Persecutions as CAH** (count 6) under Articles 7(1) (**joint criminal enterprise**) and 7(3) of the Statute (**superior responsibility**) for the same acts.[187]
Trial	- Guilty of **Persecutions as CAH** (count 6) under Article 7(1) of the Statute (**co-**

184 *Naletilić and Martinović* Trial Judgement, para. 496.

185 *Naletilić and Martinović* Trial Judgement, paras. 509, 511.

186 *Prosecutor v. Milomir Stakić*, Case No. IT-97-24-PT, Fourth Amended Indictment, 11 April 2002 ("*Stakić* Indictment"), paras. 41(2) ("Following the take-over of the [Prijedor] municipality, the execution of the above campaign included: […] (2) Causing serious bodily or mental harm to Bosnian Muslim and Bosnian Croat non-combatants during their confinement in camps, other detention facilities, and during their interrogations at police stations and military barracks when detainees were continuously subjected to or forced to witness […] rape, sexual assault […]".), 48–49 ("In the camps and detention facilities, Bosnian Serb forces and others who were given access to the camps, subjected non-combatant Bosnian Muslim and Bosnian Croat detainees from the municipalities to physical and mental abuse including […] sexual assaults and the witnessing of inhumane acts, including […] causing them serious bodily or mental harm. […] The infliction of serious bodily or mental harm on numerous Bosnian Muslims and Bosnian Croats included: […] (2) At the Omarska Camp[, f]emale detainees were raped and sexually assaulted. (3) At the Keraterm Camp[, f]emale detainees were raped. (4) At the Trnopolje Camp detainees were predominantly women, children and the elderly. […] Female detainees were raped".), 51 ("By his involvement in these acts or omissions Milomir STAKIĆ committed: **Count 1: GENOCIDE**, punishable under Articles 4(3)(a), and 7(1) and 7(3) of the Statute of the Tribunal; **OR, alternatively, Count 2: COMPLICITY IN GENOCIDE**, punishable under Articles 4(3)(e), and 7(1) and 7(3) of the Statute of the Tribunal".).

187 *Stakić* Indictment, paras. 52 ("The Prosecutor re-alleges and reincorporates by reference paragraphs 23–50 *supra* […] in Count 6".), 54(2) ("The above planning, preparation or execution of persecutions included: (2) […] rapes and sexual assaults […]".), 55 ("By his involvement in these acts or omissions **Milomir STAKIĆ** committed: **Count 6:** Persecutions, a **CRIME AGAINST HUMANITY**, punishable under Articles 5(h), 7(1) and 7(3) of the Statute of the Tribunal".).

Judgement	**perpetration**) for various acts, including rapes and sexual assaults.[188] - Not guilty of counts 1 and 2 because it was not proved that Milomir Stakić had the specific genocidal intent.[189]
Appeal Judgement	- The Appeals Chamber affirmed Milomir Stakić's conviction for persecutions (count 6) but found that the Trial Chamber erred in employing a mode of liability, co-perpetratorship, which is not valid within the jurisdiction of the Tribunal. It **set aside the finding that Milomir Stakić was responsible as a co-perpetrator and found Milomir Stakić guilty as a participant in a joint criminal enterprise – first category**.[190]
Legal and Factual Findings and/or Evidence	- Legal findings: - **Rape and sexual violence constituting genocide by causing serious bodily or mental harm:** The Trial Chamber considered that rape and sexual violence can constitute genocide by causing serious bodily or mental harm. The Trial Chamber held: "'Causing serious bodily or mental harm' in sub-paragraph (b) is understood to mean, *inter alia*, acts of torture, inhumane or degrading treatment, sexual violence including rape, interrogations combined with beatings, threats of death, and harm that damages health or causes disfigurement or injury. The harm inflicted need not be permanent and irremediable".[191] - **Rape:** The Trial Chamber adopted the definition of rape given in the *Kunarac et al.* case:[192] "The Trial Chamber concurs with the definition of the crime of rape adopted by the *Kunarac et al.* Appeals Chamber. In this context, '[f]orce or threat of force provide clear evidence of non-consent, but force is not an element *per se* of rape. [...] A narrow focus on force or threat of force could permit perpetrators to evade liability for sexual activity to which the other party had not consented by taking advantage of coercive circumstances without relying on physical force'".[193] - **Sexual assault in international criminal law:** "This Trial Chamber holds that, under international criminal law, not only rape but also any other sexual assault falling short of actual penetration is punishable. This offence embraces all serious abuses of a sexual nature inflicted upon the integrity of a person by means of coercion, threat of force or intimidation in a way that is humiliating and degrading to the victim's dignity".[194] - Factual and legal findings: - Rape during the attack against the non-Serbs on Hambarine in the Prijedor municipality: "Afterwards, two or three tanks set out from the direction of Prijedor, followed by

[188] *Prosecutor v. Milomir Stakić*, Case No. IT-97-24-T, Judgement, 31 July 2003 ("*Stakić* Trial Judgement"), paras. 234–236, 240–241, 244, 400–401, 791–806, 818, 821, 826, 872, 880–882 and Section V (Disposition), p. 253.

[189] *Stakić* Trial Judgement, para. 544–561 and Section V (Disposition), p. 253.

[190] *Prosecutor v. Milomir Stakić*, Case No. IT-97-24-A, Judgement, 22 March 2006, paras. 62, 78, 85, 104 and Section XII (Disposition), pp. 141–142.

[191] *Stakić* Trial Judgement, para. 516 (internal reference omitted).

[192] ICTY ISCC *Kunarac et al.*, see *supra* p. 528.

[193] *Stakić* Trial Judgement, paras. 755–756 (internal references omitted).

[194] *Stakić* Trial Judgement, para. 757 (internal reference omitted).

	infantry. The TO tried to defend the village, but the residents were forced to flee to other villages or to the Kurevo woods to escape the shelling. There were approximately 400 refugees, mostly women, children and elderly people, who fled Hambarine as a result of the attack that saw the Serb soldiers kill, rape and torche houses".[195] - Rape and sexual abuse at the Omarska camp: "The Trial Chamber also heard evidence of sexual abuse taking place in the Omarska camp. Witness H was raped at Omarska every night usually by three or four men. Witness H later learned that one of the men who raped her was called Pavlić or Pavić. Due to the frequent rapes, Witness H experienced severe blood loss and fell into a coma. Dr. Kosuran was summoned and he told the guard that she was weak and in danger as a result of low blood pressure. Witness H had constant painful bleeding from the rapes. One incident of sexual abuse occurred in the 'White House' on 26 June 1992. The guards tried to force Mehmedalija Sarajlic to rape a girl. He begged: 'Don't make me do it. She could be my daughter. I am a man in advanced age.' The soldiers replied: 'Well, try to use the finger.' There was a scream and beatings, and then everything was silent. A minute or two later, a guard came into the room and asked for two strong men who went to fetch the body of Mehmedalija Sarajlic. His dead body was later seen near the 'White House'".[196] - Rape at the Keraterm camp: "Rape was also committed in the Keraterm camp. A woman, Witness H, was taken to a first floor room by a guard whose name she mentioned. Then this guard raped her in a 'sort of ceremony'. He left her lying on a desk and other men came into the room. The victim could not tell the number or the names of the rapists, and she lost consciousness several times. When she awoke the next morning, she was covered in blood and thought she was dying. Later on, she was brought to the Omarska camp. Her fate there was discussed in that context. The Chamber heard convincing evidence of one incident in late July, when Witness B saw the men from Brđo, who were being kept in Room 3, outside. Half the group was naked from the waist-down and standing, and half the group was kneeling. According to Witness B: 'They were positioned in such a way as if engaged in intercourse'".[197] - Rape at the Trnopolje camp: "Both Witness F and Witness I heard that women were raped in the Trnopolje camp. Several other witnesses testified that women who were detained at the Trnopolje camp were taken out of the camp at night by Serb soldiers and raped or sexually assaulted. Dr. Idriz Merdžanić testified that there were several women who sought help at the clinic. Dr. Merdžanić was able to arrange for several of them to visit the gynaecological ward in Prijedor in order to enable them to establish that the rapes had occurred. Dr. Duško Ivić, a Serb physician, reported that all the women who went had been raped, although Dr. Merdžanić himself never saw the results of the medical examinations. If this hearsay evidence were the only evidence available, this Trial Chamber may have had reasonable doubts that rapes did occur. However the Trial Chamber did hear evidence from an individual who was herself a victim of rape in the camp and confirmed that several women and young girls, including a 13 year old one, were raped in the camp or taken out at night for this purpose. Thus, the Trial Chamber is satisfied that rapes did occur in the Trnopolje camp".[198]

195 *Stakić* Trial Judgement, para. 133 (internal references omitted).

196 *Stakić* Trial Judgement, paras. 234–236 (internal references omitted).

197 *Stakić* Trial Judgement, paras. 240–241 (internal references omitted).

198 *Stakić* Trial Judgement, para. 244 (internal references omitted).

	- Stakić's knowledge of the crimes committed in the camps and *mens rea* for persecutions: "However, this single and not finally clarified event, has no impact at all on the Trial Chamber's assessment that Dr. Stakić not only had knowledge about the existence of the camps but also actively participated in setting up and running them. For the foregoing reasons, the Trial Chamber is satisfied that, Dr. Stakić was aware that non-Serbs were detained in the camps on a discriminatory basis and that foreseeable crimes were being committed against them in the camps".[199] "The aforementioned findings lead the Trial Chamber to the conclusion that various crimes such as murder, torture, physical violence, rapes and sexual assaults were committed by the direct perpetrators with a discriminatory intent. What is crucial is that these crimes formed part of a persecutorial campaign headed *inter alia* by Dr. Stakić as (co-)perpetrator behind the direct perpetrators. He is criminally responsible for all the crimes and had a discriminatory intent in relation to all of them, whether committed by the direct perpetrator/actor with a discriminatory intent or not".[200] - Rapes and sexual assaults constituting persecutions at the Trnopolje camp: "The Trial Chamber finds that acts of rape were committed in the Trnopolje camp. It now wishes to discuss in detail one concrete case of rape, allegedly committed on Witness Q where the discriminatory intent of the direct perpetrator played an important role. The Trial Chamber is confronted with two opposing versions of the rape: one is Witness Q's own account of the event, the other is the denial by her alleged rapist who was also heard as a witness. Witness Q was arrested around 26 July 1992 and taken to Trnopolje where she stayed until 4 September 1992. After nine days in the camp, she was told that the commander wanted to see her. They took her to Slobodan Kuruzović whom she knew because he had been her brother's teacher. He started interrogating her and then said that she should move to the house where the command was located. She returned to get her children and then moved to the command house where Kurozovi[ć] was living. Witness Q testified that that first night in the house Kuruzović came in wearing sun glasses. He removed his shirt and took out his pistol. He sat down and, wearing only his undershirt, said to her: 'Come on, get up and give me a kiss'. Witness Q looked down and did not want to comply. He grabbed her face and ordered her to take her clothes off. He said: 'I want to see how Muslim women fuck'. He stripped naked and told her to do the same. He started ripping her shirt and Witness Q said: 'You'd better kill me'. He answered: 'I'm not going to kill a fine woman like you'. She asked him not to do this to her. He kissed her and started biting and hitting her. She screamed and he said: 'You are screaming in vain. There is nobody here who can help you'. He took out his penis and put it in her mouth and then raped her. She screamed but he said: 'It is better that you stay quiet or all the soldiers outside will take their turn'. She had no chance to resist him. He raped her and ejaculated into her. Then he left saying: 'See you tomorrow'. She found some clothes in the house to replace the ones which had been ruined. He returned the second night and asked: 'Who has done this to you'. She said 'some fool' and he laughed. The second night he cursed her and said: 'You know what Muslims are doing to our women'. Showing his knife, he started raping her again. She screamed and grabbed him by the neck so that she almost strangled him. He stabbed her in the left shoulder with the knife and then raped her. He left and said: 'See you tomorrow, baby'. Witness Q testified that she is still suffering from the stab wound to her left shoulder and that she cannot hold her hand up for long above her shoulder. When Kuruzović returned the

199 *Stakić* Trial Judgement, paras. 400–401.

200 *Stakić* Trial Judgement, paras. 818.

	third day, she begged him to release her brother, who was also in the camp. She wanted to kill herself and have her brother look after the children. The next day, Witness Q's brother was brought in and, when he saw her, he started to cry and said that he knew what had happened to her. Kuruzović came back the next night. He took off her clothes and pushed her down to the floor. She did not resist. When he raped her that night, she was wracked with pain. Kuruzović came to her on all but two of the nights they were in that house. This Trial Chamber had some reservations as to the accuracy of Witness Q's testimony because of one detail she mentioned that did not appear very credible: she told the Chamber that, on the first night, Kuruzović ripped her clothes off with a knife and that she had found other clothes in the house to replace the ruined ones. However, she stated that this also happened the following nights. The Chamber finds it difficult to believe that she had so many clothes with her while in detention. When questioned by the Prosecution about the people who were put in the house he used, Slobodan Kuruzović first stated that he did not use it at all except for a few days to watch television when no one was there. He then gave a list of different people who stayed at that house and remembered that there was once a group from Brdo, from Hambarine among whom was a student of his, a girl, accompanied by her mother and some other children. Asked why out of the thousands of people in the camp he put this girl in the house, he rectified his previous answer and said that she was not a girl but a woman around 30–35 years old, who was staying there with her mother and sisters. He was unable to give any particular reason why he had put her there. He wanted the Trial Chamber to believe that she had asked him for permission to stay there because he had been her teacher. When shown a photograph of Witness Q, Kuruzović said that he did not remember: 'I don't think…this is somebody who is a bit older', was his answer. Asked if she looked like the student he was talking about, but perhaps ten years older, he stated: 'She looks a bit heavier. Maybe she has gained some weight'. Slobodan Kuruzović was shown the video-tape of the testimony of Witness Q. After the video was stopped, though cautioned not to do so, he made a long statement without being prompted by any questions. He protested his innocence and expressed surprise and indignation at being accused of this act. He tried to put the blame on others ('maybe one of the Muslims had done this') or on Witness Q herself ('is she trying to denigrate the Serbian people as such?'…; 'she simply seized the opportunity or perhaps in collusion with her brother'.) He told the Trial Chamber that he had no need to do something like that because he is a 'relatively good-looking man'. He went on to say that Witness Q's story was impossible, that everybody around would have known, that she stayed there for a few days, that it would have been impossible for her to leave the camp wounded and injured ('You can't make it disappear in just several days. These are serious injuries'). He insisted that the injuries would have been impossible to hide. After listening to Kuruzović's denial and contradictions, the Trial Chamber did not believe his protestations of innocence. His alleged surprise and indignation were feigned, because he already knew of the accusation as he had been questioned on the subject when interviewed by the Office of the Prosecutor in Banja Luka. Furthermore, his insistence that it would have been impossible to hide the consequences of the rape (Witness Q's injuries) was not consistent with the fact that she was detained in Trnopolje for more than a month (26 July to 4 September 1992) and that no people were allowed access to the house he used as his headquarters. Other allegations he made were simply unconvincing, such as that he was a 'relatively good-looking man' and had no need to rape. For a woman, rape is by far the ultimate offense, sometimes even worse than death because it brings shame on her. To tell previously unknown people, such as the Judges, the Counsel of both parties and all others present in the courtroom, is undoubtedly a difficult and stressful effort. No one could have expected Witness Q to be a calm and detached witness. The Trial Chamber has come to the conclusion that her repeated account of the way she was undressed was her way of conveying her resistance to the fact that she was forcibly undressed. As the attack on her dignity was the same nightmare for her every night, Witness Q also attached the

	details of the first rape to the successive ones. Her testimony is credible and the Trial Chamber considers it proved beyond reasonable doubt that she was repeatedly raped in the Trnopolje camp. The Trial Chamber is therefore convinced that rape based on discriminatory intent was committed also in the Trnopolje camp. The Trial Chamber has already established the commission of other cases of rape and sexual assaults in the Keraterm and Omarska camps. As discussed above, these crimes were committed with a discriminatory intent".[201]

15. Blagoje **Simić *et al.*** (Case No. IT-95-9) "***Bosanski Šamac***" - Blagoje Simić: President of the Municipal Board of the Serbian Democratic Party; President of the Serb Crisis Staff (later renamed the War Presidency) in the municipality of Bosanski Šamac, located in north-eastern Bosnia and Herzegovina; he was the highest ranking civilian official in the municipality. - Miroslav Tadić: Assistant Commander for Logistics within the 4th Detachment (a Yugoslav National Army-organised territorial defence unit); Commander of the Civil Protection Staff, an *ex-officio* member of the Crisis Staff; a responsible member of the Exchange Commission in the municipality of Bosanski Šamac. - Simo Zarić: Assistant Commander for Intelligence, Reconnaissance, Morale and Information in the 4th Detachment; Chief of National Security in Bosanski Šamac from 29 April 1992 to 19 May 1992; Deputy to the President of the Civilian Council in Odžak.	
Indictment (International sex crimes (or related) charges and mode(s) of liability)	- There are no factual allegations of international sex crimes in the Indictment. However, the charge for which Blagoje Simić and Simo Zarić were tried for international sex crimes is: **Persecutions as CAH** (count 1) under Article 7(1) of the Statute.[202]
Trial Judgement	- Blagoje Simić and Simo Zarić: Guilty of **Persecutions as CAH** (count 1) under Article 7(1) of the Statute (**joint criminal enterprise – first category**) of non-Serb civilians in the municipality of Bosanski Šamac through various acts including sexual assaults of detainees constituting torture. The Trial Chamber found, Judge Per-Johan

[201] *Stakić* Trial Judgement, paras. 791–806 (internal references omitted).

[202] *Prosecutor v. Blagoje Simić et al.*, Case No. IT-95-9-T, Fifth Amended Indictment, 30 May 2002, paras. 13(d) ("From about the 17th of April 1992 to at least the 31st of December 1993, **Blagoje SIMIĆ,** both prior to, and while serving as President of the Bosanski Samac Serb Crisis Staff, and as President of the War Presidency, acting in concert with others, planned, instigated, ordered, committed, or otherwise aided and abetted the planning, preparation, or execution of the crime of persecutions as described in paragraphs 11 and 12 above, through his participation in the following acts or omissions, among others: [...] d. the cruel and inhumane treatment of Bosnian Croats, Bosnian Muslims and other non-Serb civilians including beatings, torture [...]".), 15(c) ("From about September 1991 to about the 31st of December 1992, **Simo ZARIĆ**, both prior to and while serving in various positions such as 'Assistant Commander for Intelligence, Reconnaissance, Morale and Information' of the Fourth Detachment, 'Chief of National Security Service' in Bosanski Šamac, 'Deputy to the President of the War Council for Security Matters' in Odžak, and 'Assistant Commander of the 2nd Posavina Brigade for Morale Information,' acting in concert with others, planned, instigated, ordered, committed, or otherwise aided and abetted the planning, preparation, or execution of the commission of the crime of persecutions as described in paragraphs 11 and 12 above, through his participation in the following acts or omissions, among others: [...] c. the cruel and inhumane treatment of Bosnian Croats, Bosnian Muslims and other non-Serb civilians including beatings, torture [...]""), 16 ("By these actions **Blagoje SIMIĆ** [...] and **Simo ZARIĆ,** acting in concert together and with others, planned, instigated, ordered, committed or otherwise aided and abetted the planning, preparation, or execution of: **Count 1**: Persecutions on political, racial and religious grounds, a **CRIME AGAINST HUMANITY,** punishable under Article 5(h) of the Statute of the Tribunal".).

	Lindholm dissenting, that Simo Zarić only aided and abetted the commission of the joint criminal enterprise.[203]
Appeal Judgement	- Only Blagoje Simić appealed the Trial Judgement. The Appeals Chamber **set aside**, Judge Mohamed Shahabuddeen and Judge Wolfgang Schomburg dissenting, **Blagoje Simić's conviction for Persecutions as CAH (count 1)** for the cruel and inhumane treatment of Bosnian Croat, Bosnian Muslim and non-Serb civilian detainees **insofar as the conduct underlying this conviction encompassed the acts of beatings and torture, which include the international sex crimes for which he was found guilty**.[204]
Legal and Factual Findings and/or Evidence	- <u>Factual findings:</u> - Beating detainees in their genitals or while naked and sexual assaults at the SUP (Secretariat of the Interior) in Bosanski Šamac: "When Kemal Mehinović was arrested on 27 May 1992, Stevan Todorović and his bodyguard Goran hit him and Hasan Hadžialijagić, Admir Džakić, and a man called Srna, nicknamed 'Cuba', with a truncheon, a baseball bat, and a metal bar for several hours all over their bodies and their heads. Several times, Kemal Mehinović had to spread his legs so that they could beat him in the crotch, and they told him that the Muslims should not propagate".[205] "Witness A was beaten by 'Lugar' with a police rubber baton and a rifle butt on his spine, lower back, head and hands, and 'Lugar' also kicked him with his boots in the stomach. Some days later, Witness A, Salko Hurtić, and Anto Simović were beaten by 'Laki' with a metal bar, and Witness A's eye was swollen shut. In mid-June, Witness A was beaten by 'Lugar' with a wrench on his joints, knees, elbows and hands, and Stevan Todorović beat him with a police baton on his head and kicked him in his genital area and lower abdomen".[206] "On or about 28 April 1992, Witness G was taken to a room in the SUP in which there were five men in different uniforms, among them Radulović, Nikolić, and 'Zvaka'. 'Lugar' ordered her to take off her clothes. She did so very slowly and placed them on the table. At that time she had her period. One of the men swore at her, and she was told to lie down on the table and spread her legs. 'Lugar' stood next to the table and told her to lie in such a way that his knife was resting underneath her throat. Then they beat her repeatedly with a belt and a bat. On one side a man was beating her with a belt, and on the other side another man with a bat. During this time, they insulted her. After the first stroke, the knife slipped. She was crying, and they turned up the music very loudly. One of the men said that they should cool her off, and he urinated on her. They hit her for a long time and she felt faint. At some point, she could face the door, and she saw Simo Zarić standing in the doorway. He then left, and the men continued beating her".[207] "Several Prosecution witnesses gave evidence that detainees were subjected to sexual assaults. One incident involved ramming a police truncheon in the anus of a detainee. Other incidents involved forcing male prisoners to perform oral sex on each other and on Stevan Todorović, sometimes in front of other prisoners".[208] "The Trial Chamber is satisfied that these beatings caused severe pain and suffering,

[203] *Prosecutor v. Blagoje Simić et al.*, Case No. IT-95-9-T, Judgement, 17 October 2003 ("*Blagoje Simić et al.* Trial Judgement"), paras. 697–698, 719, 728, 771–772, 1003, 1008–1010, 1015–1017, 1115, 1123.

[204] *Prosecutor v. Blagoje Simić*, Case No. IT-95-9-A, Judgement, 28 November 2006, paras. 130–131, 138, 190, 301.

[205] *Blagoje Simić et al.* Trial Judgement, para. 697 (internal reference omitted).

[206] *Blagoje Simić et al.* Trial Judgement, para. 698 (internal reference omitted).

[207] *Blagoje Simić et al.* Trial Judgement, para. 719 (internal reference omitted).

[208] *Blagoje Simić et al.* Trial Judgement, para. 728 (internal reference omitted).

	both physically and mentally, to the detainees. The Trial Chamber is also satisfied that the beatings were committed on discriminatory grounds. The evidence shows that practically all detainees who were beaten were non-Serbs. On one occasion, a victim was beaten in the crotch, and his assailants told him that Muslims should not propagate. Prisoners were regularly insulted on the basis of their ethnicity. For these reasons, the Trial Chamber finds that the beatings that were committed on discriminatory grounds constitute cruel and inhumane treatment as an underlying act of persecution. The Trial Chamber is further satisfied that the other heinous acts that witnesses testified about, including sexual assaults, the extraction of teeth, and the threat of execution, constitute torture. These acts caused severe physical and mental pain and suffering and occurred in order to discriminate on ethnic grounds against the victims".[209]

16. Dragan Nikolić (Case No. IT-94-2) "***Sušica Camp***" Commander of the Sušica Detention Camp in the municipality of Vlasenica, eastern Bosnia and Herzegovina from early June 1992 until its closure in late September 1992; also known as 'Jenki'.	
Indictment[210] (International sex crimes (or related) charges and mode(s) of liability)	- **Persecutions as CAH** (count 1) under Article 7(1) of the Statute (**committing**) for the persecutions of Muslim and non-Serb detainees at the Sušica camp by subjecting them to various acts, including rapes, by participating in sexual violence directed at women at the Sušica camp and by subjecting detainees to an atmosphere of terror created by various acts, including sexual violence.[211] - **Rape as CAH** (count 3) Under Article 7(1) of the Statute (**aiding and abetting**) for facilitating the removal of female detainees from the hangar, which he knew was for purposes of rapes and other sexually abusive conduct conducted by camp guards, special forces, local soldiers and other men and by encouraging the sexually abusive conduct.[212]

209 *Blagoje Simić et al.* Trial Judgement, paras. 771–772 (internal references omitted).

210 For the general background to the charges, see *Prosecutor v. Dragan Nikolić*, Case No. IT-94-2-S, Third Amended Indictment, 31 October 2003 ("*Dragan Nikolić* Indictment"), para. 47 ("Many of the detained women were subjected to sexual assaults, including rape. Camp guards or other men who were allowed to enter the camp frequently took women out of the hangar at night. When the women returned, they were often in a traumatised state and other detainees observed that the women were distraught".).

211 *Dragan Nikolić* Indictment, paras. 2–4, 6–7 ("From at least early June 1992 until about 30 September 1992, **DRAGAN NIKOLIĆ** persecuted the Muslim and non-Serb detainees at Sušica camp on political, racial and religious grounds. **DRAGAN NIKOLIĆ** persecuted Muslim and non-Serb detainees at the Sušica camp by subjecting them to […] rapes and torture as charged specifically in the indictment. In addition, **DRAGAN NIKOLIĆ** persecuted Muslim and non-Serb detainees by participating in sexual violence directed at women at the Susica camp as set forth in paragraphs 20 and 21 of the indictment. […] As part of the persecutions, **DRAGAN NIKOLIĆ** subjected detainees to an atmosphere of terror created by the […] sexual violence and other physical and mental abuse of detainees […]. As a result, detainees suffered severe psychological and physical trauma. **Dragan NIKOLIĆ** participated in creating and maintaining this atmosphere of terror and the inhumane conditions. By his participation in the acts or omissions described in paragraph 3-6, **DRAGAN NIKOLIĆ** is individually criminally responsible for: **Count 1:** Persecutions on political, racial and religious grounds, a **CRIME AGAINST HUMANITY**, punishable under Article 5(h) and Article 7(1) of the Statute of the Tribunal".).

212 *Dragan Nikolić* Indictment, paras. 2, 20–22 ("From early June until about 15 September 1992 many female detainees at Sušica camp were subjected to sexual assaults, including rapes and degrading physical and verbal abuse. **DRAGAN NIKOLIĆ** personally removed and otherwise facilitated the removal of female detainees from the hangar, which he knew was for purposes of rapes, and other sexually abusive conduct. The sexual assaults were committed by camp guards, special forces, local soldiers and other men. Female detainees were sexually assaulted at various locations, such as the guardhouse, the houses surrounding the camp, at the Panorama Hotel, a military headquarters, and at locations where such women were taken to perform forced labour. **DRAGAN NIKOLIĆ** allowed female detainees, including girls and elderly women, to be verbally

Sentencing Judgement	- Guilty of **Rape as CAH** (count 3) under Article 7(1) of the Statute (**aiding and abetting**) for facilitating the removal of female detainees from the hangar, which he knew was for purposes of rapes committed by camp guards, special forces, local soldiers and other men and by encouraging these rapes and **Persecutions as CAH** (count 1) under Article 7(1) of the Statute (**committing**) for the persecutions of Muslim and non-Serb detainees at the Sušica camp by participating in sexual violence directed at women at the Sušica camp and by subjecting detainees to an atmosphere of terror created by various acts, including sexual violence.[213] - Note: plea agreement: On 2 September 2003, a joint motion was filed by Dragan Nikolić and the Office of the Prosecutor informing the Trial Chamber of an agreement reached between the parties as to the entry of a guilty plea by the accused to all counts in the Indictment. On 4 September 2003, Dragan Nikolić entered a guilty plea to all counts in the Indictment and the Trial Chamber entered a finding of guilt.[214]
Appeal Judgement	N/A
Legal and Factual Findings and/or Evidence	- Legal findings: - **Sexual violence as persecutions:** The Trial Chamber held that sexual violence can constitute persecutions as CAH: "Murder, rape and torture, as set out in paragraph 4 of the Indictment, are contained within the count of persecutions and are among the crimes listed in Article 5 of the Statute. However, the Trial Chamber has to consider whether […] sexual violence […] may be taken as additional acts of persecution. The Trial Chamber reiterates what it stated in *Stakić*: 'The acts of persecution not enumerated in Article 5 or elsewhere in the Statute must be of an equal gravity or severity as the other acts enumerated under Article 5. When considering whether acts or omissions satisfy this threshold, they should not be considered in isolation but in their context and with consideration to their cumulative effect. An act which may not appear comparable to the other acts enumerated in Article 5 might reach the required level of gravity if it had, or was likely to have, an effect similar to that of the other acts because of the context in which it was undertaken.' The Trial Chamber finds that the situation in Sušica camp, as previously described, was that serious that the acts of […] sexual violence […] rise without further explanation to a level of gravity that falls within the ambit of Article 5 of the Statute".[215] "As discussed, the Trial Chamber considers that only that part of the Accused's criminal conduct set out in paragraphs 20 and 21 of the Indictment which amounts to the crime of aiding and abetting rape should be considered under Count 3. The remaining criminal conduct alleged in these paragraphs of the Indictment should be subsumed under Count 1, Persecutions".[216] - Factual findings:

subjected to humiliating sexual threats in the presence of other detainees in the hangar. **DRAGAN NIKOLIĆ** facilitated the removal of female detainees by allowing guards, soldiers and other males to have access to these women on a repetitive basis and by otherwise encouraging the sexually abusive conduct. By his aiding and abetting in the conduct described in paragraph 20 and 21, in relation to female detainees in the Sušica camp, **DRAGAN NIKOLIĆ** is individually criminally responsible for: **Count 3:** Rape, a **CRIME AGAINST HUMANITY** punishable under Article 5(g) and Article 7(1) of the Statute of the Tribunal".).

213 *Prosecutor v. Dragan Nikolić*, Case No. IT-94-2-S, Sentencing Judgement, 18 December 2003 ("*Dragan Nikolić* Sentencing Judgement"), paras. 66–68, 87–90, 117, 119, 194.

214 *Dragan Nikolić* Sentencing Judgement, paras. 35–36, 49, 117, 119.

215 *Dragan Nikolić* Sentencing Judgement, paras. 109–111 (internal references omitted).

216 *Dragan Nikolić* Sentencing Judgement, para. 90.

	- General background: "Many of the detained women were subjected to sexual assaults, including rape. Camp guards or other men who were allowed to enter the camp frequently took women out of the hangar at night. When the women returned, they were often in a traumatised state and other detainees observed that the women were distraught".[217] - Persecutions: "From early June until about 30 September 1992, Dragan Nikolić was a commander in Sušica detention camp. During his tenure as a camp commander, the Accused persecuted detainees on political, racial and religious grounds. The Accused persecuted Muslim and other non-Serb detainees by subjecting them to [...] rapes [...] as charged specifically in the Indictment. In addition, Dragan Nikolić participated in creating and maintaining an atmosphere of terror in the camp through [...] sexual violence [...]. The Accused persecuted Muslim and other non-Serb detainees by participating in sexual violence directed at the female detainees in Sušica camp".[218] - Rape and sexual violence: "The Accused abused his personal position of power especially *vis à vis* the female detainees of Sušica camp. He personally removed and returned women of all ages from the hangar, handing them over to men whom he knew would sexually abuse or rape them. Witness SU-032 believes had they resisted, they would have been liquidated. Witness SU-032 would have to agonize throughout the day, knowing what was to be her fate in the coming night".[219]

17. Ranko **Češić** (Case No. IT-95-10/1) "***Brčko***" Member of the Bosnian Serb Territorial Defence in Grčica, in the municipality of Brčko, north-eastern Bosnia and Herzegovina; from 15 May 1992, member of the Intervention Platoon of the Bosnian Serb Police Reserve Corps at the Brčko police station.	
Indictment (International sex crimes (or related) charges and mode(s) of liability)	- **Humiliating and degrading treatment as a violation of the laws or customs of war (WC)** (count 7) and **Rape as CAH** (count 8) under Article 7(1) of the Statute (**committing**) for forcing, at gunpoint, two Muslim brothers detained at Luka camp to perform sexual acts on each other in the presence of others.[220]
Sentencing Judgement	- Guilty of **Humiliating and degrading treatment as a violation of the laws or customs of war (WC)** (count 7) and **Rape as CAH** (count 8) under Article 7(1) of the Statute (**committing**) for forcing, at gunpoint, two Muslim brothers detained at Luka

217 *Dragan Nikolić* Sentencing Judgement, para. 61 (internal reference omitted).

218 *Dragan Nikolić* Sentencing Judgement, paras. 66–68 (internal references omitted).

219 *Dragan Nikolić* Sentencing Judgement, para. 194 (internal references omitted).

220 *Prosecutor v. Ranko Češić*, Case No. IT-95-10/1-PT, Third Amended Indictment, 26 November 2002 ("*Češić* Indictment"), para. 15 ("On about 11 May 1992, at Luka camp, **Ranko ČEŠIĆ** forced, at gunpoint, Muslim detainees A and B, who were brothers detained there, to beat each other and perform sexual acts on each other in the presence of others, causing them great humiliation and degradation. By these actions, **Ranko ČEŠIĆ** committed: Count 7: a **VIOLATION OF THE LAWS OR CUSTOMS OF WAR** recognized by Article 3 of the Tribunal Statute and Article 3(1)(c) (humiliating and degrading treatment) of the Geneva Conventions; Count 8: a **CRIME AGAINST HUMANITY** recognized by Article 5(g) (rape, which includes other forms of sexual assault) of the Tribunal Statute".). See also *Češić* Indictment, para. 9.

	camp to perform fellatio on each other in the presence of others on approximately 11 May 1992.[221] - Note: plea agreement: On 7 October 2003, a joint motion was filed by Ranko Češić and the Office of the Prosecutor informing the Trial Chamber of an agreement reached between the parties as to the entry of a guilty plea by the accused to all counts in the Indictment. On 8 October 2003, Ranko Češić pleaded guilty to all twelve counts in the Indictment and the Trial Chamber entered a finding of guilt.[222]
Appeal Judgement	N/A
Legal and Factual Findings and/or Evidence	- Factual findings: - Sexual assault of two Muslim brothers detained at Luka camp: "Ranko Češić admitted that, on approximately 11 May 1992, he intentionally forced, at gunpoint, two Muslim brothers detained at Luka Camp to perform fellatio on each other in the presence of others. Ranko Češić acknowledged that he was fully aware that this was taking place without the consent of the victims. Excerpts from two statements of one of the victims, dated 25 February 1995 and 7 November 2003, were annexed to the Prosecution's Brief and the full statements were confidentially filed on 18 November 2003. In the first statement, the victim relates that Ranko Češić first forced, at gunpoint, the brothers to hit each other. One of the guards considered that they were not hitting each other hard enough, so he started beating the witness himself with such strength that he was knocked over a desk. Ranko Češić fired approximately in the direction of his brother as he was moving towards the witness to help him. The bullet impacted on the wall, about 10 to 15 centimetres from his brother. Ranko Češić then forced both brothers to perform fellatio on each other and left the office after he told a guard to make sure that they would not stop until he returned. He left the door open when he went out and several guards could watch and laugh. The witness stated that the situation lasted for about 45 minutes, until Ranko Češić returned with another guard. The witness specified in both statements that Ranko Češić was his neighbour before the war and knew both brothers since before the war. He indicated in the second statement that Ranko Češić was 17 years younger than him. He described that his brother and himself were covered with bruises when they were released, on 13 and 14 May 1992 respectively. The witness still has spinal problems, which he thinks may stem from the beatings he received at Luka Camp".[223]

18. Radoslav **Brđanin** (Case No. IT-99-36) "***Krajina***" Leading political figure in the Autonomous Region of Krajina (ARK); held key positions at the municipal, regional and republic levels, including: First Vice-President of the ARK Assembly, President of the ARK Crisis Staff, later Acting Deputy Prime Minister for Production, Minister for Construction, Traffic and Utilities and acting Vice-President of the Government of the Republika Srpska.	
Indictment (International sex crimes	- **Genocide** (count 1) or, alternatively, **Complicity in genocide** (count 2) under Articles 7(1) and 7(3) of the Statute (**superior responsibility**) for various crimes, including **causing serious bodily or mental harm** to Bosnian Muslim and Bosnian Croat

[221] *Prosecutor v. Ranko Češić*, Case No. IT-95-10/1-S, Sentencing Judgement, 11 March 2004 ("*Češić* Sentencing Judgement"), paras. 4, 13–14, 33, 35–36.

[222] *Češić* Sentencing Judgement, para. 4

[223] *Češić* Sentencing Judgement, paras. 13–14 (internal references omitted).

(or related) charges and mode(s) of liability)	detainees in various camps and detention facilities by subjecting them to rapes and sexual assaults.[224] - **Persecutions as CAH** (count 3) under Articles 7(1) and 7(3) of the Statute (**superior responsibility**) for the same acts.[225] - **Torture as CAH** (count 6) and **Torture as a grave breach of the Geneva Conventions of 1949 (WC)** (count 7) under Articles 7(1) and 7(3) of the Statute (**superior responsibility**) for the same acts.[226]

224 *Prosecutor v. Radoslav Brđanin*, Case No. IT-99-36-T, Sixth Amended Indictment, 9 December 2003 ("*Brđanin* Indictment"), paras. 36, 37(2), 42, 44 ("Between about 1 April 1992 and 31 December 1992, **Radoslav BRĐANIN** acting individually or in concert with others in the Bosnian Serb leadership, planned, instigated, ordered, committed or otherwise aided and abetted in the planning, preparation, or execution of a campaign designed to destroy Bosnian Muslims and Bosnian Croats, in whole or in part, as national, ethnical, racial, or religious groups, as such, in the municipalities listed in paragraph 4 above, which formed part of the ARK, the most extreme manifestation of which took place in the municipalities of Bosanski Novi, Kljuc, Kotor Varos, Prijedor, and Sanski Most. Following the political take-overs of the municipalities listed in paragraph 4 above, the execution of the above campaign included: […] (2) causing serious bodily or mental harm to Bosnian Muslim and Bosnian Croat non-combatants during their confinement in camps, other detention facilities, and during their interrogations at police stations and military barracks when detainees were continuously subjected to or forced to witness inhumane acts including […] rape, sexual assault […]. […] In the camps and detention facilities, Bosnian Serb forces and others who were given access to the camps, subjected non-combatant Bosnian Muslim and Bosnian Croat detainees from the municipalities to physical and mental abuse including torture, beatings with weapons, sexual assaults and the witnessing of inhumane acts, including murder, causing them serious bodily or mental harm. […] The infliction of serious bodily or mental harm on numerous Bosnian Muslims and Bosnian Croats occurred throughout the indictment period in each of the municipalities listed in paragraph 4. The incidences of such infliction were widespread and often repetitive. The pattern is summarised below for each municipality. Banja Luka: […] In Mali Logor, detainees were forced to perform sexual acts upon each other. […] Manjaca received detainees from various municipalities. It was one of the major detention facilities in the area of the ARK. […] Detainees were subjected to acts of sexual degradation. […] Kotor Varos: At the Kotor Varos Police Station[, … m]ale and female detainees were forced to perform sexual acts with each other. […] At the Kotor Varos Elementary School detainees were beaten and forced to perform sexual acts with each other. […] At the Kotor Varos Sawmill the detainees were predominantly non able-bodied men, women and children. Women were systematically raped […]. Prijedor: At the Omarska Camp[,… f]emale detainees were raped and sexually assaulted. At the Keraterm Camp[, … f]emale detainees were raped. At the Trnopolje Camp[, … f]emale detainees were raped. […] Between about 1 April 1992 and 31 December 1992, **Radoslav BRĐANIN** knew or had reason to know that Bosnian Serb forces under his control were about to commit such acts or had done so, and he failed to take the necessary and reasonable measures to prevent such acts or to punish the perpetrators thereof. By his involvement in these acts or omissions **Radoslav BRĐANIN** committed: **Count 1: GENOCIDE**, punishable under Articles 4(3)(a), and 7(1) and 7(3) of the Statute of the Tribunal; **AND/OR Count 2: COMPLICITY IN GENOCIDE**, punishable under Articles 4(3)(e), and 7(1) and 7(3) of the Statute of the Tribunal".).

225 *Brđanin* Indictment, paras. 46, 47(2), 48 ("Between about 1 April 1992 and 31 December 1992, **Radoslav BRĐANIN** acting individually or in concert with others in the Bosnian Serb leadership, planned, instigated, ordered, committed or otherwise aided and abetted in the planning, preparation or execution of persecutions on political, racial or religious grounds of the Bosnian Muslim and Bosnian Croat population in the municipalities listed in paragraph 4, which formed part of the ARK. The above planning, preparation or execution of persecutions included: […] (2) […] rapes and sexual assaults […] of Bosnian Muslims and Bosnian Croats […]. Between about 1 April 1992 and 31 December 1992, **Radoslav BRĐANIN**, knew or had reason to know that Bosnian Serb forces under his control were about to commit such acts or had done so, and he failed to take the necessary and reasonable measures to prevent such acts or to punish the perpetrators thereof. By his involvement in these acts or omissions **Radoslav BRĐANIN** committed: **Count 3:** Persecutions, a **CRIME AGAINST HUMANITY**, punishable under Articles 5(h), 7(1) and 7(3) of the Statute of the Tribunal".).

226 *Brđanin* Indictment, paras. 54–56 ("Between about 1 April 1992 and 31 December 1992, **Radoslav BRĐANIN** acting individually or in concert with others in the Bosnian Serb leadership, planned, instigated, ordered, committed or otherwise aided and abetted in the planning, preparation, or execution of a campaign of terror designed to drive the Bosnian Muslim and Bosnian Croat population from the municipalities listed

Trial Judgement	- Guilty of **Torture as a grave breach of the Geneva Conventions of 1949 (WC)** (count 7) under Article 7(1) of the Statute (**aiding and abetting**) for various acts, including the rapes of a number of Bosnian Muslim women in the Keraterm camp in July 1992, in the Trnopolje camp in July 1992 and in the Omarska camp in June 1992.[227] - Guilty of **Persecutions as CAH** (count 3) under Article 7(1) of the Statute (**aiding and abetting**) of the Statute for the same acts and for additional rapes and sexual assaults. This conviction incorporates torture as CAH (count 6).[228] - Not guilty of genocide (count 1) and complicitiy in genocide (count 2) because the Trial Chamber held that the various acts, including rapes, even if they were taken together, do not allow it to legitimately draw the inference that the underlying offences were committed with the specific intent required for the crime of genocide.[229]
Appeal Judgement	- The Appeals Chamber **reversed Radoslav Brđanin's conviction for Torture as a grave breach of the Geneva Conventions of 1949 (WC)** (count 7) **insofar as he was found guilty for aiding and abetting torture in the camps and detention facilities**, which includes the rapes of a number of Bosnian Muslim women in the Keraterm camp in July 1992, in the Trnopolje camp in July 1992 and in the Omarska camp in June 1992. The Appeals Chamber considered that the Trial Chamber's finding that Brđanin aided and abetted acts of torture committed in camps and detention facilities is not one which a reasonable trier of fact could have reached. The Appeals Chamber held that there was insufficient evidence to prove beyond reasonable doubt that Brđanin's conduct constituted either encouragement or moral support to the camp personnel, which had a substantial effect on the commission of torture.[230] Consequently, the Appeals Chamber also **reversed Radoslav Brđanin's conviction for Persecutions as CAH** (count 3) **insofar as it incorporated Torture as CAH committed in the camps and detention facilities** (count 6).[231]
Legal and Factual Findings and/or	- Legal findings: **- Rape necessarily implies severe pain or suffering:** The Trial Chamber held that rape necessarily implies severe pain or suffering as requested by the definition of torture: "Some acts, like rape, appear by definition to

in paragraph 4 above, which formed part of the ARK. The execution of the above campaign included the intentional infliction of severe pain or suffering on Bosnian Muslim or Bosnian Croat non-combatants by inhumane treatment including sexual assaults, rape [...] in camps, police stations, military barracks and private homes or other locations, as well as during transfers of persons and deportations. [...] Many Bosnian Muslims and Bosnian Croats were forced to witness executions and brutal assaults on other detainees. The intentional infliction of severe pain or suffering on Bosnian Muslims and Bosnian Croats occurred throughout the indictment period in each of the municipalities listed and summarised below. [...] Prijedor: [...] Women were raped and sexually assaulted. Teslic: [...] A number of non-combatant Bosnian Muslims were raped by unidentified soldiers. Between about 1 April 1992 and 31 December 1992, **Radoslav BRĐANIN** knew or had reason to know that Bosnian Serb forces under his control were about to commit such acts or had done so, and he failed to take the necessary and reasonable measures to prevent such acts or to punish the perpetrators thereof. By his involvement in these acts or omissions **Radoslav BRĐANIN** committed: **Count 6:** Torture, a **CRIME AGAINST HUMANITY,** punishable under Articles 5 (f), 7(1) and 7(3) of the Statute of the Tribunal. **Count 7:** Torture, a **GRAVE BREACH** of the Geneva Conventions of 1949, punishable under Articles 2(b), 7(1) and 7(3) of the Statute of the Tribunal".).

227 *Prosecutor v. Radoslav Brđanin*, Case No. IT-99-36-T, Judgement, 1 September 2004 ("*Brđanin* Trial Judgement"), paras. 498, 500, 512–518, 523–524, 537–538, 1082, 1085, 1087–1088, 1152.

228 *Brđanin* Trial Judgement, paras. 1010–1011, 1013, 1018–1020, 1050, 1054–1055, 1058, 1060–1061, 1085, 1087–1088, 1152.

229 *Brđanin* Trial Judgement, paras. 989–991, 1152.

230 *Prosecutor v. Radoslav Brđanin*, Case No. IT-99-36-A, Judgement, 3 April 2007 ("*Brđanin* Appeal Judgement"), paras. 276–289 and Section X (Disposition), p. 157.

231 *Brđanin* Appeal Judgement, Section X (Disposition), p. 157.

Evidence	meet the severity threshold [of the definition of torture]. Like torture, rape is a violation of personal dignity and is used for such purposes as intimidation, degradation, humiliation and discrimination, punishment, control or destruction of a person. Severe pain or suffering, as required by the definition of the crime of torture, can be said to be established once rape has been proved, since the act of rape necessarily implies such pain or suffering".[232] **- Rape:** The Trial Chamber adopted the definition of rape given in the *Kunarac et al.* case:[233] "Under the jurisprudence of the Tribunal, it is defined as follows: 'the *actus reus* of the crime of rape in international law is constituted by: the sexual penetration, however slight: (a) of the vagina or anus of the victim by the penis of the perpetrator or any other object used by the perpetrator; or (b) the mouth of the victim by the penis of the perpetrator; where such sexual penetration occurs without the consent of the victim. Consent for this purpose must be consent given voluntarily, as a result of the victim's free will, assessed in the context of the surrounding circumstances. The *mens rea* is the intention to effect this sexual penetration, and the knowledge that it occurs without the consent of the victim.' It should be noted that the Appeals Chamber has held that force or threat of force provides clear evidence of non-consent, but is not an element *per se* of rape, since 'a narrow focus on force or threat of force could permit perpetrators to evade liability for sexual activity to which the other party had not consented by taking advantage of coercive circumstances without relying on physical force'".[234] **- Sexual assault:** The Trial Chamber adopted the definition of sexual assault given in the *Stakić* case:[235] "This offence embraces all serious abuses of a sexual nature inflicted upon the integrity of a person by means of coercion, threat of force or intimidation in a way that is humiliating and degrading to the victim's dignity".[236] **- Rapes and sexual assaults constituting persecutions:** The Trial Chamber confirmed that rapes and sexual assault can constitute persecutions: "Rape is set out as a crime against humanity under Article 5(g) of the Statute and as such is of sufficient gravity to constitute persecution".[237] "Any sexual assault falling short of rape may be punishable as persecution under international criminal law, provided that it reaches the same level of gravity as the other crimes against humanity enumerated in Article 5 of the Statute".[238] - <u>Factual findings:</u> - Beating Midho Družić, a detainee, in the genitals at Kozila camp: "Detainees at Kozila were frequently interrogated and ill-treated by the camp commander, who was either Mišo Zorić or Milan Kresoje, and by the camp guards, including Željko Branković, Zoran Salasa and Milan Knežević. On 6 July 1992, Midho Družić, one of the detainees, was taken to the camp administration office. Mišo Zorić

232 *Brđanin* Trial Judgement, para. 485 (internal references omitted).

233 ICTY ISCC *Kunarac et al.*, see *supra* p. 528.

234 *Brđanin* Trial Judgement, paras. 1008–1009 (internal references omitted).

235 ICTY ISCC *Stakić*, see *supra* p. 576.

236 *Brđanin* Trial Judgement, para. 1012 (internal reference omitted).

237 *Brđanin* Trial Judgement, para. 1008.

238 *Brđanin* Trial Judgement, para. 1012 (internal reference omitted).

	and a few other guards present called him by pejorative names, including 'Balija' and 'Mujahedin'. They asked him where he had hidden his weapons. Then they kicked him in the genitals and beat him all over his body for about an hour".[239] "The Trial Chamber is satisfied that the cruel treatment set out above, when inflicted during interrogations, was aimed at obtaining information. Other ill-treatment was aimed at intimidating and discriminating against the victims because of their ethnicity".[240] - Rapes and sexual assaults in Prijedor: "In June or July 1992, at Keraterm camp, a number of other guards raped a female inmate on a table in a dark room until she lost consciousness. The next morning, she found herself lying in a pool of blood. Other women in the camp were also raped. In August 1992, Slobodan Kuruzović, the commander of Trnopolje camp, personally arranged for a Bosnian Muslim woman to be detained in the same house in which he had his office. During the first night, Kuruzović entered her room with a pistol and a knife. He took his clothes off and told the woman that he wanted to see 'how Muslim women fuck'. She replied 'You better kill me.' When the woman started screaming, Kuruzović said 'You are screaming in vain. There's nobody here who can help you.' He started raping her, and when she started screaming, Kuruzović warned her: 'You better keep quiet. Did you see all these soldiers standing outside? They will all take their turns on you.' He left saying 'See you tomorrow'. The woman was bleeding and spent the whole night crying, wanting to kill herself. Kuruzović raped that woman nearly every night for about a month. On two occasions, he stabbed her shoulder and her leg with his knife because she resisted against being raped. There were many more incidents of rape at the Trnopolje camp between May and October 1992. Not all of the perpetrators were camp personnel. Some were allowed to visit the camp from the outside. Soldiers took out girls aged 16 or 17 from the camp and raped them on the way to Kozarac on a truck. In one case, a 13 year old Bosnian Muslim girl was raped. One rape victim was told by a member of the camp staff that it was wartime and nothing could be done about these things. The Trial Chamber also finds that at Omarska camp, there were frequent incidents of sexual assault and rape. Female detainees were often called out by camp guards and the camp commander. When they returned, those women looked absent-minded and kept silent. On 26 June 1992, Omarska camp guards tried to force Mehmedalija Sarajlić, an elderly Bosnian Muslim, to rape a female detainee. He begged them 'Don't make me do it. She could be my daughter. I am a man in advanced age.' The guards laughed and said 'Well, try to use the finger.' A scream and the sound of beatings could be heard, and then everything was silent. The guards had killed the man. The Trial Chamber, by majority, finds that the threat of rape constituted a sexual assault *vis-à-vis* the female detainee. On an unknown date after May 1992, an armed man entered the Omarska camp restaurant where detainees were eating. He uncovered the breast of a female detainee, took out a knife, and ran it along her breast for several minutes. The other detainees were holding their breath because they thought he might cut off the breast at any second. Bystanding camp guards laughed and obviously enjoyed watching this incident. The Trial Chamber concludes that rapes and sexual assaults were commonplace throughout the camps in the Prijedor area. It is satisfied that in all these incidents, the male perpetrators aimed at discriminating against the women because they were Muslim".[241]

239 *Brđanin* Trial Judgement, para. 498 (internal references omitted).

240 *Brđanin* Trial Judgement, para. 500.

241 *Brđanin* Trial Judgement, paras. 512–518 (internal references omitted).

	"At Omarska, there were frequent incidents of female detainees being called out by the camp guards and the camp commander to be raped and sexually assaulted".[242] "Females detainees were raped in Keraterm camp".[243] "Women were raped in Trnopolje camp, including by Kuruzović, the commander of the camp".[244] - Rapes in Teslić: "Over the period of July to October 1992, a number of Bosnian Muslim women were raped by members of the Bosnian Serb police and the VRS in Teslić municipality. The Trial Chamber finds that all this was intrinsically discriminatory against these women".[245] - Rapes in Kotor Varoš police station: "Outside interrogation, Bosnian Muslim and Bosnian Croat male and female detainees were forced by a Bosnian Serb policeman to perform sexual acts with each other, in front of a crowd of cheering men in police and Bosnian Serb military uniforms, some of whom were wearing red berets. Two other male detainees, at least one of whom was a Bosnian Muslim, were forced to perform *fellatio* on each other by the 'Specialists' whilst being subjected to ethnic slurs".[246] - Rapes in Kotor Varoš sawmill: "Female detainees were taken out during the night by Bosnian Serb soldiers who wore camouflage uniforms, and who were from Banja Luka, and by policemen from Kotor Varoš. At least two female detainees were raped".[247] - Rapes, sexual assaults and constant humiliation and degradation constituting persecutions: "Earlier in this judgement, the Trial Chamber established that a number of Bosnian Muslim women were raped in Prijedor and in Teslić municipalities. The Trial Chamber finds that, apart from these municipalities, rapes of Bosnian Muslim and Bosnian Croat women occurred in the municipalities of Banja Luka, Bosanska Krupa, Donji Vakuf, and in Kotor Varoš. In each incident, armed Bosnian Serb soldiers or policemen were the perpetrators. There can be no doubt that these rapes were discriminatory in fact. With regard to the requisite *mens rea*, the Trial Chamber notes that the direct perpetrators made abundant use of pejorative language. One of them made no secret that he wanted a Bosnian Muslim woman to 'give birth to a little Serb'. The Trial Chamber is satisfied beyond reasonable doubt that, in the circumstances surrounding the commission of these rapes, these acts were carried out with the intent to discriminate against the Bosnian Muslim and Bosnian Croat women on racial, religious or political grounds".[248] "The Trial Chamber finds that many incidents of sexual assault occurred, including the case of a Bosnian Croat woman who was forced to undress herself in front of cheering Bosnian Serb policemen and soldiers. In another incident, a knife was run along the

242 *Brđanin* Trial Judgement, para. 847 (internal reference omitted).

243 *Brđanin* Trial Judgement, para. 852 (internal reference omitted).

244 *Brđanin* Trial Judgement, para. 856 (internal reference omitted).

245 *Brđanin* Trial Judgement, para. 523 (internal reference omitted).

246 *Brđanin* Trial Judgement, para. 824 (internal references omitted).

247 *Brđanin* Trial Judgement, para. 835 (internal references omitted).

248 *Brđanin* Trial Judgement, paras. 1010–1011 (internal references omitted).

	breast of a Bosnian Muslim woman. Frequently, it was demanded that detainees perform sex with each other. In each incident, armed Bosnian Serb soldiers or policemen were the perpetrators. The Trial Chamber is satisfied that, evaluated in their context, these acts are serious enough to rise to the level of crimes against humanity. Moreover, the Trial Chamber is satisfied that the circumstances surrounding the commission of sexual assaults leave no doubt at all that there was discrimination in fact and discriminatory intent on the part of the direct perpetrators, based on racial, religious or political grounds".[249] "As part of the ill-treatment by camp guards, Bosnian Muslims and Bosnian Croats were also forced to beat and perform sexual acts on each other. It was announced that their mothers and sisters would be raped in front of them. Bosnian Muslims and Bosnian Croats were forced to watch other members of their group being killed, raped, and beaten. [...] There can be no doubt that these acts were discriminatory in fact. The Trial Chamber also finds that in the given situation, these acts amount to the level of gravity of crimes against humanity. With regard to the requisite *mens rea*, taking into account the circumstances surrounding the commission of these acts of humiliation and degradation, the Trial Chamber has no doubt at all that the direct perpetrators possessed the requisite discriminatory intent based on racial, religious and political grounds".[250] "To sum up, the Trial Chamber is satisfied that the persecutorial campaign against Bosnian Muslims and Bosnian Croats included [...] torture, [...] rapes and sexual assaults, constant humiliation and degradation [...]. These acts were discriminatory in fact and were committed by the perpetrators with the requisite discriminatory intent on racial, religious and political grounds".[251]

19. Miroslav **Bralo** (Case No. IT-95-17) "***Lašva Valley***" Member of the "Jokers", the anti-terrorist platoon of the 4th Military Police Battalion of the Croatian Defence Council (HVO), which operated primarily in the Lašva Valley region in central Bosnia and Herzegovina.	
Indictment (International sex crimes (or related) charges and mode(s) of liability)	- **Torture or Inhuman treatment as a grave breach of the Geneva Conventions of 1949 (WC)** (count 3), **Torture as a violation of the laws or customs of war (WC)** (count 4), **Outrages upon personal dignity as a violation of the laws or customs of war (WC)** (count 5) and **Unlawful confinement as a grave breach of the Geneva Conventions of 1949 (WC)** (count 6) under Article 7(1) of the Statute (**committing** and **aiding and abetting**) for repeatedly raping Witness A and biting her nipples while Anto Furundžija interrogated her on 15 May 1993 and for confining her in a house in the area of Nadioci where she was repeatedly raped by members of the "Jokers", with the knowledge of Miroslav Bralo, on 16 May 1993.[252]

249 *Brđanin* Trial Judgement, para. 1013 (internal references omitted).

250 *Brđanin* Trial Judgement, paras. 1018–1020 (internal references omitted).

251 *Brđanin* Trial Judgement, para. 1050.

252 *Prosecutor v. Miroslav Bralo*, Case No. IT-95-17-PT, Amended Indictment, 19 July 2005, paras. 28–31 ("Between 15 May 1993 and an unknown date in July 1993, Witness A was repeatedly raped by **MIROSLAV BRALO** and by other members of the 'Jokers'. On 15 May 1993, Witness A, a Bosnian Muslim woman, was taken to the 'bungalow' by members of the 'Jokers' where she was interrogated by Anto Furundžija and by others at his direction. At one point during her protracted interrogation by Anto Furundžija, a Bosnian Croat soldier (Victim B) who had been badly beaten, was brought into the room where she was being interrogated. Victim B was beaten in her presence by **MIROSLAV BRALO** who also threatened to kill Witness A. During the course of her interrogation, and in order to obtain information from her, **MIROSLAV BRALO**, in the presence of other soldiers, repeatedly raped Witness A, penetrating her vagina with his penis. Whilst raping Witness A, **MIROSLAV BRALO** bit Witness A about the body, including her nipples,

Sentencing Judgement	- Guilty of **Torture or Inhuman treatment as a grave breach of the Geneva Conventions of 1949 (WC)** (count 3), **Torture as a violation of the laws or customs of war (WC)** (count 4), **Outrages upon personal dignity as a violation of the laws or customs of war (WC)** (count 5) and **Unlawful confinement as a grave breach of the Geneva Conventions of 1949 (WC)** (count 6) under Article 7(1) of the Statute (**committing** and **aiding and abetting**) for repeatedly raping Witness A and biting her nipples while Anto Furundžija interrogated her in the presence of others on, or about, 15 May 1993 and for confining her in a house in the area of Nadioci where she was repeatedly raped by members of the "Jokers" with the knowledge of Miroslav Bralo between 16 May 1993 and July 1993.[253] - Note: plea agreement: On 19 July 2005, a motion was filed by the Office of the Prosecutor informing the Trial Chamber of an agreement reached between the parties as to the entry of a guilty plea by the accused to all counts in the Indictment. On the same day, Miroslav Bralo entered a guilty plea to all counts in the Indictment and the Trial Chamber accepted the guity plea and entered a finding of guilt for each of the eight counts charged in the Indictment.[254]
Appeal Judgement	N/A
Legal and Factual Findings and/or Evidence	- Factual and legal findings: - Rape of Witness A: "On yet another occasion, on or about 15 May 1993, members of the 'Jokers' took a Bosnian Muslim woman ('Witness A') to the 'bungalow,' where she was interrogated. While she was held in the 'bungalow,' she was repeatedly raped and sexually assaulted by Bralo. At one point while she was being interrogated, Bralo beat a Bosnian Croat man in her presence and threatened to kill her. He raped her in front of other soldiers and ejaculated repeatedly over her body. He also bit her about the body, including her nipples. Witness A was then taken from the 'bungalow' to another house in the Nadioci area, where she was detained by the 'Jokers,' including Bralo, until some time in July 1993. During that period she was again repeatedly raped by members of the 'Jokers,' with the knowledge of Bralo. Bralo failed to release her, even though he was in a position to effect her release".[255] "The Factual Basis for Counts 3 to 6 of the Indictment describes the horrific ordeal of a Bosnian Muslim woman—Witness A—at the hands of Bralo and other members of the 'Jokers,' over a lengthy period of time. Her brutal rape and torture, and her imprisonment for approximately two months to be further violated at the whim of her captors, are crimes of a most depraved nature. The Trial Chamber emphasises once again

and repeatedly threatened to kill her. The aforesaid Anto Furundžija was present throughout the entire incident and did nothing to stop or curtail **MIROSLAV BRALO**'s actions. On 16 May 1993, Witness A was taken from the 'bungalow' to a weekend house in the area of Nadioci where she was confined against her will by **MIROSLAV BRALO** and other members of the 'Jokers'. Whilst at that location, Witness A was repeatedly raped by members of the 'Jokers' with the knowledge of **MIROSLAV BRALO**. By the foregoing acts and omissions, **MIROSLAV BRALO** committed and aided and abetted in the execution of the following crimes: **COUNT 3:** a **GRAVE BREACH** (torture or inhuman treatment) punishable under Articles 2(b) and 7(1) of the Statute of the Tribunal; **COUNT 4:** a **VIOLATION OF THE LAWS OR CUSTOMS OF WAR** (torture) punishable under Articles 3 and 7(1) of the Statute of the Tribunal; **COUNT 5:** a **VIOLATION OF THE LAWS OR CUSTOMS OF WAR** (outrages upon personal dignity including rape) punishable under Articles 3 and 7(1) of the Statute of the Tribunal; and **COUNT 6:** a **GRAVE BREACH** (unlawful confinement) punishable under Articles 2(g) and 7(1) of the Statute of the Tribunal".).

253 *Prosecutor v. Miroslav Bralo*, Case No. IT-95-17-S, Sentencing Judgement, 7 December 2005 ("*Bralo* Sentencing Judgement"), paras. 3, 5, 15–16.

254 *Bralo* Sentencing Judgement, paras. 3, 5.

255 *Bralo* Sentencing Judgement, paras. 15–16.

	that international humanitarian law, along with basic principles of humanity, require that individuals who are detained during an armed conflict must be treated humanely, and that the rape and torture of a woman in this context is a most heinous crime requiring unequivocal condemnation. With regard to the exacerbated humiliation and degradation of Witness A by Bralo, the Trial Chamber finds that this should be considered as a factor which further aggravates the gravity of an already extremely serious offence. Bralo threatened Witness A's life while she was being interrogated, he raped her in front of an unknown number of other people over an extended period of time, and he bit her and ejaculated repeatedly over her body during his prolonged assault of her. These actions demonstrate a desire to debase and terrify a vulnerable woman, who was at the complete mercy of her captors. It is therefore incumbent upon the Trial Chamber to take into account these particular circumstances as having aggravated the gravity of his rape of Witness A".[256]

20. Ivica **Rajić** (Case No. IT-95-12) "***Stupni Do***" Commander of units of Bosnian Croat soldiers – the Croatian Defence Council (HVO) – based in Kiseljak, a town in central Bosnia and Herzegovina; also known as Viktor Andrić.	
Indictment (International sex crimes (or related) charges and mode(s) of liability)	- **Inhuman treatment as a grave breach of the Geneva Conventions of 1949 (WC)** (count 3), **Outrages upon personal dignity as a violation of the laws or customs of war (WC)** (count 4) and **Cruel treatment as a violation of the laws or customs of war (WC)** (count 6) under Articles 7(1) and 7(3) of the Statute (**superior responsibility**) for the sexual assaults of Muslim women in Stupni Do by the HVO forces under Ivica Rajić's responsibility on 23 October 1993 and for the sexual assaults of Muslim women in Vareš town by the HVO soldiers between 23 October and 3 November 1993.[257]
Sentencing Judgement	- Guilty of **Inhuman treatment as a grave breach of the Geneva Conventions of 1949 (WC)** (count 3) under Article 7(1) of the Statute for the sexual assaults of Muslim women in Stupni Do and Vareš.[258] - Note: plea agreement: On 25 October 2005, a joint motion was filed by Ivica Rajić and the Office of the Prosecutor informing the Trial Chamber of an agreement reached between the parties as to the entry of a guilty plea by the accused to four counts, including inhuman treatment as a grave breach of the Geneva Conventions of 1949 (WC) (count 3) and the withdrawal of all other counts against him. On 26 October

256 *Bralo* Sentencing Judgement, paras. 33–34.

257 *Prosecutor v. Ivica Rajić*, Case No. IT-95-12-PT, Amended Indictment, 14 January 2004, paras. 16 ("On the morning of 23 October 1993, HVO forces under **Ivica RAJIĆ's** command attacked Stupni Do. After gaining control of various parts of the village, HVO soldiers forced the civilians out of their homes and hiding places, […] sexually assaulted Muslim women […] (A list of […] the women sexually assaulted is attached as confidential Annex 1.) […]"), 20 ("During the time from 23 October to 3 November 1993, before leaving Vares town, HVO soldiers […] sexually assaulted Muslim women. (A list of the women sexually assaulted is attached as confidential Annex 2.)"), p. 7 ("By the acts and omissions charged above, **Ivica RAJIĆ, also known as Viktor Andrić,** committed: […] **Count 3: inhuman treatment** (including sexual assault), a GRAVE BREACH OF THE GENEVA CONVENTIONS OF 1949, punishable under Statute Articles 2(b), 7(1) and 7(3) (as described in Paragraphs 13, 14, 15, 16, 20) **Count 4: outrages upon personal dignity, in particular humiliating and degrading treatment** (including sexual assault), a VIOLATION OF THE LAWS OR CUSTOMS OF WAR, as recognized by Article 3(1)(c) of the Geneva Conventions, punishable under Statute Articles 3, 7(1) and 7(3) (as described in Paragraphs 13, 14, 15, 16, 20) […] **Count 6: cruel treatment,** a VIOLATION OF THE LAWS OR CUSTOMS OF WAR, as recognised by Article 3(1)(a) of the Geneva Conventions, and punishable under Statute Articles 3, 7(1) and 7(3) (as described in Paragraphs 13, 14, 15, 16, 20) […]").

258 *Prosecutor v. Ivica Rajić*, Case No. IT-95-12-S, Sentencing Judgement, 8 May 2006 ("*Rajić* Sentencing Judgement"), paras. 9, 13, 38, 49, 53.

	2005, Ivica Rajić entered a guilty plea to counts 1, 3, 7 and 9 and the Trial Chamber entered a finding of guilt. On 4 May 2006, the remaining counts were withdrawn.[259]
Appeal Judgement	N/A
Legal and Factual Findings and/or Evidence	- Factual findings: "At all times relevant to the Amended Indictment, including on 21 October 1993 and following, Ivica RAJIĆ knew that HVO units under his command, including the Maturice and Ban Josip Jelaćić Brigade, had participated in several earlier operations against Bosnian Muslims villages in Kiseljak municipality and committed crimes against Bosnian Muslims, including [...] rape [...]".[260] "In Stupni Do, HVO commanders and soldiers under Ivica RAJIĆ's command forced Bosnian Muslim civilians out of their homes and hiding places [...] and sexually assaulted Muslim women".[261] "Ivica RAJIĆ left Vareš town on 26 October 1993, leaving Boro Malbašić and Krešimir Božić in command. During the time from approximately 23 October to 3 November 1993, in Vareš town, HVO commanders and soldiers under Ivica RAJIĆ's command and control [...] sexually assaulted Muslim women".[262]

21. Momčilo **Krajišnik** (Case No. IT-00-39) "***Bosnia and Herzegovina***" A member of the Bosnian Serb (later Republika Srpska) leadership during the war – on the Main Board of the Serbian Democratic Party of Bosnia and Herzegovina (SDS) and President of the Bosnian Serb Assembly.	
Indictment (International sex crimes (or related) charges and mode(s) of	- **Genocide** (count 1) and/or **Complicity in Genocide** (count 2) under Articles 7(1) (**joint criminal enterprise**) and 7(3) of the Statute (**superior responsibility**) for various crimes, including **causing serious bodily or mental harm** to the Bosnian Muslim and Bosnian Croat detainees in various detention facilities by subjecting them to sexual violence and **deliberately inflicting conditions of life calculated to bring about their physical destruction** through sexual violence.[263]

259 *Rajić* Sentencing Judgement, paras. 8–9, 11–12.

260 *Rajić* Sentencing Judgement, para. 38.

261 *Rajić* Sentencing Judgement, para. 49.

262 *Rajić* Sentencing Judgement, para. 53.

263 *Prosecutor v. Momčilo Krajišnik and Biljana Plavšić*, Case No. IT-00-39&40-PT, Amended Consolidated Indictment, 7 March 2002 ("*Krajišnik* Indictment"), paras. 15–17 ("Between 1 July 1991 and 30 December 1992, **Momčilo KRAJIŠNIK** and **Biljana PLAVŠIĆ**, acting individually or in concert with each other and with Radovan KARADŽIĆ, Nikola KOLJEVIĆ and other participants in the joint criminal enterprise, planned, instigated, ordered, committed or otherwise aided or abetted the planning, preparation or execution of the partial destruction of the Bosnian Muslim and Bosnian Croat national, ethnical, racial or religious groups, as such, in territories within Bosnia and Herzegovina. As alleged in paragraphs 3 to 9, **Momčilo KRAJIŠNIK** and **Biljana PLAVŠIĆ** participated in a joint criminal enterprise. The objective of the joint criminal enterprise was primarily achieved through a manifest pattern of persecutions as alleged in this indictment. In some Municipalities this campaign of persecutions included or escalated to include conduct committed with the intent to destroy in part the national, ethnical, racial or religious groups of Bosnian Muslims and Bosnian Croats as such. In these municipalities a significant section of the Bosnian Muslim and Bosnian Croat groups, namely their leaderships, as well as a substantial number of the members of the groups were targeted by Bosnian Serb Forces and Bosnian Serb Political and Governmental Organs and their agents for intended destruction. The most extreme manifestations of this form of partial destruction of the Bosnian Muslims and Bosnian Croats took place in Bosanski Novi, Brčko, Ključ, Kotor Varoš, Prijedor, and Sanski Most. The destruction of these groups was effected by: [...] b. the causing of serious bodily or mental harm to Bosnian Muslims and Bosnian Croats, including leading members of their communities, during their

liability)	- **Persecutions as CAH** (count 3) under Articles 7(1) (**joint criminal enterprise**) and 7(3) of the Statute (**superior responsibility**) of Bosnian Muslims, Bosnian Croats and other non-Serbs through various acts, including sexual violence.[264]
Trial Judgement	- Guilty of **Persecutions as CAH** (count 3) under Article 7(1) of the Statute (**joint criminal enterprise**) of Bosnian Muslims, Bosnian Croats and other non-Serbs through various acts, including rapes and sexual assaults.[265] - Not guilty of genocide (count 1) and complicity in genocide (count 2) because the Trial Chamber could not make conclusive findings that any acts were committed with the specific genocidal intent to destroy, in part, the Bosnian-Muslim or Bosnian-Croat ethnic group, as such.[266]
Appeal Judgement	- The Appeals Chamber found that the trial Chamber committed an error as persecutions fell outside the original common objective of the joint criminal enterprise, which only encompassed the crimes of deportation and forcible transfer. Therefore, the Appeals Chamber **reversed Momčilo Krajišnik's conviction for Persecutions as CAH** (count 3) of Bosnian Muslims, Bosnian Croats and other non-Serbs through various acts, including sexual violence.[267]

confinement in detention facilities. The detention facilities include those that are specified in **Schedule C**. At these locations, detainees were subjected to cruel or inhuman treatment, including [...] sexual violence [...]. c. the detention of Bosnian Muslims and Bosnian Croats, including leading members of their communities, in detention facilities under conditions of life calculated to bring about their physical destruction, namely through cruel and inhuman treatment, including [...] sexual violence [...]. By these acts and omissions, **Momčilo KRAJIŠNIK** [...] participated in: **Count 1: GENOCIDE,** punishable under Articles 4(3)(a), and 7(1) and 7(3) of the Statute of the Tribunal; and/or **Count 2: COMPLICITY IN GENOCIDE**, punishable under Articles 4(3)(e), and 7(1) and 7(3) of the Statute of the Tribunal".).

264 *Krajišnik* Indictment, paras. 18–21 ("Between 1 July 1991 and 30 December 1992, **Momčilo KRAJIŠNIK** and **Biljana PLAVŠIĆ**, acting individually or in concert with each other and with Radovan KARADŽIĆ, Nikola KOLJEVIĆ and other participants in the joint criminal enterprise, planned, instigated, ordered, committed or otherwise aided and abetted the planning, preparation or execution of persecutions of the Bosnian Muslim, Bosnian Croat or other non-Serb populations of the following municipalities: Banja Luka; Bijeljina; Bileća; Bosanska Krupa; Bosanski Novi; Bosanski Petrovac; Bratunac; Brčko; Čajniče; Čelinac; Doboj; Donji Vakuf; Foča; Gacko; Hadžići; Ilidža; Ilijaš; Ključ; Kalinovik; Kotor Varoš; Nevesinje; Novi Grad; Novo Sarajevo; Pale; Prijedor; Prnjavor; Rogatica; Rudo; Sanski Most; Šipovo; Sokolac; Teslić; Trnovo; Višegrad; Vlasenica; Vogošća and Zvornik ('Muncipalities'). Bosnian Serb Forces and Bosnian Serb Political and Governmental Organs and their agents committed persecutions in the Municipalities upon Bosnian Muslim, Bosnian Croat or other non- Serb populations. The persecutions included: [...] c) cruel or inhumane treatment during and after the attacks on towns and villages in the Municipalities including torture, physical and psychological abuse, sexual violence and forced existence under inhumane living conditions; [...] g) cruel or inhumane treatment in detention facilities including those listed in **Schedule C**. This treatment included torture, physical and psychological abuse and sexual violence; [...] Beginning in March 1992, Bosnian Serb Forces and Bosnian Serb Political and Governmental Organs and their agents attacked and took control of towns and villages in the Municipalities. Before, during and after these attacks, they committed persecutory acts enumerated in paragraph 19 upon Bosnian Muslim, Bosnian Croat or other non-Serb populations. Bosnian Serb Forces and Bosnian Serb Political and Governmental Organs and their agents established and controlled detention facilities in the Municipalities. After the attacks, Bosnian Muslim, Bosnian Croat or other non-Serb populations were detained in those facilities and were subjected to persecutory acts enumerated in paragraph 19. [...] By these acts and omissions, **Momčilo KRAJIŠNIK** [...] participated in: **Count 3:** Persecutions on political, racial and religious grounds, a **CRIME AGAINST HUMANITY**, punishable under Articles 5(h) and 7(1) and 7(3) of the Statute of the Tribunal".).

265 *Prosecutor v. Momčilo Krajišnik*, Case No. IT-00-39-T, Judgement, 27 September 2006 ("*Krajišnik* Trial Judgement"), paras. 304, 306, 309, 327, 333, 372, 461, 463, 487, 490, 493, 499, 545, 547, 550, 576, 600, 606, 637–641, 652, 656, 665, 667, 679, 685, 696, 701, 800, 803–806, 877, 965–966, 972, 1105, 1126, 1182.

266 *Krajišnik* Trial Judgement, paras. 867, 869, 1125, 1181.

267 *Prosecutor v. Momčilo Krajišnik*, Case No. IT-00-39-A, Judgement, 17 March 2009 ("*Krajišnik* Appeal Judgement"), paras. 177–178, 284, 820.

Legal and Factual Findings and/or Evidence	- Factual findings: - Rapes and sexual assaults in the Batković camp and in Bijeljina in north-eastern Bosnia and Herzegovina: "From at least June 1992 until the end of the indictment period, Serbs detained Muslims and Croats in the Batković camp in Bijeljina municipality [C2.5]. The detainees originated from a large number of different municipalities, including Brčko, Ključ, Lopare, Rogatica, Sokolac, Ugljevik, Vlasenica, and Zvornik. Many had been transferred from other detention facilities, particularly Sušica camp in Vlasenica and Manjača camp in Banja Luka. In August 1992, the commander at the camp was Velibor Stojanović. At that time, around 1,280 Muslim men were detained in a single warehouse. There were also some women, children, and elderly persons detained in a separate area. [...] They were beaten three times a day, forced to beat each other, and repeatedly forced to engage in degrading sexual acts with each other in the presence of other detainees".[268] "In the months following the take-over of Bijeljina, paramilitary groups in the municipality, together with members of the local MUP, engaged in criminal activities on a massive scale. Muslim residents of Bijeljina, as well as some Serbs, were terrorized by these groups through killings, rapes, house searches, and looting".[269] "After the take-over of Bijeljina in early April [1992], paramilitary groups, in particular Arkan's men, terrorized mainly Muslims through killings, rapes, house searches, and looting".[270] - Rape and sexual assault in Brčko and in Luka camp in north-eastern Bosnia and Herzegovina: "On 21 June, a group of armed men in uniform identifying themselves as police beat and shot dead an elderly Muslim woman in her home [...]. Ranko Češić, a local Serb, then sexually abused the woman's granddaughter".[271] "Detainees at Luka camp were subjected to systematic abuse by Serb guards, particularly by Jelisić and Ranko Češić. Detainees were frequently beaten and some female detainees were raped".[272] - Sexual mutilations in the Dom Kulture building in Čelopek village in Zvornik municipality in north-eastern Bosnia and Herzegovina: "From late May 1992 onwards, Muslims were detained in the Dom Kulture building in Čelopek village [...] and subjected to severe physical and psychological abuse. [...] The Yellow Wasps, headed by the Vučković brothers, Repić and Žućo, arrived at the Dom Kulture on 11 June and killed at least five detainees. One man had his ear cut off, others had their fingers cut off, and at least two men were sexually mutilated".[273] - Sexual assaults in the police station of Kotor Varoš town and rapes at the Pilana Sawmill in Kotor Varoš municipality in north-western Bosnia and Herzegovina: "In June and July 1992, a dozen Croats and Muslims were detained in the police

268 *Krajišnik* Trial Judgement, para. 304 (internal references omitted).

269 *Krajišnik* Trial Judgement, para. 306 (internal reference omitted). See also *Krajišnik* Trial Judgement, para. 966.

270 *Krajišnik* Trial Judgement, para. 309.

271 *Krajišnik* Trial Judgement, para. 327 (internal reference omitted).

272 *Krajišnik* Trial Judgement, para. 333 (internal references omitted). See also *Krajišnik* Trial Judgement, para. 972.

273 *Krajišnik* Trial Judgement, para. 372.

	station of Kotor Varoš town [...] where they were beaten by special police officers and by Serb soldiers wearing red berets. One of them was nearly strangled while being interrogated about the activities of other SDA members. Some of them were also sexually abused by the police officers".[274] "In August 1992, approximately 1,000 women, children, and elderly civilians were detained at the Pilana sawmill [...] Many women and girls aged 13 and older were raped by Serb soldiers prior to being sent to Travnik from where they were released".[275] - Rapes and sexual assaults in the Keraterm, Omarska and Trnopolje camps in Prijedor municipality in north-western Bosnia and Herzegovina: "As stated earlier, three large detention centres were established in the municipality: men of military age were brought mostly to Keraterm [...] and Omarska [...], while women, children, elderly persons, and other men to Trnopolje [...]. Teams representing both military and civilian authorities screened detainees in Keraterm and Trnopolje in order to determine their role in the conflict. As armed conflict spread throughout the municipality in the following days, the need to process large numbers of captured persons led the municipal crisis staff to transform Keraterm into a transit centre and to establish another camp at Omarska. These three camps were guarded by soldiers, police forces, TO units, or combination thereof. Detainees were executed and subjected to severe mistreatment, which included psychological abuse, beatings, sexual assaults, and torture".[276] "Detainees in Omarska, who numbered up to 3,000 at one time, were mostly Muslims, Croats, and a dozen Serbs deemed to be on the side of Muslims. Overall, less than 40 women were detained in Omarska during the period of its operation. One of these women was repeatedly raped and beaten".[277] "Camp authorities in Trnopolje did not distribute food and, on occasion, Serb soldiers beat and killed Muslim and Croat detainees. [...] Moreover, soldiers coming from outside the camp and Slobodan Kuruzović, the camp commander, raped the female detainees".[278] "The Chamber further concludes that most of the Muslims and Croats in Prijedor municipality were detained for some period of time at one of 58 detention centres in Prijedor municipality, five of which were long-term detention camps. Particularly in the long-term detention centres at Keraterm, Trnopolje, and Omarska, detainees were subjected to severe mistreatment, which included psychological abuse, beatings, sexual assaults, rapes, and torture, often leading to death".[279] - Sexual assaults at the Hadžići sports centre and at the Hadžići civil defence headquarters in Hadžići municipality: "On 25 May 1992, Serb forces transferred some of the detainees from the garage of the municipal building to the Hadžići sports centre [...] where at that time 60 men and one woman were detained. Vidomir Banduka, a member of the crisis staff of Hadžići municipality, confirmed that it was a decision of the crisis staff to keep the Muslims

[274] *Krajišnik* Trial Judgement, para. 461 (internal reference omitted).

[275] *Krajišnik* Trial Judgement, para. 463.

[276] *Krajišnik* Trial Judgement, para. 487. See also *Krajišnik* Trial Judgement, para. 1070.

[277] *Krajišnik* Trial Judgement, para. 490 (internal reference omitted).

[278] *Krajišnik* Trial Judgement, para. 493 (internal reference omitted).

[279] *Krajišnik* Trial Judgement, para. 499.

	there. While in detention in the Hadžići sports centre, the detainees were often beaten and sexually abused by members of the paramilitary units".[280] "On 20 June 1992, Serb military police detained Witness 141 and her sister at the Hadžići civil defence headquarters [...], where they were beaten and raped by the Serb guards. In the headquarters, military policemen intimidated Witness 141 by pretending to order her execution and by handing her an active grenade. Around 25 June 1992, they were moved to the garage of the municipal building [...] where the witness's sister was sexually abused by a Serb paramilitary soldier. In mid July 1992, Ratko Radić, the SDS municipal president transferred the two women to the premises of a factory outside Hadžići [...] where they were detained together with other Muslims from Hadžići and were forced to work. At the factory, Radić raped the witness's sister regularly. Other commanders and guards stationed at the factory raped both women on many occasions".[281] "The Chamber concludes that Serb forces took over Hadžići town and parts of Hadžići municipality with the assistance of JNA forces and expelled most of the non-Serb population in May 1992. They detained mainly Muslim and Croat civilians in thirteen detention facilities under inhumane conditions, mistreated and sexually abused them".[282] - Rapes in the commune of Grbavica in Novo Sarajevo municipality: "At the end of April 1992, JNA forces shelled Sarajevo and its neighbourhoods, such as Bijelo Polje and Novo Sarajevo. From June 1992 onwards, soldiers, assigned to sniper duty, took position at the upper floors of four multi-storey buildings in the commune of Grbavica. A VRS soldier reported that he had heard sounds of gunfire coming from the upper floors and was told by the snipers that they had shot people. Members of the Serb army, the Serb police, and Šešelj's men, searched Muslim and Croat houses in the commune of Grbavica for weapons. Three women, two Muslim and one of mixed ethnicity, were raped during these house searches from June to September 1992, by an armed man, named Batko, who had come to their apartments".[283] "Around June 1992, members of the VRS and the MUP, as well as Šešelj's men, searched Muslim and Croat houses in the commune of Grbavica for weapons. Three women, two Muslim and one of mixed ethnicity, were raped during these house searches by an armed man named Batko. Biljana Plavšić stated that in June or July 1992 she was informed by people living in Grbavica that Batko and an armed group associated with him were committing crimes against non-Serbs. When she returned to Pale she had a meeting with Radovan Karadžić, the Accused, Nikola Koljević, Mićo Stanišić, and Momčilo Mandić regarding what she had heard from the people in Grbavica. The reaction was one of indifference, Mandić smiling and saying, 'Oh, Batko'".[284] - Sexual assaults in the Planjo's house in Semizovac, in Vogošća municipality: "On 8 July, the municipal secretariat for town planning, property rights, housing policy, and land register decided, upon request of the Ministry of Justice, to temporarily turn over Planjo's house [in Semizovac] to the Ministry, for use as a prison. On 17 August, a group of more than 80 Muslim men who had been in detention in a school Podlugovi, in Ilijaš municipality, were transferred by police officers in camouflage

280 *Krajišnik* Trial Judgement, para. 545 (internal references omitted).

281 *Krajišnik* Trial Judgement, para. 547 (internal references omitted).

282 *Krajišnik* Trial Judgement, para. 550.

283 *Krajišnik* Trial Judgement, para. 576 (internal references omitted).

284 *Krajišnik* Trial Judgement, para. 965 (internal reference omitted).

uniform to Planjo's house. [...] There were a total of 113 men detained at Planjo's house, most of whom were Muslims, but also some Croats and one Serb. Women and children were held in separate quarters upstairs. They were guarded by Serb soldiers and police officers in camouflage uniform, who would often severely beat them. In October, 172 people were detained here. In the period between August and November 1992, Serbs would come from Serbia on the weekends to beat the detainees and force them to perform sexually humiliating acts".[285]

"The Chamber concludes [..., a]fter the take-over of villages, Serb forces arrested Muslims and Croats and detained them in ten detention centers in the municipality under harsh conditions. [...] Until November 1992, Serbs regularly came from Serbia to beat the detainees and force them to perform sexually humiliating acts".[286]

- Rapes and sexual assaults in Foča municipality, in south-eastern Bosnia and Herzegovina:

"On 22 June 1992, all fifteen adult men from the village of Trnovača, including Witness 558's husband, were taken from the village to a bridge over the Drina river in the area of Foča called Brod, where fourteen were killed [...]. On 24 June, local Serbs took a number of women from the same village to Bukovica motel [...], where one woman was raped".[287]

"In early July 1992, local Serb soldiers, including Gojko Janković and Radomir Kovač, attacked the Muslim village of Mješaja/Trošanj. At the time of the attack, some Muslim villagers were in the woods where they spent the nights in fear of attacks. [...] At the meadow, the Serb soldiers separated the men from the women and the women were chased down a hill towards the village of Trošanj. [...] Some of the women were brought to one of the attacking soldier's apartment and were raped repeatedly by many soldiers; they were later sold. Some other women from the village of Mješaja/Trošanj were taken by Serb soldiers to a detention centre at the construction site Buk Bijela [...], where Gojko Janković was in charge. At this detention centre, Witness 295 was raped by around ten Serb soldiers until she lost consciousness. [...] Witness 295 was later transferred to the Srednja Škola [...], where women and children were being held in a classroom. Mitar Sipčić was in charge of the guards at the school. Witness 295 and nine other women were raped almost every night by local Serb soldiers either in one of the classrooms or at a location outside the school".[288]

"Between 10 April and the beginning of June 1992, large-scale arrests of Muslim civilian men and women were carried out throughout Foča and its environs. They were arrested, rounded up, separated and imprisoned or detained at several detention centres in the municipality. Some of them were [...] raped [...]. The sole reason for this treatment of the civilians was their Muslim ethnicity".[289]

"There were Muslim civilians held at Foča high school [...] and Partizan Hall [...] in intolerably unhygienic conditions, without medical care, and with insufficient food. All this was done in full view, with complete knowledge and sometimes with the direct involvement of the local authorities, particularly the police forces. The Partizan hall was in fact guarded by police officers. Serb soldiers or policemen, including the chief of Foča's police, Dragan Gagović, would come to these detention centres, select one or more women, take them out and rape them. On one occasion, when women who were being transferred from Buk Bijela to Foča high school tried to seek the protection of the police in Foča, their complaints were ignored. On another occasion, a

[285] *Krajišnik* Trial Judgement, para. 600 (internal references omitted).
[286] *Krajišnik* Trial Judgement, para. 606.
[287] *Krajišnik* Trial Judgement, para. 637 (internal reference omitted).
[288] *Krajišnik* Trial Judgement, para. 638 (internal references omitted).
[289] *Krajišnik* Trial Judgement, para. 639 (internal references omitted).

	woman who tried to seek refuge at the SJB was hit by a policeman with the butt of his rifle. Some of the women were also taken out of these two detention centres by Serb soldiers, including Dragoljub Kunarac, to privately owned apartments and houses where they had to cook, clean and serve the residents. They were also subjected to sexual assaults. During one rape, Kunarac expressed with verbal and physical aggression his view that rapes against Muslim women were one of the many ways in which the Serbs could assert their superiority and victory over the Muslims. After months of captivity, many women were transferred from the municipality or exchanged. Some of the women from Partizan Hall were at some point moved to different houses and apartments where they continued to be raped and mistreated. In particular, at 'Karaman's house' in Miljevina […], soldiers had easy access to women and girls whom they raped. Radovan Stanković was in charge at the house. Two female detainees, including a twelve-year-old girl, spent about 20 days in another apartment in the so-called Lepa Brena block in Foča during which they were constantly raped by the two occupants of the apartment and by other men who visited. In mid-November 1992, the two female detainees were taken to a house near the Hotel Zelengora. They stayed in this house for approximately 20 days during which they were continually raped by a group of soldiers. This group of soldiers subsequently took them to yet another apartment where they continued to rape them for approximately two weeks".[290] "The Chamber concludes that […] Muslim and Croat civilians were detained in nineteen detention centres under harsh conditions. Muslim women were raped or sexually abused on a regular basis and detained in private houses".[291] - Rape at the Gacko police station, in south-eastern Bosnia and Herzegovina: "From as early as April 1992, Bosnian Serbs, including paramilitary groups active in the municipality, detained mostly Muslim and Croats in Gacko in at least six locations […]. In early June, there were around 120 Muslim detainees at the Gacko police station […]. Witness 3 was arrested on 10 June 1992 and brought to the police station […] where he was held with six other Muslim men. […] On 4 July 1992, in the same police station, the witness was forced by Popić to watch the rape of his own wife by a Serb man from the Munja unit of the Red Berets assisted by two other armed Red Berets".[292] - Rapes at the Kalinovik elementary school, in south-eastern Bosnia and Herzegovina: "Between 1 and 5 August 1992, Serbs arrested, rounded up, separated and imprisoned, or detained almost all remaining Muslims men and women from Kalinovik, and also approximately 190 women, children, and elderly persons from Gacko. All detainees where subsequently taken to Kalinovik elementary school […]. During detention, […] women were raped. The sole reason for this treatment of the civilians was their Muslim ethnicity".[293] "The Chamber concludes that [… d]uring detention, […] women were raped".[294] - Rapes in the Rogatica secondary school, in south-eastern Bosnia and Herzegovina: "Later on, local Serbs under the authority of Rajko Kušić detained up to 1,100 Muslims of Rogatica in the secondary school. Guards and machine-gun nests were posted around the secondary school and the detainees were informed that the surrounding

290 *Krajišnik* Trial Judgement, paras. 640–641 (internal references omitted).

291 *Krajišnik* Trial Judgement, para. 652.

292 *Krajišnik* Trial Judgement, para. 656 (internal references omitted).

293 *Krajišnik* Trial Judgement, para. 665 (internal references omitted).

294 *Krajišnik* Trial Judgement, para. 667.

	area had been set with landmines. Serb soldiers, police officers, special unit members, and paramilitaries interrogated Muslims detained in the secondary school for periods of up to three and a half months. The guards beat, raped, and tortured the Muslim detainees".[295] "The Chamber concludes that [...] Serb forces detained mostly Muslim civilians in seven detention facilities, among them up to 1,100 at the secondary school in Rogatica where they were [...] raped in the period June to August 1992".[296] - Rapes in Višegrad municipality, in south-eastern Bosnia and Herzegovina: "On 19 May 1992, the JNA withdrew from Višegrad. Paramilitary groups stayed behind, and other paramilitaries arrived as soon as the army had left the town. Some local Serbs joined them. Those Muslims who remained in the area of Višegrad or those who had returned to their homes found themselves trapped, disarmed, and at the mercy of paramilitaries. Others were subjected to [...] rapes [...]".[297] "The Chamber finds that many civilians fled from their villages in Višegrad municipality out of fear for their lives. Those who remained or returned to their homes were humiliated, mistreated, beaten or raped".[298] - Rapes and sexual assaults constituting persecutions as CAH: "The Chamber finds that in a number of detention centres, Muslim and Croat detainees were raped or sexually abused. For example, in Batković camp [...] in Bijeljina, male detainees were forced to engage in degrading sexual acts with each other in the presence of other detainees. In several detention centres in Foča, women and young girls were raped on a regular basis, namely in Bukovica motel [...], the workers huts at Buk Bijela [...], Srednja Škola [...], and Karaman's house in Miljevina [...]. Sexual abuse also occurred in Luka camp [...] in Brčko; the civil defence headquarters [...], a factory outside the town of Hadžići [...], and the sports centre [...] in Hadžići; Kalinovik elementary school [...]; the police station [...] and Pilana sawmill [...] in Kotor Varoš; the police station [...] in Vogošća; and the Dom Kulture Čelopek [...] in Zvornik. [...] The Chamber finds that the inhumane living conditions at the detention centres, and the ill-treatment of Muslims and Croats during the attacks on towns and villages, and in detention centres, resulted in serious injuries and serious mental and physical suffering of the victims. Regarding the creation and maintenance of inhumane living conditions in detention centres, the Chamber finds that the perpetrators either had the intention to inflict serious mental and physical harm on the detainees, or that they knew that their acts or omissions was likely to cause serious mental or physical suffering or injury, or a serious attack on human dignity, and was reckless as to that result. Regarding the ill-treatment of Muslims and Croats during attacks on towns and villages and in the detention centres, the Chamber finds that the perpetrators intended to inflict such serious injuries and serious mental and physical harm. The Chamber therefore finds that all these acts and omissions constitute cruel or inhumane treatment. The victims of the cruel and inhumane treatment were exclusively Muslims and Croats [...]. While raping a woman in a Foča detention centre, Dragoljub Kunarac expressed with verbal and physical aggression his view that rapes against Muslim women were one of the many ways in which the Serbs could assert their superiority and victory over the Muslims. In this respect, the Chamber also considers the fact that Muslims and Croats were detained on discriminatory grounds [...]. In conclusion, the Chamber finds that the cruel or inhumane treatment was carried out on discriminatory grounds.

295 *Krajišnik* Trial Judgement, para. 679 (internal references omitted).

296 *Krajišnik* Trial Judgement, para. 685.

297 *Krajišnik* Trial Judgement, para. 696 (internal references omitted).

298 *Krajišnik* Trial Judgement, para. 701.

	The Chamber further finds that the victims referred to above were either captured or detained, or otherwise not taking active part in the hostilities, at the time of the cruel or inhumane treatment. The Chamber finds that the cruel or inhumane treatment was part of the widespread and systematic attack against the Muslim and Croat civilian population. The Chamber therefore finds that all above incidents of cruel and inhumane treatment constitute persecution as a crime against humanity".[299]

22. Dragan **Zelenović** (Case No. IT-96-23/2) "***Foča***" A former Bosnian Serb soldier and de facto military policeman in the town of Foča, located south-east of Sarajevo, Bosnia and Herzegovina, near the borders with Serbia and Montenegro.	
Indictment[300] (International sex crimes (or related) charges and	- **Torture as CAH** (count 5), **Rape as CAH** (count 6), **Torture as a violation of the laws or customs of war (WC)** (count 7) and **Rape as a violation of the laws or customs of war (WC)** (count 8) under Article 7(1) of the Statute for the rape of Witness FWS-75 lasting one to two hours and for the gang-rape of Witness FWS-87, a 15 year-old girl, on or about 3 July 1992 at Buk Bijela.[301]

299 *Krajišnik* Trial Judgement, paras. 800, 803–806.

300 For the general background to the charges, see *Prosecutor v. Gojko Janković et al.*, Case No. IT-96-23/2-I, Amended Indictment, 20 April 2001 (redacted version), ("*Zelenović* Indictment"), paras. 1.2–1.4 ("As soon as the Serb forces had taken over parts of Foča town, military police accompanied by local and non-local soldiers started arresting Muslim and Croat inhabitants. Until mid-July 1992 they continued to round up and arrest Muslim villagers from the surrounding villages in the municipality. The Serb forces separated men and women and unlawfully confined thousands of Muslims and Croats in various short and long-term detention facilities or kept them essentially under house arrest. During the arrests many civilians were killed, beaten or subjected to sexual assault. The Foča Kazneno-popravni Dom (hereinafter KP Dom), one of the largest prison facilities in the former Republic of Yugoslavia, was the primary detention facility for men. Muslim women, children and the elderly were detained in houses, apartments and motels in the town of Foča or in surrounding villages, or at short and long-term detention centres such as Buk Bijela, Foča High School and Partizan Sports Hall, respectively. Many of the detained women were subjected to humiliating and degrading conditions of life, to brutal beatings and to sexual assaults, including rapes. Besides the above-mentioned detention places, several women were detained in houses and apartments used as brothels, operated by groups of soldiers, mostly paramilitary".).

301 *Zelenović* Indictment, paras. 5.1–5.5, 5.9 ("Buk Bijela refers to a settlement on a hydro-electric dam construction site on the road from Brod to Miljevina by the river Drina which was turned into a local military headquarters and barracks for Bosnian Serb forces and paramilitary soldiers after the April 1992 take-over of Foča and the surrounding villages. The Buk Bijela complex consisted of workers' barracks, where about 200 to 300 soldiers were barracked, and an adjoining motel. Buk Bijela was used as a temporary detention and interrogation facility for civilian women, children and the elderly who were captured in various villages in the municipality of Foča in July 1992. On 3 July 1992, soldiers commanded by the accused **GOJKO JANKOVIĆ**, and among them […] **DRAGAN ZELENOVIĆ** […], arrested a group of at least 60 Muslim women, children and a few elderly men from Trosanj and Mjesaja, and took them to Buk Bijela. After the attack on Foča, the villages of Trosanj and Mjesaja had offered armed resistance. While detained at Buk Bijela for several hours, all the Muslim civilians were lined up along the river Drina and guarded by armed soldiers. They were threatened with being either killed or raped and were otherwise humiliated. The soldiers approached each detained civilian, and took him or her to the above-mentioned accused for questioning. The soldiers separated the women from their children. **GOJKO JANKOVIĆ**, [… and] **DRAGAN ZELENOVIĆ** interrogated the women. The interrogations focused on the hiding-places of the male villagers and weapons. The accused threatened the women with murder and sexual assault if they lied. […] **DRAGAN ZELENOVIĆ** and other soldiers acting under the control of **GOJKO JANKOVIĆ** gang-raped several women during or immediately after the interrogation who they suspected of lying. Paragraphs 5.4 to 5.7, here under, particularise some of those sexual assaults which occurred on or about 3 July 1992. A witness code named FWS-75 was interrogated by **GOJKO JANKOVIĆ** and **DRAGAN ZELENOVIĆ** about her village and whether the villagers had weapons. **GOJKO JANKOVIĆ** warned the witness not to lie, otherwise she would be raped by soldiers and killed afterwards. As FWS-75 did not answer the questions sufficiently, a

mode(s) of liability)	- **Torture as CAH** (count 13), **Rape as CAH** (count 14), **Torture as a violation of the laws or customs of war (WC)** (count 15) and **Rape as a violation of the laws or customs of war (WC)** (count 16) under Article 7(1) of the Statute for the rapes of Witnesses FWS-50, FWS-75, FWS-87, FWS-95, FWS-74 and FWS-88 at Foča High School, for the rape of Witness FWS-75 on or about 6 or 7 July 1992 at Foča High School, for the rapes in at least five occasions of Witnesses FWS-75 and FWS-87 between or about 8 July and about 13 July 1992 at Foča High School, for the gang-rape of Witness FWS-75 and the rape of Witness FWS-87 on three occasions between or about 8 July and about 13 July 1992 in an apartment building called Brena in the centre of Foča, for the rapes of Witnesses FWS-75 and FWS-87 between about 8 July and about 13 July 1992 in Brena, for the rape of Witness FWS-87 between about 8 July and about 13 July 1992 in an abandoned house of a Muslim policeman in Gornje Polje and for the numerous rapes of Witness FWS-95 between or about 8 July and about 13 July 1992 in different classrooms in the Foča High School.[302]

soldier took her to another room. There, at least ten unidentified soldiers raped her, in turn. The nature of the rape included vaginal penetration and fellatio. FWS-75 lost consciousness after the tenth soldier sexually assaulted her. The episode of sexual assault lasted between one to two hours. Another witness, FWS-87, a 15 year old, was interrogated by **DRAGAN ZELENOVIĆ** and three unidentified soldiers in a room at Buk Bijela. During the interrogation, they accused FWS-87 of not telling the truth. The interrogators removed her clothing and then, each one raped her. The nature of the rape was vaginal penetration. The first soldier also threatened her by putting a gun to her head. FWS-87 experienced severe pain during the assault, followed by heavy vaginal bleeding. [...] By the foregoing acts and omissions in relation to the victims FWS-75 and FWS-87, **DRAGAN ZELENOVIĆ** committed: **Count 5:** Torture, a **CRIME AGAINST HUMANITY** punishable under Article *5* (f) of the Statute of the Tribunal. **Count 6:** Rape, a **CRIME AGAINST HUMANITY** punishable under Article 5 (g) of the Statute of the Tribunal. **Count 7:** Torture, a **VIOLATION OF THE LAWS OR CUSTOMS OF WAR,** punishable under Article 3 of the Statute of the Tribunal and recognised by Common Article 3 (1) (a) (torture) of the Geneva Conventions. **Count 8:** Rape, a **VIOLATION OF THE LAWS OR CUSTOMS OF WAR,** punishable under Article 3 of the Statute of the Tribunal".).

302 *Zelenović* Indictment, paras. 6.1–6.11, 6.14 ("During the occupation that followed the take-over of the town of Foča, the Foča High School, situated in the Aladža area, functioned as a barracks for Serb soldiers, and as a short term detention facility for Muslim women, children and the elderly. Between 3 July and about 13 July 1992, at least 72 Muslim inhabitants of the municipality of Foča were detained in two classrooms in the Foča High School, including the women, children and the elderly who had earlier been held at Buk Bijela, mentioned above. On or about 13 July 1992, all detainees were transferred from Foča High School to the Partizan Sports Hall in Foča. At the Foča High School, the detainees were surrounded by armed Serb soldiers, who patrolled outside the Foča High School and constantly entered and left the building. There were also two armed police guards from the Foča SUP patrolling the corridor outside of the detention rooms. Many of the female detainees were subjected to sexual abuse during their detention at the Foča High School. From the second day of their detention, every evening, groups of Serb soldiers sexually assaulted, including gang-rape, some of the younger women and girls in class-rooms or apartments in neighbouring buildings. Among them were witnesses FWS-50, FWS-75, FWS-87, FWS-95, FWS-74 and FWS-88, as set forth below. The soldiers threatened to kill the women or the women's children if they refused to submit to sexual assaults. Women who dared to resist the sexual assaults were beaten. The above mentioned groups of soldiers consisted of members of the military police. They referred to themselves 'Ćosa's Guards', named for the local commander of the military police Ćosović. The accused **GOJKO JANKOVIĆ, DRAGAN ZELENOVIĆ,** Janko Janjić and Zoran Vuković were among these groups of soldiers. The physical and psychological health of many female detainees seriously deteriorated as a result of these sexual assaults. Some of the women endured complete exhaustion, vaginal discharges, bladder problems and irregular menstrual bleedings. The detainees lived in constant fear. Some of the sexually abused women became suicidal. Others became indifferent as to what would happen to them and suffered from depression. On or about 6 or 7 July 1992, **DRAGAN ZELENOVIĆ** in concert with Janko Janjić and Zoran Vuković, selected FWS-50, FWS-75, FWS- 87, FWS-95 out of the group of detainees. The accused led them to another classroom where unidentified soldiers stood waiting. Then **DRAGAN ZELENOVIĆ** decided which woman should go to which man. The women were ordered to remove their clothes. FWS-95 refused to do so and Janko Janjić slapped her and held her at gun point. Then **DRAGAN ZELENOVIĆ** raped FWS-75 (vaginal penetration). Zoran Vuković raped FWS-87

	- **Torture as CAH** (count 41), **Rape as CAH** (count 42), **Torture as a violation of the laws or customs of war (WC)** (count 43) and **Rape as a violation of the laws or customs of war (WC)** (count 44) under Article 7(1) of the Statute for the gang-rape of Witness FWS-87 in July 1992, for the gang-rape of Witness FWS-48 on or around 15 July 1992 in an empty house in the Aladža neighbourhood, for the rape of Witness FWS-48 on or around 23 July 1992 in a house close to Partizan, for the rapes of Witness FWS-48 on 12 August 1992 in a house in Donje Polje and for the rapes and gang-rape of Witness FWS-95 from July 1992 to 13 August 1992.[303]

(vaginal penetration) and Janko Janjić raped FWS-95 (vaginal penetration) within the same room. One of the other soldiers took FWS-50 to another classroom and raped her (vaginal penetration). Between or about 8 July and about 13 July 1992, in addition to the sexual assaults described under paragraph 6.6, on at least five other occasions **DRAGAN ZELENOVIĆ** led a group of soldiers that sexually abused FWS-75 and FWS-87. First the women were taken into another classroom in the Foča High School. There Zoran Vuković and **DRAGAN ZELENOVIĆ** raped FWS-75 and FWS-87 (vaginal penetration). Between or about 8 July and about 13 July 1992, on three occasions, FWS-75 and FWS-87 were taken from the Foča High School to an apartment building called Brena in the centre of Foča. The building was near the Zelengora hotel, a military headquarters of the Serb forces. The first time, the two women went to an apartment owned by **DRAGAN ZELENOVIĆ.** The accused Janko Janjić, **DRAGAN ZELENOVIĆ** and two other unidentified soldiers raped FWS-75 (vaginal and anal penetration and fellatio) while **DRAGAN ZELENOVIĆ** raped FWS-87 (vaginal penetration). Between about 8 July and about 13 July 1992, on two occasions **DRAGAN ZELENOVIĆ** and several other unidentified soldiers took FWS-75 and FWS-87 to Brena and raped them. On these occasions, the accused raped FWS-75 (vaginal and anal penetration and fellatio) and raped FWS-87 (vaginal penetration). Between about 8 July and about 13 July 1992, on another occasion, FWS-75, FWS-87 and Z.G. were taken by **DRAGAN ZELENOVIĆ** to an abandoned house of a Muslim policeman in Gornje Polje. There **DRAGAN ZELENOVIĆ** raped FWS-87 (vaginal penetration). An unidentified soldier raped Z.G. Between or about 8 July and about 13 July 1992, in addition to the acts described in paragraph 6.6, FWS-95 was sexually assaulted in different classrooms in the Foča High School. Because she had previously been beaten and threatened when sexually assaulted FWS-95 dared not resist the soldiers again. She was raped on numerous occasions by many perpetrators among them Janko Janjić, **DRAGAN ZELENOVIĆ** and **GOJKO JANKOVIĆ** (vaginal and anal penetration and fellatio). […] By the foregoing acts and omissions in relation to the victims FWS-50, FWS-75, FWS-87 and FWS-95, **DRAGAN ZELENOVIĆ** committed: **Count 13:** Torture, a **CRIME AGAINST HUMANITY** punishable under Article 5 (f) of the Statute of the Tribunal. **Count 14:** Rape, a **CRIME AGAINST HUMANITY** punishable under Article 5 (g) of the Statute of the Tribunal. **Count 15:** Torture, a **VIOLATION OF THE LAWS OR CUSTOMS OF WAR,** punishable under Article 3 of the Statute of the Tribunal and recognised by Common Article 3 (1) (a) (torture) of the Geneva Conventions. **Count 16:** Rape, a **VIOLATION OF THE LAWS OR CUSTOMS OF WAR,** punishable under Article 3 of the Statute of the Tribunal".).

303 *Zelenović* Indictment, paras. 7.1, 7.4–7.7, 7.13, 7.15, 7.17, 7.19–7.20, 7.22, 7.26 ("Partizan Sports Hall ('Partizan') functioned as a detention centre for women, children and the elderly from at least on or about 13 July 1992 until at least 13 August 1992. The detainees held at Partizan, during this time period, numbered at least 72. The detainees were all civilian Muslim women, children and a few elderly persons from villages in the municipality of Foča. […] Living conditions in Partizan were brutal. The detention was characterised by inhumane treatment, unhygienic facilities, overcrowding, starvation, physical and psychological torture, including sexual assaults. Immediately after the transfer of women to Partizan, a pattern of sexual assaults commenced. Armed soldiers, mostly in groups of three to five, entered Partizan, usually in the evenings, and removed women. When the women resisted or hid, the soldiers beat or threatened the women to force them to obey. The soldiers took the women from Partizan to houses, apartments or hotels for the purpose of sexual assault and rape. Three witnesses, identified by the pseudonyms FWS-48, FWS-95 and FWS-50, a 16 year old girl, were detained at Partizan from about 13 July until 13 August 1992. Two others, identified by the pseudonyms FWS-75 and FWS-87, a 15 year old girl, were detained in Partizan from about 13 July until 2 August 1992. Almost every night during their detention, Serb soldiers took FWS-48, FWS-95, FWS-50, FWS-75 and FWS-87 out of Partizan and sexually abused them (vaginal and anal penetration and fellatio). On or around 13 August 1992, most detainees were released from Partizan and deported to Montenegro. The women who left on the 13 August convoy received medical care for the first time in Montenegro. Many women suffered permanent gynaecological harm due to the sexual assaults. At least one woman can no longer have children. All the women who were sexually assaulted suffered psychological and emotional harm; some remain traumatised. […] In July 1992, witness FWS-87 was frequently taken out, and raped (vaginal

	- **Rape as CAH** (count 49), and **Rape as a violation of the laws or customs of war (WC)** (count 50) under Article 7(1) of the Statute for the rapes of Witnesses FWS-75, FWS-87 and the two other women into an apartment near the Fish Restaurant in Foča on or about 30 October 1992.[304]
Sentencing Judgement	- Guilty of **Torture as CAH** (count 5) and **Rape as CAH** (count 6) under Article 7(1) of the Statute for the rape of Witness FWS-75 (**aiding and abetting**) and for raping Witness FWS-87 (**committing**). - Guilty of **Torture as CAH** (count 13) and **Rape as CAH** (count 14) under Article 7(1) of the Statute for the rapes of Witness FWS-87 and two unidentified women (**co-perpetration**) and for thrice raping Witnesses FWS-75 and FWS-87 (**committing**). - Guilty of **Torture as CAH** (count 41) and **Rape as CAH** (count 42) under Article

and anal penetration and fellatio). On one occasion witness FWS-87 was gang-raped by 4 men including **DRAGAN ZELENOVIĆ** and Zoran Vuković. […] On or around 15 July 1992, **GOJKO JANKOVIĆ** led FWS-48 to an empty Muslim house in the Aladža neighbourhood. When FWS-48 arrived, about 14 Montenegrin soldiers were already present. **DRAGAN ZELENOVIĆ** then arrived with about 8 more soldiers, among them Zoran Vuković. **DRAGAN ZELENOVIĆ** took FWS-48 to a room and threatened to slash her throat if she resisted. Then, **DRAGAN ZELENOVIĆ** raped FWS-48 (vaginal penetration and fellatio) together with at least other 7 soldiers. Zoran Vuković was the 6th man who raped her. During the sexual assault, Zoran Vuković bit her nipples a number of times. Although the witness was bleeding from these bites, the 7th man squeezed and pinched her breasts as he raped her. FWS-48 fainted as a result of the pain. […] On or around 23 July 1992, **DRAGAN ZELENOVIĆ** and some unidentified soldiers took FWS-48 to a house close to Partizan. **DRAGAN ZELENOVIĆ** took her into a separate room and raped her (vaginal penetration). During this incident, he said that she would give birth to good Serbian children. After this sexual assault, an unidentified soldier took her to another room where FWS-48 saw another women being sexually assaulted. At that moment, the soldier who had taken her to that room pushed FWS-48 onto a bed and raped her. On or around 11 August 1992, **DRAGAN ZELENOVIĆ** and other soldiers took FWS-48 to the Hotel Zelengora. When she arrived, many soldiers were present, eating and drinking. Immediately thereafter, a person identified as Spomenko approached FWS-48, took her to a room upstairs and raped her (vaginal penetration). On 12 August 1992, **DRAGAN ZELENOVIĆ** and **GOJKO JANKOVIĆ** took FWS-48 together with FWS-95 and other women to a house in Donje Polje. There, **DRAGAN ZELENOVIĆ** raped FWS-48 twice. That night **DRAGAN ZELENOVIĆ** told FWS-48 that everything would end in a few days. […] From July 1992 to 13 August 1992, FWS-95 was removed to different houses and apartments, almost every night by groups of soldiers, commanded by Dragoljub Kunarac, Janko Janjić and **DRAGAN ZELENOVIĆ.** Sometimes, she was taken alone, sometimes together with other women. On each of these occasions, FWS-95 was raped, (vaginal penetration and fellatio). Sometimes, she was gang-raped. Dragoljub Kunarac, Janko Janjić, **GOJKO JANKOVIĆ** and **DRAGAN ZELENOVIĆ** were among the soldiers who frequently assaulted her. […] By the foregoing acts and omissions in relation to the victims FWS-48, FWS-87 and FWS-95, **DRAGAN ZELENOVIĆ** committed: **Count 41:** Torture, a **CRIME AGAINST HUMANITY** punishable under Article 5 (f) of the Statute of the Tribunal. **Count 42:** Rape, a **CRIME AGAINST HUMANITY** punishable under Article 5 (g) of the Statute of the Tribunal. **Count 43:** Torture, a **VIOLATION OF THE LAWS OR CUSTOMS OF WAR,** punishable under Article 3 of the Statute of the Tribunal and recognised by Common Article 3 (1) (a) (torture) of the Geneva Conventions. **Count 44:** Rape, a **VIOLATION OF THE LAWS OR CUSTOMS OF WAR,** punishable under Article 3 of the Statute of the Tribunal".).

304 *Zelenović* Indictment, paras. 9.1–9.3 ("On or about 30 October 1992, FWS-75, FWS-87 and two other women were taken from Karaman's house to Foča by **DRAGAN ZELENOVIĆ, GOJKO JANKOVIĆ** and Janko Janjić. These women continued to be detained at different houses and apartments, and continued to be subjected to sexual assaults. On or about 30 October 1992, the three above-mentioned perpetrators took FWS-75, FWS-87 and the two other women into an apartment near the Fish Restaurant in Foča. There, all four women were raped by **DRAGAN ZELENOVIĆ, GOJKO JANKOVIĆ** and Janko Janjić. By the foregoing acts and omissions, **GOJKO JANKOVIĆ, DRAGAN ZELENOVIĆ** and Janko Janjić committed: **Count 49:** Rape, a **CRIME AGAINST HUMANITY** punishable under Article 5 (g) of the Statute of the Tribunal. **Count 50:** Rape, a **VIOLATION OF THE LAWS OR CUSTOMS OF WAR,** punishable under Article 3 of the Statute of the Tribunal".).

	7(1) of the Statute for raping Witness FWS-87 (**committing**). - Guilty of **Rape as CAH** (count 49) under Article 7(1) of the Statute for the rapes of Witness FWS-75 and two unidentified women (**co-perpetration**) and for raping Witness FWS-87 (**committing**).[305] - Note: plea agreement: On 14 December 2006, a joint motion was filed by Dragan Zelenović and the Office of the Prosecutor informing the Trial Chamber of an agreement reached between the parties as to the entry of a guilty plea by the accused to seven counts, three of which charge torture as CAH (counts 5, 13 and 41) and four of which charge rape as CAH (counts 6, 14, 42 and 49) and the withdrawal of all other counts against him. On 17 January 2007, Dragan Zelenović entered a guilty plea to counts 5, 6, 13, 14, 41, 42 and 49 and the Trial Chamber entered a finding of guilt. The same day, the Prosecution withrew the remaining counts.[306]
Appeal Judgement	N/A
Legal and Factual Findings and/or Evidence	-Factual findings: -Rape of Witness FWS-75 (counts 5 and 6): "On 3 July 1992, Mr. Zelenović, along with other men, arrested a group of about 60 Muslim women, children and elderly men from Tosanj and Mjesaja and took them to a temporary detention facility called Buk Bijela. At the detention centre, Mr. Zelenović and other men separated the women from the children and interrogated the women about the hiding places of the male villagers and of weapons. The women were threatened with sexual assault and murder. On or about 3 July 1992, Mr. Zelenović and another man interrogated FWS-75 about her village and whether the villagers had weapons. FWS-75 was warned by the other man that she would be raped by soldiers, and killed afterwards, if she did not answer truthfully. In the course of her interrogation she was taken by a soldier to another room where ten soldiers raped her in turn. Mr. Zelenović knew that his action in respect of the interrogation and his omission to act with regard to the threats of rape and death, and the eventual transfer of FWS-75 to the room where she was raped, substantially assisted in the commission of the crime. Mr. Zelenović pleaded guilty to aiding and abetting this rape against FWS-75".[307] - Rapes of Witnesses FWS-87 and FWS-75 and two unidentified women (counts 13 and 14): "On or about 3 July, Mr. Zelenović and three unidentified soldiers interrogated FWS-87, a 15-year-old girl, in a room at Buk Bijela. During the interrogation, Mr. Zelenović and the three soldiers accused the girl of not telling the truth and proceeded to rape her. During the rape one of the soldiers threatened FWS-87 by putting a gun to her head. Mr. Zelenović pleaded guilty to committing this rape against FWS-87. Between 3 and 13 July 1992, the group of women, children, and elderly men who had been detained at Buk Bijela were transferred and detained together with other persons in two classrooms at Foča high school. On or about 6 or 7 July 1992, Mr. Zelenović, in concert with other men, selected four women and girls from the classrooms, among them FWS-75 and FWS-87. Mr. Zelenović led them to another classroom where soldiers were waiting. He then decided which woman should go with which soldier. Mr. Zelenović raped FWS-75, while the other co-perpetrators raped the other women and girls. Mr. Zelenović pleaded guilty to committing the rapes against the four women, as principal perpetrator and as co-perpetrator. Between 8 and 13 July 1992, on

305 *Prosecutor v. Dragan Zelenović*, Case No. IT-96-23/2-S, Sentencing Judgement, 4 April 2007 ("*Zelenović* Sentencing Judgement"), paras. 10, 13, 36, 38, 71.

306 *Zelenović* Sentencing Judgement, paras. 10, 13. See also *Zelenović* Sentencing Judgement, paras. 11–12.

307 *Zelenović* Sentencing Judgement, para. 21 (internal references omitted).

	three occasions, FWS-75 and FWS-87 were taken from Foča high school to various locations. On the first occasion, the women were taken to an apartment owned by Mr. Zelenović. There, Mr. Zelenović and three other men raped FWS-75. Mr. Zelenović also raped FWS-87 on that occasion. On the second occasion, FWS-75 and FWS-87 were taken to another apartment, where Mr. Zelenović again raped them. On the third occasion, Mr. Zelenović took FWS-75 and FWS-87 to an abandoned house in Gornje Polje where he raped FWS-87. Mr. Zelenović pleaded guilty to committing the two rapes against FWS-75 and the three rapes against FWS-87. The physical and psychological health of many of the female detainees seriously deteriorated as a result of the sexual assaults. The detainees lived in constant fear and some of the sexually abused women became suicidal. Others became indifferent as to what happened to them and suffered from depression".[308] - Rapes of Witness FWS-87 (counts 41 and 42): "On 13 July 1992, the detainees at Foča high school were transferred to Partizan Sports Hall where they were detained until 13 August 1992, after which most detainees were deported to Montenegro. The detainees, who numbered about 70, were all Muslim civilians from villages in Foča municipality. Living conditions at Partizan Sports Hall were brutal and the detention was characterized by inhumane treatment, unhygienic conditions, overcrowding, starvation, and physical and psychological torture, including sexual assaults. During July 1992, Mr. Zelenović and other men took FWS-87 away from Partizan Sports Hall and raped her. Mr. Zelenović pleaded guilty to committing this rape against FWS-87".[309] - Rapes of Witnesses FWS-87 and FWS-75 and two unidentified women (count 49): "On or about 3 August 1992, FWS-87 and FWS-75 were taken from Partizan Sports Hall and detained in a house close to Miljevina Hotel known as Karaman's house. On or about 30 October 1992, Mr. Zelenović and two men took FWS-87, FWS-75, and two other women from that house to an apartment in Foča town. There, Mr. Zelenović raped FWS-87 while the other two men raped the other women. The women remained detained at several houses and apartments, and continued to be subject to sexual assaults by various groups of soldiers. Mr. Zelenović pleaded guilty to committing the rapes against the four women, as principal perpetrator and as co-perpetrator".[310] - Gravity of the crimes committed: "The determination of the gravity of the offences also requires consideration of the particular circumstances of the case and the form and degree of the participation of the convicted person in the crimes. Of central concern when assessing the gravity of a crime is the scale of the crime, including the number of victims and its duration. The crimes which Mr. Zelenović has pleaded guilty to were part of a pattern of sexual assaults that took place over a period of several months, and in four different locations, and involved multiple victims. Mr. Zelenović took direct part in the sexual abuse of victims in a number of detention facilities, including the multiple rape of victims FWS-75 and FWS-87. Mr. Zelenović has been found guilty of personally committing nine rapes, eight of which were qualified as both torture and rape. He has also been found guilty of two instances of rape through co-perpetratorship, one of which was qualified as both torture and rape, and one instance of torture and rape through aiding and abetting. Four of the instances of sexual abuse were gang rapes, committed together with three or more other perpetrators. In one of those instances he participated

[308] *Zelenović* Sentencing Judgement, paras. 22–25 (internal references omitted).

[309] *Zelenović* Sentencing Judgement, para. 26 (internal references omitted).

[310] *Zelenović* Sentencing Judgement, para. 27 (internal references omitted).

	as aider and abettor in the rape of FWS-75 by at least ten soldiers, which was so violent that the victim lost consciousness. He participated as co-perpetrator in an incident during which the victim was threatened with a gun to her head while being sexually abused. The Trial Chamber finds that the scale of the crimes committed was large and that Mr. Zelenović's participation in the crimes was substantial. An important factor when assessing the gravity of a crime is the vulnerability of the victims. The victims in this case were arrested and detained under brutal conditions for long periods of time. They were unarmed and defenceless. The victims were therefore in a particularly vulnerable situation at the time of the commission of the crime. In addition, victim FWS-87, who was raped by Mr. Zelenović on numerous occasions, was about 15 years old at the time of the commission of the crimes. This further increases the gravity of the crimes committed against her. Mr. Zelenović was aware, and took advantage of, this vulnerability of the victims. Another important factor is the physical and mental trauma suffered by the victims, even long after the commission of the crime. In 1992, FWS-75 and FWS-87 were 25 and 15 years old, respectively. After their initial arrest, they were taken from one detention centre to another where they were repeatedly sexually abused by Mr. Zelenović and others. The victims of sexual abuse in the detention centres in Foča suffered the unspeakable pain, indignity, and humiliation of being repeatedly violated, without knowing whether they would survive the ordeal. As a result of the violent sexual assaults, the physical and psychological health of many of the victims was seriously damaged. The women and girls in the detention centres lived in constant fear of repeated rapes and sexual assaults. Some became suicidal and others became indifferent to what happened to them. The scars left from the crimes committed against them were deep and might never heal. This, perhaps more than anything, speaks about the gravity of the crimes in this case".[311]

23. Milan **<u>Martić</u>** (Case No. IT-95-11) "***Republic of Serbian Krajina***" From 4 January 1991 until August 1995, held various leadership positions, in the so-called "Serbian Autonomous District (SAO) Krajina" and the so-called "Republic of Serbian Krajina" (RSK), such as President, Minister of Defence and Minister of Internal Affairs.	
Indictment (International sex crimes (or related) charges and	- **Persecutions as CAH** (count 1) under Articles 7(1) (**joint criminal enterprise**) and 7(3) of the Statute (**superior responsibility**) of the Croat, Muslim and other non-Serb civilian population in the Serbian Autonomous District Krajina and city of Zagreb through various crimes, including repeated sexual assaults of civilian detainees.[312] - **Torture as CAH** (count 6), **Inhumane acts as CAH** (count 7), **Torture as a viola-**

[311] *Zelenović* Sentencing Judgement, paras. 38–40 (internal references omitted).

[312] *Prosecutor v. Milan Martić*, Case No. IT-95-11-PT, Amended Indictment, 9 December 2005 ("*Martić* Indictment"), paras. 21–24 ("From on or about 1 August 1991 until 31 December 1995, **Milan MARTIĆ,** acting individually or in concert with other known and unknown members of a joint criminal enterprise, planned, instigated, ordered, committed, or otherwise aided and abetted the planning, preparation, or execution of the persecutions of the Croat, Muslim and other non-Serb civilian population in the SAO Krajina and city of Zagreb in Croatia, and in the Autonomous Region of Krajina ('ARK') in Bosnia and Herzegovina, in particular in Bosanski Novi, Bosanska Gradiška, Prnjavor, and Šipovo. Throughout this period, Serb forces, comprised of JNA, VJ, VRS units, local Serb TO units and TO units from Serbia and Montenegro, local and Serbian MUP police units, including 'Martić's Police,' and paramilitary units, attacked and took control of towns, villages and settlements in the territories listed above. After the take-over, Serb forces in co-operation with the local Serb authorities, including the accused **Milan MARTIĆ**, established a regime of persecutions designed to drive the Croat, Muslim and other non-Serb civilian populations from these territories. These persecutions were based on political, racial or religious grounds and included the following: […] d. The repeated […] sexual assaults […] of Croat, Muslim and other non-Serb civilian detainees in the mentioned detention facilities. […] By these acts and omissions, **Milan MARTIĆ** committed: <u>Count 1:</u> Persecutions on political, racial, and religious grounds, a CRIME AGAINST HUMANITY, punishable under Articles 5(h), and 7(1) and 7(3) of the Statute of the Tribunal".).

mode(s) of liability)	**tion of the laws or customs of war (WC)** (count 8) and **Cruel treatment as a violation of the laws or customs of war (WC)** (count 9) under Articles 7(1) (**joint criminal enterprise**) and 7(3) of the Statute (**superior responsibility**) for various crimes, including the sexual assaults of Croat, Muslim and other non-Serb civilians detained in various detention facilities.[313]
Trial Judgement	- Guilty of **Persecutions as CAH** (count 1) under Article 7(1) of the Statute (**joint criminal enterprise – third category**) of the Croat, Muslim and other non-Serb civilian population through various crimes, including sexual abuses, forced mutual oral sex among detainees or with prison guards and mutual masturbation in the old hospital in Knin.[314] - Guilty of **Torture as CAH** (count 6), **Inhumane acts as CAH** (count 7), **Torture as a violation of the laws or customs of war (WC)** (count 8) and **Cruel treatment as a violation of the laws or customs of war (WC)** (count 9) under Article 7(1) of the Statute (**joint criminal enterprise – third category**) for various crimes, including sexual abuses assaults of Croat, Muslim and other non-Serb civilians detained in the old hospital in Knin, forced mutual oral sex among detainees or with prison guards and mutual masturbation.[315]
Appeal Judgement	- The convictions were affirmed by the Appeals Chamber.[316]
Legal and Factual Findings and/or Evidence	- Legal findings: **- Rape necessarily implies severe pain or suffering:** The Trial Chamber held that rape necessarily implies severe pain or suffering as required by the definition of torture: "In the jurisprudence of the Tribunal several acts have been listed as rising to the level of seriousness necessary to constitute torture. These acts include [...] rape [...]".[317]

313 *Martić* Indictment, paras. 38–41 ("From August 1991 until December 1992, **Milan MARTIĆ**, acting individually or in concert with other known and unknown members of a joint criminal enterprise, planned, instigated, ordered, committed, or otherwise aided and abetted the planning, preparation, or execution of the unlawful confinement or imprisonment under inhumane conditions of the Croat, Muslim and other non-Serb civilian populations in the territories listed above. Members of Martić's Police, acting in co-operation with local Serb authorities and other Serb forces, including Serbian State Security officials and JNA, arrested and detained hundreds of Croat, Muslim and other non-Serb civilians from the territories specified in the following short- and long-term detention facilities: a. Prison in Knin, SAO Krajina run by the JNA, approximately one hundred and fifty detainees. b. Old hospital in Knin, SAO Krajina run by Martić's Police, approximately one hundred and twenty detainees. c. Police station in Titova Korenica run by Martić's Police, ten detainees. d. Bosanska Kostajnica Police Station run by Serb forces, including Martić's Police, eight to ten detainees. e. Bosanski Novi Police Station run by Serb forces, including Martić's Police, at least fifty detainees. f. Sloga Shoe Factory in Prnjavor run by Serb forces, including the Wolves of Vučjak, approximately one hundred and eighty detainees. The living conditions in these detention facilities were brutal and characterised by [...] constant physical and psychological assault, including sexual assault. By these acts and omissions, **Milan MARTIC** committed: [...] Count 6: Torture, a CRIME AGAINST HUMANITY punishable under Article 5(f) and Article 7(1) and Article 7(3) of the Statute of the Tribunal. Count 7: Inhumane acts, a CRIME AGAINST HUMANITY punishable under Article 5(i) and Article 7(1) and Article 7(3) of the Statute of the Tribunal. Count 8: Torture, a VIOLATION OF THE LAWS OR CUSTOMS OF WAR as recognised by Common Article 3 (1)(a) of the Geneva Conventions of 1949, punishable under Article 3 and Article 7(1) and Article 7(3) of the Statute of the Tribunal. Count 9: Cruel treatment, a VIOLATION OF THE LAWS OR CUSTOMS OF WAR as recognised by Common Article 3 (1)(a) of the Geneva Conventions of 1949, punishable under Article 3 and Article 7(1) and Article 7(3) of the Statute of the Tribunal".).

314 *Prosecutor v. Milan Martić*, Case No. IT-95-11-T, Judgement, 12 June 2007 ("*Martić* Trial Judgement"), paras. 288 (and fn. 899), 413–414, 416, 454–455, 480, 518.

315 *Martić* Trial Judgement, paras. 288 (and fn. 899), 413–415, 454–455, 480, 518.

316 *Prosecutor v. Milan Martić*, Case No. IT-95-11-A, Judgement, 8 October 2008, para. 355.

317 *Martić* Trial Judgement, para. 76 (internal reference omitted).

	- Sexual assault constituting persecutions: The Trial Chamber confirmed that sexual assault can constitute persecutions: "The jurisprudence holds that the following acts […] may constitute the underlying acts of the crime of persecution: […] sexual assault […]".[318] - Factual findings: - International sex crimes at the old hospital in Knin: "Former detainees reported that detainees were sexually abused through forced mutual oral sex or oral sex with prison guards, and mutual masturbation […] Luka Brkić [… testified] that he heard that there had been attempts to rape men in the room next to his".[319]

24. Mile **<u>Mrkšić *et al.*</u>** (Case No. IT-95-13/1) "***Vukovar Hospital***"	
- Mile Mrkšić: Colonel in the Yugoslav People's Army (JNA) and commander of the 1st Guards Motorised Brigade and Operational Group South; after the fall of Vukovar, promoted to the rank of general in the JNA and became the commander of the 8th JNA Operational Group in the Kordun area in Croatia. - Miroslav Radić: Captain in the JNA; commanded an infantry company in the 1st Battalion of the 1st Guards Motorised Brigade. - Veselin Šljivančanin: Major in the JNA; security officer of the 1st Guards Motorised Brigade and Operational Group South in charge of a military police battalion subordinated to the 1st Guards Motorised Brigade; after the fall of Vukovar, promoted to the rank of lieutenant colonel and placed in command of the Yugoslav Army (VJ) brigade in Podgorica, Montenegro.	
Indictment (International sex crimes (or related) charges and mode(s) of liability)	All three accused were charged with: **- Persecutions as CAH** (count 1) under Articles 7(1) (**joint criminal enterprise**) and 7(3) of the Statute (**superior responsibility**) of Croats and other non-Serbs who were present in the Vukovar hospital after the fall of Vukovar for various crimes, including sexual assault.[320] **- Torture as CAH** (count 5), **Inhumane acts as CAH** (count 6), **Torture as a violation of the laws or customs of war (WC)** (count 7) and **Cruel treatment as a violation of the laws or customs of war (WC)** (count 8) under Articles 7(1) (**joint criminal enterprise**) and 7(3) of the Statute (**superior responsibility**) for various crimes committed at the Ovčara farm, including the sexual assault of one female detainee.[321]

318 *Martić* Trial Judgement, para.119 (internal reference omitted).

319 *Martić* Trial Judgement, para. 288 and fn. 899 (internal references omitted).

320 *Prosecutor v. Mile Mrkšić et al.*, Case No. IT-95-13/1-PT, Third Consolidated Amended Indictment, 15 November 2004 ("*Mile Mrkšić et al.* Indictment"), paras. 40–42 ("From or about 18 November 1991 until 21 November 1991, **Mile MRKŠIĆ, Miroslav RADIĆ,** and **Veselin ŠLJIVANČANIN**, acting alone or in concert with other known and unknown members of a joint criminal enterprise, planned, instigated, ordered, committed, or otherwise aided and abetted the planning, preparation, or execution of the persecution of Croats and other non-Serbs who were present in the Vukovar Hospital after the fall of Vukovar. This persecution was based on political, racial or religious grounds and included the following: […] b) The cruel or inhumane treatment of Croats and other non-Serbs, including […] sexual assaults […]. By these acts and omissions, **Mile MRKŠIĆ, Miroslav RADIĆ,** and **Veselin ŠLJIVANČANIN** committed: **<u>Count 1:</u>** Persecutions on political, racial, and religious grounds, a **CRIME AGAINST HUMANITY**, punishable under Articles 5(h), and 7(1) and 7(3) of the Statute of the Tribunal".).

321 *Mile Mrkšić et al.* Indictment, paras. 46, 48 ("From on or about 18 November 1991 until 21 November 1991, **Mile MRKŠIĆ, Miroslav RADIĆ,** and **Veselin ŠLJIVANČANIN**, acting individually or in concert with

Trial Judgement	- Miroslav Radić: Acquitted of all counts.[322] - Although Mile Mrkšić was found guilty of torture as a violation of the laws or customs of war (WC) (count 7) and of cruel treatment as a violation of the laws or customs of war (WC) (count 8) and Veselin Šljivančanin was found guilty of torture as a violation of the laws or customs of war (WC) (count 7),[323] the Trial Chamber found that there was no evidence of sexual assault.[324]
Appeal Judgement	- As there was no evidence or factual findings of international sex crimes at trial, the Appeal Judgement was also silent on this issue.[325]
Legal and Factual Findings and/or Evidence	N/A

25. Ramush **<u>Haradinaj *et al.*</u>** (Case No. IT-04-84)
- Ramush Haradinaj: Commander of the Kosovo Liberation Army (KLA) in the Dukagjin operational zone, located to the west of Priština/Prishtinë, which encompassed the municipalities of Peć/Pejë, Dečani/Deçan, Đakovica/Gjakovë, and parts of the municipalities of Istok/Istog and Kline/Klinë; also known as "Smajl". - Idriz Balaj: Member of the KLA, acted as the commander of the special unit known as the "Black Eagles"; subordinate to Ramush Haradinaj; also known as "Toger/Togeri" meaning "Lieutenant".

other known and unknown members of a joint criminal enterprise, planned, instigated, ordered, committed, or otherwise aided and abetted the imprisonment at the Ovčara farm of approximately three hundred Croats and other non-Serbs who were present in the Vukovar Hospital after the fall of Vukovar. The conditions at this detention facility were brutal and characterized by inhumane treatment and constant physical and psychological assault. […] At least one female detainee was sexually assaulted. […] By these acts and omissions, **Mile MRKŠIĆ, Miroslav RADIĆ,** and **Veselin ŠLJIVANČANIN** committed: **<u>Count 5:</u>** Torture, a **CRIME AGAINST HUMANITY** punishable under Article 5(f) and Article 7(1) and Article 7(3) of the Statute of the Tribunal. **<u>Count 6:</u>** Inhumane acts, a **CRIME AGAINST HUMANITY** punishable under Article 5(i) and Article 7(1) and Article 7(3) of the Statute of the Tribunal. **<u>Count 7:</u>** Torture, a **VIOLATION OF THE LAWS OR CUSTOMS OF WAR** as recognised by Common Article 3(1)(a) of the Geneva Conventions of 1949, punishable under Article 3 and Article 7(1) and Article 7(3) of the Statute of the Tribunal. **<u>Count 8:</u>** Cruel Treatment, a **VIOLATION OF THE LAWS OR CUSTOMS OF WAR** as recognised by Common Article 3(1)(a) of the Geneva Conventions of 1949, punishable under Article 3 and Article 7(1) and Article 7(3) of the Statute of the Tribunal".).

322 *Prosecutor v. Mile Mrkšić et al.*, Case No. IT-95-13/1-T, Judgement, 27 September 2007 ("*Mile Mrkšić et al.* Trial Judgement"), para. 714.

323 *Mile Mrkšić et al.* Trial Judgement, paras. 712, 714.

324 *Mile Mrkšić et al.* Trial Judgement, para. 529 ("The Indictment further alleges that at least one female detainee was sexually abused at Ovčara. There were two women among the prisoners held at Ovčara: Ružica Markobašić and Janja Podhorski. Ružica Markobašić was visibly pregnant. She was married to a man believed by the Serb forces to be a 'dangerous Ustasha'. There is no specific evidence about Janja Podhorski. The cause of death of both women was established as wounds from multiple gunshots. Only one witness gave evidence about an act of assault directed against one of the women. P022 testified that Ružica Markobašić was taken outside the hangar and a little later shot in the abdomen with a rifle by a man called Zoran from Karaburma. For reasons set out elsewhere the Chamber is unable to rely on P022's evidence unless it is confirmed by independent evidence. P022's account of Ružica Markobašić's death stands alone. The autopsy report indicates that Ružica Markobašić died from multiple gunshot wounds and, not from a single shot in the abdomen. The Chamber accepts that Ružica Markobašić was killed by shooting in the evening hours of 20 November 1991 at the mass grave. There is no evidence to establish that she was sexually abused".).

325 *Prosecutor v. Mile Mrkšić and Veselin Šljivančanin*, Case No. IT-95-13/1-A, Judgement, 5 May 2009.

<table>
<tr><td colspan="2">- Lahi Brahimaj: Member of the KLA General Staff stationed at the headquarters in Jablanica/Jabllanicë, in Đakovica/Gjakovë municipality; acted as the deputy commander in the Dukagjin area for a short period; subordinate to, and worked closely with, Ramush Haradinaj; also known as "Maxhup" or "Gypsy".</td></tr>
<tr><td>Indictment (International sex crimes (or related) charges and mode(s) of liability)</td><td>All the three accused were charged with:
- Persecutions as CAH or, in the alternative, Torture and Other inhumane acts as CAH (count 1) and Cruel Treatment, Torture, and Outrages upon personal dignity as violations of the laws or customs of war (WC) (count 2) under Article 7(1) of the Statute (joint criminal enterprise for all the three accused or, in the alternative, ordering, instigating or aiding and abetting for Ramush Haradinaj) for various crimes including stripping Witness SST7/38 naked and the sexual assault of Witness SST7/38's sister.[326]
- Persecutions as CAH or, in the alternative, Torture and Other inhumane acts (serious physical and mental injury) as CAH (count 33) and Cruel treatment and Torture as violations of the laws or customs of war (WC) (count 34) under Article 7(1) of the Statute (joint criminal enterprise for all the three accused or, in the alternative, ordering, instigating or aiding and abetting for Ramush Haradinaj and committing, planning or aiding and abetting for Idriz Balaj and Lahi Brahimaj) for various crimes, including kicking Naser Lika in the testicles while he lay on the ground.[327]
- Persecutions as CAH or, in the alternative, Torture, Rape and Other inhumane acts (serious physical and mental injury) as CAH (count 35), Rape as a violation</td></tr>
</table>

[326] *Prosecutor v. Ramush Haradinaj et al.*, Case No. IT-04-84-T, Fourth Amended Indictment, 16 October 2007 ("*Ramush Haradinaj et al.* Indictment"), paras. 54–55 ("The KLA soldiers beat Witness SST7/38's father and permitted Albanian civilians to mistreat the detainees. They stripped Witness SST7/38 naked and placed a knife against the witness' throat, forced the witness to eat a small plastic-coated book, and struck the witness on the face with a pistol. […] Over the next two days, as the convoy continued towards Djoci/Gjocaj, KLA soldiers humiliated and physically mistreated the detainees. […] KLA soldiers sexually assaulted the sister of Witness SST7/38. […] By these acts and omissions **Ramush Haradinaj**, **Idriz Balaj**, and **Lahi Brahimaj** committed as part of the JCE defined in paragraphs 26 and 27 above, the following crimes: **Count 1:** A CRIME AGAINST HUMANITY, Persecution (deportation or forcible transfer, imprisonment, torture, other inhumane acts, abduction), punishable under Article 5(h) and Article 7(1) of the Statute of the Tribunal; **In the alternative**, A CRIME AGAINST HUMANITY, Torture and Other Inhumane Acts (forcible transfer, imprisonment, serious physical and mental injury), punishable under Articles 5(1) and 5(i) and Article 7(1) of the Statute of the Tribunal; **Count 2:** A VIOLATION OF THE LAWS OR CUSTOMS OF WAR, Cruel Treatment and Torture and Outrages upon Personal Dignity, as recognised by Common Articles 3(1)(a) and 3(1)(c) of the Geneva Conventions of 1949, punishable under Article 3 and Article 7(1) of the Statute of the Tribunal. **In the alternative**, **Ramush Haradinaj** ordered, instigated, or aided and abetted the commission of the crimes described in Count 1 and Count 2".).

[327] *Ramush Haradinaj et al.* Indictment, para. 108 ("In July 1998, **Lahi Brahimaj** and other KLA soldiers again abducted Naser Lika at his house in Grabanica/Grabanicë and took him to the Jablanica/Jabllanicë KLA headquarters, where he was brought before **Ramush Haradinaj** and **Idriz Balaj**. **Ramush Haradinaj** told **Lahi Brahimaj** to go ahead with his 'job'. […] KLA soldiers kicked him in the testicles while he lay on the ground. […] By these acts and omissions **Ramush Haradinaj**, **Idriz Balaj**, and **Lahi Brahimaj** committed as part of the JCE defined in paragraphs 26 and 27 above, the following crimes: **Count 33:** A CRIME AGAINST HUMANITY, Persecution (imprisonment, torture, other inhumane acts, abduction), punishable under Article 5(h) and Article 7(1) of the Statute of the Tribunal; **In the alternative**, A CRIME AGAINST HUMANITY, Imprisonment, Torture, and Other Inhumane Acts (serious physical and mental injury), punishable under Articles 5(e), 5(f), and 5(i) and Article 7(1) of the Statute of the Tribunal. **Count 34:** A VIOLATION OF THE LAWS OR CUSTOMS OF WAR, Cruel Treatment and Torture, as recognised by Common Article 3(1)(a) of the Geneva Conventions of 1949, punishable under Article 3 and Article 7(1) of the Statute of the Tribunal. **In the alternative**, **Ramush Haradinaj** ordered, instigated, or aided and abetted the commission of the crimes described in Count 33 and Count 34; **Idriz Balaj** committed, or planned or aided and abetted the commission of, the crimes described in Count 33 and Count 34; and **Lahi Brahimaj** committed, or planned or aided and abetted the commission of, the crimes described in Count 33 and Count 34".).

	of the laws or customs of war (WC) (count 36) and **Cruel Treatment and Torture as violations of the laws or customs of war (WC)** (count 37) under Article 7(1) of the Statute (**joint criminal enterprise** for all the three accused or, in the alternative, **committing** or **planning** for Idriz Balaj) for the repeated rape of Witness SST7/02.[328]
Trial Judgement	- The Trial Chamber found that the three accused should be acquitted of all counts charging crimes against humanity, including counts 1, 33 and 35, because there was no evidence of an attack against a civilian population.[329] - Ramush Haradinaj and Idriz Balaj: Acquitted of all counts.[330] - Lahi Brahimaj: Not guilty of counts relating to international sex crimes.[331]
Appeal Judgement	- The Appeals Chamber, Judge Patrick Robinson dissenting, granted the Prosecution first ground of appeal, quashed the Trial Chamber's decision to acquit the accused on some counts and ordered that the three accused be retried on these counts, including count 34. The Appeals Chamber confirmed the acquittals of the three accused on the other counts relating to international sex crimes.[332] - The Appeals Chamber found that the Trial Chamber acted within the bounds of its discretion in finding that there was reasonable doubt as to whether Idriz Balaj raped Witness 61. Thus, it confirmed Idriz Balaj's acquittal for this crime.[333]
Legal and Factual Findings and/or Evidence	- <u>Legal findings:</u> **- Rape:** The Trial Chamber adopted the definition of rape given in the *Kunarac et al.* case:[334] "The crime of rape consists of the following elements: (a) a sexual penetration however slight: (i) of the vagina or anus of the victim by the penis of the perpetrator or by any other object used by the perpetrator; or (ii) of the mouth of the victim by the penis of the perpetrator; (b) the sexual penetration occurred without the consent of the victim. Consent for this purpose must be consent given voluntarily; and (c) the sexual

328 *Ramush Haradinaj et al.* Indictment, paras. 112–113 ("At the end of July or the beginning of August 1998, **Idriz Balaj** and four uniformed and masked KLA soldiers forced Witness SST7/01 and Witness SST7/02 to walk to the KLA headquarters in Rznić/Irzniq. **Idriz Balaj** took Witness SST7/02 into the building to interrogate her about involvement or collaboration with the Serbian Police and military forces. After interrogating her, **Idriz Balaj** ordered another KLA soldier in the room to leave them alone. **Idriz Balaj** then forced her onto a bed and repeatedly raped her. Witness SST7/02's family reported the rape to the KLA local authorities. **Idriz Balaj** told KLA soldiers that he had been ordered to commit the rape. No action was taken against him. [...] By these acts and omissions **Ramush Haradinaj, Idriz Balaj,** and **Lahi Brahimaj** committed as part of the JCE defined in paragraphs 26 and 27 above, the following crimes: **<u>Count 35:</u>** A CRIME AGAINST HUMANITY, Persecution (imprisonment, torture, rape, other inhumane acts, abduction, forcible labour), punishable under Article 5(h) and Article 7(1) of the Statute of the Tribunal; **<u>In the alternative</u>,** A CRIME AGAINST HUMANITY, Imprisonment, Torture, Rape, and Other Inhumane Acts (forcible labour, serious physical and mental injury), punishable under Articles 5(e), 5(f), 5(g), and 5(i) and Article 7(1) of the Statute of the Tribunal; **<u>Count 36:</u>** A VIOLATION OF THE LAWS OR CUSTOMS OF WAR, Rape, punishable under Article 3 and Article 7(1) of the Statute of the Tribunal; **<u>Count 37:</u>** A VIOLATION OF THE LAWS OR CUSTOMS OF WAR, Cruel Treatment and Torture, as recognised by Common Article 3(1)(a) of the Geneva Conventions of 1949, punishable under Article 3 and Article 7(1) of the Statute of the Tribunal. **<u>In the alternative</u>, Idriz Balaj** committed, or planned the commission of, the crimes described in Count 36 and Count 37".).

329 *Prosecutor v. Ramush Haradinaj et al.*, Case No. IT-04-84-T, Judgement, 3 April 2008 ("*Ramush Haradinaj et al.* Trial Judgement"), para. 122.

330 *Ramush Haradinaj et al.* Trial Judgement, paras. 122, 170, 458, 469, 476, 478, 502–503.

331 *Ramush Haradinaj et al.* Trial Judgement, paras. 122, 170, 458, 476, 478, 504.

332 *Prosecutor v. Ramush Haradinaj et al.*, Case No. IT-04-84-A, Judgement, 19 July 2010 ("*Ramush Haradinaj et al.* Appeal Judgement"), paras. 50, 377.

333 *Ramush Haradinaj et al.* Appeal Judgement, paras. 63–87, 103, 377.

334 ICTY ISCC *Kunarac et al.*, see *supra* p. 528.

	penetration was committed with intent, and with the knowledge that it occurred without the consent of the victim".[335] - Factual findings: - Cruel treatment, torture and outrages upon the personal dignity of Witness 38 and her family (count 2): The Trial Chamber held: "Based on the evidence, the Trial Chamber concludes that sometime in May 1998, KLA soldiers forced Witness 38 and her relatives to join a convoy of people. At some point, they were taken from the convoy and brought to a mill in Junik. She and her father were forced to undress. She further testified that she was kept naked for a considerable amount of time and that she was forced to re-join the convoy while still naked. […] Although the Trial Chamber is convinced that Witness 38 and Witness 58 were taken from their home, it considers that the testimonies of Witness 38 and 58 lack coherence and specificity with regard to important details. In a statement Witness 38 gave to the Serbian MUP in 2002, she stated that she was allowed to dress after half an hour, whereas in Court she testified that she was naked for about two days. Witness 58 confirmed that Witness 38 and her father were mistreated by the KLA soldier, but did not provide any details as to how they were ill-treated. Moreover, although Witness 58 was with Witness 38 for most of the time, she testified that she did not notice that Witness 38 was naked. […] Due to the significant inconsistencies and lack of corroboration on important details, the Trial Chamber is not convinced, beyond a reasonable doubt that Witness 38 or her family were subject ed to serious mental or physical suffering, or injury or to an act constituting a serious attack on human dignity. Likewise, the Trial Chamber cannot conclude that Witness 38 or her family were subjected to acts causing severe humiliation or degradation. The Trial Chamber further finds that the evidence before it is insufficient to conclude that Ramush Haradinaj was at the location where the alleged mistreatment of Witness 38 and her father took place. That a witness appeared to have difficulties in giving an adequate account of what he or she has experienced does not immediately lead the Trial Chamber to find the witness's testimony unreliable. Although the Trial Chamber gained the impression that both Witness 38 and Witness 58 had such difficulties, it considers their testimonies unreliable primarily on the basis of the objective incoherence, inconsistency, and lack of specificity on important details. For these reasons, the Trial Chamber finds that all three Accused should be acquitted of this count".[336] - Rape of Witness 61 and cruel treatment and torture of Witnesses 1 and 61 (counts 36 and 37): The Trial Chamber held: "As referred to above, the Trial Chamber has heard evidence that one night around midnight in the summer of 1998, five armed men in black uniforms with KLA insignia took Witness 61 and Witness 1 from their home to the KLA headquarters in Rznić/Irzniq. There, the witnesses were separated. Witness 1 stated that two of the five armed men put him in a well, where he was left standing in water. Witness 61 testified that two of the others took her into a room, where she was left alone with a man who interrogated her for about half an hour about whether her husband had collaborated with the Serbian police. This man placed several weapons on a table and then repeatedly subjected her to sexual penetration in the course of about one and a half hours. Witness 61 feared that he would kill her. Witness 61 and Witness 1 returned home around 3 to 4 a.m. Witness 61 told Witness 1 about what had happened to her, which Witness 56 overheard. Witness 1 told Witness 61 and Witness 56 that he had been put in a well, and they both noticed that his clothes were wet. On the basis of

335 *Ramush Haradinaj et al.* Trial Judgement, para. 130 (internal reference omitted).

336 *Ramush Haradinaj et al.* Trial Judgement, paras. 168–170.

	this evidence, the Trial Chamber is satisfied that a KLA soldier intentionally sexually penetrated Witness 61, knowing that it occurred without her consent. The Trial Chamber is furthermore convinced that this inflicted severe physical and mental suffering upon her and constituted a serious attack on her human dignity. The Trial Chamber therefore concludes that the KLA soldier committed the crimes of rape and cruel treatment against Witness 61. Considering the circumstances under which the rape was committed, in particular that Witness 61 had been interrogated for about half an hour about whether the husband had collaborated with the Serbian police, the Trial Chamber finds that the rape was aimed at punishing and/or intimidating Witness 61. The Trial Chamber therefore concludes that the KLA soldier committed torture against Witness 61. The Trial Chamber is furthermore convinced that the crimes were closely related to the armed conflict in Kosovo/Kosova. The Trial Chamber finds that it is also not established that KLA soldiers, by putting Witness 1 in a well or by any other acts, caused him serious mental or physical suffering or injury, or seriously attacked his human dignity. Consequently, the Trial Chamber is not convinced beyond a reasonable doubt that cruel treatment or torture was committed against Witness 1. […] Idriz Balaj is also charged, in the alternative, with having committed or planned the crimes described in Counts 36 and 37. Witness 1 stated that one of the five men who took him and Witness 61 from their house was 'Toger', whom Witness 1 knew from before. Witness 61 testified that one of the five men was addressed as 'Toger' by the other four. She also testified that after the incident Witness 1 told her that he had recognized one of these men as 'Toger'. The Trial Chamber finds that 'Toger' was among the men who took Witness 61 and Witness 1 from their home. Based on the whole of the evidence, the Trial Chamber is convinced that 'Toger' is Idriz Balaj. Witness 61 and Witness 1 both stated that two of the five armed men took Witness 1 to the well. Witness 61 testified that she was taken to a room in a house by two of the other men, while Witness 1 stated that Toger took her to the house. Witness 1 was not in a position to see who brought Witness 61 into the room where she was raped. The Trial Chamber finds that this evidence leaves reasonable doubt as to whether it was Toger or another KLA soldier who raped Witness 61. As she testified that it was too dark for her to see the soldiers who came to her house, it is possible that she confused Toger with someone else. Furthermore, Witness 61 did not recognize Idriz Balaj on an ICTY photo board, and stated, when seeing Idriz Balaj on television in 2005, that he did not look like the man who raped her and that he looked older. She also testified in court that she would no longer be able to recognize the man who raped her. The Trial Chamber concludes that her memory of the perpetrator is either insufficient for the purpose of identification or does not fit the likeness of Idriz Balaj. As for Witness 1, he was not in a position to know who committed the rape. Considering the doubts arising from this evidence, the Trial Chamber will not rely on the hearsay evidence according to which Toger admitted to having raped Witness 61. Based on the evidence, the Trial Chamber cannot conclude beyond a reasonable doubt that the person who raped Witness 61 was Idriz Balaj, or that he planned for anyone else to do so. Consequently, the Trial Chamber concludes that Idriz Balaj should be acquitted of committing or planning the commission of the crimes of rape, cruel treatment, and torture against Witness 61".[337] The Appeals Chamber found that the Trial Chamber acted within the bounds of its discretion in finding that there was reasonable doubt as to whether Idriz Balaj raped Witness 61. The Appeals Chamber held: "The Appeals Chamber notes that the Trial Chamber was satisfied that a KLA soldier raped and tortured Witness 61. However, it also observed that there was reasonable doubt as to the identity of this soldier. More specifically, the Trial Chamber considered, *inter alia*, that Witness 61 did not recognise Idriz Balaj when presented with an ICTY photo board; stated, after seeing Idriz Balaj on television in 2005, that he did not look like the man who raped her; and

337 *Ramush Haradinaj et al.* Trial Judgement, paras. 465–469 (internal reference omitted).

	testified that she was not able to recognise the man who raped her anymore. The Trial Chamber further observed that Witness 1 could not have known who committed the rape of Witness 61, given the broader doubts about the identification evidence before it. The Appeals Chamber is satisfied that, given the uncertainties surrounding Witness 61's identification of Idriz Balaj, the evidence of his guilt is not conclusive. The Trial Chamber thus acted within the bounds of its discretion in finding that there was reasonable doubt as to whether he raped and tortured Witness 61. The Appeals Chamber therefore rejects the Prosecution's argument".[338]

26. Rasim **<u>Delić</u>** (Case No. IT-04-83) From 8 June 1993, Commander of the Main Staff of the Army of Bosnia-Herzegovina (ABiH).	
Indictment (International sex crimes (or related) charges and mode(s) of liability)	**- Rape as a violation of the laws or customs of war (WC)** (count 3) and **Cruel treatment as a violation of the laws or customs of war (WC)** (count 4) under Article 7(3) of the Statute (**superior responsibility**) for the rape and the sexual assault of three women, Witnesses DRW-1, DRW-2 and DRW-3, detained at the Kamenica Camp.[339]
Trial Judgement	- Not guilty of count 4 for the alleged sexual assaults of Witnesses DRW-1, DRW-2 and DRW-3 because the Trial Chamber found that the evidence indicated that these victims were subjected to sexual assaults while they were detained at the Vatrostalna facility (and not at the Kamenica Camp), which was not pleaded in the Indictment.[340]

---

338 *Ramush Haradinaj et al.* Appeal Judgement, paras. 72–74 (internal references omitted).

339 *Prosecutor v. Rasim Delić*, Case No. IT-04-83-PT, Amended Indictment, 14 July 2006, paras. 48–50 ("As described in the preceding section and paragraph 40 in particular, three women, DRW 1, DRW 2 and DRW 3, were captured during the attack on Vozuća and taken to the Kamenica Camp on 11 September 1995. The women, who were kept separate from the male prisoners, were beaten and kicked, hit with metal sticks and rifle butts and subjected to sexual assaults, including rape. On or about 13 September 1995, the three female civilians were transferred from the Kamenica Camp to the Vatrostalna Building in the village of Podbrežje, near Zenica, which was serving as the headquarters of the El Mujahed Detachment. On 28 September 1995, these three women were transferred by the Military Police of the ARBiH 3rd Corps from the Vatrostalna Building to the Zenica KP Dom, where they were kept until released on 15 November 1995. The Accused **Rasim DELIĆ** was put on notice that ARBiH soldiers from the El Mujahed Detachment had a propensity to commit crimes, and particularly crimes against captured civilians and that the El Mujahed Detachment was operating at the Kamenica Camp. Nevertheless, the Accused **Rasim DELIĆ** failed to take the necessary and reasonable measures to prevent the crimes that occurred in this camp as described above. **<u>Count 3:</u> RAPE**, a **VIOLATION OF THE LAWS OR CUSTOMS OF WAR**, punishable under Articles 3 and 7(3) of the Statute of the Tribunal. **<u>Count 4:</u> CRUEL TREATMENT**, a **VIOLATION OF THE LAWS OR CUSTOMS OF WAR**, punishable under Articles 3 and 7(3) of the Statute of the Tribunal and recognized by Article 3(1)(a) of the Geneva Conventions".). On 7 December 2007, the Prosecution sought leave to withdraw count 3 of the Indictment. The Trial Chamber denied the Prosecution's request because: "The withdrawal of a count after the accused has entered a plea and on which the Prosecution has led evidence would not be in the interests of justice because the accused could be tried again on that count" and because he is entitled to a formal verdict on that count, once he has entered a plea of not guilty. See Hearing of 10 December 2007, T. 6763. On 14 February 2008, the Defence made an oral submission for acquittal in respect of count 3 of the Indictment. The Prosecution responded on the same day concurring with the Defence that Rasim Delić should be acquitted of Count 3. On 26 February 2008, in its oral judgement of acquittal (Rule 98*bis* of the Rules of Procedure and Evidence), the Trial Chamber found that Rasim Delić has no case to answer in relation to count 3 and acquitted him on this count. See Hearing of 26 February 2008, T. 6891-6893.

340 *Prosecutor v. Rasim Delić*, Case No. IT-04-83-T, Judgement, 15 September 2008 ("*Rasim Delić* Trial Judgement"), paras. 320, 596.

Appeal Judgement	- Rasim Delić died on 16 April 2010 during the appellate proceedings. On 29 June 2010, the Appeal Chamber terminated the appellate proceedings for lack of jurisdiction following the death of Rasim Delić. The Appeal Chamber held that the Trial Judgement shall be considered final.[341]
Legal and Factual Findings and/or Evidence	- Factual findings: - Sexual assault of Witnesses DRW-1, DRW-2 and DRW-3: "As described earlier, DRW-1, DRW-2 and DRW-3 originally formed part of the group of approximately 60 Bosnian Serbs who were captured on 11 September 1995. After their separation from the men, they were briefly detained at the Kesten hall. From there, one or more ABiH soldiers of the 5th Battalion took the three women towards the Battalion's IKM in Marići so that they would not fall into the hands of the Mujahedin. Near Marići, however, a group of Mujahedin took over the women from their ABiH escort. The women were blindfolded and taken away in a van. The van passed through Zavidovići. The Mujahedin eventually delivered the women to a wooden shed in a location which the Trial Chamber is satisfied was the Kamenica Camp. They remained detained in this shed for two days, blindfolded, with hands and legs tied, and without being given any food or water. On both days, Mujahedin entered the shed and beat the three women with their hands, metal sticks and rifle butts. They were also verbally abused and kicked. On the second day, the women underwent questioning by Bosnian Mujahedin, in the course of which they were beaten with fists and given electric shocks on various body parts. Not long thereafter, a Mujahedin entered the shed and threatened to kill the three women with a knife but was prevented from doing so by a Bosnian Mujahedin. In the evening of 13 or 14 September 1995, the women were taken out of the shed and put on a van which brought them to the *Vatrostalna* facility on the outskirts of Zenica, where the command of the EMD was located at the time. At *Vatrostalna*, their blindfolds were removed and their hands and legs were untied. When asked by the women what would happen to them, a Mujahedin told them that 'General Sakib would make the decision after he returns from the frontline.' The three women were interrogated but not beaten while detained there. During one interrogation, a foreign Mujahedin pulled DRW-3's track suit down to her knees and forced her to stand with her back against the wall for a couple of minutes. On a different occasion, a foreign Mujahedin forcibly lifted DRW-1's shirt, took down her pants, and touched her breasts and other private parts. On 28 September 1995, a vehicle manned by Military Police of the ABiH 3rd Corps arrived at *Vatrostalna* and transported the three women to the *KP Dom* facility in Zenica. They were eventually released from the *KP Dom* on 15 November 1995. Two of the women described that, as a result of their detention, they are still traumatised and have ongoing health problems. The Trial Chamber finds that, during their detention at Kamenica Camp, DRW-1, DRW-2 and DRW-3 were routinely subjected by EMD members to acts amounting to serious mental and physical suffering, including beatings, as well as the infliction of electric shocks. The Trial Chamber further finds that none of the victims took an active part in hostilities at the time of the mistreatment. The Trial Chamber therefore finds that the Prosecution has proved beyond reasonable doubt the elements of cruel treatment as a violation of the laws or customs of war (Count 4). In relation to this finding, it should be noted that the Indictment alleges that DRW-1, DRW-2 and DRW-3 were subjected to sexual assaults while they were detained in the Kamenica Camp. However, the evidence indicates that these victims were subjected to sexual assaults while they were detained at the *Vatrostalna* facility. Because no sexual assaults at *Vatrostalna* are alleged in the Indictment, the Trial Chamber does not base its finding concerning Count 4 on that evidence".[342]

341 *Prosecutor v. Rasim Delić*, Case No. IT-04-83-A, Decision on the Outcome of the Proceedings, 29 June 2010, paras. 8, 15–16.

342 *Rasim Delić* Trial Judgement, paras. 315–320 (internal references omitted).

<table>
<tr><td colspan="2">27. Milan <u>Milutinović et al.</u> (Case No. IT-05-87) "Kosovo"

- Milan Milutinović: From 21 December 1997 until 29 December 2002, President of Serbia and a member of the Supreme Defence Council of the Federal Republic of Yugoslavia (Serbia and Montenegro).
- Nikola Šainović: From February 1994 until November 2000, Deputy Prime Minister of the Federal Republic of Yugoslavia (Serbia and Montenegro).
- Dragoljub Ojdanić: From 24 November 1998, Chief of the General Staff of the Yugoslav Army (VJ); from 15 February 2000 until 3 November 2000, Minister of Defence of the Federal Republic of Yugoslavia (Serbia and Montenegro).
- Nebojša Pavković: From 25 December 1998 until early 2000, Commander of the Third Army of the VJ; from February 2000 until 24 June 2002, Chief of the General Staff of the VJ.
- Vladimir Lazarević: From 1998, Chief of Staff of the Priština Corps of the VJ; from 25 December 1998, Commander of the Priština Corps; from 28 December 1999, Chief of Staff of the Third Army of the VJ; from 13 March 2000, Commander of the Third Army of the VJ.
- Sreten Lukić: From May 1998, Head of the Serbian Ministry of Internal Affairs (MUP) Staff for Kosovo & Metohija; from June 1999, Assistant Chief of the Public Security Service (RJB) and the Chief of Border Administration of the Border Police in the MUP; from 31 January 2001, Assistant Minister and Chief of the RJB.</td></tr>
<tr><td>Indictment[343] (International sex crimes (or related) charges and mode(s) of liability)</td><td>All accused were charged with:
- Deportation as CAH (count 1) and Other Inhumane acts (forcible transfer) as CAH (count 2) under Articles 7(1) and 7(3) of the Statute (superior responsibility) for deliberately creating an atmosphere of fear and oppression through various crimes, including the sexual assault of Kosovo Albanian women, in order to forcibly displace and deport Kosovo Albanian civilians. These crimes include: (i) the sexual assault of Kosovo Albanian women en route from the city of Prizren and the Albanian border from 28 March 1999; (ii) the sexual assault of Kosovo Albanian women in a barn in Ćirez/Qirez in the municipality of Srbica/Skenderaj; (iii) the sexual assault of Kosovo Albanian women during forced expulsion in the town of Kosovska Mitrovica/Mitrovicë between 25 March and mid-April 1999; (iv) the sexual assault of Kosovo Albanian women during the course of forced expulsions in the city of Priština/Pristinë between 24 March and the end of May 1999; and (v) the sexual assault of three Kosovo Albanian women in a building at night in the municipality of Dečani/Deçan, on or about 29 March 1999.[344]</td></tr>
</table>

343 For the general background to the charges, see *Prosecutor v. Milan Milutinović et al.*, Case No. IT-05-87-PT, Third Amended Joinder Indictment, 21 June 2006 ("*Milan Milutinović et al.* Indictment"), para. 27 ("In addition to the deliberate destruction of property owned by Kosovo Albanian civilians, forces of the FRY and Serbia committed widespread or systematic acts of brutality and violence against Kosovo Albanian civilians in order to perpetuate the climate of fear, create chaos and a pervading fear for life. Forces of the FRY and Serbia went from village to village and, in the towns and cities, from area to area, threatening and expelling the Kosovo Albanian population. […] Many Kosovo Albanians who were not directly forcibly expelled from their communities fled as a result of the climate of terror created by the widespread or systematic beatings, harassment, sexual assaults, unlawful arrests, killings, shelling and looting carried out across the province".).

344 *Milan Milutinović et al.* Indictment, paras. 72 (b)-(c), (f)-(g), (l), 73 ("Beginning on or about 1 January 1999 and continuing until 20 June 1999, forces of the FRY and Serbia, acting at the direction, with the encouragement, or with the support of **MILAN MILUTINOVIĆ, NIKOLA ŠAINOVIĆ, DRAGOLJUB OJDANIĆ, NEBOJŠA PAVKOVIĆ, VLADIMIR LAZAREVIĆ,** Vlastimir Đorđević and **SRETEN LUKIĆ** perpetrated the actions set forth in paragraphs 25–32, which resulted in the forced deportation of approximately 800,000 Kosovo Albanian civilians. To facilitate these expulsions and displacements, forces of the FRY and Serbia deliberately created an atmosphere of fear and oppression through the use of force, threats of force and acts of violence, as described above in paragraphs 25–32. Throughout Kosovo, forces of

	- **Persecutions as CAH** (count 5) under Articles 7(1) and 7(3) of the Statute (**superior responsibility**) of Kosovo Albanian population for various crimes, including sexual assaults by forces of the Federal Republic of Yugoslavia and Serbia.[345]

the FRY and Serbia systematically [...] sexually assaulted Kosovo Albanian women. These actions were undertaken in all areas of Kosovo, and these deliberate means and methods were used throughout the province, including the following municipalities: [...] b. Prizren: [...] From 28 March 1999, in the city of Prizren, forces of the FRY and Serbia went from house to house, ordering Kosovo Albanian residents to leave. They were forced to join convoys of vehicles and persons travelling on foot to the Albanian border. En route, members of the forces of the FRY and Serbia [...] separated Kosovo Albanian women from the convoy and sexually assaulted the women. [...] c. Srbica/Skenderaj: Beginning on or about 25 March 1999, forces of the FRY and Serbia attacked and destroyed the villages of Vojnike/Vocnjak, Leocina/Lecine, Kladernica/Klladernicë, Turicevac/Turiçec and Izbica/Izbicë by shelling and burning. [...] Some women and children were taken away by members of the forces of the FRY and Serbia and held in a barn in Cirez/Qirez. The women were subjected to sexual assault [...]. At least eight of the women were killed after being sexually assaulted, and their bodies were thrown into three wells in the village of Cirez/Qirez. [...] f. Kosovska Mitrovica/Mitrovicë: beginning on or about 25 March 1999 and continuinthrough the middle of April 1999, forces of the FRY and Serbia began moving systematically through the town of Kosovska Mitrovica/Mitrovicë. They entered the homes of Kosovo Albanians and ordered the residents to leave their houses at once and go to the bus station. [...] Over a three-week period the forces of the FRY and Serbia continued to expel the Kosovo Albanian residents of the town. During this period, Kosovo Albanian women were sexually assaulted. A similar pattern was repeated in other villages in the Kosovska Mitrovica/Mitrovicë municipality, where forces of the FRY and Serbia forced Kosovo Albanians from their homes and destroyed the villages. The Kosovo Albanian residents of the municipality were forced to join convoys going to the Albanian border via the towns of Srbica/Skenderaj, Peć/Pejë, Đakovica/Gjakovëand Prizren. [...] g. Priština/Prishtinë: Beginning on or about 24 March 1999 and continuing through the end of May 1999, forces of the FRY and Serbia went to the homes of Kosovo Albanians in the city of Priština/Prishtinë and forced the residents to leave. [...] During the course of these forced expulsions, [...] several women were sexually assaulted. [...] l. Dečani/Deçan: On or about 29 March 1999, forces of the FRY and Serbia surrounded and attacked the village of Beleg, and other surrounding villages in the Dečani/Deçan municipality. Forces of the FRY and Serbia went from house to house and told villagers to leave their houses immediately. [...] Men were separated from women and children and taken to the basement of a building near the field. Women and children were ordered to go to another building. During the night at least 3 women were sexually assaulted. [...] By these acts and omissions, **MILAN MILUTINOVIĆ, NIKOLA ŠAINOVIĆ, DRAGOLJUB OJDANIĆ, NEBOJŠA PAVKOVIĆ, VLADIMIR LAZAREVIĆ,** Vlastimir Đorđević and **SRETEN LUKIĆ** planned, instigated, ordered, committed or otherwise aided and abetted the planning, preparation or execution of: **Count 1:** Deportation, a **CRIME AGAINST HUMANITY**, punishable under Article 5(d) of the Statute of the Tribunal. With respect to those Kosovo Albanians who were internally displaced within the territory of Kosovo, the Prosecutor re-alleges and incorporates by reference paragraphs 16–69, and 71–72, and, in particular, paragraph 29. By these acts and omissions, **MILAN MILUTINOVIĆ, NIKOLA ŠAINOVIĆ, DRAGOLJUB OJDANIĆ, NEBOJŠA PAVKOVIĆ, VLADIMIR LAZAREVIĆ,** Vlastimir Đorđević and **SRETEN LUKIĆ** planned, instigated, ordered, committed or otherwise aided and abetted the planning, preparation or execution of: **Count 2:** Other Inhumane Acts (Forcible Transfer), a **CRIME AGAINST HUMANITY**, punishable under Article 5(i) of the Statute of the Tribunal".).

345 *Milan Milutinović et al.* Indictment, para. 77(c) ("Beginning on or about 1 January 1999 and continuing until 20 June 1999, the forces of the FRY and Serbia, acting at the direction, with the encouragement, or with the support of **MILAN MILUTINOVIĆ, NIKOLA ŠAINOVIĆ, DRAGOLJUB OJDANIĆ, NEBOJŠA PAVKOVIĆ, VLADIMIR LAZAREVIĆ,** Vlastimir Đorđević and **SRETEN LUKIĆ**, utilised the means and methods set forth in paragraphs 25 through 32 to execute a campaign of persecution against the Kosovo Albanian population, including Kosovo Albanian civilians based on political, racial, or religious grounds. Each of the accused intended to discriminate against the Kosovo Albanian population on political, racial or religious grounds or was aware of the substantial likelihood that the forces of the FRY and Serbia would perpetrate the crimes set forth in paragraphs 25 through 32 against the Kosovo Albanian population on political, racial, or religious grounds, as is evident from, among other things, the overwhelming predominance of Kosovo Albanians of Muslim faith among the victims of crimes and the widespread use of terms derogatory to Kosovo Albanians. These persecutions included, but were not limited to, the following means: [...] c. The sexual assault by forces of the FRY and Serbia of Kosovo Albanians, in particular women, including the sexual assaults described in paragraphs 27 and 72. [...] By these acts and omissions, **MILAN MILUTI-**

Trial Judgement	- Milan Milutinović: Not guilty of all the counts in the Indictment.[346] - Nikola Šainović: Although Nikola Šainović was found guilty of counts 1 to 5 of the Indictment, the Trial Chamber found that, with respect to the sexual assault charges that were proved (in Beleg and Ćirez/Qirez), the Prosecution failed to adduce evidence that convinced the Chamber that these sexual assaults were reasonably foreseeable to Nikola Šainović. The Trial Chamber further found that Nikola Šainović lacked knowledge of sexual assaults.[347] - Dragoljub Ojdanić: Not guilty of count 5. Although Dragoljub Ojdanić was found guilty of counts 1 and 2, the Trial Chamber found that, while the forcible displacements were part of the VJ and MUP organised campaign, it was not satisfied beyond reasonable doubt that sexual assaults were intended aims of this campaign. The Trial Chamber found that it was not proved that Dragoljub Ojdanić was aware that the VJ and MUP were going into some specific crime sites in order to commit sexual assaults and, therefore, the Trial Chamber found that the mental element of aiding and abetting was not established in relation to these crimes. Moreover, the Trial Chamber did not find that information regarding the specific sexual assaults, for which it was proved that the VJ was responsible, was available to Dragoljub Ojdanić or that he had reason to know about them.[348] - Nebojša Pavković: Guilty of **Persecutions as CAH** (count 3) under Article 7(1) of the Statute (**joint criminal enterprise**) for various crimes, including the sexual assaults committed in Dečani/Deçan and in Ćirez/Qirez in the municipality of Srbica/Skenderaj.[349] - Vladimir Lazarević: Not guilty of count 5. Although Vladimir Lazarević was found guilty of counts 1 and 2, the Trial Chamber found that, while the forcible displacements were part of the VJ and MUP organised campaign, it was not satisfied beyond reasonable doubt that sexual assaults were intended aims of this campaign. The Trial Chamber found that was not proved that Vladimir Lazarević was aware that the VJ and MUP were going into some specific crime sites in order to commit sexual assaults and, therefore, the Trial Chamber found that the mental element of aiding and abetting was not established in relation to these crimes. Moreover, the Trial Chamber did not find that information regarding the specific sexual assaults, for which it was proved that the VJ was responsible, was available to Vladimir Lazarević or that he had reason to know about them.[350] - Sreten Lukić: Although Sreten Lukić was found guilty of counts 1 to 5 of the Indictment, the Trial Chamber found that, with respect to the sexual assault charges that were proved (in Beleg and Ćirez/Qirez), the Prosecution failed to adduce evidence that convinced the Chamber that these sexual assaults were reasonably foreseeable to Sreten Lukić. The Trial Chamber further found that Sreten Lukić lacked knowledge of the sexual assaults.[351] - <u>Note:</u> Judge Ali Nawaz Chowhan appended a partially dissenting opinion stating the

NOVIĆ, NIKOLA ŠAINOVIĆ, DRAGOLJUB OJDANIĆ, NEBOJŠA PAVKOVIĆ, VLADIMIR LAZAREVIĆ, Vlastimir Đorđević and **SRETEN LUKIĆ** planned, instigated, ordered, committed or otherwise aided and abetted the planning, preparation or execution of: **Count 5:** Persecutions on political, racial and religious grounds, a **CRIME AGAINST HUMANITY**, punishable under Article 5(h) of the Statute of the Tribunal".).

346 *Prosecutor v. Milan Milutinović et al.*, Case No. IT-05-87-T, Judgement, 26 February 2009 ("*Milan Milutinović et al.* Trial Judgement"), vol. III, paras. 284, 1207.

347 *Milan Milutinović et al.* Trial Judgement, vol. III, paras. 472, 476, 1208.

348 *Milan Milutinović et al.* Trial Judgement, vol. III, paras. 629, 633, 635, 1209.

349 *Milan Milutinović et al.* Trial Judgement, vol. III, paras. 766, 785, 788, 1210.

350 *Milan Milutinović et al.* Trial Judgement, vol. III, paras. 928, 933, 935, 1211.

351 *Milan Milutinović et al.* Trial Judgement, vol. III, paras. 1135, 1139, 1212.

	following: "I respectfully differ from the view expressed by the majority regarding the foreseeability of sexual assault of Kosovo Albanian women to members of the joint criminal enterprise. In a conflict like the one we are addressing, which involved able-bodied military and security forces acting pursuant to a common plan to use violence to remove large numbers of Kosovo Albanian civilians, including women, from their homes, prudence and common sense, as well as the past history of conflicts in the region, lead me to think that sexual assaults, like murders, were certainly foreseeable realities. Thus, I consider that it was foreseeable to the Accused found to have participated in the joint criminal enterprise that Kosovo Albanian women and girls would be raped and sexually assaulted in the execution of their criminal enterprise, and would find them responsible by way of the third form of joint criminal enterprise for the sexual assaults proved in the present case".[352]
Appeal Judgement	N/A (The appellate proceedings are in progress.)
Legal and Factual Findings and/or Evidence	- <u>Legal findings:</u> **- Sexual assault constituting persecutions:** The Trial Chamber confirmed that sexual assault can constitute persecutions. The Trial Chaber held: "Having been classified as falling within crimes such as 'torture' and 'inhumane acts', among others, sexual assault offences may reach the requirement of gravity equal to that of other crimes against humanity enumerated in Article 5 of the Statute, particularly since both 'torture' and 'inhumane acts' are expressly listed as underlying offences within the ambit of Article 5. The Chamber therefore concludes that 'sexual assault' is a form of persecution and thus is punishable as a crime against humanity, so long as the equal gravity requirement is satisfied. In reaching its conclusions concerning the elements of 'sexual assault' below, the Chamber has throughout been mindful of the equal gravity requirement that qualifies the offence as a form of persecution".[353] **- Elements of sexual assault:** The Trial Chamber established the elements of the crime of sexual assault as follows: "Having established that 'sexual assault' fulfils the criteria for consideration as a form of persecution, the elements of the offence that are here applied must now be clarified. As noted above, the ICTR explicitly held in *Akayesu* that '[s]exual violence is not limited to physical invasion of the human body and may include acts which do not involve penetration or even physical contact' including forced nudity. In *Brđanin*, the Trial Chamber found that the offence of sexual assault 'embraces all serious abuses of a sexual nature inflicted upon the integrity of a person by means of coercion, threat of force or intimidation in a way that is humiliating and degrading to the victim's dignity.' These cases provide some indication of the types of conduct short of sexual penetration that may be considered to constitute 'sexual assault', rather than the narrower offence of rape, which does require such penetration. However, no international treaty sets out the elements of sexual assault as an offence recognised by international law. Similarly, the elements of sexual assault in customary international law have never been elaborated. Analysis of the situation in a number of common law and civil law jurisdictions leads to the conclusion that, while the majority do not have a codified, elements-based definition of the term 'sexual assault', they do generally have provisions on the prosecution and punishment of offences similar to sexual assault. These domestic systems often provide for a range of different types of offences that could be considered to fall within the more general category of sexual assault that is here under

352 *Milan Milutinović et al.* Trial Judgement, vol. III, Partially Dissenting Opinion of Judge Chowan, p. 481.

353 *Milan Milutinović et al.* Trial Judgement, vol. I, para. 193 (internal reference omitted). See also *Milan Milutinović et al.* Trial Judgement, vol. I, paras. 183–192.

	discussion. Overall, analysis of domestic approaches to sexual assault offences shows some common elements. Generally, it is required that sexual assault be committed through the exercise of violence, force, constraint or other form of coercion on the victim. Threat to use violence against the victim or, in some cases, against a third person, can also be sufficient. However, a number of jurisdictions place the emphasis upon absence of the victim's consent rather than highlighting the use of violence or threats by the perpetrator. However, the Chamber observes that the apparent disparity in approach is of a formal nature only. As stated above, the Trial Chamber in *Brđanin* found that for a finding of the offence of sexual assault, a person must be subjected to 'coercion, threat of force, or intimidation'. In *Akayesu*, the ICTR embraced a broad understanding of coercion, holding that it may be evidenced by '[t]hreats, intimidation, extortion and other forms of duress which prey on fear or desperation' as well as be inherent 'in certain circumstances, such as armed conflict'. In this light, when a victim performed an act without giving genuine consent to the same, the necessary implication is that that person had been coerced to do so. Therefore, in this respect, domestic solutions are consonant with the existing international jurisprudence. The Statute and jurisprudence of the Tribunal only contain rape and sexual assault, rather than other categories of offences of a sexual nature. The Trial Chamber is, therefore, of the view that a broad approach to the requisite elements is appropriate, so long as the equal gravity requirement for its characterisation as a form of persecution is taken account of. Thus, the Chamber considers that 'sexual assault' may be committed in situations where there is no physical contact between the perpetrator and the victim, if the actions of the perpetrator nonetheless serve to humiliate and degrade the victim in a sexual manner. Indeed, limiting the elements of sexual assault to non-consensual touching would contradict existing jurisprudence such as in the case of *Akayesu*, where it was held that '[s]exual violence is not limited to physical invasion of the human body and may include acts which do not involve penetration or even physical contact' including forced nudity. Furthermore, the Chamber considers that it would be inappropriate to place emphasis on the sexual gratification of the perpetrator in defining the elements of 'sexual assault'. In the context of an armed conflict, the sexual humiliation and degradation of the victim is a more pertinent factor than the gratification of the perpetrator, and it is this element that provides specificity to the offence. Any form of coercion, including acts or threats of violence, detention, and generally oppressive surrounding circumstances, is simply evidence that goes to proof of lack of consent. In addition, the Trial Chamber is of the view that when a person is detained, particularly during an armed conflict, coercion and lack of consent can be inferred from these circumstances. In this regard, the force required for a sexual assault is only that which is necessary to perform the act of a sexual nature, and actual coercion is not a required element. The Chamber therefore finds that, in addition to the general requirements of crimes against humanity, and the specific requirements of persecutions, the Prosecution must prove that the following elements have been satisfied beyond a reasonable doubt, in order to establish that the underlying offence of sexual assault as a form of persecution, as a crime against humanity, has been committed: (a) The physical perpetrator commits an act of a sexual nature on another, including requiring that person to perform such an act. (b) That act infringes the victims's physical integrity or amounts to an outrage to the victim's personal dignity. (c) The victim does not consent to the act. (d) The physical perpetrator intentionally commits the act. (e) The physical perpetrator is aware that the act occurred without the consent of the victim".[354]

[354] *Milan Milutinović et al.* Trial Judgement, vol. I, paras. 194–201 (internal references omitted).

- Rape:

The Trial Chamber adopted the definition of rape given in the *Kunarac et al.* case:[355] "In this respect, the Chamber recalls that, after extensive reviews of the law pertaining to rape in international instruments and national jurisdictions, the *Furundžija* and *Kunarac et al.* Trial Chambers articulated the following definition of rape in international law: '[T]he *actus reus* of the crime of rape in international law is constituted by: the sexual penetration, however slight: (a) of the vagina or anus of the victim by the penis of the perpetrator or any other object used by the perpetrator; or (b) of the mouth of the victim by the penis of the perpetrator; where such sexual penetration occurs without the consent of the victim. Consent for this purpose must be consent given voluntarily, as a result of the victim's free will, assessed in the context of the surrounding circumstances. The *mens rea* is the intention to effect this sexual penetration, and the knowledge that it occurs without the consent of the victim'".[356]

- Factual and legal findings:

- Rapes of two Kosovo Albanian women and sexual assaults of two others in the village of Beleg, in Dečani/Deçan municipality, on the night of 29 March 1999:

"With the onset of darkness the women, including K20 and K58, were taken into two rooms and the courtyard cattle shed, or stable, of a house in Beleg. Later that evening two or three VJ soldiers and a policeman, at least one of whom spoke Albanian, entered one of the rooms where the women were being detained and said they needed some 'girls' for cleaning. Some older women volunteered, but the soldiers used torch lights to identify five younger women or girls. K20, one of the five thus selected, explained how, after offering them cigarettes and shining the torch on their faces, the soldiers told two of the girls to return to the room. The remaining three were then taken to another house. K20 was taken into a bathroom by herself and was then forcibly undressed and raped by one of the soldiers. As this was happening the policeman and other soldiers stood in the doorway occasionally illuminating the scene with a torch. Once the first soldier had finished, K20 tried to dress herself, but she was slapped by the policeman causing her to lose consciousness temporarily. She was then raped by a second soldier, and then again by a third. Although the policeman told her after the third soldier that he would be the last, a fourth soldier entered the bathroom from the hallway and also raped her. K20 could not describe the individual soldiers, but testified that they were wearing green camouflage uniforms, some with insignia, and all spoke Serbian. While K20 was being raped in the bathroom, she could hear one of the other two girls who had been taken to the house with her screaming in the next room. When K20 was allowed to leave the house, the Albanian-speaking police officer stated to her 'the [KLA] did worse than they are doing. You can handle them.' As she was leaving, she also heard the second of the other two selected girls screaming. About half an hour after she was returned to the place where the rest of the women were being detained, one of the two girls who had been taken away with her returned, followed by the other some time later. The first said that she had not been required to do anything; the second said merely that she had had to clean, but looked 'lost'. K20 concluded that these two girls had also been raped, as 'their screams were the same as my screams while they raped me.' K58 described how, while K20 and the two other girls were absent from the room, more young women were selected by 'paramilitaries', who came to the rooms about four or five times, until approximately 20 young women or girls had been taken, with the last being returned at around 5:00 a.m. These girls returned dishevelled and crying, and K58 overheard one of them telling her mother that she had been raped. K20's compelling account of her ordeal, supported by the evidence of K58, convinces the Chamber that she was raped by VJ soldiers. In the

[355] ICTY ISCC *Kunarac et al.*, see *supra* p. 528.

[356] *Milan Milutinović et al.* Trial Judgement, vol. I, para. 203 (internal reference omitted).

	circumstances described by K20 and K58, where young women were selected and taken away for lengthy periods of time throughout the night, and in light of K20's description of the screaming she heard from the other two young women who were taken away at the same time as herself, the Chamber considers that the only reasonable inference is that these two at least were also sexually assaulted and that the woman whose complaint was overheard by K58 was also raped. The women were kept in the house until around 8:00 or 9:00 the next morning, 30 March 1999, when they were told by a policeman, who was described by K20 as 'the Commander', to leave the village for Albania. K58 reported that the women were told: 'Go to Albania – you have asked for NATO'. Led by three APCs (one army and two police), the displaced villagers were then put into a convoy and made to leave along with ten of the older men [who] were allowed to go with the convoy to drive the tractors".[357]
	"The Chamber finds that on or around 28 March 1999 MUP personnel, including PJP members, and VJ personnel, including VJ 'paramilitary' reservists, arrived in Beleg and detained, harassed, and strip searched Kosovo Albanians from that village and nearby villages, physically assaulted a number of the Kosovo Albanian men, and seized the villagers' identity documents. On or around 29 March 1999 at least four of the young women who had been detained were taken by some of these VJ and MUP personnel to a building, where two were raped by them, and two others were sexually assaulted. The next day the villagers were forced to leave Beleg and go to Albania, although a number of men were kept behind. The Chamber is satisfied that the VJ and MUP were not engaged in combat with the KLA in Beleg at this time and that there were no NATO airstrikes in the area. It finds that VJ and MUP personnel operated together in Dečani/Deçan to ensure, and control the direction of, the movement of the Kosovo Albanians whom they expelled. The Chamber thus finds that the expulsion of the group of Kosovo Albanians from Beleg was carried out in an organised manner utilising forces and resources under the control of the FRY and Serbian state authorities, including the VJ and MUP".[358]
	"The Chamber has found that on or around 28 March 1999 MUP and VJ forces targeted Kosovo Albanian civilians in the village of Beleg in Dečani/Deçan. These civilians were detained, harassed, physically assaulted, and were then expelled from the village in an organised manner by MUP and VJ forces. Eventually they crossed the border and went to Albania. The Chamber is satisfied that these events amounted to an attack upon the civilian population of the village, that this attack was carried out in a systematic manner, and that it was part of a widespread and systematic attack against Kosovo Albanian civilians in at least 13 municipalities of Kosovo. These actions of VJ and MUP forces were clearly part of the broader attack on the civilian population, as identity documents were taken from the displaced people, they were mistreated, and they were ordered to go to Albania. Furthermore, the physical perpetrators, who made comments such as 'Go to Albania – you have asked for NATO', were undoubtedly aware that they were acting in the context of a larger attack upon the Kosovo Albanian population. As noted above, MUP and VJ forces operating together expelled the civilians from the village of Beleg in an organised manner. It is also clear from their comments during these expulsions that these physical perpetrators intended the Kosovo Albanians to cross the border to Albania. There was no legitimate reason for these expulsions of Kosovo Albanians who were in Beleg lawfully. The Chamber finds, therefore, that all of the elements of deportation, as a crime against humanity punishable under Article 5(d) of the Statute, are satisfied. Similarly, and in light of the various witness accounts of the violence, fear, and intimidation that these forces systematically effected in Beleg, the Chamber is convinced that the elements of the crime of other

357 *Milan Milutinović et al.* Trial Judgement, vol. II, paras. 61–65 (internal references omitted).

358 *Milan Milutinović et al.* Trial Judgement, vol. II, paras. 68–69. See also *Milan Milutinović et al.* Trial Judgement, vol. II, para. 1158.

inhumane acts (forcible transfer), punishable under Article 5(i) of the Statute, are also satisfied. The Chamber is in no doubt that at least two women who were detained in Beleg by VJ and MUP forces were subjected to sexual intercourse, and another two women were subjected to acts of a sexual nature where they plainly did not consent and those attacking them knew that they did not consent. Thus, their fundamental right to physical integrity was violated, which satisfies the elements of sexual assault. Given that the Indictment charges sexual assault only as a form of persecution, the Prosecution must prove that the perpetrators acted with the intent to discriminate against Kosovo Albanians as an ethnic group. The physical perpetrators carrying out these rapes and sexual assaults made comments such as 'the [KLA] did worse than they are doing. You can handle them.' Consequently, the Chamber concludes that they carried out the rapes and sexual assaults deliberately, with the intent to discriminate against the Kosovo Albanians as an ethnic group. Thus all of the elements sexual assault as a form of persecution, a crime against humanity punishable under Article 5(h) of the Statute, are satisfied".[359]

- Alleged sexual assault of Kosovo Albanian women en route from the city of Prizren to the Albanian border:

"The Trial Chamber heard no evidence regarding the charges in the Indictment that Kosovo Albanian women were separated from the convoy and sexually assaulted".[360]

- Sexual assaults of Kosovo Albanian women in a barn in Ćirez/Qirez in Srbica/Skenderaj municipality:

"Direct evidence relating to the charges of sexual assault in the village of Ćirez/Qirez around mid-April 1999 was given by two eye-witnesses, namely Xhevahire Rrahmani and K24. Their testimony was largely unchallenged and, aside from some discrepancies in the identification of uniforms of the perpetrators of these offences, generally consistent. The Chamber also admitted into evidence certain forensic information relevant to the fate of some of the alleged victims which is consistent with the evidence of Rrahmani and K24. The Chamber, therefore, accepts their evidence".[361]

"Direct evidence relating to the charges of sexual assault in the village of Ćirez/Qirez around mid-April 1999 was given by two witnesses, namely Xhevahire Rrahmani and K24. Although consistent on the events that took place in that village, the two women were not consistent when it came to the identification of the forces involved, as will be outlined below. The Chamber also received certain forensic information relevant to the fate of some of the women who are alleged to have been sexually assaulted".[362]

"The women were handed over to another group of men and then taken to a barn in Ćirez/Qirez. According to K24 they were handed over to three men wearing camouflage uniforms with a blend of dark green, yellow, and red marks, and with tiger badges on their sleeves, who took them to the barn. Rrahmani, however, testified that they were handed over to a group of men, two of whom then took them to the barn, while the third appeared later. The two men were older, with beards, and were wearing black and brown uniforms. Both K24 and Rrahmani were relatively consistent in their accounts of the events that took place in and outside of the barn. According to Rrahmani, once they all entered the barn the two soldiers ordered the women to hand over their money, jewellery, and identification documents, and started taking women out of the barn, in succession. The first woman to come back told Rrahmani that she was forced to take her clothes off. When Rrahmani was taken out, she was searched, asked

359 *Milan Milutinović et al.* Trial Judgement, vol. II, paras. 1184–1188.

360 *Milan Milutinović et al.* Trial Judgement, vol. II, para. 287.

361 *Milan Milutinović et al.* Trial Judgement, vol. II, para. 562.

362 *Milan Milutinović et al.* Trial Judgement, vol. II, para. 622.

	about the whereabouts of her husband, and then told to lift her blouse and her bra up. The soldier searching her touched her breasts and taunted her with sexual comments. About 20 minutes later she was told to go back into the barn. A third soldier arrived, who, according to Rrahmani, was very tall and blonde and could speak Albanian. In the next two hours or so all women, except for two elderly ones, were taken out of the barn one by one and searched in the same manner. Some, mainly the younger ones, were repeatedly taken out. K24 also stated that a tall man with blonde hair took the women out of the room and searched them one by one, forcing them to take their clothes off. Eventually, over a period of two hours, he took out five young girls a number of times. These girls were: the three sisters, Antigona, Bukurije, and Mirishahe Dibrani; Lumnie Zymeri; and Zahide Xhema. They went out one by one and came back with their clothes in disorder, terrified and not willing to speak about what had happened. One said that they were stripped naked. At one point K24 was also taken outside, where she saw the other two men with tiger badges. The blonde man ordered her to take her clothes off and dropped his trousers to his knees. He started touching her breasts and vagina, at which point she fainted. When she regained consciousness she realised that she had not been raped. She was then told to get up and start walking to the barn. Just before entering the barn, the soldier escorting her told her to sit down and rest. Some five minutes later he told her to follow him and ordered her to take off her clothes. He took off his trousers and his underwear and started touching her. The man then threatened her with a knife, but soon after lost patience and told her to go back to the barn, which she did. Both women testified that, throughout their ordeal, the men taunted them verbally, making statements such as '[s]o, you want a republic, you want independence' and 'you are asking for NATO, for Thaqi and Rugova'".[363]
	"The Chamber is satisfied that the evidence of K24, as well as of Rrahmani, is both credible and reliable. Thus, it is of the view that both K24 and Rrahmani were touched in a sexual and threatening manner around mid-April 1999. In addition, at least two other women were sexually assaulted and were then, together with another six women, thrown into three wells while still alive. All eight died as a result of drowning. The Chamber notes that these killings are not charged in the Indictment and thus will not be entering convictions in respect of the same. With respect to the perpetrators of these sexual assaults, the Chamber notes that throughout April VJ and the MUP forces were in and around Ćirez/Qirez, as confirmed by a number of April 1999 orders and combat reports of the 37th Motorised Brigade. Relying on the same orders and reports, the Chamber is satisfied that MUP forces were also present in the area and that they, as reported by Diković, were misbehaving and engaging in looting. The Chamber further recalls Diković's evidence that members of his unit had been investigated for killing Kosovo Albanians and disposing of their bodies by throwing them into wells. However, the Chamber notes that the men described as perpetrators by Rrahmani and K24 wore either black and brown uniforms, or green camouflage uniforms with red ribbons and the tiger insignia. K24 also mentioned a man in a dark blue camouflage uniform releasing her and the remaining women from the barn. In addition, Salihu testified about 'paramilitaries' being present in Ćirez/Qirez. Accepting those accounts casts doubt on the allegation that the perpetrators were members of the regular VJ. Further doubt is caused by the fact that, when they returned to Kozica/Kozhica, the women went to the VJ soldiers and told them what had happened. The soldiers then attempted to investigate and find the other eight women who, by that time, had probably already been assaulted and thrown into wells. The Chamber cannot, therefore, make any findings about precisely who it was who sexually assaulted these women, but notes that the perpetrators worked in collaboration with VJ forces present in the area at the

[363] *Milan Milutinović et al.* Trial Judgement, vol. II, paras. 630–632 (internal references omitted).

	time and that they were armed, uniformed men who formed part of the forces of the FRY and Serbia".[364] "The Chamber is in no doubt that in Ćirez/Qirez at least four women were subjected to acts of a sexual nature, infringing their physical integrity or amounting to an outrage to their personal dignity, during the course of the attack upon the Kosovo Albanian population of the municipality. Given that all these women were detained by the physical perpetrators and that some of them were later killed, it is clear that none of them consented to these sexual acts. The Chamber is also convinced that the physical perpetrators intentionally committed these acts and that they were aware that the victims did not consent. Since the women were also verbally abused by the physical perpetrators who made specific references to Kosovo Albanian leaders, the Chamber is convinced that the physical perpetrators carried out the sexual assaults with the intent to discriminate against the Kosovo Albanians as an ethnic group. Accordingly, all of the elements of sexual assault as a form of persecution, punishable as a crime against humanity under Article 5(h) are satisfied".[365] - Alleged sexual assaults of Kosovo Albanian women during the forced expulsion in the town of Kosovska Mitrovica/Mitrovicë: "The Chamber has not heard any evidence relating to sexual assault of people from Kosovska Mitrovica/Mitrovica municipality, and these charges are therefore unsupported".[366] - Rapes and gang-rapes of three Kosovo Albanian women during the forced expulsions in the city of Priština/Pristinë: "Three witnesses gave evidence relating to their experiences of being sexually assaulted in Priština/Prishtina in April and May 1999. K62, K14, and K31, all Kosovo Albanian women, gave detailed accounts of their ordeals at the hands of Serbian soldiers and police officers, which were not substantially challenged by the Defence. The Chamber finds their evidence credible and reliable. K62 testified that on 1 April 1999 she was alone in her home when three men wearing green camouflage uniforms and 'some hats and masks on their faces' arrived. Two of them started searching the apartment, while the third man pushed K62 to the floor and raped her. A second man then raped her as well, and the third one put his penis in her mouth. After the men had left, K62 managed to contact her husband with the help of a neighbour and he immediately returned home. They stayed in their apartment for two more nights after the incident until they were expelled from their home on 3 April 1999 as described above. She subsequently met a woman who told her that the same thing had happened to many other women in Priština/Prishtina at that time. K63 provided some support for his wife's account. Although he was not present when she was raped and did not see her attackers, he heard her almost contemporaneous account and told the Chamber what she said. That account was similar to the one she gave in court. K14 was in her mid-teens in May 1999 when she too was raped in Priština/Prishtina. While some of her evidence in relation to the incident was contradictory, in light of her age, the traumatic nature of the event, and the passage of time, the Chamber considers that to be entirely understandable, and finds her testimony to be generally reliable. K14 described how in late May 1999 a group of policemen came to her home. They were wearing blue and green camouflage uniforms with blue ribbons tied on their right arms. The next morning two of these policemen returned, along with a local person

364 *Milan Milutinović et al.* Trial Judgement, vol. II, paras. 689–690 (internal references omitted). See also *Milan Milutinović et al.* Trial Judgement, vol. II, para. 1164.

365 *Milan Milutinović et al.* Trial Judgement, vol. II, para. 1224.

366 *Milan Milutinović et al.* Trial Judgement, vol. II, para. 730.

	whom she knew and who was wearing a police uniform. K14 heard one of the policemen being referred to by name. All three men spoke Serbian, and two of them spoke a bit of Albanian. K14 and her sister were taken by these policemen to a car parked outside. However, her sister was allowed to return to the house before the car departed. K14 was put in the back seat with one of the policemen, who hit her on her hip with the butt of his gun. He also slapped her face, bit her on the neck, and sprayed her on her face and neck with a clear liquid contained in a small clear plastic spray bottle. After five minutes she felt relaxed and started laughing. The Trial Chamber notes that, although there is some documentary evidence to suggest that the some police forces in Kosovo were instructed to wear red ribbons on the date in question, rather than blue, this does not change its finding that K14 gave a reliable account of the incident and could identify her perpetrators as police. At the Bozhur Hotel in the centre of Priština/Prishtina K14 was taken through the basement to a room on the second floor where one of the policemen raped her. The other policeman stayed outside. Afterwards the one who had raped her told her that he would not let the other policeman in if she promised to come back on Monday and bring her sister for his friend. K14 agreed because she wanted him to leave. In the car on the way back to her house he kept reminding her to return on Monday. When she got back home, she told one of her friends what had happened to her. Her friend told K14 that the same thing had happened to her, and that she had been taken to a civilian house, had been raped by four men, and had been brought back after two days. K14 added that the following day the local person who had accompanied the policemen the previous day came back to her house and told her not to worry, that she could not become pregnant, and that, if she was frightened, she could stay in his house. That same day and the next the policeman who had raped her, and the other who had not, drove past the house several times and honked the car horn. At 4:00 a.m. the following Monday, when she was supposed to go back to the hotel, K14 and her family fled Priština/Prishtina on foot, as described above. K31, a Kosovo Albanian woman from Kačanik/Kaçanik municipality, was in her late-teens in May 1999 when she was raped by three 'Serb soldiers' at a hospital in Priština/Prishtina town. Towards the end of May 1999, she and her injured brother were taken from Kačanik/Kaçanik municipality to a hospital in Priština/Prishtina town. K31 testified that on the way one soldier sexually assaulted her in the vehicle. When they arrived at the hospital in Priština/Prishtina, K31 was taken to the basement and put in a locked, dark room with no furniture and about 10 to 15 other women inside, all Kosovo Albanian. About 20 minutes later a soldier entered and, using a torch, selected K31 and took her into another room in the basement. He and two other soldiers beat her and forced her to drink something with a bitter taste, after which she felt as if something had hit her on the head. After two of the soldiers left the room, K31 was raped by the one who had first selected her; he bit her shoulders, arms, and breasts, and covered her mouth with his hand. While K31 was still on the floor, a second soldier came into the room and raped her twice. Afterwards this soldier called the third into the room. K31 then lost consciousness. This soldier may also have raped her while she was unconscious, but the next thing she could remember was waking up naked and on her back in the empty room. When she was finally able to stand up, she left the room and went to the first floor, which was deserted".[367] "The Chamber also finds it proved that three women were raped in the course of the operation to remove large numbers of Kosovo Albanians from Priština/Prishtina town – K62 by three VJ or MUP personnel, K14 by a policeman, and K31 by three VJ soldiers".[368] "In relation to the three women who said they were raped during the course of the

[367] *Milan Milutinović et al.* Trial Judgement, vol. II, paras. 874–880 (internal references omitted).

[368] *Milan Milutinović et al.* Trial Judgement, vol. II, para. 889. See also *Milan Milutinović et al.* Trial Judgement, vol. II, para. 1167.

	attack upon the Kosovo Albanian population of Priština/Prishtina, the Chamber is in no doubt that what they meant is that they were subjected to sexual intercourse, where they plainly did not consent and those attacking them knew that they did not consent, and thus their fundamental right to physical integrity was violated, which satisfies all the elements of sexual assault. In one of these three cases the perpetrators broke-in to the home of the victim and raped her; in another case the victim was a young girl who was taken from her home, physically assaulted, and then raped in a hotel; and in the third case the victim was a young woman who had accompanied her injured brother to a hospital and was there held in a basement, before being beaten and raped several times. Given that the Indictment charges sexual assault only as a form of persecution, the Prosecution must prove that the perpetrators acted with the intent to discriminate against Kosovo Albanians as an ethnic group. However, it has failed to bring any evidence in these three cases from which such intent can be inferred. The Chamber finds, therefore, that it has not been proved by the Prosecution that sexual assault as a form of persecution was committed by forces of the FRY and Serbia in Priština/Prishtina".[369] - Alleged individual criminal responsibility of Nikola Šainović for sexual assaults: "With respect to the sexual assault charges that have been proved (in Beleg and Ćirez/Qirez), the Prosecution has failed to adduce evidence that convinces the Chamber that these sexual assaults were reasonably foreseeable to Šainović. While sexual offences were discussed at the 17 May meeting in presence of Šainović, this discussion took place after the sexual assaults in Beleg and Ćirez/Qirez. The Chamber has examined the *Krstić* and *Kvočka* Trial Chambers' findings in relation to the foreseeability of rapes in those cases. However, the particular facts of those cases with regard to foreseeability were significantly more compelling than those in relation to this case and, specifically, Šainović. Šainović's lack of knowledge about sexual assaults also leads to the conclusion that he did not plan, instigate, order, or otherwise aid and abet them. He is also not responsible for them under Article 7(3) because he did not have reason to know of them".[370] "Šainović is not responsible for all other charges alleged in the Indictment, including the sexual assault charges set out in count 5 (persecution), subject to the final paragraph of the Judgement".[371] - Alleged individual criminal responsibility of Dragoljub Ojdanić for sexual assaults: "While the forcible displacements were part of the VJ and MUP organised campaign, the Chamber is not satisfied beyond reasonable doubt that […] sexual assaults […] were intended aims of this campaign. Accordingly, although he was aware of VJ members killing Kosovo Albanians in some instances, it has not been proved that Ojdanić was aware that VJ and MUP forces were going into the specific crime sites referred to above in order to commit […] sexual assaults […]. Consequently, in Ojdanić's case, the mental element of aiding and abetting has not been established in relation to [count] 5".[372] "Ojdanić is further charged with being responsible under Article 7(3) of the Statute for [count] 5 of the Indictment. The Chamber notes that it has not been proved beyond reasonable doubt that […] sexual assaults […] were intended aims of the campaign of forcible displacement. Therefore, Ojdanić would only have reason to know that his forces were committing these crimes where information relating to the specific crimes

[369] *Milan Milutinović et al.* Trial Judgement, vol. II, paras. 1244–1245.

[370] *Milan Milutinović et al.* Trial Judgement, vol. III, para. 472 (internal references omitted).

[371] *Milan Milutinović et al.* Trial Judgement, vol. III, para. 476.

[372] *Milan Milutinović et al.* Trial Judgement, vol. III, para. 629.

	of [...] sexual assaults [...], carried out by VJ forces, was available to him. The Chamber does not consider that information regarding the specific [...] sexual assaults [...], for which it has been proved that the VJ was responsible, was available to him or that he had reason to know about them".[373] - Individual criminal responsibility of Nebojša Pavković for sexual assaults: "The Chamber, therefore, finds that Pavković was aware of specific allegations of widespread crimes, including forcible displacements within and without Kosovo [...] and sexual assaults, which were being committed against the Kosovo Albanian civilian population by members of the VJ and MUP during the NATO campaign".[374] "As described above, Pavković intended to forcibly displace part of the Kosovo Albanian population and shared this intent with other members of the joint criminal enterprise, the object of which was to forcibly displace Kosovo Albanians within and deport them from Kosovo in order to maintain control over the province. Pavković was aware of the strong animosity between ethnic Serbs and Kosovo Albanians in Kosovo during 1998 and 1999. He was aware of the context in which the forcible displacement took place. It was thus reasonably foreseeable that other crimes [...] would be committed by physical and intermediary perpetrators with intent to discriminate against Kosovo Albanians. The Chamber is of the view that Pavković's detailed knowledge of events on the ground in Kosovo in 1998 and 1999 put him on notice that [...] sexual crimes would by committed by the VJ and MUP as a result of the displacements taking place in 1999. In addition, there is specific evidence to support this conclusion. [...] A 4 April 1999 order issued by Pavković ordered the Niš Corps to prevent the population from being robbed, raped, or mistreated by conducting daily checks on deserted settlements and buildings. [...] A 10 April 1999 report from Pavković indicated that volunteers who were either convicted or awaiting sentence were deployed in Kosovo and that seven volunteers had been detained for *inter alia* killing and rape. On 25 May 1999 Pavković sent a report to the Supreme Command Staff referring to *inter alia* murder and rape committed by MUP forces against the Kosovo Albanian population. Consequently, it was reasonably foreseeable to Pavković that VJ and MUP forces would commit [...] sexual assault against Kosovo Albanians during their forcible displacement of them".[375] "The Trial Chamber therefore finds that it has been established beyond reasonable doubt that Nebojša Pavković is responsible for committing (through his participation in a joint criminal enterprise) the following crimes in the following locations: [...] Dečani/Deçan: Beleg: deportation as a crime against humanity; other inhumane acts (forcible transfer) as a crime against humanity; persecution (sexual assault) as a crime against humanity [...] Srbica/Skenderaj [...] Ćirez/Qirez: deportation as a crime against humanity; other inhumane acts (forcible transfer) as a crime against humanity; persecutions (sexual assault) as a crime against humanity [...]".[376] "Nebojša Pavković is, therefore, guilty of counts 1 through 5 of the Indictment to the extent specified above".[377] - Alleged individual criminal responsibility of Vladimir Lazarević for sexual assaults: "While the forcible displacements were part of the VJ and MUP organised campaign, the Chamber is not satisfied beyond reasonable doubt that [...] sexual assaults [...] were intended aims of this campaign. Accordingly, although he was aware of VJ

373 *Milan Milutinović et al.* Trial Judgement, vol. III, para. 633.
374 *Milan Milutinović et al.* Trial Judgement, vol. III, para. 766 (internal reference omitted).
375 *Milan Milutinović et al.* Trial Judgement, vol. III, para. 785 (internal reference omitted).
376 *Milan Milutinović et al.* Trial Judgement, vol. III, para. 788.
377 *Milan Milutinović et al.* Trial Judgement, vol. III, para. 790 (internal reference omitted).

	members killing Kosovo Albanians in some instances, it has not been proved that Lazarević was aware that VJ and MUP forces were going into the specific crime sites referred to above in order to commit [...] sexual assaults [...]. Consequently, in Lazarević's case, the mental element of aiding and abetting has not been established in relation to [count] 5".[378] "Lazarević is further charged with being responsible under Article 7(3) of the Statute for [count] 5 of the Indictment. The Chamber notes that it has not been proved beyond reasonable doubt that [...] sexual assaults [...] were intended aims of the campaign of forcible displacement. Therefore, Lazarević would only have reason to know that his forces were committing these crimes where information relating to the specific crimes of [...] sexual assaults [...], carried out by VJ forces, was available to him. The Chamber does not consider that information regarding the specific [...] sexual assaults [...], for which it has been proved that the VJ was responsible, was available to him. [... T]he Chamber does not consider that information regarding the [...] sexual assaults [...], for which it has been proved that the VJ was responsible, was available to him or that he had reason to know about them".[379] - Alleged individual criminal responsibility of Sreten Lukić for sexual assaults: "With respect to the sexual assault charges that have been proved (in Beleg and Ćirez/Qirez), the Prosecution has failed to adduce evidence that convinces the Chamber beyond reasonable doubt that these sexual assaults were reasonably foreseeable to Lukić. Lukić reported on 1 May 1999 that a MUP reservist had been detained for committing indecent assault against a Kosovo Albanian woman, indicating his knowledge, by that time, that such crimes were being committed. However, this evidence does not demonstrate that the sexual assaults committed in late March (in Beleg) and mid-April (in Ćirez/Qirez) were reasonably foreseeable to him. The Chamber has examined the *Krstić* and *Kvočka* Trial Chambers' findings in relation to the foreseeability of rapes in those cases. However, the particular facts of those cases with regard to foreseeability were significantly more compelling than those in relation to this case and, specifically, Lukić. Lukić's lack of knowledge about sexual assaults also leads to the conclusion that he did not plan, instigate, order, or otherwise aid and abet them. He is also not responsible for them under Article 7(3) because he did not have reason to know of them".[380] "Lukić is not responsible for all other charges alleged in the Indictment, including the sexual assault charges set out in count 5 (persecution), subject to the final paragraph of the Judgement".[381]

28. Vlastimir **<u>Đorđević</u>** (Case No. IT-05-87/1) "***Kosovo***" From 1 June 1997 to 30 January 2001, Assistant Minister of the Serbian Ministry of Internal Affairs (MUP) and Chief of the Public Security Department (RJB) of the MUP; responsible for all units and personnel of the RJB in Serbia, including those in Kosovo between 1 January and 20 June 1999.	
Indictment[382] (International	- **Deportation as CAH** (count 1) and **Other Inhumane acts (forcible transfer) as CAH** (count 2) under Articles 7(1) and 7(3) of the Statute (**superior responsibility**)

[378] *Milan Milutinović et al.* Trial Judgement, vol. III, para. 928.

[379] *Milan Milutinović et al.* Trial Judgement, vol. III, para. 933.

[380] *Milan Milutinović et al.* Trial Judgement, vol. III, para. 1135 (internal references omitted).

[381] *Milan Milutinović et al.* Trial Judgement, vol. III, para. 1139.

[382] For the general background to the charges, see *Prosecutor v. Vlastimir Đorđević*, Case No. IT-05-87/1-PT, Fourth Amended Indictment, 9 July 2008 ("*Đorđević* Indictment"), para. 27 ("In addition to the deliberate destruction of property owned by Kosovo Albanian civilians, forces of the FRY and Serbia committed wide-

sex crimes (or related) charges and mode(s) of liability)	for deliberately creating an atmosphere of fear and oppression through various crimes, including thesexual assaults of Kosovo Albanian women, in order to forcibly displace and deport Kosovo Albanian civilians. These crimes include: (i) the sexual assaults of Kosovo Albanian women en route from the city of Prizren to the Albanian border from 28 March 1999; (ii) the sexual assaults of Kosovo Albanian women in a barn in Cirez/Qirez in Srbica/Skenderaj municipality; (iii) the sexual assaults of Kosovo Albanian women during the course of forced expulsions in the city of Priština/Pristinë between 24 March and the end of May 1999; and (iv) the sexual assaults of three Kosovo Albanian women in a building at night in Dečani/Deçan municipality, on or about 29 March 1999.[383] - **Persecutions as CAH** (count 5) under Articles 7(1) and 7(3) of the Statute (**superior responsibility**) of Kosovo Albanian population through various crimes, including the

spread or systematic acts of brutality and violence against Kosovo Albanian civilians in order to perpetuate the climate of fear, create chaos and a pervading fear for life. Forces of the FRY and Serbia went from village to village and, in the towns and cities, from area to area, threatening and expelling the Kosovo Albanian population. […] Many Kosovo Albanians who were not directly forcibly expelled from their communities fled as a result of the climate of terror created by the widespread or systematic beatings, harassment, sexual assaults, unlawful arrests, killings, shelling and looting carried out across the province".).

383 *Đorđević* Indictment, paras. 72(b)-(c), (g), (l), 73 ("Beginning on or about 1 January 1999 and continuing until 20 June 1999, forces of the FRY and Serbia, acting at the direction, with the encouragement, or with the support of Milan Milutinović, Nikola Šainović, Dragoljub Ojdanić, Nebojša Pavković, Vladimir Lazarević, **VLASTIMIR ĐORĐEVIĆ** and Sreten Lukić perpetrated the actions set forth in paragraphs 25–32, which resulted in the forced deportation of approximately 800,000 Kosovo Albanian civilians. To facilitate these expulsions and displacements, forces of the FRY and Serbia deliberately created an atmosphere of fear and oppression through the use of force, threats of force and acts of violence, as described above in paragraphs 25–32. Throughout Kosovo, forces of the FRY and Serbia systematically […] sexually assaulted Kosovo Albanian women. These actions were undertaken in all areas of Kosovo, and these deliberate means and methods were used throughout the province, including the following municipalities: […] b. Prizren: […] From 28 March 1999, in the city of Prizren, forces of the FRY and Serbia went from house to house, ordering Kosovo Albanian residents to leave. They were forced to join convoys of vehicles and persons travelling on foot to the Albanian border. En route, members of the forces of the FRY and Serbia […] separated Kosovo Albanian women from the convoy and sexually assaulted the women. […] c. Srbica/Skenderaj: Beginning on or about 25 March 1999, forces of the FRY and Serbia attacked and destroyed the villages of Vojnike/Vocnjak, Leocina/Lecine, Kladernica/Klladernicë, Turicevac/Turiçec and Izbica/Izbicë by shelling and burning. […] Some women and children were taken away by members of the forces of the FRY and Serbia and held in a barn in Cirez/Qirez. The women were subjected to sexual assault […]. At least eight of the women were killed after being sexually assaulted, and their bodies were thrown into three wells in the village of Cirez/Qirez. […] g. Priština/Prishtinë: Beginning on or about 24 March 1999 and continuing through the end of May 1999, forces of the FRY and Serbia went to the homes of Kosovo Albanians in the city of Priština/Prishtinë and forced the residents to leave. […] During the course of these forced expulsions, […] several women were sexually assaulted. […] l. Dečani/Deçan: On or about 29 March 1999, forces of the FRY and Serbia surrounded and attacked the village of Beleg, and other surrounding villages in the Dečani/Deçan municipality. Forces of the FRY and Serbia went from house to house and told villagers to leave their houses immediately. […] Men were separated from women and children and taken to the basement of a building near the field. Women and children were ordered to go to another building. During the night at least 3 women were sexually assaulted. […] By these acts and omissions, **VLASTIMIR ĐORĐEVIĆ** planned, instigated, ordered, committed or otherwise aided and abetted the planning, preparation or execution of: **Count 1:** Deportation, a **CRIME AGAINST HUMANITY**, punishable under Article 5(d) of the Statute of the Tribunal. With respect to those Kosovo Albanians who were internally displaced within the territory of Kosovo, the Prosecutor re-alleges and incorporates by reference paragraphs 16–33, 60–64, and 71–72. By these acts and omissions, **VLASTIMIR ĐORĐEVIĆ** planned, instigated, ordered, committed or otherwise aided and abetted the planning, preparation or execution of: **Count 2:** Other Inhumane Acts (Forcible Transfer), a **CRIME AGAINST HUMANITY**, punishable under Article 5(i) of the Statute of the Tribunal".).

	sexual assaults committed by forces of the Federal Republic of Yugoslavia and Serbia.[384]
Trial Judgement	- Although Vlastimir Đorđević was found guilty of deportation as CAH (count 1), other inhumane acts (forcible transfer) as CAH (count 2) and persecutions as CAH (count 5),[385] the Trial Chamber did not base the convictions for deportation as CAH (count 1) and other inhumane acts (forcible transfer) as CAH (count 2) on findngs of sexual assault.[386] Moreover, with respect to persecutions, the Trial Chamber found that "[w]hile the victims in each of these [sexual assault] incidents were Kosovo Albanians and the perpetrators were members of the Serbian forces, considering the limited number of incidents relied on to support this underlying act of persecutions, the Chamber finds that the ethnicity of the two victims alone is not a sufficient basis to establish that the perpetrators acted with discriminatory intent" and, therefore, found that the offence of persecutions committed through sexual assaults was not established.[387]
Appeal Judgement	N/A (The appellate proceedings are in progress.)
Legal and Factual Findings and/or Evidence	- Legal findings: **- Sexual assault: definition and elements:** The Trial Chamber gave the following definition of sexual assault: "The charges of persecution set out in Count 5 of the Indictment include '[t]he sexual assault by forces of the FRY and Serbia of Kosovo Albanians, in particular women…' The Chamber will interpret the term 'sexual assault' as an offence that may include rape where there is evidence of sexual penetration, as well as other forms of sexual assault. While the narrower offence of rape requires sexual penetration, sexual violence other than rape can constitute 'sexual assault'. The ICTR found in *Akayesu* that '[s]exual violence is not limited to physical invasion of the human body and may include acts which do not involve penetration or even physical contact'. In *Brđanin*, the Trial Chamber held that the offence of sexual assault 'embraces all serious abuses of a sexual nature inflicted

[384] *Đorđević* Indictment, paras. 76, 77(c) ("The Prosecutor re-alleges and incorporates by reference paragraphs 16–33, 60–64, 72 and 75. Beginning on or about 1 January 1999 and continuing until 20 June 1999, the forces of the FRY and Serbia, acting at the direction, with the encouragement, or with the support of Milan Milutinović, Nikola Šainović, Dragoljub Ojdanić, Nebojša Pavković, Vladimir Lazarević, **VLASTIMIR ĐORĐEVIĆ** and Sreten Lukić, utilised the means and methods set forth in paragraphs 25 through 32 to execute a campaign of persecution against the Kosovo Albanian population, including Kosovo Albanian civilians based on political, racial, or religious grounds. The accused intended to discriminate against the Kosovo Albanian population on political, racial or religious grounds or was aware of the substantial likelihood that the forces of the FRY and Serbia would perpetrate the crimes set forth in paragraphs 25 through 32 against the Kosovo Albanian population on political, racial, or religious grounds, as is evident from, among other things, the overwhelming predominance of Kosovo Albanians of Muslim faith among the victims of crimes and the widespread use of terms derogatory to Kosovo Albanians. These persecutions included, but were not limited to, the following means: […] c. The sexual assault by forces of the FRY and Serbia of Kosovo Albanians, in particular women, including the sexual assaults described in paragraphs 27 and 72. […] By these acts and omissions, **VLASTIMIR ĐORĐEVIĆ** planned, instigated, ordered, committed or otherwise aided and abetted the planning, preparation or execution of: **Count 5:** Persecutions on political, racial and religious grounds, a **CRIME AGAINST HUMANITY**, punishable under Article 5(h) of the Statute of the Tribunal".).

[385] *Prosecutor v. Vlastimir Đorđević*, Case No. IT-05-87/1-T, Public Judgement with confidential annex, 23 February 2011 ("*Đorđević* Trial Judgement"), para. 2230.

[386] *Đorđević* Trial Judgement, para. 1796. See also *Vlastimir Đorđević* Trial Judgement, paras. 1791–1795, 1797.

[387] *Đorđević* Trial Judgement, paras. 1615–1704.

upon the integrity of a person by means of coercion, threat of force or intimidation in a way that is humiliating and degrading to the victim's dignity'".[388]

The Trial Chamber adopted the constituve elements of sexual assault given in the *Milutinović et al.* case:[389] "The elements of the offence of sexual assault were set out in the *Milutinović* Trial Judgement, as follows: (a) The physical perpetrator commits an act of a sexual nature on another; this includes requiring that other person to perform such an act. (b) That act infringes the victim's physical integrity or amounts to an outrage to the victim's personal dignity. (c) The victim does not consent to the act. (d) The physical perpetrator intentionally commits the act. (e) The physical perpetrator is aware that the victim did not consent to the act. The Chamber considers that these requirements correctly reflect the elements of the crime of sexual assault other than rape".[390]

- Sexual assault constituting persecutions:

The Trial Chamber confirmed that sexual assault can constitute persecutions: "'Sexual assault' *per se* is not listed in Article 5 of the Statute, while rape is listed under subparagraph (g). For those forms of sexual assault other than rape, it must be shown that the act denies or infringes upon a fundamental human right. In this respect, it is well established that sexual assault may amount to a denial of or infringement upon the fundamental right to physical integrity, depending on the specific circumstances. It has also been held that rape and sexual assault may constitute torture or cruel, inhuman or degrading treatment. In addition, sexual assault may amount to an inhumane act or to an 'outrage upon personal dignity' in the specific circumstances. Therefore, in the view of the Chamber, an act of sexual assault, in the specific circumstances, may be of equal gravity to the crimes listed in Article 5 of the Statute and may amount to persecutions, provided that the other requisite elements are established".[391]

- <u>Factual findings:</u>

- Alleged sexual assault of a Kosovo Albanian girl in Lukare/Llukar, in Priština/Prishtinë municipality:

"The Chamber has heard evidence about two incidents of alleged sexual assault in Priština/Prishtinë. Sometime in April 1999, a witness described that she saw a Kosovo Albanian girl, who was travelling with other displaced persons in a convoy from Graštica/Grashticë in the Priština/Prishtinë municipality to the town of Priština/Prishtinë, taken off a tractor in Lukare/Llukar by two men. One of the men was carrying knives and was dressed in a black sleeveless shirt and green camouflage pants. He had a shaved head tied with a scarf and three earrings in one ear. The other man, identified as a policeman, wore a blue camouflage uniform with a blue ribbon on his sleeve. The man with the shaved head took the Kosovo Albanian girl into the woods, while the policeman stood guard. When the man with the shaved head came out, the policeman went into the woods. The girl was heard from the convoy to be screaming and crying. After about half an hour the girl was brought back to the convoy. She was flushed from crying. She was barefoot, wrapped in a blanket and appeared to be naked. She had been clothed when taken to the wood. There is no direct evidence as to the events in the wood, nor is there direct evidence concerning what happened to another woman who was also seen to be taken from this convoy. In the

388 *Đorđević* Trial Judgement, para. 1766 (internal references omitted).

389 ICTY ISCC *Milutinović et al.*, see *supra* p. 619.

390 *Đorđević* Trial Judgement, paras. 1768–1769 (internal reference omitted).

391 *Đorđević* Trial Judgement, para. 1767 (internal references omitted).

	absence of further evidence, the Chamber is unable to make a finding in this instance that this woman was subjected to sexual assault".[392] - Rape of a Kosovo Albanian girl on 21 May 1999 in Priština/Prishtinë town: "The second alleged incident of sexual assault is related to events that began on 20 May 1999 in Kolevic-e-Re, a neighbourhood located in the outskirts of Priština/Prishtinë town. On this day, six Serbian men went to a house in the neighbourhood; some of the men wore the blue camouflage uniform of the police and each had a blue ribbon on the shoulder. The others wore green camouflage uniforms which is consistent with the uniforms of the PJP of the MUP or the VJ. Some of these men had numbers on their uniforms above their left chests, and had camouflage caps on their shoulders under their epaulets. They gave the family in the house, green cards to fill out, and told them that they would come the next day to take them to Hotel Bozhur to get their papers stamped. […] On the morning of 21 May 1999, two of the men in blue police uniforms came back to the same house. One of them was referred to by the other as Novica. They were armed with automatic guns. This time, they brought a 'Roma' with them who had been a road sweeper living nearby. On that day, the Roma was dressed in a police blue camouflage uniform. All three men spoke Serbian; the one called Novica and the Roma spoke a little Albanian. The men forcefully took two girls, sisters, to a red Ascona car with no registration plate, parked in front of the house. They threw one of the girls on the ground, and forced the other onto the back seat of the car with Novica on her right side. The girl was crying and Novica hit her hip with the butt of his gun, and slapped her face. Novica then grabbed her head, turned it towards him and bit and sucked on her neck. He also sprayed clear liquid resembling a perfume all over her face and neck. The girl was very scared but the spray caused her to become more calm. The girl's sister was allowed to return to the house before the car left with the girl in the back seat. The car arrived at the Bozhur Hotel where there were many Kosovo Albanians forming a queue. The girl was not allowed to join them, and was taken to a room on the second floor through the basement of the hotel. Novica went inside the room with her and he locked the door of the room. The Roma remained in the basement and the other policeman stayed outside the room. Novica ripped the girl's clothes off and made her lie naked on the bed. He then took his clothes off. He started touching and kissing her body and told her that she would not get pregnant. When the girl refused him, he slapped her. Novica put his penis inside the girl, and this lasted for a while. When he got off, the girl was bleeding and was in a great pain. When Novica opened the bedroom door, the other policeman tried to come in. The girl begged Novica not to let the other policeman do the same thing to her. Novica asked her if she would promise to come out with him on Monday and bring her sister for his friend. The girl agreed out of fear. Apparently after the girl dressed, Novica took the witness by her arm and walked her out of the room, helped by the other policeman because she could not walk. The Roma was still in the basement and Novica gave him some money. The Roma told the girl to stop crying if she wanted to go home because other Kosovo Albanians would see her. He then put a pair of sunglasses on her to cover her eyes. In the car on the way back to the house, Novica continued to kiss the girl and kept reminding her of their promise. The whole incident lasted approximately two hours. On the same day, the girl told a friend what had happened. Her friend started crying and told the girl that she had also been raped by four men in a civilian house where she had been detained for two days. On 22 May 1999, the Roma came to tell the girl not to worry about becoming pregnant and that she could stay at his house if she was frightened. On 22 and 23 May 1999, policemen drove by the girl's house several times and honked. The girl was afraid that she and her sister would be raped, and told her uncle that it would not be safe for girls

[392] *Đorđević* Trial Judgement, para. 832 (internal references omitted).

	in the house to stay there. The girl and her sister decided to flee to FYROM; they left in the early morning on 24 May 1999 and, with her aunt and her aunt's family, took the next train to FYROM. At Blace, on the border of FYROM, the witness saw a lot of Serbian police. Small groups of people were being allowed to cross into FYROM. They spent the night at the border and then continued walking on foot. When the witness and her family arrived to a refugee camp in FYROM she spoke with a representative from the ICTY. She also reported the rape to the FYROM authorities and she was given medical assistance. Authorities in Serbia were not ever notified of the rape. While the Chamber accepts that this girl was sexually assaulted, as will be discussed in more detail later in this Judgement, no finding in respects of the count of sexual assault as persecution could be established on the evidence".[393] - Rapes of several young Kosovo Albanian women in the village of Beleg, in Dečani/Deçan municipality: "The events discussed below took place in the village of Beleg and in neighbouring villages which are located in the central part of Dečani/Deçan municipality, to the east and south of Dečani/Deçan town. […] On or about 28 March 1999 people in Beleg heard shots being fired, as well as shelling and the sound of tanks approaching the village. They saw police and VJ soldiers arrive in the village. […] [The next morning at about 0600 hours] VJ soldiers and police surrounded another house in the village and opened fire on it. The people inside the house, some 100 of them, were ordered to leave the house. […] The people from this house were then taken to the basement where other people had been taken earlier, and afterwards to the yard where some of them were beaten by Serbian police forces. […] Policemen then took the men in groups of four or five, to another basement to be 'checked'. When they came back the men carried their clothes; some were in their underwear. After the men, the young girls were taken to the basement to be bodily searched and sometimes forced to remove their clothes, the women were given the same treatment. On the floor in the basement where the checking took place there was a cloth on which villagers were required to leave their valuables and personal documents. However, all golden valuables of the women were returned the following day by a policeman. […] After the checking was completed the detainees were held in the same place, or in a field, until the evening when they were moved to other buildings. The men were then taken to the second floor of the house where the checking had taken place earlier. The women and a few elderly men were taken to two rooms and a stable in another house. They were guarded by Serbian forces. At about 2200 or 2300 hours men came to one of the rooms where the women and children were taken. These men wore solid green uniforms or green camouflage. A witness testified that they had the words police written in Serbian on their arms. One of them, who spoke Albanian, told the people in the room that they needed people to help clean the house and wash the dishes. Some older women offered to help but the soldiers told them to stay in the room. The soldiers then checked the faces of the people in the room using a flashlight and took out five young women. Two returned almost immediately. The remaining three young women were taken to different rooms in a burned house nearby which was being used as a base by the soldiers. One of the soldiers took one of the young women to a bathroom without windows or doors, undressed her and raped her. The girl was screaming and the soldier put a piece of cloth against her mouth and threatened her. During the rape a police officer was standing at the door on guard, occasionally pointing his flashlight to see what was happening. When the soldier who raped the girl left, the police officer slapped her in the face and she lost consciousness. A second, third and fourth soldier, wearing green camouflage uniforms, came in and each raped the girl. After this the police officer, who spoke Albanian, told the girl to tell the others that she had been cleaning. The

[393] *Đorđević* Trial Judgement, paras. 833–838 (internal references omitted).

	screaming of the other two young women who had been taken away by soldiers could be heard during the night. After taking away the first group of young women soldiers returned to the room where the people were staying to look for more girls. This happened on four or five occasions and some 20 young women were taken away. When they were brought back they were crying and had dishevelled hair. One of them told her mother that she had been raped. On 30 March 1999 at 0800 or 0900 hours the man who appeared to the villagers to be a commander, in police uniform, arrived at the rooms where the women and children were held and ordered them to leave for Albania. At about the same time a police officer came to the second floor of the house where the men were and asked whether anyone had a tractor. Those who had tractors or other vehicles were told to take the women and children to Dečani/Deçan town and Đakovica/Gjakovë. Accordingly, shortly thereafter, a convoy of tractors and vehicles with the women and children and some men set off from Beleg. Along the way, some other displaced persons from other villages joined the convoy so that there were hundreds of Kosovo Albanians travelling on trucks and tractors. […] The convoy passed through checkpoints where the people were asked for their personal documents. The convoy crossed over the Albanian border near Kukës in the evening of 30 March 1999, or on the following day. At the border, when asked to produce their identification documents the refugees told the Serbian border authorities that their personal documents had already been taken from them. Of the approximately 60 men who were taken to the second floor of a building in Beleg on 29 March 1999, 10 were released on the following day to drive the women and children to Albania. The remaining men have not been heard of since that day and are still unaccounted for. Following the end of hostilities in the summer of 1999, when residents of the area were able to return, they observed that all houses in Beleg had been burnt down. For reasons explained in detail later in this Judgement the Chamber is satisfied that the offence of deportation has been established with respect to Beleg".[394] - Persecutions committed through sexual assault: "The Chamber has established earlier that on 21 May 1999, a young Kosovo Albanian woman was taken from her home in the municipality of Priština/Prishtinë by policemen to a hotel, physically assaulted, and then raped in a hotel by one of them. The Chamber is in no doubt that the victim was subjected to sexual intercourse, that she did not consent and that the policeman knew that she did not consent. Therefore, the Chamber finds that her right to physical integrity was violated and that the legal requirements of the crime of sexual assault are satisfied. The Chamber has heard evidence that sometime in April 1999 a Kosovo Albanian girl who was travelling in a convoy to Priština/Prishtinë was taken off a tractor and taken to the woods by men, including a policeman. The girl was heard from the convoy screaming and crying and when she was brought back to the convoy she was flushed from crying and appeared naked under the blanket that was wrapped around her body. There is no further evidence as to this incident. In the circumstances, the Chamber cannot make a finding that this sexual assault has been established. The Chamber has found that a young Kosovo Albanian woman was subjected to multiple rapes by VJ soldiers while police stood guard, in the night of 29/30 March 1999 in the village of Beleg in Dečani/Deçan municipality. The Chamber is satisfied that the offence of sexual assault has been established. The Chamber also heard that other young Kosovo Albanian women were selected and taken away by soldiers, for lengthy periods of time throughout the night of 29/30 March 1999 in Beleg. When the young women were brought back, they were crying and had dishevelled hair. One of them was heard telling her mother that she had been raped. No further evidence has been presented. In the absence of further evidence the Chamber is unable to make a finding that these two women were subjected to

[394] *Đorđević* Trial Judgement, paras. 1142, 1145, 1147–1156 (internal references omitted).

	sexual assault. In addition to the allegations about sexual assault in the municipalities of Priština/Prishtinë and Dečani/Deçan, the Indictment also contains allegations of sexual assaults in Srbica/Skenderaj municipality and Prizren municipality. No evidence to support these allegations has been presented. The allegations of sexual assault in Srbica/Skenderaj and Prizren municipalities have not been proven. The charge of sexual assault as a form of persecution requires the Prosecution to prove that the perpetrators acted with the intent to discriminate against Kosovo Albanians as an ethnic group. The Chamber has found that two incidents of sexual assault have been established. No specific evidence has been presented with respect to either of the incidents that the perpetrators acted with intent to discriminate. While the victims in each of these incidents were Kosovo Albanians and the perpetrators were members of the Serbian forces, considering the limited number of incidents relied on to support this underlying act of persecutions, the Chamber finds that the ethnicity of the two victims alone is not a sufficient basis to establish that the perpetrators acted with discriminatory intent. In the Chamber's finding the offence of persecutions committed through sexual assault has not been established".[395]

29. Jadranko **Prlić *et al.*** (Case No. IT-04-74) - Jadranko Prlić: Highest political official in the Croatian wartime entity, Herzeg-Bosna; former President of the "Croatian Community of Herceg Bosna" (HZ H-B); Prime Minister of the "Croatian Republic of Herceg-Bosna" (HR H-B). - Bruno Stojić: Head of the Department of Defence of the "Croatian Defence Council" (HVO), that body's top political and management official; in charge of the Herceg-Bosna/HVO armed forces. - Slobodan Praljak: Senior Croatian Army officer, Assistant Minister of Defence and senior representative of the Croatian Ministry of Defence to the Herceg-Bosna/HVO government and armed forces; also known as "Brada". - Milivoj Petković: Military head of the Herceg-Bosna/HVO armed forces, with the title "Chief of the HVO Main Staff"; from late July 1993, deputy overall commander of the Herceg-Bosna/HVO armed forces. - Valentin Ćorić: Deputy for Security and Commander of the HVO Military Police, later titled "Chief of the Military Police Administration" (within the HVO Department, later Ministry of Defence); in November 1993, appointed Minister of Interior in the HR H-B. - Berislav Pušić: Held a command position in the military police and was HVO liaison officer to UNPROFOR; Head of the Service for the Exchange of Prisoners and Other Persons; President of the commission in charge of all Herceg-Bosna/HVO prisons and detention facilities holding prisoners of war and detainees; member of the HVO Commission of Exchange of Prisoners; also known as "Berto" or "Berko".	
Indictment (International sex crimes (or related) charges and mode(s) of liability)	- **Persecutions as CAH** (count 1), **Rape as CAH** (count 4) and **Inhuman treatment (sexual assault) as a grave breach of the Geneva Conventions of 1949 (WC)** (count 5) under Articles 7(1) (**joint criminal enterprise**) and 7(3) of the Statute (**superior responsibility**) for various crimes, including: (i) forcing Bosnian Muslim detainees to perform sexual acts in various detention centres in Prozor Municipality; (ii) the rapes of Bosnian Muslim women confined in houses under HVO control in or about the villages of Lapsunj and Duge and in part of Prozor town called Podgrade during July and August 1993; (iii) subjecting Bosnian Muslim civilians to sexual assault in Prozor Municipality at the end of August 1993 and thereafter; (iv) sexually assaulting Bosnian Muslim civilians from West Mostar during their forced expulsions from 9 May 1993 until April 1994 and thereafter; (v) the rape of at least one Bosnian Muslim woman in September 1993 during forced evictions in the Centar 11 district in West

[395] *Đorđević* Trial Judgement, paras. 1791–1797 (internal references omitted).

	Mostar; (vi) repeatedly raping and sexually assaulting Bosnian Muslim women and girls detained at Vojno Camp; (vii) sexually assaulting Muslim women in Stupni Do on 23 October 1993; and (viii) sexually assaulting Muslim women in Vareš town from 23 October to 3 November 1993.[396]

[396] For the general background to the charges, see *Prosecutor v. Jadranko Prlić et al.*, Case No. IT-04-74-T, Second Amended Indictment, 11 June 2008 ("*Jadranko Prlić et al.* Indictment"), paras. 39 ("As part of and in the course of these actions, involving ethnic cleansing on a widespread and systematic basis, and in furtherance of the joint criminal enterprise, JADRANKO PRLIĆ, BRUNO STOJIĆ, SLOBODAN PRALJAK, MILIVOJ PETKOVIĆ, VALENTIN ĆORIĆ and BERISLAV PUŠIĆ, together with other leaders and members of the Herceg-Bosna/HVO authorities and forces, engaged in: [...] (b) *Use of Force, Intimidation and Terror:* Herceg-Bosna/HVO authorities and military and police units used force and the threat of force to dominate, suppress and persecute Bosnian Muslims. In the course of mass arrests and evictions, Bosnian Muslims were [...] sexually assaulted [...]. (d) *Detention and Imprisonment:* The accused and other members of the joint criminal enterprise, together with various members of the Herceg-Bosna/HVO authorities and forces, established, supported and operated a system of ill-treatment, involving a network of prisons, concentration camps and other detention facilities (including, without limitation, the Heliodrom Camp, Ljubuški Prison, Dretelj Prison, Gabela Prison and Vojno Camp) to arrest, detain and imprison thousands of Bosnian Muslims, including women, children and elderly. Many of the imprisoned and detained Muslims were kept in horrible conditions and deprived of basic human necessities, such as adequate food, water and medical care. Many suffered inhumane treatment and physical and psychological abuse, including beatings and sexual assaults".), 54–55 ("From spring 1993 until the end of that year, Herceg-Bosna/HVO forces arrested Bosnian Muslim men and took them to various detention centres in Prozor Municipality, including the Secondary School Centre, the Unis building, the military police building located at the fire station and the Ministry of Interior ('MUP') building. Herceg-Bosna/HVO forces physically abused the Muslim detainees, some of whom were taken away and never seen again. Beginning in July 1993, the HVO transferred some detainees to other detention facilities at Ljubuški, the Heliodrom, Dretelj and Gabela. (Annex). Herceg-Bosna/HVO forces used Bosnian Muslim detainees to perform forced labour, including construction of military fortifications and digging trenches. Some Muslim detainees died or were injured while performing forced labour. HVO soldiers often beat and humiliated Muslim detainees while they were being held or used as labourers, and on some occasions forced them to perform sexual acts. (Annex)"), 57 ("During July and August 1993, the Herceg-Bosna/HVO forces collected and confined (in houses under HVO control) several thousand Bosnian Muslim women, children and elderly in or about the villages of Lapsunj and Duge and in a part of Prozor town called Podgrade. The various locations were overcrowded and the living conditions were deplorable. [...] Members of the HercegBosna/ HVO forces often raped Bosnian Muslim women. (Annex)"), 59 ("At the end of August 1993 and thereafter, Herceg-Bosna/HVO forces continued to persecute and mistreat Bosnian Muslim civilians who remained in Prozor Municipality, subjecting them to harassment, physical and sexual assault and humiliating acts".), 99 ("From 9 May 1993 and continuing to April 1994 and thereafter, the Herceg-Bosna/HVO forces engaged in the systematic expulsion and forcible transfer of thousands of Bosnian Muslim civilians from West Mostar. During and in the course of these expulsions, often at gunpoint, Bosnian Muslims were routinely [...] sexually assaulted [...]".), 109 ("In late September 1993, the Herceg-Bosna/HVO forces engaged in another round of evictions of Bosnian Muslims from West Mostar, in the Centar 11 district. Approximately 600 Bosnian Muslim civilians were forced from their homes, and at least one Bosnian Muslim woman was raped. (Annex)"), 141 ("HVO soldiers repeatedly raped and sexually assaulted Bosnian Muslim women and girls detained at Vojno Camp. (Annex) Such episodes of sexual assault were often preceded or accompanied by beatings or threats that noncompliance would result in the woman's child (or children) being killed".), 211 ("On the morning of 23 October 1993, Herceg-Bosna/HVO forces attacked Stupni Do. After gaining control of various parts of the village, HVO soldiers forced the civilians out of their homes and hiding places, [...] sexually assaulted Muslim women [...]. (A list of the victims killed and the women sexually assaulted is part of the Annex.)"), 213 ("From 23 October to 3 November 1993, before leaving Vareš town, Herceg-Bosna/HVO forces [...] sexually assaulted Muslim women. (Annex)"), 229 ("By the foregoing acts, conduct, practices and omissions, **JADRANKO PRLIĆ, BRUNO STOJIĆ, SLOBODAN PRALJAK, MILIVOJ PETKOVIĆ, VALENTIN ĆORIĆ** and **BERISLAV PUŠIĆ** are responsible for the following crimes: **Count 1: persecutions on political, racial and religious grounds**, a CRIME AGAINST HUMANITY, punishable under Statute Articles 5(h), 7(1) and 7(3) (as alleged in Paragraphs 15–17.6, 21–41,43–59, 61–71, 73–86, 88–117, 119–134, 136–142, 144–152, 154–170, 172–185, 187–193, 195–202 and 204–216); [...] **Count 4: rape**, a CRIME AGAINST HUMANITY, punishable under Statute Articles 5(g), 7(1) and 7(3) (as alleged in Paragraphs 15–17.6, 38, 39, 57, 59, 99, 109,

Trial Judgement	N/A (The trial is in progress.)
Appeal Judgement	N/A
Legal and Factual Findings and/or Evidence	N/A

30. Jovica **Stanišić and** Franko **Simatović** (Case No. IT-03-69) - Jovica Stanišić: Head or Chief of the State Security Service (DB) of the Ministry of the Internal Affairs of the Republic of Serbia (MUP). - Franko Simatović: Initially worked on counter intelligence within the DB and then moved into the newly formed Intelligence Administration (or Second Administration) of the DB and as such was the commander of the Special Operations Unit of the DB.	
Indictment (International sex crimes (or related) charges and mode(s) of liability)	The two accused are charged with: - **Persecutions as CAH** (count 1), **Deportation as CAH** (count 4) and **Inhumane acts (forcible transfer) as CAH** (count 5) under Article 7(1) of the Statute for the unlawful forcible transfer or deportation to other countries or other areas inside the country caused by various crimes, including rapes and other forms of sexual abuse, of Croat, Bosnian Muslim, Bosnian Croat and other non-Serb civilians from locations in the SAO Krajina, SAO SBWS and territories of Bosnia and Herzegovina, in which they were lawfully present.[397]

141,211 and 213); **Count 5: inhuman treatment (sexual assault)**, a GRAVE BREACH OF THE GENEVA CONVENTIONS OF 1949, punishable under Statute Articles 2(b), 7(1) and 7(3) (as alleged in Paragraphs 15–17.6, 38, 39, 55, 57, 59, 99, 109, 141, 211 and 213)"). See also *Jadranko Prlić et al.* Indictment, paras. 60, 118, 143, 217.

397 *Prosecutor v. Jovica Stanišić and Franko Simatović*, Case No. IT-03-69-PT, Third Amended Indictment, 10 July 2008, paras. 22–25 ("From no later than 1 April 1991 until 31 December 1995, **Jovica STANIŠIĆ** and **Franko SIMATOVIĆ,** acting in concert with other members of the JCE, committed persecutions of Croats, Bosnian Muslims and Bosnian Croats and other non-Serbs within the SAO Krajina, SAO SBWS and the BiH municipalities of Bijeljina, Bosanski Šamac, Doboj, Sanski Most, Trnovo (of Muslim civilians from Srebrenica) and Zvornik. Alternatively, or in addition, **Jovica STANIŠIĆ** and **Franko SIMATOVIĆ,** planned, ordered, and/or otherwise aided and abetted the planning, preparation and/or execution of persecutions of Croats, Bosnian Muslims and Bosnian Croats and other non- Serbs within the SAO Krajina, SAO SBWS and the BiH municipalities of Bijeljina, Bosanski Šamac, Doboj, Sanski Most, Trnovo (of Muslim civilians from Srebrenica) and Zvomik. Throughout this period, special units of the Republic of Serbia DB, acting alone or in conjunction with the other Serb Forces, took control of towns and villages in the territories of Croatia and BiH referred to above (with the exception of Trnovo). After the take-over, special units of the Republic of Serbia DB, acting alone or in conjunction with the other Serb Forces, established a regime of persecutions designed to force Croats, Bosnian Muslims, Bosnian Croats and other non-Serbs to leave these territories. These persecutions were committed through discrimination on the grounds of race, religion or politics, and included: [...] b) The forcible transfer and deportation of Croat, Bosnian Muslim, Bosnian Croat and other non Serb civilians, as described in paragraphs 64 and 65 of this Indictment. By the acts and omissions described in this Indictment, **Jovica STANIŠIĆ** and **Franko SIMATOVIĆ** committed, planned, ordered, and/or otherwise aided and abetted the planning, preparation and/or execution of: **COUNT 1: PERSECUTIONS ON POLITICAL, RACIAL OR RELIGIOUS GROUNDS**, a **CRIME AGAINST HUMANITY**, punishable under Articles 5(h) and 7(1) of the Statute of the Tribunal".), 64–66 ("From no later than April 1991 until 31 December 1995, **Jovica STANIŠIĆ** and **Franko SIMATOVIĆ**, acting in concert with other members of the JCE, committed unlawful forcible transfer or deportation of thousands of Croat, Bosnian

Trial Judgement	N/A (The trial is in progress.)
Appeal Judgement	N/A
Legal and Factual Findings and/or Evidence	N/A

31. Mićo **Stanišić and** Stojan **Župljanin** (Case No. IT-08-91) "***Bosnia and Herzegovina***" - Mićo Stanišić: From 1 April 1992, Minister of the newly established Serbian Ministry of Internal Affairs in Bosnia and Herzegovina (RS MUP). - Stojan Župljanin: Chief of the Regional Security Services Centre (CSB) of Banja Luka, located in north-western Bosnia and Herzegovina; member of the Autonomous Region of Krajina (ARK) Crisis Staff, advisor on internal affairs to the President of Republika Srpska (RS).	
Indictment[398] (International	The two accused are charged with:

Muslim, Bosnian Croat and other non-Serb civilians from locations in which they were lawfully present in the SAO Krajina, SAO SBWS and territories of BiH in the municipalities of Bijeljina, Bosanski Šamac, Doboj, Sanski Most, and Zvornik to other countries or other areas inside the country. Alternatively, or in addition, **Jovica STANIŠIĆ** and **Franko SIMATOVIĆ** planned, ordered, and/or otherwise aided and abetted the planning, preparation and/or execution of unlawful forcible transfer or deportation of thousands of Croat, Bosnian Muslim, Bosnian Croat and other non-Serb civilians from locations in which they were lawfully present in the SAO Krajina, SAO SBWS and territories of BiH in the municipalities of Bijeljina, Bosanski Šamac, Doboj, Sanski Most, and Zvornik to other countries or other areas inside the country. The […] rape and other forms of sexual abuse, as well as the threat of further persecutory acts, which targeted non-Serb civilians in SAO Krajina, SAO SBWS, Bijeljina, Bosanski Šamac, Doboj, Sanski Most, and Zvornik caused the non-Serb population to flee from these areas in which they were lawfully present to other parts of Croatia and BiH and to other countries. The forcible transfer and/or deportation took different forms, including forced expulsions. By the acts and omissions described in this Indictment, **Jovica STANIŠIĆ** and **Franko SIMATOVIĆ** committed, planned, ordered, and/or otherwise aided and abetted the planning, preparation and/or execution of: **COUNT 4: DEPORTATION, a CRIME AGAINST HUMANITY,** punishable under Articles 5(d) and 7(1) of the Statute of the Tribunal. **COUNT 5: INHUMANE ACTS (FORCIBLE TRANSFER), a CRIME AGAINST HUMANITY,** punishable under Articles 5(i) and 7(1) of the Statute of the Tribunal".).

398 For the general background to the charges, see *Prosecutor v. Mićo Stanišić and Stojan Župljanin*, Case No. 09-91-T, Second Amended Consolidated Indictment, 23 November 2009 ("*Stanišić and Župljanin* Indictment"), paras. 11(f) ("**Mićo STANIŠIĆ** is criminally liable for crimes committed in the period 1 April 1992 to 31 December 1992 in the municipalities of Banja Luka, Bijeljina, Bileća, Bosanski Šamac, Brčko, Doboj, Donji Vakuf, Gacko, Ilijaš, Ključ, Kotor Varoš, Pale, Prijedor, Sanski Most, Skender Vakuf, Teslić, Vlasenica, Višegrad, Vogošća and Zvornik ('the Municipalities'). **Mićo STANIŠIĆ** participated in the JCE in one or more of the following ways: […] f) Facilitating the establishment and operation of camps and detention facilities in which Serb Forces beat, killed and sexually assaulted non-Serb detainees; […]"), 12(e) ("**Stojan ŽUPLJANIN** is criminally liable for crimes committed in the period 1 April 1992 to 31 December 1992 in the municipalities of Banja Luka, Donji Vakuf, Ključ, Kotor Varoš, Prijedor, Sanski Most, Skender Vakuf and Teslić ('the ARK Municipalities'). **Stojan ŽUPLJANIN** participated in the JCE in one or more of the following ways: […] e) Facilitating, establishing and/or operating camps and detention facilities in which Serb Forces beat, killed and sexually assaulted non-Serb detainees; […]").

sex crimes (or related) charges and mode(s) of liability)	- **Persecutions as CAH** (count 1) under Articles 7(1) and 7(3) of the Statute (**superior responsibility**) of Bosnian Muslim and Bosnian Croat populations through various crimes, including sexual violence committedin detention facilities.[399] - **Torture as CAH** (count 5), **Torture as a violation of the laws or customs of war (WC)** (count 6), **Cruel treatment as a violation of the laws or customs of war (WC)** (count 7) and **Inhumane acts as CAH** (count 8) under Articles 7(1) and 7(3) of the Statute for subjecting Bosnian Muslims and Bosnian Croats in camps, police stations, military barracks and other detention facilities to various crimes, including sexual violence.[400]

399 *Stanišić and Župljanin* Indictment, paras. 24–28 ("Between about 1 April 1992 and 31 December 1992, **Mićo STANIŠIĆ**, in concert with other members in the JCE committed, or individually instigated or otherwise aided and abetted the planning, preparation or execution of persecutions on political, racial and/or religious grounds of the Bosnian Muslim and Bosnian Croat populations in the Municipalities. Between about 1 April 1992 and 31 December 1992, **Stojan ŽUPLJANIN**, in concert with other members in the JCE committed, or individually planned, instigated, ordered or otherwise aided and abetted the planning, preparation or execution of persecutions on political, racial and/or religious grounds of the Bosnian Muslim and Bosnian Croat populations in the ARK Municipalities. The acts of persecution for which **Mićo STANIŠIĆ** is criminally responsible, which were carried out by members of Serb Forces, included: […] (d) torture, cruel treatment and inhumane acts in detention facilities, as listed in Schedule D. This treatment included […] sexual violence […] The acts of persecution for which **Stojan ŽUPLJANIN** is criminally responsible, which were carried out by members of Serb Forces, included: […] (d) torture, cruel treatment and inhumane acts in detention facilities, as listed in Schedule D.I through D.7. This treatment included […] sexual violence […] By their acts and omissions, **Mićo STANIŠIĆ** committed, instigated or otherwise aided and abetted, and **Stojan ŽUPLJANIN** committed, planned, ordered, instigated or otherwise aided and abetted, or each by knowing or having reason to know that the crimes were about to be or had been committed by their subordinates and failing to take necessary and reasonable measures to prevent them or to punish the perpetrators, **Mićo STANIŠIĆ** and **Stojan ŽUPLJANIN** are each criminally responsible for: **Count 1:** Persecutions on political, racial and religious grounds, a **CRIME AGAINST HUMANITY**, punishable under Articles 5(h), 7(1) and 7(3) of the Statute of the Tribunal".).

400 *Stanišić and Župljanin* Indictment, paras. 32–36 ("Between about 1 April 1992 and 31 December 1992, **Mićo STANIŠIĆ**, in concert with other members of the JCE committed, or individually instigated or otherwise aided and abetted in the planning, preparation or execution of torture, cruel treatment and inhumane acts inflicted by Serb Forces on the non-Serb population in the Municipalities. In the alternative, **Mićo STANIŠIĆ** knew or had reason to know that said torture, cruel treatment and inhumane acts was about to be or had been committed by Serb Forces on the non-Serb population in the Municipalities but failed to take necessary and reasonable measures to prevent such acts or to punish the perpetrators thereof. Between about 1 April 1992 and 31 December 1992, **Stojan ŽUPLJANIN**, in concert with other members of the JCE committed, or individually planned, instigated, ordered or otherwise aided and abetted in the planning, preparation or execution of torture, cruel treatment and inhumane acts inflicted by Serb Forces on the non-Serb population in the ARK Municipalities. In the alternative, **Stojan ŽUPLJANIN** knew or had reason to know that said torture, cruel treatment and inhumane acts was about to be or had been committed by Serb Forces on the non-Serb population in the ARK Municipalities but failed to take necessary and reasonable measures to prevent such acts or to punish the perpetrators thereof. Bosnian Muslims and Bosnian Croats were confined in inhumane conditions and subjected to intentional infliction of severe pain and suffering by beatings, torture, sexual violence, humiliation, harassment, and psychological abuses in camps, police stations, military barracks and other detention facilities as listed in Schedule D, as well as at the locations and on the dates listed under 2.1 and 3.4 in Schedule A, for which **Mićo STANIŠIĆ** is criminally responsible. Bosnian Muslims and Bosnian Croats were confined in inhumane conditions and subjected to intentional infliction of severe pain and suffering by beatings, torture, sexual violence, humiliation, harassment, and psychological abuses in camps, police stations, military barracks and other detention facilities within the ARK Municipalities, as listed in Schedule D.1 through D.7, as well as at the locations and on the dates listed under 2.1 and 3.4 in Schedule A, for which **Stojan ŽUPLJANIN** is criminally responsible. By their acts and omissions, **Mićo STANIŠIĆ** committed, instigated or otherwise aided and abetted, and **Stojan ŽUPLJANIN** committed, planned, ordered, instigated or otherwise aided and abetted, or each by knowing or having reason to know that the crimes were about to be or had been committed by their subordinates and failing to take necessary and reasonable measures to prevent the crimes or to punish the perpetrators, **Mićo STANIŠIĆ** and

Trial Judgement	N/A (The trial is in progress.)
Appeal Judgement	N/A
Legal and Factual Findings and/or Evidence	N/A

32. Vojislav **Šešelj** (Case No. IT-03-67) In June 1990, founded the Serbian National Renewal Party, later renamed the Serbian Chetnik Movement (SČP), which was banned by the authorities of the Socialist Federal Republic of Yugoslavia (SFRY) in December 1990; appointed President of the newly founded Serbian Radical Party (SRS) on 23 February 1991; elected as a member of the Assembly of the Republic of Serbia in June 1991.	
Indictment (International sex crimes (or related) charges and mode(s) of liability)	- **Persecutions as CAH** (count 1) under Article 7(1) of the Statute of Croat, Muslim and other non-Serb civilians by Serb soldiers during their capture and while detained through various acts, including sexual assaults.[401] - **Torture as a violation of the laws or customs of war (WC)** (count 8) and **Cruel treatment as a violation of the laws of customs of war (WC)** (count 9) under Article 7(1) of the Statute for various crimes, including sexual assaults, committed against the Muslim, Croat and other non-Serb civilians detained in various dentention facilities.[402]

Stojan ŽUPLJANIN are each criminally responsible for: **Count 5:** Torture, a **CRIME AGAINST HUMANITY**, punishable under Article 5 (f), 7(1) and 7(3) of the Statute of the Tribunal; **Count 6:** Torture, a **VIOLATION OF THE LAWS OR CUSTOMS OF WAR**, as recognised by Common Article 3 (l)(a) of the Geneva Conventions of 1949, punishable under Articles 3, 7(1) and 7(3) of the Statute of the Tribunal; **Count 7:** Cruel treatment, a **VIOLATION OF THE LAWS OR CUSTOMS OF WAR**, as recognised by Common Article 3(1) of the Geneva Conventions of 1949, punishable under Articles 3, 7(1) and 7(3) of the Statute of the Tribunal; **Count 8:** Inhumane acts, a **CRIME AGAINST HUMANITY**, punishable under Article 5(i), 7(1) and 7(3) of the Statute of the Tribunal".).

401 *Prosecutor v. Vojislav Šešelj*, Case No. IT-03-67-T, Third Amended Indictment, 7 December 2007 ("*Šešelj* Indictment"), paras. 15–16, 17(f) ("From on or about 1 August 1991 until at least September 1993, **Vojislav ŠEŠELJ,** acting individually or as a participant in a joint criminal enterprise, planned, ordered, instigated, committed or otherwise aided and abetted in the planning, preparation or execution of, or physically committed, persecutions of Croat, Muslim and other non-Serb civilian populations in the territories of the SAO SBWS (Slavonia, Baranja and Western Srem), and in the municipalities of Zvornik, 'Greater Sarajevo', Mostar, and Nevesinje in Bosnia and Herzegovina and parts of Vojvodina in Serbia. Throughout this period, the Serb forces defined in paragraph 8(a), above, including volunteers recruited and/or instigated by **Vojislav ŠEŠELJ**, attacked and took control of towns and villages in these territories. After the take-over, these Serb forces, in co-operation with the local Serb authorities, established a regime of persecutions designed to drive the non-Serb civilian population from these territories. These persecutions were committed on political, racial and religious grounds and included: […] f. Sexual assaults of Croat, Muslim and other non-Serb civilians by Serb soldiers during their capture and while detained in the said detention facilities. […] By his participation in these acts, **Vojislav ŠEŠELJ** committed: **Count 1:** Persecutions on political, racial or religious grounds, a **CRIME AGAINST HUMANITY**, punishable under Articles 5(h) and 7(1) of the Statute of the Tribunal".).

402 *Šešelj* Indictment, paras. 28–30 ("From August 1991 until September 1993, **Vojislav ŠEŠELJ,** acting individually or as a participant in a joint criminal enterprise, planned, ordered, instigated, committed or otherwise aided and abetted in the planning, preparation or execution of the imprisonment under inhumane conditions of Muslim, Croat and other non-Serb civilians in the territories listed above. Serb forces, including those volunteer units recruited and/or incited by **Vojislav ŠEŠELJ,** captured and detained hundreds of Croat,

Trial Judgement	N/A (The trial is in progress.)
Appeal Judgement	N/A
Legal and Factual Findings and/or Evidence	N/A

33. Radovan **Karadžić** (Case No. IT-95-5/18) Founding member of the Serbian Democratic Party (SDS); President of the SDS until his resignation on 19 July 1996; Chairman of the National Security Council of the so-called Serbian Republic of Bosnia and Herzegovina (later Republika Srpska – RS); President of the three-member Presidency of RS from its creation on 12 May 1992 until 17 December 1992, and thereafter sole President of Republika Srpska and Supreme Commander of its armed forces.	
Indictment (International sex crimes (or related) charges and mode(s) of	- **Genocide** (count 1) under Articles 7(1) (**joint criminal enterprise**) and 7(3) of the Statute (**superior responsibility**) for various crimes, including **causing serious bodily or mental harm** to Bosnian Muslim and/or Bosnian Croat detainees by subjecting them to rapes and other acts of sexual violence and **deliberately inflicting on them conditions of life calculated to bring about their physical destruction** through rapes and other acts of sexual violence.[403]

Muslim and other non-Serb civilians. They were detained in the following short- and long-term detention facilities: a) The Velepromet warehouse, Vukovar, SAO SBWS, November 1991, run by JNA, approximately twelve hundred detainees. b) The Ovčara farm, near Vukovar, SAO SBWS, November 1991, run by JNA, approximately three hundred detainees. […] e) The 'Standard' shoe factory, the 'Ciglana' factory, the Ekonomija farm, the Drinjača Dom Kulture, the Karakaj Technical School, Gero's slaughter-house and the Čelopek Dom Kulture in Zvornik, Bosnia and Herzegovina between April and July 1992, hundreds of detainees. […] g) The 'Iskra' warehouse in the village of Podlugovi, Ilijaš municipality, 'Planja's house' in the village of Svrake, Vogošća municipality, 'Sonja's house' in Vogošća municipality, the barracks in Semizovac village, Vogošća municipality and the tire repair garage at the Vogošća crossroad in Vogošća municipality between April 1992 and September 1993, dozens of detainees. […] j) The city mortuary in Sutina, Mostar and the stadium in Vrapčići, Mostar during June 1992, more than one hundred detainees. k) The basement of the heating factory in Kilavci, Nevesinje, the resort at Boračko Jezero, Nevesinje, the primary school in Zijemlje, Nevesinje and the SUP building in Nevesinje during June 1992, more than one hundred detainees. The living conditions in these detention facilities were brutal and characterised by […] systematic physical and psychological assault, including […] sexual assault. By his participation in these acts, **Vojislav ŠEŠELJ** committed: […] **<u>Count 8:</u>** Torture, a **VIOLATION OF THE LAWS OR CUSTOMS OF WAR** as recognised by Common Article 3(1)(a) of the Geneva Conventions of 1949, punishable under Articles 3 and 7(1) of the Statute of the Tribunal. **<u>Count 9:</u>** Cruel Treatment, a **VIOLATION OF THE LAWS OR CUSTOMS OF WAR** as recognised by Common Article 3(1)(a) of the Geneva Conventions of 1949, punishable under Articles 3 and 7(1) of the Statute of the Tribunal".).

403 *Prosecutor v. Radovan Karadžić*, Case No. IT-95-5/18-PT, Third Amended Indictment (Marked-Up), 19 October 2009 ("*Karadžić* Indictment"), para. 40(b)-(c) ("Between 31 March 1992 and 31 December 1992, Bosnian Serb Political and Governmental Organs and Serb Forces carried out the following acts against Bosnian Muslims and Bosnian Croats: […] (b) the causing of serious bodily or mental harm to thousands of Bosnian Muslims and Bosnian Croats, including leading members of these groups, during their confinement in detention facilities, including those listed in **Schedule C**. At these locations, detainees were subjected to cruel or inhumane treatment, including torture, physical and psychological abuse, rape, other acts of sexual violence and beatings; and (c) the detention of thousands of Bosnian Muslims and Bosnian Croats, including leading members of these groups, in detention facilities, including those listed in **Schedule C**, under condi-

liability)	- **Persecutions as CAH** (count 3) under Articles 7(1) (**joint criminal enterprise**) and 7(3) of the Statute (**superior responsibility**) of Bosnian Muslims and/or Bosnian Croats through various acts, including rapes and other acts of sexual violence.[404] - **Deportation as CAH** (count 7) and **Inhumane acts (forcible transfer) as CAH** (count 8) of Bosnian Muslims and/or Bosnian Croats by forcibly displacing them as a result of various acts, including rapes and other acts of sexual violence.[405]
Trial Judgement	N/A (The trial is in progress.)
Appeal Judgement	N/A
Legal and Factual Findings and/or Evidence	N/A

34. Ratko **<u>Mladić</u>** (Case No. IT-09-92) Appointed Commander of the Main Staff of the Bosnian Serb Army (VRS) on 12 May 1992 (a position he held until at least 8 November 1996); promoted to the rank of Colonel General in June 1994.	
Indictment (International sex crimes (or related)	- **Genocide** (count 1) under Articles 7(1) (**joint criminal enterprise**) and 7(3) of the Statute (**superior responsibility**) for various crimes, including **causing serious bodily or mental harm** to Bosnian Muslim and/or Bosnian Croat detainees by subjecting them to rapes and other acts of sexual violence and **deliberately inflicting on them**

tions of life calculated to bring about their physical destruction, namely through cruel and inhumane treatment, including torture, physical and psychological abuse, rape, other acts of sexual violence, inhumane living conditions, forced labour and the failure to provide adequate accommodation, shelter, food, water, medical care or hygienic sanitation facilities. **Radovan KARADŽIĆ** is criminally responsible for: **<u>Count 1:</u> GENOCIDE**, punishable under Articles 4(3)(a), and 7(1) and 7(3) of the Statute".).

404 *Karadžić* Indictment, paras. 53–54 ("During and after these takeovers and continuing until 30 November 1995, Serb Forces and Bosnian Serb Political and Governmental Organs carried out persecutory acts against Bosnian Muslims and Bosnian Croats including […] rape and other acts of sexual violence […]. Serb Forces and Bosnian Serb Political and Governmental Organs also established and controlled detention facilities in the Municipalities where Bosnian Muslims and Bosnian Croats were detained and subjected to persecutory acts including […] rape and other acts of sexual violence […]".), 60(c) ("Acts of persecution carried out by members of the Serb Forces and Bosnian Serb Political and Governmental Organs pursuant to one or more of the joint criminal enterprises included: […] (c) rape and other acts of sexual violence during and after takeovers in the Municipalities and in detention facilities in the Municipalities, including those detention facilities listed in **Schedule C**, as cruel and inhumane treatment; […] **Radovan KARADŽIĆ** is criminally responsible for: **<u>Count 3</u>:** Persecutions on Political, Racial and Religious Grounds, a **CRIME AGAINST HUMANITY**, punishable under Articles 5(h) and 7(1) and 7(3) of the Statute".).

405 *Karadžić* Indictment, paras. 71 ("Beginning in March 1992, restrictive and discriminatory measures, arbitrary arrest and detention, harassment, torture, rape and other acts of sexual violence, killing, and destruction of houses and cultural monuments and sacred sites, all targeting Bosnian Muslims and Bosnian Croats in the Municipalities, as well as the threat of further such acts, caused Bosnian Muslims and Bosnian Croats to flee in fear. Others were physically driven out".), 75 ("[…] **Radovan KARADŽIĆ** is criminally responsible for: **<u>Count 7</u>:** Deportation, a **CRIME AGAINST HUMANITY,** punishable under Articles 5(d), and 7(1) and 7(3) of the Statute; and **<u>Count 8</u>:** Inhumane Acts (forcible transfer), a **CRIME AGAINST HUMANITY,** punishable under Articles 5(i), and 7(1) and 7(3) of the Statute".).

charges and mode(s) of liability)	**conditions of life calculated to bring about their physical destruction** through rapes and other acts of sexual violence.[406] - **Persecutions as CAH** (count 3) under Articles 7(1) (**joint criminal enterprise**) and 7(3) of the Statute (**superior responsibility**) of Bosnian Muslims and/or Bosnian Croats through various acts, including rapes and other acts of sexual violence.[407] - **Deportation as CAH** (count 7) and **Inhumane acts (forcible transfer) as CAH** (count 8) of Bosnian Muslims and/or Bosnian Croats by forcibly displacing them as a result of various acts, including rapes and other acts of sexual violence.[408]
Trial Judgement	N/A (The trial has not yet started.)
Appeal Judgement	N/A
Legal and Factual Findings and/or Evidence	N/A

406 *Prosecutor v. Ratko Mladić*, Case No. IT-09-92-I, Second Amended Indictment, 1 June 2011 ("*Mladić* Indictment"), para. 39(b)-(c) ("Between 12 May 1992 and 31 December 1992, Bosnian Serb Political and Governmental Organs and Serb Forces carried out the following acts against Bosnian Muslims and Bosnian Croats: […] (b) the causing of serious bodily or mental harm to thousands of Bosnian Muslims and Bosnian Croats, including leading members of these groups, during their confinement in detention facilities, including those listed in **Schedule** C. At these locations, detainees were subjected to cruel or inhumane treatment, including torture, physical and psychological abuse, rape, other acts of sexual violence and beatings; and (c) the detention of thousands of Bosnian Muslims and Bosnian Croats, including leading members of these groups, in detention facilities, including those listed in **Schedule** C, under conditions of life calculated to bring about their physical destruction, namely through cruel and inhumane treatment, including torture, physical and psychological abuse, rape, other acts of sexual violence, inhumane living conditions, forced labour and the failure to provide adequate accommodation, shelter, food, water, medical care or hygienic sanitation facilities. **Ratko MLADIĆ** is criminally responsible for: **Count 1: GENOCIDE,** punishable under Articles 4(3)(a), and 7(1) and 7(3) of the Statute".).

407 *Mladić* Indictment, paras. 52–53 ("During and after these takeovers and continuing until 30 November 1995, Serb Forces and Bosnian Serb Political and Governmental Organs carried out persecutory acts against Bosnian Muslims and Bosnian Croats including […] rape and other acts of sexual violence […]. Serb Forces and Bosnian Serb Political and Governmental Organs also established and controlled detention facilities in the Municipalities where Bosnian Muslims and Bosnian Croats were detained and subjected to persecutory acts including […] rape and other acts of sexual violence […]".) 59(c) ("Acts of persecution carried out by members of the Serb Forces and Bosnian Serb Political and Governmental Organs pursuant to one or more of the joint criminal enterprises between 12 May 1992 and 30 November 1995 included: […] (c) rape and other acts of sexual violence during and after takeovers in the Municipalities and in detention facilities in the Municipalities, including those detention facilities listed in **Schedule C**, as cruel and inhumane treatment; […] **Ratko MLADIĆ** is criminally responsible for: **Count 3:** Persecutions on Political, Racial and Religious Grounds, a **CRIME AGAINST HUMANITY**, punishable under Articles 5(h) and 7(1) and 7(3) of the Statute".).

408 *Mladić* Indictment, paras. 70 ("Beginning in March 1992, restrictive and discriminatory measures, arbitrary arrest and detention, harassment, torture, rape and other acts of sexual violence, killing, and destruction of houses and cultural monuments and sacred sites, all targeting Bosnian Muslims and Bosnian Croats in the Municipalities, as well as the threat of further such acts, caused Bosnian Muslims and Bosnian Croats to flee in fear. Others were physically driven out".), 74 ("**Ratko MLADIĆ** is criminally responsible for: **Count 7:** Deportation, a **CRIME AGAINST HUMANITY,** punishable under Articles 5(d), and 7(1) and 7(3) of the Statute; and **Count 8:** Inhumane Acts (forcible transfer), a **CRIME AGAINST HUMANITY,** punishable under Articles 5(i), and 7(1) and 7(3) of the Statute".).

<table>
<tr><td colspan="2">35. Goran <u>Hadžić</u> (Case No. IT-04-75)

President of the Government of the self-proclaimed Serbian Autonomous District Slavonia, Baranja and Western Srem (SAO SBWS); subsequently President of the Republic of Serbian Krajina (RSK).</td></tr>
<tr><td>Indictment (International sex crimes (or related) charges and mode(s) of liability)</td><td>- Persecutions as CAH (count 1), Torture as CAH (count 6), Inhumane acts as CAH (count 7), Torture as a violation of the laws or customs of war (WC) (count 8) and Cruel treatment as a violation of the laws or customs of war (count 9) under Articles 7(1) and 7(3) of the Statute (superior responsibility) for imposing on Croat and other non-Serb civilian detainees living conditions in various detention facilities characterised by, inter alia, inhumane treatment and constant physical and psychological assault, including sexual assault.[409]</td></tr>
</table>

[409] *Prosecutor v. Goran Hadžić*, Case No. IT-04-75-I, First Amended Indictment, 22 July 2011, paras. 19 ("From no later than 25 June 1991 until the end of December 1993, **Goran HADŽIĆ**, committed in concert with others, planned, instigated, ordered, and/or aided persecutions of the Croat and other non-Serb civilian population in the SAO SBWS/RSK. In addition, **Goran HADŽIĆ** knew or had reason to know that persecutions were about to be or had been committed by his subordinates, and he failed to take the necessary and reasonable measures to prevent such acts or punish the perpetrators thereof".), 21(d) ("These persecutions were based on political, racial or religious grounds and included the following: (d) The physical and psychological mistreatment of Croat and other non-Serb civilian detainees in the mentioned detention facilities described in paragraph[s] 40 to 42, including but not limited to [...] sexual assault [...]".), 22 ("**Goran HADŽIĆ** is criminally responsible for: <u>Count 1:</u> Persecutions on politicial, racial, or religious grounds, a CRIME AGAINST HUMANITY, punishable under Articles 5(h) and 7(1) and 7(3) of the Statute of the Tribunal".), 40–43 ("From at least 25 June 1991 until the end of December 1993, **Goran HADŽIĆ** committed in concert with others, planned, instigated, ordered, and/or aided and abetted the unlawful confinement or imprisonment under inhumane conditions of members of the Croat and other non-Serb population and persons not taking an active part in the hostilities in the territories listed in paragraph 7 of this indictment. In addition, in relation to paragraph 41 (f) to (m), **Goran HADŽIĆ** knew or had reason to know that unlawful confinement or imprisonment under inhumane conditions were about to be or had been committed by his subordinates, and he failed to take the necessary and reasonable measures to prevent such acts or punish the perpetrators thereof. Serb Forces, including JNA, local Serb TO and special units of the Republic of Serbia MUP and/or DB acting in co-operation with local and Serbian police staff and local SAO SBWS authorities and authorities in Serbia, arrested and detained thousands of Croat and other non-Serb, including civilians and persons not taking an active part in the hostilities, in the following short- and long-term detention facilities: a) STAJIĆEVO agricultural farm in Serbia, approximately one thousand and seven hundred detainees. b) Agricultural complex in Begejci in Serbia, approximately two hundred and sixty detainees. c) Military barracks in Zrenjanin in Serbia, dozens of detainees. d) Military prison Sremska Mitrovica in Serbia, hundreds of detainees. e) Military prison in Šid, Serbia, approximately one hundred detainees. f) Police buildings and the hangar near the railway station in Dalj, SAO SBWS, hundreds of detainees. g) Territorial Defence training centre in Erdut, also referred to as Arkan's military base, SAO SBWS, approximately fifty-two detainees. h) Vukovar Hospital and the JNA Vukovar Barracks, SAO SBWS, at least three hundred detainees. i) Ovčara farm, near Vukovar, SAO SBWS, approximately three hundred detainees. j) Velepromet facility near Vukovar, SAO SBWS, hundreds of detainees. k) Police station in Opatovac, SAO SBWS, dozens of detainees. l) Stable or workshop in Borovo Selo, SAO SBWS, approximately ninety-two detainees. m) *Zadruga* building in Lovas, dozens of detainees. The living conditions in these detention facilities were inadequate and characterised by inhumane treatment, overcrowding, starvation, forced labour, inadequate medical care, and constant physical and psychological assault, including [...] sexual assault. **Goran HADŽIĆ** is criminally responsible under Article 7(1) in relation to all detention facilities listed in paragrpah 41, and under Article 7(3) in relation to detention facilities listes in paragraph 41 (f) to (m) for: [...] <u>Count 6:</u> Torture, a CRIME AGAINST HUMANITY punishable under Article 5(f) and Article 7 (1) and 7(3) of the Statute of the Tribunal. <u>Count 7:</u> Inhumane acts, a CRIME AGAINST HUMANITY punishable under Article 5(i) and Article 7 (1) and 7(3) of the Statute of the Tribunal. <u>Count 8:</u> Torture, a VIOLATION OF THE LAWS OR CUSTOMS OF WAR as recognised by Common Article 3 (1)(a) of the Geneva Conventions of 1949, punishable under Article 3 and Article 7 (1) and 7(3) of the Statute of the Tribunal. <u>Count 9:</u> Cruel treatment, a VIOLATION OF THE LAWS OR CUSTOMS OF WAR as recognised by Common Article 3 (1)(a) of the Geneva Conventions of 1949, punishable under Article 3 and Article 7 (1) and 7(3) of the Statute of the Tribunal".).

Trial Judgement	N/A (The trial has not yet started.)
Appeal Judgement	N/A
Legal and Factual Findings and/or Evidence	N/A

15.3. ICTR International Sex Crimes Charts

1. Jean-Paul **Akayesu** (Case No. ICTR-96-4) Bourgmestre of Taba commune, in Gitarama prefecture, from April 1993 until June 1994.	
Indictment[410] (International sex crimes (or related) charges and mode(s) of liability)	- **Genocide** (count 1) and **Complicitiy in genocide** (count 2) under Article 6(1) of the Statute as well as **Rape as CAH** (count 13), **Other inhumane acts as CAH** (count 14) and **Outrages upon personal dignity, in particular humiliating and degrading treatment, rape and indecent assault as a violation of Article 3 common to the Geneva Conventions and of Additional Protocol II (WC)** (count 15) under Articles 6(1) and 6(3) of the Statute (**superior responsibility**) for the sexual violence committed against Tutsi women by local armed militia and/or communal police near the bureau communal premises.[411]

410 For the definition of the term "sexual violence" used in the Indictment, see *Prosecutor v. Jean-Paul Akayesu*, Case No. ICTR-96-4-T, Amended Indictment, 30 June 1997 ("*Akayesu* Indictment"), para. 10.A. ("In this indictment, acts of sexual violence include forcible sexual penetration of the vagina, anus or oral cavity by a penis and/or of the vagina or anus by some other object, and sexual abuse, such as forced nudity".).

411 *Akayesu* Indictment, paras. 12.A-12.B ("Between April 7 and the end of June, 1994, hundreds of civilians (hereinafter 'displaced civilians') sought refuge at the bureau communal. The majority of these displaced civilians were Tutsi. While seeking refuge at the bureau communal, female displaced civilians were regularly taken by armed local militia and/or communal police and subjected to sexual violence, and/or beaten on or near the bureau communal premises. Displaced civilians were also murdered frequently on or near the bureau communal premises. Many women were forced to endure multiple acts of sexual violence which were at times committed by more than one assailant. These acts of sexual violence were generally accompanied by explicit threats of death or bodily harm. The female displaced civilians lived in constant fear and their physical and psychological health deteriorated as a result of the sexual violence and beatings and killings. **Jean Paul AKAYESU** knew that the acts of sexual violence, beatings and murders were being committed and was at times present during their commission. **Jean Paul AKAYESU** facilitated the commission of the sexual violence, beatings and murders by allowing the sexual violence and beatings and murders to occur on or near the bureau communal premises. By virtue of his presence during the commission of the sexual violence, beatings and murders and by failing to prevent the sexual violence, beatings and murders, **Jean Paul AKAYESU** encouraged these activities".), pp. 6–7 ("By his acts in relation to the events described in paragraphs 12–23, **Jean Paul AKAYESU** is criminally responsible for: COUNT 1: **GENOCIDE**, punishable by Article 2(3)(a) of the Statute of the Tribunal; COUNT 2: Complicity in **GENOCIDE**, punishable by Article 2(3)(e) of the Statute of the Tribunal"), pp. 9–10 ("committed: COUNT 13: **CRIMES AGAINST HUMANITY** (rape), punishable by Article 3(g) of the Statute of the Tribunal; and COUNT 14: **CRIMES AGAINST HUMANITY**, (other inhumane acts), punishable by Article 3(i) of the Statute of the Tribunal; and COUNT 15: **VIOLATIONS OF ARTICLE 3 COMMON TO THE GENEVA CONVENTIONS AND OF ARTICLE 4(2)(e) OF ADDITIONAL PROTOCOL 2**, as incorporated by Article 4(e)(outrages upon personal dignity, in particular rape, degrading and humiliating treatment and indecent assault) of the Statute of the Tribunal".). The Prosecution closed its case on 24 May 1997. However, on 16 June 1997, the Prosecution sought leave to amend the Indictment to add three further counts on international sex crimes (counts 13, 14

Trial Judgement	- Guilty of **Rape as CAH** (count 13) under Article 6(1) of the Statute for: (i) the rape of Witness JJ by an *Interahamwe* who took her from outside the bureau communal and raped her in a nearby forest (**aiding and abetting**); (ii) the multiple acts of rape of fifteen girls and women, including Witness JJ, by numerous *Interahamwe* in the cultural center of the bureau communal (**aiding and abetting**); (iii) the multiple acts of rape of ten girls and women, including Witness JJ, by numerous *Interahamwe* in the cultural center of the bureau communal (**ordering, instigating and aiding and abetting**); (iv) the rape of Witness OO by an *Interahamwe* named Antoine in a field near the bureau communal (**ordering, instigating and aiding and abetting**); (v) the rape of a woman by *Interahamwe* in between two buildings of the bureau communal (**aiding and abetting**); (vi) the rape of the younger sister of Witness NN by an *Interahamwe* at the bureau communal (**aiding and abetting**); (vii) the multiple rapes of Alexia, wife of Ntereye, and her two nieces Louise and Nishimwe by *Interahamwe* near the bureau communal (**aiding and abetting**). - Guilty of **Other inhumane acts as CAH** (count 14) under Article 6(1) of the Statute for: (i) the forced undressing of the wife of Tharcisse outside the bureau communal, after making her sit in the mud (**aiding and abetting**); (ii) the forced undressing and public marching of Chantal naked at the bureau communal (**ordering, instigating and aiding and abetting**); (iii) the forced undressing of Alexia, wife of Ntereye, and her two nieces Louise and Nishimwe, and forcing the women to perform exercises naked in public near the bureau communal (**aiding and abetting**). - Guilty of **Genocide (causing serious bodily or mental harm)** (count 1) under Article 6(1) of the Statute for the infliction of all the above-mentioned acts (**aiding and abetting**).[412] - Not guilty of outrages upon personal dignity (in particular rape, degrading and humiliating treatment and indecent assault) as a violation of Article 3 common to the Geneva Conventions and of Additional Protocol II (WC) (count 15), because the Trial Chamber found that it was not proved beyond reasonable doubt that the acts perpetrated by Jean-Paul Akayesu were committed in conunction with the armed conflict.[413]
Appeal Judgement	- The convictions were affirmed by the Appeals Chamber.[414]
Legal and Factual Findings and/or Evidence	- The Trial Judgement contains the first conviction for rape as CAH and sexual violence as genocide before the ICTR. - <u>Legal findings:</u> **- Sexual mutilation and rape can constitute genocide (imposing measures intended to prevent births within the group):** The Trial Chamber held: "For purposes of interpreting Article 2(2)(d) of the Statute,

and 15). The Trial Chamber granted the Prosecution's request and postponed the date for resumption of the trial to 22 October 1997. On that day, Jean-Paul Akayesu pleaded not guilty to each new count and the Prosecutor then proceeded to present six new witnesses. See *Prosecutor v. Jean-Paul Akayesu*, Case No. ICTR-96-4-T, Leave to Amend the Indictment, dated 17 June 1997 and filed on 8 October 1997, pp. 2–3. On appeal, Jean-Paul Akayesu submitted that the Trial Chamber committed an error of law in allowing the Prosecutor to amend the Indictment to include three new counts on international sex crimes. The Appeals Chamber rejected all the grounds of appeal related to the amendment of the Indictment. See *Prosecutor v. Jean-Paul Akayesu*, Case No. ICTR-96-4-A, Judgement, 1 June 2001 ("*Akayesu* Appeal Judgement"), paras. 102–123.

412 *Prosecutor v. Jean-Paul Akayesu*, Case No. ICTR-96-4-T, Judgement, 2 September 1998 ("*Akayesu* Trial Judgement"), paras. 449–460, 692–697, 706–707, 724, 731–734 and Section 8 (Verdict), p. 294.

413 *Akayesu* Trial Judgement, paras. 643–644 and Section 8 (Verdict), p. 294.

414 *Akayesu* Appeal Judgement, Section V (Disposition), p. 144.

	the Chamber holds that the measures intended to prevent births within the group, should be construed as sexual mutilation, the practice of sterilization, forced birth control, separation of the sexes and prohibition of marriages. In patriarchal societies, where membership of a group is determined by the identity of the father, an example of a measure intended to prevent births within a group is the case where, during rape, a woman of the said group is deliberately impregnated by a man of another group, with the intent to have her give birth to a child who will consequently not belong to its mother's group. Furthermore, the Chamber notes that measures intended to prevent births within the group may be physical, but can also be mental. For instance, rape can be a measure intended to prevent births when the person raped refuses subsequently to procreate, in the same way that members of a group can be led, through threats or trauma, not to procreate".[415] **- Rape can constitute torture and definition:** The Trial Chamber held: "Considering the extent to which rape constitute crimes against humanity, pursuant to Article 3(g) of the Statute, the Chamber must define rape, as there is no commonly accepted definition of this term in international law. While rape has been defined in certain national jurisdictions as non-consensual intercourse, variations on the act of rape may include acts which involve the insertion of objects and/or the use of bodily orifices not considered to be intrinsically sexual. The Chamber considers that rape is a form of aggression and that the central elements of the crime of rape cannot be captured in a mechanical description of objects and body parts. The Convention against Torture and Other Cruel, Inhuman and Degrading Treatment or Punishment does not catalogue specific acts in its definition of torture, focusing rather on the conceptual frame work of state sanctioned violence. This approach is more useful in international law. Like torture, rape is used for such purposes as intimidation, degradation, humiliation, discrimination, punishment, control or destruction of a person. Like torture, rape is a violation of personal dignity, and rape in fact constitutes torture when inflicted by or at the instigation of or with the consent or acquiescence of a public official or other person acting in an official capacity. The Chamber defines rape as a physical invasion of a sexual nature, committed on a person under circumstances which are coercive. Sexual violence which includes rape, is considered to be any act of a sexual nature which is committed on a person under circumstances which are coercive. This act must be committed: (a) as part of a wide spread or systematic attack; (b) on a civilian population; (c) on certained catalogued discriminatory grounds, namely: national, ethnic, political, racial, or religious grounds".[416] "In considering the extent to which acts of sexual violence constitute crimes against humanity under Article 3(g) of its Statute, the Tribunal must define rape, as there is no commonly accepted definition of the term in international law. The Tribunal notes that many of the witnesses have used the term 'rape' in their testimony. At times, the Prosecution and the Defence have also tried to elicit an explicit description of what happened in physical terms, to document what the witnesses mean by the term 'rape'. The Tribunal notes that while rape has been historically defined in national jurisdictions as non-consensual sexual intercourse, variations on the form of rape may include acts which involve the insertion of objects and/or the use of bodily orifices not considered to be intrinsically sexual. An act such as that described by Witness KK in her testimony - the Interahamwes thrusting a piece of wood into the sexual organs of a woman as she lay dying - constitutes rape in the Tribunal's view. The Tribunal considers that rape is a form of aggression and that the central elements of the crime of rape cannot be captured in a mechanical description of objects and body parts. The Tribunal

415 *Akayesu* Trial Judgement, paras. 507–508.
416 *Akayesu* Trial Judgement, paras. 596–598.

	also notes the cultural sensitivities involved in public discussion of intimate matters and recalls the painful reluctance and inability of witnesses to disclose graphic anatomical details of sexual violence they endured. The United Nations Convention Against Torture and Other Cruel, Inhuman and Degrading Treatment or Punishment does not catalogue specific acts in its definition of torture, focusing rather on the conceptual framework of state-sanctioned violence. The Tribunal finds this approach more useful in the context of international law. Like torture, rape is used for such purposes as intimidation, degradation, humiliation, discrimination, punishment, control or destruction of a person. Like torture, rape is a violation of personal dignity, and rape in fact constitutes torture when it is inflicted by or at the instigation of or with the consent or acquiescence of a public official or other person acting in an official capacity. The Tribunal defines rape as a physical invasion of a sexual nature, committed on a person under circumstances which are coercive".[417] **- Sexual violence: definition:** The Trial Chamber held: "The Tribunal considers sexual violence, which includes rape, as any act of a sexual nature which is committed on a person under circumstances which are coercive. Sexual violence is not limited to physical invasion of the human body and may include acts which do not involve penetration or even physical contact. The incident described by Witness KK in which the Accused ordered the Interahamwe to undress a student and force her to do gymnastics naked in the public courtyard of the bureau communal, in front of a crowd, constitutes sexual violence. The Tribunal notes in this context that coercive circumstances need not be evidenced by a show of physical force. Threats, intimidation, extortion and other forms of duress which prey on fear or desperation may constitute coercion, and coercion may be inherent in certain circumstances, such as armed conflict or the military presence of Interahamwe among refugee Tutsi women at the bureau communal".[418] **- Sexual violence can constitute other inhumane acts as CAH, outrages upon personal dignity (WC) and genocide (serious bodily or mental harm):** The Trial Chamber held: "Sexual violence falls within the scope of 'other inhumane acts', set forth Article 3(i) of the Tribunal's Statute, 'outrages upon personal dignity,' set forth in Article 4(e) of the Statute, and 'serious bodily or mental harm,' set forth in Article 2(2)(b) of the Statute".[419] - <u>Factual and legal findings:</u> - Rapes and sexual violence: "Having carefully reviewed the testimony of the Prosecution witnesses regarding sexual violence, the Chamber finds that there is sufficient credible evidence to establish beyond a reasonable doubt that during the events of 1994, Tutsi girls and women were subjected to sexual violence, beaten and killed on or near the bureau communal premises, as well as elsewhere in the commune of Taba. Witness H, Witness JJ, Witness OO, and Witness NN all testified that they themselves were raped, and all, with the exception of Witness OO, testified that they witnessed other girls and women being raped. Witness J, Witness KK and Witness PP also testified that they witnessed other girls and women being raped in the commune of Taba. Hundreds of Tutsi, mostly women and children, sought refuge at the bureau communal during this period and many rapes took place on or near the premises of the bureau communal - Witness JJ was taken by Interahamwe from the refuge site near the bureau communal to a

[417] *Akayesu* Trial Judgement, paras. 686–688.
[418] *Akayesu* Trial Judgement, para. 688.
[419] *Akayesu* Trial Judgement, para. 688.

	nearby forest area and raped there. She testified that this happened often to other young girls and women at the refuge site. Witness JJ was also raped repeatedly on two separate occasions in the cultural center on the premises of the bureau communal, once in a group of fifteen girls and women and once in a group of ten girls and women. Witness KK saw women and girls being selected and taken by the Interahamwe to the cultural center to be raped. Witness H saw women being raped outside the compound of the bureau communal, and Witness NN saw two Interahamwes take a woman and rape her between the bureau communal and the cultural center. Witness OO was taken from the bureau communal and raped in a nearby field. Witness PP saw three women being raped at Kinihira, the killing site near the bureau communal, and Witness NN found her younger sister, dying, after she had been raped at the bureau communal. Many other instances of rape in Taba outside the bureau communal - in fields, on the road, and in or just outside houses - were described by Witness J, Witness H, Witness OO, Witness KK, Witness NN and Witness PP. Witness KK and Witness PP also described other acts of sexual violence which took place on or near the premises of the bureau communal - the forced undressing and public humiliation of girls and women. The Chamber notes that much of the sexual violence took place in front of large numbers of people, and that all of it was directed against Tutsi women. With a few exceptions, most of the rapes and all of the other acts of sexual violence described by the Prosecution witnesses were committed by Interahamwe. It has not been established that the perpetrator of the rape of Witness H in a sorghum field and six of the men who raped Witness NN were Interahamwe. In the case of Witness NN, two of her rapists were neighbours, two were teenage boys and two were herdsmen, and there is no evidence that any of these people were Interahamwe. Nevertheless, with regard to all evidence of rape and sexual violence which took place on or near the premises of the bureau communal, the perpetrators were all identified as Interahamwe. Interahamwe are also identified as the perpetrators of many rapes which took place outside the bureau communal, including the rapes of Witness H, Witness OO, Witness NN, Witness J's daughter, a woman near death seen by Witness KK and a woman called Vestine, seen by Witness PP. There is no suggestion in any of the evidence that the Accused or any communal policemen perpetrated rape, and both Witness JJ and Witness KK affirmed that they never saw the Accused rape anyone. In considering the role of the Accused in the sexual violence which took place and the extent of his direct knowledge of incidents of sexual violence, the Chamber has taken into account only evidence which is direct and unequivocal. Witness H testified that the Accused was present during the rape of Tutsi women outside the compound of the bureau communal, but as she could not confirm that he was aware that the rapes were taking place, the Chamber discounts this testimony in its assessment of the evidence. Witness PP recalled the Accused directing the Interahamwe to take Alexia and her two nieces to Kinihira, saying 'Don't you know where killings take place, where the others have been killed?' The three women were raped before they were killed, but the statement of the Accused does not refer to sexual violence and there is no evidence that the Accused was present at Kinihira. For this reason, the Chamber also discounts this testimony in its assessment of the evidence. On the basis of the evidence set forth herein, the Chamber finds beyond a reasonable doubt that the Accused had reason to know and in fact knew that sexual violence was taking place on or near the premises of the bureau communal, and that women were being taken away from the bureau communal and sexually violated. There is no evidence that the Accused took any measures to prevent acts of sexual violence or to punish the perpetrators of sexual violence. In fact there is evidence that the Accused ordered, instigated and otherwise aided and abetted sexual violence. The Accused watched two Interahamwe drag a woman to be raped between the bureau communal and the cultural center. The two commune policemen in front of his office witnessed the rape but did nothing to prevent it. On the two occasions Witness JJ was brought to the cultural center of the bureau communal to be raped, she and the group of girls and women with her were

	taken past the Accused, on the way. On the first occasion he was looking at them, and on the second occasion he was standing at the entrance to the cultural center. On this second occasion, he said, 'Never ask me again what a Tutsi woman tastes like.' Witness JJ described the Accused in making these statements as 'talking as if someone were encouraging a player.' More generally she stated that the Accused was the one 'supervising' the acts of rape. When Witness OO and two other girls were apprehended by Interahamwe in flight from the bureau communal, the Interahamwe went to the Accused and told him that they were taking the girls away to sleep with them. The Accused said 'take them.' The Accused told the Interahamwe to undress Chantal and march her around. He was laughing and happy to be watching and afterwards told the Interahamwe to take her away and said 'you should first of all make sure that you sleep with this girl.' The Chamber considers this statement as evidence that the Accused ordered and instigated sexual violence, although insufficient evidence was presented to establish beyond a reasonable doubt that Chantal was in fact raped".[420] - Responsibility of Jean-Paul Akayesu for rapes and forced undressing of women: "The Tribunal has found that the Accused had reason to know and in fact knew that acts of sexual violence were occurring on or near the premises of the bureau communal and that he took no measures to prevent these acts or punish the perpetrators of them. The Tribunal notes that it is only in consideration of Counts 13, 14 and 15 that the Accused is charged with individual criminal responsibility under Section 6(3) of its Statute. As set forth in the Indictment, under Article 6(3) 'an individual is criminally responsible as a superior for the acts of a subordinate if he or she knew or had reason to know that the subordinate was about to commit such acts or had done so and the superior failed to take the necessary and reasonable measures to prevent such acts or punish the perpetrators thereof.' Although the evidence supports a finding that a superior/subordinate relationship existed between the Accused and the Interahamwe who were at the bureau communal, the Tribunal notes that there is no allegation in the Indictment that the Interahamwe, who are referred to as 'armed local militia,' were subordinates of the Accused. This relationship is a fundamental element of the criminal offence set forth in Article 6(3). The amendment of the Indictment with additional charges pursuant to Article 6(3) could arguably be interpreted as implying an allegation of the command responsibility required by Article 6(3). In fairness to the Accused, the Tribunal will not make this inference. Therefore, the Tribunal finds that it cannot consider the criminal responsibility of the Accused under Article 6(3). The Tribunal finds, under Article 6(1) of its Statute, that the Accused, by his own words, specifically ordered, instigated, aided and abetted the following acts of sexual violence: (i) the multiple acts of rape of ten girls and women, including Witness JJ, by numerous Interahamwe in the cultural center of the bureau communal; (ii) the rape of Witness OO by an Interahamwe named Antoine in a field near the bureau communal; (iii) the forced undressing and public marching of Chantal naked at the bureau communal. The Tribunal finds, under Article 6(1) of its Statute, that the Accused aided and abetted the following acts of sexual violence, by allowing them to take place on or near the premises of the bureau communal, while he was present on the premises in respect of (i) and in his presence in respect of (ii) and (iii), and by facilitating the commission of these acts through his words of encouragement in other acts of sexual violence, which, by virtue of his authority, sent a clear signal of official tolerance for sexual violence, without which these acts would not have taken place: (i) the multiple acts of rape of fifteen girls and women, including Witness JJ, by numerous Interahamwe in the cultural center of the bureau communal; (ii) the rape of a woman by Interahamwe in between two buildings of the bureau communal, witnessed by Witness NN; (iii) the forced undressing of the wife of Tharcisse after making her sit in the mud

[420] *Akayesu* Trial Judgement, paras. 449–452. See also *Akayesu* Trial Judgement, paras. 416–448, 453–460.

	outside the bureau communal, as witnessed by Witness KK; The Tribunal finds, under Article 6(1) of its Statute, that the Accused, having had reason to know that sexual violence was occurring, aided and abetted the following acts of sexual violence, by allowing them to take place on or near the premises of the bureau communal and by facilitating the commission of such sexual violence through his words of encouragement in other acts of sexual violence which, by virtue of his authority, sent a clear signal of official tolerance for sexual violence, without which these acts would not have taken place: (i) the rape of Witness JJ by an Interahamwe who took her from outside the bureau communal and raped her in a nearby forest; (ii) the rape of the younger sister of Witness NN by an Interahamwe at the bureau communal; (iii) the multiple rapes of Alexia, wife of Ntereye, and her two nieces Louise and Nishimwe by Interahamwe near the bureau communal; (iv) the forced undressing of Alexia, wife of Ntereye, and her two nieces Louise and Nishimwe, and the forcing of the women to perform exercises naked in public near the bureau communal. The Tribunal has established that a widespread and systematic attack against the civilian ethnic population of Tutsis took place in Taba, and more generally in Rwanda, between April 7 and the end of June, 1994. The Tribunal finds that the rape and other inhumane acts which took place on or near the bureau communal premises of Taba were committed as part of this attack. The Accused is judged criminally responsible under Article 3(g) of the Statute for the following incidents of rape: (i) the rape of Witness JJ by an Interahamwe who took her from outside the bureau communal and raped her in a nearby forest; (ii) the multiple acts of rape of fifteen girls and women, including Witness JJ, by numerous Interahamwe in the cultural center of the bureau communal; (iii) the multiple acts of rape of ten girls and women, including Witness JJ, by numerous Interahamwe in the cultural center of the bureau communal; (iv) the rape of Witness OO by an Interahamwe named Antoine in a field near the bureau communal; (v) the rape of a woman by Interahamwe in between two buildings of the bureau communal, witnessed by Witness NN; (vi) the rape of the younger sister of Witness NN by an Interahamwe at the bureau communal; (vii) the multiple rapes of Alexia, wife of Ntereye, and her two nieces Louise and Nishimwe by Interahamwe near the bureau communal. The Accused is judged criminally responsible under Article 3(i) of the Statute for the following other inhumane acts: (i) the forced undressing of the wife of Tharcisse outside the bureau communal, after making her sit in the mud, as witnessed by Witness KK; (ii) the forced undressing and public marching of Chantal naked at the bureau communal; (iii) the forced undressing of Alexia, wife of Ntereye, and her two nieces Louise and Nishimwe, and the forcing of the women to perform exercises naked in public near the bureau communal".[421] "With regard to the acts alleged in **paragraphs 12 (A) and 12 (B)** of the Indictment, the Prosecutor has shown beyond a reasonable doubt that between 7 April and the end of June 1994, numerous Tutsi who sought refuge at the Taba Bureau communal were frequently beaten by members of the Interahamwe on or near the premises of the Bureau communal. […] Numerous Tutsi women were forced to endure acts of sexual violence, mutilations and rape, often repeatedly, often publicly and often by more than one assailant. Tutsi women were systematically raped, as one female victim testified to by saying that 'each time that you met assailants, they raped you'. Numerous incidents of such rape and sexual violence against Tutsi women occurred inside or near the Bureau communal. It has been proven that some communal policemen armed with guns and the accused himself were present while some of these rapes and sexual violence were being committed. Furthermore, it is proven that on several occasions, by his presence, his attitude and his utterances, Akayesu encouraged such acts, one particular witness testifying that Akayesu, addressed the Interahamwe who were committing the rapes and said that 'never ask me again what a Tutsi woman tastes like'. In the opinion of the Chamber, this constitutes tacit encouragement to the rapes that were

421 *Akayesu* Trial Judgement, paras. 691–697.

	being committed. In the opinion of the Chamber, the above-mentioned acts with which Akayesu is charged indeed render him individually criminally responsible for having abetted in […] the infliction of serious bodily and mental harm on members of [the Tutsi] group".[422] "With regard, particularly, to the acts described in paragraphs 12(A) and 12(B) of the Indictment, that is, rape and sexual violence, the Chamber wishes to underscore the fact that in its opinion, they constitute genocide in the same way as any other act as long as they were committed with the specific intent to destroy, in whole or in part, a particular group, targeted as such. Indeed, rape and sexual violence certainly constitute infliction of serious bodily and mental harm on the victims and are even, according to the Chamber, one of the worst ways of inflict[ing] harm on the victim as he or she suffers both bodily and mental harm. In light of all the evidence before it, the Chamber is satisfied that the acts of rape and sexual violence described above, were committed solely against Tutsi women, many of whom were subjected to the worst public humiliation, mutilated, and raped several times, often in public, in the Bureau Communal premises or in other public places, and often by more than one assailant. These rapes resulted in physical and psychological destruction of Tutsi women, their families and their communities. Sexual violence was an integral part of the process of destruction, specifically targeting Tutsi women and specifically contributing to their destruction and to the destruction of the Tutsi group as a whole. The rape of Tutsi women was systematic and was perpetrated against all Tutsi women and solely against them. A Tutsi woman, married to a Hutu, testified before the Chamber that she was not raped because her ethnic background was unknown. As part of the propaganda campaign geared to mobilizing the Hutu against the Tutsi, the Tutsi women were presented as sexual objects. Indeed, the Chamber was told, for an example, that before being raped and killed, Alexia, who was the wife of the Professor, Ntereye, and her two nieces, were forced by the Interahamwe to undress and ordered to run and do exercises 'in order to display the thighs of Tutsi women'. The Interahamwe who raped Alexia said, as he threw her on the ground and got on top of her, 'let us now see what the vagina of a Tutsi woman ta[st]es like'. As stated above, Akayesu himself, speaking to the Interahamwe who were committing the rapes, said to them: 'don't ever ask again what a Tutsi woman tastes like'. This sexualized representation of ethnic identity graphically illustrates that tutsi women were subjected to sexual violence because they were Tutsi. Sexual violence was a step in the process of destruction of the tutsi group - destruction of the spirit, of the will to live, and of life itself. On the basis of the substantial testimonies brought before it, the Chamber finds that in most cases, the rapes of Tutsi women in Taba, were accompanied with the intent to kill those women. Many rapes were perpetrated near mass graves where the women were taken to be killed. A victim testified that Tutsi women caught could be taken away by peasants and men with the promise that they would be collected later to be executed. Following an act of gang rape, a witness heard Akayesu say 'tomorrow they will be killed' and they were actually killed. In this respect, it appears clearly to the Chamber that the acts of rape and sexual violence, as other acts of serious bodily and mental harm committed against the Tutsi, reflected the determination to make Tutsi women suffer and to mutilate them even before killing them, the intent being to destroy the Tutsi group while inflicting acute suffering on its members in the process. In light of the foregoing, the Chamber finds firstly that the acts described *supra* are indeed acts as enumerated in Article 2 (2) of the Statute, which constitute the factual elements of the crime of genocide, namely […] the serious bodily and mental harm inflicted on the Tutsi. The Chamber is further satisfied beyond reasonable doubt that these various acts were committed by Akayesu with the specific intent to destroy the Tutsi group, as such. Consequently, the Chamber is of the opinion that the acts alleged in paragraphs 12, 12A […] of the Indictment and

[422] *Akayesu* Trial Judgement, paras. 706–707 (internal reference omitted).

	proven above, constitute the crime of genocide, but not the crime of complicity; hence, the Chamber finds Akayesu individually criminally responsible for genocide".[423]

2. Alfred **Musema** (Case No. ICTR-96-13) Director of the Gisovu tea factory.	
Indictment (International sex crimes (or related) charges and mode(s) of liability)	- **Genocide** (count 1) or, alternatively, **Complicity in genocide** (count 2) and **Conspiracy to commit genocide** (count 3) for various crimes, including **causing serious bodily or mental harm** to Tutsis, as well as, **Other inhumane acts as CAH** (count 6), **Rape as CAH** (count 7) and **Outrages upon personal dignity as a violation of Article 3 common to the Geneva Conventions and of Additional Protocol II (WC)** (count 9) under Articles 6(1) and 6(3) of the Statute (**superior responsibility**) for raping Tutsi women and encouraging others to rape Tutsi women at various locations within the area of Bisesero and Gisovu, in the prefecture of Kibuye, throughout April, May and June 1994 and, in particular, for the rape of Annunciata, a Tutsi woman, on 14 April 1994, the rapes of Immaculee Mukankusi, a pregnant Tutsi woman, and Nyiramusugi, a Tutsi woman, on 13 May 1994.[424]

---

423 *Akayesu* Trial Judgement, paras. 731–734 (internal reference omitted).

424 *Prosecutor v. Alfred Musema*, Case No. ICTR-96-13-T, Amended Indictment, 29 April 1999, paras. 4.7–4.10 ("At various locations within the area of Bisesero and Gisovu, in the Prefecture of Kibuye, throughout April May and June 1994, Alfred Musema, committed acts of rape and encouraged others to capture, rape and kill Tutsi women, seeking refuge from attacks within the area of Bisesero in Gisovu and Gishyita communes, Kibuye Prefecture. On 14 April 1994, within the area of the Gisovu Tea Factory, Twumba Cellule, Gisovu Commune, Alfred Musema, in concert with others, ordered and encouraged the raping of Annunciata, a Tutsi woman and thereafter, ordered, that she be killed together with her son Blaise. On 13 May 1994, within the area of Bisesero, in Gisovu and Gishyita communes, Kibuye Prefecture, Alfred Musema, in concert with others, raped and killed Immaculee Mukankusi, a pregnant Tutsi and thereafter, ordered others accompanying him, to rape and kill Tutsi women seeking refugee from attacks. On 13 May 1994, within the area of Bisesero, in Gisovu and Gishyita communes, Kibuye Prefecture, Alfred Musema, acting in concert with others, raped Nyiramusugi, a Tutsi woman and encouraged others accompanying him, to rape and kill her. [...] By his acts in relation to the events referred to above, **Alfred Musema** is individually responsible for the crimes alleged below pursuant to Article 6(1) and 6(3) of the Tribunal Statute: Count 1: **Alfred Musema**, during the months of April, May and June 1994, in Gisovu and Gishyita communes, Kibuye Prefecture, in the Territory of Rwanda, is responsible for the killing or causing of serious bodily or mental harm to members of the Tutsi population with the intent to destroy, in whole or in part, an ethnic or racial group as such and has thereby committed GENOCIDE in violation of Article 2(3)(a) and punishable in reference to Articles 22 and 23 of the Statute of the Tribunal. **ALTERNATIVELY** Count 2: **Alfred Musema**, during the months of April, May and June 1994, in Gisovu and Gishyita communes, Kibuye Prefecture, in the Territory of Rwanda, is responsible for killing and causing serious bodily or mental harm to members of the Tutsi population with the intent to destroy, in whole or in part, an ethnic or racial group as such and has thereby committed **COMPLICITY IN GENOCIDE** in violation of Article 2(3)(e) and punishable in reference to Article 22 and 23 of the Statute of the Tribunal. Count 3: **Alfred Musema**, prior to his participation in the attacks and killings in Gisovu and Gishyita communes, Kibuye Prefecture, in the Territory of Rwanda, did conspire with others to kill or cause serious bodily or mental harm to members of the Tutsi population with the intent to destroy, in whole or part, an ethnic or racial group as such, and has thereby committed **CONSPIRACY TO COMMIT GENOCIDE** in violation of Article 2(3)(b) and punishable in reference to Articles 22 and 23 of the Statute of the Tribunal [...] Count 6: **Alfred Musema**, during the months of April, May and June 1994, in Gisovu and Gishyita communes, Kibuye Prefecture, in the Territory of Rwanda, did commit other inhumane acts, against a civilian population on political, ethnic, or racial grounds, and has thereby committed a **CRIME AGAINST HUMANITY** in violation of Article 3(i) and punishable in reference to Articles 22 and 23 of the Statute of the Tribunal. Count 7: Alfred Musema, during the months of April May and June 1994, in Gisovu and Gishyita communes, Kibuye Prefecture, in the territory of Rwanda, is responsible for the rape of Tutsi civilians, as part of a wide spread and systematic attack against a civilian population on political ethnic or racial grounds, and has thereby committed a **CRIME AGAINST HUMANITY** in

Trial Judgement	- Guilty of **Genocide** (count 1) under Article 6(1) of the Statute (**committing** and **aiding and abetting**) for various crimes, including raping Nyiramusugi, a young Tutsi woman, and abetting others to rape her and, therefore, **causing serious bodily and mental harm** to a member of the Tutsi group.[425] - Guilty of **Rape as CAH** (count 7) under Article 6(1) of the Statute (**committing**) for raping Nyiramusugi.[426] - Not guilty of conspiracy to commit genocide (count 3) as the Trial Chamber found the Prosecution did not bring evidence that Alfred Musema and others reached an agreement to commit the crime of genocide. Not guilty of other inhumane acts as CAH (count 6) as the Trial Chamber found that the Prosecution failed to adduce evidence of any act falling within the ambit of this crime. Not guilty of Outrages upon personal dignity as a violation of Article 3 common to the Geneva Conventions and of Additional Protocol II (WC) (count 9) as the Trial Chamber found that the Prosecution did not prove there was a nexus between the crimes and the armed conflict.[427]
Appeal Judgement	- On appeal, Alfred Musema was granted leave to file additional evidence in relation to the rape of Nyiramusugi, namely the out-of-court statements of Witnesses CB and EB. The Appeals Chamber heard these witnesses at a hearing on 17 October 2001. The Appeals Chamber found that, had the testimonies of Witnesses CB and EB been available at trial, a reasonable trier of fact would have reached the conclusion that there was a reasonable doubt as to the guilt of Alfred Musema with respect to the rape of Nyiramusugi. Thus, the Appeals Chamber **reversed his conviction for Rape as CAH** (count 7). Accordingly, although the Appeals Chamber upheld Alfred Musema's conviction for **Genocide** (count 1), **insofar as his conviction was based on the rape of Nyiramusugi, his conviction was reversed** [428]
Legal and Factual Findings	- Legal findings: **- Sexual violence and rape can constitute genocide (causing serious bodily or mental harm):**

violation of Article 3 (g) and punishable in reference to Article 22 and 23 of the Statute of the Tribunal. [...] Count 9: **Alfred Musema**, during the months of April, May and June 1994, in Gisovu and Gishyita communes, Kibuye Prefecture, in the Territory of Rwanda, did commit or order others to commit, **SERIOUS VIOLATIONS OF ARTICLE[] 3 COMMON TO THE GENEVA CONVENTIONS AND OF ADDITIONAL PROTOCOL II thereof,** in violation of Article 4(e) and punishable in reference to Articles 22 and 23 of the Statute of the Tribunal".). On 29 April 1999, the Prosecution sought leave to amend the Indictment to add one additional count of rape as crime against humanity (count 7) and to expand on the facts adduced in the original indictment in support of the new charge (paragraphs 4.7 to 4.11 of the Indictment). On 6 May 1999, the Trial Chamber acknowledged that, although the filing of the motion for leave to amend the Indictment came at a late stage in the presentation of the Prosecution's case, this did not cause prejudice to Alfred Musema. The Trial Chamber, therefore, granted the Prosecution's request. See *Prosecutor v. Alfred Musema*, Case No. ICTR-96-13-T, Decision on the Prosecutor's Request for Leave to Amend the Indictment, dated 6 May 1999, filed on 25 May 1999, pp. 2–5. On appeal, Alfred Musema submitted that the Trial Chamber committed an error of law in allowing the Prosecution to amend the Indictment. Given that the Appeals Chamber reversed Alfred Musema's conviction with respect to count 7, the Appeals Chamber did not deem it necessary to rule on the merits of this ground of appeal. However, the Appeals Chamber underscored the particularly late filing of the Prosecution's request to amend the Indictment. See *Alfred Musema v. The Prosecutor*, Case No. ICTR-96-13-A, Judgement, 16 November 2001 ("*Musema* Appeal Judgement"), paras. 342–343.

425 *Prosecutor v. Alfred Musema*, Case No. ICTR-96-13-T, Judgement and Sentence, 27 January 2000 ("*Musema* Trial Judgement"), paras. 847–861, 907–909, 933–936 and Section 7 (Verdict), p. 276. See also *Musema* Trial Judgement, Separate Opinion of Judge Pillay, paras. 1, 6–12.

426 *Musema* Trial Judgement, paras. 847–861, 966–968 and Section 7 (Verdict), p. 276. See also *Musema* Trial Judgement, Separate Opinion of Judge Pillay, paras. 1, 6–12.

427 *Musema* Trial Judgement, paras. 937–941, 959–961, 974–975 and Section 7 (Verdict), p. 276.

428 *Musema* Appeal Judgement, paras. 189–194 and Section VI (Disposition), p. 133.

and/or Evidence	The Trial Chamber held: "For the purposes of interpreting Article 2(2)(b) of the Statute, the Chamber understands the words 'serious bodily or mental harm' to include, but not limited to, acts of bodily or mental torture, inhumane or degrading treatment, rape, sexual violence, and persecution. The Chamber is of the opinion that 'serious harm' need not entail permanent or irremediable harm".[429] **- Sexual mutilation can constitute genocide (imposing measures intended to prevent births):** The Trial Chamber held: "In its interpretation of Article 2(2)(d) of the Statute, the Chamber holds that the words 'measures intended to prevent births within the group' should be construed as including sexual mutilation, enforced sterilization, forced birth control, forced separation of males and females, and prohibition of marriages. The Chamber notes that measures intended to prevent births within the group may be not only physical, but also mental".[430] **- Rape: definition given in the *Akayesu* case rather than in the *Furundžija* case:** The Trial Chamber considered the definitions of rape given in the *Akayesu* case[431] and the *Furundžija* case[432] and adopted the *Akayesu* definition. The Trial Chamber held: "Rape may constitute a crime against humanity, pursuant to Article 3(g) of the Statute. In the *Akayesu* Judgement, rape as a crime against humanity was defined as: '[...] a physical invasion of a sexual nature, committed on a person under circumstances which are coercive. Sexual violence, which includes rape, is considered to be any act of a sexual nature which is committed on a person under circumstances which are coercive. This act must be committed: (a) as part of a widespread or systematic attack; (b) on a civilian population; (c) on certain catalogued discriminatory grounds, namely: national, ethnic, political, racial, or religious grounds.' The Chamber notes that, while rape has been defined in certain national jurisdictions as non-consensual intercourse, variations on the acts of rape may include acts which involve the insertions of objects and/or the use of bodily orifices not considered to be intrinsically sexual. The Chamber also observes that in defining rape, as a crime against humanity, the Trial Chamber in the *Akayesu* Judgement acknowledged: 'that rape is a form of aggression and that the central elements of the crime of rape cannot be captured in a mechanical description of objects and body parts. The Convention against Torture and Other Cruel, Inhuman and Degrading Treatment or Punishment does not catalogue specific acts in its definition of torture, focu[]sing rather on the conceptual frame work of state sanctioned violence. This approach is more useful in international law. Like torture, rape is used for such purposes as intimidation, degradation, humiliation, discrimination, punishment, control or destruction of a person. Like torture, rape is a violation of personal dignity, and rape in fact constitutes torture when inflicted by or at the instigation of or with the consent or acquiescence of a public official or other person acting in an official capacity.' The Chamber notes that the definition of rape and sexual violence articulated in the *Akayesu* Judgement was adopted by the Trial Chamber II of the ICTY in its *Delalic* Judgement. The Chamber has considered the alternative definition of rape set forth by Trial Chamber I of the ICTY in its *Furund[ž]ija* Judgement, which relies on a detailed description of objects and body parts. In this judgement the Trial Chamber looked to national legislation and noted: 'The Trial Chamber would emphasise at the outset, that a trend can be discerned in the national legislation of a number of States of broadening the definition of rape so that it now embraces acts that were

429 *Musema* Trial Judgement, para. 156.

430 *Musema* Trial Judgement, para. 158.

431 ICTR ISCC *Akayesu*, see *supra* p. 649.

432 ICTR ISCC *Furundžija*, see *supra* p. 524.

| | previously classified as comparatively less serious offences, that is sexual or indecent assault. This trend shows that at the national level States tend to take a stricter attitude towards serious forms of sexual assault; the stigma of rape now attaches to a growing category of sexual offences, provided of course they meet certain requirements, chiefly that of forced physical penetration.' The *Furund[ž]ija* Judgement further noted that 'most legal systems in the common and civil law worlds consider rape to be the forcible sexual penetration of the human body by the penis or the forcible insertion of any other object into either the vagina or the anus'. Nevertheless, after due consideration of the practice of forced oral penetration, which is treated as rape in some States and sexual assault in other States, the Trial Chamber in that case determined as follows: '[...] The Trial Chamber holds that the forced penetration of the mouth by the male sexual organ constitutes a most humiliating and degrading attack upon human dignity. The essence of the whole corpus of international humanitarian law as well as human rights law lies in the protection of the human dignity of every person, whatever his or her gender. The general principle of respect for human dignity is the basic underpinning and indeed the very *raison d'être* of international humanitarian law and human rights law, indeed in modern times it has become of such paramount importance as to permeate the whole body of international law. This principle is intended to shield human beings from outrages upon their personal dignity, whether such outrages are carried out by unlawfully attacking the body or by humiliating and debasing the honour, the self-respect or the mental well being of a person. It is consonant with this principle that such an extremely serious sexual outrage as forced oral penetration should be classified as rape.' The Chamber concurs with the conceptual approach set forth in the *Akayesu* Judgement for the definition of rape, which recognizes that the essence of rape is not the particular details of the body parts and objects involved, but rather the aggression that is expressed in a sexual manner under conditions of coercion. The Chamber considers that the distinction between rape and other forms of sexual violence drawn by the *Akayesu* Judgement, that is 'a physical invasion of a sexual nature' as contrasted with 'any act of a sexual nature' which is committed on a person under circumstances which are coercive is clear and establishes a framework for judicial consideration of individual incidents of sexual violence and a determination, on a case by case basis, of whether such incidents constitute rape. The definition of rape, as set forth in the *Akayesu* Judgement, clearly encompasses all the conduct described in the definition of rape set forth in *Furund[ž]ija*. The Chamber notes that in the *Furund[ž]ija* Judgement, the Trial Chamber considered forced penetration of the mouth as a humiliating and degrading attack on human dignity and largely for this reason included such conduct in its definition of rape even though State jurisdictions are divided as to whether such conduct constitutes rape. The Chamber further notes, as the *Furund[ž]ija* Judgement acknowledges, that there is a trend in national legislation to broaden the definition of rape. In light of the dynamic ongoing evolution of the understanding of rape and the incorporation of this understanding into principles of international law, the Chamber considers that a conceptual definition is preferable to a mechanical definition of rape. The conceptual definition will better accommodate evolving norms of criminal justice. For these reasons, the Chamber adopts the definition of rape and sexual violence set forth in the *Akayesu* Judgement".[433]

- Indecent assault: definition:
The Trial Chamber gave the following definition of indecent assault contained in the crime of Outrages upon personal dignity, in particular humiliating and degrading treatment, rape, enforced prostitution and any form of indecent assault as a violation of Article 3 common to the Geneva Conventions and of Additional Protocol II: "The accused caused the infliction of pain or injury by an act which was of a sexual nature |

[433] *Musema* Trial Judgement, paras. 220–229 (internal references omitted).

	and inflicted by means of coercion, force, threat or intimidation and was non-consensual."[434] - Factual findings: - Alleged rape of Annunciata Mujawayezu on 14 April 1994: "The Chamber notes that the testimony of Witness I was confusing in certain respects, particularly with regard to the details of her movement and the chronology of events. However, her testimony was consistent on cross-examination, and she did provide reasonable and clear answers to the questions raised on cross-examination with regard to her various pre-trial statements. The Chamber noted the determination of the witness to clarify the distinction between what she had heard others say and what she herself witnessed. She also carefully indicated on numerous occasions what she did not see or hear, as well as what she did see or hear. With regard to her account concerning the rape and murder of Annunciata Mujawayezu, the Chamber finds Witness I to be clear and consistent and accepts her testimony. The testimony of Witness L is limited with respect to its probative value because the witness was not able to hear Musema from where he was standing. What he saw, that is Musema standing near the pergola (bungalow), Annunciata Mujawayezu standing by the fence with the others and subsequently being taken by them into the guest house, is consistent with Witness I's much more detailed account of the event. On cross-examination, the witness clearly stated that Musema did not enter the guest house. This is not inconsistent with the other accounts, all of which indicate that he remained outside and left shortly thereafter in his vehicle. It, it is clear, from Witness L's testimony, Witness I's testimony and Musema's own testimony, that Musema and Annunciata Mujawayezu were at the Guest House on 14 April 1994. It appears that Annunciata Mujawayezu was near the Guest House at the beginning but afterwards she was taken in by the back door. According to Musema's testimony to the Swiss Judge, he was inside the Guest House. The Chamber notes that Witness L places the date of this incident as around 18 April. In light of the evidence of Witness I and Musema himself that this incident took place on the 14 April, the Chamber considers that the witness is mistaken about the date, which he indicated in any event as an estimation. The testimony of Witness PP is limited with respect to its probative value because Witness PP was not present when the killing of Annunciata Mujawayezu occurred. The witness saw her body and testified that there was no clothing on the upper half of the body. This evidence would be consistent with the account of Witness I that sexual violence might have been directed to her upper body. However, Witness PP noted that he did not see injuries to the body from its position. The testimony does not make it clear whether the body was face down or on its back. For this reason, the Chamber finds that the evidence of Witness PP, while credible, is not helpful in establishing what happened other than to corroborate that Annunciata Mujawayezu was killed and that Musema was present at the factory on 14 April. The Chamber further notes that the witness testified that he saw the body of Annunciata Mujawayezu on 13 April, whereas both Witness I and Musema date the death of Annunciata Mujawayezu to 14 April. The Chamber considers that the witness is mistaken about the date. The Chamber has considered the testimony of Musema in light of the pre-trial statements he made to Swiss authorities which differ not only from his testimony but from each other in material respects. In one version of the incident, Musema tried to stop the killing of Annunciata Mujawayezu. In another version, he came too late. In each version, she was killed in a different place. In light of these gross inconsistencies, for which Musema does not have any reasonable explanation, the Chamber concludes that the only reasonable explanation for the inconsistencies is that he is not being truthful. Having considered the evidence, as set forth above, the Chamber finds that the Prosecution has established beyond a reasonable

[434] *Musema* Trial Judgement, para. 285.

	doubt that Musema ordered the rape of Annunciata Mujawayezu, a Tutsi woman, and the cutting off of her breast to be fed to her son. No evidence was introduced to indicate that he ordered her to be killed, although there is conclusive evidence that she was in fact killed. Considering Musema's high position in the *commune*, he must have known that his words would necessarily have had an important and even binding impact on his interlocutors. There is no conclusive evidence that Annunciata Mujawayezu was raped, or that her breast was cut off, although there is some evidence to support an inference that these acts were perpetrated".[435] In its legal findings, the Trial Chamber held: "[…] regarding the allegations presented under paragraph 4.8 of the Indictment, according to which Musema, in concert with others, ordered and abetted in the rape of Annunciata, a Tutsi, and thereafter ordered that she and her son be killed, the Chamber holds that even if it is proven that Musema ordered that Annunciata be raped, such order, by and of itself, does not suffice for him to incur individual criminal responsibility, given that no evidence has been adduced to show that the order was executed to produce such result, namely the rape of Annunciata. Nor has it been proven that Musema ordered that she and her son be killed".[436] On appeal, Alfred Musema challenged the legal findings of this incident. The Appeals Chamber dismissed Alfred Musema's arguments on this point as it found that the Trial Chamber did not take this incident into account as a basis for a conviction or in determining Alfred Musema's sentence. The Appeals Chamber held: "It is the understanding of the Appeals Chamber that, although the Trial Chamber made the factual finding that Musema ordered the rape of Annunciata Mujawayezu, it held that the order in itself was not sufficient for him to incur individual criminal responsibility. Consequently, the Trial Chamber did not take account of this incident, either as a basis for a conviction on the count in question, or in determining the sentence passed. Witness I, whose testimony Musema challenges, gave evidence only with respect to the rape of Annunciata Mujawayezu. Therefore, the testimony of this Witness has no bearing on the counts on which Musema was eventually convicted and sentenced, nor on the factual findings made by the Trial Chamber. Consequently, the Appeals Chamber finds that Musema's challenge to the credibility of Witness I is misguided and, accordingly, dismisses the argument on this point".[437] - Alleged rape of Immaculée Mukankuzi on 13 May 1994: "The Chamber notes that witness J is the sole witness of the rape and killing of Immaculée Mukankuzi by Musema and the rape and killing of other women by the men with him at Muyira Hill on his instruction. The Chamber found her, generally speaking, to be a balanced witness. Her evidence on direct and cross-examination was notably consistent and additional details which emerged through extensive questioning provide a clear picture of the events she was describing. Yet, the Chamber notes that the witness made several time estimates which appeared to be inaccurate. For example, she testified that the man who raped her was on top of her for four hours, saying subsequently that it felt like four hours or even a day. She testified that a distance which would take a young man five minutes to cover would take her two hours. The Chamber considers that these estimates reflect a general difficulty of the witness in measuring time which do not detract from the credibility or her testimony. On cross-examination, Defence counsel challenged the witness on several grounds. The Chamber considers that with regard to the interview she did on Radio Rwanda, that it is inaccurate to characterize the interview as 'different' from her testimony, as if it were therefore inconsistent with her testimony. Defence pointed out that she did not say

435 *Musema* Trial Judgement, paras. 823–829.

436 *Musema* Trial Judgement, para. 889. See also *Musema* Trial Judgement, Separate Opinion of Judge Aspegren, paras. 36–40.

437 *Musema* Appeal Judgement, paras. 169–171. See also *Musema* Appeal Judgement, paras. 165–168.

	everything in the interview that she said in her testimony and that she did not say everything in her testimony that she said in the interview. The witness had a reasonable explanation for these differences - the radio interview was of short duration with a specific purpose and controlled by the interviewer. The fact that she did not mention Musema is not, in the view of the Chamber, significant, particularly in light of the fact that she did not mention the killing of her children and other very significant events to which she testified. The chamber recognizes that it is especially difficult to testify about rape and sexual violence, moreover in a public forum. No inconsistencies between the radio interview and the testimony were identified. The Chamber considers that the principal inconsistency in the testimony of Witness J relates to her account of the circumstances surrounding the killing of her 19 year-old daughter by Sikubwabo and the rape and killing of her 18 year-old daughter by the young men with Musema at Muyira hill. The witness clearly testified several times that she had five children, who were aged 25, 23, 19, 12, and 9. This has further been established by documentary evidence at the request of the Chamber. She clearly testified several times that her three eldest children were killed by Sikubwabo, leaving her with two children aged 12 and 9. Yet she also testified that one of the five young women raped with her at Muyira hill was her 18 year-old daughter. On cross-examination when the question was put to her to explain how this was possible, she did not provide any answer. On re-direct examination, in reply to a specific question on this point by the Prosecutor, she provided a very general answer to the effect that Musema had ordered her children to be killed. She did not explain the apparent inconsistency. While the Chamber found the testimony of Witness J to be generally credible, it is deeply troubled by this unexplained inconsistency regarding the rape of her daughter. Without any reasonable explanation, the Chamber must question the accuracy of the account. The Chamber believes that there is likely to be a reasonable explanation, based on its evaluation of the witness. However, recalling the high burden of proof on the Prosecutor and the lack of any other evidence produced to corroborate the account of Witness J, the Chamber cannot find beyond a reasonable doubt that the allegations have been established relating to the rape and killing of Immaculée Mukankuzi by Musema and the rape and killing of others with her by his men and on his order on 13 May 1994".[438] - Rape of Nyiramusugi on 13 May 1994: "*Witness N*, a 39 year old Tutsi, testified that he sought refuge in the Bisesero area from 26 April to 13 May 1994. He stated that there were many attacks on Muyira hill on 13 May 1994 and that he stayed on Muyira hill until that date, after which he had to flee again. He testified that he knew Musema. He saw Musema arrive at Muyira hill aboard his red vehicle on 13 May 1994. He said that this was the first time that he had seen Musema during the attacks. He explained that he was able to hear Musema once the group moved to within a few metres of him. The witness testified that Musema spoke to a policeman named Ruhindura, and asked him whether a young woman called Nyiramusugi was already dead, to which the policeman answered 'no'. He stated that Musema then asked that before anything, this girl had to be brought to him. He and the *bourgmestre* fired the first shots so the others would start shooting. Ruhindura while fighting and looking for the young woman caught her. The Witness stated that he knew Nyiramusugi. He used to see her when she walked to school and he used to take his cows to graze in front of her parents' house. He said that she was a young unmarried teacher. Witness N testified that Nyiramusugi was caught around 15.30hrs. He said that he saw Ruhindura with four youths drag the young woman on the ground and take her to Musema. He said that Musema was carrying a rifle which he then handed to Ruhindura. The four people holding Nyiramusugi brought her to the ground. They pinned her down, two holding her arms and two holding her legs. The two

[438] *Musema* Trial Judgement, paras. 840–845.

	holding her legs then spread them, and Musema placed himself between them. The witness saw Musema rip off Nyiramusugi's clothes and underclothes and then took off his own clothes. The witness stated that Musema said aloud 'Today, the pride of the Tutsi shall end' and then raped the young woman. Witness N said that Nyiramusugi was a very well known Tutsi girl who was very beautiful. The witness explained that because of the echo at Muyira hill, it was possible to hear everything that was said and to recognize the voice of certain of the attackers. The Witness also explained that he was able to see the rape as he had fallen in a bush when fleeing to the top of the hill. Musema was at 40 metres, bird flight, on a little hill at Muyira, walking distance being further because to get to Musema from the Witness' position on the hill, one had to walk down and back up the other side. The witness affirmed that the victim was Tutsi and explained that Musema took her by force. He stated that during the rape, Nyiramusugi struggled until Musema grabbed one of her arms and held it against her neck. The four assailants who initially held down the victim watched from nearby while the policeman, Ruhindura, stood further away. Witness N stated that after the rape, which he estimated lasted forty minutes, Musema walked over to Ruhindura, took his rifle back and left with him. Witness N also testified that the four other men, who initially pinned down the victim, went back to the girl and took turns raping her. She was struggling and started rolling down toward the valley. He was able to see them rape Nyiramusugi until they were out of sight. During the rape, he heard the victim scream and say 'the only thing that I can do for you is only to pray for you.' Witness N added that he later saw the four attackers on the rise of the other side of the valley and saw that Nyiramusugi had been left for dead in the valley. That night, the witness and three other people went to the victim and found her badly injured. She was cut all over her body, covered with blood and nail scratches around her neck. He stated that they took her to her mother. The witness testified that the mother died the next day and that he learnt from Nyiramusugi's brother that she had been shot. On cross-examination, Defence counsel extensively questioned the witness as to how he came to testify and the circumstances of his statement which was made on 13 January 1999 to the Prosecutor. The witness explained that he had previously made a statement about Musema to the local court in 1997. The witness further testified that he was able to hear Musema as the refugees were speaking amongst themselves softly and the attackers were getting organized. Moreover, the attackers spoke loudly so that everyone could hear them. The witness was asked why Nyarimusugi was not killed after she was raped. He replied that he did not know. When asked again, he replied that what they did to her was worse than killing her. When pressed further as to whether it was not strange that she was not killed he replied that in a way they did kill her, and that sometimes they would leave people to die if they thought they had been sufficiently weakened. He added that if she had been left there without any help through the night, she would have died. The witness was asked whether he had been paid any money to come and testify, and he replied that he had not. Finally, it was put to him that he was lying, and he replied that he had not come to lie but rather to talk about what he himself had seen and that Musema would know that he was telling the truth. According to the Defence, Musema was not in Kibuye during the period covering 13 May 1994. Several letters were presented in support of the alibi. The Chamber accepts the testimony of Witness N as credible. It is clear and consistent, and nothing emerged from the cross-examination of the witness which cast any doubt on the evidence presented. In the view of the Chamber, the reasons given by witness N as to why he waited five years to come forward with this statement, namely that he reported Musema to his local court in 1997, is satisfactory. The reasons given by the witness as to how he had been able to hear Musema's exclamations are also convincing. The witness indeed explained that, *firstly*, the attacks had not yet started when Musema asked for the girl to be brought to him, *secondly*, he was able to hear Musema since the refugees were speaking amongst themselves softly and the attackers were getting organized, and *thirdly*, the attackers spoke loudly. Moreover, the witness explained that because of the echo at Muyira hill,

	it was possible for him to hear everything that was said and to recognize the voice of certain attackers, taking into account that the bush in which he was hiding was approximately at 40 metres bird flight from Musema. In the light of exhibits D7-A, D7-B and P21, Witness N's observation and description of the area of Muyira hill is convincing. Concerning the alibi, the Chamber recalls its finding in Section 5.2 above as regards mid-May attacks. The Chamber here confirms that this alibi does not stand. Based on this evidence, the Chamber finds, beyond a reasonable doubt, that Musema, acting in concert with others raped Nyiramusugi, and by his example encouraged the others to rape her on 13 May 1994".[439] "[T]he Chamber finds that it has been established beyond a reasonable doubt that on 13 May 1994, during the above-mentioned attack on Muyira Hill, Musema, having been told by a policeman called Ruhindara that a young Tutsi woman, a teacher by the name Nyiramusugi, was still alive, asked Ruhindara to catch her and to bring her to him. With the help of four young men, Ruhindara dragged the woman on the ground and brought her to Musema who had his rifle in his hand. The four young men, who were restraining Nyiramusugi, dropped her on the ground and pinned her down. Two of them held her arms, while the other two clamped her legs. The latter two opened the legs of the young woman and Musema tore her garments and undergarments, before undressing himself. In a loud voice, Musema said: 'The pride of the Tutsi is going to end today'. Musema raped Nyiramusugi. During the rape, as Nyiramusugi struggled, Musema immobilized her by taking her arm which he forcibly held to her neck. Standing nearby, the four men who initially held Nyiramusugi to the ground watched the scene. After Musema's departure, they came back to the woman and also raped her in turns. Thereafter, they left Nyiramusugi for dead. The Chamber finds that Musema incurs individual criminal responsibility under Article 6 (1) of the Statute, for having raped, in concert with others, a young Tutsi woman and for thus having caused serious bodily and mental harm to a member of the Tutsi group. The Chamber also finds that Musema incurs individual criminal responsibility under Article 6(1) of the Statute, for having abetted others to rape the girl, by the said act of rape and the example he thus set. With respect to the Prosecutor's argument that Musema could also be liable under Article 6(3) of the Statute, the Chamber notes that the Prosecutor has not established, nor even alleged, that among the assailants who attacked Nyiramusugi there were employees of the Gisovu Tea Factory or other persons who were Musema's subordinates. Therefore, the Chamber holds that Musema does not incur individual criminal responsibility under Article 6(3) of the Statute for Nyiramusugi's rape".[440] "[…] the Chamber notes that on the basis of the evidence presented, it emerges that acts of serious bodily and mental harm, including rape and other forms of sexual violence were often accompanied by humiliating utterances, which clearly indicated that the intention underlying each specific act was to destroy the Tutsi group as a whole. The Chamber notes, for example, that during the rape of Nyiramusugi Musema declared: 'The pride of the Tutsis will end today'. In this context, the acts of rape and sexual violence were an integral part of the plan conceived to destroy the Tutsi group. Such acts targeted Tutsi women, in particular, and specifically contributed to their destruction and therefore that of the Tutsi group as such. Witness N testified before the Chamber that Nyiramusugi, who was left for dead by those who raped her, had indeed been killed in a way. Indeed, the Witness specified that 'what they did to her is worse than death'".[441] "The Chamber therefore finds, that Musema is individually criminally responsible for crime against humanity (rape), pursuant to Articles 3(g) and (6)(1) of the Statute. However, the Chamber finds, that the Prosecutor has failed to prove beyond a reason-

[439] *Musema* Trial Judgement, paras. 847–861 (internal references omitted).

[440] *Musema* Trial Judgement, paras. 907–909.

[441] *Musema* Trial Judgement, para. 933.

	able doubt any act of rape that had been committed by Musema's subordinates and that Musema knew or had reason to know of this act and he failed to take reasonable measures to prevent the said act or to punish the perpetrators thereof, following the commission of such act. The Prosecutor has therefore not proved beyond a reasonable the individual criminal responsibility of Musema, pursuant to Articles 3(g) and 6(3) of the Statute, as charged in Count 7 of the Indictment".[442] On appeal, Alfred Musema was granted leave to file additional evidence in relation to the rape of Nyiramusugi, namely the out-of-court statements of Witnesses CB and EB. The Appeals Chamber heard these witnesses at a hearing on 17 October 2001. The Appeals Chamber found that Alfred Musema had failed to show that the Trial Chamber erred in its assessment of the testimony of Witness N on which this conviction is based. However, in light of the new evidence, the Appeals Chamber then proceeded to determine whether the Trial Chamber's findings were incorrect and, eventually, reversed his conviction. The Appeals Chamber held: "First of all, with respect to Witness CB, the Appeals Chamber notes that the circumstances described by this Witness differ on various points from the evidence given by Witness N at trial. Indeed, it emerges from the evidence given by Witness CB on 17 October 2001 that: Nyiramusugi was raped by one 'Mika' at the foot of Muyira Hill between 11 a.m. and 12 noon on 13 May 1994; Witness CB observed the incident from a bush located about 10 metres from the bush where Mika found Nyiramusugi; After the rape, Mika told Nyiramusugi to go and that he would be killed by other people; Witness CB left the bush in which he had taken refuge around 16.00 hours, that is, when the attack on Muyira Hill ceased, and found Nyiramusugi in the bush where she had gone to hide; At that time, Witness CB told Nyiramusugi that he had witnessed the rape and Nyiramusugi told him: 'Mika raped me'; Witness CB saw no one else rape Nyiramusugi on 13 May 1994 and asserted that it was indeed Mika that he had seen raping Mika on that day; Witness CB saw Nyiramusugi again on 13 May 1994 after 16.00 hours and again on the morning of 14 May 1994. With respect to Witness EB, the Appeals Chamber notes that the parties admitted that the Witness related the circumstances in which Musema raped Nyiramusugi on a day other than 13 May 1994 and that those facts do not appear in the Amended Indictment. Witness CB insisted on the fact that his sister Nyiramusugi had been raped and killed by Musema 'between 15 May and 15 June [1994].' The Appeals Chamber is of the opinion that the evidence presented by Witness CB is hardly reconcilable with Witness N's evidence at trial. Indeed, paragraph 852 of the Trial Judgement states that Musema raped Nyiramusugi on 13 May 1994 on Muyira Hill. For his part, Witness CB asserts that he witnessed a rape by Mika at the foot of that same hill on that same day. It is stated in paragraphs 849 and 851 of the Trial Judgement that Nyiramusugi was captured and brought to Musema around 15.30 hours on 13 May 1994 and that she was raped for about 40 minutes. Yet, Witness CB testified that he left his hiding place at 16.00 hours on 13 May, and that at that time, he found Nyiramusugi who told him: 'Mika raped me'. Witness CB did not see anyone else rape Nyiramusugi on that day and affirmed that it was, indeed, Mika that he saw. Regarding the testimony of Witness EB, the Appeals Chamber notes that the facts narrated by the Witness do not appear in the Amended Indictment. The Appeals Chamber notes, nonetheless, that it emerges from the said witness's testimony that Nyiramusugi was alive, at least until 15 May 1994, whereas it is stated in paragraph 853 of the Trial Judgement that Nyiramusugi was shot dead on 14 May 1994. Having considered the additional evidence admitted into the record on appeal, the Appeals Chamber finds that if the testimonies of Witnesses N, CB and EB had been presented before a reasonable tribunal of fact, it would have reached the conclusion that there was a reasonable doubt as to the guilt of Musema in respect of Count 7 of the Amended Indictment. Consequently, the Trial Chamber's factual and legal findings in relation to the rape of Nyiramusugi are incorrect and occasioned a miscarriage

442 *Musema* Trial Judgement, paras. 967–968.

	of justice. In accordance with the standard laid down in *Kupreskić*, the Appeals Chamber finds that the appropriate remedy in the instant case is to quash the conviction handed down by the Trial Chamber in respect of Count 7 of the Amended Indictment. Accordingly, the Appeals Chamber finds the Appellant not guilty of rape as a crime against humanity".[443]

3. Laurent **Semanza** (Case No. ICTR-97-20) Member of the *Mouvement révolutionnaire national pour la démocratie et le développement* (MRND) political party; bourgmestre of Bicumbi commune, in Kigali rural prefecture, until 1993; subsequently appointed as MRND representative to serve in the National Assembly established pursuant to the Arusha Accords of 1993.	
Indictment (International sex crimes (or related) charges and mode(s) of liability)	- **Rape as CAH** (count 8), **Violence to life, health and physical or mental well-being of persons, in particular cruel treatment such as rape as a violation of Article 3 common to the Geneva Conventions and of Additional Protocol II (WC)** (count 7) and **Outrages upon personal dignity, in particular humiliating and degrading treatment, rape, sexual abuse and other forms of indecent assault as a violation of Article 3 common to the Geneva Conventions and of Additional Protocol II (WC)** (count 9) under Articles 6(1) (**instigating**, **ordering** and **encouraging**) and 6(3) of the Statute (**superior responsibility**) for the rapes of Tutsi women and other outrages upon the personal dignity of Tutsi women committed between 6 and 30 April 1994 in Bicumbi and Gikoro communes by militiamen, in particular *Interahamwe*, and other persons over whom Laurent Semanza had superior responsibility. - **Genocide** (count 1) and **Persecutions as CAH** (count 6) under Articles 6(1) and 6(3) of the Statute (**superior responsibility**) and **Complicity in genocide** (count 3) under Article 6(1) of the Statute for various crimes, including **causing serious bodily or mental harm** to members of the Tutsi population through the above-mentioned crimes as well as the rapes and other forms of sexual violence committed against Tutsi women during the massacres at Ruhanga church and Musha church in Gikoro commune and the massacres at Mwulire hill and Mabare mosque in Bicumbi commune. - **Rape as CAH** (count 10), **Torture as CAH** (count 11) and **Violence to life, health and physical or mental well-being of persons, in particular cruel treatment such as rape and torture as a violation of Article 3 common to the Geneva Conventions and of Additional Protocol II (WC)** (count 13) under Articles 6(1) and 6(3) of the Statute (**superior responsibility**) for the rapes of two Tutsi women, Victim A and Victim B, between 7 and 30 April 1994, after inciting a small group of men in Gikoro commune to rape Tutsi women.[444]

[443] *Musema* Appeal Judgement, paras. 189–194.

[444] *Prosecutor v. Laurent Semanza*, Case No. ICTR-97-20-I, Third Amended Indictment, 12 October 1999 ("*Semanza* Indictment"), paras. 3.10–3.17 ("On or about 10 April 1994, **Laurent SEMANZA** worked in close cooperation with the Bourgmestre of Gikoro, Paul BISENGIMANA, to organize and execute the Ruhanga massacres, Gikoro commune, where thousands of persons had taken refuge to escape the killings in their sector. Between 9 and 13 April 1994, **Laurent SEMANZA** worked in close cooperation with the Bourgmestre of Gikoro, Paul BISENGIMANA, to organize and execute the massacres at Musha church, Gikoro commune, where several hundred people had taken refuge to escape the killings in their sector. On or about 13 April 1994, Laurent SEMANZA led the attack on the refugees at the Musha church and personally participated in the killings. Between 7 and 20 April 1994, **Laurent SEMANZA** organized and executed the massacres at Mwulire Hill, Bicumbi Commune, where several thousand people had taken refuge to escape the killings. On or about 16 and 18 April 1994, Laurent SEMANZA directed the attacks on the refugees at Mwulire Hill and personally participated in the killings. On or about 12 April 1994, **Laurent SEMANZA** organized and executed the massacre at Mabare mosque, Bicumbi commune, where several hundred people

had taken refuge to escape the killings. On or about 12 April 1994, **Laurent SEMANZA** directed the attacks on refugees at the Mabare mosque and personally participated in the killings. The massacres referred to in paragraphs 3.8 through 3.13 above, included killing and causing serious bodily and mental harm, including rape and other forms of sexual violence, to members of the Tutsi ethnic group. Laurent SEMANZA intended these massacres to be part of the non-international armed conflict against the RPF because he believed the Tutsi refugees to be enemies of the Government and/or accomplices of the RPF as stated in subparagraphs 3.4.2 and 3.4.3 *supra*. Between 6 April and 30 April, 1994, in Bicumbi and Gikoro Communes, Laurent SEMANZA instigated, ordered and encouraged militiamen, in particular *Interahamwe*, and other persons to rape Tutsi women or commit other outrages upon the personal dignity of Tutsi women, and such people did rape Tutsi women or commit other outrages upon the personal dignity of Tutsi women in response to the instigation, orders and encouragement of SEMANZA. Between 6 April and 30 April, 1994, in Bicumbi and Gikoro Communes, Laurent SEMANZA had *de facto* and/or *de jure* authority and control over militiamen, in particular *Interahamwe*, and other persons, including members of the Rwandan Armed Forces (FAR), communal police and other government agents, and he knew or had reason to know that such persons were about to commit acts of rape or other outrages against the personal dignity of Tutsi women, and he failed to take necessary and reasonable measures to prevent such acts, which were subsequently committed. Laurent SEMANZA intended the acts described in Paragraphs 3.15 and 3.16 to be part of the non-international armed conflict against the RPF as stated in subparagraphs 3.4.2 and 3.4.3 *supra*. Between April 7 and April 30 1994, Laurent SEMANZA spoke to a small group of men in Gikoro Commune. He told them that they had killed Tutsi women but that they must also rape them before killing them. In response to Semanza's words the same men immediately went to where two Tutsi women, Victim A and Victim B, had taken refuge. One of the men raped Victim A and two men raped and murdered Victim B. Laurent SEMANZA intended the acts described in this paragraph to be part of the non-international armed conflict against the RPF as stated in subparagraphs 3.4.2 and 3.4.3 *supra*".), pp. 4–7 ("**COUNT 1:** By his acts referred to in paragraphs 3.7 to 3.16 above, **Laurent SEMANZA** is responsible for killing and the causing of serious bodily or mental harm to members of the Tutsi population with the intent to destroy, in whole or in part, an ethnic or racial group, as such, and has thereby committed **GENOCIDE**, stipulated in Article 2(3)(a) of the Statute of the Tribunal as a crime, attributed to him by virtue of Articles 6(1) and 6(3), and punishable in reference to Articles 22 and 23 of the same Statute. [...] **COUNT 3:** By his acts in relation to the events described in paragraphs 3.7 to 3.16 above, **Laurent SEMANZA** is an accomplice to the killing and causing of serious bodily or mental harm to members of the Tutsi population and has thereby committed **COMPLICITY TO COMMIT GENOCIDE** stipulated in Article 2(3)(e) of the Statute of the Tribunal as a crime, attributed to him by virtue of Article 6(1) and punishable in reference to Articles 22 and 23 of the same Statute. [...] **COUNT 6:** By his acts in relation to the events described in paragraphs 3.7 to 3.16 above, **Laurent SEMANZA** is responsible for the **PERSECUTION** of civilians on political, racial or religious grounds as part of a widespread or systematic attack against a civilian population on political, ethnic or racial grounds, and has thereby committed a **CRIME AGAINST HUMANITY** stipulated in Article 3(h) of the Statute of the Tribunal as a crime, attributed to him by virtue of Articles 6(1) and 6(3), and punishable in reference to Articles 22 and 23 of the same Statute. **COUNT 7:** By his acts in relation to the events described in paragraphs 3.4 (subparagraphs 3.4.1 to 3.4.3), 3.6 and 3.9 to 3.16 in particular, **Laurent SEMANZA** is responsible for causing violence to life, health and physical or mental well-being of persons, in the course of a non-international armed conflict, in particular murder as well as cruel treatment such as rape, torture, mutilations or any form of corporal punishment, and has thereby committed **SERIOUS VIOLATIONS OF ARTICLE 3 COMMON TO THE GENEVA CONVENTIONS** of 12 August 1949, for the **PROTECTION OF WAR VICTIMS**, particularly paragraph (1)(a), and of **ADDITIONAL PROTOCOL II** thereto of 8 June 1977, particularly Article 4(2)(a), stipulated in Article 4(a) of the Statute of the Tribunal as a crime, attributed to him by virtue of Articles 6(1) and 6(3), and punishable in reference to Articles 22 and 23 of the same Statute. **COUNT 8:** By his acts in relation to the events described in paragraphs 3.15 and 3.16 above, **Laurent SEMANZA** is responsible for the **RAPE** of civilians as part of a widespread or systematic attack against a civilian population on political, ethnic or racial grounds, and has thereby committed a **CRIME AGAINST HUMANITY** stipulated in Article 3 (g) of the Statute of the Tribunal as a crime, attributed to him by virtue of Articles 6(1) and 6(3), and punishable in reference to Articles 22 and 23 of the same Statute. **COUNT 9:** By his acts in relation to the events described in paragraphs 3.4 (subparagraphs 3.4.1 to 3.4.3), 3.6, 3.14, 3.15 and 3.16, **Laurent SEMANZA** is responsible for causing outrages upon personal dignity of women, including humiliating and degrading treatment, rape, sexual abuse and other forms of indecent assault, in the course of a non-international armed conflict, and has thereby committed **SERIOUS VIOLATIONS OF ARTICLE 3 COMMON TO THE GENEVA CONVENTIONS** of 12 August 1949, for the **PROTECTION OF WAR VICTIMS** particularly paragraph (1)(c), and of **ADDITIONAL PROTOCOL II** thereto of 8 June 1977,

Trial Judgement	- Guilty of **Rape as CAH** (count 10) and **Torture as CAH** (count 11) under Article 6(1) of the Statute (**instigating**) for the rape of Victim A on 13 April 1994.[445] -Not guilty of violence to life, health and physical or mental well-being of persons, in particular cruel treatment such as rape and torture as a violation of Article 3 common to the Geneva Conventions and of Additional Protocol II (WC) (count 13) as the Trial Chamber, Judge Lloyd G. Williams dissenting, held that no conviction could be entered because it would constitute cumulative conviction with rape and torture as crimes against humanity charged in counts 10 and 11.[446] - Not guilty of rape as crime against humanity (count 8). The Trial Chamber refused to consider this charge because it was based solely on paragraphs 3.15 and 3.16 of the Indictment, which the Trial Chamber held to be impermissibly vague, thereby prejudicing Laurent Semanza's ability to prepare his defence.[447] - Not guilty of persecutions as crime against humanity (count 6), violence to life, health and physical or mental well-being of persons, in particular cruel treatment such as rape as a violation of Article 3 common to the Geneva Conventions and of Additional Protocol II (WC) (count 7) and outrages upon personal dignity, in particular humiliating and degrading treatment, rape, sexual abuse and other forms of indecent assault as a violation of Article 3 common to the Geneva Conventions and of Additional Protocol II (WC) (count 9) because the Trial Chamber found that the Prosecution did not introduce any evidence of rapes or other forms of sexual violence at Musha church, Mwulire hill and Mabare mosque.[448] - Although Laurent Semanza was found guilty of complicity in genocide (count 3), the Trial Chamber found that the Prosecution did not adduce any evidence of rapes or other forms of sexual violence at Musha church, Mwulire hill and Mabare mosque.
Appeal	- The convictions were affirmed by the Appeals Chamber.[449]

particularly Article 4(2)(e), stipulated in Article 4(e) of the Statute of the Tribunal as a crime, attributed to him by virtue of Articles 6(1) and 6(3), and punishable in reference to Articles 22 and 23 of the same Statute. **COUNT 10:** By his acts in relation to the events described in paragraph 3.17 above, **Laurent SEMANZA** is responsible for the **RAPE** of Victim A and Victim B as part of a widespread or systematic attack against a civilian population on political, ethnic or racial grounds, and has thereby committed **CRIMES AGAINST HUMANITY** stipulated in Article 3(g) of the Statute of the Tribunal as a crime, attributed to him by virtue of Articles 6(1) and 6(3), and punishable in reference to Articles 22 and 23 of the same Statute. **COUNT 11:** By his acts in relation to the events described in paragraphs 3.17 and 3.18 above, **Laurent SEMANZA** is responsible for the **TORTURE** of Victim A, Victim B and Victim C as part of a widespread or systematic attack against a civilian population on political, ethnic or racial grounds, and has thereby committed **CRIMES AGAINST HUMANITY** stipulated in Article 3(f) of the Statute of the Tribunal as a crime, attributed to him by virtue of Articles 6(1) and 6(3), and punishable in reference to Articles 22 and 23 of the same Statute. […] **COUNT 13:** By his acts in relation to the events described in paragraphs 3.4 (subparagraphs 3.4.1 to 3.4.3), 3.6, 3.17 and 3.18 above **Laurent SEMANZA** is responsible for causing violence to the life, health and physical or mental well-being of Victim A, Victim B and Victim C in the course of a non-international armed conflict, including murder as well as cruel treatment; to wit rape, torture and mutilation, and has thereby committed **SERIOUS VIOLATIONS OF ARTICLE 3 COMMON TO THE GENEVA CONVENTIONS** of 12 August 1949, for the **PROTECTION OF WAR VICTIMS**, particularly paragraph (1)(a), and of **ADDITIONAL PROTOCOL II** thereto of 8 June 1977, particularly Article 4(2)(a), stipulated in Article 4(a) of the Statute of the Tribunal as a crime, attributed to him by virtue of Articles 6(1) and 6(3), and punishable in reference to Articles 22 and 23 of the same Statute".).

445 *Prosecutor v. Laurent Semanza*, Case No. ICTR-97-20-T, Judgement and Sentence, 15 May 2003 ("*Semanza* Trial Judgement"), paras. 258–261, 476–479, 481–485, 488, 553.

446 *Semanza* Trial Judgement, paras. 542–545, 547–548, 551–553.

447 *Semanza* Trial Judgement, paras. 51–52, 54, 61, 474, 553.

448 *Semanza* Trial Judgement, paras. 250–251, 467–468, 474, 538–539, 553.

449 *Laurent Semanza v. The Prosecutor*, Case No. ICTR-97-20-A, Judgement, 20 May 2005 ("*Semanza* Appeal Judgement"), paras. 280–290 and Section IV (Disposition), p. 126.

Judgement	- The Appeals Chamber found that the Trial Chamber committed an error of law when it failed to enter a conviction for violence to life, health and physical or mental well-being of persons, in particular cruel treatment such as rape and torture as a violation of Article 3 common to the Geneva Conventions and of Additional Protocol II (WC) (count 13). Thus, in addition to the convictions imposed by the Trial Chamber, the Appeals Chamber, Judge Fausto Pocar dissenting, **entered a conviction for violence to life, health and physical or mental well-being of persons as a violation of Article 3 common to the Geneva Conventions and of Additional Protocol II (WC)** (count 13) under Article 6(1) of the Statute (**instigating**) for the rape of Victim A on 13 April 1994.[450]
Legal and Factual Findings and/or Evidence	- Legal findings: - **Rape: definition:** The Trial Chamber adopted the definition of rape given in the *Kunarac et al.* case:[451] "The *Akayesu* Judgement enunciated a broad definition of rape which included any physical invasion of a sexual nature in coercive circumstance and which was not limited to forcible sexual intercourse. The Appeals Chamber of the ICTY, in contrast, affirmed a narrower interpretation defining the material element of rape as a crime against humanity as the non-consensual penetration, however slight, of the vagina or anus of the victim by the penis of the perpetrator or by any other object used by the perpetrator, or of the mouth of the victim by the penis of the perpetrator. Consent for this purpose must be given voluntarily and freely and is assessed within the context of the surrounding circumstances. While this mechanical style of defining rape was originally rejected by this Tribunal, the Chamber finds the comparative analysis in *Kunarac* to be persuasive and thus will adopt the definition of rape approved by the ICTY Appeals Chamber. In doing so, the Chamber recognises that other acts of sexual violence that do not satisfy this narrow definition may be prosecuted as other crimes against humanity within the jurisdiction of this Tribunal such as torture, persecution, enslavement, or other inhumane acts. The mental element for rape as a crime against humanity is the intention to effect the prohibited sexual penetration with the knowledge that it occurs without the consent of the victim".[452] - Factual findings: - Alleged rapes and other forms of sexual violence during the Mwulire hill, Musha church and Mabare mosque massacres: "The Prosecution did not lead any evidence about rapes or other forms of sexual violence during the Mwulire Hill, Musha church, or Mabare mosque massacres. Prosecution Witness VAO was the only witness to testify about rapes during the Ruhanga massacre. The Chamber recalls that she was not an eye-witness to the alleged rapes, about which she learned from a woman whom she met at a refugee camp. The Chamber finds, therefore, that the Prosecution did not prove these allegations beyond a reasonable doubt. The Chamber notes that various assailants raped several Tutsi females, including Prosecution Witnesses VR, VAW, VAV, and VAO, at various locations in Bicumbi and Gikoro communes during April 1994. None of these women, however, was raped during the massacres referred to in paragraphs 3.8 through 3.13 of the Indictment as alleged in paragraph 3.14. These crimes appear to fall within the broad language of paragraphs 3.15 and 3.16 of the Indictment. However, the Chamber decided to disregard those paragraphs because they are impermissibly vague".[453]

450 *Semanza* Appeal Judgement, paras. 365–371 and Section IV (Disposition), p. 126. See also *Semanza* Appeal Judgement, Dissenting Opinion of Judge Pocar, paras. 1–4.

451 ICTY ISCC *Kunarac et al.*, see *supra* p. 528.

452 *Semanza* Trial Judgement, paras. 344–346 (internal references omitted).

453 *Semanza* Trial Judgement, paras. 250–251.

	- Rape of Witness VV, a Tutsi woman referred as Victim A in the Indictment, on 13 April 1994: "Prosecution Witness VV, a Tutsi woman, stated that on the morning of the attack at Musha church in April 1994 at approximately 10:00 a.m., she overheard a discussion between the Accused, Rugambage, Bisengimana, three members of the Presidential Guard, and a crowd of others from Bicumbi and Gikoro. She stated that the Accused asked the crowd how the work of killing Tutsis was progressing, to which they responded that they were busy doing their work. The witness testified that she then heard the Accused say: 'Are you sure you're not killing Tutsi women and girls before sleeping with them…. [y]ou should do that and even if they have some illness, you should do it with sticks.' The witness explained that the Accused used the Kinyarwanda word *kurongora*, which means 'to marry' and also 'to make love'. Witness VV testified that three of the men who heard the Accused's instructions came to the house where she and her cousin were hiding. She explained that one of the attackers stayed inside the house with the witness, while the two other men took her cousin outside. The witness testified that the man told her that they had permission to rape them. She stated that the man removed her clothes and had non-consensual sexual intercourse with her and told her that he would kill her if she resisted. The witness explained that she could not see what the other two attackers were doing to her cousin, but heard her cousin scream that she preferred that the attackers kill her. According to the witness, when she left the house, she found that her cousin had been killed and buried. The Accused denied any knowledge of rapes in Bicumbi commune, explaining that '[i]n Rwandan tradition or culture, rape has never existed.' Other Defence witnesses made similar broad assertions, stating either that rape is unknown in Rwanda or that they did not see or hear of any rapes in 1994. The Accused denied that he was in the area during the relevant period. The Accused also specifically denied that he ordered *Interahamwe* to do as they pleased with Tutsi women, including raping them, and noted that he was accused of being in multiple places at the same time on that date. The Chamber notes that Witness VV is referred to in the Indictment as Victim A, and that her cousin is Victim B. The Chamber has carefully reviewed and considered the transcript of the evidence of Witness VV, which was given by deposition pursuant to Rule 71. The Chamber finds her consistent and detailed evidence to be credible and reliable. Although the witness did not specify a certain date in April 1994, the Chamber notes that she testified that the event was contemporaneous with the attack at Musha church. Therefore, the Chamber finds that the attack on Witness VV occurred on or about 13 April 1994. The Chamber finds that the unsubstantiated claims of Defence witnesses that no rapes occurred in their localities or in Rwanda are not credible or reliable. The Chamber also notes that there is no reliable or credible evidence that places the Accused at another place during the meeting. The Chamber has also carefully considered the Accused's alibi in relation to these events, discussed above in Chapter III. In particular, the Chamber recalls that the Accused claimed to be in Gitarama town on 13 April 1994 which was supported by Defence Witness PFM, whose testimony, in the Chamber's opinion, is biased by her close personal relationship with the Accused. Upon considering all relevant evidence, including the alibi, the Chamber finds based on the testimony of Prosecution Witness VV that the Prosecutor proved beyond a reasonable doubt that on 13 April 1994 at approximately 10:00 a.m. the Accused directed a group of people to rape Tutsi women before killing them. The Chamber also finds beyond a reasonable doubt that Victim A was raped by one of the men in the group and that her cousin, Victim B, was taken outside and killed by two other men from the group. Witness VV did not observe what happened to her cousin after she was taken outside, but testified that she heard Victim B screaming that she would prefer to be killed. On the basis of this evidence, the Chamber is not able to conclude

	beyond a reasonable doubt that Victim B was also raped and/or tortured before she was killed".[454] "The Chamber has found, in relation to paragraph 3.17 of the Indictment, that the Accused, in the presence of commune and military authorities, addressed a crowd and asked them how their work of killing the Tutsis was progressing and then encouraged them to rape Tutsi women before killing them. Immediately thereafter, one of the men from the crowd had non-consensual sexual intercourse with Victim A, who was hiding in a nearby home. The Chamber has found that Victim B was killed by two other men from this crowd, but has had insufficient evidence to draw any conclusions about whether she had also been raped. The Chamber finds beyond a reasonable doubt that Victim A was raped by one of the assailants who heard the Accused encouraging the crowd to rape Tutsi women. In light of the generalized instructions about raping and killing Tutsis, the ethnic group targeted by the widespread attack, and the fact that the assailant arrived at Victim A's hiding place with two others who then killed Victim B, the Chamber finds that this rape was part of the widespread attack against the civilian Tutsi population and that the assailant was so aware. The Chamber therefore finds that the principal perpetrator committed rape as a crime against humanity. Having regard, *inter alia*, to the influence of the Accused and to the fact that the rape of Victim A occurred directly after the Accused instructed the group to rape, the Chamber finds that the Accused's encouragement constituted instigation because it was causally connected and substantially contributed to the actions of the principal perpetrator. The assailant's statement that he had been given permission to rape Victim A is evidence of a clear link between the Accused's statement and the crime. The Chamber also finds that the Accused made his statement intentionally with the awareness that he was influencing the perpetrator to commit the crime. The Chamber finds beyond a reasonable doubt that the Accused instigated the rape of Victim A as a crime against humanity. Therefore, the Chamber finds the Accused guilty on Count 10".[455] "The Chamber has found, in relation to paragraph 3.17 of the Indictment, that the Accused, in the presence of commune and military authorities, encouraged a crowd to rape Tutsi women before killing them. The Chamber has found that Victim A was raped immediately thereafter by one of the men from this crowd. The Chamber has found that Victim B was killed by two other men from this crowd, but has had insufficient evidence to draw any conclusions about whether she had also been raped or tortured. Noting, in particular, the extreme level of fear occasioned by the circumstances surrounding the event and the nature of the rape of Victim A, the Chamber finds that the perpetrator inflicted severe mental suffering sufficient to form the material element of torture. It is therefore unnecessary to determine whether this rape also inflicted *severe physical* pain or suffering, for which the Prosecutor only adduced evidence of the fact that non-consensual intercourse occurred. The Chamber finds that the rape was committed on the basis of discrimination, targeting Victim A because she was a Tutsi woman. The Chamber recalls that severe suffering inflicted for the purposes of discrimination constitutes torture and, therefore, finds that the principal perpetrator tortured Victim A by raping her for a discriminatory purpose. The Chamber also finds that the torture formed part of the widespread attack on the civilian population since the victim was raped because she was a Tutsi, the ethnicity targeted by the attack. The Chamber finds that the perpetrator was aware of the larger context of his actions, since he acknowledged that he was acting on the encouragement of the Accused to rape women as part of their broader work of killing Tutsis and he knew that others from the crowd were similarly targeting Tutsis for rape and murder. The Chamber therefore finds that the principal perpetrator committed torture as a crime against humanity. The Chamber finds that by encouraging a crowd to rape women

454 *Semanza* Trial Judgement, paras. 253–262 (internal references omitted).

455 *Semanza* Trial Judgement, paras. 476–479.

	because of their ethnicity, the Accused was encouraging the crowd to inflict severe physical or mental pain or suffering for discriminatory purposes. Therefore, he was instigating not only rape, but rape for a discriminatory purpose, which legally constitutes torture. The Chamber finds that his words were causally connected to and substantially contributed to the torture of Victim A because immediately after the Accused made his remarks to the crowd, the assailant went to a nearby home and tortured Victim A by raping her because she was a Tutsi woman. The Chamber notes that the Accused's general influence in the community and the fact that his statements were made in the presence of commune and military authorities gave his instigation greater force and legitimacy. The Chamber finds that the Accused acted intentionally and with the awareness that he was influencing others to commit rape for a discriminatory purpose as part of a widespread attack on the civilian population on ethnic grounds. Therefore, the Chamber finds that the Accused is criminally responsible for instigating torture as a crime against humanity. […] On the basis of the foregoing, the Chamber finds that the Accused is individually criminally responsible for torture as a crime against humanity […] for instigating the torture of Victim A. The Chamber therefore finds the Accused guilty on Count 11".[456] "The Accused, in the presence of commune and military authorities, addressed a crowd and asked them how their work of killing the Tutsis was progressing, and then encouraged them to rape Tutsi women before killing them. Three men from this crowd came to the nearby house where Victims A and B were hiding. One of these assailants had non-consensual sexual intercourse with Victim A. Two others took Victim B outside where she was killed. The *actus reus* of rape is non-consensual sexual penetration. The Chamber finds that Victim A was raped by one of the assailants who heard the Accused encourage the crowd. The *actus reus* of torture involves the intentional infliction of severe mental or physical pain for the purpose of obtaining information or a confession; or punishing, intimidating or coercing the victim or a third person; or discriminating, on any ground, against the victim or a third person. The Chamber also notes that an act of rape may constitute torture if committed for a prohibited purpose. The Chamber finds that the rape of Victim A constitutes torture because the assailant raped her because she was a Tutsi, which is a discriminatory purpose. In particular, the Chamber notes that the perpetrator acted intentionally and with this prohibited purpose because he acknowledged the Accused's discriminatory instructions to rape Tutsi women as part of their broader work of killing Tutsis. […] Prosecution Witness VV heard Victim B scream that she preferred that the two attackers who took her outside kill her and that, when the witness left the house after the assailants had left, she found Victim B dead. There is insufficient evidence to establish whether Victim B was raped or tortured. The Chamber finds, however, that Victim B was intentionally murdered by the two men. The Chamber finds that the Accused's encouragement to the crowd to rape Tutsi women as part of their work of killing Tutsis had a substantial effect on the rape and torture of Victim A […]. The assailants, who perpetrated the acts, heard the Accused speak and immediately afterwards committed the acts. The admission by Victim A's assailant, who heard the Accused speak, that he had authorisation to rape her indicates that he was acting on Accused's directions to rape Tutsi women. The Chamber also notes that the Accused's general influence in the community and the fact that he made the statement in the presence of commune and military authorities gave his encouragement greater force and seeming legitimacy. The Chamber also finds that in encouraging the crowd, the Accused acted intentionally and with the awareness that he was contributing to the commission of the crimes by the principal perpetrators. […] The Chamber finds beyond a reasonable doubt that the Accused instigated the rape and torture of Victim A […] and that the Accused committed torture […]. The majority, Judge Ostrovsky dissenting for reasons set out in his separate opinion, finds that these acts constitute violations of Article 4(a) of the Statute. Judge Williams is of

[456] *Semanza* Trial Judgement, paras. 481–485, 488.

	the view that based on the law and the facts a conviction should be entered on this Count for the reasons stated herein. However, for the reasons expressed in his separate opinion, Judge Dolenc considers that it would be impermissible to convict on Count 13 because of the apparent ideal concurrence of the crime charged therein with rape, torture, and murder as crimes against humanity charged in Counts 10, 11, and 12. Therefore, by a majority, no conviction will be entered for Count 13".[457]

4. Eliézer **Niyitegeka** (Case No. ICTR-96-14) Member of the *Mouvement démocratique républicain* ("MDR"); Chairman of the MDR in Kibuye prefecture from 1991 to 1994; Minister of Information of the Interim Government from 9 April 1994.	
Indictment (International sex crimes (or related) charges and mode(s) of liability)	- **Genocide** (count 1) or, alternatively, **Complicity in genocide** (count 2) and **Violence to life, health and physical or mental well-being of civilians as a violation of Article 3 common to the Geneva Conventions and of Additional Protocol II (WC)** (count 9) under Article 6(1) of the Statute for the rape and sexual assaults committed against Tutsi women (**ordering**, **instigating**, **encouraging** or **participating in**) and under Article 6(3) of the Statute (**superior responsibility**) for the rapes and acts of sexual violence committed against Tutsi women during attacks on Tutsi civilians, particularly in Kibuye. - **Rape as CAH** (count 7) and **Outrages upon personal dignity, in particular humiliating and degrading treatment, rape and indecent assault as a violation of Article 3 common to the Geneva Conventions and of Additional Protocol II (WC)** (count 10) under Article 6(1) of the Statute (**committing**) for the rape of a young Tutsi girl on or about 20 May 1994 and under Article 6(3) of the Statute (**superior responsibility**) for the the rapes and acts of sexual violence committed against Tutsi women during attacks on Tutsi civilians. - **Other inhumane acts as CAH** (count 8) under Article 6(1) of the Statute for ordering civilian militias to insert a piece of wood into a woman's vagina after she had been killed (**ordering**) and under Article 6(3) of the Statute (**superior responsibility**) for the rapes and acts of sexual violence committed against Tutsi women during attacks on Tutsi civilians.[458]

[457] *Semanza* Trial Judgement, paras. 542–545, 547–548, 551–552.

[458] *Prosecutor v. Éliezer Niyitegeka*, Case No. ICTR-96-14-T, Harmonised Amended Indictment, 25 November 2002, paras. 5.38 ("Furthermore, soldiers, militiamen and gendarmes raped or sexually assaulted or committed other crimes of a sexual nature against Tutsi women and girls, sometimes after having first kidnapped them".), 6.53 ("Between April and June 1994, several people found refuge at the secondary nursing school in Kabgayi, Gitarama *prefecture*, where students and staff were already located. On several occasions during this period, soldiers and *Interahamwe* militiamen abducted and raped female Tutsi students and refugees".), 6.59–6.61 ("During the events referred to in this indictment, rapes and other forms of sexual violence were widely and notoriously committed in Rwanda against the Tutsi population, in particular Tutsi women and girls [or] Hutu women married to Tutsi men. These acts were often accompanied by killing or were themselves used as a method of killing. They were perpetrated by, among others, militia men, including *Interahamwe-MRND*, soldiers and gendarmes. Members of the Interim Government generally instigated, encouraged, facilitated, or acquiesced to, among others, the militia, *Interahamwe-MRND*, sold[i]ers and gendarmes raping and sexual violating Tutsi women. Government ministers even sometimes committed these acts themselves, thereby encouraging by their own example the commission of such acts by among others, militia, *Interahamwe-MRND*, soldiers and gendarmes over whom they had *de facto* and/or *de jure* authority. For example, on or about 20 May 1994, political party affiliates and militia men working directly under the supervision of **Eliezer Niyitegeka** forced a young girl to get into his car, whereupon Eliezer Niyitegeka raped her, and when she got out of the vehicle **Eliezer Niyitegeka** himself shot and killed her. Similarly, on or about 28 June 1994 **Eliezer Niyitegeka** used his vehicle to run another vehicle off the road. The occupants of that vehicle, a man and a woman, were shot to death. **Eliezer Niyitegeka** approached the vehicle and instructed the militia men that had gathered nearby to undress the woman, cut a piece of wood, and to insert

the wood in the woman's genitalia. Rape and other forms of sexual violence, including sexual torture, degrading sexual acts and indecent exposure were integral to the genocidal policy of the conspirators that seized political power from the first moments of 7th April 1994 when political assassinations began. Not even the Prime Minister Agathe Uwiligimana was spared. Her semi-nude, lifeless body was discovered on the morning of 7 April 1994 with indicia of sexual torture and sexual degradation".), 6.69 ("**Éliezer Niyitegeka** exercised command responsibility over civilian militia that committed acts of sexual violence and sexual torture by ordering them to assist him when he committed such acts upon Tutsi women, and by encouraging such acts by his own example, and in failing to forbid or discourage such acts, or to sanction or punish the perpetrators of those acts".), pp. 60–66, 76–85 (**Count 1: GENOCIDE:** The Prosecutor of the International Criminal Tribunal of Rwanda charges **Eliézer NIYITEGEKA** with ***GENOCIDE**, a crime stipulated in Article 2(3)(a) of the Statute*, in that on or between the dates of 6 April 1994 and 17 July 1994, notably, though not exclusively, in Kibuye *préfecture*, Rwanda, **Eliézer NIYITEGEKA** did kill and cause serious bodily or mental harm to members of the Tutsi population with the intent to destroy, in whole or in part, a racial or ethnic group, as follows: *Pursuant to Article 6(1) of the Statute*: by virtue of his affirmative acts in ordering, instigating, commanding, participating in and aiding and abetting the preparation and execution of the crime charged, as set forth in paragraphs […] 5.38 […] and 6.56 to 6.71 of this indictment. Without limiting the generality of the foregoing, these acts and omissions include, but are not limited to: […] (e) ordering, instigating, encouraging or participating in rape and sexual assaults upon Tutsi women [¶6.60]; *and [p]ursuant to Article 6(3) of the Statute*: by virtue of his actual an constructive knowledge of the acts and omissions of local public officials, […] and soldiers, gendarmes, communal police, *Interahamwe*, civilian militia and civilians acting under his authority, and his failure to stop or prevent them, or to discipline and punish them, for their acts in the preparation and execution of the crime charged, as set forth in paragraphs […] 5.38 […] and 6.56 to 6.71 of this indictment. Without limiting the generality of the foregoing, these acts and omissions include, but are not limited to: […] (i) ordering, commanding or participating in generalized attacks on Tutsi civilians, particularly in Kibuye, knowing that rape and sexual violence against Tutsi women were systematically incorporated in such attacks, and failing to stop or discipline or punish the perpetrators, including soldiers, communal police, civilian militias and local residents, subject to his authority as a Minister of the Interim Government [¶¶6.59; 6.60; 6.61]; *with the intent to destroy the Tutsi ethnic group, in whole or in part, each of which acts or omissions is punishable in reference to Articles 22 and 23 of the Statute*. Or alternatively, **Count 2: COMPLICITY IN GENOCIDE:** The Prosecutor of the International Criminal Tribunal of Rwanda charges **Eliézer NIYITEGEKA** with ***COMPLICITY IN GENOCIDE**, a crime stipulated in Article 2(3)(e) of the Statute*, in that on or between the dates of 6 April 1994 and 17 July 1994, notably, though not exclusively, in Kibuye *préfecture*, Rwanda, **Eliézer NIYITEGEKA** did kill or cause serious bodily or mental harm to members of the Tutsi population with the intent to destroy, in whole or in part, a racial or ethnic group, as follows: *Pursuant to Article 6(1) of the Statute*: by virtue of his affirmative acts in planning, instigating, ordering, committing, or otherwise aiding and abetting the planning, preparation or execution of the crime charged, as set forth in paragraphs […] 5.38 […] and 6.56 to 6.71 of this indictment. Without limiting the generality of the foregoing, these acts and omissions include, but are not limited to: […] (e) ordering, instigating, encouraging or participating in rape and sexual assaults upon Tutsi women [¶6.60]; *[p]ursuant to Article 6(3) of the Statute*: by virtue of his actual and constructive knowledge of the acts and omissions of local public officials, […] and soldiers, gendarmes, communal police, *Interahamwe*, civilian militia and civilians acting under his authority, and his failure to stop or prevent them, or to discipline and punish them, for their acts in the preparation and execution of the crime charged, as set forth in paragraphs […] 5.38 […] and 6.56 to 6.71 of this indictment. Without limiting the generality of the foregoing, these acts and omissions include, but are not limited to: […] (i) ordering, commanding or participating in generalized attacks on Tutsi civilians, particularly in Kibuye, knowing that rape and sexual violence against Tutsi women were systematically incorporated in such attacks, and failing to stop or discipline or punish the perpetrators, including soldiers, communal police, civilian militias and local residents, subject to his authority as a Minister of the Interim Government [¶¶6.59; 6.60; 6.61]; *each of which acts or omissions is punishable in reference to Articles 22 and 23 of the Statute*. […] **Count 7: CRIMES AGAINST HUMANITY (Rape):** The Prosecutor of the International Criminal Tribunal of Rwanda charges **Eliézer NIYITEGEKA** with ***RAPE as a CRIME AGAINST HUMANITY**, as stipulated in Article 3(g) of the Statute*, in that on or between the dates of 6 April 1994 and 17 July 1994, notably, though not exclusively, in Kibuye *préfecture*, Rwanda, **Eliézer NIYITEGEKA** did cause women to be raped as part of a widespread or systematic attack against a civilian population on political, ethnic or racial grounds, as follows: *Pursuant to Article 6(1) of the Statute*: by virtue of his affirmative acts in planning, instigating, ordering, committing, or otherwise aiding and abetting the planning, preparation or execution of the crime charged, as set forth in paragraphs 5.38; 6.59 to 6.71 of this indictment. Without limiting the generality of the foregoing, these acts or omissions include, but are not limited to: (a) raping a young girl on or about 20 May 1994 [¶6.60]; *[p]ursuant to Article 6(3) of the Statute*: by virtue of his actual or constructive knowledge of the acts or omissions of his subordinates, including local public officials, […] and soldiers, gendarmes, communal police, *Interahamwe*, civilian militia or civilians acting under his authority, and his failure to stop or prevent them, or to discipline and punish them, for their acts in the planning, preparation or execution of the crime charged, as set forth in paragraphs 5.38; 6.59 to 6.71 of this indictment. Without limiting the generality of the foregoing, these acts or omissions include, but are not limited to: (b) ordering or leading generalized attacks upon Tutsi civilians, knowing that sexual violence against Tutsi women, particularly rape, was, or would be, systematically incorporated in such generalized attacks [¶¶5.38; 6.59; 6.60; 6.61]; *each of which acts or omissions is punishable in reference to Articles 22 and 23 of the Statute*. **Count 8: CRIMES AGAINST HUMANITY (Inhumane Acts):** The Prosecutor of the International Criminal Tribunal of Rwanda charges **Eliézer NIYITEGEKA** with ***INHUMANE ACTS as a CRIME AGAINST HUMANITY***, *as stipulated in Article 3(i) of the Statute*, in that on or between the dates of 6 April 1994 and 17 July 1994, notably, though not exclusively, in Kibuye *préfecture*, Rwanda, **Eliézer NIYITEGEKA** did commit inhumane acts upon persons as part of a widespread or systematic attack against a civilian population on political, ethnic or racial grounds, as follows: *Pursuant to Article 6(1) of the Statute*: by virtue of his affirmative acts in planning, instigating, ordering, committing, or otherwise aiding and abetting the planning, preparation or execution of the crime charged, as set forth in paragraphs […] 5.38 […] and 6.56 to 6.71 of this indictment. Without limiting the generality of the foregoing, these acts or omissions include, but are not limited to: (a) ordering civilian militias to shoot a woman and then ordering them to cut a piece of wood and insert it in her vagina [¶6.60]; *[p]ursuant to Article 6(3) of the Statute*: by virtue of his actual or constructive knowledge of the acts or omissions of his subordinates, including soldiers, gendarmes, communal police, *Interahamwe*, civilian militia or civilians acting under his authority, and his failure to stop or prevent them, or to discipline or punish them, for their acts in the planning, preparation or execution of the crime charged, as set forth in paragraphs […] 5.38 […] and 6.56 to 6.71 of this indictment. Without limiting the generality of the foregoing, these acts or omissions include, but are not limited to: (a) ordering, instigating or participating in attacks on Tutsi civilians, or on persons perceived to be politically opposed to the MRND or the Interim Government by communal police, *Interahamwe*, civilian militias or local residents in Byumba or Kibungo *prefectures*, resulting in injury, rape and death of thousands of persons [¶5.38; 6.55 to 6.71]; (b) ordering or leading generalized attacks upon Tutsi civilians, knowing that sexual violence against Tutsi women, particularly rape, was, or would be, systematically incorporated in such generalized attacks [¶¶5.38; 6.59; 6.60; 6.61]; *each of which acts or omissions is punishable in reference to Articles 22 and 23 of the Statute*. **Count 9: SERIOUS VIOLATIONS OF ARTICLE 3 COMMON TO THE GENEVA CONVENTION AND OF ADDITIONAL PROTOCOL II:** The Prosecutor of the International Criminal Tribunal of Rwanda charges **Eliézer NIYITEGEKA** with ***VIOLENCE TO LIFE, HEALTH AND PHYSICAL OR MENTAL WELL-BEING as a SERIOUS VIOLATION OF ARTICLE 3 COMMON TO THE GENEVA CONVENTION AND OF ADDITIONAL PROTOCOL II***, *as stipulated in Article 4(a) of the Statute*, in that on or between the dates of 6 April 1994 and 17 July 1994, notably, though not exclusively, in Kibuye *préfecture*, Rwanda, **Eliézer NIYITEGEKA** did cause violence to the life, health and physical or mental well-being, in particular murders and killings, of civilian non-combatants during a non-international armed conflict, as follows: *[p]ursuant to Article 6(1) of the Statute*: by virtue of his affirmative acts in planning, instigating, ordering, committing, or otherwise aiding and abetting the planning, preparation or execution of the crime charged, as set forth in paragraphs […] 5.38 […] and 6.56 to 6.71 of this indictment. Without limiting the generality of the foregoing, these acts and omissions include, but are not limited to: […] (e) ordering, instigating, encouraging or participating in rape and sexual assaults upon Tutsi women [¶6.60]; *and [p]ursuant to Article 6(3) of the Statute*: by virtue of his actual and constructive knowledge of the acts and omissions of soldiers, gendarmes, communal police, *Interahamwe*, civilian militia or civilians acting under his authority, and his failure to stop or prevent them, or to discipline or punish them, for their acts in the preparation and execution of the crime charged, as set forth in paragraphs […] 5.38 […] and 6.56 to 6.71 of this indictment. Without limiting the generality of the foregoing, these acts or omissions include, but are not limited to: […] (i) ordering, commanding or participating in generalized attacks on Tutsi civilians, particularly in Kibuye, knowing that rape and sexual violence against Tutsi women were systematically incorporated in such attacks, and failing to stop or discipline or punish the perpetrators, including soldiers, communal police, civilian militias and local residents, subject to his authority as a Minister of the Interim Government [¶¶6.59; 6.60; 6.61]; *as an offensive or defensive strategy to combat the RPF, each of which acts or omissions is punishable in reference to Articles 22 and 23 of the Statute*. **Count 10: SERIOUS VIOLATIONS OF ARTICLE 3 COMMON TO THE GENEVA CONVENTION AND OF ADDITIONAL PROTOCOL II:** The Prosecutor of the International Criminal Tribunal of Rwanda charges **Eliézer NIYITEGEKA** with ***OUTRAGES ON PERSONAL DIGNITY as SERIOUS VIOLATIONS OF ARTICLE 3***

Trial Judgement	- Guilty of **Other inhumane acts as CAH** (count 8) under Article 6(1) of the Statute for the castration of Assiel Kabanda and hanging his genitals on a spike on 22 June 1994, at Kazirandimwe hill, after he had been killed (**aiding and abetting**) and for ordering *Interahamwe* to insert a sharp piece of wood into a Tutsi woman's vagina after she had been killed (**ordering**).[459] - Although Eliézer Niyitegeka was found guilty of genocide (count 1), the underlying offences of this crime did not include international sex crimes.[460] - Not guilty of rape as CAH (count 7), because the Trial Chamber found that there was insufficient evidence to find that Eliézer Niyitegeka raped a young girl on 20 May 1994 near the Gisovu-Kibuye road.[461] - Not guilty of counts 9 and 10, because the Prosecution withdrew these counts in its final trial brief.[462]
Appeal Judgement	- The conviction was affirmed by the Appeals Chamber.[463]
Legal and Factual Findings and/or Evidence	- Factual findings: - Alleged rape of a young Tutsi girl on 20 May 1994: "The witness did not see the Accused rape the young girl. He surmised that the girl had been raped by the Accused in light of the circumstances, and because he had later heard the Interahamwe talk of the girl having been raped. The Interahamwe could not have seen the act either, since it allegedly occurred in a closed vehicle and there is no evidence that the Interahamwe had peered into the vehicle. Nor did the witness state that their reported conversation named the Accused as the perpetrator. There is insufficient evidence for a factual finding that the girl had been raped, or that the alleged rape was perpetrated by the Accused. Therefore, the Chamber finds that there is insufficient evidence to support the allegation that the Accused raped the young girl".[464] - Castration of Assiel Kabanda, a prominent Tutsi trader, on 22 June 1994:

***COMMON TO THE GENEVA CONVENTION AND OF ADDITIONAL PROTOCOL II**, as stipulated in Article 4(e) of the Statute*, in that on or between the dates of 6 April 1994 and 17 July 1994, notably, though not exclusively, in Kibuye *préfecture*, Rwanda, **Eliézer NIYITEGEKA** did cause outrages upon the personal dignity, in particular humiliating and degrading treatment, rape and indecent assault, upon civilian non-combatants during a non-international armed conflict, as follows: *[p]ursuant to Article 6(1) of the Statute*: by virtue of his affirmative acts in planning, instigating, ordering, committing, or otherwise aiding and abetting the planning, preparation or execution of the crime charged, as set forth in paragraphs [...] 5.38 [...] and 6.56 to 6.71 of this indictment. Without limiting the generality of the foregoing, these acts and omissions include, but are not limited to: (c) raping a young girl on or about 20 May 1994 [¶6.60]; *[p]ursuant to Article 6(3) of the Statute*: by virtue of his actual or constructive knowledge of the acts or omissions of his subordinates, including soldiers, gendarmes, communal police, *Interahamwe*, civilian militia or civilians acting under his authority, and his failure to stop or prevent them, or to discipline or punish them, for their acts in the planning, preparation or execution of the crime charged, as set forth in paragraphs [...] 5.38 [...] and 6.56 to 6.71 of this indictment. Without limiting the generality of the foregoing, these acts or omissions include, but are not limited to: (d) ordering or leading generalized attacks upon Tutsi civilians, knowing that sexual violence against Tutsi women, particularly rape, was, or would be, systematically incorporated in such generalized attacks [¶¶5.38; 6.59; 6.60; 6.61]; *as an offensive or defensive strategy to combat the RPF, each of which acts or omissions is punishable in reference to Articles 22 and 23 of the Statute*".).

459 *Prosecutor v. Éliezer Niyitegeka*, Case No. ICTR-96-14-T, Judgement and Sentence, 16 May 2003 ("*Niyitegeka* Trial Judgement"), paras. 312, 316, 462–467, 480.

460 *Niyitegeka* Trial Judgement, paras. 416–417, 420, 480.

461 *Niyitegeka* Trial Judgement, paras. 301, 457–458, 480.

462 *Niyitegeka* Trial Judgement, paras. 7, 468–469, 480.

463 See *Éliezer Niyitegeka v. The Prosecutor*, Case No. ICTR-96-14-A, Judgement, 9 July 2004.

464 *Niyitegeka* Trial Judgement, para. 301.

	"Based on the totality of the evidence, the Chamber finds that on 22 June 1994, sometime in the afternoon after 3.00 p.m., at Kazirandimwe Hill, the Accused was with others leading an attack against Tutsi refugees. The attackers found a prominent Tutsi trader, Assiel Kabanda, for whom attackers had been looking several days. The Accused and the others rejoiced when they found him. The Accused and others were jubilating when Kabanda was killed and subsequently decapitated and castrated, and his skull pierced through the ears with a spike. His genitals were hung on a spike, and visible to the public. Although the Accused did not personally kill Kabanda, the Chamber finds that he was part of the group that perpetrated these crimes, and rejoiced at the commission of these acts".[465] "In II.7.1.[5] above, the Chamber found that on 22 June 1994, at Kazirandimwe Hill, the Accused was participating in an attack when Assiel Kabanda was found. The Accused and the attackers were jubilant at this capture as Kabanda was a prominent Tutsi who was influential and well-liked. The Accused was rejoicing when Kabanda was killed, decapitated, castrated and his skull pierced through the ears with a spike. The skull was carried away by two men each holding one end of the spike with the skull in the middle. Kabanda's genitals were hung on a spike, and visible to the public. The Chamber finds that the jubilation of the Accused, particularly in light of his leadership role in the attack, at the decapitation and castration of Kabanda, and the piercing of Kabanda's skull, supported and encouraged the attackers, and thereby aided and abetted the commission of these crimes".[466] "The Chamber finds that the acts committed with respect to Kabanda and the sexual violence to the dead woman's body are acts of seriousness comparable to other acts enumerated in the Article, and would cause mental suffering to civilians, in particular, Tutsi civilians, and constitute a serious attack on the human dignity of the Tutsi community as a whole. [...] The Chamber finds that by his act of encouragement during the killing, decapitation and castration of Kabanda, and the piercing of his skull, and his association with the attackers who carried out these acts, and his ordering of Interahamwe to perpetrate the sexual violence on the body of the dead woman, the Accused is individually criminally responsible, pursuant to Article 6(1) of the Statute, for inhumane acts committed as part of a widespread and systematic attack on the civilian Tutsi population on ethnic grounds and as such constitute a crime against humanity, as provided in Article 3(i) of the Statute. Accordingly, the Chamber finds that the Accused is guilty of Crime against Humanity (Other Inhumane Acts) as charged in Count 8 of the Indictment".[467] - Insertion of a piece of wood into a Tutsi woman's vagina, on 28 June 1994, near the Technical training college: "Although the witness did not see the act of inserting the piece of wood into the woman's genitalia, he heard the order being issued by the Accused and later saw the woman lying on the road with wood sticking out of her genitalia. Based on the totality of the evidence, the Chamber finds that on 28 June 1994, near the Technical Training College, on a public road, the Accused ordered Interahamwe to undress the body of a woman who had just been shot dead, to fetch and sharpen a piece of wood, which he then instructed them to insert into her genitalia. This act was then carried out by the Interahamwe, in accordance with his instructions. The body of the woman, with the piece of wood protruding from it, was left on the roadside for some three days thereaf-

465 *Niyitegeka* Trial Judgement, para. 312.
466 *Niyitegeka* Trial Judgement, para. 462.
467 *Niyitegeka* Trial Judgement, paras. 465, 467.

	ter. The Accused referred to the woman as 'Inyenzi' which the Chamber is satisfied was meant to refer to Tutsi".[468] "In II.7.2.4 above, the Chamber found that on 28 June 1994, near the Technical Training College, the Accused ordered Interahamwe to undress the body of a Tutsi woman, whom he called 'Inyenzi', who had just been shot dead, to fetch and sharpen a piece of wood, which he then instructed them to insert into her genitalia. This act was then carried out by the Interahamwe, in accordance with his instructions".[469] "The Chamber finds that the acts committed with respect to Kabanda and the sexual violence to the dead woman's body are acts of seriousness comparable to other acts enumerated in the Article, and would cause mental suffering to civilians, in particular, Tutsi civilians, and constitute a serious attack on the human dignity of the Tutsi community as a whole. […] The Chamber finds that by his act of encouragement during the killing, decapitation and castration of Kabanda, and the piercing of his skull, and his association with the attackers who carried out these acts, and his ordering of Interahamwe to perpetrate the sexual violence on the body of the dead woman, the Accused is individually criminally responsible, pursuant to Article 6(1) of the Statute, for inhumane acts committed as part of a widespread and systematic attack on the civilian Tutsi population on ethnic grounds and as such constitute a crime against humanity, as provided in Article 3(i) of the Statute. Accordingly, the Chamber finds that the Accused is guilty of Crime against Humanity (Other Inhumane Acts) as charged in Count 8 of the Indictment".[470] - Genocidal intent of Eliézer Niyitegeka: "In ascertaining the intent of the Accused, the Chamber has also taken into account incidents charged elsewhere, in addition to his acts relevant to this charge. The Chamber has considered the Accused's act of ordering Interahamwe to undress a Tutsi woman, and to insert a sharpened piece of wood into her genitalia, after ascertaining that she was of the Tutsi ethnic group (see II.7.2.4 above). The body was then left, with the piece of wood protruding from it, in plain view on a public road for some three days thereafter. […] The Chamber has also considered the Accused's jubilation at the killing of Assiel Kabanda and his subsequent decapitation and castration, and the piercing of his skull through the ears with a spike. Kabanda was a prominent Tutsi whose capture was met with rejoicing by the Accused and others (see II.7.1.[5] above)".[471]

5. Juvénal **Kajelijeli** (Case No. ICTR-98-44A) Bourgmestre of Mukingo commune, in Ruhengeri prefecture, from 1988 until 1993 and from June 1994 until mid-July 1994.	
Indictment (International sex crimes (or related) charges and mode(s) of liability)	- **Conspiracy to commit genocide** (count 1), Genocide (count 2) or, alternatively, **Complicity in genocide** (count 3), **Direct and public incitement to commit genocide** (count 4), **Rape as CAH** (count 7), **Persecutions as CAH** (count 8), **Other inhumane acts as CAH** (count 9), **Violence to life, health and physical or mental well-being of civilians, in particular cruel treatment, as a violation of Article 3 common to the Geneva Conventions and of Additional Protocol II (WC)** (count 10) and **Outrages upon personal dignity, in particular humiliating and degrading treatment, rape and indecent assault as a violation of Article 3 common to the**

468 *Niyitegeka* Trial Judgement, para. 316.
469 *Niyitegeka* Trial Judgement, para. 463.
470 *Niyitegeka* Trial Judgement, paras. 465, 467.
471 *Niyitegeka* Trial Judgement, paras. 416–417.

	Geneva Conventions and of Additional Protocol II (WC) (count 11) for witnessing the rapes and other sexual assaults committed against Tutsi women.[472]

[472] *Prosecutor v. Juvénal Kajelijeli*, Case No. ICTR-98-44A-I, Amended Indictment Pursuant to the Tribunal Order Dated 25 January 2001, 25 January 2001, paras. 4.18 ("During such meetings, speeches were made by influential persons including **the Accused** and Joseph Nzirorera, inciting their audience who were predominantly members of MRND and Hutus, to assault, rape and exterminate the Tutsis who were excluded from such meetings on ac of their ethnicity".), 5.3 ("From April through July 1994, many Tutsi men, women and children were attacked, abducted, raped and massacred in their residences or at their places of shelter within the Mukingo *commune* or arrested, detained and later murdered. **The Accused** commanded, organized, supervised and participated in these attacks".), 5.5 ("**The Accused** ordered and witnessed the raping and other sexual assaults on the Tutsi females. At all times material to this indictment, **the Accused**, as a person in authority over the attackers failed to take any measure to stop these nefarious acts on the Tutsi females".), pp. 9–11 ("***Count 1: Conspiracy to commit genocide, pursuant to Article 2(3)(b) of the Statute***[:] **Juvénal Kajelijeli** by the acts or omission described in the paragraphs to which reference is made herein below: Pursuant to Article 6(1): Paragraphs […] 4.18 […], 5.3, […] 5.5 […] Pursuant to Article 6(3): Paragraphs […] 4.18 […], 5.3, […] 5.5 […] Conspired with others to kill or cause serious bodily or mental harm to members of the Tutsi population with the intent to destroy, in whole or in part, a racial or ethnic group, and thereby committed **CONSPIRACY TO COMMIT GENOCIDE**, pursuant to Article 2(3)(b) and punishable in reference to Articles 22 and 23 of the Statute of the International Criminal Tribunal for Rwanda. ***Count 2: Genocide, pursuant to Article 2(3)(a) of the Statute***[:] **Juvénal Kajelijeli** by the acts or omission described in the paragraphs to which reference is made herein below: Pursuant to Article 6(1): Paragraphs […] 4.18 […], 5.3, […] 5.5 […] Pursuant to Article 6(3): Paragraphs […] 4.18 […], 5.3, […] 5.5 […] Is responsible for killing or causing serious bodily or mental harm to members of the Tutsi population with the intent to destroy, in whole or in part, a racial or ethnic group, and thereby committed **GENOCIDE**, pursuant to Article 2(3)(a) and punishable in reference to Articles 22 and 23 of the Statute of the International Criminal Tribunal for Rwanda. ***Count 3: Complicity to commit genocide, pursuant to Article 2(3)(e) of the Statute***[:] **Juvénal Kajelijeli** by the acts or omissions described in the paragraphs to which reference is made herein below: Pursuant to Article 6(1): Paragraphs […] 4.18 […], 5.3 […], Pursuant to Article 6(3): Paragraphs […] 4.18 […], 5.3 […], Is responsible for killing and causing serious bodily and mental harm to members of the Tutsi population with the intent to destroy, in whole or in part, a racial or ethnic group, and thereby committed **COMPLICITY IN GENOCIDE**, pursuant to Article 2(3)(e) and punishable in reference to Articles 22 and 23 of the Statute of the International Criminal Tribunal of Rwanda. ***Count 4: Direct and public incitement to genocide, pursuant to Article 2(3)(c) of the Statute***[:] **Juvénal Kajelijeli** by the acts or omissions described in the paragraphs to which reference is made herein below: Pursuant to Article 6(1): Paragraphs […] 4.18 […], Pursuant to Article 6(3): Paragraphs […] 4.18 […], Is responsible for direct and public incitement to kill and cause serious bodily or mental harm to members of the Tutsi population with the intent to destroy, in whole or in part, a racial or ethnic group, and thereby committed **DIRECT AND PUBLIC INCITEMENT TO GENOCIDE**, pursuant to Article 2(3)(c) and punishable in reference to Articles 22 and 23 of the Statute of the International Criminal Tribunal of Rwanda".), pp. 13–15 ("***Count 7: Crimes against humanity-Rape, pursuant to Article 3(g) of the Statute***[:] **Juvénal Kajelijeli** by the acts or omissions described in the paragraphs to which reference is made herein below: Pursuant to Article 6(1): Paragraphs […] 4.18 […], 5.3, […] 5.5 […] Pursuant to Article 6(3): Paragraphs […] 4.18 […], 5.3, […] 5.5 […] Is responsible for the rape of Tutsi(s) as part of a widespread and systematic attack against a civilian population on political, ethnic or racial grounds, and thereby committed **CRIMES AGAINST HUMANITY**, pursuant to Article 3(g) and punishable in reference to Articles 22 and 23 of the Statute of the International Criminal Tribunal of Rwanda. ***Count 8: Crimes against humanity-Persecution on Racial, Political, Religious Grounds Pursuant to Article 3(h) of the Statute***[:] **Juvénal Kajelijeli** by the acts or omissions described in the paragraphs to which reference is made herein below: Pursuant to Article 6(1): Paragraphs […] 4.18 […], 5.3, […] 5.5 […] Pursuant to Article 6(3): Paragraphs […] 4.18 […], 5.3, […] 5.5 […] Is responsible for the persecution of Tutsi(s) as part of a widespread and systematic attack against a civilian population on political, ethnic or racial grounds, and thereby committed a **CRIME AGAINST HUMANITY**, pursuant to Article 3(h) and punishable in reference to Articles 22 and 23 of the Statute of the International Criminal Tribunal of Rwanda. ***Count 9: Crimes against humanity-Other Inhumane Acts, Pursuant to Article 3(i) of the Statute***[:] **Juvénal Kajelijeli** by the acts or omissions described in the paragraphs to which reference is made herein below: Pursuant to Article 6(1): Paragraphs […] 4.18 […], 5.3, […] 5.5 […] Pursuant to Article 6(3): Paragraphs […] 4.18 […], 5.3, […] 5.5 […] Is responsible for other inhumane acts against the Tutsi(s) as part of a widespread and systematic attack against a civilian population on political, ethnic or racial grounds, and thereby

Trial Judgement	- Not guilty of conspiracy to commit genocide (count 1).[473] - Although Juvénal Kajelijeli was found guilty of genocide (count 2) and direct and public incitement to commit genocide (count 4), the underlying offences of these crimes did not include international sex crimes.[474] - Not guilty of rape as CAH (count 7) because the Trial Chamber, Judge Arlette Ramaroson dissenting, found that the Prosecution failed to prove the responsibility of Juvénal Kajelijeli beyond a reasonable doubt under either Article 6(1) or Article 6(3) of the Statute.[475] - The charge of persecutions as CAH (count 8) was dismissed as, in its closing arguments, the Prosecution requested the Trial Chamber to withdraw this charge due to insufficient evidence. In the Trial Judgement, the Trial Chamber granted the Prosecution request for withdrawal of count 8.[476] - Not guilty of other inhumane acts as CAH (count 9) because the Trial Chamber found that the Prosecution failed to prove the responsibility of Juvénal Kajelijeli beyond a reasonable doubt under both Article 6(1) and Article 6(3) of the Statute.[477]
Appeal Judgement	- The Prosecution did not appeal Juvénal Kajelijeli's acquittal for international sex crimes.[478]
Legal and	- Legal findings:

committed **CRIMES AGAINST HUMANITY**, pursuant to Article 3(i) and punishable in reference to Articles 22 and 23 of the Statute of the International Criminal Tribunal of Rwanda. ***Count 10: Serious violations of Article 3 common to the Geneva Conventions and Additional Protocol II, pursuant to Article 4(a) of the Statute***[:] **Juvénal Kajelijeli,** during a non-international armed conflict, by his acts or omissions described in the paragraphs to which reference is made herein below: Pursuant to Article 6(1): Paragraphs […] 4.18 […], 5.3, […] 5.5 […] Pursuant to Article 6(3): Paragraphs […] 4.18 […], 5.3, […] 5.5 […] Is responsible for causing violence to life, health and physical or mental well-being of persons, in particular murder as well as cruel treatment such as torture, mutilation or any form of corporal punishment against the Tutsi(s) and has thereby committed **SERIOUS VIOLATIONS OF ARTICLE 3 COMMON TO THE GENEVA CONVENTIONS OF 12 AUGUST 1949 FOR THE PROTECTION OF WAR VICTIMS, AND OF ADDITIONAL PROTOCOL II THERETO OF 8 JUNE 1977**, pursuant to Article 4(a), a crime which is punishable in reference to Articles 22 and 23 of the Statute of the International Criminal Tribunal of Rwanda. ***Count 11: Serious violations of Article 3 common to the Geneva Conventions and Additional Protocol II, pursuant to Article 4(e) of the Statute***[:] **Juvénal Kajelijeli,** during a non-international armed conflict, by his acts or omissions described in the paragraphs to which reference is made herein below: Pursuant to Article 6(1): Paragraphs […] 4.18 […], 5.3, […] 5.5 […] Pursuant to Article 6(3): Paragraphs […] 4.18 […], 5.3, […] 5.5 […] Is responsible for causing outrages upon personal dignity, in particular humiliating and degrading treatment, rape, enforced prostitution and any form of indecent assault against the Tutsi(s) and has thereby committed **SERIOUS VIOLATIONS OF ARTICLE 3 COMMON TO THE GENEVA CONVENTIONS OF 12 AUGUST 1949 FOR THE PROTECTION OF WAR VICTIMS, AND OF ADDITIONAL PROTOCOL II THERETO OF 8 JUNE 1977**, pursuant to Article 4(e), a crime which is punishable in reference to Articles 22 and 23 of the Statute of the International Criminal Tribunal of Rwanda".). On 13 September 2002, in its Decision on Kajelijeli's Motion for Partial Acquittal Pursuant to Rule 98 *bis*, the Trial Chamber found that insufficient evidence has been presented in relation to the charges contained in counts 10 and 11 of the Indictment and acquitted Juvénal Kajelijeli on these counts. See *Prosecutor v. Juvénal Kajelijeli*, Case No. ICTR-98-44A-T, Decision on Kajelijeli's Motion for Partial Acquittal Pursuant to Rule 98 *bis*, 13 September 2002, para. 11, p. 6.

473 *Prosecutor v. Juvénal Kajelijeli*, Case No. ICTR-98-44A-T, Judgment and Sentence, 1 December 2003 ("*Kajelijeli* Trial Judgement"), paras. 794–798, 942.

474 *Kajelijeli* Trial Judgement, paras. 842–845, 856–861, 942.

475 *Kajelijeli* Trial Judgement, paras. 917–925, 943. See also *Kajelijeli* Trial Judgement, Opinion Dissidente du Juge Arlette Ramaroson.

476 *Kajelijeli* Trial Judgement, paras. 926–928, 942.

477 *Kajelijeli* Trial Judgement, paras. 934–940, 942.

478 See *Juvénal Kajelijeli v. The Prosecutor*, Case No. ICTR-98-44A-A, Judgement, 23 May 2005.

Factual Findings and/or Evidence	**- Rape and sexual violence can constitute genocide (serious bodily or mental harm):** The Trial Chamber reaffirmed that "[…] 'serious bodily harm' does not necessarily have to be permanent or irremediable, and that it included non-mortal acts of sexual violence, rape […]".[479] **- Rape: definition:** The Trial Chamber adopted the definition of rape given in the *Kunarac et al.* case:[480] "This definition substantially modified and completed by Trial Chamber II in the *Kunarac* Judgment has been endorsed by the Appeals Chamber. It reads as follow: 'The *actus reus* of the crime of rape in international law is constituted by: the sexual penetration, however slight: (a) of the vagina or anus of the victim by the penis of the perpetrator or any other object used by the perpetrator; or (b) of the mouth of the victim by the penis of the perpetrator; where such sexual penetration occurs without the consent of the victim. Consent for this purpose must be consent given voluntarily, as a result of the victim's free will, assessed in the context of the surrounding circumstances.' The *mens rea* is the intention to effect this sexual penetration, and the knowledge that it occurs without the consent of the victim. Given the evolution of the law in this area, culminating in the endorsement of the *Furundžija/Kunarac* approach by the ICTY Appeals Chamber, the Chamber finds the latter approach of persuasive authority and hereby adopts the definition as given in *Kunarac* and quoted above. The mental element of the offence of rape as a crime against humanity is the intention to effect the above described sexual penetration, with the knowledge that it was being done without the consent of the victim".[481] **- Other acts of sexual violence can constitute other inhumane acts as CAH:** "Other acts of sexual violence which may fall outside of this specific definition may of course be prosecuted, and would be considered by the Chamber under other categories of crimes for which the Tribunal has jurisdiction, such as *other inhumane acts*".[482] - <u>Factual and legal findings:</u> - Alleged speech inciting rape of Tutsi women: "The Chamber also finds that there is insufficient evidence to prove, as charged in paragraph 4.18 of the Indictment, that during the meetings which were held between 1 January and 6 April 1994 speeches were made by the Accused, inciting the audience to assault, rape or exterminate Tutsis".[483] - Rape of a Tutsi woman named Joyce, on 7 April 1994, in Rwankeri cellule: "Prosecution Witness GAO also testified that, on the morning of 7 April 1994, he and other *Interahamwe* went to Rwankeri *cellule*, on the orders of the Accused. The Witness attested that 'on that day they were telling us to exterminate those people; as well as the babies in their mothers' wombs. And I did not know exactly what their objective was.' Once they arrived at Rwankeri *cellule*, Witness GAO saw two *Interahamwe* named Gapfobo Mbonankira and Rugumire rape a Tutsi woman named Joyce. Witness GAO testified that Mbonankira and Rugumire 'rape[d] her and [then] they used a spear to pierce her side, and they also pierced her sexual organs. She was killed and

479 *Kajelijeli* Trial Judgement, para. 815 (internal reference omitted).

480 ICTY ISCC *Kunarac et al.*, see *supra* p. 528.

481 *Kajelijeli* Trial Judgement, paras. 912–915 (internal references omitted).

482 *Kajelijeli* Trial Judgement, para. 916.

483 *Kajelijeli* Trial Judgement, para. 447.

	her skirt was used to cover her.' The Chamber finds Witness GAO's testimony regarding these events reliable and therefore finds that a Tutsi woman named Joyce was raped and killed by *Interahamwe* on 7 April 1994 at Rwankeri *cellule*. Furthermore, the Chamber finds that the *Interahamwe* pierced Joyce's side and sexual organs with a spear, and then covered her dead body with her skirt".[484] - Mutilation of a Tutsi girl named Nyiramburanga by cutting off her breast, on 7 April 1994, in Rwankeri cellule: "Prosecution Witness GAO also testified that he saw the mutilation of a Tutsi girl named Nyiramburanga by two *Interahamwe* members named Ntenzireyerimye and Uyamuremye. The Witness testified that he saw Uyamuremye cut of the victim's breast and then lick it. This eyewitness testimony was corroborated by the testimony of Defence Witness RGM, who testified on cross-examination that 'Uyamuremye threw a spear towards a girl and the spear hit her on the chest. I don't know whether he cut off the girl's breast or not.' While the Chamber notes minor inconsistencies in regard to the type of weapon used by the assailant, the Chamber regards the testimonies as corroborative on the event described. The Chamber therefore finds that Ntenzireyerimye and Uyamuremye, members of the *Interahamwe*, mutilated a Tutsi girl named Nyiramburanga by cutting off her breast and then licking it, on the morning of 7 April 1994 in Rwankeri *cellule*".[485] - Rape of Witness ACM, on 7 April 1994, in Kabyaza cellule: "Additional reliable evidence of rape is found in the testimony of Prosecution Witness ACM. Witness ACM testified that, on the evening of 7 April 1994, as she was fleeing the massacre at the Busogo Parish, she was stopped at the nearby roadblock located in Kabyaza *cellule* in Nkuli *commune* and raped by two members of the *Interahamwe*. The Witness recognized the attackers and identified them as Felix and Twarayisenze. The Chamber finds the detailed testimony of Witness ACM to be reliable. The Chamber therefore finds that Witness ACM, a Tutsi woman, was raped by members of the *Interahamwe* in Kabyaza *cellule* on 7 April 1994".[486] - Rape of Witness GDO's daughter, on 7 April 1994, in Rukoma cellule: "Prosecution Witness GDO provided first-hand testimony about the rape and killing of her daughter on 7 April 1994, in Rukoma *Cellule*, Shiringo *Secteur*. The Witness attested that she took refuge in a bamboo forest, which is on her property, with her three children, including the victim, a 15 year-old handicapped girl, when a group of *Interahamwe* began to search the forest for Tutsis and found her daughter. The Witness further testified that *Interahamwe* threw the daughter on the ground, undressed her and raped her. The Witness testified that from her hiding place she could see the Accused in his vehicle with the remaining *Interahamwe*. The Witness also testified that the Accused ordered the *Interahamwe* to rape Tutsi women and specifically, that the Accused told the *Interahamwe* that 'it was necessary to look for the Tutsi women, rape them and kill them' and that 'that they should forcefully rape them and then kill them, that he had to separate the good grain from the bad ones.' The Witness testified that, concurrent with the rape of her daughter, she was subjected to beating and to stripping by the *Interahamwe* and that at one point she lost consciousness due to the beating. When the Witness regained consciousness, she saw the body of her dead daughter, with her mouth open and her legs apart. The Chamber also notes the testimonies of Defence Witnesses RHU30, RHU27 and KNWA, who testified that the

484 *Kajelijeli* Trial Judgement, para. 677 (internal references omitted).

485 *Kajelijeli* Trial Judgement, para. 678 (internal references omitted).

486 *Kajelijeli* Trial Judgement, para. 679 (internal reference omitted).

	Witness's daughter was killed by *Interahamwe* but was not raped, and that Witness GDO was not present at the site of her daughter's killing. The Chamber rejects this version of the events, noting the inconsistencies between the Defence Witnesses testimonies in relation to dates and to the age of the victim as well as the fact that Witnesses RHU27 and KNWA were not present at the events, but rather those were related to them at a later time. The Chamber finds Witness GDO's testimony credible and notes in particular her demeanour while testifying, including the emotional intensity of her recollection of the events and her breakdown during the testimony. For these reasons, the Chamber accepts the testimony of Witness GDO insofar as she alleges that her daughter was raped and killed by a group *Interahamwe* on 7 April 1994 in the Rukoma *Cellule*, Shiringo *Secteur*. However, the Chamber, by a majority, Judge Ramaroson dissenting, notes inconsistencies between the Witness's written statement (in which she located the Accused at a distance of 50 meters and recalled the time of the rape to be 4:00am) and her testimony at trial (in which she insisted that she did not know how to estimate distance in meters and recalled the time as early in the morning). The Chamber also takes note that the events took place in a forest, which, in the majority opinion of the Chamber, makes visibility and hearing more difficult. For these reasons, the Chamber finds that there is reasonable doubt as to whether the Accused was present at the scene. Consequently, the Chamber finds, by a majority, Judge Ramaroson dissenting, that the Prosecution did not prove beyond reasonable doubt that the Accused was present at the scene during the time of the rape or that he specifically instructed the rape and the killing of Witness GDO's daughter".[487] - Rape of Witness GDT, on 7 April 1994, in Susa secteur, in Kinigi commune: "Prosecution Witness GDT testified that on the morning of 7 April 1994 a group of *Interahamwe* accompanied by approximately 20 soldiers arrived at her home which is located in Susa *secteur*, Kinigi *Commune*. The Witness attested that the *Interahamwe* entered the house, and took her to the Kazi River, which is located approximately 30 or 40 steps from her home. The Witness testified that she recognized three of the people who took her to the river—named Gahamanyi, Munyarimbanje and Bugeri—and that all three were members of the *Interahamwe* in Mukingo *commune*. As soon as they reached the river, according to the Witness, the *Interahamwe* pushed her down, spread her legs and raped her. The Witness testified that after the sixth person had finished raping her she lost consciousness and therefore could not recall the exact number of *Interahamwe* who raped her. Witness GDT testified that when she regained consciousness she realised that the *Interahamwe* also cut off a part of her sexual organ, causing her permanent physical damage. The Witness alleged that the Accused was responsible for the attack. Specifically, the Witness testified that she heard her assailants subsequently say that the Accused told them 'to be quick about it and go back to where he [the Accused] was before he finished drinking his bottle of beer' and that one of the aggressors said that if an investigation was carried out in Ruhengeri to determine the main killers, the Accused would be number one. According to the Defence, the Prosecution has not produced a single witness to corroborate that the Accused was indeed at a bar, drinking beer between 9:00am and 10:00am in the morning. To the contrary, Prosecution Witnesses GAO, GBV, GBG, and ACM do not place the Accused at a bar at 10:00am on the morning of 7 April 1994. The Defence also challenges the credibility of Witness GDT insofar as the area by the River, where Witness GDT claimed to have been raped, was inaccessible at this time. In support of its allegation, the Defence relies on the testimonies of Defence Witnesses ZLG and FMB. Both Defence Witnesses stated that, as the area around the Kazi River was within a demilitarised zone until March or April 1994, it would have been impossible for any armed *Interahamwe* to go through the checkpoints. However, both Witnesses were

[487] *Kajelijeli* Trial Judgement, para. 680 (internal references omitted).

	unable to provide the Chamber with any information regarding the military status of this area after 7 April 1994. Furthermore, the Chamber finds that, considering the content of the Witness testimony and the lapse of time since the event, the fact that she was not able to specify the exact location where the rapes occurred does not affect her overall credibility. After careful consideration of the evidence presented at trial the Chamber is convinced that Witness GDT was raped by members of the *Interahamwe* on 7 April 1994 in Susa *secteur*, Kinigi *Commune*. It is not in contention that the Accused was not present at the scene of the rape of GDT. The Chamber finds, by a majority, Judge Ramaroson dissenting, that the Prosecution did not prove that the Accused issued a specific order to rape or sexually assault Tutsi women in Susa *secteur*, Kinigi *Commune* on that day".[488] - Rape of Witness GDF, on 10 April 1994, in a maize field in Susa secteur, in Kinigi commune: "Prosecution Witness GDF testified that on 10 April 1994 she was raped in a maize field near her home which is located in Susa *secteur*, Kinigi *Commune*. According to the Witness, around 10:00am that day she saw the Accused, in his red vehicle, accompanied by armed and uniformed *Interahamwe*. The Accused talked to the *Interahamwe* and got back into the vehicle at which time twelve *Interahamwe* approached her house. Shortly thereafter, a group of *Interahamwe* tracked down the Witness and her sister in their hiding place in the maize field. While at least three *Interahamwe* raped her and her sister, the other held her down, watched and mocked her. The Witness testified that before raping her, the first *Interahamwe* said, 'Allow me to have sex with a Tutsi woman to taste her.' One *Interahamwe* inserted a cigarette stub in her sexual organ and left her unconscious. According to the Witness, she and her sister still suffer both physical and mental disorders from this experience. Although she did not see her sister being raped, Witness GDF says she was close by. As 'a consequence of what happened' her sister is now 'mentally unstable' and is being treated in Ndera. The Defence challenged the credibility of the Witness on the same basis as it challenged the credibility of Witness GDT: namely, the Defence alleges that this area was inaccessible on 10 April 1994. The Chamber recalls its finding, in the previous section, about the accessibility of the area and finds the Witness to be credible and trustworthy. The Chamber is convinced that Witness GDF was raped on 10 April 1994 by members of the *Interahamwe*. The Chamber is not convinced, by a majority, Judge Ramaroson dissenting, that the Accused was present at the site of the rape during the time of the rape itself".[489] - Alleged presence of Juvénal Kajelijeli during the rapes and sexual assaults: "Pursuant to the above testimonies of Prosecution Witnesses GAO, ACM, GDO, GDT and GDF, the Chamber is convinced that members of the *Interahamwe*, including *Interahamwe* from Mukingo *commune* and neighbouring areas committed rapes and sexual assaults in the Ruhengeri *Prefecture* between 7 and 10 April 1994. The Chamber notes that the Defence does not dispute the occurrence of the said rapes and assaults. Rather, the Defence alleges that the testimonies placing the Accused at the scenes of these acts were fabricated by the Prosecution Witnesses. In addition, the Chamber notes the testimony given by Defence Witness ZLA, who said that representatives of the civic group AVEGA tried to induce her to falsely allege that the Accused raped her in 1994, in return for which testimony they will help her to recover her property and to receive assistance as a survivor. Having carefully considered the allegations and evidence set forth by both Prosecution and Defence, the Chamber

488 *Kajelijeli* Trial Judgement, para. 681 (internal references omitted).

489 *Kajelijeli* Trial Judgement, para. 682 (internal references omitted).

	finds, in the absence of corroboration of Witness ZLA's allegation, insufficient evidence to determine that subornation of perjury or intimidation attempts did in fact occur. However, the majority of the Chamber, Judge Ramaroson dissenting, is not convinced that the Accused was present during any of the said rapes and sexual assaults. Consequently, it is the finding of the majority of the Chamber that the Prosecution did not prove that the Accused was physically present during the commission of the rapes and sexual assaults by members of the *Interahamwe*".[490] - Responsibility of Juvénal Kajelijeli for rape as CAH: "The Chamber found that pursuant to an order of the Accused given at Byangabo Market on 7 April 1994 to 'exterminate the Tutsis' the *Interahamwe* went to Rwankeri cellule. The Chamber further found that at Rwankeri cellule, a Tutsi woman named Joyce was raped and killed by *Interahamwe*. The Chamber found that Witness ACM, a Tutsi woman, was raped by members of the *Interahamwe* in Busogo Parish and in Kabyaza *cellule* on 7 April 1994, after having been stopped at a roadblock. The Chamber found that the handicapped daughter of Witness GDO, a Tutsi woman, was raped and killed by members of the *Interahamwe* in Rukoma *Cellule*, Shiringo *Secteur* on 7 April 1994. The Chamber by majority, Judge Ramaroson dissenting, found that the Accused was not present at the scene of the crime, and the Chamber by majority found not proven the allegation that he specifically instructed the rape and murder of Witness GDO's daughter. The Chamber found that Witness GDT, a Tutsi woman, was raped and sexually mutilated by members of the *Interahamwe* in Susa *secteur*, Kinigi *commune* on 7 April 1994. The Chamber, by a majority, Judge Ramaroson dissenting, also found not proven the allegation that the Accused issued a specific order to rape or sexually assault Tutsi women in Susa *secteur*, Kinigi *Commune* on that day. The Chamber found that Witness GDF, a Tutsi woman, was raped by members of the *Interahamwe* in Susa *secteur*, Kinigi *Commune* on 10 April 1994. The Chamber was not convinced however that the Accused was present during the rape. The Chamber finds that between 7 April and 10 April 1994 some rapes were committed by members of the *Interahamwe* in Mukingo and Kinigi *Communes*, Ruhengeri *Préfecture*. Furthermore, given the circumstances under which these acts were committed, the Chamber finds that these rapes were committed in the course of a widespread attack upon the Tutsi civilian population. In relation to this finding, Judge Ramaroson attaches her separate and dissenting opinion. Based upon the factual findings of the Chamber set out above, the Chamber finds, by a majority, Judge Ramaroson dissenting, that the Prosecution failed to prove beyond a reasonable doubt that the Accused either planned, instigated, ordered, committed or otherwise aided and abetted in the planning, preparation or execution of the rapes which the Chamber found to have occurred. For the reasons set out in her dissenting opinion, Judge Ramaroson does not find it necessary to consider the Accused's responsibility under Article 6(3) of the Statute for Rape but rather under Article 6(1). Therefore the following findings of the Chamber in relation to Article 6(3) responsibility are by a majority decision of the Chamber. The Chamber finds by a majority that during the rapes, which the Chamber found to have been committed by members of the *Interahamwe*, the Accused was not personally present. It was not established that the Accused ever gave an order for the *Interahamwe* to rape, but rather his instructions were, in general, to kill or to exterminate. Furthermore, it is not possible on the evidence and in the circumstances to infer that the Accused knew or had reason to know that these rapes were being committed by members of the *Interahamwe*. The Chamber finds therefore by a majority that the Prosecution failed to establish beyond a reasonable doubt that the Accused knew or had reason to know about the rapes committed by members of the *Interahamwe*, which the Chamber found to have occurred in Mukingo and Kinigi *Communes* between 7 and 10 April 1994.

490 *Kajelijeli* Trial Judgement, para. 683.

	Thus, in relation to the charge of rape as a crime against humanity, the Prosecution has failed to meet the requirements of establishing individual criminal responsibility under Article 6(3) of the Statute. Thus, in relation to **Count 7** of the Indictment, the Chamber, by a majority, Judge Ramaroson dissenting, finds the Accused NOT GUILTY of RAPE AS A CRIME AGAINST HUMANITY".[491] - Responsibility of Juvénal Kajelijeli for other inhumane acts as CAH: "The Chamber found that, at Rwankeri cellule on 7 April 1994, the *Interahamwe* raped and killed a Tutsi woman called Joyce. Furthermore, the Chamber found that they pierced her side and her sexual organs with a spear, and then covered her dead body with her skirt. The Chamber found that, at Rwankeri cellule on 7 April 1994, a Tutsi girl named Nyiramburanga was mutilated by an *Interahamwe* who cut off her breast and then licked it. The Chamber finds that these acts constitute a serious attack on the human dignity of the Tutsi community as a whole. Cutting a woman's breast off and licking it, and piercing a woman's sexual organs with a spear are nefarious acts of a comparable gravity to the other acts listed as crimes against humanity, which would clearly cause great mental suffering to any members of the Tutsi community who observed them. Furthermore, given the circumstances under which these acts were committed, the Chamber finds that they were committed in the course of a widespread attack upon the Tutsi civilian population. There was no evidence, however, that the Accused was present during these acts, or gave an order for them to be committed. Thus, the Chamber finds that the Prosecution failed to prove beyond a reasonable doubt that the Accused either planned, instigated, ordered, committed or otherwise aided and abetted in the planning, preparation or execution of these inhumane acts. The Chamber finds that during these other inhumane acts, which the Chamber found to have been committed by members of the *Interahamwe*, the Accused was not personally present. The Chamber finds that it was not established that the Accused ever gave an order for the *Interahamwe* to commit these acts, but rather his instructions were, in general, to kill or to exterminate. Furthermore, it is not possible on this evidence and in the circumstances to infer that the Accused knew or had reason to know that these other inhumane acts were being committed by members of the *Interahamwe*. The Chamber finds therefore that the Prosecution failed to establish beyond a reasonable doubt that the Accused knew or had reason to know about these other inhumane acts committed by members of the *Interahamwe*, which the Chamber found to have occurred in Mukingo *Commune* on 7 April 1994. Thus, in relation to the charge of other inhumane acts as a crime against humanity, the Chamber finds that the Prosecution has failed to meet the requirements of establishing individual criminal responsibility under Article 6(3) of the Statute. Thus, in relation to Count 9 of the Indictment, the Chamber finds the Accused NOT GUILTY of OTHER INHUMANE ACTS AS A CRIME AGAINST HUMANITY".[492]

6. Ferdinand **Nahimana *et al.*** (Case No. ICTR-99-52) "***Media***"

- Ferdinand Nahimana: Founded a *Comité d'initiative* (Steering Committee) with others in 1992 in order to set up the company *Radio television libre des milles collines S.A.* (RTLM); member of the *Mouvement révolutionnaire national pour la démocratie et le développement* (MRND) party.
- Jean-Bosco Barayagwiza: Founding member of the *Coalition pour la défense de la République* (CDR) party, which was formed in 1992; member of the Steering Committee responsible for the establishment of the company RTLM S.A.; concurrently, Director of Political Affairs in the Ministry of Foreign

[491] *Kajelijeli* Trial Judgement, paras. 917–925 (internal references omitted).

[492] *Kajelijeli* Trial Judgement, paras. 934–940 (internal references omitted).

Affairs. - Hassan Ngeze: Founder and editor of the newspaper *Kangura*; founding member of the CDR party.	
Indictment (International sex crimes (or related) charges and mode(s) of liability)	- Ferdinand Nahimana: **Direct and public incitement to commit genocide** (count 3) under Article 6(3) of the Statute (**superior responsibility**) and **Persecutions as CAH** (count 5) under Articles 6(1) and 6(3) of the Statute (**superior responsibility**) for slandering and denigrating Tutsi women over RTLM airwaves.[493] - Jean-Bosco Barayagwiza: **Direct and public incitement to commit genocide** (count 4) and **Persecutions as CAH** (count 7) under Articles 6(1) and 6(3) of the Statute (**superior responsibility**) for slandering and denigrating Tutsi women over RTLM airwaves.[494]

493 *Prosecutor v. Ferdinand Nahimana*, Case No. ICTR-96-11-I, Amended Indictment, 15 November 1999, paras. 5.28 ("Furthermore, soldiers, militiamen and gendarmes raped or sexually assaulted or committed other crimes of a sexual nature against Tutsi women and girls, sometimes after having first kidnapped them".), 6.9 ("Between January and July 1994, other reporters such as Valérie Bemeriki, Kantano Habimana, Gaspard Gahigi and Noël Hitimana also incited the population and the *Interahamwe* to exterminate the Tutsis and moderate Hutus. The same reporters slandered and denigrated Tutsi women over the RTLM airwaves".), pp. 27–28 ("COUNT 3: DIRECT AND PUBLIC INCITEMENT TO COMMIT GENOCIDE: By the acts and omissions described in paragraphs 4.1 to 6.27 and more specifically in the paragraphs to which reference is made hereinbelow: Ferdinand Nahimana: [...] pursuant to Article 6(3), paragraphs [...] 6.9 [...]; is responsible for direct and public incitement to kill and cause serious bodily or mental harm to members of the Tutsi population, with intent to destroy in whole or in part, that ethnic or racial group as such, and thereby committed Direct and Public Incitement to Commit Genocide, stipulated in Article 2(3)(c) of the Statute as a crime, for which he is individually responsible pursuant to Article 6, and which is punishable in reference to Articles 22 and 23 of the Statute of the Tribunal. [...] COUNT 5: CRIME AGAINST HUMANITY: PERSECUTION[:] By the acts and omissions described in paragraphs 4.1 to 6.27 and more specifically in the paragraphs to which reference is made hereinbelow: Ferdinand Nahimana: pursuant to Article 6(1), paragraphs [...] 6.9 [...]; pursuant to Article 6(3), paragraphs [...] 6.9 [...]; is responsible for persecution on political or racial grounds, as part of a widespread or systematic attack against a civilian population, on political, ethnic or racial grounds, and thereby committed a Crime Against Humanity, stipulated in Article 3(h) of the Statute as a crime, for which he is individually responsible pursuant to Article 6, and which is punishable in reference to Articles 22 and 23 of the Statute of the Tribunal".).

494 *Prosecutor v. Jean-Bosco Barayagwiza*, Case No. ICTR-97-19-I, Amended Indictment, 14 April 2000, paras. 5.25 ("Furthermore, soldiers, militiamen and gendarmes raped or sexually assaulted or committed other crimes of a sexual nature against Tutsi women and girls, sometimes after having first kidnapped them".), 6.9 ("Between January and July 1994, other reporters, broadcasters or announcers, such as Valérie Bemeriki, Kantano Habimana, Gaspard Gahigi and Noël Hitimana also incited the population and the *Interahamwe* to exterminate the Tutsis and moderate Hutus. The same reporters slandered and denigrated Tutsi women over the RTLM airwaves".), pp. 26–28 ("**COUNT 4:** By the acts and omissions described in paragraphs 5.1 to 7.13 and more specifically in the paragraphs referred to below: **JEAN-BOSCO BARAYAGWIZA:** -pursuant to Article 6(1), according to paragraphs: [...] 6.9 [...] -pursuant to Article 6(3), according to paragraphs [...] 6.9 [...] is responsible for direct and public incitement to kill and cause serious bodily or mental harm to members of the Tutsi population, with intent to destroy in whole or in part, a racial or ethnic group, and thereby committed **DIRECT AND PUBLIC INCITEMENT TO COMMIT GENOCIDE**, a crime stipulated in Article 2(3)(c) of the Statute of the Tribunal, for which he is individually responsible pursuant to Article 6 of the Statute and which is punishable in reference to Articles 22 and 23 of the Statute. [...] **COUNT 7:** By the acts and omissions described in paragraphs 5.1 to 7.13 and more specifically in the paragraphs referred to below: **JEAN-BOSCO BARAYAGWIZA:** -pursuant to Article 6(1), according to paragraphs: [...] 6.9 [...] -pursuant to Article 6(3), according to paragraphs [...] 6.9 [...] is responsible for **persecution** on political, racial or religious grounds, as part of a widespread and systematic attack against a civilian population on political, ethnic or racial grounds, and thereby committed a **CRIME AGAINST HUMANITY**, a crime stipulated in Article 3(h) of the Statute of the Tribunal, for which he is individually responsible pursuant to Article 6 of the Statute and which is punishable in reference to Articles 22 and 23 of the Statute".).

	- Hassan Ngeze: **Direct and public incitement to commit genocide** (count 4) under Article 6(1) of the Statute for inciting militiamen to commit rape and sexual assault against Tutsi women and girls in Gisenyi prefecture.[495]
Trial Judgement	Although the Trial Chamber's factual findings are unclear, it seems as if the convictions for persecutions as CAH include sexual attacks against Tutsi women: - Ferdinand Nahimana: Guilty of **Persecutions as CAH** (count 5) under Articles 6(1) and 6(3) (**superior responsibility**) of the Statute for advocating ethnic hatred or inciting violence against the Tutsi population through RTLM broadcasts in 1994, including articulating a framework that negatively portrayed Tutsi women, making sexual attacks against Tutsi women a foreseeable consequence of the role attributed to them. - Jean-Bosco Barayagwiza: Guilty of **Persecutions as CAH** (count 7) under Article 6(3) (**superior responsibility**) of the Statute for advocating ethnic hatred or inciting violence against the Tutsi population through RTLM broadcasts in 1994, including articulating a framework that negatively portrayed Tutsi women, making sexual attacks against Tutsi women a foreseeable consequence of the role attributed to them. - Hassan Ngeze: Guilty of **Persecutions as CAH** (count 6) under Article 6(1) of the Statute for advocating ethnic hatred or inciting violence against the Tutsi population through the *Kangura* newspaper, including articulating a framework that negatively portrayed Tutsi women, making sexual attacks against Tutsi women a foreseeable consequence of the role attributed to them.[496] - Although Ferdinand Nahimana, Jean-Bosco Barayagwiza and Hassan Ngeze were found guilty of direct and public incitement to commit genocide, it does not seem that these convictions encompass the incitement to sexually attack Tutsi women.[497]
Appeal Judgement	- The Appeals Chamber **reversed Ferdinand's conviction for persecutions as CAH** (count 5) **under Article 6(1) of the Statute** on account of RTLM broadcasts after 6 April 1994 but **affirms**, Judge Meron dissenting, **his conviction for persecutions as CAH** (count 5) **under Article 6(3) of the Statute** because it found that he did not take the necessary and reasonable measures to prevent or punish the acts of persecution and instigation to persecution committed by RTLM staff after 6 April 1994.[498] - The Appeals Chamber **set aside part of Jean-Bosco Barayagwiza's conviction for persecution as CAH (insofar as his conviction is based on account of RTLM broadcasts)** (count 7) under Article 6(3) of the Statute because it found that he could not be held responsible as a superior for the crimes committed by RTLM staff after 6

495 *Prosecutor v. Hassan Ngeze*, Case No. ICTR-97-27-I, Amended Indictment, 22 November 1999, paras. 5.31 ("Furthermore, soldiers, militiamen and gendarmes raped or sexually assaulted or committed other crimes of a sexual nature against Tutsi women and girls, sometimes after having first kidnapped them".), 7.10 ("Between April and July 1994, **Hasan Ngeze**, one of *interahamwe* leaders in Gisenyi, incited the militiamen to commit rape and sexual assault against Tutsi women and girls in Gisenyi prefecture".), pp. 23–24 ("**COUNT 4:** By the acts or omissions described in paragraphs 5.1 to 7.15 and more specifically in the paragraphs referred to below: **HASSAN NGEZE:** -pursuant to Article 6(1), according to paragraphs: […] 7.10 […] is responsible for direct and public incitement to kill and cause serious bodily or mental harm to members of the Tutsi population with the intent to destroy, in whole or in part, a racial or ethnic group, and thereby committed **DIRECT AND PUBLIC INCITEMENT TO COMMIT GENOCIDE**, a crime stipulated in Article 2(3)(c) of the Statute of the Tribunal, for which he is individually responsible pursuant to Article 6 of the Statute and which is punishable in reference to Articles 22 and 23 of the Statute".).

496 *Prosecutor v. Ferdinand Nahimana et al.*, Case No. ICTR-99-52-T, Judgement and Sentence, dated 3 December 2003 and filed on 5 December 2003 ("*Ferdinand Nahimana et al.* Trial Judgement"), paras. 187–188, 1079–1084, 1092–1094.

497 *Ferdinand Nahimana et al.* Trial Judgement, paras. 1092–1094.

498 *Ferdinand Nahimana et al. v. The Prosecutor*, Case No. ICTR-99-52-A, Judgement, 28 Novemebr 2007 ("*Ferdinand Nahimana et al.* Appeal Judgement"), para. 996 and Section XVIII (Disposition), p. 345. See also *Ferdinand Nahimana et al.* Appeal Judgement, Partly Dissenting Opinion of Judge Meron, para. 19.

	April 1994 and because it found that it could not conclude that RTLM broadcasts before 6 April 1994 had substantially contributed to persecutions.[499] - The Appeals Chamber **reversed Hassan Ngeze's conviction for persecution as CAH** (count 6) under Article 6(1) of the Statute because it found that: (i) he could not be convicted on the basis of *Kangura* publications prior to 1994; (ii) *Kangura* was not published between 6 April and 17 July 1994; and (iii) the article published in *Kangura* between 1 January and 6 April 1994 amounted to acts of persecutions as a crime against humanity.[500]
Legal and Factual Findings and/or Evidence	- Factual and legal findings: - The sexual attack against Tutsi women as a foreseeable consequence of the content of the newspaper *Kangura*: "The Chamber notes that the editorials and articles reviewed above consistently portrayed the Tutsi as wicked and ambitious, using women and money against the vulnerable Hutu. These themes echo the message of the *The Ten Commandments*. In some articles, such as the article in *Kangura* No. 11, "If One Asks Generals Why They're Favoring Tutsis", information about Tutsi privilege and Hutu disadvantage was conveyed in a manner that appears as though intended to raise consciousness regarding ethnic discrimination against the Hutu. In many other articles, however, the intent, as evidenced by the vitriolic language, was to convey a message of ethnic hatred, and to arouse public hostility towards the Tutsi population. In articles such as "A Cockroach Cannot Give Birth to a Butterfly" the Tutsi were portrayed as innately evil. The presentation of Tutsi women as *femmes fatales* focused particular attention on Tutsi women and the danger they represented to the Hutu. This danger was explicitly associated with sexuality. By defining the Tutsi woman as an enemy in this way, Kangura articulated a framework that made the sexual attack of Tutsi women a foreseeable consequence of the role attributed to them".[501] - Inserting the metal rods of an umbrella into the vagina of a Tutsi woman in Gisenyi on 7 April 1994: "The Chamber finds that Hassan Ngeze ordered the *Interahamwe* in Gisenyi on the morning of 7 April 1994 to kill Tutsi civilians and prepare for their burial at the *Commune Rouge*. Many were killed in the subsequent attacks that happened immediately thereafter and later on the same day. Among those killed were Witness EB's mother, brother and pregnant sister. Two women, one of whom was Ngeze's mother, inserted the metal rods of an umbrella into her body. The attack that resulted in these and other killings was planned systematically, with weapons distributed in advance, and arrangements made for the transport and burial of those to be killed".[502] - Responsibility of the accused for persecutions as CAH: "The Chamber notes that Tutsi women, in particular, were targeted for persecution. The portrayal of the Tutsi woman as a *femme fatale*, and the message that Tutsi women were seductive agents of the enemy was conveyed repeatedly by RTLM and *Kangura. The Ten Commandments*, broadcast on RTLM and published in *Kangura*, vilified and endangered Tutsi women, as evidenced by Witness AHI's testimony that a Tutsi woman was killed by CDR members who spared her husband's life and told him "Do not worry, we are going to find another wife, a Hutu for you". By defining the Tutsi woman as an enemy in this way, RTLM and *Kangura* articulated a framework

499 *Ferdinand Nahimana et al.* Appeal Judgement, para. 997.

500 *Ferdinand Nahimana et al.* Appeal Judgement, paras. 1011–1014 and Section XVIII (Disposition), p. 346.

501 *Ferdinand Nahimana et al.* Trial Judgement, paras. 187–188.

502 *Ferdinand Nahimana et al.* Trial Judgement, para. 836.

	that made the sexual attack of Tutsi women a foreseeable consequence of the role attributed to them. The Chamber notes that persecution when it takes the form of killings is a lesser included offence of extermination. The nature of broadcasts, writings, and the activities of CDR is such, however, that the same communication would have caused harm of varying degrees to different individuals. An RTLM broadcast, *Kangura* article, or CDR demonstration that led to the extermination of certain Tutsi civilians inflicted lesser forms of harm on others, constituting persecution. The Chamber considers that these actions by the Accused therefore constitute multiple and different crimes, for which they can be held separately accountable. The responsibility of Ferdinand Nahimana for the broadcasts of RTLM is set forth above in paragraphs 970–974. For RTLM broadcasts in 1994 advocating ethnic hatred or inciting violence against the Tutsi population, the Chamber finds Nahimana guilty of crimes against humanity (persecution) under Article 3(h), pursuant to Article 6(1) and Article 6(3) of the Statute. The responsibility of Jean-Bosco Barayagwiza for the broadcasts of RTLM is set forth above in paragraph 973. For RTLM broadcasts in 1994 advocating ethnic hatred or inciting violence against the Tutsi population, the Chamber finds Barayagwiza guilty of crimes against humanity (persecution) under Article 3(h), pursuant to Article 6(3) of the Statute of the Tribunal. [...] The responsibility of Hassan Ngeze for the content of *Kangura* is set forth above in paragraphs 977 and 978. For the contents of this publication that advocated ethnic hatred or incited violence, as well as for his own acts that advocated ethnic hatred or incited violence against the Tutsi population, as set forth in paragraph 1039. The Chamber finds Ngeze guilty of crimes against humanity (persecution) under Article 3(h), pursuant to Article 6(1) of the Statute of the Tribunal".[503]

7. Jean de Dieu **Kamuhanda** (Case No. ICTR-99-54A) Minister of Higher Education and Scientific Research in the Interim Government from 25 May until mid-July 1994.	
Indictment (International sex crimes (or related) charges and mode(s) of liability)	- **Conspiracy to commit genocide** (count 1), **Genocide** (count 2) or, alternatively, **Complicity in genocide** (count 3), **Rape as CAH** (count 6), **Other inhumane acts as CAH** (count 7), **Outrages upon personal dignity, in particular humiliating and degrading treatment, rape and indecent assault as a violation of Article 3 common to the Geneva Conventions and of Additional Protocol II (WC)** (count 8) and **Violence to health and to the physical or mental well-being of civilians as a violation of Article 3 common to the Geneva Conventions and of Additional Protocol II (WC)** (count 9) under Articles 6(1) and 6(3) of the Statute (**superior responsibility**) for the rapes of Tutsi women committed during various attacks, including the attack on the school in Gikomero, in Kigali-rural prefecture, on or about 12 April 1994.[504]

503 *Ferdinand Nahimana et al.* Trial Judgement, paras. 1079–1082, 1084 (internal reference omitted).

504 *Prosecutor v. Jean de Dieu Kamuhanda*, Case No. ICTR-99-54A-I, Indictment, 15 November 2000, paras. 5.39 ("Furthermore, soldiers, militiamen and gendarmes raped or sexually assaulted or committed other crimes of a sexual nature against Tutsi women and girls, sometimes after having first kidnapped them".), 6.45–6.46 ("Furthermore, **Jean de Dieu Kamuhanda** personally led attacks of soldiers and Interahamwe against Tutsi refugees in Kigali-Rural préfecture, notably on or about April 12th at the parish church and adjoining school in Gikomero. On that occasion **Jean de Dieu Kamuhanda** arrived at the school with a group of soldiers and Interahamwe armed with firearms and grenades. He directed the militia into the courtyard of the school compound and gave them the order to attack. The soldiers and Interahamwe attacked the refugees. Several thousand persons were killed. During the attack on the school in Gikomero the militia also selected women from among the refugees, carried them away and raped them before killing them".), 6.81–6.82, 6.84 ("During the events referred to in this indictment, rapes and other forms of sexual violence were widely and

notoriously committed in Rwanda against the Tutsi population, in particular Tutsi women and girls or Hutu women married to Tutsi men. These acts were often accompanied by killing or were themselves used as a method of killing. They were perpetrated by, among others, militiamen, including *Interahamwe*-MRND, soldiers and gendarmes. Members of the Interim Government generally instigated, encouraged, facilitated, and acquiesced to, among others, the *Interahamwe-MRND,* soldiers, and gendarmes raping and sexual violating Tutsi women. Government ministers even sometimes committed these acts themselves, thereby encouraging by their own example the commission of such acts by, among others, militia, *Interahamwe-MRND,* soldiers and gendarmes over whom they had *de facto* and *de jure* authority. […] Rape and other forms of sexual violence, including sexual torture, degrading sexual acts and indecent exposure were integral to the genocidal policy of the conspirators that seized political power from the first moments of 7th April, 1994 when political assassinations began. Not even the Prime Minister Agathe Uwiligimana was spared. Her body was discovered on the morning of 7 April 1994 with indicia of sexual torture and sexual degradation".), pp. 65–67 ("**COUNT 1:** By the acts or omissions described in paragraphs 5.1 to 6.90 and more specifically in the paragraphs referred to below: **Jean de Dieu Kamuhanda:** -pursuant to Article 6(1), according to paragraphs: […] 6.46, […] 6.79 to 6.90. -pursuant to Article 6(3), according to paragraphs: […] 6.46, […] 6.79 to 6.90. conspired with others to kill and cause serious bodily or mental harm to members of the Tutsi population with the intent to destroy, in whole or in part, a racial or ethnic group, and thereby committed **CONSPIRACY TO COMMIT GENCODE**, a crime stipulated in Article 2(3)(b) of the Statute of the Tribunal, for which he is individually responsible pursuant to Article 6 and which is punishable in reference to Articles 22 and 23 of the Statute. **COUNT 2:** By the acts or omissions described in paragraphs 5.1 to 6.90 and more specifically in the paragraphs referred to below: **Jean de Dieu Kamuhanda:** -pursuant to Article 6(1), according to paragraphs: […] 6.46, […] 6.79 to 6.90. -pursuant to Article 6(3), according to paragraphs: […] 6.46, […] 6.79 to 6.90. is responsible for killing and causing serious bodily or mental harm to members of the Tutsi population with the intent to destroy, in whole or in part, a racial or ethnic group, and thereby committed **GENOCIDE**, a crime stipulated in Article 2(3)(a) of the Statute of the Tribunal, for which he is individually responsible pursuant to Article 6 and which is punishable in reference to Articles 22 and 23 of the Statute. **Or, alternatively COUNT 3***:* By the acts or omissions described in paragraphs 5.1 to 6.90 and more specifically in the paragraphs referred to below: **Jean de Dieu Kamuhanda:** -pursuant to Article 6(1), according to paragraphs: […] 6.46, […] 6.79 to 6.90. -pursuant to Article 6(3), according to paragraphs: […] 6.46, […] 6.79 to 6.90. is responsible for killing and causing serious bodily or mental harm to members of the Tutsi population with the intent to destroy, in whole or in part, a racial or ethnic group, and thereby committed **COMPLICITY IN GENOCIDE**, a crime stipulated in Article 2(3)(e) of the Statute of the Tribunal, for which he is individually responsible pursuant to Article 6 and which is punishable in reference to Articles 22 and 23 of the Statute".), pp. 70–73 ("**COUNT 6:** By the acts or omissions described in paragraphs 5.1 to […] 6.90 and more specifically in the paragraphs referred to below: **Jean de Dieu Kamuhanda:** -pursuant to Article 6(1), according to paragraphs: […] 5.39, […] 6.46, […] 6.79 to 6.90. -pursuant to Article 6(3), according to paragraphs: […] 5.39, […] 6.46, […] 6.79 to 6.90. is responsible for rape as part of a widespread and systematic attack against a civilian population on political, ethnic or racial grounds, and thereby committed a **CRIME AGAINST HUMANITY**, a crime stipulated in Article 3(g) of the Statute of the Tribunal, for he is individually responsible pursuant to Article 6 of the Statute and which is punishable in reference to Articles 22 and 23 of the Statute. **COUNT 7:** By the acts or omissions described in paragraphs 5.1 to 6.90 and more specifically in the paragraphs referred to below: **Jean de Dieu Kamuhanda:** -pursuant to Article 6(1), according to paragraphs: […] 6.46, […] 6.79 to 6.90. -pursuant to Article 6(3), according to paragraphs: […] 6.46, […] 6.79 to 6.90. is responsible for inhumane acts against persons as part of a widespread and systematic attack against a civilian population on political, ethnic or racial grounds, and thereby committed a **CRIME AGAINST HUMANITY**, a crime stipulated in Article 3(i) of Statute of the Tribunal, for which he is individually responsible pursuant to Article 6 of the Statute and which is punishable in reference to Articles 22 and 23 of the Statute. **COUNT 8:** By the acts or omissions described in paragraphs 5.1 to 6.90 and more specifically in the paragraphs referred to below: **Jean de Dieu Kamuhanda:** -pursuant to Article 6(1), according to paragraphs: […] 6.46, […] 6.79 to 6.90. -pursuant to Article 6(3), according to paragraphs: […] 6.46, […] 6.79 to 6.90. is responsible for outrages upon personal dignity, in particular humiliating and degrading treatment, rape and indecent assault, as part of an armed internal conflict, and thereby committed **SERIOUS VIOLATIONS OF ARTICLE 3 COMMON TO THE GENEVA CONVENTIONS AND OF ADDITIONAL PROTOCOL II**, a crime stipulated in Article 4(e) of the Statute of the Tribunal, for which he is individually responsible pursuant to Article 6 of the Statute and which is punishable in reference to Articles 22 and 23 of the Statute. **COUNT 9:** By the acts or omissions described in paragraphs 5.1 to 6.90 and more specifically in the paragraphs referred to below: **Jean de Dieu Kamuhanda:** -pursuant to Article 6(1), according to paragraphs: […] 6.46, […] 6.79 to 6.90. -pursuant to Article 6(3), according to paragraph: […]

Trial Judgement	- Although Jean de Dieu Kamuhanda was found guilty of genocide (count 2), the underlying offences of this crime did not include rapes of Tutsi women.[505] - Not guilty of rapes as CAH (count 6), other inhumane acts as CAH (count 7), outrages upon personal dignity, in particular humiliating and degrading treatment, rape and indecent assault as a violation of Article 3 common to the Geneva Conventions and of Additional Protocol II (WC) (count 8) and violence to health and to the physical or mental well-being of civilians as a violation of Article 3 common to the Geneva Conventions and of Additional Protocol II (WC) (count 9) because the Trial Chamber found that there was insufficient evidence of the alleged rapes.[506]
Appeal Judgement	- The Prosecution did not appeal Juvénal Kajelijeli's acquittals for international sex crimes.[507]
Legal and Factual Findings and/or Evidence	- Legal findings: **- Rape and sexual violence can constitute genocide (serious bodily or mental harm):** The Trial Chamber reaffirmed that: "Trial Chambers of the Tribunal have held that what is 'bodily' or 'mental' harm should be determined on a case-by-case basis and have further held that 'serious bodily harm' does not necessarily have to be permanent or irremediable, and that it includes non-mortal acts of sexual violence, rape […]".[508] **- Rape: definition:** The Trial Chamber adopted the definition of rape given in the *Kunarac et al.* case:[509] "This definition substantially modified and completed by Trial Chamber II in the *Kunarac* Judgment has been endorsed by the Appeals Chamber. It reads as follow: 'The *actus reus* of the crime of rape in international law is constituted by: the sexual penetration, however slight: (a) of the vagina or anus of the victim by the penis of the perpetrator or any other object used by the perpetrator; or (b) of the mouth of the victim by the penis of the perpetrator; where such sexual penetration occurs without the consent of the victim. Consent for this purpose must be consent given voluntarily, as a result of the victim's free will, assessed in the context of the surrounding circumstances.' The *mens rea* is the intention to effect this sexual penetration, and the knowledge that it occurs without the consent of the victim. Given the evolution of the law in this area, endorsed in the *Furundžija/Kunarac* approach by the ICTY Appeals Chamber, the Chamber finds the latter approach of persuasive authority and hereby

6.46, […] 6.79 to 6.90. is responsible for killing and causing violence to health and to the physical or mental well-being of civilians as part of an armed internal conflict, and thereby committed **SERIOUS VIOLATION OF ARTICLE 3 COMMON TO THE GENEVA CONVENTIONS AND ADDITIONAL PROTOCOL II**, a crime stipulated in Article 4(a) of the Statute of the Tribunal, for which he is are individually responsible pursuant to Article 6 of the Statute and which is punishable in reference to Articles 22 and 23 of the Statute".). On 20 August 2002, in its Decision on Kamuhanda's Motion for Partial Acquittal Pursuant to Rule 98 *bis* of the Rules of Procedure and Evidence, the Trial Chamber found that insufficient evidence was presented in relation to the charges contained in count 1 of the Indictment and acquitted Jean de Dieu Kamuhanda of conspiracy to commit genocide. See *Prosecutor v. Jean de Dieu Kamuhanda*, Case No. ICTR-99-54A-T, Decision on Kamuhanda's Motion for Partial Acquittal Pursuant to Rule 98 *bis* of the Rules of Procedure and Evidence, 20 August 2002, para. 23, p. 6.

505 *Prosecutor v. Jean de Dieu Kamuhanda*, Case No. ICTR-99-54A-T, Judgment and Sentence, dated 22 January 2004 and filed on 23 January 2004 ("*Kamuhanda* Trial Judgement"), paras. 495–497, 507, 646–647, 651–652, 750.

506 *Kamuhanda* Trial Judgement, paras. 495–497, 507, 711–713, 719–720, 746, 748, 750.

507 See *Jean de Dieu Kamuhanda v. The Prosecutor*, Case No. ICTR-99-54A-A, Judgement, 19 September 2005.

508 *Kamuhanda* Trial Judgement, para. 634 (internal reference omitted).

509 ICTY ISCC *Kunarac et al.*, see *supra* p. 528.

	adopts the definition as given in *Kunarac* and quoted above. The mental element of the offence of rape as a Crime against Humanity is the intention to effect the above described sexual penetration, with the knowledge that it was being done without the consent of the victim".[510] **- Other acts of sexual violence can constitute other inhumane acts as CAH:** "Other acts of sexual violence which may fall outside of this specific definition may of course be prosecuted, and would be considered by the Chamber under other categories of crimes for which the Tribunal has jurisdiction, such as *other inhumane acts*".[511] - <u>Factual and legal findings:</u> - Alleged rapes during the attack on the Gikomero parish compound on 12 April 1994: "With respect to the allegations of rape, the Chamber has noted that the Defence stated that Prosecution Witness GAG testified that during the attack of 12 April 1994 she had seen women taken away by assailants to be raped. The Chamber observes that GAG did not Witness the rapes, but learned from her daughter and two victims about them after the war. The Chamber further notes that the Defence highlighted the testimony of Prosecution Witness GEP who asserted that during the massacres some girls were selected and led away in a vehicle while the massacres continued. The Witness specified that the Accused left after the departure of the girls. The Witness added that no more than 20 girls were picked. She indicated that she did not know any of these girls, but later learnt at the camp where the *Inkotanyi* took those who escaped the massacres, that all the girls except one were raped and killed by the attackers. The Chamber observes that Witness GEP did not Witness the rapes but learnt about them after the events. The Chamber recalls that on 20 August 2002, it denied a Defence Motion to enter a judgement of acquittal with respect to Count 6 of the Indictment, Crimes Against Humanity (Rape), finding that at that stage of the proceeding, the evidence adduced was not *prima facie* insufficient for a conviction. Having analysed all the evidence presented, the Chamber finds that the testimonies of both Witnesses GAG and GEP are credible but that the hearsay nature of the evidence adduced by these Witnesses is not sufficient to sustain a rape charge against the Accused. The Chamber finds therefore that there is insufficient evidence for a conviction of Rape as a Crime against humanity".[512] "The Chamber does not find the hearsay evidence adduced by the Prosecution to demonstrate alleged rapes committed during the attack at the Gikomero Parish Compound on 12 April 1994 sufficient to implicate the Accused, as alleged in paragraph 6.46 of the Indictment".[513]

8. Sylvestre **<u>Gacumbitsi</u>** (Case No. ICTR-01-64) Bourgmestre of Rusumo commune, in Kibungo prefecture, until April 1994.	
Indictment (International sex crimes (or related) charges and	- **Genocide** (count 1) under Articles 6(1) and 6(3) of the Statute (**superior responsibility**) or, alternatively, **Complicity in genocide** (count 2) under Article 6(1) of the Statute for **causing serious bodily or mental harm** to members of the Tutsi population through various crimes, including the rapes and acts of sexual violence committed against Tutsi women in Rusumo commune and for circulating throughout Rusumo

[510] *Kamuhanda* Trial Judgement, paras. 707–709 (internal references omitted).
[511] *Kamuhanda* Trial Judgement, para. 710.
[512] *Kamuhanda* Trial Judgement, paras. 495–497 (internal reference omitted).
[513] *Kamuhanda* Trial Judgement, para. 507.

mode(s) of liability)	commune in a vehicle announcing by megaphone that Tutsi women should be raped and sexually degraded, including on, or about, 17 April 1994 when he exhorted the population along the Nyarubuye road to "rape Tutsi girls that had always refused to sleep with Hutu".[514] - **Rape as CAH** (count 5) under Articles 6(1) and 6(3) of the Statute (**superior responsibility**) for: (i) luring Tutsi women to a certain location on, or about, 17 April 1994, by announcing over a megaphone that Tutsi women would be spared and, when a number of Tutsi women gathered, for their rapes, including the insertion of objects in their vaginas; and (ii) travelling along the Nyarubuye road in a caravan of vehicles on, or about, 17 April 1994, announcing by megaphone that "Tutsi girls that have always refused to sleep with Hutu should be raped and sticks placed in their genitals".[515]

514 *Prosecutor v. Sylvestre Gacumbitsi*, Case No. ICTR-01-64-I, Indictment, 20 June 2001 ("*Gacumbitsi* Indictment"), pp. 1–2 ("**Count 1: GENOCIDE** The Prosecutor of the International Criminal Tribunal of Rwanda charges **Sylvestre GACUMBITSI** with ***GENOCIDE,*** *a crime stipulated in Article 2(3)(a) of the Statute,* in that on or between the dates of 6 April 1994 and 30 April 1994 in Kibungo *prefecture,* Rwanda, **Sylvestre GACUMBITSI** was responsible for killing or causing serious bodily or mental harm to members of the Tutsi population with the intent to destroy, in whole or in part, a racial or ethnic group; *Pursuant to Article 6(1) of the Statute:* by virtue of his affirmative acts in ordering, instigating, commanding, participating in and aiding and abetting the preparation and execution of the crime charged; ***and*** *Pursuant to Article 6(3) of the Statute:* by virtue of his actual or constructive knowledge of the acts and omissions of soldiers, gendarmes, communal police, *Interahamwe,* civilian militia and civilians acting under his authority, and his failure to take necessary and reasonable measures to stop or prevent them, or to discipline and punish them, for their acts in the preparation and execution of the crime charged; ***or alternatively,*** **Count 2: COMPLICITY IN GENOCIDE** The Prosecutor of the International Criminal Tribunal of Rwanda charges **Sylvestre GACUMBITSI** with ***COMPLICITY IN GENOCIDE,*** *a crime stipulated in Article 2(3)(e) of the Statute,* in that on or between the dates of 6 April 1994 and 30 April 1994 in Kibungo *préfecture,* Rwanda, **Sylvestre GACUMBITSI** was responsible for killing or causing serious bodily or mental harm to members of the Tutsi population with the intent to destroy, in whole or in part, a racial or ethnic group, as follows: *Pursuant to Article 6(1) of the Statute:* by virtue of his affirmative acts in ordering, instigating, commanding, participating in and aiding and abetting the preparation and execution of the crime charged".), paras. 20–21 ("Sexual violence against Tutsi women was systematically incorporated in the generalized attacks against the Tutsi. In leading, ordering and encouraging the campaign of extermination in Rusumo *commune,* **Sylvestre GACUMBITSI** knew, or should have known, that sexual violence against civilian Tutsi was, or would be, widespread or systematic, and that the perpetrators would include his subordinates or those that committed such acts in response to his generalized orders and instructions to exterminate the Tutsi. Furthermore, **Sylvestre GACUMBITSI** circulated about Rusumo *commune* in a vehicle announcing by megaphone that Tutsi women should be raped and sexually degraded. For example, on or about 17 April 1994 **Sylvestre GACUMBITSI** exhorted the population along the Nyarubuye road to '*rape Tutsi girls that had always refused to sleep with Hutu ...*' and to '*search in the bushes, do not save a single snake ...*'. Attacks and rapes of Tutsi women immediately followed".), 24 ("By virtue of his positions of leadership of the MRND and the *Interahamwe,* particularly as derived from his status as *bourgmestre* of Rusumo, **Sylvestre GACUMBITSI** ordered or directed or otherwise authorized government armed forces, civilian militias and civilians to persecute rape and kill or facilitate the killing of civilian Tutsi. By virtue of that same authority **Sylvestre GACUMBITSI** had the ability and the duty to halt, prevent, discourage or sanction persons that committed, or were about to commit, such acts, and did not do so, or only did so selectively".).

515 *Gacumbitsi* Indictment, p. 8 ("**Count 5: RAPE as a CRIME AGAINST HUMANITY:** The Prosecutor of the International Criminal Tribunal of Rwanda charges **Sylvestre Gacumbitsi** with ***RAPE as a CRIME AGAINST HUMANITY*** *as stipulated in Article 3(g) of the Statute,* in that on or between the dates of 6 April 1994 and 30 **April** 1994 in Kibungo *préfecture,* Rwanda, **Sylvestre Gacumbitsi** did cause women to be raped as part of a widespread or systematic attack against a civilian population on political, ethnic or racial grounds, as follows: *Pursuant to Article 6(1) of the Statute:* by virtue of his affirmative acts in planning, instigating, ordering, committing, or otherwise aiding and abetting the planning, preparation or execution of the crime charged; ***and*** *Pursuant to Article 6(3) of the Statute:* by virtue of his actual or constructive knowledge of the acts or omissions of his subordinates, including soldiers, gendarmes, communal police, *Interahamwe,* civilian militia or civilians acting under his authority, and his failure to take necessary and reasonable measures to stop or prevent them, or to discipline and punish them, for their acts in the planning,

Trial Judgement	- Guilty of **Genocide** (count 1) and **Rape as CAH** (count 5) under Article 6(1) of the Statute for the rapes of Witness TAQ and seven other Tutsi women and girls by attackers (**instigating**).[516]
Appeal Judgement	- The convictions were affirmed by the Appeals Chamber.[517]
Legal and Factual Findings and/or Evidence	- Legal findings: **- Non-consent and knowledge thereof as constitutive elements of the crime of rape:** The Appeals Chamber clarified the constitutive elements of rape. It held: "In the *Kunarac* case, the ICTY Appeals Chamber defined rape as follows: 'the *actus reus* of the crime of rape in international law is constituted by: the sexual penetration, however slight: (a) of the vagina or anus of the victim by the penis of the perpetrator or any other object used by the perpetrator; or (b) the mouth of the victim by the penis of the perpetrator; where such sexual penetration occurs without the consent of the victim. Consent for this purpose must be consent given voluntarily, as a result of the victim's free will, assessed in the context of the surrounding circumstances. The *mens rea* is the intention to effect this sexual penetration, and the knowledge that it occurs without the consent of the victim.' However, it immediately emphasized that 'the circumstances giving rise to the instant appeal and that prevail in most cases charged as either war crimes or crimes against humanity will be almost universally coercive. That is to say, true consent will not be possible.' The Appeals Chamber adopts and seeks to further elucidate the position expressed by the ICTY Appeals Chamber in the *Kunarac et al.* Appeal Judgement. Two distinct questions are posed. First, are non-consent and the knowledge thereof elements of the crime of rape, or is consent instead an affirmative defence? Second, if they are elements, how may they be proved? With respect to the first question, *Kunarac* establishes that non-consent and knowledge thereof are elements of rape as a crime against humanity. The import of this is that the Prosecution bears the burden of proving these elements beyond reasonable doubt. If the affirmative defence approach were taken, the accused would bear, at least, the burden of production, that is, the burden to introduce evidence providing *prima facie* support for the defence. As the Prosecution points out, Rule 96 of the Rules does refer to consent as a

preparation or execution of the crime charged"), paras. 37–40 ("During April, May and June of 1994, there were widespread or systematic rapes and sexual violence of Tutsi women. The sexual assaults were often a prelude to murder, and was sometimes the cause of death of a number of civilian Tutsi. On one particular occasion, on or about 17 April 1994, **Sylvestre GACUMBITSI** lured Tutsi women to a certain location by announcing over a megaphone that Tutsi women would be spared, and that only Tutsi men would be killed. When a number of Tutsi women gathered in response to **Sylvestre GACUMBITSI's** exhortations, they were surrounded by several attackers, raped, and then killed. Attackers also sexually degraded a number of Tutsi women by inserting objects in their genitals. On or about 17 April 1994, **Sylvestre GACUMBITSI** travelled along the Nyarubuye road in a caravan of vehicles, announcing with a megaphone '*Search in the bushes, do not save a single snake .... Hutu that save Tutsi should be killed Tutsi girls that have always refused to sleep with Hutu should be raped and sticks placed in their genitals...*' After **Sylvestre GACUMBITSI** drove by, a group of men attacked Tutsi women that were hiding nearby and raped several of the women. One of the women was killed and a stick was thrust in her genitals. The sexual violence was so widespread, and conducted so openly, and was so integrally incorporated in generalized attacks against civilian Tutsi, that **Sylvestre GACUMBITSI** must have known, or should have known, that it was occurring, and that the perpetrators were his subordinates, subject to his authority and control, and acting under his orders. This is especially so since the perpetrators of sexual violence were often the same individuals that organized and led or participated in the generalized attacks against the Tutsi that **Sylvestre GACUMBITSI** had ordered".).

516 *Prosecutor v. Sylvestre Gacumbitsi*, Case No. ICTR-01-64-T, Judgment, 17 June 2004 ("*Gacumbitsi* Trial Judgement"), paras. 224–228, 259, 292–293, 321–334.

517 *Sylvestre Gacumbitsi v. The Prosecutor*, Case No. ICTR-01-64-A, Judgement, 7 July 2006 ("*Gacumbitsi* Appeal Judgement"), paras. 99–108, 126–146, 207.

	'defence'. The Rules of Procedure and Evidence do not, however, redefine the elements of the crimes over which the Tribunal has jurisdiction, which are defined by the Statute and by international law. The Appeals Chamber agrees, moreover, with the analysis of the Trial Chamber in the *Kunarac* case: 'The reference in the Rule [96] to consent as a 'defence' is not entirely consistent with traditional legal understandings of the concept of consent in rape. Where consent is an aspect of the definition of rape in national jurisdictions, it is generally understood [...] to be *absence of consent* which is an *element* of the crime. The use of the word 'defence', which in its technical sense carries an implication of the shifting of the burden of proof to the accused, is inconsistent with this understanding. The Trial Chamber does not understand the reference to consent as a 'defence' in Rule 96 to have been used in this technical way.' Rather than changing the definition of the crime by turning an element into a defence, Rule 96 of the Rules must be read simply to define the circumstances under which evidence of consent will be admissible. Thus, it speaks to the second part of the present inquiry: how may non-consent be proven? The answers both Tribunals have given to this second question resolve as a practical matter the objections raised by the Prosecution with respect to the elements approach. The Prosecution can prove non-consent beyond reasonable doubt by proving the existence of coercive circumstances under which meaningful consent is not possible. As with every element of any offence, the Trial Chamber will consider all of the relevant and admissible evidence in determining whether, under the circumstances of the case, it is appropriate to conclude that non-consent is proven beyond reasonable doubt. But it is not necessary, as a legal matter, for the Prosecution to introduce evidence concerning the words or conduct of the victim or the victim's relationship to the perpetrator. Nor need it introduce evidence of force. Rather, the Trial Chamber is free to infer non-consent from the background circumstances, such as an ongoing genocide campaign or the detention of the victim. Indeed, the Trial Chamber did so in this case. Under certain circumstances, the accused might raise reasonable doubt by introducing evidence that the victim specifically consented. However, pursuant to Rule 96(ii) of the Rules, such evidence is inadmissible if the victim: '(a) Has been subjected to or threatened with or has had reason to fear violence, duress, detention or psychological oppression; or (b) Reasonably believed that if the victim did not submit, another might be so subjected, threatened or put in fear.' Additionally, even if it admits such evidence, a Trial Chamber is free to disregard it if it concludes that under the circumstances the consent given was not genuinely voluntary. As to the accused's knowledge of the absence of consent of the victim, which as *Kunarac* establishes is also an element of the offence of rape, similar reasoning applies. Knowledge of non-consent may be proven, for instance, if the Prosecution establishes beyond reasonable doubt that the accused was aware, or had reason to be aware, of the coercive circumstances that undermined the possibility of genuine consent".[518] - <u>Factual and legal findings:</u> - Paragraph 38 of the Indictment: "The Chamber notes that no evidence was tendered to sustain the allegations contained in paragraph 38 of the Indictment. Thus, it shall not make any finding on such allegations".[519] - Instigating rapes and insertions of sticks into Tutsi women and girls' vaginas: "Regarding paragraphs 21 and 39 of the Indictment, and in light of the evidence admitted above, the Chamber finds that it is established that the Accused publicly

[518] *Gacumbitsi* Appeal Judgement, paras. 151–157 (internal references omitted).

[519] *Gacumbitsi* Trial Judgement, para. 199.

| | instigated the rape of Tutsi girls, by specifying that sticks be inserted into their genitals in case they resisted. The Chamber finds that the rapes and other acts of sexual violence recounted by Prosecution Witness TAQ, the consequence of the instigation against Tutsi girls, are established".[520]

- Alleged widespread character of the acts of sexual violence:
"Regarding paragraph 40 of the Indictment, the Chamber finds that acts of sexual violence were part of a systematic and widespread attack against Tutsi civilians in Rusumo *commune* during the events of April 1994. Although it is possible that many rapes were committed in Rusumo *commune*, the evidence tendered covered only a few cases of rape and acts of sexual violence. Thus, the Chamber cannot make a finding on the widespread character of such crimes. Nor can the Chamber find that the Accused knew or had reason to know that such acts were being perpetrated because of their widespread character. However, as the Chamber has already found that the Accused instigated such acts of violence, he thereby clearly demonstrated his intent to see them committed".[521]

- Rapes recounted by Witnesses TAQ, TAO, TAS and TAP:
"The Chamber finds that the rapes recounted by Prosecution Witnesses TAQ, TAO, TAS and TAP are established. In light of the closeness in time and space between the instigation by the Accused on 17 April 1994 and the rapes committed against Witness TAQ and other women and girls, the mode of commission of which amounted to instigation, the Chamber finds that the rapes were a direct consequence of instigation. However, the Chamber is unpersuaded that there is a sufficient nexus between such instigation and the other rapes, the commission of which has been proved beyond a reasonable doubt. Although it is true that Prosecution Witness TAS testified that an attacker told her that he was acting in accordance with the Accused's instructions, the Chamber has not found any evidence that this part of her account is reliable".[522]

- Sylvestre Gacumbitsi's knowledge that rapes were being committed:
"With regard to paragraphs 20 and 37 of the Indictment, and in light of the evidence adduced in respect of paragraphs 39 and 40 of the same Indictment, the Chamber finds that the Prosecutor has established beyond a reasonable doubt that, from April to June 1994, in Rusumo *commune*, rapes and other acts of sexual violence were committed as part of a widespread and systematic attack against Tutsi civilians. The Chamber finds that the Accused knew or had reason to know that such rapes were being committed because he instigated the attack against Tutsi civilians".[523]

- Responsibility of Sylvestre Gacumbitsi for rapes constituting genocide:
"With regard to paragraph 21 of the Indictment, the Chamber has already found that the Accused publicly instigated the rape of Tutsi women and girls, and that the rape of Witness TAQ and seven other Tutsi women and girls by attackers who heeded the instigation was a direct consequence thereof. The Chamber finds that these rapes caused serious physical harm to members of the Tutsi ethnic group. Thus, the Chamber finds that, as to the specific crime of serious bodily harm, Sylvestre Gacumbitsi incurs responsibility for the crime of genocide by instigating the rape of Tutsi women and girls. Accordingly, the Chamber finds Sylvestre Gacumbitsi GUILTY of GENO- |

[520] *Gacumbitsi* Trial Judgement, para. 224.

[521] *Gacumbitsi* Trial Judgement, para. 225.

[522] *Gacumbitsi* Trial Judgement, paras. 226–227.

[523] *Gacumbitsi* Trial Judgement, para. 228.

	CIDE, pursuant to Article 2(3)(a) and (b), as charged under Count 1 of the Indictment".[524] - Responsibility of Sylvestre Gacumbitsi for rapes as CAH: "The Chamber is of the opinion that any penetration of the victim's vagina by the rapist with his genitals or with any object constitutes rape, although the definition of rape under Article 3(g) of the Statute is not limited to such acts alone. In the case at bench, the Chamber has already found that Witness TAQ was raped at the same time as seven other Tutsi women and girls; that the rapists either penetrated each victim's vagina with their genitals or inserted sticks into them; that Witness TAO's wife was raped, with the rapist penetrating the victim's vagina with his genitals; that Witness TAS was raped in a similar manner, as well as Witness TAP and her mother. The Chamber finds that all these acts fall within the definition of rape. The Chamber reiterates its previous findings on the existence of a widespread and systematic attack against civilians in Rusumo in April 1994. In its factual findings, the Chamber held, on the one hand, that the widespread and systematic attack targeted specifically Tutsi civilians and, on the other hand, that Prosecution Witnesses TAQ, TAP and TAS, the wife of Prosecution Witness TAO, the mother of Prosecution Witness TAP, and seven Tutsi women and girls were all raped, as testified to by Prosecution Witness TAQ. The evidence shows that all these victims are civilians. The Chamber finds that these victims of rape were chosen because of their Tutsi ethnic origin, or because of their relationship with a person of the Tutsi ethnic group, which is the case with Prosecution Witness TAS. The Chamber finds that the order given by the Accused to attackers to attack and select rape victims was discriminatory in character. Under such circumstances, the utterances made by the Accused to the effect that in case of resistance the victims should be killed in an atrocious manner, and the fact that rape victims were attacked by those they were fleeing from, adequately establish the victims' lack of consent to the rapes. The Prosecutor submits that the Accused planned, instigated, ordered, committed or otherwise aided and abetted in the planning, preparation or perpetration of the rape of the above-mentioned victims. The Chamber finds that the evidence adduced establishes that Sylvestre Gacumbitsi, through such utterances as were heard by Prosecution Witness TAQ, also instigated the rape of Tutsi women and girls. On her part, Prosecution Witness TAS also testified that she heard those who raped her say that the Accused had ordered them to rape Tutsi women and girls, but her uncorroborated hearsay evidence is not such as to prove the involvement of the Accused. The Chamber recalls that, immediately after the utterances made by the Accused instigating the rape of Tutsi women and girls, while he was crossing the bridge between Kankobwa and Nyarubuye *secteurs* on his way to Nyarubuye, Prosecution Witness TAQ and seven other Tutsi women and girls were raped by young men who, being in the neigbourhood, heard the *bourgmestre*'s instigation. The Chamber finds that these rapes, as recounted by Prosecution Witness TAQ, resulted directly from the instigation of the Accused. On the contrary, the Chamber finds no evidence establishing a link between the rape of Prosecution Witness TAS and the possible utterances of the Accused and therefore the Accused cannot incur responsibility in that respect. The same applies to the rape of the wife of Prosecution Witness TAO, and the rape of the mother of Prosecution Witness TAP. However, the Chamber[] finds that these rapes are established as part of the widespread and systematic attack against Tutsi civilians in Rusumo. Pursuant to Article 6(1) of the Statute, the Chamber finds Sylvestre Gacumbitsi criminally liable for instigating the rape of Witness TAQ and seven other Tutsi women and girls, thereby also committing a crime against humanity. As to the other forms of criminal participation, the Prosecution has not adduced evidence to show that they are applicable to the Accused. Having found the Accused

524 *Gacumbitsi* Trial Judgement, paras. 292–293.

	criminally liable under Article 6(1) of the Statute for instigating others to commit rape in Rusumo *commune* in April 1994, the Chamber does not deem it necessary to *enquire* whether he is equally responsible pursuant to Article 6(3) of the Statute, given the similarity of the acts charged and the lack [of] evidence of a superior-subordinate relationship between the Accused and the perpetrators of the rapes. Thus, with regard to Count 5, the Chamber finds Sylvestre Gacumbitsi GUILTY OF RAPE AS A CRIME AGAINST HUMANITY".[525]

9. Mikaeli **Muhimana** (Case No. ICTR-95-1B) Conseiller of Gishyita secteur, in Gishyita commune, in Kibuye prefecture.	
Indictment (International sex crimes (or related) charges and mode(s) of liability)	- **Rape as CAH** (count 3) under Article 6(1) of the Statute for: (i) the rapes committed after a meeting held at his residence in Gishyita town on or around 7 April 1994; (ii) raping two Tutsi women, Gorretti Mukashyaka and Languida Kamukina, in his house in Gishyita town on or about 7 April 1994 and inviting *Interahamwe* and civilians to look at their vaginas; (iii) raping a Tutsi woman, Esperance Mukagasana, at his house in Gishyita town on, or about, 14 April 1994 and offering her to an *Interahamwe* named Gisambo, who raped her in Mikaeli Muhimana's presence; (iv) raping a Tutsi woman, Witness AX-K, on two occasions in Gishyita town towards the end of April 1994; (v) raping Witness AV-K in the vicinity of a cemetery located between Mubuga parish and Mubuga dispensary on or around 15 April 1994; (vi) instructing *Interahamwe* to rape two Tutsi women, Colette and Alphonsine, at Mubuga parish on or around 15 April 1994; (vii) raping, in concert with others, three Tutsi women, Josiana, Mariana Gafurafura and Martha Gafurafura, in Gishyita commune between 14 and 16 April 1994; (viii) raping, in concert with *Interahamwe*, Tutsi women, including Mukasine Kajongi, in one of the halls of the Mugonero medical school on 16 April 1994; (ix) raping collectively two Tutsi women, Mukasine and Murekatete, and a Hutu woman, Witness BJ-K, at Mugonero hospital on 16 April 1994 and for subsequently apologising to the Hutu woman for the "mistake" as he thought she was a Tutsi; (x) raping, collectively with *Interahamwe*, three Tutsi women, Johaneta, Theresa Mukabutera and Eugenia, in the surgical ward in the Mugonero hospital on 16 April 1994; (xi) raping a Tutsi woman, Witness AU-K, while *Interahamwe* raped two Tutsi women, Immaculate Mukabarore and Josephine Mukankwaro, in the operating room of the medical school in the Mugonero complex on 16 April 1994; (xii) raping a Tutsi woman, Bahati Nyiransengimana, and physically assaulting two other Tutsis, Helen Mugiraneza and Drocella who was nine year-old, at a pub in Ngoma in May 1994; (xiii) permitting an armed civilian named Mugonero to detain and keep a Tutsi woman, Witness BG-K, in his house where he repeatedly raped her for several weeks from on or around 22 April 1994; (xiv) instructing an *Interahamwe* named Ngabonzina to rape a Tutsi woman, Virginie Gasherebuka, at Katbatwa hill Bisesero area and subsequently sexually assaulting her by inserting instruments in her vagina; (xv) raping, in concert with an *Interahamwe* named Gisambo, a Tutsi woman named Pascasie Mukarema at Nyakiyabo hill in Bisesero towards the end of May 1994; and (xvi) raping, in concert with armed civilians, including a man named Ngabonzina, a Tutsi woman, Felicite Kankuyu, at Gitwa hills in the Bisesero area around June 1994.[526]

525 *Gacumbitsi* Trial Judgement, paras. 321–333 (internal references omitted).

526 *Prosecutor v. Mikaeli Muhimana*, Revised Amended Indictment, 29 July 2004 ("*Muhimana* Indictment"), para. 6 ("**Count III: RAPE as a CRIME AGAINST HUMANITY** Between 6 April and 30 June 1994 **Mikaeli Muhimana** committed rape as part of a widespread or systematic attack against Tutsi women civilians and other women perceived to be Tutsi in Gishyita sector, Mugonero church, hospital and nursing school, and in the Bisesero area. **Events in Gishyita Sector, Gishyita Commune** (a) On or about 7 April 1994, **Mikaeli Muhimana** held a meeting at his residence in Gishyita town, Gishyita sector, Gishyita commune, with,

	- There are no factual allegations in the Indictment of rapes constituting genocide. However, according to the Trial Chamber, the accused was also charged for **Genocide** (count 1) or, alternatively, **Complicity in genocide** (count 2) under Article 6(1) of the Statute for the rapes commited at the Mugonero complex.[527]
Trial Judgement	- Guilty of **Genocide** (count 1) under Article 6(1) of the Statute for various crimes, including the rapes of Tutsi women at Mugonero complex.[528]

amongst others, the Gishyita Bourgmestre Charles Sikubwabo and a businessman Obed Ruzindana. Shortly thereafter killings, rape and other atrocities commenced in Gishyita commune. (i) On or about 7 April 1994 in Gishyita town[,] Gishyita sector, Gishyita commune, **Mikaeli Muhimana** brought two civilian women Gorretti Mukashyaka and Languida Kamukina into his house and raped them. Thereafter he drove them naked out of his house and invited *Interahamwe* and other civilians to come and see how naked Tutsi girls looked like. **Mikaeli Muhimana** then directed the *Interahamwe* to part the girls' legs to provide the onlookers with a clear view of the girls' vaginas. (ii) On or about 14 April 1994 in Gishyita town[,] Gishyita sector, Gishyita commune, at his residence, **Mikaeli Muhimana** raped a Tutsi women Esperance Mukagasana and offered her to an *Interahamwe* named Gisambo, for the same purpose. The said Gisambo raped Esperance Mukagasana at **Mikaeli Muhimana** residence and within his presence. (iii) Towards the end of April 1994, **Mikaeli Muhimana** raped a Tutsi civilian woman, **AX-K** on two occasions, at the Bureau commune in Gishyita town[,] Gishyita sector, Gishyita commune. **Events at Mubuga Parish, Mubuga Sector** (b) On or around 15 April 1994, at Mubuga parish, **Mikaeli Muhimana** in concert with others, including *Interahamwe* named Kigana, Theophil and Byamwenga took Tutsi civilian women named Colette a girl from Mubuga, Agnes Mukagatare an employee of Mubuga dispensary and Alphonsine from Mubuga dispensary to the vicinity of a cemetery located between Mubuga parish and Mubuga dispensary where **Mikaeli Muhimana** raped **AV-K**. (i) On or around 15 April 1994, at Mubuga parish, *Interahamwe* raped two women named Colette a girl from Mubuga and Alphonsine on instructions and within the presence of **Mikaeli Muhimana**. **Events at the Mugonero Complex, Gishyita Commune** (c) Between 14 and 16 April 1994, **Mikaeli Muhimana** in concert with, amongst others, Charles Sikubwabo and an *Interahamwe* named Gisambo took three civilian Tutsi women Josiana, Mariana Gafurafura, and Martha Gafurafura from Mugonero complex where they had sought refuge, to Gishyita commune where they continually raped them. (i) On 16 April 1994, at the Mugonero complex, **Mikaeli Muhimana** in concert with two *Interahamwe* raped civilian Tutsi women in one of the halls of the Mugonero medical school. **Mikaeli Muhimana** raped one Mukasine Kajongi while brutally assaulting her and removing her clothing so that passers by could view her sexual organs. (ii) On 16 April 1994, at the Mugonero complex, **Mikaeli Muhimana** and *Interahamwe* collectively raped civilian Tutsi women Mukasine and Murekatete staff maids at Mugonero hospital, and a civilian Hutu lady **BJ-K**. **Mikaeli Muhimana** subsequently apologised to **BJ-K** for the 'mistake' of raping her as he initially thought she was Tutsi. (iii) On 16 April 1994, in the surgical wardroom in the Mugonero hospital, **Mikaeli Muhimana**, in concert with two *Interahamwe* collectively raped Tutsi women Johaneta, Theresa Mukabutera and Eugenia, verbally insulting them in the process. (iv) On 16 April 1994, at the Mugonero complex, **Mikaeli Muhimana**, acting in concert with *Interahamwe* went to one of the operating rooms in the medical school building in the Mugonero complex and collectively raped Tutsi women **AU-K**, Immaculate Mukabarore, Josephine Mukankwaro. In Particular **Mikaeli Muhimana** raped **AU-K**. (v) In May 1994, in a pub in Ngoma, **Mikaeli Muhimana**, acting in concert with others, including a soldier named Gikeri and one Obed Ruzindana, raped a Tutsi woman Bahati Nyiransengimana, Tutsi women Helen Mugiraneza and Drocella, aged 9 years. **Events in Bisese[r]o area, Gishyita and Gisovu Communes** (d) On or around 22 April 1994, **Mikaeli Muhimana** permitted an armed civilian, one Mugonero to detain and keep a Tutsi woman **BG-K** in his house where he repeatedly raped her for several weeks. (i) Towards the end of April 1994, at Kabatwa hill Bisesero area, and *Interahamwe* named Ngabonzina raped a Tutsi civilian woman Virginie Gasherebuka on instructions of **Mikaeli Muhimana**. Acting on orders of **Mikaeli Muhimana**, Ngabonzina undressed Virginie Gasherebuka, laid her on the ground, parted her legs and **Mikaeli Muhimana** and Ngabonzina jointly assaulted her sexually in her vaginal area with machetes and other instruments. (ii) Towards the end of May 1994, at Nyakiyabo hill in the Bisesero area **Mikaeli Muhimana**, in concert with an *Interahamwe* named Gisambo, raped Pascasie Mukarema. (iii) Around June 1994, at Gitwa hills in the Bisesero area, **Mikaeli Muhimana** in concert with armed civilians, including one Ngabonzina, raped a civilian Tutsi woman named Felicite Kankuyu".).

527 *Muhimana* Indictment, pp. 1–4, paras. 4–5.

528 *Prosecutor v. Mikaeli Muhimana*, Case No. ICTR-95-1B-T, Judgement and Sentence, dated 28 April 2005 and filed on 26 May 2005 ("*Muhimana* Trial Judgement"), paras. 269–275, 300–304, 513(c), 517–519, 585.

	- Guilty of **Rape as CAH** (count 3) under Article 6(1) of the Statute (**committing**) for raping: (a) Gorretti Mukashyaka and Languida Kamukina in his house, in Gishyita town, on 7 April 1994; (b) Esperance Mukagasana several times, in his house, during the first week after the eruption of hostilities; (c) Agnes Mukagatere, in a cemetery near Mubuga church, on 15 April 1994; (d) Mukasine Kajongi, in the basement of Mugonero hospital, at Mugonero complex, on 16 April 1994; (e) Witness AU twice, in a room of the basement of Mugonero hospital, at Mugonero complex, on 16 April 1994; and (f) Witness BJ, a young Hutu girl, whom he mistook for a Tutsi, in the basement of Mugonero hospital, at Mugonero complex, on 16 April 1994; and (**aiding and abetting**) for the rapes of: (a) the daughters of Amos Karera by two soldiers, in the basement of Mugonero hospital, on 16 April 1994; (b) Murekatete and Mukasine by two men accompanying Mikaeli Muhimana, in the basement of Mugonero hospital, on 16 April 1994; and (c) Witness BG several times over a period of two days by an *Interahamwe* named Mugonero, in Mugonero's residence, between 22 and 24 April 1994.[529]
Appeal Judgement	- The Appeals Chamber, Judge Mohamed Shahabuddeen and Judge Wolfgang Schomburg dissenting, **reversed Mikaeli Muhimana's conviction for Rape as CAH** (count 3) **insofar as the conviction was based on the rapes of Gorretti Mukashyaka and Languida Kamukina**.[530] - The Appeals Chamber dismissed all the other grounds of appeal raised by Mikaeli Muhimana with respect to the other rapes and **affirmed his conviction for Rape as CAH** (count 3) **in all other respects**.[531]
Legal and Factual Findings and/or Evidence	- Legal findings: - **Rape: definition:** The Trial Chamber took "the view that the *Akayesu* definition and the *Kunarac* elements are not incompatible or substantially different in their application. Whereas *Akayesu* referred broadly to a 'physical invasion of a sexual nature', *Kunarac* went on to articulate the parameters of what would constitute a physical invasion of a sexual nature amounting to rape. On the basis of the foregoing analysis, the Chamber endorses the conceptual definition of rape established in *Akayesu*, which encompasses the elements set out in *Kunarac*".[532] - Factual and legal findings: - Rapes of Languida Kamukina and Gorretti Mukashyaka in Gishyita town on 7 April 1994: "The Prosecution relies on the testimony of Witness AP in support of the allegation of the rapes of Languida Kamukina and Gorretti Mukashyaka. The Chamber finds the evidence of Witness AP to be internally consistent. Moreover, her testimony was not shaken by extensive cross-examination by the Defence. The Chamber is satisfied that the witness knew the Accused at the time of the events and accepts her explanation as to why she was in close proximity to the rapes when they occurred. The Chamber notes that, although she was visibly disturbed in recounting the events of 7 April 1994, her answers were straightforward and she did not exaggerate the evidence. Thus, the

529 *Muhimana* Trial Judgement, paras. 22–33, 102–108, 191–204, 269–275, 282–292, 300–304, 318–323, 552–553, 558–563, 585.

530 *Mikaeli Muhimana v. The Prosecutor*, Case No. ICTR-95-1B-A, Judgement, 21 May 2007 ("*Muhimana* Appeal Judgement"), paras. 49–53 and Section XIX (Disposition), p. 81. See also *Muhimana* Appeal Judgement, Joint Partly Dissenting Opinion of Judge Shahabuddeen and Judge Schomburg, paras. 1–4.

531 *Muhimana* Appeal Judgement, paras. 14–21, 94–105, 116–124, 133–140, 148–192 and Section XIX (Disposition), p. 81.

532 *Muhimana* Trial Judgement, paras. 550–551. See also *Muhimana* Trial Judgement, paras. 537–549.

	Chamber finds her evidence credible and reliable. The Defence points out that Witness AP's testimony is at odds with the 'Amended Indictment' with respect to the age of the two victims. The Chamber finds this challenge to be irrelevant, since the Revised Amended Indictment does not mention the victims' ages. The Chamber finds that the mere fact that several Defence witnesses did not hear of rapes committed by the Accused in his house on 7 April 1994 does not mean that they could not have occurred. The witnesses advanced no reason to support the implied assertion that, if the Accused had committed rapes, they would have heard of them. The Chamber does not find this argument persuasive. The Chamber does not accept the contention that under Rwandan culture it is impossible for a man to rape a woman in the matrimonial home. The Chamber accepts that in any society such behaviour would be considered unacceptable. However, this fact does not preclude the possibility that it could occur. Although Witness DQ testified that Languida was not in Gishyita during the events of 1994, the Defence did not provide further evidence to substantiate this allegation. The Chamber also notes the contradiction between the evidence of Witness DQ, who stated that Languida was not in Gishyita during the events of 1994, and Witness DI, who stated that Languida sought refuge in Mubuga Church. The Chamber has considered the Defence submission that whereas in the Indictment and the Witness Statement of Witness AP, it is alleged that the two girls who were raped are called Goretti Mukashyaka and Languida Kamukina, Witness AP in her testimony gives the names as Immaculée Mukakayiro and Languida Kamukina. The Prosecution contends that the witness gave an adequate explanation for this discrepancy. In her statement of 30 August 1999, Witness AP refers to the two raped girls as Languida Kamukina and Gorretti Mukashyaka, the daughters of Ruhigira. In her testimony she referred to Immaculée Mukashyaka and Languida Kamukina, the daughters of Ruhigira. However, she also stated that 'I may have made a mistake about their names because it's a long time ago. When people are dead you can forget their names, but you always have an image of these people in your head'. The Chamber notes that Witness AP is related to Ruhigira by marriage and knew the victims well. The Chamber accepts the witness' explanation that the passage of time has led to some confusion as to the exact names of the two sisters, and is satisfied that, where in her testimony Witness AP referred to Immaculée Mukashyaka, or where the surname was given as Mukakayiro, she was referring to the sister of Languida Kamukina and daughter of Ruhigira, that is, Gorretti Mukashyaka. The Chamber has also noted the Defence challenge to Witness AP's credibility that she is related to the current *conseiller* of Gishyita *Secteur*, who replaced the Accused, and that her testimony is therefore biased, and part of a plot against the Accused by the *conseiller* to deprive the Accused of his property. The Chamber notes that the Defence never put this allegation of bias to the witness during cross-examination. Moreover, in assessing the credibility of Witness AP, the Chamber has taken note of this allegation of bias and is satisfied that it does not in any way discredit her testimony. Consequently, the Chamber dismisses the Defence challenges to Witness AP's credibility. Although Witness AP was not an eyewitness to the rape of Goretti and Languida, the Chamber infers that the Accused raped them on the basis of the following factors: the witness saw the Accused take the girls into his house; she heard the victims scream, mentioning the Accused's name and stating that they 'did not expect him to do that' to them; finally the witness saw the Accused lead the victims out of his house, stark naked, and she noticed that they were walking 'with their legs apart'. The Chamber also finds that, following the rapes, the Accused further humiliated the girls by inviting others to come and see 'what *Tutsi* girls look like'".[533]
	- Rapes committed after a meeting held at Mikaeli Muhimana's residence in Gishyita town in April 1994:

[533] *Muhimana* Trial Judgement, paras. 22–33 (internal references omitted).

	"The Chamber finds that there is insufficient evidence to prove the allegations contained in Paragraph 6 (a) of the Indictment and Paragraph 40 of the Pre-Trial Brief that the Accused and others held meetings at which plans to attack *Tutsi* civilians were made. On the basis of Witness AQ's testimony, the Chamber finds that a meeting of officials was held at the Accused's residence during mid-April 1994. However, there is nothing to suggest that the meeting was held for an unlawful purpose, and the Prosecution has failed to establish a link between the meeting and the killings, rapes, and other atrocities that allegedly occurred afterwards".[534] - Rape of Esperance Mukagasana in mid-April 1994: "The Chamber finds the testimony of Prosecution Witness AQ credible. The Chamber is satisfied that Witness AQ, who lived in the Accused's house, was an eyewitness to the rape of Esperance. She gave a detailed description of how the Accused raped Esperance several times. The Witness did not exaggerate her evidence and was prepared to admit that she was not able to see the alleged rape of Esperance by Gisambo, because he closed the door. The Chamber accepts Witness AQ's testimony that she and the victim lived in the Accused's house at the time of the rape, and that she saw Esperance raped several times. The witness was able to see what the Accused did to the victim because the door to the room was open, and he was always completely naked. The witness stated that, on the first occasion, 'about a week after the war erupted', she saw the victim being dragged to the room, struggling to be released. The Accused pushed her on to the bed, stripped her naked, and raped her. The Chamber also finds that the witness' approximation of the date of the first rape corresponds to the date alleged in Paragraph 6(a) (ii) of the Indictment. The Chamber has already found that, even though some Defence witnesses testified that they did not hear of rapes committed by the Accused in his house on 7 April 1994, it does not follow that such rapes did not occur. The Chamber rejects the testimony of Defence witnesses who testified that it was not possible for the Accused to rape women in his own house, where his wife lived. These witnesses did not advance any convincing reason for this assertion. Regarding the allegation in the Indictment that the Accused offered Esperance to an *Interahamwe* named Gisambo, who raped her in the Accused's house and in his presence, the Chamber notes that no evidence was led to support the allegation that Esperance was offered to Gisambo by the Accused or that she was raped in his presence. Furthermore, although Witness AQ testified to seeing Gisambo drag Esperance into the Accused's house as she screamed, the witness was not able to see the alleged rape because Gisambo closed the door behind him. Accordingly, the Chamber finds that the Prosecution has failed to prove the allegation that the Accused offered Esperance to Gisambo and that he raped her in the Accused's presence. The Chamber is mindful of the Defence submission regarding the partiality of Witness AQ and has, accordingly, considered her testimony with the necessary caution. Nevertheless, the Chamber finds her recollection of the events credible and reliable. The Chamber will address the allegation of the witness' rape by the Accused in the Facts Not Pleaded Section of this Judgement. Based on the eyewitness testimony of Witness AQ, the Chamber finds that the Prosecution has proved beyond reasonable doubt the allegation in Paragraph 6 (a) (ii) of the Indictment that the Accused raped Esperance Mukagasana in his residence".[535] - Rapes of Colette, Alphonsine and Agnes at Mubuga parish cemetery on 15 April 1994: "The Prosecution relies on the evidence of Witness AV to support its allegations that

534 *Muhimana* Trial Judgement, para. 88 (internal reference omitted).

535 *Muhimana* Trial Judgement, paras. 102–108 (internal reference omitted).

	the Accused raped Agnes Mukagatare, and that two other girls were raped by the *Interahamwe* in his presence. The Defence contends that the rape of Agnes Mukagatare by the Accused, to which Witness AV testified, is not alleged in the Indictment. Therefore, the Accused cannot be expected to prepare a defense against such an allegation. It submits that actual witness testimony cannot serve as an amendment to the Indictment. An analysis of Paragraph 6 (b) of the Indictment (including sub-paragraph 6(b) (i)) reveals that the Accused is charged with personally raping one *Tutsi* woman in the cemetery on 15 April 1994, Witness AV, and ordering the rape of two others. The evidence speaks to the rape not of Witness AV by the Accused, but to the rape of one of the abducted girls by the Accused. The Chamber notes that on 27 February 2004, upon filing its Pre-Trial Brief, the Prosecution placed the Defence on notice that Witness AV-K (later Witness AV) was not in fact raped as alleged in Paragraph 6 (b) of the Indictment, but rather that she witnessed the rape of the women mentioned in that paragraph: Colette from Mubuga, Agnes Mukagatare and Alphonsine from Mubuga. The Chamber further notes that in the Annex to the Pre-Trial Brief, the Prosecution gives the following details in its summary of the anticipated witness testimony of Witness AV: 'On 15 April 1994, Muhimana working in common purpose with *Interahamwe* Kigana, Theophil and Byamwenge, took away *Tutsi* women, including one Colette and a girl called Agnes Mukagatere, an employee at Mubuga dispensary to an isolated area of a cemetery located between the Parish and the dispensary. Muhimana indicated that it would not be proper to kill the girls without first raping them. Muhimana violently raped Agnes. Muhimana ordered the *Interahamwe* to rape the other girls and kill them by opening up their bellies.' Before closing its case, the Prosecution made an oral request before the Chamber to rectify a 'typographical error' in the Indictment, to amend the name of the woman allegedly raped by the Accused in Paragraph 6 (b) of the Indictment from 'AV-K' to 'Agnes'. The Prosecution explained that the error had occurred in the drafting of the Indictment as Witness AV-K and 'Agnes' share the same first name, which had at the time of drafting caused some confusion. However, the Prosecution submitted that the Defence had been given notice of this typographical error since the Pre-Trial Brief was filed. The Bench proceeded to enquire from the Defence whether it had any objection to the amendment, and the Defence replied that it did not see any reason to object. However the Defence made a reservation that it wished to verify the information, since it did not have the relevant document at hand. Unfortunately, the Chamber did not return to the matter after the commencement of the Defence case. The Chamber notes that the Accused was given notice, from the time of the Indictment, of the time and place where he is alleged to have raped a *Tutsi* woman. The Indictment specified the names of all three girls that the Accused and others were alleged to have abducted and taken to the cemetery. One of the three girls mentioned is Agnes Mukagatare, the girl that Witness AV alleges in her testimony to have been raped. The Chamber also notes that the Prosecution Pre-Trial Brief gave accurate details of Witness AV's anticipated testimony in sufficient time for the Accused to prepare his defence. The Chamber concludes that the Defence suffered no prejudice in its ability to meet the Prosecution evidence on this matter, and in fact presented several witnesses to rebut the Prosecution evidence. Consequently, the Chamber finds that the defect in the Indictment was cured by timely, clear, and consistent information. The Chamber has already found Witness AV to be a credible and reliable witness. Furthermore, the Chamber notes that, during the events in the cemetery, she clearly recognised the Accused and had a clear and unobstructed view of the events. On the basis of Witness AV's testimony, the Chamber finds that, on 15 April 1994, the Accused, accompanied by a group of *Interahamwe*, abducted six *Tutsi* girls and led them to a cemetery near Mubuga Church. The Accused informed the *Interahamwe* that '[n]obody should kill [these] girls before we've raped them.' He then grabbed Agnes Mukagatere, and forced her to undress and lie down. Following this, he climbed on top of her and raped her violently, while she screamed and pleaded with him to stop. After raping her, the Accused pushed his naked victim towards the *Inte-*

	rahamwe and told them, 'Now you should kill her, but before killing her take time to see her guts, to see what she looks like'. He then ordered the *Interahamwe* to continue with their 'work' on the other girls, and instructed them that they should disembowel the girls before killing them. The Chamber received hearsay evidence as to what happened to the girls, but finds that this evidence lacks sufficient indicia of reliability to prove that they were raped following the Accused's instruction. The Chamber finds the Defence evidence presented in rebuttal of this allegation that the Accused raped Agnes Mukagatere to be unconvincing. Witnesses DAA, DC, DA, and DL testified that they did not hear of any rapes committed at the cemetery. In the opinion of the Chamber, this might be true, but it does not make it impossible that these events occurred. Furthermore, the Chamber recalls its finding that Witness DA is not a credible witness. Witnesses DG and DF described incidents they witnessed or heard about involving girls being taken to the cemetery, where neither the Accused was present nor were any girls raped. Witness DF mentioned different names to those mentioned by Witness AV, and in any case could not remember the date on which this happened. It is difficult to conclude that the witnesses are recalling the same event. The Defence presented evidence regarding the death of the Accused's son, the mourning period, and the funeral on 10 April 1994. However, for reasons already noted, the alibi is not persuasive. It does not render the Accused's presence elsewhere impossible. Indeed, as has already been noted, both Prosecution Witnesses AV and AF, and Defence Witness DC, place the Accused at Mubuga Church on 15 April 1994. Consequently, the Chamber finds that the Prosecution has proved beyond reasonable doubt the allegation in Paragraph 6 (b) of the Indictment and the relevant sections of the Pre-Trial Brief, that, on 15 April 1994, the Accused, acting in concert with a group of *Interahamwe*, abducted a group of *Tutsi* girls, and led them to a cemetery near Mubuga Church. The Accused then raped one of the abducted girls, Agnes Mukagatere. The Chamber finds insufficient evidence to establish the allegation that two *Tutsi* girls, called Alphonsine and Colette, were raped by the *Interahamwe* in the presence of and on the instructions of the Accused. Consequently, the Chamber dismisses the allegation in Paragraph 6 (b) (i) of the Indictment".[536] - Alleged rapes of Josiana, Martha and Mariana in mid-April 1994: "The Chamber accepts the evidence that the Accused, Sikubwabo, and Gisambo took Josiana, Martha, and Mariana away in a vehicle. However, the Chamber finds insufficient evidence to prove that the Accused raped any of the women. A single witness, Witness BI, testified about the alleged rapes of the three women. He was not an eyewitness to the alleged rapes. The women told the witness that they had been raped but did not give any information as to who raped whom or provide any details as to the circumstances under which the rapes had occurred. The Chamber finds that the Prosecution has failed to prove that the Accused participated in the alleged abduction and rape of three civilian *Tutsi* women from Mugonero Complex. Consequently, the Chamber dismisses the allegations in Paragraph 6 (c) of the Indictment".[537] - Rape of Mukasine Kajongi at Mugonero complex on 16 April 1994: "On the basis of inconsistent information contained in Witness AT's out-of-court written statements of 1996, 1999, and 2002, in regard to the number and the identity of victims allegedly raped by the Accused, the Defence asserts that the witness is not reliable or credible. After a careful review of the written statements and the oral testimony of Witness AT, the Chamber finds that the inconsistencies relate only to minor details and do not undermine the overall credibility of Witness AT's account of the

536 *Muhimana* Trial Judgement, paras. 191–205 (internal references omitted).

537 *Muhimana* Trial Judgement, paras. 223–225 (internal reference omitted).

	acts of rapes. The Defence points out that Witness AT recollected the rape of Mukasine Kajongi for the first time in his written statement of 12 November 1999. The Defence contends that the omission of this rape in the prior 1996 statement affects the credibility of the witness' testimony. The Chamber notes the witness' explanation, during cross-examination, that the 1996 statement focused on the attack itself, not on particular incidents which occurred during the course of the attack. The Chamber further notes that, in his later out-of-court statements of 1999 and 2002, as well as in his oral testimony, the witness was consistent in his description of the rape of Mukasine Kajongi. The Chamber therefore is of the view that the omission of the rape of Mukasine Kajongi in the 1996 statement does not, in and of itself, affect the witness' credibility. The Defence contends that Witness AT's testimony did not provide a credible account of the location of the room in the surgical theatre in Mugonero Hospital, where he allegedly hid and witnessed rapes committed by the Accused and others. In support of its argument, the Defence refers to the testimony of its Witness AR1 that there were not many rooms in the surgical theatre and that the rooms for post-surgery patients were far from the surgery ward. The Chamber notes that Witness AT did not assert that the surgical theatre consisted of many rooms. Rather, the witness testified only that there were more than two rooms in the surgical area, located in the basement of the hospital. The Defence also points to inconsistencies between the witness' testimony before the Chamber and his evidence presented in the *Ntakirutimana* case about the location of his hiding place in the surgical theatre. In light of the trauma which the witness experienced at the time of the events, the passage of time, as well as the witness' prior lack of familiarity with the surgical theatre, the Chamber finds that the inconsistency with regard to the witness' location in Mugonero Hospital does not undermine the credibility of the witness' testimony. The Chamber also accepts Witness AT's account of how he hid under corpses and that from his position he could see the Accused and the other alleged perpetrators of the crimes. The Chamber finds credible Witness AT's testimony that he was approximately four and half metres away when the Accused 'took his gun, … hit Mukasine on her body with the butt of the gun … opened up her legs forcefully, … took his penis and thrust it into the vagina of his victim.' On the basis of the witness' detailed description of the rapes, his proximity to the crimes, and his plausible explanation that the Accused and the other perpetrators could not see him as he lifted his head up and down from his hiding place because 'they were busy raping those young girls,' the Chamber finds the witness' account of the rape to be credible and reliable. The Chamber has already found Witness AT to be credible. On the basis of her testimony, the Chamber finds that the Accused told Mukasine Kajongi to undress and that, upon her refusal, and notwithstanding her plea for mercy, threw her on the floor, undressed her forcefully and took off her underwear. He then hit her with the butt of his gun, parted her legs forcefully, and thrust his penis into her vagina. At the same time and in the same area where the Accused raped Mukasine Kajongi in the basement of Mugonero Hospital, two soldiers, in his presence, raped the daughters of Amos Karera. By his presence during these rapes, and by his own actions in raping Mukasine, the Accused encouraged the two soldiers to rape Amos Karera's daughters. The Chamber therefore finds that the Prosecution has proved beyond reasonable doubt the allegations in Paragraph 6 (c) (i) of the Indictment".[538] - Rapes of Johaneta, Teresa Mukabutera and Eugenia at Mugonero hospital on 16 April 1994: "The Prosecution relies solely on the evidence of Witness BH in support of the allegations in Paragraph 6 (c) (iii) of the Indictment. The Chamber recalls its finding in relation on the credibility of Witness BH in relation to the attack on Mugonero Com-

538 *Muhimana* Trial Judgement, paras. 269–275 (internal reference omitted).

	plex. Similarly, the Chamber finds that Witness BH's testimony in relation to the alleged rapes of Johaneta, Theresa Mukabutera, and Eugenia lacks credibility. Consequently, the Chamber dismisses the allegation in Paragraph 6 (c) (iii) of the Indictment".[539] - Rapes of Witness BJ, Mukasine and Murekatete at the Mugonero complex on 16 April 1994: "The Prosecution relies on the evidence of Witness BJ to establish the allegation that the Accused and *Interahamwe* collectively raped her and two *Tutsi* staff maids from Mugonero Hospital, Mukasine and Murekatete. The Chamber has found Witness BJ credible and reliable. This finding is based on her straightforward and detailed testimony and her demeanour in Court. The Defence challenges Witness BJ's credibility on the grounds that, when the Accused, in the hospital basement, said that he wanted to see the private parts of a *Tutsi* woman, she did not disclose her *Hutu* ethnicity. The Chamber accepts the witness' explanation that she did not realise that only *Tutsi* were being targeted but thought, at that time, that all Rwandans were the same, as they had taken refuge in the same place. The Chamber accepts the witness' explanation and does not find the Defence contention persuasive. The Chamber finds that, on 16 April 1994, in the basement of Mugonero Hospital, at Mugonero Complex, the Accused raped Witness BJ, a young *Hutu* girl, whom he mistook for a *Tutsi*. At the same time, the two men who were accompanying the Accused raped the two other girls, named Mukasine and Murekatete, whose ethnicity is unknown. Consequently, the Chamber finds that the Prosecution has proved beyond reasonable doubt the allegation in Paragraph 6 (c) (ii) of the Indictment".[540] - Rapes of Witness AU, Immaculee Mukabarore, Josephine Mukankwaroa and Bernadette at Mugonero hospital on 16 April 1994: "The Prosecution relies on the testimony of Witness AU to establish the allegation in Paragraph 6 (c) (iv) of the Indictment that the Accused and *Interahamwe* collectively raped *Tutsi* women AU, Immaculate Mukabarore, and Josephine Mukankwaro. Specifically, the Prosecution alleges that the Accused raped Witness AU. The Defence challenges the credibility of Witness AU on the basis of alleged inconsistencies in her testimony concerning the identities of other rape victims and her failure to recall their full names. On the basis of Witness AU's testimony, which the Chamber has found credible, the Chamber finds that on 16 April 1994, in the basement of Mugonero Hospital, at Mugonero Complex, the Accused raped Witness AU twice. The Prosecution also charges the Accused with the collective rape of Immaculee Mukabarore and Josephine Mukankwaro. By virtue of her location, and the fact that she was being violently raped at the time, the Chamber finds that she may not have been in a position to observe what was being done to other girls in the hallway. Consequently, the Chamber finds proved beyond reasonable doubt the allegation in Paragraph 6 (c) (iv) of the Indictment that the Accused personally raped Witness AU on 16 April 1994 in a room in the basement of Mugonero Hospital. However, the Chamber finds that the Prosecution has failed to prove the allegation that the *Interahamwe* raped Immaculee Mukabarore and Josephine Mukankwaro in the presence of the Accused".[541] - Rape of Witness BG on 22 April 1994: "In light of the evidence and submissions of the Parties, the Chamber finds credible Witness BG's testimony that the Accused allowed an *Interahamwe*, Mugonero, to

539 *Muhimana* Trial Judgement, paras. 281–282 (internal reference omitted).

540 *Muhimana* Trial Judgement, paras. 288–292 (internal reference omitted).

541 *Muhimana* Trial Judgement, paras. 300–304.

	abduct and rape her. The Chamber accepts Witness BG's testimony that, on 22 April 1994, on a Bisesero Hill, she and other refugees who were in hiding were found by the Accused, Mugonero, and a group of *Interahamwe*. Mugonero asked the Accused if he could take away the witness so that he could 'smell the body of a *Tutsi* woman'. It is apparent to the Chamber, from the witness' testimony, that Mugonero's words meant that he wanted to rape her. The Chamber finds that the Accused granted his request, following which Mugonero took the witness to his house in Muramba. There, the witness was kept in a locked room, with *Interahamwe* standing guard on the outside of the room, where the witness was raped several times until she escaped on 24 April 1994. The Chamber notes the Defence contention that the witness voluntarily 'married' Mugonero, who gave her protection. In support of this version of the incident, the Defence relied on the evidence of Witness DAC, whom the Chamber finds not to be a credible witness. The Defence also challenges Witness BG's credibility because of her inability to describe the vehicle in which she was taken to Mugonero's house, her description of the size of the window in the room in which she was detained, and her escape through a window in the house, which was surrounded by *Interahamwe*. Having considered the evidence and the Parties' submissions, the Chamber finds Witness BG's account of her abduction and rape credible and reliable. In light of the coercive circumstances prevailing in the Bisesero area at this time, the Chamber is not persuaded by the testimonies of Defence Witnesses DAB and DAC that Witness BG consented to 'marry', or cohabit with Mugonero, an *Interahamwe*, who had participated in killing other refugees who had been in hiding with the witness. The Chamber finds the testimony of Witnesses DAB and DAC implausible. In the Chamber's view, the inconsistencies in Witness BG's account of her abduction and rape, such as the circumstances surrounding her detention and eventual escape, are insignificant, and do not undermine the credibility and reliability of her evidence. Accordingly, the Chamber finds that the Accused permitted Mugonero to take away Witness BG, knowing that he wanted to rape her. The Chamber further finds that Mugonero raped Witness BG several times in his house, as alleged in Paragraph 6 (d) of the Indictment".[542] - Rape of Witness AX in May 1994: "The Prosecution relies on the testimony of Witness AX in support of the allegation that the Accused raped her on two occasions 'towards the end of April 1994'. Witness AX was visibly traumatized whilst recalling before the Chamber what happened to her family and her. Apart from her own injuries, Witness AX lost her mother, her four children, and her husband during the events of 1994. Despite this tragedy, her testimony was clear, straightforward, and convincing. The Chamber finds her to be a credible witness. The Chamber rejects Witness DS's opinion that it is impossible for a married man to commit rape. The Chamber does not accept Witness DS's testimony that he never heard of any rapes in Gishyita *Commune*, in the light of abundant testimony to the contrary. The testimony of many witnesses that Gishyita *Secteur* had no official *secteur* office is inconsequential. Witness AX testified that she was taken to a building which the Accused used as his office. Whether that building was the *commune* office or the *secteur* office is immaterial. The Chamber accepts Witness AX's testimony that she was raped twice by the Accused after he summoned her to his office, once in May 1994, and again in June 1994. Unfortunately, the Prosecution pleaded in the Indictment that the rapes occurred during April 1994. The witness' testimony cannot therefore be reconciled with the allegations contained in the Indictment. Moreover, the Prosecution failed to provide the Defence with clear and consistent notice of the material facts in support of this allegation. Consequently, the Chamber dismisses the allegations contained in Paragraph 6 (a) (iii) of the Indictment".[543]

[542] *Muhimana* Trial Judgement, paras. 318–323.

[543] *Muhimana* Trial Judgement, paras. 385–390 (internal reference omitted).

	- Alleged rape of Pascasie Mukamera in mid-May 1994: "The Prosecution alleges that the actions of the Accused, in cutting open Pascasie Mukaremera from her breasts to her vagina, constitute rape, as alleged in Paragraph 6 (d) (ii) of the Indictment. The Chamber will consider this argument in the Legal Findings Chapter".[544] "The Chamber finds that the Accused bears no criminal responsibility for the rape of Pascasie Mukaremera. In its factual findings, the Chamber has found that the Accused disembowelled Pascasie Mukaremera by cutting her open with a machete from her breasts to her vagina. The Chamber has carefully considered the Prosecution's submission to consider this act as rape, and concludes that such conduct cannot be classified as rape. Although the act interferes with the sexual organs, in the Chamber's opinion, it does not constitute a physical invasion of a sexual nature".[545] - Rape of Félicité Kankuyu in mid-May 1994: "The Chamber accepts the testimony of Witness AW as credible. The witness testified to the rape and murder of Félicité Kankuyu, whom the witness knew, which occurred about an hour after the disembowelment of Pascasie Mukaremera. The witness testified that, after the death of Pascasie, the assailants found Félicité and alerted the Accused and Sikubwabo. The latter ordered that she be brought to them, and the assailants complied. The witness testified that Sikubwabo called the Accused to come and 'have intercourse' with this woman. The Accused then took the woman, undressed and raped her, after which the Accused invited the five *Interahamwe* to rape and kill her 'because she's also an Inyenzi'. The *Interahamwe* duly complied, in the Accused's presence, and then thrust pieces of wood into her genitals until she died. While the Chamber accepts Witness AW's testimony on the chain of events, as described above, the Chamber notes that Paragraphs 6 (d) (iii) and 7 (d) (ii) of the Indictment charge these events as two separate incidents, occurring a month apart and in two different locations. The Chamber observes that Witness AW neither mentions Ngabonzina nor indicates that Félicité was raped in Gitwa Hills. The time and the location of the alleged crimes, as set out in Paragraphs 6 (d) (iii) and 7 (d) (ii) of the Indictment, are clearly at variance with the evidence. Consequently, the Chamber finds that the Prosecution has failed to prove the allegations contained in Paragraphs 6 (d) (iii) and 7 (d) (ii) of the Indictment".[546] - Responsibility of Mikaeli Muhimana for rapes constituting genocide: "The Chamber finds that, through personal commission, the Accused killed and caused serious bodily or mental harm to members of the *Tutsi* group: By taking part in attacks at Mugonero Complex, where he raped *Tutsi* women and shot at *Tutsi* refugees. Many *Tutsi* refugees died or were injured in the attack".[547] "The Accused targeted *Tutsi* civilians during these attacks by shooting and raping *Tutsi* victims. He also raped a young *Hutu* girl, Witness BJ, whom he believed to be *Tutsi*, but later apologised to her when he was informed that she was *Hutu*. During the course of some of the attacks and rapes, the Accused specifically referred to the *Tutsi* ethnic identity of his victims. Thus, the Chamber finds that the Accused's participation in the attacks, and his words and deeds demonstrate his intent to destroy, in whole or

544 *Muhimana* Trial Judgement, para. 408.

545 *Muhimana* Trial Judgement, para. 557.

546 *Muhimana* Trial Judgement, paras. 409–411.

547 *Muhimana* Trial Judgement, para. 513(c) (internal reference omitted).

	in part, the *Tutsi* group. The Chamber therefore finds the Accused, Mika Muhimana, GUILTY of GENOCIDE, as charged under Count 1 of the Indictment".[548] - Responsibility of Mikaeli Muhimana for rape as CAH: "On the basis of the above analysis, the Chamber finds that, during the months of April and May 1994, the Accused committed rape: (a) On 7 April 1994, in Gishyita town, the Accused took two women, Gorretti Mukashyaka and Languida Kamukina, into his house and raped them. Thereafter he drove them out of his house naked and invited *Interahamwe* and other civilians to see what naked *Tutsi* girls looked like; (b) During the first week after the eruption of hostilities, the Accused pushed Esperance Mukagasana onto his bed, stripped her naked, and raped her. He raped her in his home several times; (c) On 15 April 1994, the Accused, acting in concert with a group of *Interahamwe*, abducted a group of *Tutsi* girls and led them to a cemetery near Mubuga Parish Church. The Accused then raped one of the abducted girls, Agnes Mukagatere; (d) On 16 April 1994, in the basement of Mugonero Hospital, at Mugonero Complex, the Accused raped Mukasine Kajongi; (e) On 16 April 1994, in a room of the basement of Mugonero Hospital, at Mugonero Complex, the Accused raped Witness AU twice; (f) On 16 April 1994, in the basement of Mugonero Hospital, at Mugonero Complex, the Accused raped Witness BJ, a young *Hutu* girl, whom he mistook for a *Tutsi*. He later apologised to her for the rape, when he was informed by an *Interahamwe* that BJ was not a *Tutsi*. The Chamber finds that the Accused also abetted in the commission of rapes by others: (a) On 16 April 1994, at the same time and in the same area where the Accused raped Mukasine Kajongi in the basement of Mugonero Hospital, two soldiers, in his presence, raped the daughters of Amos Karera. The presence of the Accused during the rape of Amos Karera's daughters coupled with his own action of raping Mukasine, encouraged the two soldiers to rape Amos Karera's daughters. This encouragement contributed substantially to the commission of these rapes; (b) On 16 April 1994, while the Accused was raping Witness BJ in the basement of Mugonero Hospital, two men, who accompanied him, were also raping two other girls named Murekatete and Mukasine. The Accused, by his actions, encouraged the other men to commit the rapes of Murekatete and Mukasine. This encouragement contributed substantially to the commission of these rapes; (c) On 22 April 1994, the Accused permitted an *Interahamwe* named Mugonero to take Witness BG away so that he could 'smell the body of a *Tutsi* woman'. The witness was raped several times in Mugonero's residence over a period of two days. The Chamber finds that by allowing Mugonero to take Witness BG home, the Accused encouraged him to rape Witness BG. This encouragement contributed substantially to the commission of the rape. The Chamber finds insufficient evidence to prove the allegations that the Accused bears criminal responsibility for: (a) the collective rape of Immaculee Mukabarore and Josephine Mukankwaro, who, according to the Prosecution, were raped by *Interahamwe* at the same time that the Accused raped Witness AU; (b) killings, rapes, and other atrocities which the Prosecution alleges were linked to a meeting held in the Accused's residence on 7 April 1994; (c) abetting the rape of Esperance Mukagasana in the Accused's house, by offering her to an *Interahamwe* named Gisambo; (d) the rape of Josiana, Mariana Gafurafura and Martha Gafurafura in Gishyita, following their abduction on 13 April 1994; (e) the rape of Johaneta, Teresa Mukabutera and Eugenia at the Mugonero hospital on 16 April 1994. The Chamber also finds that the Accused bears no criminal responsibility for the rape of Felicité Kankuyu, because the evidence led by the Prosecution did not support the facts as pleaded in the Indictment. The Chamber finds that the Accused bears no criminal responsibility for the rapes of Witness AX, because the Prosecution failed to plead the material fact of the dates of the crime accurately, thus rendering the Indictment defective. The Chamber has exam-

548 *Muhimana* Trial Judgement, paras. 517–519.

	ined the Prosecution's Pre-Trial Brief and the witness statements and finds that this defect was not cured by clear and consistent notice. The Chamber finds that the Accused bears no criminal responsibility for the rape of Pascasie Mukaremera. In its factual findings, the Chamber has found that the Accused disembowelled Pascasie Mukaremera by cutting her open with a machete from her breasts to her vagina. The Chamber has carefully considered the Prosecution's submission to consider this act as rape, and concludes that such conduct cannot be classified as rape. Although the act interferes with the sexual organs, in the Chamber's opinion, it does not constitute a physical invasion of a sexual nature. However, the Chamber will return to consider this incident under its legal findings on murder. The Chamber recalls its finding that a discriminatory, widespread and systematic attack was carried out against a group of *Tutsi* civilians in Gishyita *Commune*, between the months of April and June 1994. The Chamber recalls its finding that the Accused participated in attacks against *Tutsi* during April, May, and June 1994 and that in doing so, he intended to destroy the *Tutsi* ethnic group. Consequently, the Chamber finds that the Accused knew that all of these rapes were part of a discriminatory, widespread, and systematic attack against *Tutsi* civilians. The Chamber finds that the Accused chose his rape victims because he believed that they were *Tutsi*. Whether the victims were in fact *Tutsi* is irrelevant in the determination of the Accused's criminal responsibility. The Chamber concludes, on the basis of the Accused's conduct, that he raped his victims with the knowledge that the rapes formed part of a widespread and systematic attack on the *Tutsi* civilian population. Accordingly, the Chamber finds the Accused Mika Muhimana criminally liable for committing and abetting the rapes charged, as part of a widespread and systematic attack against a civilian population. Consequently, the Chamber finds the Accused Mika Muhimana GUILTY of RAPE AS A CRIME AGAINST HUMANITY, under Count 3 of the Indictment".[549] However, the Appeals Chamber reversed Mikaeli Muhimana's conviction for rape insofar as it concerns the rapes of Gorretti Mukashyaka and Languida Kamukina: "The Trial Chamber found that, on 7 April 1994, the Appellant raped two Tutsi women, Languida Kamukina and Goretti Mukashyaka, in his home and, as a result, convicted him of rape as a crime against humanity. In making this finding, the Trial Chamber relied on the evidence of Prosecution Witness AP, holding as follows: 'Although Witness AP was not an eyewitness to the rape of Goretti and Languida, the Chamber infers that the Accused raped them on the basis of the following factors: the witness saw the Accused take the girls into his house; she heard the victims scream, mentioning the Accused's name and stating that they 'did not expect him to do that' to them; finally the witness saw the Accused lead the victims out of his house, stark naked, and she noticed that they were walking 'with their legs apart'.' The Appellant submits that the Trial Chamber erred in law and in fact in relying on Witness AP's uncorroborated circumstantial evidence of the rapes, in assessing Witness AP's credibility, and in assessing Defence evidence. Recalling the elements of rape as defined in the *Kunarac et al.* case at the ICTY, the Appellant alleges that, because Witness AP was not an eyewitness, she was not in a position to establish the *actus reus* of rape. The Prosecution responds that any crime under the jurisdiction of the Tribunal may be established through circumstantial evidence and that there is no rule requiring direct evidence to prove the *actus reus* of rape. Moreover, the Prosecution submits that Witness AP gave both direct and circumstantial evidence, which was 'detailed, credible and 'internally consistent'.' The Appeals Chamber recalls that it is permissible to base a conviction on circumstantial evidence and that a Trial Chamber has the discretion to decide in the circumstances of each case whether corroboration of evidence is necessary. The Trial Chamber's finding that the Appellant raped Languida Kamukina and Goretti Mukashyaka is based on the testimony of Witness AP who described their

549 *Muhimana* Trial Judgement, paras. 552–563 (internal references omitted).

	maltreatment. In such circumstances, the Appeals Chamber can identify no factual error on the part of the Trial Chamber in concluding that these two women were raped in the Appellant's home. The above-quoted text, in particular coupled with the evidence of widespread rape committed in the course of the crimes perpetrated by the Appellant, provides a sufficient basis for this conclusion. However, it is apparent from Witness AP's testimony that the Appellant was not alone with the young women in the house at the relevant time. Witness AP testified that '[a]mongst the voices coming from inside the house, the witness also recognised the voice of *Bourgmestre* Sikubwabo, telling the girls to 'shut up'.' Consequently, the Appeals Chamber is not persuaded that the Trial Chamber acted reasonably in determining that it was the Appellant who raped the two women, rather than another person present in the house, such as Sikubwabo. Accordingly, the Appeals Chamber finds, Judge Shahabuddeen and Judge Schomburg dissenting, that the Trial Chamber erred in fact in convicting the Appellant for committing rape based on this event and reverses this factual finding. Even if Witness AP's evidence, as accepted by the Trial Chamber, demonstrated that the Appellant could bear criminal responsibility for the rapes of these women as an aider and abettor, the Prosecution did not charge this form of criminal responsibility in connection with these rapes, and, therefore, it would not be appropriate for the Appeals Chamber to uphold the conviction on this basis. The Trial Chamber's error of fact, however, did not occasion a miscarriage of justice because no conviction on any count of the Indictment rested solely on these rapes. The Appellant's conviction for rape as a crime against humanity, for which he was sentenced to life imprisonment, rests on his commission of or complicity in the rapes of ten other individuals. Accordingly, the Appeals Chamber is not satisfied that its finding of error on the part of the Trial Chamber with respect to the rape of Languida Kamukina and Goretti Mukashyaka is sufficient to impugn his conviction for rape as a crime against humanity. The Appeals Chamber is also not satisfied that this error affects the Appellant's sentence of imprisonment for the remainder of his life in view of the other crimes and the appropriateness of considering this event in aggravation. Accordingly, the Appeals Chamber finds no basis for disturbing the Appellant's conviction or sentence due to this error of fact".[550]

10. Jean **Mpambara** (Case No. ICTR-01-65) Bourgmestre of Rukara commune, in Kibungo prefecture.	
Indictment (International sex crimes (or related) charges and mode(s) of liability)	- **Genocide** (count 1) or, alternatively, **Complicity in genocide** (count 2) under Article 6(1) of the Statute (**aiding and abetting by omission** or, alternatively, **joint criminal enterprise – third category**) for the acts of sexual violence committed against Tutsi women between 6 and 16 April 1994, including: (i) the rape of a Tutsi woman by two attackers in Gahini secteur, in Rukara commune, on or about 8 April 1994; (ii) the rape of a pregnant Hutu woman married to a Tutsi man by multiple attackers in Nyawera secteur, in Rukara commune, on or about 11 April 1994; and (iii) the rapes of a number of Tutsi women by soldiers during the attacks on Rukara parish between 7 and 16 April 1994.[551]

[550] *Muhimana* Appeal Judgement, paras. 46–53 (internal references omitted).

[551] *Prosecutor v. Jean Mpambara*, Case No. ICTR-01-65-I, Amended Indictment, 7 March 2005, p. 2 ("**Count 1: GENOCIDE** The Prosecutor of the International Criminal Tribunl for Rwanda charges **Jean MPAMBARA** with **GENOCIDE**, a crime stipulated in Article 2(3)(a) of the Statute, in that on or between the dates of 6 April 1994 and 16 April 1994, particularly in Rukara Commune and generally in Kibungo Prefecture, **Jean MPAMBARA** was responsible for killing or causing serious bodily or mental harm to members of the Tutsi racial or ethnic group, with intent to destroy, in whole or in part, a racial or ethnic group, as such, as outlined in paragraphs 1 through 20. ***Alternatively*** **Count 2: COMPLICITY IN GENOCIDE** The Prosecu-

Trial Judgement	- Jean Mpambara was found not guilty of all charges.[552]
Appeal Judgement	N/A (The Prosecution did not appeal the acquittal.)
Legal and Factual Findings and/or Evidence	N/A (There are no legal or factual findings on international sex crimes in the Trial Judgement.)

11. Tharcisse **Muvunyi** (Case No. ICTR-00-55A) Lieutenant-Colonel in the Rwandan Army stationed at *Ecole des sous-officiers* (ESO).	
Indictment (International sex crimes (or related) charges and mode(s) of liability)	- **Genocide** (count 1) or, alternatively, **Complicity in genocide** (count 2) and **Rape as CAH** (count 4) under Article 6(3) of the Statute (**superior responsibility**) for the rapes – including gang-rapes, multiple rapes, rapes of virgin girls, rapes of daughters in front of their mothers or other family members, which involved violence and degrading treatment – and sexual assaults of Tutsi women and girls committed by *Interahawe* and soldiers of the Ngoma Camp at Ngoma parish in Ngoma commune, at Matyazo dispensary in Matyazo, at Kibeho parish in Mugusa commune, at Beneberika convent in Sovu in Huye commune, at *groupe scolaire* in Ngoma, at *economat general* in Gatare commune and at Muslim quarters in Ngoma commune.[553]

tor of the International Criminal Tribunal for Rwanda charges **Jean MPAMBARA** with **COMPLICITY IN GENOCIDE**, a crime stipulated in Article 2(3)(e) of the Statute, in that on or between the dates of 6 April 1994 and 16 April 1994, particularly in Rukara Commune and generally in Kibungo Prefecture, **Jean MPAMBARA** was responsible for killing or causing serious bodily or mental harm to members of the Tutsi racial or ethnic, with intent to destroy, in whole or in part, a racial or ethnic group, as such, or with knowledge that other people intended to destroy, in whole or in part, the Tutsi racial or ethnic group, as such, and that his assistance would contribute to the crime of genocide, as outlined in paragraphs 1 through 20".), para. 20 ("Between 6 and 16 April 1994, Tutsi women were often victims of sexual violence. The sexual assaults were a prelude to murder, and were often the cause of death. The sexual violence was widespread, conducted openly, and was integrally incorporated in generalized attacks against Tutsi civilians, that **Jean MPAMBARA** knew, or should have known, that it was occurring, and the perpetrators were his subordinates, subject to his authority and control, or acting under his orders or those of the other participants in the joint criminal enterprise. Alternatively, **Jean MPAMBARA** knew, or should have known, that the perpetrators' actions were a foreseeable outcome of the objectives and implementation of the joint criminal enterprise. For example: (i) on or about 8 April 1994, a Tutsi woman in Gahini *secteur*, Rukara *commune*, was beaten and raped by two attackers. The two attackers each raped her, beat her with a hoe until her teeth fell out, and then attacked her with machetes; (ii) on or about 11 April 1994, a Hutu pregnant woman married to a Tutsi man was raped, in Nyawera *secteur*, Rukara Commune, by multiple attackers and, as a result, lost her Tutsi baby. One of the rapists was the leader of the attackers who attacked and destroyed her house two days earlier; (iii) between 7 and 16 April 1994, soldiers who reinforced the Interahamwe during attacks on Rukara Parish raped a number of Tutsi women at or near the Parish complex".).

552 *Prosecutor v. Jean Mpambara*, Case No. ICTR-01-65-T, Judgement, dated 11 September 2006 and filed on 12 September 2006, para. 175.

553 *Prosecutor v. Tharcisse Muvunyi*, Case No. ICTR-00-55A-I, Indictment, 23 December 2003, paras. 3.40–3.41(i) ("During the event referred to in this indictment, thousands of civilians, mostly Tutsi, in Butare *prefecture*, were massacred, including at the following locations: *-Ngoma parish, Ngoma Commune –Matyazo Duspensary, Matyazo –Kibeho parish, Mugusa Commune –Beneberika Convent, Sovu, Huye Commune –Groupe Scolaire, Ngoma –Economat Generale, Ngoma Commune –Nyumba parish, Gatare Commune –Muslim Quarters, Ngoma commune*. During the course of the acts referred to in Paragraphs 3.40 above, many women and girls were raped and sexually violated in these locations or were taken by force or coerced

Trial Judgement	- Not guilty of rape as CAH (count 4) because the Trial Chamber found that the evidence heard that soldiers from ESO Camp committed rape does not support the specific allegation in the Indictment that soldiers from Ngoma Camp committed rape and, therefore, it would be prejudicial and unfair to hold this evidence against Tharcisse Muvunyi.[554] - Although Tharcisse Muvunyi was convicted for genocide, the underlying offences of this crime did not include rapes or sexual assaults.[555]
Appeal Judgement	- The Appeals Chamber dismissed the Prosecution's ground of appeal challenging Muvunyi's acquittal for rape as CAH (count 4) and confirmed his acquittal.[556]
Legal and Factual Findings and/or Evidence	- Legal findings: **- Rape: definition:** The Trial Chamber held: "In *Muhimana* this Tribunal expressed the view that the *Akayesu* and *Kunarac* definitions of rape are not incompatible and noted that '[w]hereas *Akayesu* referred broadly to a 'physical invasion of a sexual nature', *Kunarac* went on to articulate the parameters of what would constitute a physical invasion of a sexual nature amounting to rape.' The Chamber agrees with the above analysis and considers that the underlying objective of the prohibition of rape at international law is to penalise serious violations of sexual autonomy. A violation of sexual autonomy ensues whenever a person is subjected to sexual acts of the genre listed in *Kunarac* to which he/she has not consented, or to which he/she is not a voluntary partici-

to other locations, where they were raped and subjected to acts of sexual violence by *Interahamwe* and soldiers from the Ngoma Camp. Lieutenant Colonel **MUVUNYI** by reason of his position of authority and the widespread nature of these acts, knew or had reason to know, that these acts were being committed and he failed to take measures to prevent, or to put an end to these acts, or punish the perpetrators. In most cases the rapes were aggravated by circumstances of gang rape, multiple rape, rape of virgin girls, rape of daughters in front of their mothers or other family members, which involved violence and degrading treatment to the persons involved. Most of these acts of sexual violence were accompanied by the killing of the victim".), 3.51 ("The accused […] equally intended the various acts of sexual violence and incitement to sexual violence described above in paragraphs 3.47 to 3.47(i) as actions contributing to the non-international armed conflict against the RPF and the fulfilment of the aims of the Rwandan Government in defeating the enemy and its accomplices".), pp. 15–17 (**COUNT 1:** By the acts or omissions described specifically in the paragraphs to which reference is made herein below: **Tharcisse MUVUNYI** pursuant to Article 6(1) paragraphs […] 3.41–3.41(i) […] pursuant to Article 6(3) paragraphs […] 3.35–3.43, […] is responsible for killing and causing serious bodily and mental harm to members of the Tutsi population, with the intent to destroy, in whole or in part, an ethnic or racial group as such, and thereby committed **GENOCIDE**, stipulated in Article 2(3)(a) as a crime, for which he is individually responsible, and which is punishable in reference to Articles 22 and 23 of the Statute of the Tribunal **ALTERNATIVELY COUNT 2:** By the acts or omissions described specifically in the paragraphs to which reference is made herein below: **Tharcisse MUVUNYI** pursuant to Article 6(1) paragraphs […] 3.41–3.41(i) […] pursuant to Article 6(3) paragraphs […] 3.41–3.41(i) […] is responsible for killing and causing serious bodily and mental harm to members of the Tutsi population with the intent to destroy in whole or in part, a racial or ethnic group, and thereby committed **COMPLICITY IN GENOCIDE**, stipulated in Article 2(3)(e) as a crime, for which he is individually responsible, and which is punishable in reference to Articles 22 and 23 of the Statute of the Tribunal. […] **COUNT 4:** By the acts or omissions described specifically in the paragraphs to which reference is made herein below: **Tharcisse MUVUNYI** pursuant to Article 6(3) paragraphs paragraphs 3.41 and 3.41(i) is responsible for rape as part of a widespread and systematic attack against a population, on political, ethnic or racial grounds, and thereby committed a **CRIME AGAINST HUMANITY** stipulated in Article 3(g) as a crime, for which he is individually responsible, and which is punishable in reference to Articles 22 and 23 of the Statute of the Tribunal".).

554 *Prosecutor v. Tharcisse Muvunyi*, Case No. ICTR-00-55A-T, Judgement and Sentence, dated 12 September 2006 and filed on 18 September 2006 ("*Muvunyi* Trial Judgement"), paras. 400–409, 526, 531.

555 *Muvunyi* Trial Judgement, paras. 400–409, 526, 531.

556 *Prosecutor v. Tharcisse Muvunyi*, Case No. ICTR-00-55A-A, Judgement, 29 August 2008 ("*Muvunyi* Appeal Judgement"), paras. 160–169, 171.

	pant. Lack of consent therefore continues to be an important ingredient of rape as a crime against humanity. The fact that unwanted sexual activity takes place under coercive or forceful circumstances may provide evidence of lack of consent on the part of the victim. The Chamber considers that in their result, both the *Akayesu* and *Kunarac* definitions of rape reflect this objective of protecting individual sexual autonomy and therefore are not incompatible. The broad language in *Akayesu* that rape constitutes 'physical invasion of a sexual nature', when properly interpreted, could include 'sexual penetration' as stipulated in *Kunarac*. The Chamber therefore concludes that the offence of rape exists whenever there is sexual penetration of the vagina, anus or mouth of the victim, by the penis of the perpetrator or some other object under, circumstances where the victim did not agree to the sexual act or was otherwise not a willing participant to it. The *mens rea* consists of the intent of the perpetrator to effect such sexual penetration with knowledge that it occurs without the consent of the victim".[557] - <u>Factual and legal findings:</u> - Pleading of rape in the Indictment: "The Indictment alleges that many women and girls were raped and sexually assaulted by *Interahamwe* and soldiers from the Ngoma Camp. At Paragraph 82 of its Pre-Trial Brief, however, the Prosecution stated that the acts of rape were committed by *Interahamwe* as well as soldiers from the Ngoma and ESO Camps and the *gendarmerie*. Similarly, during its Opening Statement, the Prosecution indicated that it would lead evidence to show that soldiers from the ESO and Ngoma Camps under the command of the Accused committed rape. The question to be considered is whether by including the ESO soldiers in the Pre-Trial Brief and its Opening Statement, the Prosecution discharged its obligation to give clear and timely notice in order to put the Defence on alert in respect of this charge. Pursuant to Article 20(4)(a) of the Statute, an accused has the right to be informed of the nature and cause of the charges against him. According to the Appeals Chamber, when considered in light of Rule 47(C), this provision translates into a prosecutorial obligation 'to state the material facts underpinning the charges in the indictment, but not the evidence by which such material facts are to be proven.' The Chamber notes that the evidence of Witnesses AFV and QY that they were raped by soldiers from ESO does not support the very clear and specific allegation in the Indictment that soldiers from Ngoma Camp and *Interahamwe* were responsible for the said rapes. In the Chamber's view, the allegation that ESO soldiers committed rape in Butare in 1994 is a material fact that should have been pleaded in the Indictment, not a mere evidential detail that could be introduced at a later stage. It is clear from the jurisprudence of the *ad hoc* Tribunals that in certain limited circumstances the Prosecution may cure a defective indictment by giving timely, clear and consistent notice to the Defence through subsequent communications such as the Pre-Trial Brief, witness statements, or the opening statement. Thus, a vague or otherwise defective indictment can be cured through these means if it merely fails to set out the particulars of the Prosecution case with sufficient specificity. As stated by the ICTY Appeals Chamber, 'the question whether an indictment is pleaded with sufficient particularity is dependent upon whether it sets out the material facts of the Prosecution case with enough detail to inform a defendant clearly of the charges against him so that he may prepare his defense.' In the instant case, however, the Chamber is confronted with a very different problem. With respect to the rape charge, the Chamber is of the view that the Indictment is not vague. On the contrary, the Indictment clearly states that soldiers from Ngoma Camp committed rape. This is a clear and straightforward charge. There is no ambiguity in this. A careful consideration of all the charges contained in the Indictment reveals that the Prosecution clearly distinguished between

[557] *Muvunyi* Trial Judgement, paras. 520–522 (internal references omitted).

	the criminal acts attributed to soldiers from the Ngoma Camp and those attributed to ESO soldiers. There is specific reference to the Ngoma and ESO Camps in some charges while other charges refer only to one Camp and not to the other. Therefore, it cannot be said that it was a mistake on the part of the Prosecution to have listed only the Ngoma Camp under the rape charge. When the evidence was presented in Court during the trial, however, it turned out that it was not the soldiers from Ngoma Camp but those from the ESO Camp who had committed these acts. Lack of evidence to prove a charge does not make the charge defective. For the Prosecution to turn around in its Pre-Trial Brief and state that the ESO soldiers as well as soldiers from Ngoma Camp and *Interahamwe* committed rape could be interpreted as a radical transformation of the Prosecution case. It is clear that the Accused did not have the opportunity to defend himself against such a fundamentally different case. The Chamber therefore considers that it would be prejudicial to consider the evidence of rape by ESO soldiers in light of the allegation in the Indictment. It is clear from the Rules that the Prosecution cannot amend an existing charge in an indictment or introduce a new charge without following the proper procedure. Rule 50 deals with the amendment of indictments. Once the indictment is confirmed it can be amended only with leave of the Confirming Judge or the Trial Chamber, as the case may be. If new charges are added when the accused has already made an initial appearance before a Trial Chamber, a further appearance shall be held in order to enable the accused to enter a plea on the new charges. These provisions would be null and void if the Prosecution could amend existing charges merely by giving notice in the opening statement or Pre-Trial Brief. As mentioned earlier, if the existing charge were merely vague or otherwise defective, such defects could be cured by providing timely, clear, and consistent notice. However, when these are new charges, the matter has to be referred to the Chamber to have the indictment amended. It is generally alleged in the Indictment that the Accused was Interim Commander of ESO from about 7 April 1994. Thus the issue of his responsibility for the alleged criminal acts of his subordinates is an important matter that needs to be clearly spelt out in the Indictment, not a mere detail that can be added later at the convenience of the Prosecution. The Chamber recalls that the Prosecution sought leave to amend the Indictment, including a specific prayer to drop the rape charge, but its motion for amendment was denied on the ground, *inter alia*, that it came just before the commencement of the trial and that further delay in the opening of trial would prejudice the rights of the Accused. The matter went up to the Appeals Chamber, which proceeded to elaborate on the distinctions between a new charge and the material facts underpinning an existing charge. It should be noted, however, that the Prosecution did not seek in that instance to amend the rape charge. To establish the rape charge, the Prosecution presented the evidence of three witnesses, viz, AFV, QY and TM, all alleged victims of rape. The Prosecution also presented Witnesses YAI, CCP and YAK to show that the Accused knew or should have known that the widespread rape of Tutsi women was taking place in Butare. The Defence did not present any witness to challenge the evidence on rape but argued that the Prosecution witnesses were not credible. The Chamber has carefully considered the testimonies of Prosecution Witnesses AFV, QY and TM, and finds that their accounts of the rapes they endured are reliable. The Chamber fully understands the unique circumstances of rape victims and sympathises with them. However, in light of the very specific nature of the rape charge contained in the Indictment, and the nature of the evidence adduced at trial, the Chamber is of the view that the Prosecution has not proved beyond reasonable doubt that the Accused can be held responsible for the crime of rape as charged in Count 4 of the Indictment".[558]
	"The evidence provided in this case shows that Tutsi women as young as 17 years old were raped by soldiers during the months of April and May 1994 in the Butare and Gikongoro *préfectures*. The evidence before the Chamber establishes that Witnesses

[558] *Muvunyi* Trial Judgement, paras. 400–409 (internal references omitted).

	TM, QY and AFV were raped at various locations in Butare between April and May 1994. In each case, the evidence points to sexual penetration of the victim's vagina under circumstances in which they did not consent to such penetration. Moreover, each of these events took place in the context of widespread attacks against civilians in Butare in 1994. The legal requirements for the offence of rape as a crime against humanity have therefore been satisfied. However, in order to hold the Accused culpable, the Prosecution must also prove that he aided or abetted the commission of these rapes, or otherwise bore superior responsibility for their commission. Having concluded that the evidence heard by the Chamber does not support the specific allegation in the Indictment that soldiers from Ngoma Camp committed rape, and that it would be prejudicial and unfair to hold this evidence against the Accused, the Chamber hereby finds the Accused NOT GUILTY of rape under Count 4 of the Indictment".[559] - Alleged error related to the pleading of rape in the Indictment: "Paragraph 3.41 of the Indictment alleges that *Interahamwe* and soldiers from the Ngoma Camp raped and sexually violated women during the course of several attacks in Butare Prefecture and places responsibility on Muvunyi for failing to prevent or to punish these crimes. At trial, in support of this allegation, the Prosecution presented evidence from Prosecution Witnesses AFV, QY, and TM that ESO Camp soldiers committed rapes, but did not present any evidence of rapes committed by Ngoma Camp soldiers. The Trial Chamber held that the evidence did not support the charge of rape as pleaded, as it related to rapes committed by different perpetrators. The Trial Chamber further concluded that because of this Muvunyi did not have an adequate opportunity to defend himself against the charge and that, therefore, it would be prejudicial to hold this evidence against him. Consequently, the Trial Chamber found that the charge of rape against Muvunyi was not proven beyond reasonable doubt. The Prosecution submits that the Trial Chamber erred in law in failing to enter a conviction against Muvunyi for rape as a crime against humanity. In this respect, the Prosecution argues that the Trial Chamber erred in finding that its attempts to cure the defect in the Indictment by giving subsequent notice of its intent to hold Muvunyi responsible for rapes committed by ESO soldiers amounted to introducing a new legal charge, which would have required a formal amendment of the Indictment. The Prosecution submits that its failure to plead the rapes by ESO Camp soldiers constituted a defect in pleading a material fact which was subsequently cured by the Pre-Trial Brief, Opening Statement, and the Schedule of Particulars; that Muvunyi suffered no prejudice; and that, consequently, a conviction should be entered against him for these rapes. Muvunyi responds that the allegation that ESO Camp soldiers committed rapes was a 'material transformation' of the Prosecution's case that constituted a new charge and, as such, should have been pleaded in the Indictment. He adds that, throughout the case, the Prosecution's position was that he had authority over Ngoma Camp soldiers and *Interahamwe* and that he based his defence strategy on this. A review of the Trial Judgement reveals that the Trial Chamber considered the allegation implicating ESO Camp soldiers under Muvunyi's authority in rape as a material fact which should have been pleaded in the Indictment, which the Prosecution concedes. After noting that a defective indictment could be cured with subsequent timely, clear, and consistent notice, the Trial Chamber explained that this approach would not be appropriate with respect to this new allegation. Bearing in mind the specific nature of the charge of rape in the Indictment – attributing responsibility to Muvunyi for rapes committed by *Interahamwe* and Ngoma Camp soldiers – the Trial Chamber viewed the allegation pertaining to rapes committed by ESO Camp soldiers as a 'radical transformation' of the Prosecution case. The Trial Chamber concluded that Muvunyi did not have an opportunity to defend himself against this 'fundamentally different case' and consid-

559 *Muvunyi* Trial Judgement, paras. 524–526.

	ered that it would be prejudicial to hold against him the evidence of the rapes allegedly committed by ESO Camp soldiers. The Trial Chamber then observed that the proper method of bringing this allegation would have been to request an amendment of the Indictment, intimating that the addition of this material fact amounted to a new charge. Finally, the Trial Chamber noted that, when the Prosecution sought to amend the Indictment at the outset of the trial, it requested the removal of the rape count as opposed to adding this further allegation. The Appeals Chamber cannot identify any legal error in the approach taken by the Trial Chamber that would invalidate its decision not to hold the allegation or evidence of rapes committed by ESO Camp soldiers against Muvunyi. The Appeals Chamber has held that an accused cannot be convicted of a crime on the basis of material facts omitted from an indictment or pleaded with insufficient specificity, unless the Prosecution has cured the defect by providing timely, clear, and consistent information detailing the factual basis underpinning the charges against him or her. However, the principle that a defect in an indictment may be cured is not without limits. In this respect, the Appeals Chamber has previously emphasized: '[T]he 'new material facts' should not lead to a 'radical transformation' of the Prosecution's case against the accused. The Trial Chamber should always take into account the risk that the expansion of charges by the addition of new material facts may lead to unfairness and prejudice to the accused. Further, if the new material facts are such that they could, on their own, support separate charges, the Prosecution should seek leave from the Trial Chamber to amend the indictment and the Trial Chamber should only grant leave if it is satisfied that it would not lead to unfairness or prejudice to the Defence.' The Appeals Chamber agrees with the Trial Chamber that the addition of the rape allegation implicating ESO Camp soldiers amounted to a radical transformation of the Prosecution's case on this count. This is not a case where the Indictment pleaded the alleged perpetrators in a general or vague manner, which the Prosecution then sought to cure through timely, clear, and consistent information. Indeed, the perpetrators of the rapes set out in paragraph 3.41 of the Indictment are specifically identified as *Interahamwe* and soldiers from the Ngoma Camp. Paragraph 3.41 makes no mention of soldiers from the ESO Camp. The scope of the transformation of the Prosecution's case in respect of the rape charge is particularly illustrated by the fact that the Prosecution did not present evidence of acts of rape committed by *Interahamwe* and soldiers from the Ngoma Camp, but instead presented evidence of rapes allegedly committed by ESO Camp soldiers. As the Appeals Chamber previously observed in this case, '[i]t is to be assumed that an Accused will prepare his defence on the basis of material facts contained in the indictment, not on the basis of all the material disclosed to him that may support any number of additional charges, or expand the scope of existing charges.' Consequently, the Trial Chamber did not err in law by finding that it would be prejudicial to consider the evidence of rape by ESO Camp soldiers in light of the rape allegation in the Indictment. In any event, even if this defect in the Indictment could have been remedied, the Appeals Chamber is not satisfied that the Prosecution provided timely, clear, and consistent information of this new material fact to Muvunyi. In this respect, the Appeals Chamber is not convinced that the Pre-Trial Brief, Opening Statement, and the Schedule of Particulars cured the defect in the Indictment, as the Prosecution suggests. Though the Pre-Trial Brief and Opening Statement appear to implicate ESO Camp soldiers in acts of rape, the purported notice provided in these passing references does not signal the Prosecution's intention to hold Muvunyi responsible for these acts in a clear and consistent manner. In particular, around the same time the Prosecution filed its Pre-Trial Brief on 25 January 2005 and made its Opening Statement on 28 February 2005, it sought leave to amend the Indictment on 19 January 2005, including a specific prayer to remove the charge of rape in its entirety, and, on 28 February 2005, appealed against the Trial Chamber's decision denying its request to amend the indictment. In addition, contrary to the Prosecution's submissions, the Schedule of Particulars does not provide additional notice, but rather leads to further confusion. The paragraph in the Schedule of

	Particulars referred to by the Prosecution mentions Muvunyi's position as a superior of ESO Camp soldiers only as a basis for his knowledge of the acts of rape alleged in paragraph 3.41 of the Indictment. However, the operative paragraph in the Schedule of Particulars, outlining which perpetrators actually committed the rapes, mirrors the Indictment and implicates only *Interahamwe* and soldiers from the Ngoma Camp. This is telling as the sole purpose of the Schedule of Particulars was to remedy the deficiencies in the Prosecution's pleading of the material facts in the Indictment. Accordingly, the Prosecution's Second Ground of Appeal is dismissed".[560]

12. Siméon **Nchamihigo** (Case No. ICTR-01-63) Deputy Prosecutor in Cyangugu.	
Indictment (International sex crimes (or related) charges and mode(s) of liability)	- **Other inhumane acts as CAH** (count 4) under Article 6(1) of the Statute for ordering or instigating *Interahamwe* to remove the genitals of a Tutsi man, Jean-Fidele Murekezi before killing him near Cyangugu prison on or about 16 April 1994 (**ordering** or **instigating**).[561]
Trial Judgement	- Although Siméon Nchamihigo was found guilty for other inhumane acts (count 4), the Trial Chamber found that no evidence was led on the allegation of the mutilation of Jean-Fidele Murekezi's genitals, as the Prosecution conceded.[562]
Appeal Judgement	N/A (This issue was not part of the Appeal Judgement.)[563]
Legal and Factual Findings and/or	N/A (There are no legal or factual findings on international sex crimes in the Trial Judgement.)

560 *Muvunyi* Appeal Judgement, paras. 160–169 (internal references omitted).

561 *The Prosecutor v. Siméon Nchamihigo*, Case No. ICTR-01-63-T, Second Revised Amended Indictment (In conformity with Trial Chamber III Decision dated 07 December 2006), 11 December 2006, paras. 66 ("**COUNT 4: CRIME AGAINST HUMANITY: OTHER INHUMANE ACTS** The Prosecutor of the International Criminal Tribunal for Rwanda charges **SIMEON NCHAMIHIGO** of **other inhumane acts a a crime against humanity**, a crime stipulated in Article 3(i) of the Statute, in that between 6 April and 17 July 1994, throughout Rwanda, particularly in Cyangugu Prefecture, **SIMEON NCHAMIHIGO** was responsible for committing inhumane acts against Tutsi civilians or of people considered as Tutsi, and of Hutu opponents, as part of a widespread or systematic attack against a civilian population on political, ethnic or racial grounds, as outlined in paragraphs 67 through 70 of this indictment".), 70 ("On 16 April 1994 or thereabouts, **SIMEON NCHAMIHIGO** and other members of the prefecture security council, including Lieutenant Samuel Imanishimwe and Christophe Nyandwi, removed from Karampaka Stadium about 15 Tutsi and 1 Hutu woman by the name of Marianne Baziruwiha, and took them to a place near the prison after dropping off Marianne Baziruwiha at the gendarmerie camp. Among the 15 Tutsi who were removed from the stadium by **SIMEON NCHAMIHIGO** and others, were Jean-Fidele Murekezi, Albert Twagiramumgu and Gapfumu. **SIMEON NCHAMIHIGO** then ordered or instigated the *Interahamwe* whom he had brought along with him from Mutongo Centre earlier the same day, including Bizimungu Anasthase, to kill the 15 Tutsi. Following **SIMEON NCHAMIHIGO**'s order or instigation, the *Interahamwe* killed the 15 Tutsi near Cyangugu prison and threw their dead bodies into a latrine in Gapfumu's compound; before doing so the *Interahamwe* removed the genitals of Jean-Fidele Murekezi and Albert Twagiramungu and the heart of Gapfumu".).

562 *Prosecutor v. Siméon Nchamihigo*, Case No. ICTR-01-63-T, Judgement and Sentence, 12 November 2008, paras. 221, 381.

563 See *Siméon Nchamihigo v. The Prosecutor*, Case No. ICTR-01-63-A, Judgement, 18 March 2010.

Evidence	

13. Simon **Bikindi** (Case No. ICTR-01-72) A composer and singer; worked at the Ministry of Youth and Association Movements of the Government of Rwanda.	
Indictment (International sex crimes (or related) charges and mode(s) of liability)	- **Genocide** (count 2) under Articles 6(1) (**ordering, instigating** or **aiding and abetting**) and 6(3) of the Statute (**superior responsibility**) or, in the alternative, **Complicity in genocide** (count 3) under Article 6(1) of the Statute (**ordering, instigating** or **aiding and abetting**) for various crimes, including the rapes and acts of sexual violence committed by *Interahamwe* under his effective control against Tutsi women (including the rape of a woman named Ancilla), in the course of the execution of his orders to kill all Tutsi in Rubavu area.[564]

564 *Prosecutor v. Simon Bikindi*, Case No. ICTR-01-72-I, Amended Indictment Pursuant to Decisions of 11 May 2005 and 10 June 2005, 15 June 2005, pp. 6–7 ("**Count 2: GENOCIDE:** The Prosecutor of the International Criminal Tribunal of Rwanda charges **Simon BIKINDI** with ***GENOCIDE****, a crime stipulated in Article 2(3)(a) of the Statute*, in that on or between the dates of 7 April 1994 and 14 July 1994 throughout Rwanda, particularly in Kigali-ville and Gisenyi *prefectures*, **Simon BIKINDI** was responsible for killing or causing serious bodily or mental harm to members of the Tutsi population with intent to destroy, in whole or in part, a racial or ethnic group, as such; *Pursuant to Article 6(1) of the Statute*: by virtue of his affirmative acts in planning, instigating, ordering, committing, or otherwise aiding and abetting the planning, preparation or execution of the crime charged; and *Pursuant to Article 6(3) of the Statute*: by virtue of his actual or constructive knowledge of the acts or omissions of his subordinates, including *Interahamwe* and civilian militias, particularly *Interahamwe* members of his Irindiro Ballet, and his failure to take necessary and reasonable measures to stop or prevent them, or to discipline and punish them, for their acts in the planning, preparation or execution of the crime charged; ***or alternatively***, **Count 3: COMPLICITY IN GENOCIDE:** The Prosecutor of the International Criminal Tribunal of Rwanda charges **Simon BIKINDI** with ***COMPLICITY IN GENOCIDE****, a crime stipulated in Article 2(3)(e) of the Statute*, in that on or between the dates of 1 January 1994 and 14 July 1994 throughout Rwanda, particularly Kigali-ville and Gisenyi *prefectures*, **Simon BIKINDI** was responsible for killing or causing serious bodily or mental harm to members of the Tutsi population with intent to destroy, in whole or in part, a racial or ethnic group, as such, as follows: *Pursuant to Article 6(1) of the Statute*: by virtue of his affirmative acts in planning, instigating, ordering, committing, or otherwise aiding and abetting the planning, preparation or execution of the crime charged"), para. 29 ("Sexual violence against Tutsi women was systematically incorporated in the generalized attacks against the Tutsi. In leading, ordering and encouraging the campaign of extermination in Gisenyi *prefecture*, **Simon BIKINDI** knew, or should have known, that sexual violence against civilian Tutsi was, or would be, widespread or systematic, and that the perpetrators would include his subordinates or those that committed such acts in response to his generalized orders and instructions to exterminate the Tutsi. For example, in late June 1994, at about 6pm, **Simon BIKINDI** led a group of *Interahamwe*, including Jean KAVUNDERI (Noel's younger brother), PASCAL, CARI, SELAMANI, KABULIMBO, and SENDEGEYA to Rubavu, and ordered them to kill all of the Tutsis in the area. In the course of executing **Simon BIKINDI's** orders, the *Interahamwe* under his effective control also committed rapes of Tutsi women, of which **Simon BIKINDI** was aware, or ought to have been aware by his presence and effective supervision of the killing and rape operations of the *Interahamwe*. Notably, the *Interahamwe* called SENDEGEYA boasted in the hearing of other persons in the vicinity of the crimes, including **Simon BIKINDI**, after the rape and murder of ANCILLA that he 'had always dreamt of sleeping with a Tutsi woman and now his dream had come true'. During the killings and rape perpetrated by the *Interahamwe* in **Simon BIKINDI's** company and to whom he gave orders, including the perpetrators named above, **Simon BIKINDI** stood by the road near the home of ANCILLA to ensure his orders were carried out by the *Interahamwe*. By ordering the *Interahamwe* under his effective control to commit acts of violence against Tutsis in Rubavu commune, which included acts of killing and sexual violence, and by effectively staying on the road close to the scene of these crimes to ensure his orders were followed, **Simon BIKINDI** was aware, or ought to have been aware of the acts of rape and sexual violence committed by the *Interahamwe* under his effective control, notably SENDEGEYA, on ANCILLA. Notably still, when the said *Interahamwe* boasted in the hearing of other persons in the vicinity of the crimes, including **Simon**

Trial Judgement	- Not guilty of counts 2 and 3 because the Prosecution did not prove these charges beyond reasonable doubt.[565]
Appeal Judgement	- The Prosecution did not appeal Simon Bikindi's acquittals for counts 2 and 3.[566]
Legal and Factual Findings and/or Evidence	- Factual findings: - Alleged rape of Ancilla: "There are also significant discrepancies between the accounts of the incident provided by the Prosecution witnesses. In particular, the evidence of Witnesses AJZ and AJY is contradictory as to whether Ancilla was raped before she was killed. Witness AJY testified that he learnt that Ancilla had been raped immediately afterwards from those who had just come out of her house. Witness AJZ, allegedly present when Ancilla was taken out from her house, did not even allude to Ancilla's rape. The Chamber finds it difficult to accept the witnesses' discrepancy on such a significant matter. While both witnesses were alleged eye-witnesses to Ancilla being brought out of her house, their testimony differed on other significant aspects. One stated that Bikindi came into the house with the rest of the group, the other testified that Bikindi was outside on the road. One stated that Ancilla attempted to save her child, the other did not. One testified that Bikindi and Noël took Ancilla and her child to be killed, the other only stated that Ancilla and her child were subsequently killed. One suggested it occurred in the morning, the other in the evening. In further support of its allegation, the Prosecution entered Bikindi's 'personal file' from the Rugerero *cellule* Gacaca court into the record as Exhibit P80. This document dated 9 March 2005 is signed by seven judges and indicates that Bikindi was suspected of participating in the murder of Ancilla and her child. Kabulimbo is mentioned therein as one of the co-perpetrators. The Defence also adduced as Exhibit D110 an alleged attestation from members of the same Rugerero *cellule* Gacaca court obtained by Co-Counsel Momo, which contains a list of those who participated in Ancilla's death. Bikindi is not listed among them, but Kabulimbo is. The attestation is neither signed nor stamped and the Chamber questions the probative value of Co-Counsel Momo's *affidavit* attached therewith. The Chamber observes that Exhibits P80 and D110 referred to different people as officials of the court. Whatever the authenticity and reliability of those two exhibits may be, the Chamber considers that the mere fact that the allegation brought before the Tribunal is also the subject of proceedings in Rwanda is not sufficient for a proof beyond reasonable doubt that the Accused indeed participated in the crime with which he is charged. Even considered together with the questionable evidence of Witnesses AJZ and AJY, Exhibit P80 does not prove Bikindi's responsibility in the killing of Ancilla and her daughter. In assessing the Prosecution's evidence, the Chamber has also considered the evidence given by Witnesses DFA and JTX related to the killing of Ancilla, which it found to be of very limited probative value. The Chamber has no doubt that Ancilla was killed during the genocide. However, given the serious reservations the Chamber has on the credibility of Witnesses AJY and AJZ and the divergence in their accounts of the incident, the Chamber does not find that their evidence, even considered in light of Exhibit P80, prove beyond reasonable doubt that Bikindi, Noël or anyone under Bikindi's command participated in the killing or rape of Ancilla or the killing of her

BIKINDI, after the rape of ANCILLA that he 'had always dreamt of sleeping with a Tutsi woman and now his dream had come true', by these specific actions, **Simon BIKINDI** ordered, instigated and aided and abetted in these rapes, notably, in the rape of ANCILLA".).

565 *Prosecutor v. Simon Bikindi*, Case No. ICTR-01-72-T, Judgement, 2 December 2008 ("*Bikindi* Trial Judgement"), paras. 337–350, 365–366, 408–416, 441.

566 See *Prosecutor v. Simon Bikindi*, Case No. ICTR-01-72-A, Judgement, 18 March 2010.

	daughter as alleged by the Prosecution in paragraphs 23, 28, 29, 30(g), 46 and 47(f) of the Indictment".[567] - Alleged sexual violence against Tutsi women in Rubavu: "Under paragraph 29 of the Indictment, the Prosecution alleges that Bikindi is responsible for the acts of sexual violence committed by *Interahamwe* against Tutsi women in the course of the execution of his orders to kill all Tutsi in Rubavu area. The Chamber observes that, save for the specific incident concerning Ancilla discussed above, the Prosecution failed to adduce evidence in support of its allegation. Accordingly, the Chamber dismisses this allegation without discussing it any further".[568]

14. Théoneste **Bagosora *et al.*** (Case No. ICTR-98-41) - Colonel Théoneste Bagosora: *Directeur de cabinet* of the Rwandan Ministry of Defence from June 1992 until 14 July 1994, acting in fact as the Minister of Defence from 6 to 9 April 1994. - General Gratien Kabiligi: Head of the G-3 Operational Bureau (military operations) of the Rwanda Army general staff from September 1993 until 17 July 1994. - Major Aloys Ntabakuze: Commander of the elite Para-Commando Battalion at Camp Kanombe from June 1988 until 3 July 1994. - Colonel Anatole Nsengiyumva: Commander of the Gisenyi Operational Sector from 13 June 1993 until 17 July 1994.	
Indictment (International sex crimes (or related) charges and mode(s) of liability)	- Théoneste Bagosora: **Conspiracy to commit genocide** (count 1), **Genocide** (count 2), **Complicity in genocide** (count 3), **Rape as CAH** (count 7), **Persecutions as CAH** (count 8), **Other inhumane acts as CAH** (count 9), **Violence to health and to the physical or mental well-being of civilians as a violation of Article 3 common to the Geneva Conventions and of Additional Protocol II (WC)** (count 10) and **Outrages upon personal dignity, in particular humiliating and degrading treatment, rape and indecent assault as a violation of Article 3 common to the Geneva Conventions and of Additional Protocol II (WC)** (count 12) under Article 6(3) of the Statute (**superior responsibility**) for various crimes, including: (i) the rapes, sexual assaults and other crimes of a sexual nature committed against Tutsi women and girls throughout Rwanda, including in Gisenyi and at the secondary nursing school in Kabgayi, in Gitarama prefecture; and (ii) the sexual assault of Prime Minister Agathe Uwilingiyimana.[569]

[567] *Bikindi* Trial Judgement, paras. 345–350.

[568] *Bikindi* Trial Judgement, paras. 365–366.

[569] *Prosecutor v. Théoneste Bagosora*, Case No. ICTR-96-7-I, Amended Indictment, 12 August 1999, paras. 5.45 ("Furthermore, soldiers, militiamen and gendarmes raped, sexually assaulted and committed other crimes of a sexual nature against Tutsi women and girls, sometimes having first kidnapped them".), 6.8–6.9 ("In the morning of 7 April, another meeting of the FAR officers was held at the *Ecole Supérieure Militaire* (ESM) [...]. The meeting was chaired by **Colonel Théoneste Bagosora**. He reiterated his position, maintaining that the military should take power. For the third time, **Colonel Théoneste Bagosora** refused that the Prime Minister be consulted, adding that he did not know if she was still alive. [...] While this meeting was going on, Prime Minister Agathe Uwilingiyimana was tracked down, arrested, sexually assaulted and killed by Rwandan Army personnel, more specifically, members of the Presidential Guard, the Para-Commando Battalion and the Reconnaissance Battalion".), 6.59 ("Furthermore, on the 7 April 1994, Anatole Nsengiyumva received a telegram from Kigali ordering him to start the massacres. Between 7 April and mid-July 1994, in Gisenyi, Anatole Nsengiyumva ordered militiamen and soldiers to exterminate the civilian Tutsi population and its 'acomplices'. Between April and July 1994, the militiamen, on the orders of Anatole Nsengiyumva, hunted down, abducted and killed several members of the Tutsi and moderate Hutu population in Gisenyi. Furthermore, several of those militiamen commit[t]ed rapes, sexual assaults and other crimes

of sexual nature against Tutsi woman and girls".), 6.60 ("Between April and June 1994, several people found refuge at the secondary nursing school in Kabgayi, Gitarama *prefecture*, where students and staff were already located. On several occasions during this period, soldiers and *Interahamwe* militiamen abducted and raped female Tutsi students and refugees. Minister of Defense Augustin Bizimana and the General Staff of the Rwandan Army were informed of this situation but did not take any effective steps to end the crimes once and for all".), 6.65 ("During the events referred to in this indictment, rapes, sexual assaults and other crimes of a sexual nature were widely and notoriously committed throughout Rwanda. These crimes were perpetrated by, among others, soldiers, militiamen and gendarmes against the Tutsi population, in particular Tutsi women and girls".), pp. 54–56, 58–60, 62–63 ("**COUNT 1:** By the acts or omissions described in paragraphs 5.1 to 6.73 and more specifically in the paragraphs referred to below: **Théoneste Bagosora:** [...] - pursuant to Article 6(3), according to paragraphs 5.44, 5.45, 6.9, 6.18, 6.20, 6.22, 6.23, 6.27, 6.28, 6.30, 6.31, 6.34, 6.35, 6.37 to 6.39, 6.42 to 6.55, 6.57 to 6.66 conspired with Anatole Nsengiyumva, Gratien Kabiligi, Aloys Ntabakuze and others to kill and cause serious bodily or mental harm to members of the Tutsi population with the intent to destroy, in whole or in part, a racial or ethnic group, and thereby committed **CONSPIRACY TO COMMIT GENOCIDE**, a crime stipulated in Article 2(3)(b) of the Statute of the Tribunal, for which he is individually responsible pursuant to Article 6 and which is punishable in reference to Articles 22 and 23 of the Statute. **COUNT 2:** By the acts or omissions described in paragraphs 5.1 to 6.73 and more specifically in the paragraphs referred to below: **Théoneste Bagosora:** [...] -pursuant to Article 6(3), according to paragraphs 5.44, 5.45, 6.9, 6.18, 6.20, 6.22, 6.23, 6.27, 6.28, 6.30, 6.31, 6.34, 6.35, 6.37 to 6.39, 6.42 to 6.55, 6.57 to 6.66 is responsible for killing and causing serious bodily or mental harm to members of the Tutsi population with the intent to destroy, in whole or in part, a racial or ethnic group, and thereby committed **GENOCIDE,** a crime stipulated in Article 2(3)(a) of the Statute, for which he is individually responsible pursuant to Article 6 and which is punishable in reference to Articles 22 and 23 of the Statute. **COUNT 3:** By the acts or omissions described in paragraphs 5.1 to 6.73 and more specifically in the paragraphs referred to below: **Théoneste Bagosora:** [...] -pursuant to Article 6(3), according to paragraphs 5.44, 5.45, 6.9, 6.18, 6.20, 6.22, 6.23, 6.27, 6.28, 6.30, 6.31, 6.34, 6.35, 6.37 to 6.39, 6.42 to 6.55, 6.57 to 6.66 is responsible for killing and causing serious bodily or mental harm to members of the Tutsi population with the intent to destroy, in whole or in part, a racial or ethnic group, and thereby committed **COMPLICITY IN GENOCIDE,** a crime stipulated in Article 2(3)(e) of the Statute, for which he is individually responsible pursuant to Article 6 and which is punishable in reference to Articles 22 and 23 of the Statute. [...] **COUNT 7:** By the acts or omissions described in paragraphs 5.1 to 6.73 and more specifically in the paragraphs referred to below: **Théoneste Bagosora:** -pursuant to Article 6(3), according to paragraphs: 4.2, 4.3, 4.4, 5.1, 5.45, 6.59, 6.60, 6.65 is responsible for rape as part of a widespread and systematic attack against a civilian population on political, ethnic or racial grounds, and thereby committed a **CRIME AGAINST HUMANITY**, a crime stipulated in Article 3(g) of [the] Statute of the Tribunal, for which he is individually responsible pursuant to Article 6 of the Statute and which is punishable in reference to Articles 22 and 23 of the Statute. **COUNT 8:** By the acts or omissions described in paragraphs 5.1 to 6.73 and more specifically in the paragraphs referred to below: **Théoneste Bagosora:** [...] -pursuant to Article 6(3), according to paragraphs: 5.44, 5.45, 6.9, 6.18, 6.20, 6.22, 6.23, 6.27, 6.28, 6.30, 6.31, 6.34, 6.35, 6.37 to 6.39, 6.42 to 6.55, 6.57 to 6.66 is responsible for persecution on political, racial or religious grounds, as part of a widespread and systematic attack against a civilian population on political, ethnic or racial grounds, and thereby committed a **CRIME AGAINST HUMANITY**, a crime stipulated in Article 3(h) of [the] Statute of the Tribunal, for which he is individually responsible pursuant to Article 6 of the Statute and which is punishable in reference to Articles 22 and 23 of the Statute. **COUNT 9:** By the acts or omissions described in paragraphs 5.1 to 6.73 and more specifically in the paragraphs referred to below: **Théoneste Bagosora:** [...] -pursuant to Article 6(3), according to paragraphs: 5.44, 5.45, 6.9, 6.18, 6.20, 6.22, 6.23, 6.27, 6.28, 6.30, 6.31, 6.34, 6.35, 6.37 to 6.39, 6.42 to 6.55, 6.57 to 6.66 is responsible for inhumane acts against persons as part of a widespread and systematic attack against a civilian population on political, ethnic or racial grounds, and thereby committed a **CRIME AGAINST HUMANITY,** a crime stipulated in Article 3(i) of [the] Statute of the Tribunal, for which he is individually responsible pursuant to Article 6 of the Statute and which is punishable in reference to Articles 22 and 23 of the Statute. [...] **COUNT 10:** By the acts or omissions described in paragraphs 5.1 to 6.73 and more specifically in the paragraphs referred to below: **Théoneste Bagosora:** [...] -pursuant to Article 6(3), according to paragraphs: 5.44, 5.45, 6.9, 6.18, 6.20, 6.22, 6.23, 6.27, 6.28, 6.30, 6.31, 6.34, 6.35, 6.37 to 6.39, 6.42 to 6.55, 6.57 to 6.66 is responsible for [...] and causing violence to health and to the physical or mental well-being of civilians as part of an armed internal conflict, and thereby committed **SERIOUS VIOLATION OF ARTICLE 3 COMMON TO THE GENEVA CONVENTIONS AND ADDITIONAL PROTOCOL II**, a crime stipulated in Article 4 (a) of the Statute of the Tribunal, for which he is individually responsible pursuant to Article 6 of the Statute and which is punishable in reference to Articles 22 and 23

	- Gratien Kabiligi and Aloys Ntabakuze: **Conspiracy to commit genocide** (count 1), **Genocide** (count 2), **Complicity in genocide** (count 3), **Rape as CAH** (count 6), **Persecutions as CAH** (count 7), **Other inhumane acts as CAH** (count 8), **Violence to health and to the physical or mental well-being of civilians as a violation of Article 3 common to the Geneva Conventions and of Additional Protocol II (WC)** (count 9) and **Outrages upon personal dignity, in particular humiliating and degrading treatment, rape and indecent assault as a violation of Article 3 common to the Geneva Conventions and of Additional Protocol II (WC)** (count 10) under Article 6(3) of the Statute (**superior responsibility**) for various crimes, including: (i) the rapes, sexual assaults and other crimes of a sexual nature committed against Tutsi women and girls throughout Rwanda, including at the secondary nursing school in Kabgayi, in Gitarama prefecture; and (ii) the sexual assault of Prime Minister Agathe Uwilingiyimana. - Anatole Nsengiyumva: **Conspiracy to commit genocide** (count 1), **Genocide** (count 2), **Complicity in genocide** (count 3), **Rape as CAH** (count 7), **Persecutions as CAH** (count 8), **Other inhumane acts as CAH** (count 9), **Violence to health and to the physical or mental well-being of civilians as a violation of Article 3 common to the Geneva Conventions and of Additional Protocol II (WC)** (count 10) and **Outrages upon personal dignity, in particular humiliating and degrading treatment, rape and indecent assault as a violation of Article 3 common to the Geneva Conventions and of Additional Protocol II (WC)** (count 11) under Article 6(3) of the Statute (**superior responsibility**) for various crimes, including the rapes, sexual assaults and other crimes of a sexual nature committed against Tutsi women and girls in various locations in Gisenyi, including at Nyundo parish.[570]

of the Statute. **COUNT 12:** By the acts or omissions described in paragraphs 5.1 to 6.73 and more specifically in the paragraphs referred to below: **Théoneste Bagosora:** -pursuant to Article 6(3), according to paragraphs: 4.2, 4.3, 4.4, 5.1, 5.45, 6.59, 6.60, 6.65 is responsible for outrages upon personal dignity, in particular humiliating and degrading treatment, rape and indecent assault, as part of an armed internal conflict, and thereby committed **SERIOUS VIOLATIONS OF ARTICLE 3 COMMON TO THE GENEVA CONVENTIONS AND OF ADDITIONAL PROTOCOL II**, a crime stipulated in Article 4 (e) of the Statute of the Tribunal, for which he is individually responsible pursuant to Article 6 of the Statute and which is punishable in reference to Articles 22 and 23 of the Statute".).

570 *Prosecutor v. Anatole Nsengiyumva*, Case No. ICTR 96-12-I, Amended Indictment, 12 August 1999, paras. 5.32 ("Furthermore, soldiers, militiamen and gendarmes raped, sexually assaulted and committed other crimes of a sexual nature against Tutsi women and girls, sometimes having first kidnapped them".), 6.34 ("During the events referred to in this indictment, rapes, sexual assaults and other crimes of a sexual nature were widely and notoriously committed throughout Rwanda. These crimes were perpetrated by, among others, soldiers, militiamen and gendarmes against the Tutsi population, in particular Tutsi women and girls".), pp. 36–38, 40–44 ("**COUNT 1:** By the acts or omissions described in paragraphs 5.1 to 6.37 and more specifically in the paragraphs referred to below: **Anatole Nsengiyumva:** […] -pursuant to Article 6(3), according to paragraphs: 5.31, 5.32, 6.16, 6.17, 6.20 to 6.24, 6.26, 6.28, 6.29, 6.32, 6.34, 6.36 conspired with Th[é]oneste Bagosora, Gratien Kabiligi, Aloys Ntabakuze and others to kill and cause serious bodily or mental harm to members of the Tutsi population with the intent to destroy, in whole or in part, a racial or ethnic group, and thereby committed **CONSPIRACY TO COMMIT GENOCIDE**, a crime stipulated in Article 2(3)(b) of the Statute of the Tribunal, for which he is individually responsible pursuant to Article 6 and which is punishable in reference to Articles 22 and 23 of the Statute. **COUNT 2:** By the acts or omissions described in paragraphs 5.1 to 6.37 and more specifically in the paragraphs referred to below: **Anatole Nsengiyumva:** […] -pursuant to Article 6(3), according to paragraphs: 5.31, 5.32, 6.16, 6.17, 6.20 to 6.24, 6.26, 6.28, 6.29, 6.32, 6.34, 6.36 is responsible for killing and causing serious bodily or mental harm to members of the Tutsi population with the intent to destroy, in whole or in part, a racial or ethnic group, and thereby committed **GENOCIDE,** a crime stipulated in Article 2(3)(a) of the Statute, for which he is individually responsible pursuant to Article 6 and which is punishable in reference to Articles 22 and 23 of the Statute. **COUNT 3:** By the acts or omissions described in paragraphs 5.1 to 6.37 and more specifically in the paragraphs referred to below: **Anatole Nsengiyumva:** […] -pursuant to Article 6(3), according to paragraphs: 5.31, 5.32, 6.16, 6.17, 6.20 to 6.24, 6.26, 6.28, 6.29, 6.32, 6.34, 6.36 is responsible for killing and

Trial Judgement	- Théoneste Bagosora: guilty of **Genocide (causing serious bodily or mental harm)** (count 2) under Article 6(1) of the Statute (**ordering**) for various crimes, including for ordering the crimes at Kigali area roadblocks, which included rapes and acts of sexual violence (he was also found liable for these crimes under Article 6(3) of the Statute) and under Article 6(3) of the Statute (**superior responsibility**) for various crimes, including the rape of a woman and the stripping of female Tutsi refugees at the Saint Josephite Centre on 8 April 1994 and the rapes and acts of sexual violence committed in Gikondo parish on the morning of 9 April 1994.[571] Guilty of **Rape as CAH** (count 7) and **Outrages upon personal dignity as a violation of Article 3 common to the Geneva Conventions and of Additional Protocol II (WC)** (count 12) under Article 6(3) of the Statute (**superior responsibility**) for the rapes committed between 7 and 9 April 1994 at Kigali area roadblocks, the Saint Josephite centre and Gikondo parish.[572] Guilty of **Persecutions as CAH** (count 8) under Article 6(1) of the Statute (**ordering**)

causing serious bodily or mental harm to members of the Tutsi population with the intent to destroy, in whole or in part, a racial or ethnic group, and thereby committed **COMPLICITY IN GENOCIDE,** a crime stipulated in Article 2(3)(e) of the Statute, for which he is individually responsible pursuant to Article 6 and which is punishable in reference to Articles 22 and 23 of the Statute. [...] **COUNT 7:** By the acts or omissions described in paragraphs 5.1 to 6.37 and more specifically in the paragraphs referred to below: **Anatole Nsengiyumva:** -pursuant to Article 6(3), according to paragraphs: 4.2 to 4.4, 5.32, 6.29, 6.34 is responsible for rape as part of a widespread and systematic attack against a civilian population on political, ethnic or racial grounds, and thereby committed a **CRIME AGAINST HUMANITY**, a crime stipulated in Article 3(g) of [the] Statute of the Tribunal, for which he is individually responsible pursuant to Article 6 of the Statute and which is punishable in reference to Articles 22 and 23 of the Statute. **COUNT 8:** By the acts or omissions described in paragraphs 5.1 to 6.37 and more specifically in the paragraphs referred to below: **Anatole Nsengiyumva:** [...] -pursuant to Article 6(3), according to paragraphs: 5.31, 5.32, 6.16, 6.17, 6.20 to 6.24, 6.26, 6.28, 6.29, 6.32, 6.34, 6.36 is responsible for persecution on political, racial or religious grounds, as part of a widespread and systematic attack against a civilian population on political, ethnic or racial grounds, and thereby committed a **CRIME AGAINST HUMANITY**, a crime stipulated in Article 3(h) of [the] Statute of the Tribunal, for which he is individually responsible pursuant to Article 6 of the Statute and which is punishable in reference to Articles 22 and 23 of the Statute. **COUNT 9:** By the acts or omissions described in paragraphs 5.1 to 6.37 and more specifically in the paragraphs referred to below: **Anatole Nsengiyumva:** [...] -pursuant to Article 6(3), according to paragraphs: 5.31, 5.32, 6.16, 6.17, 6.20 to 6.24, 6.26, 6.28, 6.29, 6.32, 6.34, 6.36 is responsible for inhumane acts against persons as part of a widespread and systematic attack against a civilian population on political, ethnic or racial grounds, and thereby committed a **CRIME AGAINST HUMANITY**, a crime stipulated in Article 3(i) of [the] Statute of the Tribunal, for which he is individually responsible pursuant to Article 6 of the Statute and which is punishable in reference to Articles 22 and 23 of the Statute. **COUNT 10:** By the acts or omissions described in paragraphs 5.1 to 6.37 and more specifically in the paragraphs referred to below: **Anatole Nsengiyumva:** [...] -pursuant to Article 6(3), according to paragraphs: 5.31, 5.32, 6.16, 6.17, 6.20 to 6.24, 6.26, 6.28, 6.29, 6.32, 6.34, 6.36 is responsible for killing and causing violence to health and to the physical or mental well-being of civilians as part of an armed internal conflict, and thereby committed **SERIOUS VIOLATION OF ARTICLE 3 COMMON TO THE GENEVA CONVENTIONS AND ADDITIONAL PROTOCOL II**, a crime stipulated in Article 4 (a) of the Statute of the Tribunal, for which he is individually responsible pursuant to Article 6 of the Statute and which is punishable in reference to Articles 22 and 23 of the Statute. **COUNT 11:** By the acts or omissions described in paragraphs 5.1 to 6.37 and more specifically in the paragraphs referred to below: **Anatole Nsengiyumva:** [...] -pursuant to Article 6(3), according to paragraphs: 4.2 to 4.4, 5.32, 6.29, 6.34 is responsible for outrages upon personal dignity, in particular humiliating and degrading treatment, rape and indecent assault, as part of an armed internal conflict, and thereby committed **SERIOUS VIOLATION OF ARTICLE 3 COMMON TO THE GENEVA CONVENTIONS AND ADDITIONAL PROTOCOL II**, a crime stipulated in Article 4 (e) of the Statute of the Tribunal, for which he is individually responsible pursuant to Article 6 of the Statute and which is punishable in reference to Articles 22 and 23 of the Statute".).

571 *Prosecutor v. Théoneste Bagosora et al.*, Case No. ICTR-98-41-T, Judgement and Sentence, dated 18 December 2008 and filed on 9 February 2009 ("*Théoneste Bagosora et al.* Trial Judgement"), paras. 938–939, 988–989, 1920–1924, 2123–2126, 2129, 2132–2135, 2158, 2258.

572 *Théoneste Bagosora et al.* Trial Judgement, paras. 938–939, 988–989, 1920–1924, 2201–2203, 2252–2254, 2258.

	for various crimes, including for ordering the crimes at Kigali area roadblocks, which included rapes (he was also found liable for these crimes under Article 6(3) of the Statute) and under Article 6(3) of the Statute (**superior responsibility**) for various crimes, including the rapes committed at the Saint Josephite centre and Gikondo parish.[573] Guilty of **Other inhumane acts as CAH** (count 9) under Article 6(3) of the Statute (**superior responsibility**) for the insertion of a bottle into Prime Minister Agathe Uwilingiyimana's vagina after her death and for the stripping of Tutsi female refugees at the Saint Josephite Centre.[574] Although Théoneste Bagosora was found guilty of violence to health and to the physical or mental well-being of civilians as a violation of Article 3 common to the Geneva Conventions and of Additional Protocol II (WC) (count 10), this conviction only encompassed killings.[575] Not guilty of conspiracy to commit genocide (count 1) because the Trial Chamber found that the Prosecution did not prove beyond reasonable doubt that the four accused conspired among themselves or with others to commit genocide before it unfolded on 7 April 1994.[576] Not guilty of complicity in genocide (count 3) because the Prosecution indicated that this count should be dismissed in the event of a finding of guilt on the count of genocide.[577] - Gratien Kabiligi: Acquitted of all counts, including the international sex crimes charges because the Trial Chamber did not find that he was directly involved in any of the specific criminal events alleged. Moreover, the evidence did not show that his subordinates committed crimes when Kabiligi exercised effective control over them.[578] - Aloys Ntabakuze: Although Aloys Ntabakuze was found guilty of genocide (count 2), persecutions as CAH (count 7), other inhumane acts as CAH (count 8) and violence to health and to the physical or mental well-being of civilians as a violation of Article 3 common to the Geneva Conventions and of Additional Protocol II (WC) (count 9), none of these convictions included international sex crimes.[579] Not guilty of conspiracy to commit genocide (count 1) because the Trial Chamber found that the Prosecution did not prove beyond reasonable doubt that the four accused conspired among themselves or with others to commit genocide before it unfolded on 7 April 1994.[580] Not guilty of complicity in genocide (count 3) because the Prosecution indicated that this count should be dismissed in the event of a finding of guilt on the count of genocide.[581] Not guilty of rape as CAH (count 6) and outrages upon personal dignity as a violation of Article 3 common to the Geneva Conventions and of Additional Protocol II (WC) (count 10).[582] - Anatole Nsengiyumva: Although Anatole Nsengiyumva was found guilty of genocide (count 2), persecutions as CAH (count 8), other inhumane acts as CAH (count 9) and violence to health and to the physical or mental well-being of civilians as a viola-

573 *Théoneste Bagosora et al.* Trial Judgement, paras. 938–939, 988–989, 1920–1924, 2201–2203, 2210–2213, 2258.

574 *Théoneste Bagosora et al.* Trial Judgement, paras. 720, 723–724, 938–939, 2219–2224, 2258.

575 *Théoneste Bagosora et al.* Trial Judgement, paras. 2243–2245, 2258.

576 *Théoneste Bagosora et al.* Trial Judgement, paras. 2113, 2258. See also *Théoneste Bagosora et al.* Trial Judgement, paras. 2092–2112.

577 *Théoneste Bagosora et al.* Trial Judgement, paras. 2162, 2258.

578 *Théoneste Bagosora et al.* Trial Judgement, paras. 2005, 2056, 2258.

579 *Théoneste Bagosora et al.* Trial Judgement, paras. 2128, 2135–2139, 2160, 2210–2212, 2215, 2220–2223, 2226, 2243–2244, 2247, 2258.

580 *Théoneste Bagosora et al.* Trial Judgement, paras. 2113, 2258. See also *Théoneste Bagosora et al.* Trial Judgement, paras. 2092–2112.

581 *Théoneste Bagosora et al.* Trial Judgement, paras. 2162, 2258.

582 *Théoneste Bagosora et al.* Trial Judgement, paras. 2205, 2256, 2258.

	tion of Article 3 common to the Geneva Conventions and of Additional Protocol II (WC) (count 10), none of these convictions included international sex crimes.[583] Not guilty of conspiracy to commit genocide (count 1) because the Trial Chamber found that the Prosecution did not prove beyond reasonable doubt that the four accused conspired among themselves or with others to commit genocide before it unfolded on 7 April 1994.[584] Not guilty of complicity in genocide (count 3) because the Prosecution indicated that this count should be dismissed in the event of a finding of guilt on the count of genocide.[585] Not guilty of rape as CAH (count 7) and outrages upon personal dignity as a violation of Article 3 common to the Geneva Conventions and of Additional Protocol II (WC) (count 11).[586]
Appeal Judgement	N/A (The appellate proceedings are in progress.)
Legal and Factual Findings and/or Evidence	- <u>Legal findings:</u> **- Rape and sexual violence can constitute genocide (causing serious bodily or mental harm):** The Trial Chamber held: "The term 'causing serious bodily harm' refers to acts of sexual violence, serious acts of physical violence falling short of killing that seriously injure the health, cause disfigurement, or cause any serious injury to the external or internal organs or senses. Serious mental harm refers to more than minor or temporary impairment of mental faculties. The serious bodily or mental harm, however, need not be an injury that is permanent or irremediable. This harm can include crimes of sexual violence, including rape".[587] **- Rape: definition:** The Trial Chamber adopted the definition of rape given in the *Kunarac et al.* case:[588] "Rape as a crime against humanity requires proof of the non-consensual penetration, however slight, of the vagina or anus of the victim by the penis of the perpetrator or by any other object used by the perpetrator, or of the mouth of the victim by the penis of the perpetrator. Consent for this purpose must be consent given voluntarily and freely and is assessed within the context of the surrounding circumstances. Force or threat of force provides clear evidence of non-consent, but force is not an element *per se* of rape. The *mens rea* for rape as a crime against humanity is the intention to effect the prohibited sexual penetration with the knowledge that it occurs without the consent of the victim".[589] - <u>Factual and legal findings:</u> - Sexual assault of the Prime Minister Agathe Uwilingiyimana, in Kigali, on 7 April 1994: "Witness AE stated that he ordered his soldiers back to their positions at ESM and then heard gunshots a few minutes later. The Prime Minister's naked and bullet ridden body was seen lying openly in the compound with a bottle shoved into her vagina. Soldiers from several units including the Presidential Guard, ESM, the Reconnais-

[583] *Théoneste Bagosora et al.* Trial Judgement, paras. 2140–2142, 2146–2152, 2154, 2155–2157, 2161, 2210–2212, 2216, 2220–2223, 2227, 2243–2244, 2248, 2258.

[584] *Théoneste Bagosora et al.* Trial Judgement, paras. 2113, 2258. See also *Théoneste Bagosora et al.* Trial Judgement, paras. 2092–2112.

[585] *Théoneste Bagosora et al.* Trial Judgement, paras. 2162, 2258.

[586] *Théoneste Bagosora et al.* Trial Judgement, paras. 2206, 2257, 2258.

[587] *Théoneste Bagosora et al.* Trial Judgement, para. 2117 (internal references omitted).

[588] ICTY ISCC *Kunarac et al.*, see *supra* p. 528.

[589] *Théoneste Bagosora et al.* Trial Judgement, paras. 2199–2200 (internal references omitted).

	sance Battalion and the Huye Battalion, were seen walking around the property. Around 1.00 to 1.30 p.m., Dallaire travelled from the Ministry of Defence to the UNDP compound passing by the Prime Minister residence. He saw blood and bullet holes on the walls of the compound, but explained that the Prime Minister's body had been taken away".[590] "With respect to the killing of Prime Minister Uwilingiyimana, the Chamber considers that Witnesses XXO and AE provided credible and convincing first-hand accounts of what transpired at her residence from 6 to 7 April 1994. Both witnesses were in a position to closely follow the events, and the Defence generally does not dispute the accuracy of their evidence. From their accounts, it clearly follows that elements of the Presidential Guard and Reconnaissance Battalion participated in the attack on the Prime Minister's residence as well as her murder and sexual assault".[591] "In the Chamber's view, however, the attack on the Prime Minister's residence in Kiyovu was an organised military operation. The Chamber notes the proximity in time of the attack to the killing of other moderate politicians in the Kimihurura area nearby (III.3.3.3). Furthermore, the use of armoured vehicles and the build-up of soldiers during the course of the night, including elite units of the Rwandan army, also strongly suggest an organised military operation. Moreover, the Chamber simply cannot accept in this context that elite units of the Rwandan army would spontaneously engage in sustained gun and grenade fire with Rwandan gendarmes and United Nations peace-keepers, arrest these individuals, and then brutally murder and sexually assault the Prime Minister of their country unless it formed part of a military operation. The fact that Witness AE observed some soldiers who did not wish to pursue this ultimate course of action in the overall context does not detract from the Chamber's finding".[592] "[...] the Chamber has found that Bagosora had authority over the Rwandan army at the time of the attack (IV.1.2). The organised attack, involving elite units of the Rwandan army, targeted a senior government official. In the Chamber's view, the order for such an assault could only have come from the highest military authority, which at the time was Bagosora. In this respect, the Chamber also bears in mind his refusal to consult with the Prime Minister, his suspicions that she was involved in an attempted *coup d'état*, and his awareness that UNAMIR wanted her to address the nation. The Chamber has not heard sufficient evidence directly implicating Kabiligi, Ntabakuze or Nsengiyumva in this crime".[593] - Rape at Saint Josephite centre, in Kigali, on 8 April 1994: "Based on Witness DBJ's testimony, the Chamber finds beyond reasonable doubt that, on 8 April, soldiers wearing black berets and militiamen attacked and killed a number of Tutsi refuges at the Saint Josephite Centre. Many female victims were forced to undress before being killed. During the course of the attack, at least one Tutsi woman was raped by a soldier. The Chamber, however, is not satisfied that the witness's testimony convincingly demonstrates that the soldiers were members of the Presidential Guard as opposed to another unit of the army. The witness did not know if there was any difference between the uniform of the Presidential Guard and other units. The Chamber has found that Bagosora had authority over the Rwandan army at the time of the attack (IV.1.2). There is no evidence directly showing that Bagosora was aware of the specific attack at the [Saint Josephite Centre]. However, given the widespread killing throughout Kigali perpetrated by or with the assistance of soldiers, the Chamber is convinced that Bagosora was aware that soldiers under his authority were partic-

590 *Théoneste Bagosora et al.* Trial Judgement, para. 705 (internal references omitted).

591 *Théoneste Bagosora et al.* Trial Judgement, para. 717 (internal reference omitted).

592 *Théoneste Bagosora et al.* Trial Judgement, para. 720.

593 *Théoneste Bagosora et al.* Trial Judgement, paras. 723–724.

	ipating in killings. The Chamber has not heard sufficient evidence directly implicating Kabiligi or Ntabakuze in this crime".[594] "On 8 April, soldiers wearing black berets and militiamen attacked and killed a number of Tutsi refugees at the Saint Josephite Centre. The assailants initially asked to see the refugees' identity cards, and Hutus were asked to leave. During the course of the attack, some of the women were asked to undress before being killed and at least one woman was raped by a soldier. […] Considering the nature of how the attacks unfolded, the Chamber finds that soldiers, gendarmes or *Interahamwe* participating in the events intentionally killed Tutsis during these events. Furthermore, the acts of rape, sexual violence and mistreatment constituted serious bodily or mental harm. The Chamber heard extensive evidence about the killing of Tutsi civilians throughout Kigali area and in other parts of Rwanda in the days immediately after the death of President Habyarimana. In the course of many of the attacks, the assailants checked the identity cards of the victims or asked Hutus to leave. In these circumstances, the only reasonable conclusion is that the assailants who physically perpetrated the killings possessed the intent to destroy, in whole or in substantial part, the Tutsi group. The Chamber concluded that Bagosora bears superior responsibility for the crimes committed in […] the Saint Josephite Centre […]. In the circumstances of the attacks, described above, Bagosora […] also would have been fully aware of the participants' genocidal intent".[595] "The Chamber has found that acts of rape occurred during attacks on civilians at […] the Saint Josephite Centre (III.3.5.5) […]. It is clear that, given the circumstances surrounding these attacks, there could have been no consent for these acts of sexual violence and that the perpetrators would have known this fact. The Chamber has determined that the crimes at these locations were committed as part of a widespread and systematic attack on ethnic and political grounds (IV.3.2). Bagosora bears superior responsibility for the crimes committed at […] the Saint Josephite Centre […]. As noted above, the assailants and the Accused were aware that these attacks formed part of widespread and systematic attacks against the civilian population on ethnic and political grounds (IV.3.2). The Chamber finds Bagosora guilty of rape as a crime against humanity (Count 7) for the rapes committed between 7 and 9 April 1994 […] at the Saint Josephite Centre […] under Article 6 (3)".[596] - Rapes and sexual assaults at Gikondo parish, in Kigali, on 9 April 1994: "According to the military observers, the Rwandan army blocked off access to the area that morning, and then gendarmes, carrying lists, moved methodically through it escorting or sending Tutsis to the church. Other Tutsis also fled to the church. The priests and military observers, who were at the residence, heard screams from the church and walked over to investigate. The gendarmes seized them and held them against the wall with gun barrels pressed to their throats. The gendarmes compared identity cards of the Tutsi refugees to the lists that they were carrying. The identity cards were then burned as the *Interahamwe* entered the church and began killing the refugees over the course of the next several hours. Beardsley recounted the crimes in detail: 'Pregnant women had their stomachs slashed open, foetuses on the floor. Even a foetus was smashed. I remember -- just from the time I was there, I remember looking down, a woman obviously had tried to protect her baby. Somebody had rolled her off the baby. The baby was still alive and trying to feed on her breasts. She'd been -- her clothes had been ripped off. The killing that was done was not done, in their opinion, to kill the people immediately; it had been done to kill them slowly. Women's breasts, women vaginas had been cut with machetes; men's scrotum areas cut with

594 *Théoneste Bagosora et al.* Trial Judgement, paras. 938–939 (internal reference omitted).

595 *Théoneste Bagosora et al.* Trial Judgement, paras. 2129, 2133–2135 (internal reference omitted).

596 *Théoneste Bagosora et al.* Trial Judgement, paras. 2201–2203 (internal reference omitted).

	machetes. Men had been hamstrung behind their Achilles' tendons so that they couldn't walk, but they would have to watch what was happening to their families. There was rape that had taken place in addition to the killings, and the murder. The priests and military observers were forced to watch, and the gendarmes beat them with rifle butts if they averted their eyes from the killing. After a few hours, the gendarmes and militiamen became tired of the killing and left'".[597] "The Chamber finds beyond reasonable doubt that the Rwandan army, gendarmerie and *Interahamwe* conducted a joint operation to seal off the Gikondo area, to identify specific Tutsis there and to kill them along with all other Tutsi at the parish, a traditional place of refuge. Lists were used in ensuring that specific Tutsis were killed. The perpetrators also engaged in sexual assault and rape during the attack. The Chamber has found that Bagosora had authority over the Rwandan army at the time of the attack (IV.1.2). There is no evidence directly showing that Bagosora was aware of the attack on the parish. However, given the widespread killing throughout Kigali perpetrated by or with the assistance of military personnel, the Chamber is satisfied that Bagosora was aware that personnel under his authority were participating in killings. The Chamber, however, has not heard sufficient evidence directly implicating Kabiligi, Ntabakuze or Nsengiyumva in this crime".[598] "During an attack on Gikondo Parish on the morning of 9 April, the army sealed off the Gikondo area, and gendarmes moved systematically through the neighbourhood with lists, sending Tutsis to the parish. The gendarmes checked the identity cards of the Tutsis there against their lists and burned the identity cards. The *Interahamwe* then proceeded to kill the more than 150 Tutsi refugees in an atrocious manner. The parish priests and UNAMIR military observers were forced to watch at gunpoint. Major Brent Beardsley of UNAMIR arrived shortly after the attack and described the terrible scene, which bore witness of killing, mutilation and rape. The *Interahamwe* returned later that night to finish off the survivors. Considering the nature of how the attacks unfolded, the Chamber finds that soldiers, gendarmes or *Interahamwe* participating in the events intentionally killed Tutsis during these events. Furthermore, the acts of rape, sexual violence and mistreatment constituted serious bodily or mental harm. The Chamber heard extensive evidence about the killing of Tutsi civilians throughout Kigali area and in other parts of Rwanda in the days immediately after the death of President Habyarimana. In the course of many of the attacks, the assailants checked the identity cards of the victims or asked Hutus to leave. In these circumstances, the only reasonable conclusion is that the assailants who physically perpetrated the killings possessed the intent to destroy, in whole or in substantial part, the Tutsi group. The Chamber concluded that Bagosora bears superior responsibility for the crimes committed in […] Gikondo Parish (IV.1.2). […] In the circumstances of the attacks, described above, Bagosora […] also would have been fully aware of the participants' genocidal intent".[599] "The Chamber has found that acts of rape occurred during attacks on civilians at […] Gikondo Parish (III.3.5.8). It is clear that, given the circumstances surrounding these attacks, there could have been no consent for these acts of sexual violence and that the perpetrators would have known this fact. The Chamber has determined that the crimes at these locations were committed as part of a widespread and systematic attack on ethnic and political grounds (IV.3.2). Bagosora bears superior responsibility for the crimes committed at […] Gikondo Parish (IV.1.2). As noted above, the assailants and the Accused were aware that these attacks formed part of widespread and systematic attacks against the civilian population on ethnic and political grounds (IV.3.2). The

597 *Théoneste Bagosora et al.* Trial Judgement, para. 976 (internal reference omitted).

598 *Théoneste Bagosora et al.* Trial Judgement, paras. 988–989.

599 *Théoneste Bagosora et al.* Trial Judgement, paras. 2132–2135.

	Chamber finds Bagosora guilty of rape as a crime against humanity (Count 7) for the rapes committed […] at […] Gikondo Parish under Article 6 (3)".[600] - Alleged rapes of Tutsi women refugees from *École technique officielle* (ESO) while being forced to walk to Nyanza hill, in Kigali, on 11 April 1994: "Alison Des Forges, an expert in Rwandan history, testified that, after UNAMIR peacekeepers withdrew from ETO on 11 April 1994, militiamen attacked the 2,000 refugees there forcing them to flee. The refugees were stopped by members of the Para Commando Battalion at the Sonatube junction where they were held for approximately an hour before being marched towards Nyanza. A Belgian officer recognised and greeted Ntabakuze at the intersection. The officer was concerned for the refugees, but was unable to alert his superiors over the radio network. Des Forges made reference to written records from the Belgian peacekeeping contingent as part of the basis of her testimony. As the military and militiamen marched the refugees towards Nyanza, assailants pulled women from the column and raped them, sometimes killing them in the bushes. The refugees were stopped at the top of Nyanza hill, where they sat down for approximately 30 minutes. A truck carrying military personnel arrived, and the military fired at the refugees, giving the signal to the militiamen to begin the attack. Des Forges did not specify which unit of the military accompanied the refugees to Nyanza but said that the operation was carried out 'jointly through cooperation between paracommando, gendarme and militia'. The killing continued throughout the night, and assailants returned the following day to loot and finish off survivors. Nearly all the refugees were killed. According to Des Forges, they were killed at Nyanza because it was 'a place remote from observation, unlike the Sonatube intersection, which would not be an appropriate place for a massacre'".[601] "Based primarily on the evidence of Witness AR, the Chamber finds that the column of refugees arrived at Nyanza hill around 5.00 p.m. where they were met by 15 to 20 soldiers, most of whom were wearing camouflage berets, which had passed them on their way in a Toyota pickup truck. The Chamber is satisfied that the soldiers escorting the refugees and in the pickup truck were primarily members of the Para Commando Battalion since, as discussed above, they left from the Para Commando position at the Sonatube junction and because of their camouflage uniforms and camouflage berets. Des Forges mentioned that some of the refugees were raped as they were marched to Nyanza. She was not specifically questioned by the parties on this point, her evidence does not indicate the identity of the perpetrators, and there was no corroboration by direct evidence in the present case".[602] - Rapes in the Kiyovu neighbourhood, in Kigali, from mid-April 1994: Prosecution Witness DAS testified as follows: "After Zigiranyirazo left around 15 or 16 April, and without his knowledge, the *Interahamwe* and soldiers, including Corporal Irandemba, would take away young Hutu and Tutsi women and rape them at a property located in front of Zigiranyirazo's residence, referred to as the 'Chinese house'. Rapes also occurred inside Zigiranyirazo's plot. Women were locked inside the Chinese house property, fed by *Interahamwe* and prevented from escaping. The witness mentioned five such women who were later rescued by the RPF: Goretti, Mutesi from the post office, Epiphany at Electrogaz, Immaculate, a businesswoman, and Davita".[603] The Trial Chamber found: "The main question for the Chamber is whether Bagosora

[600] *Théoneste Bagosora et al.* Trial Judgement, paras. 2201–2203 (internal reference omitted).

[601] *Théoneste Bagosora et al.* Trial Judgement, paras. 1324–1325 (internal references omitted).

[602] *Théoneste Bagosora et al.* Trial Judgement, para. 1354.

[603] *Théoneste Bagosora et al.* Trial Judgement, para. 1469 (internal reference omitted).

	or Nsengiyumva visited a roadblock in Kiyovu between mid-April and the end of June 1994 and encouraged the crimes committed there. Witness DAS provided the only first-hand account to this effect. The Chamber accepts that he lived and worked in Kiyovu in 1994 and therefore would have been familiar with the events in the area, including the killing and rape of persons apprehended at the roadblock".[604] "The Chamber also accepts Witness DAS's testimony that, after 15 or 16 April, *Interahamwe* and soldiers at the roadblock would take young Hutu and Tutsi women and house them nearby. The assailants would then rape them. The witness was present at the roadblock when this happened and it further is consistent with the pattern of sexual violence, which occurred in connection with roadblocks (III.5.1). In sum, the Chamber is satisfied that roadblocks were established by soldiers and civilians in the Kiyovu neighbourhood between 7 and 9 April 1994. At least from 12 April, the assailants at them killed Tutsi civilians. From 15 or 16 April, young women were stopped at them and raped nearby. The evidence reflects active coordination between the military and civilian assailants. The Prosecution, however, has not proven beyond reasonable doubt that Bagosora and Nsengiyumva were present at the roadblocks or that Bagosora distributed weapons at them".[605] - Sexual violence in Gisenyi prefecture: "It is well known that rape and other forms of sexual violence were widespread in Rwanda during the events in 1994. This follows in part from Prosecution Expert Witness Binaifer Nowrojee. The Chamber has determined that these acts were committed open and notoriously at Kigali area roadblocks (III.5.1; III.4.1.7), the Kabgayi religious centre (III.4.4.1), and during the attacks at the Saint Josephite Centre (III.3.5.5) and Gikondo Parish (III.3.5.8). Furthermore, the case law of this Tribunal has shown that sexual violence was widespread. The question here is whether Nsengiyumva is responsible for specific acts of rape committed in Gisenyi prefecture as alleged by Witnesses ZF and Serushago. The Prosecution presented two main witnesses in order to prove allegations of rape or other forms of sexual violence in Gisenyi prefecture during the relevant events. Witness ZF provided the only testimony on the existence of the rape house allegedly used by militiamen in Gisenyi. His testimony is largely second-hand, although he claims that he visited the house with Lieutenant Bizumuremyi. It is also uncorroborated. Furthermore, he also did not witness any specific crimes of sexual violence there. His testimony concerning Nsengiyumva's alleged visit to the *Commune Rouge* is similarly uncorroborated. The Prosecution did not examine Serushago, who Witness ZF saw there, on this alleged incident. The Chamber has elsewhere expressed concern about the credibility of other aspects of Witness ZF's testimony (III.2.7–9; III.3.6.1). The Chamber views his testimony concerning the rape house with caution. The Chamber therefore declines to accept Witness ZF's testimony on these points without corroboration. Serushago testified generally about rape committed by militiamen and soldiers at the *Commune Rouge*. He provided only one example of rape committed there, referring to a rape involving an alleged military reservist named Migendo who was also an intelligence officer. No detail was provided about this incident, and it is not clear whether Serushago has direct knowledge of the incident. The Chamber notes the difference between his testimony and his statement in February 1998 to Tribunal investigators where he said Migendo had left the military. Serushago claimed that his statement was not properly interpreted. However, this explanation is not entirely convincing, in particular since the investigator confirmed Migendo's status with Serushago during the interview. Serushago is the sole witness to testify about rapes committed by Munyagishari. His evidence on this point is second-hand and lacking in any detail. Serushago is an alleged accomplice

604 *Théoneste Bagosora et al.* Trial Judgement, para. 1489.

605 *Théoneste Bagosora et al.* Trial Judgement, paras. 1504–1505.

of Nsengiyumva, who has been convicted of genocide. The Chamber views his evidence with caution. In view of these concerns, the Chamber declines to accept these parts of his testimony without corroboration. The Nsengiyumva Defence also points to the evidence of Witnesses CF-1 and NR-1, attesting to Serushago boasting about rapes he committed, to attack his credibility. In view of the Chamber's findings, it is not necessary to assess these second-hand allegations in detail. Accordingly, the Prosecution has not established beyond reasonable doubt the allegations connecting Nsengiyumva to sexual violence in Gisenyi prefecture. The Chamber held during the trial that Nsengiyumva had adequate notice of his alleged role in these crimes. It is therefore not necessary to revisit the Defence's challenges to the notice provided for these incidents in the Indictment".[606]

- Rapes at Kabgayi religious centre, in Gitarama prefecture, between April and June 1994:

"Witness DAZ, a Tutsi, was a refugee at the nursing school at the Kabgayi religious centre in Gitarama prefecture from April until June 1994. Her written statement was admitted pursuant to Rule 92 *bis,* and she was cross-examined by the Defence in relation to Kabgayi. The witness estimated that approximately 3,000 refugees were at the centre during this period. A group of two or three soldiers and 10 to 15 *Interahamwe* came to the school around three times a week, usually between 10.00 and 11.00 a.m., to abduct young men and intellectuals. Sometimes these assailants carried lists and searched for specific individuals. The persons taken from the school were never seen again by the witness. The assailants also abducted women in order to rape them. In addition, there were wounded soldiers at the school who would rape the female refugees at night. The witness saw around four dead bodies every morning. Two soldiers raped Witness DAZ on 26 May around 7.00 p.m. in one of the rooms at the nursing school. The soldiers beat her with their guns as they took her to the room. When they arrived, the soldiers asked her if she was Tutsi. After she said 'yes', a soldier raped her while calling her an *Inyenzi.* The soldiers also said that they were raping her because she was a Tutsi. Another soldier raped her in the same room on 28 May, calling her an *Inyenzi* and telling her that she must suffer because of her kinsmen. The witness was able to identify the perpetrators as soldiers because they wore uniforms. However, she acknowledged that she could not distinguish between soldiers by their unit or rank and that she had never seen a gendarme. Witness UT, a Tutsi, was a refugee at the Kabgayi religious centre. Her statement was admitted pursuant to Rule 92 *bis*. She was cross-examined by the Defence in connection with the events at Gikondo Parish, but was not questioned on Kabgayi. The witness stated that soldiers and *Interahamwe* abducted injured refugees, including her husband, and killed them. Soldiers also came at night to take young women. The women would return the next morning and speak about suffering repeated rapes by multiple soldiers. They wore camouflage uniforms and various types of head gear. The witness stated that she could distinguish between soldiers and gendarmes by the color of their berets, but was not able to identify a particular unit".[607]

"There are a number of facts related to the events at the Kabgayi religious centre that are not disputed. From 7 April to 2 June 1994, thousands of mostly Tutsi refugees gathered at the centre, fleeing ethnic violence in surrounding areas as well as the resumed hostilities. Several soldiers from the Gitarama military camp were stationed there or nearby. There was also a gendarmerie post two kilometres away. During this period, wounded soldiers received treatment at the Kabgayi hospital, including some

606 *Théoneste Bagosora et al.* Trial Judgement, paras. 1728–1733 (internal references omitted).

607 *Théoneste Bagosora et al.* Trial Judgement, paras. 1757–1759 (internal references omitted).

	members of the Para Commando Battalion. In addition, some women, including Witness DAZ, were raped by individuals in military uniform".[608] "Turning to the evidence of other crimes at the Kabgayi religious centre, it follows from the unchallenged evidence from Witnesses DAZ and UT that individuals in military uniforms and *Interahamwe* repeatedly raped some Tutsi women at the complex. Some of these assailants were wounded military personnel being treated at the Kabgayi hospital. In the case of Witness DAZ, the assailants said that they were raping her because she was a Tutsi. Their evidence also reflects that groups of assailants periodically abducted refugees, sometimes using lists. While the evidence of Witness DI-35 suggests that there were no crimes committed in the centre, this testimony is not convincing in light of the evidence of Witnesses DAZ and UT. In addition, Witness DI-35's evidence covers a limited period, given his transfer to Kigali on 4 May. Therefore, he was not in a position to know what transpired at the centre after that date. The Chamber notes, however, that there is little evidence indicating whether the military personnel were part of the army or the gendarmerie and no evidence as to their unit. The evidence of Witnesses DAZ, UT and Des Forges about the individual crimes committed at the centre is too general for the Chamber to make any specific findings on their scope. There is insufficient evidence demonstrating that Bagosora, Kabiligi and Ntabakuze were aware of or otherwise connected to the specific crimes committed at Kabgayi or in Gitarama prefecture in general. The Chamber has not found that Bagosora had authority over the Rwandan military after 9 April when the Minister of Defence returned (IV.1.2). Similarly, the Prosecution did not establish that Kabiligi exercised command over the army (IV.1.3). The evidence also does not show that either of them were at Kabgayi during the relevant events or had any specific involvement in the crimes committed there or elsewhere in the prefecture. As discussed above, it was not proven that Ntabakuze came to the centre. While there were some wounded members of the Para Commando Battalion at Kabgayi, there is not a sufficient basis to determine that they were involved in the rape or killing of refugees there".[609] - Rapes at Kigali roadblocks: "The Chamber also received other evidence about crimes at such roadblocks. Witness XAB, a Tutsi member of the Third Company of the Para Commando Battalion, heard from a member of the First Company that its soldiers were raping Tutsi women along with *Interahamwe* at Sobolirwa position. Witness DBQ, a Hutu, who was purportedly a member of the Para Commando Battalion, described *Interahamwe* and soldiers manning roadblocks in the vicinity of Ntabakuze's command post at the Giporoso junction in Remera. He claimed that people were stopped at these roadblocks and taken away and killed. Ntabakuze denied that members of his battalion manned roadblocks with *Interahamwe* or committed rapes at their positions".[610] "Civilian roadblocks were usually run by a soldier, policeman, gendarme or a civilian armed with a gun. The leader might also have grenades and, occasionally, a hand-held Motorola radio. The roadblocks manned by militia appeared to be the most dangerous, in particular after 8 or 9 April 1994. These locations were sites of open and notorious slaughter and sexual assault. Several witnesses, including Dallaire and Beardsley, observed dead men and women around roadblocks throughout Kigali, including children. The bodies of the dead were frequently piled near the roadblocks and at times were collected by local officials. Female victims were left lying on their back with their legs spread and stained with semen. Dallaire saw objects crushed or implanted in vaginas, breasts cut off, stomachs opened and the mutilated genitals of men. The only

608 *Théoneste Bagosora et al.* Trial Judgement, para. 1767 (internal reference omitted).

609 *Théoneste Bagosora et al.* Trial Judgement, paras. 1775–1776 (internal reference omitted).

610 *Théoneste Bagosora et al.* Trial Judgement, para. 1906 (internal references omitted).

	uniformed soldier among the dead whom Dallaire observed at a roadblock was one of his military observers".[611] "The evidence clearly demonstrates that civilian roadblocks manned by militia were sites of slaughter and sexual assault from 7 April. In view of the accounts, in particular of UNAMIR personnel, the Chamber does not accept that anyone travelling in Kigali in the early period of conflict would not have seen the crimes being committed at roadblocks. The Chamber is mindful though of the testimony of Major MacNeil, an operations officer for UNAMIR's humanitarian cell, who stated that most of the bodies had been removed when he arrived on 20 April. There is evidence, in particular from MacNeil, that the RPF was daily infiltrating behind the Rwandan government's front line. A roadblock is in principle designed to combat such infiltration. However, the scope of the violence inflicted at these installations, which included sexual assault and the killing of the elderly and children, cannot be justified by the threat of infiltration. The main question for the Chamber is whether the Accused bear responsibility for the crimes which occurred at these sites. The Chamber does not have direct evidence of an explicit order emanating from the military or government to establish or man roadblocks. There is Prosecution and Defence evidence that suggests that the roadblocks were erected spontaneously and were under no one's control. The Chamber does not exclude that some of the roadblocks in Kigali at various places and points in time fell into this category. Nevertheless, the Chamber observes that there was an extensive network of roadblocks throughout Kigali. They were mounted from 7 April at the same time that the Rwandan military was publicly asking civilians to stay home (IV.1.2). Some of these were manned by both civilian and military personnel. Rwandan military and government vehicles had little difficulty passing through them while UNAMIR and other civilians frequently had difficulty, absent written authorisation from the Rwandan authorities. High ranking army officers, including Bagosora, served as points of contact to facilitate movement through them. The Chamber also recalls that, during a meeting with UNAMIR on 17 May 1994, Bagosora referred to the civilians manning roadblocks as being responsible for the civil defence of Kigali (III.2.6.2). Therefore, as a general matter, in view of this evidence as well as the strategic importance of Kigali in the war against the RPF, the Chamber is satisfied that a majority of the roadblocks in Kigali were established and operated at the behest of or with the blessing of government or military authorities as part of its defensive effort (III.2.6.2). In view of this, the Chamber does not accept the Defence submission that the army was unable to put an end to the violence occurring at roadblocks. The evidence of Alison Des Forges that militia groups acted increasingly on their own as the conflict progressed, as well as that of Major MacNeil concerning the evacuation of orphans in mid-May, however, demonstrates that this control was not always effective, even when high-ranking army and gendarmerie personnel were involved. Nevertheless, there is no doubt that civilian and military authorities exercised some degree of control or influence over them. As for Bagosora's responsibility, the Chamber recalls that he was the main authority in the Ministry of Defence from 6 to 9 April, with control over the Rwandan army and gendarmerie (IV.1.2). It is inconceivable in view of the open and notorious slaughter at roadblocks that he would be unaware of the crimes being committed at them or the presence of military personnel at some of the primarily civilian ones, notwithstanding his denial to the contrary. In the Chamber's view, Bagosora is responsible for the crimes committed at roadblocks in the Kigali area during this period. This does not mean that other authorities are not also culpable for their role in establishing and operating them. With respect to Ntabakuze, there is no evidence that Ntabakuze participated in the wider system of primarily civilian roadblocks throughout Kigali. In addition, it has not been shown that members of the Para Commando Battalion were present at civilian roadblocks. Witness XAB testified that he heard that members of the Para Commando Battalion were raping women at a

611 *Théoneste Bagosora et al.* Trial Judgement, para. 1908 (internal references omitted).

	military check point at the Sobolirwa position and killing those who resisted. His testimony is uncorroborated and second-hand, and the Chamber declines to accept Witness XAB's evidence on this point. […] Based on the foregoing, the Chamber is not convinced beyond reasonable doubt that members of the Para Commando Battalion committed rapes at the Sobolirwa military position or that members of that battalion and *Interahamwe* together committed killings at the roadblocks in the Remera-Giporoso area. The Kabiligi Defence has presented an alibi that Kabiligi was outside of Rwanda until 23 April (III.6.2). Furthermore, the Chamber has not found that he had operative authority over Rwandan army personnel (IV.1.3). The Prosecution has not proven beyond reasonable doubt that Kabiligi bears responsibility for crimes committed at roadblocks".[612] "Roadblocks manned primarily by civilians, at times with a soldier or gendarme at its head, proliferated throughout Kigali, beginning on 7 April 1994. The civilians were mostly members of political party militias or local inhabitants who volunteered or were pressed into service at them as part of the "civil defence" efforts (III.2.6.2). The roadblocks were used to check the identities of passers-by. Tutsis, persons without identification documents, and Hutu members of opposition parties were singled out. These roadblocks were sites of open and notorious slaughter and sexual assault from 7 April. The Chamber finds that, considering the purpose of roadblocks, the assailants at them intentionally killed Tutsis. The Chamber also finds that the acts of rape, sexual violence and mistreatment of Tutsis there constituted serious bodily or mental harm. The Chamber heard extensive evidence about the killing of Tutsi civilians throughout the Kigali area at roadblocks immediately after the death of President Habyarimana. The assailants checked the identity cards of the victims and targeted mainly Tutsis along with Hutus suspected of being sympathetic to the RPF. In these circumstances, the only reasonable conclusion is that the assailants who physically perpetrated the killings possessed the intent to destroy, in whole or in substantial part, the Tutsi group. The Chamber has considered, as the only reasonable inference, that Bagosora in the exercise of his authority between 6 and 9 April 1994 ordered the crimes at Kigali area roadblocks (III.2.6.2). In the context of the open and notorious targeting and slaughter of Tutsis at them, he was aware of the genocidal intent of the perpetrators and shared it".[613] "The Chamber has found that acts of rape occurred during attacks on civilians at Kigali area roadblocks (III.5.1) […]. It is clear that, given the circumstances surrounding these attacks, there could have been no consent for these acts of sexual violence and that the perpetrators would have known this fact. The Chamber has determined that the crimes at these locations were committed as part of a widespread and systematic attack on ethnic and political grounds (IV.3.2). Bagosora bears superior responsibility for the crimes committed at Kigali area roadblocks between 7 and 9 April […]. As noted above, the assailants and the Accused were aware that these attacks formed part of widespread and systematic attacks against the civilian population on ethnic and political grounds (IV.3.2). The Chamber finds Bagosora guilty of rape as a crime against humanity (Count 7) for the rapes committed between 7 and 9 April 1994 at Kigali area […] under Article 6 (3)".[614]

15. Emmanuel **Rukundo** (Case No. ICTR-01-70)

Priest and military chaplain for the Rwandan Armed Forces in Ruhengeri and Gisenyi military sectors from February 1993 until May 1994 and in Kigali from May 1994.

[612] *Théoneste Bagosora et al.* Trial Judgement, paras. 1920–1925, 1927–1928 (internal references omitted).

[613] *Théoneste Bagosora et al.* Trial Judgement, paras. 2123–2126.

[614] *Théoneste Bagosora et al.* Trial Judgement, paras. 2201–2203 (internal reference omitted).

Indictment (International sex crimes (or related) charges and mode(s) of liability)	- **Genocide** (count 1) under Article 6(1) of the Statute for various crimes, including for **causing serious mental harm** to a young Tutsi woman by sexually assaulting her at the Saint Léon Minor Seminary on or about 15 May 1994.[615]
Trial Judgement	- By majority, Judge Seon Ki Park dissenting, guilty of **Genocide** (count 1) under Article 6(1) of the Statute (**committing**) for various crimes, including for sexually assaulting Witness CCH, a young Tutsi woman, at the Saint Léon Minor Seminary **causing her serious mental harm**.[616]
Appeal Judgement	- The Appeals Chamber, Judge Fausto Pocar dissenting, **reversed Emmanuel Rukundo's conviction for genocide** (count 1) **insofar as it concerned the sexual assault of Witness CCH at the Saint Léon Minor Seminary**.[617]
Legal and Factual Findings and/or Evidence	- Factual and legal findings: - Sexual assault of Witness CCH at the Saint Léon minor seminary on or about 15 May 1994: "The Indictment alleges that, on or about 15 May 1994, at the St. Léon Minor Seminary, Rukundo took a young Tutsi woman into his room, locked the door and sexually assaulted her, therefore causing her serious mental harm. Witness CCH, the alleged victim, is the only witness who testified in support of the Prosecution's case. Rukundo denied the allegation. Witness CCH's testimony is that, in the later part of May 1994, Rukundo came to the St. Léon Minor Seminary. Witness CCH greeted Rukundo, introduced herself and asked him if he could hide her. Rukundo responded that he could not help her. He said that her entire family had to be killed because her relative was an *Inyenzi*. Nevertheless, Witness CCH assisted him in carrying some items to his room, in the hope that he would change his mind and hide her. While in the room, Rukundo locked the door, placed his pistol on the table next to the bed and began to caress the witness. He forced her onto the bed, opened the zipper on his trousers and

615 *Prosecutor v. Emmanuel Rukundo*, Case No. ICTR-01-70-PT, Amended Indictment, 6 October 2006, pp. 3–4 ("**Count 1: GENOCIDE** The Prosecutor charges **Emmanuel RUKUNDO** with **GENOCIDE**, a crime stipulated in Article 2(3)(a) of the Statute, in that from 6 April through 17 July 1994, in Rwanda, notably in Gitarama and Cyangugu Prefectures, **Emmanuel RUKUNDO** was responsible for killing or causing serious bodily or mental harm to members of the Tutsi racial or ethnic group with the intent to destroy, on whole or in part, a racial or ethnic group, as such, as outlined in paragraphs 3 through 22 below. Pursuant to Article 6(1) of the Statute, the accused, **Emmanuel RUKUNDO**, is individually responsible for the crime of Genocide because he planned, instagted, ordered, committed or otherwise aided and abetted in the planning, preparation or execution of this crime, with the object, purpose, and foreseeable outcome being the commission of genocide against the Tutsi racial or ethnic group, and persons identified as Tutsis, in Gitarama and Cyangugu Prefectures, Rwanda. With respect to the commission of this crime, **Emmanuel RUKUNDO**, relying on the authority due to his position as a priest and military chaplain in the RAF, ordered, instigated, or aided and abetted soldiers, armed civilians and the *interahamwe* militia, for at least the period of 6 April through 17 July 1994, to do the acts described below in this indictment. The particulars that give rise to his individual criminal responsibility are set forth in paragraphs 3 through 22 below".), para. 14 ("On one occasion on or about 15 May 1994, at the Saint Léon Minor Seminary, **Emmanuel RUKUNDO**, armed and escorted by an armed soldier, took a young Tutsi refugee woman into his room, locked the door, and sexually assaulted her. These acts of **Emmanuel RUKUNDO** caused her serious mental harm".).

616 *Prosecutor v. Emmanuel Rukundo*, Case No. ICTR-01-70-T, Judgement, dated 27 February 2009 and filed on 13 March 2009 ("*Rukundo* Trial Judgement"), paras. 372–389, 574–576, 591. See also *Rukundo* Trial Judgement, Dissenting opinion of Judge Park, paras. 1–7.

617 *Emmanuel Rukundo v. The Prosecutor*, Case No. ICTR-01-70-A, Judgement, 20 October 2010 ("*Rukundo* Appeal Judgement"), paras. 227–238, 270. See also *Rukundo* Appeal Judgement, Partially Dissenting Opinion of Judge Pocar, paras. 1–13.

	lay on top of her. He tried to spread her legs and have sexual intercourse, but she resisted. Following Witness CCH's continued resistance, Rukundo gave up trying to have intercourse, but rubbed himself against her until he ejaculated. Witness CCH said that she could not escape since he was on top of her, holding her down. He was also in a position of authority and had a gun. Rukundo admitted to visiting the St. Léon Minor Seminary on 21 May 1994, but maintained that he did not see Witness CCH. He further stated that he had no access to any room at the Seminary since he was not a resident. If he wanted access to a room, he would have needed to obtain a key from the bursar. The Defence argues that since Witness CCH is the only person to allege sexual assault by Rukundo, her story should not be believed. The Defence further claims that the witness has a motive to make false allegations against the Accused because she believes that Rukundo is responsible for the death of one of her relatives. The Defence argues that Witness CCH's testimony is improbable and that, even if believed, the elements of the alleged crime have not been established. Witness CCH denied the proposition that she had made up the allegation of sexual assault to avenge the death of her relative. Witness CCH stated that she did not attribute her relative's death to Rukundo and she did not hear that Rukundo may have been responsible for the death, although she knew Rukundo wanted that relative dead. Witness CCH confirmed that she never told anyone of the incident because, as a young girl, one could not report an attempted rape, especially to a close relative. The Chamber finds Witness CCH to be a credible witness and believes her evidence. This conclusion is supported by her consistent and detailed evidence, by the Accused's admission that he visited the St. Léon Minor Seminary on 21 May 1994 and by Witness SLA's confirmation of the existence of a small room at the Seminary where Rukundo kept his belongings. Finally, the Chamber finds that the allegation that Witness CCH had a motive to give false testimony against the Accused in respect of the sexual assault is not tenable. The Chamber notes, in particular, that the witness only testified that Rukundo attempted to have sexual intercourse with her, rubbed himself against her but did not touch her vagina. She could very well have testified that Rukundo had raped her, but she did not. She could have done so under the witness protection scheme, affording her a pseudonym and protection from public view. In light of the foregoing, the Chamber finds that Rukundo assaulted Witness CCH, as described in her testimony. The Chamber recalls that rape and sexual violence 'constitute genocide in the same way as any other act as long as they were committed with the specific intent to destroy, in whole or in part, a particular group, targeted as such.' Sexual violence was broadly defined in *Akayesu* as '…any act of a sexual nature which is committed on a person under circumstances which are coercive. Sexual violence is not limited to physical invasion of the human body and may include acts which do not involve penetration or even physical contact.' In order for the act of sexual violence to constitute genocide pursuant to Article 2(2)(b) of the Statute, it must have caused serious bodily or mental harm to members of the group. From the evidence adduced in this case, the Chamber considers it proper to proceed as follows. First, the Chamber will determine whether the act in question was of a sexual nature. Second, the Chamber will determine whether there existed coercive circumstances. Third, the Chamber will determine whether the act, if sexual and committed under coercive circumstances, caused Witness CCH serious mental harm, as alleged by the Prosecution. The actions in question were clearly of a sexual nature: Rukundo forced sexual contact with her by opening the zipper of his trousers, trying to remove her skirt, forcefully lying on top of her and caressing and rubbing himself against her until he ejaculated and lost his erection. Rukundo's actions and words, such as telling her that if she made love with him he would never forget her, support the Chamber's finding that his actions were of a sexual nature. In *Akayesu*, the Trial Chamber stated that, '… coercive circumstances need not be evidenced by a show of physical force. Threats, intimidation, extortion and other forms of duress which prey on fear or desperation may constitute coercion, and coercion may be inherent in certain circumstances, such as armed conflict or the military presence of

	Interahamwe among refugee Tutsi women at the bureau communal.' When it was put to Witness CCH in cross-examination that Rukundo did not use any threat or force to convince her to have sexual intercourse with him, she replied that '[y]ou don't need to use a gun to threaten somebody. He definitely did not point his gun at me. But, remember that he's the one who pushed me to the bed, and he took into account the weakness – the weak point from which I was. That was also a disguised threat …' She further testified that she drank a beer with Rukundo to acknowledge his position of authority and that she ultimately thought he was taking advantage of his position. The Chamber notes that Witness CCH testified that the situation surrounding the Tutsi refugees at the St. Léon Minor Seminary from April until June 1994 was dangerous. Other witnesses testified that many Tutsi refugees were regularly abducted from the St. Léon Minor Seminary and killed. Witness CCH further testified that, fearing for her life, she implored the Accused to hide her. Rukundo compounded her fear by indicating that she and her family must be killed because her relative was an *Inyenzi*. At all material times, Rukundo was armed with a gun. After Witness CCH assisted Rukundo to bring some of his belongings to a small room, he locked her inside the room alone with him; and, placing a pistol on a nearby table, he proceeded to force himself upon her, while she struggled to free herself from his control. The Chamber finds that these events, taken together, clearly constitute coercive circumstances. The Appeals Chamber has also stated that the element of non-consent in the crime of rape [or sexual violence] can be proved beyond reasonable doubt when the Prosecution demonstrates the existence of coercive circumstances under which meaningful consent is not possible. A Trial Chamber, however, is still entitled to admit evidence under certain special circumstances that the victim specifically consented. Although the Defence denied that Witness CCH's consent of sexual assault was in issue, in cross-examination, questions were put to her by Defence Counsel regarding the possible interpretation of her behaviour as consent. After examining the evidence, the Chamber concludes that the coercive circumstances, as found above, indeed vitiated Witness CCH's ability to consent to the sexual assault in question. The Chamber has already expressed the general standard required to find serious mental harm with regards to the allegation at the Bishopric. Although the mental harm suffered must be more than a minor or temporary impairment of mental faculties, it need not be permanent or irremediable. Additionally, the Trial Chamber in *Kamuhanda* stated that serious mental harm could be found when there is a non-mortal act, such as sexual assault, combined with the threat of death. It has further been held that 'rape and sexual violence certainly constitute infliction of serious bodily and mental harm on the victims and are even […] one of the worst ways of inflicting harm on the victim as he or she suffers both bodily and mental harm.' The evidence of Witness CCH, which the Chamber has accepted, describes a young Tutsi woman fearing for her life and seeking protection from a member of the clergy, known to her, who was in a position of authority. Instead of providing protection, Rukundo abused Witness CCH by sexually assaulting her under coercive circumstances. The Chamber acknowledges that it has not had the benefit of any direct evidence on Witness CCH's mental state, following the sexual assault, apart from her testimony that she could not tell anyone about the incident. The Chamber, however, recalls that it may draw inferences from the evidence presented. The Chamber finds it necessary to look beyond the sexual act in question and finds it particularly important to consider the highly charged, oppressive and other circumstances surrounding the sexual assault on Witness CCH. The Chamber notes in particular the following circumstances: 1) Members of her ethnic group were victims of mass killings; 2) She and her family, fearing death in this way, sought refuge in a religious institution; 3) Upon seeing a familiar and trusted person of authority and of the church, *i.e.* the Accused, she requested protection for herself; 4) When the Accused refused her the protection she had requested, he specifically threatened her – that her family was to be killed for its association with the '*Inyenzi*'; 5) Rukundo had a firearm; 6) Still hoping to be protected, Witness CCH sought to ingratiate herself to

	Rukundo by assisting him to carry his effects into a nearby room; 7) The Accused locked her in the room with him, put his firearm down nearby and proceeded to physically manhandle her in a sexual way; and 8) At the time of the incident, Witness CCH was sexually inexperienced. In light of the established jurisprudence and the totality of the evidence, in particular the surrounding circumstances of the sexual assault, the Chamber finds, Judge Park dissenting, that the only reasonable conclusion is that Witness CCH suffered serious mental harm as a consequence of Rukundo's actions".[618] "The Chamber has found that Rukundo sexually assaulted Witness CCH, a young Tutsi woman. The Chamber has further found, Judge Park dissenting, that Witness CCH suffered serious mental harm as a consequence of Rukundo's conduct. Considering the general context of mass violence against the Tutsi in Gitarama *préfecture* and in Kabgayi, and, specifically, Rukundo's words spoken prior to assaulting Witness CCH, that her entire family had to be killed for assisting the *Inyenzi*, the Chamber finds that Rukundo possessed the intent to destroy, in whole or in substantial part, the Tutsi ethnic group. Accordingly, the Chamber finds, Judge Park dissenting, that Rukundo is guilty on Count 1 of the Indictment, under Article 6(1), for committing genocide, through his sexual assault of a young Tutsi woman at the St. Léon Minor Seminary in May 1994".[619] However, the Appeal Chamber reversed this conviction: "The Trial Chamber convicted Rukundo of committing genocide by causing serious mental harm to Witness CCH when he sexually assaulted her towards the end of May 1994 at the Saint Léon Minor Seminary. The Trial Chamber found Witness CCH's account of the incident to be credible, which it described in pertinent part as follows: 'Witness CCH's testimony is that, in the later part of May 1994, Rukundo came to the [Saint] Léon Minor Seminary. Witness CCH greeted Rukundo, introduced herself and asked him if he could hide her. Rukundo responded that he could not help her. He said that her entire family had to be killed because her relative was an *Inyenzi*. Nevertheless, Witness CCH assisted him in carrying some items to his room, in the hope that he would change his mind and hide her. While in the room, Rukundo locked the door, placed his pistol on the table next to the bed and began to caress the witness. He forced her onto the bed, opened the zipper on his trousers and lay on top of her. He tried to spread her legs and have sexual intercourse, but she resisted. Following Witness CCH's continued resistance, Rukundo gave up trying to have intercourse, but rubbed himself against her until he ejaculated. Witness CCH said that she could not escape since he was on top of her, holding her down. He was also in a position of authority and had a gun.' The Trial Chamber considered that Witness CCH's account was corroborated, in part, by Rukundo's admission of visiting the seminary on 21 May 1994 as well as Defence Witness SLA's testimony that Rukundo maintained a small room there for his personal items. Rukundo submits that the Trial Chamber erred in convicting him of this crime. In this section, the Appeals Chamber need only consider whether the Trial Chamber erred in assessing the legal elements of the crime of genocide by causing serious mental harm. Rukundo submits that, even if the Trial Chamber's findings on this incident were accepted, it erred in finding that his actions amounted to the commission of genocide by causing serious mental harm. He argues that serious mental harm requires 'grave and long-term disadvantage'. Rukundo submits that the Trial Chamber's findings on the harm suffered by Witness CCH were based exclusively on circumstantial evidence. He points to several errors in its analysis, which, in his view, demonstrate that she did not suffer long-term psychological trauma. Rukundo argues that Witness CCH's fear of death was not based on his conduct since she willingly followed him to his room after his remarks and he did not use

[618] *Rukundo* Trial Judgement, paras. 372–389 (internal references omitted).

[619] *Rukundo* Trial Judgement, paras. 574–576.

	his gun to threaten her. He contends that, at most, Witness CCH suffered only disappointment since he was not ultimately able to protect her. Rukundo further submits that the harm resulting from sexual abuse must be 'inflicted upon the integrity of a person by means of coercion, threat of force or intimidation in a way that is humiliating and degrading to the victim's dignity'. In this respect, he contends that 'the sexual humiliation and degradation of the victim is a more pertinent factor than the gratification of the perpetrator, and it is this element that provides specificity to the offence.' Rukundo argues that Witness CCH was not subjected to degrading or humiliating treatment as part of a campaign against Tutsis and that the incident was also insufficiently grave. Rather, 'he treated her with consideration, like a woman one is trying to seduce.' To illustrate, Rukundo points to evidence that he first invited her to share a beer with him, told her that he would like to help her, but could not, then asked if he could make love to her, and immediately stopped when she resisted his advances. He emphasizes that the incident occurred in private, that he did not touch her 'private parts', that she remained clothed, and that the two allegedly shared more beer before parting amicably. Finally, Rukundo argues that the Trial Chamber erred in finding that he intentionally inflicted serious harm with genocidal intent since, in the circumstances described above, it was unreasonable to find that he targeted Witness CCH based on her ethnicity or acted with knowledge that there was no consent on her part since she did not show her fear. In Rukundo's view, the Trial Chamber, in fact, did not examine the issue of his knowledge of her lack of consent, which is evident from the summary of Witness CCH's testimony. The Prosecution responds that the Trial Chamber reasonably considered that Rukundo's conduct resulted in serious mental harm and that he possessed genocidal intent. The Appeals Chamber recalls that genocidal intent may be inferred, *inter alia*, from evidence of other culpable acts systematically directed against the same group. In this case, the Trial Chamber found that Rukundo possessed genocidal intent in relation to the sexual assault of Witness CCH based on the 'general context of mass violence' against Tutsis in Gitarama Prefecture as well as his assertion, prior to the incident, that Witness CCH's 'entire family had to be killed for assisting the *Inyenzi*'. Central to the Trial Chamber's finding of genocidal intent was Rukundo's assertion that Witness CCH's family had to be killed because one of her relatives was assisting the '*Inyenzi*'. While evidence concerning the use of expressions such as '*Inyenzi*' can, in some circumstances, suffice to establish genocidal intent, the Appeals Chamber recalls that inferences drawn from circumstantial evidence must be the only reasonable inference available. In this particular context, the Appeals Chamber, Judge Pocar dissenting, considers that genocidal intent is not the only reasonable inference to be drawn from Rukundo's assertion. In particular, the Appeals Chamber, Judge Pocar dissenting, observes that Rukundo's language can plausibly be interpreted as expressing anger that a former friend was affiliated with the '*Inyenzi*', without signifying a personal desire to destroy Tutsis. This interpretation is supported by the fact that Rukundo's statement did not frighten Witness CCH; according to her evidence, she only became frightened when Rukundo locked her in his room prior to assaulting her. The Appeals Chamber also notes that, after they entered the room together, Rukundo told Witness CCH that if he could have hidden her, he would have done so. The Appeals Chamber, Judge Pocar dissenting, also considers that the 'general context of mass violence' cited by the Trial Chamber is insufficient to justify a finding of genocidal intent with respect to this incident. The Appeals Chamber, Judge Pocar dissenting, observes that the crime committed against Witness CCH was qualitatively different from the other acts of genocide perpetrated by Rukundo. In its analysis of events at Saint Joseph's College and the Saint Léon Minor Seminary, the Trial Chamber relied on the systematic, repeated searches for Tutsis on the basis of identity cards or lists, and the subsequent killing or assault of those individuals removed, to conclude that the perpetrators, including Rukundo, had genocidal intent. By contrast, the Appeals Chamber, Judge Pocar dissenting, considers that Rukundo's sexual assault of Witness CCH appears to have been unplanned and spontaneous. In this context, the

	Appeals Chamber, Judge Pocar dissenting, finds that his act could reasonably be construed as an opportunistic crime that was not accompanied by the specific intent to commit genocide. While this analysis does not alter the highly degrading and non-consensual nature of the act committed, the Appeals Chamber, Judge Pocar dissenting, considers that it supports the inference that Rukundo's sexual assault, while taking place during a genocide, was not necessarily a part of the genocide itself. In light of this equivocal evidence, the Appeals Chamber, Judge Pocar dissenting, finds that no reasonable trier of fact could find that the only reasonable inference available from the evidence was that Rukundo possessed genocidal intent in relation to the sexual assault of Witness CCH. Consequently, the Appeals Chamber does not need to address Rukundo's remaining arguments under this ground of appeal. Accordingly, the Appeals Chamber, Judge Pocar dissenting, grants Rukundo's Eighth Ground of Appeal and reverses his conviction for genocide, in part, for causing serious mental harm to Witness CCH".[620]

16. Tharcisse **Renzaho** (Case No. ICTR-97-31) Prefect of Kigali-Ville prefecture.	
Indictment (International sex crimes (or related) charges and mode(s) of liability)	- **Genocide** (count 1) or, alternatively, **Complicity in genocide** (count 2) and **Rape as CAH** (count 4) and **Rape as a violation of Article 3 common to the Geneva Conventions and of Additional Protocol II (WC)** (count 6) under Article 6(3) of the Statute (**superior responsibility**) for: (i) the rapes of Tutsi women by *Interahamwe*, soldiers and other individuals under the effective control of Tharcisse Renzaho on April 16 and on diverse unknown dates between April and June 1994; (ii) compelling Tutsi women to provide Father Munyeshyaka and *Interahamwe* under the effective control of Tharcisse Renzaho with sexual pleasures in exchange for their safety on diverse unknown dates between April and June 1994; and (iii) maintaining Tutsi women at houses in central Kigali compelling them to provide *Interahamwe*, soldiers and armed civilians under the effective control of Tharcisse Renzaho with sexual pleasures in exchange for their safety on diverse unknown dates between April and June 1994.[621]

620 *Rukundo* Appeal Judgement, paras. 227–238 (internal references omitted).

621 *Prosecutor v. Tharcisse Renzaho*, Case No. ICTR-97-31-I, Second Amended Indictment, 16 February 2006, p. 4 ("**Count I: GENOCIDE** The Prosecutor of the International Criminal Tribunal for Rwanda charges **Tharcisse RENZAHO** with **GENOCIDE**, a crime stipulated in Article 2(3)(b) of the Statute, in that on or between the dates of 7 April 1994 and 17 July 1994 throughout Rwanda, particularly in Kigali-*ville Préfecture*, **Tharcisse RENZAHO** was responsible for killing or causing serious bodily or mental harm to members of the Tutsi racial or ethnic group, including acts of sexual violence, with intent to destroy, in whole or in part, a racial or ethnic group, as such, as outlined in paragraphs 6 through 43. ***Alternatively*, Count II: COMPLICITY IN GENOCIDE** The Prosecutor of the International Criminal Tribunal for Rwanda charges **Tharcisse RENZAHO** with **COMPLICITY IN GENOCIDE**, a crime stipulated in Article 2(3)(e) of the Statute, in that on or between the dates of 7 April 1994 and 17 July 1994 throughout Rwanda, particularly in Kigali-*ville Préfecture*, **Tharcisse RENZAHO** was responsible for killing or causing serious bodily or mental harm to members of the Tutsi racial or ethnic group, including acts of sexual violence, with intent to destroy, in whole or in part, a racial or ethnic group, as such, or with knowledge that other people intended to destroy, in whole or in part, the Tutsi racial or ethnic group, as such, and that his assistance would contribute to the crime of genocide, as outlined in paragraphs 6 through 43".), paras. 41–43 ("Tutsi women were raped by *Interahamwe* militia, soldiers and other individuals under the effective control of **Tharcisse RENZAHO** on April 16 and diverse unknown dates during the months of April, May and June 1994. *Conseillers* under the direct command and authority of **Tharcisse RENZAHO** reported on a regular basis about the rape of Tutsi women by *Interahamwe* militia, soldiers and other individuals under the effective control of **Tharcisse RENZAHO**. **Tharcisse RENZAHO** failed or refused to take the necessary or reasonable measures to prevent such rapes or to punish the perpetrators thereof. Father MUNYESHYAKA and *Interahamwe*, under the

effective control of **Tharcisse RENZAHO**, compelled Tutsi women to provide them with sexual pleasures in exchange for the woman's safety at Ste. Famille during the period in which Tutsi sought refuge at Ste. Famille in the months of April, May and June 1994. **Tharcisse RENZAHO** knew or had reason to know that these acts were being perpetrated against Tutsi women and he failed or refused to prevent or to punish the perpetrators against Tutsi women and he failed or refused to prevent or to punish the perpetrators of these forced sexual acts at Ste. Famille. *Interahamwe*, soldiers, and armed civilians under the effective control of **Tharcisse RENZAHO** maintained Tutsi women at houses in central Kigali, where they compelled the women [to] provide them with sexual pleasures in exchange for the women's safety on diverse unknown dates during the months of April, May and June 1994. **Tharcisse RENZAHO** knew or had reason ro know that these acts were being perpetrated against Tutsi women and he failed or refused to prevent or to punish the perpetrators of these forced sexual acts".), pp. 14–15 ("**Count IV: RAPE as a CRIME AGAINST HUMANITY** The Prosecutor of the International Criminal Tribunal for Rwanda charges **Tharcisse RENZAHO** with **RAPE as a CRIME AGAINST HUMANITY**, a crime stipulated in Article 3(g) of the Statute, in that on [or] between 7 April 1994 and 17 July 1994 throughout Rwanda, particularly in Kigali-*ville Préfecture*, **Tharcisse RENZAHO**, members of the Tutsi racial or ethnic group or persons identified as Tutsi were raped by subordinates of **Tharcisse RENZAHO** as part of a widespread or systematic attack against that civilian population on racial and ethnic grounds, as set forth in paragraphs 52 through 55".) paras. 52–55 ("Pursuant to Article 6(3) of the Statute, the accused, **Tharcisse RENZAHO**, is responsible for the rape as a crime against humanity because specific criminal acts were committed by subordinates of the accused and the accused knew or had reason to know that such subordinates were about to commit such acts before they were committed or that such subordinates had committed such acts and the accused failed to take the necessary and reasonable measures to prevent such acts or to punish the perpetrators thereof. These subordinates included leaders and members of the FAR; the Presidential Guard; the *Interahamwe*; the 'Civil Defense Forces'; communal police; civilian militias; local administrative officials; other soldiers and militiamen; other known participants, such as Father Wenceslas MUNYESHYAKA; and other unknown participants. The particulars that give rise to the accused's individual criminal responsibility are set forth in paragraphs 53 through 55. Tutsi women were raped by *Interahamwe* militia, soldiers and other individuals under the effective control of **Tharcisse RENZAHO** on April 16 and diverse unknown dates during the months of April, May and June 1994. *Conseillers* under the direct command and authority of **Tharcisse RENZAHO** reported on a regular basis about the rape of Tutsi women by *Interahamwe* militia, soldiers and other individuals under the effective control of **RENZAHO**. **Tharcisse RENZAHO** failed or refused to take the necessary or reasonable measures to prevent such rapes or to punish the perpetrators thereof. Father MUNYESHYAKA and *Interahamwe*, under the effective control of **Tharcisse RENZAHO** compelled Tutsi women to provide them with sexual pleasures in exchange for the wom[e]n's safety at Ste. Famille in the period in which Tutsi sought refuge at Ste. Famille in the months of April, May and June 1994. **Tharcisse RENZAHO** knew or had reason to know that these acts were being perpetrated against Tutsi women and he failed or refused to punish the perpetrators of these forced sexual acts at Ste. Famille. *Interahamwe*, soldiers, and armed civilians under the effective control of **Tharcisse RENZAHO** maintained Tutsi women at houses in central Kigali, where they compelled the women provide them with sexual pleasures in exchange for the women's safety on diverse unknown dates during the months of April, May and June 1991. **Tharcisse RENZAHO** knew or had reason to know that these acts were being perpetrated against Tutsi women and he failed or refused to punish the perpetrators of these forced sexual acts".), pp 17–18 ("**Count VI: RAPE AS A VIOLATION OF ARTICLE 3 COMMON TO THE GENEVA CONVENTIONS OF 1949** The Prosecutor of the International Criminal Tribunal for Rwanda charges **Tharcisse RENZAHO** with **RAPE AS A VIOLATION OF ARTICLE 3 COMMON TO THE GENEVA CONVENTIONS OF 1949 AND ADDITIONAL PROTOCOL II OF 1977**, a crime stipulated in Article 4(e) of the Statute, in that **Tharcisse RENZAHO** was responsible for the rape of non-combatant Tutsi women during the period between 7 April 1994 and 17 July 1994 when throughout Rwanda, particularly in Kigali-*ville Préfecture*, there was a non-international armed conflict within the meaning of Articles 1 and 2 of Protocol II Additional to the Geneva Convention[s] of 1949, and the raping of the victims was closely related to the hostilities or committed in conjunction with the armed conflict and the victims were persons taking no part in that conflict; all as set forth in paragraphs 61 through 65".), paras. 61–65 ("Pursuant to Article 6(3) of the Statute, the accused, **Tharcisse RENZAHO**, is responsible for rape as a violation of Article 3 common to the Geneva Conventions of 1949 and Additional Protocol II of 1977 because specific criminal acts were committed by subordinates of the accused and the accused knew or had reason to know that such subordinates were about to commit such acts before they were committed or that such subordinates had committed such acts and the accused failed to take the necessary and reasonable measures to prevent such acts or to punish the perpetrators thereof. These subordinates included leaders and members of the FAR; the Presidential Guard; the *Interahamwe*, such as Odette NYIRA-

Trial Judgement	- Guilty of **Genocide** (Count 1), **Rape as CAH** (count 4) and **Rape as a violation of Article 3 common to the Geneva Conventions and of Additional Protocol II (WC)** (count 6) under Article 6(3) of the Statute (**superior responsibility**) for his failure to prevent the rapes of Witnesses AWO and AWN as well as Witness AWN's sister.[622]
Appeal Judgement	- The Appeals Chamber **reversed Tharcisse Renzaho's convictions for Genocide** (Count 1), **Rapes as CAH** (count 4) and **Rape as a violation of Article 3 common to the Geneva Conventions and of Additional Protocol II (WC)** (count 6) under Article 6(3) of the Statute (**superior responsibility) for his failure to prevent the rapes of Witnesses AWO and AWN as well as Witness AWN's sister** because the Appeals Chamber found that Tharcisse Renzaho's reason to know of the rapes of Witness AWO, Witness AWN, and Witness AWN's sister was not pleaded in the Indictment, nor communicated by the Prosecution in a manner sufficient to give notice to Tharcisse Renzaho and that Tharcisse Renzaho was materially prejudiced by this defect.[623]
Legal and Factual Findings and/or Evidence	- Legal findings: **- Rape: definition:** The Trial Chamber adopted the definition of rape given in the *Kunarac et al.* case:[624] "Rape as a crime against humanity requires proof of the non-consensual penetration, however slight, of the vagina or anus of the victim by the penis of the perpetrator or by any other object used by the perpetrator, or of the mouth of the victim by the penis of the perpetrator. Consent for this purpose must be consent given voluntarily and freely and is assessed within the context of the surrounding circumstances. Force or threat of force provides clear evidence of non-consent, but force is not an element *per se* of rape. The *mens rea* for rape as a crime against humanity is the intention to effect the

BAGENZI; the 'Civil Defense Forces'; communal police; civilian militias; local administrative officials; other soldiers and militiamen; other known participants, such as Father Wenceslas MUNYESHYAKA; and other unknown participants. The particulars that give rise to the accused's individual criminal responsibility pursuant to Article 6(3) are set forth in paragraphs 62 through 65. During the relevant periods of 7 April 1994 through 4 July 1994, the FAR occupied central areas of Kigali, including Nyarugenge commune and the area around Ste. Famille Church. The FAR trained and armed the *Interahamwe*, and were supported in the conflict by the *Interahamwe*, the *gendarmerie*, *préfectural* communal police, and armed civilians. Tutsi women were raped by *Interahamwe* militia, soldiers and other individuals under the effective control of **Tharcisse RENZAHO** on April 16 and diverse unknown dates during the months of April, May and June 1994. *Conseillers* under the direct command and authority of **Tharcisse RENZAHO** reported on a regular basis about the rape of Tutsi women by *Interahamwe* militia, soldiers and other individuals under the effective control of **Tharcisse RENZAHO**. **Tharcisse RENZAHO** failed or refused to take the necessary or reasonable measures to prevent such rapes or to punish the perpetrators thereof. Father MUNYESHYAKA and other *Interahamwe* under the effective control of **Tharcisse RENZAHO** compelled Tutsi women to provide them with sexual pleasures in exchange for the wom[e]n's safety at Ste. Famille in the period in which Tutsi sought refuge at Ste. Famille in the months of April, May and June 1994. **Tharcisse RENZAHO** knew or had reason to know that these acts were being perpetrated against Tutsi women and he failed or refused to prevent or punish the perpetrators of these forced sexual acts at Ste. Famille. *Interahamwe*, soldiers, and armed civilians under the effective control of **Tharcisse RENZAHO** maintained Tutsi women at houses in central Kigali, where they compelled the women provide them with sexual pleasures in exchange for the women's safety on diverse unknown dates during the months of April, May and June 1994. **Tharcisse RENZAHO** knew or had reason ro know that these acts were being perpetrated against Tutsi women and he failed or refused to prevent or punish the perpetrators of these forced sexual acts".).

622 *Prosecutor v. Tharcisse Renzaho*, Case No. ICTR-97-31-T, Judgement and Sentence, dated 14 July 2009 and filed on 14 August 2009 ("*Renzaho* Trial Judgement"), paras. 709–718, 774–779, 793–794, 810–812.

623 *Tharcisse Renzaho v. The Prosecutor*, Case No. ICTR-97-31-A, Judgement, 1 April 2011 ("*Renzaho* Appeal Judgement"), paras. 109–129, 622.

624 ICTY ISCC *Kunarac et al.*, see *supra* p. 528.

prohibited sexual penetration with the knowledge that it occurs without the consent of the victim".[625]

- Factual findings:

- Support of rapes in Rugenge sector:

"Two Tutsi refugees provided first-hand evidence that Renzaho encouraged rapes during meetings in Rugenge sector, attended by *Conseiller* Odette Nyirabagenzi and *Interahamwe*. Witness AWO testified that she was repeatedly raped in the ruins of her home after Renzaho's visit with *Interahamwe* to the Sisters of Saint Teresa of Calcutta orphanage around 10 or 11 April 1994, where he described Tutsi women as 'food items'. When the witness was subsequently identified as an '*Inkotanyi*' during the so-called pacification meeting near Nyirabagenzi's home, Renzaho stated that she should not be killed because she was a woman and was 'food for the militiamen'. Having been forced to attend that meeting by *Interahamwe*, the witness was returned to her house where *Interahamwe*, soldiers and policemen 'who lived in Nyirabagenzi's house' continued to rape her until she fled to Sainte Famille, about seven or eight weeks after she left the orphanage for her home. Similarly, Witness AWN was forced to go to the Rugenge sector office around the third or fourth week of May 1994. Among those present were Odette Nyirabagenzi, her brother called Munarira, and *Interahamwe*. When Renzaho, arriving with persons in military attire carrying firearms, heard that the witness had refused Munanira's advances, he said that it was 'time to show Tutsi women that the Hutus are strong and can do whatever they wanted to do with them'. After he left, Nyirabagenzi subsequently reinforced Renzaho's statement by promising Munanira that she would ensure that the witness would beg to have sex with him. The witness and her sister were then repeatedly raped by Munanira and other *Interahamwe* at their headquarters until they arrived at Sainte Famille three to four weeks later. Differences in the location, timing and substance of the meetings demonstrate that Witnesses AWO and AWN testified about distinct incidents wherein Renzaho encouraged the rape of Tutsi women. The Chamber assesses the merits of each testimony in sequence. Witness AWO's account was, at times, confusing. Elements of her description of the attack on the orphanage were not coherent. She also testified that Renzaho organised meetings in Rugenge sector virtually daily, but her basis for saying so was not solid, as she only attended one. Furthermore, her evidence about when she was sexually assaulted and the sequence of events sometimes lacked clarity. However, to the extent the witness did not provide testimony in a cohesive, narrative form, this is reasonably explained by the passage of time and the extremely traumatic nature of the events. The witness was raped on a daily basis for nearly eight weeks by several different men, including *Interahamwe*, policemen and soldiers. Given her ethnicity and the prevalence of roadblocks, she was unable to flee. She therefore remained in the ruins of her former home, in an area where there was fighting. Towards the end of her stay there, the witness, who was eight months pregnant, asked one of her attackers to kill her but he refused. Instead he promised to arrange it so that no one else would rape her and stabbed her in the lower abdomen and ankle with a bayonet. As a result of this incident the witness's baby was stillborn. By then, she could no longer close her legs or stand on her feet. The witness still has health problems caused by the assault. Witness AWN stated that she was abducted and raped by Munanira a few days or possibly two weeks after she was forced to meet at the sector office. The Defence referred to her statement to Tribunal investigators in October 2004, which suggests that the assault took place 'one month' after the meeting. The witness repeatedly explained that she could not remember the date with precision, as 10 years had elapsed between the incident and the time that she was interviewed. The Chamber finds this explanation reasonable and notes that the state-

[625] *Renzaho* Trial Judgement, paras. 791–792 (internal references omitted).

	ment suggests that she was taken away at the end of May. This is generally in conformity with her testimony, which places her abduction in the end of May or early June. Furthermore, and contrary to the Defence assertion, there is no inconsistency between the statement and her testimony as to whether Renzaho arrived at the Rugenge sector office before or after her. The witness reaffirmed her testimony that he arrived later, and the statement does not say otherwise. Finally, notwithstanding the traumatic nature of the events she described, her testimony appeared measured and unexaggerated. Her explanations for her observations were clear and logical. Defence Witness HIN suggested that, in view of the RPF shelling in the area, it would have been equivalent to killing people to organise a meeting in Rugenge sector between 7 and 18 April. However, he conceded that such shelling did not occur on a daily basis, that he only knew of four houses being hit, and that Nyirabagenzi's house remained standing at the time of his testimony. In the Chamber's view, his evidence does not cast doubt on Witnesses AWO and AWN's accounts that meetings indeed took place. The testimonies of the two Prosecution witnesses contained similar elements, in particular that Tutsi women existed to feed or to be handled by Hutus at their discretion. They therefore provide a degree of mutual corroboration. Furthermore, the record as a whole contains circumstantial support for their evidence. In particular, their description of the authority exercised by Renzaho is consistent with other evidence in the case, showing that Renzaho provided instruction to *conseillers* and that his orders were followed (II.2 and 3). The Chamber is satisfied with the identifications of Renzaho by Witnesses AWO and AWN. Their physical descriptions of him were consistent and adequate. Witness AWN recognised him because he had been pointed out to her as the prefect during *conseiller* elections approximately two years earlier. Compared to the extensive Prosecution evidence implicating Renzaho in the meetings described by the two witnesses, his denials that he was present during the attack against the orphanage and at subsequent meetings where Tutsi women were referred to as 'food', carry limited weight. Although it is clear from the evidence that he attended other meetings and carried out other activities in the same period, this does not raise doubt that he was present at the meetings described by them. Having assessed all the evidence, the Chamber accepts the fundamental aspects of Witness AWO's testimony. During a meeting, which took place after about 10 or 11 April, attended by *Conseiller* Odette Nyaribagenzi and *Interahamwe*, Renzaho said that the witness should not be killed because she was 'food for the militiamen'. After this instruction, the witness continued to be raped by *Interahamwe*, policemen and soldiers who either lived in Nyaribagenzi's home, or at least, worked in coordination with her. The Chamber also finds the main elements of Witness AWN's testimony established beyond reasonable doubt. In May 1994, she was brought to the Rugenge sector office. Renzaho, accompanied by persons in military attire carrying firearms, stated that it was 'time to show Tutsi women that the Hutus are strong and can do whatever they wanted to do with them'. After he left, Nyirabagenzi reinforced Renzaho's statement by promising Munanira that she would ensure that the witness would beg to have sex with him. Subsequently the witness was raped repeatedly by Munanira and other *Interahamwe* at their headquarters for three to four weeks. Her sister and Tutsi neighbour were also raped repeatedly there".[626] "In its factual findings, the Chamber found that, at a meeting which occurred after 10 or 11 April 1994, attended by *Conseiller* Odette Nyrirabagenzi and *Interahamwe*, Renzaho said that Witness AWO, a Tutsi, should not be killed because she was 'food for the militiamen'. After this, the witness was repeatedly raped by *Interahamwe*, policemen and soldiers who either lived in Nyaribagenzi's home or worked with her (II.13). In addition, the Chamber concluded that Munanira, an *Interahamwe* and the brother of *Conseiller* Nyirabagenzi, as well as other militimen, repeatedly raped Witness AWN and her sister, both Tutsis, over the couse of several weeks at the

626 *Renzaho* Trial Judgement, paras. 709–718 (internal references omitted).

	assailants' headquarters. This followed an incident at the Rugenge sector office where Renzaho in the presence of Witness AWN, Nyaribagenzi and Munanira stated it was 'time to show Tutsi women that the Hutus are strong and can do whatever they wanted to do with them'. After Renzaho's departure Nyirabagenzi promised Munanira that she would ensure that the witness would beg to have sex with him (II.13). The Chamber considers that these acts of rape constituted serious bodily or mental harm. Given the witnesses' Tutsi ethnicity, their public identification as such, as well as the extensive evidence of the targeting of other members of the Tutsi group in Kigali at the time, it follows that these rapes were committed with genocidal intent. The Prosecution seeks convinction for these crimes solely through Article 6 (3) of the Statute. The Chamber has concluded that Renzaho is the superior of urban police. Furthermore, in the context of both of these incidents, the Chamber is equally satisfied that Renzaho was the superior of the militiamen. The Chamber observes that they worked closely with *Conseiller* Nyirabagenzi, a de facto subordinate of Renzaho, and in some cases received accommodation from her. Therefore, these militiamen were closely linked with government authorities. In any event, even if the militiamen could not be considered as his subordinates, he would still remain liable for his subordinate *Conseiller* Nyirabagenzi's role in facilitating the crimes. In particular, her acquiescing presence during Renzaho's encouragement of the rapes, as well as her further encouragement and support of the assailants, substantially assisted and thus aided and abetted the crimes. Similarly, the Chamber is also convinced that soldiers who engaged in rapes of Witness AWO were Renzaho's de facto subordinates Renzaho given his rank, instructions and their attacks on the witness. Renzaho's conduct in relation to both incidents clearly reflected that he had knowledge that the crimes would occur and condoned them. Therefore, there is no question that he failed in his duty to prevent the crimes. [...] The Chamber further finds Renzaho guilty of genocide (Count I) under Article 6 (3) based on his failure to prevent the rapes of Witnesses AWO and AWN as well as Witness AWN's sister".[627] "The Prosecution has also charged the crimes committed against Witnesses AWO, AWN and Witness AWN's sister as rape as a crime against humanity. The Chamber has already determined that these rapes constituted serious bodily and mental harm as genocide. On the same basis, the Chamber is satisfied that they were conducted on ethnic grounds. The Chamber has found that Renzaho bears responsibility for these rapes as a superior under Article 6 (3) of the Statute. The Chamber finds Renzaho guilty of rape as a crime against humanity (Count IV) as a superior under Article 6 (3) of the Statute for the crimes committed against Witnesses AWO, AWN and Witness AWN's sister".[628] "The Prosecution has charged the crimes committed against Witnesses AWO, AWN and Witness AWN's sister as rape as a serious violation of Article 3 Common to the Geneva Conventions and of Additional Protocol II. The Chamber has already found that these rapes constituted serious bodily and mental harm as genocide and rape as a crime agasint humaity. The Chamber has also determined that Renzaho bears responsibility for these rapes as a superior under Article 6 (3) of the Statute. The Chamber finds Renzaho guilty of rape as a serious violation of Article 3 Common to the Geneva Conventions and of Additional Protocol II (Count VI) as a superior under Article 6 (3) of the Statute for the crimes committed against Witnesses AWO, AWN and Witness AWN's sister".[629] However, the Appeals Chamber reversed Tharcisse Renzaho's convictions for rapes: "The Trial Chamber found Renzaho guilty of genocide, crimes against humanity, and serious violations of Article 3 common to the Geneva Conventions and of Additional

[627] *Renzaho* Trial Judgement, paras. 774–779.

[628] *Renzaho* Trial Judgement, paras. 793–794.

[629] *Renzaho* Trial Judgement, paras. 810–811.

Protocol II under Article 6(3) of the Statute based on his failure to prevent the rapes of Prosecution Witnesses AWO and AWN, as well as Witness AWN's sister. In particular, the Trial Chamber found that Witness AWO was repeatedly raped by *Interahamwe*, policemen, and soldiers after Renzaho stated that Tutsi women were 'food for the militiamen', and that Witness AWN and her sister were repeatedly raped by *Interahamwe* after Renzaho stated that it was 'time to show Tutsi women that the Hutus are strong and can do whatever they wanted to do with them'. Renzaho claims that the Indictment was defective, as it lacked detailed information on the dates, locations, and names of victims and perpetrators of rapes underlying the charges. He contends that, in holding him responsible for the rapes committed in Rugenge sector, the Trial Chamber went beyond the charge of superior responsibility and convicted him on the basis of facts not pleaded in the Indictment, namely, that he incited or instigated the commission of rapes. He argues that these facts support a theory of individual responsibility which the Prosecution chose not to pursue, likely because of lack of evidence. The Prosecution responds that the Indictment provided Renzaho with sufficient information alleging his responsibility as a superior for the rapes of Tutsi women in Kigali-Ville on various dates. It submits that although Rugenge sector was not specifically mentioned, Renzaho admitted that it was one of Kigali-Ville's 19 sectors. In addition, the Prosecution submits that the Indictment alleges that between 6 April and 17 July 1994, Tutsi women and girls were raped throughout Kigali-Ville by sufficiently identified subordinates who maintained Tutsi women at houses in central Kigali and compelled them to provide sexual pleasures in exchange for their safety. It further submits that Renzaho received clear, consistent, and timely information detailing the factual basis underpinning the charges against him. The Prosecution contends that Renzaho's arguments therefore lack merit and should be dismissed. In reply, Renzaho argues that the Indictment does not conform to the jurisprudence of the Tribunal, as it does not provide sufficient details on the identity of the victims and the circumstances of the crimes, including their time frame and location. He further contends that as the Prosecution Pre-Trial Brief was filed before the Indictment, it could not have cured the defects in the Indictment. The Appeals Chamber observes that the Trial Chamber did not specify which paragraphs of the Indictment underpin Renzaho's conviction for the rapes of Witness AWO, Witness AWN, and Witness AWN's sister. However, a review of the Trial Judgement suggests that paragraphs 43, 55, and 65 of the Indictment are pertinent. These paragraphs provide: '*Interahamwe,* soldiers, and armed civilians under the effective control of **Tharcisse RENZAHO** maintained Tutsi women at houses in central Kigali, where they compelled the women [to] provide them with sexual pleasures in exchange for the women's safety on diverse unknown dates during the months of April, May and June 1994. **Tharcisse RENZAHO** knew or had reason to know that these acts were being perpetrated against Tutsi women and he failed or refused to prevent or to punish the perpetrators of these forced sexual acts.' The Appeals Chamber notes that Renzaho was charged as a superior under Article 6(3) of the Statute with regard to the facts alleged in paragraphs 43, 55, and 65 of the Indictment. When an accused is charged pursuant to Article 6(3) of the Statute, four categories of material facts must be pleaded in the Indictment: '(i) that the accused is the superior of sufficiently identified subordinates over whom he had effective control – in the sense of a material ability to prevent or punish criminal conduct – and for whose acts he is alleged to be responsible; (ii) the criminal acts committed by those others for whom the accused is alleged to be responsible; (iii) the conduct of the accused by which he may be found to have known or had reason to know that the crimes were about to be committed or had been committed by his subordinates; and (iv) the conduct of the accused by which he may be found to have failed to take necessary and reasonable measures to prevent such acts or to punish the persons who committed them.' The Appeals Chamber considers that the Indictment adequately pleaded the material facts relating to three of these categories. In relation to the first category, the Appeals Chamber recalls that a superior need not necessarily know the exact identity of his or

	her subordinates who perpetrate crimes in order to incur liability under Article 6(3) of the Statute. The Appeals Chamber has held that the physical perpetrators of the crimes can be identified by category in relation to a particular crime site. The Appeals Chamber considers that the perpetrators of the rapes of Witness AWO, Witness AWN, and Witness AWN's sister were adequately pleaded by category. In relation to the second category, the criminal act of rape was clearly pleaded. In relation to the fourth category, the Appeals Chamber recalls that it will be sufficient in many cases to plead that the accused did not take any necessary and reasonable measure to prevent or punish the commission of criminal acts. The Appeals Chamber finds the Indictment sufficient in this respect. However, in relation to the third category, the Appeals Chamber recalls that Renzaho was found by the Trial Chamber to have reason to know of the rapes due to his vocal encouragement of them. The conduct by which Renzaho was found to have reason to know that the rapes were about to be committed was therefore not pleaded in the Indictment. The failure to include this material fact in the Indictment renders it defective. The Appeals Chamber will therefore consider whether this defect was cured by the provision of clear, consistent, and timely information by the Prosecution. To support its contention that 'post-indictment communications' provided Renzaho with clear, consistent, and timely notice, the Prosecution relies on its Pre-Trial Brief and two written statements disclosed in February 2005. However, these documents were filed *before* the Second Amended Indictment came into force on 16 February 2006. Renzaho contends that the Prosecution Pre-Trial Brief cannot cure a defect in the Indictment, relying on the *Karera* Appeal Judgement. The Appeals Chamber recalls that in the *Karera* case, the pre-trial brief, which was filed seven days before the amended indictment, was found to be incapable of curing a particular defect therein relating to a murder charge because, among other things, it was unclear which version of the indictment the pre-trial brief was referring to, creating further confusion. In the present case, the Appeals Chamber notes that the proposed Second Amended Indictment was attached to the Motion to Amend filed on 19 October 2005. On 31 October 2005, the Prosecution filed its Pre-Trial Brief, specifying that 'references to the 'Indictment' herein are to the proposed Second Amended Indictment'. Further, the Prosecution Pre-Trial Brief and the attached summaries of anticipated witness testimony were clear about which paragraphs of the proposed Second Amended Indictment they referred to. Once the Trial Chamber accepted the Second Amended Indictment on 16 February 2006, nearly one year before the commencement of Renzaho's trial, its link to the Prosecution Pre-Trial Brief was consolidated. Since there were no subsequent amendments to the Indictment or the Prosecution Pre-Trial Brief, the Appeals Chamber considers that the Prosecution Pre-Trial Brief in this case is capable of curing defects in the Indictment. Turning to whether the Prosecution's communications in fact cured the defect in the Indictment, the Appeals Chamber notes that the Prosecution Pre-Trial Brief emphasized that the receipt of reports of rapes from Renzaho's subordinates constituted his reason to know about the rapes. Although the Prosecution Pre-Trial Brief also noted Renzaho's encouragement of rapes, it did so in respect of only two of the relevant Counts. The Appeals Chamber further considers that this new element of the Prosecution's case was not highlighted in a manner sufficient to give clear notice to Renzaho that his encouragement now formed the basis for his criminal liability as a superior. The Prosecution Pre-Trial Brief notably failed to clarify that the Prosecution was relying on Renzaho's acts of encouragement to infer his *mens rea*. Absent any indication that Renzaho's encouragement was the basis for his reason to know about particular rapes, it is difficult to conclude that the Defence would have understood that this material fact was the key element of the Prosecution's case. Moreover, the Prosecution Pre-Trial Brief did not provide consistent notice that Renzaho's encouragement of rapes constituted his reason to know, as conceded by the Prosecution on appeal. While the summaries of Witnesses AWO's and AWN's anticipated testimony annexed to the Prosecution Pre-Trial Brief describe the circumstances of their rapes and those of Witness AWN's sister in detail, Witness AWN's summary

	attributed Renzaho's statement encouraging rapes to another individual. It was only during her testimony that Witness AWN clarified that it was Renzaho who made the statement. The Prosecution Pre-Trial Brief and the summary of Witness AWN's anticipated testimony therefore did not provide the 'unambiguous information' required to cure a defect in the Indictment. While the summary of Witness AWO's anticipated evidence did allege that Renzaho stated that Tutsi women were food for the soldiers, given the ambiguity contained in the Prosecution Pre-Trial Brief concerning the import of Renzaho's encouragement, the Appeals Chamber finds this one witness statement insufficient to cure the defect in the Indictment. Consequently, Renzaho received neither clear nor consistent notice of the conduct by which he had reason to know of the rapes. The Appeals Chamber recalls that a defect in the Indictment, not cured by timely, clear, and consistent notice, constitutes a prejudice to the accused. The defect may only be deemed harmless through a demonstration that the accused's ability to prepare his or her defence was not materially impaired. When an appellant raises a defect in the indictment for the first time on appeal, the appellant bears the burden of showing that his or her ability to prepare his or her defence was materially impaired. When, however, an accused has previously raised the issue of lack of notice before the Trial Chamber, the burden rests on the Prosecution to prove on appeal that the ability of the accused to prepare his or her defence was not materially impaired. The Appeals Chamber therefore turns to consider this issue. In the pre-trial stage, Renzaho challenged the Indictment on the basis of vagueness, a challenge that was dismissed by the Trial Chamber. Although Renzaho did not object to Witnesses AWO's and AWN's evidence that he encouraged rapes upon the filing of the Prosecution Pre-Trial Brief or at the time of their testimony, the Appeals Chamber considers that Renzaho's confusion regarding the import of this evidence, discussed below, reasonably explains his failure to object. Further, in his Closing Brief, Renzaho renewed his challenge to the Indictment on the basis that it failed to plead the material facts necessary to establish his superior responsibility. Renzaho also contended that the charges alleging his responsibility for sexual violence were impermissibly vague, and noted that the evidence that he made encouraging statements about rapes was not included in the Indictment. The Appeals Chamber therefore finds that Renzaho raised an adequate objection to the failure to properly plead his reason to know. Consequently, the Prosecution has the burden of establishing that Renzaho's defence was not materially impaired by the defect in the Indictment. The Appeals Chamber finds that the Prosecution has not met its burden. It notes that, when Witness AWN testified that it was Renzaho who encouraged rapes, rather than another individual, the Defence did not object to the introduction of the new material fact. At the Appeal Hearing, the Defence indicated that it failed to do so because it 'did not make the link at that time' and suffered prejudice from the introduction of this new material fact because it did not understand that this evidence was relevant to the charge under Article 6(3) of the Statute. The strategy adopted at trial by the Defence and in particular the cross-examination of Witnesses AWO and AWN convinces the Appeals Chamber that Renzaho understood that he was to defend himself against knowledge of rapes through receipt of reports as pleaded in the Indictment. He was therefore prejudiced by the Prosecution's failure to cure the defect in the Indictment through adequate notice. The Appeals Chamber also notes with concern that the relevant paragraphs of the Indictment are extremely broad, and fail to specify the dates and locations of the meetings at which Renzaho encouraged the rapes; the dates and locations of the rapes; and the names of the victims. The provision of these material facts only in post-indictment documents impacts upon the ability of the accused to know the case he or she has to meet and to prepare his or her defence, and is particularly troubling when the Prosecution was in a position to include them in the Indictment. The Appeals Chamber therefore finds that Renzaho's reason to know of the rapes of Witness AWO, Witness AWN, and Witness AWN's sister was not pleaded in the Indictment, nor communicated by the Prosecution in a manner sufficient to give notice to Renzaho. Further, Ren-

	zaho was materially prejudiced by this defect. Accordingly, the Appeals Chamber finds that the Trial Chamber erred in convicting Renzaho and reverses his convictions for genocide, crimes against humanity, and serious violations of Article 3 common to the Geneva Conventions and of Additional Protocol II under Article 6(3) of the Statute based on these rapes".[630] - Responsibility for sexual violence at Sainte Famille: "Several Prosecution witnesses testified that women who had sought refuge at Sainte Famille were raped or abused. Witness AWN stated that she saw Father Munyeshyaka lead away two girls called Hyacinthe Rwanga and Nyiratunga when she arrived at Sainte Famille near the end of June. She also heard that he had raped them. According to Witness HAD, Munyeshyaka made sexual advances towards Hyacinthe Rwanga; he had made one female his sex slave; and he would abuse young girls. Witness KBZ, who fled to Sainte Famille in early July, said that she was raped by two *Interahamwe* behind the church when she could not produce an identification card. Witness HAD explained that rape was prevalent during her stay at Sainte Famille from 22 April to around 19 or 20 June 1994, and that *Interahamwe* took girls away to be raped and executed. Witness AWX also gave evidence about rape and mentioned that some women subsequently died. Of these five Tutsi refugees, only Witness AWX suggested that Renzaho played a direct role in an operation at Sainte Famille that resulted in rapes. Around 24 May, she saw him arrive in a vehicle with armed soldiers. He asked them to do their job, and the soldiers entered the church. Father Munyeshyaka called out names of Tutsi refugees and said that Renzaho had ordered those identified to step forward. The selected men and women were separated. Approximately three hours after Renzaho's arrival, the witness, her sister and her cousin were led away by soldiers to a house approximately five minutes away. The witness was locked in a room for two days, where she was raped twice by a soldier. The women were returned to Sainte Famille but then removed by the same soldiers on 15 June and raped again over the course of two days. The witness was released, as well as her cousin, whereas she saw her sister's body around 18 June, while Renzaho was overseeing the burial of corpses after an attack on Sainte Famille that day (II.11). Witness AWX provided the only testimony about Renzaho working in coordination with soldiers and Munyeshyaka in separating Tutsi refugees at Sainte Famille in late May. There are some differences between her evidence and a statement she gave to Tribunal investigators in February 2005. According to the statement, presidential guards removed the witness, her older sister and cousin and kept her in the house for three days (not two), raped her three times (not two), and this was done by two such guards (not one). In the Chamber's view, these discrepancies do not affect her credibility. Although they describe serious acts, the differing numbers are comparably minor in nature, and may stem from communication problems, or be explained by the traumatic nature of the events and the time that has passed since then. The Chamber considers that the fundamental features of Witness AWX's evidence regarding her abduction from Sainte Famille and subsequent rapes were coherent, compelling and consistent with her prior accounts to Tribunal investigators. The testimonies of Defence Witnesses PER, TOA, BDC and UT were of a general character and did not discredit her account. Witness PER was not permanently positioned at Sainte Famille. Moreover, given his close working relationship with Father Munyeshyaka, it is not surprising that victims, who at a minimum suspected Munyeshyaka as being involved in sexual assaults, did not confide in him about the abuse they suffered. Witness TOA's opinion – that overcrowding and unhygienic conditions at Sainte Famille would have prevented rapes from occurring there – fails to address the allegations that victims were often removed from Sainte Famille and raped elsewhere. His suggestion that rapes would have been

630 *Renzaho* Appeal Judgement, paras. 109–129 (internal references omitted).

	reported to the Red Cross or UN journalists is speculative. Given the vast number of refugees present, the Chamber has doubts that the witness, a man, would have been privy to reports of such a private nature. Witness BDC's testimony about not having received reports of sexual assaults was equivocal. Moreover, while Witness UT said that he never received complaints about rapes at Sainte Famille, he did read of such claims in the press. Based on the evidence, it is clear that Witness AWX, her sister and cousin were abducted from Sainte Famille by soldiers around 24 May and again about 15 June 1994. The Chamber finds it established that Witness AWX was raped multiple times during these episodes before being released. She was returned to Sainte Famille each time. Regarding the alleged rapes of her cousin and sister, there is no direct evidence. It follows from the witness's testimony that her sister and cousin were raped after having been led away from Sainte Famille, but she did not provide an explicit basis for this view. This said, her first-hand observations of soldiers working in parallel, separating the women from other refugees, and holding them for the same time period, leads to the only reasonable conclusion that her sister and cousin were subject to sexual assaults similar to those suffered by the witness. These two women were of no strategic importance to the military operations being carried out on Sainte Famille or elsewhere. That the sister was seen dead in June, and the cousin contracted AIDS and died in 2001, lend support to this conclusion. The question remains whether Renzaho can be found responsible for the rapes of Witness AWX, her sister and her cousin. While the witness's testimony reflects that the soldiers arrived with Renzaho during the operation in May, it also suggests that she, her sister and cousin were removed by these soldiers three hours afterwards. Moreover, her account indicates that Renzaho left quickly after the separation of refugees began, and there is no evidence that the women were removed on his orders or with his knowledge. Similarly, there is no indication that Renzaho was present when the women were taken away in the middle of June. It is also noteworthy that Witness AWX's statement to Tribunal investigators makes no link between Renzaho's alleged role in the attack by *Interahamwe* in May 1994 and the abduction of the witness, her sister and cousin by soldiers. Even though the document reflects that she saw him with military personnel, he is described as instructing the *Interahamwe* to attack, as opposed to soldiers or, more specifically, presidential guards. The statement does reflect the witness's belief that Renzaho wielded enough power that, had he 'ordered perpetrators of rapes and killings to stop they would have obeyed him', but the absence of such a specific link between Renzaho's attack coordinated with *Interahamwe* and the rapes by the soldiers leads to a lack of clarity. Given that the evidence fails to demonstrate that Renzaho's participation in separating the refugees led to the witness's alleged rape in May, the Chamber also has reasonable doubt that Renzaho was involved in or aware of the rapes that the witness, her cousin, and her sister, who ultimately died, allegedly suffered in June. The Chamber now turns to Witness KBZ, who testified that she was raped by two *Interahamwe* behind a church when she arrived at Sainte Famille in early July. Her testimony was precise and largely consistent with her prior statement given to Tribunal investigators in August 2004. The Defence seeks generally to refute the allegation that women were raped at Sainte Famille. As mentioned above, this is not convincing, in view of the solid Prosecution evidence. The Chamber finds that Witness KBZ was indeed raped by two unidentified *Interahamwe* in early July 1994. This said, there is no specific evidence linking this event to Renzaho. No witness observed him at Sainte Famille in July, and there is no indication that he was informed of this incident. Under these circumstances, the Chamber cannot find beyond reasonable doubt that when Witness KBZ was raped by two *Interahamwe* he was specifically involved. In the circumstances, it is not established that Renzaho was involved in this event, that those who committed the rapes were his subordinates, or that Renzaho had sufficient information to establish criminal liability for the crimes. The Chamber has considered the allegations implicating Father Wenceslas Munyeshyaka in rapes and sexual assaults. No witness in the present case provided direct evidence about this. The

accounts by Witnesses AWN and HAD were second-hand. Although the Defence testimonies, discussed above, did not fully refute the Prosecution evidence, the Chamber does not have a sufficient basis to find that Father Munyeshyaka committed rape or other sexual assaults at Sainte Famille".[631]

- Rapes in Kimihurura:

"Only Witness KBZ testified that she and four other women, who were stopped at a roadblock on 28 May 1994, were taken to the abandoned house of Jean-Michel in Kimihurura sector. This happened after the *Interahamwe* had spoken with the *conseiller* of Kimihurura. According to the militiamen, he had given instructions that they should ask Renzaho what to do with the women. The following day, they said that the prefect had said that they should not be killed until after the burial of President Habyarimana. An *Interahamwe* called Jerôme Rwemarika then took her to his home and raped her. In the Chamber's view, the witness's account that she was raped appeared coherent and convincing. It was generally consistent with her statement to Tribunal investigators of August 2004. However, her evidence implicating Renzaho was second-hand, provided to her by the *Interahamwe* who kidnapped and raped her. Her August 2004 statement creates further doubt about Renzaho's alleged involvement. Although it reflects that the *conseiller* directed the *Interahamwe* to seek advice from Renzaho before taking action, the statement does not indicate that they did so. In the Chamber's view, this omission is material. The witness also testified that the other women were taken away from the abandoned house. She believed they were raped although they did not talk about it. This account was second-hand, and her basis for knowledge was insufficiently precise to establish that rape occurred. No information was given about the purported victims and perpetrators, location or time of the crime. Consequently, the evidence is inconclusive. The Chamber concludes that Witness KBZ was raped by an *Interahamwe* in late May 1994. However, it is not established beyond reasonable doubt that Renzaho was involved in this event, that those who committed the rapes were his subordinates, or that Renzaho had sufficient information to be held criminally liable in relation to their acts".[632]

- Renzaho's general knowledge of rapes in Kigali-Ville prefecture:

"In addition to alleging that Renzaho was involved in specific incidents of rape, as addressed above, the Prosecution also seeks to establish his general knowledge of rapes occurring in Kigali-Ville prefecture from April to July 1994. It relies on Witnesses AWE and UB, both local officials, who purportedly shared their reports about rapes in their areas with Renzaho. The Chamber recalls that, when giving evidence, Witness AWE was awaiting trial in Rwanda for genocide, whereas Witness UB's appeal against his genocide conviction was pending. Both were accused of crimes implicating Renzaho and were, at the time of their testimony, detained in the same prison. The Chamber views their evidence with caution as it may be influenced by their desire to distance themselves from responsibility. Defence Witness AIA stated that reports about rapes were not made to Renzaho, but to the *conseiller* for whom the witness worked. This official ignored such reports and even encouraged and engaged in acts of rape. As mentioned elsewhere (II.3), the Chamber has doubts about the reliability of certain aspects of this witness's account. Nevertheless, the evidentiary situation about the reporting of rape is unclear. Renzaho admitted that, during a meeting on 21 April 1994, he received information about rapes taking place within Kigali-Ville prefecture. His statements on Radio Rwanda on 24 April and 10 May further demonstrate that he had knowledge that rapes were being committed in that area. The

[631] *Renzaho* Trial Judgement, paras. 719–728 (internal references omitted).

[632] *Renzaho* Trial Judgement, paras. 729–732 (internal references omitted).

	Indictment alleges that he is responsible as a superior for such acts. However, as set forth above (subsections (II.13.3.2) and (II.13.3.3)), the Chamber has doubt that rapes were being committed by Renzaho's subordinates over whom he exercised effective control. Furthermore, and notwithstanding the testimonies summarised here, the overall evidence of Renzaho's knowledge is insufficient to make a finding of criminal liability with respect to general evidence about rape and sexual violence in Kigali-Ville prefecture".[633]

17. Ildephonse **Hategekimana** (Case No. ICTR-00-55B) Lieutenant in the Rwandan Armed Forces; member of the Butare prefecture Security Council and Commander of the Ngoma Military Camp in Butare prefecture.	
Indictment (International sex crimes (or related) charges and mode(s) of liability)	- **Genocide** (count 1) or, alternatively, **Complicity in genocide** (count 2) and **Rape as CAH** (count 4) under Article 6(1) of the Statute (**joint criminal enterprise**) for: (i) ordering his soldiers at Ngoma Camp to rape Tutsi women before killing them, in accordance with an agreement made at *Ecole des Sous Officiers* (ESO) on or about 7 April 1994 and for the subsequent rapes of Tutsi women in and around Butare town by soldiers, *Interahamwe* and armed civilians participating in the joint criminal enterprise between 7 April and 31 May 1994; (ii) kidnapping Tutsi women and keeping them against their will at his house, where he raped them between 7 April and 31 May 1994; and (iii) the rape of Nura Sezirahiga by soldiers led by him during the attack against her house in Ngoma on or about 23 April 1994; and under Article 6(3) of the Statute (**superior responsibility**) for failing to prevent or punish: (i) the rapes of Tutsi women by soldiers from Ngoma Camp, *Interahamwe* and armed civilians under his effective control at diverse unknown dates from or after 7 April 1994; (ii) the rapes of Tutsi women maintained at houses in and around Butare town by soldiers under his effective control on diverse unknown dates between 7 April and 31 May 1994; and (iii) the rape of Nura Sezirahiga by soldiers led by him during the attack against her house in Ngoma on or about 23 April 1994.[634]

633 *Renzaho* Trial Judgement, paras. 733–735 (internal reference omitted).

634 *Prosecutor v. Ildephonse Hategekimana*, Case No. ICTR-00-55B-I, Amended Indictment, 1 October 2007, p. 2 ("**COUNT I: GENOCIDE** The Prosecutor of the International Criminal Tribunal for Rwanda charges **ILDEPHONSE HATEGEKIMANA alias BIKOMAGO** with **GENOCIDE**, a crime stipulated in Article 2(3)(a) of the Statute, in that on or between the dates of 7 April and 31 May 1994 throughout Butare Prefecture, and in Butare Town in particular, **ILDEPHONSE HATEGEKIMANA alias BIKOMAGO** was responsible for killing and/or causing serious bodily or mental harm to members of the Tutsi racial or ethnic group and those perceived to be their sympathisers with intent to destroy, in whole or in part, the Tutsi racial or ethnic group, as such, details of which are set out in paragraphs 6 to 33 below. ALTERNATIVELY, **COUNT II: COMPLICITY IN GENOCIDE** The Prosecutor of the International Criminal Tribunal for Rwanda charges **ILDEPHONSE HATEGEKIMANA alias BIKOMAGO** with **COMPLICITY IN GENOCIDE**, a crime stipulated in Article 2(3)(e), in that on or between the dates of 7 April and 31 May 1994 throughout Butare Prefecture, and in Butare Town in particular, **ILDEPHONSE HATEGEKIMANA alias BIKOMAGO** was an accomplice to the killing and/or causing of serious bodily or mental harm to members of the Tutsi ethnic or racial group, which acts were carried out with the intent to destroy, in whole or in part, the Tutsi ethnic or racial group, as such, and **ILDEPHONSE HATEGEKIMANA alias BIKOMAGO** acted as an accomplice to these acts with knowledge thereof. Details of the Accused's complicity in genocide are set out in paragraphs 6 to 33 below".), paras. 7–8 ("On or about 7 April 1994, **ILDEPHONSE HATEGEKIMANA alias BIKOMAGO** attended a meeting of military officials at ESO in Butare, along with Colonel Tharcisse MUVUNYI, Lieutenant Ildephonse NIZEYIMANA, Major Cyriaque HABYARATUMA and other senior officers of the FAR and the Gendarmerie. At this meeting a decision was taken that all Tutsi should be killed and that Tutsi women should be raped before being killed. Following this meeting, **ILDEPHONSE HATEGEKIMANA alias BIKOMAGO** returned to Ngoma Camp and ordered his soldiers to kill Tutsi and to rape Tutsi women before killing them, in accordance with the agreement made at

ESO. As a result of these orders, between 7 April and at least 31 May 1994 Tutsi were killed and Tutsi women were raped, and thereby caused serious bodily or mental harm. Such acts took place in and around Butare town and were carried out by soldiers, Interahamwe and armed civilians who were participants in the joint criminal enterprise referred to in paragraph 6 above. By his actions described herein **ILDEPHONSE HATEGEKIMANA alias BIKOMAGO** planned, ordered, instigated, and committed genocide. On diverse unknown dates between 6 April and 31 May 1994, soldiers from Ngoma Camp led by and including **ILDEPHONSE HATEGEKIMANA alias BIKOMAGO** kidnapped Tutsi women and kept them against their will at the house of **ILDEPHONSE HATEGEKIMANA alias BIKOMAGO**, where they were raped by **ILDEPHONSE HATEGEKIMANA alias BIKOMAGO**, thereby causing them serious bodily and/or mental harm. By his actions described herein, **ILDEPHONSE HATEGEKIMANA alias BIKOMAGO** committed genocide".), 17 ("On or about 23 April 1994, soldiers and Interahamwe led by the Accused, **ILDEPHONSE HATEGEKIMANA alias BIKOMAGO**, went to the house of Sadiki SEZIRAHIGA in Ngoma where they attacked the inhabitants. During the attack, Michel MURIGANDE ordered one of the soldiers present to rape Nura SEZIRAHIGA. She was raped and then killed. By his actions referred to herein, **ILDEPHONSE HATEGEKIMANA alias BIKOMAGO** instigated, committed or otherwise aided and abetted genocide".), 32–33 ("Tutsi women were raped by soldiers from Ngoma Camp, Interahamwe and armed civilians under the military command or effective control of **ILDEPHONSE HATEGEKIMANA alias BIKOMAGO**, at diverse unknown dates from or after 7 April 1994. Soldiers under the military command or effective control of **ILDEPHONSE HATEGEKIMANA alias BIKOMAGO** boasted about their exploits and the Accused knew or had reason to know that these acts of sexual violence were taking place and he failed or refused to take any necessary or reasonable measures to prevent such acts of sexual violence or to punish the perpetrators thereof. Soldiers under the military command or effective control of **ILDEPHONSE HATEGEKIMANA alias BIKOMAGO** maintained Tutsi women at houses in and around Butare town where they were raped by the said soldiers on diverse unknown dates between 7 April and 31 May 1994, and thereby caused them serious bodily or mental harm. **ILDEPHONSE HATEGEKIMANA alias BIKOMAGO** knew or had reason to know that such acts were about to take place or had taken place and failed to take necessary or reasonable measures to prevent or punish such acts".), p. 12 ("**COUNT IV: RAPE AS A CRIME AGAINST HUMANITY** The Prosecutor of the International Criminal Tribunal for Rwanda charges **ILDEPHONSE HATEGEKIMANA alias BIKOMAGO** with **RAPE AS A CRIME AGAINST HUMANITY**, a crime stipulated in Article 3(g) of the Statute, in that on and between 7 April and 31 May 1994 in Butare Prefecture, **ILDEPHONSE HATEGEKIMANA alias BIKOMAGO** was responsible for the rape of members of the Tutsi ethnic or racial group or persons identified as Tutsi or presumed to support the Tutsi, as part of a widespread and/or systematic attack against the Tutsi civilian population on racial, ethnic and/or political grounds, as set out in paragraphs 42 to 45 below".), paras. 42–49 ("Pursuant to Article 6(1) of the Statute, the Accused, **ILDEPHONSE HATEGEKIMANA alias BIKOMAGO**, is individually criminally responsible for rape as a crime against humanity because he planned, ordered, instigated, committed or otherwise aided and abetted in the planning, preparation and/or execution of this crime. With regard to the commission of this crime, the Accused in addition wilfully and knowingly participated in a joint criminal enterprise whose common purpose was the commission of rape as a crime against humanity against the Tutsi racial or ethnic group and/or persons identified as Tutsi and/or […] those perceived to be their sympathisers throughout Rwanda and in Butare Prefecture in particular. To fulfil this criminal purpose, the Accused acted with leaders and members of the FAR, including Colonel Tharcisse MUVUNYI, Lieutenant Ildephonse NIZEYIMANA, Lieutenant Fabien NIYONTEZE, Sergeant MUSABIMANA, Sergeant NGIRINSHUTI, Corporal MPARANIYE, Corporal Anastase RUTANIHUBWOBA, Captain NKURUNZIZA, 'PACIFIQUE', 'ISMAEL', 'GATWAZA', 'MAHORO', and 'SHITANI'; the Presidential Guard; soldiers from ESO; leaders and members of the Gendarmerie including Major Cyriaque HABYARATUMA; political leaders such as President Théodor SINDIKUBWABO, Prime Minister Jean KAMBANDA, Callixte KALIMANZIRA, and Eliezer NIYITEGEKA; the Interahamwe, including Jean Claude MUREKEZI alias 'Fils', Deo MUREKEZI, Janvier NTASONI and 'NDEKO'; Communal Police; armed civilians; local administrative officials including Préfet Sylvain NSABIMANA, Conseiller Jacques HABIMANA; other known participants such as Félix SEMWAGA; and other unknown participants. The Accused and the aforementioned participants in this joint criminal enterprise shared a common intent to destroy the Tutsi ethnic group by raping members of that group as alleged in paragraphs 43 to 45 below. Alternatively the common purpose of the joint criminal enterprise was the destruction in whole or in part of the Tutsi racial or ethnic group; the participants in this joint criminal enterprise, including the Accused, were aware that the commission, by one or more participants in the joint criminal enterprise, of rape as a crime against humanity was a natural and foreseeable consequence of effecting their common purpose, and the accused willingly took the risk that this might occur. The particulars which give rise to the Accused's individu-

Trial Judgement	- Guilty of **Rape as CAH** (count 4) under Article 6(3) of the Statute (**superior responsibility**) for the rape of Nura Sezirahiga by a soldier from Ngoma Military Camp, during an attack led by Ildephonse Hategekimana, on 23 April 1994.[635] - Although Ildephonse Hategekimana was found guilty of genocide (count 1), the Trial Chamber found that the evidence did not establish that Nura Sezirahiga was a Tutsi or

al criminal responsibility, including his participation in a joint criminal enterprise, are set out in paragraphs 43 to 45 below. On 7 April 1994, **ILDEPHONSE HATEGEKIMANA alias BIKOMAGO** attended a meeting of military officials at ESO in Butare, along with Colonel Tharcisse MUVUNYI, Lieutenant Ildephonse NIZEYIMANA, Major Cyriaque HABYARATUMA and other senior officers of the FAR and the Gendarmerie. At this meeting a decision was taken that Tutsi women should be raped before being killed. Following this meeting, **ILDEPHONSE HATEGEKIMANA alias BIKOMAGO** returned to Ngoma Camp and ordered his soldiers to rape Tutsi women before killing them, in accordance with the agreement made at ESO. As a result of these orders, between 7 April and at least 31 May 1994 Tutsi women were raped in Butare town and elsewhere in Butare prefecture by soldiers, Interahamwe and armed civilians who were participants in the joint criminal enterprise referred to in paragraph 42 above. By his actions described herein **ILDEPHONSE HATEGEKIMANA alias BIKOMAGO** planned, ordered, instigated, and committed rape as a crime against humanity. On diverse unknown dates between 7 April and 31 May 1994, soldiers from Ngoma Camp led by and including **ILDEPHONSE HATEGEKIMANA alias BIKOMAGO** kidnapped Tutsi women and kept them against their will at the house of **ILDEPHONSE HATEGEKIMANA alias BIKOMAGO**, where they were raped by **ILDEPHONSE HATEGEKIMANA alias BIKOMAGO**. **ILDEPHONSE HATEGEKIMANA alias BIKOMAGO** thereby committed rape as a crime against humanity. On or about 23 April 1994 soldiers and Interahamwe led by the Accused, **ILDEPHONSE HATEGEKIMANA alias BIKOMAGO**, went to the house of Sadiki SEZIRAHIGA in Ngoma where they attacked the inhabitants. During the attack, Michel MURIGANDE ordered one of the soldiers present to rape Nura SEZIRAHIGA. She was raped and then killed. By his actions referred to herein, **ILDEPHONSE HATEGEKIMANA alias BIKOMAGO** instigated, committed or otherwise aided and abetted rape as a crime against humanity. Pursuant to Article 6(3) of the Statute, the Accused, **ILDEPHONSE HATEGEKIMANA alias BIKOMAGO** is responsible for rape as a crime against humanity because specific criminal acts were committed by subordinates of the Accused over whom he exercised effective control, as part of a widespread and/or systematic attack on the Tutsi civilian population on racial, ethnic and/or political grounds, and the Accused knew or had reason to know that such subordinates were about to commit such acts before they were committed, or that such subordinates had committed such acts, and the Accused failed to take [the] necessary and reasonable measures to prevent such acts or to punish the perpetrators thereof. The subordinates over whom **ILDEPHONSE HATEGEKIMANA alias BIKOMAGO** exercised effective control included soldiers under his command at Ngoma Camp, Interahamwe, and armed civilians. The particulars that give rise to the Accused's individual criminal responsibility pursuant to Article 6(3) are set forth in paragraphs 47 to 49 below. On and between 7 April and 31 May 1994 Tutsi women were regularly raped by soldiers and Interahamwe under the military command or effective control of **ILDEPHONSE HATEGEKIMANA alias BIKOMAGO** in and around Butare town. **ILDEPHONSE HATEGEKIMANA alias BIKOMAGO** knew or had reason to know that such rapes were about to take place or had taken place and failed to take [the] necessary or reasonable measures to prevent or punish such acts. Soldiers under the military command or effecive control of **ILDEPHONSE HATEGEKIMANA alias BIKOMAGO** maintained Tutsi women at houses in and around Butare town where they were raped by the said soldiers on diverse unknown dates between 7 April and 31 May 1994. **ILDEPHONSE HATEGEKIMANA alias BIKOMAGO** knew or had reason to know that such acts were about to take place or had taken place and failed to take [the] necessary or reasonable measures to prevent or punish such acts. On or about 23 April 1994, soldiers and Interahamwe under the military command or effective control of **ILDEPHONSE HATEGEKIMANA alias BIKOMAGO**, were led by him to the house of Sadiki SEZIRAHIGA in Ngoma where they attacked the inhabitants. During the attack, Michel MURIGANDE ordered one of the soldiers present to rape Nura SEZIRAHIGA. She was raped and then killed. **ILDEPHONSE HATEGEKIMANA alias BIKOMAGO** knew or had reason to know that such acts were about to take place or had taken place and failed to take [the] necessary or reasonable measures to prevent or punish such acts".).

635 *Prosecutor v. Ildephonse Hategekimana*, Case No. ICTR-00-55B-T, Judgement and Sentence, dated 6 December 2010 and filed on 14 February 2011 ("*Hategekimana* Trial Judgement"), paras. 459–464, 665, 725–730.

	that she was raped with genocidal intent. Therefore, Ildephonse Hategekimana's conviction for genocide does not encompass this rape.[636]
Appeal Judgement	N/A (The appellate proceedings are in progress.)
Legal and Factual Findings and/or Evidence	- Factual findings: - Alleged defect of the Indictment with respect to rapes: "The Defence also asserts that, apart from the rape of Nura Sezirahiga in Ngoma on 23 April 1994, the allegations of rape in paragraphs 8, 32, 33, 44, 47 and 48 are imprecise in relation to the location of the crimes, the identity of the victims and perpetrators as well as the time frame in which the rapes occurred. In the Chamber's view, the identification of the alleged locations and perpetrators of the rapes are sufficiently precise, within the context of the entire Indictment, for the Defence to pursue investigations. While the time frame of the alleged rapes spans a two-month period, the Chamber reiterates that a broad date range, in itself, does not invalidate a paragraph of an indictment. In this respect, the Appeals Chamber has stated that, in certain circumstances, the sheer scale of the alleged crimes makes it impracticable to require a high degree of specificity in such matters as the dates of the commission of the crimes and the identity of the victims. One example, according to the Appeals Chamber, is where the accused participated as a member of a military force 'in an extensive number of attacks on civilians that took place over a prolonged period of time and resulted in large numbers of killings.' In light of the large scale of the alleged rapes in and around Butare town, the Chamber accepts that the Prosecution was not necessarily in a position to provide greater specificity about either the dates or the victims of the crimes. Therefore, the Chamber considers that the Indictment is not defective with respect to the time frame, the location and the identification of the perpetrators or the victims of the rapes alleged in paragraphs 32, 33, 44, 47 and 48 of the Indictment".[637] - Alleged order to rape Tutsi women following the meeting at ESO military camp, in Ngoma commune, in Butare prefecture: "The Defence submits that Hategekimana was absent from Butare at the time of the alleged officers' meeting in the morning of 7 April 1994 at the ESO Camp. As discussed above, the Chamber does not believe Hategekimana's alibi. The Prosecution led no evidence regarding Hategekimana's participation in any decision reached during the alleged meeting of Butare military officers at the ESO Camp on 7 April 1994. While Witness BUR testified that Hategekimana attended this meeting, which was held inside the command office, the witness did not attend the meeting and did not hear any of the discussion. Witness BUR's evidence does not establish what role, if any, Hategekimana played at the alleged meeting beyond his mere presence in the command office. Witness BUR's allegations about the officers' meeting at the ESO Camp are uncorroborated. Indeed, Defence Witnesses BJ3 and CBB, both ESO Camp soldiers in April 1994, denied that a Butare military officers' meeting was held at the ESO Camp on 7 April. Witness BUR claims to have seen Hategekimana arrive at the ESO Camp to attend the meeting. The witness also claims to have heard Captain Nizeyimana issue instructions to soldiers assembled at the ESO Camp to rape and kill *Tutsis*, shortly following the officers' meeting. However, the witness' conclusion that a decision to kill and rape *Tutsis* was taken at the officers' meeting is speculative, and his testimony that Hategekimana issued those same instructions at the Ngoma Camp is hearsay. The Chamber considers that such evidence should be treated with caution. Witness BUR's testimony that he saw Hategekimana arrive at the ESO Camp, in the morning of 7 April 1994, in a green Toyota pickup is supported by the account of

[636] *Hategekimana* Trial Judgement, paras. 30, 697, 730.
[637] *Hategekimana* Trial Judgement, paras. 61–62 (internal references omitted).

	Prosecution Witness BRS that Hategekimana left the Ngoma Camp, on the same morning, 'in a green double-cabin Toyota.' However, in the Chamber's view, Witness BRS's testimony offers only limited corroboration of Witness BUR's account. Taken together, their evidence does not directly link the Accused to the killing of *Tutsis* and the rape of *Tutsi* women, before killing them, pursuant to a decision taken at the Butare officers' meeting. Consequently, owing to the lack of sufficient and reliable evidence, the Chamber does not find that the Prosecution has proven the allegations, set forth in paragraphs 7 and 43 of the Indictment, that Hategekimana attended a meeting of military officials at the ESO Camp, on or about 7 April 1994, or that he issued orders to Ngoma Camp soldiers to kill *Tutsis* and to rape *Tutsi* women before killing them".[638] - Rapes in Butare: "There is no dispute that rapes were committed in Butare as part of a series of attacks perpetrated against *Tutsis* and moderate *Hutus* during the 1994 events in Rwanda. Indeed, the Chamber has heard evidence from both the Prosecution and the Defence that such rapes were notorious".[639] - Alleged rapes at Ildephonse Hategekimana's residence: "Witness BUR testified about the alleged rapes of the *Préfet*'s wife and four *Tutsi* girls at Hategekimana's home. Although the witness was physically present at the site of the alleged crimes, while he was on patrol in the Taba neighbourhood, he did not see any victim raped. Rather, Witness BUR's testimony that Hategekimana raped *Préfet* Habyarimana's wife and other *Tutsi* girls was based on accounts that he received from members of Hategekimana's escort, as well as inferences drawn from his own observations. His evidence about the *actus reus* of these rapes is therefore hearsay. The Chamber considers that such evidence should be treated with caution. In this respect, the Chamber notes inconsistencies in Witness BUR's evidence regarding his stated reason for being at *Préfet* Habyarimana's house when he saw Hategekimana abduct the *Préfet*'s wife, Joséphine. The witness, an ESO Camp soldier, testified that he and other soldiers in his unit had been instructed to watch the house of the *Préfet*, who was a *Tutsi*, in order to ensure that the *Préfet* did not leave. However, on cross-examination, the witness denied having been assigned to guard the *Préfet*'s house, claiming rather that he happened to pass by the *Préfet*'s house while patrolling the neighbourhood. Later, the witness contradicted himself again, stating that he left the *Préfet's* house as soon as Hategekimana abducted the *Préfet's* wife because 'our mission was accomplished [...] so we didn't have any reason to remain there.' The Chamber also observes an inconsistency in Witness BUR's testimony in relation to his identification of Hategekimana's house and his knowledge of the officers' residences. When the witness was asked during trial how he knew that the *Préfet's* wife had been taken to Hategekimana's house, he first stated, 'All the residences of the officers were in Taba and I knew those houses.' The witness specified that he was able to identify the home as Hategekimana's because he 'saw the *Préfet's* wife' and 'members of his escort there.' In the Chamber's view, the basis for Witness BUR's recognition of Hategekimana's residence appears to be speculative. Later in his testimony, the witness contradicted his initial claim to know 'all the residences of the officers' in the Taba neighbourhood, and acknowledged that he was unable to identify the homes of General Gatsinzi and Colonel Muvunyi, the commanding officers of the ESO Camp, where he was stationed. The Chamber considers it doubtful that Witness BUR would have been able to identify the home of an officer of the Ngoma Camp but not know the

638 *Hategekimana* Trial Judgement, paras. 133–137 (internal reference omitted).

639 *Hategekimana* Trial Judgement, para. 165 (internal reference omitted).

	residences of his own ESO commanders. The Chamber finds the inconsistency to be significant and questions the reliability of the witness's uncorroborated identification of Hategekimana's residence, which is a site of the rapes alleged in paragraphs 8 and 44 of the Indictment. The Chamber also notes a discrepancy between Witness BUR's testimony and his statement of August 2006 to Tribunal investigators regarding the identification of individuals in Hategekimana's escort. During trial, Witness BUR specifically named the members of the escort whom he saw outside of Hategekimana's residence with *Tutsi* women in April 1994, while he was on patrol. However, in his out-of court statement, the witness declared that he did 'not know the names of [...] the soldiers in the Bikomago escort. I did not see them ever again and I no longer remember their names.' When questioned about this matter, Witness BUR acknowledged that he did not know the individuals' identities in 1994 but subsequently remembered their names while he was in exile in the Congo in 2004. When asked on cross-examination why he did not provide the escorts' names to ICTR investigators in 2006, the witness stated that he did not retain the names after hearing them in exile in 2004 but recalled them only after meeting a member of Hategekimana's escort in 2007. The witness further testified, 'I believe that I have already told the Tribunal investigators that I knew those names, but they did not want to include the names in my written statement. They suggested to me that I mention those names here before the Trial Chamber.' In the Chamber's view, the witness' explanation raises doubts about the reliability of his identification of the members of Hategekimana's escort. Witness BUR's testimony provides some support for the allegation that Hategekimana ordered Ngoma Camp soldiers to rape *Tutsi* women. However, the witness' uncorroborated testimony is second-hand and circumstantial, based largely on his inference that Ngoma Camp soldiers received the same instructions to rape as did he and other ESO Camp military staff. The witness specifically testified that ESO Camp soldiers received orders from their superiors 'to rape the *Tutsi* women and kill them afterwards' and that 'we followed the instructions that were given.' The witness stated that he did not intervene to assist the rape victims because he could not disobey orders. The witness also emphasised that neither he nor any other soldier could disobey the orders issued to them to rape and kill *Tutsi* women. When questioned about whether he participated in rapes, the witness answered, '[I]f I had committed such acts, then the *Gacaca* courts would have convicted me, and I would currently be serving a prison sentence.' The Chamber does not consider this answer to negate the possibility that Witness BUR also might have committed rapes and thus may have been an accomplice, particularly in light of his repeated assertions that instructions to rape and kill could not have been disobeyed. In view of these problematic aspects of Witness BUR's testimony and of the fact that he may have been under duress, the Chamber declines to rely on his evidence, without further corroboration, in respect of the alleged rapes of the *Préfet*'s wife and four *Tutsi* girls at Hategekimana's residence. Therefore the Chamber does not find it established beyond reasonable doubt that soldiers from the Ngoma Camp kept *Tutsi* women against their will at Hategekimana's residence, where he raped them, as pleaded in paragraphs 8 and 44 of the Indictment".[640] - Alleged rape at Queen Gicanda's home: "Witness BUR testified that he saw a girl being raped by Ngoma Camp soldiers, under the command of Sergeant Ngirinshuti, at Queen Gicanda's home. As discussed above, the Chamber has reservations about the reliability of Witness BUR's evidence, without credible corroboration. In particular, the Chamber recalls the possibility that Witness BUR, or soldiers in his own unit, might also be implicated in the rapes that he has

[640] *Hategekimana* Trial Judgement, paras. 167–172 (internal references omitted).

	described. Therefore, the Chamber dismisses the allegation that Ngoma Camp soldiers raped a *Tutsi* girl at the home of Queen Gicanda".[641] - Alleged rapes of Witness BUQ: "Witness BUQ testified about being gang raped repeatedly in her employers' home for three consecutive nights immediately following the death of President Habyarimana. She identified the perpetrators as soldiers, but could not recognise any of them except for Rubaga, whom she recognised as being from the ESO Camp. It was not until the third day that another soldier, unknown to her, introduced himself as Ndererimana, one of Hategekimana's escorts from the Ngoma Camp. According to Witness BUQ, the Ngoma Camp soldier kept her as a sexual slave in a nearby residence for approximately two weeks. The Chamber notes that Witness BUQ's testimony concerning one named Ngoma Camp soldier provides the only relevant evidence linking Hategekimana to the crimes of rape perpetrated against Witness BUQ. The Chamber finds Witness BUQ's timeline of events to be problematic. Specifically, the Chamber is concerned about the inconsistency in the Prosecution and Defence evidence about the date on which Witness BUQ's employers left their home in the Taba neighbourhood. In the absence of corroborative evidence, the Chamber has serious reservations about the veracity of Witness BUQ's testimony that her employers left Butare at 10.00 p.m. on 6 April 1994. Similarly, the Chamber doubts that Witness BUQ was raped on the night of 6 to 7 April 1994, within hours of her employers' departure, by soldiers who had already received orders to rape and kill *Tutsi* women. For instance, Prosecution Witness BRS, a soldier stationed at the Ngoma Camp in April 1994, testified that Ngoma Camp soldiers were not notified of the President's death until 2.00 or 3.00 a.m. on 7 April 1994 by Second Lieutenant Niyonteze. The Chamber also observes that no testimony was offered or evidence tendered during trial identifying any Ngoma Camp soldier by the name of Ndererimana. A doubt therefore subsists as to whether the named soldier identified by Witness BUQ served under Hategekimana's command. Thus, the Chamber finds that the Prosecution has not established that the soldier who raped Witness BUQ was one of Hategekimana's subordinates. In light of the problems discussed above, the Chamber finds that it cannot rely on the evidence of Witness BUQ without credible corroboration. Indeed, the Prosecution evidence has not established Hategekimana's alleged Superior responsibility for the rapes perpetrated in houses and other places throughout Butare, as alleged in paragraphs 47 and 48 of the Indictment. The Prosecution has not led any evidence to suggest that Hategekimana knew that the named Ngoma Camp soldier detained and raped Witness BUQ at a house in Butare. The Chamber recalls that Witness BUQ testified that her captor did not want others to know that he was hiding a *Tutsi* woman and that he visited the house where she was detained 'without the knowledge of other people.' The witness stated that 'if it had been known that he was hiding a *Tutsi* in that house, he would have had negative consequences.' Accordingly, the Prosecution has not proven beyond reasonable doubt that Hategekimana raped *Tutsi* women in his home and that he knew of the perpetration of rapes on *Tutsi* women by Ngoma Camp soldiers, *Interahamwe* and armed civilians under his effective control in houses and other locations in and around Butare town. The Chamber therefore dismisses the allegations in paragraphs 8, 32, 33, 44, 47, 48 of the Indictment".[642] - Rape of Nura Sezirahiga in Ngoma commune, in Butare prefecture, on or about 23 April 1994: "Sezirahiga is the only eyewitness to the rape of his daughter Nura. From a distance of

641 *Hategekimana* Trial Judgement, para. 173 (internal reference omitted).

642 *Hategekimana* Trial Judgement, paras. 174–178 (internal references omitted).

	four metres, he saw Michel Murigande 'deliver' his daughter to a soldier from Ngoma Camp and *Interahamwe*. The soldier raped her while Murigande was immobilizing her. Thereafter, she was killed. After assessing the evidence, the Chamber cannot determine exactly whether Hategekimana was at Sezirahiga's residence when Nura was being raped. According to the witness, Hategekimana dropped off Michel Murigande and a reinforcement of soldiers at the scene in the night of 23 April and then left, as the attackers remained and continued 'to kill people together.' The Chamber notes that Witness BTN also testified about the presence of Murigande among the assailants at Sezirahiga's home. The Defence contends that 'nothing identifies the rapist in the testimony of [Sadiki Sezirahiga]. In the circumstances, there is no basis for linking that unknown soldier, if he ever existed, to Ngoma Camp.' The Chamber however notes that it found that Ngoma Camp soldiers were present during the attack, as was Hategekimana. Consequently, the only possible deduction is that it is a soldier from Ngoma Camp who raped Nura. On cross-examination, the Defence raised the contradiction between Sezirahiga's court testimony and his prior statement of 2 November 1997. In that statement, Sezirahiga said that Michel Murigande had raped his daughter; while during the trial, he said that Murigande had delivered his daughter to soldiers and *Interahamwe*. And then one of the soldiers had raped her while Michel Murigande purportedly immobilized her. The witness explained the discrepancy between the two versions by saying that, whether it was Murigande or the soldier, they were together and Michel Murigande had immobilized his daughter. The Chamber finds that there is no major discrepancy between the two versions. And since testimony under oath has more probative value than prior statements, the Chamber finds that Nura was raped by a soldier. Although QCO witnessed the murder of Sezirahiga's children, she did not mention that she saw Nura being raped. Taking into account the place where QCO was and the number of soldiers and *Interahamwe* surrounding the victims, the Chamber is of the view that she might not have witnessed the rape of Nura. However, the fact that she did not witness the rape of Nura does not negatively affect the credibility and reliability of Sezirahiga's direct testimony. Furthermore, the Chamber is convinced that, as a father, Sezirahiga could not have fabricated the rape of his own daughter. The Chamber observed that, during his testimony, Witness Sezirahiga was sincere when he was talking about the rape of his daughter. After carefully considering Prosecution evidence, the Chamber is convinced beyond reasonable doubt that Nura was raped during the attack at his house on 23 April 1994 by a soldier from Ngoma Camp. As concerns Hategekimana's responsibility, the Chamber is convinced that he was present at Sezirahiga's home in the night of the attack and that he brought a reinforcement of soldiers there and they were involved in the rape and murder of Nura Sezirahiga. Consequently, the Chamber is convinced beyond reasonable doubt that soldiers from Ngoma Camp, led by the Accused, and in concert with *Interahamwe* and armed civilians, participated in the rape and murder of Nura Sezirahiga".[643] "In its Factual Findings the Chamber also determined that, shortly after Hategekimana arrived with four military reinforcements from the Ngoma Camp to assist assailants in attacking the Sezirahiga home, one of these soldiers raped Nura Sezirahiga. The Chamber heard credible evidence to demonstrate Hategekimana's effective control over the soldier who committed the rape. In the Chamber's view, this incident, similar to the massacres at the Ngoma Parish and the *Maison Généralice,* as well as the killings of Rugomboka and the three *Tutsi* women, demonstrates Hategekimana's effective control over Ngoma Camp soldiers, but not over other assailants".[644] - Responsibility of Ildephonse Hategekimana for the rape of Nura Sezirahiga in Ngo-

[643] *Hategekimana* Trial Judgement, paras. 459–464 (internal references omitted).

[644] *Hategekimana* Trial Judgement, para. 665.

	ma commune, in Butare prefecture, on or about 23 April 1994: "The Chamber has found that Nura Sezirahiga was singled out, raped and killed on the night of 23 April 1994. Within the context of the crimes established by the evidence in this case, the Chamber finds that the rape was part of a discriminatory, widespread and systematic attack against *Tutsi* civilians and *Hutu* moderates. Nura Sezirahiga was *Hutu*, but she was raped and killed because of the perceived political affiliation of her father. The evidence establishes that the assailants who attacked the Sezirahiga home were searching for firearms or other objects to show that her father, Sadiki Sezirahiga, was an *Inkotanyi* accomplice. The Chamber has already found that Hategekimana was present during the attack on Sezirahiga's house, following which his wife and son were brutally assaulted and left for dead and his daughter raped and killed. Sadiki Sezirahiga, the one eyewitness to the crime, whom the Chamber found credible and reliable, did not see Hategekimana during the rape of his daughter Nura Sezirahiga. However, on the basis of his evidence, the Chamber found that one of the four Ngoma Camp soldiers who accompanied Hategekimana to the site raped Nura Sezirahiga. The soldier raped her in the presence of other soldiers and the same *Interahamwe* and armed civilians who had attacked the residents of the Sezirahiga home. Hategekimana came with his subordinates, four Ngoma Camp soldiers, to attack Sezirahiga's house. He was present when Nura and her family were forced from their home and when the *Interahamwe* and armed civilians brutally attacked the residents. The rape was perpetrated as one of several crimes against family members, which were not charged in the Indictment, specifically the battery of Nura's mother, the murder of her brother and her own murder. Nura died immediately after the rape. In the Chamber's view, even if Hategekimana was not present during the rape, he had reason to know that one or more of the soldiers were about to commit such an offence or had done so. Hategekimana took no necessary nor reasonable measures to prevent the rape or to punish the perpetrator. The Chamber finds that Hategekimana had effective control over the soldiers under his command. Insofar as the evidence establishes that the rape was committed by one of the Ngoma Camp soldiers, and not by any other assailant, the Chamber has determined that Hategekimana is responsible as a superior. Accordingly, the Chamber finds Hategekimana guilty, as a superior, for the rape of Nura Sezirahiga, committed by a soldier from the Ngoma Camp, as a crime against humanity (Count IV) under Article 6 (3) of the Statute".[645]

18. Jean-Baptiste **Gatete** (Case No. ICTR-00-61) Director within the Ministry of Women and Family Affairs since April 1994.	
Indictment[646] (International sex crimes (or related) charges and mode(s) of liability)	- **Genocide** (count 1) or, alternatively, **Complicity in genocide** (count 2) and **Rape as CAH** (count 6) under Article 6(1) of the Statute for: (i) transporting a convoy of armed *Interahamwe* to Akarambo cellule where he ordered, commanded or incited the *Interahawe* to rape Tutsi civilians during the morning of 7 April 1994 and for the subsequent rape of Witness BAT at her house in Akarambo by two *Interahamwe* on or about 8 April 1994 and the rape of AVO on or about 9 April 1994 as a result of his actions; (ii) inciting the local population in Rwankuba to rape Tutsi civilians on or about 7 April 1994; (iii) ordering, supervising and participating in the rapes of Tutsi

645 *Hategekimana* Trial Judgement, paras. 725–729 (internal references omitted).

646 For the general background to the charges, see *Prosecutor v. Jean-Baptiste Gatete*, Case No. ICTR-00-61-I, Indictment, 7 July 2009 ("*Gatete* Indictment"), para. 8 ("**Jean-Baptiste GATETE**, acted individually or in concert with other members of the joint criminal enterprise in the following ways: […] b. Trained, indoctrinated, encouraged, provided intelligence to, transported and distributed arms to members of the *Interahamwe*, the *Arnahindure*, 'Civil Defence Forces,' and other militiamen who murdered, caused serious bodily and mental harm, raped and pillaged Tutsi group members".).

	civilians at Kiziguro parish complex on or about 11 April 1994; (iv) transporting armed soldiers and *Interahamwe* to Mukarange parish, where Tutsis were raped as a result of his actions on or about 10 to 11 April 1994; (v) commanding the *Interahamwe* to rape Tutsi women at Kayonza commune office on or about 10 to 15 April 1994 and for the subsequent rapes as a result of his actions; (vi) ordering and instigating *Interahamwe* to rape Tutsis in Nyarusage, Nkamba and Giparara secteurs and for the subsequent rapes as a result of his actions; and (vii) ordering the *Interahamwe* to rape Tutsis in Rukira commune in mid to late April 1994 and for the subsequent rapes as a result of his actions.[647]

[647] *Gatete* Indictment, paras. 10–11 ("**Counts 1 – 2 GENOCIDE, *or alternatively* COMPLICITY IN GENOCIDE** The Prosecutor charges **Jean-Baptiste GATETE** with GENOCIDE, *a crime stipulated in Article 2(3)(a) and Article 6(1) of the Statute*, in that on or between the dates of 6 – 30 April 1994, in Byumba and Kibungo *prefectures*, Rwanda, **Jean-Baptiste GATETE**, with intent to destroy, in whole or in part, the Tutsi racial or ethnical group, or knowing that other people intended to destroy, in whole or in part, the Tutsi racial or ethnical group, planned, instigated, ordered, committed or otherwise aided and abetted those other people in the planning, preparation, or execution of killing or causing serious bodily or mental harm to members of the Tutsi group, as outlined in the factual paragraphs below: ***Alternatively*** The Prosecutor charges **Jean-Baptiste GATETE** with COMPLICITY IN GENOCIDE, *a crime stipulated in Article 2(3)(e) and Article 6(1) of the Statute*, in that on or between the dates of 6 – 30 April 1994, in Byumba and Kibungo *prefectures*, Rwanda, **Jean-Baptiste GATETE**, with intent to destroy, in whole or in part, the Tutsi racial or ethical group, or knowing that other people intended to destroy, in whole or in part, the Tutsi racial or ethnical group, and knowing that his assistance would contribute to the crime of genocide, planned, instigated, ordered, committed, or otherwise aided and abetted those other people in the planning, preparation or execution of the killing or causing serious bodily or mental harm to members of the Tutsi group, as outlined in the factual paragraphs below".), 15–16 ("During the morning of 7 April 1994, **Jean-Baptiste GATETE** facilitated the transport of the *Interahamwe* through various Murambi *commune secteurs* and *cellules*, including Akarambo, Gakoni, Nyabisindu, Kiramuruzi, and Rwankuba, and commanded the *Interahamwe*, some of whom were RUPIA, Serena GAUFRAMA and RWASIBO, to kill the civilian Tutsi. Some examples, **Jean-Baptiste GATETE**, with Murambi *bourgmestre*, Jean de Dieu MWANGE, transported a convoy of armed *Interahamwe* to Akarambo *cellule* where **GATETE** ordered the *Interahamwe* to burn, loot and pillage Tutsi homes and to rape and kill civilian Tutsi. BCS's family was killed in their Akarambo home by the *Interahamwe* on the orders of **Jean-Baptiste GATETE**, who was also present during the killings. Also killed was Aisha MUREKEYISONI, a Tutsi from Kiramurzi. Then on or about 8 April 1994, BAT was raped at her house in Akarambo by two *Interahamwe*, one being the son of NYAMUHARA and the other KAREMERA. The *Interahamwe raped* and killed Tutsi as a result of the actions of **Jean-Baptiste GATETE**. On or about 7 April 1994, in Rwankuba, **Jean-Baptiste GATETE** with Jean BIZIMUNGU and Gerard KAYONZA, the local President of the *Interahamwe*, incited the local population to pillage Tutsi homes and attack, rape and murder civilian Tutsi".), 19 ("On or about 1 April 1994, **Jean-Baptiste GATETE** ordered, supervised and participated in the killings and rapes of civilian Tutsi at Kiziguro *paroisse* complex, a church and hospital where thousands of civilian Tutsis had taken refuge".), 22–25 ("On or about 10 to 11 April 1994, **Jean-Baptiste GATETE**, with Kayonza *bourgmestre* Celestin SENKWARE, transported armed soldiers, and the *Interahamwe*, to Mukarange *paroisse* compound. Together they attacked the Mukarange *paroisse* compound where Tutsi refugees were located Tutsi were raped and killed as a result of **Jean-Baptiste GATETE**'s actions. […] On or about and between 10 April to 15 April 1994, **Jean-Baptiste GATETE** arrived in Kayonza *commune* with a group of armed *Interahamwe*, **Jean-Baptiste GATETE**, with Kayonza *bourgmestre* Célestin SENKWARE, instigated a crowd assembled in the *bureau communal* courtyard. Present in the courtyard were local residents, including a number of Tutsi women, and the recently arrived *Interahamwe*. To instigate those *Interahamwe* present, **Jean-Baptiste GATETE** reported that Tutsi populations in other areas had been decimated, and he commanded the *Interahamwe* to rape and then kill Tutsi. On or about and between 10 April to 15 April 1994, **Jean-Baptiste GATETE** with a group of armed *Interahamwe* at the Kayonza *bureau communal* courtyard ordered the segregation of Tutsi and commanded that the Tutsi be taken to a mass grave. At the grave, **Jean-Baptiste GATETE** karate kicked GATARE's knee breaking it through **Jean-Baptiste GATETE** then ordered the Interahamwe to kill GATARE, which they did. Tutsi were raped and killed at that location as a result of **Jean-Baptiste GATETE**'s actions. After the rapes and the killings described in the preceding paragraph, the *Interahamwe* returned to the Kayonza *bureau communal* courtyard where **Jean-Baptiste GATETE** addressed them again, ordering, […] and instigating them to go to the adjoining *secteurs* of Nyarusage, Nkamba and Giparara to rape and exterminate the remaining Tutsi. Both

Trial Judgement	- Not guilty of rape as CAH (count 6) as none of the allegations of rape were proved.[648] - Although Jean-Baptiste Gatete was found guilty of genocide (count 1), the Trial Chamber found that none of the allegations of rape were proved.[649]
Appeal Judgement	N/A (The appellate proceedings are in progress.)
Legal and Factual Findings and/or Evidence	- Factual findings: - Alleged orders to rape Tutsi in Akarambo cellule: "Witness BAT was the sole Prosecution witness to testify that on 8 April, sometime between 9.00 and 11.00 a.m., Gatete arrived at the business centre in Akarambo *cellule* in a vehicle carrying *Interahamwe*. They joined *Interahamwe* who were already gathered on the road there. Shortly after, the witness was raped by two *Interahamwe*. The following day, she and other women were raped by other *Interahamwe*. The Chamber considers points raised by the Defence to undermine the witness's impartiality. The Chamber does not consider that her membership of Twisungane, a subsidiary of Avega, a genocide survivors group for widows, necessarily undermines her impartiality, as suggested by the Defence. However, that she holds Gatete responsible for the alleged imprisonment and subsequent banishment of her brother in 1990, suggests a possible motive to testify against the Accused, and the Chamber therefore exercises

Jean-Baptiste GATETE and Célestin SENKWARE provided their vehicles to the *Interahamwe* to facilitate the attacks. Tutsi were raped and killed as a result of **Jean-Baptiste GATETE**'s actions. Mid to late April 1994, **Jean-Baptiste GATETE** arrived in Rulenge, Rukira *commune* with a caravan of armed Murambi communal police, civilian militias and the *bourgmestre* of Kabarondo and Kigarama *communes*. **Jean-Baptiste GATETE** publicly castigated the local residents for not massacring the Tutsi. **Jean-Baptiste GATETE** ordered the *Interahamwe* to rape and kill Tutsi in Rukira, including women and children. The following morning, those *Interahamwe*, some of whom were Emmanuel RUKIRAMAKUBA, EPHRAIM, FABIEN, and RWABIREKEZI, destroyed Tutsi homes and raped and killed Tutsi civilians in Rukira".), 39–43 ("**Count 6 RAPE** The Prosecutor charges **Jean-Baptiste GATETE** with RAPE as a CRIME AGAINST HUMANITY, *as stipulated in Article 3(a) and Article 6(1) of the Statute*, in that on or between 6 April and 30 April 1994, in Byumba and Kibungo *prefectures*, Rwanda, **Jean-Baptiste GATETE**, with the intention that rape occur, planned, instigated, ordered, committed or otherwise aided and abetted in the planning, preparation or execution or killing of any civilian population as part of a widespread or systematic attack against that civilian population on national, political, racial, religious or ethnic grounds, as outlined in the factual paragraphs below: On or about 8 and 9 April 1994, **Jean-Baptiste GATETE** facilitated the transport of his civilian militias to the center of Akarambo *cellule*. **Jean-Baptiste GATETE** commanded and incited the *Interahamwe* to attack and rape Tutsi women. On or about 8 April, 1994, BAT was raped by two *Interahamwe*, the son of NYAMUHARA and KAREMERA. On or about 9 April 1994, AVO was raped by an *Interahamwe* named KARERANGABO. The *Interahamwe* raped Tutsi women in Akarambo *cellule*. On or about 10 to 11 April 1994, **Jean-Baptiste GATETE**, with Kayonza *bourgmestre* Celestin SENKWARE, transported armed soldiers, and the *Interahamwe*, to the Mukarange *paroisse* compound. Together they attacked the Mukarange *paroisse* compound where Tutsi refugees were located. Tutsi were raped and killed as a result of **Jean-Baptiste GATETE**'s actions. On or about and between 10 – 15 April 1994, in Kayonza, **Jean-Baptiste GATETE**, with Célestin SENKWARE, Kayonza *bourgmestre*, commanded the *Interahamwe* to rape Tutsi women assembled in the bureau comm[unal] courtyard. Tutsi women were dragged off by the *Interahamwe* and raped. After the rapes and the killings described in the preceding paragraph, the *Interahamwe* returned to the Kayonza *bureau communal* courtyard where **Jean-Baptiste GATETE** addressed them again, ordering and instigating them to go to the adjoining *secteurs* of Nyarusage, Nkamba and Giparara to rape and exterminate the remaining Tutsi. Both **Jean-Baptiste GATETE** and Célestin SENKWARE provided their vehicles to the *Interahamwe* to facilitate the attacks. Tutsi were raped and killed as a result of **Jean-Baptiste GATETE**'s actions".).

648 *Prosecutor v. Jean-Baptiste Gatete*, Case No. ICTR-00-61-T, Judgement and Sentence, 31 March 2011 ("*Gatete* Trial Judgement"), paras. 554 ("[… The Chamber] need not address the charge of rape as a crime against humanity (Count VI), as none of the allegations in support of this count were proven".), 668.

649 *Gatete* Trial Judgement, paras. 554, 668.

| | caution when assessing her evidence. Moreover, the Defence submits that Witness BAT did not mention Gatete when she testified before the Gacaca courts on the 1994 events. It argues that this omission is particularly worrying, given the witness's position. She did, however, testify with respect to Gatete's actions in 1990. The witness explained that she did not come forward to testify about events in 1994 because she believed that it was not necessary, as she was to testify in the current proceedings against Gatete before this Tribunal. The Chamber has doubts about this explanation. Nevertheless, while the Chamber has reservations about the reliability of Witness BAT's evidence, ultimately, it does not consider that the only reasonable inference to be drawn from her testimony is that Gatete ordered *Interahamwe* to kill and rape Tutsis, and that the *Interahamwe* who raped her, were acting pursuant to Gatete's orders. In reaching this conclusion, the Chamber has also considered other evidence in the record, in particular, the testimonies of Witnesses BBR and AIZ, that Gatete issued orders to *Interahamwe* in Rwankuba sector to kill Tutsis. While it is possible that Gatete would also have issued orders to kill Tutsis, as well as rape Tutsi women, the following day in Akarambo *cellule*, in the Chamber's view, it is not the only reasonable inference. Accordingly, while the Chamber does not doubt the traumatic events which Witness BAT experienced on 8 and 9 April, it finds the evidentiary record insufficient to find beyond reasonable doubt, that Gatete came to Akarambo *cellule* on 8 April and issued orders to kill and rape Tutsis, and that *Interahamwe* raped Witness BAT pursuant to his orders".[650]

- Alleged orders to rape Tutsi at Kiziguro parish:
"The Indictment alleges that Gatete ordered, supervised and participated in the rapes of Tutsi women at Kiziguro parish complex, a church and hospital where thousands of Tutsi civilians had taken refuge. The Prosecution led no evidence with respect to an attack and subsequent rapes at Kiziguro hospital. Nor did it present evidence suggesting that Gatete participated in rapes. It relies on the testimonies of Witnesses BUY and BVS, who testified that women and girls were raped by *Interahamwe* at Kiziguro parish. The Defence denies the allegation and points to the evidence of Witnesses LA84, LA27, Jean-Damascène Kampayana and LA32. Turning first to the Prosecution case, Witness BUY saw *Interahamwe* take women and girls to a place not far from the refugees. She subsequently heard screams coming from that location but did not look in that direction. She concluded from the screams that the women and girls had been raped. One woman, who had been taken away, subsequently told the witness what had happened to her. However, further details were not elicited with respect to what the witness was told. The Chamber finds Witness BUY's brief evidence to be of limited probative value. She did not see any rapes being committed, nor did she testify that Gatete issued orders to the *Interahamwe* or other assailants to rape women and girls. Nor did she suggest that he was he present when they were taken away, or during the alleged rapes. Although Witness BVS testified that she saw girls being raped by *Interahamwe* at Kiziguro parish, she did not state that Gatete was present, or that he issued orders for rapes to be committed. Her evidence was also extremely brief and vague on this point, and the Chamber finds it insufficient for the purposes of supporting findings beyond reasonable doubt. The Chamber has also considered the Defence evidence which suggests that women and girls were taken aside and killed at a later time. The Chamber finds this troubling. However, ultimately the Prosecution evidence is insufficient to establish beyond reasonable doubt that Gatete ordered, supervised, participated, or played any role in the rape of women and young girls at Kiziguro parish. In reaching this conclusion, it has also considered its findings with respect to Gatete ordering killings at Kiziguro parish. While it is possible that he also issued |

[650] *Gatete* Trial Judgement, paras. 201–205 (internal references omitted).

	orders to rape Tutsi women and girls, in the Chamber's view, it is not the only reasonable conclusion based on the evidence".[651] - Alleged rapes at Mukarange parish: "The Prosecution also presented no evidence that rapes took place at Mukarange parish".[652] - Alleged rapes at Kayonza communal office resulting from Jean-Baptiste Gatete's actions: "The Indictment alleges that sometime between about 10 and 15 April 1994, Gatete arrived in Kayonza commune, in Kibungo prefecture, with a group of armed *Interahamwe* and Kayonza commune *Bourgmestre* Célestin Senkware. Local residents, including Tutsi women, and recently arrived *Interahamwe*, had assembled in the Kayonza commune office courtyard. Gatete reported to the *Interahamwe* that Tutsis in other areas had been 'decimated' and ordered that they also rape and kill Tutsis. He further ordered that the Tutsis be segregated and that they be taken to a mass grave. It is alleged that Tutsis were raped and killed at that location as a result of Gatete's actions. The Prosecution relies on the first-hand accounts of Witnesses BAQ and BAR, who both sought refuge at the Kayonza commune office, and recounted the arrival of Gatete, as well as his subsequent orders to *Interahamwe* to rape and kill Tutsis there. Both witnesses further testified that they were raped by *Interahamwe* at the commune office. Through the accounts of Witnesses LA66, Denise Dusabe, LA44 and LA50, the Defence disputes that killings and rapes occurred at the Kayonza commune office in April 1994 and submits that Witnesses BAQ and BAR did not seek refuge there at that time. It further points to the testimony of Prosecution Witness BAY, who did not see any refugees at the Kayonza commune office on 13 April. Turning first to the Prosecution evidence, the Chamber notes a number of similarities in the accounts of Witnesses BAQ and BAR. Both testified that they fled to the Kayonza commune office following the onset of attacks in their areas, after the President's death. Both recounted Gatete's arrival in a vehicle at the commune office, in the company of *Interahamwe*. They further recalled the presence of *Bourgmestre* Senkware and communal policeman Ntaganda. Both recounted that when Gatete arrived, he spoke to Senkware, enquiring after the refugees and subsequently issued instructions to the *Interahamwe* to 'sleep' with the women. Witness BAQ further recalled Gatete's orders to kill the refugees. Both testified that Tutsis were raped and killed following Gatete's orders and that they themselves were raped by *Interahamwe*. Notwithstanding these similarities, the evidence of Witnesses BAQ and BAR diverges with respect to the date of the attack. While a variance of a few days may, in some instances, be explained by the passage of time, on this occasion, both witnesses precisely recalled their movements during the days following the President's death, up until they arrived at the Kayonza commune office, suggesting that they went there on different days. Witness BAQ recalled that she went to the Kayonza commune office on the Saturday following the President's death which would have been 9 April and that Gatete arrived there the same day, when the alleged killings and rapes also occurred. Witness BAR, on the other hand, specifically recounted that killings in her area commenced on the Friday after the President's death, which would have been 8 April. She consequently hid in a banana plantation but returned home on the following Wednesday, which would have been 13 April. The following Friday, which was 15 April, she sought refuge at the Kayonza commune office, and the same day, Gatete arrived and the alleged killings and rapes took place. In any event, the Chamber must

651 *Gatete* Trial Judgement, paras. 343–346 (internal references omitted).

652 *Gatete* Trial Judgement, para. 418 (internal reference omitted). See also *Gatete* Trial Judgement, para. 386.

	examine the individual merits of the witnesses' testimonies to assess whether either, or both, sufficiently supports findings beyond reasonable doubt. At the outset, the Chamber has doubts about both witnesses' ability to identify Gatete in April 1994. Although Witness BAQ testified that she saw him once prior to 9 April, her previous sighting of him was extremely brief as he 'passed like a lightening', and on that occasion, her knowledge of him was based on hearsay. The Chamber has similar doubts with respect to Witness BAR. She testified that she did not know Gatete in April 1994 and had not seen him prior to the day she purportedly saw him at the Kayonza commune office. Her knowledge of him on that occasion was also second-hand. Consequently, the basis of both witnesses' identification of the Accused is hearsay and, thus, requires that the Chamber approach it with caution. Moreover, the Chamber notes that Witnesses BAQ and BAR are closely related and gave statements to Tribunal investigators together at the same place. Both admitted that they had discussed the events with each other. The Chamber is, thus, mindful of the possibility of collusion between the two witnesses, which warrants additional caution when weighing their evidence. Regarding the individual merits of the witnesses' testimonies, the Chamber notes that, despite being related to Witness BAR, Witness BAQ was initially evasive when asked whether she knew any other women who had been victims of rape at Kayonza commune office. Considering that her identification of the Accused was based on hearsay, and recalling her close links to Witness BAR, as well as her evasiveness under cross-examination, the Chamber does not find Witness BAQ's evidence sufficiently reliable for the purposes of supporting findings beyond reasonable doubt. With respect to Witness BAR, the Defence points to her unwillingness to cooperate during cross-examination. While the Chamber acknowledges that witnesses may have difficulties when questioned in court about traumatic events, in this instance, Witness BAR was uncooperative when asked by Defence counsel about matters unrelated to the attack at the Kayonza commune office. Moreover, her account was internally inconsistent. For instance, she initially clearly stated that she knew no women who were raped at the commune office and who had survived, but later named Witness BAQ as a survivor, and accepted that they had met to discuss the events. In sum, given the concerns about Witness BAR's ability to identify Gatete, her close links with Witness BAQ, as well as concerns about the merits of her evidence, the Chamber finds her testimony insufficient to support findings beyond reasonable doubt. The Chamber has also considered the Defence evidence, as well as the testimony of Witness BAY. While it considers this evidence to be of limited probative value, ultimately, the testimonies of Witnesses BAQ and BAR are insufficient to support findings beyond reasonable doubt. Consequently, the Prosecution has not proven that Gatete arrived at the Kayonza commune office sometime between 10 and 15 April 1994, and ordered *Interahamwe* to rape and kill Tutsis there. Nor is it proven that he ordered the segregation of Tutsis and that they be taken to a mass grave. In addition, it has not been established that Tutsis were raped and killed at that location as a result of Gatete's actions".[653] - Alleged orders to rape in Rukira commune: "No evidence was led by the Prosecution in relation to orders to rape Tutsis […]".[654] "Accordingly, it has not been established that in mid to late April 1994, Gatete instructed *Interahamwe* in Rulenge sector, in Rukira commune, to rape and kill Tutsi civilians […]".[655]

19. Augustin **Ndindiliyimana *et al.*** (Case No. ICTR-00-56) "***Military II***"

[653] *Gatete* Trial Judgement, paras. 440–448 (internal references omitted).
[654] *Gatete* Trial Judgement, para. 522.
[655] *Gatete* Trial Judgement, para. 534.

<table>
<tr><td colspan="2">- Major General Augustin Ndindiliyimana: Chief of staff of the Gendarmerie nationale.
- Major General Augustin Bizimungu: Commander of Operations for Ruhengeri secteur; Chief of Staff of the Rwandan Army after 19 April 1994.
- Major François-Xavier Nzuwonemeye: Commander of the elite Reconnaissance (RECCE) Battalion.
- Captain Innocent Sagahutu: Commander of Squadron A of the RECCE Battalion.</td></tr>
<tr><td>Indictment (International sex crimes (or related) charges and mode(s) of liability)</td><td>- Augustin Bizimungu: Rape as CAH (count 6) and Rape, humiliating and degrading treatment as a violation of Article 3 common to the Geneva Conventions and of Additional Protocol II (WC) (count 8) under Article 6(3) of the Statute (superior responsibility) for failing to prevent or to punish the rapes of Tutsi women and girls committed by: (a) soldiers of the Rwandan Army, in the vicinity of the office of the conseiller of Kicukiro in Kigali, on a daily basis in April and May 1994; (b) soldiers from the A squad of the Reconnaissance battalion in the kiosks at the entrance of the hospital of Kigali during April, May and June 1994; (c) soldiers of the Rwandan Army, in the rooms reserved for injured soldiers or in nearby places and woods near the Kabgayi primary school, in Gitarama prefecture, between April and June 1994; (d) soldiers of the Rwanda Army, in places and woods nearby the Musambira commune office and dispensary, in Gitarama prefecture, in April and May 1994; (e) soldiers of the Rwanda Army, in neighbouring places to the Trafipreo centre in Gitarama, in April and May 1994; (f) soldiers of the Rwanda Army, in the prefecture office, the Episcopal church of Rwanda (EER), the Gishamvu church and the Nyumba parish, in Butare, starting on 19 April 1994; and (g) soldiers of the Rwanda Army, at Kamarampaka stadium, in Cyangugu, during the months of April and May 1994. There are no factual allegations of rapes constituting genocide in the Indictment. However, according to the Trial Chamber, Augustin Bizimungu was also charged with Genocide (count 2) or, alternatively, Complicity in genocide (count 3) under Article 6(3) of the Statute (superior responsibility) for the rapes committed at the locations pleaded in paragraphs 68 and 69 of the Indictment.[656]
- François-Xavier Nzuwonemeye and Innocent Sagahutu: Rape as CAH (count 6) and Rape, humiliating and degrading treatment as a violation of Article 3 common to the Geneva Conventions and of Additional Protocol II (WC) (count 8) under Article 6(3) of the Statute (superior responsibility) for failing to prevent or to punish the rapes committed by soldiers from the A squad of the Reconnaissance battalion, led by Innocent Sagahutu and under the command of Major François-Xavier</td></tr>
</table>

656 *Augustin Ndindiliyimana et al.* Indictment, pp. 10–12, paras. 68–70. See also *Prosecutor v. Augustin Ndindiliyimana et al.*, Case No. ICTR-00-56-T, Judgement and Sentence, dated 17 May 2011 and filed on 17 June 2011 ("*Augustin Ndindiliyimana et al.* Trial Judgement"), paras. 1038–1039 ("The Chamber notes that paragraphs 68 and 69 of the Indictment allege that soldiers under Bizimungu's command committed murders and caused serious bodily and mental harm to Tutsi through 'acts of violence' at these locations. The Chamber recalls that for the purposes of genocide, the notion of 'causing serious bodily harm' refers to acts of physical violence falling short of killing that seriously injure the health, cause disfigurement, or cause any serious injury to the external or internal organs or senses. According to the Appeals Chamber, 'the quintessential examples of serious bodily harm are torture, rape, and non-fatal physical violence that causes disfigurement or serious injury to the external or internal organs.' Serious mental harm refers to more than minor or temporary impairment of mental faculties. The serious bodily or mental harm, however, need not be an injury that is permanent or irremediable. Although paragraphs 68 and 69 of the Indictment do not specifically allege that soldiers committed rapes at the locations identified therein, it is well established that rape falls within the notion of 'serious bodily and mental harm' to which the Prosecution refers in paragraph 68. Indeed, the Appeals Chamber has noted that 'nearly all convictions for the causing of serious bodily or mental harm involve rapes or killings.' The Chamber therefore finds that Bizimungu had sufficient notice that the alleged 'acts of violence' causing 'serious bodily or mental harm' in paragraphs 68 and 69 of the Indictment included rapes. Accordingly, the Chamber will consider the evidence of killings and rapes committed by soldiers at the locations specified in paragraph 69 in assessing the charges of genocide against Bizimungu".).

	Nzuwonemeye, in the kiosks at the entrance of the hospital of Kigali during April, May and June 1994.[657]
Trial Judgement	- Augustin Bizimungu: Guilty of **Genocide** (count 2) under Article 6(3) of the Statute for various crimes, including for the rapes committed at *École des Sciences infirmières* (ESI) and in the nearby woods in Kabgayi, TRAFIPRO and the Musambira commune office and dispensary in Gitarama during April and May 1994.[658] Guilty of **Rape as CAH** (count 6) under Article 6(3) of the Statute (**superior responsibility**) for the

[657] *Prosecutor v. Augustin Ndindiliyimana et al.*, Case No. ICTR-00-56-I, Amended Indictment (Joinder), 23 August 2004 ("*Augustin Ndindiliyimana et al.* Indictment"), paras. 110–117 ("**COUNT 6: CRIMES AGAINST HUMANITY (Rape)** The Prosecutor of the International Criminal Tribunal for Rwanda charges **Augustin Bizimungu**, **François-Xavier Nzuwonemeye** and **Innocent Sagahutu** with **Rape**, as a Crime against Humanity, an offence punishable under Article (3)(g) of the Statute, in that, in 1994, in Rwanda, **Augustin Bizimungu**, **François-Xavier Nzuwonemeye** and **Innocent Sagahutu** were responsible for several rapes committed against Tutsi civilians by soldiers under their command or by civilians over whom they had authority, as part of widespread or systematic attacks against a civlian population, on national, racial, ethnic, or political grounds, as follows: **Pursuant to Article 6(3) of the Statute:** in that the Accused knew or had reason to know that their subordinates had committed or were about to commit the rapes referred to in paragraphs 111 to 117, in respect of **Augustin Bizimungu**, in paragraph 112 in respect of **Innocent Sagahutu** and **François-Xavier Nzuwonemeye**, and did not take reasonable and necessary measures to prevent such crimes or to punish the perpetrators thereof. In April and May 1994, soldiers from the Rwandan Army went daily to the office of the *conseiller* of Kicukiro in Kigali, to abduct Tutsi women and young girls whom they raped in the vicinity of the office. During the months of April, May and June 1994, soldiers from the A squad of the Reconnaissance battalion, led by **Innocent Sagahutu** and under the command of Major **François-Xavier Nzuwonemeye**, who guarded the *Centre hospitalier de Kigali*, and their *Interahamwe* accomplices abducted several Tutsi women from the hospital who had come to seek treatment or simply to seek refuge; they raped them or mistreated them. Those rapes often took place inside the kiosks at the entrance [of] the hospital. Between April and June 1994, several persons sought refuge at Kabgayi primary school in Gitarama *prefecture*. Throughout that period, soldiers from the Rwandan Army and *Interahamew* militiamen selected and abducted Tutsi women and young girls that they took to the rooms reserved for injured soldiers or in nearby places and woods where they raped them. In April and May 1994, at the Musambira *commune* office and dispensary, in Gitarama *prefecture*, soldiers from the Rwandan Army and militiamen frequently abducted Tutsi women and young girls to take them to nearby places and woods where they raped them. Those rapes were often accompanied by humiliating and degrading treatment. In April and May 1994, at the Trafipro centre in Gitarama, soldiers from the Rwandan Army and militiamen abducted Tutsi women that they led to neighbouring places where they raped them. Those rapes were often accompanied by humiliating and degrading treatment. In Butare, starting on 19 April 1994, soldiers from the Rwandan Army and *Interahamwe* militiamen went on a regular basis to the *prefecture* office, the Episcopal church of Rwanda (EER), to Gishamvu church and Nyumba parish to abduct the female refugees and rape them. Those rapes were often accompanied by humiliating and degrading treatment. In Cyangugu, during the months of April and May 1994, soldiers from the Rwanda Army and *Interahamwe* regularly abducted Tutsi refugee women at Kamarampaka stadium and raped them and assaulted them morally".), 119 ("**COUNT 8: VIOLATION OF ARTICLE 3 COMMON TO THE GENEVA CONVENTIONS AND ADDITIONAL PROTOCOL II (Rape, humiliating and degrading treatment)** The Prosecutor of the International Criminal Tribunal for Rwanda charges **Augustin Bizimungu**, **François-Xavier Nzuwonemeye** and **Innocent Sagahutu** with Rape and other humiliating and degrading treatment, an offence punishable under Article 3 common to the Geneva Conventions and Additional Protocol II, under Article 4(e) of the Statute, in that, in 1994, in Rwanda, soldiers from the Rwandan Army, under their authority, in concert with militiamen, raped several Tutsi civilian women, in the context of a non-international armed conflict inasmuch as those Rwandan civilians were categorized by their tormentors as being virtual members of the RPF or accomplices of that movement; **Pursuant to Article 6(3) of the Statute:** in that the Accused knew or had reason to know that their subordinates had committed or were about to commit the rapes referred to in paragraphs 111 to 117, in respect of **Augustin Bizimungu**, and 112, in respect of **François-Xavier Nzuwonemeye** and **Innocent Sagahutu**, and did not take reasonable and necessary measures to prevent such crimes or to punish the perpetrators thereof".).

[658] *Augustin Ndindiliyimana et al.* Trial Judgement, paras. 1038–1039, 1184, 1192, 1196–1197, 1205, 1220, 2160, 2163.

	rapes committed at Cyangugu Stadium during April and May 1994, and at the prefecture office and the Episcopal church of Rwanda (EER) in Butare starting on 19 April 1994 and of **Rape as a violation of Article 3 common to the Geneva Conventions and of Additional Protocol II (WC)** (count 8) under Article 6(3) of the Statute (**superior responsibility**) for the rapes committed at ESI and in the nearby woods in Kabgayi, TRAFIPRO and the Musambira commune office and dispensary in Gitarama during April and May 1994, at the prefecture office and EER in Butare starting on 19 April 1994 and at Cyangugu Stadium during April and May 1994.[659] - François-Xavier Nzuwonemeye and Innocent Sagahutu: Not guilty of rape as CAH (count 6) and rape, humiliating and degrading treatment as a violation of Article 3 common to the Geneva Conventions and of Additional Protocol II (WC) (count 8).[660]
Appeal Judgement	N/A (The appellate proceedings are in progress.)
Legal and Factual Findings and/or Evidence	- Legal findings: **- Rape: definition:** The Trial Chamber adopted the definition of rape given in the *Kunarac et al.* case:[661] "Rape as a crime against humanity requires proof of the non-consensual penetration, however slight, of the vagina or anus of the victim by the penis of the perpetrator or by any other object used by the perpetrator, or of the mouth of the victim by the penis of the perpetrator. Consent for this purpose must be consent given voluntarily and freely and is assessed within the context of the surrounding circumstances. Force or threat of force provides clear evidence of non-consent, but force is not an element *per se* of rape. The *mens rea* for rape as a crime against humanity is the intention to effect the prohibited sexual penetration with the knowledge that it occurs without the consent of the victim".[662] - Factual findings: - Rapes at the Josephite Brothers compound on 8 April 1994: "The Chamber recalls that Witness DBJ gave evidence that during the attack of 8 April 1994, one of the soldiers raped a female refugee aged about 20. The witness gave evidence that on the following day, he saw the dead body of the girl but had no information on who killed her. The witness was cross-examined at length regarding his vantage point as he witnessed the alleged rape. According to the Defence, the witness testified that he saw the soldier rape the girl as he passed by the building where the soldier had taken the girl. However, in his pre-trial statement dated 28 July 1999, the witness stated that he observed the alleged rape while he was seated in the Josephite Brothers compound. The witness explained that the discrepancy may have resulted from a misunderstanding between himself and the investigators of the Tribunal. In particular, he stated that the investigators may have misconstrued his statement that the soldier ordered the girl to strip while at the compound to mean that he raped her at that compound. The Chamber accepts this as a plausible explanation of the discrepancy between the witness's evidence and his pre-trial statement. Having considered Witness DBJ's evidence, the Chamber is satisfied that the witness gave a credible account that a soldier raped a young girl during the attack at the Josephite Brothers compound on 8 April 1994. The Chamber therefore finds that the Prosecution has proved beyond reasonable doubt that soldiers of the Rwandan Army committed crimes against Tutsi

659 *Augustin Ndindiliyimana et al.* Trial Judgement, paras. 1180, 1182–1184, 1186–1188, 1192–1196, 1450–1452, 1518–1520, 1895–1896, 1899, 2124–2128, 2160–2163.

660 *Augustin Ndindiliyimana et al.* Trial Judgement, paras. 1897, 2163.

661 ICTY ISCC *Kunarac et al.*, see *supra* p. 528.

662 *Augustin Ndindiliyimana et al.* Trial Judgement, paras. 2122–2123 (internal references omitted).

	civilians at the Josephite Brothers compound on 8 April 1994 as alleged in paragraphs 68 and 69 of the Indictment. The Chamber notes, however, that the crimes alleged at the Josephite Brothers compound on 8 April 1994 took place before Bizimungu became Chief of Staff of the Rwandan Army and therefore fall outside the time period prescribed in paragraphs 68 through 70 of the Indictment. Consequently, the Chamber will not consider these allegations in assessing Bizimungu's superior responsibility for genocide".[663] - Alleged rapes at the *Centre hospitalier de Kigali* (CHK) between April and June 1994: "In regard to the allegations of rape, the Chamber recalls that Witness DAR is the only Prosecution witness to have testified about rapes perpetrated by soldiers against Tutsi girls at CHK. The witness admitted that he did not witness the rapes, nor was he informed by any of the victims of their ordeal at the hands of the soldiers at CHK. His evidence on the rapes by soldiers is based entirely on his observations of the sad demeanour of the Tutsi girls when they returned to CHK after having been abducted by soldiers. The Chamber is not satisfied that Witness DAR's *post hoc* inferences based on the demeanour of those girls alone are sufficient to support a finding beyond reasonable doubt that soldiers committed rapes against Tutsi girls at CHK. Furthermore, the Chamber has serious concerns about the overall credibility of Witness DAR in light of his claim that he was not aware of the arrival of the dead bodies of the Belgian UNAMIR soldiers at CHK in the evening of 7 April 1994. The Chamber finds it inexplicable that the witness, who claims to have been present at CHK for a period of five to six weeks starting from 7 April and who also testified that he was informed of numerous events of a lesser gravity occurring at CHK at the time, would not have heard of the arrival of the bodies of the Belgian soldiers at CHK in the evening of 7 April and their removal in the afternoon of 8 April. […] For these reasons, the Chamber is not satisfied that the Prosecution has adduced sufficient evidence to prove that soldiers under the command of Bizimungu committed crimes against Tutsi civilians at CHK from April to June 1994".[664] - Rapes at *École des Sciences infirmières* (ESI) and in the nearby woods, in Kabgayi, during April and May 1994: "The witness also saw soldiers rape and then kill a female refugee in front of 'everybody' inside ESI. […] The Chamber recalls that Witness EZ also testified that soldiers regularly and repeatedly raped female Tutsi refugees. The overwhelming majority of the victims were raped in the nearby woods, but some were raped inside the ESI compound. The witness was herself raped by soldiers on a number of occasions during her stay at ESI during April and May 1994. She also witnessed the rape of numerous other women and girls during that period, and she was able to identify four of those women and girls by name. During cross-examination, counsel for the Defence questioned Witness EZ on the reasons why she failed to report the rapes to the doctor whom she claims to have visited twice while she was at ESI. The witness explained that reporting those incidents of rape would not have done anything to improve the situation at ESI. In the Chamber's view, the reasons why a victim might fail to report a crime can be manifold. Considering the chaotic situation at ESI and in Rwanda at large when these incidents took place, the fact that the perpetrators remained at ESI along with the witness, and the physical and psychological damage suffered by rape victims, the Chamber considers the witness's explanation for her failure to report these rapes to be plausible. The Chamber finds that the witness's failure to report these rapes does

663 *Augustin Ndindiliyimana et al.* Trial Judgement, paras. 1138–1142 (internal references omitted).

664 *Augustin Ndindiliyimana et al.* Trial Judgement, paras. 1174–1175, 1177 (internal references omitted).

	not undermine the credibility of her eyewitness account of the events at ESI and her own personal experience. The Chamber therefore considers this Defence submission to be without merit. For these reasons, the Chamber finds that soldiers raped a number of Tutsi refugee women at ESI and in the nearby woods during April and May 1994".[665] - Rapes at the Musambira commune office and dispensary: "The Chamber notes that Witness DBA sought refuge at the Musambira dispensary and surrounding areas soon after her flight from her home following the President's death on 6 April 1994. The witness stated that a number of soldiers took her and other female refugees from the Musambira dispensary and then raped them nearby. Witness DBA's evidence was largely consistent and the Chamber finds it to be credible. However, the incidents that she described took place before Bizimungu assumed the position as Chief of Staff of the Rwandan Army and therefore fall outside the time period prescribed in paragraphs 68 to 70 of the Indictment. Consequently, the Chamber will not consider the testimony of Witness DBA in assessing Bizimungu's superior responsibility for genocide. The Chamber will now turn its attention to the evidence of Prosecution Witnesses DBH and DBB, who testified to crimes committed by soldiers of the Rwandan Army at Musambira *commune* office and dispensary during late April and May 1994, when Bizimungu was Chief of Staff of the Rwandan Army. Witness DBH stated that following the President's death on 6 April, she hid in a banana plantation for approximately one week before seeking refuge at the Musambira *commune* office. The Chamber infers from this evidence that Witness DBH arrived at the Musambira *commune* office on or around 14 April. The witness recalled that soon after she arrived, *Interahamwe* and soldiers killed a large number of male Tutsi refugees at the *commune* office, and the survivors of the massacre, mainly women and children, were then forced to bury the dead bodies in a mass grave located close to the *commune* office. Witness DBH estimated that they buried between 7,000 and 8,000 bodies. While the Chamber considers it unlikely that the number of victims was as high as that estimated by Witness DBH, the Chamber is satisfied that a large number of Tutsi were killed in the manner described by the witness. She also testified that she was subsequently raped by soldiers on two occasions at the *commune* office and that a number of other women were also raped by soldiers".[666] "Having carefully considered the evidence in its totality, the Chamber finds that Rwandan soldiers committed killings at the Musambira *commune* office and dispensary in Gitarama *préfecture* during April and May 1994. The Chamber also finds that soldiers committed rapes at the Musambira *commune* office during this period".[667] - Rapes at TRAFIPRO in April and May 1994: "In support of its allegation that soldiers under the command of Bizimungu perpetrated acts of violence toward Tutsi civilians at TRAFIPRO during April and May 1994, the Prosecution relies on the evidence of Witnesses DBE, DBD and DBB. Witness DBE testified that she arrived at TRAFIPRO in mid-May and remained there for approximately one month. She recalled that during her stay at TRAFIPRO, soldiers raped and murdered a number of Tutsi refugees there. Witness DBE was herself raped on several occasions and she witnessed a number of killings, including that of her 15-year-old son. She also testified that soldiers came to TRAFIPRO regularly to select and remove refugees to be killed. Her evidence is corroborated by Witnesses DBD and DBB, who also testified about rapes and killings perpetrated by soldiers at TRAFIPRO during this period. Witnesses DBD and DBB were both raped by soldiers on two occasions at

665 *Augustin Ndindiliyimana et al.* Trial Judgement, paras. 1180, 1182–1184 (internal references omitted).

666 *Augustin Ndindiliyimana et al.* Trial Judgement, paras. 1186–1188 (internal reference omitted).

667 *Augustin Ndindiliyimana et al.* Trial Judgement, para. 1192.

	TRAFIPRO. Both witnesses also saw soldiers come to TRAFIPRO each day to select and remove Tutsi refugees, and both witnesses testified that the selected refugees did not generally return. According to Witness DBD, 'Some women would return but the men who were selected were shot dead on the spot.' The Chamber notes in particular that Witnesses DBD and DBE provided corroborative evidence in relation to the visit of Prime Minister Kambanda at TRAFIPRO and the large-scale attack on Tutsi refugees shortly thereafter. The Chamber considers this corroboration to be indicative of the truthfulness of the witnesses' testimony. The Chamber has also considered the Defence submissions in relation to these witnesses. In regard to Witness DBB, the Chamber had already found this witness to be credible when discussing her evidence on the events at the Musambira dispensary. In regard to Witness DBD, the Defence argues that the witness's failure to report the alleged rapes to officials undermines her credibility. For the reasons outlined above in relation to Witness EZ, the Chamber rejects this argument in its entirety. The Defence also contends that the inconsistency between Witness DBD's pre-trial statement and her testimony regarding the identity of the assailants who raped her on the second occasion while at TRAFIPRO undermines the credibility of her testimony. The Chamber is not persuaded by this submission. The Chamber finds that Witness DBD was consistent both in her pre-trial statements and her in-court testimony that soldiers raped Tutsi refugees, including herself, at TRAFIPRO. The fact that the witness also implicated *Interahamwe* in these rapes does not diminish the credibility of her evidence in relation to soldiers' participation in these rapes. Therefore, the Chamber finds that there is clear and corroborated evidence that proves beyond reasonable doubt that Rwandan soldiers committed systematic acts of violence, namely killings and rapes, against Tutsi refugees at the TRAFIPRO complex during April and May 1994".[668] - Alleged rapes at Gishamvu church and Nyumba parish in Butare prefecture: "The Chamber notes that the Indictment also alleges that soldiers and *Interahamwe* committed abductions, murders and rapes at Gishamvu Church and Nyumba Parish in Butare *préfecture*. However, the Prosecution did not lead any evidence regarding the alleged crimes at those locations".[669] - Rapes at the Butare prefecture office and at the Episcopal church of Rwanda (EER): "Witnesses LN, XY and QBP all testified about rapes committed against female refugees at the Butare *préfecture* office during late April and May 1994. Witness XY testified that soldiers and *Interahamwe* came to the *préfecture* office every day and night to pick up refugees. The female refugees subsequently returned, often wounded, and told the other refugees that they had been raped. Witness XY saw soldiers and *Interahamwe* take her friend Marie from the *préfecture* office, and when Marie returned she was wounded in the head and she told Witness XY that soldiers had raped her in the woods nearby. Similarly, Witness QBP testified that assailants came to the *préfecture* office at night to rape the female refugees. She also testified about an incident when Minister Nyiramasuhuko came to the office and, on Nyiramasuhuko's instructions, soldiers and *Interahamwe* raped a number of refugees. Witness LN testified that he witnessed the rape of a young female refugee in broad daylight in front of the *préfecture* office, in full view of a number of soldiers. Witnesses XY and QBP also testified that soldiers and *Interahamwe* raped a number of female refugees at EER during late April and May 1994. Witness XY was herself raped by a soldier about three weeks after she arrived at EER. Witness QBP saw a number of girls taken out of EER by soldiers and *Interahamwe*, and when they returned they were 'in a pitiful

668 *Augustin Ndindiliyimana et al.* Trial Judgement, paras. 1193–1196 (internal reference omitted).
669 *Augustin Ndindiliyimana et al.* Trial Judgement, para. 1148.

	state' and they had difficulty walking. Three of the rape victims, including a girl named Suzanne, were the daughters of Witness QBP's neighbour. The Chamber notes that the evidence of Witnesses XY, QBP and LN regarding the rapes of female refugees in Butare *préfecture* is broadly consistent and the Chamber considers it to be credible".[670] - Rapes at Cyangugu stadium: "Witnesses LBC and LAV testified about a number of incidents where soldiers selected female refugees at Cyangugu Stadium, took them outside and raped them, and then brought them back inside the stadium. Witness LBC testified that she was raped more than once by soldiers guarding the stadium and that she personally saw a number of other women being raped by those soldiers. The Chamber considers that Witnesses LBC and LAV provided consistent and credible evidence concerning the rapes committed by soldiers at the stadium. Both witnesses referred to a girl named Fifi, and Witness LAV provided the names of three other women who she said were also rape victims. Based on the evidence of these two witnesses, the Chamber finds that soldiers raped a number of Tutsi refugee women at Cyangugu Stadium during April and May 1994. Regarding the involvement of *Interahamwe* in the rapes, the Chamber recalls that Witness LAV initially testified that both soldiers and *Interahamwe* took women outside the stadium and then brought them back in again. For the remainder of her testimony, however, the witness described only the role of soldiers in raping women at the stadium, without repeating her earlier statement about the role of *Interahamwe* in those rapes. When asked whether women at the stadium were raped by 'other civilians apart from the soldiers', the witness responded, 'No, just soldiers did that.' The Chamber also recalls that Witness LAV did not mention the presence of *Interahamwe* inside the stadium in her statement to ICTR investigators in 1999 and that she appeared uncertain when cross-examined on this point. Given that Witness LBC did not testify about rapes committed by *Interahamwe* in the stadium and that the testimony of Witness LAV appeared equivocal on this point, the Chamber considers that there is insufficient evidence to find that *Interahamwe* raped women at Cyangugu Stadium".[671] - Responsibility of Augustin Bizimungu for rapes: "Count 6 of the Indictment charges Bizimungu, Nzuwonemeye and Sagahutu with rape as a crime against humanity pursuant to Article 3(g) of the Statute. In support of the allegations of rape as a crime against humanity set out in paragraphs 111 to 117 of the Indictment, the Prosecution relies upon the same underlying conduct and evidence that it led in relation to the allegations of genocide (and complicity in genocide in the alternative) and murder as a crime against humanity. The Chamber notes that the allegations against Bizimungu of rape as a crime against humanity in Butare and Cyangugu are closely related to the allegations of murder as a crime against humanity at those locations. Accordingly, the Chamber considered the allegations of rape in Butare and Cyangugu in conjunction with the corresponding allegations of murder in its factual findings for murder as a crime against humanity. As set out in that section, the Chamber has found that the allegations of rapes at the *préfecture* office and EER in Butare and the allegations of rapes at Cyangugu Stadium have been proved beyond reasonable doubt against Bizimungu. In its factual findings for genocide, the Chamber set out in detail the evidence that underlies the allegations against Bizimungu of rapes committed at CHK in Kigali, ESI/Kabgayi Primary School, Musambira *commune* office and dispensary, and TRAFIPRO in Gitarama. The Chamber will not repeat that evidence at this point. The Chamber found that the allegations of rapes at ESI/Kabgayi

670 *Augustin Ndindiliyimana et al.* Trial Judgement, paras. 1450–1452 (internal references omitted).

671 *Augustin Ndindiliyimana et al.* Trial Judgement, paras. 1518–1520 (internal references omitted).

	Primary School, the Musambira *commune* office and dispensary, and TRAFIPRO have been proved beyond reasonable doubt in relation to the charges of genocide against Bizimungu. The Chamber notes that paragraph 112 of the Indictment alleges that Bizimungu, Nzuwonemeye and Sagahutu are responsible as superiors for rapes committed by soldiers of the RECCE Battalion against Tutsi women at CHK. In its factual findings for genocide, the Chamber found that the Prosecution had not presented sufficient evidence to prove that soldiers of the Rwandan Army committed rapes against Tutsi women at CHK. It follows from this finding that the allegation of rape as a crime against humanity in paragraph 112 of the Indictment has not been proved beyond reasonable doubt against Bizimungu, Nzuwonemeye and Sagahutu. The Chamber also considered, in its factual findings for genocide, the allegation of rapes at the Kicukiro *conseiller's* office. The Chamber found that the Prosecution presented no evidence to support this allegation. Therefore, the Chamber finds that the Prosecution has proved beyond reasonable doubt the allegations against Bizimungu of rape as a crime against humanity at ESI/Kabgayi Primary School, Musambira *commune* office and dispensary, and TRAFIPRO in Gitarama, at the *préfecture* office and EER in Butare, and at Cyangugu Stadium. The Chamber will analyse Bizimungu's superior responsibility for these crimes in detail in the legal findings section of the Judgement".[672] "Count 8 of the Indictment charges Bizimungu, Nzuwonemeye and Sagahutu with rape as a violation of Article 3 common to the Geneva Conventions and of Additional Protocol II under Article 4(e) of the Statute. In support of this charge, the Prosecution relies upon the same underlying conduct and evidence that it led in relation to the allegations of genocide and rape as a crime against humanity. The specific incidents that underlie this charge are pleaded in paragraphs 111 to 117 of the Indictment. The Chamber has already set out the evidence relating to these incidents in its factual findings for genocide and rape as a crime against humanity, and it will not repeat that evidence at this point. In the legal findings section of the Judgement, the Chamber will analyse whether this evidence supports the charges of rape as a violation of Article 3 common to the Geneva Conventions and of Additional Protocol II, in addition to the charges of genocide and rape as a crime against humanity as alleged by the Prosecution".[673] "Following the death of President Habyarimana on 6 April 1994, approximately 4,000 to 5,000 members of the civilian Tutsi population sought refuge at Cyangugu Stadium. The Chamber has found that soldiers raped a number of Tutsi refugee women at Cyangugu Stadium during April and May 1994. In addition, several hundred Tutsi civilians sought refuge at the *préfecture* office and EER in Butare during late April and May 1994. The Chamber has found that soldiers and *Interahamwe* raped a number of female refugees at these locations during this period. Given the circumstances surrounding these attacks, it is clear that there was no consent for these acts of sexual violence and that the perpetrators would have been aware of this fact. The Chamber has determined that the crimes at these locations were committed as part of a widespread and systematic attack on ethnic and political grounds. The Chamber has also concluded that Bizimungu bears superior responsibility for these crimes under Article 6(3). As noted above, the direct perpetrators and the Accused were aware that these attacks formed part of widespread and systematic attacks against the civilian population on ethnic and political grounds. The Chamber finds Bizimungu guilty of rape as a crime against humanity as a superior under Article 6(3) for the rapes committed at Cyangugu Stadium during April and May 1994, and at the *préfecture* office and EER in Butare".[674]

672 *Augustin Ndindiliyimana et al.* Trial Judgement, paras. 1894–1899 (internal references omitted).

673 *Augustin Ndindiliyimana et al.* Trial Judgement, paras. 1908–1909 (internal references omitted).

674 *Augustin Ndindiliyimana et al.* Trial Judgement, paras. 2124–2128 (internal references omitted).

	"In its legal findings for genocide and rape as a crime against humanity, the Chamber has found Bizimungu responsible as a superior under Article 6(3) for the rape of women at ESI, TRAFIPRO and the Musambira *commune* office and dispensary in Gitarama during April and May 1994, at the *préfecture* office and EER in Butare starting on 19 April 1994 and at Cyangugu Stadium during April and May 1994. It follows that these rapes also amount to rape under Article 4(e) of the Statute. As discussed above, it is clear from the circumstances of these attacks that the perpetrators were aware that the victims were not taking an active part in the hostilities. Furthermore, each of these crimes had a nexus to the non-international armed conflict between the Rwandan government and the RPF. The Chamber finds Bizimungu guilty under Article 6(3) of the Statute for violations of Article 3 common to the Geneva Conventions and Additional Protocol II for the rape of women at ESI, TRAFIPRO and the Musambira *commune* office and dispensary in Gitarama during April and May 1994, at the *préfecture* office and EER in Butare starting on 19 April 1994 and at Cyangugu Stadium during April and May 1994".[675]

20. Pauline **<u>Nyiramasuhuko *et al.*</u>** (Case No. ICTR-98-42) "***Butare***" - Pauline Nyiramasuhuko: Minister of Family and Women's Development under the Interim Government. - Arsène Shalom Ntahobali: Son of Pauline Nyiramasuhuko, student and part-time manager of Hotel Ihuliro in Butare. - Sylvain Nsabimana: Prefect of Butare prefecture from 19 April until 17 June 1994. - Alphonse Nteziryayo: Director of communal police matters in the Ministry of Interior and Communal Development from September 1991 until 17 June 1994; then Prefect of Butare prefecture. - Joseph Kanyabashi: Bourgmestre of Ngoma commune in Butare prefecture from April 1974 until July 1994. - Élie Ndayambaje: Bourgmestre of Muganza commune in Butare prefecture from 10 January 1983 until October 1992 and from 18 June 1994 until 7 July 1994.	
Indictment[676] (International sex crimes (or related) charges and mode(s) of liability)	- Pauline Nyiramasuhuko and Arsène Shalom Ntahobali: **Genocide** (count 2) or, alternatively, **Complicity in genocide** (count 3) and **Persecutions as CAH** (count 8), **Other inhumane acts as CAH** (count 9) and **Violence to life, health and physical or mental well-being as a violation of Article 3 common to the Geneva Conventions and of Additional Protocol II (WC)** (count 10) under Articles 6(1) and 6(3) of the Statute (**superior responsibility**) for forcing Tutsi victims to undress completely before forcing them into vehicles and taking them to their deaths and **Rape as CAH** (count 7) and **Outrages upon personal dignity as a violation of Article 3 common to the Geneva Conventions and of Additional Protocol II (WC)** (count 11) under Article 6(3) of the Statute (**superior responsibility**) for Pauline Nyiramasuhuko and

675 *Augustin Ndindiliyimana et al.* Trial Judgement, paras. 2160–2162 (internal references omitted).

676 For the general background to the charges, see *Prosecutor v. Pauline Nyiramasuhuko and Arsène Shalom Ntahobali*, Case No. ICTR-97-21-I, Amended Indictment, 1 March 2001 ("*Nyiramasuhuko and Ntahobali* Indictment"), paras. 5.18 ("Furthermore, soldiers, militiamen and gendarmes raped, sexually assaulted and committed other crimes of a sexual nature against Tutsi women and girls, sometimes having first kidnapped them".), 6.53 ("During the events referred to in this indictment, rapes, sexual assaults and other crimes of a sexual nature were widely and notoriously committed throughout Rwanda. These crimes were perpetrated by, among others, soldiers, militiamen and gendarmes against the Tutsi population, in particular Tutsi women and girls".). See also *Prosecutor v. Sylvain Nsabimana and Alphonse Nteziryayo*, Case No. ICTR-97-29-I, Amended Indictment, 12 August 1999, paras. 5.18, 6.58; *Prosecutor v. Joseph Kanyabashi*, Case No. ICTR-96-15-I, Amended Indictment, 11 June 2001, paras. 5.18, 6.63; *Prosecutor v. Élie Ndayambaje*, Case No. ICTR-96-8-I, Amended Indictment, 11 August 1999, paras. 5.18, 6.55.

	under Articles 6(1) and 6(3) of the Statute (**superior responsibility**) for Arsène Shalom Ntahobali for the rapes of Tutsi women.[677]

677 *Nyiramasuhuko and Ntahobali* Indictment, paras. 6.31 ("When abducting their victims, **Pauline Nyiramasuhuko** and **Arsène Shalom Ntahobali** often forced them to undress completely before forcing them into vehicles and taking them to their deaths".), 6.37 ("Furthermore, aside from his attacks on members of the Tutsi population during this period, **Arsène Shalom Ntahobali**, assisted by unknown 'accomplices', participated in the kidnapping and raping of Tutsi women".), pp. 38–40 ("**COUNT 2: Pauline Nyiramasuhuko:** -pursuant to Article 6(1), according to paragraphs: […] 6.31, […] 6.53, […] -pursuant to Article 6(3), according to paragraphs […] 6.31, […] 6.53, […] **Shalom Ntahobali:** -pursuant to Article 6(1), according to paragraphs: […] 6.31, […] 6.53, […] -pursuant to Article 6(3), according to paragraphs […] 6.31, […] 6.53, […] are responsible for killing and causing serious bodily or mental harm to members of the Tutsi population with the intent to destroy, in whole or in part, a racial or ethnic group, and thereby committed **GENOCIDE**, a crime stipulated in Article 2(3)(a) of the Statute of the Tribunal, for which they are individually responsible pursuant to Article 6 and which is punishable in reference to Articles 22 and 23 of the Statute. **OR, ALTERNATIVELY: COUNT 3: Pauline Nyiramasuhuko:** -pursuant to Article 6(1), according to paragraphs: […] 6.31, […] 6.53, […] -pursuant to Article 6(3), according to paragraphs […] 6.31, […] 6.53, […] **Shalom Ntahobali:** -pursuant to Article 6(1), according to paragraphs: […] 6.31, […] 6.53, […] -pursuant to Article 6(3), according to paragraphs […] 6.31, […] 6.53, […] are responsible for killing and causing serious bodily or mental harm to members of the Tutsi population with the intent to destroy, in whole or in part, a racial or ethnic group, and thereby committed **COMPLICITY IN GENOCIDE**, a crime stipulated in Article 2(3)(e) of the Statute of the Tribunal, for which they are individually responsible pursuant to Article 6 and which is punishable in reference to Articles 22 and 23 of the Statute".), 42–45 ("**COUNT 7: Pauline Nyiramasuhuko:** -pursuant to Article 6(3), according to paragraphs 6.37, 6.53, and 6.56, **Shalom Ntahobali:** -pursuant to Article 6(1), according to paragraphs: 6.37, 6.53, and 6.56, -pursuant to Article 6(3), according to paragraphs 6.37, 6.53, and 6.56, are responsible for rape as part of a widespread and systematic attack against a civilian population on political, ethnic or racial grounds, and thereby committed a **CRIME AGAINST HUMANITY**, a crime stipulated in Article 3(g) of the Statute of the Tribunal, for which they are individually responsible pursuant to Article 6 of the Statute and which is punishable in reference to Articles 22 and 23 of the Statute. **COUNT 8: Pauline Nyiramasuhuko:** -pursuant to Article 6(1), according to paragraphs: […] 6.31, […] 6.53, […] -pursuant to Article 6(3), according to paragraphs […] 6.31, […] 6.53, […] **Shalom Ntahobali:** -pursuant to Article 6(1), according to paragraphs: […] 6.31, […] 6.53, […] -pursuant to Article 6(3), according to paragraphs […] 6.31, […] 6.53, […] are responsible for persecution on political, racial or religious grounds, as part of a widespread and systematic attack against a civilian population on political, ethnic or racial grounds, and thereby committed a **CRIME AGAINST HUMANITY**, a crime stipulated in Article 3(h) of the Statute of the Tribunal, for which they are individually responsible pursuant to Article 6 of the Statute and which is punishable in reference to Articles 22 and 23 of the Statute. **COUNT 9: Pauline Nyiramasuhuko:** -pursuant to Article 6(1), according to paragraphs: […] 6.31, […] 6.53, […] -pursuant to Article 6(3), according to paragraphs […] 6.31, […] 6.53, […] **Shalom Ntahobali:** -pursuant to Article 6(1), according to paragraphs: […] 6.31, […] 6.53, […] -pursuant to Article 6(3), according to paragraphs […] 6.31, […] 6.53, […] are responsible for inhumane acts against persons as part of a widespread and systematic attack against a civilian population on political, ethnic or racial grounds, and thereby committed a **CRIME AGAINST HUMANITY**, a crime stipulated in Article 3(i) of the Statute of the Tribunal, for which they are individually responsible pursuant to Article 6 of the Statute and which is punishable in reference to Articles 22 and 23 of the Statute. **COUNT 10: Pauline Nyiramasuhuko:** -pursuant to Article 6(1), according to paragraphs: […] 6.31, […] 6.53, […] -pursuant to Article 6(3), according to paragraphs […] 6.31, […] 6.53, […] **Shalom Ntahobali:** -pursuant to Article 6(1), according to paragraphs: […] 6.31, […] 6.53, […] -pursuant to Article 6(3), according to paragraphs […] 6.31, […] 6.53, […] are responsible for killing and causing violence to health and to the physical or mental well-being of civilians as part of an armed internal conflict, and thereby committed **SERIOUS VIOLATION OF ARTICLE 3 COMMON TO THE GENEVA CONVENTIONS AND ADDITIONAL PROTOCOL II**, a crime stipulated in Article 4(a) of the Statute of the Tribunal, for which they are individually responsible pursuant to Article 6 of the Statute and which is punishable in reference to Articles 22 and 23 of the Statute. **COUNT 11: Pauline Nyiramasuhuko:** -pursuant to Article 6(1), according to paragraphs: […] 6.31, […] 6.53, […] -pursuant to Article 6(3), according to paragraphs […] 6.31, 6.37, […] 6.53, […] **Shalom Ntahobali:** -pursuant to Article 6(1), according to paragraphs: […] 6.31, 6.37, […] 6.53, […] -pursuant to Article 6(3), according to paragraphs […] 6.31, 6.37, […] 6.53, […] are responsible for outrages upon personal dignity, in particular humiliating and degrading treatment, rape and indecent assault, as part of an armed internal conflict, and thereby

Trial Judgement	- Pauline Nyiramasuhuko: Guilty of **Rape as CAH** (count 7) and **Outrages upon personal dignity as a violation of Article 3 common to the Geneva Conventions and of Additional Protocol II (WC)** (count 11) under Article 6(3) of the Statute (**superior responsibility**) for ordering *Interahamwe* under her effective control to rape Tutsi women at the Butare prefecture office between the end of April and the first half of June 1994.[678] Although Pauline Nyiramasuhuko was found guilty of genocide (count 2), persecutions as CAH (count 8) and violence to life, health and physical or mental well-being as a violation of Article 3 common to the Geneva Conventions and of Additional Protocol II (WC) (count 10), the Trial Chamber found that the Prosecution provided insufficient notice of its intention to pursue rape as genocide, persecutions as CAH and violence to life, health and physical or mental well-being as a violation of Article 3 common to the Geneva Conventions and of Additional Protocol II (WC). Therefore, it decided not enter a conviction for these counts on the basis of rapes.[679] Not guilty of other inhumane acts as CAH (count 9) because the Trial Chamber found the Prosecution provided insufficient notice of its intention to pursue rape as other inhumane acts as CAH and adduced insufficient evidence to prove that Pauline Nyiramasuhuko forced her victims to undress completely before forcing them into vehicles and taking them to their deaths.[680] - Arsène Shalom Ntahobali: Guilty of **Rape as CAH** (count 7) and **Outrages upon personal dignity as a violation of Article 3 common to the Geneva Conventions and of Additional Protocol II (WC)** (count 11) under Article 6(1) of the Statute for: (i) raping (**committing**) a young Tutsi girl at the roadblock near Hotel Ihuliro around the end of April 1994;[681] and (ii) raping (**committing**) Tutsi women, ordering *Interahamwe* to rape Tutsi women (**ordering**) and aiding and abetting the rapes of further Tutsi women at the Butare prefecture office between the end of April and the first half of June 1994 (**aiding and abetting**).[682] Although Arsène Shalom Ntahobali was found guilty of genocide (count 2), persecutions as CAH (count 8) and violence to life, health and physical or mental well-being as a violation of Article 3 common to the Geneva Conventions and of Additional Protocol II (WC) (count 10), the Trial Chamber found that the Prosecution provided insufficient notice of its intention to pursue rape as genocide, persecutions as CAH and violence to life, health and physical or mental well-being as a violation of Article 3 common to the Geneva Conventions and of Additional Protocol II (WC). Therefore, it decided not to enter a conviction for these counts on the basis of rapes.[683] Not guilty of other inhumane acts as CAH (count 9) because the Trial Chamber found the Prosecution provided insufficient notice of its intention to pursue rape as other inhumane acts as CAH and adduced insufficient

committed **SERIOUS VIOLATION OF ARTICLE 3 COMMON TO THE GENEVA CONVENTIONS AND ADDITIONAL PROTOCOL II**, a crime stipulated in Article 4(e) of the Statute of the Tribunal, for which they are individually responsible pursuant to Article 6 of the Statute and which is punishable in reference to Articles 22 and 23 of the Statute".).

678 *Prosecutor v. Pauline Nyiramasuhuko et al.*, Case No. ICTR-98-42-T, Judgement and Sentence, dated 24 June 2011 and filed on 14 July 2011 ("*Pauline Nyiramasuhuko et al.* Trial Judgement"), paras. 2072, 2773, 2781–2782, 6087–6088, 6093, 6182–6183, 6186.

679 *Pauline Nyiramasuhuko et al.* Trial Judgement, paras. 5828–5837, 5857–5865, 5911, 6076, 6085, 6089, 6180, 6186 and fn. 14709, 14726.

680 *Pauline Nyiramasuhuko et al.* Trial Judgement, paras. 6134–6135, 6137, 6145, 6186 and fn. 14709, 14726.

681 *Pauline Nyiramasuhuko et al.* Trial Judgement, paras. 3132–3135, 6077–6080, 6094, 6184–6185, 6186.

682 *Pauline Nyiramasuhuko et al.* Trial Judgement, paras. 2644, 2653, 2773, 2781–2782, 6086, 6094, 6184–6185, 6186. The Trial Chamber also found that Arsène Shalom Ntahobali was liable under Article 6(3) of the Statute (superior responsibility) for the rapes committed by the *Interahamwe* and took this into account in sentencing. See *Pauline Nyiramasuhuko et al.* Trial Judgement, para. 6086.

683 *Pauline Nyiramasuhuko et al.* Trial Judgement, paras. 5828–5837, 5857–5865, 5911, 6076, 6085, 6089, 6180, 6186 and fn. 14709, 14726.

	evidence to prove that Arsène Shalom Ntahobali forced his victims to undress completely before forcing them into vehicles and taking them to their deaths.[684]
Appeal Judgement	N/A (The appellate proceedings are in progress.)
Legal and Factual Findings and/or Evidence	- It is the first case before the ICTR in which a woman was convicted for rape as CAH. - Legal findings: - **Rape: definition:** The Trial Chamber adopted the definition of rape given in the *Kunarac et al.* case:[685] "The *actus reus* of rape involves the non-consensual penetration, however slight, of the vagina or anus of the victim by the penis of the perpetrator or any other object used by the perpetrator, or of the mouth of the victim by the penis of the perpetrator. Consent for this purpose must be given voluntarily, as a result of the victim's free will, assessed in the context of the surrounding circumstances. The *mens rea* is the intention to effect this sexual penetration, and the knowledge that it occurs without the consent of the victim. Force or threat of force provides clear evidence of non-consent, but force is not an element *per se* of rape".[686] - **Forcing victims to undress can constitute other inhumane acts as CAH:** "Paragraph 6.31, also pled in support of other inhumane acts, alleges that Nyiramasuhuko and Ntahobali 'often forced [their victims] to undress completely before forcing them into vehicles and taking them to their deaths. In the Chamber's view, this serves as an example of sufficient notice that would suffice for the charge of other inhumane acts. Reading the Indictment as a whole, the Chamber concludes that the Indictment provides notice that Nyiramasuhuko and Ntahobali allegedly forced their victims to undress, and that this constituted another inhumane act".[687] - Factual and legal findings: - Defect of the Indictment with respect to rapes at the Butare prefecture office (BPO): "On behalf of Nyiramasuhuko, the Ntahobali Defence asserts that the Chamber permitted the amendment of the Indictment to add the count of rape against Nyiramasuhuko without performing the requisite evaluation of the existence of *prima facie* evidence to support such a charge. In this regard, the Chamber recalls that on 10 August 1999, it granted leave to the Prosecutor to add a count of rape as a crime against humanity and to add Article 6 (3) responsibility to certain counts against Nyiramasuhuko. The Chamber recalls that in 1999, Rule 50 did not require the Chamber to make a *prima facie* determination in considering a motion to amend the indictment. This *prima facie* requirement was added to Rule 50 in 2004. Therefore, the Chamber was not required to make a *prima facie* determination in considering the Prosecution's Motion to add a count of rape against Nyiramasuhuko in 1999. Furthermore, the Nyiramasuhuko Defence did not appeal the Chamber's decision to grant leave to amend the Indictment or seek reconsideration by the Trial Chamber. Finally, after the completion of the Prosecution's case, the Chamber found that the Prosecution presented sufficient evidence that could sustain a conviction for the crime of rape against Nyiramasuhuko based on Article 6 (3). Therefore, the Chamber finds that Ntahobali's assertion on behalf of Nyiramasuhuko is unfounded, untimely and moot.

684 *Pauline Nyiramasuhuko et al.* Trial Judgement, paras. 6134–6135, 6137, 6145, 6186 and fn. 14709, 14726.

685 ICTY ISCC *Kunarac et al.*, see *supra* p. 528.

686 *Pauline Nyiramasuhuko et al.* Trial Judgement, para. 6075 (internal reference omitted).

687 *Pauline Nyiramasuhuko et al.* Trial Judgement, paras. 6134–6135 (internal reference omitted).

	Superior-Subordinate Relationship The Ntahobali Defence also asserts, on behalf of Nyiramasuhuko, that the Indictment was defective for failing to specifically plead a superior-subordinate relationship to support the charge of rape under Article 6 (3) against Nyiramasuhuko. It asserts the Prosecution failed to state whether Ntahobali was alleged to be Nyiramasuhuko's subordinate. The Chamber recalls that the indictment should plead that the accused is the superior of subordinates sufficiently identified, over whom she had effective control and for whose acts she is alleged to be responsible. Nonetheless, a superior need not necessarily know the exact identity of his or her subordinates who perpetrate crimes, in order to incur liability under Article 6 (3) of the Statute. In this regard, Paragraph 6.54 of the Indictment asserts that Nyiramasuhuko, among others, aided and abetted her subordinates in carrying out the massacres of the Tutsi population. However, the Indictment does not identify her subordinates. With regard to the attacks at the BPO, the Nyiramasuhuko and Ntahobali Indictment states that Nyiramasuhuko and Ntahobali were accompanied by *Interahamwe* militiamen and soldiers to abduct Tutsi refugees, assault and kill them. Paragraph 6.30 does not specify that Nyiramasuhuko was superior to the *Interahamwe* or soldiers or that she directed them in the BPO attacks. Therefore, the Indictment was defective for failing to specify that Nyiramasuhuko was superior to the *Interahamwe* or soldiers. The Chamber notes that a holistic reading of the Indictment demonstrates that numerous paragraphs pled in support of Article 6 (3) responsibility identify Nyiramasuhuko's alleged subordinates. These paragraphs provide that Nyiramasuhuko is alleged to be superior to *Interahamwe*, including Ntahobali, soldiers, *commune* police and civilians. Even were this not the case, the Chamber notes that the Prosecution Pre-Trial Brief, filed after the operative Indictment, specifically alleges that Nyiramasuhuko supervised *Interahamwe*, militiamen and soldiers. Similarly, the witness summaries appended to the Pre-Trial Brief confirm that Nyiramasuhuko was an alleged superior to Ntahobali, *Interahamwe* and the *commune* police. The Prosecution Pre-Trial Brief included the summaries of 14 witnesses, each of whom asserted that Nyiramasuhuko ordered *Interahamwe* and soldiers to rape and kill Tutsis at the BPO. Furthermore, the witness statements of Witnesses SS, SU, TA and TK, disclosed on 4 November 1998, each stated that Nyiramasuhuko gave orders to the *Interahamwe* in the attacks at the BPO or that she was their superior. The statements of Witnesses QBP and QBQ, disclosed on 1 December 1999, contained similar information. Under these circumstances, the Chamber considers that Nyiramasuhuko received sufficient notice that she was charged with superior responsibility for the alleged acts of the following persons: *Interahamwe*, Ntahobali, militiamen, soldiers and *commune* police. *Failure to Plead Crimes of* [...] *Rape* On behalf of Ntahobali and Nyiramasuhuko, the Ntahobali Defence asserts that the Indictment failed to plead factual allegations directly implicating them and that, as a matter of law, such failure cannot be cured by subsequent disclosures. The Chamber applies the settled principles of pleading in evaluating whether the Indictments were defective for failing to plead material facts and whether such defects were cured. The Chamber recalls the Prosecution has an obligation to state the material facts underpinning the charges in the indictment, but not the evidence by which such facts are to be proven. As to the abduction of persons at the BPO, the Nyiramasuhuko and Ntahobali Indictment alleges that Nyiramasuhuko and Ntahobali were accompanied by *Interahamwe* and soldiers when they went to the BPO to abduct Tutsi refugees. Those who resisted were assaulted and sometimes killed outright at locations such as the EER woods. The Indictment provides that Nyiramasuhuko and Ntahobali often made the refugees undress before forcing them onto vehicles and taking them to their deaths. Therefore, the crimes of abduction and killing at the BPO were clearly pled in the Indictment. As to the crime of rape, Paragraph 6.37 of the Nyiramasuhuko and Ntahobali indictment states that aside from the attacks on Tutsis, Ntahobali was assisted by accomplices in kidnapping and raping Tutsi women. The Chamber recalls that an indictment paragraph should be read in conjunction with the entire indictment as a whole. Read in this way, the crimes of kidnapping and rape

	were separately pled to the attacks occurring throughout the rest of the *préfecture*, including the attacks and abductions at the BPO. Nonetheless, the information in Paragraph 6.37 lacked necessary details, including specific dates, locations and the names of victims, to put Ntahobali and Nyiramasuhuko on notice that they were being charged with raping women or were responsible as a superior for rapes occurring at the BPO. The Indictment was therefore defective in this regard. The Chamber notes the Prosecution set forth in its Pre-Trial Brief that members of the Interim Government (such as Pauline Nyiramasuhuko) and Ntahobali committed, ordered, and aided and abetted their subordinates and others in the carrying out of rapes, sexual assaults and massacres of the Tutsi population. The Appendix to the Pre-Trial Brief included the summaries of numerous witnesses who were to testify as to rape allegations against Ntahobali and Nyiramasuhuko occurring at the BPO, including Witnesses TA, FAP, QBP, QBQ, QZ, RE, RF, RJ and SW. In its opening statement, the Prosecution reiterated allegations that Nyiramasuhuko was responsible for numerous rapes. Based upon the large volume of timely, clear and consistent materials disclosed to Nyiramasuhuko and Ntahobali indicating that they participated in rapes at the BPO, the Chamber finds they had adequate notice to prepare a defence. The Chamber, therefore, finds this defect in the Indictment was cured. Moreover, the Accused suffered no prejudice as a result of the defect in the Indictment. *Pleading Facts Regarding Particular Victims* On behalf of Nyiramasuhuko and Ntahobali, the Ntahobali Defence argues that the Prosecution failed to plead multiple factual allegations in the Indictment. As to the allegations against Nyiramasuhuko at the BPO, it argues that the Prosecution failed to plead that she: (1) ordered the abduction of Mbasha's wife and her children; (2) ordered that a woman named Trifina be killed; (3) abducted two persons named Semanyezi and Annonciata in order to kill them; and (4) ordered *Interahamwe* or soldiers to rape Tutsi girls and women at night. As to the allegations against Ntahobali at the BPO, the Ntahobali Defence argues that the Prosecution failed to plead that he: (1) abducted Mbasha's wife and her children in order to kill them; (2) raped and killed Tutsi refugees at a specific place with soldiers or *Interahamwe*; and (3) raped and killed a Tutsi woman named Immaculée. The Appeals Chamber has recognised that there may be instances where the sheer scale of the crimes alleged makes it impracticable to require a high degree of specificity in such matters as the identity of the victims and the dates for the commission of crimes. However, '[t]he Prosecution cannot simultaneously argue that the accused killed a named individual yet claim that the 'sheer scale' of the crime made it impossible to identify that individual in the indictment.' The Appeals Chamber has held that the identification of a particular *location* itself refutes the argument that identifying it was somehow impracticable. The same logic would apply to the identification of a particular *victim*. Further, the Appeals Chamber has advised that, '[s]ince the identity of the victim is information that is valuable to the preparation of the defence case, if the Prosecution is in a position to name the victims, it should do so.' A failure to plead the names of particular victims where they are known may render the indictment defective on that charge. Such a defect may be remedied by the provision of clear, consistent and timely disclosures. In the present case, the Indictment was not clear as to how many Tutsis were raped, abducted and killed at the BPO. However, the Pre-Trial Brief and witness statements disclosed to the Defence clearly set forth the Prosecution's case: that there were between several hundred and several thousand Tutsis seeking refuge at the BPO; that these persons were taken away by *Interahamwe*, soldiers and the Accused by repeatedly loading pickup trucks; and that the refugees were killed elsewhere. The Chamber considers that in view of the sheer scale of the attacks, rapes and killings alleged to have taken place at the BPO, it is impractical to require the Prosecution to name each of the alleged victims of this course of conduct. Therefore, there was no defect in the Indictment for failing to name each of the alleged victims at the BPO. However, the Chamber also notes that the names Immaculée, Mbasha, Trifina, Caritas, Semanyenzi and Annonciata did not appear in the Indictment even though this information was available to the Prosecution

	in the witness statements of Witnesses TA and TK. The Prosecution was under an obligation to disclose this information to the Defence. The question is whether the Defence was prejudiced by any delay in disclosing the names of these alleged victims. The witness statements of Witnesses TA and TK were disclosed on 4 November 1998 and 1 December 1999. These statements provided additional information underpinning the specific allegations as to the location, sequence of events and the Accused involved. The names of the relevant victims were redacted in those disclosures to the Defence. However, the Prosecution disclosed the unredacted witness statements of Witnesses TA and TK, which provided notice of the specific named victims, on 23 April 2001. This was six months prior to the beginning of Witness TA's testimony on 24 October 2001 and one year prior to the testimony of Witness TK which began on 20 May 2002. In addition, the Prosecution Pre-Trial Brief listed the first 12 witnesses the Prosecution intended to call to testify, which included Witnesses TA and TK. Nonetheless, the victims' names did not appear in the Indictment, the Pre-Trial Brief, its Appendix or the Prosecution opening statement. The disclosure of the victims' names in four witness statements occurred less than two months prior to trial and without any further indication to the Defence that this new information was being provided to them. Therefore, the Chamber finds the late disclosure of these victims' names accorded bias to the Defence in preparing its case. The Chamber will not convict the Accused, if established by the evidence, for alleged crimes against Trifina, Mrs. Mbasha, Annonciata, Semanyenzi, Caritas or Immaculée. Nonetheless, the Chamber will consider the evidence of these named individuals for other permissible purposes (for example, as background information, circumstantial evidence in support of other allegations, to demonstrate a special knowledge, opportunity, or identification of the accused). The other abductions, rapes and killings occurring at the BPO will be considered by the Chamber in support of counts as the Defence had adequate notice of these allegations of large-scale criminal conduct".[688]
	- Rapes of Tutsi women by Arsène Shalom Ntahobali, Pauline Nyiramasuhuko, *Interahamwe* and soldiers on various occasions, between mid-May and the end of May 1994, at the Butare prefecture office (BPO): "As a preliminary matter, the Chamber notes it is not disputed that there were a large number of refugees at the BPO compound between April and June 1994. These people consisted mainly of women and children in poor physical condition; many of them had visible skin ailments and were malnourished. The Chamber recalls the testimony of Alexandre Bararwandika, a doctor working for the Belgian Red Cross, who described the persons around the BPO as ill, emaciated and wearing torn clothing. Witness TQ described the conditions at the BPO as very poor, noted the refugees wore torn, smelling clothes and were apparently abandoned. The Chamber notes that the evidence was clear and consistent that these people had fled other *communes* and *préfectures* to escape violence and the threat of death. The Chamber also notes that all of the Prosecution witnesses who testified as to their experiences at the BPO were Tutsis. Witness TA testified that she saw Nyiramasuhuko during one night in mid-May 1994. Nyiramasuhuko was accompanied by 10 *Interahamwe*, including her son, Shalom. This was the first time Witness TA saw Shalom. Nyiramasuhuko and Shalom arrived together in the same Hilux pickup and told the *Interahamwe* who should be forced to board the bed of the pickup. Nyiramasuhuko wore a *kitenge* cloth. The truck's lights were illuminated. Nyiramasuhuko was standing in the courtyard of the BPO pointing out Tutsi refugees to the *Interahamwe*, saying as she pointed, '[t]his is another one, and another one and another one, and why are you leaving that one?' Those Tutsis were refugees. Witness TA testified that those Tutsis were beaten up and forced onto the pickup. Nyiramasuhuko pointed at three refugees who had been cut up and ordered that they

688 *Pauline Nyiramasuhuko et al.* Trial Judgement, paras. 2157–2172 (internal references omitted).

	be loaded onto the vehicle. Shalom ordered the *Interahamwe* to stop killing refugees, as the number of dead people was in excess as to what could be loaded in the vehicle. Witness TA described Nyiramasuhuko's clothing and quoted her as ordering the *Interahamwe* to attack certain individuals. Therefore, Witness TA was close enough to hear what Nyiramasuhuko was saying and identified her as the mother of Shalom. For these reasons, the Chamber finds this identification to be reliable. Witness TA said Shalom and other *Interahamwe* raped her. Nyiramasuhuko and her son arrived together in the same Hilux pickup and indicated to the *Interahamwe* who to force to board the bed of the pickup. Shalom was wearing trousers and a shirt made of *kitenge*. Over the course of the events, Witness TA saw Shalom on more than eight occasions at the BPO. Further, she stated that Shalom raped her on two occasions and took her by the arm to *Interahamwe* in order to be raped on multiple occasions. Therefore, Witness TA had numerous opportunities to view Shalom up close. Although the attacks at the BPO occurred at night, Witness TA stated there was moonlight behind the BPO on several of those occasions. In addition, there was occasionally some public lighting from the lamp posts that reached the area from the other side of the road near *Chez* Venant. Witness TA did not describe the truck as being camouflaged. However, she was never questioned on this issue. In addition, Witness FAP testified that Shalom came in a black camouflage-coloured vehicle. The Chamber considers these to be minor discrepancies. Of particular importance, Witness TA testified that she observed Shalom leading an *Interahamwe* training exercise one morning in June 1994. Therefore, she saw Shalom during broad daylight. Witness TA provided substantial detail regarding the events of the rape. She stated that Shalom moved through the refugees cutting and slashing people with his machete. She said that when Shalom got to where she was, he took her by the hand and hit her with his machete on the arm and hand. She said Shalom picked her up from the ground and pulled her towards the ORINFOR, behind the BPO buildings. Shalom removed Witness TA's clothes saying he would kill her if she refused. He removed her underwear, laid her on the ground and raped her. Then he invited some eight other *Interahamwe* to rape her, including one named Ngoma. Ngoma remained at the BPO to oversee the refugees when they were asleep, but assisted the *Interahamwe* during the attacks. One of the *Interahamwe* that raped her put his machete on her leg, telling her that if she moved he would kill her. While being raped, Witness TA saw two other women nearby who were also being raped by the *Interahamwe*. Nsabimana provided a statement to Des Forges which was consistent with Witness TA's testimony, remarking to Des Forges that during this time, soldiers and others were coming to take away women to rape them and other people were being selected to be killed. Witness TA was not acquainted with Shalom prior to encountering him at the BPO. She only knew Ntahobali's given name, Shalom. However, this does not detract from the reliability of her identification. She learned of the familial relationship between Nyiramasuhuko and Ntahobali from other refugees. She did not merely identify the Accused as 'Shalom,' as suggested by the Ntahobali Defence. She identified him as Shalom, the son of Pauline Nyiramasuhuko, who was the Minister of Women's Affairs. The Chamber is convinced that Witness TA was referring to Shalom Ntahobali throughout her testimony when she referred to 'Shalom.' Witness TA also stated that the *Interahamwe* arriving on the Toyota Hilux were holding sticks, while Ntahobali was holding a machete covered in blood and had a hammer on his belt. Witnesses TK, RE, FAP, QY and QBQ corroborated the fact that the *Interahamwe* arriving with Ntahobali at the BPO were carrying traditional weapons such as machetes, clubs and knives. The Chamber recalls some apparent inconsistencies in the testimony of Witness TA in relation to her prior statement. Witness TA stated in testimony that she had not been raped anally. However, she was cross-examined on a prior statement in which she stated that she was raped in her anus as well as her vagina. The Chamber considers that based upon the obvious intensity of experiencing multiple gang rapes at the hands of *Interahamwe*, this discrepancy is understandable and does not adversely affect the Chamber's credibility assessment of

	the witness. Witness TA was very precise in her testimony that on two occasions, there were eight *Interahamwe* who arrived at the BPO with Ntahobali. She later testified that she could not recall the number of *Interahamwe* accompanying Ntahobali on the fifth and sixth occasions he came to the BPO. The Chamber accepts that it would have been difficult to count and remember the exact number of assailants at the BPO on each night. Therefore, the Chamber finds her estimate of eight *Interahamwe* on two occasions to be credible. Witness TA testified that she reported to the authorities in her home *préfecture* that she had been raped by other assailants but did not report the rape by Shalom because he had fled and was out of the country. Considering the trauma and potential shame associated with these events, the Chamber also accepts this testimony. The Chamber notes that it may accept hearsay as the basis of knowing Ntahobali's identity. In addition, the Chamber finds Witness TA's identification of Ntahobali during this event reliable for the following reasons: (1) at times, there was some public lighting from lamp posts that reached the area from the other side of the road; (2) there was moonlight behind the BPO where Witness TA said she was raped by Ntahobali; (3) *Interahamwe* used torches to search through the refugees; and (4) Witness TA provided significant details as to what Ntahobali was carrying, stated what he was wearing, and Ntahobali was in close proximity to Witness TA when he grabbed her hand and raped her. Further, she had also previously seen him in daylight. […] The Chamber recalls its analysis of the Accused's alibis for mid-May 1994. The Chamber found that even if true, Nyiramasuhuko's assertion that she was in Murambi until 1 June 1994 for government meetings does not raise a reasonable doubt as to Nyiramasuhuko's presence in Butare due to the relatively close proximity of Murambi to Butare. Furthermore, Nyiramasuhuko admitted to being present in Butare on 14 to 16 May 1994. She claimed to be bed-ridden with malaria, although the Chamber did not find her credible in this respect. Ntahobali's alibi for this time period was that he stayed at Hotel Ihuliro operating the generator at Hotel Ihuliro. The Chamber did not find this alibi to be credible. Therefore, neither alibi raises a reasonable doubt as to the culpability of the Accused for crimes at the BPO around mid-May 1994. The Chamber finds the Prosecution has proven beyond a reasonable doubt through the testimony of Witness TA that one night in mid-May 1994, Nyiramasuhuko, Ntahobali and about 10 *Interahamwe* came to the BPO aboard a camouflaged pickup. Nyiramasuhuko ordered the *Interahamwe* to force Tutsi refugees onto the pickup. Ntahobali and about eight other *Interahamwe* raped Witness TA. Some of the *Interahamwe* raped two other Tutsi women. The pickup left the BPO, abducting Tutsi refugees in the process, some of whom were forced to undress as alleged in Paragraphs 6.30 and 6.31 of the Nyiramasuhuko and Ntahobali Indictment".[689] "In addition to the above incident, Witness TA testified that seven days after the first attack, which corresponds with the third week of May 1994, the *Interahamwe* arrived at the BPO in the same vehicle and started beating, cutting with machetes and killing people. Ntahobali woke up Witness TA, dragged and pushed her behind the BPO and raped her. He hit her with a hammer, causing her head to swell. By this time, Witness TA had previously seen Ntahobali. Furthermore, she was close enough to Ntahobali to identify him as they were in direct contact. Witness TA was confronted with a prior statement in which she said she was in view of the other refugees when she was raped on this occasion. She maintained in her testimony that she was taken behind the BPO. At the same time, the *Interahamwe* took six other women and raped them near her. She stated that the number of refugees had been reduced by this time due to the daily killings by the *Interahamwe*. Witness TA testified that during one of the rapes, Ntahobali hit her on the face with a hammer. In a prior statement, she said that Ntahobali only showed her the hammer and did not hit her. She acknowledged in testimony that the prior statement was incorrect and that she did in fact suffer a blow from the hammer. She said that the investigator taking the statement may have misun-

689 *Pauline Nyiramasuhuko et al.* Trial Judgement, paras. 2627–2638, 2643–2644 (internal references omitted).

	derstood her and thought that she did not suffer a blow since the injury was minor. The Chamber considers that this is a minor discrepancy. Four days later, at night, a group of eight *Interahamwe* including Shalom arrived in the same vehicle and started beating and cutting up people at the BPO. Shalom came to the BPO and gave Witness TA to a group of seven *Interahamwe* who dragged her to the same location, removed her clothes and raped her. He told them to do it quickly so that the *Inkotanyi* would not get to a roadblock first. While she was being raped, she saw Shalom raping a girl named Caritas who was being raped about five to six metres away from her. These men were armed with machetes, hammers, clubs, big sticks and Rwandan clubs (clubs with nails in them). Although the Chamber will not convict Ntahobali for the rape of Caritas, the details of her rape provide circumstantial evidence to support the fact that *Interahamwe* and Ntahobali raped many women, including Witness TA at the BPO. By this time, Witness TA had already suffered the same treatment at the hands of Ntahobali. Witness TA was again in contact with Ntahobali as he handed her over to a group of *Interahamwe*. Therefore, the Chamber considers this identification to be reliable. Witness SD corroborated important aspects of each of these attacks. She testified that during her stay at the BPO, each night a vehicle covered with mud would come to fetch people. Witness SD was told that Shalom, the son of Nyiramasuhuko, drove the vehicle, although she did not see him. The *Interahamwe* who were present and who took people to vehicles told them that if Shalom were to come he would deliver them to their death. Girls and women were taken away to be raped and other people were taken away and never seen again. Witness SD said before she left towards Kibilizi, Shalom attacked the BPO, and when she got back from Kibilizi, the attacks continued. Kibilizi *secteur* is on the road to Nyange *secteur* in Nyaruhengeri *commune*. Therefore, Witness SD testified that there were attacks by Shalom both prior to and after the transfer to Nyange in early June 1994. The Chamber is convinced that Witness SD was at the BPO prior to the Nyange transfer in early June 1994. While her testimony was not specific as to what occurred during each attack, she identified the distinctive features of the vehicle, namely that it was covered in mud and contained Nyiramasuhuko, Ntahobali and *Interahamwe*. Therefore, her testimony provides corroboration for Witness TA's testimony as to the attacks by Ntahobali. Ntahobali's alibi for this time period was that he stayed at Hotel Ihuliro operating the generator at Hotel Ihuliro. The Chamber did not find this alibi to be credible. Therefore, Ntahobali's alibi does not raise a reasonable doubt as to his presence at the BPO around 7 and 11 days after the first attack in mid-May 1994. The Chamber finds the Prosecution has proven beyond a reasonable doubt that around 7 and 11 days after the first attack in mid-May 1994, Ntahobali and *Interahamwe* came to the BPO on two more occasions. Ntahobali violently raped Witness TA, hitting her on the head with a hammer. *Interahamwe*, following the orders of Ntahobali, raped six other women. In a subsequent attack during this same time period, Ntahobali ordered about seven other *Interahamwe* to rape Witness TA".[690] - Pauline Nyiramasuhuko's order to rape Tutsi women at the Butare prefecture office (BPO) at the end of May 1994: "While Nyiramasuhuko stood by the door of the car, she told the *Interahamwe* and soldiers who were carrying weapons to 'start from one side and take the young girls and women and go and rape them because they refused to marry you.' Witness SS said that Nyiramasuhuko was in charge of the attacks committed against Tutsi refugees at the BPO. After Nyiramasuhuko spoke, the *Interahamwe* and soldiers got out of the vehicle and raped Tutsi women. They approached the Tutsi refugees and loaded them on the pickup. While people were being loaded onto the pickup, Nyiramasuhuko was standing next to it. [...] Witness QBQ testified that Nyiramasuhuko and the *Inte-*

690 *Pauline Nyiramasuhuko et al.* Trial Judgement, paras. 2645–2653 (internal references omitted).

	rahamwe got out of the vehicle. She corroborated Witness SS' observation that Nyiramasuhuko stood next to the vehicle and gave orders to the *Interahamwe* to '[r]ape the women and the girls and kill the rest.' The *Interahamwe* wore ordinary civilian clothes and used flashlights to find people. The *Interahamwe* were close to Nyiramasuhuko when she gave her orders. […] Witness RE's testimony also lended support to Witnesses SS' and QBQ's testimony that Nyiramasuhuko was giving orders to rape in this time period. She testified that Nyiramasuhuko came to the BPO with President Sindikubwabo one day. During this visit, Nyiramasuhuko said, the people should be killed and the young girls among them raped. Although given at a different time than the event now in question, this evidence shows a level of planning and intent on Nyiramasuhuko's part. Witness FAP testified that during the first attack Nyiramasuhuko wore a military uniform. Witness FAP was lying on the ground and thus could only see Nyiramasuhuko's top. Nyiramasuhuko stood by the vehicle and told the *Interahamwe* to take the young girls and the women who were not old, and to rape and kill them because they had refused to marry Hutus. […] In sum, several witnesses knew Nyiramasuhuko before the April to July 1994 events including Witnesses SU, SD, SS and SJ. They had an opportunity to identify her in the conditions of calm prior to the commencement of large-scale violence. Nyiramasuhuko was widely known as the Minister in charge of Women's Affairs and therefore would likely be recognisable. Several other witnesses had an adequate opportunity to observe Nyiramasuhuko at the BPO from close proximity, including Witnesses TA, QJ, TK, RE, FAP, QY and QBQ. Furthermore, numerous witnesses maintained that she was wearing a military shirt and *kitenge* cloth skirt or just a military shirt. The Chamber is therefore convinced that Nyiramasuhuko was at the BPO during this attack, ordered *Interahamwe* and soldiers to rape Tutsi women, and to kill other refugees. Witness QBQ testified that upon hearing Nyiramasuhuko's order, the *Interahamwe* immediately attacked the people on the veranda and took them away by pulling them by their noses. Many women were raped while Nyiramasuhuko was still on the spot. The *Interahamwe*, Nyiramasuhuko and Shalom subsequently loaded the Tutsi refugees onto the vehicle and took them to Kumukoni to be killed and dumped into a ditch there. This was corroborated by Witness FAP who testified that Nyiramasuhuko's orders to rape given on her first trip to the BPO were carried out; during the first visit of Nyiramasuhuko and Ntahobali, Tutsi women and girls were raped behind the BPO under the avocado trees. Upon return to the courtyard of the BPO, one of these girls said that it was better to be killed than to be raped by four or more men. Likewise, Witness SS testified that while some women were beaten and taken away in a vehicle, others were beaten and taken to the back of the BPO to be abused. The women and girls had been undressed and they were only wearing their undergarments. Other young girls and women were taken away and would return to the BPO two or three days later. Witness SS told them she thought they had been killed to which they replied, '[w]hat they subjected us to was worse than death. Imagine if six persons had a turn each on you!' Witness SS understood that these women had been raped. She did not know the names of the women who were raped. Nyiramasuhuko's alibi for this time period was that she was either in Murambi or Muramba attending Interim Government meetings. She admitted to being in Butare on 31 May 1994, but she claimed not to leave Hotel Ihuliro that night. The Chamber found that this alibi was not reasonably possibly true. Therefore, based upon the consistency and corroboration of the substantive evidence, the Chamber finds that Nyiramasuhuko was in fact present at the BPO during this attack. She ordered *Interahamwe* to rape refugees because they were Tutsis. The *Interahamwe* beat, abused and raped many Tutsi women".[691]

691 *Pauline Nyiramasuhuko et al.* Trial Judgement, paras. 2688, 2693, 2695–2696, 2698–2702 (internal references omitted).

	- Rapes of Tutsi women at the Butare prefecture office (BPO) during the first half of June 1994: "The Chamber notes that Witness TA testified that Immaculée Mukagatare was raped at the BPO during the fourth attack Witness TA observed at the BPO. This corresponds with the first or second week of June 1994. Witness QBP likewise testified that during the attack by Nyiramasuhuko, she observed the rape of a woman named Immaculée Mukagatare who died after the war. Therefore, the Chamber is convinced that Witness TA's evidence of this attack corresponds with the attack described by Witness QBP which allegedly occurred in June 1994. Witness SU testified that one night after the three attacks, she again saw Nyiramasuhuko come to the BPO on a pickup and order *Interahamwe* to rape Tutsi women. Witness SS corroborated this account. Insofar as Witness SU stated this event occurred after the night of three attacks, and the refugees were transferred to Rango around 17 June 1994, the Chamber finds it established that these additional attacks occurred in the first half of June 1994. Witnesses QBP and SU testified that Nyiramasuhuko returned to the BPO a subsequent night and ordered that Tutsi women be raped. One night after the night of three attacks, Witness SU saw a Volkswagen driven by Emmanuel Rekeraho arrive at the BPO at around 10.00 p.m. Rekeraho got out of the Volkswagen and into the Sovu ambulance at the BPO. Nyiramasuhuko then arrived at the BPO in the same Hilux vehicle, this time wearing a military shirt and a *kitenge*. When Witness SU was questioned as to her statement of 3 December 1996, in which she said that Pauline came in a white van painted with green colours rather than a Hilux vehicle, she testified that Rekeraho arrived in a van belonging to the Sovu Health Centre, but that Nyiramasuhuko arrived in a Hilux. Nyiramasuhuko summoned the *Interahamwe* present at the BPO. She told them to load people onto the vehicle. She also shouted at the *Interahamwe* to 'choose the young girls and the women that are still useful.' She ordered that the women be raped because they refused to marry Hutus and then to be loaded onto the Hilux to be killed. Witness SU was about nine metres away from Nyiramasuhuko. Immediately following Nyiramasuhuko's instruction, after the vehicle had left, one of the *Interahamwe* named Muzungu took and raped a girl whom the witness knew. Witness SU testified that the *Interahamwe* became animals and raped women. There was no respect of human beings at that time. At the same time, another *Interahamwe* whom the witness identified as Ruhengeri raped a girl in the presence of the witness. Witness SU also identified Ngoma, Ribanza and Mbote as *Interahamwe* who committed rapes. The *Interahamwe* lined up women next to the vehicle to choose whom to rape, including Witness SU. The *Interahamwe* shined a torch on Witness SU. Witness SU showed them her aged breasts to discourage the men from raping her as she was very thin. The *Interahamwe* then took the women and girls they had chosen behind the ORINFOR and into abandoned vehicles to rape them. Witness SS corroborated this account, stating an *Interahamwe* hit her sister, Witness SU, with a machete between the shoulders. One night, an *Interahamwe* woke up Witness SU who removed her clothes, showed him her breasts and told him, '[p]lease, don't take me with you, I'm an old lady and my breasts are falling.' Witness SU's identification of Nyiramasuhuko was based on prior knowledge; she knew Nyiramasuhuko because Witness SU often walked past Nyiramasuhuko's home in Ndora *commune* when Witness SU went to visit relatives. Witness SU arrived at the BPO on or about 28 May 1994 and had several opportunities to observe Nyiramasuhuko in broad daylight and from close range; on the first occasion, Nyiramasuhuko, was four metres away from the witness whereas on the second occasion Witness SU saw Nyiramasuhuko arrive at the BPO, Witness SU was nine metres away. Witness SU saw Nyiramasuhuko summon the *Interahamwe* present at the BPO and order them to select young Tutsi women and girls to be loaded on the vehicles, raped and then killed. The Chamber finds Witness SU's identification of Nyiramasuhuko reliable considering she previously knew Nyiramasuhuko, and she saw her at the BPO during the day from close proximity. Witness SU testified that she did not have any clothes therefore she could not ap-

	proach Nyiramasuhuko. She later clarified that she was only wearing clothes that had been given to her and she was not dressed to the same standard as Nyiramasuhuko. Asked why she stayed at the BPO despite having a signed affidavit indicating that she was Hutu, Witness SU stated that she attempted to seek shelter with some nuns, but once they saw she was injured it was determined that it would not be safe such that she was obliged to go to the BPO. It was also dangerous in case she ran into someone who knew her. At the time of her testimony Witness SU was not living with her sister, although they visited one another. She never discussed the events of 1994 or the events at the BPO with her sister. She also met a woman with the same first name as Witness QBP at the BPO. After the war she chanced upon Witness QBP's sister at the *commune* office where they were searching for their identity documents. They exchanged greetings but did not discuss the events of 1994 at the BPO. Witness SU said that she had problems with her eyes and needed eyeglasses. At the time of the war she could see without any problems. After the war she had eyesight problems because of an illness. She was not able to recognise what was shown in Prosecution Exhibit 23A as the photo was projected on a screen. The Chamber considers Witness SU's vision problems at the time of her testimony did not adversely affect her ability to identify Ntahobali during the events in 1994. Witness QBP named four women who had been raped, two of whom died after the war. She admitted not witnessing with her own eyes the alleged rapes in the rear of the BPO as there was no longer any light. However, she asserted that the *Interahamwe* and soldiers had just been encouraged to do something specific to these Tutsi women by Nyiramasuhuko and only a child would not understand what was going to happen to these women. Witness QBP testified during the night in which she observed the rape of Immaculée Mukagatare, 'Nyiramasuhuko told the soldiers and *Interahamwe* that there's still a lot of dirt at the *préfecture*, such as these Tutsi women, who previously were arrogant and did not want to marry Hutu men. Now it's up to you to do whatever you want with them.' Witness QBP testified that she knew Nyiramasuhuko because they lived in the same *commune* until Nyiramasuhuko got married and moved to Butare. She was aware that Nyiramasuhuko had been appointed Minister. After the witness returned from Nyange [early June], she saw Nyiramasuhuko coming to the BPO on board a camouflaged vehicle that she heard was smeared with old motor oil or cow dung. She was accompanied by *Interahamwe* and soldiers. Nyiramasuhuko was wearing a military shirt and a skirt and spoke to the soldiers and *Interahamwe* when the witness was nearby. Witness QBP said she was able to see clearly because there were lights coming from the houses surrounding the BPO. Therefore, Witness QBP's evidence corroborates that Nyiramasuhuko was wearing a mix of military and civilian clothing and arrived at the BPO in a mud-covered vehicle. Although she observed Nyiramasuhuko at night, the view was enhanced by surrounding lights. Based on these factors, the Chamber finds Witness QBP's identification of Nyiramasuhuko to be both credible and reliable. Although Witness QBP did not observe the rapes, she saw Nyiramasuhuko give the orders and watched the *Interahamwe* choose women to drag behind the BPO before the lights went out and she hid herself. Witness QBP also saw soldiers and *Interahamwe* dragging refugee women to the back of the BPO and loading other refugees aboard a double-cabin Toyota pickup that had accompanied Nyiramasuhuko's vehicle to the BPO. Witness QBP managed to hide in the bushes in the rear of the BPO when the lights went off. Witness QBP's testimony that she was at the BPO during mid-May 1994 was corroborated by Nyiramasuhuko Defence Witness WMCZ; he saw Witness QBP at the BPO among 1,000 refugees and she asked him for money. One of her children had disappeared and he later learned that child had died. On cross-examination, it was put to Witness SU that she had not been at the BPO during the time she said and that she was instead at someone's house from 27 May 1994 until the end of the war. Witness SU said that six people had been discovered at that man's house and were killed as was the man himself. Therefore, she only spent three days in his home. Witness QBP's credibility was brought into question by Witnesses WUNJN

	and WUNHF. Witness WUNJN testified that he saw Witness QBP from a drinking establishment; she was at her parent's home. For the reasons stated above, the Chamber does not find Witness WUNJN's testimony to be credible. As to Witness WUNHF, he notes that Witness QBP disappeared for five to seven days during May and, rather than worry about her safety, he speculated that she had travelled to Nyange to farm. The Chamber notes that it was uncontested that the number of roadblocks in Butare in May was considerable, restricting ease of movement. Yet Witness WUNHF suggests that Witness QBP continued to farm through May and June 1994. The picture created by WUNHF, that Witness QBP and others were free to move about and farm during the genocide, was not at all believable. Therefore, the Chamber does not find his testimony to undermine Witness QBP's credibility regarding abductions at the BPO. Witness QBP testified that on the night when Immaculée Mukagatare was raped, Nyiramasuhuko had given the order to attack Tutsi refugees. She testified that Immaculée Mukagatare was raped at the BPO and later died. Witness QBP admitted not witnessing with her own eyes the alleged rapes in the rear of the BPO, but this rape allegedly occurred in the open. Witness TA testified that she was also an eyewitness to the rape of Immaculée Mukagatare. Eighteen to 20 days after the first attack, a group of eight *Interahamwe*, including Shalom arrived at the BPO in the same vehicle and attacked the refugees with machetes, hammers, Rwandan clubs and sticks. On this occasion, Shalom again handed Witness TA over to the *Interahamwe* and told them to be quick, after which seven *Interahamwe* raped her. When Witness TA returned to where she usually slept at the BPO after being raped, she watched Ntahobali take another Tutsi refugee woman named Immaculée to rape her. Immaculée had three children with her, including a child of about one and a half to two years old that was still being breast fed. Immaculée tried to fight Shalom and asked him to let her go back to her children. Ntahobali took the youngest child from Immaculée's arms and threw the child to the side, before raping Immaculée. Witness TA picked up the child and consoled it to keep it quiet. After raping Immaculée, Shalom placed two heavy logs on her legs, one above the knee and one below knee, and, according to Immaculée, Shalom said, '[l]et's see if you can get out of that.' After Immaculée had been raped, she asked Witness TA to help remove the logs. Witness TA testified that she went to visit Immaculée at a hospital and Immaculée told Witness TA that she had contracted AIDS during the 1994 events. Immaculée died in January 2001. Witness TA later testified that the rape of Immaculée occurred on the fifth occasion that Ntahobali visited the BPO, on which occasion Witness TA was not personally raped. Given the traumatic nature of the incident, and the amount of time that has passed since this rape, the Chamber does not consider this discrepancy to be serious or such as to undermine Witness TA's overall credibility as to this account. Witness TK also corroborated Witness TA's testimony regarding additional attacks. Apart from the night of three attacks, Witness TK testified that she saw Shalom very often at the BPO. He came on a number of evenings, accompanied by *Interahamwe* or disabled soldiers who were staying at the *Groupe Scolaire*. Those soldiers hit people with their crutches. He came to mock the refugees. On some occasions, he abducted women who were then raped. He also came to determine whether there were any men left, who were then taken away to be killed. She testified that Shalom committed crimes on each evening he came to the BPO. He would say to the *Interahamwe*, '[b]e firm in your actions,' when he meant, 'kill all of them.' The *Interahamwe* surrounded Ntahobali and called him '*Shalom, chef*.' Witness TK also saw Shalom at the BPO on a few occasions during the day. Nyiramasuhuko came alone to the BPO on other occasions, but she did not see Pauline when these rapes occurred. The Chamber finds Witness TK's description of Ntahobali coming to the BPO along with soldiers from the *Groupe Scolaire* to be credible. The Chamber recalls Ntahobali's proffered alibi for June 1994 that he never left Hotel Ihuliro at night. The Chamber has found that this alibi was not reasonably possibly true. The Chamber also recalls Nyiramasuhuko's alibi that she was in Muramba attending Interim Government meetings on 6 and 10 June 1994 which the

	Chamber found to be reasonably possibly true. Nonetheless, her alibis for 7 to 9 June 1994 and from 11 to 19 June 1994 were not credible. Further, she admitted to being in Butare Town on the night of 11 June 1994. Although she claimed she did not leave Hotel Ihuliro that night, the Chamber found this not reasonably possibly true. Therefore, the Chamber finds it established beyond a reasonable doubt, based on the testimony of Witnesses TA, QBP and TK that, in addition to those attacks described above, Ntahobali, injured soldiers and *Interahamwe* came to the BPO in June 1994 to rape women and abduct refugees. During one of these attacks Ntahobali again handed Witness TA over to about seven *Interahamwe* to rape Witness TA. It further finds that in June 1994, Nyiramasuhuko ordered *Interahamwe* to rape Tutsi women at the BPO and that as a result, numerous women were raped at that location. Although Nyiramasuhuko could not have been present on 6 and 10 June 1994, she had ample opportunity to perpetrate these crimes on 7 to 9 June and 11 to 19 June 1994".[692] - Summary of factual findings with respect to the rapes committed at the Butare prefecture office (BPO) and of Pauline Nyiramasuhuko and Arsène Shalom Ntahobali's actions: "In sum, having fully considered the alibis of Nyiramasuhuko and Ntahobali and the evidence adduced against them with regard to the allegations of criminal conduct occurring at the BPO between 19 April 1994 and the end of June 1994, the Chamber makes the following factual findings. The Chamber finds the Prosecution has proven beyond a reasonable doubt that: between 19 April and late June 1994 Nyiramasuhuko, Ntahobali, *Interahamwe* and soldiers went to the BPO to abduct hundreds of Tutsis; the Tutsi refugees were physically assaulted and raped; and the Tutsi refugees were killed in various locations throughout Ngoma *commune*, including the following specific incidents: i. In mid-May 1994, Nyiramasuhuko, Ntahobali and about 10 *Interahamwe* came to the BPO aboard a camouflaged pickup. Nyiramasuhuko ordered the *Interahamwe* to force Tutsi refugees onto the pickup. Ntahobali and about eight other *Interahamwe* raped Witness TA. Some of the *Interahamwe* raped two other Tutsi women. The pickup left the BPO, abducting Tutsi refugees in the process, some of whom were forced to undress. ii. During the last half of May 1994, Ntahobali and *Interahamwe* came to the BPO on two more occasions. Ntahobali violently raped Witness TA, hitting her on the head. *Interahamwe* following the orders of Ntahobali raped six other women. In a subsequent attack during this same time period, Ntahobali ordered about seven other *Interahamwe* to rape Witness TA. iii. Around the end of May to the beginning of June 1994, Ntahobali, Nyiramasuhuko and *Interahamwe* came to the BPO on board a camouflaged pickup three times in one night. They abducted Tutsi refugees each time, some of whom were forced to undress, taking them to other sites in Butare *préfecture* to be killed. Nyiramasuhuko ordered *Interahamwe* to rape refugees because they were Tutsi. The *Interahamwe* beat, abused and raped many Tutsi women. [...] v. In the first half of June 1994, Nyiramasuhuko ordered *Interahamwe* to rape Tutsi women at the BPO and that as a result numerous women were raped at that location. Ntahobali, injured soldiers and *Interahamwe* came to the BPO to rape women and abduct refugees. During at least one of these attacks Ntahobali again handed Witness TA over to about seven *Interahamwe* to rape Witness TA. The Prosecution did not prove the following allegations beyond a reasonable doubt: (1) Ntahobali abducted 30 Tutsi refugees on 28 April 1994; and (2) based on the evidence of Witness QY, Ntahobali and Nyiramasuhuko abducted raped and killed Tutsi refugees at the BPO in late April or early May 1994. Likewise, the Chamber does not enter any conviction for the abduction, killing and/or rape of the following persons due to

[692] *Pauline Nyiramasuhuko et al.* Trial Judgement, paras. 2750–2773 (internal references omitted).

	the notice violation of the Prosecution: Mbasha's wife and children, Trifina, Immaculée, Semanyenzi, Caritas and Annonciata".[693] - Alleged meeting attended by Sylvain Nsabimana, Pauline Nyiramasuhuko and Interim President Sindikubwabo around 10 June 1994 at which Pauline Nyiramasuhuko said that young Tutsi girls should be raped: "Witness RE gave evidence about the alleged meeting between Nsabimana, Nyiramasuhuko and President Sindikubwabo. She testified that she saw Nyiramasuhuko arrive at the BPO with Sindikubwabo and said to him, '[i]s that dirt still here? In Butare they have not worked.' The Chamber notes an inconsistency between Witness RE's testimony and her prior statement. The witness did not mention in her statement that Nyiramasuhuko referred to the refugees as dirt or that Nyiramasuhuko said that young girls should be raped. Witness RE's statement indicates that Nyiramasuhuko asked '[w]hat are these people doing here and why don't they kill them?' Further, the Chamber considers Witness RE's testimony was not sufficiently detailed. For example, she did not give any precise time frame about this event, she failed to mention Nyiramasuhuko and Sindikubwabo's form of transport, and she could not recall the time of day of the visit to the BPO. In light of the foregoing, the Chamber finds this evidence insufficient to establish that around 10 June 1994, Nsabimana met with Interim President Sindikubwabo and Nyiramasuhuko at the BPO at which time Nyiramasuhuko asked why Tutsis at the BPO had not been killed. Thus, the Chamber finds this allegation has not been proven beyond a reasonable doubt".[694] - Defect of the Indictment with respect to rapes at Arsène Shalom Ntahobali's house and at the roadbloack in front of Pauline Nyiramasuhuko's residence in Butare: "Lastly, the Ntahobali Defence submits that the allegations that between 21 and 25 April 1994, Ntahobali abducted and confined seven Tutsi girls in his house, including Witness TN, in order to rape them, and that around 28 April 1994, Ntahobali arrested and sexually assaulted a Tutsi girl near the EER were not pled in the Indictment. The Chamber notes that Paragraph 6.27 of the Nyiramasuhuko and Ntahobali Indictment does not mention rape with respect to crimes alleged to have taken place at the roadblock at the Ntahobali residence, nor is Paragraph 6.27 listed in support of the count of rape in the Nyiramasuhuko and Ntahobali Indictment. However, Paragraphs 6.37 and 6.53 of the Indictment, which are listed in support of the charge of rape against Ntahobali, state that Ntahobali, assisted by unknown accomplices, participated in the kidnapping and raping of Tutsi women. Further, it is alleged that during the events referred to in the Indictment, rapes and sexual assaults were widely and notoriously committed throughout Rwanda. The Chamber finds these paragraphs unduly vague and not sufficient to put Ntahobali on notice of the Prosecution's intention to adduce evidence that Ntahobali abducted a Tutsi girl at the roadblock and raped her at the EER; nor do they specifically point to Ntahobali's abduction and raping of Witness TN and other Tutsi girls in his house, in April 1994. Thus, the Indictment was defective in this respect. The Chamber will now consider whether this defect was cured by subsequent Prosecution disclosures. The Prosecution Pre-Trial Brief reiterates the language from Paragraph 6.53 of the Indictment, and adds that Nyiramasuhuko and Ntahobali committed, ordered, aided and abetted their subordinates and others in the carrying out of rapes and sexual assaults of Tutsis. The Chamber also notes that the Prosecution opening statement mentioned rape being used as a tool against Tutsi women. In particular in relation to rape, the Prosecution submitted that Nyiramasuhuko encouraged her son, Ntahobali, to rape Tutsi women. Furthermore, the summary of

693 *Pauline Nyiramasuhuko et al.* Trial Judgement, paras. 2780–2782.

694 *Pauline Nyiramasuhuko et al.* Trial Judgement, paras. 2901–2902 (internal references omitted).

	Prosecution Witness TN's expected evidence contained in the Appendix to the Prosecution Pre-Trial Brief, states that the witness was raped by Ntahobali; that Hutu soldiers penetrated women's vaginas with sticks; that Ntahobali authorised the soldiers to kill anyone they wanted; and that one soldier called Alex took Witness TN as his wife and they fled to Burundi. Witness TN's prior statement of 11–12 March 1998 is consistent with this account. The witness described that on 21 April 1994 Ntahobali, after ordering that six girls—including Witness TN and Philippe's daughter Lillian Umubyeyi—had to go to his house, raped them, one by one. The same night, Witness TN was forced to have sex with soldiers. A few days later, she was raped again by Ntahobali, this time using a handle stick. During the five days the girls were kept in the house, they were repeatedly raped. On 25 April 1994, Shalom told the soldiers they could choose the girls to be their wives, or they were allowed to kill them. Each of the soldiers chose a girl to be his wife. A soldier named Alexis took Witness TN and forced her to go to a refugee camp in Burundi, saying the RPF soldiers were coming. Witness TN described Ntahobali as black, fat and not very tall. She added that he was heavy when he laid on her. The witness explained that she probably could not recognise Shalom if she saw him again, but confirmed Shalom was the person in charge of their hostage while at the house and he ordered their rapes. The Chamber has carefully analysed all the above material and notes that the Prosecution was in receipt of Witness TN's prior statement of 11–12 March 1998 at the time of the Amended Indictment, on 1 March 2001. The Chamber considers that the Prosecution should have been more diligent and included in the Nyiramasuhuko and Ntahobali Indictment the specific details regarding Ntahobali's involvement in the abduction and rape of girls in his compound and house. Nonetheless, the Chamber considers that the evidence contained in Witness TN's summary in the Appendix to the Pre-Trial Brief and in Witness TN's prior statement, which was disclosed in redacted and unredacted forms on 4 November 1998 and 23 April 2001 respectively, provided timely, clear and consistent information and resolved any ambiguity or vagueness in the Indictment. It was also disclosed on 23 May 2001. The Chamber considers that this information did not amount to an expansion of the charges against Ntahobali and provided sufficient notice to enable the Ntahobali Defence to prepare his defence without prejudice, in regard to this allegation. The Chamber therefore finds the defect in the Nyiramasuhuko and Ntahobali Indictment was cured with respect to the allegation that Ntahobali abducted, confined and raped seven Tutsi girls in his house, including Witness TN. In addition, the witness summaries for Prosecution Witnesses SX and TB contained in the Appendix to the Prosecution Pre-Trial Brief set forth allegations that Ntahobali raped Tutsi women at the roadblock in front of his parents' residence. Specifically, the summary of Witness SX's anticipated testimony states that Ntahobali took a girl from the roadblock near his mother's house and raped her about 10 metres away from the EER building. Witness SX provided similar information in his statement of 2 December 1997, disclosed on 4 November 1998, nearly six years before the witness was called to testify. The summary provided for Witness TB in the Appendix to the Prosecution Pre-Trial Brief, sets forth that on about 28 April 1994, Witness TB saw Ntahobali and two soldiers take a girl into the forest near the EER, rape and kill her. In Witness TB's previous statement of 5 December 1997, disclosed to the Defence on 15 November 2000, over three years before the witness was called to testify, Witness TB provided a similar, detailed account of this event. The information provided by Witnesses SX and TB's summaries contained in the Appendix to the Prosecution Pre-Trial Brief, together with their previous statements, sufficiently put the Ntahobali Defence on notice with respect to the allegation that Ntahobali abducted a Tutsi girl at the roadblock and raped her near the EER. In addition, the Chamber finds these Prosecution disclosures were timely, clear and consistent. In light of the foregoing, the Chamber concludes that the

	defect in the Nyiramasuhuko and Ntahobali Indictment as to this allegation was cured and did not prejudice the Defence in the preparation of its case".[695] - Rapes of Tutsi women, including Witness TN, allegedly committed by Arsène Shalom Ntahobali at his house on 21 and 25 April 1994: "The Chamber observes that Witness TN is the only witness who implicates Ntahobali in the abduction and rape of seven Tutsi girls in his house and compound. The Chamber is mindful that Witness TN is a single witness and exercises caution in its analysis of her testimony. The Chamber considers that Witness TN, although a single witness on this event, was a truthful witness, who was brave enough to attend court and give a detailed account of the horrendous rape and abduction allegedly inflicted on her and the other girls by Ntahobali and said soldiers. In the Chamber's view, it is clear from the witness' testimony that these girls were raped by soldiers. What is for the Chamber to determine is whether it was established that Ntahobali played a role in this incident. The witness testified that she and the other girls were abducted from the *secteur* office, where they were guarded by Shalom, and were taken to his house. The witness did not give any further detail concerning the location or the description of the house. As to the identification of Ntahobali, the Chamber notes that in her prior statement, Witness TN explained that on the day of the rape, her abductor was identified by others as 'Shalom'. In the statement, she described Shalom as being of average height, average size, black and of dark skin. The witness however explained that she would not be able to identify Ntahobali if she saw him again, given the circumstances of her encounter with him. Accordingly, when asked to identify Ntahobali in court, Witness TN pointed to a security guard. Although in the Chamber's view Ntahobali's said features could not have changed in any extreme way between 1994, between the time of the alleged rape, and 2002, the time of the witness' testimony in court, it is nevertheless understandable that, after nearly eight years from the abduction and rape, Witness TN was not able to identify Ntahobali in court. In any event, the Chamber notes that the security officer that the witness mistakenly identified as Ntahobali had similar features as those of Ntahobali. Taking all the above circumstances into account, although the Chamber does not discredit Witness TN's testimony, particularly in light of the detailed description of her traumatic experience, it nevertheless finds the evidence insufficient to establish beyond a reasonable doubt that the perpetrator of the alleged abduction and rape was Ntahobali or that the rape actually occurred at Ntahobali's house. The Chamber therefore considers that the Prosecution has not discharged its burden of proof beyond a reasonable doubt in regard to the allegation that Ntahobali abducted seven Tutsi girls to his house in April 1994; that Ntahobali raped at least four of these Tutsi girls personally and instructed and caused the rape of the seven girls by soldiers".[696] - Rape of a Tutsi girl by Arsène Shalom Ntahobali near the roadblock around 28 April 1994: "The Chamber considers that the testimony provided by Prosecution Witness SX with regard to the rape and murder of a Tutsi girl at the roadblock is detailed and believable. Further, it was corroborated by Prosecution Witness TB's testimony which was equally detailed. Both witnesses testified that the girl arrived in a yellow Daihatsu, and that a certain Jean-Pierre was with Ntahobali at the time of the incident. They also stated that the car was stopped at the roadblock and the people inside the car were asked to show their identity cards. Witness TB further testified that she saw Ntahobali drag a girl with braids, who had been in the vehicle, into the woods from her vantage

695 *Pauline Nyiramasuhuko et al.* Trial Judgement, paras. 2933–2942 (internal references omitted).

696 *Pauline Nyiramasuhuko et al.* Trial Judgement, paras. 3129–3131 (internal references omitted).

	point on the main road near the roadblock, and subsequently saw her dead body with vaginal injuries near a tree in the woods, later that evening. Witness SX also witnessed the rape from his hiding place, about 20 metres away from Ntahobali and the victim. The witnesses' descriptions regarding the subsequent burial of the body are also consistent. Witness SX testified that about four days after the girl's death he and some others buried her body in a wooded lot. Similarly, Witness TB testified that the girl's body was later buried by three people, one of whom she identified as Witness SX. As to the time period when this crime allegedly occurred, both Witnesses SX and TB refer to a few days after the roadblock in front of Hotel Ihuliro was erected. In this regard, the Chamber recalls its previous finding that the roadblock was mounted at the end of April 1994. In light of all of the foregoing, the Chamber finds Witnesses TB and SX credible with respect to this allegation, and finds the evidence establishes beyond a reasonable doubt that Ntahobali raped and murdered the young woman who arrived at the roadblock in a yellow Daihatsu, around the end of April 1994".[697] - Rapes committed at the roadblock outside Hotel Ihuliro: "The Chamber was presented with compelling evidence indicating that at the roadblock outside Hotel Ihuliro crimes were committed against Tutsis by the *Interahamwe*. The testimonies of Prosecution Witnesses FA, QCB, SX, TB and TG support the allegation that people were beaten and killed at the roadblock. Further, Witnesses TN, SX and TB also gave evidence of rapes being carried out in the vicinity of the roadblock. The Chamber observes that these were all eyewitnesses. […] Having considered all the evidence before it, the Chamber finds it has been established beyond a reasonable doubt that crimes, in particular beatings, rapes and killings, were carried out against mostly Tutsis, at the roadblock outside Hotel Ihuliro".[698] - Defect of the Indictment with respect to rapes committed by Arsène Shalom Ntahobali at *École évangéliste* of Rwanda (EER) in Butare between mid-May and early June 1994: "The Ntahobali Defence asserts that the allegation that Ntahobali abducted, raped and killed Tutsi refugees on unspecified dates at the EER together with Presidential Guard soldiers, and/or soldiers and/or *Interahamwe* was not pled in the Indictment. The Chamber notes that the Prosecution led evidence through Witness QY at trial that she was raped by soldiers at the EER. Paragraph 6.30 of the Nyiramasuhuko and Ntahobali Indictment alleges that after Nyiramasuhuko and Ntahobali attacked the refugees at the BPO between 19 April and late June 1994, the surviving refugees were taken to various locations in the *préfecture* to be executed, notably in the woods next to the EER. Significantly there is no mention of Ntahobali's involvement in or responsibility for rapes at or near the EER. However, Paragraph 6.37 of the Nyiramasuhuko and Ntahobali Indictment alleges that Ntahobali, assisted by unknown 'accomplices', participated in kidnapping and raping Tutsi women. Insofar as Paragraph 6.37 fails to include any details as to where or when Ntahobali was allegedly involved in such rapes, the Chamber finds this paragraph defective. The Chamber notes that the summary of anticipated evidence for Witness QY in the Appendix to the Prosecution Pre-Trial Brief states only that Witness QY saw Ntahobali beat people and appoint soldiers to take away five people at the EER. It makes no reference to her being raped at the EER by soldiers nor does it outline any role that Ntahobali may have played. Accordingly, the Chamber will not make any finding as to Ntahobali's alleged role in the rape of Witness QY at or near the EER".[699]

697 *Pauline Nyiramasuhuko et al.* Trial Judgement, paras. 3132–3135 (internal references omitted).

698 *Pauline Nyiramasuhuko et al.* Trial Judgement, paras. 3141, 3144 (internal references omitted).

699 *Pauline Nyiramasuhuko et al.* Trial Judgement, paras. 3842–3845 (internal references omitted).

	- Rapes at *École évangéliste* of Rwanda (EER) in Butare: "With respect to allegations of rape, Witness QY testified that one night, after soldiers and *Interahamwe* selected young men and girls, and took them to the woods, some soldiers remained behind and selected girls, among them Witness QY. Witness QY provided compelling and detailed testimony that she was raped at the EER by a corporal. Although corroboration of Witness QY's testimony concerning her rape is not required, Witness RE's testimony provided corroboration that young girls were raped at the EER and that those who refused to be raped were killed. Witness QBQ also testified that refugees were raped by soldiers from the ESO at the EER. Although Des Forges was called as an expert witness and not a witness of fact, her testimony recounting her interviews with Nsabimana nevertheless corroborates that rapes occurred at the EER. The Chamber notes Witness QY did not mention her rape in her first or second statements. When it was put to her that she first mentioned being raped at the EER by a soldier in May 1994 in her third statement of 11/13 March 1998, Witness QY explained that she did not previously have the courage to discuss such crimes, nor had she been asked about it by the investigators. The Chamber notes that Witness QY gave her first statement in January 1997 whereas Ntahobali was only later charged with rape in the Indictment issued on 16 May 1997. Accordingly, the Chamber accepts Witness QY's explanation that she was not asked about rapes by the investigators at the time of her first statement. Insofar as her second statement given in September 1997 also failed to mention any account of rape, although by this time Ntahobali had been charged with rape in the Indictment of 16 May 1997, the Chamber accepts her explanation that she did not have the courage to discuss such crimes with the Tribunal investigators. In view of the fact that the Chamber considers Witness QY's testimony with respect to the transfer to the EER and the attacks to have been largely consistent with the testimony of other Prosecution witnesses, and therefore credible, the Chamber accepts Witness QY's explanation for failing to discuss her rape at the time of giving her first and second statements. When Witness QY was also questioned as to why she had not confronted her attacker during his trial in Rwandan courts, Witness QY was unable to give any explanation. Witness QY also testified that her rape at the EER was her first sexual experience and the only time she was raped at the EER. When it was put to her that her fourth prior statement of 24 July 2000 said she had been previously raped by two soldiers in April 1994 near Kibeho Parish, she declined to answer whether she had been previously raped. She subsequently disowned the content of that statement and later testified that she was not raped at Kibeho. Accordingly, the Chamber does not accept Witness QY's testimony as to the Kibeho rape. Nevertheless, the Chamber considers Witness QY's contradictory account about the Kibeho rape does not undermine the reliability of her testimony with respect to her rape at the EER. Witness QY was cross-examined about the details of her rape at the EER. It was put to Witness QY that her third statement said that a soldier found her in an EER classroom at night and raped her at the compound of the EER school after taking her skirt, whereas her testimony was that soldiers took her from the veranda around 6.00 p.m. and took her to woods nearby where they forced her to completely undress. The Chamber has had regard to these alleged inconsistencies and does not consider they go to the root of her account such as to undermine the credibility of her overall account that she was a victim of rape. As to the testimony presented by the Defence that no attacks occurred at the EER, the Chamber finds this testimony to be not credible. The Chamber has found the Prosecution evidence as to the attacks at the EER to be both credible and reliable. Further, most of the Defence witnesses who testified in this respect were either relatives or friends of Ntahobali such that they were residing in the hotel belonging to Maurice Ntahobali during the events between April and July 1994, for which reason the Chamber considers these witnesses may have had a motive to lie. Having regard to the foregoing, the Chamber finds it established beyond a reasonable doubt that between mid-May and the beginning of June 1994: soldiers escorted and

	beat the refugees on the way to the EER; Ntahobali was involved in and led *Interahamwe* in attacks against, and abductions of, Tutsi refugees during their stay at the EER; soldiers, both alone and accompanied by Ntahobali, came to the EER and were also involved in abductions of refugees during the same period; soldiers raped women and young girls at or near the EER school; Ntahobali, *Interahamwe* and soldiers killed the abducted Tutsi refugees in the woods near the EER school complex. However, the Chamber does not find it established beyond a reasonable doubt that Ntahobali led the soldiers to the EER".[700] - Defect of the Indictment with respect to rapes at Nyange: "However, with respect to Witness QBP's testimony regarding rapes at Nyange, the Chamber notes that neither Paragraph 6.38 of the Nsabimana and Nteziryayo Indictment, nor Paragraph 6.41 of the Kanyabashi Indictment which concern the allegation of the refugees' transfer to Nyange, mention rape as one of the acts carried out upon refugees at Nyange. In the Chamber's view, to base a finding on the evidence of Witness QBP's testimony would amount to an expansion of charges against the Accused which would prejudice the Accused. As such, the Chamber considers the matter of rapes at Nyange falls outside the scope of the Indictments and will not make any finding in this respect".[701] - Rapes at Nyange: "Witness QBP is the sole Prosecution witness to testify first-hand about events at Nyange. Witness QBP testified that upon arriving at Nyange in the afternoon, the bus drivers and *Interahamwe* threw the passengers out of the bus like 'dirt'. She testified that there seemed to be a plan because there was an armed *commune* policeman on the spot with nothing to guard and that immediately after they arrived, people came from everywhere shouting, '[p]ower! Power!' and proceeded to strip the refugees of their clothes and belongings. Witness QBP testified that at nightfall the *Interahamwe* started killing and raping the refugees, and she was also raped. With respect to rapes at Nyange, Witness QBP testified that the *Interahamwe* started killing and raping the refugees at nightfall. In cross-examination, Witness QBP was asked about her prior statement where Witness QBP said that the *Interahamwe* started raping women without wasting much time after they arrived at Nyange. The Chamber considers that Witness QBP's testimony that attacks and rapes at Nyange commenced at nightfall is consistent with her testimony that they arrived at Nyange 'at the end of the afternoon'. This further corresponds with the testimony of Witness SD who said that the buses arrived at the BPO at 6.00 p.m., as well as the testimony of Prosecution Witnesses QY and RE that they left the BPO and arrived at Nyange in the early evening. Therefore, the Chamber finds Witness QBP's testimony is credible. Nonetheless, recalling the Chamber's previous finding that rapes at Nyange falls outside the scope of Paragraph 6.38 of the Nsabimana and Nteziryayo Indictment, and Paragraph 6.41 of the Kanyabashi Indictment which concern the allegation of the refugees' transfer to Nyange, the Chamber will not make any finding in this respect. Witness QBP was also questioned as to her prior written statement, in which she stated she was taken back to Butare by the *Interahamwe* who had raped her. Witness QBP explained that the *Interahamwe* who had raped her accompanied her from the hill to the road and then showed her a young refugee man who was supposed to help her with carrying one of her children. The Chamber finds this explanation credible […] In light of the foregoing evidence, the Chamber finds it established beyond a reasonable doubt that the refugees who left the

700 *Pauline Nyiramasuhuko et al.* Trial Judgement, paras. 3959–3965 (internal references omitted).

701 *Pauline Nyiramasuhuko et al.* Trial Judgement, para. 4057 (internal reference omitted).

	BPO by bus on day one were attacked and raped by *Interahamwe* at Nyange and all but a handful of those refugees were killed".[702] - Defect of the Indictment with respect to the distribution of condoms by Pauline Nyiramasuhuko: "The Chamber notes that as submitted by the Ntahobali Defence, the allegation that Nyiramasuhuko handed out two boxes of condoms in Cyarwa-Sumo *secteur*, Ngoma *commune* in early June 1994, and requested that the condoms be distributed among the young Hutu men to rape the Tutsi women and then kill them, is not specifically pled in the Nyiramasuhuko and Ntahobali Indictment. The Chamber therefore finds the Indictment to be defective in this regard. Recalling the principles of notice previously articulated in this Judgement (2.5.4), the Chamber will now determine whether the Indictment has been cured of these defects through subsequent Prosecution disclosures. The Chamber observes that the witness summary grid in the Appendix to the Prosecution Pre-Trial Brief lists one witness, Witness FAE, who was expected to testify that in Cyarwa-Sumo *secteur*, she saw Nyiramasuhuko with a gun, accompanied by four men. One of these men handed over a box of condoms to another woman, and instructed her to give them to their young supporters so that they could use them when raping the Tutsi women. The witness summary further states that Nyiramasuhuko told this woman that Tutsi women were to be killed 'because they are taking their husbands'. The Chamber notes that the summary of the intended evidence of Witness FAE provided in the Appendix to the Prosecution Pre-Trial Brief provides adequate details as to the location where this event purportedly occurred, but does not specify a time. The Chamber observes that the prior statement of Witness FAE, dated 7 May 1999, was disclosed to the Defence on 15 November 2000, 13 December 2001 and again on 21 December 2001. This statement made further specific references to the location, and specifically mentioned the time frame as 'early June 1994'. These disclosures were made well before the start of Witness FAE's testimony on 17 March 2004. The Chamber finds that the substance of Witness FAE's previous statement is consistent with the summary of her anticipated testimony contained in the Appendix to the Pre-Trial Brief regarding Nyiramasuhuko's presence in Cyarwa-Sumo *secteur* and her actions and statements in distributing the condoms and inciting others to rape and kill Tutsi women. For the foregoing reasons, the Chamber considers that the defect in the Nyiramasuhuko and Ntahobali Indictment is cured by the disclosure of clear, consistent and timely information. Consequently, Nyiramasuhuko was reasonably able to understand the nature of the charges against her and there was no prejudice to the preparation of her defence".[703] - Distribution of condoms by Pauline Nyiramasuhuko to be used in the raping of Tutsi women in Cyarwa-Sumo secteur at the beginning of June 1994: "The issues at hand are whether Nyiramasuhuko was present at Cyarwa-Sumo *secteur* in the beginning of June 1994, and whether she in fact came to distribute condoms intended for distribution to the *Interahamwe*. Witness FAE is the only Prosecution eyewitness to testify as to the allegation that Nyiramasuhuko came to Cyarwa-Sumo *secteur*, Ngoma *commune*, in the beginning of June 1994 and distributed condoms for the *Interahamwe*, to be used in the raping and killing of Tutsi women in that *secteur*. She provided extensive testimony on Nyiramasuhuko's arrival in Cyarwa-Sumo *secteur*. She knew Nyiramasuhuko from when she worked at the University, when she went to MRND meetings with her husband, and when Nyiramasuhuko took her mother to hospital to be treated. She described her vehicle as a white double-cabin vehicle,

702 *Pauline Nyiramasuhuko et al.* Trial Judgement, paras. 4183–4185, 4192 (internal references omitted).
703 *Pauline Nyiramasuhuko et al.* Trial Judgement, paras. 4923–4929 (internal references omitted).

	and delineated and identified the passengers in the vehicle and the order in which they were sitting. Witness FAE described that Nyiramasuhuko wore a camouflage military uniform with the sleeves rolled up. Furthermore, the witness provided a coherent analysis of the events that occurred. She avers that only the driver, Doctor Ndindabahizi and Remera, who was sitting in the front next to the driver, alighted from the vehicle, while the three remaining passengers stayed within the vehicle. The witness also proffered that the boxes handed over were khaki-coloured, with a drawing of a condom upon them, and the word '*Prudence*' marked on its surface. She was able to describe the dimensions of the boxes as well, comparing them to the screen before her during her testimony at trial. The witness also provided detailed excerpts of what was said by the relevant actors at this point. She stated that Ndindabahizi gave the first box to her female neighbour and said, '[g]ive this to our young *Interahamwe* for them to use when they rape the Tutsi, so that they are not contaminated with HIV or AIDS.' The Chamber notes that Witness FAE provided inconsistent testimony as to who gave the second box of condoms to the woman. Initially she said that Sibomana, who was sitting next to Nyiramasuhuko in the back seat of the car, handed Nyiramasuhuko a box which she gave to the woman. Nyiramasuhuko then said: 'Go and distribute these condoms to your young men, so that they use them to rape Tutsi women and to protect themselves from AIDS, and after having raped them they should kill all of them. Let no Tutsi woman survive because they take away our husbands.' Witness FAE stated that she could hear these words clearly because the vehicle in which Nyiramasuhuko sat was located close to the window through which she was watching the events unfold. The witness also testified that Nyiramasuhuko gave the box to Sibomana, who in turn gave the box through the window to the woman. Witness FAE then reiterated that Nyiramasuhuko handed the box to the lady, explaining that she could see that the sleeves of Nyiramasuhuko's shirt were rolled up when she handed the box through the window. The Chamber notes inconsistencies between Witness FAE's prior statement and her testimony at trial. The prior statement declared that Nyiramasuhuko was seated in the front of the car with a gun between her legs. However, she did not describe the presence of a gun at any point in her testimony. The witness responded that she merely answered questions posed by the Prosecution and did not improvise or preempt with information that was not specifically requested. Witness FAE's statement and testimony were also inconsistent as to the order of seating in the vehicle among the passengers. In her prior statement, Witness FAE stated that Nyiramasuhuko was seated in the front of the vehicle. However, in her testimony, she said Nyiramasuhuko was seated in the back. She justified this discrepancy by offering an explanation as to the dynamics of a double-cabin vehicle of this type. She claimed that the front part of the vehicle encompasses a cabin and the back is the bed of the truck, in which no one sits. Nyiramasuhuko was sitting in the back seat of the front cabin of the vehicle. The witness explained that the inconsistencies occurred because of her inability to master the French language, which also prevented her from correcting the inconsistencies at the time. She asserted that she gave this prior statement in French without an interpreter present, which accounted for these discrepancies. The Chamber accepts Witness FAE's explanation with regard to the aforementioned discrepancies, which the Chamber does not consider, in any case, to be material. Witness WZNA provided a detailed description of Witness FAE's sitting room window, overlooking the road, and what could be viewed from that standpoint. Witness WZNA stated that the front side of the neighbouring house could be seen but that the front door was not visible. Although this does not provide corroboration to Witness FAE's testimony that she was at the window when she viewed the events in front of her neighbour's house, it does confirm that Witness FAE would have been able to see both the car and the passengers seated within. Witnesses MNW, WZNA and WNMN all denied that Nyiramasuhuko was present during this time in Cyarwa-Sumo *secteur*. Witness MNW lived at the crossroads and so would have seen any vehicle that would have passed during that time. However, Witness MNW's theory as to why Nyiramasuhuko did not visit the *secteur*

	in June 1994 is based on the fact that she did not hear about it from others or her husband's boss. She had a 'drinking joint' in her house and claimed that if Nyiramasuhuko had come or said these things, she would have heard about it from her patrons. However, Witness MNW conceded that the bar she operated was closed from the first few days of June 1994 for the rest of the month due to lack of supplies. The Chamber therefore considers that the testimony of Witness MNW in this regard is of limited value. Not only is the witness unreliable in terms of Nyiramasuhuko's whereabouts during that period, but she did not demonstrate first-hand knowledge of the situation. Witness WZNA stated that his friend Sibomana, who according to Witness FAE was in the vehicle with Nyiramasuhuko on that day, would have told him about delivering condoms in the presence of Nyiramasuhuko. This would have been an unusual turn of events, considering that he was in the company of a minister. Witness WZNA also claimed to have seen Witness FAE and her children in their house in June 1994. The witness based his conclusion that Nyiramasuhuko was not present at that time and did not distribute condoms, on the fact that Sibomana did not inform him of its occurrence. His evidence in this regard is neither compelling nor conclusive. Witness WNMN was a native of Mpare *secteur*, but lived with his sister in Cyarwa-Sumo *secteur* while he was teaching. In 1994, the academic year did not follow the normal timetable due to the war. He testified that after the Easter holidays, classes resumed during the first two weeks of the month of May 1994, and he taught for about two weeks and three or five days. During this time, the witness went to his sister's house each day as the road to his school passed in front of her house. He would go from his parents' house in Mpare *secteur*. The witness averred that after this period, he saw refugees coming in from other *communes* and the school was forced to shut down because there were too many refugees. After the classes stopped he went home to his parents' house. He also stated that he met Witness FAE at his sister's home towards the end of June 1994, when he spent four days there. The Chamber notes that Witness WNMN was not present in Cyarwa-Sumo *secteur* during the time of this incident, as he claimed to have been at his parents' house. He may have visited Cyarwa-Sumo *secteur*, but these visits may have been sporadic. Therefore Witness WNMN would not have been in a position to provide eyewitness testimony or direct knowledge of the whereabouts of Nyiramasuhuko. Each of the Defence witnesses provided their own hypotheses as to why Nyiramasuhuko could not have possibly distributed condoms and ordered rapes. Witness MNW initially testified that she had not heard any news of condom distribution in her *secteur*, which she claimed she was in a prime position to hear because of the bar in her house. Under cross-examination, it arose that Witness MNW had heard people talk about condoms and had even seen pictures of condoms. However, she did not elaborate as to whether the condoms she had heard of were linked back to Nyiramasuhuko. On the contrary, she claimed that this allegation against Nyiramasuhuko was untrue because as a mother, a married Rwandan woman, and a Minister of a high post, Nyiramasuhuko would not risk distributing condoms for fear of being labelled an 'uneducated person'. Witness WZNA stated that, due to her ministerial position, Nyiramasuhuko would not have had the time to complete such tasks. However, Witness WNMN recognised that he was not in a position to report as to Nyiramasuhuko's actions or words from April to 4 July 1994. Defence Witnesses MNW, WZNA and WNMN testified as to when they saw Witness FAE between April and June 1994. Witness MNW stated that she did not see Witness FAE in June 1994. Witness WZNA testified that between April and July 1994 he visited Witness FAE's house on multiple occasions and confirmed that both Witness FAE and her children were inside the house on these occasions. Witness WNMN stated that he saw Witness FAE twice in May 1994 and again towards the end of June 1994, at his sister's home. The Defence witnesses are not consistent as to when they saw Witness FAE. However, the Chamber notes that they may have seen her at different times and on different occasions. Witness FAE testified that she was only away from her house from 23 April 1994 to early June 1994. Nonetheless, the Chamber finds it unbelievable that during

	that time, Witness FAE would be openly at home with her children or that she would be visiting Witness WNMN's sister, who was a Hutu. Witness FAE testified that between April and July 1994, Tutsis were being pursued and she was hiding in various locations. The Chamber therefore finds Witnesses WZNA and WNMN not credible on this point. Nyiramasuhuko admitted she knew Witness FAE, but testified that the present allegation was implausible. She would not have sat in a vehicle along with Doctor Ndindabahizi, the leader of the PSD Party in Butare, and would not have gone with him to distribute condoms. The Chamber notes that Defence Witnesses MNW, WZNA and WNMN all provided hearsay accounts as to why the allegation is implausible, without any convincing and detailed analyses. Indeed, among the Defence witnesses there are inconsistencies as to when they saw Witness FAE. Witness MNW testified that she did not see Witness FAE in June 1994, whereas Witnesses WZNA and WNMN both testified as to seeing Witness FAE in June 1994. The Chamber considers it impossible to rely on these witnesses to establish that Witness FAE was not in the area in June 1994 or that Nyiramasuhuko did not visit the area at that time. The Nyiramasuhuko Defence relied on Witness WNMN in submitting that Witness FAE was a 'militant' member of the Association of Genocide Survivors, an association run by *Ibuka* and known for fabricating testimony against accused at the ICTR. Prosecution Witness FAE was asked during cross-examination whether the survivors association that she belonged to had a custom of character destruction. She responded: 'We are telling you what we saw and we are telling you about things that we heard with our own ears.' When asked whether they denounced people in order to be requited with scholarships for their children, she responded that she, and no one else, paid for her children's studies. Taking into account the foregoing, the Chamber finds that Witness WNMN's assertions about Witness FAE were not sufficiently credible or convincing to undermine the veracity of Witness FAE's testimony under oath. The Chamber recalls that Prosecution Witness FAE is the only Prosecution witness to implicate Nyiramasuhuko in the events at Cyarwa-Sumo *secteur*. The Chamber recalls that it may rule on the basis of a single testimony if, in its opinion, that testimony is relevant and credible (2.7.3.3). It is not disputed that Witness FAE knew Nyiramasuhuko prior to the events and that she identified the Accused clearly in court and as being present at the time of the alleged events. Although there were slight inconsistencies in her testimony, the Chamber determines that Witness FAE was a reliable witness who provided credible testimony with regard to this allegation. Her proximity to the location where the incident occurred placed her in a strong position to have witnessed the distribution of condoms as specified. The Chamber recalls Nyiramasuhuko's alibi evidence for early June 1994 (3.6.19.3.2.1). The Chamber has considered this evidence with regard to the present allegation and finds that the Prosecution has discharged its burden of proof. Regardless of whether Nyiramasuhuko was staying in Murambi, Gitarama *préfecture*, from 12 April to 5 June 1994, the short distance between Butare and Murambi would have permitted Nyiramasuhuko to be present in Cyarwa-Sumo *secteur*, for the distribution of condoms at this time (3.6.19.4.1). The Chamber notes that the analysis regarding Nyiramasuhuko's other alibi evidence in relation to June 1994, is equally relevant to this allegation (3.6.19.4.1). Therefore, Nyiramasuhuko's alibi evidence does not raise a reasonable doubt that she was present at Cyarwa-Sumo *secteur* in early June 1994. The Chamber finds that the testimony of Prosecution Witness FAE, provides sufficient and unchallenged detail so as to establish beyond a reasonable doubt the allegation that Nyiramasuhuko came to Cyarwa-Sumo *secteur*, Ngoma *commune*, in the beginning of June 1994 and distributed condoms for the *Interahamwe*, to be used in the raping and killing of Tutsi women in that *secteur*. The Chamber further finds that Nyiramasuhuko ordered the woman to whom she distributed the condoms to '[g]o and distribute these condoms to your young men, so that they use them to rape Tutsi women and to protect themselves from AIDS, and

	after having raped them they should kill all of them. Let no Tutsi woman survive because they take away our husbands'".[704] - Defect in the Pauline Nyiramasuhuko and Arsène Shalom Ntahobali Indictment of pleading the rapes committed at the roadblock near Hotel Ihuliro as genocide, persecutions as CAH, other inhumane acts as CAH and violence to life, health and physical or mental well-being as a violation of Article 3 common to the Geneva Conventions and of Additional Protocol II (WC): "As a preliminary matter, the Chamber notes that Paragraph 6.27 of the Nyiramasuhuko and Ntahobali Indictment, which pertains to the allegations at the Hotel Ihuliro roadblock, and which was pled in support of the count of genocide, does not allege that rape was perpetrated during the abductions and killings of Tutsis at this location. This Indictment paragraph was not pled in support of the count alleging rape as a crime against humanity or outrages upon personal dignity. Paragraph 6.53 of the Indictment, pled in support of both genocide and rape as a crime against humanity and outrages upon personal dignity, alleges that rapes were widely committed throughout Rwanda. However this paragraph does not identify any location in Butare *préfecture* where these alleged rapes occurred. The crime of rape features prominently in Paragraph 6.37 of the Indictment, which alleges that Ntahobali kidnapped and raped Tutsi women. Given this allegation, the Chamber considers it significant that it was not pled in support of genocide, but was instead pled in support of rape as a crime against humanity and outrages upon personal dignity. Reading the Indictment as a whole, the Chamber cannot conclude that the Prosecution pled rapes in support of genocide. In particular, the Chamber notes that the paragraph concerning the Hotel Ihuliro roadblock omitted any reference to rape. Moreover, the paragraph that explicitly ties Ntahobali to rape was not pled as genocide. The Indictment is therefore defective in failing to plead rape as genocide. The Chamber recalls that defects in the Indictment can be cured if the Prosecution provides information that is timely, consistent and clear (2.5.4). Although the Prosecution Pre-Trial Brief and opening statement make reference to rape as genocide, these indications do not clarify whether the Prosecution intended to pursue this allegation against the Accused. Similarly, the Appendix to the Pre-Trial Brief provides witness summaries that are pled in support of genocide and that allege various rapes and killings, but there is no clear indication of whether the rapes themselves are intended to support this charge in addition to the killings. The Chamber also recalls that on 17 August 1998 the Prosecution filed a request for leave to amend the Indictment a second time. In its request, the Prosecution submitted that '[t]he new charges contained in the proposed amended indictment, accurately reflect the totality of the accused['s] alleged criminal conduct and allows the Prosecutor to present the full scope of available, relevant evidence'. This proposed Indictment added various charges, including rape as a crime against humanity pled against Nyiramasuhuko. No mention was made of pleading rape as genocide. The Chamber granted the Prosecution request on 10 August 1999. While there is ample notice that Nyiramasuhuko and Ntahobali were being charged with rapes under the counts of rape as crime against humanity, and of outrages upon personal dignity as a serious violation of Article 3 common to the Geneva Conventions and of Additional Protocol II thereto, the Prosecution provided insufficient notice of its intention to pursue rape as genocide. Under the present circumstances, the Chamber concludes that the Prosecution did not provide sufficient notice that could be capable of curing the defects in the Indictment. Because it would be prejudicial to hold the Accused responsible for a charge of which they had insufficient notice, the Chamber will not enter a conviction for genocide on the basis of any rapes that occurred at the Hotel Ihuliro roadblock. The Chamber notes, however, that it will mention rapes in the course of its legal findings on genocide. This

704 *Pauline Nyiramasuhuko et al.* Trial Judgement, paras. 4965–4985 (internal references omitted).

	will be done to convey the entire set of facts in a coherent fashion, and will not be taken into account by the Chamber in assessing genocide. Instead, they will be considered when assessing the counts of rape as a crime against humanity, and outrages upon personal dignity as a serious violation of Article 3 common to the Geneva Conventions and of Additional Protocol II thereto".[705] "For similar reasons, the Chamber will not address rapes when considering persecution and other inhumane acts as crimes against humanity, and violence to life, health and physical or mental well-being of persons as a serious violation of Article 3 common to the Geneva Conventions and of Additional Protocol II thereto".[706] - Responsibility of Arsène Shalom Ntahobali for rapes committed at the roadblock near Hotel Ihuliro: "In April 1994 Ntahobali manned the roadblock near Hotel Ihuliro. With the assistance of soldiers and other unknown persons he utilised the roadblock to abduct and kill members of the Tutsi population. Towards the end of April 1994, Ntahobali personally raped and murdered one Tutsi girl, and instructed the *Interahamwe* to kill Léopold Ruvurajabo, who was subsequently killed, at the roadblock near Hotel Ihuliro. It was established that various crimes, in particular beatings, rapes and killings, were carried out mostly against Tutsis at this roadblock during the relevant time period (3.6.23.4). The Chamber recalls that it will not take into account rapes when assessing genocide. Instead, they will be considered when assessing the counts of rape as a crime against humanity, and outrages upon personal dignity as a serious violation of Article 3 common to the Geneva Conventions and of Additional Protocol II thereto. The Chamber finds that Ntahobali intentionally committed the mentioned crimes".[707] - Defect in the Pauline Nyiramasuhuko and Arsène Shalom Ntahobali Indictment of pleading the rapes committed at the Butare prefecture office (BPO) as genocide, persecutions as CAH, other inhumane acts as CAH and violence to life, health and physical or mental well-being as a violation of Article 3 common to the Geneva Conventions and of Additional Protocol II (WC): "The Chamber notes that Paragraph 6.30 of the Nyiramasuhuko and Ntahobali Indictment which pertains to the allegations at the Butare *préfecture* office, and which was pled in support of the count of genocide, does not allege that rape was perpetrated during the attacks, abductions, and killings of Tutsis there. This Indictment paragraph was not pled in support of the count alleging rape as a crime against humanity or outrages upon personal dignity. As discussed above (4.2.2.3.11), Paragraph 6.53 of the Indictment, pled in support of both genocide and rape as a crime against humanity and or outrages upon personal dignity, alleges that rapes were widely committed throughout Rwanda. However this paragraph does not identify any location in Butare *préfecture* where these alleged rapes occurred. The crime of rape features prominently in Paragraph 6.37 of the Indictment, which alleges that Ntahobali kidnapped and raped Tutsi women. Given this allegation, the Chamber considers it significant that it was not pled in support of genocide, but was instead pled in support of rape as a crime against humanity and outrages upon personal dignity. Reading the Indictment as a whole, the Chamber cannot conclude that the Prosecution pled rapes in support of genocide. In particular, the Chamber notes that the paragraphs concerning the Butare *préfecture* office omitted any reference to rape. Moreover, the paragraph that explicitly ties Ntahobali to rape was not pled as genocide. The Indictment is therefore defective in failing to plead rape as genocide. The Chamber recalls that defects in the Indictment

705 *Pauline Nyiramasuhuko et al.* Trial Judgement, paras. 5828–5837 (internal references omitted).

706 *Pauline Nyiramasuhuko et al.* Trial Judgement, fn. 14709.

707 *Pauline Nyiramasuhuko et al.* Trial Judgement, paras. 5842–5844.

can be cured if the Prosecution provides information that is timely, consistent and clear (2.5.4). Although the Prosecution Pre-Trial Brief and opening statement make reference to rape as genocide, these indications do not clarify whether the Prosecution intended to pursue this allegation against the Accused. Similarly, the Appendix to the Pre-Trial Brief provides witness summaries that are pled in support of genocide and that allege various rapes and killings, but there is no clear indication of whether the rapes themselves are intended to support this charge in addition to the killings. The Chamber also recalls that, on 17 August 1998, the Prosecution filed a request for leave to amend the Indictment a second time. In its request, the Prosecution submitted that '[t]he new charges contained in the proposed amended indictment, accurately reflect the totality of the accused['s] ... alleged criminal conduct and allows the Prosecutor to present the full scope of available, relevant evidence ....'. This proposed Indictment added various charges, including rape as a crime against humanity pled against Nyiramasuhuko. No mention was made of pleading rape as genocide. The Chamber granted the Prosecution request on 10 August 1999. While there is ample notice that Nyiramasuhuko and Ntahobali were being charged with rapes under the counts of rape as crime against humanity, and of outrages upon personal dignity as a serious violation of Article 3 common to the Geneva Conventions and of Additional Protocol II thereto, the Prosecution provided insufficient notice of its intention to pursue rape as genocide. Under the present circumstances, the Chamber concludes that the Prosecution did not provide sufficient notice that could be capable of curing the defects in the Indictment. Because it would be prejudicial to hold the Accused responsible for a charge of which they had insufficient notice, the Chamber will not enter a conviction for genocide on the basis of any rapes that occurred. The Chamber notes, however, that it will mention rapes in the course of its legal findings on genocide. This will be done to convey the entire set of facts in a coherent fashion, including that the intensity and repeated nature of the attacks provides evidence that rape was, in fact, utilised as a form of genocide. The Chamber will not take this into account in assessing genocide, but instead will consider this for the counts of rape as a crime against humanity and outrages upon personal dignity as a serious violation of Article 3 common to the Geneva Conventions and of Additional Protocol II thereto".[708]

"For similar reasons, the Chamber will not take rapes into account when considering persecution and other inhumane acts as crimes against humanity, and violence to life, health and physical or mental well-being or persons as a serious violation of Article 3 common to the Geneva Conventions and of Additional Protocol II thereto".[709]

- Rapes committed at the Butare prefecture office (BPO):

"As an introduction, the Chamber notes that, as the violence in other parts of Rwanda pushed people to seek refuge in places they considered safe like churches and government offices, numerous already traumatised, mainly Tutsi, civilians went to the Butare *préfecture* office seeking refuge. Hoping to find safety and security, they instead found themselves subject to abductions, rapes and murder. The evidence presented by these survivors, and accepted by the Chamber, is among the worst encountered by this Chamber; it paints a clear picture of unfathomable depravity and sadism. Between mid-May and mid-June 1994 Nyiramasuhuko, Ntahobali, *Interahamwe* and soldiers went to the BPO to abduct hundreds of Tutsis; the Tutsi refugees were physically assaulted and raped; and were killed in various locations throughout Butare *préfecture*. In mid-May 1994, Nyiramasuhuko, Ntahobali and about 10 *Interahamwe* came to the BPO aboard a camouflaged pickup. Nyiramasuhuko pointed out Tutsi refugees to the *Interahamwe*, ordering them to force the refugees onto the pickup (3.6.19.4.6; 3.6.19.4.11). Ntahobali also gave the *Interahamwe* orders, telling them to stop loading

708 *Pauline Nyiramasuhuko et al.* Trial Judgement, paras. 5857–5865 (internal references omitted).

709 *Pauline Nyiramasuhuko et al.* Trial Judgement, fn. 14726.

| | the truck because it could not accept anymore dead. The refugees were taken to other locations in Butare to be killed. Therefore, both Nyiramasuhuko and Ntahobali were responsible for ordering the killings of numerous Tutsi refugees who were forced on board the pickup. Furthermore, Witness TA and two other women were raped during this mid-May attack. […] Witness TA was brutally raped by a gang of about eight *Interahamwe* in addition to Ntahobali. At least two other Tutsi women were raped on this occasion by the *Interahamwe*. This was the first of many such attacks from mid-May until mid-June 1994 during which Tutsi women, including Witness TA were raped (3.6.19.4.6; 3.6.19.4.11). […] The Chamber recalls that it will not take rapes into account in assessing genocide, but instead will consider them for charges that were properly pled. There was no evidence of Nyiramasuhuko's direct involvement in ordering the rape of Witness TA or the other Tutsi women on this occasion in mid-May 1994. Nonetheless, the *Interahamwe* were acting under the orders of Ntahobali and Nyiramasuhuko to load the truck with people. The *Interahamwe* accompanied Ntahobali and Nyiramasuhuko who were in the cabin of the vehicle as it transported the *Interahamwe* to the BPO. This assisted, encouraged or lent moral support to the perpetration of the rapes and had a substantial effect on the realisation of these crimes. Therefore, Nyiramasuhuko, by her presence and position of authority, is guilty of aiding and abetting the rapes at the BPO. […] Likewise, Nyiramasuhuko issued instructions to rape the women. […] During the last half of May 1994, Ntahobali and *Interahamwe* came to the BPO on two more occasions. Ntahobali violently raped Witness TA, hitting her on the head. *Interahamwe* following the orders of Ntahobali raped six other women. In a subsequent attack during this same time period, Ntahobali ordered about seven other *Interahamwe* to rape Witness TA (3.6.19.4.11). As discussed above, the Chamber considers the bodily harm or the mental harm inflicted on the Tutsi refugees at the BPO in the perpetration of these rapes was of such a serious nature as to threaten the destruction in whole or in part of the Tutsi ethnic group. These Tutsis were entirely helpless and consisted mainly of women and children. The only reasonable conclusion is that Ntahobali and his co-perpetrators possessed genocidal intent in committing these rapes. However, as stated above, the Chamber will not take rapes into account in assessing genocide, but instead will consider them for charges that were properly pled. Around the end of May to the beginning of June 1994, Ntahobali, Nyiramasuhuko and *Interahamwe* came to the BPO on board a camouflaged pickup on three occasions in one night. They abducted Tutsi refugees each time, some of whom were forced to undress, and took them to other sites in Butare *préfecture* to be killed. Nyiramasuhuko ordered *Interahamwe* to rape refugees (3.6.19.4.7; 3.6.19.4.11). This evidences Nyiramasuhuko's intent to destroy, in whole or in part, the Tutsi group. The *Interahamwe* beat, abused and raped many Tutsi women. As discussed above, the Chamber considers the bodily harm or the mental harm inflicted on the Tutsi refugees at the BPO in the perpetration of these rapes was of such a serious nature as to threaten the destruction in whole or in part of the Tutsi ethnic group. They were all committed with genocidal intent. Therefore, the acts of Nyiramasuhuko and Ntahobali constitute genocide. The Chamber again recalls that it will not take rapes into account in assessing genocide, but instead will consider them for charges that were properly pled. In the first half of June 1994, Nyiramasuhuko ordered *Interahamwe* to rape Tutsi women at the BPO and as a result numerous women were raped at that location. Ntahobali, injured soldiers, and *Interahamwe* came to the BPO to rape women and abduct refugees. During at least one of these attacks, Ntahobali again handed Witness TA over to about seven *Interahamwe* to rape Witness TA (3.6.19.4.9; 3.6.19.4.11). Each of these attacks constitutes the *actus reus* of genocide. Likewise, as discussed above, the Chamber finds Nyiramasuhuko and Ntahobali possessed genocidal intent. Moreover, the Chamber finds that Ntahobali aided and abetted the rapes of Witness TA. The *Interahamwe* who raped Witness TA on this occasion possessed genocidal intent, and Ntahobali knew of their intent. He specifically acted to assist and encourage their rape of Witness TA, and his actions substantially |

	contributed to these rapes. Regardless of this conclusion, the Chamber recalls that it will not take rapes into account in assessing genocide, but instead will consider them for charges that were properly pled".[710] - Responsibility of Pauline Nyiramasuhuko and Arsène Shalom Ntahobali for the rapes committed at the Butare prefecture office (BPO): "The Chamber also finds that the evidence establishes that Ntahobali committed rapes, that Nyiramasuhuko aided and abetted rapes, and that they both ordered rapes. However, for the reasons explained above, the Chamber will not take rapes into account in assessing genocide, but instead will consider them for the counts of rape as a crime against humanity and outrages upon personal dignity as a serious violation of Article 3 common to the Geneva Conventions and of Additional Protocol II thereto".[711] "As set out above, throughout the events at the BPO, Nyiramasuhuko and Ntahobali issued orders to *Interahamwe* and the *Interahamwe* complied with these orders and perpetrated the acts asked of them, which included abductions, rapes and killings. In view of these findings, and considering the evidence in its entirety, the Chamber has no doubt that Nyiramasuhuko and Ntahobali wielded effective control over the *Interahamwe* at the BPO. The only reasonable conclusion is that Nyiramasuhuko and Ntahobali had a superior-subordinate relationship over these *Interahamwe*. The Chamber likewise finds that their orders demonstrate that they knew that the *Interahamwe* were about to commit a crime and had later done so, and that they failed to prevent the crimes. It is also clear from that evidence that they did not punish the *Interahamwe* for obeying their orders. Accordingly, the Chamber finds beyond a reasonable doubt that Nyiramasuhuko and Ntahobali bear superior responsibility pursuant to Article 6 (3) for the acts of the *Interahamwe* at the BPO, including their abductions, rapes and killings. As the Chamber has found that Nyiramasuhuko and Ntahobali are criminally responsible pursuant to Article 6 (1) of the Statute, their superior responsibility will only be considered in sentencing, and the Chamber will not enter a conviction based on their superior responsibility for these actions. Although the Chamber has found that soldiers played a role in the events at the BPO, no evidence has been led to establish any relationship between the soldiers and Nyiramasuhuko or Ntahobali. Accordingly, the Chamber finds that Nyiramasuhuko and Ntahobali do not bear superior responsibility for the acts of soldiers at the BPO".[712] - Responsibility of Sylvain Nsabimana for the rapes committed at the Butare prefecture office (BPO): "The evidence does not support an argument that Nsabimana committed, planned, ordered, or instigated the crimes perpetrated at the BPO. The Chamber will therefore address only whether he aided and abetted these crimes. An accused may be responsible for aiding and abetting in two different manners: (1) by positive acts including, providing tacit approval and encouragement; or (2) by omission, namely failing to discharge a legal duty to act. Aiding and abetting by tacit approval and encouragement appears to require the presence of the accused at or near the scene of the crime. Here, it was not contested that Nsabimana was absent from the BPO at night when the attacks were perpetrated by Nyiramasuhuko, Ntahobali and *Interahamwe*. Therefore, aiding and abetting by tacit approval or encouragement is inapplicable to Nsabimana's conduct. However, aiding and abetting by omission may serve as a basis for liability even where the accused is not present at or near the scene of the crime. Pursuant to this form of responsibility, the failure to discharge a legal duty must assist, encourage or

710 *Pauline Nyiramasuhuko et al.* Trial Judgement, paras. 5866–5870, 5872–5875 (internal references omitted).

711 *Pauline Nyiramasuhuko et al.* Trial Judgement, para. 5877.

712 *Pauline Nyiramasuhuko et al.* Trial Judgement, paras. 5884–5887.

	lend moral support to the perpetration of a crime and have a substantial effect on the realisation of that crime. This implicitly requires that the accused had the ability to act, such that the means were available to the accused to fulfil his or her duty. The aider and abettor must know that his or her omission assists in the commission of the crime of the principal perpetrator and must be aware of the essential elements of the crime which was ultimately committed by the principal perpetrator. The Prosecution argues that Nsabimana is responsible for the abductions, rapes and killings at the BPO when those taking refuge there should have been under his protection. The Prosecution referred to the Rwandan Organic Law which, it argued, gives the *préfet* a legal duty to ensure the peace, public order and security of persons and property, including those taking refuge at the BPO. A prerequisite of criminal liability for aiding and abetting by omission is a legal duty to act. The Chamber notes that the Rwandan Penal Code imposes an obligation on every Rwandan citizen to provide assistance to persons in danger where it would not cause risk to oneself, and failure to do so is a criminal offence. This obligation was considered by the Trial Chamber in *Rutaganira* at sentencing. Although the Rwandan Penal Code provides a justification for failure to act, namely where there is risk to oneself, the *Rutaganira* Trial Chamber held that '[v]iolence to physical well-being suffered by thousands of people during the said events affects the very fundamental interests of Humanity as a whole, and the protection of such interests cannot be counterbalanced by the mere personal risk that may have been faced by any person in a position of authority who failed to act in order to assist people whose lives were in danger.' In *Rutaganira*, the Chamber considered that the accused in that case 'was under a duty to provide assistance to people in danger.' Likewise, in the present case, the Chamber finds that *Préfet* Nsabimana was under a duty to provide assistance to people in danger, pursuant to Article 256 of the Rwandan Penal Code. Further, under Rwandan domestic law, Nsabimana had an obligation to ensure the tranquillity, public order, and security of people and property within his *préfecture*. […] The Chamber further notes that a legal duty to act may also be imposed by the laws and customs of war. In *Mrkšić & Šljivančanin*, the ICTY Appeals Chamber held that Article 13 of Geneva Convention III imposes a duty to protect prisoners of war. Likewise, the *Blaskić* Appeals Judgement noted that Article 27 of Geneva Convention IV imposes a legal duty to protect civilians against acts of violence. More specifically, it held that Blaskić was under a duty imposed by the laws or customs of war to care for protected persons put in danger, and to intervene and alleviate that danger. Article 13 of Geneva Convention III and Article 27 of Geneva Convention IV are limited in application to armed conflict of an international nature. However, Additional Protocol II to the Geneva Conventions contains similar obligations and is applicable to non-international armed conflicts. The Chamber notes that Article 7 of Additional Protocol II to the Geneva Conventions provides: 'All the wounded, sick and shipwrecked, whether or not they have taken part in the armed conflict, *shall be* respected and *protected.*' In addition, Article 13 of Additional Protocol II states: '1. The civilian population and individual civilians *shall enjoy general protection* against the dangers arising from military operations. To give effect to this protection, the following rules shall be observed in all circumstances. 2. The civilian population as such, as well as individual civilians, *shall not be the object of attack.* Acts or threats of violence the primary purpose of which is to spread terror among the civilian population are prohibited.' It was clear that the Tutsis taking refuge at the BPO were civilians and that many of them were sick and injured. Although these provisions do not explicitly reference individual criminal liability, the Chamber considers they are applicable to the situation prevailing at the BPO from the end of April to mid-June 1994. The Chamber recalls the ICTY Appeals Chamber's holding that 'customary international law imposes criminal liability for serious violations of common Article 3, as supplemented by other general principles and rules of protection on the protection of victims of internal armed conflict'. The Chamber considers the criminalisation of individual conduct, includes, but is not limited to Article 3 common

	to the Geneva Conventions. As the ICTY Appeals Chamber held in *Delalić et al.*: 'Common Article 1 thus imposes upon State parties, upon ratification, an obligation to implement the provisions of the Geneva Conventions in their domestic legislation. *This obligation clearly covers the Conventions in their entirety* and this obligation thus includes common Article 3.' In the Chamber's view, the criminalisation of individual conduct encompasses the Geneva Conventions in their entirety, including Articles 7 and 13 of Additional Protocol II. Therefore, these provisions impose a legal duty on the Accused to protect civilians, including the wounded and sick, against acts or threats of violence. The Chamber has found that Nyiramasuhuko, Ntahobali, *Interahamwe* and soldiers were responsible for raping numerous Tutsi women and for killing hundreds of Tutsi refugees abducted from the BPO from mid-May until mid-June 1994. Nsabimana was the *préfet* of Butare during this time period. Although many people took refuge at the BPO precisely because they thought the *préfet* would protect them, Nsabimana refused to help. His attitude in this respect was evidenced by Witness TQ who approached Nsabimana at the BPO asking for help in burying the bodies of orphans that had been killed at the school complex. Nsabimana told Witness TQ that he was a madman. By refusing to take action in the midst of the continuing attacks at the BPO, Nsabimana assisted Nyiramasuhuko, Ntahobali and the *Interahamwe* in the perpetration of their attacks. Further, his failure to act had a substantial effect on the realisation of these crimes. Witness SS described an incident in which soldiers prevented attacks at the BPO. Had Nsabimana posted *gendarmes* or soldiers sometime prior to 5–15 June 1994, he could have prevented the mass killing and rape, at least in part, at the BPO. Pursuant to Rwandan Law, the *préfet* has the power to request the intervention of the Armed Forces to restore public order. In addition, the *préfet* may verbally request the intervention of the National *Gendarmerie* pursuant to the Rwandan Law on the creation of the *Gendarmerie*. Nsabimana in fact requisitioned forces around 5–15 June 1994. At that time, 5–6 soldiers were seconded to the BPO under the command of a female lieutenant. The evidence establishes that these soldiers forestalled attacks against those taking refuge at the Butare *préfecture* office. This shows that Nsabimana, pursuant to his powers as *préfet*, had the ability to requisition forces that could forestall the attacks. Despite this, Nsabimana failed to take any steps to prevent the ongoing attacks at the BPO for a significant period between the end of April and mid-June 1994. Even if the soldiers' presence may not have been able to stop the attacks altogether, the evidence establishes that their presence would have alleviated the situation of recurring abductions, rapes and killings. These means were available to Nsabimana to fulfil his duty and to forestall these harms, but he did nothing. Nsabimana knew that those taking refuge at the BPO were Tutsis and on multiple occasions, they asked him directly for protection from the ongoing attacks. He knew that they were being abducted, raped and killed. [...] Furthermore, the Chamber concludes that Nsabimana also knew that his failure to act assisted in the commission of the crimes. Nsabimana knew the attacks were occurring at night when he was not at the BPO and when there were likely to be fewer witnesses. Moreover, he testified that after he learned of the massacres, he would go home at night fearing that the refugees would not be at the BPO when he returned in the morning. Yet, the perpetrators of these attacks were given free reign to repeatedly attack the BPO for a significant period between the end of April and mid-June 1994. In sum, Nsabimana failed to take action to stop the massacres at the BPO during his tenure as *préfet*. Although Nsabimana posted *gendarmes* or soldiers at the BPO around 5–15 June 1994, he was responsible [...] for failing to discharge his duty to protect civilians until that time".[713] - Defect in the Pauline Nyiramasuhuko and Arsène Shalom Ntahobali Indictment of pleading the rapes committed at *École évangeliste* of Rwanda (EER) as genocide:

[713] *Pauline Nyiramasuhuko et al.* Trial Judgement, paras. 5890–5906 (internal references omitted).

	"The Chamber notes that the paragraph of the Nyiramasuhuko and Ntahobali Indictment that concerns the EER, Paragraph 6.30, is the same as that concerning the Butare *préfecture* office. For the same reasons as explained above (4.2.2.3.13), the Chamber will not enter a conviction for genocide on the basis of any rapes that occurred at the EER. Instead, these rapes will be considered in the sections addressing rape as a crime against humanity and outrages upon personal dignity as a serious violation of Article 3 common to the Geneva Conventions and of Additional Protocol II thereto".[714] - Alleged responsibility of Pauline Nyiramasuhuko for distributing condoms in early June 1994: "The Chamber has found beyond a reasonable doubt that Nyiramasuhuko came to Cyarwa-Sumo *secteur*, Ngoma *commune*, in the beginning of June 1994 and distributed condoms for the *Interahamwe*, to be used in the raping and killing of Tutsi women in that *secteur*. The Chamber further found that Nyiramasuhuko ordered the woman to whom she distributed the condoms to: 'Go and distribute these condoms to your young men, so that they use them to rape Tutsi women and to protect themselves from AIDS, and after having raped them they should kill all of them. Let no Tutsi woman survive because they take away our husbands' (3.6.47.4). The Chamber lacks sufficient reliable evidence to show a link between Nyiramasuhuko's actions in distributing the condoms on this occasion, in addition to her utterances evincing her clear intent to target Tutsi women, and actual rapes committed against said Tutsi women. Therefore, the requirement of the commission of the actual crime, namely the rapes as a result of this distribution, has not been met in this instance".[715] "The Chamber has found beyond a reasonable doubt that Nyiramasuhuko came to Cyarwa-Sumo *secteur*, Ngoma *commune*, in the beginning of June 1994 and distributed condoms for the *Interahamwe*, to be used in the raping and killing of Tutsi women in that *secteur*. The Chamber further found that Nyiramasuhuko ordered the woman to whom she distributed the condoms to: 'Go and distribute these condoms to your young men, so that they use them to rape Tutsi women and to protect themselves from AIDS, and after having raped them they should kill all of them. Let no Tutsi woman survive because they take away our husbands' (3.6.47.4). The Chamber observes that this is not a vague or indirect suggestion and cannot be considered ambiguous within the context of the rapes and parallel large-scale massacres being committed throughout Butare *préfecture* and Rwanda at this time. However, the Chamber is not satisfied that the 'public' element of this crime has been established. The evidence shows that Nyiramasuhuko directed her speech to one woman, in the presence of four other men. In order to possess the requisite *mens rea* for the crime of direct and public incitement, the audience must be much broader than that found in the present circumstance. Here, Nyiramasuhuko's statements are more akin to a 'conversation', consistent with the definition of private incitement found in the *travaux préparatoires* of the Genocide Convention. There is no indication in the record that anyone other than those cited was present. The Chamber is therefore not satisfied that the evidence reasonably supports the Prosecution charge of direct and public incitement. Therefore, the Chamber does not find Nyiramasuhuko guilty of the crime of direct and public incitement to commit genocide for distributing condoms in Cyarwa-Sumo *secteur*, Ngoma *commune*, in the beginning of June 1994, to be used in the raping and killing of Tutsi women in that *secteur*. Accordingly the Chamber acquits Nyiramasuhuko of direct and public incitement to commit genocide. However, the Chamber finds that this circumstantial evidence shows Nyiramasuhuko's intent to destroy, in whole or in substantial part, the Tutsi group".[716]

714 *Pauline Nyiramasuhuko et al.* Trial Judgement, para. 5911 (internal reference omitted).

715 *Pauline Nyiramasuhuko et al.* Trial Judgement, paras. 5938–5939.

716 *Pauline Nyiramasuhuko et al.* Trial Judgement, paras. 6014–6018 (internal references omitted).

	"The Chamber lacks sufficient reliable evidence to show a link between Nyiramasuhuko's actions in distributing the condoms, and actual rapes committed against said Tutsi women. Therefore, the requirement of the commission of the actual crime, namely the rapes as a result of this distribution, has not been met in this instance. Therefore, the Chamber is not satisfied that the evidence reasonably supports the Prosecution charge of rape as a crime against humanity. Therefore, the Chamber does not find that these events constitute rape as a crime against humanity".[717] - Responsibility of Arsène Shalom Ntahobali for the rapes committed at the roadblock near Hotel Ihuliro in late April 1994: "The Chamber has found beyond a reasonable doubt that Ntahobali personally raped one Tutsi girl at the roadblock near Hotel Ihuliro, around the end of April 1994 (3.6.23.4.5). The Chamber is satisfied that Ntahobali intentionally committed this crime. Further, the Chamber considers the circumstances surrounding this offence, namely that before perpetrating the rape Ntahobali dragged the girl into the woods. It was also established that her dead body was later found with vaginal injuries. The Chamber is satisfied this event occurred without the consent of the victim. The Chamber also finds that Ntahobali intended to effect the sexual penetration in the knowledge that it occurred without this consent. The Chamber has already found that there was a widespread or systematic attack against the civilian population and that the Accused knew that their acts formed part of this attack (4.3.2). Therefore, the Chamber finds this offence constitutes rape as a crime against humanity, and that Ntahobali is responsible as a principal perpetrator for committing it. The Chamber recalls that it was also proven beyond a reasonable doubt that during the time when Ntahobali manned the roadblock, other crimes including rapes were committed against members of the Tutsi population (3.6.23.4.7). The Chamber has found that Ntahobali bore superior responsibility over the *Interahamwe* at this roadblock (4.2.2.3.11). However, because there is insufficient evidence to establish beyond a reasonable doubt that the *Interahamwe* committed rapes at or near this roadblock, the Chamber does not find that Ntahobali is responsible as a superior for the rapes that occurred near this roadblock. This alleged responsibility, therefore, will not be taken into account in sentencing".[718] "Ntahobali raped a Tutsi girl near the Hotel Ihuliro roadblock. […] The Chamber has found that th[is] act[] constitute[s] rape as a crime against humanity (4.3.5.4). Based on the same reasoning, the Chamber finds Ntahobali guilty of committing, ordering, and aiding and abetting outrages upon personal dignity as a serious violation of Article 3 common to the Geneva Conventions and of Additional Protocol II".[719] - Responsibility of Pauline Nyiramasuhuko for the rapes committed at the roadblock near Hotel Ihuliro roadblock in late April 1994: "The Chamber has also found that Nyiramasuhuko was present at the roadblock near Hotel Ihuliro on occasions during the period of time when crimes were carried out, but recalls that she was not found to be present when any crime was perpetrated there (3.6.23.4.7). Moreover, the evidence is insufficient to conclude that she played any role in relation to the rapes there, or that she bears superior responsibility for them. Therefore, the Chamber finds Nyiramasuhuko not guilty of rape as a crime against humanity, in relation to the rapes carried out at the roadblock near Hotel Ihuliro".[720] - Responsibility of Arsène Shalom Ntahobali for the rapes committed at Butare prefec-

717 *Pauline Nyiramasuhuko et al.* Trial Judgement, paras. 6091–6092.
718 *Pauline Nyiramasuhuko et al.* Trial Judgement, paras. 6077–6082.
719 *Pauline Nyiramasuhuko et al.* Trial Judgement, paras. 6184–6185.
720 *Pauline Nyiramasuhuko et al.* Trial Judgement, paras. 6083–6084.

	ture office (BPO) between the end of April and the first half of June 1994: "The Chamber is satisfied that the rapes of Witness TA and many other unnamed Tutsi women at the BPO were conducted on ethnic grounds. The Chamber finds that Ntahobali bears responsibility as a principal perpetrator for committing these acts, for ordering *Interahamwe* to commit rapes, and also for aiding and abetting rapes. Similarly, the Chamber considers that Ntahobali bears superior responsibility for the rapes committed by the *Interahamwe*, and will take this into account in sentencing".[721] "Ntahobali […] raped Tutsi women at the Butare *préfecture* office, ordered *Interahamwe* to rape Tutsis there, and aided and abetted the rapes of a Tutsi there. The Chamber has found that these acts constitute rape as a crime against humanity (4.3.5.4). Based on the same reasoning, the Chamber finds Ntahobali guilty of committing, ordering, and aiding and abetting outrages upon personal dignity as a serious violation of Article 3 common to the Geneva Conventions and of Additional Protocol II".[722] - Responsibility of Pauline Nyiramasuhuko for the rapes committed at Butare prefecture office (BPO) between the end of April and the first half of June 1994: "Nyiramasuhuko was only charged with rape as a crime against humanity pursuant to Article 6 (3) of the Statute, which the Chamber considers to be a serious omission on the part of the Prosecution. The Chamber has already found that Nyiramasuhuko ordered *Interahamwe* to rape Tutsi women at the BPO (3.6.19.4.11). Nyiramasuhuko had a superior-subordinate relationship with the *Interahamwe* who accompanied her to the BPO. Her effective control over them was evidenced by the fact that she brought them to the BPO with her son Ntahobali and the fact that her orders to rape were obeyed. She knew of, and failed to prevent or punish, these rapes. Therefore, Nyiramasuhuko bears responsibility as a superior for the rapes perpetrated by the *Interahamwe* at the BPO".[723] "Nyiramasuhuko ordered *Interahamwe* to rape Tutsis at the Butare *préfecture* office (3.6.19.4.11). Although this could have been charged pursuant to Article 6 (1) of the Statute, the Chamber notes that Paragraph 6.37, concerning rapes, was pled only in support of Nyiramasuhuko's superior responsibility. Under these circumstances, and taking into account the Chamber's discussion of this paragraph and of notice, above (4.2.2.3.13), the Chamber will only consider whether Nyiramasuhuko bears superior responsibility for events at the Butare *préfecture* office. The Chamber has found, in the context of rape as a crime against humanity, that Nyiramasuhuko bears superior responsibility for these events (4.3.5.3.2). For the same reasons, the Chamber finds Nyiramasuhuko guilty, pursuant to Article 6 (3) of the Statute, of outrages upon personal dignity as a serious violation of Article 3 common to the Geneva Conventions and of Additional Protocol II".[724] - Alleged responsibility of Pauline Nyiramasuhuko and Arsène Shalom Ntahobali for the rapes committed at, or near, the *École évangeliste* of Rwanda (EER) in early June 1994: "The Chamber has found that soldiers raped women and girls at or near the EER (3.6.36.4.3.6). Although Ntahobali was implicated in some of the attacks at the EER, it has not been established that he is responsible for rapes that occurred during this general time period. The Chamber has also found that Nyiramasuhuko's alleged

721 *Pauline Nyiramasuhuko et al.* Trial Judgement, para. 6086.

722 *Pauline Nyiramasuhuko et al.* Trial Judgement, paras. 6184–6185.

723 *Pauline Nyiramasuhuko et al.* Trial Judgement, paras. 6087–6088.

724 *Pauline Nyiramasuhuko et al.* Trial Judgement, paras. 6182–6183.

	involvement in the events at the EER, including rapes, has not been established beyond a reasonable doubt".[725]

21. Casimir **Bizimungu *et al.*** (Case No. ICTR-99-50) "***Government II***" - Casimir Bizimungu: Minister of Health in the Interim Government from 9 April until mid-July 1994. - Justin Mugenzi: Minister of Trade and Industry in the Interim Government from 9 April until mid-July 1994. - Jérôme-Clément Bicamumpaka: Minister of Foreign Affairs and Cooperation in the Interim Government from 9 April until mid-July 1994. - Prosper Mugiraneza: Minister of the Civil Service in the Interim Government from 9 April until mid-July 1994.	
Indictment[726] (International sex crimes (or related) charges and mode(s) of	- Casimir Bizimungu: **Genocide** (count 2) or, alternatively, **Complicity in genocide** (count 3) and **Rapes as CAH** (count 8) as well as **Outrages upon personal dignity as a violation of Article 3 common to the Geneva Conventions and of Additional Protocol II (WC)** (count 10) under Article 6(3) of the Statute (**superior responsibility**) for failing to prevent or to punish the rapes of Tutsi women and students committed by soldiers and *Interahamwe* at the secondary nursing school in Kabgayi, in Gitarama prefecture.[727]

725 *Pauline Nyiramasuhuko et al.* Trial Judgement, para. 6090.

726 For the general background to the charges, see *Prosecutor v. Casimir Bizimungu et al.*, Case No. ICTR-99-21-I, Indictment as confirmed, 16 August 1999 ("*Casimir Bizimungu et al.* Indictment"), paras. 5.37 ("Furthermore, soldiers, militiamen and gendarmes raped, sexually assaulted and committed other crimes of a sexual nature against Tutsi women and girls, sometimes having first kidnapped them".), 6.65 ("During the events referred to in this indictment, rapes, sexual assaults and other crimes of a sexual nature were widely and notoriously committed throughout Rwanda. These crimes were perpetrated by, among others, militiamen including *Interahamwe*-MRND, soldiers and gendarmes against the Tutsi population, in particular Tutsi women and girls".).

727 *Casimir Bizimungu et al.* Indictment, para. 6.56 ("Between April and June 1994, several people found refuge at the secondary nursing school in Kabgayi, Gitarama *préfecture*, where students and staff were already located. On several occasions during this period, soldiers and *Interahamwe* militiamen abducted and raped female Tutsi students and refugees. [...] **Casimir Bizimungu**, Minister of Health, did not take any steps to stop the crimes being committed in the Kabgayi School of Nursing or punish the perpetrators".), pp. 63, 65, 67 ("**COUNT 2:** By the acts or omissions described in paragraphs 5.1 to 6.68 and more specifically in the paragraphs referred to below: **Casimir Bizimungu:** -pursuant to Article 6(1), according to paragraphs [...] 6.56 [...] -pursuant to Article 6(3), according to paragraphs: [...] 6.56 [... is] responsible for killing or causing serious bodily or mental harm to members of the Tutsi population with the intent to destroy, in whole or in part, a racial or ethnic group, and thereby committed **GENOCIDE**, a crime stipulated in Article 2(3)(a) of the Statute of the Tribunal, for which [he is] individually responsible pursuant to Article 6 and which is punishable in reference to Articles 22 and 23 of the Statute. **OR, ALTERNATIVELY COUNT 3:** By the acts or omissions described in paragraphs 5.1 to 6.68 and more specifically in the paragraphs referred to below: **Casimir Bizimungu:** -pursuant to Article 6(1), according to paragraphs [...] 6.56 [...] -pursuant to Article 6(3), according to paragraphs: [...] 6.56 [... is] responsible for killing or causing serious bodily or mental harm to members of the Tutsi population with the intent to destroy, in whole or in part, a racial or ethnic group, and thereby committed **COMPLICITY IN GENOCIDE**, a crime stipulated in Article 2(3)(e) of the Statute of the Tribunal, for which [he is] individually responsible pursuant to Article 6 and which is punishable in reference to Articles 22 and 23 of the Statute".), pp. 74–76 ("**COUNT 8:** By the acts or omissions described in paragraphs 5.1 to 6.68 and more specifically in the paragraphs referred to below: **Casimir Bizimungu:** -pursuant to Article 6(1), according to paragraphs [...] 6.56 [...] -pursuant to Article 6(3), according to paragraphs: [...] 6.56 [... is] responsible for rape as part of a widespread and systematic attack against a civilian population on political, ethnic or racial grounds, and thereby committed a **CRIME AGAINST HUMANITY**, a crime stipulated in Article 3(g) of [the] Statute of the Tribunal, for which [he is] individually responsible pursuant to Article 6 of the Statute and which is punishable in reference to Articles 22 and 23

liability)	- Although the Indictment charges Justin Mugenzi, Jérôme-Clément Bicamumpaka, and Prosper Mugiraneza with rapes as CAH (count 8) and outrages upon personal dignity as a violation of Article 3 common to the Geneva Conventions and of Additional Protocol II (WC) (count 10) under Articles 6(1) and 6(3) of the Statute (superior responsibility), there is no material fact with respect to rapes linked to them in the Indictment.[728]
Trial Judgement	N/A (The trial is in progress.)
Appeal Judgement	N/A
Legal and Factual Findings and/or Evidence	N/A

22. Édouard **Karemera** and Mathieu **Ngirumpatse** (Case No. ICTR-98-44) "***Government I***" - Édouard Karemera: Minister of the Interior in the Interim Government from 25 May until July 1994; First Vice-President of the *Mouvement révolutionnaire national pour la démocratie et le développement* (MRND) political party; member of the MRND's Steering Committee. - Mathieu Ngirumpatse: President of the MRND political party; member of the MRND's Steering Committee.	
Indictment (International sex crimes (or related) charges and mode(s) of liability)	- Édouard Karemera and Mathieu Ngirumpatse: **Genocide** (count 3) or, alternatively, **Complicity in genocide** (count 4) and **Rape as CAH** (count 5) under Articles 6(1) (**joint criminal enterprise – third category**) and 6(3) of the Statute (**superior responsibility**) for the rapes and sexual assaults of Tutsi women and girls committed by *Interahamwe* and militiamen throughout Rwanda, including in Ruhengeri prefecture during early and mid-April 1994, in Kigali-ville prefecture during April 1994, in Butare prefecture during mid- and late April 1994, in Kibuye prefecture during May and June 1994, and in Gitarama prefecture during April and May 1994.[729]

of the Statute".), pp. 78, 80 ("**COUNT 10:** By the acts or omissions described in paragraphs 5.1 to 6.68 and more specifically in the paragraphs referred to below: **Casimir Bizimungu:** -pursuant to Article 6(1), according to paragraphs [...] 6.56 [...] -pursuant to Article 6(3), according to paragraphs: [...] 6.56 [... is] responsible for outrages upon personal dignity, in particular humiliating and degrading treatment, rape and indecent assault, as part of an armed internal conflict, and there by committed **SERIOUS VIOLATIONS OF ARTICLE 3 COMMON TO THE GENEVA CONVENTIONS AND OF ADDITIONAL PROTOCOL II**, a crime stipulated in Article 4(e) of the Statute of the Tribunal, for which [he is] individually responsible pursuant to Article 6 of the Statute and which is punishable in reference to Articles 22 and 23 of the Statute".).

728 See *Casimir Bizimungu et al.* Indictment, pp. 74–76, 78–80.

729 *Prosecutor v. Édouard Karemera and Mathieu Ngirumpatse*, Case No. ICTR-98-44-T, Amended Indictment of 23 August 2010, 23 August 2010, p. 14 ("**Count 3: Genocide** The Prosecutor charges **Édouard KAREMERA**, and **Mathieu NGIRUMPATSE** with **Genocide** pursuant to Articles 2, 6(1) and 6(3) of the Statute of the Tribunal in that during the period 1 January – 17 July 1994 they were responsible for killing or causing serious bodily or mental harm to members of the Tutsi population, or deliberately inflicting conditions of life upon the Tutsi population that were calculated to bring about its physical destruction, with the intent to destroy, in whole or in part, the Tutsi racial or ethnic group, committed as follows: ***Or alternatively*** **Count 4: Complicitiy in Genocide** The Prosecutor charges **Édouard KAREMERA**, and **Mathieu NGIRUMPATSE** with **Complicity in Genocide** pursuant to Articles 2 and 6(1) of the Statute of the Tribunal in that during the period 1 January – 17 July 1994 they instigated or provided means to other persons to kill or

Trial Judgement	N/A (The trial is in progress.)
Appeal Judgement	N/A
Legal and Factual Findings and/or Evidence	N/A

23. Augustin **Ngirabatware** (Case No. ICTR-99-54) Minister of Planning in the Interim Government from 9 April until mid-July 1994.	
Indictment (International sex crimes (or related) charges and	- **Rape as CAH** (count 6) under Article 6(1) of the Statute (**joint criminal enterprise – third category**) for the rapes of Bonishance, Denise Nyirabunori and Chantal Murazemariya committed by members of the *Interahamwe*, acting in concert with Faustin Bagango, the Bourgmestre and *Interahamwe* Chairman throughout Nyamyumba commune, in Gisenyi prefecture, in April 1994.[730]

cause serious bodily or mental harm to members of the Tutsi population, or to deliberately inflict conditions of life upon the Tutsi population that were calculated to bring about its physical destruction, knowing that those other persons intended to destroy, in whole or in part, the Tutsi racial or ethnic group, committed as follows:"), para. 66 ("In Ruhengeri *prefecture* during early-mid April 1994, Kigali-ville *préfecture* during April 1994, Butare *préfecture* during mid-late April 1994, Kibuye *préfecture* during May – June 1994, and Gitarama *préfecture* during April and May 1994, and throughout Rwanda, *Interahamwe* and militiamen raped and sexually assaulted Tutsi women and girls throughout Rwanda, causing them serious bodily or mental harm. Such serious bodily or mental harm inflicted upon Tutsi women and girls was intended to destroy the capacity of persons of Tutsi ethnic or racial identity to sustain themselves physically or psychologically as a group, or to reproduce themselves as a group. **Édouard KAREMERA**, **Mathieu NGIRUMPATSE**, and Joseph NZIRORERA were aware that rape was the natural and foreseeable consequence of the execution of the joint criminal enterprise and knowingly and wilfully participated in that enterprise".), p. 22 ("**Count 5: Rape as a Crime Against Humanity** The Prosecutor charges **Édouard KAREMERA**, and **Mathieu NGIRUMPATSE** with **Rape as a Crime Against Humanity** pursuant to Articles 3, 6(1) and 6(3) of the Statute of the Tribunal in that on or between the dates of 6 April and 17 July 1994, throughout the territory of Rwanda, they were responsible for raping persons or causing persons to be raped, as part of a widespread or systematic attack against a civilian population on political, ethnic, or racial grounds, committed as follows:"), paras. 67–70 ("Between 6 April 1994 and 17 July 1994 throughout Rwanda there were widespread or systematic attacks against a civilian population based on Tutsi ethnic or racial identification or politicial opposition to the MRND and 'Hutu power' politicial parties, as described in detail in paragraphs 34 through 66. As part of these widespread or systematic attacks, *Interahamwe* and other militiamen raped Tutsi women and girls in Ruhengeri *préfecture* during early-mid April 1994, Kigali-ville *préfecture* during April 1994, Butare *préfecture* during mid-late April 1994, Kibuye *préfecture* during May – June 1994, and Gitarama *préfecture* during April and May 1994. These rapes were the natural and foreseeable consequences of the object of the joint criminal enterprise to destroy the Tutsi as a group. **Édouard KAREMERA**, **Mathieu NGIRUMPATSE**, and Joseph NZIRORERA were aware that rape was the natural and foreseeable consequence of the execution of the joint criminal enterprise and knowingly and wilfully participated in that enterprise. Rape against Tutsi women between 6 April and 17 July 1994 was so widespread and so systematic that **Édouard KAREMERA**, **Mathieu NGIRUMPATSE**, and Joseph NZIRORERA knew or had reason to know that *Interahamwe* and other militiamen were about to commit these crimes or that they had committed them. The accused had the material capacity to halt or prevent the rapes, or to punish or sanction those that committed these crimes, but failed to take the necessary and reasonable measures to prevent the rapes or to punish the perpetrators".).

730 *Prosecutor v. Augustin Ngirabatware*, Case No. ICTR-99-54-T, Amended Indictment, 14 April 2009, p. 15 ("**COUNT 6: RAPE AS A CRIME AGAINST HUMANITY** The Prosecutor of the International Criminal

mode(s) of liability)	
Trial Judgement	N/A (The trial is in progress.)
Appeal Judgement	N/A
Legal and Factual Findings and/or Evidence	N/A

24. Ildephonse **Nizeyimana** (Case No. ICTR-00-55) Captain in the Rwandan Armed Forces (FAR); S2/S3, in charge of intelligence and military operations, at the *École des Sous Officiers* (ESO) in Butare prefecture during April and part of May 1994.	
Indictment (International sex crimes (or related) charges and mode(s) of liability)	- **Genocide** (count 1), **Rape as CAH** (count 4) and **Rape as a violation of Article 3 common to the Geneva Conventions and of Additional Protocol II (WC)** (count 6) under Articles 6(1) and 6(3) of the Statute (**superior responsibility**) for: (i) ordering FAR soldiers, gendarmes and officers stationed at both Ngoma Camp and ESO to rape Tutsi women and for the subsequent rapes (**ordering**); and for (ii) ordering or instigating soldiers from the FAR, ESO, Ngoma Camp, Butare *Gendarmerie* Camp and *Interahamwe* militia to rape Tutsi women at Butare Hospital, Butare University and at various locations in Butare prefecture, including the residence of Rosalie Gicanda, and for the subsequent rapes, including the multiple rapes and gang-rapes of MKA, ZBL, BUQ, BJW and DCO (**ordering** or **instigating**).[731]

Tribunal for Rwanda charges **Augustin NGIRABATWARE** with **RAPE as a CRIME AGAINST HUMANITY**, a crime stipulated in Article 3(g) of the Statute of the Tribunal, in that between 1 January and 17 July 1994 throughout Rwanda **Augustin NGIRABATWARE** was responsible for the rape of persons as part of a widespread or systematic attack against the civilian population on political, ethnic or racial grounds and thereby committed **a CRIME AGAINST HUMANITY**, as stipulated in Article 3(g) of the Statute".), paras. 61–63 ("Around April 1994, in Nyamyumba Commune, Gisenyi Prefecture, members of the *Interahamwe*, acting in concert with Faustin BAGANGO, the Bourgmestre and *Interahamwe* Chairman in Nyamyumba commune, and who were engaged in a joint criminal enterprise with **Augustin NGIRABATWARE** to exterminate the civilian Tutsi population, raped BONISHANCE, a Tutsi woman, as part of a widespread and systematic attack against the Tutsi population on eth[n]ic grounds. Around April 1994, in Nyamyumba Commune, Gisenyi Prefecture, members of the *Interahamwe*, acting in concert with Faustin BAGANGO, the Bourgmestre and *Interahamwe* Chairman in Nyamyumba commune, who were engaged in a joint criminal enterprise with **Augustin NGIRABATWARE** to exterminate the civilian Tutsi population, raped Denise NYIRABUNORI a Tutsi woman who was hiding in the house of **Augustin NGIRABATWARE**'s brother, Alphonse BANANYIE, as part of a widespread and systematic attack against the Tutsi population on ethnic grounds. Around April 1994, in Nyamyumba Commune, Gisenyi Prefecture, members of the *Interahamwe*, including JUMA and MAKUZE acting in concert with Faustin BAGANGO, the Bourgmestre and *Interahamwe* Chairman in Nyamyumba commune, and who were engaged in a joint criminal enterprise with **Augustin NGIRABATWARE** to exterminate the civilian Tutsi population, repeatedly raped Chantal MURAZEMARIYA, a Tutsi woman, as part of a widespread and systematic attack against the Tutsi population on ethnic grounds".).

731 *Prosecutor v. Ildephonse Nizeyimana*, Case No. ICTR-00-55-PT, Second Amended Indictment (Filed pursuant to Trial Chamber Order dated 15 December 2010), 17 December 2010, p. 3 ("**Count I: GENOCIDE** The Prosecutor of the International Criminal Tribunal for Rwanda charges **Ildephonse NIZEYIMANA** with **GENOCIDE**, a crime stipulated in Article 2(3)(a) of the Statute, in that on or between the dates of 7 April 1994 and 17 July 1994 throughout Rwanda, particularly in Butare *préfecture*, **Ildephonse NIZEYIMANA**

was responsible for killing or causing serious bodily or mental harm to members of the Tutsi ethnic group, including acts of sexual violence, with intent to destroy, in whole or in part, an ethnic group, as such, as outlined in paragraphs 5 through 35 herein".), paras. 8 ("On or about 7 April 1994, following the death of President Habyarimana, **Ildephonse NIZEYIMANA** convened a meeting of FAR officers and soldiers at the ESO where he personally spoke and ordered soldiers to kill Tutsi civilians and to rape Tutsi women. Many of the FAR officers and soldiers in attendance were members of the joint criminal enterprise referred to in paragraph 5 herein. It was this same initiating order that was subsequently followed by the Accused's subordinates during the period of 7 April 1994 through mid July 1994, with respect to the crimes committed in Butare *préfecture*. This initiating order was never rescinded and subsequent orders by the Accused were consistent with and flowed from the course set by this order".), 14(ii) ("From on or about 16 April 1994, **Ildephonse NIZEYIMANA** ordred and instigated soldiers from the FAR, ESO, Ngoma Camp and Butare *Gendarmerie* Camp, and *Interahamwe* who were members of the joint criminal enterprise referred to in paragraph 5 herein to kill many Tutsi civilians at Butare University, with words to the effect that no Tutsi should remain. In greater particular: […] (ii) on or about 19 April 1994, attacks occurred at the University against students identified as Tutsi, during which gunshots were fired and female victims were targeted by soldiers from the FAR, ESO, Ngoma Camp and Butare *Gendarmerie* Camp, and *Interahamwe* militia who were members of the joint criminal enterprise referred to in paragraph 5 herein committing crimes of sexual violence"), 30–35 ("Beginning the night of 6 April 1994, the Accused issued orders to FAR soldiers stationed in Butare prefecture at both Ngoma camp and ESO, to kill Tutsis generally but specifically to rape Tutsi women and then kill them. That same order was repeated the following day near mid-day, on the premises of ESO, directed to an audience of FAR gendarmes, soldiers and officers from Ngoma camp and ESO, including Lieutenant Hategekimana of Ngoma camp, Majory Cyriaque Habyarabatuma of the Butare *Gendarmerie*, Sous-Lieutenants Gatsinzi and Bizimana of ESO and many other officers from the region, including Gikongoro and Nyanza. Between 6 April 1994 and 17 July 1994, soldiers from the FAR, ESO, Ngoma Camp and Butare *Gendarmerie* Camp, and other participants of the joint criminal enterprise […] acting on the orders or at the instigation of **Ildephonse NIZEYIMANA** raped Tutsi women at Butare Hospital, Butare University and at various other locations in Butare prefecture, including the residence of Rosalie Gicanda. In greater particular: (i) in April 1994 at the residence of Rosale Gicanda more than one dozen FAR soldiers were present during the rape of a female civilian identified as Tutsi of approximately age 18–20. The soldiers were all from Ngoma camp or ESO and included Sergeant Ngirinshuti; […] (iii) During the period of late April and mid-May 1994, MKA and other women were raped by FAR soldiers at the Hospital on several occasions. On the first occasion five FAR soldiers entered a maternity ward at the Hospital and raped several patients, including MKA. On a second occasion approximately 3 days later MKA was again raped by a FAR soldier. On a third occasion, in early to mid-May after MKA had given birth she was raped by an unknown male in the presence of four other women who were also being raped by unknown men in the same maternity ward. (iv) Towards the end of May 1994 ZBL was repeatedly raped by two FAR soldiers at the Hospital, in a room where she was kept for three days. ZBL was raped by an *Interahamwe* behind the hospital in the presence of another woman who was also raped by an *Interahamwe* and later killed. [A]ll of which was within the *de facto* and *de jure* operational region, command and influence of the Accused. Between 6 April 1994 and 9 April 1994, approximately 14 FAR soldiers from both the ESO and Ngoma Camps acting under the authority or on the orders of **Ildephonse NIZEYIMANA** raped BUQ and two other women multiple times over the course of three days in a house near the ESO camp: (i) Late on the night of 6 April 1994, approximately 6 soldiers came from the homes of the Accused and Lieutenant Ildephonse Hateg[e]kimana, forcibly entered the home where BUQ, ALAB and CEL were present, and told the victims 'We have received order from our superiors to rape all Tutsi women and girls and kill them.' One of the perpetrators was named Rubaga and known to be a driver who was stationed at the ESO; (ii) The following day, four more soldiers forcibly entered the home and committed multiple rapes, ordering the victims not to move from the premises; (iii) The next day, three more soldiers came to the house and spent many hours committing multiple rapes; (iv) On the morning of the fourth day, a soldier who identified himself as Innocent Ndererimana, stationed at Ngoma camp as an escort to Lieutenant Hateg[e]kimana, took BUQ into his custody and held her in a nearby but different home for approximately two weeks, during which time he repeatedly committed multiple rapes; all of which was within the *de facto* and *de jure* operational region, command and influence of the Accused. During April 1994, unknown FAR soldiers who were members of the joint criminal enterprise […] acting under the authority or on the orders of **Ildephonse NIZEYIMANA** raped BJW. On or about 18 April 1994, BJW was raped in her parent's home in Butare by a FAR soldier who said his name was Alexis Karemera, and who was in command of at least two other FAR soldiers in the operational zone of Rusatira commune, within the *de facto* and *de jure* operational region, command and influence of the Accused. On or about 23 April 1994, at approximately 11 pm, unknown FAR soldiers who were members of the joint criminal enter-

Trial Judgement	N/A (The trial is in progress.)
Appeal Judgement	N/A
Legal and Factual Findings and/or Evidence	N/A

25. Bernard **Munyagishari** (Case No. ICTR-05-89)

Secretary General of the *Mouvement révolutionnaire national pour la démocratie et le développement* (MRND) political party for Gisenyi town; President of the *Interahamwe* for Gisenyi prefecture.

---

prise […] acting under the authority or on the orders or at the instigation of **Ildephonse NIZEYIMANA** raped two young girls in Butare prefecture, near Butare town, in Ngoma commune, near the Muslim quarter, in the house of a woman whose husband had just been killed. The precise identities of the rape victims and the precise identities of the rape perpetrators are unknown, except that the victims' Rwandan mother had just been killed and their European father lived abroad, and that the perpetrators were FAR soldiers of low rank, in the operational zone of Ngoma commune, and were known by and under the instructions of FAR soldier Ismael Rubayiza, and were thus within the *de facto* and *de jure* operational region, command and influence of the Accused. Between May and July 1994, soldiers from the FAR, ESO and Ngoma Camp who were members of the joint criminal enterprise […] acting under the authority or on the orders of **Ildephonse NIZEYIMANA** regularly raped DCO and other women on several occasions in various locations on the Butare Hospital premises: (i) From the beginning of May, the FAR soldiers came more frequently to the Hospital, demanding to see identity cards, selecting only Tutsi and killing them just outside the ward, generally after raping the less educated women; (ii) Approximately mid-May, three FAR soldiers entered a Hospital ward where care was being given to a sick child, forcibly removed DCO and then one of the soldiers took DCO outside to a nearby mass grave, raping her on the ground; (iii) Sometime during the month of June, four FAR soldiers came into the Hospital ward and forcibly removed four women, including DCO, took the victims outside behind the maternity unit and raped them on the ground in the open; (iv) In early July, in the belief that RPF troops were nearby, DCO and others were asked to leave the Hospital, and when DCO went just outside the premises she was apprehended by four FAR soldiers, one of whom immediately began to rape her; these repetitive crimes occurred within the *de facto* and *de jure* operational region, command and influence of the Accused".), p. 18 ("**Count IV: RAPE as a CRIME AGAINST HUMANITY** The Prosecutor of the International Criminal Tribunal for Rwanda charges **Ildephonse NIZEYIMANA** with **RAPE as a CRIME AGAINST HUMANITY**, a crime stipulated in Article 3(g) of the Statute, in that between 6 April 1994 and 3 July 1994 in Butare *préfecture*, **Ildephonse NIZEYIMANA**, with the intention that rape of members of the Tutsi ethnic group or persons identified as Tutsi occur, was responsible for the rape of Tutsi as part of a widespread or systematic attack against that civilian population on ethnic grounds, as set forth in paragraphs 47 though 50 herein".), paras. 48 ("Paragraphs 8 and 30 through 35 above are incorporated by reference herein".), 50 ("Paragraphs 8 and 30 through 35 above are incorporated by reference herein".), p. 22 ("**Count VI: RAPE AS A VIOLATION OF ARTICLE 3 COMMON TO THE GENEVA CONVENTIONS OF 1949 AND ADDITIONAL PROTOCOL II OF 1977** The Prosecutor of the International Criminal Tribunal for Rwanda charges **Ildephonse NIZEYIMANA** with **RAPE as a violation of Article 3 Common and Protocol II**, a crime stipulated in Article 4(e) of the Statute, in that **Ildephonse NIZEYIMANA** was responsible for the rape of non-combatant Tutsi women during the period 6 April 1994 through 3 July 1994 when in Butare *préfecture*, there was a non-international armed conflict within the meaning of Articles 1 and 2 of Protocol II Additional to the Geneva Convention of 1949, and the rape of victims was closely related to the hostilities or committed in conjunction with the armed conflict and the victims were persons taking no part in that conflict, all as is set forth in paragraphs 55 through 58 herein".), paras. 56 ("Paragraphs 8 and 30 through 35 above are incorporated by reference herein".), 58 ("Paragraphs 8 and 30 through 35 above are incorporated by reference herein".).

Indictment (International sex crimes (or related) charges and mode(s) of liability)	- **Genocide** (count 2) or, alternatively, **Complicity in genocide** (count 3) and **Rape as CAH** (count 5) under Article 6(1) of the Statute for: (i) ordering or instigating a special corps of young *Interahamwe* called the '*Ntarumikwa*' to rape Tutsi women and girls (**ordering** or **instigating**); (ii) for instigating his wife Zainabou and the female group of *Interahamwe* she headed to sexually torture Tutsi women (**instigating**); and (iii) raping a young Tutsi student named Françoise during the three weeks she was held captive in his house (**committing**); and under Article 6(3) of the Statute (**superior responsibility**) for: (i) the rape of a young Tutsi student named Françoise by two *Interahamwe* under his effective control during the three weeks she was held captive in his house; and (ii) the crimes committed by his wife Zainabou and the female group of *Interahamwe* she headed, who were under his effective control, including sexually torturing Tutsi women, forcing iron rods into Tutsi women's vaginas and asking Tutsi women to produce milk from their bodies.[732]

[732] *Prosecutor v. Bernard Munyagishari*, Case No. ICTR-05-89-I, Indictment, 9 June 2005, pp. 7–8 ("**COUNT 2: GENOCIDE** The Prosecutor charges **Bernard Munyagishari** with **GENOCIDE**, a crime stipulated in Article 2(3)(a), of the Statute in that on or between the dates of 7 April 1994 and 17 July 1994 in Gisenyi *prefecture*, Rwanda, **Bernard Munyagishari** was responsible for killing or causing serious bodily or mental harm to members of the Tutsi population, including acts of sexual violence, with intent to destroy, in whole or in part, a racial or ethnic group as such, as outlined in paragraphs 27 through 46 of this indictment. ***OR ALTERNATIVELY*** **COUNT 3: COMPLICITY IN GENOCIDE** The Prosecutor charges **Bernard Munyagishari** with **COMPLICITY IN GENOCIDE**, a crime stipulated in Article 2(3)(e) of the Statute, in that on or between the dates of 7 April 1994 and 17 July 1994 in Gisenyi *prefecture*, Rwanda, **Bernard Munyagishari** was responsible for killing or causing serious bodily or mental harm to members of the Tutsi population, including acts of sexual violence, with knowledge that others intended to destroy, in whole or in part, a racial or ethnic, group as such, and that his assistance would contribute to the crime of genocide, as outlined in paragraphs 27 through 46 of this indictment".), paras. 37 ("During the period of 7 April 1994 to 17 July 1994, **Bernard Munyagishari** created a special corps of young *Interahamwe* called the '*Ntarumikwa*', to rape and kill the Tutsi women. **Bernard Munyagishari** ordered or instigated these young *Interahamwe* openly to rape Tutsi women and girls before killing them, **Bernard Munyagishari** also instigated his wife and fellow *Interahamwe*, Zainabou, and a female group that she headed, to sexually torture female Tutsis before killing them".), 43 ("During the period from April 1994 to July 1994, rape, sexual assaults and other crimes of a sexual nature were widely and notoriously committed throughout Gisenyi. These crimes were perpetrated by *Interahamwe* who were subordinates of **Bernard Munyagishari**, against the Tutsi, in particular against Tutsi women and girls. **Bernard Munyagishari** knew or had reason to know that his *Interahamwe* had committed such crimes and failed to prevent the acts or punish the perpetrators".), 45–46 ("Between April and July 1994, **Bernard Munyagishari** abducted a young Tutsi student named Françoise, daughter of one Emmanuel, telling her that she was being protected from the massacres that were going on in Gisenyi at the time. In the three weeks she was held captive in the house of **Bernard Munyagishari**, two of **Bernard Munyagishari**'s *Interahamwe*, Damas and Michel raped the young Françoise. The girl was later killed and her body disposed at a place called '*Mu Makoro*' in Gisenyi. **Bernard Munyagishari** knew or had reason to know that his *Interahamwe* had raped and killed Françoise and failed to prevent the acts or punish the perpetrators. During the period from 7 April to 17 July 1994, the wife of **Bernard Munyagishari** named Zainabou, headed a female group of *Interahamwe* who were subordinate to **Bernard Munyagishari**. This group was notorious for sexually torturing Tutsi women before killing them. This group forced iron rods into the genitals of the Tutsi women. They also asked Tutsi women to produce milk from their bodies if they were true Tutsi. Those Tutsi women were then tortured to death. These acts constituted rape and **Bernard Munyagishari** knew or had reason to know that his subordinates had committed such crimes and failed to prevent the acts or punish the perpetrators".), p. 13 ("**COUNT 5: RAPE AS A CRIME AGAINST HUMANITY** The Prosecutor charges **Bernard Munyagishari** with **RAPE AS A CRIME AGAINST HUMANITY**, a crime stipulated in Article 3(g) of the Statute, in that on or between the dates of 1 January 1994 and 17 July 1994 throughout Rwanda, **Bernard Munyagishari** with the intention of raping members of the Tutsi racial or ethnic group or persons identified as Tutsis, was responsible for the rape of Tutsis as part of a widespread or systematic attack against that civilian population on ethnic or racial grounds".), paras. 55–56 ("During the period from 7 April 1994 to 17 July 1994, **Bernard Munyagishari** created a special corps of young *Interahamwe* called the '*Ntarumikwa*', to rape and kill the Tutsi women. **Bernard Munyagishari** ordered or instigated these young *Interahamwe* to rape Tutsi women and girls before killing them. **Bernard**

Trial Judgement	N/A (The trial is in progress.)
Appeal Judgement	N/A
Legal and Factual Findings and/or Evidence	N/A

26. Augustin **Bizimana** (Case No. ICTR-98-44) Minister of Defence in the Interim Government.	
Indictment[733] (International sex crimes (or related) charges and	- **Genocide** (count 2) or, alternatively, **Complicitiy in genocide** (count 3) and **Rape as CAH** (count 7), **Persecutions as CAH** (count 8), **Other inhumane acts** (count 9) and **Outrages upon personal dignity as a violation of Article 3 common to the Geneva Conventions and of Additional Protocol II (WC)** (count 11) under Article 6(3) of the Statute (**superior responsibility**) for the rapes of Tutsi women committed by

Munyagishari also instigated his wife and fellow *Interahamwe*, Zainabou, and a female group that she headed, to sexually torture female Tutsis before killing them. Between 7 April and 17 July 1994, **Bernard Munyagishari** abducted a young Tutsi student named Françoise, daughter of one Emmanuel, telling her that she was being protected from the massacres that were going on in Gisenyi at the time. For three weeks she was held captive in the house of **Bernard Munyagishari**. **Bernard Munyagishari** raped Françoise. The girl was later killed and her body disposed of at a place called '*Mu Makoro*' in Gisenyi".), 58–60 ("During the period from April 1994 to July 1994, rape, sexual assaults and other crimes of sexual nature were widely and notoriously committed throughout Gisenyi. These crimes were perpetrated by *Interahamwe* who were subordinates of **Bernard Munyagishari**, against the Tutsi, in particular against Tutsi women and girls. **Bernard Munyagishari** knew or had reason to know that his *Interahamwe* had committed such crimes and failed to prevent the acts or punish the perpetrators. Between April and July 1994, **Bernard Munyagishari** abducted a young Tutsi student named Françoise, daughter of one Emmanuel, telling her that she was being protected from the massacres that were going on in Gisenyi at the time. In the three weeks she was held captive in the house of **Bernard Munyagishari**, two of **Bernard Munyagishari**'s *Interahamwe*, Damas and Michel, raped Françoise. The girl was later killed and her body disposed of at a place called '*Mu Makoro*' in Gisenyi. **Bernard Munyagishari** knew or had reason to know that his *Interahamwe* had raped Françoise and failed to prevent the acts or punish the perpetrators. During the period from April to 17 July 1994, **Bernard Munyagishari** named Zainabou, headed a female group of *Interahamwe* that was subordinate to **Bernard Munyagishari** and notorious for sexually torturing Tutsi women before killing them. This group forced iron rods into the genitals of the Tutsi women. They also asked Tutsi women to produce milk from their bodies if they were true Tutsis. Those Tutsi women were then tortured to death. These acts constituted rape and **Bernard Munyagishari** knew or had reason to know that his subordinates had committed such crimes and failed to prevent the acts or punish the perpetrators".).

733 For the general background to the charges, see *Prosecutor v. Augustin Bizimana et al.*, Case No. ICTR-98-44-I, Amended Indictment, 21 November 2001 ("*Augustin Bizimana et al.* Indictment"), paras. 5.47 ("Furthermore, soldiers, militiamen and gendarmes raped or sexually assaulted or committed other crimes of a sexual nature against Tutsi women and girls, sometimes after having first kidnapped them".), 6.101 ("During the events referred to in this indictment, rapes, sexual assaults and other crimes of a sexual nature were widely and notoriously committed throughout Rwanda. These crimes were perpetrated by, among others, militiamen including *Interahamwe*-MRND, soldiers and gendarmes against the Tutsi population, in particular Tutsi women and girls".).

mode(s) of liability)	soldiers and *Interahamwe* militiamen at the secondary nursing school in Kabgayi, in Gitarama prefecture between April and June 1994.[734]
Trial Judgement	N/A (Still at large)
Appeal Judgement	N/A
Legal and Factual Findings and/or Evidence	N/A

[734] *Augustin Bizimana et al.* Indictment, para. 6.91 ("Between April and June 1994, several people found refuge at the secondary nursing school in Kabgayi, Gitarama *préfecture*, where students and staff were already located. On several occasions during this period, soldiers and *Interahamwe* militiamen abducted and raped female Tutsi students and refugees. Minister of Defense **Augustin Bizimana** and the General Staff of the Rwandan Army were informed of this situation but did not take any effective steps to end the crimes once and for all".), pp. 74, 77–78, 80 ("**COUNT 2:** By the acts or omissions described in paragraphs 5.1 to 6.104 and more specifically in the paragraphs referred to below: **Augustin Bizimana:** […] -pursuant to Article 6(3), according to paragraphs: […] 6.91 [… is] responsible for killing or causing serious bodily or mental harm to members of the Tutsi population with the intent to destroy, in whole or in part, a racial or ethnic group, and thereby committed **GENOCIDE**, a crime stipulated in Article 2(3)(a) of the Statute of the Tribunal, for which [he is] individually responsible pursuant to Article 6 and which is punishable in reference to Articles 22 and 23 of the Statute. **COUNT 3:** By the acts or omissions described in paragraphs 5.1 to 6.104 and more specifically in the paragraphs referred to below: **Augustin Bizimana:** […] -pursuant to Article 6(3), according to paragraphs: […] 6.91 [… is] responsible for killing or causing serious bodily or mental harm to members of the Tutsi population with the intent to destroy, in whole or in part, a racial or ethnic group, and thereby committed **COMPLICITY IN GENOCIDE**, a crime stipulated in Article 2(3)(e) of the Statute of the Tribunal, for which [he is] individually responsible pursuant to Article 6 and which is punishable in reference to Articles 22 and 23 of the Statute".), 90–91, 93–94, 96–97, 100–101 ("**COUNT 7:** By the acts or omissions described in paragraphs 5.1 to 6.104 and more specifically in the paragraphs referred to below: **Augustin Bizimana:** […] -pursuant to Article 6(3), according to paragraphs: […] 6.91 [… is] responsible for rape as part of a widespread and systematic attack against a civilian population on political, ethnic or racial grounds, and thereby committed a **CRIME AGAINST HUMANITY**, a crime stipulated in Article 3(g) of [the] Statute of the Tribunal, for which [he is] individually responsible pursuant to Article 6 of the Statute and which is punishable in reference to Articles 22 and 23 of the Statute. **COUNT 8:** By the acts or omissions described in paragraphs 5.1 to 6.104 and more specifically in the paragraphs referred to below: **Augustin Bizimana:** […] -pursuant to Article 6(3), according to paragraphs: […] 6.91 [… is] responsible for persecution on political, racial or religious grounds, as part of a widespread and systematic attack against a civilian population on political, ethnic or racial grounds, and thereby committed a **CRIME AGAINST HUMANITY**, a crime stipulated in Article 3(h) of [the] Statute of the Tribunal, for which [he is] individually responsible pursuant to Article 6 of the Statute and which is punishable in reference to Articles 22 and 23 of the Statute. **COUNT 9:** By the acts or omissions described in paragraphs 5.1 to 6.104 and more specifically in the paragraphs referred to below: **Augustin Bizimana:** […] -pursuant to Article 6(3), according to paragraphs: […] 6.91 [… is] responsible for inhumane acts against persons as part of a widespread and systematic attack against a civilian population on political, ethnic or racial grounds, and thereby committed a **CRIME AGAINST HUMANITY**, a crime stipulated in Article 3(h) of [the] Statute of the Tribunal, for which [he is] individually responsible pursuant to Article 6 of the Statute and which is punishable in reference to Articles 22 and 23 of the Statute".), 104–105, 107 ("**COUNT 11:** By the acts or omissions described in paragraphs 5.1 to 6.104 and more specifically in the paragraphs referred to below: **Augustin Bizimana:** […] -pursuant to Article 6(3), according to paragraphs: […] 6.91 [… is] responsible for outrages upon personal dignity, in particular humiliating and degrading treatment, rape and indecent assault, part of an armed internal conflict, and thereby committed **SERIOUS VIOLATIONS OF ARTICLE 3 COMMON TO THE GENEVA CONVENTIONS AND OF ADDITIONAL PROTOCOL II**, a crime stipulated in Article 4(e) of the Statute of the Tribunal, for which he is individually responsible pursuant to Article 6 of the Statute and which is punishable in reference to Articles 22 and 23 of the Statute".).

<table>
<tr><td colspan="2">27. Protais Mpiranya (Case No. ICTR-00-56)

Commander of the Presidential Guard Battalion within the High Command of the Rwandan Army.</td></tr>
<tr><td>Indictment[735] (International sex crimes (or related) charges and mode(s) of liability)</td><td>- Genocide (count 2) or, alternatively, Complicitiy in genocide (count 3) and Rape as CAH (count 7), Persecutions as CAH (count 8) and Other inhumane acts as CAH (count 9) under Article 6(3) of the Statute (superior responsibility) for: (i) the sexual assault of the Prime Minister Agathe Uwilingiyimana by members of the Presidential Guard under the command of Protais Mpiranya; and (ii) the gang-rapes, rapes and other degrading acts committed against young Tutsi women and girls by soldiers, including those of the Presidential Guard, on a daily basis at locations nearby the conseiller's compound in Kicukiro, particularly empty houses and to a forest nearby.[736]</td></tr>
</table>

735 *Prosecutor v. Augustin Bizimungu et al.*, Case No. ICTR-00-56-I, Indictment (Amended in conformity with Trial Chamber II Decision dated 25 September 2002), 23 October 2002 ("*Mpiranya* Indictment"), paras. 4.40 ("Furthermore, soldiers, militiamen and gendarmes abducted some Tutsi women and girls, and took them to other locations, where they raped or sexually assaulted them or committed other crimes of a sexual nature against them. These acts were commonly accompanied by verbal abuses, physical assault, degrading treatments and several cases of murder. Those crimes resulted in serious mental and physical injuries, permanent disabilities, including destruction of reproductive organs, unwanted pregnancies and sexually transmitted diseases, including AIDS".), 5.71 ("During the events referred to in this indictment, rapes, sexual assaults and other crimes of a sexual nature were systematically and widely committed throughout Rwanda. These crimes were perpetrated by, among others, soldiers, militiamen and gendarmes against the Tutsi population, in particular against Tutsi women and young girls".).

736 *Mpiranya* Indictment, paras. 5.7 ("While this meeting was going on, Prime Minister Agathe Uwilingiyimana was tracked down, arrested, sexually assaulted and killed by Rwandan Army personnel, more specifically, by members of the Presidential Guard under the command of **Major Protais Mpiranya** […]".), 5.19 ("As from 7 April 1994, massacres of the Tutsi population, which included on many occasions, rapes, sexual assaults and other crimes of a sexual nature, and the murder of numerous political opponents were perpetrated throughout the territory of Rwanda. These crimes, which had been planned and prepared for a long time by prominent civilian and military figures who shared the extremist Hutu ideology, were carried out by militiamen, military personnel and gendarmes on the orders and directives of some of these authorities, including […] **Major Protais Mpiranya** […]".), 5.43 ("From April to July 1994, by virtue of their position, their statements, the orders they gave and their acts, […] **Major Protais Mpiranya** […] exercised authority over members of the *Forces Armées Rwandaises*, their officers and militiamen. The military, gendarmes and militiamen, as from 6 April 1994, committed massacres of the Tutsi population and of moderate Hutu and other crimes such as rapes and sexual assaults and other crimes of a sexual nature, which extended throughout the territory of Rwanda with the knowledge of […] **Major Protais Mpiranya** […]".), 5.45 ("From April to July 1994, in all the regions of the country, members of the Tutsi population who were fleeing from the massacres in their areas sought refuge in locations they believed would be safe, often on the recommendation of the local civil and military authorities. […] Furthermore, in many of those places, soldiers and militiamen abducted, killed and raped or sexually assaulted Tutsi women. […] **Protais Mpiranya**, in his capacity of Commander of the Presidential Guard, […] knew or had reasons to know and that their subordinates were about to commit or had committed crimes and did nothing to prevent such crimes or to punish the perpetrators".), 5.48 ("As of 7 April, in Kigali, elements of the Rwandan Army, Gendarmerie and *Interahamwe* perpetrated massacres of the civilian Tutsi population often in collaboration with one another. Numerous massacres of the civilian Tutsi population took place in places where they had sought refuge, and included on many occasions, sexual violence and rape of Tutsi women. […] **Protais Mpiranya**, in his capacity of Commander of the Presidential Guard, […] knew or had reasons to know and that their subordinates were about to commit or had committed crimes and did nothing to prevent such crimes or to punish the perpetrators".), 5.54 ("During April and May 1994, soldiers, including those of the Presidential Guard, and *Interahamwe* came to the *Conseiller's* compound in Kicukiro on a daily basis and abducted young Tutsi women and girls to nearby locations, particularly empty houses and to a forest nearby, where they subjected them to gang-rapes, rapes and other degrading acts. Those who showed any resistance were killed".), pp. 30–32 ("**COUNT 2:** By the acts or omissions described in the paragraphs referred to below: […] 3) **Protais Mpiranya** : pursuant to Article

Trial Judgement	N/A (Still at large.)
Appeal Judgement	N/A
Legal and Factual Findings and/or Evidence	N/A

15.4. SCSL International Sex Crimes Charts

1. Alex Tamba **Brima *et al.*** (Case No. SCSL-04-16) "***AFRC***"

- Alex Tamba Brima: Member of the Supreme Council of the Armed Forces Revolutionary Council (AFRC), the highest decision-making body of the military junta, since May 1997; Principal Liaison Officer (PLO) 2 in the AFRC government; overall Commander of the AFRC force since December 1998.
- Brima Bazzy Kamara: Member of the Supreme Council of the AFRC since May 1997; PLO 3 in the AFRC government; Deputy Commander of the AFRC force since December 1998.
- Santigie Borbor Kanu: Member of the Supreme Council of the AFRC since May 1997; Chief of Staff of the AFRC force since December 1998.

6(1), paragraphs: […] 5.43, 5.45 pursuant to Article 6(3), paragraphs: […] 5.7, […] 5.45, 5.48, […] 5.54, [… is] responsible for killing and causing serious bodily or mental harm to members of the Tutsi population with the intent to destroy, in whole or in part, a racial or ethnic group, and thereby committed **GENOCIDE**, a crime stipulated in Article 2(3)(a) of the Statute of the Tribunal, for which [he is] individually responsible pursuant to Article 6 and which is punishable in reference to Articles 22 and 23 of the Statute. **ALTERNATIVELY TO COUNT 2, COUNT 3:** By the acts or omissions described in the paragraphs referred to below: […] 3) **Protais Mpiranya** : pursuant to Article 6(1), paragraphs: […] 5.43 pursuant to Article 6(3), paragraphs: […] 5.7, […] 5.45, 5.48, […] 5.54 [… is] responsible for killing and causing serious bodily or mental harm to members of the Tutsi population with the intent to destroy, in whole or in part, a racial or ethnic group, and thereby committed **COMPLICITY IN GENOCIDE,** a crime stipulated in Article 2(3)(e) of the Statute of the Tribunal, for which [he is] individually responsible pursuant to Article 6 and which is punishable in reference to Articles 22 and 23 of the Statute".), 34–36 ("**COUNT 7:** By the acts or omissions described in the paragraphs referred to below: […] 2) **Protais Mpiranya**: pursuant to Article 6(3), paragraphs: 5.7, 5.54 [… is] responsible for rape as part of a widespread and systematic attack against a civilian population on political, ethnic or racial grounds, and thereby committed a **CRIME AGAINST HUMANITY**, a crime stipulated in Article 3(g) of Statute of the Tribunal, for which [he is] individually responsible pursuant to Article 6 of the Statute and which is punishable in reference to Articles 22 and 23 of the Statute. **COUNT 8:** By the acts or omissions described in the paragraphs referred to below: 3) **Protais Mpiranya** : pursuant to Article 6(1), paragraphs: […] 5.43, 5.45 […] pursuant to Article 6(3), paragraphs: […] 5.7, […] 5.45, 5.48, […] 5.54 [… is] responsible for persecution on political, racial or religious grounds, as part of a widespread and systematic attack against a civilian population on political, ethnic or racial grounds, and thereby committed a **CRIME AGAINST HUMANITY**, a crime stipulated in Article 3(h) of Statute of the Tribunal, for which [he is] individually responsible pursuant to Article 6 of the Statute and which is punishable in reference to Articles 22 and 23 of the Statute. **COUNT 9:** By the acts or omissions described in the paragraphs referred to below: […] 3) **Protais Mpiranya** : pursuant to Article 6(1), paragraphs: […] 5.43, 5.45 pursuant to Article 6(3), paragraphs: […] 5.7, […] 5.45, 5.48 […] 5.54 [… is] responsible for inhumane acts against persons as part of a widespread and systematic attack against a civilian population on political, ethnic or racial grounds, and thereby committed a **CRIME AGAINST HUMANITY**, a crime stipulated in Article 3(i) of Statute of the Tribunal, for which [he is] individually responsible pursuant to Article 6 of the Statute and which is punishable in reference to Articles 22 and 23 of the Statute".).

Indictment (International sex crimes (or related) charges and mode(s) of liability)	All three accused were charged with: - **Rape as CAH** (count 6), **Sexual slavery and any other form of sexual violence as CAH** (count 7), **Other inhumane acts as CAH** (count 8) and **Outrages upon personal dignity as a violation of Article 3 common to the Geneva Conventions and of Additional Protocol II (WC)** (count 9) under Articles 6(1) and 6(3) of the Statute (**superior responsibility**) for: (i) the rapes of hundreds of women and girls; and (ii) the abductions of an unknown number of women and girls for using them as sex slaves and/or forcing them into 'marriages' and/or subjecting them to other forms of sexual violence.[737] - **Acts of terrorism as a violation of Article 3 common to the Geneva Conventions and of Additional Protocol II (WC)** (count 1) and **Collective Punishment as a violation of Article 3 common to the Geneva Conventions and of Additional Protocol II (WC)** (count 2) under Articles 6(1) and 6(3) of the Statute (**superior**

[737] *Prosecutor v. Alex Tamba Brima et al.*, Case No. SCSL-04-16-PT, Further Amended Consolidated Indictment, 18 February 2005 ("*Alex Tamba Brima et al.* Indictment"), paras. 51–57 ("Widespread sexual violence committed against civilian women and girls included brutal rapes, often by multiple rapists, and forced 'marriages'. Acts of sexual violence included the following: **Kono District** Between about 14 February 1998 and 30 June 1998, members of AFRC/RUF raped hundreds of women and girls at various locations throughout the District, including Koidu, Tombodu, Kissi-town (or Kissi Town), Foendor (or Foendu), Tomendeh, Fokoiya, Wondedu and AFRC/RUF camps such as 'Superman camp' and Kissi-town (or Kissi Town) camp. An unknown number of women and girls were abducted from various locations within the District and used as sex slaves and/or forced into 'marriages' and/or subjected to other forms of sexual violence. The 'wives' were forced to perform a number of conjugal duties under coercion by their 'husbands'; **Koinadugu District** Between about 14 February 1998 and 30 September 1998, members of AFRC/RUF raped an unknown number of women and girls in locations in Koinadugu District, such as Kabala, Koinadugu, Heremakono and Fadugu. In addition an unknown number of women and girls were abducted and used as sex slaves and/or forced into 'marriages' and/or subjected to other forms of sexual violence. The 'wives' were forced to perform a number of conjugal duties under coercion by their 'husbands'; **Bombali District** Between about 1 May 1998 and 31 November 1998, members of the AFRC/RUF raped an unknown number of women and girls in locations in Bombali District, including Mandaha and Rosos (or Rosors or Rossos). In addition, an unknown number of abducted women and girls were used as sex slaves and/or forced into 'marriages' and/or subjected to other forms of sexual violence. The 'wives' were forced to perform a number of conjugal duties under coercion by their 'husbands'; **Kailahun District** At all times relevant to this Indictment, an unknown number of women and girls in various locations in the District were subjected to sexual violence. Many of these victims were captured in other areas of the Republic of Sierra Leone, brought to AFRC/RUF camps in the District, and used as sex slaves and/or forced into 'marriages' and/or subjected to other forms of sexual violence. The 'wives' were forced to perform a number of conjugal duties under coercion by their 'husbands'; **Freetown and the Western Area** Between 6 January 1999 and 28 February 1999, members of AFRC/RUF raped hundreds of women and girls throughout the City of Freetown and the Western Area, and abducted hundreds of women and girls and used them as sex slaves and/or forced them into 'marriages' and/or subjected them to other forms of sexual violence. The 'wives' were forced to perform a number of conjugal duties under coercion by their 'husbands'; **Port Loko District** About the month of February 1999, AFRC/RUF fled from Freetown to various locations in the Port Loko District. Between February 1999 and April 1999, members of the AFRC/RUF raped an unknown number of women and girls in various locations in the District. In addition, an unknown number of women and girls in various locations in the District were used as sex slaves and/or forced into 'marriages' and/or subjected to other forms of sexual violence by members of the AFRC/RUF. The 'wives' were forced to perform a number of conjugal duties under coercion by their 'husbands'; By their acts or omission in relation to these events, **ALEX TAMBA BRIMA, BRIMA BAZZY KAMARA and SANTIGIE BORBOR KANU**, pursuant to Artice 6.1. and, or alternatively, Article 6.3. of the Statute, are individually criminally responsible for the crimes alleged below: **Count 6:** Rape, a **CRIME AGAINST HUMANITY**, punishable under Article 2.g. of the Statute; And: **Count 7:** Sexual slavery and any other form of sexual violence, a **CRIME AGAINST HUMANITY**, punishable under Article 2.g. of the Statute; And: **Count 8:** Other inhumane act, a **CRIME AGAINST HUMANITY**, punishable under Article 2.i. of the Statute; In addition, or in the alternative: **Count 9:** Outrages upon personal dignity, a **VIOLATION OF ARTICLE 3 COMMON TO THE GENEVA CONVENTIONS AND OF ADDITIONAL PROTOCOL II**, punishable under Article 3.e. of the Statute".).

	responsibility) for committing the same crimes of sexual violence as those pleaded in counts 6 to 9 as part of a campaign to terrorise the civilian population and to punish the civilian population for allegedly supporting the elected government and factions aligned with that government, or for failing to provide sufficient support to the AFRC/RUF.[738]
Trial Judgement	- Alex Tamba Brima: Guilty of **Rape as CAH** (count 6) under Article 6(3) of the Statute (**superior responsibility**) and **Outrages upon personal dignity as a violation of Article 3 common to the Geneva Conventions and of Additional Protocol II (WC)** (count 9) under Article 6(1) of the Statute (**planning the commission**) for the crimes of rapes and sexual slavery committed in Bombali District and the Western Area.[739] Guilty of **Acts of terrorism as a violation of Article 3 common to the Geneva Conventions and of Additional Protocol II (WC)** (count 1) and **Collective Punishment as a violation of Article 3 common to the Geneva Conventions and of Additional Protocol II (WC)** (count 2) under Article 6(3) of the Statute (**superior responsibility**) for the various crimes, including rapes and sexual slavery in Bombali District and the Western Area, committed as part of a campaign to terrorise the civilian population and in order to punish the civilian population for allegedly supporting the elected government and factions aligned with that government.[740] The Trial Chamber did not enter a conviction for Sexual slavery and any other form of sexual violence as CAH (count 7) or Other inhumane act as CAH (count 8).[741] - Brima Bazzy Kamara: Guilty of **Rape as CAH** (count 6) under Article 6(3) of the Statute (**superior responsibility**) and **Outrages upon personal dignity as a violation of Article 3 common to the Geneva Conventions and of Additional Protocol II (WC)** (count 9) under Article 6(1) of the Statute for the crimes of rapes committed in Bombali District and in Freetown and sexual slavery committed in Kono.[742] Guilty of

738 *Alex Tamba Brima et al.* Indictment, paras. 41 ("Members of the AFRC/RUF subordinate to and/or acting in concert with **ALEX TAMBA BRIMA, BRIMA BAZZY KAMARA and SANTIGIE BORBOR KANU**, committed the crimes set forth below in paragraphs 42 through 79 and charged in Counts 3 through 14, as part of a campaign to terrorize the civilian population of the Republic of Sierra Leone, and did terrorize that population. The AFRC/RUF also committed the crimes to punish the civilian population for allegedly supporting the elected government of President Ahmed Tejan Kabbah and factions aligned with that government, or for failing to provide sufficient support to the AFRC/RUF. By their acts or omissions in relation to these events, **ALEX TAMBA BRIMA, BRIMA BAZZY KAMARA and SANTIGIE BORBOR KANU**, pursuant to Article 6.1. and, or alternatively, Article 6.3. of the Statute, are individually criminally responsible for the crimes alleged below: **Count 1:** Acts of Terrorism, a **VIOLATION OF ARTICLE 3 COMMON TO THE GENEVA CONVENTIONS AND OF ADDITIONAL PROTOCOL II**, punishable under Article 3.d. of the Statute; And: **Count 2:** Collective Punishments, a **VIOLATION OF ARTICLE 3 COMMON TO THE GENEVA CONVENTIONS AND OF ADDITIONAL PROTOCOL II**, punishable under Article 3.b. of the Statute".), 51–57.

739 *Prosecutor v. Alex Tamba Brima et al.*, Case No. SCSL-04-16-T, Judgement, 20 June 2007 ("*Alex Tamba Brima et al.* Trial Judgement"), paras. 1041, 1068, 1145, 1170, 1188, 1744, 1810, 1833, 1835, 2104, 2113–2114.

740 *Alex Tamba Brima et al.* Trial Judgement, paras. 1546, 1567, 1571–1573, 1633–1634, 1744, 2104, 2113.

741 *Alex Tamba Brima et al.* Trial Judgement, paras. 95, 714, 2116.

742 *Alex Tamba Brima et al.* Trial Judgement, paras. 1041, 1068, 1109, 1188, 1928, 1950, 1976, 2105, 2117–2118; *Prosecutor v. Alex Tamba Brima et al.*, Case No. SCSL-04-16-T, Corrigendum to Judgement Filed on 21 June 2007, 19 July 2007 ("*Alex Tamba Brima et al.* Trial Judgement Corrigendum"), para. 12. Although the disposition of the *Alex Tamba Brima et al.* Trial Judgement convicts Brima Bazzy Kamara for Outrages upon personal dignity as a violation of Article 3 common to the Geneva Conventions and of Additional Protocol II (WC) (count 9) under Article 6(1) of the Statute for sexual slavery committed in Kono, the Trial Chamber's factual and legal findings clearly show that the Trial Chamber found him guilty under Article 6(3) of the Statute (superior responsibility) and not under Article 6(1) of the Statute. See also *Prosecutor v. Alex Tamba Brima et al.*, Case No. SCSL-04-16-A, Judgment, 22 February 2008 ("*Alex Tamba Brima et al.* Appeal Judgement"), paras. 239–240 and Section X (Disposition), p. 106.

	Acts of terrorism as a violation of Article 3 common to the Geneva Conventions and of Additional Protocol II (WC) (count 1) and **Collective Punishment as a violation of Article 3 common to the Geneva Conventions and of Additional Protocol II (WC)** (count 2) under Article 6(3) of the Statute (**superior responsibility**) for the various crimes, including rapes in Bombali District and Freetown and sexual slavery in Kono, committed as part of a campaign to terrorise the civilian population and in order to to punish the civilian population for allegedly supporting the elected government and factions aligned with that government.[743] The Trial Chamber did not enter a conviction for Sexual slavery and any other form of sexual violence as CAH (count 7) or Other inhumane act as CAH (count 8).[744] - Santigie Borbor Kanu: Guilty of **Rape as CAH** (count 6) under Article 6(3) of the Statute (**superior responsibility**) and **Outrages upon personal dignity as a violation of Article 3 common to the Geneva Conventions and of Additional Protocol II (WC)** (count 9) under Article 6(1) of the Statute (**planning the commission**) for the crimes of rapes and sexual slavery committed in Bombali District and the Western Area.[745] Guilty of **Acts of terrorism as a violation of Article 3 common to the Geneva Conventions and of Additional Protocol II (WC)** (count 1) and **Collective Punishment as a violation of Article 3 common to the Geneva Conventions and of Additional Protocol II (WC)** (count 2) under Article 6(3) of the Statute (**superior responsibility**) for the various crimes, including rapes in Bombali District and Freetown and sexual slavery in Kono, committed as part of a campaign to terrorise the civilian population and in order to to punish the civilian population for allegedly supporting the elected government and factions aligned with that government.[746] The Trial Chamber did not enter a conviction for Sexual slavery and any other form of sexual violence as CAH (count 7) or Other inhumane act as CAH (count 8).[747]
Appeal Judgement	The convictions were affirmed by the Appeals Chamber.[748] - Brima Bazzy Kamara: with respect to **Brima Bazzy Kamara's conviction for Outrages upon personal dignity as a violation of Article 3 common to the Geneva Conventions and of Additional Protocol II (WC)** (count 9) under Article 6(1) of the Statute, **the Appeals Chamber substituted Article 6(3) of the Statute (superior responsibility) for Article 6(1) of the Statute**. The Appeals Chamber found that the Trial Chamber's factual and legal findings clearly show that the Trial Chamber found Brima Bazzy Kamara guilty under Article 6(3) of the Statute (superior responsibility) but mistakenly stated in its disposition that he was guilty under Article 6(1) of the Statute.[749]

743 *Alex Tamba Brima et al.* Trial Judgement, paras. 1546, 1567, 1571–1573, 1633–1634, 1928, 2105, 2118; *Alex Tamba Brima et al.* Trial Judgement Corrigendum, paras. 12–13.

744 *Alex Tamba Brima et al.* Trial Judgement, paras. 95, 714, 2120.

745 *Alex Tamba Brima et al.* Trial Judgement, paras. 1041, 1068, 1145, 1170, 1188, 2044, 2080, 2096, 2106, 2121–2122; *Alex Tamba Brima et al.* Trial Judgement Corrigendum, para. 14.

746 *Alex Tamba Brima et al.* Trial Judgement, paras. 1546, 1567, 1571–1573, 1633–1634, 2044, 2106, 2122; *Alex Tamba Brima et al.* Trial Judgement Corrigendum, paras. 14–15.

747 *Alex Tamba Brima et al.* Trial Judgement, paras. 95, 714, 2123.

748 *Alex Tamba Brima et al.* Appeal Judgement, Section X (Disposition), pp. 105–106.

749 *Alex Tamba Brima et al.* Appeal Judgement, paras. 239–240 ("The Appeals Chamber has considered Kamara's Grounds Two, Three and Four where the substance of complaint is that the Trial Chamber erred in fact in finding that Kamara planned the crimes alleged in Counts 9, 12 and 13. Having scrutinised the Record on Appeal the Appeals Chamber concludes that the Grounds of Appeal were misconceived. The Trial Chamber in its findings had not found that Kamara planned the crimes set out in Counts 9, 12 and 13. However, the Appeals Chamber has noted that the Trial Chamber in its Disposition had mistakenly stated that Kamara was guilty of the crimes in Counts 9, 12 and 13 pursuant to Article 6(1) of the Statute when it should have been Article 6(3). Accordingly, the Appeals Chamber revises the Trial Chamber's Disposition by substituting Article 6(3) for Article 6(1) in respect of Counts 9, 12 and 13".) and Section X (Disposition), p. 106.

	- Santigie Borbor Kanu: with respect to Santigie Borbor Kanu's conviction for Outrages upon personal dignity as a violation of Article 3 common to the Geneva Conventions and of Additional Protocol II (WC) (count 9) under Article 6(1) of the Statute (planning the commission) for the crimes of sexual slavery committed in the Western Area, the Appeals Chamber found that that Trial Chamber erred in failing to convict Santigie Borbor Kanu for aiding and abetting those crimes. However, the Appeals Chamber upheld the conviction for planning the commission of sexual slavery in the Western Area and found that the question of convicting him on the basis of aiding and abetting does not arise as he has already been convicted of planning those crimes.[750]
Legal and Factual Findings and/or Evidence	- Legal findings: **- Rape:** The Trial Chamber adopted the definition of rape given in the *Kunarac et al.* case:[751] "In addition to the chapeau requirements of Crimes against Humanity pursuant to Article 2 of the Statute, the Trial Chamber adopts the following elements of the crime of rape: 1. The non-consensual penetration, however slight, of the vagina or anus of the victim by the penis of the perpetrator or by any other object used by the perpetrator, or of the mouth of the victim by the penis of the perpetrator; and 2. The intent to effect this sexual penetration, and the knowledge that it occurs without the consent of the victim. Consent of the victim must be given voluntarily, as a result of the victim's free will, assessed in the context of the surrounding circumstances. Force or threat of force provides clear evidence of non-consent, but force is not an element per se of rape and there are factors other than force which would render an act of sexual penetration non-consensual or non-voluntary on the part of the victim. This is necessarily a contextual assessment. However, in situations of armed conflict or detention, coercion is almost universal. 'Continuous resistance' by the victim, and physical force, or even threat of force by the perpetrator are not required to establish coercion".[752] The Trial Chamber further held: "Children below the age of 14 cannot give valid consent".[753] The Trial Chamber held that the *actus reus* of rape can be proved through circumstantial evidence: "The Trial Chamber acknowledges that the very specific circumstances of an armed conflict where rapes on a large scale are alleged to have occurred, coupled with the social stigma which is borne by victims of rape in certain societies, render the

[750] *Alex Tamba Brima et al.* Appeal Judgement, paras. 305–306 ("Finally, the Appeals Chamber finds that the evidence led before the Trial Chamber warrants an examination of Kanu's responsibility for aiding and abetting the commission of sexual slavery […] in Newton in the Western Area. The Appeals Chamber notes that witness TF1-334, whom the Trial Chamber found to be credible and reliable, stated that Kanu was responsible for the women and girls in the camp at Newton. AFRC soldiers reported to Kanu if they had any problems with the women and girls. The Trial Chamber found that while the women were helping with the cooking, 'the 'girls' were sleeping with the 'commanders'.' The Appeals Chamber is satisfied that in this position of responsibility regarding the women and girls at Newton, Kanu provided practical assistance to a system of sexual slavery and forced labour. The Appeals Chamber is further satisfied that Kanu was aware that his acts would assist in the implementation of this system of sexual slavery […]. In light of the above evidence, the Appeals Chamber is satisfied that Kanu aided and abetted the commission of sexual slavery […] in the Western Area. Thus, the Appeals Chamber finds that the Trial Chamber erred in failing to convict Kanu for aiding and abetting the commission of sexual slavery […] in the Western Area. The Appeals Chamber upholds the conviction of Kanu for planning the commission of sexual slavery in the Bombali District and upholds the conviction of Kanu for planning the commission of sexual slavery in the Western Area […]. The Appeals Chamber furthermore finds that there is sufficient evidence that Kanu aided and abetted the commission of the said crimes. However, as he has already been convicted of planning those crimes the question of convicting him on the basis of aiding and abetting does not arise" (internal references omitted)).

[751] ICTY ISCC *Kunarac et al.*, see *supra* p. 528.

[752] *Alex Tamba Brima et al.* Trial Judgement, paras. 693–694 (internal references omitted).

[753] *Alex Tamba Brima et al.* Trial Judgement, para. 694 (internal reference omitted).

	restrictive test set out in the elements of the crime difficult to satisfy. Circumstantial evidence may therefore be used to demonstrate the *actus reus* of rape".[754] **- Duplicity in pleading sexual slavery and any other form of sexual violence:** The Trial Chamber, Judge Teresa Doherty dissenting, found that count 7 (Sexual slavery and any other form of sexual violence as CAH) violated the rule against duplicity and dismissed that count in its entirety.[755] The Appeals Chamber held: "In its Judgment, the Trial Chamber revisited Count 7 and endorsed Justice Sebutinde's Rule 98 Opinion that the Count offended the rule against duplicity. It adopted her Rule 98 Opinion that Article 2.g of the Statute 'encapsulates five distinct categories of sexual offences [...] each of which is comprised of separate and distinct elements.' It held that Count 7 of the Indictment charged the Appellant with two distinct crimes against humanity in one count, namely 'sexual slavery' and 'any other form of sexual violence.' [...] The Appeals Chamber agrees with the Trial Chamber that Article 2.g of the Statute provides for five distinct crimes against humanity, each of which is of a sexual nature, among which are 'sexual slavery' and 'any other form of sexual violence.' 'Sexual slavery' requires the exercise of rights of ownership over the victim, which is not the case for 'other forms of sexual violence.' Consequently, Count 7 of the Indictment, which charges the commission of 'sexual slavery and any other form of sexual violence,' offends the rule against duplicity by charging two offences in the same count. The dispositive question, therefore, is not whether the rule was violated, but what are the consequences. [...] The Appeals Chamber holds that the rule against duplicity applies to international criminal tribunals such that the charging of two separate offences in a single count renders the count defective, although a single count may charge different means of committing the same offence. Accordingly, Count 7 of the Indictment, which charges the commission of 'sexual slavery and any other form of sexual violence,' violates the rule against duplicity. [...] Upon its finding that Count 7 violated the rule against duplicity, the Trial Chamber dismissed the count in its entirety. The Trial Chamber's choice of remedy was premised on its finding that any proceedings on the basis of a duplicitous count would render the trial unfair to the Appellants. The duplicitous pleading of Count 7 placed the Appellants in the position of having to defend two crimes in the same count. The residual nature of the crime of 'any other form of sexual violence' requires clarification of the conduct the Prosecution would rely upon to prove the offence. [...] In light of the foregoing, the Appeals Chamber considers that the remedies available to the Trial Chamber included: (i) quashing the count; (ii) ordering that the Indictment be amended; (iii) directing the Prosecution to elect to proceed on the basis of one of the two offences in the duplicitous count; (iv) upon a review of the entire case, determining which of the two offences charged in the count the Appellant had defended fully, having regard to the manner in which the defence case had been conducted; and (v) refusing to consider evidence of one of the two charges so as to eliminate the duplicity of Count 7. Each case is to be considered on its own merits. In the instant case, from the evidence accepted by the Trial Chamber and the findings it had made, it should have chosen the option to proceed on the basis that the offence of sexual slavery had been properly charged in Count 7, return appropriate verdict on that Count in respect of the crime of sexual slavery and struck out the charge of 'any other form of sexual violence.' Although the Trial Chamber had not chosen that option, no miscarriage of justice has resulted therefrom. It is not necessary for the Appeals Chamber to substitute a conviction for sexual slavery as the Trial Chamber relied upon the evidence of

[754] *Alex Tamba Brima et al.* Trial Judgement, para. 695 (internal reference omitted).

[755] *Alex Tamba Brima et al.* Trial Judgement, para. 95. See also *Alex Tamba Brima et al.* Trial Judgement, Partly Dissenting Opinion of Justice Doherty on Count 7 (Sexual Slavery) and Count 8 ('Forced Marriages').

sexual slavery to enter convictions for Count 9 which charged the offence of 'outrages upon personal dignity.'"[756]

- Other inhumane acts for international sex crimes:

The Trial Chamber held: "The offence of 'other inhumane acts' pursuant to Article 2(i) of the Statute is a residual clause which covers a broad range of underlying acts not explicitly enumerated in Article 2(a) through (h) of the Statute. In light of the exhaustive category of sexual crimes particularised in Article 2(g) of the Statute, the offence of 'other inhumane acts', even though residual, must logically be restrictively interpreted as applying only to acts of a non-sexual nature amounting to an affront to human dignity".[757]

The Appeals Chamber found that the Trial Chamber erred in law and overturned the Trial Chamber's reasoning. The Appeals Chamber held: "The jurisprudence of the international tribunals shows that a wide range of criminal acts, including sexual crimes, have been recognised as 'Other Inhumane Acts.' These include forcible transfer, sexual and physical violence perpetrated upon dead human bodies, other serious physical and mental injury, forced undressing of women and marching them in public, forcing women to perform exercises naked, and forced disappearance, beatings, torture, sexual violence, humiliation, harassment, psychological abuse, and confinement in inhumane conditions. Case law at these tribunals further demonstrates that this category has been used to punish a series of violent acts that may vary depending upon the context. In effect, the determination of whether an alleged act qualifies as an 'Other Inhumane Act' must be made on a case-by-case basis taking into account the nature of the alleged act or omission, the context in which it took place, the personal circumstances of the victims including age, sex, health, and the physical, mental and moral effects of the perpetrator's conduct upon the victims. The Trial Chamber therefore erred in law by finding that 'Other Inhumane Acts' under Article 2.i must be restrictively interpreted. A tribunal must take care not to adopt too restrictive an interpretation of the prohibition against 'Other Inhumane Acts' which, as stated above, was intended to be a residual provision. At the same time, care must be taken not to make it too embracing as to make a surplusage of what has been expressly provided for, or to render the crime nebulous and incapable of concrete ascertainment. An overbroad interpretation will certainly infringe the rule requiring specificity of criminal prohibitions. Furthermore, the Appeals Chamber sees no reason why the so-called 'exhaustive' listing of sexual crimes under Article 2.g of the Statute should foreclose the possibility of charging as 'Other Inhumane Acts' crimes which may among others have a sexual or gender component. As an ICTY Trial Chamber has recognised, '[h]owever much care [was] taken in establishing a list of all the various forms of infliction, one would never be able to catch up with the imagination of future torturers who wish to satisfy their bestial instincts; and the more specific and complete a list tries to be, the more restrictive it becomes.' The Trial Chamber therefore erred in finding that Article 2.i of the Statute excludes sexual crimes".[758]

- "Forced marriages" as other inhumane acts and sexual slavery:

The Trial Chamber, Judge Teresa Doherty dissenting, found: "As described above, the crime of 'other inhumane acts' exists as a residual category in order not to unduly restrict the Statute's application with regard to crimes against humanity. 'Forced marriage' as an 'other inhumane act' must therefore involve conduct not otherwise

756 *Alex Tamba Brima et al.* Appeal Judgement, paras. 90, 102–103, 105–106, 108–110 (internal references omitted).

757 *Alex Tamba Brima et al.* Trial Judgement, para. 697 (internal reference omitted).

758 *Alex Tamba Brima et al.* Appeal Judgement, paras. 184–186 (internal references omitted).

	subsumed by other crimes enumerated under Article 2 of the Statute. At the Motion for Acquittal Stage, the Trial Chamber found that there was *prima facie* evidence of a non-sexual nature relating to the abduction of women and girls forced to submit to 'marital' relationships and to perform various conjugal duties. Having now examined the whole of the evidence in the case, the Trial Chamber by a majority is not satisfied that the evidence adduced by the Prosecution is capable of establishing the elements of a non-sexual crime of 'forced marriage' independent of the crime of sexual slavery under article 2(g) of the Statute".[759] The Trial Chamber found: "The Prosecution evidence in the present case does not point to even one instance of a woman or girl having had a bogus marriage forced upon her in circumstances which did not amount to sexual slavery. Not one of the victims of sexual slavery gave evidence that the mere fact that a rebel had declared her to be his wife had caused her any particular trauma, whether physical or mental. Moreover, in the opinion of the Trial Chamber, had there been such evidence, it would not by itself have amounted to a crime against humanity, since it would not have been of similar gravity to the acts referred to in Article 2(a) to (h) of the Statute. The Trial Chamber finds that the totality of the evidence adduced by the Prosecution as proof of 'forced marriage' goes to proof of elements subsumed by the crime of sexual slavery. [...] so-called 'forced marriages' involved the forceful abduction of girls and women from their homes or other places of refuge and their detention with the AFRC troops as they attacked and moved through various districts. The girls and women were taken against their will as 'wives' by individual rebels. The evidence showed that the relationship of the perpetrators to their 'wives' was one of ownership and involved the exercise of control by the perpetrator over the victim, including control of the victim's sexuality, her movements and her labour; for example, the 'wife' was expected to carry the rebel's possessions as they moved from one location to the next, to cook for him and to wash his clothes. Similarly, the Trial Chamber is satisfied that the use of the term 'wife' by the perpetrator in reference to the victim is indicative of the intent of the perpetrator to exercise ownership over the victim, and not an intent to assume a marital or quasi-marital status with the victim in the sense of establishing mutual obligations inherent in a husband wife relationship. In fact, while the relationship of the rebels to their 'wives' was generally one of exclusive ownership, the victim could be passed on or given to another rebel at the discretion of the perpetrator. None of the witnesses gave evidence that they considered themselves to be in fact 'married'. (One witness testified that she had been 'married' to her rebel 'husband' in a ceremony, but no consent could be inferred given the environment of violence and coercion.) Rather, the repeated assertion of the witnesses was that they had been 'taken as wives'. They were held against their will and a number tried to escape. There was no evidence that any of the women taken as 'wives' stayed on with their rebel 'husbands' following the end of hostilities. In light of the foregoing, the Trial Chamber finds, by a majority, that the evidence adduced by the Prosecution is completely subsumed by the crime of sexual slavery and that there is no lacuna in the law which would necessitate a separate crime of 'forced marriage' as an 'other inhumane act'. In view of the Trial Chamber's findings that Count 7 is bad for duplicity, the Trial will in the interests of justice consider the evidence of Sexual Slavery under Count 9. The Trial Chamber further finds that alleged offences of a residual, non-sexual nature do not belong under the part of the Indictment entitled 'Counts 6–9: Sexual Violence'. The Trial Chamber finds by a majority that Count 8 is redundant insofar as the crime of sexual slavery

[759] *Alex Tamba Brima et al.* Trial Judgement, paras. 703–704 (internal references omitted). See also *Alex Tamba Brima et al.* Trial Judgement, Separate Concurring Opinion of the Hon. Justice Julia Sebutinde Appended to Judgement Pursuant to Rule 88 (C); *Alex Tamba Brima et al.* Trial Judgement, Partly Dissenting Opinion of Justice Doherty on Count 7 (Sexual Slavery) and Count 8 ('Forced Marriages').

	will be dealt with in Count 9. Other residual crimes of a non-sexual nature are dealt with in Count 11. Count 8 is therefore dismissed".[760] The Appeals Chamber found that the Trial Chamber erred and overturned the Trial Chamber's reasoning. The Appeals Chamber held: "The trial record contains ample evidence that the perpetrators of forced marriages intended to impose a forced conjugal association upon the victims rather than exercise an ownership interest and that forced marriage is not predominantly a sexual crime. There is substantial evidence in the Trial Judgment to establish that throughout the conflict in Sierra Leone, women and girls were systematically abducted from their homes and communities by troops belonging to the AFRC and compelled to serve as conjugal partners to AFRC soldiers. They were often abducted in circumstances of extreme violence, compelled to move along with the fighting forces from place to place, and coerced to perform a variety of conjugal duties including regular sexual intercourse, forced domestic labour such as cleaning and cooking for the 'husband,' endure forced pregnancy, and to care for and bring up children of the 'marriage.' In return, the rebel 'husband' was expected to provide food, clothing and protection to his 'wife,' including protection from rape by other men, acts he did not perform when he used a female for sexual purposes only. As the Trial Chamber found, the relative benefits that victims of forced marriage received from the perpetrators neither signifies consent to the forced conjugal association, nor does it vitiate the criminal nature of the perpetrator's conduct given the environment of violence and coercion in which these events took place. The Trial Chamber findings also demonstrate that these forced conjugal associations were often organised and supervised by members of the AFRC or civilians assigned by them to such tasks. A 'wife' was exclusive to a rebel 'husband,' and any transgression of this exclusivity such as unfaithfulness, was severely punished. A 'wife' who did not perform the conjugal duties demanded of her was deemed disloyal and could face serious punishment under the AFRC disciplinary system, including beating and possibly death. In addition to the Trial Chamber's findings, other evidence in the trial record shows that the perpetrators intended to impose a forced conjugal association rather than exercise mere ownership over civilian women and girls. In particular, the Appeals Chamber notes the evidence and report of the Prosecution expert Mrs. Zainab Bangura which demonstrates the physical and psychological suffering to which victims of forced marriage were subjected during the civil war in Sierra Leone. […] In light of all the evidence at trial, Judge Doherty, in her Partly Dissenting Opinion, expressed the view that forced marriage involves 'the imposition, by threat or physical force arising from the perpetrator's words or other conduct, of a forced conjugal association by the perpetrator over the victim.' She further considered that this crime satisfied the elements of 'Other Inhumane Acts' because victims were subjected to mental trauma by being labelled as rebel 'wives'; further, they were stigmatised and found it difficult to reintegrate into their communities. According to Judge Doherty, forced marriage qualifies as an 'Other Inhumane Acts' causing mental and moral suffering, which in the context of the Sierra Leone conflict, is of comparable seriousness to the other crimes against humanity listed in the Statute. Furthermore, the Appeals Chamber also notes that in their respective Concurring and Partly Dissenting Opinions, both Justice Sebutinde and Justice Doherty make a clear and convincing distinction between forced marriages in a war context and the peacetime practice of 'arranged marriages' among certain traditional communities, noting that arranged marriages are not to be equated to or confused with forced marriage during armed conflict. Justice Sebutinde goes further to add, correctly in our view, that while traditionally arranged marriages involving minors violate certain international human rights norms such as the Convention on the Elimination of all Forms of Discrimination against Women (CEDAW), forced marriages which involve the abduction and detention of women and girls and their use for sexual and other purposes is clearly criminal in nature. Based on the evidence on

[760] *Alex Tamba Brima et al.* Trial Judgement, paras. 710–714 (internal references omitted).

	record, the Appeals Chamber finds that no tribunal could reasonably have found that forced marriage was subsumed in the crime against humanity of sexual slavery. While forced marriage shares certain elements with sexual slavery such as non-consensual sex and deprivation of liberty, there are also distinguishing factors. First, forced marriage involves a perpetrator compelling a person by force or threat of force, through the words or conduct of the perpetrator or those associated with him, into a forced conjugal association with a another person resulting in great suffering, or serious physical or mental injury on the part of the victim. Second, unlike sexual slavery, forced marriage implies a relationship of exclusivity between the 'husband' and 'wife,' which could lead to disciplinary consequences for breach of this exclusive arrangement. These distinctions imply that forced marriage is not predominantly a sexual crime. The Trial Chamber, therefore, erred in holding that the evidence of forced marriage is subsumed in the elements of sexual slavery. In light of the distinctions between forced marriage and sexual slavery, the Appeals Chamber finds that in the context of the Sierra Leone conflict, forced marriage describes a situation in which the perpetrator through his words or conduct, or those of someone for whose actions he is responsible, compels a person by force, threat of force, or coercion to serve as a conjugal partner resulting in severe suffering, or physical, mental or psychological injury to the victim".[761] The Appeals Chamber further held: "The Appeals Chamber agrees with the Prosecution that the notion of 'Other Inhumane Acts' contained in Article 2.i of the Statute forms part of customary international law. As noted above, it serves as a residual category designed to punish acts or omissions not specifically listed as crimes against humanity provided these acts or omissions meet the following requirements: (i) inflict great suffering, or serious injury to body or to mental or physical health; (ii) are sufficiently similar in gravity to the acts referred to in Article 2.a to Article 2.h of the Statute; and (iii) the perpetrator was aware of the factual circumstances that established the character of the gravity of the act. The acts must also satisfy the general *chapeau* requirements of crimes against humanity. The Appeals Chamber finds that the evidence before the Trial Chamber established that victims of forced marriage endured physical injury by being subjected to repeated acts of rape and sexual violence, forced labour, corporal punishment, and deprivation of liberty. Many were psychologically traumatised by being forced to watch the killing or mutilation of close family members, before becoming 'wives' to those who committed these atrocities and from being labelled rebel 'wives' which resulted in them being ostracised from their communities. In cases where they became pregnant from the forced marriage, both they and their children suffered long-term social stigmatisation. In assessing the gravity of forced marriage in the Sierra Leone conflict, the Appeals Chamber has taken into account the nature of the perpetrators' conduct especially the atmosphere of violence in which victims were abducted and the vulnerability of the women and girls especially those of a very young age. Many of the victims of forced marriage were children themselves. Similarly, the Appeals Chamber has considered the effects of the perpetrators' conduct on the physical, moral, and psychological health of the victims. The Appeals Chamber is firmly of the view that acts of forced marriage were of similar gravity to several enumerated crimes against humanity including enslavement, imprisonment, torture, rape, sexual slavery and sexual violence. The Appeals Chamber is also satisfied that in each case, the perpetrators intended to force a conjugal partnership upon the victims, and were aware that their conduct would cause serious suffering or physical, mental or psychological injury to the victims. Considering the systematic and forcible abduction of the victims of forced marriage, and the prevailing environment of coercion and intimidation, the Appeals Chamber finds that the perpetrators of these acts could not have been under any illusion that their conduct was not criminal. This conclusion is fortified by the fact that the acts described as forced marriage may

761 *Alex Tamba Brima et al.* Appeal Judgement, paras. 190–196 (internal references omitted).

have involved the commission of one or more international crimes such as enslavement, imprisonment, rape, sexual slavery, abduction among others. The Appeals Chamber has carefully given consideration to whether or not it would enter fresh convictions for 'Other Inhumane Acts' (forced marriage). The Appeals Chamber is fully aware of the Prosecution's submission that entering such convictions would reflect the full culpability of the Appellant. The Appeals Chamber is also aware that the Trial Chamber relied upon the evidence led in support of sexual slavery and forced marriage to enter convictions against the Appellants for 'Outrages upon Personal Dignity' under Count 9 of the Indictment. Since 'Outrages upon Personal Dignity' and 'Other Inhumane Acts' have materially distinct elements (in the least, the former is a war crime, and the latter a crime against humanity) there is no bar to entering cumulative convictions for both offences on the basis of the same facts. However, in this case the Appeals Chamber is inclined against entering such cumulative convictions. The Appeals Chamber is convinced that society's disapproval of the forceful abduction and use of women and girls as forced conjugal partners as part of a widespread or systematic attack against the civilian population, is adequately reflected by recognising that such conduct is criminal and that it constitutes an 'Other Inhumane Act' capable of incurring individual criminal responsibility in international law".[762]

- Sexual slavery:

The Trial Chamber found that the prohibition of sexual slavery is a norm of *jus cogens*: "Sexual slavery is a specific form of slavery. The prohibition against slavery is a customary norm of international law and the establishment of enslavement as a crime against humanity is firmly entrenched. Thus, slavery for the purpose of sexual abuse is a *jus cogens* prohibition in the same manner as slavery for the purpose of physical labour".[763]

With respect to the elements of the crime, the Trial Chamber held: "In addition to the chapeau requirements of Crimes Against Humanity pursuant to Article 2 of the Statute, the elements of the crime of sexual slavery are as follows: 1. The perpetrator exercised any or all of the powers attaching to the right of ownership over one or more persons, such as by purchasing, selling, lending or bartering such a person or persons, or by imposing on them a similar deprivation of liberty; 2. The perpetrator caused such person or persons to engage in one or more acts of a sexual nature; 3. The perpetrator committed such conduct intending to engage in the act of sexual slavery or in the reasonable knowledge that it was likely to occur. The powers of ownership listed in the first element of sexual slavery are non-exhaustive. There is no requirement for any payment or exchange in order to establish the exercise of ownership. Deprivation of liberty may include extracting forced labour or otherwise reducing a person to servile status. Further, ownership, as indicated by possession, does not require confinement to a particular place but may include situations in which those who are captured remain in the control of their captors because they have no where else to go and fear for their lives. The consent or free will of the victim is absent under conditions of enslavement".[764]

- Outrages upon personal dignity:

The Trial Chamber found: "Article 3(e) of the Statute safeguards the highly important value of human dignity by prohibiting '[o]utrages upon personal dignity, in particular humiliating and degrading treatment, rape, enforced prostitution and any form of indecent assault'. The crime of outrages upon personal dignity must be interpreted in

762 *Alex Tamba Brima et al.* Appeal Judgement, paras. 198–202 (internal references omitted).

763 *Alex Tamba Brima et al.* Trial Judgement, para. 705 (internal references omitted).

764 *Alex Tamba Brima et al.* Trial Judgement, paras. 708–709 (internal references omitted).

light of the purpose behind Common Article 3 of the Conventions, which is: 'to uphold the inherent human dignity of the individual'; or to safeguard 'the principles of humane treatment.' The said crime is formulated in a manner which ensures broad and flexible interpretation. The list of offences subsumed under outrages against personal dignity constitutes a 'non-exhaustive list of conduct', with humiliating and degrading treatment, rape, enforced prostitution and indecent assaults of any kind given by way of example. The *ICRC Commentary on the Fourth Geneva Convention* notes that: '[i]t seems useless and even dangerous to attempt to make a list of all the factors that make treatment 'humane'' and that treatment which degrades human dignity can take innumerable forms. The crime of outrages upon personal dignity was first articulated in the 1949 Geneva Conventions and is firmly entrenched in customary international law. In addition to the chapeau requirements of Violations of Article 3 Common to the Geneva Conventions and of Additional Protocol II pursuant to Article 3 of the Statute, the Trial Chamber adopts the following elements of the crime of outrages upon personal dignity: 1. The perpetrator committed an outrage upon the personal dignity of the victim; 2. The humiliation and degradation was so serious as to be generally considered as an outrage upon personal dignity; 3. The perpetrator intentionally committed or participated in an act or omission which would be generally considered to cause serious humiliation, degradation or otherwise be a serious attack on human dignity; and 4. The perpetrator knew that the act or omission could have such an effect".[765]

- Rape, sexual slavery, and any other form of sexual violence as outrages upon personal dignity:

The Trial Chamber held: "Rape […] is an offence which is specified in Article 3(e) of the Statute as being an outrage upon personal dignity. As stated by the ICTR Trial Chamber in *Akayesu*, '[l]ike torture, rape is used for such purposes as intimidation, degradation, humiliation, discrimination, punishment, control or destruction of a person. Like torture, rape is a violation of personal dignity'. With reference to the elements of sexual slavery set out […] above, the Trial Chamber is similarly satisfied that sexual slavery is an act of humiliation and degradation so serious as to be generally considered an outrage upon personal dignity. The Trial Chamber in *Kvočka* held that 'perform[ing] subservient acts,' and 'endur[ing] the constant fear of being subjected to physical, mental or sexual violence' in camps were outrages upon personal dignity. Sexual slavery, which may encompasses rape and/or other types of sexual violence as well as enslavement, entails a similar humiliation and degradation of personal dignity. 'Any other form of Sexual Violence' in the context of crimes against humanity is a residual category of sexual crimes listed under Article 2(g) of the Statute, and may encompass an unlimited number of acts. The Trial Chamber agrees with the conclusion of the ICTY Trial Chamber in *Kvočka* that 'sexual violence is broader than rape'. The prohibition embraces all serious abuses of a sexual nature inflicted upon the physical and moral integrity of a person by means of coercion, threat of force or intimidation. The Indictment fails to provide any particulars as to the specific form of sexual violence alleged. One of the fundamental rights guaranteed to an accused under Article 17(4)(a) of the Statute is the right to be informed 'of the nature and cause of the charge against him'. An Indictment is defective if it does not state the material facts underpinning the charges with enough detail to enable an accused to prepare his or her defence. In the present case, given the broad scope of the offence of 'any other form of sexual violence', it was essential for the Indictment to clearly identify the specific offence or offences which the Accused are required to answer. The Trial Chamber finds that the Indictment is defective in this respect because it fails to plead material facts with sufficient specificity. For this reason[], the charge of 'any other form of sexual violence' is dismissed and thus will not be considered additional-

[765] *Alex Tamba Brima et al.* Trial Judgement, paras. 715–716 (internal references omitted).

	ly or alternatively under Count 9. Finally, as Count 8 has been dismissed for redundancy, the Trial Chamber will not consider it additionally or alternatively under Count 9".[766] **- Sexual slavery constituting acts of terrorism as a violation of Article 3 common to the Geneva Conventions and of Additional Protocol II (WC) and collective punishment as a violation of Article 3 common to the Geneva Conventions and of Additional Protocol II (WC):** The Trial Chamber held: "As a preliminary observation, the Trial Chamber is of the opinion that the purpose behind an individual act of violence may not necessarily correspond with that of the campaign in which it simultaneously occurs. It follows that certain acts of violence, even when committed in the context of other acts of violence the primary purpose of which may be to terrorise the civilian population, may not have been committed in furtherance of such a campaign. The Trial Chamber is of the opinion that this is the case with regards to certain acts of violence underlying Counts 3 through 14 of the Indictment, as outlined below".[767] "The Trial Chamber has found that many women abducted by the AFRC troops were detained for many months, repeatedly raped and forced to do domestic work such as cooking, washing clothes and to carry loads. Many women were told by the perpetrators that they were now their 'wives'. Witness TF1-334 testified that at Rosos, civilians were captured by 'rebels' from the surrounding villages. Those who tried to escape were executed. Women – particularly the young and beautiful ones – were placed under the full control of 'commanders'; they became their 'wives'. As their 'wives' the women cooked for the rebels and the other soldiers in Kono. They were also 'used sexually.' This was an open practice. The Witness testified that he and other soldiers all 'had sexual intercourse' with captured women. Witness TF1-133 testified that all the women who were captured at the same time as her were given to men as their wives which meant that the women had to have sex with the men. She testified further that in Krubola, the captured women cooked and 'had sex' with the rebels and were forced to be their 'wives'. The Witness stated that when a women was 'betrothed' to a man, she became his 'wife' which according to the Witness, meant that 'whoever you were with would have sex with you.' The Witness testified that when the rebels captured women, they would have sex with them before bringing them to where the rebels were based. When the captured women were taken to the base, they would be handed over to a person who would have sex with that woman all the time. The 'bosses and stronger guys' all had wives who were captured but the subordinates were not allowed to have wives. The subordinates would be sent to the front and they would always bring back captured civilians, including women. The practice of sexual slavery was regulated by the AFRC troops through a system of ownership and punishment for transgressing the rules. Witness TF1-094 testified that she believed that if she refused to have sex with her captor, she would have been killed. Some women were transferred as 'wives' between two or more different soldiers. The Trial Chamber therefore finds that in the particular factual circumstances before it, the primary purpose behind commission of sexual slavery was not to spread terror among the civilian population, but rather was committed by the AFRC troops to take advantage of the spoils of war, by treating women as property and using them to satisfy their sexual desires and to fulfil other conjugal needs. As with evidence of the other enslavement crimes, namely the abduction and use of child soldiers and forced labour therefore, even where sexual slavery occurred simultaneously with other acts of violence examined by this Chamber with regards to the crime of terror, the Trial Chamber is of the

[766] *Alex Tamba Brima et al.* Trial Judgement, paras. 718–722 (internal references omitted).

[767] *Alex Tamba Brima et al.* Trial Judgement, para. 1445.

	opinion that such acts cannot be considered to have been committed with the primary purpose to terrorise the civilian population".[768] - Factual and legal findings: - Rapes in Koinadugu District (14 February 1998 – 30 September 1998): In Kabala: "Defence witness DAB-156 testified that after the AFRC was overthrown in Freetown in February 1998 but before the rainy season, she was raped by 'Junior Lion' in Kabala. He held her, raped her, banged her on the forehead where she still has a scar, and knocked out some of her teeth. The Trial Chamber is satisfied that the actus reus and mens rea of rape are satisfied on the basis of this evidence".[769] In Koinadugu Town: "Witness TF1-209 testified that she was 'in Kabala in Koinadugu Town' in August of 1998 when the witness heard and saw 'rebels' carrying guns shooting outside her home. The 'rebels' were dressed in combat and civilian clothes with pieces of red and white cloth tied around their heads. The witness fled. The next day, the witness was at her mother's farm when she, her husband, her six year old child and some neighbours were attacked by 'rebels'. The Trial Chamber notes that the witness testified in chief that the timeframe of these events was August 1998 but that on cross-examination, when asked whether she remembered when she was captured, she stated that she was not sure of the dates because she had never been to school, and that she could not remember the year. When asked if she remembered August 1998, the witness stated that she remembered August was in the rainy season and that was the time in which she was captured. The Trial Chamber notes, in light of the repeated evidence and references before it, that the annual rainy season in Sierra Leone extends from May to September. The Trial Chamber accepts that witness TF1-209 has little formal education and that her indication of August is not inconsistent with the Chamber's determination of the rainy season. The Trial Chamber is therefore satisfied that it can rely upon the timeframe adduced of August 1998. The witness described the persons who attacked her as 'rebels and soldiers' and as 'juntas'. They were armed. The witness saw four rebels arrive; two went towards a neighbouring farm and two remained at the witness's mother's farm. Two rebels raped the witness in the presence of her husband. The two rebels told her to 'bow down' and they removed her 'pants' and 'lappa'. The witness stated that the rebels and raped her 'as their wife.' The witness was pregnant at the time of the rapes. She stated that her 'pregnancy was wasted' which the Trial Chamber understands to mean that she miscarried as a result of the rapes. The witness testified that the rebels beat her husband to death with a mortar pestle and shot her child dead. A rebel cut the witness's hand with a knife when she tried to hold on to her child. The witness also testified that she saw the rebels rape other women and children during the attack. She was unable to estimate how many persons were raped. She estimated that the children who were raped were approximately nine to ten years old. After the attack, the rebels looted some belongings, such as rice, and forced civilians to carry those belongings to town. In town, the witness learned that the men who raped her belonged to Superman and SAJ Musa's groups. The Trial Chamber notes that the witness's testimony was unclear with regards to her location at the time of the attacks. She testified that she was 'in Kabala in Koinadugu' at the time that she first saw rebels in August 1998, but then continued to respond to the Prosecutor's questions with regards to 'Koinadugu.' She also testified that the rebels she saw at this time told her they were going to Kabala. On cross-examination, the witness clarified that in August 1998 in the rainy season she was not in Kabala, but in Koinadugu. On the second occasion the witness saw rebels, at the time that according to her testimony she was raped, the witness testified she had fled to her mother's farm but did not give the precise location of the farm. She subsequently testified that

768 *Alex Tamba Brima et al.* Trial Judgement, paras. 1455–1459 (internal references omitted).

769 *Alex Tamba Brima et al.* Trial Judgement, para. 986 (internal references omitted).

	after the attack she was brought 'to town' by the rebels. Although she did not explicitly specify which town she was referring to, the Trial Chamber infers, as discussed below, that she was taken to Koinadugu Town. The Trial Chamber similarly infers that witness's mother's farm is located in the environs of Koinadugu Town. The Trial Chamber finds the witness's evidence with regards to this attack credible and not significantly shaken on cross-examination. From the description of her attackers as armed 'rebels and soldiers', as 'juntas', and as members of 'Superman' and SAJ Musa's groups, known commanders of the RUF and the AFRC respectively, the Trial Chamber is satisfied that the perpetrators of the attack belonged to either the AFRC or the RUF. The Trial Chamber infers from the context of violence and coercion that the witness did not and could not have validly consented to the sexual intercourse. The Trial Chamber is thus satisfied that the *actus reus* and *mens rea* elements of rape are met with regards to this incident".[770] "Witness TF1-209 was abducted and brought to Koinadugu Town in approximately August, 1998, by members of the AFRC/RUF. In Koinadugu Town she stayed first with a certain 'Jabie' for a period of three months and subsequently with a certain 'Allusein' for one month. The Trial Chamber is satisfied that the witness's identification of 'Jabie' as one of the persons present when she was attacked at her mother's farm; her description of attackers at her mother's farm as armed 'rebels and soldiers', 'juntas'; and her description of 'Jabie' as being a member of SAJ Musa's group or Superman's group; are consistent with a finding that 'Jabie' was a member of the AFRC or RUF. The Trial Chamber is satisfied from the repeated references to Koinadugu Town and the witness's detailed descriptions of events that occurred there in her presence, that she was held by 'Jabie' in Koinadugu Town. Finally, the Trial Chamber is satisfied on the basis of the testimony of the witness that 'Jabie' repeatedly had sex with her and that given the context of violence, to wit, the previous attacks against the witness, the death of her husband and her child at the hands of 'Jabie', her abduction and her subsequent confinement, that the witness could not have validly consented to the repeated acts of sexual intercourse. The Trial Chamber is thus satisfied that the *actus reus* and *mens rea* elements of rape are met with regards to this incident".[771] In Fadugu: "With regards to the attack in September, the Trial Chamber has carefully reviewed the testimony of witness DAB-078 who also testified that he was in Fadugu Town when ECOMOG forces in the town were attacked on 11 September 1998. The witness testified that he hid during the attack and when the gunfire subsided he ran to a house. When he arrived he found four men who were attempting to rape a girl. The witness described two of the men as wearing soldier's uniforms and two in civilian clothes. Three of the men were armed with guns. The Trial Chamber is satisfied from this description and from the context of the attack that the men were members of the AFRC or RUF. The men detained the witness and forced him to watch as they raped the girl. The witness testified that the girl died from the rape due to excessive bleeding. After the attack, the witness did not see the men again. The witness later met a woman in the bush who told him that the rebels had called a meeting where 'Savage' introduced himself as the commander of the attack. His second in command was 'Ishmael'. The witness knew that 'Savage' and 'Ishmael' were SLAs 'from the discussion with the men.' The Trial Chamber finds the testimony of witness DAB-078 to be detailed, consistent and credible and that the *actus reus* and *mens rea* of rape are satisfied with regards to this incident".[772] "By virtue of the foregoing the Trial Chamber is satisfied that the elements of rape are established in relation to Koinadugu District".[773]

[770] *Alex Tamba Brima et al.* Trial Judgement, paras. 989–996 (internal references omitted).

[771] *Alex Tamba Brima et al.* Trial Judgement, paras. 1006–1009.

[772] *Alex Tamba Brima et al.* Trial Judgement, paras. 1022–1023 (internal references omitted).

[773] *Alex Tamba Brima et al.* Trial Judgement, para. 1026.

	- Rapes in Bombali District (1 May 1998 – 30 November 1998): In Rosos: "Prosecution witness TF1-269 testified that she was living in Rosos during the war when, during the rainy season, 'rebels' entered the town and captured her. The Trial Chamber is satisfied that the time period described by the witness is May through July 1998. The witness testified that some of the rebels were wearing vests and some were wearing combat. Three of the rebels raped her. One of the rebels had a gun and the other had a knife. After they had raped her, a rebel pushed her to the ground and cut her in the back of the neck. The existence of a scar on the witness's body was noted by the Chamber. The witness testified that two of the rebels convinced the others not to kill her. The three rebels spoke to the witness in Temne and asked her to show them where the other civilians were hiding. The witness took them to a nearby area; however the civilians were not there. Rather, there were only more rebels. One of these rebels, whom the witness described as wearing a T-shirt, told the witness to take his penis in her mouth. She refused and the rebel said he would have her killed. The rebel put his penis in her mouth and tried to rape her vaginally. When the witness resisted the rebel brought her over to another group of rebels. The witness testified that some of these rebels were armed with guns, some with sticks and some with knives and they were wearing a mix of combat and civilian clothes. One of these rebels hit the witness's head and left shin with a stick. The witness was unable to walk and her leg remains scarred. The scar on the witness's left shin was noted by the Trial Chamber. After she was beaten the witness was raped twice more. The witness described the last rebel who raped her as wearing civilian dress. Altogether, the witness was raped by five rebels. The Trial Chamber finds the evidence of witness TF1-269 to be detailed and consistent. The Defence was unable to adduce any major inconsistencies in her testimony during cross-examination. As such, the Trial Chamber finds the evidence described to be credible and that the *actus reus* and *mens rea* of rape are satisfied on the basis of her evidence".[774] "Prosecution witness TF1-267 testified that she was at her home in Rosos in 1998, during the time when farms were being burnt in the countryside, when people from the neighbouring village came and told her and the other villagers that 'rebels' were attacking the area and urged them to leave. The witness left Rosos with her family and hid in the bush. Several days later, when the witness and her family were drying their belongings after a 'big rain' in a nearby area called Rotu, rebels and soldiers attacked. The witness testified that one of the attackers wore a soldier's fatigue cap, another wore trousers and combat fatigue, and another had 'big shoes that they wore'. On cross-examination, the witness stated that she was able to identify SLA soldiers even though she had not seen them before and she clarified that one of the soldiers was wearing a cap and trousers which were both 'military fatigue' and that others were wearing big black boots. The witness explained that others wore civilian clothes. The witness tried to run away, but a soldier kicked her and she fell down. The soldier tore off all her clothes, including her 'knicker' - which the Trial Chamber understands to mean underwear - and brutally raped her. The witness stated, 'he took his penis and thrust it into my vagina and started pounding me like he was pounding mud…he did not sex me as people do normally. He did it abnormally'. The witness was then raped by another rebel. She tried to fight him but he pinned her back on the ground. A third rebel - who was armed, came and told the witness, 'If you open your mouth, I will shoot you dead' and then raped her. The witness testified that she experienced great pain. A fourth rebel came and the witness tried to get up, but as she bent to rise 'somebody' pushed her back down onto her back. The fourth rebel also raped the witness. She was afraid he would kill her and she could not resist. The witness testified that the last rape was particularly painful. She stated, 'it seem[ed] at though all my guts were

[774] *Alex Tamba Brima et al.* Trial Judgement, paras. 1031–1033 (internal references omitted).

	coming out.' When the rebels left, the witness tried to get up but she fell back down again as she was so weak. The Trial Chamber is satisfied on the basis of this evidence that the *actus reus* and *mens rea* of rape are proven. The witness testified further that when the rebels left the village, her daughter ran to her and told her that she too had been raped by two rebels from the same group – the only group of rebels to come to Rosos that day. The witness's daughter told her that 'they' stuffed her mouth with cloth and raped her one after the other. The witness saw that her daughter was bleeding from her vagina. Prior to this incident, her daughter was a virgin. The Trial Chamber notes that in her evidence-in-chief, the witness refers to her daughter alternately as her 'sibling', 'daughter' and 'lady'. On cross-examination the witness adopted prior statements which use the term 'daughter'. The Trial Chamber notes that the witness testified in Krio which was translated into English. The Chamber is satisfied that the various terms used do not undermine the credibility of the witness and that a girl that the witness knew very well was raped that day. The Trial Chamber finds the evidence given by witness TF1-267 in chief to be highly detailed and coherent and the witness was not shaken on cross-examination. The Trial Chamber therefore finds the evidence to be credible and is satisfied on the basis of this evidence that the *actus reus* and *mens rea* of rape are satisfied".[775] "By virtue of the foregoing the Trial Chamber is satisfied that the elements of rape are established in relation to Bombali District".[776] - Rapes in Freetown and the Western Area (6 January 1999 – 28 February 1999): At the State House: "Witness TF1-334 testified that on 6 January 1999, he saw 'soldiers' bring an unknown number of abducted women to rooms within the State House and rape them there. He testified that the most beautiful ones were brought to the senior commanders, including 'Gullit', 'Bazzy' and '55'. Witness TF1-334 saw 'Gullit' with a girl who told the witness that she was in Form Two; that is, approximately 12 years old. The witness did not see 'Gullit' abduct the girl. The girls with '55' and 'Bazzy' were also very young school girls. The girl with Bazzy was approximately 12–15 years old. Gullit was with his girl up to Makeni; '55' stayed with his girl until the retreat from Freetown; and 'Bazzy' was with his girl until Westside. The Trial Chamber has previously considered general issues of credibility with regards to witness TF1-334 and finds the evidence given by him with regards to rapes at the State House to be reliable. However, the Trial Chamber finds this evidence insufficient to prove the *actus reus* and *mens rea* of rape. The evidence of witness TF1-334 is generally supported by that of witness TF1-024 who testified that on 8 January 1999, he was captured by a group of rebels and soldiers. The Trial Chamber notes that the witness describes his abductors variously as 'rebels and soldiers [...] combin[ed] together', as 'rebel boys', as 'rebels and soldiers [...] all mixed together'. The witness also describes them as wearing 'ECOMOG' uniforms and speaking Liberian English. The rebels and soldiers took the witness to State House where he was detained for four nights in a kitchen on the ground level. Through the kitchen window, the witness testified that he could see women and girls being raped by 'Gullit's boys' every night in the compound. He heard the women cry and heard the girls saying 'We do not agree. We are school-going girls.' ('A no de gri. Mi na small pikin.') The witness testified that he saw 'Gullit' twice at the State House. The rebels called him 'Honorable Gullit' and he was 'commanding his boys.' When ECOMOG forces approached the State House, 'Gullit' ordered the rebels to leave and left together with them. The Trial Chamber notes that on cross-examination, the witness testified that the girls who were raped were given 5000 leones, but that this was not pay. The Trial Chamber finds that given the overwhelmingly coercive environment and the suggestion of the young

775 *Alex Tamba Brima et al.* Trial Judgement, paras. 1034–1037 (internal references omitted).

776 *Alex Tamba Brima et al.* Trial Judgement, para. 1041.

	age of the victims, no attribution of consent to the sexual acts can be derived from this payment. The Trial Chamber is of the opinion that the testimony of witness TF1-024 is detailed and coherent. The witness was not shaken on this evidence on cross-examination. The Trial Chamber accepts this evidence as credible. The Trial Chamber is satisfied that the *actus reus* and *mens rea* elements of rape are satisfied on the basis of this evidence".[777] "By virtue of the foregoing, and without predetermining the individual criminal responsibility of the three Accused, the Trial Chamber is satisfied that the elements of rape are established in relation to Freetown and the Western Area".[778] - Sexual slavery as outrages upon personal dignity in Kono District (14 February 1998 – 30 June 1998): "The Trial Chamber is of the opinion that witness TF1-334's testimony that women were captured; that captured civilians who tried to escape were executed; that captured women were place under the 'full control' of commanders and became their 'wives'; and that these women cooked for the commanders and other soldiers is indicative of the deprivation of the captured women's liberty and the exercise of ownership over them by members of the AFRC. The Trial Chamber is also satisfied on the evidence of the witness, namely that the women were 'used sexually' and that soldiers, including himself, had sexual intercourse with captured women, that acts of sexual violence were committed against the captured women. The Trial Chamber infers from the environment of violence and coercion that the women did not consent to these sexual acts. The Trial Chamber is thus of the opinion that the *actus reus* and *mens rea* elements of the crime of sexual slavery are satisfied on the basis of this evidence. The evidence of witness TF1-334 is generally supported by that of witness DAB-101 who testified that after hearing on the radio about 'Operation No Living Thing' he was captured and released three times by the RUF in Kono District. The 'rebels' were based at Mortema at this time. The witness was captured, together with two other civilians, by the RUF a fourth time. The rebels were armed and were wearing civilian clothing. The rebels told the witness that they would release him if he agreed to turn over two of his nieces to them to be their 'wives'. The witness testified that the nieces advised him to accept the offer so he did. The girls were 15 and 17 years old at the time. The witness then went back to the 'bush'. The witness saw the girls again after the war. The girls told the witness their 'ordeal'; they said they were beaten but did not tell the witness anything else. The Trial Chamber is of the opinion that girls aged 15 and 17 years of age, in the context of coercion and violence, could not have validly consented to 'marriage'. Witness DAB-101 also testified that, generally, women that were captured by the rebels were transformed into their 'wives'. They were usually sent to spy for the rebels or to find food. In Mortema, the witness did not hear about any rapes. He also never heard the name of the Accused Brima. The evidence of witness TF1-334 is also generally supported by that of witness DAB-125 who testified that around Wordu Town, if 'they' saw a young girl they would hold and turn her into their wife. By virtue of the foregoing the Trial Chamber is satisfied that the elements of sexual slavery are established in relation to Kono District".[779] - Sexual slavery as outrages upon personal dignity in Koinadugu District (14 February 1998 – 30 September 1998): "As examined, *supra*, in the evidence by witness section, witness TF1-094 testified that in August of 1998 she was abducted by a certain 'Andrew' from her village,

[777] *Alex Tamba Brima et al.* Trial Judgement, paras. 1045–1048 (internal references omitted).

[778] *Alex Tamba Brima et al.* Trial Judgement, para. 1068.

[779] *Alex Tamba Brima et al.* Trial Judgement, paras. 1105–1109 (internal references omitted).

	Bambukura, Koinadugu District. The Trial Chamber is satisfied from the witness's description of 'Andrew' as an 'SLA' dressed in combat that Andrew was a member of the AFRC or the RUF. The witness testified that after Andrew abducted her, he repeatedly raped her. The witness became pregnant within the first month of being with Andrew. She testified that she had to do his laundry and other chores and that Andrew considered the witness to be his 'wife'. The witness was taken with the troops as they travelled to Bombali District. They reached Rosos when the witness was four months pregnant. The Trial Chamber is of the opinion that the witness's testimony of her forcible abduction; the murder of her parents in her presence which established an context of fear and violence; her fear that she too would be killed if she did not have sex with 'Andrew'; the extraction of her forced labour by 'Andrew', namely laundering and other chores; the use of the term 'wife'; and her detention with the troops for approximately four to five months as they travelled through Koinadugu District to Bombali District are all indicative of the deprivation of her liberty and the exercise of ownership over her person by 'Andrew' which together with acts of sexual violence, namely, 'Andrew's repeated rape of the witness and her subsequent pregnancy, satisfies the *actus reus* and *mens rea* elements of the crime of sexual slavery".[780]
	"Prosecution witness TF1-133 testified that captured women in Koinadugu District were forced to be 'wives' to members of the AFRC or RUF and that she was present in Krubola for a period of seven months and Serekolia for a period of three months during which time 'forced marriages' were supervised and organised by herself for members of the AFRC and RUF. The witness testified that in Kumala, in April 1998, at the time that the villagers were 'getting ready to make [their] farms' at the end of the dry season, she, her siblings and one of her husband's other wives, were captured by four 'rebels' whom the witness named as 'Mohammed the Killer', 'Trouble', 'Arpick' and 'Cyborg'. Some of the rebels were in uniform and some were in civilian dress. The witness and her family members, together with some other captured civilians known to the witness – Bamba Jalloh and Sialo Kamara - were taken by the rebels on a path towards Woronbiai. Before they reached town, 'Mohammed the Killer', who was armed, raped the witness. The witness testified that she was unable to refuse. At the same time, another rebel – whom the witness named as 'RPG' - raped the witness's husband's other wife. The witness was kept with the rebels at Woronbiai for eight days. There the witness learned that Mohammed the Killer's commander was named 'Cobra'. Other commanders at Woronbiai were 'Colonel Tee' who was SLA; 'Pa Mani' who was SLA; and 'Rambo'. 'Rambo' and 'Pa Mani' were the overall commanders at Woronbiai. At Woronbiai, 'Mohammed the Killer' wanted to marry the witness to 'Cobra'. The witness refused. 'Mohammed the Killer' said the witness should be killed and he wounded her with a bayonet. The witness was injured on her hip and buttocks. The witness was led away by a rebel to be killed, however, 'Rambo' intervened. 'Rambo' and 'Pa Mani' punished 'Mohammed the Killer' by having him beaten. 'Cobra' said 'You have brought this woman for me. If she says she doesn't love me, leave her alone'. The witness was treated for her injuries. For the eight days she was in Woronbiai, the witness lived with 'Cobra'. All of the women who were captured at the same time as the witness were given to 'men' as their 'wives' which meant that the women had to have sex with the men. The witness's husband's other wife was given to a 'rebel' named Komba; Bamba Jalloh was given to a Mende 'rebel' named Yubao. Sialo Kamara was made to work for the wives of the rebels. She laundered clothes and washed dishes. The Trial Chamber notes that in its Final Brief, the Prosecution cites the proceeding testimony of witness TF1-133 as evidence of crimes committed in Woronbiai, *Kono* District. The Trial Chamber finds that this is a mistaken assertion. Witness TF1-133 clearly testified that she was in the bush outside of Kumala, near Alikalia, when she was captured, and that she was raped in the bush on the way to Woronbiai. She also testified that immediately prior to the attack on Kuma-

[780] *Alex Tamba Brima et al.* Trial Judgement, paras. 1113–1114.

	la, Yiffin had been attacked. The Trial Chamber has no doubt that the proceeding events the witness describes took place in Koinadugu District. Witness TF1-133 testified that then she and an unknown number of other women who had been captured by 'rebels' were taken with the rebels - including 'Cobra' and 'Brigadier' Mani - to Krubola where they stayed for seven months. At Krubola, they 'met' another group of rebels which included a 'fighter' named 'Savage', a 'rebel' named 'Komba Gbundema', and a 'rebel' named 'Superman'. There were other men there, but the witness did not know their names. The men at Krubola were all 'under' Komba Gbundema. The Trial Chamber is satisfied on the basis of this evidence that the rebels present at Krubola at this time were both members of the AFRC and RUF. In Krubola, the captured women cooked and 'had sex' with the rebels and were forced to be their 'wives'. The witness stated that when a women was 'betrothed' to a man, she became his 'wife' which according to the witness, meant that 'whoever you were with would have sex with you.' The witness testified that when the rebels captured women, they would have sex with them before bringing them to where the rebels were based. When the captured women were taken to the base, they would be handed over to a person who would have sex with that woman all the time. The 'bosses and stronger guys' all had wives who were captured but the subordinates were not allowed to have wives. The subordinates would be sent to the front and they would always bring back captured civilians, including women. The witness testified that in her presence the 'elders' and 'bosses' including 'Rambo', 'Colonel Tee' and 'Pa Mani' made a law that whoever was given a woman would be the sole owner over her and that a man should not covet his colleague's wife. 'If you were caught, you will be killed'. Captured children were made to work for the captured 'wives' of the rebels. On cross-examination, the witness testified that the children were captured *because* older civilians wanted them to work for them. At the time that groundnuts were about to be harvested the rebels moved to Serekolia, Koinadugu District. On the way, the rebels travelled through Mongo which 'was captured'. The rebels that moved included Kombo Gbundema's group, 'Superman', 'Savage', 'Colonel Tee' and 'Pa Mani'. They remained in Serekolia for three months. While they were there the civilians voted for the witness to represent them. She was appointed the 'Mammy Queen' by 'Pa Mani', 'Colonel Tee' and their clerk Alhaji. As the Mammy Queen, the witness would investigate captured civilians who had been mistreated and cases where husbands or wives had sex with someone else's spouse. If a woman was found guilty of having sex with someone else's husband she could be given 200 lashes. If a man raped another man's wife, he could be killed. The Prosecution asserts that the witness's position as a 'Mammy Queen' did not in any way help her or the other 'wives'' plight, as it did not affect the powers of the men over their abducted 'wives', or afford them any liberty to leave or refuse to engage in acts of a sexual nature with their so called husbands. The Prosecution also asserts that witness TF1-133 was not discredited on cross-examination and that her evidence has not been challenged by any Defence evidence and as such, the Prosecution version of events should be accepted. The Trial Chamber is satisfied on the evidence of witness TF1-133 that women captured in Koinadugu District were subject to repeated rape by members of the AFRC/RUF; were made to labour for members of the AFRC/RUF, namely to cook, launder clothes and wash dishes; were labelled as 'wives', in this context a label of possession, and placed in exclusive relationships of ownership by certain rebels; were punished with physical violence if the exclusive sexual relationship was violated; and were detained at rebel bases in Krubola and Serekolia and made to travel together with the troops; are all indicative of the deprivation of liberty and the exercise of ownership over captured women together with acts of sexual violence satisfying the *actus reus* and *mens rea* of the crime of sexual slavery".[781] "As found by the Trial Chamber, *supra,* Prosecution witness TF1-209 was raped at her

[781] *Alex Tamba Brima et al.* Trial Judgement, paras. 1115–1126 (internal references omitted).

	mother's farm outside of Koinadugu Town by two members of the AFRC/RUF in or about August, 1998. Following this attack the rebels brought her to Koinadugu Town where over a period of three months she was repeatedly raped by 'Jabie', a member of the AFRC. In addition to these findings, the Trial Chamber also relies upon the evidence of witness TF1-209 that when she and other captured civilians were brought to Koinadugu Town, they were taken to the 'MP's' office where their names were recorded by a person to whom the witness referred as 'Mongo.' The witness testified that this was done so that the captured civilians would not go missing. The witness described 'Mongo' as dressed in combat and stated that he was the boss of the Military Police. The witness testified that following this registration process she was taken by the 'person' who captured her to 'Jabie's house where she cooked and laundered for him. The witness testified that he turned her into his 'wife' which she explained meant that he would have sex with the witness whenever he felt like it. The witness also testified that with the exception of excursions during the day to farms in the bush, she stayed in the same house with 'Jabie' in Koinadugu Town for three months until he was killed. The Trial Chamber is satisfied that the witness's testimony of her forcible capture; the registration of her name by 'Mongo' when she arrived in Koinadugu Town and her perception that this was done to prevent her and other captured civilians from 'going missing'; the extraction of her forced labour by 'Jabie', namely cooking and laundering; the use of the term 'wife', in this context a label of possession; and her detention in the same house as 'Jabie' is indicative of the deprivation of her liberty and the exercise of ownership over her person which together with acts of sexual violence, namely, 'Jabie's repeated rape of the witness found previously by the Trial Chamber satisfies the *actus reus* and *mens rea* elements of the crime of sexual slavery".[782] "The evidence of Prosecution witnesses TF1-094, TF1-133, and TF1-209 is generally supported by that of Defence witnesses DAB-156 and DAB-079. As found by the Trial Chamber with regards to Count 6, *supra*, Defence witness DAB-156 was raped by 'Junior Lion' in Kabala sometime after the AFRC was overthrown in Freetown in February 1998 but before the rainy season. The witness also testified that he took her as his 'wife' by force and that he abducted her in Yuromia Town, near Foday Street. Witness DAB-079 testified that he did not receive any information about sexual violence in Kabala Town by the SLAs, although there were rumours of 'bush wives' in the interior. The witness was part of a CDF information network of 1000–1700 people and was receiving weekly reports from Kabala, Koinadugu, Yiffin, Geberefe and other locations".[783] "By virtue of the foregoing the Trial Chamber is satisfied that the elements in relation to sexual slavery are established in relation to Koinadugu District".[784] - Sexual slavery as outrages upon personal dignity in Bombali District (1 May 1998 – 30 November 1998): "In coming to its findings in Bombali District, the Trial Chamber relies on the evidence of Prosecution witnesses TF1-334, TF1-094 and TF1-033 and Defence witness DAB-095. Witness TF1-334 testified that he and other 'soldiers' under the command of 'Woyoh' captured approximately 35 civilian women during the attack on Karina in June of 1998. The women were initially stripped naked but were later permitted to dress. When the soldiers left Karina they stopped at a temporary base in the jungle. There, Woyoh handed the women over to 'Five-Five' who was the Chief of Staff. 'Five-Five' distributed the women among the soldiers under his command by requiring them to 'sign for' a woman. 'Five-Five' stated that if there were any problems the soldiers should immediately report directly to him. He also stated that if the soldiers

782 *Alex Tamba Brima et al.* Trial Judgement, paras. 1127–1130 (internal references omitted).

783 *Alex Tamba Brima et al.* Trial Judgement, paras. 1131–1132 (internal references omitted).

784 *Alex Tamba Brima et al.* Trial Judgement, para. 1133.

	'disturbed' the women, they would be removed from the soldier's control. The women were 'wives to the soldiers' and they remained with their 'husbands' until the soldiers invaded Freetown. Witness TF1-334 testified that the AFRC troops arrived in Rosos at the beginning of the rainy season in 1998 and stayed there for three months, leaving in September. 'Five-Five' was in charge of overseeing that the captured women were trained for combat. 'Five-Five' continued to regulate the 'marriages' of the women abducted in Karina at Camp Rosos. 'Gullit' appointed a 'Mammy Queen' – a woman at the camp who looked after women's affairs, including pregnancy, birth and sickness. 'Five-Five' issued a 'disciplinary order' regulating the conduct of women which was explained to supervisors in the camp and to the Mammy Queen. According to this order, women who were unfaithful to their husbands should be punished. Soldiers and their 'wives' reported problems directly to 'Five-Five' and if 'Five-Five' determined that the woman deserved punishment this could be delegated to the Mammy Queen. Women found by 'Five-Five' to have misbehaved could be beaten or given lashes. Women were also locked for long periods of time in a box meant for transporting rice. In one instance, witness TF1-334 observed a Staff Sergeant named 'Junior' a.k.a 'General Bagehgeh' report to 'Five-Five' that he suspected his 'wife' of misbehaving. 'Five-Five' called the woman before him and found her guilty. He ordered that she be sent to the Mammy Queen, be given a dozen lashes and be locked in the box. The witness escorted her to the box. The Trial Chamber considers the evidence of Prosecution witness TF1-334 together with that of Prosecution witness TF1-033 who testified to having been taken along with AFRC troops to Rosos during the rainy season in 1998. He testified that rape was widespread throughout the time he was in captivity with the AFRC troops and that the only thing done about sexual violence committed by ARFC troops by 'the commanders' occurred at Rosos. The witness testified that according to the 'jungle justice' rules at that time, any fighter who raped another fighter's abducted and forcefully married wife would be put to death. The witness specifically recalled an incident in which Alhaji Kamanda alias 'Gunboot' killed an AFRC fighter for raping another fighter's forcefully abducted and married wife. The evidence of Prosecution witnesses TF1-334 and TF1-033 is supported by that of Prosecution witness TF1-094, found by the Trial Chamber to have been subject to sexual slavery in Koinadugu District, who also testified that during the period of her sexual slavery, she was brought by the troops to Rosos. The Trial Chamber is satisfied that the testimony of Prosecution witnesses TF1-334, TF1-033 and TF1-094 that women captured by the AFRC/RUF were distributed to soldiers to be their 'wives'; that captured women were brought to Rosos where they were subject to physical and psychological violence as a form of punishment; and that the women were detained with their 'husbands' until the soldiers invaded Freetown is indicative of the deprivation of the captured women's liberty and the exercise of ownership over her person which taken together with acts of sexual violence committed against them, namely, rape at the hands of their rebel 'husbands' or at the hands of other fighters satisfies the *actus reus* and *mens rea* elements of the crime of sexual slavery. The Trial Chamber finds further that this was a practice tolerated and regulated by the AFRC/RUF commanders".[785] "By virtue of the foregoing, and without predetermining the individual responsibility of the three Accused, the Trial Chamber is satisfied that the elements in relation to sexual slavery are established in relation to Bombali District".[786] - Sexual slavery as outrages upon personal dignity in Freetown and the Western Area (6 January 1999 – 28 February 1999): "In coming to its findings in relation to Freetown and the Western Area, the Trial

[785] *Alex Tamba Brima et al.* Trial Judgement, paras. 1136–1141 (internal references omitted).

[786] *Alex Tamba Brima et al.* Trial Judgement, para. 1145.

	Chamber relies on the evidence of Prosecution witnesses TF1-023, TF1-334, TF1-094 and Defence witnesses DBK-113 and DBK-126. Prosecution witness TF1-023 testified that she was 16 when the AFRC invaded Freetown in January 1999. She and her family tried to hide; however, she was captured by 'rebels' in Calaba Town on 22 January 1999. She was taken by the rebels first to Allen Town and then back to Calaba Town. At Calaba town, she was given to an AFRC rebel, hereinafter 'the Captain' to be his 'wife'. The Captain told the witness he would not take her as his 'wife' as he had already been given another woman – the witness's cousin – and could not take care of two women at the same time. Instead, the Captain handed the witness over to a known AFRC Colonel, hereinafter 'Colonel X', who took her as his 'wife'. There was no ceremony and he did not ask her consent. The witness was afraid. That night, Colonel X came into the room where the witness was instructed to sleep. He told her to undress, threatened her and had sex with her without her consent. Prior to this incident, the witness was a virgin. After that night, the witness was taken along with the rebels as they attempted to evade ECOMOG attacks, travelling to Allen Town, Waterloo, Benguema, Lumpa and Four Mile. At Benguema, the witness saw a man whom the soldiers said was the senior commander, Brigadier 'Gullit'. At Four Mile the witness spent three weeks with Colonel X. During this time Colonel X and the witness lived together and he continued to have sex with her frequently. He did not ask her consent when he had sex with her; he said she was his 'wife'. Colonel X asked the witness to cook for him, but she did not because she did not know how. The witness felt there was no way for her to escape from Colonel X. She was unfamiliar with the area in which she was being held and Colonel X sent an armed escort with her wherever she went. She was afraid. There were approximately 400 armed rebels at Four Mile and the witness knew that those who tried to escape were caught and beaten by the rebels. The witness testified that Colonel X told her that the senior commander at Four Mile was Brigadier 'Bazzy'. She would see Brigadier 'Bazzy' regularly when he would visit Colonel X. There were other women given to soldiers as wives in Four Mile. In Lumpa, for example, the witness knew ten other women who had been captured and given as 'wives' to AFRC rebels. Some were given to lieutenants and some were given to ordinary soldiers. The Prosecution asserts that this evidence was not challenged in cross-examination. As the 'wife' of a commander, the witness was accorded certain privileges. The Trial Chamber notes that in chief the witness stated that she was not forced to do 'anything'. She clarified on cross-examination that she was not forced to do any work; she was not forced to cook or clean, for example. The witness testified that 'people of lower ranks' respected her and deferentially called her 'De Mammy' because of the Colonel. The Prosecution submits that this did not change the status of the witness who remained under sexual slavery because she had no way of leaving as an armed person watched over her and those who attempted to escape were caught and beaten. The Trial Chamber agrees with this submission. The fact that some individual abductees were treated less harshly than others does not, in our opinion, detract from the fact that they were forcibly taken and subjected to sexual slavery. Colonel X left the witness in Four Mile and went to Makeni. In his absence, Colonel X left her in the care of another AFRC captain, hereinafter 'Captain Y', whom the witness accepted on cross-examination tried to look after her and to ensure that she did not come to any harm. The witness travelled with Captain Y and the rebels to Mile 38, Port Loko District and then to Magbeni where later, in August of 1999, the witness was able to escape. The witness was in the custody of Captain Y for approximately five months. During this time, Colonel X did not return. The witness saw 'Bazzy' several times in Mile 38. 'Bazzy' was the overall commander in Magbeni. In June or July, the witness also saw 'Gullit' in Magbeni. The Prosecution submits that the evidence of the witness remained consistent and was unsuccessfully challenged in cross-examination. The Trial Chamber is satisfied that the witness's testimony of her forcible capture; the use of the term 'wife', in this context a label of possession; her detention with the troops as they travelled through the Western Area; her detention

	with Colonel X for three weeks in Four Mile at which time she felt that she could not escape for fear of being beaten or killed by him; and her subsequent detention by Colonel X and the other rebels for a period of several months, are all indicative of the deprivation of her liberty and the exercise of ownership over her person which, together with acts of sexual violence committed against her, namely 'Colonel X's repeated rape of the witness, satisfies the *actus reus* and *mens rea* of the crime of sexual slavery. The Trial Chamber notes that the witness testified that as the 'wife' of Colonel X she was accorded certain benefits, for example, she was not forced to cook or clean and was deferentially called 'De Mammy'. The Trial Chamber is of the opinion that this is a relative benefit only and does not in any way undermine the absolute seriousness of the crime committed against the witness".[787]
	"The evidence of Prosecution witness TF1-023 is generally supported by that of Prosecution witness TF1-334 who testified that after the invasion of Freetown on 6 January 1999, a number of soldiers who did not 'have women' before had new 'wives'. The soldiers gave the women food and clothing and the women cooked for the soldiers. Prosecution witness TF1-334 testified that civilians abducted during the retreat from Freetown were brought with the rebels to Benguema where the rebels were based for approximately one month. There were approximately 300 civilians at Benguema – men, women and children. During this time, the civilians that were abducted were 'well-secured' meaning that they could not escape. Most of the young girls who were abducted from Freetown became the 'wives' of 'various commanders' meaning that they had sex with the commanders. In the Kissy area, where the witness knew some of the captured girls, they told the witness 'what they would do with the men who captured them'; sometimes the witness would 'see with my own eyes'. The 'wives' were also required to help with the cooking. Witness TF1-334 testified that 'families', which the witness explained refers to the captured civilians travelling with the troops, travelled with the troops from Waterloo to Newton where they all stayed for about a month. The only civilians with the 'troops' at Waterloo and Newton were those who arrived with them. The 'women' were helping with the cooking and the 'girls' were sleeping with the 'commanders'. The 'commanders' would call them their 'wives'. 'Five-Five' was responsible for the women and girls in the camp at Newton. The soldiers would report problems with the women to 'Five-Five'. The Trial Chamber is of the opinion that witness TF1-334's testimony that civilian women were captured from Freetown and brought with the retreating troops to the Western Area, were held in Benguema for approximately one month and were taken to Kissy, Waterloo and Newton; that during their detention in Benguema the civilians were well secured so they could not escape; that young girls became the 'wives' of various commanders; and that the 'wives' were required to cook for the soldiers is credible and is indicative of the deprivation of the captured women's liberty and the exercise of ownership over them by members of the AFRC/RUF. The Trial Chamber is also satisfied that acts of sexual violence described by the witness, namely that the 'wives' had sex with the various commanders, were committed against the captured women. The Trial Chamber infers from the environment of violence and coercion that the women did not consent to these sexual acts. The Trial Chamber is thus of the opinion that the *actus reus* and *mens rea* elements of the crime of sexual slavery are satisfied on the basis of this evidence".[788]
	"The Trial Chamber also relies on the evidence of Prosecution witness TF1-094, found by the Trial Chamber to have been subject to sexual slavery in Koinadugu District, that during the period of her sexual slavery, she was brought by the troops to Freetown during the AFRC invasion of 6 January 1999 and was present during the retreat through the Western Area. Defence witness DBK-113 testified that he was with the

[787] *Alex Tamba Brima et al.* Trial Judgement, paras. 1152–1160 (internal references omitted).
[788] *Alex Tamba Brima et al.* Trial Judgement, paras. 1161–1165 (internal references omitted).

troops during the invasion of Freetown in January, 1999. He testified that after SAJ Musa died, he remained with the troops in Hastings for three to four days. From Hastings, the witness passed through Allen Town, Wellington and Kissi and, on January 6th, he came as far as Hill Cot Road. The witness cannot recall that a 'Mammy Queen' was appointed during the move to Freetown. The Trial Chamber finds the evidence of witness DBK-113 to be credible and consistent. However, the fact that the witness could not recall a 'Mammy Queen' does not raise a reasonable doubt with regards to the evidence of Prosecution witnesses TF1-023, TF1-094 and TF1-334 whose evidence indicates numerous incidents of sexual slavery following the 6 January 1999 invasion. The Trial Chamber has also carefully examined the evidence of witness DBK-126 who testified that when the AFRC entered Freetown, all the soldiers were with their wives. Only the detainees did not have wives. The Trial Chamber finds that in the face of overwhelming evidence to the contrary this statement is not credible. Witness DBK-126 also testified that she had a 'boyfriend' who was a commander of a mortar platoon. The witness testified that from the time she and her 'boyfriend' were in Kono at Masingbi Road, he had repeatedly proposed to her. He went to 'Junior Lion' whom the witness referred to as 'the Chief' and told him he wanted the witness. 'Junior Lion' told the witness 'this is your husband.' She agreed because she had no option. They have a son together. After they left the bush, the witness told her 'boyfriend' that she did not want him anymore. In Freetown, the witness was called a 'rebel wife', but she testified that she does not consider herself a 'rebel wife', as she was with the SLA and not the RUF. Although the witness also stated she had not heard the term 'forced marriage' the Trial Chamber is satisfied that her evidence shows the *actus reus* and *mens rea* of sexual slavery".[789]

"By virtue of the foregoing, and without predetermining the individual responsibility of the three Accused, the Trial Chamber is satisfied that the elements in relation to sexual slavery are established in relation to Freetown and the Western Area".[790]

- Sexual slavery as outrages upon personal dignity in Port Loko District (February 1999 – April 1999):

"In coming to its findings in Port Loko District, the Trial Chamber relies upon the evidence of Prosecution witnesses TF1-282 and TF1-285 and Defence witness DAB-156. Witness TF1-282 testified that during the dry season in early 1999, 'rebels' entered her village in Port Loko District. The Trial Chamber notes that the witness testified in chief that the time period was 'early in 1999' and in the 'dry season'. On cross-examination the witness accepted that the correct month was January but she could not say if it was towards the beginning or end of January. The witness hid in an uncultivated area outside of the village. As she was hiding, the 'rebels', whom the witness described as some wearing civilian attire, some in combat, and some with guns, came a second time and captured the witness along with other civilians hiding in the uncultivated area. Witness TF1-282 was 14 at the time. The Trial Chamber notes that the witness stated that she was born in 1985 but on cross-examination testified that she does not know how old she was when she was captured. The Trial Chamber accepts that the witness is innumerate and finds that this does not undermine her credibility. The witness testified that the civilians were made to sit on the ground and were surrounded by the rebels. The witness watched as an armed rebel selected a woman from the group and led her away to another area. The rebel brought the woman back a short while later and then selected the witness and led her along the same route where a man the witness referred to as '55' and another armed rebel were waiting. The witness testified that she knew the man was called '55' because the rebel who brought her to the area called the name '55' and nodded at him. '55' told the witness to undress

[789] *Alex Tamba Brima et al.* Trial Judgement, paras. 1166–1169 (internal references omitted).

[790] *Alex Tamba Brima et al.* Trial Judgement, para. 1170.

	and to lie down and then he raped her. After the rape the witness was light-headed and was unable to get up for some time. '55' told her to stand up and brought her back to the group of civilians. Witness TF1-282 testified that she later heard '55' giving orders to fire and to move to Sumbuya, although on cross-examination she admitted that she did not hear '55' give these orders directly. The witness also stated that she was later told by her rebel husband, whose name was given in closed session and hereinafter referred to as 'Rebel A', that '55' was the 'big man' in Sumbuya and gave orders to loot. On cross-examination the witness stated that she only saw '55' once, when he raped her, and could not describe him. The Kanu Defence submits that witness TF1-282 is highly unreliable. In cross-examination, the witness was presented with a prior statement in which she described the person 'Five-Five' who raped her as 'tall, slim, and fair in complexion, which means not too black.' When presented with this account of her description of 'Five-Five' the witness recanted stating that she was not able to describe the man who raped her, as she only saw him once, and that she did not describe him as tall, slim and fair in complexion. The Trial Chamber finds that the witness's identification evidence is therefore inconsistent and cannot be relied upon. The Trial Chamber makes no findings on the basis of this evidence with regards to the Accused Kanu. After she was raped, the rebels, some of whom the witness described as wearing civilian attire and some of whom were in combat and who had guns took the witness to Sumbuya, a two day march. On the way, 'Rebel A' told the witness that he 'wanted' her. When they arrived at Sumbuya, the named rebel took the witness to a house where he raped her. After that, the named rebel asked the witness to be his 'wife'. The witness testified that she said 'yes' because saying no in the circumstances would make no difference and she was afraid she might have been killed. In cross-examination, a prior statement of witness TF1-282 was put to her in which she stated that the man who took her had asked the witness' brother to go and inform her parents that he had taken her as a wife and that after the war, he would go and see them. The witness testified that she could not remember saying this. It is the case of the Prosecution that, even if she had said so, it did not change the situation of the witness being in sexual slavery or forced 'marriage'. The Trial Chamber agrees that such retroactive action does not diminish the seriousness of the acts. The witness testified that the named rebel continued to rape her everyday. The witness and the named rebel lived in the house with two other rebels; all three rebels were armed. There were also many other rebels in Sumbuya. The witness was afraid of the named rebel and did not try to escape for fear of what he might do to her. The witness was kept in Sumbuya by the named rebel for less than a month. On cross examination, the witness stated that she did not know if she was with the rebels in Sumbuya during February. The Brima Defence asserts that the testimony of witness TF1-282 is not reliable as she testified on cross that by giving evidence at the Special Court her lifestyle had changed for the better. The Trial Chamber does not share this opinion. Any benefit received by the witness related to her short-term accommodation during the Trial and in no way changes the witness's overall lifestyle. The Trial Chamber is satisfied that the witness's testimony of her forcible capture; her detention in a house with her rebel husband and two other rebels for under a month; her feeling that she could not escape for fear of what her rebel husband might do to her; and the use of the term 'wife', in this context a label of possession; is indicative of the deprivation of her liberty and the exercise of ownership over her person which, together with acts of sexual violence committed against her, namely repeated rapes committed by her rebel husband, satisfies the *actus reus* and *mens rea* of the crime of sexual slavery".[791] "The Trial Chamber also relies on the evidence of Prosecution witness TF1-085, examined by the Trial Chamber, *supra*, that she was abducted from Wellington, Western Area by persons found by the Chamber to belong to the AFRC/RUF sometime shortly after the 6th of January 1999. She was forced by the rebels to carry a load and

[791] *Alex Tamba Brima et al.* Trial Judgement, paras. 1173–1183 (internal references omitted).

	taken to Allen Town where a rebel, present at the time of the witness's abduction and whose name was given to the Court in closed session [hereinafter 'named rebel'], raped her and told her she was his 'wife.' The witness was taken with the troops during the retreat from Freetown to Waterloo and then Masiaka, Port Loko District, where the named rebel continued to repeatedly rape her. The witness became pregnant and miscarried twice as a result of the rapes. In Masiaka, the named rebel 'married' the witness in a ceremony, although the Trial Chamber has held that given the environment of coercion, there could be no valid consent on the part of the witness and therefore, this 'marriage' could not have been legal. The witness was not forced to do any work for the named rebel, but she was detained against her will for several months and punished and threatened with death by the named rebel when she tried to escape. The Trial Chamber is satisfied on the basis of the evidence above that the named rebel exercised ownership over the witness and committed acts of sexual violence against her. As such, the Trial Chamber is satisfied that the *actus reus* and *mens rea* of the crime of sexual slavery are satisfied with regards to the evidence of witness TF1-085".[792] "By virtue of the foregoing, and without predetermining the individual responsibility of the three Accused, the Trial Chamber is satisfied that the elements in relation to sexual slavery are established in relation to Port Loko District".[793] - General conclusion on sexual slavery as outrages upon personal: "By virtue of the foregoing and of the Trial Chamber's findings with regards to Count 6 and the chapeau elements of war crimes, the Trial Chamber is satisfied that the elements in relation to Count 9 (Outrages on Personal Dignity) are established in Kono, Koinadugu, Bombali, Freetown and Western Area and Port Loko Districts".[794] - Rapes constituting acts of terrorism as a violation of Article 3 common to the Geneva Conventions and of Additional Protocol II (WC) and collective punishment as a violation of Article 3 common to the Geneva Conventions and of Additional Protocol II (WC) in Bombali District: "The Trial Chamber has found that acts of violence were committed against protected persons in Bornoya (Unlawful Killings); Karina (Unlawful Killings); Mateboi (Unlawful Killings); Gbendembu (Unlawful Killings); and Rosos (Rape, Physical Violence)".[795] "The Trial Chamber has found that while the troops were at Camp Rosos, at least three civilians were raped in or near Rosos and that one was gang-raped and was badly beaten and stabbed during the attack".[796] "On this basis, the Trial Chamber is satisfied that the acts of violence committed by members of the AFRC against protected persons or the property in Bornoya, Mateboi, Mandaya, Karina, Gebendembu and Rosos can only reasonably be inferred to have been carried out with the primary purpose to spread terror among the civilian population. The Trial Chamber is further satisfied that the crimes committed also served as a punishment against protected persons. No evidence has been adduced to indicate whether the protected persons targeted in these attacks did or did not in fact support the elected government of President Ahmed Tejan Kabbah or factions aligned with that government. The Trial Chamber has held that the material element in the *actus reus* of the crime of collective punishment is not whether the acts were actually com-

792 *Alex Tamba Brima et al.* Trial Judgement, paras. 1184–1185 (internal references omitted).
793 *Alex Tamba Brima et al.* Trial Judgement, para. 1187.
794 *Alex Tamba Brima et al.* Trial Judgement, para. 1188.
795 *Alex Tamba Brima et al.* Trial Judgement, para. 1546.
796 *Alex Tamba Brima et al.* Trial Judgement, para. 1567 (internal references omitted).

	mitted or not by the victims, but whether the perpetrator indiscriminately and collectively punished these individuals for acts that they might or might not have committed. The Trial Chamber is satisfied, on the basis of the evidence specified above, that protected persons were collectively punished for allegedly supporting the President Ahmed Tejan Kabbah by members of the AFRC/RUF".[797] "By virtue of the foregoing and of the Trial Chamber's findings with regards to the Chapeau elements of war crimes, the Trial Chamber is satisfied that the elements in relation to Count 1 (Terror) are established. By virtue of the foregoing and of the Trial Chamber's findings with regards to the Chapeau elements of war crimes, the Trial Chamber is satisfied that the elements in relation to Count 2 (Collective Punishment) are established".[798] - Individual criminal responsibility of Alex Tamba Brima for sexual slavery constituting outrages upon personal dignity: "The Trial Chamber heard that sexual slavery was systemic amongst the perpetrators. Abducted women were distributed to soldiers and commanders who signed for them. There were disciplinary measures regulating the conduct of sexual slaves and their rebel 'husbands'. This system was overseen by commanders who appointed a 'Mammy Queen' to assist them. At Camp Rosos, abducted young women were forced to provide sexual services and to perform domestic tasks. [...] Based on the large scale, continuous and organised nature of the enslavement crimes, the Trial Chamber is satisfied that the only reasonable inference is that a substantial degree of planning and preparation were required to commit the crimes. [...T]he Trial Chamber is further satisfied that the Accused Brima, alone or with others, designed the commission of [...] sexual slavery [...] and that although these crimes were largely committed by his subordinates, his contribution was substantial. [...] Throughout the conflict women and young girls were treated as war bounty, abducted from their homes and repeatedly raped. [...] Given his authority, the Accused was in a position to shut down this system of exploitation entirely, to deter the excesses committed by his troops, and to alleviate the plight of the victims. On the evidence adduced the Trial Chamber finds that he failed to do so. The Trial Chamber stresses that the above evidence relates entirely to enslavement crimes committed in Bombali and the Western Area. The Trial Chamber has found that the Accused Brima was not involved in the commission of crimes in Bo, Kenema, Kailahun, Kono, Koinadugu and Port Loko Districts. The Trial Chamber is satisfied that the Accused planned, ordered, organised and implemented the system to abduct and enslave civilians which was in fact committed by AFRC troops in Bombali and Western Area. It is further satisfied that the Accused had the direct intent to set up and implement the system of exploitation involving [...] sexual slavery [...]. On the basis of the foregoing, the Trial Chamber is satisfied beyond reasonable doubt that the Accused Brima is individually criminally responsible under Article 6(1) of the Statute for planning the commission of the crime of outrages on personal dignity in Bombali District and Freetown and the Western Area".[799] - Individual criminal responsibility of Santigie Borbor Kanu for sexual slavery constituting outrages upon personal dignity: "The Trial Chamber has found that the Accused Kanu was Chief of Staff and commander in charge of abducted civilians in Bombali District and the Western Area. As the AFRC troops depended heavily on these civilians for a multitude of tasks, the Accused Kanu's position was a critical one. In Bombali District the Accused Kanu

797 *Alex Tamba Brima et al.* Trial Judgement, paras. 1571–1573 (internal references omitted).

798 *Alex Tamba Brima et al.* Trial Judgement, paras. 1633–1634 (internal references omitted).

799 *Alex Tamba Brima et al.* Trial Judgement, paras. 1823, 1826–1827, 1832–1835 (internal references omitted).

	designed and implemented a system to control abducted girls and women. All abducted women and girls were placed in the custody of the Accused. Any soldier who wanted an abducted girl or woman to be his 'wife' had to 'sign for her'. The Accused informed his fighters that any problems with the women were to be immediately reported back to him, and that he would then monitor the situation. The Accused issued a disciplinary instruction ordering that any woman caught with another woman's husband should be beaten and locked in a box. In one instance, Witness TF1-334 observed a Staff Sergeant reporting to Kanu that he suspected his 'wife' of misbehaving and the Accused Kanu called the woman before him and found her guilty. He ordered that she be sent to the Mammy Queen, be given a dozen lashes and be locked in the box. […] The Trial Chamber […] is further satisfied that the Accused Kanu had the direct intent to establish and implement the system of exploitation involving […] sexual slavery […]. On the basis of the foregoing, the Trial Chamber is satisfied beyond reasonable doubt that the Accused Kanu is individually criminally responsible under Article 6(1) of the Statute for planning the commission of the crime of sexual slavery in Bombali District and the Western Area".[800]

2. Moinina **Fofana and** Allieu **Kondewa** (Case No. SCSL-04-14) "***CDF***" - Moinina Fofana: National Director of War of the Civil Defence Forces (CDF) – a security force comprised mainly of "Kamajors", traditional hunters – and, as such, one of the top leaders of the CDF; second in command of the CDF. - Allieu Kondewa: High Priest of the CDF and, as such, one of the top leaders of the CDF.	
Indictment (International sex crimes (or related) charges and mode(s) of liability)	- There are no factual allegations or charges of international sex crimes in the Indictment.[801]
Trial Judgement	N/A
Appeal Judgement	N/A
Legal and Factual Findings and/or Evidence	- Legal findings: **- Amendment of the Indictment to include charges on sexual violence:** The Prosecution did not include any allegations or charges of international sex crimes in the *Fofana and Kondewa* Indictment. Prior to the start of the trial, the Prosecution's request to include such charges – namely rape, sexual slavery and other inhumane acts like forced mariage as crimes against humanity and outrages upon personal dignity as a war crime – was dismissed by the Trial Chamber in a decision issued just before the start of the trial. On appeal, the Prosecution alleged that the Trial Chamber committed an error of law and fact in dismissing its request for leave to amend the *Fofana and Kondewa* Indictment to include charges of sexual violence. As a remedy, the Prosecution only sought a reversal by the Appeals Chamber of the Trial Chamber's legal reasoning and a

800 *Alex Tamba Brima et al.* Trial Judgement, paras. 2091–2092, 2095–2096 (internal references omitted).

801 *Prosecutor v. Samuel Hinga Norman et al.*, Case No. SCSL-04-14-PT, Indictment, 5 February 2004 ("*Fofana and Kondewa* Indictment").

	declaration to that effect. The Prosecution did not request the Appeals Chamber to substitute any additional conviction or to order any trial proceedings.[802] The Appeals Chamber held: "In the instant case, the Prosecution merely requests the Appeals Chamber to declare that the Indictment Amendment Decision contains an error of law and or of fact. The Prosecution notes that, '[i]f the present Ground of Appeal is upheld, in order for any verdict to be reached on the individual responsibility of the Accused for the additional counts of gender crimes, the Appeals Chamber would [...] have to remit the case to the Trial Chamber for further trial proceedings on those counts.' The Prosecution 'accepts that this would not be practicable,' and therefore, does not seek any other remedy than a finding that the Trial Chamber erred in the impugned decision. In view of the scope of the Prosecution's request and its failure to seek any remedy other than a mere finding of an error of law in the Indictment Amendment Decision, coupled with the fact that the alleged errors under this ground of appeal do not relate to Counts contained in the Indictment upon which the verdict was made, the Appeals Chamber finds that the Prosecution has not shown that the error of law would invalidate the decision or that an error of fact would lead to a miscarriage of justice. The findings in the Trial Judgment were made upon the charges brought by the Prosecution in the Indictment. The Trial Chamber's decision refusing leave to amend the Indictment does not, as such, affect any of the legal and factual findings set forth in the Trial Judgment. It is also recalled that the amendment of the Indictment sought by the Prosecution was aimed at including new and additional charges based on various acts of sexual violence. Denying the amendment did not preclude the Prosecution from charging the Accused with these crimes, since it is within the Prosecution's discretion to bring, alongside the original indictment, a separate indictment regarding the new allegations it intended to bring in the case. In view of the foregoing, the Appeals Chamber finds that the consideration of this Ground of Appeal would be an academic exercise. The Appeals Chamber, Justice Winter dissenting, concludes that the Prosecution's Eighth Ground of Appeal is an unnecessary exercise and that it fails in its entirety".[803] In her dissenting opinion, Justice Winter held: "I hold that a review by the Appeals Chamber of the merits of the Prosecution's submissions against the Indictment Amendment Decision cannot be regarded as an 'academic exercise.' [...] In addressing whether to grant leave to amend an indictment, the overall consideration for a Trial Chamber is to ensure the accused's right to a fair hearing. The scope and nature of the amendments, their effect on the case and the consequences on the trial proceedings shall be considered in light of the rights of the accused to be tried without undue delay and to have adequate time to prepare his/her defense, as enshrined in Article 17 of the Statute. Further, international criminal tribunals examine whether the amendment may help to 'ensure that the real issues in the case will be determined.' As the ICTY Appeals Chamber held, 'the timeliness of the Prosecutor's request for leave to amend the indictment must be measured within the framework of the overall requirement of the fairness of the proceedings.' In this respect, I consider that the principle of fairness of the proceedings and of equality of arms applies to both, the Defence and the Prosecution which 'acts on behalf of and in the interest of the community, including the interest of the victims of the offence charged. In this case, the proposed amendments to the indictment included new charges based on various acts of gender-based violence, extended the timeframe of certain allegations and added new locations to others. Although the proposed amendments altered the case geographically, temporally and in terms of the nature of the charges against the Accused, I do not consider that the Defense's statutory rights would have been breached so as to render the trial unfair for

[802] *Prosecutor v. Moinina Fofana and Allieu Kondewa*, Case No. SCSL-04-14-A, Judgment, 28 May 2008 ("*Fofana and Kondewa* Appeal Judgement"), paras. 410, 415 (internal references omitted).

[803] *Fofana and Kondewa* Appeal Judgement, paras. 425–427 (internal references omitted).

the following reasons: [...] I further believe that, in deciding whether to grant leave to amend the indictment, consideration must be given to the impact on and significance of prosecuting the material facts alleged in the amended indictment. In the present case, the denial of the amendments precluded that any of the gender-based violence allegedly committed against women and girls by the Kamajors/CDF during the armed conflict could be prosecuted. Article 15(4) of the Statute specifically addresses the need for the Prosecution to consider employment of prosecutors and investigators specialised in gender-based violence. The Trial Chamber itself stated in another context that this provision 'underscore[s] the necessity for international criminal justice to highlight the high profile nature of the emerging domain of gender offences with a view to bringing the alleged perpetrators to justice.' It follows in my view that denying the Prosecution to prosecute acts of gender-based violence committed against women and girls during the armed conflict in Sierra Leone impeded the Special Court's fulfilment of its mandate. Finally, the approach adopted by the Majority of the Trial Chamber prevented victims of gender-based violence from seeing their case adjudicated before the Special Court. I consider that when an international forum is established to adjudicate gross violations of human rights, it has an inherent duty to fulfil its mandate by providing the victims with proper access to justice. This consideration is particularly relevant in the context of the prosecution of crimes committed in Sierra Leone during the armed conflict since the victims might be prevented from seeking remedy before the national courts in view of the Amnesty included in the Lomé Agreement. For the above reasons, I consider that in denying the Prosecution's request for leave to amend the Indictment in order to add charges of gender-based violence, the Trial Chamber committed a discernable error of fact and of law in finding that the Prosecution did not act with due diligence and in failing to balance the rights of the accused with other factors, including the rights and duties of the Prosecution and the overall mandate of the Court".[804]

- Admissibility of evidence on sexual violence:

At trial, the Trial Chamber decided that evidence on crimes of a sexual nature and forced marriage was not admissible under existing Counts 3 and 4 of the Indictment in light of the Trial Chamber's decision denying the Prosecution's request for leave to amend the Indictment to add four new counts relating to sexual violence. The Trial Chamber found that because the allegations of sexual violence were not specifically pleaded in the Indictment, to admit evidence of sexual violence would infringe upon the Accused's rights under Article 17(2) and (4) of the Statute, either because the Accused would not have been properly informed of the nature of the case against him or the admission of such evidence would require a lengthy delay in the trial proceedings, thus violating the Accused's right to a fair and expeditious trial. The Trial Chamber further held that the admission of evidence of sexual violence would prejudice the rights of the accused because: (i) Counts 3 and 4 of the Indictment contained no specific factual allegations concerning sexual violence, and therefore, evidence cannot be properly adduced; (ii) admitting the disputed evidence at that very late and crucial stage of the trial, derogates significantly from Article 17(4)(a) of the Statute, which guarantees every accused the right to be informed promptly and in detail in a language which he understands of the nature and cause of the charges against him; and (iii) "nothing in the record[] seems to support the Prosecution's assertion that evidentiary material under reference had been disclosed to the Defence in 'some form' over 12 months ago", especially in light of the fact that specific allegations are not contained in

804 *Fofana and Kondewa* Appeal Judgement, Section VII (Partially Dissenting Opinion of Honourable Justice Renate Winter), paras. 73, 82–83, 85–86.

	the Indictment. The Trial Chamber denied the Prosecution's request to appeal the Trial Chamber's decision.[805] In the *Fofana and Kondewa* Trial Judgement, the Trial Chamber held: "In its Admissibility Decision, the Trial Chamber dismissed evidence of sexual violence that the Prosecution attempted to adduce at trial in support of Counts 3–4. The Chamber held that it would be prejudicial to the Accused to allow such evidence to be admitted, as acts of sexual violence were not plead in the Indictment under these Counts, and the Accused had therefore not been put on notice that they were facing such charges. In line with the reasoning in this Decision, the Chamber has considered only those acts which are listed in the Indictment in relation to Counts 3 and 4 (mental suffering). The Chamber will therefore consider only the following acts for the purposes of its legal findings on Counts 3 and 4: (i) screening for collaborators; (ii) unlawfully killing suspected collaborators, often in plain view of friends and relatives; (iii) illegal arrest and unlawful imprisonment of collaborators; (iv) the destruction of homes and other buildings; (v) looting and threats to unlawfully kill, destroy or loot".[806] On appeal, the Prosecution alleged that the Trial Chamber committed an error of law and fact in denying its request to lead and adduce evidence of sexual violence under Count 3 (other inhumane acts as a crime against humanity) and Count 4 (violence to life, health and physical or mental well-being as a war crime) of the *Fofana and Kondewa* Indictment.[807] "The Prosecution submits that it is settled law that a defective indictment can be cured where there has been timely, clear and consistent information provided to the accused detailing the factual basis of the charges against him. Furthermore, it submits that, as a matter of law, the war crime of violence to life, health and physical and mental well being of persons, in particular cruel treatment can include crimes of a sexual nature. In light of these legal principles, the Prosecution contends that had the Trial Chamber exercised its discretion correctly and applied the correct legal principle it would have found that the Prosecution did provide timely, clear and consistent information that crimes of a sexual nature were being alleged under Counts 3 and 4 of the Indictment, over twelve months before it sought to lead evidence of sexual violence, through its pre-trial, supplemental pre-trial briefs, and opening statement. To the extent that the Trial Chamber found that 'nothing in the record seems to support the Prosecution's assertion that the evidentiary material under reference had been disclosed to the Defence 'in some form' over 12 months ago,' the Prosecution contends that the Trial Chamber erred in fact".[808] The Appeals Chamber held: "The Appeals Chamber is of the opinion that acts of sexual violence may constitute 'other inhumane acts' as alleged in Count 3 of the Indictment as well as 'cruel treatment,' as alleged in Count 4 of the Indictment. Counts 3 and 4 of the Indictment do not explicitly list the acts of sexual violence that amounts either to an 'other inhumane act' under Article 2.i. of the Statute or 'cruel treatment' under Article 3.a. of the Statute. The Indictment on its face was defective with respect to allegations relating to sexual violence. However, case law at the *ad hoc* Tribunals recognizes that in limited circumstances, a defect in the indictment may be 'cured' if the Prosecution provides the accused with timely, clear and consistent information

805 See *Fofana and Kondewa* Appeal Judgement, paras. 430–434 (internal reference omitted).

806 *Prosecutor v. Moinina Fofana and Allieu Kondewa*, Case No. SCSL-04-14-T, Judgement, 2 August 2007 ("*Fofana and Kondewa* Trial Judgement"), para. 48 (internal references omitted), referring to *Prosecutor v. Sam Hinga Norman et al.*, Case No. SCSL-04-14-T, Reasoned Majority Decision on Prosecution Motion for a Ruling on the Admissibility of Evidence, 22 June 2005. See also *Prosecutor v. Sam Hinga Norman et al.*, Case No. SCSL-04-14-T, Decision on the Urgent Prosecution Motion Filed on the 15th of February 2005 for a Ruling on the Admissibility of Evidence, 23 May 2005; *Prosecutor v. Sam Hinga Norman et al.*, Case No. SCSL-04-14-PT, Decision on Prosecution Request for Leave to Amend the Indictment, 20 May 2004.

807 *Fofana and Kondewa* Appeal Judgement, paras. 428, 435 (internal references omitted).

808 *Fofana and Kondewa* Appeal Judgement, para. 436 (internal references omitted).

	detailing the factual basis underpinning the charge. While a vague indictment not cured by timely, clear and consistent notice causes prejudice to the accused, the defect may be deemed harmless if the Prosecution can demonstrate that the accused's ability to prepare his defence was not materially impaired. Factors to be considered in this respect include, among others, information provided in the Prosecution's pre-trial brief or its opening statement, the timing of the communications, the importance of the information to the ability of the accused to prepare his defence and the impact of the newly-disclosed material facts on the Prosecution's case. The Appeals Chamber adopts these principles. The Appeals Chamber notes that the Prosecution's Pre-Trial Brief, filed on 2 March 2004, clearly notes that in relation to Bonthe District, '[t]he evidence will demonstrate that their daughters and wives [civilians] were systematically raped and held in sexual slavery.' The Prosecution's Supplemental Pre-Trial Brief, filed on 22 April 2004, alleged that under Counts 3 and 4 of the Indictment, in relation to Bonthe District, both Fofana and Kondewa were being held responsible pursuant to Article 6(1) of the Statute for subjecting women and girls to 'sexual assaults, harassment, and non-consensual sex, which resulted in widespread proliferation of sexually transmitted diseases, unwanted pregnancies and severe mental suffering [...],' as well as for 'committing unlawful physical violence and mental harm or suffering through sexual assaults as well as other acts during the attacks in Bonthe District.' Furthermore, the Prosecution's opening statement, delivered on 3 June 2004, referred to the testimony of several witnesses relating to evidence of sexual violence or forced marriage. The Appeals Chamber therefore is satisfied that by the time the Prosecution filed its Admissibility of Evidence Motion, the Accused had timely and consistent notice for nearly one year that acts of sexual violence were being alleged in relation to Bonthe District under Counts 3 and 4 of the Indictment. Fofana argues that the Trial Chamber was correct in refusing to admit evidence of sexual violence because the 'evidence sought to be adduced would be prejudicial to the interest of the accused persons. Such evidence would cast a cloak of doubt on the image of innocence that the Accused enjoys under law, until the contrary is proved.' The Appeals Chamber is of the view that the right to a fair trial enshrined in Article 17 of the Statute cannot be violated by the introduction of evidence relevant to any allegation in the trial proceedings, regardless of the nature or severity of the evidence. The Appeals Chamber concludes that evidence of sexual violence was relevant to charges in the Indictment and that the Trial Chamber was in error in prospectively denying the admittance of such evidence. Further, the accused were put on notice of such evidence, which is not prejudicial in itself".[809]

3. Issa Hassan **<u>Sesay *et al.*</u>** (Case No. SCSL-04-15) "***RUF***" - Issa Hassan Sesay: Senior officer and commander in the Revolutionary United Front (RUF) Junta and AFRC/RUF forces. - Morris Kallon: Senior officer and commander in the RUF Junta and AFRC/RUF forces. - Augustine Gbao: Senior officer and commander in the RUF Junta and AFRC/RUF forces.	
Indictment (International sex crimes (or related) charges and mode(s) of liability)	All three accused were charged with: - **Rape as CAH** (count 6), **Sexual slavery and any other form of sexual violence as CAH** (count 7), **Other inhumane act as CAH** (count 8) and **Outrages upon personal dignity as a violation of Article 3 common to the Geneva Conventions and of Additional Protocol II (WC)** (count 9) under Articles 6(1) and 6(3) of the Statute (**superior responsibility**) for: (i) the rapes of hundreds of women and girls; and (ii) the abductions of an unknown number of women and girls for using them sex as slaves

[809] *Fofana and Kondewa* Appeal Judgement, paras. 441–446 (internal references omitted).

	and/or forcing them into 'marriages' and/or subjecting them to other forms of sexual violence.[810] **- Acts of terrorism as a violation of Article 3 common to the Geneva Conventions and of Additional Protocol II (WC)** (count 1) and **Collective Punishment as a violation of Article 3 common to the Geneva Conventions and of Additional Protocol II (WC)** (count 2) under Articles 6(1) and 6(3) of the Statute (**superior responsibility**) for committing the same crimes of sexual violence as those pleaded in counts 6 to 9 as part of a campaign to terrorise the civilian population and to punish the civilian population for allegedly supporting the elected government and factions aligned with that government, or for failing to provide sufficient support to the AFRC/RUF.[811]

810 *Prosecutor v. Issa Hassan Sesay et al.*, Case No. SCSL-04-15-PT, Corrected Amended Consolidated Indictment, 2 August 2006 ("*Issa Hassan Sesay et al.* Indictment"), paras. 54–60 ("Widespread sexual violence committed against civilian women and girls included brutal rapes, often by multiple rapists, and forced 'marriages'. Acts of sexual violence included the following: **Kono District** Between about 14 February 1998 and 30 June 1998, members of AFRC/RUF raped hundreds of women and girls at various locations throughout the District, including Koidu, Tombodu, Kissi-town (or Kissi Town), Foendor (or Foendu), Tomendeh, Fokoiya, Wondedu and AFRC/RUF camps such as 'Superman camp' and Kissi-town (or Kissi Town) camp. An unknown number of women and girls were abducted from various locations within the District and used as sex slaves and/or forced into 'marriages'. The 'wives' were forced to perform a number of conjugal duties under coercion by their 'husbands'; **Koinadugu District** Between about 14 February 1998 and 30 September 1998, members of AFRC/RUF raped an unknown number of women and girls in locations in Koinadugu District, such as Kabala, Koinadugu, Heremakono and Fadugu. In addition an unknown number of women and girls were abducted and used as sex slaves and/or forced into 'marriages' and/or subjected to other forms of sexual violence. The 'wives' were forced to perform a number of conjugal duties under coercion by their 'husbands'; **Bombali District** Between about 1 May 1998 and 31 November 1998, members of the AFRC/RUF raped an unknown number of women and girls in locations in Bombali District, including Mandaha and Rosos (or Rosors or Rossos). In addition, an unknown number of abducted women and girls were used as sex slaves and/or forced into 'marriages' and/or subjected to other forms of sexual violence. The 'wives' were forced to perform a number of conjugal duties under coercion by their 'husbands'; **Kailahun District** At all times relevant to this Indictment, an unknown number of women and girls in various locations in the District were subjected to sexual violence. Many of these victims were captured in other areas of the Republic of Sierra Leone, brought to AFRC/RUF camps in the District, and used as sex slaves and/or forced into 'marriages'. The 'wives' were forced to perform a number of conjugal duties under coercion by their 'husbands'; **Freetown and the Western Area** Between 6 January 1999 and 28 February 1999, members of AFRC/RUF raped hundreds of women and girls throughout the City of Freetown and the Western Area, and abducted hundreds of women and girls and used them as sex slaves and/or forced them into 'marriages' and/or subjected them to other forms of sexual violence. The 'wives' were forced to perform a number of conjugal duties under coercion by their 'husbands'; **Port Loko District** About the month of February 1999, AFRC/RUF fled from Freetown to various locations in the Port Loko District. Between February 1999 and April 1999, members of the AFRC/RUF raped an unknown number of women and girls in various locations in the District. In addition, an unknown number of women and girls in various locations in the District were used as sex slaves and/or forced into 'marriages' and/or subjected to other forms of sexual violence by members of the AFRC/RUF. The 'wives' were forced to perform a number of conjugal duties under coercion by their 'husbands'; By their acts or omission in relation to these events, **ISSA HASSAN SESAY, MORRIS KALLON and AUGUSTINE GBAO**, pursuant to Artice 6.1. and, or alternatively, Article 6.3. of the Statute, are individually criminally responsible for the crimes alleged below: **Count 6:** Rape, a **CRIME AGAINST HUMANITY**, punishable under Article 2.g. of the Statute; And: **Count 7:** Sexual slavery and any other form of sexual violence, a **CRIME AGAINST HUMANITY**, punishable under Article 2.g. of the Statute; And: **Count 8:** Other inhumane act, a **CRIME AGAINST HUMANITY**, punishable under Article 2.i. of the Statute; In addition, or in the alternative: **Count 9:** Outrages upon personal dignity, a **VIOLATION OF ARTICLE 3 COMMON TO THE GENEVA CONVENTIONS AND OF ADDITIONAL PROTOCOL II**, punishable under Article 3.e. of the Statute".).

811 *Issa Hassan Sesay et al.* Indictment, paras. 44 ("Members of the AFRC/RUF subordinate to and/or acting in concert with **ISSA HASSAN SESAY, MORRIS KALLON and AUGUSTINE GBAO**, committed the crimes set forth below in paragraphs 45 through 82 and charged in Counts 3 through 14, as part of a cam-

Trial Judgement	- Issa Hassan Sesay: Guilty of **Rape as CAH** (count 6) under Article 6(1) of the Statute (**joint criminal enterprise**) for the rapes committed in Koidu Town, Bumpeh, Tombodu, Penduma, Bomboafuidu, Sawao and Wendedu in Kono District.[812] Guilty of **Sexual slavery as CAH** (count 7) and **Other inhumane acts as CAH** (count 8) under Article 6(1) of the Statute (**joint criminal enterprise**) for the crimes of sexual slavery and forced marriages committed in Koidu Town and Wendedu in Kono District and in locations in Kailahun District.[813] Guilty of **Outrages upon personal dignity as a violation of Article 3 common to the Geneva Conventions and of Additional Protocol II (WC)** (count 9) under Article 6(1) of the Statute (**joint criminal enterprise**) for the crimes of rapes, sexual slavery and forced marriages committed in Koidu Town, Bumpeh, Tombodu, Penduma, Bomboafuidu, Sawao and Wendedu in Kono District and in locations in Kailahun District.[814] Guilty of **Acts of terrorism as a violation of Article 3 common to the Geneva Conventions and of Additional Protocol II (WC)** (count 1) under Article 6(1) of the Statute (**joint criminal enterprise**) for the various crimes, including the above-mentioned international sex crimes set forth in counts 6 to 9 committed in Koidu Town, Bumpeh, Tombodu, Penduma, Bomboafuidu, Sawao and Wendedu in Kono District and in locations in Kailahun District.[815] - Morris Kallon: Guilty of **Rape as CAH** (count 6) under Article 6(1) of the Statute (**joint criminal enterprise**) for the rapes committed in Koidu Town, Bumpeh, Tombodu, Penduma, Bomboafuidu, Sawao and Wendedu in Kono District.[816] Guilty of **Sexual slavery as CAH** (count 7) and **Other inhumane acts as CAH** (count 8) under Article 6(1) of the Statute (**joint criminal enterprise**) for the crimes of sexual slavery and forced marriages committed in Koidu Town and Wendedu in Kono District and in locations in Kailahun District, and under Article 6(3) of the Statute (**superior responsibility**) for the crimes of sexual slavery and forced marriages committed in Kissi Town in Kono District.[817] Guilty of **Outrages upon personal dignity as a violation**

paign to terrorize the civilian population of the Republic of Sierra Leone, and did terrorize that population. The AFRC/RUF also committed the crimes to punish the civilian population for allegedly supporting the elected government of President Ahmed Tejan Kabbah and factions aligned with that government, or for failing to provide sufficient support to the AFRC/RUF. By their acts or omissions in relation to these events, **ISSA HASSAN SESAY, MORRIS KALLON and AUGUSTINE GBAO**, pursuant to Article 6.1. and, or alternatively, Article 6.3. of the Statute, are individually criminally responsible for the crimes alleged below: **Count 1:** Acts of Terrorism, a **VIOLATION OF ARTICLE 3 COMMON TO THE GENEVA CONVENTIONS AND OF ADDITIONAL PROTOCOL II**, punishable under Article 3.d. of the Statute; And: **Count 2:** Collective Punishments, a **VIOLATION OF ARTICLE 3 COMMON TO THE GENEVA CONVENTIONS AND OF ADDITIONAL PROTOCOL II**, punishable under Article 3.b. of the Statute".), 54–60.

812 *Prosecutor v. Issa Hassan Sesay et al.*, Case No. SCSL-04-15-T, Judgement, 2 March 2009 ("*Issa Hassan Sesay et al.* Trial Judgement"), paras. 1152–1153, 1171, 1180–1181, 1185, 1191–1195, 1206, 1208, 1286–1290, 2091–2092 and Section IX (Disposition), p. 700.

813 *Issa Hassan Sesay et al.* Trial Judgement, paras. 1154–1155, 1178–1179, 1291–1297, 1406–1413, 1460–1473, 2090–2092, 2161–2163 and Section IX (Disposition), p. 700.

814 *Issa Hassan Sesay et al.* Trial Judgement, paras. 1152–1155, 1171, 1178–1181, 1185, 1191–1195, 1205–1208, 1286–1297, 1299, 1302–1309, 1406–1413, 1460–1475, 2090–2092, 2161–2163 and Section IX (Disposition), p. 700.

815 *Issa Hassan Sesay et al.* Trial Judgement, paras. 1152–1155, 1171, 1178–1181, 1185, 1191–1195, 1205–1208, 1353–1356, 1406–1413, 1460–1473, 1493, 2090–2092, 2161–2163 and Section IX (Disposition), p. 699.

816 *Issa Hassan Sesay et al.* Trial Judgement, paras. 1152–1153, 1171, 1180–1181, 1185, 1191–1195, 1206, 1208, 1286–1290, 2099, 2101–2103 and Section IX (Disposition), p. 704.

817 *Issa Hassan Sesay et al.* Trial Judgement, paras. 1154–1155, 1178–1179, 1211–1214, 1291–1297, 1300–1301, 1406–1413, 1460–1473, 2101–2103, 2146, 2148, 2150–2151, 2161–2163 and Section IX (Disposition), p. 704.

	of Article 3 common to the Geneva Conventions and of Additional Protocol II (WC) (count 9) under Article 6(1) of the Statute (**joint criminal enterprise**) for the crimes of rapes, sexual slavery and forced marriages committed in Koidu Town, Bumpeh, Tombodu, Penduma, Bomboafuidu, Sawao and Wendedu in Kono District and in locations in Kailahun District, and under Article 6(3) of the Statute (**superior responsibility**) for the crimes of sexual slavery and forced marriages committed in Kissi Town in Kono District.[818] Guilty of **Acts of terrorism as a violation of Article 3 common to the Geneva Conventions and of Additional Protocol II (WC)** (count 1) under Article 6(1) of the Statute (**joint criminal enterprise**) for the various crimes, including the above-mentioned international sex crimes set forth in counts 6 to 9 committed in Koidu Town, Bumpeh, Tombodu, Penduma, Bomboafuidu, Sawao and Wendedu in Kono District and in locations in Kailahun District, and under Article 6(3) of the Statute (**superior responsibility**) for a crime of sexual slavery set forth in count 7 committed in Kissi Town in Kono District.[819] - Augustine Gbao: Guilty of **Rape as CAH** (count 6) under Article 6(1) of the Statute (**joint criminal enterprise**) for the rapes committed in Koidu Town, Bumpeh, Tombodu, Penduma, Bomboafuidu, Sawao and Wendedu in Kono District.[820] Guilty of **Sexual slavery as CAH** (count 7) and **Other inhumane acts as CAH** (count 8) under Article 6(1) of the Statute (**joint criminal enterprise**) for the crimes of sexual slavery and forced marriages committed in Koidu Town and Wendedu in Kono District and in locations in Kailahun District.[821] Guilty of **Outrages upon personal dignity as a violation of Article 3 common to the Geneva Conventions and of Additional Protocol II (WC)** (count 9) under Article 6(1) of the Statute (**joint criminal enterprise**) for the crimes of rapes, sexual slavery and forced marriages committed in Koidu Town, Bumpeh, Tombodu, Penduma, Bomboafuidu, Sawao and Wendedu in Kono District and in locations in Kailahun District.[822] Guilty of **Acts of terrorism as a violation of Article 3 common to the Geneva Conventions and of Additional Protocol II (WC)** (count 1) under Article 6(1) of the Statute (**joint criminal enterprise**) for the various crimes, including the above-mentioned international sex crimes set forth in counts 6 to 9 committed throughout Kailahun District.[823]
Appeal Judgement	- The convictions were affirmed by the Appeals Chamber.[824]
Legal and Factual Findings and/or	- <u>Legal findings:</u> - **Rape:** The Trial Chamber adopted the following definition of rape: "Thus, the Chamber has

[818] *Issa Hassan Sesay et al.* Trial Judgement, paras. 1152–1155, 1171, 1178–1181, 1185, 1191–1195, 1205–1208, 1211–1214, 1286–1297, 1299–1309, 1406–1413, 1460–1475, 2099, 2101–2103, 2146, 2148, 2150–2151, 2161–2163 and Section IX (Disposition), p. 704.

[819] *Issa Hassan Sesay et al.* Trial Judgement, paras. 1152–1155, 1171, 1178–1181, 1185, 1191–1195, 1205–1208, 1211–1214, 1291, 1294, 1297, 1300–1301, 1353–1356, 1406–1413, 1460–1473, 1493, 2099, 2101–2103, 2146, 2148, 2150–2151, 2161–2163 and Section IX (Disposition), pp. 702–703.

[820] *Issa Hassan Sesay et al.* Trial Judgement, paras. 1152–1153, 1171, 1180–1181, 1185, 1191–1195, 1206, 1208, 1286–1290, 2104–2110 and Section IX (Disposition), p. 707.

[821] *Issa Hassan Sesay et al.* Trial Judgement, paras. 1154–1155, 1178–1179, 1291–1297, 1406–1413, 1460–1473, 2104–2110, 2167–2168, 2171–2172 and Section IX (Disposition), pp. 707–708.

[822] *Issa Hassan Sesay et al.* Trial Judgement, paras. 1152–1155, 1171, 1178–1181, 1185, 1191–1195, 1205–1208, 1286–1297, 1299, 1302–1309, 1406–1413, 1460–1475, 2104–2110, 2167–2168, 2171–2172 and Section IX (Disposition), p. 708.

[823] *Issa Hassan Sesay et al.* Trial Judgement, paras. 1406–1413, 1460–1473, 1493, 2167–2168, 2171–2172 and Section IX (Disposition), p. 706.

[824] *Prosecutor v. Issa Hassan Sesay et al.*, Case no. SCSL-04-15-A, Judgment, 26 October 2009 ("*Issa Hassan Sesay et al.* Appeal Judgement"), Section XII (Disposition), pp. 463–466.

Evidence	held that the constitutive elements of rape are as follows: (i) The Accused invaded the body of a person by conduct resulting in penetration, however slight, of any part of the body of the victim or of the Accused with a sexual organ, or of the anal or genital opening of the victim with any object or any other part of the body; (ii) The invasion was committed by force, or by threat of force or coercion, such as that caused by fear of violence, duress, detention, psychological oppression or abuse of power against such person or another person or by taking advantage of a coercive environment, or the invasion was committed against a person incapable of giving genuine consent; (iii) The Accused intended to effect the sexual penetration or acted in the reasonable knowledge that this was likely to occur; and (iv) The Accused knew or had reason to know that the victim did not consent. The first element of the *actus reus* defines the type of invasion that is required to constitute the offence of rape and covers two types of penetration, however slight. The first part of the provision refers to the penetration of any part of the body of either the victim or the Accused with a sexual organ. The 'any part of the body' in this part includes genital, anal or oral penetration. The second part of the provision refers to the penetration of the genital or anal opening of the victim with any object or any other part of the body. This part is meant to cover penetration with something other than a sexual organ which could include either other body parts or any other object. This definition of invasion is broad enough to be gender neutral as both men and women can be victims of rape. The second element of the *actus reus* of rape refers to the circumstances which would render the sexual act in the first element criminal. The essence of this element is that it describes those circumstances in which the person could not be said to have voluntarily and genuinely consented to the act. The use or threat of force provides clear evidence of non-consent, but it is not required. The ICTY Appeals Chamber has emphasised that the circumstances 'that prevail in most cases charged as either war crimes or crimes against humanity will be almost universally coercive. That is to say, true consent will not be possible.' The last part of this element refers to those situations where, even in the absence of force or coercion, a person cannot be said to genuinely have consented to the act. A person may not, for instance, be capable of genuinely consenting if he or she is too young, under the influence of some substance, or suffering from an illness or disability. The Chamber observes that the very specific circumstances of an armed conflict where rapes on a large scale are alleged to have occurred, coupled with the social stigma which is borne by victims of rape in certain societies, render the restrictive test set out in the elements of the crime difficult to satisfy. Circumstantial evidence may therefore be used to demonstrate the *actus reus* of rape. The *mens rea* requirements for the offence of rape are that the invasion was intentional and that it was done in the knowledge that the victim was not consenting".[825] **- Sexual slavery:** The Trial Chamber held: "The specific offence of sexual slavery was included for the first time as a war crime and a crime against humanity in the ICC Statute. The offence is characterised as a crime against humanity under Article 2(g) of the Statute and the Indictments before the Special Court were the first to specifically indict persons with the crime of sexual slavery. By this assertion, the Chamber does not suggest that the offence is entirely new. It is the Chamber's view that sexual slavery is a particularised form of slavery or enslavement and acts which could be classified as sexual slavery have been prosecuted as enslavement in the past. In the *Kunarac* case, for instance, the Accused were convicted of the offences of enslavement, rape and outrages on personal dignity for having detained women for months and subjected them to rape and other sexual acts. In that case, the ICTY Appeals Chamber emphasised that 'it finds that enslavement, even if based on sexual exploitation, is a distinct offence from that of

[825] *Issa Hassan Sesay et al.* Trial Judgement, paras. 145–150 (internal references omitted).

	rape.' The Chamber opines that the prohibition of the more particular offences such as sexual slavery and sexual violence criminalises actions that were already criminal. The Chamber considers that the specific offences are designed to draw attention to serious crimes that have been historically overlooked and to recognise the particular nature of sexual violence that has been used, often with impunity, as a tactic of war to humiliate, dominate and instil fear in victims, their families and communities during armed conflict."[826] The Trial Chamber found that the prohibition of sexual slavery is a norm of *jus cogens*: "this Chamber takes the view that the offence of enslavement is prohibited at customary international law and entails individual criminal responsibility. The Chamber is satisfied that this would equally apply to the offence of sexual slavery which is 'an international crime and a violation of *jus cogens* norms in the exact same manner as slavery'".[827] With respect to the elements of the crime, the Trial Chamber held: "Consistent with the Rule 98 Decision, the Chamber has held that the relevant constitutive elements of sexual slavery are: (i) The Accused exercised any or all the powers attaching to the right of ownership over one or more persons, such as by purchasing, selling, lending or bartering such a person or persons, or by imposing on them a similar deprivation of liberty; (ii) The Accused caused such person or persons to engage in one or more acts of a sexual nature; and (iii) The Accused intended to exercise the act of sexual slavery or acted in the reasonable knowledge that this was likely to occur. This Chamber considers that the *actus reus* of the offence of sexual slavery is made up of two elements: first, that the Accused exercised any or all of the powers attaching to the right of ownership over a person or persons (the slavery element) and second, that the enslavement involved sexual acts (the sexual element). In determining whether or not the enslavement element of the *actus reus* has been established, the Chamber notes that the list of actions that reflect the exercise of a power of ownership that is included in the element is not exhaustive. The Chamber adopts the following indicia of enslavement identified by the ICTY in *Kunarac et al.*: 'control of someone's movement, control of physical environment, psychological control, measures taken to prevent or deter escape, force, threat of force or coercion, duration, assertion of exclusivity, subjection to cruel treatment and abuse, control of sexuality and forced labour.' The Chamber also notes that the expression 'similar deprivation of liberty' may cover situations in which the victims may not have been physically confined, but were otherwise unable to leave as they would have nowhere else to go and feared for their lives. To convict an Accused for this offence, the Prosecution must also prove that the Accused caused the enslaved person to engage in acts of a sexual nature. The acts of sexual violence are the additional element that, when combined with evidence of slavery, constitutes sexual slavery. The Chamber emphasises that the lack of consent of the victim to the enslavement or to the sexual acts is not an element to be proved by the Prosecution, although whether or not there was consent may be relevant from an evidentiary perspective in establishing whether or not the Accused exercised any of the powers attaching to the right of ownership. The Chamber subscribes to the statement of the ICTY Appeals Chamber that 'circumstances which render it impossible to express consent may be sufficient to presume the absence of consent.' The duration of the enslavement is not an element of the crime, although it may be relevant in determining the quality of the relationship".[828] **- Other inhumane acts for international sex crimes:** The Trial Chamber held: "The Appeals Chamber has emphasised that the crime of

[826] *Issa Hassan Sesay et al.* Trial Judgement, paras. 154–156 (internal references omitted).

[827] *Issa Hassan Sesay et al.* Trial Judgement, para. 157 (internal references omitted).

[828] *Issa Hassan Sesay et al.* Trial Judgement, paras. 158–163 (internal references omitted).

	other inhumane acts is designed to be 'inclusive in nature, intended to avoid unduly restricting the Statute's application to crimes against humanity.' The Chamber noted that a wide range of criminal or violent acts, including sexual crimes, have been recognised as other inhumane acts in the jurisprudence of international tribunals and concluded that the offence of other inhumane acts cannot be limited to exclude crimes with a sexual or gender component or nature".[829] **- Duplicity in pleading sexual slavery and any other form of sexual violence:** The Trial Chamber found that count 7 (Sexual slavery and any other form of sexual violence as CAH) violated the rule against duplicity: "Guided by the Appeals Chamber's finding that Count 7 in the AFRC Indictment was duplicitous for having charged separate and distinct offences, 'sexual slavery' and 'any other form of sexual violence', in the same Count, the Chamber finds that Count 7 of the RUF Indictment, which reflects the same wording as Count 7 of the AFRC Indictment, is bad for duplicity. The Chamber has considered the remedies available to it as outlined by the Appeals Chamber. In so doing, we have taken into account the Prosecution's Notice re Count 7 of the Indictment in which the Prosecution requested permission to proceed on the basis of the offence of sexual slavery and not on the offence of any other form of sexual violence. It is the considered view of this Chamber that the Prosecution cannot unilaterally elect upon which crime to proceed. However, in light of all of the circumstances of this trial and the evidence that has been led, the Chamber is satisfied that the appropriate remedy is to proceed on the basis that the offence of sexual slavery is properly charged within Count 7 and to strike out the charge of 'any other form of sexual violence'. As a result, the Chamber will only consider whether or not the offence of sexual slavery has been established in this case".[830] **- Rape, sexual slavery and "forced marriages" constituting outrages upon personal dignity:** "The Chamber finds that the acts of rape, sexual slavery and 'forced marriage,' as described above, also constitute in each case a severe humiliation, degradation and violation of the dignity of the victims and the perpetrators knew or ought to have known that that their acts would produce this effect".[831] **- Rape, sexual slavery, "forced marriages" and outrages upon personal dignity constituting acts of terrorism as a violation of Article 3 common to the Geneva Conventions and of Additional Protocol II (WC):** "In making its Legal Findings on sexual violence as an act of terrorism committed against the civilian population, the Chamber has considered the body of evidence adduced in relation to the various Districts of Sierra Leone as charged in the Indictment. The Chamber observes that sexual violence was rampantly committed against the civilian population in an atmosphere in which violence, oppression and lawlessness prevailed. The Chamber finds that the nature and manner in which the female population was a target of the sexual violence portrays a calculated and concerted pattern on the part of the perpetrators to use sexual violence as a weapon of terror. These fighters employed perverse methods of sexual violence against women and men of all ages ranging from brutal gang rapes, the insertion of various objects into victims' genitalia, the raping of pregnant women and forced sexual intercourse between male and female civilian abductees. In one instance, the wife of TF1-217 was raped by eight rebels as he and his children were forced to watch. TF1-217 was ordered to count each rebel as they consecutively raped his wife, 'he had no power not to' as the rapists

829 *Issa Hassan Sesay et al.* Trial Judgement, para. 166 (internal references omitted).
830 *Issa Hassan Sesay et al.* Trial Judgement, paras. 457–458 (internal references omitted).
831 *Issa Hassan Sesay et al.* Trial Judgement, para. 1298 (internal reference omitted).

	laughed and mocked him. After the ordeal, her rapists took a knife and stabbed her in front of the entire family. The Chamber is satisfied that the manner in which the rebels ravaged through villages targeting the female population effectively disempowered the civilian population and had a direct effect of instilling fear on entire communities. The Chamber moreover finds that these acts were not intended merely for personal satisfaction or a means of sexual gratification for the fighter. We opine that the savage nature of such conduct against the most vulnerable members of the society demonstrates that these acts were committed with the specific intent of spreading fear amongst the civilian population as a whole, in order to break the will of the population and ensure their submission to AFRC/RUF control. We note that the physical and psychological pain and fear inflicted on the women not only abused, debased and isolated the individual victim, but deliberately destroyed the existing family nucleus, thus undermining the cultural values and relationships which held the societies together. Victims of sexual violence were ostracised, husbands left their wives, and daughters and young girls were unable to marry within their community. The Chamber finds that sexual violence was intentionally employed by the perpetrators to alienate victims and render apart communities, thus inflicting physical and psychological injury on the civilian population as a whole. The Chamber finds that these effects of sexual violence were so common that it is apparent they were calculated consequences of the perpetrators' acts. The Chamber recalls the testimony of TF1-029 describing the general perception among the rebels that 'soldiers who captured civilians had a right to rape them and make them their wives.' The Chamber considers this statement indicative of the atmosphere of terror and helplessness that the rebel forces created by systematically engaging in sexual violence in order to demonstrate that the communities were unable to protect their own wives, daughters, mothers, and sisters. Rebels invaded homes at random and raped women. In this way the AFRC and RUF extended their power and dominance over the civilian population by perpetuating a constant threat of insecurity that pervaded daily life and afflicted both women and men. The Chamber has further found that countless women of all ages were routinely captured and abducted from their families, homes and communities and forced into prolonged exclusive conjugal relationships with rebel as 'wives.' The practice of 'forced marriages' and sexual slavery stigmatised the women, who lived in shame and fear of returning to their communities after the conflict. The Chamber finds that the pattern of sexual enslavement employed by the RUF was a deliberate system intended to spread terror by the mass abductions of women, regardless of their age or existing marital status, from legitimate husbands and families. In light of the foregoing, the Chamber finds that rape, sexual slavery, 'forced marriages' and outrages on personal dignity, when committed against a civilian population with the specific intent to terrorise, amount to an act of terror. The Chamber considers that the evidence on the record establishes that members of the AFRC/RUF regularly committed such acts of sexual violence as part of a campaign to terrorise the civilian population of Sierra Leone".[832] **- Cumulative convictions for rape and sexual slavery:** "The Chamber considers that the crime charged under Count 7 (sexual slavery) requires a distinct element from the crime of rape (Count 6). The offence of rape requires sexual penetration, whereas sexual slavery requires the exercise of powers attaching to the right of ownership and acts of sexual nature. As the acts of a sexual nature do not necessarily require sexual penetration, and rape does not require that the right to ownership is exercised, the Chamber finds that sexual slavery is distinct from rape. Where the commission of sexual slavery, however, entails acts of rape, the Chamber finds that the act of rape is subsumed by the act of sexual slavery. In such a

[832] *Issa Hassan Sesay et al.* Trial Judgement, paras. 1346–1352 (internal references omitted).

case, a conviction on the same conduct is not permissible for rape and sexual slavery".[833]

- Cumulative convictions for rape and "forced marriages":

"The Chamber considers that the crime charged under Count 8 ('forced marriage') as an other inhumane act requires a distinct element from the crime of rape (Count 6), and *vice versa*. The offence of rape requires sexual penetration, whereas 'forced marriage' requires a forced conjugal association based on exclusivity between the perpetrator and victim. Therefore, the Chamber finds that it is permissible to convict on both counts".[834]

- Cumulative convictions for sexual slavery and "forced marriages":

"The Chamber considers that the conduct charged under Count 8 is distinct from the charges of sexual slavery under Count 7 (sexual slavery). The Appeals Chamber has explicitly held that 'forced marriage' is not subsumed by sexual slavery. The distinct elements are a forced conjugal association based on exclusivity between the perpetrator and victim. Therefore a conviction on both Counts 7 (sexual slavery) and 8 (other inhumane acts) is permissible".[835]

- The issue of consent in establishing the *actus reus* of sexual slavery and "forced marriages":

The Appeals Chamber found that the absence of consent is neither an element of sexual slavery nor of "forced marriages". In particular, the Appeals Chamber found that, when the legal requirements of the crimes have been proved, then consent is impossible and, therefore, not a relevant consideration. The Appeals Chamber held: "In paragraphs 1465 through 1473 of the Trial Judgment, the Trial Chamber found that the circumstances surrounding the sexual relations and marriages included that (i) the women and girls were 'forcefully captured and abducted' from 'throughout Sierra Leone' and taken to Kailahun District, (ii) that these abductions took place 'in the context of a hostile and coercive war environment,' (iii) that the women and girls could not leave for fear of being killed or sent into armed conflict, and (iv) that women and girls were subjected to 'threats, intimidation, manipulation and other forms of duress which were predicated on the victims' fear and their desperate situation.' The Trial Chamber found that the hostile and coercive circumstances were such that '*genuine consent was not possible*,' and it concluded that '[i]n light of the foregoing and given the violent, hostile and coercive environment in which these women suddenly found themselves … the sexual relations with the rebels … *was*, in [the] circumstances, *not consensual* because of the state of uncertainty and subjugation in which they lived in captivity.' The Trial Chamber's reasoning led to a finding of the exercise of rights of ownership and of the force, threats of force and coercion used to compel victims. In part, the reasoning results in a finding of the absence of consent, not a presumption thereof, however, the absence of consent is neither an element of sexual slavery nor of forced marriage. Sexual slavery, a form of enslavement, 'flows from claimed rights of ownership' to which consent is impossible. With respect to forced marriage, the Appeals Chamber recalls that the offence 'describes a situation in which the perpetrator[,] … compels a person by force, threat of force, or coercion to serve as a conjugal partner.' The conduct must constitute an 'other inhumane act,' which entails that the perpetrator: (i) inflict great suffering, or serious injury to body or to mental or physical health; (ii) sufficiently similar in gravity to the acts referred to in

833 *Issa Hassan Sesay et al.* Trial Judgement, para. 2305.

834 *Issa Hassan Sesay et al.* Trial Judgement, para. 2306 (internal reference omitted).

835 *Issa Hassan Sesay et al.* Trial Judgement, para. 2307 (internal references omitted).

	Article 2.a through Article 2.h of the Statute; and that (iii) the perpetrator was aware of the factual circumstances that established the character of the gravity of the act. As a crime against humanity, the offence also requires that the acts of the accused formed part of a widespread or systematic attack against the civilian population, and that the accused knew that his crimes were so related. The Appeals Chamber considers that where the Prosecution has proved the legal requirements of the offence, that is, that an accused, by force, threat of force, or coercion, or by taking advantage of coercive circumstances, causes one or more persons to serve as a conjugal partner, and the perpetrator's acts are knowingly part of a widespread or systematic attack against a civilian population and amount to the infliction of great suffering, or serious injury to body or to mental or physical health sufficiently similar in gravity to the enumerated crimes against humanity, then consent is impossible and therefore is not a relevant consideration. As found by the Trial Chamber, 'given the violent, hostile and coercive environment in which these women suddenly found themselves … the sexual relations with the rebels … could not [be], and was, in [the] circumstances, not consensual because of the state of uncertainty and subjugation in which they lived in captivity.' Such captivity in itself would have vitiated consent in the circumstances under consideration. After finding the absence of consent, the Trial Chamber went on to opine generally that, in circumstances such as the ones it had just found, 'there *should be* a presumption of absence of genuine consent to having sexual relations or contracting marriages with the said RUF fighters.' This additional statement did not provide the framework for its analysis and nothing suggests that it informed its findings on the elements of the offences. Rather, it is precatory, conditional, and follows the Trial Chamber's analysis of the circumstances that eliminated the possibility of genuine consent. The impugned statement is therefore an *obiter dicta*. The Appeals Chamber finds no error of law in the Trial Chamber's approach. […] The Trial Chamber's findings were sufficient to establish the *actus reas* of sexual slavery and forced marriage. Having thus found, *inter alia*, that the victims were subject to enslavement, force and coercion, the Trial Chamber did not have to examine the issue of consent, and in particular to have assessed whether every victim did not consent. Sesay's argument is thus without merit".[836] - <u>Factual and legal findings:</u> - Rapes in Koidu Town in Kono District: "TF1-217 was in Koidu during the attack by the AFRC/RUF forces in February/March 1998. The rebels forcibly entered civilian houses during the night on a regular basis and stabbed people, took property and raped women. On those mornings when news spread of such events from the previous evenings, TF1-217 would go to the local hospital. He stated that: '[On arrival at the hospital] we met young women that were raped and young people – men that were damaged. And it happened many times.' AFRC/RUF fighters also regularly raped women who were being used to carry loads in the Guinea Highway area of Koidu in March 1998".[837] "The Chamber recalls the testimony of TF1-217 and TF1-141 that an unknown number of women were 'raped' in Koidu during the February/March 1998 attack by AFRC/RUF rebels. The Chamber observes that an atmosphere of violence prevailed in Koidu during the attack, noting the lootings, burnings and killings occurring simultaneously. The Chamber finds that in such violent circumstances the women were not capable of genuine consent. The Chamber accordingly finds that an unknown number of women were raped in Koidu, as charged in Count 6".[838]

836 *Issa Hassan Sesay et al.* Appeal Judgement, paras. 733–737, 740 (internal references omitted).

837 *Issa Hassan Sesay et al.* Trial Judgement, paras. 1152–1153 (internal references omitted).

838 *Issa Hassan Sesay et al.* Trial Judgement, paras. 1286–1287 (internal references omitted).

	- Rape of a woman by Staff Alhaji in Tombodu, in Kono district: "In Tombodu, in mid-April 1998, TF1-197 watched Staff Alhaji point a gun at the head of a woman carrying a child and command her to put the child down and undress. The woman did so and Staff Alhaji 'began pointing and touching the private of the woman. Then he told the woman to lie down […] and he, Alhaji, came and used the woman […] he had sex with the woman'".[839] "The Chamber recalls the evidence that in Tombodu, Staff Alhaji pointed a gun at a woman, ordered her to lie down and then had sex with her. The Chamber finds that the elements of rape as charged in Count 6 are proved beyond reasonable doubt in respect of this incident".[840] - Rapes in Sawao, in Kono district: "Some weeks after the Intervention in February 1998, TF1-195 was captured in the bush between Kainako and Gandorhun by two rebels - one of whom was wearing a soldier's uniform and armed with a gun, while the other was dressed in civilian clothes and carrying a stick to which a red piece of cloth was attached. The rebel with the gun pointed it at TF1-195 and said 'You, come out here.' He ordered her to undress, and she stripped to her underwear. The rebel with the gun ordered her to remove her underwear and to lie down and she did so. The rebel with the gun lowered his trousers and told TF1-195 to open her legs so he could have sex with her. While the rebel was having sex with her, another man arrived, also with a stick. The two men watched the rebel have sex with TF1-195. They then took turns having sex with the witness, while the rebel with the gun remained standing over her".[841] "The rebels divided the female civilians into two groups. The youngest girls, believed to be virgins, were in one group and TF1-195 and five older women were in the second group. The young girls were taken away in one direction, whilst the witness's group was subsequently taken towards Benguema Fiama by a group of rebels armed with guns and sticks. The women were told to undress and lie down. TF1-195 was raped by two different rebels and the second rebel inserted a stick into her vagina. The witness did not consent to these acts, and since this maltreatment has experienced physical pain for five years".[842] "The Chamber recalls its findings that: (i) sexual acts were perpetrated on TF1-195 five times and an unknown number of times on five other women by rebels in Sawao […]. The Chamber is satisfied from the evidence in respect of each of these incidents that the *actus reus* of rape is established. The perpetrators' acts occurred in the context of armed rebels capturing groups of civilians, and threatening, killing or physically injuring them. The Chamber is satisfied that in such circumstances the women did not consent and were in fact incapable of genuine consent. The Chamber accordingly finds that each of these acts constitute rape as charged in Count 6".[843] - Rapes in Penduma, in Kono district: "In April 1998 a large number of rebels wearing jeans and military fatigues and led by Staff Alhaji surrounded Penduma. TF1-217, who was present, knew Staff Alhaji personally from their childhood in Koidu. He also knew many of the other rebels, including Junior from Tombodu, who was not an SLA soldier but a 'vigilante';

[839] *Issa Hassan Sesay et al.* Trial Judgement, para. 1171 (internal reference omitted).
[840] *Issa Hassan Sesay et al.* Trial Judgement, para. 1288 (internal reference omitted).
[841] *Issa Hassan Sesay et al.* Trial Judgement, paras. 1180–1181 (internal references omitted).
[842] *Issa Hassan Sesay et al.* Trial Judgement, para. 1185 (internal references omitted).
[843] *Issa Hassan Sesay et al.* Trial Judgement, paras. 1289–1290 (internal reference omitted).

Tamba Joe, who was an AFRC fighter; and Lieutenant Jalloh. Rebels shot at civilians who tried to escape Penduma. TF1-217 and his family were captured, along with many other civilians. The leader of the group separated the civilians into three groups. The first group comprised children, pregnant women and nursing mothers, while the remaining women made up the second group. The men formed a third group and were ordered into three separate lines. Staff Alhaji sat on a tree stump and signalled to each of his men to select a woman. The men came forward and took women. Some women were taken inside houses and some men raped their selected woman outside in view of the civilians. TF1-217's wife was raped by eight fighters, including Junior and Tamba Joe: 'Some of them, they bow her down, some of them laid her down and take the feet up. This is how they raped my wife.' Men holding guns ordered him to watch and to count the men raping his wife. His children, sitting in the other group, were also watching. As the men raped his wife, they told TF1-217: 'They only told me that I don't know how to do it, they knew how to do it, they were laughing, they shouted.' After raping his wife, Tamba Joe stabbed and killed her. Other women were also killed after being raped. TF1-217 saw the corpses of about six women, including the one of his wife".[844]

"The Chamber recalls its findings that: […] (ii) sexual acts were perpetrated on TF1-217's wife eight times and on an unknown number of other women by rebels in Penduma […]. The Chamber is satisfied from the evidence in respect of each of these incidents that the *actus reus* of rape is established. The perpetrators' acts occurred in the context of armed rebels capturing groups of civilians, and threatening, killing or physically injuring them. The Chamber is satisfied that in such circumstances the women did not consent and were in fact incapable of genuine consent. The Chamber accordingly finds that each of these acts constitute rape as charged in Count 6".[845]

- Rapes, sexual violence and outrages upon personal dignity in Bumpeh, in Kono district:

"In March 1998, rebels captured a group of civilians in Bumpeh, stripped them naked and forced them into a line. The rebels commanded them to laugh and told them that their lives had ended. A rebel ordered a couple to have sexual intercourse in front of the other captured civilians, stating that he would kill them if they did not comply. The rebels then forced the man's daughter to wash her father's penis. The rebels questioned TF1-218 about the whereabouts of her husband. When TF1-218 answered that he had been killed, the rebel responded that 'since your husband is not here, I am going to have sexual intercourse with you.' He pushed her to the ground, putting his gun on one side and his knife on the other, lifted her feet, opened her legs and started forcing her to have sex with him under threat of death. TF1-218 was then raped by another rebel. She described her condition after the two rapes: 'I was trembling, so I got up. I stood there for some time trembling.' TF1-218 managed to escape but not before the rebels had shot her hand. She said 'I was naked. Everywhere blood was oozing out of me […] from my vagina, and also from my hand'".[846]

"The Chamber recalls its findings that: […] (iii) sexual acts were perpetrated on TF1-218 twice by rebels in Bumpeh […]. The Chamber is satisfied from the evidence in respect of each of these incidents that the *actus reus* of rape is established. The perpetrators' acts occurred in the context of armed rebels capturing groups of civilians, and threatening, killing or physically injuring them. The Chamber is satisfied that in such circumstances the women did not consent and were in fact incapable of genuine con-

844 *Issa Hassan Sesay et al.* Trial Judgement, paras. 1191–1195 (internal references omitted).

845 *Issa Hassan Sesay et al.* Trial Judgement, paras. 1289–1290 (internal reference omitted).

846 *Issa Hassan Sesay et al.* Trial Judgement, paras. 1205–1206 (internal references omitted).

	sent. The Chamber accordingly finds that each of these acts constitute rape as charged in Count 6".[847] "The Chamber recalls that in February/March 1998, rebels in Bumpeh ordered a couple to have sexual intercourse in the presence of the other captured civilians and their daughter. After the enforced rape they forced the man's daughter to wash her father's penis. The Chamber recalls its finding that conduct which constitutes 'any other form of sexual violence' may form the basis for charges of outrages upon personal dignity. The Chamber observes, however, that the Prosecution did not particularise the conduct that constitutes other forms of sexual violence. The Prosecution also restricted its pleadings on sexual violence in the Indictment to crimes committed against 'women and girls,' thereby excluding male victims of sexual violence. The Prosecution therefore failed to adequately plead material facts which it then relied on as evidence of crimes, rendering the Indictment defective. The Chamber must therefore determine whether this defect in the Indictment was cured by clear, timely and consistent notice of the material facts to the Accused. The Prosecution disclosed a witness statement of TF1-218 in which it is alleged that rebels forced a couple to have sexual intercourse in public and abused the couple's 10 year old daughter. As this statement was disclosed prior to the start of the Prosecution case on 5 July 2004, the Chamber finds that this constitutes adequate notice of the material particulars of the form of sexual violence alleged. The Chamber finds that the defect in the Indictment was cured by clear, timely and consistent notice to the Defence. The Chamber is satisfied that these acts severely humiliated the couple and their daughter and violated their dignity. Given the nature of these acts and the public context in which they occurred, the Chamber further finds that the perpetrators possessed full knowledge that their actions degraded the personal dignity of the victims. The Chamber accordingly finds that AFRC/RUF rebels committed two outrages upon personal dignity, as charged in Count 9 of the Indictment".[848] - Rapes, sexual violence and outrages upon personal dignity in Bomboafuidu, in Kono district: "TF1-192 and 20 other civilians were captured in Bomboafuidu at the beginning of the 1998 rainy season, by about 50 armed men mostly in combat uniform. The civilians were ordered to undress. Male and female captives were paired up and ordered to have sex with each other. The sexual violence was combined with sexual mutilations, with the rebels slitting the private parts of several male and female civilians with a knife. The men also inserted a pistol into the vagina of one of the female captives where it remained overnight".[849] "The Chamber recalls its findings that: [...] (iv) rebels inserted a pistol in the vagina of a female civilian in Bomboafuidu. The Chamber is satisfied from the evidence in respect of each of these incidents that the *actus reus* of rape is established. The perpetrators' acts occurred in the context of armed rebels capturing groups of civilians, and threatening, killing or physically injuring them. The Chamber is satisfied that in such circumstances the women did not consent and were in fact incapable of genuine consent. The Chamber accordingly finds that each of these acts constitute rape as charged in Count 6".[850] "The Chamber finds that the conduct of AFRC/RUF rebels in forcing approximately 20 captive civilians to have sexual intercourse with each other and slitting the genitalia of several male and female civilians constituted a severe degradation, harm and viola-

847 *Issa Hassan Sesay et al.* Trial Judgement, paras. 1289–1290 (internal reference omitted).

848 *Issa Hassan Sesay et al.* Trial Judgement, paras. 1302–1306 (internal references omitted).

849 *Issa Hassan Sesay et al.* Trial Judgement, paras. 1207–1208 (internal references omitted).

850 *Issa Hassan Sesay et al.* Trial Judgement, paras. 1289–1290 (internal reference omitted).

tion of the victims' personal dignity. The Chamber is satisfied that the perpetrators knew their actions would have this effect and so intended. Again, the Chamber observes that the Prosecution did not particularise the conduct that constitutes other forms of sexual violence and did not plead forms of sexual violence committed against male victims. However, the Chamber finds that the Prosecution adequately notified the Defence of the material fact of this allegation by the disclosure of such information in the witness statement of TF1-192. Therefore, the Chamber finds that the defect in the Indictment was cured in a timely, clear and consistent manner causing no material prejudice to the Defence in the preparation of their case. The Chamber therefore finds that AFRC/RUF rebels in Bomboafuidu committed outrages upon the personal dignity of an unknown number of civilians, as charged in Count 9".[851]

- Sexual slavery and "forces marriages" in Koidu, in Kono district:

"In February and March 1998, as the Junta troops travelled to Kono, many civilian women and girls from villages along the road were forcibly abducted by the fighters. Some women were forced into marriage, used as domestics to do cooking or housework, and others were raped. Following the capture of Koidu in February/March 1998, TF1-071 saw women being forcibly taken from their husbands, parents and home villages, particularly from Sewafe to Koidu. Some were raped and others, especially the beautiful ones, became the wives of the Commanders. These women were under the control of the Commanders and were responsible for cooking for them and 'serving them as their wives,' meaning that the rebels used the women for sexual purposes".[852]

- Sexual slavery and "forced marriages" in Wendedu, in Kono district:

"After ECOMOG and the Kamajors forces retook control of Koidu in April 1998, TF1-217 fled to Wendedu along with many other civilians. The AFRC/RUF were also in Wendedu and one day he saw five young girls, aged between about 13 and 16 years of age, sitting inside vehicles with AFRC/RUF rebels. One of the girls was weeping. One of the Junta boys then captured TF1-217's 16 year old sister and declared 'This is Captain Bai Bureh's wife'. Captain Bai Bureh said 'Yes, this is a beautiful lady.' Among the other Commanders present, TF1-217 also recognised Lieutenant Jalloh. TF1-217 begged for the release of his sister, but the rebels said 'Your life, your sister, which of the two do you want?' TF1-217 left his sister and did not see her again until after disarmament. While TF1-015, an abducted civilian, was in Wendedu camp, he heard women in the camp screaming at night '[l]eave me, leave me, leave me alone. You did not bring me for this. I'm not your wife.' He spoke to some women who said that they were forced to have sex with the rebels at night. The Commanders claimed that captured women were their wives, stating that 'there is no wedlock from the family. Just because of gun, you've taken her to be your wife, using her as your wife'".[853]

- "Forced marriages" of TF1-016 and her daughter and outrages upon personal dignity in Kissi Town, in Kono district:

"Following the carving incident described in the previous paragraph, TF1-016, her daughter and the other civilian women were forced to accompany the RUF on foot to Kissi Town, carrying rice on their heads. When they arrived, the rebels gave the rice to their leader, Alpha. The RUF then distributed the female captives among themselves, with each rebel saying 'this is my own wife'. Both TF1-016 and her daughter were

[851] *Issa Hassan Sesay et al.* Trial Judgement, paras. 1307–1309 (internal references omitted).

[852] *Issa Hassan Sesay et al.* Trial Judgement, paras. 1154–1155 (internal references omitted).

[853] *Issa Hassan Sesay et al.* Trial Judgement, paras. 1178–1179 (internal references omitted).

	given to rebels as wives in this fashion. TF1-016 was given to Kotor, a member of the RUF. TF1-016 explained that she did not consent to this arrangement: '[It was] not my wish, because somebody is not your husband and you are just taken and given to the person. I was not really happy about it.' TF1-016 was required to live with Kotor in his house. Alpha also lived in the house and was always armed with a gun. Kotor was a palm tree tapper and made palm wine for the RUF and he did not carry a gun. In cross-examination, TF1-016 agreed with the proposition that this made him a civilian, but she clearly emphasised that Kotor worked for the RUF. TF1-016 performed domestic chores for Kotor: she cooked for him, washed his clothes, cleaned his house and pounded rice for him: 'I did everything... I used to do all this work up to an extent all my hands were all blistered.' Kotor also made TF1-016 have sex with him on a daily basis, whenever he wished, despite her attempts to tell him that she did not consent. She also made it clear that she complained about it. TF1-016 explained that she was too afraid to attempt an escape, because armed rebels were throughout Kissi Town and 'if we attempt to go somewhere, they will do something bad with us.' There were many other captured civilians, men and women, in Kissi Town. On three occasions while TF1-016 was in Kissi Town, the RUF went out and returned with large numbers of captured civilians. After spending a month in Kissi Town, her 'husband' Kotor took TF1-016 to Njagbema, where she continued working for him and he continued to force her to have intercourse with him. TF1-016's daughter was also brought to Njagbema with her rebel 'husband'. Her daughter told her that on one occasion, Alpha forced her to have sex with him, even though she was crying and other men had to hold her down. TF1-016 told her daughter to be patient because 'this is the war' and there was nothing that the women could do about it. TF1-016 was held captive with Kotor for a period of one year and three months. She did not make any attempt to talk to other civilians outside of her house, because it was not permitted and the rebels punished such behaviour by death. On one occasion, a number of captives attempted to escape from Kissi Town and TF1-016 was summoned and accused of inciting them to do so. The rebels threatened to kill her for this. Eventually, TF1-016, her daughter and her other children were released in Kono when the head of the rebels announced that a ceasefire had been concluded and all civilians were be permitted to leave".[854] "The Chamber recalls its finding that RUF member Kotor forcibly married TF1-016 in Kissi Town. Although the Chamber finds that Kotor was not an RUF fighter, we hold that war crimes may be committed by persons who are not members of a party to a conflict, as long as a functional relationship existed between the act and the conflict. The Chamber recalls that Kotor worked for the RUF over a period of many months, that he was among a group of RUF rebels who were offered an abducted 'wife,' and that he lived in a residence with armed RUF fighters from whom his 'wife' was too afraid to attempt escape. The Chamber is satisfied from this evidence that Kotor enjoyed a close relationship with the RUF which permitted him to force TF1-016 into a 'marriage'. The Chamber thus finds that a clear functional relationship existed between Kotor's conduct and the armed conflict, such that Kotor's acts constitute an outrage on the personal dignity of TF1-016, as charged in Count 9".[855] - Legal findings on sexual slavery and "forced marriages" in Koidu, Wendedu and Kissi Town, in Kono district: "The Chamber recalls its findings that: (i) an unknown number of women were taken as 'wives' by AFRC/RUF fighters in Koidu in February and March 1998; (ii) an unknown number of women were forcibly kept as 'wives' by RUF fighters in the civilian camp at Wendedu; and, (iii) TF1-016 and her daughter were forcibly 'married' to RUF members in Kissi-Town. In relation to the finding that TF1-217's sister was

[854] *Issa Hassan Sesay et al.* Trial Judgement, paras. 1211–1214 (internal references omitted).

[855] *Issa Hassan Sesay et al.* Trial Judgement, paras. 1300–1301 (internal references omitted).

	taken as a 'wife' by Captain Bai Bureh in Wendedu, the Chamber observes that the Prosecution did not adduce evidence to prove the course of events after the rebels captured TF1-217's sister. In the absence of further detail, the Chamber finds that the Prosecution has not established beyond reasonable doubt the elements of Counts 7 and 8 in respect of this specific incident. However, the Chamber has taken this evidence into account to corroborate its finding that an unknown number of women were taken as wives and held as sex slaves by AFRC/RUF rebels in Wendedu in this time frame. The Chamber concludes from the evidence pertaining to Koidu and Wendedu that a consistent pattern of conduct existed towards women who were forced into conjugal relationships. These 'wives' were 'married' against their will, forced to engage in sexual intercourse and perform domestic chores, and were unable to leave their 'husbands' for fear of violent retribution. The Chamber is satisfied that the 'husbands' were aware of the power exercised over their 'wives' and therefore were aware that their 'wives' did not genuinely consent to the 'marriage' or perform conjugal 'duties' including sexual intercourse and domestic labour of their own free volition. The Chamber is accordingly satisfied that the perpetrators intended to deprive the women of their liberty by exercising powers attaching to the right of ownership over them, including by forcing the women to engage in acts of a sexual nature. The Chamber thus finds that in February to May 1998, the AFRC/RUF rebels forced an unknown number of women into sexual slavery in Koidu; that RUF rebels forced an unknown number of women into sexual slavery in Wendedu; and that an RUF member forced TF1-016 and her daughter into sexual slavery in Kissi-Town, as charged in Count 7. In relation to Count 8, the Chamber is satisfied that the conduct described by numerous reliable witnesses that rebels captured women and 'took them as their wives' in Koidu and Wendedu satisfies the *actus reus* of 'forced marriage,' namely the imposition of a forced conjugal association. We consider that the phenomenon of 'bush wives' was so widespread throughout the Sierra Leone conflict that the concept of women being 'taken as wives' was well-known and understood. The Chamber observes that the conjugal association forced upon the victims carried with it a lasting social stigma which hampers their recovery and reintegration into society. This suffering is in addition to the physical injuries that forced intercourse commonly inflicted on women taken as 'wives'. The Chamber thus finds that the perpetrators' actions in taking 'wives' in Koidu inflicted grave suffering and serious injury to the physical and mental health of the victims, and that the perpetrators were aware of the gravity of their actions. The Chamber is therefore satisfied that AFRC/RUF rebels forced an unknown number of women into marriages in Koidu; that AFRC/RUF rebels forced an unknown number of women into marriages in Wendedu; and that an RUF member forcibly married TF1-016 in Kissi-Town, which crimes constitute inhumane acts as charged in Count 8".[856] - Legal findings on outrages upon personal dignity in Koidu, Tombodu, Sawao, Penduma, Bumpeh, Bomboafuidu and Wendedu, in Kono district: "The Chamber finds that the acts of rape, sexual slavery and 'forced marriage,' as described above, also constitute in each case a severe humiliation, degradation and violation of the dignity of the victims and the perpetrators knew or ought to have known that that their acts would produce this effect. The Chamber thus finds that, as charged in Count 9, AFRC/RUF rebels committed outrages on personal dignity in respect of an unknown number of civilians in Koidu; that Staff Alhaji committed an outrage on the personal dignity of a civilian woman in Tombodu; that AFRC/RUF rebels committed outrages on personal dignity in respect of six women in Sawao, TF1-217's wife and an unknown number of other women in Penduma, TF1-218 in Bumpeh, and a woman in Bomboafuidu; that RUF rebels committed outrages on

856 *Issa Hassan Sesay et al.* Trial Judgement, paras. 1291–1297 (internal references omitted).

	personal dignity in respect of an unknown number of women in Wendedu; and that an RUF rebel committed an outrage on the personal dignity of TF1-016's daughter".[857] - Rape, sexual slavery, "forced marriages" and outrages upon personal dignity constituting acts of terrorism as a violation of Article 3 common to the Geneva Conventions and of Additional Protocol II (WC), in Kono district: "The Chamber recalls that an unknown number of civilians were raped in Koidu sometime in February and March 1998. These rapes were committed on a regular basis by rebels who forcibly entered random civilian homes at night. The Chamber is satisfied on this basis that the perpetrators of these acts of violence against civilians used rape as a deliberate tactic to terrorise the civilian population of Koidu. The Chamber accordingly finds that AFRC/RUF rebels committed an unknown number of acts of terrorism in Koidu in February and March 1998 as charged under Count 1 of the Indictment. We find that the rape by Staff Alhaji in Tombodu, the rapes in Sawao, Penduma, Bumpeh and Bomboafuidu and the outrages on personal dignity committed in Bumpeh and Bomboafuidu reflect a consistent pattern of conduct openly exhibited by the rebel forces in their encounters with civilians. The Chamber notes that in each case the rapes were committed in front of other civilians. In Penduma, women were lined up and rebels selected their victim one by one. A husband was forced at gun point to witness the rape of his wife. In Bumpe, victims were forced to laugh and told their lives were over prior to being compelled to have intercourse with each other. In Sawao, as in Penduma, the rapes of multiple women were committed at the same time as men were killed or had their limbs amputated. In Bomboafuidu, a husband and wife and their daughter were openly selected from a group of civilians as the rebels' victims. The Chamber is satisfied from this evidence that the public nature of the crimes was a deliberate tactic on the part of the perpetrators to instil fear into the civilians. Given the geographic and temporal proximity of these crimes to each other, and to the killings and amputations in Kono District, the Chamber finds that the rebels regularly used rape and other forms of sexual violence to spread terror among the civilian population of Kono District. We accordingly find that these crimes constitute acts of terrorism as charged in Count 1 of the Indictment. The Chamber recalls its general considerations on sexual violence as acts of terrorism. As found above, the Chamber is satisfied that because of the consistent pattern of conduct demonstrated in the exercise of the sexual violence the above findings of sexual slavery and 'forced marriage' were committed with the requisite and specific intent to terrorise the civilian population. Accordingly, we find that the Prosecution has proven Count 1 beyond reasonable doubt in relation to these acts".[858] - Rape, sexual slavery, "forced marriages" and outrages upon personal dignity constituting collective punishment as a violation of Article 3 common to the Geneva Conventions and of Additional Protocol II (WC), in Kono district: "The Prosecution has not adduced evidence to prove beyond reasonable doubt that AFRC/RUF rebels who committed the crimes of rape, sexual slavery, 'forced marriage,' outrages upon personal dignity, enslavement and pillage in Kono District did so with the specific intent of collectively punishing the victims for acts for which some or none of them may have been responsible. The Chamber therefore finds that these crimes did not constitute acts of collective punishment as charged in Count 2. The Chamber accordingly makes no finding under Count 2 in relation to these crimes".[859]

[857] *Issa Hassan Sesay et al.* Trial Judgement, paras. 1298–1299 (internal reference omitted).

[858] *Issa Hassan Sesay et al.* Trial Judgement, paras. 1353–1356 (internal references omitted).

[859] *Issa Hassan Sesay et al.* Trial Judgement, paras. 1378–1379 (internal references omitted).

	- Sexual slavery and "forced marriages" in various locations, in Kailahun district: "The Chamber heard evidence of numerous incidents of sexual violence in Kailahun District and notes that sexual violence was widespread both prior to and throughout the Indictment period. Although evidence of rapes and other forms of sexual violence committed by RUF fighters was adduced, the Chamber recalls that the Prosecution did not plead these crimes in respect of Kailahun District. Accordingly, the Chamber's findings on such acts are limited to their occurrence within the context of 'forced marriages' and sexual slavery".[860] - Sexual slavery and "forced marriages" of Witness TF1-314 in Kailahun district: "In 1994, TF1-314 was abducted and twice raped by RUF fighters. The RUF fighter who raped her the second time took her as his 'wife'. From 1994 to 1998, TF1-314 was in Buedu as part of the Small Girl Unit ('SGU'). She cooked and did laundry for her rebel 'husband' and lived in his house. She was also forced to have sexual intercourse with him at night. Other girls between 10 and 15 years of age were also taken as 'wives' by rebels in Buedu. The girls cooked, did laundry and other domestic chores and at night had sex with their rebel 'husbands'. TF1-314 testified that she remained in Buedu because civilians who attempted to escape were liable to be killed or fall into the hands of Kamajors, who would kill anyone who came from a rebel zone".[861] "The Chamber recalls TF1-314's testimony that she was abducted from Masingbi in Tonkolili District at age 10 and taken to Buedu in Kailahun District where she lived from 1994 to 1998. The Chamber concludes from her evidence that she was raped twice before being 'married' to a rebel Commander in Buedu. As the Commander's 'wife' TF1-314 was forced to engage in domestic chores and to have sexual intercourse with him. The Chamber is satisfied that TF1-314 remained as the 'wife' of the Commander as she feared that, if she were to escape, she could be captured and fall into the hands of Kamajors who would kill her because she came from a rebel zone. The Chamber finds that TF1-314 did not consent to her 'marriage' and that, moreover, genuine consent was not possible in such coercive circumstances. Based upon the foregoing, the Chamber is satisfied that the Commander intended to exercise powers attaching to the right of ownership over TF1-314 and that he deliberately forced her into a conjugal partnership. The Chamber thus finds that the elements of sexual slavery and the other inhumane act of 'forced marriage' have been established, as charged under Counts 7 and 8 of the Indictment".[862] - Sexual slavery and "forced marriages" of Witness TF1-093 in Kailahun district: "In the rainy season of 1996, at the age of 15, TF1-093 was raped in Njala, Moyamba District, by two of Superman's bodyguards. While the rebels were fighting over her, one stabbed her foot and her 'private'. After the rape, Superman treated her wounds and 'offered' to marry her. TF1-093 accepted as she did not want to die. TF1-093 then moved with the RUF to Kailahun District. While travelling with the RUF, she observed the abductions of many other women who were forced to become the 'wives' of Commanders. As Superman's wife, TF1-093 was forced to have sexual intercourse with him. She also cooked and did laundry for him. Superman habitually gave her drugs, including cannabis sativa, tablets and also gunpowder to eat".[863] "The Chamber recalls that during the rainy season of 1996, TF1-093 was raped by

[860] *Issa Hassan Sesay et al.* Trial Judgement, para. 1405 (internal reference omitted). See also *Issa Hassan Sesay et al.* Trial Judgement, para. 1459.

[861] *Issa Hassan Sesay et al.* Trial Judgement, paras. 1406–1407 (internal references omitted).

[862] *Issa Hassan Sesay et al.* Trial Judgement, paras. 1460–1461 (internal reference omitted).

[863] *Issa Hassan Sesay et al.* Trial Judgement, para. 1408 (internal references omitted).

	Superman's bodyguards in Moyamba District. As this rape was committed outside of the temporal jurisdiction of the Special Court and in a District not pleaded in the Indictment for sexual violence, the Accused are not charged for this act committed in Moyamba District. The Chamber concludes that TF1-093 was taken after the rainy season of 1996 to Kailahun District where she was forced into an exclusive conjugal relationship with Superman and was forced to become his 'wife'. The Chamber is satisfied that TF1-093 was incapable of giving her genuine consent and became Superman's 'wife' because she feared she would have been killed. As Superman's wife, she cooked and did laundry for him and had sex with him, all of which caused her to endure physical and mental suffering. The Chamber further finds that Superman exercised the rights of ownership over TF1-093 by virtue of this exclusive conjugal relationship with the victim. The Chamber also finds that Superman gave drugs to TF1-093 which reflects his intention to further abuse and exercise control over her. Based upon the foregoing, the Chamber finds that the elements of sexual slavery and of 'forced marriage' as an other inhumane act have been established beyond reasonable doubt. We therefore find that the 'forced marriage' of TF1-093 constitutes sexual slavery and an other inhumane act, as charged under Counts 7 and 8 of the Indictment".[864] - Sexual slavery and "forced marriages" of an unknown number of women in Kailahun district: "The Chamber heard evidence from insider witnesses and witnesses who had been 'bush wives' who testified to the widespread rebel practice of abducting women and forcing them to act as 'wives' in Kailahun District. Many of the women interviewed by expert witness TF1-369, who authored Exhibit 138, the *Expert Report on Forced Marriages*, were school children and petty traders who were abducted from Koinadugu, Tonkolili, Pujehun, Kono, Bonthe, Bo, Freetown and Kenema and taken to Kailahun. The RUF routinely captured women during combat operations on villages in Kailahun District. Upon entering a village, the fighters moved from house to house, forcibly entering and removing the civilians. If the rebels were repelled by a counter-attack, the captured civilians were forced to retreat with them. Many of the abducted women were then assigned as 'wives' to RUF Commanders. A senior RUF Commander explained the practice as follows: 'A Commander who hasn't a wife, somebody to take care of him domestically, take care of his domestic needs, go [sic] to a particular town on combat mission, and he is the head of that mission. He happens to conquer that particular territory, and abduct young girls that found it extremely difficult to escape with the opposing troop, and that Commander sees a young lady that he is interested in [...] The combatants, the other combatant are subjected to him. It is up to him, I mean at his discretion, to tell lady A, Fatmata, you are supposed to be with the CO, I mean, the commanding officer. The young lady has no -- I mean, has no option, in terms of negotiating whether in fact he [sic] want or not. So that lady automatically become the wife of that Commander.' Many Commanders including Bockarie had a captured 'wife'. Dennis Koker, the MP Adjutant in Kailahun District between 1998 and 1999, testified that it was regular practice for women to be forcibly taken as 'wives' and some Commanders had five or six 'wives.' A woman's status as a married woman was no bar to abduction as married women were forced to leave their legitimate husbands and become 'bush wives' to the RUF rebels. The thousands of young women thus captured had no option but to submit to a 'husband' as they were in no position to negotiate their freedom. The abducted women could not escape for fear of being killed. A rebel 'wife' was expected to carry out certain functions for her 'husband' in return for his protection. These functions included carrying the rebel's possessions when he was deployed, engaging in sexual intercourse on demand, per-

[864] *Issa Hassan Sesay et al.* Trial Judgement, paras. 1462–1464 (internal references omitted).

	forming domestic chores and showing undying loyalty to the rebel in return for his 'protection'. If the women refused sexual intercourse with their 'husbands,' they were sent to the front line. Many 'wives' bore children to their rebel 'husbands'".[865] "The Chamber has found that RUF rebels forcefully captured and abducted an unknown number of women and girls from locations throughout Sierra Leone and took them to Kailahun District. The Chamber concludes that it was common practice for rebels to keep captured women subject to their control as sex slaves and to force conjugal relationships on women who unwillingly became their 'wives.' The Chamber finds that acts of sexual violence were intentionally committed against women and girls in the context of a hostile and coercive war environment in which genuine consent was not possible. The Chamber also finds that when the rebels forcefully took victims as 'wives' they intended to deprive them of their liberty. The Chamber finds that the use of the term 'wife' by the rebels was deliberate and strategic, with the aim of enslaving and psychologically manipulating the women and with the purpose of treating them like possessions. The Chamber is satisfied that many fighters had 'bush wives', who, similarly to the cases of TF1-314 and TF1-093 discussed above, were intentionally forced to have sex with the rebels. The Chamber also finds that the perpetrators intended to exercise control and ownership over their victims who were unable to leave or escape for fear that they would be killed or sent to the front lines as combatants. Accordingly, the Chamber finds that young girls and women were intentionally forced into conjugal relationships with rebels. We also find that many women were forced into marriage by means of threats, intimidation, manipulation and other forms of duress which were predicated on the victims' fear and their desperate situation. In relation to the sexual offences alleged in the Indictment, the Chamber notes that the Accused have canvassed the defence of consent and contend that the women and girls who they captured and abducted during attacks, and who were victims of those offences, willingly consented to the alleged marriages and sexual relationships. The Defence also contends that the marriages which were so contracted were conducted with the requisite consent of the parties involved. The Chamber observes, however, that parental and family consent to the so-called marriages of these sexually enslaved and abused women was conspicuously absent. In light of the foregoing and given the violent, hostile and coercive environment in which these women suddenly found themselves, the Chamber first of all considers that the sexual relations with the rebels, notwithstanding the contention of the Defence to the contrary, and on the basis of very credible and compelling evidence, could not, and was, in circumstances, not consensual because of the state of uncertainty and subjugation in which they lived in captivity. In this regard, the Chamber is of the opinion and so holds, that in hostile and coercive circumstances of this nature, there should be a presumption of absence of genuine consent to having sexual relations or contracting marriages with the said RUF fighters. The Chamber is satisfied that 'bush wives' were not only forced into exclusive conjugal sexual relationships but were also expected to perform domestic chores and to bear children. The Chamber is therefore satisfied that all the elements of sexual slavery and of 'forced marriage' as an other inhumane act have been established. We conclude that an unknown number of women were subjected to sexual slavery and 'forced marriages' in Kailahun District, as charged under Counts 7 and 8 of the Indictment".[866] - Outrages upon personal dignity in various locations in Kailahun district: "The Chamber is satisfied that the acts of sexual violence in respect of which findings were made under Counts 6 to 8 resulted in the humiliation, degradation and violation of the dignity of the victims. The Chamber is satisfied that the victims of sexual slavery and 'forced marriage' endured particularly prolonged physical and mental suffer-

865 *Issa Hassan Sesay et al.* Trial Judgement, paras. 1409–1413 (internal references omitted).

866 *Issa Hassan Sesay et al.* Trial Judgement, paras. 1465–1473 (internal reference omitted).

	ing as they were subjected to continued sexual acts while living with their captors under difficult and coercive circumstances. Due to the social stigma attached to them by virtue of their former status as 'bush wives' and the effects of the prolonged forced conjugal relationships to which they were subjected, these women and girls were too ashamed or too afraid to return to their communities after the conflict. Accordingly, many victims were displaced from their home towns and support networks. The Chamber finds that these violations were serious and that the perpetrators were aware of their degrading effect. We accordingly find that TF1-093, TF1-314 and an unknown number of other women were subjected to outrages upon their personal dignity in Kailahun District, as charged in Count 9 of the Indictment".[867] - Sexual slavery and "forced marriages" constituting acts of terrorism as a violation of Article 3 common to the Geneva Conventions and of Additional Protocol II (WC), in Kailahun district: "The Chamber recalls its general observations on sexual violence as acts of terrorism. The Chamber is satisfied that the consistent pattern of conduct as demonstrated in our findings on sexual slavery and 'forced marriage' were committed with the requisite specific intent to terrorise the civilian population in Kailahun District. Accordingly, we find that these acts constitute acts of terrorism as charged in Count 1".[868] - Rape, sexual slavery, "forced marriages" and outrages upon personal dignity constituting collective punishment as a violation of Article 3 common to the Geneva Conventions and of Additional Protocol II (WC), in Kailahun district: "The Prosecution has not adduced evidence to prove beyond reasonable doubt that AFRC/RUF rebels who committed the crimes of rape, sexual slavery, 'forced marriage,' outrages upon personal dignity and enslavement in Kailahun District did so with the specific intent of collectively punishing the victims for acts for which some or none of them may have been responsible. The Chamber therefore finds that these crimes did not constitute acts of collective punishment as charged in Count 2".[869] - General factual findings on sexual violence during the attack on Freetown: "Many abducted women and girls were subjected to sexual violence. Expert Witness TF1-081 testified that of 1,168 patients examined between March and December 1999, 99% had been abducted following the 6 January 1999 invasion, the 'vast majority' of whom originated from Freetown. Out of these patients, 274 (23.4%) had been beaten for refusing to engage in sexual relations or carry heavy looted goods; 648 (58.5%) of the abductees had been subjected to rape, some by more than two and up to 30 men; 281 (24.1%) complained of vaginal discharge and 327 (27.9%) had pelvic inflammatory disease, both of which are transmitted through sexual intercourse; and 200 (17.1%) were pregnant, over 80% of whom were girls between the ages of 14 and 18".[870] - Rapes committed in Freetown and the Western Area: "On 6 January 1999, the rebels took women to State House where they were raped. Each of the senior Commanders, and many of the troops, had captured women at their disposal. Many of these women remained with the fighters during and after the withdrawal from Freetown".[871]

867 *Issa Hassan Sesay et al.* Trial Judgement, paras. 1474–1475 (internal references omitted).

868 *Issa Hassan Sesay et al.* Trial Judgement, para. 1493 (internal reference omitted).

869 *Issa Hassan Sesay et al.* Trial Judgement, para. 1495.

870 *Issa Hassan Sesay et al.* Trial Judgement, para. 1520 (internal references omitted).

871 *Issa Hassan Sesay et al.* Trial Judgement, para. 1523 (internal references omitted).

	"TF1-093 and the fighters under her command burned houses and killed and raped civilians in the Upgun and Fourah Bay Road areas and around the Eastern Police Station".[872] "On 21 January 1999, TF1-097, a family member and two neighbours were at the witness's house in Kissy when Captain Blood and another rebel entered the compound and threatened to set the house on fire. The two neighbours managed to escape. […] Later that night, from his hiding place, TF1-097 observed a rebel rape a number of women. He met other civilians who had been subjected to amputation, one of whom told him of his sister's rape".[873] - Rapes of an unknown number of women and "forced marriages" of a 10-year old girl, TF1-023 and TF1-029 in Freetown and the Western Area: "On 22 January 1999 in Kissy, TF1-022 heard gunshots and saw many houses in the vicinity on fire. A rebel ran to TF1-022's gate and shouted for money. At the same time, TF1-022 heard gunshots as a woman was shot by rebels. TF1-022's brother-in-law ran outside and was himself shot and injured. While TF1-022 and five youths were carrying his injured brother-in-law to Connaught Hospital, they were captured by seven rebels, who took them to a group of other captured civilians, including a 10-year old girl who was taken as a 'wife' by one of the rebels".[874] "On 22 January 1999, an afternoon attack on Wellington forced TF1-023 to flee to Calaba Town where she was captured with another six unarmed civilians by a group of approximately 200 armed rebels. TF1-023 and the others were taken to Allen Town where they were told that the rebels intended to use them as human shields, but that no harm would come to them. […] After Allen Town, TF1-023 was taken together with her cousin to Calaba Town for three days by a named AFRC fighter. Her cousin stayed with that fighter and TF1-023 was handed over to an AFRC Commander as a 'wife'. TF1-023 did not consent, but accepted the role because 'they had the say.' That night she was forced to strip and to have sexual intercourse with her 'husband'. As his 'wife' she continued to be forced to have sexual intercourse with the AFRC Commander, although it was against her will. At some point in February 1999, the AFRC troops moved to Newton/Four Mile and TF1-023 had to follow her 'husband'. At Four Mile she was expected to cook, as well as to continue sexual relations with her 'husband'. TF1-023 was unable to escape from Four Mile as, on the orders of her 'husband,' she was continuously shadowed by armed guard. Approximately 400 fighters were stationed at Four Mile and any civilians who attempted to escape were punished with beatings. TF1-023 knew of ten other women who were forced into 'marriages' with the troops at Four Mile Base to officers and soldiers. TF1-023 was only able to escape from the troops in August 1999".[875] "On 22 January 1999, TF1-029, aged 16 at the time, was abducted in Wellington with 50 other civilians by a group of rebels who identified themselves as SLA (AFRC) and RUF fighters. The mixed group of rebels included both young children and older fighters. TF1-029 estimated the younger fighters to be between 13 and 16 years of age. The abducted civilians were forced to march from Wellington to Calaba Town and the AFRC and RUF killed people and torched houses en route. At Calaba Town, Major Arif took TF1-029 as his wife and she was forced to have sex with him. TF1-029 testified that 'thousands' of women were taken and raped by the AFRC and RUF rebels. She was told that 'soldiers who captured civilians had a right to rape them and make them their wives.' […] After remaining in Calaba Town for about two weeks,

872 *Issa Hassan Sesay et al.* Trial Judgement, para. 1529 (internal reference omitted).

873 *Issa Hassan Sesay et al.* Trial Judgement, para. 1556 (internal references omitted).

874 *Issa Hassan Sesay et al.* Trial Judgement, para. 1553 (internal references omitted).

875 *Issa Hassan Sesay et al.* Trial Judgement, paras. 1558, 1560–1561 (internal references omitted).

the group moved to Benguema where a further 100 civilians were captured. On the march from Calaba Town to Benguema, the AFRC and RUF killed babies as they did not want their cries to disclose their position. TF1-029 remained at Benguema until 10 March 1999, during which time she was raped ten times by Major Arif. She learned that other girls were also subjected to rape by the rebels and at least one civilian was killed. Throughout February 1999, roughly 300 civilians captured from Freetown were held by AFRC rebels at Benguema, Four Mile and Newton. Most of the young girls were forced to be the 'wives' of various AFRC Commanders and were expected to care for their needs by cooking their food and having sexual relations with them, while abducted young boys were trained to be SBUs. Male captives were expected to carry out household chores, while those women who had not been taken as 'wives' also cooked".[876]

- Legal findings on rapes, sexual slavery, "forced marriages" and outrages upon personal dignity committed in Freetown and the Western Area:

Rapes: "The Chamber recalls the expert evidence of TF1-081 that as many as 648 of the 1,168 patients treated after the attack on Freetown were raped. The Chamber is satisfied that the vast majority of these rapes were committed by the rebel forces and considers that this evidence further corroborates our specific findings of rape. The Chamber recalls its findings that: (i) an unknown number of women were raped at State House; (ii) a large number of civilians under the control of witness TF1-093 were raped; (iii) an unknown number of women at Benguema and Calaba Town were raped by AFRC rebels throughout February 1999; and (iii) an unknown number of women were raped in Kissy. The Chamber is satisfied that the use of the term 'rape' by credible witnesses describes acts of forced sexual penetration consistent with the *actus reus* of the offence of rape. The Chamber observes that an atmosphere of extreme violence prevailed during the attack on the Freetown peninsula, noting the lootings, burnings, amputations and killings that occurred simultaneously. The Chamber finds that in such circumstances the individuals who were forced to have intercourse were incapable of genuine consent. The Chamber is satisfied that the perpetrators of each of these acts knew or had reason to know that the victims did not consent. The Chamber accordingly finds that these acts constitute rape as charged under Count 6 of the Indictment".[877]

Sexual slavery and "forced marriages": "The Chamber recalls its findings that: (i) rebels abducted a 10 year-old girl and, in the presence of TF1-022, gave the girl to one rebel to be his 'wife;' (ii) TF1-023 and ten other women were given as 'wives' to AFRC Commanders and fighters, with TF1-023 being forced to have sexual intercourse with her 'husband' on multiple occasions; and (iii) TF1-029 was forced into a 'marriage' with Major Arif and forced to have sexual relations with him. The Chamber further finds, recalling the testimony of TF1-334 that the practice of taking women, including young girls, to become the 'wives' of various Commanders and to perform sexual acts and domestic chores for their 'husbands' was widespread, that an unknown number of other women were forced into 'marriages' in Freetown and the Western Area. The Chamber is satisfied that rebels forced a conjugal relationship on these 'wives' in an atmosphere of extreme violence and terror. From the foregoing the Chamber concludes that the perpetrators had knowledge that the women did not consent. These women were abducted and deprived of their liberty and coerced to perform sexual duties and domestic chores for their 'husbands'. The perpetrators controlled their movement and prohibited their escape on fear of death. On the basis of these indicia, the Chamber finds that the perpetrators exercised powers attaching to the right of ownership over these women. The Chamber therefore finds that these acts

[876] *Issa Hassan Sesay et al.* Trial Judgement, paras. 1562, 1564–1565 (internal references omitted).

[877] *Issa Hassan Sesay et al.* Trial Judgement, paras. 1575–1578 (internal references omitted).

	constitute sexual slavery and 'forced marriages,' as charged under Counts 7 and 8 of the Indictment".[878] Outrages upon personal dignity: "The Chamber finds that these crimes of rape, sexual slavery and 'forced marriage' constitute in each case a severe humiliation, degradation and violation of the dignity of the victims and the perpetrators knew that their acts would have this effect. The Chamber accordingly finds that AFRC rebels committed outrages on personal dignity in respect of an unknown number of civilians in Freetown and the Western Area between 6 January 1999 and 28 February 1999. These acts constitute the crime […] charged in Count 9 of the Indictment".[879] - Sexual slavery and "forced marriages" constituting acts of terrorism as a violation of Article 3 common to the Geneva Conventions and of Additional Protocol II (WC), in Freetown and the Western Area: "The Chamber also considers the testimony of TF1-029 regarding the claim of rebels that 'soldiers who captured civilians had a right to rape them and make them their wives.' Coupled with our findings in relation to Count 6 above, the Chamber finds that the widespread and systematic rape of women instilled fear and a sense of insecurity among the civilian population. The deliberate and concerted campaign to rape women constitutes an extension of the battlefield to the women's bodies, a degrading treatment that inflicts physical, mental and sexual suffering to the victims and to their community. We find that widespread and systematic sexual violence, including rape, constitutes an act of terrorism as charged under Count 1 of the Indictment. The Chamber accordingly finds that the perpetrators of the crimes committed in Freetown acted with the intent to spread terror among the civilian population. For the foregoing reasons, the Chamber finds that the […] sexual violence […] described above constitute acts of terrorism as charged in Count 1 of the Indictment".[880] - <u>Evidence:</u> **- Using the term "rape" without clarifying the use of the term and the conduct entailed by it:** - In its legal findings, the Trial Chamber held: "As an observation pertinent to the evidence on Count 6 in respect of all Districts, the Chamber notes that numerous witnesses used the term 'rape' without the Prosecution seeking to clarify the use of the term and the conduct entailed by it. We are cognisant that it is natural for some witnesses to be reticent to provide explicit details of sexual violence, especially in Sierra Leonean society where stigma often attaches to victims of such crimes. Nonetheless, we consider it an unfortunate reality in post-conflict Sierra Leone that 'rape' is a commonly understood concept. The Chamber is therefore of the view that the use of the term 'rape' by reliable witnesses describes acts of forced or non-consensual sexual penetration consistent with the *actus reus* of the offence of rape. This approach may be reinforced by circumstantial evidence of violence or coercion".[881]

4. Charles **<u>Taylor</u>** (Case No. SCSL-03-01)

Leader or Head of the National Patriotic Front of Liberia (NPFL), an organised armed group; President of the Republic of Liberia from 2 August 1997 until about 11 August.

[878] *Issa Hassan Sesay et al.* Trial Judgement, paras. 1579–1582 (internal references omitted).
[879] *Issa Hassan Sesay et al.* Trial Judgement, para. 1583 (internal reference omitted).
[880] *Issa Hassan Sesay et al.* Trial Judgement, para. 1602–1604 (internal reference omitted).
[881] *Issa Hassan Sesay et al.* Trial Judgement, para. 1285 (internal reference omitted).

Indictment (International sex crimes (or related) charges and mode(s) of liability)	- **Rape as CAH** (count 4), **Sexual slavery as CAH** (count 5) and **Outrages upon personal dignity as a violation of Article 3 common to the Geneva Conventions and of Additional Protocol II (WC)** (count 6) under Articles 6(1) and 6(3) of the Statute (**superior responsibility**) for the rapes and the abductions of an unknown number of women and girls and for using them as sex slaves.[882] - **Acts of terrorism as a violation of Article 3 common to the Geneva Conventions and of Additional Protocol II (WC)** (count 1) under Articles 6(1) and 6(3) of the Statute (**superior responsibility**) for committing the same crimes of sexual violence as those pleaded in counts 4 to 6 as part of a campaign to terrorise the civilian population of the Republic of Sierra Leone.[883]
Trial Judgement	N/A (The Trial Judgement has not been issued yet.)
Appeal Judgement	N/A
Legal and Factual Findings and/or Evidence	N/A

[882] *Prosecutor v. Charles Taylor*, Case No. SCSL-03-01-PT, Prosecution's Second Amended Indictment, 29 May 2007 ("*Taylor* Indictment"), paras. 14–17 ("**SEXUAL VIOLENCE – COUNT 4:** Rape, a **CRIME AGAINST HUMANITY**, punishable under Article 2.g. of the Statute; And: **COUNT 5:** Sexual slavery, a **CRIME AGAINST HUMANITY**, punishable under Article 2.g. of the Statute; In addition, or in the alternative: **COUNT 6:** Outrages upon personal dignity, a **VIOLATION OF ARTICLE 3 COMMON TO THE GENEVA CONVENTIONS AND OF ADDITIONAL PROTOCOL II**, punishable under Article 3.e. of the Statute. **PARTICULARS:** Between about 30 November 1996 and about 18 January 2002, members of RUF, AFRC, AFRC/RUF Junta or alliance, and/or Liberian fighters, assisted and encouraged by, acting in concert with, under the direction and/or control of, and/or subordinate to the **ACCUSED**, committed widespread acts of sexual violence against civilian women and girls, including the following: **<u>Kono District</u>** Between about 1 February 1998 and about 31 December 1998, raped an unknown number of women and girls in various locations, including Koidu, Tombodu or Tumbodu, Wondedu and AFRC and/or RUF camps such as 'Superman Ground', 'Guinea Highway' and 'PC Ground'; abducted an unknown number of women and girls from various locations within the District, or brought them from locations outside the District, and used them as sex slaves; **<u>Kailahun District</u>** Between about 30 November 1996 and about 18 January 2002, raped an unknown number of women and girls in locations throughout Kailahun District; abducted many victims from other areas of the Republic of Sierra Leone, brought them to locations throughout the District, and used them as sex slaves; **<u>Freetown and Western Area</u>** Between about 21 December 1998 and about 28 February 1999, raped an unknown number of women and girls throughout Freetown and Western area, and abducted an unknown number of women and girls and used them as sex slaves".).

[883] *Taylor* Indictment, paras. 5 ("**TERRORIZING THE CIVILIAN POPULATION – Count 1:** Acts of Terrorism, a **VIOLATION OF ARTICLE 3 COMMON TO THE GENEVA CONVENTIONS AND OF ADDITIONAL PROTOCOL II**, punishable under Article 3.d. of the Statute. **PARTICULARS:** Members of the Revolutionary United Front (RUF), Armed Forces Revolutionay Council (AFRC), AFRC/RUF Junta or alliance, and/or Liberian fighters, including members and ex-members of the NPFL (Liberian fighters), assisted and encouraged by, acting in concert with, under the direction and/or control of, and/or subordinate to the **ACCUSED**, [...] and committed the crimes set forth below in paragraphs 6 through 31 and charged in Counts 2 through 11, as part of a campaign to terrorize the civilian population of the Republic of Sierra Leone".), 14–17.

INDEX

D

E

F

G

H

I

J

K

L

M

T

U

V

W

Y

Z

TORKEL OPSAHL ACADEMIC EPUBLISHER

Editors
Professor Morten Bergsmo, Editor-in-Chief
Professor Olympia Bekou
Professor CHEAH Wui Ling
Mr. Håkan Friman
Dr. Kishan Manocha

Editorial Assistants
Mr. Alf Butenschøn Skre, Senior Editorial Assistant
Mr. Mats Benestad
Ms. Kiki A. Japutra

Principal Scientific Advisers of the Torkel Opsahl Academic EPublisher
Professor Dan Sarooshi, Principal Scientific Adviser for International Law
Professor Andreas Zimmermann, Principal Scientific Adviser for Public International Law
Professor Kai Ambos, Principal Scientific Adviser for International Criminal Law
Dr.h.c. Asbjørn Eide, Principal Scientific Adviser for International Human Rights Law

Editorial Board
Dr. Xabier Agirre, International Criminal Court
Dr. Claudia Angermaier, Austrian judiciary
Dr. Markus Benzing, Freshfields Bruckhaus Deringer, Frankfurt
Professor Margaret deGuzman, Temple University
Ms. Cecilie Hellestveit, Norwegian Centre for Human Rights
Dr. Pablo Kalmanovitz, Columbia University
Mr. Sangkul Kim, Korea University
Professor Jann K. Kleffner, Swedish National Defence College
Dr. Kjetil Mujezinovic Larsen, Norwegian Centre for Human Rights
Mr. Salím A. Nakhjavání, University of Cape Town
Dr. Hector Olasolo, University of Utrecht
Ms. Maria Paula Saffon, Columbia University
Ms. Torunn Salomonsen, Norwegian Ministry of Justice
Professor Carsten Stahn, Leiden University
Professor Jo Stigen, University of Oslo
Ms. Philippa Webb, Legal Consultant

Advisory Board
Mr. Hirad Abtahi, Legal Adviser of the Precidency of the International Criminal Court
Professor Kai Ambos, Georg-August-Universität Göttingen and State Court Göttingen
Professor Emeritus M. Cherif Bassiouni, DePaul University
Professor Jon Bing, University of Oslo
Mr. Gilbert Bitti, International Criminal Court
Research Professor J. Peter Burgess, PRIO

Judge Advocate General Arne Willy Dahl, Norway
Professor Emeritus Yoram Dinstein, Tel Aviv University
Professor Jon Elster, Columbia University and Collège de France
Mr. James A. Goldston, Open Society Institute Justice Initiative
Mr. Richard Goldstone, former Chief Prosecutor,
International Criminal Tribunal for the former Yugoslavia
Judge Hanne Sophie Greve, Gulating Court of Appeal, formerly
European Court of Human Rights
Dr. Fabricio Guariglia, Senior Appeals Counsel, Office of the Prosecutor,
International Criminal Court
Dr. Franz Guenthner, Ludwig-Maximilians-Universität
Mr. Christopher Keith Hall, Amnesty International
Professor Emeritus Frits Kalshoven, Leiden University
Judge Hans-Peter Kaul, International Criminal Court
Judge Erkki Kourula, International Criminal Court
Professor Claus Kress, Director of the Institute for Criminal Law and Criminal Procedure,
Cologne University
Professor David Luban, Georgetown University
Mr. Juan E. Méndez, Special Adviser to the ICC Prosecutor on Crime Prevention, former
President, ICTJ
Dr. Alexander Muller, Director, The Hague Institute for the Internationalisation of Law
Judge Erik Møse, European Court of Human Rights, former President,
International Criminal Tribunal for Rwanda
Dr. Gro Nystuen, University of Oslo and Norwegian Defence Command and Staff College
Mr. William Pace, Convener, Coalition for the International Criminal Court
Ms. Jelena Pejić, International Committee of the Red Cross
Mr. Robert Petit, former International Co-Prosecutor,
Extraordinary Chambers in the Courts of Cambodia
Maj-Gen (ret'd) Anthony P.V. Rogers, Cambridge University
Professor William A. Schabas, National University of Ireland, Galway
Professor James Silk, Yale Law School
Professor Emeritus Otto Triffterer, Salzburg University
Professor Marcos Zilli, University of Sao Paulo

ALSO IN THE FICHL PUBLICATION SERIES

Morten Bergsmo, Mads Harlem and Nobuo Hayashi (editors):
Importing Core International Crimes into National Law
Torkel Opsahl Academic EPublisher
Oslo, 2010
FICHL Publication Series No. 1 (Second Edition, 2010)
ISBN 978-82-93081-00-5

Nobuo Hayashi (editor):
National Military Manuals on the Law of Armed Conflict
Torkel Opsahl Academic EPublisher
Oslo, 2010
FICHL Publication Series No. 2 (Second Edition, 2010)
ISBN 978-82-93081-02-9

Morten Bergsmo, Kjetil Helvig, Ilia Utmelidze and Gorana Žagovec:
The Backlog of Core International Crimes Case Files in Bosnia and Herzegovina
Torkel Opsahl Academic EPublisher
Oslo, 2010
FICHL Publication Series No. 3 (Second Edition, 2010)
ISBN 978-82-93081-04-3

Morten Bergsmo (editor):
Criteria for Prioritizing and Selecting Core International Crimes Cases
Torkel Opsahl Academic EPublisher
Oslo, 2010
FICHL Publication Series No. 4 (Second Edition, 2010)
ISBN 978-82-93081-06-7

Morten Bergsmo and Pablo Kalmanovitz (editors):
Law in Peace Negotiations
Torkel Opsahl Academic EPublisher
Oslo, 2010
FICHL Publication Series No. 5 (Second Edition, 2010)
ISBN 978-82-93081-08-1

Morten Bergsmo, César Rodríguez Garavito, Pablo Kalmanovitz and Maria Paula Saffon (editors):
Distributive Justice in Transitions
Torkel Opsahl Academic EPublisher
Oslo, 2010
FICHL Publication Series No. 6 (2010)
ISBN 978-82-93081-12-8
Also available in Spanish:
Justicia distributiva en sociedades en transición
ISBN 978-82-93081-10-4

Morten Bergsmo (editor):
Complementarity and the Exercise of Universal Jurisdiction for Core International Crimes
Torkel Opsahl Academic EPublisher
Oslo, 2010
FICHL Publication Series No. 7 (2010)
ISBN 978-82-93081-14-2

Morten Bergsmo (editor):
Active Complementarity: Legal Information Transfer
Torkel Opsahl Academic EPublisher
Oslo, 2011
FICHL Publication Series No. 8 (2011)
ISBN 978-82-93081-55-5

Sam Muller, Stavros Zouridis, Morly Frishman and Laura Kistemaker (editors):
The Law of the Future and the Future of Law
Torkel Opsahl Academic EPublisher
Oslo, 2010
FICHL Publication Series No. 11 (2011)
ISBN 978-82-93081-27-2

All volumes are freely available as e-books on the FICHL homepage www.fichl.org. Printed copies may be ordered online at www.amazon.co.uk.

www.ingramcontent.com/pod-product-compliance
Lightning Source LLC
Chambersburg PA
CBHW071338230926
51849CB00006B/513/J
* 9 7 8 8 2 9 3 0 8 1 2 9 6 *